INTRODUCIN GEOGR/

Introducing Human Geographies is a 'travel guide' into the academic subject of human geography and the things that it studies. The coverage of the new edition has been thoroughly refreshed to reflect and engage with the contemporary nature and direction of human geography.

This updated and much extended fourth edition includes a diverse range of authors and topics from across the globe, with a completely revised set of contributions reflecting contemporary concerns in human geography. Presented in four parts with a streamlined structure, it includes over 70 contributions written by expert international researchers addressing the central ideas through which human geographers understand and shape their subject. It maps out the big, foundational ideas that have shaped the discipline past and present; explores key research themes being pursued in human geography's various sub-disciplines; and identifies emerging collaborations between human geography and other disciplines in the areas of technology, justice and environment. This comprehensive, stimulating and cutting-edge introduction to the field is richly illustrated throughout with full colour figures, maps and photos.

The book is designed especially for students new to university degree courses in human geography across the world and is an essential reference for undergraduate students on courses related to society, place and culture.

Kelly Dombroski is a Rutherford Discovery Fellow and Associate Professor in the School of People, Environment and Planning at Te Kunenga ki Pūrehuroa | Massey University, Aotearoa New Zealand.

Mark Goodwin is Emeritus Professor of Human Geography at the University of Exeter, UK.

Junxi Qian is Associate Professor in the Department of Geography, The University of Hong Kong, Hong Kong SAR.

Andrew Williams is Senior Lecturer in Human Geography at Cardiff University, Wales.

Paul Cloke was Emeritus Professor of Human Geography at the University of Exeter, UK.

4th Edition

INTRODUCING HUMAN GEOGRAPHIES

EDITED BY KELLY DOMBROSKI, MARK GOODWIN, JUNXI QIAN, ANDREW WILLIAMS AND PAUL CLOKE

Routledge
Taylor & Francis Group

LONDON AND NEW YORK

Designed cover image: © Inge Flinte

Fourth edition published 2024
by Routledge
4 Park Square, Milton Park, Abingdon, Oxon, OX14 4RN

and by Routledge
605 Third Avenue, New York, NY 10158

Routledge is an imprint of the Taylor & Francis Group, an informa business

First edition published by Hodder Arnold 1999
Second edition published by Hodder Arnold 2005
Third edition published by Routledge 2014

British Library Cataloguing-in-Publication Data
A catalogue record for this book is available from the British Library

Library of Congress Cataloging-in-Publication Data
Names: Dombroski, Kelly, editor. | Goodwin, Mark, editor. |
Qian, Junxi, editor. | Williams, Andrew, editor. | Cloke, Paul J., editor.
Title: Introducing human geographies / Edited by Kelly Dombroski,
Mark Goodwin, Junxi Qian, Andrew Williams, and Paul Cloke.
Description: Fourth edition. | Abingdon, Oxon ; New York, NY :
Routledge, 2024. | Includes bibliographical references and index.
Identifiers: LCCN 2023042054 (print) | LCCN 2023042055 (ebook) |
ISBN 9780367211752 (hardback) | ISBN 9780367211769 (paperback) |
ISBN 9780429265853 (ebook)
Subjects: LCSH: Human geography.
Classification: LCC GF41 .I56 2024 (print) |
LCC GF41 (ebook) | DDC 304.2--dc23/eng/20230912
LC record available at https://lccn.loc.gov/2023042054
LC ebook record available at https://lccn.loc.gov/2023042055

ISBN: 978-0-367-21175-2 (hbk)
ISBN: 978-0-367-21176-9 (pbk)
ISBN: 978-0-429-26585-3 (ebk)

DOI: 10.4324/9780429265853

Access the Instructor and Student Resources at www.routledge.com/cw/dombroski

Typeset in Stone Serif, Avenir and Rockwell
by KnowledgeWorks Global Ltd.

Printed and bound in Great Britain by Bell & Bain Ltd, Glasgow

For Paul Cloke

Contents

Figures

Tables

Contributors

Editors

Paul Cloke was Emeritus Professor of Human Geography at the University of Exeter, UK.

Kelly Dombroski is a Rutherford Discovery Fellow and Associate Professor in the School of People, Environment and Planning at Te Kunenga ki Pūrehuroa | Massey University, Aotearoa New Zealand.

Mark Goodwin is Emeritus Professor of Human Geography at the University of Exeter, UK.

Junxi Qian is Associate Professor in the Department of Geography, The University of Hong Kong, Hong Kong SAR.

Andrew Williams is Senior Lecturer in Human Geography at Cardiff University, Wales.

Contributors

Benjamin Adams is Associate Professor of Computer Science at the University of Canterbury, Aotearoa New Zealand.

Peter Adey is Professor in Human Geography at Royal Holloway, University of London, UK.

Ning An is Associate Professor in Political Geography and Cultural Geography at South China Normal University, China.

Ben Anderson is Professor of Human Geography at Durham University, UK.

Rachel Bayer is a PhD Researcher studying asexual geographies at University College Dublin, Éire/Ireland.

Franz Bernhardt is a Postdoctoral Researcher in the Department of Culture and Learning at Aalborg University, Denmark.

Joe Blakey is Lecturer in Human Geography at the University of Manchester, UK.

Carl Bonner-Thompson is an Assistant Professor of Urban Injustice in the Department of Human Geography and Spatial Planning at Utrecht University, the Netherlands.

Kath Browne is a Professor in the School of Geography at University College Dublin, Éire/Ireland.

Laklak Burarrwanga is Elder for the Datiwuy people and a caretaker for the Gumatj clan and is an Honorary Associate of Geography and Planning at Macquarie University.

Jenny Cameron is co-chair of the Community Economies Institute.

Aline Carrara is an independent scholar and activist for social and environmental justice.

Noel Castree is a Professor of Geography at the University of Manchester, and Professor of Society & Environment at the University of Technology, Sydney.

Ritodhi Chakraborty is a Lecturer in the Department of Environmental Management at Lincoln University, Aotearoa New Zealand.

T.C. Chang is Associate Professor of Geography at the National University of Singapore.

David Conradson is Professor of Human Geography at the University of Canterbury, Aotearoa New Zealand.

Lara Daley is a Research Fellow in Geography and Environmental Studies at the University of Newcastle, Australia.

Jessica Dempsey is Associate Professor and Associate Head of Undergraduate Program in the Department of Geography at the University of British Columbia, Canada.

Ben Derudder is a Research Professor of Urban Studies at KU Leuven, Belgium.

Luke Drake is Associate Professor in the Department of Geography and Environmental Studies at California State University, USA.

Bianca Elkington is General Manager Education and Employment for Te Rūnanga o Toa Rangatira, in Aotearoa New Zealand.

Kajsa Ellegård is Professor emerita in Technology and Social Change, Department of Thematic Studies, Linköping University, Sweden.

Sara Fregonese is Associate Professor of Political Geography at the University of Birmingham, UK.

Banbapuy Ganambarr is from the clan Gapiny and her moiety is Dhuwa, teaches at Yirrkala School and is an Honorary Associate of Geography and Planning at Macquarie University in Australia.

Ritjilili Ganambarr is Elder for the Datiwuy people and a caretaker for the Gumatj clan and is an Honorary Associate of Geography and Planning at Macquarie University in Australia.

Merrkiyawuy Ganambarr-Stubbs is a proud Yolŋu woman and leader from northeast Arnhem Land, Principal of Yirrkala Community School and is an Honorary Associate of Geography and Planning at Macquarie University in Australia.

Menelaos Gkartzios is Professor of Planning at the Izmir Institute of Technology in Turkey and Reader in Planning and Rural Development at Newcastle University in the UK.

Enrico Gualini is Professor of Planning Theory and Urban-Regional Policy Analysis, Technische Universität Berlin (Berlin University of Technology), Germany.

Prince K Guma is a Research Associate at the Urban Institute, University of Sheffield, UK.

Sophie Hadfield-Hill is Professor of Human Geography at the University of Birmingham, UK.

Rogério Haesbaert da Costa is Professor in the Department of Geography, Fluminense Federal University, Rio de Janeiro state, Brazil, and at the University of Buenos Aires, Argentina.

Sarah Hall is Professor of Economic Geography, University of Nottingham, UK, and Deputy Director of UK in a Changing Europe.

Sam Halvorsen is Reader in Human Geography in the School of Geography, Queen Mary University of London, UK.

Camilla Hawthorne is Associate Professor in the Department of Sociology at University of California, Santa Cruz, USA.

Kersty Hobson is Reader in Human Geography in the School of Geography and Planning, Cardiff University, Wales.

Paul Hodge is Senior Lecturer in the School of Environmental and Life Sciences (Geography and Environmental Studies), University of Newcastle, Australia.

Julian Holloway is a Senior Lecturer in Human Geography at Manchester Metropolitan University, UK.

Donna Houston is Professor of Geography and Planning at Macquarie University, Australia.

Gengzhi Huang is Professor of Human Geography in the School of Geography and Planning at Sun Yat-sen University, China.

Lynda Johnston is Professor of Geography and Assistant Vice-Chancellor Sustainability at the University of Waikato, Aotearoa New Zealand.

Rebecca Kiddle (Ngāti Porou and Ngāpuhi) is Director of Te Manawahoukura Centre of Rangahau (Research), Te Wānanga o Aotearoa, Aotearoa New Zealand.

Jana Kleibert is Professor of Economic and Social Geography at the University of Hamburg, Germany.

Elise Klein is Associate Professor of Public Policy in the Crawford School, Australian National University, Australia.

Regan Koch is Senior Lecturer in Human Geography and Director of the City Centre at Queen Mary University of London, UK.

Peter Kraftl is Professor of Human Geography at the University of Birmingham, UK.

Soren Larsen is Professor of Geography at the University of Missouri, USA.

Maggi W.H. Leung is Professor in the Department of Human Geography, Planning and International Development Studies, University of Amsterdam, the Netherlands.

Yurui Li is Professor of Human Geography and Rural Development at the Institute of Geographic Sciences and Natural Resources Research (IGSNRR), University of the Chinese Academy of Sciences, Beijing, China.

Chen Liu is an Associate Professor of Cultural Geography in the School of Geography and Planning, Sun Yat-sen University, China.

Kate Lloyd is Professor in Geography and Planning, School of Social Sciences at Macquarie University, Australia.

Julie MacLeavy is Professor of Economic Geography at the University of Bristol, UK.

Juliana Mansvelt is a Professor of Human Geography at Te Kunenga ki Pūrehuroa | Massey University, Aotearoa New Zealand.

Uncle Bud Marshall is a Waambung man of the Baga baga bari on Gumbaynggirr Country. He is a senior cultural advisor to Gumbaynggirr Jagun in Australia and co-leads Yandaarra, a research collaboration with the University of Newcastle on Gumbaynggirr Country.

Jon May is Professor of Geography, Queen Mary University of London, UK.

Djawundil Maymuru works for Bawaka Cultural Experiences and is Honorary Associate of Geography and Planning, Macquarie University, Australia.

Andrew McGregor is Associate Professor in Human Geography at Macquarie University, Australia.

Katharine McKinnon is Director of the Centre for Sustainable Communities at the University of Canberra, Australia, and a member of the Community Economies Institute.

Ocean Ripeka Mercier (Ngāti Porou) is an Associate Professor in Māori studies, Victoria University of Wellington, Aotearoa New Zealand.

Melissa Nursey-Bray is Professor in the School of Social Sciences at the University of Adelaide, Australia.

Emily O'Gorman is Associate Professor and Australian Research Council Future Fellow at Macquarie University, Australia.

Nelson Oppong is Lecturer in African Studies and International Development at the Centre of African Studies, University of Edinburgh, Scotland.

Rhacel Salazar Parreñas is the Doris Stevens Professor in Women's Studies and Professor of Sociology and Gender and Sexuality Studies at Princeton University, USA.

Meg Parsons is Associate Professor in Environment at the University of Auckland, Aotearoa New Zealand.

Joseph Pierce is Senior Lecturer of Human Geography, University of Aberdeen, Scotland.

Gabriel Popescu is Professor of Geography in the Department of Political Science at Indiana University South Bend, USA.

Emma R. Power is Associate Professor in Geography and Urban Studies in the School of Social Sciences at Western Sydney University, Australia.

Steven Ratuva is Distinguished Professor, Pro-Vice Chancellor Pacific and Director of the Macmillan Brown Centre for Pacific Studies at Te Whare Wānanga a Waitaha | University of Canterbury, in Aotearoa New Zealand.

Jennifer Robinson is Professor and Chair of Human Geography at University College London, UK.

Amanda Rogers is an Associate Professor in Human Geography at Swansea University, UK.

Michael (Mike) Dennis Ross (Tainui) is a Senior Lecturer in Te Kawa a Māui | The School of Māori Studies at Te Herenga Waka | Victoria University of Wellington, Aotearoa New Zealand.

Gianne Sheena Sabio is a graduate student in the Department of Sociology at the University of Southern California. She studies migration and medical sociology.

Chie Sakakibara is Associate Professor of Geography & the Environment and Native American & Indigenous Studies at Syracuse University, USA.

Joris Schapendonk is Associate Professor of Human Geography in Radboud University, the Netherlands.

Benedikt Schmid is Postdoctoral Researcher at the Institute of Environmental Social Sciences and Geography at the University of Freiburg, Germany.

Amba J. Sepie is Lecturer in Sociology, Anthropology and Human Services at Te Whare Wānanga o Waitaha | University of Canterbury, Aotearoa New Zealand.

Pasang Yangjee Sherpa is Assistant Professor of Lifeways in Indigenous Asia in the Department of Asian Studies and Critical Indigenous Studies at the University of British Columbia, Canada.

Paul Simpson is Associate Professor of Human Geography at the University of Plymouth.

Jennie Smeaton (Ngāti Toa Rangatira) is the Pou Rātonga/Chief Operating Officer of Te Runanga o Toa Rangatira, in Aotearoa New Zealand.

Aunty Shaa Smith is a Gumbaynggirr woman, artist, cultural facilitator, co-founder of Gumbaynggirr Jagun and leads Yandaarra, a research collaboration with the University of Newcastle on Gumbaynggirr Country.

Neeyan Smith is a Gumbaynggirr woman and co-founder of Gumbaynggirr Jagun and is project coordinator of Yandaarra, a research collaboration with the University of Newcastle on Gumbaynggirr Country.

Thomas S.J. Smith is a postdoctoral researcher in the Department of Geography at the Ludwig Maximilian University of Munich, Germany.

Angharad Closs Stephens is an Associate Professor in Human Geography at Swansea University, UK.

Sandie Suchet-Pearson is Professor in Geography and Planning and Australian Research Council Future Fellow in the School of Social Sciences at Macquarie University, Australia.

Juanita Sundberg is Associate Professor in the Department of Geography at the University of British Columbia, Canada.

Callum Sutherland is Lecturer in Human Geography at the School of Geographical & Earth Sciences, University of Glasgow, Scotland.

Amanda Thomas is a Pākehā/white researcher working as Senior Lecturer in Environmental Studies at Te Herenga Waka | Victoria University of Wellington, Aotearoa New Zealand.

Charlotte Veal is Lecturer in Landscape at Newcastle University, UK.

Suliasi Vunibola is Research Fellow in the Macmillan Brown Centre for Pacific Studies at Te Whare Wānanga o Waitaha | University of Canterbury, Aotearoa New Zealand.

Richard J. White is Reader in Human Geography at Sheffield Hallam University, UK.

Miriam J. Williams is a Senior Lecturer in Geography and Planning at Macquarie University, Australia.

Heather Winlow is a Senior Lecturer in Human Geography at Bath Spa University, UK.

Orlando Woods is an Associate Professor of Geography and Lee Kong Chian Fellow at the College of Integrative Studies, Singapore Management University.

Sarah Wright is a Professor of Geography and Development Studies and Australian Research Council Future Fellow at the University of Newcastle in Australia.

John Wylie is Professor of Cultural and Historical Geographies at the University of Bristol, UK.

J.J. Zhang is Assistant Professor in Human Geography at the National Institute of Education, Nanyang Technological University, Singapore.

Acknowledgements

A book this large and with this many contributors is clearly a team effort, but there are a few more people who require some special acknowledgement. Firstly and foremostly, we would like to acknowledge our students. Our geography students at Cardiff University, the University of Hong Kong, Massey University, the University of Canterbury and the University of Exeter have provided us with the impetus to better connect the world of geographical research with the world of geographical education. Their curiosity, questions, clarifications, conversations, emails and responses to our teaching work have enabled us to revise and update this fourth edition for contemporary times.

Secondly, we thank the team that have shepherded us through the entire process of producing this new edition. At Routledge, Andrew Mould regularly prompted us to think about a fourth edition, and the reviews he commissioned of the third edition guided us with the extensive revisions we undertook and, indeed, guided the make-up of the new editorial team. We are very grateful to him, as we are to Claire Maloney, also at Routledge, who piloted us through all the different stages of submission and helped get the book ready for production, and Kalie Hyatt at KnowledgeWorks Global Ltd, who steered the book through the production process itself. We also thank photographer Inge Flinte for sourcing and collating the final images and author information, and the Rutherford Discovery Fellowship of Te Aparangi Royal Society of New Zealand for the funding that enabled this, and Kelly Dombroski's time on the project.

Thirdly, we thank our contributors. We began working on this book a few months before the COVID-19 pandemic hit, and all of us faced many challenges getting this book together. Many of our contributors wrote their chapters while facing unprecedented online teaching loads. Others came in to fill in for authors who had to withdraw. We especially appreciate the care and attention to detail that the contributors brought to this project, and the many messages of encouragement we received from you all during these challenging times.

The most significant challenge we faced during the writing of the book was the sudden death of our friend, colleague and co-editor Paul Cloke. Paul was a mentor to us all, and he was the guiding light and inspiration behind this edition – as indeed he was for all the previous editions of the book. It was Paul who was determined to diversify the backgrounds of co-editors and authors to decentre and decolonise the production of geographical knowledge, who brought us all together for this revised edition, who led us through the process of developing the prospectus, and who chaired and organised our editorial meetings. He had high hopes for this revised version, and throughout his work on the book, he showed his customary care and consideration for the *Introducing Human Geographies* project.

Just before his death Paul was awarded the Victoria Medal by the Royal Geographical Society (with IBG), the UK's learned and professional body for geography. When Paul was interviewed by the RGS-IBG, he was asked what he considered his greatest achievement. After mentioning the founding of a journal, and some of his academic work, Paul also named the impact of this textbook, which as he said 'continues to encourage many new geography students around the world to develop their own critical scholarship'. While he was not able to be here to see the project coming to fruition, we know he would be happy that it did get there in the end, and we also know that the final version is full of his indomitable spirit and love for geography. We acknowledge Paul's good-humoured care and attention while he was working on the book, and we have missed him very much indeed over the last year. Paul was, and continues to be, an inspiration for young and old geographers alike, and we have dedicated the book to him.

On a personal note, we would like to thank those who have supported us (particularly given the many early mornings or late nights on international zoom calls): Viv Cloke, with Liz and Will; Travis, Imogen, Analiese, Emmaus and Casimir Dombroski; Anne Barlow and Rosa and Sylvie Goodlow; John, Lynda, Paul and Stephen Williams and Jen Clemence for looking after Andy when he was sick with preseptal cellulitis and facial palsy in Autumn 2022 (plus the doctors and nurses in Heath Hospital) and his colleagues in Cardiff and fellow co-editors who covered work on his phased return to work; Shenjing He, He Wang, Jin Zhu, Xingjian Liu and other friends, Yanheng Lu, Zuyi Lyu, Han Zhang and other students, for providing emotional support while Junxi was moored in Hong Kong and away from his family during the pandemic. They have all shared in this project and have all helped in so many ways to bring it to fruition.

Preface: A guide to introducing human geographies

Introducing Human Geographies is a 'travel guide' into the academic subject of human geography and the things that it studies. Now in an updated and much extended fourth edition, the book is designed especially for students new to university degree courses. In guiding you through the subject, *Introducing Human Geographies* maps out the big, foundational ideas that have shaped the discipline past and present; explores key research themes being pursued in human geography's various sub-disciplines; and identifies some emerging collaborations between human geography and other disciplines that are helping to shape the future horizons of the subject.

This fourth edition differs quite considerably from its predecessors and is centred on some core priorities. We have refreshed the coverage, making the book relevant to the contemporary nature and direction of human geography. Only ten authors from the third edition remain, because we have sought to incorporate significantly stronger representation of authors and editors from beyond UK and American universities. In addition to this we have broadened the content with significant additions to the text that are relevant to the Majority World, and we have introduced a completely new final section which provides forward-thinking ideas about how geographical knowledges can be 'put to work' collaboratively in pursuit of contemporary issues of ethical responsibility and transformation. But crucially we remain committed to the idea expressed by Paul Cloke that this book is designed to encourage you, as new geography students, to develop your own critical ideas about the discipline of human geography and its subject matter.

One way to make a start on this is for you to engage with research literatures through academic journals and books. This is an important part of degree level study, and there is a reason why in the UK we still refer to 'reading' for a degree. The debates going on within them are exciting, challenging us not only to think about new subjects but also to think in new ways. However, it can take some time to get to grips with that published research. It is huge and diverse. It is dynamic, so that as a new student you can feel like you are coming into conversations halfway through, trying to figure out what people are talking about, why they are interested in it, and how come they are so animated about things. Academic publications are also by and large addressed to other researchers, deploying what may feel like rather arcane vocabularies as communicational shorthand. So not only has the conversation already begun, but it can also sound like it is in a foreign language. The ethos of *Introducing Human Geographies* is to make that cutting edge of contemporary human geography accessible; to map out key areas of study and debate; to guide you on forays into its somewhat daunting collections of ideas and interests; and to help students such as yourself participate in its conversations.

The human geography you will be introduced into here feels very different to some of the popular images of the subject. It is not a dry compendium of facts about the world, such as countries and capital cities. Apologies in advance if this book is of limited help in getting the geography questions right in a quiz or television game show! Of course, knowing geographical facts and information is useful and important in all kinds of ways. But it is not enough. Human geography today casts information in the service of two larger goals. On the one hand, it seeks out the realities of people's lives, places and environments in all their complexity. Geography is a subject that lives outside the classroom, outside the statistical dataset or the abstract model, and it gains its strength from its encounters with what (somewhat comically) we academics have a tendency to call 'the world out there'. On the other hand, human geographers are also acutely aware that this worldly reality is not easy to discern. The nature of the world is not laid out before our eyes, waiting for us to venture out blinking from the dark lecture theatre or library so that we can 'see' it. 'Reality' only emerges through the carefully considered ways of thinking and investigating that we sometimes call 'theory'. As the contributions to this book show, human geography is characterised by a refusal to oppose 'reality' and 'theory', or to oppose worldly engagement with contemplative, creative thought. Both are needed if we are to describe, explain, understand, question and maybe even improve the world's human geographies. This book will introduce you to both.

We have used the metaphor of a travel guide to describe this book. Guidebooks are not designed to be read from front to back in one go. They set scenes, provide contexts, and then as a reader we dip into them, dependent on our interests and our travel schedules. This new edition of *Introducing Human Geographies* is the same. It is designed to accompany and guide you as you find your way around human geography. Exactly how you read it, which parts you spend most time in and so on, will depend on your own intellectual itinerary and your programme of studies. The format we have created for the book, with a large number of comparatively short chapters organised into parts and sections, supports that kind of tailored reading 'on the go'.

Structure of the book

Nonetheless, it may be helpful to explain the book's structure. The 73 chapters are organised into four parts – an Introductory section, followed by Foundations, Themes and Collaborations (see Figure 0.1). The two introductory chapters trace the evolution of human geography and set out a clear account of what it means to be 'doing' human geography at university level. The 11 chapters in Foundations give you the latest thinking on some of the 'big questions' that have long shaped the thinking of human geographers. In setting out our foundations we have eschewed two common approaches: on the one hand, a narrative or episodic history of the subject; and on the other, abstract summaries of key theoretical approaches or '-isms'. (Often these are offered in combination; a chronology of different theoretical schools, dated on the basis of when they became influential within human geography.) There are excellent books that adopt variants of such approaches (for example, Livingstone, 1992, Nayak and Jeffrey, 2011, Cresswell, 2013, Johnston and Sidaway, 2016) that we would encourage you to read, but for our purposes here we wanted to avoid a division of theoretical foundations from the relational geographies we live with every day. The foundations presented here therefore weave together conceptual ideas with examples and illustrations. This may mean that the chapters in this section will not match with particular, substantive lectures in a taught course and don't always exist as easily locatable debates in the discipline's journals. The topics discussed here crop up everywhere because in many ways they deal with some of the most important ideas to think about as a new human geography student. They are designed to provide a clear, contextualised focus on some (but not all) of the core foundational ideas that underpin many of the substantive human geography topics that are covered later in the book.

Those substantive areas of the subject are turned to directly in the next and largest part of the book, Themes. It has 48 chapters, divided into six sections, addressing major thematic 'sub-disciplines' of human geography: in alphabetical order, areal geographies, cultural geographies, economic geographies, environmental geographies, political geographies and social geographies. Each of these sections begins with a thematic overview chapter written by two of the editors, setting out both the key concerns of the sub-disciplinary field and how the following chapters engage with them. This part of the book provides you with thought-provoking arguments on the key issues currently being debated within sub-disciplines, as well as giving you a feel for the distinctive kind of human geography undertaken within each.

As we discuss further in Chapter 1, thematic sub-disciplines are one of the major ways in which teaching curricula are organised and research activity structured, to the extent that geographers are often labelled according to these specialisms (as economic geographers, political geographers, and so on). However, the world we live in is (unsurprisingly) resistant to these neat classifications. Economy and politics and **culture** and environment (and so on) all interweave with each other. You can't go out and find something that is purely 'economic' (or purely political, cultural or environmental). In fact, a lot of the most innovative work in human geography goes on in the border zones between these sub-disciplinary territories, and in the zones between geography and other disciplines. Accordingly, the final part of the book concentrates on these collaborations, especially those that are emerging between human geography and other disciplines or agendas in the search for ethical transformation and **ecological**, social and technical responsibility. This section of the book delves deeper into three particular areas of collaboration, which we contend are having profound impacts on the current directions of human geography – collaborations for the **Anthropocene,** collaborations with technology and collaborations with justice. These three areas are under intense scrutiny right now both within human geography and in society more generally. The period known as 'the Anthropocene' marks a historical epoch where much of human society is under threat due to the effects of modern industrialisation on the planet. We are seeing new ethically challenging technological advances, particularly in geospatial **big data, artificial intelligence** and internet connected objects and cities. And we are seeing continued battles for justice, particularly in the wake of momentous events in recent history highlighting the ongoing oppression brought by racism, sexism, homophobia and more. This final section seeks to highlight work where geographers are contributing to both 'understanding' and 'doing' in these areas.

Stylistically, while every chapter has its own authorial signature, all the contributions combine discussions of challenging ideas and issues with accessible presentation. Unfamiliar academic terminology is kept to a minimum, but where central to an argument and not explained fully at the time it is marked in bold type and defined in the glossary of terms. Chapters include periodic summaries of key points, enabling you to pull out the central lines of argument as you go through the chapter. Potential discussion points are given at the end of chapters, offering options for group debates or individual essay plan development. Generally, *Introducing Human Geographies* aims to make you think and to challenge you intellectually, but to do that through being lively and engaging. Scholarly knowledge doesn't have to be dry and self-obsessed. Our

Introduction

1. Understanding human geographies

2. Doing human geographies

Foundations

3. Scale 4. Time 5. Place 6. Landscape 7. More-than-human 8. More-than-representation 9. Majority and Minority Worlds 10. Indigeneity 11. Mobilities 12. Gender and sexuality 13. Ethnicity and race

Area geographies	Cultural geographies	Economic geographies	Environmental geographies	Political geographies	Social geographies
14. Knowing area geographies	22. Knowing cultural geographies	30. Knowing economies	39. Knowing environments	46. Knowing political geographies	54. Knowing social geographies
15. Urban theory	23. Imaginative geographies	31. Money and finance	40. Global and local environmental problems and activism	47. Territory	55. Social inequality
16. Global cities	24. Affect and emotion	32. Consumption	41. Climate change	48. Nationalism and nation-states	56. Stigma and exclusion
17. Comparative urban studies	25. Performance and the performing arts	33. Work	42. Sustainability	49. Colonisation and colonialism	57. Migration and diaspora
18. Rurality	26. Materialities	34. Informal economies	43. Nature culture	50. Borders	58. Identity and difference
19. Comparative ruralities	27. Travel and tourism	35. Economic globalisation	44. Political ecology	51. Critical geopolitics	59. Age and the geographies of childhood and youth
20. Region	28. Religion	36. Global economies of care	45. Rethinking environmental governance	52. Neoliberalism	60. Health and wellbeing
21. Lived regions	29. Spectral geography	37. New economic geographies of development		53. Activism and protest	61. Care and responsibility
		38. Innovation for the pluriverse			

Collaborations

62. Anthropocene collaborations 63. Environmental humanities 64. Postcapitalist geographies 65. Commons 66. Big data 67. Participatory cartographies for social change 68. Smart cities and everyday urbanism 69. Ordinary technologies of everyday life 70. Black geographies 71. Decolonisation 72. Queer geographies 73. Spiritual activism and postsecularity

Afterword: Going forward with human geography

Figure 0.1
A visualisation of the book structure

chapters are deliberately short and punchy, but there is guidance for how to develop and deepen your knowledge via suggested further readings included at the end of each chapter.

The mention of further readings marks an appropriate place for us to stop this preface. Like any guidebook, the intention of *Introducing Human Geographies* is to take you around the subject so you can experience it for yourself. We rarely read guidebooks without travelling; the book is a companion on a journey not a destination in and of itself. Likewise, you shouldn't read this book without moving on from it to experience more directly the areas of research and debate it guides you towards. Studying a subject means getting to know it, figuring out what you like about it and what you don't. In other words, see what happens when not only are you introduced to human geography but human geography is introduced to you. We hope that you will use this book as a guide both to reading about human geography and to doing it yourself by thinking geographically.

The editors, June 2023.

References

Cresswell, T. (2013). *Geographic Thought: A Critical Introduction*. Chichester: Wiley-Blackwell.

Johnston, R., and Sidaway, J. (2016). *Geography and Geographers: Anglo-American Human Geography Since 1945*. London: Routledge.

Livingstone, D. N. (1992). *The Geographical Tradition*. Oxford: Basil Blackwell.

Nayak, A., and Jeffrey, A. (2011). *Geographical Thought: An Introduction to Ideas in Human Geography*. Harlow: Pearson.

PART ONE

INTRODUCTION

1 Understanding human geographies

*Mark Goodwin, Kelly Dombroski,
Junxi Qian and Andrew Williams*

In the Preface we used the idea that this book can be seen as a 'travel guide' to the subject of human geography. In this opening chapter we set out the broad terrain the guide covers by introducing you to the contents of the subject and to its evolution. As you will have noticed, especially if you are reading (and carrying around…) the hard copy of the book, this fourth edition of *Introducing Human Geographies* has a lot in it. Its contents are diverse. But that is because the academic subject of human geography is itself diverse. We contend that this diversity and breadth is one of the attractions, and indeed one of the strengths, of the subject. How did this come to be the case, and how did human geography come to be the subject that it is today? Answering these questions lies at the core of this chapter, which does two main things. First, we focus on what unites this variety by addressing head on the question 'What is human geography?'. Second, we expand on the kinds of approaches and styles of thought that have shaped the subject as it has evolved across the years. Putting these two elements together should give you an understanding not just of what human geography is but also of how it is a subject that is actively made and shaped by those who practice and study it. We want to get away from the notion that there is a neat, delineated body of knowledge that is called human geography, which can be learnt by successive generations of students, and introduce the idea that human geography is constantly shaped and reshaped by new waves of ideas and knowledges, which are built on what has gone before. This is why this is the fourth edition of this book, and why each edition is different from the one before. This is also why human geography is such an exciting subject to study.

What is human geography?

A common exercise for an initial human geography tutorial or seminar is a request to mine a week's news coverage and to come back with an example of something that seems to you to be 'human geography'. Have a go at doing this now. Think about the last week's news. Draw up a shortlist of two or three stories that strike you as the kinds of things that human geographers would study or that you think are 'human geography'. Then reflect on how you decided on these and what you thought was 'geographical' about them. What does your selection tell you about what human geography means to you?

DOI: 10.4324/9780429265853-2

The word 'geography' can be traced back to ancient Greece over 2200 years ago. Specifically, it was Eratosthenes of Kyrene (ca. 288–205 BC), Librarian at Alexandria, who wrote the first scholarly treatise that established geography as an intellectual field, the three-volume *Geographika* (Roller, 2010). In Greek, geography means 'earth (*geo*) writing (*graphy*)'. Writing the earth was what geographers did two millennia ago, and it still describes what geographers do today. In all kinds of ways, it is a wonderful definition of the subject. It speaks to geography as a fundamental intellectual endeavour concerned with understanding the world in which we live and upon which our lives depend. It expresses how geography is all around us, a part of our everyday lives. It suggests that geography is not just confined to academic study but includes a host of more popular forms of knowledge through which we come to understand and describe our world. It also raises questions, in particular about breadth and coherence. To return to that exercise of reviewing the week's news for examples of human geography, if what we were looking for were cases of 'earth writing', then an awful lot of stuff could fit that brief in some way. Most of the news is about things happening on the Earth.

How do we deal with that breadth, with that seeming absence of specialisation in geography? We would suggest there are three sorts of responses: to recognise the underpinning intellectual commitments built into the very notion of geography; to embrace the diverse topics and events to which these relate; and to recognise the ways in which different areas of geography are defined and organised. Let us take these in turn.

First, then, we need to think a little more directly about the 'geo' in geo-graphy, about what we mean by the *earth* in earth writing. This word is not just a general designation of everything around us but signals two interconnected cores to human geography's interests (Cosgrove, 1994): what we might call an 'earthiness' and a 'worldliness'; or, to use more current academic vocabulary, the relations between society and nature and between society and **space** (see Figure 1.1). In terms of 'earthiness', the 'geo' in geography signifies 'the living planet Earth', the biophysical environments composed of land, sea, air, plants and animals that we live in and with. These are central concerns for geographers. The relations between human beings and the 'nature' which we are also part of have been a consistent preoccupation of human geography. There is a second meaning to 'geo' as well, though, that is equally central, one we use when we talk about 'the whole Earth' or 'the world'. Here, to write the Earth means to explore its extents, to describe its areas, places and people, and to consider how and why these may have distinctive qualities. Human geographers have long been fascinated with how various parts of the Earth's surface differ, with the relations between them, and with ways of knowing such things (such as mapping and exploring). Geography endeavours to know the world and its varied

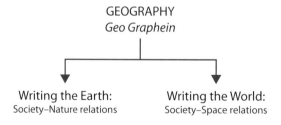

Figure 1.1
Human geography: Writing the earth and writing the world

features, both near to home and far away. The 'geo' in geography designates this commitment to world knowledge.

The precise forms such concerns with 'earth' and 'world' have taken in geography have varied over time of course, but both are central to the project of human geography today. Thus, human geographers lead debates over what are now often called the relations between society and nature, on environmental understandings and values, on the causes and responses to climate and environmental change, and they do so at a variety of scales, from global concerns with climate change to local debates over particular environments and landscapes. Human geographers are also concerned with how human lives, and our relations to nature, vary across the surface of the Earth. Everything happens somewhere and human geographers argue that this matters. A variety of central geographical notions reflect this: space, place, region, location, **territory**, distance, scale, for example, all try to express something about the 'where-ness' of things in the world. In contemporary parlance, human geographers emphasise the relations between society and space or what can be called **spatiality**. They argue both that human life is shaped by 'where it happens' and that 'where it happens' is socially shaped. The world and its differences are not innate; they are made. Human geographers study that making.

Our argument, then, is that human geography today still lives up to the original meaning in its name, revolving around both 'writing the earth' (in contemporary academic parlance the relations between society and nature) and 'writing the world' (in contemporary academic parlance the relations between society and space). However, and this is the second point we want to develop, these core concerns are developed through a vast range of substantive topics. In this book you will find subject matters that range from the contested meanings of development and innovation to how we organise care, from the international financial system to tourism, from the use of '**big data**' and **artificial intelligence** to urban **gentrification**, from global climate change to shopping. It is quite common to have mixed feelings about this range. Many people choose to study geography because of it, appreciating the wider understanding of human life such breadth seems to offer in comparison to the narrowness of many academic disciplines. In contrast, some react against it, worrying that geographers seem to be 'jacks of all trades' and 'masters of none'; complaining that human geography today seems to study things that 'aren't really geography'.

In our view, the diversity of human geography is a strength not a weakness, for at least two reasons. First, it reflects how geography existed well before, and exists well beyond, the kinds of specialisation promoted by academic institutions over the last century or so (Bonnett, 2008). Geography is notable for how it challenges the divisions that have come to characterise academic organisations, spanning as it does the natural sciences, the social sciences and the arts and humanities. The world doesn't present itself to us in those categories and geography resists being confined within them. As an academic discipline, geography has a healthy scepticism towards the disciplining of knowledge. Its diversity embodies that. Second, we would also encourage you to embrace the diversity of human geography in the spirit of being open to what might matter in the world. It is important that our thinking and our academic disciplines are not defined by inertia, pursuing topics simply because those are the subjects that we have traditionally pursued. Convention is not a good way to define and delimit what counts as human geography. You may find some of the subjects discussed in *Introducing Human Geographies* more familiar to you – for example, economic **globalisation** – some less so – the idea of 'emotional geographies', perhaps – but all of them represent how human geography today is pursuing its tasks of 'writing the Earth and the world'. Knowing the traditions of human geography is enormously valuable, but one of the crucial lessons we learn from that history is that what counts as human geography has always been subject both to change and to contestation (see Livingstone (1992) for an excellent, sustained analysis of this). For instance, shaped by the social worlds in which it was being produced, for much of its history, human geography largely ignored over half the world's human beings. It reduced human to man. Even well into the latter half of the twentieth century, economic geographers largely ignored the domestic work done by women at home; development geographers paid too little attention to the **gendered** nature of development problems and practice; issues and understandings that were seen as feminine were routinely trivialised and cast as less worthy of academic attention. Human geography was **masculinist** (Women and Geography Study Group (WGSG), 1997, Domosh and Seager, 2001). Countering this involved introducing into geography many novel topics and ideas. The issue for us, then, is not whether a topic is familiar as geography but whether attending to it is part of 'writing the earth' in ways that have value. It is also the case that for a long time, much of what counts as legitimate geographical knowledge was produced by universities and research institutes in the Minority World, and in the latter half of the nineteenth century, geography was seen as 'the science of **imperialism** par excellence' (Livingstone, 1992: 170). In this new edition we have sought to give much more space to Indigenous knowledges, and to viewpoints from the Majority World than in the previous three editions – again a reflection of how what counts as geography can be challenged and contested, and ultimately changed (with still further to go).

Generally, then, *Introducing Human Geographies* presents a diverse and dynamic subject and poses questions for you about what might count as valuable forms of geographical knowledge. There is, however, also a third response to the diversity inherent in geography's intellectual remit: to organise it into various 'subdisciplines' and research specialisms. The very idea of human geography already manifests this response, reflecting the widespread division between physical geography (placed in the natural sciences) and human geography (located in the social sciences and humanities). Contemporary research literatures and curricula take the process of dividing and specialising much further, organising human geography itself into the kind of subdisciplines and themes we present later in the book (cultural geographies, economic geographies, environmental geographies, social geographies, political geographies and so on). These each possess their own research literatures (via their specialist journals) and, indeed, their own introductory textbooks. Quite often these sub-disciplinary designations form the basis of how human geography is taught within universities. Subdisciplines are helpful in a number of ways. They map out the diversity of geography into recognisable areas of work. They promote the development of expertise. They focus on geographers' engagements with other academic disciplines (political geographers engaging with political science and international relations, cultural geographers with cultural studies and so on). But they can also be problematic. If one gets too hung-up on subdisciplines, one can lose the holism that is one of the strengths of the subject. The much discussed 'divide' between physical and human geography is a case in point, and it is notable that at a time when issues of sustainability and climate change are so pressing, research and education in these areas often crosses this divide. Furthermore, sub-disciplinary labels bear the imprint of university bureaucracy and job titling; we academics are very used to them, but outside of universities they don't much help people relate to the geography that we do. So, the useful foci provided by the various subdivisions of geography need to be accompanied by an ongoing commitment to seeing the distinctively geographical contribution that they make to understanding our worlds. At its best, Human Geography has a strong intellectual coherence, but applies it with an invigorating catholicism.

Summary

- Geography means 'earth writing'. As a subject with that aim, geography is notable for its wide-ranging concerns and interests.
- The first meaning of the 'geo' in geography is 'the earth'. The first of human geography's main intellectual contributions is to understand the relations between human beings and the natural world of which we are a part.
- The second meaning of the 'geo' in geography is 'the world'. The second of human geography's main intellectual contributions is to understand the world both near and far. More abstractly, this means recognising how all facets of human societies – the economic, the environmental, the political and so forth – are bound up with questions of 'spatiality'.
- These fundamental concerns of human geography are pursued across diverse and changing subject matters. We would encourage you to be open to that diversity and change; resist restricting your human geography to topics and approaches with which you are already familiar.

Approaching human geography today

Up to this point we have been outlining what human geography is about, emphasising its foci on both 'the earth' (human–nature relations) and 'the world' (society–space relations). Now we turn to how human geographers approach these issues and the kinds of knowledge that they try to create. Our interest is not in well-defined schools of thought or even intellectual paradigms but in the looser sensibilities that shape how human geography is done today.

At the outset, it is important to note that the approaches of human geography have changed over time and differ from place to place. Human geography in the 1920s or 1960s was different to human geography today. The approaches to human geography in Germany, Brazil or China are not identical to those in Britain. Even individual university departments can have their own distinctive research cultures, often dependent on the specialisms of the staff working there. In fact, the situation is more complex still; as you may find in your own courses, at any one time and in any one place there are likely to be different kinds of human geography being done. There is not a single agreed view on what kinds of knowledge human geography should produce. *Introducing Human Geographies* contains some of that variety; it does not present a single version of the subject. But it does reflect and support some recurrent emphases that, in our view, characterise much of human geography today. We see these as commitments to six kinds of knowledge: *description, experience, interpretation, explanation, critique* and *possibility* (see Table 1.1). Not all of these are equally endorsed by all human geographers, indeed they are often argued over; but they are commitments you will find frequently evidenced both in this book and in the course of your studies. Let us elaborate on each in turn.

First, then, human geography looks to describe the world. Sometimes dismissed with the epithet 'mere', in fact, description has a very special value. Geographical description is not synonymous with dry compendia of information about a region or place. It involves attending to the

Table 1.1 Approaches to human geography today: a schema

Type of knowledge	Approach	Illustrative examples
Description	Paying close attention to, and finding ways to represent, geographies that we normally struggle to perceive.	Statistical descriptions, GIS visualisations and maps; tracings of spatial networks and associations; detailed evocations of particular places.
Experience	Understanding geographies as part of human experience.	The emphasis is placed on the experiential knowledge generated by fieldwork; humanistic concerns with understanding other people's diverse experiences of the world.
Interpretation	Recognising and engaging with the meanings of the world's geographies.	Work focusing on geographical representations and on the discourses of which they are a part. Often associated with the so-called cultural turn.
Explanation	Explaining why the world's geographies exhibit the forms and processes that they do.	Geographical explanations range from spatial science's search for spatial laws to (more commonly today) socio-spatial analyses of causal processes.
Critique	Rigorously evaluating and judging the world's geographies, as well as one's own and others' understandings of them.	Critique can be understood as a broad stance to geographical knowledge. It has also come to be associated with bodies of work that explicitly designate themselves as forms of 'critical geography'.
Possibility	To set out how our geographies might be different.	Drawing on geographical knowledge to put forward different possibilities for organising society and economy, often working together with a range of partners from outside the academy.

world unusually carefully. The nature of that attention can vary. It might mean, for example, fashioning and mapping forms of statistical data (perhaps using **geographical information systems** [GIS]) that allow us to describe things that we can't fully see with our own eyes – spatial differences in wealth or access to services perhaps. It might involve tracing out the often hidden networks of connections linking people and places, as when human geographers 'follow' the things that people routinely consume (our food or clothes, for example) to see how they came to be, where they come from and what kinds of trade govern their movements (e.g. Cook, 2004). Or it might mean being peculiarly observant in person. Think, for example, about how we normally move around the world, head often down, taking our surroundings somewhat for granted. Now contrast that to a more geographical engagement with place, perhaps a public square, where we look to document the details of the built environment, its history, the people who are present and absent, the kinds of action going on. Here, to describe a place geographically is to bear witness to its material textures and the forms of life that unfold through it. Our argument, then, is that human geography is an attentive discipline. It describes in order to reveal what we might otherwise overlook and to bring into focus what we might otherwise only vaguely perceive. It crafts ways of presenting the fruits of this attention, using forms of description that range from maps to statistics, and from prose to drawings, photography and film/video-making.

Second, human geography also commits to understand the world experientially. In part we see this in the discipline's commitment to fieldwork. Geography places a value on trying to understand issues not just from afar but through actually being there, in a place, amongst the action, conversing with people, getting a feel for things. The status of this kind of first-hand field knowledge is philosophically complex, but human geography tends to view understanding gained only from more 'remote' sorts of sensing with some suspicion. It is not a subject that is comfortable with being confined to the lab or library. Important here too are the people-centred approaches trumpeted initially under the label **humanistic geography** (for exemplary early collections, see Ley and Samuels (1978) and Meinig (1979); for a more recent revisiting of such humanistic work, see Holloway and Hubbard (2000)). Humanistic geography emphasises engaging with people's real lives, their values and beliefs, their daily preoccupations, their hopes and dreams, their loves and hates, what they think about things, the ways they feel about and sense their surroundings. Human geographers are thus not only interested in experiencing places for themselves; they want to understand other people's geographical experiences and thoughts in all their variety.

A commitment to interpreting the meaningful nature of the world is apparent here too. Geographies are not just brute realities: it is fundamentally human to invest the world with meaning. We don't only sense the world; we make sense of it. Human geography is concerned with interpretation insofar as it recognises the importance of the meanings of things. Think, for example, about the interest geography has in 'the earth' and human–nature relations. The things we call 'natural', indeed the very notion of the 'natural', are deeply imbued with meanings. Reflect for a few seconds on geographical notions like 'wilderness' or 'rainforest' or 'the tropics'. These words are not narrowly factual; they come with a host of (often complex and even conflicting) meanings and connotations. The same is true of how we describe the world's different spaces. Consider what geographical designations such as 'urban', 'suburban' and 'rural' might mean to you and others; or the continents (Europe, Asia, Africa, Antarctica ...); or a seemingly simple geographical label like 'The West' or 'The Western World'. All these terms are, to use a colloquialism, 'heavily loaded'. Human geography's approaches here are informed by wider bodies of thought in the humanities on interpretation and meaning (with great names like 'hermeneutics', 'semiotics' and 'iconography'). They are also often identified with what has been called 'the cultural turn' taken within the discipline since the 1990s (Barnes and Duncan, 1992). Prominent is a focus on **representation**, with research teasing out the meanings given to geographies in forms both obviously imaginative (literature, the arts, film and television drama and so on) and less obviously so (maps, documentaries, news reports, policy documents etc.). Interpreting these representations is important because they are not just an imaginative gloss that we humans add to our worlds, a subjective filter that obscures objective reality; representations shape how we see things, think about them and act with and upon them. They partly make our worlds. They are part of reality. In academic terminology, by interpreting what things mean we engage with the **discourses** that produce the world as we know it. As an interpretive endeavour, human geography both looks to understand those discourses and to present other ways of seeing, describing and acting upon our geographies.

So far, we have outlined that when human geographers undertake their 'earth writing' (geo-graphy), they look to describe, experience and interpret. A fourth commitment has flickered in and out of these discussions: to explain. Human geography is concerned not only with what the geographies of the world are but also with how they came to be. The nature of geographical explanation has varied over time and is subject to much debate. Divergent views are underpinned by different understandings of both the world 'out there' and the sorts of knowledge required to grasp it. For some, human geography should be a **spatial science**, formulating and testing theories of spatial organisation, interaction and distribution in order to establish universal spatial laws about why geographical objects are located where they are and how they relate to each other. Emerging in the 1960s, spatial science distinguished itself from earlier regional geographies, criticising them for being overly descriptive and lacking the explanatory power of scientific analysis. However, other approaches in human geography resist the equation of explanation with spatial science. They are wary of its kind of 'social physics'. Historical geographers, for instance, emphasise how forms of historical narrative can have explanatory power; to put it crudely, a historical approach explains the world today by drawing on understandings of past events and processes. More generally, most human geography is wary of explaining things via reference only to spatial factors (what is called 'spatial reductionism'), emphasising instead the two-way relations between 'space and society'. Aspects of society – the modern **nation-state**, for example, or the **capitalist** economy – are seen both to shape the nature of space and themselves to have spatial dimensions. Thus, there are no universal spatial laws that can explain our geographies; any explanation must recognise the socially produced nature of spatiality. There is also a concern about seeking universal laws as explanations; instead, a range of theories – most visibly represented by an approach known as 'critical realism' (Sayer, 2010) – have sought to understand causality in relation both to more abstract powers and more concrete, contingent, contextual factors. As you have probably gathered by now, it is hard to do justice to these sorts of complex debates in a brief introduction (sorry!). But, in essence, our view is that human geography today widely exhibits a commitment to explain the geographical phenomena it studies but generally undertakes that explanation through nuanced accounts that weave together underlying tendencies/forces with more contextually specific factors.

Fifth, contemporary human geography is concerned with 'critique'. It is easy to misunderstand this word. In everyday speech, when we say someone is being critical what we often mean is that they are being negative or finding fault. But that is not what we have in mind here. True critical thought is as much about seeing strengths as weaknesses. Critique, then, means exercising judgement. For human geography, a commitment to critique means that the subject not only describes, experiences, interprets and explains but also rigorously evaluates the world's geographies. A general consequence of this commitment is that the 'rightness' of our answers to geographical questions is not given. There is room for debate and argument. Critique is not just a matter of expressing one's opinion, but its reasoned judgement involves values, beliefs, evidence and perspectives. For all of us, as students of human geography, there are not often agreed correct answers that we simply have to remember. Doing human geography involves developing rigorous analyses of issues, evaluating both information and arguments and thereby figuring out not only what the answers are but also what the most important questions might be. This means not taking things for granted, questioning the assumptions held by others and, crucially, ourselves. Critical thought – and this is a tricky balance – combines a determined, questioning scepticism with a profound openness to unfamiliar ideas and voices.

These general critical attitudes have shaped distinctive bodies of philosophy, theory and practice that take them forward. Within human geography, 'critical geography' has emerged as a designation that folds in earlier appeals to radicality – as seen in the foundation in the 1970s of the 'radical journal of geography', *Antipode* – and the 'dissident geographies' of **feminist**, **Marxist** and **postcolonial** writers (Blunt and Wills, 2000, Barnes and Sheppard, 2019). The words of *ACME*, an open access online journal of 'critical geography', give a sense of this; for this journal, critical analyses are understood 'to be part of the praxis of social and political change aimed at identifying and challenging systems of domination, oppression and exploitation, and dismantling the relations of power that sustain them' (ACME, 2023). A range of work discussed in this fourth edition of *Introducing Human Geographies* would fit that definition in some part, but **critical thinking** in the more general sense is not necessarily signed up to particular political colours. Critique can be taken as a more general stance, committed to questioning, reasoned judgement, and that stance can be usefully adopted within your own studies and writing of human geography.

Critique also points us to the final type of knowledge we can identify, that concerned with possibility and the hopeful search for possible better futures. Many human geographers look to move their work beyond critique, by explicitly putting forward alternatives to the current ways of doing things. This type of approach has a long history in the discipline, dating back to the **anarchist** work of Reclus and Kropotkin in the late nineteenth century. For Kropotkin, writing in 1885, geography 'must teach us, from our earliest childhood, that we are all brethren, whatever our nationality. In our times of wars, of national self-conceit, of national jealousies and hatreds ably nourished by people who pursue their own egoistic, personal or **class** interests, geography must be... a means of dissipating those prejudices and of creating other feelings more worthy of humanity' (Livingstone, 1992: 254). Writing this chapter some 140 years later, it is uncanny how the concerns of Kropotkin – wars, national self-conceit and national jealousies and hatreds – continue to be stoked by those who pursue their own 'egoistic, personal and class interests', and how the role of geography and geographers in helping to overcome these concerns and prejudices remains as pertinent as ever. In the intervening period, geographers of many theoretical persuasions have been involved in the search for alternatives to what has been labelled as 'status quo' geography (see Pickerill, 2019, for a review), and it could be argued that in the face of global threats such as climate change, environmental damage and biodiversity loss, not to mention continuing social and economic inequalities, the search for possible alternatives is more pressing than ever (Roelvink et al., 2015).

Writing a fuller history of human geography?

The outline we have given on the development of human geography as a discipline reflects the formal history of the subject as it has been conceived and practised in the universities and research centres of the Global North. Craggs and Neate (2019: 32) note how much of this formal history 'has meant the foregrounding of the experiences of Europe and the superpowers – and the geographies and geographers of these areas – over those of the majority world'. As part of the wider imperative we noted above to 'decolonise' the discipline, there have been growing calls for 'the broadening of disciplinary histories, which remain Anglo-American and exclusionary' (Craggs and Neate, 2020: 900), and for studies which address the multiple ways geographical research – past and present – is enmeshed in logics of **coloniality** (see Ferretti, 2020, for a review of work which has begun to do just this).

While drawing the work of Indigenous and non-white scholars into the stories of geography's past is a vital endeavour, Keighren (2020: 166) points out that 'just as we have a moral obligation to narrate plurality in geography's past, so we must encourage that plurality in the telling of our disciplinary present'. In this fourth edition, we have attempted to recognise this plurality by including the work of Indigenous and under-represented scholars, and by broadening the set of topics covered beyond those present in the third edition. In doing so, we have sought to avoid the risk identified by Essen et al. (2017: 386) when they stated that in seeking to decolonise geographical knowledges 'geographers run the risk of speaking not for but *instead of* those not only willing and able, but eager and equipped, to speak for themselves'. In this edition, many people 'speak for themselves' on topics such as indigeneity, **colonialism**, postcolonialism, **decolonisation**, Black geographies, the Global South and **more-than-human** geographies.

This exclusionary writing of history and production of knowledge is part of what Walter Mignolo has characterised as the 'colonial matrix of power' (see also Chapter 37). Describing the work of Anibal Quijano, Mignolo (2007; 156) talks about a 'colonial matrix of power', which includes the control of **subjectivity** and knowledge. Breaking with this 'colonial matrix of power' involves what decolonial theorists call analytic and political 'de-linking' from entrenched expressions of (racialised) institutional **power**. Such 'de-linking' attempts to create alternative social worlds not founded on colonial differentiations and hierarchies (Mignolo, 2007). Here we come back to the type of geographical knowledge that we termed 'possibility', through which geographers work with others to help produce different possibilities for organising societies and economies (Gibson-Graham, 2016, Gilmore, 2022).

Above, we have outlined various commitments that shape human geography today – to description, experience, interpretation, explanation, critique and possibility. Whilst keyed into wider debates over forms of knowledge and the interests they pursue, including postcolonial histories of the discipline, these six categories are, inevitably, something of a heuristic device. They are not exhaustive. Neither are they mutually exclusive; many kinds of geographical descriptions might also see themselves as interpreting and/or explaining, and vice versa, for example. But, with those caveats, we believe that this schema conveys some of the principal rationales for why human geography undertakes its 'earth writing' and a sense of what you can achieve by studying it. In the next chapter, we will now turn to discuss in a bit more detail just what the study of human geography at the university level entails.

Summary

- Human geography undertakes its 'earth writing' for a number of reasons. It is helpful to reflect on these reasons as you develop your own geographical imagination.
- We have suggested six undertakings that shape human geography today. We termed these: description, experience, interpretation, explanation, critique and possibility.
- This is not an exhaustive list of all the rationales that underpin human geography but one, some or all of these commitments shape a great deal of the scholarship that you will be introduced to in this book.

Discussion points

- Look at a newspaper from last week. Identify three stories that seem to you to address human geography topics. Explain your choices and why you think they are 'geographical'.
- What makes human geography a distinctive subject?
- 'Human geography is a down-to-earth subject concerned with facts not theories'. Discuss this assertion from a number of different perspectives.
- Why does human geography as a discipline show a commitment to six types of knowledges?

References

ACME (2023). *Homepage for ACME: An International E-Journal for Critical Geographers*. Available at https://acme-journal.org/index.php/acme (last accessed 6 June 2023).

Barnes, T., and Duncan, J. (eds.) (1992). *Writing Worlds: Discourse, Text and Metaphor in the Representation of Landscapes*. London: Routledge.

Barnes, T., and Sheppard, E. (eds.) (2019). *Spatial Histories of Radical Geography: North America and Beyond*. Chichester: Wiley.

Blunt, A., and Wills, J. (2000). *Dissident Geographies: An Introduction to Radical Ideas and Practice*. London: Longman.

Bonnett, A. (2008). *What Is Geography?* London: Sage.

Cook, I. (2004). Follow the thing: papaya. *Antipode* 36: 642–664.

Cosgrove, D. (1994). Contested global visions: one-world, whole-earth and the Apollo space photographs. *Annals of the Association of American Geographers* 84: 270–294.

Craggs, R., and Neate, H. (2019). Post-colonial careering and the discipline of geography: British geographers in Nigeria and the UK, 1945-1990. *Journal of Historical Geography* 66: 31–42.

Craggs, R., and Neate, H. (2020). What happens if we start from Nigeria? Diversifying histories of geography. *Annals of the American Association of Geographers* 110(3): 899–916.

Domosh, M., and Seager, J. (2001). *Putting Women in Place: Feminist Geographers Make Sense of the World*. New York: Guildford Press.

Essen, J., Noxolo, P., Baxter, R., Daley, P., and Byron, M. (2017). The 2017 RGS-IBG chair's theme: decolonising geographical knowledges or reproducing coloniality? *Area* 49(3): 384–388.

Ferretti, F. (2020). History and philosophy of geography I: Decolonising the discipline, diversifying archives and historicising radicalism. *Progress in Human Geography* 44(6): 1161–1171.

Gibson-Graham, J. K. (2016). 'Optimism', Place and the Possibility of Transformative Politics. In *The Palgrave Handbook of Gender and Development*, ed. W. Harcourt. Basingstoke: Palgrave Macmillan, 359–363.

Gilmore, R. W. (2022). *Abolition Geography: Essays Towards Liberation*. London: Verso Books.

Holloway, L. and Hubbard, P. (2000). *People and Place: The Extraordinary Geographies of Everyday Life*. London: Routledge.

Keighren, I. (2020). History and philosophy of geography III: the haunted, the reviled and the plural. *Progress in Human Geography* 44(1): 160–167.

Ley, D., and Samuels, H. (eds.) (1978). *Humanistic Geography: Prospects and Problems*. London: Croom Helm.

Livingstone, D. N. (1992). *The Geographical Tradition*. Oxford: Basil Blackwell.

Meinig, D. (ed.) (1979). *The Interpretation of Ordinary Landscapes*. Oxford and New York: Oxford University Press.

Mignolo, W. (2007). Coloniality of power and de-colonial thinking. *Cultural Studies* 21(2–3): 155–167.

Pickerill, J. (2019). Radical Geography. In *International Encyclopedia of Geography: People, the Earth, Environment and Technology*, eds. D. Richardson, N. Castree, M. F. Goodchild, A. Kobayashi, W. Liu, and R. A. Marston. https://doi.org/10.1002/9781118786352.wbieg0506.pub2

Roelvink, G., St. Martin, K., and Gibson-Graham, J. K. (2015). *Making Other Worlds Possible: Performing Diverse Economies*. Minneapolis, MN: University of Minnesota Press.

Roller, D. W. (ed.) (2010). *Eratosthenes' Geography*. Princeton, NJ: Princeton University Press.

Sayer, A. (2010). *Method in Social Science: A Realist Approach*. Second edition. London: Routledge.

Women and Geography Study Group (WGSG) (1997). *Feminist Geographies: Explorations in Diversity and Difference*. London: Longman.

Further reading

There are a number of other texts that fulfil different functions to this book but offer valuable complementary overviews and resources that help introduce human geography. These include the following:

Bonnett, A. (2008). *What Is Geography?* London: Sage.
In this book Alastair Bonnett develops his personal response to the question 'what is geography?'. His answer is thoughtful and thought-provoking, casting geography not as just another academic subject but as 'one of humanity's big ideas'. The book covers the two central foci identified in this chapter (what we called 'writing the earth and the world'); geographical interests in cities and mobilities; the doing of geography in forms of exploration, mapping, connection and engagement; and the institutionalisation of geography within and beyond universities.

Castree, N., Kitchin, R., and Rogers, A. (2013). *A Dictionary of Human Geography*. Oxford: Oxford University Press.
A concise offer of over 2000 accessible definitions of human geography terms. From basic terms and concepts to biographical entries, acronyms, organisations, and major periods and schools in the history of human geography.

Cresswell, T. (2013). *Geographic Thought: A Critical Introduction*. Chichester: John Wiley & Sons.
An accessible and engaging journey through the history of geographical theory to present day. An excellent introduction for students new to Marxist, feminist, postmodern, poststructural, relational and more-than-human geographies.

Gregory, D., Johnston, R. J., Pratt, G., Watts, M. J., and Whatmore, S. (eds.) (2009). *The Dictionary of Human Geography* (5th edn.). Chichester: Wiley-Blackwell.
This dictionary has concise but comprehensive definitions and explanations relevant to almost every aspect of human geography. As a reference tool it is invaluable and has no better. Human geography can be hard to engage with because of the density of its specialist terms. This is a book you will be able to use throughout your time studying human geography as you look to master that specialist vocabulary.

Livingstone, D. (1992). *The Geographical Tradition*. Oxford: Blackwell.
A scholarly rendition of the history of human geography, a topic we pay comparatively little attention to in this book. Livingstone concentrates on the longer term history of the subject rather than on its recent developments. Throughout, one gets fascinating insights into how the concerns of human geographers have run in parallel with wider social currents.

Doing human geographies

Kelly Dombroski, Mark Goodwin,
Junxi Qian and Andrew Williams

Introduction

Geography remains a subject deeply engaged with the world around us. It uses theory and thinks deeply about the nature of the world, but it still connects back to *doing* something – whether it is *doing* the work of thinking geographically, *doing* critical analysis or reflection or *doing* fieldwork and writing in geographical study. In writing the world and writing the Earth (see Chapter 1), human geographers combine *understanding* and *doing* in multifaceted and mutually reinforcing ways. In many ways, understanding and doing are deeply interwoven: for it is in the doing of geography that further understanding comes, and it is in seeking understanding that we might do things differently. We each approach geography from a different standpoint, and in this chapter, we invite you to bring yourself into geography – your place in the world, your history and ancestry, your experiences and blind spots. What will doing geography look like for you, and how can this book enable and support your geography journey? Take some time to reflect on this using the exercise in Box 2.1.

Like you, the editors of this book are all situated in different places and with different bodies, experiences and relationships. Of course, this affects the way we write this book, and it will no doubt affect how it connects (or not) with yourself, as reader. I (Kelly) am in Aotearoa New Zealand, in a half-empty university hollowed out by shifts in student learning preference following the COVID-19 pandemic. Most of the students in my school now study online and by distance, even though this university was originally founded as an agricultural university focused on teaching practical skills alongside academic subjects. Many staff also work from home. I prefer to cycle the 5 or 6 kilometres out of town to the university alongside a river bike path. Where am I? I'm writing in a south-facing office in a refurbished room in a tower built to 'Brutalist' aesthetics of the 1960s (see Figure 2.1). In the southern hemisphere, the south side of the building gets little sun. But if it gets warm enough to open the window, I can hear native Tui birds in the nearby bush (NZ English for 'forest'), and the loud hum of a rooftop air-conditioning unit heating a different building. I can hear my colleague on a zoom meeting through the wall, and the conversation of Pacific Island students and staff in the 'talanoa' discussion space next door.

That's where I am. But where have I come from? In many formal settings in Aotearoa New Zealand, we now introduce ourselves using the Māori custom of *pepeha*, short introductions

DOI: 10.4324/9780429265853-3

BOX 2.1
BRINGING YOURSELF TO GEOGRAPHY

Where are you right now? Look around you and think about how where you are is both similar and different from others who have come before you or who are studying alongside you. Are you working from home or from a university or in a café or outdoors – and how has this changed in recent years? Are you studying online, reading this book online, linked to an online learning system? Or have you picked up the large volume in the library or bookstore – and how does this compare to how your lecturers studied or how people study in other parts of the world? Are you in a cold or warm climate, and how has it changed? What noises can you hear, and which of these annoy or distract you, and which ones are more comforting? What can you see around you, and what does it represent of your life? Who is near you and who do you wish was near you? What does your body feel like right now, and how does that compare to other times? Take a deep breath, and let it out – what thoughts come to mind and how do these relate (or not!) to what you are reading? How might where you are, and the context you're in, help to shape your approach to the study of geography?

situating ourselves in the landscape and with our ancestors. My pepeha changes depending on what I want to emphasise in each situation, but the basics are the same: I grew up in view of the Remutaka ranges and Ruamāhanga River in south Wairarapa, a rural area of New Zealand in the traditional lands of Ngāti Kahungungu and Rangitāne peoples. My ancestors come from Scotland, England, Ireland, Germany, some as many as nine generations ago. I am a person here by the Treaty of Waitangi, Te Tiriti, our founding document signed between the British Crown and the iwi or tribes of the islands of Aotearoa. My surname is Polish – I adopted it when I married my husband who descends from Polish immigrants.

Figure 2.1
Winter view from Kelly's third story office in Palmerston North, New Zealand

Source: Photo credit: Kelly Dombroski

This way of introducing oneself is inherently geographical: it tells a story of the relationship between people and place, between the landscape and the humans who relate to it, between different societies and the places and histories they have emerged from. The purpose of such introductions is to build connection – to emplace those we are meeting with, and to work out what ancestral or wider relationship we might have with them already, in order to build on that. Even within our editorial team, we have built such connections: as a team we were brought together by Professor Paul Cloke, who organised this fourth edition in response to a comprehensive review of the previous editions. Our cross-cutting relationships with Paul, the different places we connected with him and each other are not peripheral to a book like this but central to it. It is how we built trust and worked together over three years, through a global pandemic and, sadly, through Paul's sudden death in May 2022.

Our relationships also extend back to our ancestors and places of origin: Junxi is a Mainland Chinese man living in Hong Kong, where the relationship with Britain was one of **colonialism**, framing the identity of those from Hong Kong. Andy grew up in Swansea and now lives and works in Cardiff, Wales, a country again with a complex history – of cultural violence, underdevelopment and resource extraction at the hands of its bigger neighbour and as a perpetrator and beneficiary of Empire itself (as he explains in the section introduction to social geography) – yet with the shared privileges that **cisgendered** male whiteness often brings. Mark also has the privileges of whiteness, and maleness but was born on a farm and grew up in a small village in rural Norfolk, geographically, socially and economically distant from the centres of metropolitan power in the UK. We have studied geography in different parts of the world: Kelly in Australia, China and southeast Asia as well as her home country of NZ; Junxi studied urban and regional planning in China and geography in Scotland, UK, and researched widely across different provinces in Mainland China, and to a lesser extent, Hong Kong; both Andy and Mark have studied in England and worked in England and Wales, and Mark has researched in Sweden. Although we did our best to bring together authors from all over the world, there is no doubt that all these things, and more, have affected the way we have put this book together, and the way we have engaged with one another, the subject of human geography, and you, the reader.

In many of the academic settings we have worked in (and perhaps you the reader have found yourself in), bringing this full self and its pre-existing connections into our work is not always accepted, despite the ubiquity of such relational networks and their effect on academic texts such as this. Clearly, there are dangers to leaning too fully into our idiosyncratic histories and positionalities: our awareness of our own positionalities could be understood as pointless navel gazing unless it is also accompanied by critical analysis. Here we come up against two key ideas important to the 'doing' of human geography: **positionality** and **critical thinking**. In what follows we first reflect on these two core ideas, then move on to think about how they affect the ways we approach doing human geography with others, and what comes beyond geography.

Summary

- Doing human geography requires us to recognise how place, culture and society shape us and therefore the way we approach a topic or task.

Positionality and critical thinking in doing geography

Positionality refers to how your identity and experiences shape your perspective and position in the world. It's like looking at the world through your own unique lens that is shaped by your background, beliefs, **culture** and experiences. Throughout your studies in geography and related subjects, you will be exposed to different perspectives and viewpoints. These perspectives can be influenced by various factors, such as the author's background, the historical context or the cultural biases of the time. Your own positionality can also impact how you interpret and analyse the information you're studying. **Feminist** scholars have contributed significantly to the concept of positionality, emphasising how one's social location (including **gender**, **race**, **class** and other intersecting identities) influences our perspectives and experiences. Feminist scholars like Donna Haraway (Haraway, 1988), bell hooks (hooks, 1981) and Kimberlé Crenshaw (Crenshaw, 1989), among others, have discussed the importance of positionality in understanding power dynamics, social inequality and the complexities of identity. Crenshaw also introduced the concept of **intersectionality**, which refers to the compounding effects of overlapping identities on one's life experience – for example, being a Black lesbian woman in America will entail a very different life experience from being a white woman or a Black man or a gay person there or elsewhere. Positionality and intersectionality affect both how we view things in the world and relate to it but also how we are viewed and thus acted upon and experience the world.

In this book, our positionalities as editors have shaped what we chose to include and what we chose to excise from the text. Although it is a long book, we still had to leave a lot out. We all had our own preferences and interests and different political and social standpoints from which we were thinking. To help us step outside of our own positionality and think more about those of you who will use the book, we started by considering feedback from reviews of previous editions of the book. These reviews helped Paul and Mark put together the new editorial team to include people from different parts of the world and with different life experiences in order to address some of the blind spots that the previous editions had not been able to overcome. Yet there is no doubt that we will have introduced other blind spots! The reviews also helped us understand what kinds of blind spots we should be wary of and give us confidence in changing the book quite radically based on the feedback from readers and users of the text. We also had our own personal connections and academic standing that shaped who would accept our invitations to participate in this project. On top of that, we worked on this book during some of the most difficult times of the COVID-19 pandemic, and this affected many of our contributors, some of whom could not complete their chapters due to the ongoing effects of long Covid or changes to their work and home lives. We are very grateful to those who have stepped in at later moments in the project, but again, these are more likely to be people we know and are even more shaped by our positionality and relationships.

Why is all this important? By being aware of our and your positionalities, you can critically evaluate the information you're learning and recognise potential biases or limitations. Our discussion of positionality is meant to help you approach your studies with a more open mind and develop a nuanced understanding of the subject matter. It helps you to bring your own full self to your studies and recognise what you have to offer, and what your blind spots might be. You'll also be better equipped to recognise diverse perspectives and appreciate the complexity of different viewpoints. As we wrote this book, we tried to imagine you the reader: are you a first-year student, fresh out of secondary school and embarking on a degree majoring in geography? That is the usual audience imagined for a textbook such as this, most likely with some unspoken stereotypes – perhaps as white, cisgendered, in the UK? But we know that this is not the only or even the main audience. We have also therefore imagined students in other parts of the world and of other ages and experiences and ethnicities. The study of geography varies considerably between different country contexts. The weight given to particular topics and approaches, the relationships between different subdisciplines will take different meanings based on where you live.

We have tried to think about all of you as we have developed this text, and we hope too, that you will think about each other. How is your experience of the environment different from someone in a different hemisphere or continent from you? How do global political geographies affect what you study and how it is funded? What difference does it make studying in a place with state-funded education and a place with state austerity or with a dominance of private universities? What kinds of resources do other students have in different parts of the world and how does that differ from where you live? What kind of worldview or belief system are you a part of and how does that compare to elsewhere and other people? We would love to hear more about your stories of studying geography, to help us think about our audience further, to help us critically evaluate our next edition.

Critical thinking is the second key concept in doing human geographies. The whole point of thinking about positionality is to enable us to think critically about our own perspective on the world and that of others. Critical thinking is a skill you will no doubt be working on throughout your university degree. It is an open and curious approach to thinking, bringing a degree of scepticism to any topic, questioning the underlying assumptions and the logical coherence of any argument or framework. Critical thinking will be informed by theory as well as informing theory. In human geography, critical thinking might mean bringing critical perspectives emerging from positionalities on to the subject at hand: for example, the healthcare system of a particular place. Critical thinking drawing on feminist theory might ask questions about whether women's health issues are given the same weighting as those of men in the training of doctors in that place. Critical thinking drawing on social justice thinking might ask whether the ethnic demographics of doctors matches the ethnic demographics of the population they serve, and what effects this might have on healthcare quality. Critical thinking drawing on critical GIS (**geographic information systems**) might map out key health providers alongside income level, average age, bus routes and school and rest-home locations to think critically about which populations are better serviced by accessible health care (see also Box 2.2). Critical thinkers will then test and adjust their theories, including theories of change, based on what information they find.

Critical thinking can be uncomfortable. As different issues are weighted with different importance to different people, things can get heated. As editors, we had moments of discomfort in putting this book together, many of which we learned from. In an early outline, we had a section on 'Indigenous geographies' at the end of the book, in the section on collaborations with justice. We meant to indicate that this was an important emerging area of global research. But when we invited an Indigenous author to contribute to that section, she applied critical thinking to our table of contents – why wasn't the concept of Indigeneity itself a foundational concept rather than an emerging one? Hadn't geographers been engaging with this topic in different ways for a very long time? We took that opportunity to reflect on our assumptions, as a group of non-Indigenous co-editors, and invite others' perspectives on the matter too. This resulted in a change in the book. Sometimes when we are challenged in our thinking, we might feel uncomfortable and ashamed or angry and misunderstood. This is where critical thinking intersects with positionality, but it also intersects with compassion and empathy. The best critical thinkers are those who can step outside their own interests and think clearly and critically about social structures, places, behaviours, texts, landscapes, concepts and more with other people, beings and places in mind. As you work through this book, you will come across many fine examples of critical thinking from the authors who have contributed. What can you do to learn not just the content from these texts, but the skill of critical thinking?

There are three important aspects to critical thinking here that will help. Firstly, critical thinking involves analysis and evaluation of arguments – are the arguments presented consistent, coherent and logical? Or do they demonstrate biases, fallacies and inconsistencies? Secondly, critical thinking involves examining evidence. Do the arguments presented in the chapters use evidence to make their points? And is the evidence reliable? How can you tell? Reliable evidence is usually evidence that has gone through some form of quality control, such as examination, editorial feedback or peer review – a process where research is examined by another expert in the area, often 'double blind' (neither the reviewer nor the writer knows the identity of the other). The reviewers will highlight problems with the methodology of the study or the logic and accuracy of the work – but you must also think critically about these things as you read. Thirdly, critical thinking involves maintaining a stance of open-mindedness and receptivity to new ideas. It involves being willing to consider different perspectives and be willing to change your assumptions and preconceived ideas about the world. None of these things are easy to do, and it takes practice. We often take short cuts in critical thinking: aligning ourselves with a certain **ideological** standpoint or thinker rather than engaging in the hard work of thinking critically for ourselves. But critical thinking cannot just be the mechanical application of another person's ideas. It must involve evaluating the reliability and validity of evidence, considering context and complexity and being aware of potential ethical implications as well. Critical thinkers think *with* theory, using it to explore perspectives and ideas (see Box 2.2). Critical thinkers do not live in a world by themselves but with others – as we will discuss next.

BOX 2.2
DOING THEORY IN AND WITH GEOGRAPHY

Theory is inescapable. We all have a framework through which we understand and analyse the world. Theory can be an explanation of a phenomenon. It is important for sharpening analysis, addressing shortcomings and blind spots, questioning assumptions and connecting disparate entities. One of the big steps from school to university level study of human geography is the ability to synthesise and evaluate different theoretical perspectives. At first, it might feel like learning a new language ('*Geog-ish*') and can feel detached from your real interests. What's the point?

Let us take an example – homelessness – to illustrate how and why geographers engage with different theoretical perspectives to reveal different aspects of the injustice of homelessness. A Radical/**Marxist** perspective, for instance, might focus on cycles of investment and disinvestment that lead to **gentrification** and unaffordable housing; the development of vastly polarised global cities and anti-homelessness by-laws in public spaces to sanitise and beautify urban space to successfully attract middle-class consumers and footloose global capital; or the ways housing vulnerability is built into **capitalist** systems of housing and labour (see Smith, 1996 and Chapter 56).

Anarchist perspectives might focus on the ways people self-organise to provide mutual aid, shelter or build alternative housing projects that deliberately eschew the corporatisation of the nonprofit sector (Jensen, 2018). This might include a focus on community self-determination and survival (Heynen, 2010, Giles, 2021) or the ways homeless people organise themselves in different places across the world to demand justice (Mould et al., 2022).

Meanwhile, feminist, and queer, geographies might highlight the overlooked gendered experiences of homelessness and the different social identities people enact and negotiate in everyday life. Analysis might turn to how senses of 'home' are constructed, fluid and compromised (see Little, 2017, on home, rurality and domestic violence) or draw on analysis of intersectionality to highlight the distinct nexus of racialisation and hetero- and cis-normativity in shaping **embodiment** and housing pathways (see England, 2022 on trans people's experiences of homelessness).

Seen through the lens of **Critical Race Theory** and Black geographies (Hawthorne, 2019), attention might turn to the historic and contemporary causes of racial disparities in homelessness (Fowle, 2022) including its connections to racialised economic dispossession and violence – from slavery, redlining and segregation, home foreclosure, to the disproportionate criminalisation, surveillance and imprisonment of racialised populations (Gilmore, 2007). Emphasis is given to how communities find ways of resisting and exposing capitalist logics of carcerality, white supremacy and housing precarity (Vilenica et al., 2022) and foreground ways in which Black- and Indigenous-led movements offer routes towards housing justice and the **decolonisation** of land (Ramírez, 2020).

Similarly, a **postcolonial** lens might help us focus in on how colonial thinking – past and present – shapes homelessness management in different places across the world, especially with regard to racialised constructions of poverty, citizenship and borders that shape what support is available, if any (see Chapters 50 and 55). You could take a historical perspective to analyse how colonial authorities classified and governed 'vagrant' populations; the use of disciplinary welfare apparatus as a means of cementing settler colonial power (Chapter 49); or follow the flows of money, ideas and people – and relations of extraction – that gave rise to the British Welfare State and other charitable **infrastructures** across the world (Midgley and Piachaud, 2011, Bhambra, 2022).

From this example, we can get a sense of how theory can illuminate – and conceal – different geographies of homelessness. But why not do this exercise yourself? When overwhelmed with abstract theory, pick something you deeply care about (*angerdd* in Welsh) – be it climate change, ecological destruction, Indigenous rights, **uneven development**, women's health – and use theory as a kaleidoscope to reveal different worlds.

Summary

- Positionality and critical thinking are two important concepts in doing human geography.
- Geographers use theory to help them recognise positionality and do critical thinking.

Doing geography with others

Geography is a collaborative discipline that has multiple connections to other disciplines. A 'discipline' in an academic context means an area of study, research and teaching, usually including a shared area or broad topic of study and shared methodologies of doing research. It is also possible to think about a discipline as a practice, using the word in the same way as we might use it to say the 'spiritual discipline' of meditation or prayer, or the 'sporting discipline' of an athlete. In this usage, discipline indicates training and returning one's attention to the same thing over and over again. Just as the meditator might be distracted and look elsewhere but then return their attention to their practice, a geographer might range broadly across many ideas and traditions of thinking but return their practice to the core concerns of people and place, humans and environment. But many researchers work across a range of fields and in and between disciplines, including geographers.

As a student, this might mean that your geography classes cover some of the same material or ideas as your classes in environmental science, anthropology, politics, psychology, development studies, sociology, philosophy, literature and many other disciplines. You might note some differences in approaches between these disciplines. One thing that many geographers have noted over the years is that geography does not have a 'core canon' of authors that most students are trained in, like some other disciplines might. A lot of geographers read outside the discipline, as such trends and 'turns' in other disciplines influence geography. But there are also geographers who have made significant contributions to fields outside of geography, for example, some of the scholars featured in the book *Key Thinkers on Space and Place* (Hubbard and Kitchin, 2010). What distinguishes geographers, in many ways, is an acute attention to place, spatial variation and patterns, and the particularities of place.

What does this mean for you, as you 'do geography'? When you are assigned work to do in your geographical study, you might be tempted just to throw your assignment topic into a Google search to get some references or ideas. But often this will bring an overwhelming range of options from disciplines both near and far – we have seen many students become overwhelmed and then write an essay that reads as confused and contradictory. A discipline is helpful in that it narrows the range of things you are focusing on (at least for the period of the assignment). Because of this, it is worth beginning an assignment by following up on the readings and recommendations of your lecturers in geography, and the further reading suggested in this book. This is part of the 'discipline' of geography: returning your attention to the themes and concerns of geography in your work in this area. It is an opportunity to go deeper in your understanding and practice of geography.

While getting a sense of the discipline is important, collaboration outside the discipline is very important too, and many of the chapters in this book demonstrate collaborations with other disciplines and studies, especially the final section on collaborations for justice and environment and with technology. In some ways, this period of study is for 'disciplining' oneself into a way of thinking and learning, an attention to place and **space**, then later periods of study are for opening up to cross-disciplinary, interdisciplinary and multidisciplinary collaborations. Core areas of collaboration and attention in geography include collaboration with different justice-seeking groups. Diverse perspectives, voices and knowledge systems can enrich our understanding of human geographies and promote social and environmental justice. Feminist geographies, Black geographies, Indigenous geographies and queer geographies are good examples of this attention to the specific justice struggles for certain groups. In this book we have featured these geographies in various ways throughout the book as well as in the final section on collaborations. But there are other important justice-seeking projects, such as inequality between Majority and Minority Worlds, between humans and non-human or '**more-than-human**' entities, between urban and rural, between abled and disabled people. In academic research and practice, it is often the intersections between disciplines where new and interesting things might happen. In your everyday life as you move on from university study, you might find the intersections between your disciplinary knowledges and real-world experiences a source of innovation and new critical thought.

Summary

- Doing geography is a 'discipline' in the active sense of returning one's attention to the same things over and over again.
- Human geography assignments often involve reading mainly within the discipline.
- Doing geography is interdisciplinary and involves collaboration with other ways of doing research as well.

Constructing geographical knowledges: on methodology and methods

All the different types of knowledges referred to in the previous section have to be actively constructed so that they can be made use of by human geographers (see Cloke et al., 2004). They are not pre-ordained or pre-given, just waiting in the world for the geographer to come along and make use of them. This construction takes place through the deployment of particular methodologies and methods, which between them will provide the information and data that can be used to address particular research questions. By methodology we mean the broad approach taken to answering any particular question or the 'overall "principles of reasoning" which specify both how questions are to be posed... and the answers are to be determined' (Cloke et al., 2004: 5). In this sense, the methodology that someone deploys will cover the concepts and philosophies they use to underpin and frame their research, as well as their research design and analysis. There are no methodologies which are necessarily better than others; there are just those that are more appropriate and relevant for addressing the research questions under consideration. Those deployed to understand, for instance, how children use the spaces of playgrounds, will differ from those seeking to understand why particular businesses locate where they do. A difference is often drawn between intensive and extensive research methodologies. The former focus on an in-depth analysis of a single case study, or small number of case studies, designed to uncover the properties operating to cause particular events. The latter generates large data sets in order to identify statistical patterns and regularities (see Sayer, 1992). Typically, the search by **spatial science** for universal spatial laws relied on extensive research, while **humanistic geography's** investigation of people's values and beliefs tends to use intensive research. In more recent times (particularly after the COVID-19 pandemic), there have also been large collaborations of geographers doing intensive research individually but working together to write more extensively (Gibson et al., 2018, Dombroski et al., 2020, Rogers et al., 2020).

While *methodology* points us to the broad approach taken by a researcher to construct their data, research *methods* refer to a much narrower set of practices and techniques through which data are obtained. As might be expected from a subject as diverse as human geography, the methods used to generate appropriate data are equally diverse. Again, the key word is 'appropriate' – methods in and of themselves are neither good nor bad, but the trick is to use appropriate methods that allow the researcher to construct relevant data in order to address their particular research questions. At their very essence, research methods can be boiled down to three different ways of obtaining information – talking to people, watching and observing, and using what for now we'll loosely call 'documents'. Imagine, for instance, arriving in an unfamiliar city late at night and looking for accommodation. You can either ask someone (talking to people), walk around looking for a hotel (watching and observing) or consult a guidebook or an online travel guide (using documents). Of course, things are never this simple, and when you read a geography methods textbook (see Cloke et al., 2004, Clifford et al., 2016, Lovell et al., 2023) or take a methods course, you will quickly realise that these three basic ways of obtaining information break down into a multiplicity of specific methods.

Talking to people, for instance, might involve asking a set of people the same questions via a questionnaire survey, or it could involve interviewing five people at the same time as part of a focus group or one person at a time as one respondent to a semi-structured interview. Watching and observing might involve participant observation, where you watch events and activity that you are part of, or more covert observation, where you watch from a distance. It could involve drawing a map, or making a sketch of a landscape, or of the architectural styles in a street of housing. Using documents for information may involve looking at formal textual sources, such as official census reports, or company reports, or minutes of meetings; at more informal textual documents such as a diary or a novel; or watching a film, or reading a blog, or an online discussion group. In reality, the possible sources of geographical information are almost endless, but there will always be a rigorous research method that can be used to access these sources in order to construct the data needed to address a particular set of research questions. To complicate matters still further, once all these potential pieces of useful information have been obtained, they must be analysed and interpreted before they can be used as research data – and here yet more methods come into play.

A basic distinction can be drawn between the methods used to analyse and interpret quantitative and qualitative data. Put simply, quantitative data are data that express the numerical quantities of those phenomena that are being studied, while qualitative data 'reveal the "qualities" of certain phenomena, events and aspects of the world under study' (Cloke et al., 2004: 17). Box 2.3 describes the distinction in more detail. Quantitative data tend to be analysed using comparative, descriptive or statistical methods (see Kitchin and Tate, 2000, Bryman, 2016, for more details), while qualitative data are amenable to a broader set of analytical and interpretative methods, including textual and discourse analysis of written documents, interpretative analysis of visual sources, coding of interview transcripts and focus group transcripts, analysis of notes made by the researcher when acting as a participant observer, archival research on historical documents, scaping data from web sources, such as discussion groups, blogs and twitter feeds (see DeLyser et al., 2010, Hay and Cope, 2021 for more details).

BOX 2.3
QUALITATIVE AND QUANTITATIVE DATA

Qualitative data are data that reveal the 'qualities' of certain phenomena, events and aspects of the world under study, chiefly through the medium of verbal descriptions which try to convey in words what are the characteristics of those data. These can be the words of the researcher, describing a given people and place in his or her field diary, or they can be the words found in a planning document, a historical report, an interview transcript or whatever (in which case the words are in effect themselves the qualitative data). Sometimes these data can be visual, as in the appearance of a landscape observed in the field, or as in paintings, photographs, videos and films. *Quantitative data* are data that express the

quantities of those phenomena, events and aspects of the world amenable to being counted, measured and thereby given numerical values, and the suggestion is that things which are so amenable will tend to be ones which are immediately tangible, distinguishable and hence readily counted (1, 2, 3...) or measured (an area of 200 m^2; a population of 20,000 live there; a per capita earning of £100,000). It should be underlined that such counts and measurements are still only descriptions of the things concerned, albeit descriptions which are arguably more accurate and certain than are qualitative attributions (chiefly because they allow a common standard of comparing different items of data, and also the possibility of repeating this form of describing data: i.e. other researchers would count the same number of things or measure the same areas, population levels, per capita incomes, etc.). The use of quantitative data is hence commonly reckoned to be more *objective* (allowing researchers to deal with data in an accurate, certain and therefore unbiased manner), while qualitative data are commonly reckoned to be more *subjective* (leaving researchers prone to injecting too much of their own 'biases' in their dealings with data)... we do not agree with such a conclusion because it forgets about the countless other issues which militate against the possibility of complete objectivity (which means that being quantitative is no convincing guarantee of objectivity).

Cloke et al., 2004: 17

Although we do not have the space here to go into further details about either research methodology or research methods, we hope to have given you a flavour of how the data used by human geographers are constructed, and we also hope you will have gained some appreciation of the huge breadth and diversity of the sorts of information that geographers use in their research. To a certain extent, this brings us back to the six types of knowledges we discussed in the previous chapter, as different methodologies and methods will be more or less appropriate for generating different kinds of knowledges. This book is packed with examples of human geographical research which utilise a huge range of different methodologies and methods. We hope they give you a sense of the richness of what makes up the discipline of human geography and of the very different kinds of human geographies that are constantly being made and remade as people go about their daily lives across the globe. Writing these different worlds remains the prime task of human geography.

SUMMARY

- Methodologies and methods should be appropriate to the research question we are interested in examining.
- There are intensive methodologies and extensive methodologies, and qualitative and quantitative methods. There are also more mixed approaches to collecting data.
- Once data are collected, it has to be analysed. Different approaches require different analytical methods. The chapters in this book use many different methodological approaches.

Conclusion: beyond geography

In these times of socio-ecological challenge and crisis, geographers are in demand for their ability to think and work across difference: understanding of physical and human landscapes, attention to place and its specificities, experience of working in groups to solve interdisciplinary problems. Recent students of ours have ended up in city councils supporting place-making activity, transport planning roles at both national and city levels, non-government environmental organisations, geospatial companies, regional environmental governance, international development organisations, research roles and more (see also statistics on the Royal Geographical Society website for UK). The skills of collaboration and critical thinking, with attention to positionality, are crucial in addressing the problems we face globally today – climate change, loss of biodiversity, widespread inequality, global health and disease challenges. People with training in geography are often valued for their skills, and even those of you who major in other disciplines might find your geography takes you places! In a meeting with the New Zealand government's long-term economic planning team, Kelly's research team was pleased to note that many economists on the team also had studied geography at one time or another. Their ability to think both with and beyond the discipline of economics had clearly benefited their careers and perhaps contributed in some way to New Zealand's shift towards wellbeing-led budgeting as well as new thinking on food and economic resilience in New Zealand in changing times.

The point is, your study in human geography might be just beginning, but it is already connecting you with the future: the future of the place in which you find yourself now, the future in places where you might end up living and working and the future in a more global sense. Doing human geography is about more than just learning a university subject but about preparing yourself for contributing to both people and planet in a range of ways throughout your life. We ourselves are inspired by what our students end up doing with their geography learning. From BBC journalists to environmental consultancy and homeless organising, the status or job title matters little. Human geography is ethics-shaping – a space for critical reflection and debate over what type of world we want to live in and what kind of people we wish to become. The rest of this book introduces you to some of the very best of this critical reflection and debate, beginning with a Part One introducing foundational concepts, Part Two detailing a range of themes from the subdisciplines and Part Three pointing towards important collaborations with key concerns and fields both inside and outside the discipline of geography.

Summary

- Geographers are in demand for their ability to think critically across environments, society and place.
- Doing geography out in the workplace and society looks different depending on where you end up but offers important perspectives on contemporary issues whatever your everyday activity.

Discussion points

- What aspects of 'doing human geography' seem the most interesting to you? Which aspects seem tricky or less interesting at this point?
- If you must introduce yourself using a *pepeha*, what mountains, rivers, lakes or other physical geography landmarks would feature in your introduction?
- How does where you are in the world and in life affect the way you think about the world? How have your perspectives changed over time depending on where you are situated?
- What do you hope to 'do' with your geography learning in the future?

References

Bhambra, G. K. (2022). Relations of extraction, relations of redistribution: empire, nation, and the construction of the British welfare state. *The British Journal of Sociology* 73: 4–15.

Bryman, A. (2016). *Social Research Methods*. London: Oxford University Press.

Clifford, N., Cope, M., Gillespie, T., and French, S. (2016). *Key Methods in Geography*. London: Sage.

Cloke, P., Cook, I., Crang, P., Goodwin, M., Painter, J., and Philo, C. (2004). *Practising Human Geography*. London: Sage.

Crenshaw, K. (1989). Demarginalizing the intersection of race and sex: a black feminist critique of anti-discrimination doctrine, feminist theory and antiracist politics. *University of Chicago Legal Forum* 1989(1): 139–168.

DeLyser, D., Herbert, S., Aitken, S., Crang, M., and McDowell, L. (2010). *The Sage Handbook of Qualitative Geography*. London: Sage.

Dombroski, K., Diprose, G., Sharp, E., Graham, R., Lee, L., Scobie, M., Richardson, S., Watkins, A., and Martin-Neuninger, R. (2020). Food for people in place: reimagining resilient food systems for economic recovery. *Sustainability* 12: 9369–9386.

England, E. (2022). 'Homelessness is a queer experience': utopianism and mutual aid as survival strategies for homeless trans people. *Housing Studies* 1–18.

Fowle, M. Z. (2022). Racialized homelessness: a review of historical and contemporary causes of racial disparities in homelessness. *Housing Policy Debate* 32: 940–967.

Gibson, K., Astuti, R., Carnegie, M., Chalernphon, A., Dombroski, K., Haryani, A. R., Hill, A., Kehi, B., Law, L., Lyne, I., McGregor, A., McKinnon, K., McWilliam, A., Miller, F., Ngin, C., Occeña-Gutierrez, D., Palmer, L., Placino, P., Rampengan, M., Than, W. L. L., Wianti, N. I., and Wright, S. (2018). Community economies in monsoon Asia: keywords and key reflections. *Asia Pacific Viewpoint* 59(1): 3–16.

Giles, D. B. (2021). *A Mass Conspiracy to Feed People: Food Not Bombs and the World-Class Waste of Global Cities*. Durham: Duke University Press.

Gilmore, R. W. (2007). *Golden Gulag: Prisons, Surplus, Crisis, and Opposition in Globalizing California*. Berkeley: University of California Press.

Haraway, D. (1988). Situated knowledges: the science question in feminism and the privilege of partial perspective. *Feminist Studies* 14(3): 575–599.

Hawthorne, C. (2019). Black matters are spatial matters: Black geographies for the twenty-first century. *Geography Compass* 13: e12468.

Hay, I., and Cope, M. (2021). *Qualitative Research Methods in Human Geography*. London: Wiley.

Heynen, N. (2010). Cooking up non-violent civil-disobedient direct action for the hungry: 'Food Not Bombs' and the resurgence of radical democracy in the US. *Urban Studies* 47: 1225–1240.

hooks, b. (1981). *Ain't I a Woman? Black Women and Feminism*. Boston: South End Press.

Hubbard, P., and Kitchin, R. (2010). *Key Thinkers on Space and Place*. London: Sage.

Jensen, P. R. (2018). 'People can't believe we exist!': social sustainability and alternative nonprofit organizing. *Critical Sociology* 44: 375–388.

Kitchin, R., and Tate, N. (2000). *Conducting Research in Human Geography: Theory, Methodology and Practice*. Harlow: Prentice Hall.

Little, J. (2017). Understanding domestic violence in rural spaces: a research agenda. *Progress in Human Geography* 41: 472–488.

Lovell, S., Coen, S. E., and Rosenberg, M. (2023). *Handbook of Methodologies in Human Geography*. Abingdon: Routledge.

Midgley, J., and Piachaud, D. (2011). *Colonialism and Welfare: Social Policy and the British Imperial Legacy*. Cheltenham: Edward Elgar.

Mould, O., Cole, J., Badger, A., and Brown, P. (2022). Solidarity, not charity: learning the lessons of the COVID-19 pandemic to reconceptualise the radicality of mutual aid. *Transactions of the Institute of British Geographers* 47(4): 866–879.

Ramírez, M. (2020). Take the houses back/take the land back: Black and Indigenous urban futures in Oakland. *Urban Geography* 41(5): 682–693.

Rogers, D., Herbert, M., Whitzman, C., McCann, E., Maginn, P. J., Watts, B., Alam, A., Pill, M., Keil, R., and Dreher, T. (2020). The city under COVID-19: podcasting as digital methodology. *Tijdschrift voor economische en sociale geografie* 111(3): 434–450.

Sayer, A. (1992). *Method in Social Science: A Realist Approach*. London: Routledge.

Smith, N. (1996). *The New Urban Frontier: Gentrification and the Revanchist City*. London: Routledge.

Vilenica, A., McElroy, E., Lancione, M., and Thompson, S. (2022). Carcerality, housing precarity, and abolition. *Radical Housing Journal* 4(1): 1–8.

Online materials

- How to do a human geography assessment. https://throwntogetherness.com/2023/06/14/university-skills-doing-your-first-geography-assessment/. This post was originally written as a box for this chapter, but we ran out of room! It gives you some tips for getting your first human geography assessment under way.
- Intersectionality, explained. https://www.vox.com/the-highlight/2019/5/20/18542843/intersectionality-conservatism-law-race-gender-discrimination. This article gives the background on ideas of intersectionality, and some of the debates and misunderstandings around the term.
- Royal Geographical Society, choose geography at university. https://www.rgs.org/choose-geography/choose-geography-at-university. This online resource gives some tips to doing geography at university from the UK Royal Geographical Society. You can find similar sites in many other countries in the world, such as the Association for American Geographers and the Institute of Australian Geographers.
- Your Library! Check out the resources provided by your geography liaison librarian, the databases your library subscribes to (many of which are much better than google scholar) and any short training events on essay writing, researching material and more.

Further reading

Cloke, P., Cook, I., Crang, P., Goodwin, M., Painter, J., and Philo, C. (2004). *Practising Human Geography*. London: Sage.
This book focuses on how research in human geography is done, covering both the production of geographical materials or 'data' and the production of varying kinds of geographical 'interpretations' of these data. This and other books on geographical research methods provide invaluable links between the kinds of materials introduced in this volume and the opportunities that exist for you to undertake your own geographical investigations in project work and independent dissertations.

Hay, I. (2012). *Communicating in Geography and the Environmental Sciences*. Oxford: Oxford University Press.
This book teaches you the basics of communicating your work in geography and environmental sciences, including how to write a report, an essay, do a presentation and more.

Hay, I., and Cope, M. (eds.) (2021). *Qualitative Research Methods in Human Geography* (5th edn.). Oxford: Oxford University Press.
This book is aimed at students using qualitative methods in human geography and provides practical contributions for getting a project going.

Hubbard, P., and Kitchin, R. (2010). *Key Thinkers on Space and Place*. London: Sage.
This book introduces key thinkers in space and place, many of whom are people 'doing geography'. Keep an eye out for the forthcoming revised version.

Kneale, P. (2011). *Study Skills for Geography, Earth, and Environmental Science Students* (3rd edn.). London: Hodder Education.
A guide to the study skills that geography students need and use at university level.

Rosenberg, M., Lovell, S., and Coen, S. E. (2023). *Handbook of Methodologies in Human Geography*. London: Routledge.
This book covers a wide range of methodologies used by geographers in 'doing' human geography. Chapters are written by a wide range of expert contributors.

PART TWO

FOUNDATIONS

3 Scale

Joe Blakey

Introduction

'Scale' is so self-evidently central to Geography, yet to *just* take it at face value would overlook its complex disciplinary history. Both the meaning and function of scale have frequently been debated by human geographers, especially since the 1980s. Consider the following questions that have animated much of this scholarship: 'How should we think about and research scale?', 'Do scales exist in a vertical or horizontal sense?', 'What scales are significant and most worthy of study?', 'What scales are overlooked?', 'Is scale something that exists "naturally" or is it something we have socially imagined?', and 'How does the concept of scale shape or constrain our understanding of social processes and politics?'. Some scholars even went as far as to ask: 'Is human geography better off without scale?'. These critical questions also reflect the twists and turns the discipline has taken. Scale is therefore a useful 'way in' for those wanting to understand the recent history of human geography and for those wanting to understand the significance of philosophical and theoretical positions on geographical thought. In this chapter, I will chart the key contours of these debates, considering (i) approaches in the 1970s and early 1980s, (ii) the subsequent move to understanding the so-called politics of scale and its **socially constructed** nature, (iii) different imaginaries of what scale is (e.g. as vertical, horizontal, hierarchical, or like a network), (iv) and finally how some have moved away from scale in favour of more 'site-based' approaches.

Early approaches to scale

Scale is derived from the Latin *scalae*, meaning ladder or rung (Herod, 2011). It is therefore unsurprising that scale was understood as a form of hierarchy over **space**. In the 1970s, geographers commonly took aim at particular scales, such as 'the national' or 'the local', as a means to examine phenomena, seldom asking critical questions about the nature and meaning of scale as a concept (Herod, 2011). Many drew upon approaches stemming from the philosopher Immanuel Kant's work. For such scholars, space, time, and by extension scale were not 'real', material things 'out there' that serve as a container for social activity but mental constructs that shape how we encounter and make sense of the world. Scale was treated, often unreflexively, as something hard-wired into our minds.

The early 1980s, however, marked a shift towards a more critical interpretation of the concept and the formation of particular scales. Peter Taylor (1982) is perhaps the earliest example. Taylor

DOI: 10.4324/9780429265853-5

argued that scales were not simply built into our minds but *produced* under conditions of **capitalism**. Taylor sought to extend the historical sociologist Immanuel Wallerstein's world-systems theory which argued that contemporary society can only be understood in relation to global capitalism. In doing so, he added a spatial accent, describing the emergence and nature of 'three scales [that] have different prime roles in the world economy' (1981: 6). This included the global scale, 'the scale of reality', as he put it, an 'all-embracing' and unavoidable scale defining the characteristics of the other scales (Taylor, 1981: 7). He argued that national is the scale we are socialised in to, where we develop sentiments around nationalism or patriotism; thus, he talks of it as the 'scale of **ideology**'. Finally, he suggests that the urban scale is the 'scale of experience' – where we live our lives (1981: 6).

It is Neil Smith, however, who has since been credited with both revolutionising disciplinary approaches to scale and sparking a lively discussion about the nature and role of scale in the discipline (Jones III et al., 2017). Smith was a **Marxist** geographer, and his early work was motivated by the question of how uneven geographical development occurs. Like Taylor, he saw scales as produced. He argued that considering their roots, ends, and nature can serve as a window through which we can understand **uneven development** under capitalism. For Smith (2010 [1984]), capitalism was not simply organised by a mosaic of spaces but a multi-scale system that attempts to 'fix' capital in certain privileged locations. He similarly identified the urban, national, and global as the scales where uneven development can be observed. This would become a highly influential intervention that prompted Marxist geographers to investigate the **political economy** of how scales are shaped and how their role changes over space and time (Sheppard and McMaster, 2008).

Summary

- In the 1970s, scale was considered to be 'hard-wired' into our minds, with geographers seldom asking critical questions of 'the local' or 'the national'.
- In the 1980s, the likes of Peter Taylor and Neil Smith offered a more critical interpretation, considering scales as produced under the conditions of capitalism.
- Neil Smith considered the role of scale in organising uneven development over space, prompting Marxist geographers to think explicitly about the political and economic conditions that shape scales.

The politics and social construction of scale

Smith himself felt that these early theorisations of scale, driven by a Marxist concern for uneven development under capitalism, were a little bit 'wooden' (Smith, 2011: 262). To invite a wider discussion, in the early 1990s, he coined the term 'the politics of scale' in the afterword to the second edition of his book, *Uneven Development: Nature, Capital, and the Production of Space* (2010 [1984]). It was an attempt to move beyond considering scale in relation to capitalism, to think more generally about the role of scale in relation to **power** and struggles.

Figure 3.1
A park bench in present-day Tompkins Square Park in the East Village of New York City

Source: Photo credit: James Andrews/iStock Photo

Smith's own writings on the politics of scale focused on resistance to **gentrification** by the homeless community in Manhattan's Lower East Side. New York City adopted a two-pronged strategy to dealing with the effects of long-term disinvestment in the 1970s and 1980s. First, they aimed to crack down on drugs in view of making it 'safe' again for the middle classes, whilst second, aiming to 'clean up' the parks which had become used by a growing homeless population. Of note was Tompkins Square Park (Figure 3.1), where a 1 a.m. curfew was imposed to 'take back control' of the park from several hundred predominantly African-American and Latino homeless residents. Many groups organised against this discriminatory curfew, with solidarity squats appearing over the Lower East Side with 'Tompkins Square Everywhere' as their slogan. For Smith, the example highlighted the role of scale in the struggle to gain control of space. The struggle initially focused on the scale of the park but through the slogan and solidarity squats 'jumped scale' to make it a neighbourhood-wide concern, 'elevat[ing] themselves to the next scale in the hierarchy' (Smith, 2010 [1984]: 232).

For Smith, the politics of scale captures not only how scale can 'contain and control' events and people but also how scales can be claimed, redefined, and transformed. He saw scale as caught between political control and political resistance, and this understanding was subsequently adopted by geographers over numerous struggles (cf. Jonas, 1994, Swyngedouw, 1996, 1997, Agnew, 1997, Herod, 1997, Leitner, 1997). Scholars frequently focused on the processes through which scales were redefined, such as scale jumping as outlined above; scale bending where assumptions about what activities belong at which scales were challenged; or glocalisation which describes restructuring from the national scale in both upwards (global) and downwards

Figure 3.2
Crowds passing in front of McDonald's in Delhi, India. The only country in the world where it does not offer beef on its menu

Source: Photo credit: Paul Prescott/iStock Photo

(local) directions simultaneously (Swyngedouw, 1997). As a simple example of the latter, consider how McDonald's restaurants operate globally but adjust their menu according to local cultural contexts, for instance removing beef from their products in India when they expanded there in 1996 (Figure 3.2).

With these interventions around the politics of scale, the literature was gravitating towards an acceptance that scale was not 'an external fact awaiting discovery but a way of framing conceptions of reality' (Delaney and Leitner, 1997: 94–95). In other words, an acceptance that there was 'nothing ontologically given' about scale (Smith, 1992: 73). The term **ontology** is often seen as intimidating, complex, and even academic jargon. Yet it need not be, and it is important to grasp to understand the disagreements surrounding scale that would unfold in the early 2000s. The word comprises two Greek words: *ontos* meaning the general state of being and *logos* meaning to provide a reason. Taken together, ontology refers to attempts to reason what existence *is*. It is an attempt to grapple with what the building blocks of reality are. Ontology is therefore what philosophers concern themselves with. So here Smith and others are arguing that scale is resolutely not one of these ontological building blocks of reality. Instead, scale was a **social construction**, something that was imagined but it was not merely rhetorical – it had very real and tangible material consequences on everyday life (Marston, 2000).

Despite the general acceptance of the social construction of scale, the 1990s scale literature was preoccupied with questions of capitalism and the state and ended up as a result telling 'only part of a much more complex story' (Marston, 2000: 233). Sallie Marston (2000), for instance, draws attention to the oversight of the household scale and how power and resources are unequally distributed based on sex and **gender**. Marston (2000) discusses how urban middle-class women in the USA embarked upon a politics of scale as they extended their influence beyond the home, challenging cultural ideas about their 'proper place' in social life. The progressive broadening of scale was not met by universal acceptance, with Neil Brenner offering a response to Marston that made the case for 'a more precise and hence analytically narrower conception of geographical scale' (2001: 593). Fearing that the analytical and conceptual sharpness of scales was being blunted, Brenner sought to limit the definition of scale to 'relations of hierarchization and rehierarchization among vertically differentiated spatial units' (Brenner, 2001: 603).

Summary

- The term 'politics of scale' was first coined by Smith in the early 1990s to invite wider discussion beyond the Marxist concern for uneven development under capitalism.
- The politics of scale considers (i) the relation between scale and power, where it contains and controls events, people, and things, and (ii) the relation between scale and political resistance, where scales can be claimed, redefined, and transformed.
- The literature on the politics of scale gravitated towards understanding scale as a 'social construction' rather than an 'ontological' fact.
- The 1990s literature on scale was preoccupied with questions of capitalism and the state, prompting **Feminist** scholars such as Marston to draw attention to the oversight of other scales such as the household.

Competing imaginaries of scale

Amidst these debates, scale has been conceptualised in a host of different ways, drawing upon different imaginaries of what scale *is* (Herod, 2011). As Howitt (1998) notes, metaphors are often central to our understandings of scale, and Herod (2011) identifies three of note: the ladder, concentric circles, and Matryoshka dolls. Consider first the ladder metaphor (Figure 3.3a), where one 'climbs up' the rungs from the local level to the global level. This implies verticality, hierarchy, and power as if those scales that are 'higher up' can surveil scales beneath them with a 'God's eye view' (Herod, 2011). A good example of a 'vertical' approach to scale is Taylor's (1982) work, which as we have seen identified the three 'levels' of the global (scale of reality), the state (scale of ideology), and the urban (scale of experience). Taylor's work was an explicit attempt to rectify what he detected as an overly horizontal approach to space in Wallerstein's world-systems theory (Jones III, 2017).

One might contrast this vertical imaginary with a series of nested concentric circles (Figure 3.3b), where more local scales are enclosed and encompassed by 'larger' scales, often spanning from the local (the smallest, innermost circle) to the global scale (the largest, all-encompassing circle). This instead connotes a more horizontal understanding, as an areal spanning of space. Within this concentric approach, there remains a sense of hierarchy: the outermost scales are typically considered to be the most powerful given that they are 'all encompassing'.

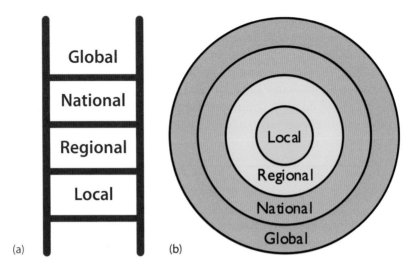

Figure 3.3
Scale as a ladder versus scale as concentric circles

Source: Illustration by Joe Blakey

A related analogy is that of Matryoshka (or Russian) dolls (Figure 3.4), a set of wooden dolls of decreasing size that can be placed inside one another. This similarly suggests the idea that scales can be nested. However, as Herod writes, 'what most distinguishes this metaphor is that each individual scale fits together as part of a whole in a much more rigidly conceived progression

Figure 3.4
Scale as Matryoshka dolls

Source: Photo credit: Rahib Yaqubov/Pexels

than in either the concentric circle or ladder metaphor' (2011: 47). Adopting the Matryoshka doll metaphor, it is hard to conceive of the local, for instance, containing the global (such as glocalisation might suggest).

Howitt (1998) offered a contrasting and rather unique metaphor: musical scales. He did so to reject both a nested and hierarchal understanding of scale, instead arguing for a more *relational* interpretation. In music, scales are a sequence of tones with a relationship to each other. Musical compositions frequently vary in scale, and even if the notes used are consistent, changing scale alters the relationship between the elements being brought together. Thinking through musical scales, therefore, encourages scholars to think in terms of *relations*. Therefore, for Howitt, when we change geographical scale, we do not change elements or things within the landscape but 'the relationships that we perceive between them' (1998: 55).

But what does it really *mean* to think about relations? Arguably Howitt's intervention was an earlier glimmer of a wider 'relational turn' in human geography that would come into force in the early 2000s. As Amin suggests, relational thinking 'defies easy summarizing' (2007: 103) yet it quickly became 'the mantra of the early twenty-first century in human geography' (Jones, 2009: 488, Darling, 2009). For relational thinkers, 'what counts is connectivity' (Thrift, 2004: 59), in that they see the world as woven together through a series of connections. It was a rejection of 'absolute' understandings of space associated with the philosopher Euclid (Euclidean approaches), that understood it as a 'neutral' container within which things happen. Instead, relational understandings see 'space as undergoing continual construction as a result of things encountering each other in more or less organized circulations' (Thrift, 2003: 96). Space is no longer seen as a container or even a discrete 'thing' that can be disentangled and pointed to. Space is something that is constantly remade, and like all other objects, can only be understood in relation to other things (Jones, 2009). Space, then, along with politics and place, became increasingly understood as 'encountered, performed, and fluid' (Jones, 2009: 492).

This relational understanding necessarily disrupts the more Euclidean, bounded, and hierarchical understandings seen in the metaphors of scale as a ladder, concentric circles, or a Matryoshka doll (Jones, 2009). Perhaps the most common metaphors for relational thinkers would become the network and the rhizome. Thinking through networks evokes a vision of relations as intersecting and interconnected lines, as Castree et al. put it, one that is 'fibrous, thread-like, wiry, stringy, ropy and capillary' (2008: 314). Kevin Cox (1998) was an early trailblazer of this networked approach. Cox adopted a networked rather than areal approach to argue that scales emerge out of relations that connect different actors and different spaces of engagement, to avoid involving 'discrete arena[s]' (1998: 20). Moving from one scale to another was a matter of actors developing different associations to engagement in different places.

Alan Latham (2002) made a network-based intervention and termed it a 'topological' approach to scale. He drew upon this wider body of relational thinking in human geography, as well as on the **actor-network theory** developed by social theorist Bruno Latour which argues that the human and non-human world exists in an ever-shifting network of relations (Latour, 1996). He offered a key distinction for horizontal approaches. Topo*graphical* approaches view scales as non-overlapping boundary lines enclosing absolute space, much like contour lines on a map, and exemplified well by the concentric circle metaphor. Topo*logical* approaches, meanwhile, express scale using lines and nodes and do not enclose absolute space (Figure 3.5) (Latham, 2002, Herod, 2011). Latham (2002) sought to highlight how places can be both global and local without necessarily being wholly either and to emphasise 'how social structure and hierarchy are

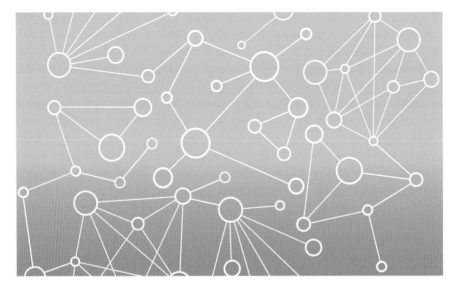

Figure 3.5
Topological or networked approaches to scale

Source: Image by Pete Linforth/Pixabay

built and maintained through more complex and heterogeneous **assemblages** than is usually realized' (2002: 116).

One might also think through the metaphor of the rhizome (Figure 3.6), which also falls within this camp of non-hierarchical, relational, and topological approaches (Herod, 2011). This metaphor is derived from the work of philosophers Giles Deleuze and Felix Guattari (1987), who

Figure 3.6
Topological or networked approaches to scale

Source: Illustration by Joe Blakey

also critique 'vertical, tree-like' modes of thinking which offer 'totalizing principles and binary thought' (Springer, 2014: 402). In place of this 'arborescent' way of thinking (a botanical term meaning tree-like), they offer the contrasting horizontal or 'flat' idea of the 'rhizome'. In botany, a rhizome is a horizontal plant stem that creeps along underground and produces new roots and shoots. For Deleuze, Guattari, and their followers, meanwhile, it describes how objects and ideas can 'link up in non-hierarchical patterns of association' (Springer, 2014: 402).

Summary

- Scale has been conceptualised in different ways and often in relation to metaphors.
- Three commonly used metaphors for scale are the ladder, concentric circles, and Matryoshka dolls, each conveying a different understanding of space and hierarchy.
- The relational turn in human geography prompted some scale theorists to move away from verticality and 'fixed' understandings to instead think about scales in a manner that emphasised fluidity, horizontality, and connectivity.
- The network and the rhizome are common metaphors used by relational thinkers.

Human geography with or without scale?

Whilst the 2000s would see a deepening of human geography's scale debate, a highly influential contribution came a couple of years earlier from Katherine Jones (1998), one of the scholars rejecting ontological approaches to scale and making the case for approaching scale as a contested **representational** device. Jones made the powerful critique that scale was an **epistemology** (where *episteme* means knowledge), *a way of* understanding the world rather than a building block 'of' the world (ontology). For Jones (1998), when we assume scales to be ontological, we uncritically treat them as something 'that just is' and, in doing so, fail to analyse the effects of how scales are deployed to represent various spatial processes and activities. In doing so, Jones laid the foundations for a later series of debates around not only how we can avoid reifying scale in ontology but also around who is doing so and its effects on our understanding of politics (Blakey, 2021).

Scholars quickly adopted the idea of 'scale as epistemology', treating scale as a representational or **discursive** device (Kurtz, 2003). They often took the form of more horizontal, networked-based approaches (see for instance Leitner et al., 2002, Bulkeley, 2005, Collinge, 2006). Scale frames tended to be seen as '[a]lways emergent' rather than something fixed, and capable of shifting 'sociospatial boundaries and relations' (Moore, 2008: 221). They offered grounded and practice-based understandings of the ways in which scale is very actively represented and invoked rather than trying to analyse 'existing scales' (Moore, 2008). It is here, however, that some of the deeper divides of the scale debate began to show.

These more practice-based perspectives took issue with scholarship that saw socially constructed scales as 'inherited': something that precedes and shapes the events being analysed. They considered this to be granting a problematic 'ontological priority to scales themselves'

(Herod, 2001: 46). The question of when we are ontologising scale (i.e. making fundamental and philosophical assumptions), and how this limits our understanding of political and social processes, was becoming a central concern. Others were sympathetic to the idea that social processes are shaped by 'inherited scales', contesting the position that this necessarily equates to a problematic ontologising of scale. Robert Kaiser and Elena Nikiforova (2008), for instance, argue for more focus on both (i) the historical study of how our shared understandings of scale come into being and (ii) the performative effects of scale (i.e. what these understandings of scale *do*).

However, perhaps the most influential intervention was a 2005 paper by Sallie Marston, John Paul Jones III, and Keith Woodward, where even the understanding of scale as an epistemological construct would be disputed. They provocatively titled their paper 'Human Geography without Scale' (Marston et al., 2005). Noting the vast divergence in conceptual imaginaries of what scale is that we have discussed, they deemed the concept to be 'chaotic'. For these scholars, even more networked and relational approaches, which had become seen as a solution to the more assumptive – and therefore problematic – nested, hierarchical approaches, got in the way of properly understanding how social and political processes occur 'on the ground'. For Marston et al. (2005: 422), networked approaches merely replaced 'one ontological-epistemological nexus (verticality) with another (horizontality)'.

Moreover, even integrating vertical and networked approaches, as the likes of Brenner (1998) had advocated, was still seen to offer an ontologically reified understanding of scale. For the authors including scale in human geography's conceptual repertoire ultimately provided more unhelpful distraction than interpretive utility. Scale, no matter how it was conceptualised, was seen as an ontological 'predetermination' (Marston et al., 2005: 422), narrowing opportunities for understanding political alternatives 'by pre-assigning to it a cordoned register for resistance' in the form of scale (2005: 427). As Springer (2014: 408) later concurred:

> scale [...] represents a theoretical distraction, a drawing away from the grounded particularities of the everyday [...where we] soar off into an abstract sky, only to touch down on the immediate materiality of everyday life when and where it becomes convenient to our argument.

What, then, did Marston et al. (2005) propose should replace scale? In short, the relational and rhizomatic approach to thinking through phenomena introduced earlier – just without scale. They termed this a 'flat' or site-based ontology, again informed by actor-network theory. They encouraged casting off predetermined categories, including scale, and focusing instead on the unfolding set of relations with a focus on 'specific social sites of interaction' (Moore, 2008: 207). Such an approach, they argue, can better attend to practices and processes occurring on the ground, and enable geographers to deconstruct representational tropes such as scale without ontologising or otherwise reifying them.

Many welcomed this intervention and the advancement of the flat ontology and the political and research possibilities it pointed to (Collinge, 2006, Escobar, 2007, Springer, 2014). Some, however, stopped short of abandoning the concept entirely (Escobar, 2007, Springer, 2014). Others sought to defend scale, with Leitner and Miller (2007) suggesting that it is necessary to take stock of pre-existing scales if we are to develop strategies of resistance. Smith himself argued that whilst scale is not an ontological category, flat approaches overlook our existing, contingent, and shared understandings of scale, amounting to 'wishful thinking' (2015: 964). It is for this reason that Kaiser and Nikiforova (2008) suggest that abolishing notions of scale only reinforces existing unequal power relations.

There have subsequently been attempts to reunify these divides. Moore (2008) suggests that we can take Marston et al.'s (2005) concerns about the risk of ontologising scale and imposing it on our analyses seriously without eradicating the concept. He suggests that we should avoid treating scale as a 'category of analysis' and instead focus on how scalar ideas become embedded 'in consciousness and practice' (Moore, 2008: 214). Mackinnon (2010), meanwhile, made two interventions. First, he suggests that scholarship is rarely squarely 'about' scale, so he advocates 'scalar politics' to capture this. Second, he suggests that the charge of 'ontological **reification**' has been too forcefully applied, instead advocating a vision of 'scalar structures' as both inherited and contested (2010: 33) whilst attempting to remain 'receptive to poststructural insights concerning the importance of scalar practices and narratives' (2010: 32).

Blakey (2021) suggests that there can be no 'one-size fits all solution' to the scale debate. His reason is that how scholars approach the scale debate depends on the philosophical positions that they subscribe to. As we saw in Chapter 1, human geographers draw upon myriad philosophies, all prompting (at least slightly) different understandings of both sociospatial processes and the boundaries and inner content of what ontology 'is'. He instead offers a reading of scale from an as-yet unexplored angle. Drawing upon a theory of **aesthetics** developed by political thinker Jacques Rancière, he suggests that scale is a 'common sense' idea that we share that affects how we make sense of the world. To avoid reifying or presupposing an understanding of scale, Blakey (2021) suggests we should instead focus on moments of dissensus. By this, he means critically interpreting moments where popular scalar imaginaries (be they vertical, horizontal, or anything else) are met with alternative visions on the ground. Doing so, he argues, enables an understanding of how common-sense concepts like scale order space, whilst avoiding reifying it in ontology and remaining sensitive to alternative political orders.

Perhaps, then, it is impossible to offer a definitive conclusion or position on the scale debate. Scale nonetheless offers a fascinating window into the various twists and turns of the discipline since the 1980s, whilst today's divisions mark the vibrancy of perspectives in contemporary human geography. Consider, for instance, how different understandings of scale allow us to trace the dominance of Marxist political economy in the late 1980s, the influx of feminist and post-structural insights in the 1990s, and the relational turn as the discipline approached the millennium. Whilst there are many approaches to scale, others still avoid it. Arguably Marston et al.'s (2005) *Human Geography without Scale* was one antecedent to the body of work termed non-representational thinking (see also Chapter 8) which has since gained much traction in cultural geography. This literature tasks itself with developing approaches to researching and writing the world without dampening its messiness and liveliness into overly totalising concepts (Barron and Blakey, 2023). However, even with such an understanding, one need not necessarily cast off scale. As Anderson (2019) has stressed, **non-representational theorists** can be very much concerned with what representations *do* – they just avoid treating them as pregiven. Scale, then, remains a fascinating, albeit occasionally divisive, concept within the discipline, and what appears at first glance to be a deceptively simple concept, turns out to be a very complex one.

Summary

- Katherine Jones (1998) critiques the idea of approaching scale as an ontological building block of the world and instead argues for approaching scale as a contested representational device and an epistemology (a way of understanding the world).
- Scholars quickly adopted the idea of 'scale as epistemology', viewing scale as a representational or discursive device, often taking the form of more horizontal, networked-based approaches. These perspectives see scales as always emergent and
  capable of shifting sociospatial boundaries and relations.
- Marston et al. (2005) take issue with all formulations of scale, calling for a 'Human
  Geography without Scale'. They consider the concept of scale to be chaotic and view its
  inclusion in human geography as a theoretical distraction that narrows opportunities for
  understanding political alternatives.
- In its place, the scholars propose a 'flat' or 'site-based' ontology, informed by actor-
  network theory, as a replacement for scale. They argue this approach allows geographers
  to deconstruct representational tropes like scale without ontologising or reifying them.
  Some have welcomed this proposal while others have defended the concept of scale.

Discussion points

- How are vertical, horizontal, hierarchical, and networked approaches to scale similar and
  different?
- What are the reasons for and against keeping scale as a core concept within human
  geography?
- What is meant by a 'flat ontology' and why do some scholars see it as favourable over scale?

References

Agnew, J. (1997). The dramaturgy of horizons: geographical scale in the 'reconstruction of Italy' by the
   new Italian political parties, 1992–95. *Political Geography* 16(2): 99–121.

Amin, A. (2007). Re-thinking the urban social. *City* 11: 100–114.

Anderson, B. (2019). Cultural geography II: the force of representations. *Progress in Human Geography*
   43(6): 1120–1132.

Barron, A., and Blakey, J. (2023). Representation(al). In *Concise Encyclopedia of Human Geography*, eds.
   L. Lees and D. Demeritt. Cheltenham: Edward Elgar, 343–347.

Blakey, J. (2021). The politics of scale through Rancière. *Progress in Human Geography* 45(4): 623–640.

Brenner, N. (1998). Between fixity and motion: accumulation, territorial organization and the historical geography of spatial scales. *Environment and Planning D: Society and Space* 16(4): 459–481.

Brenner, N. (2001). The limits to scale? Methodological reflections on scalar structuration. *Progress in
   Human Geography* 25(4): 591–614.

Bulkeley, H. (2005). Reconfiguring environmental governance: towards a politics of scales and networks. *Political Geography* 24(8): 875–902.

Castree, N., Featherstone, D., and Herod, A. (2008). Contrapuntal Geographies: The Politics of Organizing across Sociospatial Difference. In *The Sage Handbook of Political Geography*, eds. K. Cox, M. Low, and J. Robinson. London: Sage, 305–321.

Collinge, C. (2006). Flat ontology and the deconstruction of scale: a response to Marston, Jones and Woodward. *Transactions of the Institute of British Geographers* 31(2): 244–251.

Cox, K. R. (1998). Spaces of dependence, spaces of engagement and the politics of scale, or: looking for local politics. *Political Geography* 17(1): 1–23.

Darling, J. (2009). Thinking beyond place: the responsibilities of a relational spatial politics. *Geography Compass* 3(5): 1938–1954.

Delaney, D., and Leitner, H. (1997). The political construction of scale. *Political Geography* 16(2): 93–97.

Deleuze, G., and Guattari, F. (1987). *A Thousand Plateaus: Capitalism and Schizophrenia*. Minneapolis, MN: University of Minnesota Press.

Escobar, A. (2007). The 'ontological turn' in social theory. A commentary on 'Human geography without scale', by Sallie Marston, John Paul Jones II and Keith Woodward. *Transactions of the Institute of British Geographers* 32(1): 106–111.

Herod, A. (1997). Labor's spatial praxis and the geography of contract bargaining in the US east coast longshore industry. *Political Geography* 16(2): 145–169.

Herod, A. (2001). *Labor Geographies: Workers and the Landscapes of Capitalism*. New York: Guilford.

Herod, A. (2011). *Scale*. London: Routledge.

Howitt, R. (1998). Scale as relation: musical metaphors of geographical scale. *Area* 30(1): 49–58.

Jonas, A. (1994). The scale politics of spatiality. *Environment and Planning D: Society and Space* 12(3): 257–264.

Jones III, J. P. (2017). Scale and Anti-Scale. In *The International Encyclopedia of Geography: People, the Earth, Environment, and Technology*, eds. D. Richardson, N. Castree, M. F. Goodchild, A. Kobayashi, W. Liu, and R. A. Marston. New York, NY: Wiley Blackwell, 1–9.

Jones III, J. P., Leitner, H., Marston, S. A., and Sheppard, E. (2017). Neil Smith's scale. *Antipode* 49: 138–152.

Jones, K. T. (1998). Scale as epistemology. *Political Geography* 17(I): 25–28.

Jones, M. (2009). Phase space: geography, relational thinking, and beyond. *Progress in Human Geography*, 33(4): 487–506.

Kaiser, R. J., and Nikiforova, E. (2008). The performativity of scale: the social construction of scale effects in Narva, Estonia. *Environment and Planning D: Society and Space* 26(3): 537–562.

Kurtz, H. E. (2003). Scale frames and counter-scale frames: constructing the problem of environmental injustice. *Political Geography* 22(8): 887–916.

Latham, A. (2002). Retheorizing the Scale of Globalization: Topologies, Actor-Networks, and Cosmopolitanism. In *Geographies of Power: Placing Scale*, eds. A. Herod and M. W. Wright. Oxford: Blackwell, 115–144.

Latour, B. (1996). On actor-network theory: a few clarifications. *Soziale Welt* 47: 369–381.

Leitner, H. (1997). Reconfiguring the spatiality of power: the construction of a supranational migration framework for the European Union. *Political Geography* 16(2): 123–143.

Leitner, H., and Miller, B. (2007). Scale and the limitations of ontological debate: a commentary on Marston, Jones and Woodward. *Transactions of the Institute of British Geographers* 32(1): 116–125.

Leitner, H., Pavlik, C., and Sheppard, E. (2002). Networks, Governance, and the Politics of Scale: Inter-urban Networks and the European Union. In *Geographies of Power: Placing Scale*, eds. A. Herod and M. W. Wright. Oxford: Blackwell. 274–303.

MacKinnon, D. (2010). Reconstructing scale: towards a new scalar politics. *Progress in Human Geography* 35(1): 21–36.

Marston, S. A. (2000). The social construction of scale. *Progress in Human Geography* 24(2): 219–242.

Marston, S. A., Jones, J. P., and Woodward, K. (2005). Human geography without scale. *Transactions of the Institute of British Geographers* 30(4): 416–432.

Moore, A. (2008). Rethinking scale as a geographical category: from analysis to practice. *Progress in Human Geography* 32(2): 203–225.

Sheppard, E., and McMaster, R. B. (2008). *Scale and Geographic Inquiry: Nature, Society, and Method.* London: John Wiley and Sons.

Smith, N. (1992). Geography, Difference and the Politics of Scale. In *Postmodernism and the Social Sciences*, eds. J. Doherty, E. Graham, and M. Malek. London: Palgrave Macmillan, 57–79.

Smith, N. (2010 [1984]). *Uneven Development: Nature, Capital, and the Production of Space.* Georgia: University of Georgia Press.

Smith, N. (2011). Uneven development redux. *New Political Economy* 16(2): 261–265.

Smith, N. (2015). The future is radically open. *ACME* 14(3): 954–964.

Springer, S. (2014). Human geography without hierarchy. *Progress in Human Geography* 38(3): 402–419.

Swyngedouw, E. (1996). Reconstructing citizenship, the rescaling of the state and the new authoritarianism: closing the Belgian mines. *Urban Studies* 33(8): 1499–1521.

Swyngedouw, E. (1997). Neither Global nor Local: 'glocalization' and the Politics of Scale. In *Spaces of Globalization. Reasserting the Power of the Local*, eds. K. R. Cox. New York: Guilford Press, 137–166.

Taylor, P. J. (1981). Geographical scales within the world-economy approach. *Review (Fernand Braudel Center)* 5(1): 3–11.

Taylor, P. J. (1982). A materialistic framework for political geography. *Transactions of the Institute of British Geographers* 7(1): 15–34.

Thrift, N. (2003). Space: The Fundamental Stuff of Human Geography. In *Key Concept in Geography*, eds. S. Hollaway, S. Rice, and G. Valentine. London: SAGE, 95–107.

Thrift, N. (2004). Intensities of feeling: towards a spatial politics of affect. *Geografiska Annaler: Series B, Human Geography* 86(1): 57–78.

Online materials

- This is a blog post on IKEA and 'glocalisation', noting how they operate globally yet shape their offering according to specific local conditions: https://www.marketingsociety.com/the-library/watch-out-%E2%80%98ikea-effect%E2%80%99
- This article discusses how cities are acting in a networked way to drive forward an international green agenda whilst the national scale fails to take action on the climate crisis: https://theconversation.com/mayors-of-94-cities-are-taking-the-green-new-deal-global-as-states-fail-to-act-on-climate-crisis-125282
- The World Health Organisation's Age-Friendly Cities Network is an example of a networked approach, where cities are acting in a networked way to champion an international age-friendly agenda: https://extranet.who.int/agefriendlyworld/who-network/

Further reading

Herod, A. (2011). *Scale*. London: Routledge.

To date, this is the only single-authored volume on geography and scale, and it is highly accessible to students. It provides a detailed account of the scale debate up to the date of publication, offering insight into both metaphors of scale (e.g. concentric circles versus a network) and particular scales that have frequently been deployed (such as 'the regional' or 'the global').

Jones III, J. P., Leitner, H., Marston, S. A., and Sheppard, E. (2017). Neil Smith's scale. *Antipode* 49: 138–152.
This paper, published as part of a special issue acknowledging the scholarship of the late Neil Smith, traces the important contributions Smith made to the geographic understanding of scale over the course of his career.

Jones, K. T. (1998). Scale as epistemology. *Political Geography* 17(I): 25–28.
This paper by Katherine Jones rejects ontological approaches to scale and makes the case for approaching scale as an epistemology and treating it as a contested representational device.

MacKinnon, D. (2010). Reconstructing scale: towards a new scalar politics. *Progress in Human Geography* 35(1): 21–36.
In this paper, Danny MacKinnon offers a defence of scale and scalar thinking. He does so in the wake of Marston, Jones and Woodward's (2005) intervention (below) which argued that human geography may be better off without scale.

Marston, S. A., Jones, J. P., and Woodward, K. (2005). Human geography without scale. *Transactions of the Institute of British Geographers* 30(4): 416–432.
This paper is perhaps the most radical intervention in the scale debate. Taking stock of scale theorising at the time, they argue that all approaches to scale presuppose too much about the world and that the concept has become chaotic. They propose eliminating scale and instead suggest a site-based approach that renders the concept unnecessary.

4 Time

Kajsa Ellegård

Introduction

Where were you yesterday? Where have you been today and where are you now? Will you stay where you are now for a while, or will you go somewhere else? These are simple questions about the flow of time and the movements between places, which are two interrelated and fundamental aspects of human life – and thereby important in human geography. The importance of an approach which emphasises the flow of time has been recognised for centuries, ever since the Greek philosopher Heracles conceived the well-known saying: 'You cannot step twice into the same river; for fresh waters are ever flowing in upon you' (quoted in Russell, 1961: 63).

Wherever you are located now, what you see around you is a mix of objects, which exist there at this precise moment. Some objects at this place have been located there for a period, and taken together they help you to recognise the place and maybe make you feel attached to it. As time goes by, the appearance of this place alters. Some objects remain, new objects appear, other objects change while still others are replaced. Think of your childhood home: your toys may be given away to younger relatives; your old books might be in the attic, while your room is changed into a guest room. Even if your parents still live there, the process has resulted in a new mix of objects and your attachment to your old home might change. Similar processes of change, though at a macro scale, appear in the outdoor landscape, in rural as well as urban areas.

Time is embedded in human existence – just think of all the mundane words that signal the flow of time: now, then, future, past, move, fast, slow, tomorrow, before, after, in the meantime, next, late, early, to mention just a few related to everyday life. There are also words relating to the rhythms of activities in human life, whether in the day (i.e. meal times, time for study and work, bedtime, free time), week (workday, weekend), year (school term, working periods, holidays) and life (childhood, adolescence adulthood, old age). Additionally, you find processual words like change, growth and shrink, all of which signal that something is going on over time. In geography, a longer term perspective of change is often linked to studies of geological time scales or historical geography.

In daily life, most people take time for granted, and established human conceptualisations of time, into hours, weeks, months and years, are means to order, communicate about and coordinate both everyday activities and long-term projects. Various kinds of clocks and calendars are invented and utilised to measure the flow of time and to organise and control an increasingly complex **modern** society; planning the production of goods and services involves logistics solutions wherein time and place are vital. Time is also essential for understanding processes in the natural environment, such as climate change and biological diversity. In short, time influences

48

DOI: 10.4324/9780429265853-6

most aspects of peoples' daily life, and this chapter considers how change over time is a fundamental component of an understanding of the past, present and future in geography.

Time can be seen as a means for understanding events that have already gone (past), are currently ongoing (what happens now), what might appear in time to come (future) and how events interrelate over any given period (including past, now and future). Studies of interrelations over time claim that time is seen as process, where the 'now-moment' (the 'now') is steadily flowing along a time dimension. Just as the now-moment moves into what previously was the future, it leaves what has passed behind. Hence, the now (the now-moment) has a unique property: it is always on the move and thereby constitutes a continuous transformation of future into the past. This is visualised in the upper part of Figure 4.1, where the time dimension is on the vertical axis, indicating the ongoing move of the now from below and upward. The now-moment is symbolised by the horizontal 'now-line', and is defined as the precise moment when future is transformed into past: now is steadily moving along the time-axis in a continuous pace, in the figure this is indicated by the small arrows under the 'now'. Along the time dimension, the displayed clock-time period may vary and periods from parts of seconds to eons can be shown.

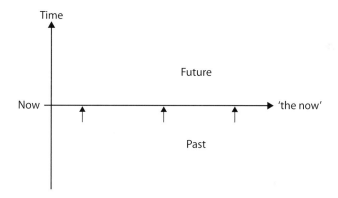

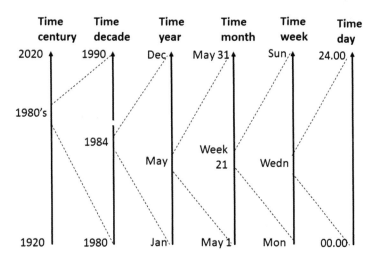

Figure 4.1
The continuous transformation of time

Source: Upper figure is inspired by Hägerstrand (2009), and lower figure is inspired by Ellegård (1983). Figure credit: Kajsa Ellegård

The lower part of Figure 4.1 exemplifies periods of various length. The time-scale of a day, of course, will give a more detailed picture of events than a time-scale of the week, decade or lifetime.

While the future includes various opportunities for people to act, the past consists of frozen events (already performed activities) that cannot be undone (even though events can be regretted and reinterpreted). This will be further elaborated on later in this chapter.

Time is the focal concept for this chapter, but, as indicated, place is as important, and the theoretical approach of time-geography foregrounds the simultaneous movements of people and things in time and **space**; geographic movements between places take time, while movements solely over time only appear when things and people are stationary (Hägerstrand, 1970, 1976, 1985, 2009).

Summary

- Time is embedded in human existence and can be conceptualised as a constant flow between past, now and future.
- Geographers have developed the theoretical approach of time-geography to explore simultaneous movements in time and space.

Objectified and experienced time: on how to communicate about time

You can discuss with your friends about precisely when a certain event occurred, but since you have different experiences of the event, your respective subjective ideas about when it happened are likely to be diverse. However, if you relate what happened to clock-time, your opportunities for agreement increase. Clock-time is a societal construction, which can be utilised as an objectification of time, to which your subjective experience of when the disputed event appeared can be related and an agreement eventually reached.

In geography, the construction of maps is based on agreements about rules and criteria, for example longitude and latitude, legend and scale, and therefore, maps are useful for communication between people about the location of places of mutual interest. Clock-time is the agreed upon means to communicate about time; what happened when, and what was the duration of the event. Time is, in its everyday immaterial appearance, less obvious and more elusive than that of a material place. While maps are images of locations in the material world, clocks are used to present an objectified image of the immaterial time.

However, in daily life, what the map and the clock show does not always correspond with the subjective experiences of people. Students who discuss a certain lecture they experienced together, located in the same place during the same time, may have different views of how long it lasted. They might have had divergent feelings during the lecture; a student lacking interest in the topic insists that the lecture lasted a long time and was protracted, while a student with deep interest in the content of the lecture says that it was over far too quickly. Each student's individual experiences of the duration of the event cannot be disputed, and their subjective ideas are, of course, correct from their own respective perspective. Such a subjective orientation to time can be labeled an everyday perspective of time.

Table 4.1 Contrasting perspectives on time (inspired by Ellegård, 2019a)		
Aspect	Everyday perspective	Analytical perspective
How are the two perspectives used?	Time is used without reflecting on it, for almost everybody it goes without saying	Time is used for systematic description, comparison and analysis
What is the relation between time and activity?	Time and activity are closely integrated and very hard to disentangle	Time and activity are looked upon as different entities. Time is used as a tool to describe activities in processes
Which is given priority, time or activity?	Activity has priority over the time it takes to perform it (you are done when your task is completed)	Time has priority over the activity performed (you are done when the time set of for the task is out)
How are traditions and repetition handled?	Focusing on repetition as a central part in forming traditions (re-occurring events may imply a circular view of time)	Process-oriented (past-present-future) and linear. Thereby, the same event is not repeated, instead similar events may appear in sequence (like your 1st, 2nd and 3rd birthdays and new year's eve of 2020, 2021, 2022 etc.)
What is meant by 'now'?	'Now' is the timespan that one can control and oversee	'Now' is a steadily forthcoming and disappearing moment, it is the continuous transformation of future to past
What is meant by 'future'?	'Future' is the time coming after time one can oversee	'Future' is the time that eventually will be transformed into 'now'. A prism of possibilities in the future can be revealed from 'now'
What is meant by 'past'?	'Past' events are located in the archive of memory	'Past' is about historical facts that cannot be changed (but re-evaluated)

But there are frequent occasions when it is important to pinpoint the start, duration and finish of an event, and then such subjective views may lead to misunderstandings and unexpected consequences. Just think of the importance of a schedule coordinating classes, so students and lecturers come together, or a correct timetable for the bus to get to the university in time. Hence, there is a need to relate events to a set of agreed upon tools to measure and communicate time, and clock-time is the social agreement which makes it possible for people with different subjective impressions to relate their respective experiences to a common ruler. In this way, we can draw a contrast between an analytical perspective based on objectified time, and an everyday perspective, based on experienced time (Table 4.1).

Time as self-evident and neglected – a day and a life perspective

Most of us use the everyday perspective on time in our daily life. From this perspective, the phenomenon of time is largely taken for granted, both in daily life and over a lifetime. In the day perspective, the regular appearance of the various activities a person performs in the course of the day is constrained by physiological needs, especially eating and sleeping. In a life perspective, a person's opportunities over the lifetime are shaped by the prevailing societal structures and arrangements, which clearly distinguish the experiences of people from different generations. This section presents ways to describe how physiological needs create rhythms in human daily life and how societal reforms create different life opportunities for people of different generations.

The day perspective: daily routines performed as time goes by

Wherever you are located, time goes by, as 'the now' moves along the time axis (see Figure 4.1). Where you are located has an influence on what you can do, since resources are unevenly spread, both socially and geographically. What you do now at this place is a result of a combination of what you want to do, what resources you have at your disposal and what other people and organisations do. For example, most people will coordinate their activities with family members, friends, work and study timetables, opening hours of shops, timetables of public transportation etc. There is, however, an even stronger restriction influencing the opportunities to perform activities, namely, the need to satisfy basic physiological needs. Eating and sleeping activities, then, are not negotiable if you want to stay healthy, and eating activities must be spread over the day. You must sleep for a period each day to make your body rest. How time-geography represents the rhythm of eating and sleeping events in the day and week perspective is shown in Figure 4.2. Time set aside several times daily for eating and drinking has a relatively short duration. Sleeping usually appears just once and has a comparatively long duration (at least for healthy people). In the day perspective (as in the right part of Figure 4.2), however, sleep might seem to appear twice, once in the late evening and again in early morning. This is an effect of the chosen time scale (day). With the time scale of a week (left part of Figure 4.2), it is obvious that the sleep period is unbroken.

For many people, the rhythm of meeting these physiological needs influences the opportunity to perform other activities, while for others their other activities (night shift work, for example) will constrain when physiological needs are met. For most people, these other activities will be valued more highly than the mundane ones of eating and sleeping, for example study, work, shopping, socialising, theatre, sport and other recreational activities. In order to get a deeper understanding of the rhythm of peoples' daily life, time-geographers have carried out empirical studies of different people and different social groups in different places (see Ellegård, 2019b, for an edited collection).

The life perspective: as the society changes, generations experience different opportunities

The lifetime of every human being can be analysed on the time dimension from the moment of birth until death. What the individual is exposed to during childhood, adolescence, adulthood and at old age strongly relate to the opportunities provided by the society at that time. For example, for those born before World War II in western Europe, education opportunities were limited, as was access to welfare benefits and paid holidays. Figure 4.3 shows how a longer time perspective allows us to compare the life experiences of two individuals (A and B) from different generations in Sweden. They are born 60 years apart, which means their life opportunities differ substantially. Individuals growing up after the introduction of social benefits take them

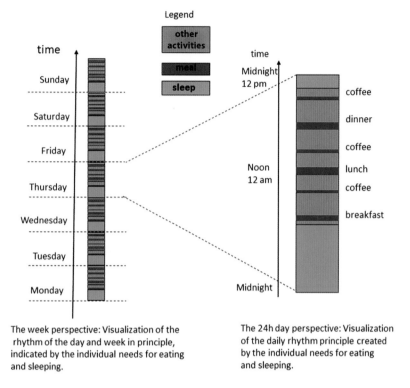

Figure 4.2
The rhythms of a day (right) and a week (left) as formed by the physiological needs for eating and sleeping

Source: Developed from Ellegård (1999 and 2019a). Figure credit: Kajsa Ellegård

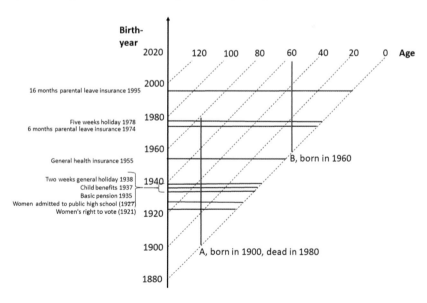

Figure 4.3
Influence of birth year on life experience for A, born 1900 and died 1980, and B, born 1960

Source: Inspired by Hägerstrand (1972) and Ellegård (2019a). Figure credit: Kajsa Ellegård

for granted, while people who grew up before welfare reforms experienced huge improvements during their lives. In Sweden today, it is obligatory for all pupils to spend at least nine years in school, but in the early twentieth century, women were not allowed any access to the public high school system. For younger generations, this is strange, and social welfare rights are taken for granted, while for older people these reforms represent the outcome of political struggles for improved welfare.

Summary

- Time geographers draw a distinction between objectified time and experienced time.
- Their studies have revealed the way the use of time revolves around the meeting of basic physiological needs.
- These studies can be carried out over any relevant timescale – a day, or part of the day, a week, a year, a lifetime or several centuries.

Time-space movements – individual paths and prisms

The individual path – to visualise an individual's movements in the past

This section presents a tool for following people's movements in space over time, called an individual path. Such a path illustrates the activities someone has undertaken and their location in time-space. Following Hägerstrand (1970) and Mårtensson (1979), a person's activities are constrained by physical and psychological abilities, resources and knowledges (*capability constraints*); prevailing laws, rules and conventions (*authority constraints*); and the opportunities to be in the right place at the right time, either to meet other people or to be located at the same place as important objects (a bus, or a school, for instance) (*coupling constraints*). The study of capacity and authority constraints is common across the social sciences, while the analysis of coupling constraints appears in time-geography to underline the importance of time-space coordination in order to be successful in fulfilling plans and achieving goals.

Every human being has, at every moment in time, a unique location in time-space. The visualisation of time-space is a combination of the time-dimension and a place-dimension, and all geographical movements performed by a person can be visualised on an individual path, which moves along time and place dimensions.

To simplify this concept, Figure 4.4 shows two students who live at the same address and two stationary buildings (home and the university). Student (1) remains in the home all day and consequently the individual path describing this student's movements is parallel to the time-axis the whole day. The other student (2) is initially stationary in the home, then s/he moves to the university where s/he attends lectures, before moving back home. When student (2) moves geographically, the individual path describing her/his movements illustrates these moves by altering the angle both to the time-axis and to the place axis. We can see that student (2) is stationary

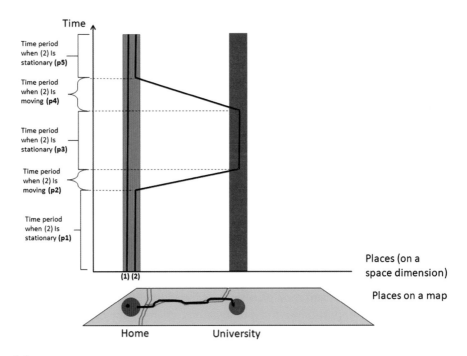

Figure 4.4
The principle of visualising movements of students (1) and (2) in time-space with the time dimension along the y-axis and a space dimension along the x-axis

Source: Figure credit: Kajsa Ellegård

in the home twice during the day (p1 and p5), moves twice (p2 and p4) and is stationary at the university once (p3). Also, the figure shows that it takes more time for (2) to move back from the university in the afternoon (p4) since s/he is not in as much hurry as when rushing to get to the lecture (p2).

It is important to underline that an individual path does not represent the more complex subjective experiences of time and only shows the time-space movements of the person (for a debate about this see Buttimer, 1976, Rose, 1993, Hägerstrand, 2006). So, both students, (1) and (2), might have had rich experiences, even though student (1) was at home all day.

This is a very simple example to illustrate the principles behind the approach, but applying these analytical principles has given rise to a whole set of very rich empirical studies tracing people's differential movements across time and space, uncovering for instance differences in **gendered** and racialised uses of space, in accessibility to work and childcare opportunities and in commuting patterns and shopping behaviour (see Ellegård, 2019b for an anthology of time-geographic studies drawn from different countries). Others have shown how time-space movements are connected to a persons' experiences (Dijst, 2019). Based on interviews (utilising the everyday time perspective), people can relate their subjective experiences to their activities and objectified time-space location over the visualised period (based on the analytical time perspective). Such approaches have been used by occupational- and physio-therapists when helping patients to overcome difficulties in pursuing their daily activities. (Orban et al., 2012, Bredland et al., 2015, Anaby et al., 2020.)

The individual path – on how to visualise a person's possible movements in the future

An individual path illustrates what has happened in the past, and located in the time-space position 'now', people partly plan their future activities based on their wishes, resources and experiences from the past. The realisation of future planned activities often involves a trip to another place. But what opportunities does a person have to move geographically from their current location to other places for performing these desired activities? Given their location right now in time-space the person can, in principle, move in any geographical direction. However, there are, of course, restrictions influencing any individual's ability to realise future activities located at other places. One hindrance concerns the distance from the current location to the desired location. Another hindrance concerns the speed of any available means of transportation. These restrictions are visualised in Figure 4.5. The slower the speed of the means of transportation (right-hand side of the figure), the smaller the area within reach (called *potential path area*) of the individual. Note that this is a theoretical illustration and that transport systems and land use in the real world are other important restrictions, as are individual's own financial resources (see Lenntorp, 1976). In urban and rural planning, such restrictions must be taken into account when discussing peoples' opportunities to go to locations where planned activities take place.

   Most people have a home where they sleep after spending time at work or education, and the need for movements between the home and other places is the rationale for the *principle of return* (Hägerstrand, 1970, Lenntorp, 1976). This principle implies that people return to their home to sleep (in the day perspective) or go back to their work place after having lunch elsewhere (in the working hours perspective). This mirrors the rhythm of the physiological needs described earlier in Figure 4.2. Figure 4.6 visualises the principle of return, where a combination of a time-space prism and the potential path area on a map shows how far away student (2) can go from

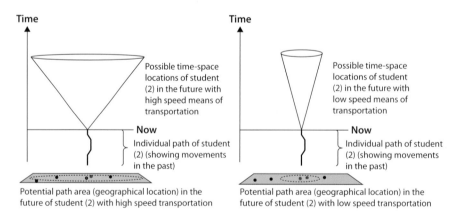

Potential path area (geographical location) in the future of student (2) with high speed transportation

Potential path area (geographical location) in the future of student (2) with low speed transportation

Figure 4.5
Principle showing the possibility for a person to move to other places given her/his location now in time-space. Blue dot = home, red dot = university and black dots = other places. Left: high-speed transportation. Right: low speed transportation. The individual path illustrates the movements of student (2) (from Figure 4.4) until now, and the cone indicates the possible locations of student (2) in the future. Within the cone, student (2) can be located at just one place at a time as the now moves into the future

Source: Figure credit: Kajsa Ellegård

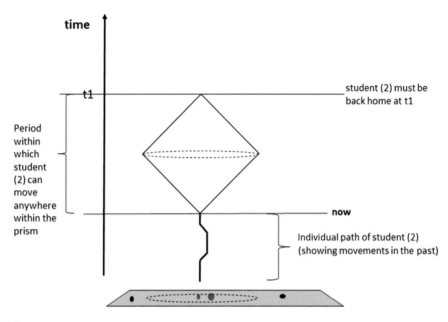

Figure 4.6
The principle of return is illustrated by a prism, and it shows how far away the student (2) can move before s/he has to turn back in order to be back home again at t1. Blue dot = home, red dot = university and black dots = other places. Dotted oval line on the map = potential path area

Source: Figure credit: Kajsa Ellegård

her/his location at 'the now' within a specific period, before s/he has to be back home. The prism is shown in the upper part of Figure 4.6 and the potential path area is shown in the lower part of the same figure (see also Miller, 1991, 2005, Farber et al., 2013).

The prism is a visual image of a person's opportunities to reach other places, based on objectified clock-time. There are, however, also subjective aspects of the prism. Maybe a part of the route is known to be dangerous, and if so, this section is passed quickly and on high alert, or is avoided. Kwan (2008), for instance, has documented the restricted movement pattern of Muslim women in the US after the 9-11 attacks, and comparisons between the prism and the subjective experience of reachable places can serve as a point of departure for planning and providing safer outdoor environments.

Summary

- An individual path shows a person's geographic locations in sequence over time in the past.
- Empirical studies can reveal the differential use of space and time by different individuals and social groups.
- A prism can be used to illustrate potential opportunities to move to other places in the future – and as the now-moment (see Figure 4.1) moves up the time axis, the future prism will also move up but will change its form.

Conclusion

History is full of technological and organisational inventions and innovations aiming at reducing the (human) time it takes to perform activities, whether in the household or in the production of goods and services (Lenntorp, 2008). The wheel, steam engine, electricity systems, telegraph/telephone, radio/TV, social media and information and communication technology (ICT) have all had immense influence on daily life since they were invented, leading to the creation of new kinds of jobs and benefits for some people, while others have lost employment and income. Such attempts to reduce the constraints of time and space have resulted in automation, migration, urbanisation and **gentrification**, along with social, cultural and political movements.

The technically embedded potential in ICT to reshape the organisation of study, work and retail activities became a savior for many during the COVID-19 pandemic. Lock-downs forced people to stay at home almost all the time, and time previously used for commuting was erased. People having ICT equipment in their home, and with appropriate jobs, could go on with their work and study activities, albeit remotely. The individual paths describing their daily life movements before and during the pandemic lock-downs differed considerably, and their daily prisms shrank, while time with other household members in the same space increased.

Some have gone so far as to claim that ICT implies the 'death of distance' (Cairncross, 1997) while others have talked about an increasing **time-space compression** (Giddens, 1984, Warf, 2017). However, geographic distance remains relevant and after all, the Earth is the same size as before – even if the internet has brought the other side of the world within reach in a split second. Indeed, from an analytical perspective on time, the concept of compressed time might be problematic since it could be interpreted as if time itself is being compressed. What is actually happening is that the material processes we use are becoming faster, whether in transportation or information technology and communication, while time flows at the same pace as before.

Taking time explicitly into consideration in human geography allows a host of important issues about the use of space and time to be revealed and analysed, whether at individual, household or societal levels. It also allows us to understand environmental as well as social issues, over timescales stretching from a second to a millennium and beyond. The current attention paid to climate change (see Chapter 41), for instance, is underpinned by the notion of change over time. The tools presented here help us to reveal and understand the hidden constraints embedded in our structures and systems, constraints which must be tackled if we are to improve our living environments and create a more equitable use of time and space.

Discussion points

- Write a short version of your activities yesterday, in sequence from midnight to midnight (what time did you do what activity, where, together with whom, what resources did you use and how did you feel doing this activity). Draw your individual path based on the principles set out in Figure 4.4. Write, by the side of the path, what activity you performed each time you change from one activity to another. Reflect on these questions, and on how your use of time and space was constrained:

What places did you visit during the day? How long did you stay at the place(s)? Did you visit the same place more than once?
Whom did you meet during the day?
How did your need for sleep and food influence the timing of the activities you performed?
Was there any activity that you had planned to do that you could not perform? What constraints hindered you in undertaking that activity (capability, authority and/or coupling constraints)?

- How do you think time-geography can be used to uncover gendered differences in the use of space?
- How might we use empirical studies of people's daily paths to improve our understanding of the lived environment?
- How might those looking to improve transport systems make use of time-geography?

References

Anaby, D., Vrotsou, K., Kroksmark, U., and Ellegård, K. (2020). Changes in participation patterns of youth with physical disabilities following the pathways and resources for engagement and participation intervention: a time-geography approach. *Scandinavian Journal of Occupational Therapy* 27(5): 364–372.

Bredland, E., Magnus, E., and Vik, K. (2015). Physical activity patterns in older men. *Physical & Occupational Therapy in Geriatrics* 33(1): 87–102.

Buttimer, A. (1976). Grasping the dynamism of the lifeworld. *Annals of the American Association of Geographers* 66: 277–292.

Cairncross, F. (1997). *The Death of Distance: How the Communications Revolution Will Change Our Lives.* London: Orion Business.

Dijst, M. (2019). A Relational Interpretation of Time-Geography. In *Time-Geography in the Global Context*, ed. K. Ellegård. Abingdon and New York: Routledge.

Ellegård, K. (1983). *Människa – Produktion. Tidsbilder av ett produktionssystem.* Meddelanden från Göteborgs universitets Geografiska institutioner, serie B, nr 72, 1983.

Ellegård, K. (1999). A time-geographical approach to the study of everyday life of individuals—a challenge of complexity. *GeoJournal* 48(3): 167–175.

Ellegård, K. (2019a). *Thinking Time Geography. Concepts, Methods and Applications.* London: Routledge.

Ellegård, K. (ed.) (2019b). *Time Geography in the Global Context.* London: Routledge.

Farber, S., Neutens, T., Miller, H. J., and Li, X. (2013). The social interaction potential of metropolitan regions: a time-geographic measurement approach using joint accessibility. *Annals of the Association of American Geographers* 103(3): 483–504.

Giddens, A. (1984). *The Constitution of Society: Outline of the Theory of Structuration.* Berkeley: University of California Press.

Hägerstrand, T. (1970). What about people in regional science? *Papers of the Regional Science Association* 24(1970): 7–21.

Hägerstrand, T. (1972). Om en konsistent individorienterad samhällsbeskrivning för framtidsstudiebruk. In *Ds Ju*. Stockholm: Justitiedepartementet, 25.

Hägerstrand, T. (1976). Geography and the study of interaction between nature and society. *Geoforum* 7: 329–344.

Hägerstrand, T. (1985). Time-Geography: Focus on the Corporeality of Man, Society, and Environment. In *The Science and Praxis of Complexity*. Tokyo: United Nations University, 193–216.

Hägerstrand, T. (2006). Foreword by Torsten Hägerstrand. In *By Northern Lights: On the Making of Geography in Sweden*, eds. A. Buttimer and T. Mels. Aldershot: Ashgate, xi–xiv

Hägerstrand, T. (2009). In *Tillvaroväven*, eds. K. Ellegård and U. Svedin. Stockholm: Formas.

Kwan, M-P. (2008). From oral histories to visual narratives: re-presenting the post-September 11 experiences of Muslim women in the USA. *Social & Cultural Geography* 9(6): 653–669.

Lenntorp, B. (1976). Paths in space-time environments. A time-geographic study of movement possibilities of individuals. Meddelanden från Lunds universitets Geografiska institutioner. Diss. LXXVII.

Lenntorp, B. (2008). Innovation Diffusion as Spatial Process (1953): Torsten Hägerstrand. In *Key Texts in Human Geography*, eds. P. Hubbard, R. Kitchin, and G. Valentine. Thousand Oaks: Sage Publications, 1–8.

Mårtensson, S. (1979). *On the Formation of Biographies in Space-Time Environments*. Lund: Diss. University of Lund, Department of Geography.

Miller, H. J. (1991). Modelling accessibility using space-time prism concepts within geographical information systems. *International Journal of Geographical Information Systems* 5(3): 287–301.

Miller, H. J. (2005). Place-Based versus People-Based Accessibility. In *Access to Destinations*, eds. D. M. Levinson and K. J. Krizek. Amsterdam and Boston: Elsevier, 63–89.

Orban, K., Edberg, A.-K., and Erlandsson, L.-K. (2012). Using a time-geographical diary method in order to facilitate reflections on changes in patterns of daily occupations. *Scandinavian Journal of Occupational Therapy* 19: 249–259.

Rose, G. (1993). *Feminism and Geography: The Limits of Geographical Knowledge*. Cambridge: Polity Press.

Russell, B. (1961). *The History of Western Philosophy*. New York and London: Simon & Schuster/George Allen & Unwin.

Warf, B. (2017). *Time-Space Compression*. Oxford Bibliographies. https://www.oxfordbibliographies.com/view/document/obo-9780199874002/obo-9780199874002-0025.xml#obo-9780199874002-0025-bibItem-0005

Online materials

- Kajsa Ellegård, Time Geography, in Oxford Bibliographies https://www.oxfordbibliographies.com/display/document/obo-9780199874002/obo-9780199874002-0161.xml?rskey=L7AclH&result=229
- Vardagboken, a diary application. Search for it on your mobile phone (either iPhone or Android). So far just in Swedish but soon to be also released in English.
- Daily Life, a diary application. Download it from https://liu.se/en/employee/kajel11

Further reading

Try to read a selection of these, as they all provide empirical studies of the use of time geography.

Ellegård, K. (2019). *Thinking Time Geography. Concepts, Methods and Applications*. Routledge. https://www.taylorfrancis.com/books/oa-mono/10.4324/9780203701386/thinking-time-geography-kajsa-elleg%C3%A5rd

Kwan, M.-P. (2008). From oral histories to visual narratives: re-presenting the post-September 11 experiences of Muslim women in the USA. *Social & Cultural Geography* 9(6): 653–669.

Li, C., and Zhang, Y. (2022). The time geography response to the digital transition of everyday life. *Progress in Human Geography* 41(1): 96–106.

Magnus, E. (2019). The Time-Geographic Diary Method in Studies of Everyday Life. In *Time Geography in the Global Context. An Anthology*, ed. K. Ellegår. Routledge. Free download: https://www.taylorfrancis.com/chapters/oa-edit/10.4324/9780203701393-7/time-geographic-diary-method-studies-everyday-life-eva-magnus

Nishimura, Y., Okamoto, K., and Boulibam, S. (2010). Time-geographic analysis on natural resource use in a village of the Vientianne Plain. *Southeast Asian Studies* 47: 426–450.

Orban, K., Edberg, A-K., Thorngren-Jerneck, K., Önnerfält, J., and Erlandsson, L.-K. (2014). Changes in parents' time use and its relationship to child obesity. *Physical & Occupational Therapy in Pediatrics* 34(1): 44–61.

Shaw, S.-L. (ed.) (2012). Special issue: time geography. *Journal of Transport Geography* 23: 1–4

Thulin, E., and Vilhelmson, B. (2022). Pacesetters in contemporary telework: how smartphones and mediated presence reshape the time–space rhythms of daily work. *New Technology, Work and Employment* 37(2): 250–269.

5 Place

Soren Larsen

Introduction: the paradox of place

Place is a paradox. It is so close to our everyday awareness that, like the nose on your face, it is difficult to see. It is so fundamental as a context for meaning and action that we take it for granted. Geographers have long pointed to the ways place structures and enables our experience of the world. They have underscored the social and political importance of our engagements with place. For some, place runs deeper, underpinning the very foundation of our being. As philosopher Edward Casey (1996) has argued, the world never appears as a whole but rather comes to us through places. Without place, we could not know the world at all.

Despite—or perhaps because of—its elusiveness, place is one of the most common concepts in human geography. It has been the focus of study in many other disciplines as well, from anthropology, sociology, and history to architectural studies, planning, and public health. If we move beyond academia, we will find other disciplinary traditions of place. Indigenous peoples, for example, have developed some of the most robust place-based systems in the world. This chapter introduces you to the ways academic geographers have studied place and then will step outside the academy to look at the concept's broader purview in Indigenous and other non-Western intellectual traditions. Taken together, the concepts in this introduction provide a basis not just for those of you wishing to study place as an academic pursuit but also for anyone interested in becoming a more skilled 'student of place' in everyday life.

How can we get a handle on such a slippery concept as place? Geographer John Agnew (2011) provides a helpful starting point by conceptualising place in terms of three dimensions:

- Location
- Locale
- Sense of place

All places have location, or a position in space. Keep in mind that the 'space' of place is not limited to the physical but includes the social and cultural as well. For example, we can think of the place a person occupies in society, that is, their social position, or the imagined places of novels, films, video games, and virtual realities. Locale, by contrast, designates place as the context for human-environment interaction and social relations. In this sense, place is the setting in which things happen or 'take place', to use the common phrase in literal terms. Finally, place is nothing if not meaningful. Geographer Yi-Fu Tuan described places as 'centers of felt value' (1977: 4) that emerge as people invest meaning and emotion into undifferentiated space, creating a world of

DOI: 10.4324/9780429265853-7

places and senses of place, or the experiential knowledge of what it means and feels like to be there. As you can see, part of place's complexity stems from the fact that it underpins the entire range of human experience and social life, from the material to the symbolic.

Place and placelessness

Another way to get a handle on place is to look at the history of the concept in the academic field of geography. With some notable exceptions, place was not a primary concept when geography was getting established as a university discipline in the late nineteenth century. Most of the discipline was focused instead on developing a theory of environmental determinism that used the natural world to explain global spatial variations in social organisation and cultural behaviour—at least as perceived by Western observers within a Eurocentric framework of development and progress. Although geography's disciplinary focus shifted temporarily to regional description in the early twentieth century, the quest for spatial theory reappeared after World War II. In the 1950s and 1960s, many geographers sought to transform geography into a **spatial science**. This came out of postwar optimism in the power of science and technology, advances in computing, and the development of more sophisticated forms of quantitative analysis and spatial modeling. The so-called quantitative revolution in geography focused on uncovering the spatial regularities that govern human behaviour and environmental interactions.

In the 1970s, **humanistic geographers** pushed back against the quantitative revolution. These geographers emphasised the meaningfulness of human experience from a subjective point of view which could not be reduced to abstract regularities. Anne Buttimer (1976) explored the geographies of the 'lifeworld', or the preconscious rhythms and flows of lived experience, and Edward Relph's *Place and Placelessness* (1976) argued that mass communication and consumer culture were transforming our experiences of place into existential 'outsideness'—that is, not belonging anywhere. A popular depiction of the supposed placelessness of late twentieth-century society in the West is James Kunstler's *Geography of Nowhere* (1993), which criticises the homogenising effects of postwar suburbs, shopping malls, and interstate highways. The sentiment of placelessness got radio play in 1982 when the English-American rock group The Pretenders released 'My City Was Gone'. In the first verse, vocalist Chrissie Hynde sings about the experience of returning from a years long stint in England to her hometown of Akron, Ohio, United States. In her years overseas, Akron had been developed into a landscape of shopping malls, urban plazas, and parking lots (Figure 5.1). All her favourite places had disappeared, and the city, for her, was 'gone'.

Summary

- Place is a complex concept that underpins the entire range of human experience and social life.
- Places can be described in terms of objective location, context or 'locale', and subjective meaning, or 'sense of place'.
- Humanistic geography was one of the first formal academic approaches to focus on the study of place, emerging in the 1970s as part of a broader social response to the perceived 'placelessness' of industrialised society.

Figure 5.1
Cascade Plaza in Akron, Ohio, USA, built in the late 1960s as part of the urban renewal that razed the predominately African-American business district on Howard Street, which The Pretenders lamented in the 1982 hit song, 'My City Was Gone'

Source: Photo credit: Sleepydre/Wikimedia Commons

Critical approaches to place

The late twentieth century saw the rise of a range of reactionary political movements based around place, for example those which focused on anti-immigration sentiments, white nationalism, and some forms of **regionalism** and separatism. These movements thought of place in an inward-looking way—nostalgic, provincial, even xenophobic—a retreat from the globally interconnected world. Analytically, the challenge for geographers became how to think about place not in this inward way, but in relation to global flows and connections. This task was taken up in the 1980s by **Marxist** geographers, and Doreen Massey (1991), for example, argued that a historical-materialist analysis helps us see place not as a bounded location, but as a 'meeting place' where global social relations converge. This creates unique localities that reflect (and can become sites of resistance against) global inequalities in capital, power, and mobility. Using the example of Kilburn High Road in northwest London, close to where she lived, Massey points to a landscape of people, goods, and images from around the world, all meeting in this particular place. There's a Muslim newsagent lamenting the war in the Persian Gulf, pamphlets on sale from the Irish Free State, advertisements for concerts by English musician Morrissey and Indian composer Anand Miland, to say nothing of all the foods and goods on offer from around the world. Kilburn is not simply an English shopping district in northwest London, but the 'coming together' of the world in one location, like a set of threads being woven together. This sort of outward-looking, politically progressive 'global sense of place' raises important scholarly and political questions about how global movements, flows, and networks get worked out in local contexts where place is a site of struggle, resistance, and socio-political change.

Historical materialism is part of a broader tradition in Western philosophy known as critical theory, which orients intellectual analysis toward social critique and political change. In geography, critical theory reintroduced questions about the notion of place via the study of **ideology**, or the systems of ideas that underpin and 'map' social practices, institutions, and worldviews (Jackson, 1989, Mitchell, 2000). From a critical perspective, ideologies require critique to expose, challenge, and ultimately change the systems of social inequality and environmental exploitation they depend on. Place is a key **ideological** 'category' in this work because often it makes the partial judgments of the dominant group appear *natural*, just the way things are. Some values, practices, and people are designated as 'in place', whereas others are marked as 'out of place', an ideological delineation that is enforced through social and material practices on the ground.

Tim Cresswell's *In Place/Out of Place* (1996) is an important book on the relationship between ideology and place. One of the empirical studies from the book concerns the Greenham Common Women's Peace Camp, established in 1981 outside the fence of the Greenham Common air base on the outskirts of Newbury, Berkshire, England. The women were protesting against the presence of U.S. cruise missiles and nuclear warheads on the base, angered by the location of weapons of mass destruction in the English countryside. The women had left their homes and were living in polythene structures known as 'benders' arranged into a motley bunch of 'higgledy-piggledy camps'. Soon, some Newbury residents and members of the English press began criticising the women's activism. On what grounds? Existing outside the private, domestic space of the English home, town authorities and members of the press deemed the women 'out of place'. While the women were protesting about the presence of weapons of mass destruction in the countryside (itself an ideological struggle over place), the broader political question became the place of women in English society.

You can see how ideologies of place play out close to home—just look at the university or college campus where many of you are studying. Campuses are places that reflect changing ideologies over time and project those ideologies into everyday life. Think about the values embodied in the architectural styles of campus buildings. On some campuses, the highly stylised towers and spires of Gothic structures, originally intended to draw the eye toward the heavens, project the almost divine authority of the educational mission, whereas on others the symmetry of Classical Revival buildings expresses Enlightenment values of rationalism, secularism, and order. The drab functionalism of **Modernist** concrete office buildings embodies the post-World War faith in efficiency and technology, whereas **postmodern** architecture playfully combines images and gestures of past styles into commodifiable forms—such as new, privately owned student housing complexes made to look like 'lodges' or 'villas'. Now, turn your eye to the broader landscape. Most campuses have green space—yards, quadrangles, or lawns—and some are set in park-like environments that create an **atmosphere** conducive to a mind-opening liberal arts education shielded from the drab, regimented spaces of industrial society. Comb through your university's regulations, however, and you will likely find campus restrictions on motorised vehicles, public gatherings, and camping overnight. These green spaces simultaneously model and manage human behaviour. University authorities can invoke such regulations to exclude or manage alternative uses of campus space, for example by student protesters, motorised scooter companies, skateboarders, or the local unhoused population. Campuses, in other words, are not just

Figure 5.2
In a 2015 protest against racism on the University of Missouri campus, the Student group Concerned Student 1950 turned one of the quadrangles into a tent camp for Jonathan Butler's hunger-strike, disrupting the ideological order of this space

Source: Photo credit: Bill Greenblatt/Alamy

places where you go to university. They are also ideological constructions that enfranchise the activities and values of certain social groups while excluding others, whose presence is marked as inappropriate or even disruptive to the order and appearance of the place itself (see Figure 5.2).

Placemaking

Critical scholarship has given us a deeper understanding of the politics of place, or the ways in which people struggle over the meanings and uses of places, often as part of political activism and social movements. In this sense, place is more than location, locale, and meaning; it is the *process* through which material and cultural realities are formed on the ground in the context of societies divided by **class**, **race**, sex, **gender** identity, **ethnicity**, age, and so on. Such politics of place are especially evident in new studies of placemaking, which examine how people construct places in support of broader organisational goals and actions. In her study of Minneapolis, Minnesota, United States, Deborah Martin (2003) used the concept of 'collective action frames' to understand how local community organisations 'framed' their neighbourhoods in ways that rallied diverse (and often, disinterested) residents around a common vision and agenda. Place, you could say, was being used as a motivational tool by neighbourhood organisers, but there was more to it than that: the Minneapolis neighbourhoods Martin studied were actively being made through the political process of organising residents into collective action.

Studies of placemaking have also contributed to our understanding of place and emotion. The edited book *Emotional Geographies* (Davidson et al., 2005) is a good starting point for new understandings of emotion as more than something individuals experience in their own minds. This research looks instead at how emotions are generated through the spatial interaction of people, places, and things. These interactions create a 'field' that gives a certain emotional 'charge' to the places we experience and engage in everyday life. Emotions, in other words, are dynamic *spatial* experiences, not simply the way we feel in our heads. This understanding departs from the humanistic approach of the 1970s, which typically approached meaning from the perspective of the individual. By contrast, contemporary research on place and emotion can be understood as 'post-humanist' because it considers the entire spatial 'field' from which individual emotions and feelings emerge.

A related development in the post-humanist scholarship on place is the recent 'creative turn' in geography. This approach uses creative methodologies (e.g. art, poetry, music, dance, storytelling) not just to engage and understand the world—something artists have been doing for millennia—but also to create original, **embodied** forms of geographic knowledge that challenge ideological constructions and envision alternative worlds. In 2009, geographer Harriet Hawkins set out to do an **ethnographic** study of *Caravanserai*, a participatory arts project run by artist Annie Lovejoy at the Porthscatho campsite, Cornwall, United Kingdom. Soon, she found herself pulled into the group's creative practice, ultimately collaborating with Lovejoy on an artist's book called *insites*. Hawkins (2015) identifies how 'creative doings' such as her drawing practice in the field became a way of knowing place through creative practice, despite her own admission that she is 'bad' at drawing! Her point is that, for geographers, the artistic product matters less than the ways in which art engages us in knowing and making place. Such creative engagements are political, raising important questions about inclusion and accessibility in arts practice as well as the potential for creative expression as a means of social critique and political intervention. In asking how place-based art can fashion alternative worlds and speculative futures, geographers in the 'creative turn' are combining the creative and the critical into a geographic praxis that is finely attuned to the power of place (see Figure 5.3).

Summary

- In the 1980s, critical geographers oriented the study of place toward social critique and political change by investigating the ideologies, or systems of meaning and power, that shape material and social reality.
- Place is a key ideological 'category' because it often makes the partial judgments of the dominant group appear universal, natural, and therefore incontestable.
- Critical scholarship also has focused on the study of placemaking, or the ways in which people construct and struggle over the meaning and uses of places, often in the context of political activism and social change.
- Recent developments in critical scholarship have highlighted the formative role of place in 'spatialising' emotion and creativity—that is, 'decentering' the human subject showing how emotion and creativity are not the product of the individual mind but rather are a property of place.

Figure 5.3
Undergraduate art student Hayley Portell makes art in place on the shore of Cheslatta Lake for a children's book project authored in collaboration with Elders from the Cheslatta Carrier Nation, British Columbia, Canada

Source: Photo credit: Soren Larsen

The power of place

The idea that place has **power** is found early in the Western intellectual tradition. Place was a primary concept for Greek philosophers—from Archytas, whose axiom 'To be (at all) is to be in (some) place' situated place at the bedrock of being, to Aristotle, who argued that place is prerequisite for change and movement and therefore **space** and time (Casey, 1998). In the European Medieval period, place fell out of favor among philosophers, who developed new systems of thought based on the divine expansiveness and hierarchies of space (and time) over the distributed particularities of place. By the time of the scientific revolution and Isaac Newton, whose model of absolute space contained the laws of the universe and everything in it, place had been reduced to the status of mere location. The preference for space over place in Western philosophy continued into the twentieth century, which also helps explain why it was not until after World War II that place finally gained traction as a core concept in human geography.

What about non-Western traditions, though? Here again, we find the power of place. In Japanese philosophy, for example, place, or *basho*, has been an important theme since the Medieval period, perhaps most fully developed in the early twentieth-century philosophy of Kitarō Nishida and his 'Kyoto School', which understands place as the emptiness that paradoxically provides ground for subjective and objective realities and their 'logics'. Around the world, Indigenous philosophies of place have persisted despite centuries of past and ongoing

colonialism, and a current generation of Indigenous scholars is orienting such 'place thought' toward the future survival of human and nonhuman relatives in the **Anthropocene**, an era of climate change and species extinction. As Eve Tuck and Marcia McKenzie pointed out in their introduction to *Place in Research*, '...one major outgrowth of the increased attention to Indigenous perspectives and methodologies in academic discourse is the recognition that alternative, long-held, comprehensive and theoretically sophisticated understandings of place exist outside, alongside, against, and within the domain of the Western philosophical tradition' (2014: 11. See also Chapters 10, 43, 45, 71 for further examples of Indigenous scholarship).

To understand the power of place from an Indigenous perspective, we must shift from a Western conceptualisation of place as location, locale, meaning, or even process. Summarising the basic principle found in many North American Indigenous philosophies, Vine Deloria, Jr., and Daniel Wildcat offer a simple equation: power and place produce personality. Power refers to the living energy of the universe, whereas place denotes the relationship of things to each other. Personality, or the uniqueness of things, is the energy of the universe expressed through the relationships of place. As Deloria, Jr., and Wildcat write, 'This equation simply means that the universe is alive, but it also contains within it the very important suggestion that the universe is personal and, therefore, must be approached in a personal way' (2001: 23). Place situates us within relationships that have intrinsic moral content, enjoining us to focus on the results of our own thoughts and actions. While this particular 'equation' comes from a North American context, similar forms of Indigenous place thought can be found around the world.

An educational relationship with place

Indigenous perspectives suggest a distinctively educational relationship with place that guides us in seeking out and reciprocating the personal relationships that sustain social and **ecological** well-being and coexistence. A core part of a place-based education involves dismantling ideological systems that promote inequality, exclusion, and oppression, whether social or environmental. In part, this is what it means to be a student of place: cultivating the 'relationship of things' in opposition to ideologies that exclude and erase. Tuck and McKenzie conceptualised this approach to education and research as 'critical place inquiry' which, among other things, understands places as mobile and shifting over time, interactive and dynamic, possessing their own **agency** to pull human and nonhuman beings into the realities of relationship (2015: 19). In pursuing a 'relational ethics of accountability to people and place', critical place inquiry supports a politics that dismantles structures of colonialism and settler colonisation while expanding the 'social' to include nonhuman communities and the land itself.

As critical place inquiry suggests, our relationship with place is not only educational but political as well. In his essay 'Place Against Empire' (2010), Dene scholar Glen Coulthard demonstrates how the relationships of place are central in Indigenous resistance against colonialism, settler-state sovereignty, and **capitalist** accumulation. Colonialism is, at root, an ongoing act of *displacement* that physically and symbolically removes Indigenous peoples from their places to make land available for settler society in the form of property. Drawing on the work of Peter Kukchyksi, Coulthard sees a fundamental difference between radical Western and Indigenous activisms in this respect. From a Marxist perspective, the **alienation** of workers is expressed in terms of the theft of their *time*, which is coopted for wage labour, whereas for the colonised, alienation is expressed in the spatial terms of dispossession, or the theft of their *places*. This difference helps explain how radical Western activists can inadvertently promote colonial structures even as they seek partnerships and alliances in support of Indigenous social movements: in privileging time and history over place and land, Western activism can be as ethnocentric as the systems it resists, without questioning the broader Western ideologies that have subjugated the political importance of place to the supposed universalities of time and space.

How to move beyond this impasse? Coulthard is quick to point out that place guides potentially *all* of us toward less oppressive realities by holding us accountable to the relationships of land, that is, all the relationships that sustain us physically, mentally, socially, and spiritually. Place decolonises by guiding us and holding us accountable to these relationships. Indigenous academics and thinkers from around the world have underscored this specific 'agency of place'. For example, Vanessa Watts (2013) described how Anishinaabe 'place thought' unravels claims of settler ownership of land, and the book *Imagining Decolonisation* (Kiddle et al., 2020) draws from a Māori 'tūrangawaewae (standing place) of thought' to envision new paths forward in decolonising Aotearoa New Zealand. In my own work with Jay T. Johnson, we discovered the agency of place at work in social movements that brought the Indigenous and non-Indigenous activists' relationships with place to the fore, helping them work through the broken relationships of colonialism while developing place-based imaginaries of allied resistance and shared

Figure 5.4
A hikoi (march) involving Māori and Pākehā (non-Native people) in opposition to Statoil's offshore seismic oil exploration arrives at Te Tii Marae to coincide with the Prime Minister's visit for Waitangi Day in Aotearoa New Zealand, 2015

Source: Photo credit: Soren Larsen

futures. Their activism never resulted in total agreement or alignment: place supports plural ways of being and knowing that, while distinct and irreducible to one another, also exist in relationship to one another. The place-based activist movements we studied were grounded in this deeper reality—and challenge—of being-together-in-place (see Figure 5.4).

Summary

- There are many examples of place-based study outside of the academic world, including Western, non-Western, and Indigenous intellectual traditions.
- Although irreducible to any single account, Indigenous philosophies typically emphasise the creative and moral power, or 'agency', of place as the source of life-supporting relationships.
- Critical place inquiry is a contemporary Indigenous-led effort to decolonise academic scholarship through a research practice of relational accountability to people and place.

Indigenous and other non-Western scholarship is pluralising academic forms of knowing in geography, but it should be noted that there is a growing appreciation of alternative traditions of place coming from the West. Thomas Moore's (1996) work, for instance, builds on the ancient Greek idea of *temenos* to imagine place as a sanctuary in the modern-day re-enchantment of everyday life, while Bobbi Patterson's (2019) studies of contemplative monastic Christianity underscore the centuries-long power of place in silence and reflection. Even mainstream science is studying the role of place in physical and mental health by identifying neurobiological responses to different environments; a fantastic summary of this science can be found in Esther Sternberg's book, *Healing Spaces* (2009). All this is to say that 'Western', 'non-Western', and 'Indigenous' are labels that can obscure the intellectual heterogeneity within these categories. Recognising this heterogeneity and embracing thinking alternative to our own provide opportunities for dialogue and exchange across diverse cultural traditions of place.

In the end, place is our human heritage, connecting us to one another and the more-than-human world. You need not become an academic geographer to explore place—far from it! As human beings, we all are students of place, so much so that Edward Casey (1996: 19) put it this way: 'More even than Earthlings, we are placelings'. Digging deeper into place will enrich your understanding of social and environmental realities while helping you discover orientation, direction, and relationship in your own life.

Discussion points

- Identify a place that evokes a strong feeling or emotion in you. What explains this sense of place? Do other people have similar experiences there? Why or why not?
- What does Doreen Massey mean by a 'global sense of place'? Identify a landscape or social group that exemplifies a global sense of place, using evidence to support your claim.

- Why is place an important ideological category? Identify and discuss one example of how place makes certain worldviews, values, and realities seem more 'natural' or valid than others.
- What kind of creative practice (e.g. art, music, dance, film) would you most enjoy using to represent a place or relationship with place? Why?
- What are the differences between Western and Indigenous philosophies of place? What are some potential connections between these two broad philosophical traditions?

References

Agnew, J. (2011). Space and Place. In *The SAGE Handbook of Geographical Knowledge*, eds. J. Agnew and D. Livingstone. London: SAGE, 316–330.

Buttimer, A. (1976). Grasping the dynamism of lifeworld. *Annals of the Association of American Geographers* 66(2): 277–292.

Casey, E. (1996). How to Get from Space to Place in a Fairly Short Stretch of Time: Phenomenological Prolegomena. In *Senses of Place*, eds. S. Feld and K. Basso. Santa Fe: School of American Research Press, 13–52.

Casey, E. (1998). *The Fate of Place: A Philosophical History*. Berkeley: University of California Press.

Coulthard, G. (2010). Place against empire: understanding Indigenous anti-colonialism. *Affinities: A Journal of Radical Theory* 4(2): 79–83.

Cresswell, T. (1996). *In Place/out of Place: Geography, Ideology, and Transgression*. Minneapolis: University of Minnesota Press.

Davidson, J., Bondi, L., and Smith, M. (eds.) (2005). *Emotional Geographies*. Aldershot: Ashgate Publishing.

Deloria, V., and Wildcat, D. (2001). *Power and Place: Indian Education in America*. Golden: Fulcrum.

Hawkins, H. (2015). Creative geographic methods: knowing, representing, intervening. On composing place and page. *Cultural Geographies* 22(2): 247–268.

Jackson, P. (1989). *Maps of Meaning: An Introduction to Cultural Geography*. London: Unwin Hyman.

Kiddle, R., Jackson, M., Elkington, B., Mercier, O. R., Ross, M., and Smeaton, J. (2020). *Imagining Decolonisation*. Wellington: Bridget Williams Books.

Kunstler, J. (1993). *The Geography of Nowhere: The Rise and Decline of America's Man-Made Landscape*. New York: Simon & Schuster.

Martin, D. (2003). 'Place-framing' as place-making: constituting a neighborhood for organizing and activism. *Annals of the Association of American Geographers* 93(3): 730–750.

Massey, D. (1991). A global sense of place. *Marxism Today* June: 24–29.

Mitchell, D. (2000). *Cultural Geography: A Critical Introduction*. Malden: Blackwell.

Moore, T. (1996). *The Re-Enchantment of Everyday Life*. New York: HarperCollins.

Patterson, B. (2019). *Building Resilience Through Contemplative Practice: A Field Manual for Helping Professionals and Volunteers*. London: Routledge.

Relph, E. (1976). *Place and Placelessness*. London: Pion.

Sternberg, E. (2009). *Healing Spaces: The Science of Place and Well-Being*. Cambridge, MA: Harvard University Press.

Tuan, Y-F. (1977). *Space and Place: The Perspective of Experience*. Minneapolis: University of Minnesota Press.

Tuck, E., and McKenzie, M. (2014). *Place in Research: Theory, Methodology, and Methods*. New York: Routledge.

Watts, V. (2013). Indigenous place-thought & agency amongst humans and non-humans (First Woman and Sky Woman go on a European world tour!). *Decolonization: Indigeneity, Education & Society* 2(1): 20–34.

Online materials

- Patterson, B. (2021). 'Contemplation, Place, and Resilience'. *Mind and Life* (podcast), episode 31, December 3. https://podcast.mindandlife.org/bobbi-patterson/
  In this podcast, Professor Bobbi Patterson discusses her work on the relationship between contemplative practice and place.

- Steinberg, E. (2012). 'The Science of Healing Places'. *On Being with Krista Tippett* (podcast), September 27. https://onbeing.org/programs/esther-sternberg-the-science-of-healing-places/
  In this podcast, author Esther Steinberg discusses her book, *Healing Spaces*, which describes recent research on the connection between place and health.

- *Strong Sense of Place* (podcast). https://strongsenseofplace.com/podcasts/
  In this collection, each podcast takes you to a fascinating place on Earth, using great books to evoke the strong sense of place there.

- http://placeness.com
  A website by Edward (Ted) Relph that explores 'place, sense of place, spirit of place, placemaking, placelessness and non-place, and almost everything to do with place and places'.

- https://www.pps.org/
  The website of the Project for Public Spaces, a nonprofit organisation based in New York City that has worked with 3,500 communities in 50 countries on a variety of 'placemaking' projects.

- https://annielovejoy.net/projects/caravanserai/
  The webpage for *Caravanserai*, a residency project initiated by Annie Lovejoy and Mac Dunlop at Treloan, a camping site on the Roseland peninsula in Cornwall, United Kingdom.

- https://teara.govt.nz/en/maori-new-zealanders
  An entry in Te Ara, the web-based encyclopedia of New Zealand, on Māori place-based culture. Click the links to learn more about Māori place knowledge and relations.

Further reading

Agnew, J. (2011). Space and Place. In *The SAGE Handbook of Geographical Knowledge*, eds. J. Agnew and D. Livingstone. London: SAGE, 316–330.
This book understands place as emerging from location, locale and sense of place. It is a frequently cited classic definition of place in Anglophone geographies.

Larsen, S. C., and Johnson, J. T. (2017). *Being Together in Place: Indigenous Coexistence in a More than Human World*. Minneapolis: University of Minnesota Press.
In this book, we go into more depth into the arguments in this chapter, understanding place as something that draws people together and acts.

Tuan, Y-F. (1977). *Space and Place: The Perspective of Experience*. Minneapolis: University of Minnesota Press.
This book heralded the beginning of more humanistic understandings of place and space, and is a classic in the field.

Tuck, E., and McKenzie, M. (2014). *Place in Research: Theory, Methodology, and Methods*. New York: Routledge.

This volume explores how researchers around the globe are coming to terms—both theoretically and practically—with place in the context of settler colonialism, globalisation, and environmental degradation.

Watts, V. (2013). Indigenous place-thought & agency amongst humans and non-humans (First Woman and Sky Woman go on a European world tour!). *Decolonization: Indigeneity, Education & Society* 2(1): 20–34.

This article describes how Anishinaabe 'place thought' unravels claims of settler ownership of land.

6 Landscape

John Wylie

Introduction

Anyone writing about landscape almost immediately encounters a set of difficulties relating to definition and scope. Here is a list of just some of the ways in which the word 'landscape' is used and understood in Anglophone settings:

- A landscape is a particular type of painting.
- The landscape is whatever you see in front of you at any given moment (especially if it's a view of fields, hills etc.).
- A landscape is an area of the Earth's surface that has been shaped, gardened – *landscaped* – so as to be pleasing to the eye; made to look neat and trim.
- A landscape doesn't have to be spectacular or scenic, or even 'rural'. The gardens, streets and houses of the suburbs are a landscape and so is the city centre – the urban landscape.
- Landscape is a page format.
- A landscape is a certain size of area, bigger than a place or a location but smaller than a country.
- The landscape is whatever's outside – the outdoor world.
- The surface of the Earth is a mosaic or jigsaw of different landscapes, some 'natural', some the product of interactions between people and their environment.
- The landscape isn't just the view, something 'out there' which you appreciate visually from a distance – it's the world all around you, the world you live in and are part of and the world you inhabit with all of your senses.

As this list hopefully shows, landscape can mean many different things, at least some of which are likely to be already familiar. If I had a more specialist term to write about – **spatiality**, say, or **globalisation** – I could more easily start from scratch, and say to the reader, 'in this chapter I will explain what this term means'. But landscape is a word in everyday use, in multiple ways. I very much doubt if any reader of this chapter – someone who I am assuming is near the start of university-level geographical study, could come to it completely free of preconceived ideas of what a landscape is. So, landscape arrives already gilded – or perhaps tarnished – by a wide range of associations. Certainly, in my experience, students in the UK will commonly offer definitions such as those above, when prompted to do so at the start of a set of classes on landscape. Associations with countryside, scenery and painting are usually prominent.

DOI: 10.4324/9780429265853-8

Human geographies of landscape

The issue I've highlighted might solve itself if I could say, at this point, please forget all those pre-existing definitions; when *human geographers* talk about landscape they mean something different altogether. But that wouldn't be true, exactly. Human geographers have approached landscape in diverse ways, and 'landscape' has been a key context and reference point for nearly a hundred years now – especially for cultural geography (see Chapter 22). For example, for much of the twentieth-century human geographers defined landscape as the outcome of how different human cultures interacted with and were influenced by, natural environmental conditions – by soil, terrain, vegetation and climate. Landscape was understood as the imprint of human culture upon the Earth. And this chimes quite closely with one of my initial bullet points above, the idea that the surface of the Earth presents a mosaic of different types of landscape, reflecting both the so-called natural environment and human cultural diversity, in terms of differences in agriculture, architecture, belief systems and so on.

My focus in this chapter will be upon more recent geographical understandings of landscape – but here, too, everyday meanings and associations creep back in. One influential and productive line of enquiry argues that landscape is a particular *way of seeing* the world (for pioneering examples, see Cosgrove, 1985, Cosgrove and Daniels, 1988). In other words, landscape is a certain format or framework for visualising and depicting the world. It is a standard visual technology, almost like a map or a telescope or microscope. As a way of seeing, a visualisation, landscape takes the form of paintings and photographs – thus, *these* are the landscapes to be studied by geographers. This understanding might not be the approach that most people might associate with geography but to say that a landscape is a type of painting is commonplace.

Another strand of current thinking argues that landscape needs to be understood as a term which connotes how humans (principally) inhabit and dwell in the world. Partly this involves understanding landscape as the accretion, over time and **space**, of local customs, knowledges, traditions and laws (see Olwig, 2002). Partly also it is about understanding that human landscapes and 'lifeworlds' emerge and are sustained through everyday practices of inhabitation – through moving, interacting, working, playing, remembering and dreaming (see Seamon and Mugerauer, 1985, Ingold, 2000). To link back to my initial bullet points, the landscape is thus the world we live in, the world we're immersed in through our senses. In this conception, a landscape is a lived, always-evolving web of pathways and dwelling places.

In this way, the definitions of landscape that human geographers mostly work with today *do* still connect with 'everyday' understandings. However, two important differences must be noted. First, cultural geographers consistently stress the role of **power** in the making and perception of landscape. Who owns and controls the landscape – whose purposes does it serve? Who has the power to influence and direct how we see landscape? How do landscapes reflect and reinforce power relations between different groups in society? And how can we as geographers make these processes more visible? Second, cultural geographers – and others – have come to understand landscape in terms of **performance**. Landscape has often been conceived as a rather static background phenomenon, or to adopt a theatrical metaphor, as the inert scenery against which the actors perform. Recent work, though, emphasises landscape as both scene *and* performance and thus advances a more dynamic account of landscape-as-performance – both in terms of everyday actions and artistic performances.

That concludes my introduction to landscape. In what follows, I want to work in detail through two landscape 'examples', two images, to flesh out the points I've made so far, and more fully introduce recent understandings of landscape. An alternative structure for the chapter would be to recount the story of how the study of landscape in geography has evolved and changed over time. But this would involve compressing and vacuum-packing a mass of often technical arguments into a short space, and in addition, there are already several sources available which tell such a 'story' of landscape (see, for example, Wylie, 2007, 2010).

Summary

- Human geographers have approached landscape in various ways.
- A common approach for much of the twentieth century emphasised the notion of the 'cultural landscape' – the human imprint upon the natural world.
- More recently, landscape has been understood both as a particular 'way of seeing' and as designating how people 'inhabit' and 'dwell' in the world.
- These approaches to landscape are currently developed with emphases placed on issues of power and performance.

The UK national ecosystem assessment

Images of landscape, painted or photographic may express not just a sense of locality but of nationality too. This link between landscapes and national identity has long been a key topic of study for geographers and others (see notably Daniels, 1993, Schama, 1995, Matless, 1998). It is crucial to note that the focus of such work has *not* been upon which landscapes 'best' or most 'accurately' depict a given nation. Instead, the *critical* focus is upon how certain types of landscape imagery communicate and reinforce certain senses of nationhood and often elite visions of the nation. So, this imaging of the nation via landscape is not an innocent or consequence-free process. No: it is a process in which *particular*, national ideas and values are reinforced and elevated over others. This example is drawn from the UK – other countries will have different **representations** of landscape that are used to draw this connection with identity. And especially pertinent is the point that this very particular vision of an 'idealised' landscape was one the British imposed on many parts of the world they colonised (see Chapters 49 and 71), with real material effects (see Seed, 1995, Mar and Edmonds, 2010). It is used here as an example of the way such images can be read, not as the embodiment of some ideal vision.

In order to critically understand how certain national values are expressed *via* landscape, we thus need to keep two sets of questions in mind. First, what is included in the image and what is excluded? Who is there, and who is not? What belongs and is at home – and what apparently does not belong? Second, how is the natural world being 'nationalised' in such imagery? Landscape art often pictures relationships between culture and nature. In this specific case, we can argue that landscape involves the creation and depiction of a 'national nature'. So, how are nature, topography, flora and fauna enrolled by landscapes into the project of expressing a sense of national identity?

Figure 6.1
Front cover of the UK National Ecosystems Assessment, 2011

Source: UK National Ecosystem Assessment

Figure 6.1 is the front cover of a UK government document – the UK National Ecosystem Assessment (UKNEA) (2011). A lengthy, detailed report, compiled by a large number of academics, experts and stakeholders, the UKNEA provided an audit of the health of the UK's ecosystems and the 'services' they provide to humans. It is thus a kind of 'state of the nation' report, an assessment of how the UK's ecosystems stand and of what the future might hold. In this context, the landscape imagery found in the report has a particular national resonance, which is why I am using it as an example here.

The front cover we see here, and the report as a whole, was designed by a company called NatureBureau. It is not, obviously, a picture of a real scene. Rather, it is a stylised ideogram intended to depict, in some way, the key motifs of the UK landscape and ecosystems addressed by the report. It is, however, very much a *landscape*, in the popular sense of presenting a scenic view of, for the most part, the countryside. In this way, the image works by drawing upon a visual landscape 'format' that readers in the UK will very likely be familiar with, to the point of almost not noticing it. So, what image of the UK does this landscape depict?

First, the UK is pictured here as a *rural* nation. Even though the UK, even when the report was written, was one of the world's most urbanised countries, at some point, a decision was taken to place the UKNEA Report within this very traditional, rural landscape frame. This landscape thus suggests that – or appeals to a sense that – the heart of the UK remains in the countryside. There *is* a city pictured here, as you can see, and industry too. And just one little car, on an otherwise-empty road. But these features take their place snugly within the landscape instead of dominating, or clashing, they are placed, unthreateningly, in the comfortable middle distances. City, industry and transport are pictured at home, so to speak, within this rural landscape. In this way, we can see that the image reproduces and perpetuates a characteristically rural landscape **ideology** when it comes to the senses of national identity in the UK. What difference would it have made if the UKNEA frontispiece had depicted a busy city scene? To whom does a rural vision of the UK appeal – whose values does it endorse and confirm?

In addition to rurality, another national landscape framing at work here is the *coast*. Clearly, this image has been designed so as to include as many key 'ecosystem' elements as possible. Thus, we see the city and the country, industry and agriculture, work and leisure, humans and non-humans. In this context, the inclusion of the coastline – and of what looks like a working fishing boat – might simply be taken as a visual acknowledgement of the role of marine ecosystems. But the symbolic placing of the coastline right at the visual centre of this landscape demands that we pay further attention here. The coast is an important signifier of national identity in the UK beyond being a physical feature it appeals to a sense of being an 'island nation' – an independent and autonomous place, a place made distinctive and strong *through* its 'islandness'. This sense of a separate island nation was writ large in the political debates around Brexit, when the UK voted to leave the European Union in 2016.

And what about the people of the UK? Crucially, here we have a *family*. Placed in the foreground of the image, in conformity with the visual conventions of Western landscape painting, we see a man, woman and child – a normative nuclear family unit. Just as we see stock representatives of 'nature' here (birds, insects), we are presented with what is almost a caricature of an 'average family'. Their **ethnicity** is indeterminate, but they are clearly a heterosexual family. And this family has chosen to go for a walk in the countryside, to interact healthily with the ecosystems. They are not obese. The parents (if we assume this role) stick responsibly to the path, while the child strays playfully onto the grass. But this is an acceptable transgression – interacting with 'nature' is good for children, the UKNEA claims. More widely, this family unit embodies the nation just as the whole landscape does, and like the 'islandness' of Britain, this is a politically contested vision of an 'ideal' family. Indeed, for parties on the right of the political spectrum, the nuclear family denotes continuity, solidity and domesticity – like the countryside. As citizens, they inherit the national landscape and assume some measure of stewardship of it. The child denotes the future of the nation – for whose sake the UK's ecosystems must be sustained and preserved. This family, in sum, adds visual focus, coherence and meaning to the landscape and helps to make it very much a picture of an idealised nation.

A 'naturalised' family unit takes centre stage here, but other emblems of nature are also placed carefully in the landscape. A bird sails through a summer sky – a symbol here of nature 'free' and unmanaged, though still, by implication, in need of recognition and protection. Elsewhere, a lonely cow faces a low fence and represents perhaps the one troubling feature of this otherwise highly composed scene. Cows and sheep are stereotypical elements of pastoral British landscape art. But, after Bovine spongiform encephalopathy (BSE) and the foot-and-mouth epidemic of 2001, the cow in the British landscape today connotes potential disaster as much as placid harmony. It conjures a sense of humans and nature worryingly out of kilter, of a once supposedly 'green and pleasant land' despoiled by the 'unnatural' practices of intensive agriculture, animal transportation, global commodity markets and so on. However, if the cow is an uneasy presence here – placed awkwardly on the surface of the landscape, like fuzzy felt, rather than nestled within it – then some reassurance can be found elsewhere, and especially perhaps on the right-hand edge of the frame, where a tree, an oak-tree maybe, confidently stands. The oak is one of the most enduring symbols of an 'English nature' and Its presence here acts as a kind of visual reassurance – a sort of promise that, however, the UK landscape might develop and change, some elements of familiar character will endure.

Lastly, we should ask, where is this landscape? It seeks to visually represent and express the UK as a nation. It communicates themes core to a normative **discourse** of UK nationhood: rurality, tradition, islandness and family. But because it is in landscape format, it must represent somewhere in particular. As we've seen, this is a stylised landscape, designed to include a series of key elements. But despite such stylisation, the landscape presented still has a particular topographic quality. It recalls most specifically the landscape of southern England, and of coastal counties such as Devon, Dorset or Sussex for example. The landscape is not just 'rural' – it is a quite specific rural vision. It is not the highlands of Scotland – or the mountains, uplands and moors of northern and western UK generally. Nor is it the flatlands of eastern England or much of the midlands. Instead, the varied landscapes of the UK – of England, Scotland, Wales and Northern Ireland – are represented here from a specifically English, southern and rural point of view. *This type of landscape is the one chosen to symbolise the nation as a whole.*

The choice might seem unremarkable and unproblematic. The landscape might even strike the casual viewer as a 'typical' or 'normal' British scene. But this is only because of a centuries-old ideology through which the rural southern 'shires' of England have been claimed to be the heart of, or the most essential expression of, the UK national landscape. This pastoral vision of British national identity stands in opposition to that of the cities and the uplands (see Cosgrove, 1985). Intentionally or not, in choosing such a landscape for the front cover of a UK-wide official report, the UKNEA bought into and reinforced a vision of rural southern England as the essential UK landscape – the one best suited to symbolising the nation.

Summary

- Landscapes and national identities are often linked. National values are expressed via landscape, and human geographers have increasingly sought to critically analyse these national landscape expressions.
- We can ask questions about who and what is included in such expressions, and consider how forms of 'nature' are enrolled into national 'culture' through landscape.
- In the example shown in Figure 6.1, the landscape picture on the front cover of the 2011 UKNEA Report, we see the reproduction of a particularly emblematic way of constructing the UK's national landscape.

Figure 6.2
'Don't trip'

Source: Photo credit: Bradley Garrett

Figure 6.2 'Don't trip' shows us another landscape, but one very different to that considered in the previous section. Here, in contrast to the conventional perspectives and comfortable, perhaps even safe scenery offered to the viewer in the UKNEA example, we find ourselves occupying an extreme, vertiginous viewpoint. We are looking down, in fact, from the very top of the Shard, London's tallest building.

To make sense of this landscape, we first need to know something about its origins. The image was posted on the Place Hacking website on April 7, 2012, but the photo itself was taken several months earlier. The photographer is, in fact, the figure we see in the image – this is thus a self-portrait, among other things. This figure is Bradley Garrett, the author/editor/owner of Place Hacking, and a well-established cultural and urban geographer. Among other things, Garrett studies, and practices, contemporary urban exploration – the exploration, by small and often anonymous groups of people, of derelict, forgotten, hidden and forbidden city spaces, such as abandoned underground tunnels, inaccessible rooftops or securitised building sites (see Garrett 2014). The ascent to the top of the Shard is thus a good example of the ethos and agendas of urban exploration. The aim is to subvert the usual ordering and policing of the urban landscape, to get past security, to access unusual or extreme locations and then to document and thus evidence the event in published photographs.

What we see documented in this landscape, therefore, is a deliberate act of *trespass*. The ascent of the Shard might seem simply a prank or publicity stunt. But a long tradition links landscape and trespass in the UK, insofar as landscape has historically been deeply implicated in issues of ownership, property and rights of access. The best known example of this in the UK is the Kinder Scout mass trespass, in the Derbyshire Peak District in 1932, when a group of ramblers, mostly working class and from the industrial cities of northern England, trespassed upon the estates of the Duke of Devonshire, leading to a pitched battle with gamekeepers and subsequent arrests and convictions. Despite this apparent defeat, however, the Kinder trespass is today seen as a victory, insofar as it became pivotal to the later establishment of legal rights of access to the countryside in the UK.[1]

Both the Kinder trespass, and the ascent of the Shard pictured in *Don't trip*, may therefore be understood as *forms of landscaping*, or direct action, which deliberately set out to contest and unsettle official spatial zonings, demarcations and claims to ownership. What we see here is landscape expressed, openly, in terms of conflict and contestation. I am stressing this point because it connects with my introductory argument that geographers commonly and critically understand landscapes in terms of power relations. In my first example of the UKNEA Report, it took a critical reading to draw this out and make visible the ways in which power was at work, as the landscape implicitly reinforced certain senses of what is acceptable, what is 'normal' and so on. But in this second example, the landscape is explicitly configured as an act of opposition and subversion. This cuts usefully against any tendency to consider landscape as inherently conformist and conservative. As Tim Cresswell (2003: 269) writes, the whole notion of landscape can seem to be 'too much about the already-accomplished'; the word itself 'altogether too quaint'. A first key message, though, of *Don't trip*, is that it need not always be so.

If *Don't trip* enables us to conceive landscape in terms of trespass, rather than encouraging us to conform to the country (or city) code, then more widely a second message here is that landscape is something kinetic and dynamic. Again, this is to cut against a common precon-ception. Because a 'landscape' is often understood as something fixed and stable – or as a view from a fixed point – it can have a static, motionless connotation. Like a map, or like an archi-tectural plan – visual forms to which landscape art is, in fact, related – a classical landscape painting imposes a static grid upon the world; all the better, it seems, to produce a picture that people will naively accept as 'objective' and 'real'. Putting this in terms of the human body, and its moods, landscape is more usually commonly associated with calm contemplation, rather than involved or intense action. And even here, with *Don't trip*, what do we see? A cer-tain moment, frozen.

Much recent work by cultural geographers and others, however, has explored an alternative perspective, one in which landscape is understood as mobile, as dynamic and as **performative**. If you read the paragraph above and thought, no, sometimes when I'm walking/cycling/driving/canoeing/skateboarding etc., the landscape *does* seem intense and alive, and I'm fully involved with it, then you may already have an intuitive sense of what this perspective might mean. To go back to the introduction again, the task is to set aside any idea of landscape as simply the stage upon which a performance is enacted – and think instead of landscape-as-performance. The ascent of the Shard documented in *Don't trip* certainly helps convey a sense of how landscape is articulated by, or *comes alive through*, moving, living bodies. The landscape is energised though, and in actuality made to exist by, the ascent itself. Rather than being the static backdrop to action, the landscape here is realised in and through action. Think of *parkour*, for example, the practice of 'urban free running', in which participants seek to jump across rooftops, or appropriate and use walls, ramps, stairwells and so on, in ways more dynamic and expressive than that intended (see Saville, 2008).

The sense of landscape here is one of engagement, involvement and immersion – a landscape sensibility in which the whole body, and not just the eyes, participates. And it is important to note that this understanding of landscape in terms of our mobile and sensory inhabitation of the world is *not* one that only applies to extreme or unusual situations and events. Rather, the argument is that such situations help bring to the fore the fact that humans – *all* human bodies, of every **gender**, young or old, able-bodied or otherwise, of all ethnicities and creeds – *always* find themselves embedded within ongoing contexts of engagement with landscape and with other bodies. This insight – that the term landscape names the world in which we move and dwell – shapes many contemporary cultural geographies of landscape.

I've got this far without making what might seem to be the most obvious point about *Don't trip*. It works as an image, it makes an impact, precisely because the perspective is so vertiginous and alarming. You take a first, quick and casual look – and then you look again. *How high up is he?* Another, closer look – and now you begin to feel a sense of fear, literally feel it, in your hands (holding on tight), as you imagine yourself in the situation of the figure in the image. But then you can relax, I imagine, because in all likelihood you're looking and reading from somewhere fairly safe and secure – a library, a bedroom.

There is a name for this odd mixture of fear and fascination, this 'pleasurable dread' as it's sometimes called – it's called *the sublime*. If notions of sublimity, of vast, wild and potentially dangerous beauty, have traditionally been associated with 'natural' landscapes – with mountain ranges, polar ice caps, towering cliffs, raging seas – then today we can also clearly see a contemporary urban and technological sublime at work. This surfaces in our awe (or revulsion) before the New York or Dubai skylines, in the popularity of superhero movies and apocalyptic sci-fi scenarios, and in the devastated urban landscapes of many video console games. And this, we can argue, is the tradition that *Don't trip* fits into and draws upon for its appeal. Just as the UKNEA image drew on pastoral landscape traditions, so here the sublime provides the aesthetic framework – the context according to which we comprehend the landscape as striking, beautiful and so on. Here, we look downward into an abyssal, sublime depth – but also outwards, out and over a glittering urban surface to a far horizon. The human figure in the foreground supplies both drama and scale, but it's very much a picture of the city too, in all its awful night-time glory.

But before we get too carried away, one final, crucial point must be made. The contemporary London skyline, with its Gherkins and Shards, may have some striking visual appeal, but this is also of course a landscape founded on, and expressive of, inequalities at many levels. With skyscrapers erected on the back of property speculation and ballooning land and rental values, it reflects the current dominance of finance and banking sectors in many Western economies and societies and the grotesque disparities in wealth and power that consequently arise. It is also undeniably a phallic landscape, symbolic of a certain conception of masculine might and potency. As **feminist** geographers have noted and discussed, the urban landscape, with its skyscrapers and statues, is often coded as a masculine space and is more widely reflective of long-standing patriarchal discourses, though which differences of power between genders, ages and social classes are maintained (Bondi,1992, Rose, 1993). The ascent of the Shard in *Don't trip* is perhaps a commentary on the absurdly inflated sense of entitlement that the rich and wealthy in society possess today, as well as being an exercise in landscape subversion. Does it also – or should it also – ironically comment upon itself? An heroic 'first ascent', by a band of brothers, with a gung-ho motto: 'explore everything'?

Summary

- Landscape is political not only because it can reinforce what is understood to be normal and acceptable but also because acts of 'landscaping', such as trespass, can contest these norms.
- Landscape is increasingly approached not only as something that is understood to be fixed and stable but also as mobile, dynamic and performative, formed in the relations of living bodies to their environments.
- The interpretation of urban exploration developed here illustrates how we can usefully roll together different understandings of landscape: as a way of dwelling and a way of seeing; as a powerful expression of inequalities and as a resistant practice.

Conclusion

My aim in this chapter has been twofold. First, to outline some of the major lines of enquiry being pursued today by cultural geographies of landscape. And second to illustrate and contextualise these, by presenting them through two extended landscape examples. In conclusion, I also want to do two things. Inevitably, in a chapter of this length, much has to be left out, and it is important to at least highlight some missing elements – I will focus here upon the role of time and memory in relation to landscape. I will then briefly return to some of the more conceptual issues flagged up in the introduction, regarding how cultural geographers understand and use the term landscape.

Through the UKNEA frontispiece and '*Don't trip*' I've explored some key issues which currently cluster around landscape. Issues such as how entrenched systems of identity and power are enacted and reproduced through landscape. And how landscape, as an influential and widespread form of visualising and picturing, acts to frame and direct our understanding of what is 'natural', what is 'beautiful' and what is 'normal'. And how landscape may also be approached and understood in terms of dwelling and inhabitation – in terms of the moving, sensing and performing body.

If we take a long-term view of landscape depiction, both examples I have worked through are quite contemporary. Although I have sought to show how both draw significantly upon long-established discourses, for instance visual and aesthetic traditions like the pastoral and the sublime, I am still left with a slight worry – a feeling that I've underplayed here the extent to which many geographers emphasise the ***historicity*** and ***temporality*** of landscape. For an archaeologist or geologist, an earthly landscape is physically composed of time, layers of time stacked successively on top of each other. In this sense, time seems to be speeding up, as climate change and economic activity are causing sea level rise, deforestation, shifting river-scapes, large-scale flooding and landslides, resulting in rapidly changing landscapes across the globe. Equally though, geographers often stress the role of time and memory in the cultural composition of landscape. For example, landscapes of heritage and collective memory play an important role in the performance of identity, especially national identity, and these also require a critical reading alert to issues of power and authority (e.g. see Tolia-Kelly's (2011) work on Hadrian's Wall). The temporality of landscape – the fact that it has been shaped and created, often over millennia, by the interaction of human and non-human forces – also needs to be critically stressed for a different reason. Because a landscape can often appear to be, or masquerade as, a slice of a fixed, pre-given 'nature', whose human histories are invisible, or at least not readily apparent. In other words, landscapes are entwined with forgetting and with absenting, and one task for cultural geographers is to critically remember, to conjure up the ghosts and traces of those who have seemingly vanished into the landscape (Wylie, 2009). Lastly, issues of time and memory are central to an understanding of landscape as dwelling-in-the-world. In my examples, I've stressed, as others have, the role of the moving, sensing body in performing landscape. But thinking of landscape as dwelling – as a gradual and always-evolving web of dwellings and pathways, in which land and human life are very closely intertwined – must involve paying attention also to how, sometimes, landscapes and lifeworlds can grow, and decay, over long durations.

This takes me back to my introduction, where I noted that two major approaches in cultural geography understand landscape as either a way of seeing the world or as dwelling in the world. A few years ago, it might have been common to see these approaches as opposed to each other, as indeed something of an either/or choice – a choice between, for instance, a critical visual analysis *of* landscape and an **embodied** engagement *with* landscape. To adopt my own phrase (Wylie, 2007), there are certainly creative tensions here. But perhaps these tensions have proved to be creative and productive. Certainly, at present in cultural geography there is a range of landscape writing which enrols together the key issues I have sought to associate with landscape in this chapter: visuality, power, identity, memory, materiality, embodiment and performance. These are the issues I would stress as central for anyone seeking a better and deeper understanding of landscape.

Discussion points

- What were your understandings of 'landscape' before you read this chapter? How have they featured, or not, within the discussion here?
- What does it mean to understand 'landscape as a way of seeing'?
- What does it mean to understand 'landscape as dwelling'?
- How does power have a role in the making and perception of landscape, and how might this vary between countries?
- Take a particular landscape and consider how it rolls together issues of visuality, power, identity, memory, embodiment and performance.

Note

1. The 80th anniversary of the Kinder trespass led to a number of commentaries and commemorations. For more details, see the news section of https://kindertrespass.org.uk/blog/

References

Bondi, L. (1992). Gender symbols and urban landscapes. *Progress in Human Geography* 16(2): 157–170.

Cosgrove, D., and Daniels, S. (eds.) (1988). *The Iconography of Landscape*. Cambridge: CUP.

Cosgrove, D. (1985). Prospect, perspective and the evolution of the landscape idea. *Transactions of the Institute of British Geographers, New Series* 10(1): 45–62.

Cresswell, T. (2003). Landscape and the Obliteration of Practice. In *Handbook of Cultural Geography*, eds. K. Anderson, D. Domosh, S. Pile, and N. Thrift. London: Sage.

Daniels, S. (1993). *Fields of Vision: Landscape Imagery and National Identity*. Cambridge: Polity Press.

Garrett, B. (2014). *Explore Everything: Place-hacking the City*. London: Verso Books.

Ingold, T. (2000). *The Perception of the Environment: Essays in Livelihood, Dwelling and Skill*. London: Routledge.

Mar, T. B., and Edmonds, P. (2010). *Making Settler Colonial Space*. London: Macmillan.

Matless, D. (1998). *Landscape and Englishness*. London: Reaktion.

Olwig, K. (2002). *Landscape, Nature and the Body Politic*. Madison: University of Wisconsin Press.

Rose, G. (1993). *Feminism and Geography*. Cambridge: Polity Press.

Saville, S. (2008). Playing with fear: parkour and the mobility of emotion. *Social & Cultural Geography* 9(8): 891–914.

Schama, S. (1995). *Landscape and Memory*. London: Harper Collins.

Seamon, D., and Mugerauer, R. (eds.) (1985). *Dwelling, Place, Environment: Toward a Phenomenology of Person and World*. Amsterdam: Nijhoff.

Seed, P. (1995). *Ceremonies of Possession in Europe's Conquest of the New World, 1492–1640*. Cambridge: Cambridge University Press.

Tolia-Kelly, D. P. (2011). Narrating the postcolonial landscape: archaeologies of race at Hadrian's wall. *Transactions of the Institute of British Geographers* 36: 71–88.

UK National Ecosystem Assessment (UKNEA). (2011). *The UK National Ecosystem Assessment: Synthesis of the Key Findings*. Cambridge: UNEP-WCMC.

Wylie, J. (2007). *Landscape*. London: Routledge.

Wylie, J. (2009). Landscape, absence and the geographies of love. *Transactions of the Institute of British Geographers* 34: 275–289.

Wylie, J. W. (2010). Landscape. In *The SAGE Handbook of Geographical Knowledge*, eds. J. Agnew and J. Duncan. London: Sage, 300–315.

Online materials

*   'Some Landscapes', a blog maintained by Andrew Ray, is a really rich resource of landscape-related materials, including posts by Ray, and also many links to other blogs, information sources and the work of various artists and writers. The general emphasis is upon landscape in Western art and literature.
    https://some-landscapes.blogspot.com/

*   The website and pages of the UK-based Landscape Research Group offer a range of resources and links regarding landscape beyond cultural geography contexts: https://landscaperesearch.org/

Further reading

Cosgrove, D. (1985). Prospect, perspective and the evolution of the landscape idea. *Transactions of the Institute of British Geographers* New Series 10(1): 45–62.
A classic essay on 'landscape as a way of seeing'.

DeLue, R., and Elkins, J. (eds.) (2008). *Landscape Theory*. London: Routledge.
A more advanced and conceptual, but still accessible text on landscape. Comprises numerous short essays on landscape, plus a full transcription of a seminar discussion on landscape by a group of leading experts.

Howard, P., Thompson, I., Waterton, E., and Atha, M. (eds.) (2018). *The Routledge Companion to Landscape Studies* (2nd edn.). London: Routledge.
This voluminous collection of essays offers perspectives on landscape research from a wide range of academic disciplines, including geography.

Ingold, T. (2000). The Temporality of Landscape. In *The Perception of the Environment: Essays on Livelihood, Dwelling and Skill*. London: Routledge, 189–208.
A classic essay on 'landscape as dwelling'.

Rose, G. (1993). Looking at Landscape: The Uneasy Pleasures of Power. In *Feminism and Geography*. Cambridge: Polity Press, 86–112.
A classic essay/chapter on landscape and gender relations, in geography and beyond.

Thompson, I. (2009). *Rethinking Landscape: A Critical Reader*. London: Routledge.
This is a compendium of numerous classic essays on landscape, with commentaries from the author/editor, Ian Thompson. It is a very valuable resource for more in-depth landscape study.

Wylie, J. (2007). *Landscape: Key Ideas in Geography*. London: Routledge.
My own textbook on landscape is a detailed study of how, and why, cultural geographers and others have defined landscape in different ways (i.e. as a way of seeing and as dwelling) and gives numerous grounded examples of landscape research.

7 More-than-human

Gay'wu Group of Women and Yandaarra including Laklak Burarrwanga, Ritjilili Ganambarr, Merrkiyawuy Ganambarr-Stubbs, Banbapuy Ganambarr, Djawundil Maymuru, Uncle Bud Marshall, Aunty Shaa Smith, Neeyan Smith, Sarah Wright, Lara Daley, Kate Lloyd, Sandie Suchet-Pearson and Paul Hodge

Introduction

More-than-human is a term that you will hear more and more in your studies in geography. It is a term that acknowledges that the world we live in is not just a human world. The concept of more-than-human enables geographers to describe and critically engage with the many beings and entities that humans share the planet (and cosmos) with. These include plants, animals, lands, waters, seas, skies, songs, stories and much more. While deeper engagement with more-than-human beings, connections and relationships has been taken up in Western scholarship relatively recently, such engagements are foundational within many Indigenous knowledge systems, including through Indigenous law/lore and governance.

In this chapter, we share some thoughts about the meanings and importance of the more-than-human in geography. The knowledges and perspectives we share come from our different places and responsibilities as Indigenous and non-Indigenous people working together on unceded Indigenous lands in what is now known as Australia.

We're writing this together as a big group, two collectives. One is the Gay'wu Group of Women and the other is Yandaarra. The collectives are from two different Aboriginal **Countries** in so-called Australia. **Country**, in this context, is a term used to speak about place and all the beings, belongings and relationships that make up place. Country is land, water, air and sky; it is people and non-human animals; it is environmental and technological processes; it is plants and story and ancestors, and it is all the patterns that hold us together. In this chapter, we're led by Yolŋu and Gumbaynggirr Elders and knowledge holders and by the more-than-human beings, relationships and responsibilities of Yolŋu and Gumbaynggirr Countries. The human members

DOI: 10.4324/9780429265853-9

are a part of the interconnected beings, relationships and responsibilities of these collectives, and include eight Yoḻŋu and Gumbaynggirr Elders and knowledge holders. Their names are Dr Laklak Burarrwanga, Ritjilili Ganambarr, Merrkiyawuy Ganambarr-Stubbs, Banbapuy Ganambarr and Djawundil Maymuru from Bawaka in north-east Arnhem Land, northern Australia, and Uncle Bud Marshall, Aunty Shaa Smith and Neeyan Smith from Gumbaynggirr Country, mid-north coast of New South Wales in Australia. The collective also includes five ŋäpaki/yirraali (non-Indigenous) geographers who have been invited in and placed as part of family and Countries through our work together. The non-Indigenous authors have been brought into relationships of responsibility and connection with Custodians and Country, but this doesn't mean they can speak for or take the knowledges shared – they must always and can only ever act from their own place.

In talking about what more-than-human means and why it is so important, we draw on the teachings of Country, of place and homeland and of many diverse more-than-human beings that make up Country. And we draw from many inspiring Indigenous scholars, community members and activists who have shared teachings with us in person and through different articles and outlets. These teachings, both human and more-than-human, show how everything in the world is connected and in relation. They show that many of the beings that are assumed to be passive, without knowledge and/or non-living within mainstream Western accounts, are active and sentient beings. More-than-human beings like animals, rocks and waters have their own responsibilities, relationships and ways of communicating with humans and each other. They can act with intention and awareness, following rules and protocols that govern and ensure the well-being of Country. Acknowledging and engaging both human and more-than-human communities of place and Country are fundamental to ethical engagement with the world. It is also important to recognise ourselves as embedded and connected in more-than-human webs of relationships so that we can act responsibly as humans to ensure the well-being and flourishing of ourselves, each other and the Earth (see also Chapter 43).

The term 'more-than-human' is by no means a perfect term, but over the last 20 years, it has sparked a range of conversations in Western academia as it raises important questions around **power**, knowledge and **agency**. When we talk about more-than-human beings having agency, we mean that they have the ability and will to act, that they can intentionally carry out action, that they have rules that they follow, that their actions have meaning, purpose and that these actions have effects. It is not only humans who can act or think. So, engaging with 'more-than-human' thinking means asking questions such as – who and what can know and who and what has agency, what is knowledge and who or what has it, who and what can act and exert influence in the world?

The *more* in more-than-human is an effort to avoid setting up a binary between sentient humans and non-sentient non-humans. We are talking here not only of animals, but also environmental and technological processes, all beings and things both tangible and intangible. Neither is there any absolute border to any human body, action or thought. It is an act of humility to try and decentre humans from the centre of knowledge systems and to recognise sentience and agency beyond 'the human'. Speaking of more-than-human is an effort to recognise, respect and respond to intense, intimate and unavoidable relationality.

While this term is relatively new in academia, the concept is not a new one. It is important to recognise that Western knowledges often fail to acknowledge that what is currently understood as quite radical in academia – recognition of more-than-human worlds and agencies – is fundamental to many Indigenous peoples' **epistemologies**; diverse relational ways of knowing being and doing have been ongoing for millennia, embedded in Indigenous legal and political knowledge systems and in their ongoing more-than-human **sovereignties**.

As we move through this chapter, we focus on more-than-human agencies and follow the intentional actions of some wonderful birds and other inspiring beings to discuss what more-than-human agencies can be and mean. We go on to talk about the concept of relationality before considering how this thinking can reshape thought and action around more-than-human responsibilities and sovereignties. Unlike a lot of Western scholarship on this subject, we do not focus here specifically on technologies as more-than-human agents although technologies and things that are 'human-made' are also, always, part of Country (see for example Whatmore, 2002).

Summary

- This chapter is written by two Indigenous-led collectives.
- Many Indigenous peoples around the world have epistemologies based on relationality which recognise and value the active agencies of non-human worlds.
- Indigenous scholars, community members and activists are generously sharing their teaching around more-than-human relationality and it is important that academia recognises and values this.
- The concept of 'more-than-human' recognises the ability of non-human beings to know, act and feel, to shape and enable their worlds and works against a strict division between active, knowledgeable humans on the one hand and a passive place, Country and non-human beings on the other.

More-than-human agencies

More-than-humans have their own knowledge. Thinking of a bird, they know how to look after their young, know how to build their house, can traverse the very planet, finding their way, spreading seeds, regenerating forests, understanding the seasons; they may know loyalty through familial bonds; they may know intricate construction techniques. They know these things in ways that are radically different from the ways humans know them, with different colours, wider forms of vision and with completely different sensorial modes and maps. The male Australian brush turkey builds a mound to incubate the mother's eggs, thermally regulating the mound to keep the temperature just so. Birds learn and teach, as does the ibis in Sydney, learning to thrive in Australia's biggest city by feeding from rubbish bins, learning from a local population of ibis who used to live in the city's zoo (see Figure 7.1) or as does many a crow in Australia who has learnt to flip the toxic and invasive cane toad to eat its innards safely. These birds know, do, sense, move, think and act in ways well beyond human knowledge. And they don't do any of this in an unconnected way. They are part of a web and are part of more-than-human communities. They interact and communicate with each other and with humans.

Attending to some of the knowledges of animals is part of embracing and recognising more-than-human agency. Animals are not voiceless, not passive; they have knowledge, and they have law. It is not only animals either, although perhaps this is the most easily relatable example. It is also plants, rocks, winds, seasons, soils, waters and more. These beings send messages out into the world; they talk to each other, and they talk to humans. They shape and enable what

Figure 7.1
Ibis feeding from a bin in Sydney, Australia

Source: Photo credit: Alamy/Sheldon Levis

happens in their worlds, in the worlds that are brought into being together. This is what we mean by agency – the ability to act and shape the world.

Non-humans act and shape within their own communities, with each other, and in ways that connect to the many worlds that humans live in. This is something that has long been understood, respected and celebrated in many Indigenous cultures. Acclaimed Potawatomi scientist, author and mother Robin Wall Kimmerer evocatively and powerfully shares the agencies of numerous plants which nourish Turtle Island (what is now known as North America), shaping and caring, connecting and teaching, reciprocating and healing, imbuing the world with gratitude and generosity (Kimmerer, 2013). She speaks, for example, of sweetgrass, *wiingaashk* in the Potawatomi language, as a teacher, a sacred and healing plant, that heals open land, binding and nourishing the soil, that heals people with its spiritual and ceremonial qualities, its beautiful odour, the sweet, shining hair of Mother Earth that is, in turn, healed and helped by gentle harvesting, by ceremony, by its relationships with Potawatomi people.

Uncle Bud Marshall, Gumbaynggirr Custodian and one of the senior members of our writing collaboration, speaks of relationships and more-than-human interactions that guide. He explains that mullet, a type of fish, come with the seasons. The melaleuca flowers, butterflies and hairy grubs tell when the mullet is running along the coast and into the Nambucca River. It is then that it is time to fish for mullet. The mullet, seasons, plants and insects are all related (see Figure 7.2). As the Bawaka Collective has shared (Burarrwanga et al., 2012: 19):

> The animals are always looking for messages and sending them out too. When it's burning time and they see the grass on fire, the birds tell each other about it. One bird might sing, flying over and telling the others and then they tell others, all spreading the message. They tell the snakes, dingoes and goannas. They fly around saying, 'Let's find a safe place to stay where there's no fire'. And then they fly to a safe place, like a billabong. *Dhum'thum*, the kangaroo, runs to the billabong for safety too. They all know the language. Nature knows the language.

Figure 7.2
The dawn sun shines through silhouetted faces on a sculpture created by Uncle Bud Marshall and artist
Nick Warfield with Yandaarra at Nambucca Heads, NSW. The sculpture depicts the interconnections
between the seasonal mullet run and other beings of Country, including flowering wattle and
Gumbaynggirr people as they face in the direction of their elders

Source: Photo credit: Nick Warfield

To hear these messages, to be aware of them, we need to attend with great care. Our sweat will
tell us that fruit is ripening. As Dr Laklak Burarrwanga, senior member of the Bawaka Collective,
with whom we write with here, has explained, we know when it is hot there will be fruits to eat.
The thirst in our bodies is linked to the trees that give fruit. Humans know and the tree knows,
the fruit bat knows too. Our bodies are linked with each other and the tree, an embodied connectivity and knowing; as our body receives and also sends messages. In our heart and soul, we feel
the season unfolding. The messages, the connections are part of our very being.

We recognise and acknowledge that the land, the water, animals (including humans),
the weather, rocks, songs, fires and the charcoal in the ground contribute to our more-than-
human thoughts and actions, and they are part of our writing and thinking group. That is

why we acknowledge more-than-human beings as part of our authorship in this chapter. A wind may bring about a change in topic, a fire can teach about climate change, food can teach about the way it's hunted or caught, pathways and roads guide us to certain places; all these things and so much more contribute to what we talk about, to what we are saying. They communicate, inform what we do, guide thinking, shape and enable our more-than-human work together.

Animals, plants, all the beings of place and of Country are far from being passive, in the background, unthinking, separate from humans, beneath human notice. Rather, they protect and look after each other. As Dr Burarrwanga et al. explain (Burarrwanga et al., 2012: 19):

> If you were hunting *maranydjalk*, stingray, for example, a Yolŋu hunter might rub the sweat from under his armpits all over your body and head. This is for your protection so that Country will recognise you, so that Country will acknowledge and know you. Country will protect you then. *Maranydjalk*, the stingray, will recognise the local scent and won't hurt you. You see, Country and animals have an active part to play in that relationship. You must ask permission from them, respect the relationships and behave correctly. They decide. The world looks different if you see it that way.

We have talked up to now about specific beings. As Dr Burarrwanga's quote shows, Country and place are also active and knowledgeable. Country can recognise and protect; it is active within relationships. Understanding Country and place as sentient is foundational for many Indigenous people. Yolŋu man, Bakaman Yunupingu, points out that this is one of the first learnings children are encouraged to understand. He says, 'Land to us is a being. We feel bound to it. We feel related to it. That ties in with our singing, our dancing, our stories. It all relates. It is true. We believe in it. We know it's true' (The Yirrkala Film Project, 1986).

The understanding of place as active resonates with many Indigenous thinkers. For Anishnaabe and Haudenosaunee woman Vanessa Watts, 'Place-Thought is based upon the premise that land is alive and thinking and that humans and non-humans derive agency through the extensions of these thoughts' (2013: 21) (see also Chapter 5).

Place is kin, place teaches and guides, place has its own stories and histories, intent and integrity (RiverOfLife et al., 2020). Place has its own memory. Some of its tellings are the fossils that speak of sea level rise, of lives lived, the charcoal in the ground from the fires of Indigenous people over thousands of years, the tree rings that tell of seasons hard and abundant. And different memories too, ones recognised in Indigenous song, ceremony and conversation (Poelina et al., 2020, RiverOfLife et al., 2020). And place is not some romantic illusion of wilderness where human presence has been violently erased (Watts, 2013). Place is loved and cared for, violated and mourned. Place is farmland and national park, beach and moor, mine site and industrial zone. Place is city and village, church yard and university (Rey and Harrison, 2018).

There is an increasing interest in this idea of place agency, of vitalism, across different threads of geography, whether as posthumanism, in cultural geography through ideas of relationality and embodiment and in work that begins to engage with Indigenous **ontologies**. Such approaches recognise that non-humans, and place itself, are alive, vital and communicative (see Barad, 2007, Bennett, 2010, Ghosh, 2021). This interest has been sparked, in part, by the activism and leadership of Indigenous people and a growing awareness of the destructive potential of an understanding of the world that centres always only (certain) humans, relegating non-humans as background, as expendable. This work recognises that non-humans can and do make change. Nancy Tuana's work, for example, looks at the way Hurricane Katrina, as a more-than-human phenomenon, actively reconfigured New Orleans (see Tuana, 2008). Disentangling the natural, human-made, social and biological was simply not possible as the hurricane changed the city physically, through the lives of those humans and more-than-humans who lived there, their bodies, the city's racial politics, the political landscape, even spelling, potentially, the beginning of the end for the President of the USA.

To listen closely, to hear and understand even the beginnings of **non-human agency** requires many to relate to the world in a different way and to understand themselves in a different way. And once they/we do that, they/we have to act in a different way, with a different kind of ethics. This means seeing the ways that humans live as part of more-than-human worlds, they/we are not separate from them. Neither are animals and winds, dirt, roads or rubbish, rocks or tides or stars, separate, distinct from each other or from us. These things make us who we are. We make them who they are. This is deep but it is practical too, tangible. Where is the border of the self, when there is air coming through our lungs, bacteria in our gut and when that same air is wind and stirs the sand and sings a song through the leaves of a tree, guides the migrating bird, stirs the river and makes rain? Here then comes the term more-than-human to draw out our co-constitution, the ways we are bound in relations of responsibility.

Lauren Tynan, a trawlwulwuy woman and researcher of Tebrakunna Country, Australia, writes eloquently about more-than-human relationships in her doctoral research. Not only does she remind geographers that our research is always embedded in more-than-human family relationships – thesis as 'the sis', as sister, as kin, but she shares a more-than-human understanding of the thesis as 'a more-than-human collaborator' as the thesis also asks – 'thesis askin' (thesis asking), the thesis is an agential being prompting ethical obligations of reciprocity for researchers (Tynan, 2020: 164). This work is critically important in making visible the ongoing presence and power of more-than-human relationships and agency. It calls out and challenges the power dynamics created through enlightenment science, **capitalism** and **neoliberalism**. These power dynamics are built on an illusion of a separation between certain self-defined superior human beings and inferior **others** (nature, 'the environment', women, non-Western peoples). This illusion is not only anathema, abhorrent, to Indigenist paradigms but is used to justify devastatingly violent, exploitative and destructive colonising processes (Martin, 2008, Watts, 2013). These processes continue to resonate through the world, be it through the opulent wealth of neoliberal corporations, stolen and accumulated in the heart of the United Kingdom, the internal colonising processes which constructed the United Kingdom in the first place or the ongoing imposition of Eurocentric political, legal, welfare, education and academic systems which ignore and attempt to silence existing more-than-human sovereignties. This web of connectiveness, these intimate relationships, show that there can be no move to innocence, that everyone is differentially enveloped in the uneven power relations which can subsume, extract and violate.

However, recognition of this relationality also brings to the fore opportunities and indeed obligations to respond, care and heal. For many Indigenous peoples through multiple times and places, the world has always come into being through its relationality.

Summary

- Embracing and recognising more-than-human agency requires an openness to the relational agency of non-humans and attending to their diverse knowledges, agencies and sovereignties.
- The idea of 'more-than-human' relates to animals as well as other agents including place itself. The understanding of place as active has resonances with many Indigenous thinkers.
- There has been an increasing interest in the idea of more-than-human agency in geography, often sparked by the activism and leadership of Indigenous people, and a growing awareness of the destructive potential of an understanding of the world that centres always only (certain) humans.
- The drive to deny agency of non-human beings is connected to many violences including environmental destruction and processes of ongoing **colonisation**.
- Acknowledging relationality brings to the fore obligations to respond, care and heal.

More-than-human presences, sovereignties and responsibilities

Diverse Indigenous peoples and nations have prior and distinct place-based knowledges of how to live sustainably and in more balanced relationships with their more-than-human kin. For geographers and geography students it is critical to respectfully acknowledge these ongoing knowledges and relationships. Treating entities such as the Earth, sea or sky as devoid of existing knowledges and relationships is a form of violence as is denying the existing sophisticated knowledges of Indigenous people. Métis/otipemisiw scholar, Zoe Todd, from Amiskwaciwâskahikan (Edmonton), Canada, critiques the way that much posthumanist and more-than-human scholarship around climate change treats the climate as *aer nullius*, 'a blank commons to be populated by very Euro-Western theories of resilience, the **Anthropocene**, **Actor Network Theory** and other ideas that dominate the anthropological and climate change arenas of the moment' (2016: 8). Todd's critique highlights the way that Western scholarship has a tendency to ignore and sideline many important more-than-human knowledges and relations within Indigenous lifeworlds, treating entities such as the climate and weather as empty or null (Wright and Tofa, 2021). This runs the danger of further colonising beings and places, violently and arrogantly attempting to make many beings and their histories, presences and actions, invisible and inferior.

With the agency of non-humans comes sovereignty, the ability, the right, the obligation of more-than-human communities to make decisions and govern themselves. Birds, animals, non-humans and Country have rules; they have law of their own that they follow; they have belongings and connections and obligations that must be respected. These relations, where we write in so-called Australia, are underpinned by Aboriginal and Torres Strait Islander sovereignties, relationships of land, law/lore and people. To properly acknowledge Indigenous and more-than-human sovereignties, it is necessary to respect and tune in to the boundaries and limitations to certain knowledges and places.

It is thus critically important to engage with the more-than-human sovereignties of Indigenous peoples and knowledges. Culture, nature and politics are inseparable and on Bawaka and Gumbaynggirr Countries, each being, human or otherwise, has its own relationships and obligations to uphold. As Dr Burarrwanga says:

> We were created together and we live that creation together today. We are all part of the Law, we are bound together by the Law and as that Law continues, the stories and the songs and our communication continue… it tells you that how you interact with animals [and Country] makes you who you are. If you see yourself as separate from them, you deny something fundamental about life and about interconnectedness. If you treat them with disrespect, if you neglect them, imagine them as nothing but a tool for you, if you deny them their own Law, their own creativity, their own life, you are disrespecting yourself and the world in all its bounty.

Burarrwanga et al., 2012: 22 (see Figure 7.3)

Figure 7.3

Djirikitj (1998) artwork by the four sisters' mum, Gaymala Yunupiŋu. Djirikitj is the quail and Gaymala's artwork shows renewal and sacred fire. The six baby quails on her screenprint are the four sisters, their brother, Djali and their oldest sister, Wulara, who passed away as a little girl. To Gaymala, her children are the new generation

Source: Artwork credit: Gaymala Yunupingu, courtesy of the Buku Art Centre

This means that certain knowledge belongs to specific people and places. While it is important to engage with the knowledges that are offered by Indigenous peoples and places, you cannot just take the knowledges and make them your own. People and Country can also say, no, when asked to share. This no can be a silence, or a question left unanswered by an Elder. It could be a thunderstorm making it hard for you to remain in a particular place (Yandaarra et al., 2022).

Respectfully engaging more-than-human sovereignties means radically shifting current geographical thinking, practices and methodologies to be in respectful relationship with Indigenous knowledges, ways of being and ongoing political struggles. This is no small task but there are steps that can be taken. For example, Anja Kanngieser and Zoe Todd (2020) write about shifting away from the environmental 'case study' to a more Indigenous-led 'kin study'. In their view, case studies as a way of researching have been disassociated from the specific places in which they arise and used to create generalisable knowledge that can be lifted out of place and applied elsewhere. Whereas kin studies aim to acknowledge the multiple relations of more-than-human place, attending to 'the separations that case studies insert between place, thought and relations' (p. 387). This notion of kin studies offers a deeper engagement with Indigenous ways of knowing and being, treating Indigenous knowledges and relations as valuable to the production of knowledge on their own kinship-centred terms, rather than as an add-on to Western ways of thinking and doing.

Geographers and students from different places and positions each have different roles and responsibilities in respecting and engaging more-than-human sovereignties. This includes those of us living in places like the United Kingdom, where wealth has been built on colonising and exploitative practices. This is not at a distance, as in all our places we are each differently connected to histories and presents of colonisation and extractivism. The diversity of this is important, humans and histories are not all the same and we must speak and respond from our different places and relationships. Being led by Bawaka Country, the Gay'wu Group of women encourage enacting responsibility through *response-ability-as*. This is to say that we each have our own different *ability* to *respond as* our different positions and places. On Bawaka Country, this is responding within and *as* the more-than-human relations and **co-becomings** of Country (Bawaka Country, 2013, 2019).

On Gumbaynggirr Country, Aunty Shaa Smith also acknowledges that we are each different in our abilities to respond yet we each have a flame to nurture within us (see Figure 7.4). She invites students to challenge what is 'normal' and to go beyond the taken-for-granted ways of doing and learning. She invites students to think about studying geography – people, Earth, place and the environment – as an invitation to enter into relationships and to reflect on what we can each bring to those relationships. On Gumbaynggirr Country, there isn't a static way of living in the Dreaming (Gumbaynggirr creation, our ways of knowing the world and how it constantly comes into being). As Aunty Shaa says, 'We do not talk of Dreaming to imply we were, or are, asleep, but rather to share this story as part of the creation time, that exists now' (Smith et al., 2020: 942). In vital more-than-human creative energy, Dreaming is forever being, becoming, changing, transforming and transporting. We all have the potential within us to relate in this way as part of an ongoing creation. This is the flame inside us that Aunty Shaa invites us to nurture, to keep alight and grow in deepening connections with the ourselves, the Earth and each other.

Figure 7.4
Aunty Shaa Smith nurtures more-than-human connections and knowledges with her grandson, Zeek, at Yarriabini, NSW

Source: Photo credit: Sarah Wright

Summary

- Engaging with 'new' ideas and debates in geography means acknowledging the already existing knowledges, legal and political orders of Indigenous peoples, their lands and **territories** and more-than-human kin.
- Certain knowledge belongs to specific people and places. While it is important to engage with the knowledges that are offered by Indigenous peoples and places, you cannot just take the knowledges and make them your own. There are limits to academic knowing.

- An example of how to embrace the more-than-human in geography can be through recognising how case studies have been disassociated from the specific places in which they arise, whereas kin studies aim to acknowledge the multiple relations of more-than-human place.
- Geographers and students from different places and positions have different roles and responsibilities in respecting and engaging more-than-human sovereignties.
- Studying geography – people, Earth, place and the environment – can be an invitation to enter into relationships and to reflect on what we can each bring to those relationships.

Discussion points

- What are some diverse humans, non-humans, histories, stories and Countries that should be recognised, respected and valued in your situation?
- How are non-humans (animals, weather, plants, water) present in and influencing your interactions and what would this mean for you and your ethics?
- What are the histories of your place and your relationship with it, including histories of colonisation, dispossession and diverse ways of being?
- Which humans and non-humans are you emerging with in this particular time and place?
- What responsibilities arise from your more-than-human relationships, interactions and communications?
- How can you develop your abilities to respond to your more-than-human worlds – your response-abilities?

References

Barad, K. (2007). *Meeting the Universe Halfway: Quantum Physics and the Entanglement of Matter and Meaning*. Durham: Duke University Press.

Bawaka Country including Suchet-Pearson, S., Wright, S., Lloyd, K., and Burarrwanga, L. (2013). Caring as country: towards an ontology of co-becoming in natural resource management. *Asia Pacific Viewpoint* 54(2): 185–197.

Bawaka Country including Suchet-Pearson, S., Wright, S., Lloyd, K., Tofa, M., Sweeney, J., Burarrwanga, L., Ganambarr, R., Ganambarr-Stubbs, M., Ganambarr, B., and Maymuru, D. (2019). Goŋ Gurtha: enacting response-abilities as situated co-becoming. *Environment and Planning D: Society and Space* 37(4): 682–702.

Bennett, J. (2010). *Vibrant Matter: A Political Ecology of Things*. Durham: Duke University Press.

Burarrwanga, L., Ganambarr, R., Ganambarr-Stubbs, M., Ganambarr, B., Maymuru, D., Wright, S., Suchet-Pearson, S., and Lloyd, K. (2012). They Are Not Voiceless. In *The 2013 Voiceless Anthology*, ed. J. M. Coetzee. Australia: New South Wales: Allen & Unwin, 22–39.

Ghosh, A. (2021). *The Nutmeg's Curse: Parables for a Planet in Crisis*. Chicago: University of Chicago Press.

Kanngieser, A., and Todd, Z. O. E. (2020). From environmental case study to environmental kin study. *History and Theory* 59(3): 385–393.

Kimmerer, R. (2013). *Braiding Sweetgrass: Indigenous Wisdom, Scientific Knowledge and the Teachings of Plants*. Milkweed editions.

Martin, K. L. (2008). *Please Knock Before You Enter: Aboriginal Regulation of Outsiders and the Implications for Researchers*. Teneriffe: Post Pressed.

Poelina, A., Wooltorton, S., Harben, S., Collard, L., Horwitz, P., and Palmer, D. (2020). Feeling and hearing country. *PAN: Philosophy Activism Nature* (15): 6–15. Retrieved from http://panjournal.net/issues/15

Rey, J., and Harrison, N. (2018). Sydney as an indigenous place: 'Goanna walking' brings people together. *AlterNative: An International Journal of Indigenous Peoples* 14(1): 81–89.

RiverOfLife, M., Poelina, A., Bagnall, D., and Lim, M. (2020). Recognizing the Martuwarra's first law right to life as a living ancestral being. *Transnational Environmental Law* 9(3): 541–568.

Smith, A. S., Smith, N., Wright, S., Hodge, P., and Daley, L. (2020). Yandaarra is living protocol. *Social & Cultural Geography* 21(7): 940–961.

The Yirrkala Film Project. (1986). *We believe in it … We know it's true*. Filmmaker Ian Dunlop. National Film and Sound Archive of Australia.

Todd, Z. (2016). An Indigenous feminist's take on the ontological turn: 'Ontology' is just another word for colonialism. *Journal of Historical Sociology* 29(1): 4–22.

Tuana, N. (2008). Viscous Porosity: Witnessing Katrina. In *Material Feminisms*, eds. S. Alaimo and S. J. Hekman. Bloomington: Indiana University Press, 188–213.

Tynan, L. (2020). Thesis as kin: living relationality with research. *AlterNative: An International Journal of Indigenous Peoples* 16(3): 163–170.

Tynan, L. (2021). What is relationality? Indigenous knowledges, practices and responsibilities with kin. *Cultural Geographies* 28(4): 597–610.

Watts, V. (2013). Indigenous place-thought & agency amongst humans and non-humans (First Woman and Sky Woman go on a European world tour!). *Decolonization: Indigeneity, Education & Society* 2(1): 20–34.

Whatmore, S. (2002). *Hybrid Geographies: Natures Cultures Spaces*. London: Sage.

Wright, S., and Tofa, M. (2021). Weather geographies: talking about the weather, considering diverse sovereignties. *Progress in Human Geography* 45(5): 1126–1146.

Yandaarra with Gumbaynggirr Country including, Aunty Shaa Smith, Uncle Bud Marshall, Neeyan Smith, Sarah Wright, Lara Daley, and Paul Hodge. (2022). 'Ethics and consent in more-than-human research: Some considerations from/with/as Gumbaynggirr Country, Australia'. *Transactions of the Institute of British Geographers* 47: 709–724

Online materials

- https://bawakacollective.com/ The Bawaka collective's website describes their work and includes links to videos and publications.
- https://bawakacollective.com/handbook/ The Bawaka Collective's Intercultural Communication Handbook which inspired the discussion points for this chapter.
- https://www.gumbaynggirrjagun.org/ is an Aboriginal organisation that has the aim of 'maintaining the integrity of the Gumbaynggirr Dreaming and its place in the world while strengthening cultural practice in a way that is relevant for today, and for the purpose of sharing wisdom of growing relationships with self, each other and the earth'. The website includes resources and links to the work of Gumbaynggirr Jagun and Yandaarra.
- https://civiclaboratory.nl/ Civic Laboratory for Environmental Action Research (CLEAR) is a feminist, anti-colonial space nurturing interdisciplinary natural and social science work and resources around good land relations.
- https://criticalposthumanism.net/posthumanism-and-the-question-of-race-or-posthumanisation-in-the-colonial-anthropocene/ is a great blog situating posthumanism in the context of **colonialism** and **race** and has some excellent references.

Further reading

Bawaka Country including Suchet-Pearson, S., Wright, S., Lloyd, K., Tofa, M., Sweeney, J., Burarrwanga, L., Ganambarr, R., Ganambarr-Stubbs, M., Ganambarr, B., and Maymuru, D. (2019). Goŋ Gurtha: enacting response-abilities as situated co-becoming. *Environment and Planning D: Society and Space* 37(4): 682–702.

Led by the Goŋ Gurtha songspiral, the Bawaka Collective discusses the concept of response-ability-as. Centring Indigenous Bawaka-led ways of knowing, being and doing, this paper discusses the ethics associated with understanding ourselves as part of our worlds.

Kanngieser, A., and Todd, Z. (2020). From environmental case study to environmental kin study. *History and Theory* 59(3): 385–393.

This paper rethinks the geographical method of a case study and embodies and embeds geographical ways of doing in an Indigenous-led, relational way of understanding the world based on kinship.

Todd, Z. (2016). An Indigenous feminist's take on the ontological turn: 'Ontology' is just another word for colonialism. *Journal of Historical Sociology* 29(1): 4–22.

An influential paper from Métis/otipemisiw scholar, Zoe Todd, that powerfully critiques the tendency of much mainstream work within Euro-Western academia to ignore the Indigenous lineages of much critical work, including posthumanist thought around nature-society relations.

Tynan, L. (2021). What is relationality? Indigenous knowledges, practices and responsibilities with kin. *Cultural Geographies* 28(4): 597–610.

This fabulous paper, written by trawlwulwuy woman, Lauren Tynan, discusses Indigenous understandings of relationality. Many examples, stories and lessons from Country are woven throughout the paper to help the reader better understand relationality in practical ways.

Watts, V. (2013). Indigenous place-thought & agency amongst humans and non-humans (first woman and sky woman go on a European world tour!). *Decolonization: Indigeneity, Education & Society* 2(1): 20–34.

This powerful paper speaks of agency in human and more-than-human worlds. Anishnaabe and Haudenosaunee scholar Vanessa Watts shares an Indigenous conception of Place-Thought and critiques the processes of colonisation that construct ideas of agency so it is perceived as something only belonging to humans.

Yandaarra with Gumbaynggirr Country including, Aunty Shaa Smith, Uncle Bud Marshall, Neeyan Smith, Sarah Wright, Lara Daley, and Paul Hodge. (2022). 'Ethics and consent in more-than-human research: Some considerations from/with/as Gumbaynggirr Country, Australia'. *Transactions of the Institute of British Geographers* 47: 709–724. https://doi.org/10.1111/tran.12520

This paper, written by Yandaarra, a Gumbaynggirr and non-Gumbaynggirr research collective from Gumbaynggirr Country in so-called Australia, considers what ethical research practice should look like when more-than-human agency is taken into account. The collective discusses a less human-centric approach to ethics and shares some stories around how research might centre Country, more-than-human agencies, knowledges and sovereignties.

8 More-than-representation

Paul Simpson

Introduction

Think about a recent time you went out with your friends. That might have been going to your University's Student Union, a bar, or a nightclub; you might have gone to a gig or a concert; it might have been a trip to the cinema, a cafe, or shopping. You might have just gone to their house or apartment. There are probably a host of things that are memorable about that and a range of things that made it enjoyable. I'm betting at least one of you took at least one photo: a group selfie before heading out, one of you stood in front of a mirror in your room, a photo of your food or the 'latte art' on top of your coffee, and so on. Afterwards, I'm guessing that one of you picked one, applied an appropriate filter/animation/sticker, and posted it on a social media site. For many, that social media feed acts as a record of life, allowing you to remember fun times you had with people who have become an important part of this stage of life.

Those photos can tell us a lot of things. You might have 'tagged' the people you were with or where the photo was taken. We might be able to identify when the image was taken by the date it was posted. And we'll get a general sense of what was going on – smiling faces will suggest fun, poses might suggest activities undertaken (singing, dancing, drinking, eating, etc.), and various objects or other background features of the scene will give clues on what you were doing. It'd be fair to say, though, that these images almost certainly do not capture a lot of what made the events depicted enjoyable. They are a partial or imperfect record of what happened and of the experiences that you had with your friends. That partiality exists because such photos are a literal snapshot of one view at one moment in time. They don't capture the unfolding events of that day or night. Additionally, they miss key aspects of your experience in that moment. We can't straightforwardly see what you were thinking or how you were feeling, for example. Facial expressions might act as a 'tell' here, but only so much (Figure 8.1). We can't hear the music you were dancing to, the sound of the music in the room that was so loud you could feel it in the pit of your stomach (Simpson, 2014). We can't see the alcohol (or other recreational substances) that affected your mood (and judgement?), changing your attitude towards those around you (Latham and McCormack, 2004). We only get a loose sense of the 'buzz' or 'vibe' emanating from the motion and proximity of bodies dancing as part of a crowd (McCormack, 2008). We can't smell the food you were eating or the perfumes and aftershaves of the people you were with. And equally, what we see might present but one version of the reality of what

DOI: 10.4324/9780429265853-10

Figure 8.1
A snapshot of a night out

Source: Photo credit: Hinterhaus Productions/Getty images

was going on here, the one you want to remember or want others to see. We don't see the tears running down an emotional friend's cheeks as you consoled them over an ended relationship. We don't see the anxiety that might have been felt in the pit of your stomach as you walked home through the dark streets of an unfamiliar town or city.

While the above hopefully resonates in some way with your experiences of university life so far, you'd be justified in asking what this has to do with human geography. A lot of what I've written departs from the sort of things human geography has concerned itself with for a long time. However, a fundamental concern for human geographers is the relation people have with the environments they live in and move through. So, the key hook for this chapter is the following: our relationships with such environments are made up of something more than might be captured in the images we have or make of those environments. In this chapter I'm going to explore some of the ways in which such environments become meaningful in (inter)action and practice (see Simpson, 2021), and, as a result, how they are made and re-made through the activities that people engage in within them. Various forms of **representation** like the images mentioned above play a part in that, but there is more to it than that.

Summary

- The meaningfulness of environments cannot be fully grasped through textual representation.
- Geographers are increasingly interested in the fluid and multisensory aspects of environments.

More-than what?

Geographers became concerned with something that we might describe as 'more-than-representational' in the late 1990s. Before this, during the 1980s and 1990s, geographers had asked critical questions about representations of the world and the image of the people and places shown in them. Photographs, paintings, documents, statues, buildings, movies, song lyrics, amongst other things, were questioned based on the image of the world they played a part in (re)producing (Cosgrove and Daniels, 1988, Barnes and Duncan, 1992). A representation is, in simple terms, something that stands for something else. It re-presents something, taking it from one place and bringing it into another, telling a story in the process. The photos mentioned earlier are a clear example where a place and time is captured in freeze frame, and then circulated and narrated. There are other examples we can think of here. Think of the prospectuses or other marketing materials that you may have flicked through when considering where to apply for university study. Those documents likely contained a combination of images and text which try to represent something of the nature and character of the university that produced it – its 'unique selling point' – as well as the students studying there and the place where that university is located.

Geographers asked questions about who it was that made such representations and what agendas they had in making them. Sticking with the university marketing materials, it's clear that these are produced by marketing departments who are trying to attract students to study at their institution. This means that a very particular version of that university will be presented. Think about it: how many images showed sunshine and how many images were taken on a rainy day in autumn or winter? I'm betting that you didn't see many images of students braced against horizontal rain on the way to their Monday 9 am lecture in the depth of Winter, did you? Geographers also asked questions about who was present in these representations, or equally who was absent from them. Again, thinking about our prospectuses, you'll likely see a range of students covering a diverse demography. But how representative are these images when it comes to that university's actual student body? Not all university campuses will be as diverse as these images suggest, or certain bodies feature more in the images than others do. Further, geographers explored how people were portrayed and the impression that creates of their circumstances. Think about these students and what they are and aren't doing in these images. How many are sat hungover at the back of a lecture theatre in wet trainers and damp clothing on that wet Monday morning? How many are smiling and laughing with friends on a sunny campus green space or are engaged dynamically amid some sort of sporting activity? How many are doing some exciting looking science experiment in a modern looking laboratory, or performance in an arts studio, or are intensely engaged in some sort of small-group discussion or debate? And how many are huddled in the rain and wind on a remote hillside struggling to hear what their geography lecturer is telling them about the field site they are visiting? (see Figure 8.2). Finally, geographers were concerned with where these images circulated and who their audience may (or may not) be. Again, who is brought into these images and positioned as a potential member of that student body and who might never end up seeing them? What social structures and inequalities curtail the likelihood of some people going to university at all, while ensuring a place at an elite, selective institution for others?

—

Figure 8.2a and b
Idealised images versus the reality of Geography fieldwork?

Source: Photo credit: Paul Simpson

In Figure 8.2a we see the sort of thing you might encounter in the marketing of a University Geography programme: students engaged in discussion and taking photos of Mt St Helens in Washington State, USA during a field trip. Figure 8.2b, taken three years later, is unlikely to make it into the university promotional materials. These cold and damp students did not see the crater of Mt St Helens due to the low cloud cover during their trip.

—

These are all important questions when it comes to understanding how our knowledge of the world comes into being and is perpetuated. These representations are not necessarily accurate reflections of the world around us and so aren't neutral objects that simply reflect reality back to us; they are produced to work in shaping our understanding of ourselves and others (Mitchell, 1996).

However, alongside representation and meaning, geographers began to ask: isn't there more to the world than these representations of it? Or to put it in slightly different terms, don't our ongoing interactions in the world *also* shape our understanding of the world and those who live in it? Or more technically, Nigel Thrift (1996: 5) suggested that in geography at the end of the twentieth century:

> A hardly problematised sphere of representation [was] allowed to take precedence over lived experience and materiality, usually as a series of images or texts which a theorist contemplatively deconstructs thus implicitly degrading practice.

In response, Thrift (1996) proposed that geographers should pay greater attention to those lived experience of the world, to the 'doing' of our day-to-day lives. Thrift argued that this was important as these are fundamental to how humans relate to each other and the world around them. What this meant was a focus on the '**non-representational**' dimension of these geographies, to our *actual doing* of various things that continually (re)shape our understandings of our place in the world. To ask such questions came to be known as a 'non-representational' way of thinking about geography that focused on:

> How life takes shape and gains expression in shared experiences, everyday routines, fleeting encounters, embodied movements, pre-cognitive triggers, practical skills, affective intensities, enduring urges, unexceptional interactions and sensuous dispositions … which escape from the established academic habit of striving to uncover meanings and values that apparently await our discovery, interpretation, judgement and ultimate representation.
>
> *Lorimer (2005: 84)*

What Lorimer describes here is a whole geography of day-to-day living which 'foreground[s] those less-tangible, temporal dynamics of experience which are often overlooked' (Barron, 2021: 603). For example, when we walk, take the bus/train, drive, or cycle to our university campus (or place of work), we move amongst a host of other commuters as part of a complex, coordinated daily migration of thousands of bodies from home to work (see Bissell, 2010, Wilson, 2011, Simpson, 2017). In that our relation to our surroundings will vary depending on the mood we're in, the time of day we undertake the journey, the experiences we've had the previous day/week/month, and what we're headed to that day. We might feel a sense of dread as we approach an exam or a feeling of anxiety for the discussion seminar we're not fully prepared for. We might be excited in anticipation of a social plan for later in the day or to see someone we'd really like to see more of. We might feel lethargic or indifferent as we approach another lecture on a topic we find less than inspiring, the caffeinated beverage in hand yet to have made a dent in your downbeat disposition. We might think about the events of the night before. We might walk and talk with others, becoming lost in conversation. And we might be bluntly brought back to the present as we mistime the crossing of a street: a horn sound, and a stride is interrupted. We might not have heard the approaching vehicle due to that absorbing conversation, or it might have been the music we listen to on headphones which mediate our relationship with our surroundings (drowning out some sounds, make us walk in time to the beat, and so on). In this scene a host of relationships with people and environment unfolds as part of our day-to-day lives. Much of that gets very little thought because it is so routine. But again, it's fundamental to our inhabitation of the world (see Simpson, 2021).

As part of such a focus on our unfolding relationship with the world around us, those interested in this non-representational thinking argued that we need to recognise how both ourselves and the world around us are constantly emerging and changing through the relations that we engage in within it. Those relations include a very wide range of constituent elements: think of the vast array of 'stuff' that we engage with as part of our everyday lives, ranging from the (**more-than-human**) social and economic networks that we are a part of, which sustain us (Wilson, 2017); to the complex technological **infrastructures** that we constantly (sometimes unthinkingly or unknowingly) rely on for performing the most basic of tasks (Kinsley, 2014); to the bio-chemical changes that unfold within our bodies as they encounter as host of things in our environments, shaping our moods and dispositions (McCormack, 2007). This all has an ability to shape how the world around us appears to us and impacts our experience of, and place in, that world.

Summary

- Geographers have long questioned representations of the world and the agendas behind them, examining the images and texts used to construct narratives about people, places, and institutions.
- Non-representational thinking emerged as a response, emphasising the importance of lived experiences, day-to-day interactions, and materiality in shaping our understanding of the world, highlighting the dynamic and ever-changing relationships between individuals and their environments.

Animating places

Place is a key concept for geographers (see Chapter 5). Geographers commonly define places as spaces which have come to be inscribed with meaning (for better or worse) over time. That word 'inscribed' is important here. We and those around us are the authors of a host of meaningful experiences when it comes to our relations to place. Think of the stories about where we're from and things that have happened there that we tell others. Consider the reminiscence we engage in with friends and family. Think of the stories we tell about ourselves through the ways we shape those spaces (decorating, covering them with pictures, and so on). There are, though, other registers on which places come to impact upon us and which shape our relationship with them that aren't just about the representation of that place (see Barron, 2021). We (hopefully) *feel* comfortable in them. We might have an emotional attachment to these places. At times that's not easily put into words; a place just feels like home (or not). We're affected by the accumulated **encounters** we've had there in a way that might make us relax (or tense). Pulling into a familiar street, seeing the place name on the train station platform as it comes into view, smelling the smell of our home (which is different to other people's homes), can all act to change how we feel in that moment; tensions might ease (or tighten), stresses might dissipate (or coalesce), our concerns about the world 'out there' might seem that little bit more distant (or all too close).

Building on that, there will likely be sites in your hometown that say something about that place's past that are more than just personal to you. There might be statues, monuments, or some other sort of memorial to people and events that have some connection to that locality, or the broader regional/national context in which it falls. That extends from gravestones and park benches with name plaques on them, to streets and buildings named after important people, to memorials to national and international conflicts. Again, these all tell stories about a place, a people, and its past. They do this through words engraved on them but also through the symbols they include or the forms they take. But again, in addition to reading that cultural landscape and interpreting what is said, we can relate to it on other registers that aren't just about representation (Hoelscher and Alderman, 2004). You might well up when visiting the grave of a deceased family member, becoming overwhelmed by an upwelling of sentiment and sensation which you have little control over. In this sort of situation, we can experience a 'weight' of feeling that completely changes how we feel and how the world around us appears to us at that moment (see Box 8.1). That might be unrelated to the various representations you encounter, or it may well be heightened by them; reading the inscription on a headstone might trigger something or amplify what you were feeling. Or you might be entirely unaffected by the meaningless names and dates that you walk by day-on-day, year-on-year because they have become part of the background of your daily habits (walking to school, work, or shop) which you carry out without giving them a second thought (Harrison, 2000). Whichever the case, there are 'situational affective contexts of heritage' in these places operating here where our past or that of a broader people impinge upon our relationships with place in a particular experiential way (Waterton, 2014: 824).

That all got quite heavy in talking about death, memorials, and other relatively profound things. There are other ways that we can think about this animation of places which are lighter and more mundane. Returning to the day or night out we started the chapter with, there are lots of things that with might imagine as being a part of a 'club night'. We can think of a venue that looks a certain way and has certain features – seating areas, a dance floor, a bar, and so on. That will be decorated in a way that means something – it might try to look sleek and classy by using certain materials and lighting. It might be 'themed', having various clichéd objects and images fitting that. For example, in an Australian themed bar, there'll be Australian flags, perhaps inflatable animals like kangaroos, cork hats hanging on the wall, and so on. Through your repeated frequenting of that representation-filled venue, a host of memories and records of experiences will accumulate and circulate, making it meaningful to you and your friends.

Moving beyond that largely representation-based framing of your relationship with that place built through a combination of symbolism, iconography, and story (re)telling, we can think a little bit more about your experiences here. A lot of what animates the sorts of places you visit

BOX 8.1
DENSITIES OF FEELING

The sort of felt impact where something weighs upon us heavily mentioned above comes through nicely in Emma Waterton's account of visiting a memorial museum which documents the bombing of Hiroshima during World War II. As she says:

> For me, the clearest memory of experiencing such a density of feeling occurred in September 1999, when I visited the Hiroshima Peace Memorial Museum. Part of that museum houses the relocated remains of a small section of wall and two adjoining stone steps. Both the wall and steps are marked with visible reminders of heat and trauma but impressed into their fabric there is something else: a smudge, a smear, a shadow. It is all that is left of a man who was sitting on those steps waiting for the Sumitomo Bank to open at the precise moment an atomic bomb was unleashed onto the city. I remember it taking me a few heartbeats to register, and recognize, what I was seeing – to really understand. I remember, too, being bodily interrupted in ways I hesitate to put into words. I have carried that **atmosphere** with me ever since. It has a lived duration. Indeed, it haunts me at times, though it is more muted now than it was.
>
> *Waterton (2014: 823)*

We can see clearly here the power of an encounter with something in the world to 'affect' us at any given time. The impact here was something that went beyond the realms of representation and storytelling in the first instance, with Emma noting that she had to take a moment to realise what was going on, what she was encountering, having been affected by it before it made sense or could (falteringly) be put into words. Unfortunately, there are lots of examples of this sort of situation where we encounter these sorts of emotive prompts. That might be in the routine holding of silences at memorial services such as those that happen around VE Day or on the anniversary of events like terrorist attacks. Here the 'weight' of that silence may bear down upon us, becoming a tangible presence that impacts upon how we feel. Or equally, we might struggle to tune into the feelings of those around us, not being sure how to act or feeling awkward for not being a part of something (see Closs Stephens et al., 2017) (Figure 8.3). Or it might be that we're affected by an encounter with a meaningful symbolic object related to these events which impacts upon our mood or disposition for however long – from the duration of a ceremony to years depending on your relationship with them and what they symbolise. These symbols can be meaningful *and* affective at national or international levels, like the poppies that are worn in remembrance of those killed in armed conflict. Or they might come to operate at more local levels, like the 'worker bees' that circulated around Manchester after the arena bombing (see Merrill et al., 2020). A combination of symbolism *and* individual or collective feelings characterise the work that such objects do in bringing people together around a shared relation to a past event.

Figure 8.3
Commuters and employees take part in a 1-minute silence

Source: Photo credit: Kawai Tang/Getty

comes at the level of the specific **embodied** relationship you have with them on a night out. You have to be there, in the midst of that encounter with a place and people for it to really make sense. That's often because each night out isn't the same. Sometimes you might have a great time, being affected positively by the range of encounters you have. Other times, you might not, being affected negatively for reasons you can't always put your finger on. Sometimes the atmosphere might not quite be the same as it was the last time you were there, though you might not be sure why. There might be a catalysing event that shapes how the event unfolds this time: an argument, a breakup, an unpleasant encounter with a stranger, and so on. But it might be less obvious. Perhaps the music just didn't sit quite right with your mood. It's rarely possible to exactly reproduce the exact buzz that emerged on a previous good night, even though so much might have been similar in terms of people and place (Ash, 2010). The experiences we have and the buzz we may or may not get are fleeting and temporary. There is often a fine line between what might be a good night out and one that leaves us cold, and this all unfolds in the 'doing' of that night out whereby your experience of that place and time is (re)made again and again on each occasion.

Summary

- Places can evoke intense feelings and affect us beyond representation, shaping our relationships and experiences through embodied encounters.
- Non-representational theory highlights the importance of embodiment, materiality, and **affective** atmospheres in shaping how worlds are made and re-made.

Conclusion

This chapter has introduced geography's recent concern with something that we might call 'more-than-representational'. In doing so it introduced the idea that a well-established concern for geographers is how people and environments are represented through a host of media. There are lots of questions that can be asked about such representations related to their production, the partial or incomplete image of the world they present to us, and how they circulate in the world and so reproduce certain visions of the things they depict. However, geographers have argued that there might be more going on here that warrants geographic scrutiny. As well as reflecting on how people and environments are represented, we might also think about how such environments are lived in, related to, and (re)produced in practical, embodied action. This focus on something more-than representational 'foregrounds the process, change and the constant reshuffling of relations' in our unfolding inhabitation of the world (Barron, 2021: 606). In many ways there is a desire here to think about how places are animated through the things we do in living in them. That's not to say that representations shouldn't be studied by geographers or that they do not matter. Rather, the point here was to think about representations (both their production and consumption) differently, as forming one part of this broader practice-orientated concern with how we live in the world and relate to the environments we inhabit.

Discussion points

- Go and find a public space near to where you live or study: a city square, a public park, a shopping centre food court, or a pedestrianised shopping street. Find a place where you can stand or sit for a while undisturbed.
- In your chosen space, begin by establishing what sort of baseline 'feel' the space has. Is it vibrant with the bustle of activity? Or is the bustle overwhelming and oppressive? Is it calm and quiet? Or is it uninspiring and 'dead'? What word best captures the nature of the scene unfolding in front of you?
- Having tried to initially identify a baseline tone, think about what it is that is going on here to give this place that specific character. Consider:
    - Who is using the space and what are they doing? Can you spot any patterns in this?
    - What is shaping that activity? Are there benches, ledges, paving, grass areas, and so on? Are there other technologies present that are impacting on what people are doing?
    - Are there any non-human participants in this space? Are there animals and what are they doing? What role is the broader climate/weather playing?
    - How does the space sound/smell? Where is that coming from? Are there 'natural' sounds or are there artificially introduced sounds (recordings of messages or music)?
    - What representations can you see and what are they doing in shaping people's actions? Is there signage which mixes words and symbols? How much are people paying attending to them and how much are they ignoring them?

Once you've made your observations, try to draw a diagram of the space and map what is happening there. Think about the objects present but also the flows of bodies through the space.

Think about the background architecture/scene as well as those humans and non-humans using it. Then return to the space at a different time on a different day and repeat the exercise. What differences and what continuities can you identify? Why might that be the case? What difference does this make to the character of the space you've observed?

References

Ash, J. (2010). Architectures of affect: anticipating and manipulating the event in processes of videogame design and testing. *Environment and Planning D: Society and Space* 28: 653–671.

Barnes, T. J., and Duncan, J. S. (1992). *Writing Worlds: Discourse, Text and Metaphor in the Representation of Landscape*. London: Routledge.

Barron, A. (2021). More-than-representational approaches to the life-course. *Social & Cultural Geography* 22: 603–626.

Bissell, D. (2010). Passenger mobilities: affective atmospheres and the sociality of public transport. *Environment and Planning D: Society and Space* 28: 270–289.

Closs Stephens, A., Hughes, S., Schofield, V., and Sumartojo, S. (2017). Atmospheric memories: affect and minor politics at the ten-year anniversary of the London bombings. *Emotion, Space and Society* 23: 44–51.

Cosgrove, D., and Daniels, S. J. (eds.) (1988). *The Iconography of Landscape*. Cambridge: Cambridge University Press.

Harrison, P. (2000). Making sense: embodiment and the sensibilities of the everyday. *Environment and Planning D: Society and Space* 18: 497–517.

Hoelscher, S., and Alderman, D. H. (2004). Memory and place: geographies of a critical relationship. *Social & Cultural Geography* 5: 347–355.

Kinsley, S. (2014). The matter of 'virtual' geographies. *Progress in Human Geography* 38: 364–384.

Latham, A., and McCormack, D. (2004). Moving cities: rethinking the materialities of urban geographies. *Progress in Human Geography* 28: 701–724.

Lorimer, H. (2005). Cultural geography: the busyness of being 'more-than-representational'. *Progress in Human Geography* 29: 83–94.

McCormack, D. P. (2008). Geographies for moving bodies: thinking, dancing, spaces. *Geography Compass* 2: 1822–1836.

McCormack, D. P. (2007). Molecular affects in human geographies. *Environment and Planning A: Economy and Space* 39(2): 359–377.

Merrill, S., Sumartojo, S., Closs Stephens, A., and Coward, M. (2020). Togetherness after terror: the more or less digital commemorative public atmospheres of the Manchester Arena bombing's first anniversary. *Environment and Planning D: Society and Space* 38: 546–566.

Mitchell, D. (1996). *The Lie of the Land: Migrant Workers and the California Landscape*. Minneapolis: University of Minnesota Press.

Simpson, P. (2014). Spaces of Affect. In *The Ashgate Research Companion to Media Geography*, eds. P. Adams, J. Craine, and J. Dittmer. Aldershot: Ashgate, 329–346.

Simpson, P. (2017). A sense of the cycling environment: felt experiences of infrastructure and atmospheres. *Environment and Planning A* 49: 426–447

Simpson, P. (2021). *Non-Representational Theory*. Abingdon: Routledge.

Thrift, N. (1996). *Spatial Formations*. London: Sage.

Waterton, E. (2014). A more-than-representational understanding of heritage? The 'past' and the politics of affect. *Geography Compass* 8(11): 823–833.

Wilson, H. F. (2011). Passing propinquities in the multicultural city: the everyday encounters of bus passengering. *Environment and Planning A* 43: 634–649.

Wilson, H. F. (2017). On geography and encounter. *Progress in Human Geography* 41: 451–471.

Online materials

'Woodstock' was a music and arts festival that took place in 1969 in Bethel, New York, on the site of a large dairy farm. This festival is generally considered to be a key moment in the history of both popular music and counter-cultural imaginations. It has come to represent 'hippy' values of peace, love, and freedom.

Now, watch the following three videos:

- Performance of 'Soul Sacrifice' by the band Santana (https://vimeo.com/231111863). Here the band's multi-cultural mix of members get lost in extended solo passages, performing under the influence of mind-altering substances.
- Netflix documentary called 'Trainwreck: Woodstock 99' (https://www.imdb.com/title/tt21217912/). It tells the story of the Woodstock anniversary festival organised in 1999 on a disused military base. The narrative centres on the greed of the organisers and the eruption of large-scale violence.
- The performance of 'Break Stuff' by Limp Bizkit, a Nu-Metal band, said to have had a catalysing effect in bringing about this 'trainwreck' (see https://www.youtube.com/watch?v=YPk7-fCvbao).

Now, consider how various factors and relations led to Woodstock 1999 becoming something of a war zone:

- What role did the style of music play?
- What other factors played a role? A lack of shade from intense heat; lack of affordable water and food (on top of expensive tickets); poor sanitation provision, amongst other factors, quickly impacted upon the tone of proceedings, leading to acts of violence and vandalism by increasingly frustrated attendees.

The lyrics of Break Stuff clearly fitted the collective mood, focusing on disenchantment, violent sentiments, and general aggression. However, there was more going on here than this simple messaging which tipped things over from sentiment to action. Tapping into the collective discontent evident in the crowd, the band's singer Fred Durst can be seen here overtly amplifying this darkening mood, literally talking the crowd into breaking stuff. The circumstances of the performance here and the specific space-time in which it took place mattered; it's hard to image those in the audience acting the manner they did having listened to the song by themselves at home, for example. Instead, there is an affective entrainment whereby members of the crowd were swept along in the moment as part of a wider wave of anger and frustration.

From this example we can see how a particular coming together of material circumstances, social relations, embodied dispositions, practical actions, and symbolic content produced a troubling space-time of festival experience: a trainwreck.

Further reading

Anderson, B., and Harrison, P. (eds.) (2010). *Taking-Place: Non-Representational Theories and Geography*. Farnham: Ashgate.
Another comprehensive introduction to non-representational theory but written by 16 academics exploring various aspects of non-representational theory, including life, representation, ethics, and politics. The introductory chapter also provides a clear genealogy of the emergence of non-representational theory and addresses a number of critiques.

Bissell, D. (2019). On Edge: Writing Non-Representational Journeys. In *Non-Representational Theory and the Creative Arts*, eds. C. P. Boyd and C. Edwardes. Singapore: Palgrave Macmillan, 351–358. https://doi.org/10.1007/978-981-13-5749-7_23
A reflective piece written about a car journey Bissell took as child in Norfolk. The chapter and others in the edited collection show one of the ways academics engage the creative arts to write about the richness of the world.

Doughty, K., and Drozdzewski, D. (2022). Sonic methods, sonic affects. *Emotion, Space and Society* 42: 100867.
A special issue that explores how sound makes us feel, how we encounter it and its spatial and social affects.

Lorimer, H. (2005). Cultural geography: the busyness of being 'more-than-representational'. *Progress in Human Geography* 29(1): 83–94.
A good introduction to those new to non-representational theory wanting to understand the implications for research in cultural geography.

Simpson, P. (2021). *Non-Representational Theory*. Abingdon: Routledge.
An accessible introduction to non-representational theory with chapters organised around key concepts such as practice, affect, materiality, landscape, and performance. The book also reflects on methodological challenges going about researching non-representational aspects of everyday life.

9 Majority and Minority Worlds

Nelson Oppong and Kelly Dombroski

Introduction

Geographers have long sought to divide the world up into its component parts, and much of the discipline's foundational terminology comes from such categorisation. Sometimes this is done with reference to landmass, such as dividing the world up into continents, or into meteorological zones such as the polar regions and the tropics. At other times, as we shall see in this chapter, this has been done by referring to political blocs or stages of economic development. New categories are emerging all the time, and in some of your university courses, you may have come across the terms 'Majority' and 'Minority' Worlds and have wondered what these mean. While at the time of publication, these terms have been in use for at least a decade, they are less visible outside of academia, where popular media continues to use terms like 'Global South' and 'Global North', or 'developed' and 'developing' world countries (as many chapters do in this volume). Aid agencies like the World Bank and International Monetary Fund (IMF) have also popularised other terms to distinguish countries based on economic indicators, such as 'high income', 'middle-income', and 'low-income'. As we will discuss in this chapter, the terms 'Majority' and 'Minority' Worlds have been proposed because they recognise and allow us to talk about global inequality and differences, but in less **teleological** ways than the words used in popular media and the development sector. Instead, they feed into a broader critique of how powerful organisations depict regions outside of Western Europe and North America as less civilised, backward, or poor based on false hierarchies and misconceptions of wealth and **power**. The terms also enable us to gain a deeper understanding of the histories, patterns, dynamics and data around changes in global inequality, where super-rich people can be found in all parts of the world, even as many countries continue to record relatively high rates of poverty. In short, 'Majority World' refers to the majority of people in the world, who live in previously colonised, lower and middle-income nations, but who do not have access to the elite lifestyles of the richest people in their home countries, or elsewhere in this globalised world. 'Minority World' refers to the minority of people in this world, including those who live in high-income countries and also those who have access to elite consumerist lifestyles from anywhere in the world. The concept was proposed by Bangladeshi photographer Shahidul Alam in the early 1990s. As Gibson-Graham, Cameron, and Healy summarise:

> Rather than representing the majority of humankind in terms of what they lack, Alam suggested that we replace the terms 'third world' and 'LDCs' [Less Developed Countries] with

DOI: 10.4324/9780429265853-11

the less judgmental, more descriptive term 'Majority World'. In this categorization, 'Minority World' refers to that fraction of humankind that is relatively well off.

2013, 9

But what is wrong with representing people with reference to what they lack? How did geographers and others in the field known as 'development studies' come to see their representation of the majority of the world as judgmental? Given the intractable reality of global inequality, surely it comes as no surprise that people need to distinguish between the 'haves' and the 'have-nots' geographically?

In January 2023, a damning report on inequality was released by Oxfam International, a global non-government organisation, the aim of which is to 'tackle the inequality that keeps people poor' (https://www.oxfam.org/en). The report is titled 'Survival of the Richest', and it begins with a set of disappointing facts: In 2022, poverty increased for the first time in 25 years globally, with a cost-of-living crisis meaning tens of millions of people are facing hunger, while hundreds of millions of people are unable to cope with price rises in basic goods and home heating (Christensen et al. 2023). The Oxfam report opens with two statistics that illustrate not only the issue of income but also the issue of tax:

> Elon Musk, one of the world's richest men, paid a 'true tax rate' of just over 3% from 2014 to 2018.
>
> Aber Christine, a market trader in Northern Uganda who sells rice, flour and soya, makes $80 a month in profit. She pays a tax rate of 40%.
>
> *Christensen et al., 2023: 7, see also page 26*

The report continues, with other new and shocking statistics on the rise in inequality since 2020, the year the global COVID-19 pandemic began:

> Since 2020, the richest 1% have captured almost two-thirds of all new wealth – nearly twice as much money as the bottom 99% of the world's population.
>
> *Christensen et al., 2023: 7*

The global COVID-19 pandemic made this much worse: since 2020, for every dollar the bottom 90% of income earners in the world have gained, billionaires have gained $1.7m (Christensen et al., 2023: 15).

But are scholars referring to this 99% and 1% as described by Oxfam's report when they use the terms Majority World and Minority World? Not quite. As we will discuss in this chapter, the 'Minority World' is a shorthand term for those people, wherever in the world they are, who fall into the top percentage of indicators for income and other indicators of wealth and wellbeing. Most of these people will live in the higher income countries of the world. In Figure 9.1, you can see the different countries of the world coloured differently depending on their gross national income (GNI) per capita. The countries coloured darker green are the ones considered high-income countries under the World Bank classification system in 2021. In terms of both population and land area, they are a smaller group than the remaining countries on low, lower middle, upper middle incomes. The countries in purple have higher rates of poverty but are still home to a small percentage of elite wealthy people.

■ Low income ■ Lower middle income ■ Upper middle income ■ High income

Figure 9.1
World Bank map showing GNI per capita

Source: Figure credit: World Bank. (See https://databank.worldbank.org/source/world-development-indicators)

The remainder of this chapter traces the global divisions of Majority and Minority Worlds through three different **discursive** regimes – 'three worlds', 'global north and south', and majority/minority. It will explain how these terms came to be used by geographers, and what implications the different terms we use have for our geographical study and research, as well as our thinking and acting in the world more broadly.

Summary

- The terms 'Majority World' and 'Minority World' were coined by Shahidul Alam in the 1990s to describe countries in the 'Global South' without judgement.
- Majority World refers to the people in previously colonised, lower income, and middle-income nations and those who lack access to the affluent lifestyles and power found in their own countries or elsewhere in the globalised world (often including Indigenous peoples in settler-colonial places).
- Minority World refers to people in high-income regions and also those in other places who have access to privileged consumerist lifestyles globally.
- These terms, popularised by human geographers and scholars in political science and development studies, challenge concepts like modernisation theory and terms such as 'developing' or 'low-income' that depict Global South countries as impoverished and backward, emphasising the need for development to be more like the Global North.

Three worlds

You may have heard people refer to things ironically as 'first world problems', and to the notion of 'the Third World', usually in reference to poverty or a failure of infrastructure, often collected under the generic terminology of 'Third World conditions'. What do these terms mean, and where do they come from? The terms date back to the Second World War (1939–1945), as a new world order started to emerge where the United States dominated economically and politically, with stiff competition from the Union of Soviet Socialist Republics (USSR). In July 1944, as the Allied Powers looked set to secure victory, economic specialists, and dignitaries from over 40 countries met at Bretton Woods, a resort in New Hampshire, USA, to devise a new international monetary system. To rebuild the vast swathes of Europe that were ruined during the War and prevent failures in international trade that led to the Great Recession, the Bretton Woods Conference set up the International Monetary Fund and World Bank:

> In the wake of the greatest economic collapse and most catastrophic war in history the representatives of the United Nations sought world peace, freedom, and security. Global economic growth integrating countries in a world market would be the means to achieve these goals – growth based on the 'axiom' of infinite natural resources feeding limitlessly increasing prosperity. The Bretton Woods institutions, the World Bank and the IMF, would be the critical instrumentalities.
>
> *Rich, 1994: 55*

The Fund and Bank were dominated by US finances and leadership and were key instruments of the post-war political and economic order. US concerns about the spread of communism inspired them to adopt more generous lending criteria within Europe, which culminated with the Marshall Plan, a US foreign aid programme which transferred $20 billion to support European reconstruction between 1948 and 1961. The United States later expanded its lending to the newly independent nations that were emerging in the post-war period across Africa and Asia. During this time, divisions increased and solidified between the US-led allies of the 'West' and the 'East' led by the USSR. The mutual suspicions and tensions led to an arms race and competition for global dominance by these two powerful forces and their allies, which became known as the Cold War. The United States and the Western allies formed a military alliance, called the North Atlantic Treaty Organisation (NATO), to rival the military threat posed by the 'East'. They sought to contain the spread of communism in non-aligned nations that were not officially part of either set of allies (see Figure 9.2). The USSR responded by implementing a binding military treaty with other Eastern and Central European countries under the Warsaw Pact. The Cold War also entailed an **ideological** campaign between the principles of **capitalism** and free market, which were espoused by Western countries, and the ideas of the socialism and state-led development advanced by the USSR.

It was these non-aligned states that were originally labelled the 'Third World', to denote their reluctance to take sides between the two different worlds of the superpowers. Both the United States and the USSR sought to influence the Third World, and while the major powers avoided direct military confrontations, the Cold War period was certainly hot in places like Vietnam,

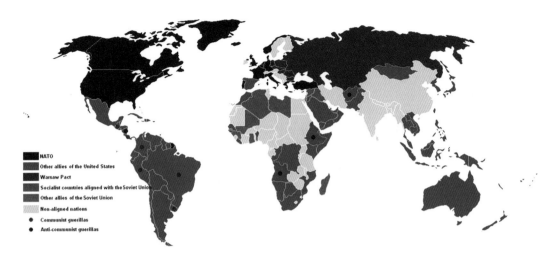

Figure 9.2
Map of allies in the time of the Cold War

Source: Figure credit: Aivazovsky, Wikimedia Commons

Cambodia, and Afghanistan, where proxy wars were fought, and in places like the Congo, where elected leaders were assassinated (Robarge 2014). As non-aligned countries became the battle-grounds for this super-power rivalry and its threats of new **imperialism**, a group of leaders and activists from newly independent nations pushed for a different set of global norms that respected their rights to self-determination, sovereignty, and social justice. Notably, in 1955, a conference was held in Bandung, Indonesia, which aimed to promote coalition building among African and Asian nations, and to push back against the **neocolonialism** of European powers, the United States, and the USSR (see also Chapter 37). The conference

> Was agreed in declaring that **colonialism** in all its manifestations was an evil, and that free-dom and independences must be granted to all such peoples…it expressed itself in favour of universal disarmament and effective international control to ensure it and, in particular, was in favour of disarmament and the prohibition of the production or use or experimentation with nuclear and thermos-nuclear weapons.
>
> *Appadorai, 1955: 214*

Participants at the Bandung Conference did not align with either the 'First' or 'Second' worlds of the United States or USSR, and they represented 1.4 billion people, an estimated two thirds of the world's population at that time, and a quarter of the world's land surface (Appadorai 1955). The conference inspired the creation of the Non-Aligned Movement in 1961 and other movements for solidarity among the nations of Africa, Asia, and Latin America, such as the Tricontinental conference in Cuba, in 1966, which led to the founding of the anti-colonial and radical Organization of Solidarity with the Peoples of Asia, Africa, and Latin America. The latter first introduced the concept of the 'Global South', and these solidarity movements added greater impetus to the influence of 'Global South' countries on the global stage. In May 1974, the UN adopted a Resolution, the Declaration of a New International Economic Order. This resolution called for an urgent programme of action that would address inequality in trade and techno-logical progress, promote accelerated socio-economic development, and remove the 'remaining vestiges of alien and colonial domination, foreign occupation, racial discrimination, apartheid and neo-colonialism in all its forms' (United Nations General Assembly 1974).

While the foundation of the Third World as a unifying concept was in solidarity and shared action for change, the Third World increasingly became seen primarily as 'underdeveloped' by powerful global organisations such as the World Bank. This view was premised on models of devel-opment that placed various countries on different stages of growth and modernisation. Notably, theorists such as Walt Rostow understood development to be a linear progress from 'traditional' to 'industrialising' to 'high mass consumption' and inspired various international development organisations to produce rankings of countries based on how 'developed' they were according to such understandings of progress. The discourse shifted from one which emphasised solidarity and cooperation among the non-aligned, to one where the Third World was understood by powerful actors as a problem that had to be fixed. Between the 1960s and mid-80s, for instance, the term 'Third World' was used by some prominent French sociologists and others to refer to 'backward' or 'uncivilised' or 'under-developed' places and societies (Bratman, 2011). Geographer Doreen Massey critiques this understanding of the world as being a kind of imaginary 'historical queue' where some countries are 'in front' and others are 'behind', where the assumption is that those in the rear can 'catch up' with properly applied development advice (Massey 2005). She insists that geography (and history) matters and such a historical queue does not account for the diversity of places and trajectories of change globally (Massey and Allen 1984, Massey 2005).

For thinkers such as Arturo Escobar, the 'making' of the Third World was a violent process of development and active *under*development, where vast areas of the world came to be impov-erished through world orders set up to benefit the most powerful nations (Escobar, 1995). For Escobar and others (see also Chapter 37), the Third World can also be understood as having been *produced* as underdeveloped through increasing debt, through teleological understandings of development based on First World notions of capitalist industrialisation, through restructur-ing that removed social protections such as health care and education, and through deliber-ate disruptions to Third World politics (sometimes through CIA interventions) and economies (through trade rules that benefited the First World). For many in the First World, the Third World became associated with a set of problems – poverty and violence – or as a kind of exotic place of premodern tradition (Williams et al., 2014). This tension is evident in two influential reports from the 1980s, which subsequently shaped global economic relations, discussed next.

Summary

- The terms 'First World' and 'Third World' emerged during the Second World War and Cold War, representing the divide between the US-led capitalist bloc (First World) and the Soviet Union-led communist bloc (Second World), with non-aligned nations (Third World) in between.
- The Third World, consisting of non-aligned countries, aimed to promote self-determi-nation, sovereignty, and social justice, advocating for disarmament, independence from colonial powers, and an end to neocolonialism.

> • Over time, the 'Third World' became associated with being 'underdeveloped' by global organisations, based on linear development models that ranked countries by progress and modernisation. This perception reduced the Third World to a problem to be solved rather than recognising their **agency** for change.

Global South and Global North

Since the 1980s, two main influential reports have proven pivotal for shaping key ideas and approaches about the Third World. The Brandt Report and the Berg Report were both intended to address unequal patterns of development and propose solutions. They introduced the ideas of Global North and South and represented different understandings of the causes of poverty.

In 1980, the Brandt Report was published by the Independent Commission on International Development Issues, led by Willy Brandt (later released as a book; see Brandt et al., 1982). The report focused on the disparities in wealth and development between the rich and poor countries and proposed a global economic partnership between developed and developing countries. In the report, 'the Brandt line' was used to divide the world into two broad groups based on economic development, with the developed countries of the Global North located above the line, and the developing countries of the Global South located below the line (see Figure 9.3). The Brandt Report reiterated the need for a new international economic order that would promote greater cooperation between Global North and Global South. It called for a redistribution of wealth from the rich to the poor and proposed measures to improve the living conditions of the poorest people in the world. The report also proposed measures to address issues such as food

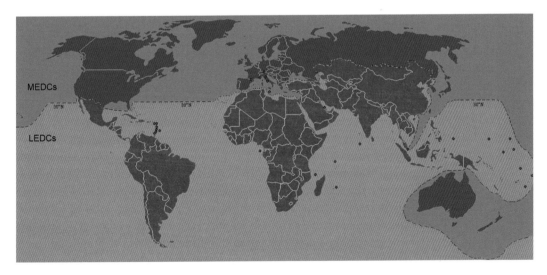

Figure 9.3
'The Brandt line' shows the divisions between Global North and Global South, labelled here as MEDC ('most economically development countries') and LEDC ('least economically developed countries')

Source: Figure credit: Bramfab, Wikimedia Commons

security, energy, and the environment. In sum, it located the problems of development and poverty as being located *outside* the Global South, or at least, a shared responsibility.

The Berg Report, titled 'Accelerated Development in Sub-Saharan Africa', was published by the World Bank in 1981 and was named after the chairman of the commission that produced it, Elliot Berg. The report aimed to address the crisis in international debt and proposed measures to promote economic growth in developing countries. The proposed measures centred around three major policy actions, namely, free trade and flexible exchange rate, efficiency of resources in the public sector, and improvements in agricultural productivity (World Bank, 1981, p3). In sum, it saw the problem of development and poverty as being located *within* the nations of the Global South and proposed measures that sought to roll back the state from the economy and facilitate private sector participation in the economy (Loxley, 1983). In the 1980s, the Brandt and Berg reports provided the intellectual precursors for the adoption of the **Structural Adjustment Programmes** (SAPs), through which the World Bank and IMF led countries to undertake comprehensive reforms aimed at securing medium-term macroeconomic stabilisation measures and 'unleash' the markets through support for free trade and private sector growth, in exchange for access to concessionary loans (Mkandawire and Soludo, 1998). While the SAPs proved beneficial in reversing overall decline in economic output, especially in terms of GDP growth, critics argue that their social costs (in terms of rising poverty levels and crippling effects on social investment) far outweighed their benefits.

Across the Global South, the fallout from the adjustment decade fed into three main approaches to research and practice of international development. Firstly, the rise of sustainability as an important development concept was captured by the World Commission on Environment and Development (also known as the Brundtland report) in 1987. The report called on humanity to make development respond to the needs of the present, without compromising the ability of future generations to meet their own needs (United Nations, 1987). Secondly, development scholars (such as Paul Streeten and Amartya Sen) began to emphasise the limits of economic growth and an expanded view of economic development to include opportunities and investments that support individual wellbeing in the form of health, nutrition, education, and improved standard of living. The third dynamic emerged largely from a wave of campaigns by **transnational** activists, such as the Jubilee 2000 Campaign and the protests at the 1999 World Trade Organisation's Seattle meeting, which marked a renewed focus on the negative effects of terms of the global trade and debt owed to countries of the North by countries in the Global South.

The turn of the twenty-first century has therefore brought into sharp focus the need to adopt a multidimensional approach to our understanding of the causes and solutions to international development and inequality. This evolving consensus has informed the growing prominence of key measures such as the Human Development Index and the United Nations Millennium Development Goals, which were replaced by the Sustainable Development Goals. And, while the North-South divide continues to be useful, especially in locating the spaces for social and political solidarity, this evolving consensus has raised fundamental questions about the relevance of linear models and depictions in popular media that confine development to simplistic notions of economic and technological growth. This pushback has also been led by a critical group of scholars, like Edward Said, who proposed a critical use of the term **Orientalism,** and popular literary icons like Chimamanda Adichie, who have pointed to the dangers of depicting the Global South based on imperialist tropes and exaggerations of '**otherness**'. We therefore need words to accurately describe and understand inequality without them becoming terms of oppression and exoticism. How do we do that?

Summary

- The Brandt Report and the Berg Report in the 1980s shaped ideas on the Third World, addressing unequal development and proposing solutions.
- The Brandt Report called for global economic partnership, improving living conditions in the Global South, wealth redistribution, and greater cooperation.
- The Berg Report aimed to promote economic growth in developing countries through free trade, private sector involvement, and macroeconomic stabilisation but faced criticism for social costs and negative impacts on poverty and social investment.

Majority and Minority Worlds

Shahidul Alam's works highlight how expressions and images shape people's cultural consciousness and convey complex truths and untruths, particularly in the areas that are often depicted in popular culture as the Third World. He therefore deployed the terms 'Majority' and 'Minority' Worlds as a pushback against the negative connotations usually associated with depictions of countries that have been colonised, and continue to be colonised, through globalised forms of control, as 'Third World' or 'Developing World' or 'Least Developed Countries' (LDCs) (Alam, 2008: 89). As he observed,

> the expressions have strong negative connotations that reinforce the stereotypes about poor communities and represent them as icons of poverty. They hide their histories of oppression and continued exploitation. The labels also hinder the appreciation of the cultural and social wealth of these communities.
>
> *Alam, 2008: 89*

By seeking to recast the 'Third World' as 'Majority World', Alam's goal was to highlight the fact that persons living in countries labelled as such are the majority of humankind, compared to the wealthy and powerful who represent a 'tiny fraction of humankind' but, nonetheless, made decisions affecting the majority of the world's population.

The terms have subsequently gained currency among various scholars in human geography, development studies, political science, and social anthropology, not only to question teleological and linear ideas and approaches to international development and social wellbeing but also to flip the script on where to find the sort of problems usually associated with the third world or the Global South. This work has moved us beyond generalised categories that ignore contextual differences both across and within countries. Eve Bratman, for instance, has identified the conditions of what she labels as 'third worldality' – such as political exclusion, inequality and socio-economic segregation, and unhealthy environments – and found that they persist in the very heart of the 'First World', in places that often fall outside the scope of traditional development geography. She specifically observes that while Washington DC expresses the ideals of democracy, equality, and opportunity in America, the city suffers from its own contradictions in terms of its inequality, environmental quality, and social segregation (Bratman, 2011).

Work such as this underscores how problematic geographically-determined dichotomies and hierarchies undermine deeper understandings and actions in international development or change. In this sense, the criticism invites us to search for alternative viewpoints and pathways from the Global South and to incorporate the voice and concerns of minority groups, including minority **gendered**, racialised, and Indigenous communities.

While the terms Minority and Majority Worlds remain an important alternative frame, they have not gone unchallenged. On one hand, some critics have argued that undue attention to numbers downplays the asymmetries of wealth and power which continue to influence interactions and outcomes of development around the world. Notably, there is reasonable confusion about what the terms ignore in terms of the historical basis of inequality within and across nations, and how descriptors like 'minority' and 'majority' play into the sense of inferiority and superiority and the problematic 'othering' which they seek to address (Khan et al., 2022). On the other hand, some scholars have argued that although 'Third World' was a historical construct that was used to erase the historical, cultural, political, and social realities of the non-Western world, it still retains symbolic and discursive value, which can be used to make sense of conditions of deprivation and inequality around the world (Bratman, 2011).

Summary

- The terms 'Majority World' and 'Minority World' were introduced by Shahidul Alam as alternatives to 'Third World' and 'Developing World', aiming to challenge negative connotations and stereotypes associated with impoverished communities.
- These terms highlight that the majority of the world's population resides in places often considered marginalised or insignificant, emphasising their importance and pushing back against hierarchical notions of development.
- While the use of 'Majority World' and 'Minority World' has been critiqued for overlooking wealth and power asymmetries and perpetuating notions of inferiority/superiority, the terms provide a framework to understand global inequalities and the need for diverse voices in development discussions.

Emerging terms

In recent times, an emerging cohort of ecological economists has experimented with other kinds of language to group **nation-states** according to their ability to keep within the planetary boundaries (measured on a per capita basis) and to keep human wellbeing within a certain set of parameters (largely overlapping with the SDGs). The Doughnut Economics Action Lab has developed an indicator framework based on planetary boundaries and human wellbeing or 'the social floor'. Recently, they have mapped the nations of the world, combining all this information with 'meeting the needs of all people' on the Y axis, and 'within the means of the planet' on the X axis. On this graph, they have identified three cohorts of nations that are somewhat different from Majority and Minority Worlds but with some overlaps (see Figure 9.4). They identified that some nations need to work primarily on meeting the needs of all people, including working together to provide for water, food, health, education, peace and justice, gender equality, social

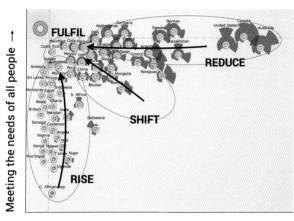

No nation is living within the Doughnut

Every nation is on a journey of transformation.

What's the best way to name or characterize each cluster of nations?

 goodlife.leeds.ac.uk

Figure 9.4
Doughnut Economics Action Lab proposed categories of nation-states

Source: Figure credit: Andrew Fanning

equity, housing, political voice, energy, and communications. These nations are collectively referred to as 'Rise' nations, where the action of 'rise' refers to strategies for bringing people up above the 'social floor' in ways that stay within planetary boundaries.

Other nations need to 'reduce' – these are ones which are broadly able to meet the needs of their people but are living well beyond the planetary boundaries: the settler colonies of Australia, Canada, Aotearoa New Zealand, and the United States are prominent overshooters, yet there is also need for further 'reduce' strategies for Scandinavian countries such as Sweden and Norway and many others that are consuming resources way beyond what the planet can sustain. For example, Aotearoa New Zealand is vastly overshooting in phosphorus use, while the United States is performing poorly on all indicators for climate change (see https://doughnuteconomics. org/). Finally, there are a set of nations whose primary action could be 'Reorient' – these are nations that are accelerating up both axes of meeting human needs and overshooting the planet. Reorientation would be shifting focus towards innovation for continuing to improve in meeting human needs but steering clear of planetary overshoot.

In many ways, the story we have told here is a tension between using 'descriptive' and 'normative' frameworks for thinking about global inequality. The terms Third World, Global South and North, and Majority-Minority World tried to be primarily descriptive (in terms of non-allied nations, inequality between North and South, and reframing the majority and minority to highlight the relative problems of each). Low-, middle-, and high-income countries are another way of describing differences without prescribing normative change. Terminologies, such as 'less-developed nations', 'developing world', and 'underdeveloped', presume a normative direction and method of change: development has a certain trajectory and includes certain things such as higher income, access to communications, industrialisation, and **globalisation**.

All these terms have been critiqued by many human geographers as imposing a certain kind of 'development' on the world that also normalises inequality, high mass consumption, environmental destruction, and accumulation of wealth by the few. Yet with the Doughnut Action Lab and the Sustainable Development Goals, we see a new kind of normative terminology: the actions of Rise, Reorient and Reduce label sets of nations with actions they might take to live within the 'sweet spot' between planetary boundaries and the social floor. Similarly, the indicators for the Sustainable Development Goals seek to group *all* nations together in the tasks of addressing the world's current human and planetary challenges. Moreover, because these new normative categorisations use a set of indicators for change that are based less on economic generalisations and more on holistic wellbeing indicators for social and planetary health, it may be that they help all of us to articulate and work together on the necessary transformations needed to address the stark inequalities *and* the planetary destruction and resource extraction processes that have accompanied the contemporary age of 'development'.

Summary

- Ecological economists introduced alternative categorisations of nation-states based on planetary boundaries and human wellbeing: Rise, Reduce, and Reorient nations.
- Rise nations focus on meeting needs within boundaries. Reduce nations meet needs but exceed boundaries. Reorient nations balance needs and boundaries.
- These categorisations promote sustainable development, holistic wellbeing indicators, and necessary transformations for addressing inequalities and environmental challenges.
- An important part of current debates in academic scholarship and policy practice is the question of how best to describe and approach solutions to poverty and inequality across different countries in ways that are more accurate and do not stigmatise.
- Ongoing debates in human geography include questions about how we describe and think about solutions to poverty and poverty across different countries that are more accurate and do not stigmatise 'others' based on imperialist or orientalist tropes.

Discussion points

- Why are words like 'developing', 'developed', 'Global North', 'Global South', 'Low Income', 'Middle Income', and 'High Income' often dismissed by some geographers as problematic?
- How did the Cold War influence the ways in which policy makers, activists, and scholars around the world viewed, and indeed used, the idea of the 'Third World'?
- Compare and contrast the key observations of the Brandt and Berg Reports. How do you think these reports shaped debates and policy interventions about the 'Third World'?
- What are the main strengths and shortcomings of the terms 'Majority' and 'Minority' Worlds?
- Use the links in the online materials listed below to review the categories of countries based on the Sustainable Development Goals outcomes and the principles espoused by the Doughnut Economics Action Lab. Do you consider these plausible alternatives to the categories of Majority/Minority Worlds?

References

Alam, S. (2008). Majority world: challenging the West's rhetoric of democracy. *Amerasia Journal* 34(1): 88–98.

Appadorai, A. (1955). The Bandung conference. *India Quarterly* 11: 207–235.

Brandt, W., Al-Hamad. A. Y., and Botero Montoya, R. Commission indépendante sur les problèmes de développement. (1982). *North South: a Programme for Survival*. Cambridge: MIT Press.

Bratman, E. (2011). Development's paradox: is Washington DC a Third World city? *Third World Quarterly* 32(9): 1541–1556.

Christensen, M.-B., Hallum, C., Maitland, A., Parrinello, Q., and Putaturo, C. (2023). *Survival of the Richest: How We Must Tax the Super-Rich Now to Fight Inequality*. Oxford: Oxfam.

Escobar, A. (1995). *Encountering Development: the Making and Unmaking of the Third World*. Princeton: Princeton University Press.

Gibson-Graham, J. K., Cameron, J., and Healy, S. (2013). *Take Back the Economy: An Ethical Guide for Transforming Our Communities*. Minneapolis: University of Minnesota Press.

Khan, T., Abimbola, S., Kyobutungi, C., and Pai, M. (2022). How we classify countries and people—and why it matters. *BMJ Global Health*, 7(6), e009704.

Loxley, J. (1983). The Berg Report and the Model of Accumulation in Sub-Saharan Africa. *R* Bangladeshi photographer Shahidul Alam in the early 1990s. *Review of African Political Economy*, 197–204.

Massey, D. (2005). *For Space*. Los Angeles, London, New Delhi, Singapore, Washington: Sage.

Massey, D., and Allen, J. (1984). *Geography Matters!: A Reader*. Cambridge: Cambridge University Press.

Mkandawire, P. T., and Soludo, C. C. (1998). *Our Continent, Our Future: African Perspectives on Structural Adjustment*. New Jersey: Africa World Press.

Rich, B. (1994). *Mortgaging the Earth*. Abingdon: Earthscan.

Robarge, D. (2014). CIA's covert operations in the Congo, 1960–1968: insights from newly declassified documents. *Studies in Intelligence* 58: 1–9.

United Nations. (1987). *Report of the World Commission on Environment and Development: Our Common Future*. United Nations: New York.

United Nations General Assembly. (1974). *Declaration on the Establishment of a New International Economic Order*. Geneva: United Nations.

Williams, G., Meth, P., and Willis, K. (2014). *Geographies of Developing Areas: The Global South in a Changing World*. Abingdon: Routledge.

World Bank. (1981). *Accelerated Development in Sub-Saharan Africa: An Agenda for Action*. Washington: The World Bank.

Online materials

- https://www.oxfam.org/en/research/survival-richest
  Oxfam global inequality report January 2023

- https://doughnuteconomics.org/
  The Doughnut Economics site has resources for calculating planetary overshoot and social issues.

- Here, you can read about the different SDGs and progress made against them.
  United Nations Sustainable Development Goals. https://sdgs.un.org/goals

- Human Development Index
  https://hdr.undp.org/data-center/human-development-index#/indicies/HDI

- This talk by Chimamanda Ngozi Adichie'emphasises 'the danger of a single story'
  https://www.ted.com/talks/chimamanda_ngozi_adichie_the_danger_of_a_single_story?utm_campaign=tedspread&utm_medium=referral&utm_source=tedcomshare

- Take a look at the World Bank Interactive Income Map to find out more about how different places compare.
  https://databank.worldbank.org/source/world-development-indicators

Further reading

Alam, S. (2008). Majority world: challenging the West's rhetoric of democracy. *Amerasia Journal* 34(1): 88–98.
Alam was one of the original advocates for the new idea of the Majority World, and this was a key article in the spreading of the term.

Chang, H.-J. (2002). *Kicking Away the Ladder: Development Strategy in Historical Perspective*. London: Anthem Press.
The title refers to the 'kicking away' of the ladder by which rich countries have climbed to the top of the world order, and the book examines the strategies which the west has looked to impose on rest of the world as it tries to follow their path.

Ferguson, J. (2006). *Global Shadows: Africa in the Neoliberal World Order*. Durham (North Carolina): Duke University Press.
This wide-ranging book examines Africa's changing position within the world order, and interrogates the idea of Africa as a place of crisis and failure.

Raworth, K. (2017). *Doughnut Economics: Seven Ways to Think Like a 21st-Century Economist*. Chelsea Green Publishing.
A new type of economics, advocating development which stresses economic, social and environmental sustainability.

Said, E. W. (1978). *Orientalism*. New York: Pantheon Books.
This is the book which proposed and explained the critical use of the term 'orientalism'.

Sen, A. (1999). *Development as Freedom*. Oxford: OUP.
In this book, the Nobel Prize winning economist links economic development to ethical considerations based around ideas of choice, freedom, and political rights.

10 Indigeneity

*Pasang Yangjee Sherpa,
Ritodhi Chakraborty
and Aline Carrara*

Introduction

In Khumbu, there is a mountain that protects the people. Its body rises from the twin-villages of Khumjung and Khunde. It stands tall and looks over the villages down below from its elevated vantage point (see Figure 10.1). The mountain does not begin or end with the visible dark rock for the Sherpa people who live on its lap. It extends to the surrounding hills, valleys, villages, people and streams. It connects the Earth to the sky. This mountain is known as the Khumbi-Yullha. In the Sherpa language, this name identifies it as the village deity, or Yullha, of Khumbu. The deity resides in the physical mountain that our eyes are able to see. The deity Je-gyal Tri-tsen Nyen is depicted as being white and radiant, his body dressed in white silk and his head adorned with a white silk turban. His image is placed on altars of Khumbu families, showing him riding a red horse and holding a lance with red silk ribbons in his right hand and a red lasso in his left. This mountain is considered too sacred to climb. To set foot on its upper flanks is a spiritually polluting act that may result in sickness, death and destruction. Sherpas are careful not to disturb the deity who lives there or his associates (called 'khor'), which include the Yeti, yaks, goats and sheep.

Local residents make incense offerings to the Yullha every morning. The smoke is believed to rise to the sky to reach the deity. Sherpas also perform the lhapsang ritual annually, each village with its own slight variations, to appease the deity and to request continued protection from him. The relationship between the Yullha and the villagers requires constant effort to remain strong. It cannot be taken for granted.

A childhood memory of my maternal grandmother offering incense to Khumbi-Yullha connects me spiritually to the place I call home. I used to wake every morning to the sound of her repeating the Buddhist mantra, Om Mane Padme Hung. I watched her take embers from the hearth, lay them on dried juniper leaves and blow air into them. The barely lit kitchen would fill with smoke as she walked out to place the brass burner in her front yard. The grey smoke rose towards the mountain, and the scent lingered around us. To talk about this mountain is to talk about home. It is to talk about how Sherpas belong to Khumbu. It is to understand the vitality of the old soul it represents. It is to acknowledge the countless life forms it has continued to support. It is to recognise the brief human presence in comparison to its existence over the ages.

–Pasang Yangjee Sherpa

DOI: 10.4324/9780429265853-12

Figure 10.1
Mount Khumbila, Nepal

Source: Photo credit: Un Sherpa

Speaking of Indigeneity

Indigeneity is about Indigenous ways of being and knowing, how Indigenous peoples live their Indigenous traditions in their everyday lives (Perley, 2014). So, Sherpa Indigeneity is distinct. Similarly, the Indigeneity of another Indigenous people is distinct. Each Indigenous people have their own histories, stories, songs, dances, food, protocols and traditions that shape the complexities of their lives. To speak of Indigeneity is thus to speak of our plural and parallel existences. It is to recognise more than one way of being and knowing. It is not about a hierarchy of being or knowing. It is about relationality.

Indigeneity as a concept offers a way to relate to each other. It offers a way to be in relationship with each other. It opens up our senses to relational meaning-making and expands the possibilities of responsible worlding. Stories and storytelling offer the tools through which cultural nuances can be transmitted, holding ourselves accountable to the ancestors that have come before us and ones that will follow.

In this chapter, three authors have come together to share how the concept of Indigeneity allow us to recognise multiple ways of knowing and being. We show how Indigeneity can be approached from different angles, instead of defining it. Before we do that, we introduce ourselves and explain our positionalities because who we are has an impact on how we see and engage with Indigeneity. Through Indigeneity, we practice relational accountability. We begin to do so by telling our stories of where we come from. We close this chapter by highlighting what Indigeneity means.

Summary

- Indigeneity is about Indigenous ways of being and knowing, how Indigenous peoples live their Indigenous traditions in their everyday lives.
- Each Indigenous people have their own histories, stories, songs, dances, food, protocols and traditions that shape the complexities of their lives.
- Indigeneity as a concept offers a way to relate to each other. It opens up our senses to relational meaning-making and expands the possibilities for better worlds.

Where we come from

Pasang Yangjee is a Sherpa mother from Pharak in north-eastern Nepal, currently based in Vancouver, Canada. The word Sherpa is derived from the Sherpa word *Sharwa*, which means the easterners. She is also an anthropologist, who studies Indigeneity, human dimensions of climate change and the Sherpa **diaspora**. She uses **ethnographic** methods to study everyday concerns of Himalayan people in order to normalise their experiences and represent them as equal partners in decision-making spaces. Her work is guided by the belief that the sustainability of Indigenous Himalayan people in the wake of climate change depends on keeping their stories about people, places and things alive for the next generation.

Ritodhi Chakraborty is a parent, scholar and activist from India who works in solidarity with a variety of rural, immigrant and Indigenous communities on issues of social and environmental justice. In the past he has worked in Bhutan and Southwest China and continues to work in Himalayan India and more recently in Aotearoa New Zealand. His professional and personal achievements have been enabled by a significant set of caste, **gender** and educational privileges which are unfairly inaccessible to most others. His current research explores the politics of climate knowledge production and the responses of rural Himalayan youth to social-ecological change.

Aline Carrara, from Brazil, is a mother, artist, storyteller and activist. She is a broadly trained environmental social scientist and for the past 20 years has engaged at the intersections of human rights, justice, development, environmental change and land management issues in Latin America. Most (but not all) of her ancestors came from Europe and were/are settler-colonists in Brazil. She has some privilege from being a white-passing settler in a country where afro-descendant and Indigenous communities continue to be politically and culturally oppressed. Her current research focuses on Indigenous economies and **territorial** aspirations beyond the developmental state in Brazil.

We began with stories of ourselves, we now turn to telling the story of geography, as a discipline, and its relationship with Indigeneity and Indigenous peoples.

Geography and Indigeneity

Geography is unquestionably a colonial science. It was meant to document places and people who were in the path of empire.

Curley and Smith (2020: 39)

We began with stories of ourselves, we now turn to telling the story of geography, as a discipline, and its relationship with Indigeneity and Indigenous peoples. Geography as a discipline, as articulated in the quote above, has a problematic past. Associated with European colonial powers, geographers were complicit in the colonial domination of communities and **ecologies** across the world, and the discipline continues to be rooted in tools of knowledge production which oppress certain ways of understanding the world (Curley and Smith, 2020). The discipline has been challenged by a variety of provocations, seeking to reform and, if possible, transform since the middle of the twentieth century (Shaw et al., 2006). These critiques have emerged from scholars and activists embedded within a diversity of **feminist** and queer movements, **postcolonial** perspectives, post-structuralism and **Marxist** economics, to name a few (see also Chapters 12, 33, 38, 49, 65, 71 and 72). For decades, they have been 'pointing to both the limited forms of mainstream knowledge and the socially unequal peopling of geography departments, societies and publishing arenas' (Panelli, 2008: 802). Efforts to pluralise and democratise the discipline have yielded results. While some describe the discipline as, 'both distinctive and exceedingly vibrant' (Castree et al., 2022: 3), others argue that **coloniality** continues to structure it (de Leeuw and Hunt, 2018). It should also be noted that human geography and physical geography have matured and pursued different pathways of knowledge production (Colven and Thomson, 2019). The tools and strategies from geography are now increasingly practiced beyond the conceptual and material boundaries of the discipline by a wide variety of individuals and communities ranging from scholars and activists to artists and policymakers (Gregory and Castree, 2012).

Given the contentious history of the discipline, geography's engagement with Indigeneity as a term, concept and practice has been quite varied across **space** and time. Some point to the spaces of radical and critical geography scholarship of the 1960s which nurtured Indigenous geographies, pursued by both Indigenous and non-Indigenous individuals. Within English language geographical scholarship, this small but powerful sub-discipline of Indigenous geography has been juxtaposed to the overwhelming presence of colonial and elite **epistemologies** (theories on how we know the world) and **ontologies** (theories on what that world consists of and how it works) (Hunt, 2016). Additionally, there has been greater advocacy for the presence of Indigenous geographers within the academy. Since the 1990s, such mobilisations have catalysed the creation of spaces nurturing and supporting Indigeneity within prominent associations of geographers. Examples include the Indigenous Peoples Speciality Group in the Association of American Geographers, the Indigenous Peoples Working Group of the Canadian Association of Geographers, the Indigenous Peoples Knowledge and Rights Study Group of the Institute of Australian Geographers and the work towards highlighting Indigenous issues in the International Geographical Union. Driven by the dual aspiration of self-determination and representation, such manifestation of Indigeneity in the institutional setting have challenged the ethical architecture of the discipline, interrogating its use of exclusionary and extractive methods (Coombes et al., 2012, 2013, 2014, McCreary and Milligan, 2018). Despite such forays, Indigeneity, both as an intellectual driver and as a political project, remains on the peripheries.

There is a growing consensus among geographers that the discipline needs to listen to and work with the many relational insights of Indigeneity if it is to decolonise itself and to ensure that the aspirations of historically marginalised communities and ecologies are included, as it has claimed (de Leeuw and Hunt, 2018, Radcliffe and Radhuber, 2020, Sundberg, 2014). So, a question that can be asked here is, *what difference does Indigeneity make to the discipline of geography?* (Radcliffe, 2020) While there are quite a few different ways in which this question can be answered, one way of addressing it is by categorising some complementary objectives.

First, geography as a discipline can be quite diverse, both in terms of its research and teaching. However, this breadth of focus, made possible in part by avoiding intellectual and pedagogical orthodoxy, can be difficult to sustain if it is not grounded in the material needs of both human and non-human beings. Indigeneity provides such grounding. Indigeneity is often chastised for its inability to speak to a 'universal subject' and the relationships of such a subject/s with a dynamic environment. The specificity of Indigeneity, however, allows geography as a discipline to challenge the universals that are often colonial in nature. You will note that all the chapters in this textbook that touch on Indigeneity in some way refuse to claim universality (see Chapters 7, 43, 45 and 71, among others). The concept of Indigeneity confronts static Black and white binaries, as it is built on a critique of simplistic understandings of relationships between structural processes, subjects and ideas. It highlights both the plurality of such relationships and their 'unfinished' and dynamic character. As an example, see the attempts at domesticating the process of **colonisation**, the state and the settler culture as shown in the A'uwe Uptabi (Xavante) case study below.

Second, as geography enters the twenty-first century, there is an increasing demand for the discipline (and others) to actively challenge their historical separation from the 'real world'. Many Indigenous scholars and activists have questioned whether true **decolonisation** can be achieved within the walls of elite educational systems. The questions about the emancipatory potential of 'expert knowledge production' are not unique to geography and are increasingly more resonant across a variety of institutions. Complicating things is the fact that as the project of decolonisation grows in popularity, Indigeneity is being wielded 'metaphorically' and/or hijacked by subjects and institutions. Addressing the many complicated issues of inequality, ethnic **othering**, **neoliberal** state building, climate change, **patriarchy** and the COVID-19 pandemic, among others, requires geography as a discipline to eschew its search for internal 'unity' and instead informed by Indigeneity, pursue allyship with a politics of plurality. Such an objective deviates from oppressive and static tools of description. It advocates for sitting with the discomfort of the messy, seemingly paradoxical, hybrid entities emerging from the ongoing **encounters** between elite and non-elite knowledge production processes. These emerging hybrid subjects and institutions allow for a politics of recognition that release Indigenous communities and their many relationalities from artificial, essentialised, conceptual categories to emerge.

We are witnessing the shift in disciplinary focus towards what is most needed: building solidarity across disciplines, departments, fields, regions and aspirations, in an effort to subvert and dismantle the ongoing violence of processes such as colonisation, slavery, white supremacy, **capitalism**, casteism and patriarchy. There is also the unfinished project of widening the scope of academic research through place-based Indigenous engagements to make geography more connected to community needs and aspirations (Curley et al., 2022). The 'Skin of Chitwan' case study below explores place-based Indigenous Tharu life entanglements.

Summary

- Given the contentious history of the discipline, geography's engagement with Indigeneity as a term, concept and practice has been quite varied across space and time.
- There is a growing consensus among geographers that the discipline needs to listen to and work with the many relational insights of Indigeneity if it is to decolonise itself and

to ensure that the aspirations of historically marginalised communities and ecologies are included, as it has claimed.

- The disciplinary focus is shifting towards what is most needed: building solidarity across disciplines, departments, fields, regions and aspirations, in an effort to subvert and dismantle the ongoing violence of processes such as colonisation, slavery, white supremacy, capitalism, casteism and patriarchy.

Explore: case studies

In the following case studies, you will explore Indigeneity and the complexities of Indigenous worlds. Each case is different and yet they are connected through commonalities of their struggles. The first case study is an online exhibition of *The Skin of Chitwan* (see Figure 10.2). The exhibition illuminates the concept of Indigeneity. It invites us to think about Tharu Indigeneity from southern Nepal and with that reflect on our lives and the habitability of the planet Earth. The second case study titled *Taming the Waradzu (white man)* explores settler/Indigenous relations with the A'uwe Uptabi (Xavante) community from Mato Grosso, Brazil.

Figure 10.2
Installation shot of the 'Skin of Chitwan' exhibition, Kathmandu, Nepal

Source: Photo credit: Shikhar Bhattarai

The skin of Chitwan

The first thing the audience will experience in this exhibition is the whooshing sound of the winds as two still images reveal the skin of Chitwan. The skin has scales and scars. It is marked with use and abuse. In that surface condition, what we are able to see is life. The ground is all there is. And on that ground, we find accounts of ways the familiar world has been made unfamiliar. The landscape contains traces of life entanglements that came before. These traces, the ghosts of our ecologies, keep those present today on that ground to sense the land's unresolved histories. The exhibition then pulls the audience to reflect on how we have forgotten to belong to a particular soil and how the ghosts tell us to be terrestrial. And reminds us that the main story is still about the habitability of Earth.

The exhibition talks about Indigeneity as being oriented to a particular place. The curators show Indigeneity as 'knowing how to find one's way and how to pace oneself in order to make or avoid encounters with other acknowledged beings who share this space'. The Indigenous Tharu people of this place, now called Chitwan, have shrines of forest deities and phantoms they share the ground with. These shrines serve as coordinates for them to find their bearings in this space. Stories and memories of gods, ghosts and animals are a frame of reference for them to connect with the place across time that allow participation in the present and the future. Today, the connection to the ground, the coordinates of this place and the co-habitants of this land find themselves having to navigate a whole network of new itineraries and directions that have been grafted onto the landscapes of Chitwan.

This vision of the Nepali **nation-state's** economic development, framed as progress, has come charging towards Chitwan with new machines for churning the earth. Contemporary Nepalis regard Chitwan as a wild space for viewing the wilderness. The chronicle of mounting ecological crises in the home of the Tharu people are masked. Large-scale deforestation, intensification of land use, contamination, species extinction, destruction of homes and habitat are hidden in plain sight from the public, but it is intensely felt on Indigenous bodies. Stories and songs archive these crises ensuring that they are not erased from public memory just as the people themselves struggle to remain alive on their own terms. The experience of the Tharu people in Nepal is nested within the **Anthropocene** and is not detached from the present human condition of ecological precarity. It is an example of the ways in which humanity's unmitigated economic ambitions have gone so far as to engineer the conditions of life and death on Earth, penetrating the planet's core geophysical dynamics.

Taming the Waradzu (white man): exploring economies, urbanisms and identities with the A'uwe Uptabi (Xavante)

Barra do Garças is a frontier city in Mato Grosso State, Brazil. Currently, Mato Grosso leads the Brazilian cattle and soy production. Within this ocean of ranches, which have devoured the Brazilian savannah, are state recognised Indigenous territories, floating like disconnected islands of Indigeneity.

One such Indigenous territory near Barra do Garças is home to the A'uwe Uptabi Indigenous peoples (known by non-Indigenous as Xavante), who comprise the largest Indigenous population of the state. Before the 1950s, the A'uwe were nomadic people who occupied a vast territory. They embody a cosmology which understands territory as a fluid, continuous and limitless space, open to mobility, known as *zomori*. *Zomori* (a condition defined by constant walking) is considered as part of the A'uwe Uptabi's cosmological wellbeing and a vital element for their cultural and physical reproduction through the act of walking long distances for hunting and gathering. It is during these long walks that they pass all knowledge down through the generations, and where the identification of places unfolds in A'uwe Uptabi territoriality, occupying spaces which are defined as territory (Ró). Ró can be understood as a **representation** of the A'uwe Uptabi's concept of a territorial world, which configures spatially through concentric circles, in a spatial organisation that goes from the village to the territory or the 'outside' world. It has spatial distinctions, which operate and interact with each other in a fluid manner, making it a spatial continuum. There is always an order when A'uwe Uptabi describe the Ró *as* the 'space', starting with the Aldeia as the most interior, moving to the crops and then to the world, together with all the animals, plants and the spirits.

Since colonial contact, through the ongoing influence of the Christian church and the extractive policies of the settler state and capitalism, the A'uwe's access to and presence in the region is heavily regulated. However, the A'uwe are not passive victims but, in their own words, have been engaged in 'domesticating the waradzu (white man)' since first contact. These strategies are on open display in the city of Barra.

A'uwe are omnipresent in Barra do Garças, walking in the streets, shopping at stores, supermarkets and pharmacies, eating in restaurants, sitting in public squares, entering banks, hotels and hospitals. Despite this constant presence, the non-Indigenous population of the city treat them as invisible, constantly questioning the validity of their Indigeneity while also reducing them to historically negative stereotypes.

A'uwe engage with the city to ensure access to institutional networks, engaging through a knowledge of tools and gatekeepers which/who act as translators and intermediaries between 'worlds'. One A'uwe woman said, mulling over her experience with the state health services that treated her daughter's sickness:

> I want to move here. Living in the city will allow me to study and I can have a job. I want to become a nurse to help the people in my village. Maybe I become a nutritionist because I heard it is easier to get in college for that profession. That would also help my people. Everybody there has problems caused by the food. You know, the food from waradzu.
>
> *Interview with Aline Carrara, 2017*

Along with resisting exploitation by state institutions, A'uwe also challenge their exclusion from the city, by being corporeally present in that space. The map below shows (Figure 10.3) the presence of A'uwe 'bodies' in various places, engaging in forms of consumption (see Chapter 32). Some Waradzu consider such engagements as antithetical to A'uwe Indigeneity. For the A'uwe, however, this is an attempt at reclaiming their territory and also to domesticate both capitalism and the colonial state. However, such a project is incredibly difficult and the results of their strategies remain mixed as evidenced by the ongoing problems with physical health, food insecurity, intra-communal violence, limited political representation and increasing threats to their Indigenous territory (for further reading see Carrara, 2020).

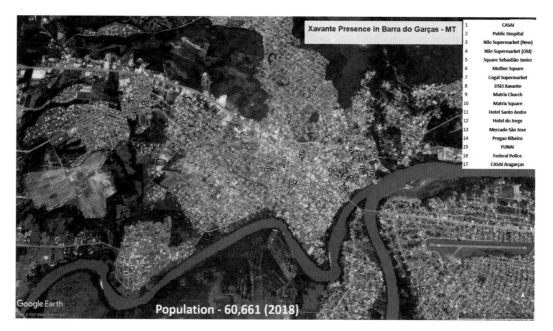

Figure 10.3
A map visualising the presence of A'uwe in Barra do Garças

Source: By Aline Carrara using a Google Earth image

Summary

- The case studies from Nepal and Brazil explore Indigeneity and the complexities of Indigenous worlds, emphasising their struggles and interconnectedness.
- The exhibition 'The Skin of Chitwan' highlights the significance of Indigeneity as rooted in a particular place, as well as the challenges faced by the Tharu people in Nepal due to ecological crises and economic development.
- The A'uwe Uptabi (Xavante) community in Barra do Garças, Brazil, is seeking to resist and engage with the settler state and capitalist systems while reclaiming their territory and challenging exclusion.

What does Indigeneity mean in the twenty-first century?

Indigenous environmental justice responses to questions of sustainability and the Anthropocene (see Chapter 62) bring into sharp focus the enduring presence of colonial caricatures of Indigenous communities. These caricatures attempt to trap Indigenous communities within simplistic ecological and economic ideologies, at once threatening the much-needed project of sovereignty and thwarting just and equitable responses to socio-ecological change. Geography has a fundamental interest in understanding the dynamic relationships between humans and the environment and is now responding to the growing calls for reckoning with its colonial, elite and **hegemonic** past, in emerging collaboration with a variety of communities and institutions (see Chapter 71). Geographers can support the dismantling of such caricatures while studying (and hopefully suggesting) more just and inclusive ways of being.

People working with the tools of geography and/or interested in the discipline more broadly should look for certain emerging conversations. Some of the political and **ideological** flash-points include the ways in which different Indigenous and historically marginalised subjects/institutions are presenting their aspirations and the questions embedded within material and cultural reparations of colonisation in settler colonies.

Indigeneity centres Indigenous peoples. It is about how Indigenous peoples live their everyday lives following their Indigenous traditions. It is about Indigenous ways of knowing and being. As a concept, Indigeneity offers ways to reveal the complexities of Indigenous worlds as shown in the case studies. Indigeneity as a methodological tool has opened up institutional spaces for more representation of Indigenous bodies within geography (see Chapter 71). It has encouraged relational adjustments in the discipline to extend beyond Indigenous concerns to those of other historically politically subjugated groups. Indigeneity thus aids the unfinished project of decolonising the discipline of geography. Lastly, meaningful engagement with Indigeneity requires operating with relationality, not hierarchy, between our plural and parallel experiences. Only then will the rocky mountain in Khumbu, known as Khumbi-Yullha to the Sherpa, cease to appear as just another geological feature in the Himalayas to be replaced by one that is also imbued with knowledge, wisdom and power.

Summary

- Indigenous environmental justice challenges colonial caricatures and seeks sovereignty and equitable responses to socio-ecological change.
- Geographers are addressing the colonial past of their discipline, collaborating with communities and promoting just and inclusive ways of being.
- Indigeneity focuses on Indigenous peoples' traditions, ways of knowing and being and aids in decolonising geography while fostering relational adjustments and representation of historically marginalised groups.

Discussion points

- How does Indigeneity offer us a way to relate to the world around us?
- How does Indigeneity keep us accountable to everyone that surrounds us in the human form or not?
- What safeguards can be created which ensure against the hijacking of the emancipatory potential of Indigeneity by certain elite groups to pursue their own objectives?

- What forms of intellectual and political bridges can be created between geography and Indigeneity to ensure that despite diverging goals they can continue to engage in conversation with each other?
- In what ways does the discipline of geography informed by Indigeneity help us address the emerging impacts of complicated challenges such as climate change or global pandemic?

References

Carrara, A. F. A. (2020). *The Struggle for Indigenous Territories in the Brazilian Amazon* (Doctoral dissertation, University of Florida).

Castree, N., Leszczynski, A., Stallins, J. A., Schwanen, T., and Patel, Z. (2022). Reconstituting geography for the 21st century. *Environment and Planning F* 1(1): 3–6. https://doi.org/10.1177/26349825211005376

Colven, E., and Thomson, M. J. (2019). Bridging the divide between human and physical geography: potential avenues for collaborative research on climate modeling. *Geography Compass* 13(2): 1–15. https://doi.org/10.1111/gec3.12418

Coombes, B., Johnson, J. T., and Howitt, R. (2012). Indigenous geographies I: mere resource conflicts? The complexities in Indigenous land and environmental claims. *Progress in Human Geography* 36(6): 810–821.

Coombes, B., Johnson, J. T., and Howitt, R. (2013). Indigenous geographies II: the aspirational spaces in postcolonial politics–reconciliation, belonging and social provision. *Progress in Human Geography* 37(5): 691–700.

Coombes, B., Johnson, J. T., and Howitt, R. (2014). Indigenous geographies III: methodological innovation and the unsettling of participatory research. *Progress in Human Geography* 38(6): 845–854.

Curley, A., and Smith, S. (2020). Against colonial grounds: geography on colonial lands. *Dialogues in Human Geography* 10(1): 37–40.

Curley, A., Gupta, P., Lookabaugh, L., Neubert, C., and Smith, S. (2022). Decolonisation is a political project: overcoming impasses between Indigenous sovereignty and abolition. *Antipode* 54(4): 1043–1062. https://doi.org/10.1111/anti.12830

de Leeuw, S., and Hunt, S. (2018). Unsettling decolonizing geographies. *Geography Compass* 12(7): 1–14. https://doi.org/10.1111/gec3.12376

Gregory, D., and Castree, N. (2012). Editors' Introduction: Human Geography. In *Human Geography*, eds. D. Gregory and N. Castree. London: SAGE Publications Ltd, xxv–lxxix.

Hunt, S. (2016). Indigeneity. *International Encyclopedia of Geography: People, the Earth, Environment and Technology*, 1–9.

McCreary, T., and Milligan, R. (2018). The limits of liberal recognition: racial capitalism, settler colonialism, and environmental governance in Vancouver and Atlanta. *Antipode* 53(3): 724–744. https://doi.org/10.1111/anti.12465

Panelli, R. (2008). Social geographies: encounters with Indigenous and more-than-White/Anglo geographies. *Progress in Human Geography* 32(6): 801–811. https://doi.org/10.1177/0309132507088031

Perley, B. (2014). Living Traditions: A Manifesto for Critical Indigeneity. In *Performing Indigeneity*, eds. L. R. Graham and H. G. Penny. Nebraska: UNP, 32.

Radcliffe, S. A. (2020). Geography and Indigeneity III: co-articulation of colonialism and capitalism in Indigeneity's economies. *Progress in Human Geography* 44(2): 374–388.

Radcliffe, S. A., and Radhuber, I. M. (2020). The political geographies of D/decolonization: variegation and decolonial challenges of/in geography. *Political Geography* 78. https://doi.org/10.1016/j.polgeo.2019.102128

Shaw, W. S., Herman, R. D., and Dobbs, R. G. (2006). Encountering Indigeneity re-imagining and decolonizing geography. *Geografiska Annaler B* 88(B (3)): 267–276.

Sundberg, J. (2014). Decolonizing posthumanist geographies. *Cultural Geographies* 21(1): 33–47. https://doi.org/10.1177/1474474013486067

Online materials

- The Skin of Chitwan: https://skinofchitwan.nepalpicturelibrary.org
  Visit the virtual installation Skin of Chitwan.

- Indigenous Cartography in Amazonia from Acre, Brazil: https://notanatlas.org/maps/indigenous-cartography-in-acre
  The experience reported here refers to the Pro-Indian Commission of Acre (CPI/AC)1, which has been working to produce 'Indigenous Cartography' with Indigenous Agroforestry Agents (IAAFs) as a means for managing their territories. In mapping natural resources, morphology, environmental conflicts, cultural historical elements and many other aspects of the landscape and life, with the effective participation of Indigenous peoples, it is becoming an important tool for territorial and environmental management of Indigenous lands in Acre.

- This Place: 150 years retold: https://www.cbc.ca/books/thisplace
  Explore the past 150 years through the eyes of Indigenous creators in this groundbreaking graphic novel anthology. Beautifully illustrated, these stories are a wild ride through magic realism, serial killings, psychic battles and time travel. See how Indigenous peoples have survived a post-apocalyptic world since Contact.

Further reading

Hunt, S. (2014). Ontologies of Indigeneity: the politics of embodying a concept. *Cultural Geographies* 21(1): 27–32.
This is useful to work towards understanding Indigenous ontologies, as differentiated from western ontologies of Indigeneity.

Perley, B. (2014). Living Traditions: A Manifesto for Critical Indigeneity. In *Performing Indigeneity*, eds. L. R. Graham and H. G. Penny. Nebraska: UNP, 32–54.
This helps us understand that 'every day practices of critical Indigeneity are engaged practices of self-determination against the daily traumas of colonial domination of Indigenous Peoples in the twenty-first century'.

Shaw, W. S., Herman, R. D., and Dobbs, R. G. (2006). Encountering Indigeneity re-imagining and decolonizing geography. *Geografiska Annaler B* 88(B (3)): 267–276.
This article discusses 'Indigenous geographies' as a potential research trajectory within the discipline of geography in its active movement away from its colonising project.

11 Mobilities

Peter Adey

Introduction

Mobility is an important fact of geography. We move in and through **space** albeit very differently. The airport terminal might seem an exemplar of our increasingly, but unevenly so, mobile world (Figure 11.1). It is truly a global place, and it has become a common focus of geographical and social scientific research which focuses on the study of mobilities. A perspective known as the 'new mobilities paradigm' – postured first by sociologists such as Mimi Sheller and John Urry (2006) and geographers such as Tim Cresswell (2006, 2010) – presupposes that the social world is constituted by mobilities of people and objects, flows of information and materials, all entangled together. Contemporary relations and obligations, such as employment and services, or structures, such as the family, all depend upon mobilities in order to constitute and produce them.

Somewhere like the airport resembles the flux of this sort of mobile global condition. The airport sees all manner of mobilities for all different sorts of reasons: a package holiday to Florida; short-haul commutes in France banned by the government in 2022 in order to cut carbon emissions; one worker's journey among 35 million others during China's Chunyun spring festival; a return from Birmingham to Poland to see family for a while; travellers arriving at Kuala Lumpur's low-cost terminal KLIA2 for budget airlines such as AirAsia for work and leisure in Malaysia, Thailand and Southeast Asia; not to mention the dance of movements behind the scenes at airports: tracing lost baggage, pushing back planes from the gate; clearing debris from the runway. At Jakarta's international airport, many workers (check-in personnel and gate agents) are already mobile, having moved to Java from the Indonesian archipelago. From commuting to tourism, to migration, the airport encompasses not only different transport modes but a variety of different kinds of mobility, from the more fleeting to the more permanent. Mobile societies give these kinds of movements certain sorts of values and significance. In the airport, all options seem open to us – the world is your oyster; any destination is possible.

Mobilities like this are regularly portrayed in novels and literature and films and music videos. Perhaps this is the kind of air-world expressed in Jason Reitman's film *Up in the Air* (2009), based on the novel by Walter Kirn. It is all about smoothness, a quality George Clooney radiates as Ryan Bingham, an executive for Career Transitions Corporation (CTC). Or perhaps it's the kind of globetrotting lifestyle exuded in the aeromobile sheen of rap artists transporting their retinue of staff across cities and borders. These kinds of portrayals show mobility as easy and uninhibited. Life on the move inhabiting a world of surfaces and distance. Swipe, click, click, swipe, swivel. Nod, smile, greet and glide. Indeed, for the international music star, the airport may be bypassed altogether as the private jet appears to have captivated the mobile ideals of rap artists,

DOI: 10.4324/9780429265853-13

Figure 11.1
Everywhere but no place to go

Source: Photo credit: Inge Flinte

musicians and other celebrities, appearing to subvert international borders entirely. The rapper Drake even finds himself in the **gendered** private jet cockpit in 'Started from the Bottom' as a symbol of his upward mobility and is playfully ticked off by the male pilot for daring to touch the controls.

These ways of seeing mobility are deeply positioned and problematic, mainly because this kind of experience of the airport, air travel (and mobility more generally) is highly unequal and in many ways unlikely – in the case of Drake's music video, hugely sexist too. Weightless travel is accentuated here. There are few realisations of the breakdown, frustration and delay that may constitute air travel. Or the borders and mobility regimes that prevent many from crossing, such as visa regimes and the requirement for international papers; security practices reliant on data; and biometric information (Amoore, 2006). And of course, the distanced (in time and space) consequences of air travel are reliant on highly polluting energy-intensive aircraft fuels, and the massive semi-urban complexes of airports, and many are still structured through the efficiency and convenience of the private car. Indeed, as we learn more about Bingham's (the businessman in *Up in the Air) life*, we find that it is not actually all that fun or fulfilling. It is disorientating, tiring, and as we focus on the bodily practices of mobility, it is telling of how life on the move is deeply unequal. His experience of mobility is highly westernised, middle-class and privileged, and highly gendered.

Many experiences of airport mobility are likely to be much less smooth than Bingham's initially seem to be: perhaps more choppy or stressful from a struggle with overtired and hungry children, or by delays, queues at check-in or passport control, jockeying for position to grab unassigned seats, arrival at/transit via an airport that seems remarkably distant from our desired destination, marked by mixtures of excitement, stress and so on. The global COVID-19 pandemic has illustrated the fragility of air travel mobilities to massive disruption, global health measures and, in some cases, almost complete societal 'lock-down' (Adey et al., 2021). Airports have featured highly as key centres of attack within geopolitical conflict and war; and as key sites of democratic protest movements to claim political dissensus, such as in Hong Kong as pro-democracy protestors occupied the airport in 2019, denouncing the police and the Chinese and Hong Kong authorities; and as key logistics hubs for international and humanitarian aid within disasters and environmental catastrophe, such as the 2015 Nepal earthquake (Harris, 2021).

Wider tensions often intrude on and shape spaces of mobility, not only in the airport. While racism and abuse are common in spaces of public transport, there are now countless research articles exploring race- and gender-based violence, harassment and intolerance perpetrated on public transport: in the press of a packed bus or subway train; through to assault, groping, exposure and unwanted attention for women, young girls and trans and gender minority people; and even in the intimate proximities of aircraft seats (Evans et al., 2021) for bigger, fat or so-called obese bodies hyperpresent for fat-phobic passengers. In different contexts, so-called pink trains or carriages have been introduced into public transport systems in Rio de Janeiro and Mumbai, and the *joseisenyōsha* subway carriages in Japan, for instance, in order to recognise and reduce male violence against women (Figure 11.2).

The kind of approaches developed to understand mobility, or the plural 'mobilities', can help us unpack the airport and other places of mobility in order to understand their complex human geographies, their social and cultural relations and their politics. Attending to the geographies of mobilities takes the question of life on the move seriously, opening movement up to

Figure 11.2
Women's only carriage, Kyoto, Japan

Source: Photo credit: Michael Runkel/Alamy

critical purchase. Studies within human geography have addressed a number of kinds of every-day mobility, in different contexts: including not only airports but also cars and auto-mobility (Merriman, 2009), including auto-rickshaws, e-scooters, so-called e-mobilities, as well as running (MacGahern, 2019, Cook, 2021), cycling (Spinney, 2006, 2009), public rail transport (Bissell, 2009, 2010), budget airlines and migration (Burrell, 2011) and urban walking (Middleton, 2011) but also through writing, through music, musical instruments and other cultural practices (Nóvoa, 2012, Kielman, 2022); and in the techno-mobility-mediated transformations changing our experiences of public space via the mobile phone (Andrade, 2020). Growing attention has been given to the ways that policies, knowledge and policy practices may move and transform between and in places and networks (Baker et al., 2016) as 'policy mobilities'. Equally, the shifts towards platform and gig economy labour, for example, in global growth of Uber, Deliveroo and Airbnb (Christensen, 2023, Allis and Machado, 2023) ride-sharing and on-demand transport apps such as GoJek and Uber (Pollio, 2021) in Singapore or India, or the stretched and discon-nected lifestyles of fly-in-fly-out (FIFO) workers in Australia (Bissell et al., 2020), have concen-trated research interests in mobilities.

The aim of this chapter is to focus on some of the key questions that have animated these more specific studies. To that end, we will explore mobilities in two main ways. We start by exploring how mobilities intersect with *politics*. Second, the chapter looks at how mobility is *practised*, or in other words how it is done and experienced, and researched.

Summary

- The 'new mobilities paradigm' argues that social worlds are constituted through flows of people, objects and information.
- We often imagine these flows to be smooth, creating worlds of easy movement and lives that float above the constraints of place. Images of airports and air travel often represent such ideas.
- In reality, mobilities are varied, shaped by and shaping forms of **power** and privilege.

Politics

There is a politics to mobility. Mobilities are not innate. They are both **socially constructed** – shaped by social relations of various sorts – and socially constitutive – shaping our social worlds. In a formative essay on the politics of mobility, Tim Cresswell suggests that mobilities 'involve the production and distribution of power' (Cresswell, 2010: 21) and gives three ways in which we might think about this. First, we might consider how mobilities are given meaning in **represen-tations**. What do mobilities mean as they are expressed in popular culture, stories and language? Second, how do we imagine mobility? What qualities do we associate various forms of mobility with? Third, we can consider how there are multiple mobilities, keyed into forms of social dif-ference and inequality. Looking at the mobilities of an airport, for example, we might ask, does everyone move in the same way within it? 'Who moves furthest? Who moves fastest? Who moves most often?' (Cresswell, 2010: 21), who has the capacity to move or not (Bissell, 2016). Indeed, the so-called pink carriages discussed above distribute complicated consequences around mobility. Do they simply segregate certain kinds of public space without dealing with the root causes of sexism and misogyny which may happen still in other spaces of movement and transport, and apportion blame and victimhood? In what way might 'women' only carriages essentialise gender across different normative categories of gender and bodily ability and serve to exclude lesbian, bisexual, non-binary and transgender women who experience frequent harassment too (Lubitow et al., 2017, Lewis et al., 2021) but also those with hidden or more overt disabilities (Kusters, 2019).

Generally, research on mobilities has sought to move beyond the kinds of ways of thinking about place that imagine it as local, closed, static, bounded, which in part situates some of the xenophobic and racist abuse mentioned above. Places shape mobilities and mobilities shape places. Work focused on place has also sought to question simplistic oppositions between it and mobility. Whilst being attuned to how such an opposition may be mobilised in representations of places, geographers are used to thinking more critically about notions of place which are articulated as somehow authentic, pure, immobile and marked by stasis. Influentially, Doreen Massey (2005) suggests that our notions of place should become more extroverted, progressive and global, viewing them as comings-together, coagulations of flows. Politically, Massey advocates a more porous, open sense of place rather than a defensive one where mobilities are seen as a threat to a place's integrity, whilst being careful not to fall into the **romanticised** approaches that valorise mobility as universally experienced that were mentioned above in relation to the airport.

Emergencies can highlight the stark differences that pervade mobility. We do not have equal access to it. Neither do we have equal ability to choose to be mobile or immobile. Current events might point us to evacuation mobilities from conflict and at large scales of population movement: such as Russia's war on Ukraine, where once again evacuation of civilians and onward migration has led to vast population movements within Europe, especially across the Polish-Ukrainian border. Moreover, the Belarussian-Polish and Belarusian-Lithuanian borders have become sites of the pushback and detention of migrants seeking to reach Europe through Belarus, a form of what some European states have called 'Hybrid aggression' given Belarus's alignment with Moscow. Neither is mobility itself such an easy signal of apparent 'freedoms'. Europe's own migration regime utilises mobility as a way of keeping refugees and those seeking asylum in 'motion', some seeking to evade mobile border patrols and state officials, others shuttled between detainment sites and quasi-carceral processing camps and centres (Tazzioli, 2020) (Figure 11.3).

Many different ways of approaching such a 'politics of mobility' have also evolved in human geography, in some contexts around notions of justice which, as Mimi Sheller (2018) has set out, encourages us to consider mobility and immobility in the context of multi-scalar conditions and effects, where it may be very difficult to assess just how 'just' mobility is, and for what and for whom? Attentiveness to transport as an important form of carbon emissions is crucial to consider the multi-faceted complications of moving by car or plane, even for academics (Hopkins et al., 2019). Mobilities are often carbon-intensive with localised air pollution, they rely on the supply chains of component resources, such as rare-earth elements that go into mobile materials such as cars, which may be dependent in-turn upon mobilities and migration perhaps towards labour opportunities, and for workers who have perhaps been forced to move as a consequence of drought and climate change (Parsons, 2019). These differential (in)justices at multiple times and scales may mean those who have the least access to mobility – or perhaps a choice over mobility, which could include long-term marginalised racial and ethnic communities, and in

Figure 11.3
Immigration Removal Centre Campsfield in Kidlington near Oxford, United Kingdom. Originally a youth offenders institution, Campsfield House re-opened as a Immigration Detention Centre in November 1993. In 2018, the centre was closed following years of protests, riots, fires, hunger strikes, and two suicides. However, the Home Office plans to reopen Campsfield in 2024 as a 400-bed detention facility to 'support' its plan of sending asylum seekers and anyone 'entering the UK illegally' to Rwanda

Source: Photo credit: Anadolu/Getty

some cases Indigenous First Nations people (Suliman et al., 2019) – are often the most affected, disempowered and even dispossessed by and through mobility and immobility.

Summary

- There is a politics to mobility. Mobilities are implicated in the production and distribution of power.
- One way to see the politics of mobility is to focus on questions of 'difference': how mobilities differ; and how these differences key into wider forms of social difference such as **class**, **race**, dis/ability and gender.

Practices

Rather than assuming its qualities, however, or making general associations (for example, between mobility and freedom), we can investigate specific acts of mobility, asking questions such as 'How is mobility **embodied**? How comfortable is it? Is it forced or free?' (Cresswell, 2010: 22). Mobility or mobilities involve, of course, practices. Practice is a word we might use to describe many different kinds of mobile actions, such as doings, habits, routines which are constitutive of different things that we often think of as mobility: such as travel, leisure, tourism, migration, commuting and transportation that make up our social and cultural worlds.

Many practices are politicised in interesting and difficult ways. We mentioned emergencies above and the experience of Hurricane Katrina in 2005 in New Orleans and Louisiana saw difficult differences in who was able to evacuate and leave the area from the flood waters, scarce food and electricity, which saw both state and private security firms, police and military personnel reinforcing class and racial divides by criminalising desperate people without food and water. Sarah Kaufman (2006) picks up on a story from the *New York Times* which compared news reports over two images which contained people wading through shoulder-high waters laden with foodstuff taken from a supermarket. The first image was a picture of a Black African-American; reports described his actions as 'looting a grocery' store. The second image was of a white couple; stories described their movements after 'finding bread and soda from a local grocery store'. The operative word here is, of course 'looting', as opposed to 'finding'. Looting became admonished as the worst kind of behaviour. Victims of the flooding became the problem. However, describing the store as 'local' to the white couple implies some forms of belonging and ownership not afforded to the 'Black looter'.

These are quite specific but culturally and politically significant readings of different representations of mobility. But there are other ways of understanding mobile practices in more-than-representational ways, to ask what bodily skills and capacities make mobile practices possible but also what mobility might feel like, how is it sensed and perceived, registered and felt? What does it mean to move together in a shared **atmosphere** of encounter and togetherness, for example (Crang and Zhang, 2012)? Other mobile practices such as riding a train to work or to meet someone are not entirely unconscious but involve habits and routines we may not need to think about much but require the evolution of skills to navigate public space, such as bus travel or taxi ride-sharing in Cape Town (Rink, 2022), and even, as we discussed above, to negotiate unwanted attention and threat such as on the Sao Paulo metro (Moreira and Ceccato, 2021) in micro-political **encounters**. Indeed, researchers of mobility have been showing how and why these practices and structures of practices around other social obligations and lifestyles are not so easily shifted or even resilient to the changes that might be required to reduce carbon emissions, such as a greater reliance on public transport, for example (Cass and Faulconbridge, 2016).

A wide attention of research in this area has developed approaches and research methods – sometimes called mobile methodologies – to understanding these practices, sometimes involving approaches more attentive to physical mobility, or being-there and with mobile practices (Merriman, 2014). These approaches have led to a wide variety of research methods ranging from more traditional approaches to archives to explore mobilities in the past, to examining the data flows that enable some mobilities, towards smartwatch- and wrist-strap-style tracking technologies towards the moving-with-style high-resolution GoPro video and even eye-monitoring. It should be recognised, however, that mobilities are not always so easily *there* for researchers to study. They are already patterned by existing inequalities, such as anti-Muslim acts in public spaces, which may mean some research methods – such as the go-along walking interview – may not be appropriate. In her research with Muslim women, Warren (2017) has argued that mobile methods should be careful in how marginalised individuals and groups are engaged, especially in spaces and situations where multiple barriers, from the perceptual to the psychological, as well the more obviously physical, can be a barrier to moving with participants in public space.

Summary

- Human mobilities are done and experienced in embodied ways.
- Mobile methods are a significant research 'practice' but no less political.

Conclusion

Perhaps it is because mobility is too self-evident that it has escaped serious analysis. We might overlook it because of its apparent ordinariness. It is the flights high in the air above us, the underground subway line beneath our feet, the journey that brings a visitor or a loved one to our door, the habits and routines we take for granted as we move around places. However, human geographers and other social scientists are now opening up multiple mundane mobilities to scrutiny while realising how these seemingly normal movements are conditioned by complex multi-scalar power relations which shape our capacities to move or not move. First, there is a politics of mobility, including how various people are differently mobile, with distinctive kinds of relationships and reactions to places. Second, mobility does not just happen, it is practised, and there is a need to understand the different sorts of experiences and doings of mobility.

Discussion points

- In what ways is mobility 'political'?
- Why are romanticised and hyper-stylised representations of mobility by elites and the rich problematic?
- In what ways is your own everyday life shaped by practices and experiences of mobility?

References

Adey, P., Hannam, K., Sheller, M., and Tyfield, D. (2021). Pandemic (im)mobilities. *Mobilities* 16(1): 1–19.

Allis, T., and Machado, A. C. P. (2023). After the #Stayhome, 'Live Like a Local': Towards Alternative Urban Tourism Mobilities? In *Alternative (Im)mobilities*, ed. M. A. Nogueira. London: Routledge, 138–153.

Amoore, L. (2006). Biometric borders: governing mobilities in the war on terror. *Political Geography* 25: 336–351.

Andrade, L. A. (2020). Is It More 'Pokémon' Than 'Go'? New Mobilities Paradigm in Locative Gaming. In *Brazilian Mobilities*, eds. M. A. D. F. Nogueira and C. M. dos Santos Moraes. London: Routledge, 116–129.

Baker, T., Cook, I. R., McCann, E., Temenos, C., and Ward, K. (2016). Policies on the move: the transatlantic travels of tax increment financing. *Annals of the American Association of Geographers* 106(2): 459–469.

Bissell, D. (2009). Visualising everyday geographies: practices of vision through travel-time. *Transactions of the Institute of British Geographers* 34: 42–60.

Bissell, D. (2010). Passenger mobilities: affective atmospheres and the sociality of public transport. *Environment and Planning D: Society and Space* 28: 270–289.

Bissell, D. (2016). Micropolitics of mobility: public transport commuting and everyday encounters with forces of enablement and constraint. *Annals of the American Association of Geographers* 106(2): 394–403.

Bissell, D., Straughan, E. R., and Gorman-Murray, A. (2020). Losing touch with people and place: labor mobilities, desensitized bodies, disconnected lives. *Annals of the American Association of Geographers* 110(6): 1891–1906.

Burrell, K. (2011). Going steerage on Ryanair: cultures of migrant air travel between Poland and the UK. *Journal of Transport Geography* 19: 1023–1030.

Cass, N., and Faulconbridge, J. (2016). Commuting practices: new insights into modal shift from theories of social practice. *Transport Policy* 45: 1–14.

Christensen, M. D. (2023). Doing digital discipline: how Airbnb hosts engage with the digital platform. *Mobilities* 18(1): 70–85.

Cook, S. (2021). Geographies of run-commuting in the UK. *Journal of Transport Geography* 92: 103038.

Crang, M., and Zhang, J. (2012). Transient dwelling: trains as places of identification for the floating population of China. *Social & Cultural Geography* 13(8): 895–914.

Cresswell, T. (2006). *On the Move: Mobility in the Modern Western World*. New York: Routledge.

Cresswell, T. (2010). Towards a politics of mobility. *Environment and Planning D: Society and Space* 28(1): 17–31.

Cresswell, T., and Merriman, P. (eds.) (2011). *Geographies of Mobilities: Practices, Spaces and Subjects*. Aldershot: Ashgate.

Evans, B., Bias, S., and Colls, R. (2021). The dys-appearing fat body: bodily intensities and fatphobic sociomaterialities when flying while fat. *Annals of the American Association of Geographers* 111(6): 1816–1832.

Harris, T. (2021). Air pressure: temporal hierarchies in Nepali aviation. *Cultural Anthropology* 36(1): 83–109.

Hopkins, D., Higham, J., Orchiston, C., and Duncan, T. (2019). Practising academic mobilities: bodies, networks and institutional rhythms. *The Geographical Journal* 185(4): 472–484.

Kaufman, S. (2006). The criminalization of New Orleanians in Katrina's Wake. *Understanding Katrina: Perspectives from the Social Science*. https://items.ssrc.org/understanding-katrina/the-criminalization-of-new-orleanians-in-katrinas-wake/

Kielman, A. (2022). *Sonic Mobilities: Producing Worlds in Southern China*. Chicago: University of Chicago Press.

Kusters, A. (2019). Boarding Mumbai trains: the mutual shaping of intersectionality and mobility. *Mobilities* 14(6): 841–858.

Lewis, S., Saukko, P., and Lumsden, K. (2021). Rhythms, sociabilities and transience of sexual harassment in transport: mobilities perspectives of the London underground. *Gender, Place and Culture* 28(2): 277–298.

Lubitow, A., Carathers, J., Kelly, M., and Abelson, M. (2017). Transmobilities: mobility, harassment, and violence experienced by transgender and gender nonconforming public transit riders in Portland, Oregon. *Gender, Place and Culture* 24(10): 1398–1418.

Massey, D. (2005). *For Space*. London: Sage.

McGahern, U. (2019). Making space on the run: exercising the right to move in Jerusalem. *Mobilities* 14(6), 890–905.

Merriman, P. (2009). Automobility and the geographies of the car. *Geography Compass* 3: 586–599.

Merriman, P. (2014). Rethinking mobile methods. *Mobilities* 9(2): 167–187.

Middleton, J. (2011). Walking in the city: the geographies of everyday pedestrian practices. *Geography Compass* 5: 90–105.

Moreira, G. C., and Ceccato, V. A. (2021). Gendered mobility and violence in the São Paulo metro, Brazil. *Urban Studies* 58(1): 203–222.

Nóvoa, A. (2012). Musicians on the move: mobilities and identities of a band on the road. *Mobilities* 7(3): 349–368.

Parsons, L. (2019). Structuring the emotional landscape of climate change migration: towards climate mobilities in geography. *Progress in Human Geography* 43(4): 670–690.

Pollio, A. (2021). Uber, airports, and labour at the infrastructural interfaces of platform urbanism. *Geoforum* 118: 47–55.

Rink, B. (2022). Capturing amaphela: negotiating township politics through shared mobility. *Geoforum* 136: 232–241.

Sheller, M., and Urry, J. (2006). The new mobilities paradigm. *Environment and Planning A* 38(2): 207–226.

Spinney, J. (2006). A place of sense: a kinaesthetic ethnography of cyclists on Mont Ventoux. *Environment and Planning D: Society and Space* 24: 709–732.

Spinney, J. (2009). Cycling the city: movement, meaning and method. *Geography Compass* 3: 317–335.

Suliman, S., Farbotko, C., Ransan-Cooper, H., McNamara, K. E., Thornton, F., Mcmichael, C., and Kitara, T. (2019). Indigenous (im)mobilities in the Anthropocene. *Mobilities* 14(3): 298–318.

Tazzioli, M. (2020). Governing migrant mobility through mobility: containment and dispersal at the internal frontiers of Europe. *Environment and Planning C: Politics and Space* 38(1): 3–19.

Warren, S. (2017). Pluralising the walking interview: researching (im)mobilities with Muslim women. *Social & Cultural Geography* 18(6): 786–807.

Online materials

- These two short videos by Prof Tim Cresswell introduce mobilities as a field of study and introduce transition to low carbon mobilities:

  - Mobility between movement, meaning and practice – Tim Cresswell – YouTube https://www.youtube.com/watch?v=EXo0gdlVvNU
  - Transitioning toward low-carbon mobility: a holistic approach to transition policy – YouTube https://www.youtube.com/watch?v=ogS3qoeX69Q

- An animation produced by Stacy Bias with Dr Bethan Evans (University of Liverpool) that centres the voices of fat travellers as they explain their experiences of flying while fat.

  - Flying While Fat Animation – Stacy Bias – Fat Activist and Freelance Animator in London, UK https://flyingwhilefat.com/

Further reading

Adey, P. (2017). *Mobility*. London: Routledge.
This is a textbook that presents mobility as a key idea in geography. It addresses mobility as both a ubiquitous facet of the 'world out there' and as a way of engaging with that world analytically. It provides deeper and wider consideration of the meanings, practices and politics of mobility highlighted in this chapter.

Cresswell, T. (2006). *On the Move: Mobility in the Modern Western World*. New York: Routledge.
One of the first book length treatments of mobility in human geography. Cresswell understands mobility as central to what it is to be human, a fundamental of geographical existence. The first two chapters in the book discuss how to define and approach mobility. The other chapters are case studies that apply this approach in a range of contexts from the workplace, to immigration, to the dance hall. Chapter 9 examines the mobilities at Schiphol Airport, Amsterdam, arguing against its reduction to a 'non-place'. The Epilogue gives an early response to Hurricane Katrina's impact on New Orleans.

Cresswell, T., and Merriman, P. (eds.) (2011). *Geographies of Mobilities: Practices, Spaces and Subjects*. Aldershot: Ashgate.
This edited collection rethinks how geographers have approached mobilities in the light of the 'new mobilities paradigm'. It suggests that focusing on mobilities allows connections to be made between previously distinct sub-disciplinary fields such as migration, transport and tourism.

Sheller, M. (2018). *Mobility Justice: The Politics of Movement in an Age of Extremes*. London: Verso.
An already influential book that presents a manifesto for 'mobility justice'. The book deploys different and interlinked concepts of justice to advance a set of principles and approaches to mobility which is multi-scalar and relational.

Gender and sexuality

Lynda Johnston

Introduction

Gender, sexuality, **space**, and place are inextricably linked. In this chapter I define what is meant by the terms 'gender' and 'sexuality' and show the ways in which gender and sexuality are part of place and space, and vice versa. A geographical focus on gender and sexuality across all spatial scales has been led by the rich human geography sub-fields of **feminist** and queer geography. Now a well-established sub-field, feminist geography only gained attention in 1970s – and during the rise of social movements – when Wilbur Zelinsky (1973) wrote 'The strange case of the missing female geographer'. A decade later, feminist geographers Janice Monk and Susan Hanson (1982) wrote an article called 'On not excluding half of the human in human geography'. It took another decade, in 1994, before a specialist journal *Gender, Place and Culture: A Journal of Feminist Geography* was launched. As a discipline, then, human geography has a history of excluding subjects explicitly about gender and sexuality. Geography – like many Western academic knowledges – has been dominated by masculinity, heterosexuality, white, and able-bodied cis-men, and this is reflected in the form and content of geographical knowledge (see Figure 12.1, showing the dominance of male names as scholarly authors). What human geography is, and who does it, continues to be contested territory.

In what follows I first provide definitions of gender and sexuality, followed by a brief overview of the different stages of feminist and queer geography. Second, the space of the home is presented as a way to understand how gender and sexualities are linked to – and/or excluded from – home (private) spaces. Third, the chapter broadens the spatial scale to investigate public monuments. Here it becomes obvious that monuments represent spatially specific cultures of gender and sexuality.

What are gender, sex, and sexuality? What are feminist and queer geographies?

The definition and conceptualisation of gender and sexuality has become more nuanced in recent geographical work. Gender and sexuality, like other identity categorisations, are an outcome of human thoughts and actions. Geographers argue that place, space, gender, and sexuality are linked (Johnston and Longhurst, 2010). Our gendered and sexual bodies are constantly being mapped and remapped across cultural and social landscapes.

DOI: 10.4324/9780429265853-14

Figure 12.1
Word cloud of first names of authors published in top five journals 2005–2020

Source: David Ubilava

The famous statement on the construction of gender by Simone de Beauvoir (1974: 301) – 'one is not born a woman, but rather becomes one' – rejects the notion of a natural or biological sex. Several decades later, feminist and queer theorist Judith Butler (1990, 1993) extends de Beauvoir's gender construction. In the book *Gender Trouble*, Butler (1990: 24–25) insists that becoming a woman, or a man, is a constant practice. Gender, therefore, is an ongoing process. Gender is something we do, rather than something we are born with. For **cisgender** people, their gender identity aligns with the sex identity they were assigned at birth. They perform gender throughout their life course.

Butler shows that gender, as well as sexuality, is a **social construction** and that we are 'girled' or 'boyed':

> Consider the medical interpellation which … shifts an infant from 'it' to a 'she' or a 'he', and in that naming, the girl is 'girled', brought into the domain of language and kinship through the interpellation of gender.
>
> *Butler, 1993: 7*

Throughout a human's life, and even before birth with ultra-sound technologies and gender reveal parties, bodies are 'girled' or 'boyed'. During our life course we perform versions of femininity and/or masculinity, and this 'gender performance' is – for the most part – regulated by binary gender norms. Gender identities are repeated performances to an extent to which the gender identity is not questioned; rather, it is considered normal and natural.

The term sex tends to be used to depict biological differences, and gender, in contrast, to describe **socially constructed** characteristics. We know, however, that biological categorisations do not sit outside of social thought and actions. The binary sex/gender is mutually

153

constitutive. Binary understandings of sex/gender exclude an array of diverse gender and sex identities, such as:

> transgender, transsexual, transvestite, cross-dresser, trans women, trans feminine, trans man, trans masculine, genderqueer, non-binary, gender fluid, agenda, pangender, non-gender, bi-gender, demi-gender, gender diverse, third gender, drag king and drag queen, to name a few.
>
> *Johnston, 2019: 7–8*

Moreover, non-Western gender categories, for example those of Indigenous peoples, do not necessarily align with Western understandings of gender.

Insights from feminist and queer geographers (Johnston, 2018) show that the **performance** (or the 'doing') of gender and sexuality is regulated due to **patriarchy**. Patriarchy is male control over women through a system of social structures and practices. There are many spaces in which men dominate, oppress, and exploit women and girls. Patriarchy, and other oppressive structures, such as '**colonialism**, homophobia, transphobia, gender norms, racism, ableism and more – either individually or, even less often, in mutual constitution – take and shape place' (Oswin, 2020: 10).

Institutions, laws, family, and communities influence the creation and maintenance of a gender hierarchy and a performance of 'naturalised' heterosexuality (or **heteronormativity**). Sexual identities, therefore, may be connected to gender but are also a distinct identity category. Sexualities are many and varied, and as queer geographers have demonstrated, places too are sexualised (see Browne et al., 2007, Johnston and Longhurst, 2010).

The term 'sexuality' refers to one's sexual desires and actions and is often connected to one's sexual identity or **subjectivity**. Heterosexuals are closely aligned to the binary gender construct of male/female, with one gender being attracted to their opposite gender. Homosexuals (for example gays and lesbians) are attracted to those of the same gender. Bisexuals are attracted to both the opposite and the same gender. Yet, in reality, these identities are never this clearly defined. One might identify as heterosexual, yet also have sex with people of the same gender. Sexual identities are multiple, fluid, and changing. Like gender, our sexuality is influenced by culture and **ethnicity**. There is nothing innate or natural to either place and space or sex and sexualities.

> Sex and sexualities are created in, through and by space, place and environment. Moreover, how space and place are organized and used is directly related to sex and sexualities. Space/place are usually understood as heterosexual and meant to be used by two people who are unambiguously sexed (man or woman), exhibit proper gendered behaviours (femininity and masculinity) that are mapped on to that unambiguous physical body and sexual interests that are directed toward the clearly differentiated 'opposite sex'. Heteronormativity refers to the ways in which sexuality, sex and gender are intertwined in ways that are presumed to be natural. It is usually based on particular **class**, race and able-bodied ideals.
>
> *Browne and Brown, 2016: 1*

Due to patriarchy, heterosexuality is deemed to be the norm and 'natural' and, therefore, often goes unnoticed. Heterosexual couples holding hands, for example, are unremarkable and considered 'normal' in most public Western spaces and places. In contrast, those who upset or trouble these norms are detected and often repudiated, with accompanying threats of verbal and physical violence.

A key way through which sexual identities are performed and/or regulated is through private and public spaces. At the level of the state, some countries regulate to eliminate certain sexual acts, practices, and relationship forms, in the hope to move them to only domestic spaces. The home, however, is not always a haven and may itself be a place where lesbians, gays, bisexuals, transgender people, intersex people, queers, and others (LGBTIQ+) experience oppression, **alienation**, and discrimination from their parental families, other household residents, the neighbours, and tradespeople. Examples of private (home) and public (monuments) are included later in this chapter. The two sub-fields that consider gender and sexuality are feminist geography and queer geography.

Feminist geography brings feminist theories and methodologies to human geography. It is a critical approach that investigates, challenges, and changes inequitable gendered divisions across a range of spatial scales. Queer geography brings queer theories and methodologies of human geography. It too is a critical approach that investigates, challenges, and changes inequitable sexual divisions across a range of spatial scales. Both approaches may be used together, or separately, to analyse the social co-construction of gender, sexuality, space, and place.

The taken-for-granted notion of geography (and who is considered a geographer) is linked to ideas of masculinity. As geographers we bring our gender and sexual identities to our workplace (even when we may hide our gender and/or sexual identity), and we notice if our identity is in a minority, is subject to derision, or is completely missing. In the 1970s and 1980s feminist geographers pointed out that the demography of the discipline was dominated by men and topics related to a narrow understanding of masculinity. As more women and non-heterosexual people joined the discipline, new questions were asked about geographies relating to women, mothers, children, gays, and lesbians, for example. Excluding topics about women's experiences is called '**masculinist**'. Excluding topics about LGBTIQ+ experiences is called '**heteronormative**'. Many feminist and queer geographers have critiqued human geography's masculinist and **cis-heteronormative** foundations.

Summary

- Gender refers to a person's social and personal identity as female, male, or another gender that may be non-binary. One's gender identity and/or gender expression is **performative**. A person's gender may differ from the sex recorded at their birth. A person's gender may change over time, space, and place.
- Sex is a category used to describe characteristics such as chromosomes, hormones, and reproductive organs. Usually, one's sex characteristics are observed and recorded at birth and during infancy. A person's sex can change over the course of their lifetime and may differ from their sex recorded at birth.
- Feminist geographers now consider gender and sex via a focus on **embodied** performance.
- Sexual orientation refers to the expression and performance of one's sexuality and is related to three key aspects: identity, attraction, and behaviour.

- Sexual identity concerns how a person thinks and feels about their sexuality and the terms they identify with, including lesbian, gay, straight, asexual, bisexual, pansexual. These terms do not always translate to non-Western sexual identities such as takatāpui (Māori) and fa'afafine (Samoan).
- Queer geographers argue there is nothing natural or innate to space, place and environment or sex, gender and sexualities (see Chapter 72).

From then to now: changing geographies of gender and sexualities

Up until the 1970s, human geography was dominated by cisgender men, and narrow definitions of masculinity and heterosexuality. Adding women into the discipline is often called the first strand of feminist geography (a geography of women), and this grew from the women's liberation movement of the 1960s and 1970s.

Moving into the 1980s and 1990s – often called the second strand of feminist geography – there was a focus on gender, work, place, and space, known as 'socialist feminist geography' (Gregory et al., 2009). The intersection of gender and class (patriarchy and **capitalism**) received a great deal of interest, particularly in the UK (see debates in the journal *Antipode*).

Doreen Massey's (1994) book *Space, Place and Gender* highlights the tensions of the times, such as gender versus class, economic versus cultural, feminine versus masculine, local versus global, space versus time, and political versus academic. **Postmodernism** and a focus on difference and inclusion shaped the third stand of feminist geography. From the mid-1990s, (mainly white) feminist geographers, joined by queer geographers, produced a substantial amount of research focused on the intersection of place and space with embodied identities such as gender (with growing attention to masculinities), sexuality, age, ethnicity, and disability. Some foundational publications are *Places through the Body* (Nast and Pile, 1998), *Mind and Body Spaces: Geographies of Illness, Impairment and Disability* (Butler and Parr, 1999), and *Bodies: Exploring Fluid Boundaries* (Longhurst, 2001). These reshaped human geography, along with landmark publications on sexuality, place, and space, such as *Mapping Desire* (Bell and Valentine, 1995).

This literature pointed out how our bodies make a difference to our experience of spaces and places. Our size, shape, health, appearance, dress, comportment, ethnicity, sexuality, and sexual practices affect how we respond to the environment around us, and how we respond to others and how other people respond to us. We appear to live in the 'era of the body' and sometimes it can seem as though we are obsessed with bodies and bodily appearance. This body fixation can be seen in a number of examples such as tattoos and body modifications, eating disorders, plastic surgery, and an obsession with exercise. Geographers' interest in the body is clearly part of a much wider societal interest. Erin Clancy (2022: 15) says:

> Feminist geographers are well-positioned to contribute to this matter since the field has established the body itself as multi-scalar: a lived site conceptualized as spatially and historically situated, relational and shifting, and co-constituted with other bodies, practices, and emotions.

A focus on the body allows geographers to recognise the body as a space that is messy, material, and whose gender and sexual identities may change. Think about the term 'transgender'. It is usually understood (in Western countries) as an umbrella term and often shorthand for a vast array of gender identities, for example transsexual, transvestite, cross-dresser, genderqueer, non-binary, gender fluid, agender, non-gendered, third gender, trans woman, trans man, drag king and drag queen, to name a few. Non-Western gender categories, for example those in the Pacific – such as fa'afafine – do not necessarily align with Western understandings of transgender (Johnston, 2019).

It is crucial, therefore, to think about space, place, and **intersectionality**, that is, how bodies have multiple identities that intersect with each other. We are all gendered, sexed, raced, aged, and so on. For many years I have been heavily involved in organising queer events for my region's LGBTIQ+ communities. This means working with and for communities with diverse genders, sexualities, and ethnicities. Most significant, however, was (and still is) the imperative of this work to acknowledge the Indigenous politics of Māori sovereignty of Aotearoa New Zealand. Doing queer political action and research in a **postcolonial** settler society means that gender and sexual subjectivities are always entangled with **race**, ethnicity, and postcoloniality. Considering this intersection of identities allows for an examination of why and how some bodies are subject to prejudice, discrimination, and oppression, while other bodies are not.

Summary

- Feminist geographical perspectives emerged in the 1970s.
- By the end of the 1990s these had gained an institutional presence in human geography.
- Three distinctive phases of feminist and queer geography can be identified as follows: geographies of women, socialist feminist geographies, and geographies of difference (including embodied, gender diverse, and queer geographies).
- Indigenous people's gender and sexuality may differ from Western identity categories and lived experiences.

Gendered and sexualised geographies of home

The geography of home and domestic space is an excellent example of work by feminist and queer geographers. The work on the home started in the 1970s by **humanistic geographers**. The home was deemed to be an idealised place where one created a sense of belonging in an often 'outside' chaotic world. This largely affirmative work tended to exaggerate the positive emotional geographies of the home. The 'home as haven' idea has been subject to sustained critique from the 1990s onwards. Alison Blunt and Robyn Dowling (2022) investigate 'critical geographies of home'. Home, they note, is both material and imagined, that is, it is a physical place to reside in yet also an imaginative and emotional space of belonging. Home is a place where identities are formed according to age, gender, sexuality, ethnicity, and class. Often thought of as a private space, it is, however, porous and a place where the public and private intersect. Home is politicised, spatialised, and crucial to embodied identities.

Back in the 1980s feminist geographers argued that gender identities and gender roles related to home spaces developed in conjunction with public life. For example, a new division of labour emerged in the UK during the nineteenth century, with men considered to be public 'bread-winners' and integral to waged employment beyond the home. Women, however, became 'homemakers' with roles that were constructed around creating the home as a domestic haven and private. This is a good example of how gender roles are relational, that is, they involve power relations between different genders and places. Further, when considering masculine roles that are associated with **power** and dominance and the production of inequalities, this is understood as patriarchy. Gender inequalities – produced in and through the home – show the interrelations between patriarchy, identities, bodies, space, and place. These gendered spaces are historically and geographically distinct, changing over time, and across different places and cultures.

In the 1990s and through to the 2000s, feminist geographers developed thinking on home, addressing the limits of home, but also the possibilities of home. Home may be an everyday site of inequality and ongoing power dynamics. It takes on different meanings when it is a site where one is 'beaten, abused, or raped, away from the scrutiny of others' (Johnston and Longhurst, 2010: 45). Home may also be a place of resistance for Black women (hooks, 1991) away from white city spaces. As an everyday lived expression, home may be oppressive and alienating as well as supportive and comfortable. These multiple feelings were exacerbated by public health responses to COVID-19 lockdowns of 2020 and 2021. During this period, people may have felt like they were under 'house arrest', especially people experiencing poverty and poor housing conditions. In relation to sexuality, feelings of alienation were experienced by some LGBTQ+ young people in heteronormative parental homes (Blunt and Dowling, 2022).

This feminist and queer geography research shows that homes are understood as heteronormative spaces. A combination of government policies, housing design, and ingrained social and cultural norms means that homes – particularly homes of white people – are conflated with the nuclear family. One of my first research projects was about homes and lesbians (Johnston and Valentine, 1995), and it highlights the power of heteronormative space, as well as how to disrupt it. Gill Valentine (researching UK lesbians and homes) and I (researching New Zealand lesbians and homes) combined our studies. We found that lesbians' experiences of living in and visiting parental homes were complicated, particularly if lesbians were not **'out'** to their parents about their sexuality. If parents visited lesbian homes, then the occupants might 'de-dyke the house', that is, remove all material traces – books, posters, art – that would reveal their lesbian identity to their heteronormative parent(s).

> 'This like Macho Sluts [book] would go down like a cup of cold sick. I freak out and run around and de-dyke the whole place' (Joanne, New Zealand lesbian).
>
> *Johnston and Valentine, 1995: 103*

They also consider how their bodies might 'give away' their lesbian identity when in their parents' homes:

> I cover my tattoos up when I go home, especially if mum and dad have company coming over. I do that, it doesn't worry me, that's it.
>
> *Jackie New Zealand lesbian*

> I dress more conservatively … kind of straight and less scruffy (Hayley, New Zealand lesbian).
>
> *Johnston and Valentine, 1995: 103*

Home, then, may be a source of tension for lesbians. It is also a place where one may find security and freedom to be one's self (see Figure 12.2).

It is a site where lesbians may be under surveillance by parents or other visitors, such as tradespeople. To avoid discomfort, lesbians change the performance of the house according to the identity of the visitor.

The last research example I offer here is about homes and transgender identities. Consider the following advertisement for a housemate/flatmate in Box 12.1.

Some cisgender heterosexuals, commenting on sites such as Reddit, were outraged that the advertisement marginalised them, claiming heterophobia and cisphobia. As shown above, the home is a key site for the construction and reconstruction of one's identities. In a recent study of gender variant geographies (Johnston, 2019), I found that the home becomes an ambivalent **closet** space because of cisgender binaries and heteronormativity. For participants who experience socio-economic precarity, their homes were modest, shared, or – for periods of time – they lived without homes.

Figure 12.2
Portrait of a lesbian home

Source: Photo credit: Lynda Johnston

BOX 12.1
AN ONLINE ADVERTISEMENT THAT CAUSED A GREAT DEAL OF PUBLIC INTEREST IN AOTEAROA NEW ZEALAND

Four-bedroom house with one bathroom
Warm, sunny insulated old villa on Wilson St.
Queer, Transgender, Vegetarian household.
Large double room with good carpet, wardrobe, and wood burner/enclosed firm
(queen bed, drawers, and large desk avail if wanted) …
A home, not a party house

We are two feminist/politically switched on adults who work and have busy lives and come home to chill, one primary school kid who goes to school and spends every 2nd weekend away, and one cat who likes humans but not other cats or dogs. We want to live with someone who is relaxed, motivated, grown up, reliable, considerate, child friendly, LGBTQIA+, paying the board on time with no stress. Vegetarian or vegan. Smoking strictly outside. We don't want to live with a couple, a heterosexual person, or someone who is loud at night or drinks/does drugs/parties a lot. We also don't want to live with someone who is racist, sexist, homophobic, transphobic, fatphobic, hates sex workers, hates migrants, or is otherwise a jerk (Trade Me listing for a flatmate/housemate, 21 January 2016).

The thought of 'coming out' as transgender at home was discussed by most participants. When I asked Sally, a transgender woman, Pākehā (white New Zealander), in her 70s, about her feelings and experiences of home, she responded:

> I never had the guts to come out. I had a lot of things to lose at this stage. I had six children, I had a wife, I had my mother. You know a lot of people were involved. Um so that continued on for a long, for a long time really just, it just continued on and on, yeah, it was just unpleasant.
>
> *Johnston, 2019: 48*

The home is a site of personalities and feelings of (not)belonging in which people's gender – as well as age, sexuality, ethnicity, and class – become meaningful. Homes are the spaces within which we say to others who and what we are.

Summary

- Homes are key places where people's lived and embodied experiences do not always match idealised meanings of home.
- Homes may be sites of oppression, marginalisation, and violence rather than a haven.
- One might leave a childhood home and seek/create other spaces, more accepting of gender and/or sexual difference within homes.

- Homes may be 'transitional' spaces where we can explore our gendered and sexual identities.
- How the home is experienced often depends on who has the power to determine household social relations.

Monumental representations of bodies, gender, sexuality, space, and place

City monuments communicate what and who are considered important to particular places. In a city where I lived for many years – Hamilton (Aotearoa New Zealand's fourth largest city with approximately 160,000 residents) – two monuments stand out as highly significant to its identity. At the northern edge of the city sits the 'Ordinary Farming Family' monument.

The intention of the monument is to celebrate 'ordinary farming families' and 'unsung heroes'. The family is Pākehā (an Indigenous Māori term for white settlers) and heterosexual. A man (presumably a husband) carries a toddler on his shoulders. A woman (presumably a wife) carries a baby near her breasts. There's also a cow, a sheep, and a dog. This 'ordinary' monument – as the plaque notes – is not only deeply colonialist (erasing Māori as first peoples and farmers of the region); it is also **heteronormative** through its assumption that ordinary means heterosexual. This monument was the subject to our 'rainbow yarn bombing' in 2011 as part of the annual Hamilton Pride Festival (Figure 12.3). By placing rainbow knitted scarves and flags on the 'ordinary farming family', we attempted to bring attention to other forms of families beyond the heteronormative.

In Hamilton's city centre we have a statue of Riff Raff a cross-dressing butler from the cult film and musical *The Rocky Horror Picture Show* (www.riffraffstatue.org) (Figure 12.4).

The film was written by Richard O'Brien, who grew up in Hamilton and plays Riff Raff, the butler. *The Rocky Horror Picture Show* is about Frank-N-Furter, 'a sweet transvestite from transsexual Transylvania'. It illustrates the ways in which bodies become sexualised, included, or excluded depending upon place and time. The decision for Hamilton to support a statue of Riff Raff was bold and contested, yet gained enough support for the statue to be erected in 2004. The Riff Raff statue is provocative and unusual in that not only does it queer the streets of Hamilton but also it upsets the idea that city statues must be heteronormative, and commemorate and celebrate conservative family values. The significance of the statue goes beyond the city of Hamilton. It has become a site of pilgrimage for tourists. Annually, on the International Transgender Day of Remembrance (20 November), we gather at Riff Raff to lay flowers, light candles, and remember and honour transgender and non-binary people who are subject to gender bashing, have been killed, or have taken their own lives because of abuse and discrimination.

These two examples of Hamilton's monuments illustrate some spatial politics of gender, sexuality, and place. Across the globe in Greenwich Village in New York City, is a gay and lesbian monument (created by George Segal) (Figure 12.5).

Four figures – two men and two women – stand in Christopher Park. This gay liberation monument is a positive symbol of queer lives yet it also marks the site of violence against homosexuality, where on the night of June 27, 1969, police – once again – raided a gay bar called the Stonewall Inn. Word of the raid and the resistance to it soon spread, and the next day hundreds gathered to protest

161

Figure 12.3
Farming family statue with rainbow yarn bombing in Hamilton, Aotearoa New Zealand

Source: Photo credit: Lynda Johnston

Figure 12.4
Riff Raff Statue in Hamilton, Aotearoa New Zealand

Source: Photo credit: Lynda Johnston

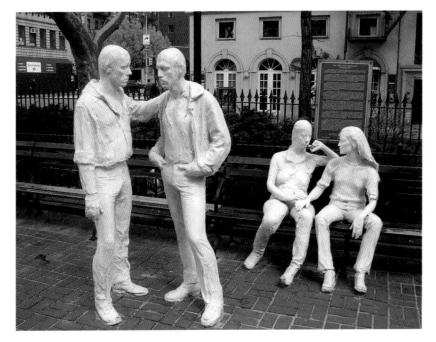

Figure 12.5
Gay liberation monument in Christopher Park, New York City, USA

Source: Photo credit: Lynda Johnston

and advocate for gay rights. Three days and two nights of rioting became emblematic of defiance of compulsory heterosexuality. At this time a group of activists organised the first gay and lesbian march in New York City, from Washington Square to Stonewall. The anniversary is marked, in most Western cities around the world, by gay pride festivals and parades. The assertion and creation of a new sense of identity was produced, one based on being proud of being gay.

These monuments show that gender and sexuality (who we are, what we do, and what we talk about) are always filtered through various cultural and social landscapes. Bodies and places are mutually constitutive. It matters whether we are trans, non-binary, and/or gay, are in England, or Aotearoa New Zealand, or somewhere else, are on a rugby field or in a gay bar. Longhurst and Johnston (2014: 268) note that gender and sexuality 'is lived in and through bodies, ranging across various scales such as homes, workplaces, cities, regions and nations'.

Summary

- Public monuments portray gender and sexual identities.
- Most cities' monuments celebrate male war heroes.
- The Farming Family monument is cis-heteronormative and celebrates white families of the region.
- Riff Raff (Hamilton, Aotearoa New Zealand) and the Gay Liberation Monument (New York City) are notable exceptions to embodied 'norms'.

Conclusion

Feminist and queer geography has made a significant impact on human geography. Taken together or separately, these sub-fields have profoundly challenged and changed the way in which we understand people, places, and spaces. Feminist and queer analyses and critiques of gender and sexuality norms are crucial to understanding gendered, sexualised, racialised, aged, and other social identities and places.

Places and spaces are not neutral; rather, they are expressions of geographically specific structural differences and inequalities. Places are gendered. They are also sexualised. The sub-fields of feminist and queer geography mean that now human geographers have the theoretical tools and empirical evidence to critically understand how places shape people and vice versa. These sub-fields, starting in the 1970s, showed how human geography is masculinist and heteronormative (excluding women, transgender, and non-heterosexual geographers). The discipline has been reshaped to include women, LGBTIQ+, Black, Indigenous, and disabled geographers, but only to some extent. There is still much more work to do to have a human geography discipline that is truly inclusive and diverse.

Two places are offered as examples of feminist and queer geography in action. The home is gendered and often reflects heteronormative nuclear families and cisgender roles. Homes may be sites of violence, and they may also be sites of comfort and belonging. How the home is experienced depends on who has power to create the social dynamics and relations within it. Often considered a private space, it is heavily influenced by the outside public world.

Cities use statues and monuments to reflect place identities. Public spaces are gendered, and most monuments pay tribute to male war heroes. Yet, in Hamilton, Aotearoa New Zealand, there are the 'Farming Family' and 'Riff Raff' statues. One reinforces cisgender and heterosexual white families as the norm for the region, while the other celebrates difference in the form of a cross-dressing butler from the *Rocky Horror Picture Show*. Where there are monumental expressions of inequalities, there is resistance.

Discussion points

- Consider the images that you share online about yourself and some of your everyday geographies. These might be your home, family spaces, your transport spaces, leisure and sport places, workplaces, and/or study spaces. How is gender and sexuality represented in these places? What are some similarities and differences in the way that men, women, and/or gender diverse people are encouraged to evaluate and manage their bodies? Which sexualities are represented and which ones are missing? What places are associated with embodied identities such as gender, sexuality, age, ethnicity, class, disability? How do these images make you feel about your body and the places you go (or don't go)? Thinking through **representations** allows us to consider how embodied experiences, beliefs, and identities affect the way in which we understand places and spaces.
- Think about the home or homes where you grew up. What were some of the gendered 'home rules' you remember? Think about the social relations, identities, and different spaces and times of the home(s) you were in as a child. In what ways did you conform to these rules

and or resist them? How did you create a feeling of belonging in the home (or parts of it)? How do these home rules compare to where you live now?

- Take a moment to make a list of the monuments and statues in your city/region. Who do they represent and why? Which genders and sexualities are prominent (or assumed)? Which genders and sexualities are absent?

References

Bell, D., and Valentine, G. (eds.) (1995). *Mapping Desire: Geographies of Sexualities*. London: Routledge.

Blunt, A., and Dowling, R. (2022). *Home* (2nd edn.). London: Routledge.

Browne, K. and Brown G. (2016). An Introduction to the Geographies of Sex and Sexualities. In *The Routledge Companion to Geographies of Sex and Sexualities*, eds. G. Brown and K. Browne. London: Routledge, 1–10.

Browne, K., Lim, J., and Brown, G. (eds.) (2007). *Geographies of Sexualities: Theory, Practice and Politics*. London: Ashgate.

Butler, J. (1990). *Gender Trouble: Feminism and the Subversion of Identity*. London and New York: Routledge.

Butler, J. (1993). *Bodies That Matter: On the Discursive Limits of 'Sex'*. New York and London: Routledge.

Butler, R., and Parr, H. (eds.) (1999). *Mind and Body Spaces: Geographies of Illness, Impairment and Disability*. London: Routledge.

Clancy, E. (2022). 'I feel fat when I feel fat': affective forces of trauma in anorexia and bulimia. *Gender, Place and Culture* 29(3): 303–322.

de Beauvoir, S. (1974). *The Second Sex* (trans. H. M. Parshely). New York: Vintage.

Fortin, J. (2017). Toppling monuments, a visual history. *The New York Times*. Available online: https://www.nytimes.com/2017/08/17/world/controversial-statues-monuments-destroyed.html

Gregory, D., Johnston, R., Pratt, G., Watts, M., and Whatmore, S. (eds.) (2009). *Dictionary of Human Geography* (5th edn.). Chichester: Wiley-Blackwell.

hooks, b. (1991). *Yearning: Race, Gender, and Cultural Politics*. London: Turnaround.

Johnston, L. (2018). Intersectional feminist and queer geographies: a view from 'down-under'. *Gender, Place and Culture* 25(4): 554–564.

Johnston, L. (2019). *Transforming Space, Place and Sex: Gender Variant Geographies*. London: Routledge.

Johnston, L., and Longhurst, R. (2010). *Space, Place and Sex: Geographies of Sexualities*. Lanham: Rowman and Littlefield.

Johnston, L., and Valentine, G. (1995). 'Where Ever I Lay My Girlfriend That's My Home': Performance and Surveillance of Lesbian Identity in Home Environments. In *Mapping Desires: Geographies of Sexualities*, eds. D. Bell and G. Valentine. London: Routledge, 99–113.

Longhurst, R. (2001). *Bodies: Exploring Fluid Boundaries*. London: Routledge.

Longhurst, R., and Johnston, L. (2014). Bodies, gender, place and culture: 21 years on. *Gender, Place and Culture* 21(3): 267–278.

Massey, D. (1994). *Space, Place and Gender*. Minneapolis: University of Minnesota Press.

Monk, J., and Hanson, S. (1982). On not excluding half of the human in human geography. *Professional Geographer* 34(1): 11–23.

Nast, H., and Pile, S. (eds.) (1998). *Places Through the Body*. London: Routledge.

Oswin, N. (2020). An other geography. *Dialogues in Human Geography* 10(1): 9–18.

Zelinsky, W. (1973). The strange case of the missing female geographer. *The Professional Geographer* 25(2): 101–105.

Online materials

- Go here: https://www.stats.govt.nz/news/new-sexual-identity-wellbeing-data-reflects-diversity-of-new-zealanders to view a short video that explains the importance of including diverse gender and sexuality identities in Aotearoa New Zealand's official statistical information.
- See also the Australian Human Rights Commission's video 'Let's talk about bodies, identity and sexuality': https://humanrights.gov.au/lets-talk-about-bodies-identity-and-sexuality
- This link to a short video about the Riff Raff Statue gives some more history to its place in Hamilton: https://www.youtube.com/watch?v=1bE7DF6ENn0
- Consider ethnicities, colonial and slavery histories in relation to monuments. Have any monuments in your city/region been 'toppled' (see the Toppling Monuments Movement (Fortin, 2017)). See this Toppling Monuments, a Visual History, in *The New York Times*: https://www.nytimes.com/2017/08/17/world/controversial-statues-monuments-destroyed.html

Further reading

All the following reading explores the topics covered in this chapter in more detail:

Brown, G., and Browne, K. (eds.) (2016). *The Routledge Companion to Geographies of Sex and Sexualities*. London: Routledge, 1–10.

Datta, A., Hopkins, P., Johnston, L., Olsen, E., and Silva, J. M. (eds.) (2020). *Routledge Handbook of Gender and Feminist Geographies* (1st edn.). London: Routledge.

Johnston, L. (2019). *Transforming Space, Place and Sex: Gender Variant Geographies*. London: Routledge.

Johnston, L., and Longhurst, R. (2010). *Space, Place and Sex: Geographies of Sexualities*. Lanham: Rowman and Littlefield.

Sullivan, C. T. (2018). Majesty in the city: experiences of an aboriginal transgender sex worker in Sydney, Australia. *Gender, Place and Culture* 25(12): 1681–1702.

13 Ethnicity and race

Heather Winlow

Introduction

Individual feelings about being 'in place' or 'out of place' (see Chapter 5) are influenced by identities and personal experiences, and by the ways in which identity categories have been constructed and represented by society. The ways in which a place is experienced are also influenced by the histories (*his*-stories) which dominate our cultural landscapes – which continue to reflect colonial (and exclusionary/exploitative) pasts and exclude parts of the story (see Chapter 6). To understand these exclusions, it is critical to have an understanding of the ways in which social identities, including **gender**, **race**, **class** and national identity, have been constructed and imagined over **space** and time. This chapter considers definitions of race and **ethnicity** and the contested nature of these categories; outlines the ways in which ideas about difference and later 'race' have developed historically in science and society; and explores some ongoing debates around the **decolonisation** of public histories.

Social construction of race and ethnicity

Ethnicity and race are forms of social identity which are now widely understood by human geographers (and other social scientists) as **'socially constructed'** rather than fixed and unchanging (or innate) entities (Jackson, 1989, Kobayashi, 2003, Barnes, 2009) – an idea which can also be applied to other identity categories. In relation to gender, for example, the dominant nineteenth-century European view of gender roles was that women should have domestic roles at home and it was perceived as unnatural to take on public roles, while twenty-first-century gender roles are much more diverse, with both men and women taking on multiple responsibilities. Gender identities have also become more fluid (Chapters 12 and 72) reflecting cultural shifts in attitudes over time. Historically human society has always had a concern with difference from a perceived 'norm', so that one group is considered as belonging and other groups are seen as outsiders. In the Greek and Roman periods, those living outside an urban metropolis were understood as living in the 'wilderness' and considered wild and savage. In the medieval period, when only three continents were known to Europeans, manuscripts and maps displayed images of monstrous peoples at the edges of the known world, partly reflecting the medieval craving for the bizarre and fantastic (Sharpe, 2008, Winlow, 2020). The idea of difference beyond the known world existed in advance of European **colonialism** and influenced

DOI: 10.4324/9780429265853-15

the ways in which 'new' worlds were perceived. Thus, ideas of difference had a long history before more recent concepts of 'race' emerged.

Definitions of race and ethnicity are complex and overlapping and our current understandings have been heavily influenced by nineteenth-century ideas. The term 'race' is associated with the idea that there exist a number of discrete and measurable biological groups. The emergence of the idea of race is outlined further below. Ethnicity as a term is often associated with belonging to a cultural group, and aspects of ethnicity may include religious traditions, language use, belief systems and cultural practices (such as culinary and musical traditions), but ethnicity can also include ancestry (therefore overlapping with ideas about race) and may also overlap with concepts of national identity. Nash (2012, 2013, 2015) argues that labels associated with race, ethnicity and national identity are used in overlapping and contradictory ways in relation to both popular and scientific discourse around ancestry. A brief consideration of the UK and US modern census categorisations (Figures 13.1a and 13.1b) serves to illustrate the ways in which race, ethnicity and nationality categories are used – and demonstrates that these identity categories are socially constructed.

Geographical imagination and representations of difference

Influenced by colonial expansion and global economic dominance, by the late sixteenth-century Europeans had developed a sense of themselves as culturally superior in comparison with other parts of the world (Wintle, 1999). This idea was reinforced by **imaginative geographies** (Chapter 23) through which **representations** of other parts of the globe were portrayed to readers in Europe, using different modes of representation such as travellers' accounts, artwork, maps and later photography (Mills, 1993, Driver 1994, 2004, Morin 1998, Ryan 1998, Winlow, 2020). As more geographical 'discoveries' were made, a European cartographic tradition emerged, which placed Europe visually at the centre of the world map. This is clearly demonstrated through Mercator's still widely used 1569 projection, which also distorts the northern latitudes, with the result that Africa and South America appear considerably smaller than in reality.

Edward Said's influential text *Orientalism* (first published in 1978) evaluates the ways in which Europeans imagined the East, or the Orient, through an examination of European travellers' accounts, novels and historical and political texts from the eighteenth and nineteenth centuries (Sharp, 2023, Morrissey, 2014). Through analysing these texts, Said introduced the concept of the '**other**' as a binary category, where the peoples of the Orient were stereotypically viewed by Europeans as the opposite of the white western European 'self' – with ideas of the exotic, mystical or despotic Easterner viewed as different to the rational and scientific European. The **cultures** of the Orient were seen as one homogenous culture and not recognised for their diversity. Said (1978) argued that there was not a cut-off point for these representations – *Orientalism*, or otherness, is still widely reflected in the way different cultural groups are represented today.

Before the 'discovery' of the Americas, there already existed in European consciousness a conception of 'otherness' which included myths about 'wild' environments, populated by monstrous peoples, man-eating cannibals, Amazonian females and untold wealth. These myths influenced

Individual questions — continued

11 If you were not born in the United Kingdom, when did you most recently arrive to live here?

⤷ Do not count short visits away from the UK

Month   Year
☐☐   ☐☐☐☐

⤷ If you arrived before 21 March 2020 ➡ GO TO **13**

⤷ If you arrived on or after 21 March 2020 ➡ GO TO **12**

12 Including the time you have already spent here, how long do you intend to stay in the United Kingdom?

☐ Less than 12 months

☐ 12 months or more

13 One year ago, what was your usual address?

⤷ If you had no usual address one year ago, state the address where you were staying

☐ The address on the front of this questionnaire

☐ Student term-time or boarding school address in the UK, write in term-time address below

☐ Another address in the UK, write in below

☐☐☐☐☐☐☐☐☐☐☐☐☐☐☐☐☐☐

☐☐☐☐☐☐☐☐☐☐☐☐☐☐☐☐☐☐

☐☐☐☐☐☐☐☐☐☐☐☐☐☐☐☐☐☐

Postcode
☐☐☐☐☐☐☐☐

☐ OR outside the UK, write in country

☐☐☐☐☐☐☐☐☐☐☐☐☐☐☐☐☐☐

14 How would you describe your national identity?

⤷ Tick all that apply

☐ British

☐ English

☐ Welsh

☐ Scottish

☐ Northern Irish

☐ Other, write in

☐☐☐☐☐☐☐☐☐☐☐☐☐☐☐☐☐☐

15 What is your ethnic group?

⤷ Choose **one** section from A to E, then **tick one box** to best describe your ethnic group or background

A White

☐ English, Welsh, Scottish, Northern Irish or British

☐ Irish

☐ Gypsy or Irish Traveller

☐ Roma

☐ Any other White background, write in

☐☐☐☐☐☐☐☐☐☐☐☐☐☐☐☐☐☐

B Mixed or Multiple ethnic groups

☐ White and Black Caribbean

☐ White and Black African

☐ White and Asian

☐ Any other Mixed or Multiple background, write in

☐☐☐☐☐☐☐☐☐☐☐☐☐☐☐☐☐☐

☐☐☐☐☐☐☐☐☐☐☐☐☐☐☐☐☐☐

C Asian or Asian British

☐ Indian

☐ Pakistani

☐ Bangladeshi

☐ Chinese

☐ Any other Asian background, write in

☐☐☐☐☐☐☐☐☐☐☐☐☐☐☐☐☐☐

D Black, Black British, Caribbean or African

☐ Caribbean

☐ African background, write in below

☐ Any other Black, Black British or Caribbean background, write in

☐☐☐☐☐☐☐☐☐☐☐☐☐☐☐☐☐☐

E Other ethnic group

☐ Arab

☐ Any other ethnic group, write in

☐☐☐☐☐☐☐☐☐☐☐☐☐☐☐☐☐☐

Page 5

Figure 13.1a
Individual questions 14 and 15 from Census Questionnaire for England 2021

Source: Office for National Statistics, UK 2021

8. **Is Person 1 of Hispanic, Latino, or Spanish origin?**

☐ **No**, not of Hispanic, Latino, or Spanish origin

☐ Yes, Mexican, Mexican Am., Chicano

☐ Yes, Puerto Rican

☐ Yes, Cuban

☐ Yes, another Hispanic, Latino, or Spanish origin – *Print, for example, Salvadoran, Dominican, Colombian, Guatemalan, Spaniard, Ecuadorian, etc.* ↗

9. **What is Person 1's race?**

*Mark ☒ one or more boxes **AND** print origins.*

☐ White – *Print, for example, German, Irish, English, Italian, Lebanese, Egyptian, etc.* ↗

☐ Black or African Am. – *Print, for example, African American, Jamaican, Haitian, Nigerian, Ethiopian, Somali, etc.* ↗

☐ American Indian or Alaska Native – *Print name of enrolled or principal tribe(s), for example, Navajo Nation, Blackfeet Tribe, Mayan, Aztec, Native Village of Barrow Inupiat Traditional Government, Nome Eskimo Community, etc.* ↗

☐ Chinese   ☐ Vietnamese   ☐ Native Hawaiian

☐ Filipino   ☐ Korean   ☐ Samoan

☐ Asian Indian   ☐ Japanese   ☐ Chamorro

☐ Other Asian – *Print, for example, Pakistani, Cambodian, Hmong, etc.* ↗   ☐ Other Pacific Islander – *Print, for example, Tongan, Fijian, Marshallese, etc.* ↗

☐ Some other race – *Print race or origin.* ↗

Figure 13.1b

Questions 8 and 9 from US National Census 2020

Source: US Census Bureau 2020

the first explorers to the Americas. The word 'canibal' appeared in Columbus' log of 1492 (after encountering a tribe who were very fearful of another tribe who they appeared to call 'canibale'), and on encountering a fierce looking individual a few months later, the idea of the 'island of canibales' was born and used to justify genocide against both the Carib and Arawak tribes in the Caribbean (Motohashi, 1999). Ideas about savage man-eating tribes were later applied to whole swathes of South America, perpetuated both in travel accounts, repeated and republished in different European languages, and through cartography – images of cannibals appeared in South America in Mercator's 1569 atlas (Figure 13.2). Whilst over time the lingering medieval ideas of the existence of monstrous others receded as a result of colonial encounters with real Indigenous groups, the ideas of difference, inferiority or savagery remained and influenced the development of a specifically racialised discourse.

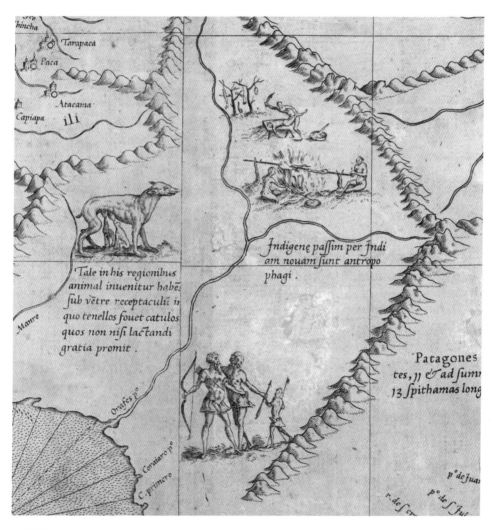

Figure 13.2
Extract from Mercator's Map of the World in Atlas

Source: Mercator, 1569. gallica.bnf.fr/Bibliothèque nationale de France (Public domain/open source)

Summary

- Ethnicity and race are not fixed entities but categories which have been socially constructed in different times and places.
- Categories of race, ethnicity and national identity are overlapping and labels are often used interchangeably.
- Throughout the colonial period different forms of representation were used to construct Europeans as dominant, in relation to a perceived inferior overseas 'Other'.

A brief history of 'race'

Modern ideas about racial difference have their roots in the eighteenth century, when scientists assumed a link between observed colour difference and different physical environments (Appiah, 2016). This idea of colour difference between human groups ('white', 'yellow', 'Negro' and 'red') as well as assumptions about the supposed superiority of white groups was evident in the work of Immanuel Kant, who also first used the term 'race' (Elden, 2009). Kobayashi (2003) notes that Kant's stress on the links between skin colour and distance from the equator fed into new ways of thinking about race. In his *Systema Naturae* (1735), Carl Linneaus was the first to identify modern humans as 'homo' within the group of quadrupeds, adding *Homo sapiens* to his system of binominal (two-part) classification in the 1750s (Appiah 2016, The Linnean Society of London, 2023). The first nine editions of his book (1735–1756) divided humanity into four 'varieties': 'European white', 'American red', 'Asian tawny' and 'African black'. These initial divisions were associated with the known four continents at that time, with differences in skin colour assumed to be linked to climate, not biology. During the 1750s Linneaus broadened his classifications and the 10th edition of his book suggested links between the varieties and the four 'temperaments or humours' (accepted in the eighteenth century) as well as adding other moral attributes to his scheme. While he is not known to have used the term 'race', this marked a departure from purely geographic or environmental factors and partly paved the way for the emergence of **'scientific racism'** (The Linnean Society of London, 2023). These assumptions around geography and difference were also reflected in other eighteenth-century work. For example, travelogues widely constructed the Tropics as having a climate which was not conducive to work and inhabitants were frequently portrayed as lazy (Livingstone, 1992, Driver, 1994).

As the evidence for species evolution amassed, a number of evolutionary theories were proposed and circulated in Europe in the early nineteenth century (Livingstone, 1992). However, it was only after the publication of Charles Darwin's *Origin of Species* in 1859, which outlined his theory of natural selection, that evolutionary theories began to receive widespread public acceptance. Alfred Russell Wallace had independently come to the same conclusions about species evolution. During this same time period, many of the fields that we recognise today as separate academic disciplines were becoming established in universities (including geography, anthropology, biology, the sub-disciplines of zoology and physiology) and as scientific societies.

Science and society influence one another and the development of scientific ideas does not take place in a void. Geographers and anthropologists collected extensive amounts of data from across the globe in attempts to classify and map supposed racial 'types' associated with different regions of the world – measuring and mapping traits such as head size, stature and pigmentation. Colonial pre-cursors to this idea of racial measurement include the doctrine of 'blood purity' developed by the Spanish Empire which led to a hierarchical division of groups based on recent ancestry, including the categories of mestizo and mulatto (Kosek, 2009). Systems of division by blood were later used in both the US and in Australia.

Many data charts and maps were published in anthropological and geographical journals in the late nineteenth and early twentieth centuries, and a diversity of racial classifications were proposed. As all the measured characteristics exist on a continuous scale, quite different conclusions could, and indeed were, drawn. Within Europe for example, and drawing on the widespread data that had been collected across the region, anthropologists variously argued for the existence of one European race, three European races and ten European races (Winlow, 2006). Social Darwinism, which encompassed many forms, many with no direct association with Darwin's theories, led to widespread commentary among nineteenth- and early twentieth-century scientists on the assumed links between physical and mental or intellectual traits. In Europe, this led to claims of racial hierarchy, with white Europeans at the top. Many geographers strongly supported the concept of environmental determinism (see Chapter 39), which assumed that societal (and racial) development was determined solely by the environment. A pseudo-science based on flawed assumptions about race became widespread (Gould, 1981). While some individual scientists, including geographers, were careful to reject ideas of a racial hierarchy, this was the exception rather than the rule.

In addition to physical characteristics, data related to ethnicity was widely collected by geographers and anthropologists. **Ethnographic** and linguistic maps were used to justify national boundaries and to consolidate national **territories**. The mapping of ethnic territories played a role in political discourse in nineteenth-century Russia. Imperial policies on the organisation of territory coincided with the development of Russian science, with work on ethnic demarcation progressing in parallel with developments in geography, ethnography and cartography (Petronis, 2007). The Russian Geographical Society established in 1845 (becoming the Imperial Russian Geographical Society in 1850) focused on the mapping of the western and northwestern parts of the Russian Empire, which included a wide mix of ethnicities, and linguistic groups. Initially the area was largely perceived as Polish, but after a Polish uprising in 1830–1831, policies of de-Polinisation were put into practice. This included the production of ethnographic maps which divided the area into dominant Belarusian, Lithuanian and Polish ethnicities and later enabled these groups to use the maps to develop their own nationalist agendas.

Photography was also widely used to reinforce ideas about race and ethnicity. Photography developed in the late nineteenth century at a time when interest in cataloguing race types was prominent and photographic techniques were quickly put to use (Ryan, 1998). Photographs were extensively used to classify racial type, alongside the collection of physical measurements – such as head size using callipers – both within and outside Europe. Francis Galton, for example, promoted photographic techniques for classifying criminal, supposedly degenerate, types within the British population. Ideas about otherness were thus applied to segments of the British population. Ideas about exotic difference were also reinforced through photography. Photography was widely used to catalogue different tribal groups and traditional lifestyles. Figure 13.3, a staged

Figure 13.3
Konyak Nagas in Assam, East India Source: E.T.D. Lambert, 1935–1936
Source: Photo credit: Royal Geographical Society picture library

photograph of members of the Konyak Nagas group from Assam from 1935 to 1936, provides an example. The catalogue label is telling – no named individuals are listed, but keywords that were catalogued include 'ethnic', 'tree', 'body decoration', 'eccentric', 'exotic' and 'primitive'. Photography was widely used to gather data on Indigenous groups who it was assumed would die out – this 'salvage motif' was evident in the work of Edward Curtis (Library of Congress, 2023) in the US. Such stereotyped images of passive Indigenous groups have increasingly been challenged by the work of Indigenous photographers.

The idea of racial groups as separate biological entities has been disproved by late twentieth-century genetic discoveries. By 2000 85% of the human genome had been mapped and it is now accepted that humans are 99% similar at a genetic level, with surface differences such as skin colour making up the last 1% (Malik, 2008). As such, race does not exist. Yet ideas about race and ethnicity are remarkably persistent both in society and in science, as demonstrated through census categories, equal opportunities monitoring surveys, prescribing of drugs based on assumed ethnicity, ancestry testing and ongoing racial discrimination. Scholars, including human geographers, working in areas of **critical race theory**, ethnic studies and cultural studies now understand race as having no universal form and being produced differently in different times and places (see Chapter 70). Some scholars have moved away from using the term race and moved 'beyond race' in order to deny any overarching integrity or coherence to the concept, while still being attentive to the ways in which racisms are a lived reality (Kosek, 2009).

Summary

- Initial ideas about human difference around the globe were linked to observed colour difference seen in different geographical locations.
- Racial categories and hierarchies were reinforced through 'scientific racism' and different modes of representation including maps and photography.
- Race does not exist. Some scholars use the term 'beyond race' to recognise this, while still recognising the lived experience of individuals.

Decolonising public histories

Currently there is a focus in higher education institutions and in the heritage sector on 'decolonising' public histories and decolonising educational curricula in order to tell more inclusive histories and create more inclusionary and accessible environments (including recent debates in human geography, Noxolo, 2017, Radcliffe 2022, see also Indigenous Peoples Speciality Group of Association of American Geographers, 2023). Ongoing debates surround repatriation of artefacts taken by European societies from overseas cultures, how museums represent and label or display artefacts taken from other societies in the colonial past, whose histories are represented in the cultural landscape (e.g. through public monuments and memorials), and which histories are represented and repeated in high school and university curricula. How often is school history about white male heroes? How often are the negative aspects of colonialism discussed?

In May 2020 Black American George Floyd was killed in broad daylight by white police officer Derek Chauvin in Minnesota, an event which drew global media attention to the ongoing issues of police brutality and discrimination in the US, leading to international support for the Black Lives Matter (BLM) movement through a series of anti-racist demonstrations. One of these protests took place in Bristol, UK, on 7 June 2020 when the statue of Transatlantic slave-trader Edward Colston was removed from its plinth and pushed into Bristol Harbour by protestors (Siddique and Skopeliti, 2020, Choksey, 2021). In the months that followed, Bristol renamed several schools, removing the name Colston and replacing this with alternatives. Following a public campaign, Colston Hall (now Bristol Beacon), the city's largest music venue, agreed to change its name in 2017 but only removed the old lettering from its building a few days after the Colston statue removal (see also Chapter 29). In Bristol there had been recognition of Colston's role in the slave trade since at least the 1990s and several earlier calls from residents for his statue to be removed, but, as in other locations, the death of George Floyd acted as a catalyst for public action to take place.

In South Africa, The Rhodes Must Fall movement has focused on the decolonisation of education. The movement originated amongst a group of staff and students at the University of Cape Town in 2015 with an initial focus on the removal of a statue of British imperialist Cecil Rhodes at the University of Cape Town which was seen as a symbol of repression and institutional racism. Later actions focused on issues of access to accommodation for Black students, the disparity in the numbers of Black professors at the institution and on the transformation of the curriculum (Mangcu, 2017). The movement led to the emergence of allied student movements around the globe, including at other universities in South Africa, as well as in the US and the UK. Following a council vote at the university, the statue was removed on 9 April 2015, but public opinion on the issue remained divided. At Oriel College Oxford, another statue of Rhodes was the subject of controversy in 2015 (Ahmed, 2020) where students called for the removal of the statue, but university donors threatened to remove large-scale financial support if this occurred. Following the death of George Floyd, two large protests took place outside the college. Following legal consultation, the college decided against removal of the statue and now a new contextual plaque (Grierson and Gale, 2021) has been installed next to the statue (Figures 13.4a and 13.4b). This case reflects some of the public debate in the UK about whether statues should be removed, or be re-contextualised through extra labelling to recognise the negative impacts of those represented.

The continued imagining of the British countryside as a white space has been challenged by academics, artists and activists for several decades (Pollard, 1988, 2022, Muslim Hikers Network, 2022). Recently there has been a significant recognition by the National Trust in the UK of the role of historic slavery and colonialism in its collections, with a new focus on telling more inclusive histories through its colonial countryside project (Huxtable et al., 2020). This has faced challenges from right-wing media, politicians and a break-off group, Restore Trust, who prefer a more sanitised version of the past (Hinsliff, 2021, Lester 2021).

Figure 13.4a
Statue of Cecil Rhodes, Oriel College, Oxford

Source: Photo credit: Heather Winlow

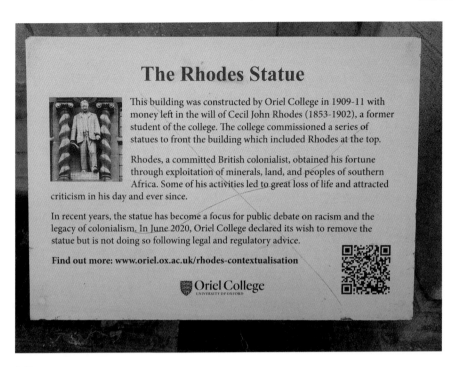

Figure 13.4b
Recontextualisation plaque, Oriel College, Oxford

Source: Photo credit: Heather Winlow

Heritage interpretations, like any form of representation, are selective. Recent critical examinations of a number of plantation museums in the Southeastern United States reveal how the tour narratives and landscapes whitewash slavery and also fail to acknowledge the genocide of native peoples who made these spaces available for incorporation into the Atlantic slave economy (Inwood et al., 2020).

Summary

- There are ongoing debates in contemporary society about how colonial pasts should be represented.
- Selective histories of the past remain in our urban landscapes, our school and university curricula and at heritage sites.

Conclusion

Recent genetic developments have disproved the existence of discrete racial groups, yet historical racial categorisations are still widely used both in science and society. Some social scientists have moved 'beyond race', while retaining a focus on interrogating systems of exclusion and discrimination which continue to impact everyday lived experiences. As human geographers, part of our role involves questioning the accepted status quo in relation to identities and inequalities. This includes challenging the ways in which assumed identity categories, including race and ethnicity, are linked to systematic forms of exclusion and discrimination. We need to continue to critique the reasons why particular groups are excluded from access to particular places, institutions and services, as well as making improvements to access. But these exclusions cannot be adequately addressed without considering the wider power dynamics operating in society, where critical **postcolonial** histories are often still rejected or simply overlooked.

Issues of race and ethnicity as a focus of research were largely ignored within geography following the widespread rejection of racism after World War II and during the mid-twentieth-century domination of the discipline by **spatial science**. Some focus on race and spatial inequalities was undertaken in the 1960s and 1970s, but it is only since the late 1980s and the critical turn in geography, when race as a social construct was accepted, that a diverse range of critical work in this area has taken place. This has included a focus on whiteness (Bonnett, 2000, 2022), on the creation of **hegemonic** landscapes (Cosgrove and Daniels, 1988, Whelan, 2014, Inwood et al., 2020, Parnell, 2020) and on the ways in which historical modes of representation reinforced ideas of otherness (Driver, 1994, 2004). In the last decade there has been an increasing body of work both in Indigenous geographies and Black geographies, emphasising the **agency** of Indigenous and Black spatial thought and the voice of Indigenous and Black geographers with wider critical links to key global challenges such as climate change and access to resources (Chapters 10, 41 and 42). Work on decolonising geography as a discipline is also taking place, which includes a recognition of how the discipline has been, and still is, shaped by colonial pasts, as well as finding ways to integrate more inclusive representation and curricula (see Chapter 71).

Discussion points

- Consider the US 2020 census questions 8 and 9 (Figure 13.1b). Why does question 8 ask about Hispanic, Latino or Spanish origin? Why might the categories used in US census question 9 be problematic? Do you view the categories used as 'race' categories? For both the UK and US censuses would all participants be able to easily select a category to which they 'belong'? Discuss and provide examples.
- What does otherness mean? What examples of otherness have you seen applied to groups within contemporary society? Do historical ideas about difference still influence perceptions of the Global South?
- Using the maps produced by the Centre for the Study of the Legacies of British Slavery, explore the financial and embodied connections between the British countryside and slavery https://www.ucl.ac.uk/lbs/ How did profits from the slave trade and slave ownership shape the British countryside?
- During your time at school which histories did you learn? To what extent were the impacts of colonialism discussed?

References

Ahmed, A. K. (2020). #Rhodes must fall: how a decolonial student movement in the global South inspired epistemic disobedience at the University of Oxford. *African Studies Review*, 63:2, 281–303.

Appiah, K. A. (2016). Mistaken identities: Colour, BBC Reith Lecture Podcast https://www.bbc.co.uk/sounds/play/b080t63w

Barnes, T. (2009). Social Construction. In *Dictionary of Human Geography*, eds. D. Gregory, R. Johnson, G. Pratt, M. Watts, and S. Whatmore (5th edn.). Chichester: Wiley-Blackwell, 690–691.

Bonnett, A. (2000). *White Identities: Historical and International Perspectives*. Harlow: Prentice Hall.

Bonnett, A. (2022). *Multiracism: Rethinking Racism in Global Context*. Cambridge: Polity Press.

Choksey, L. (2021). Colston falling. *Journal of Historical Geography* 74: 77–83.

Cosgrove, D., and Daniels, S. (eds.) (1988). *The Iconography of Landscape*. Cambridge: Cambridge University Press.

Curtis Collection, Library of Congress. (2023). http://www.loc.gov/pictures/collection/ecur/

Driver, F. (1994). *Geography, Empire, and Visualization: Making Representations*. Research Paper 1. London: Department of Geography, Royal Holloway, University of London.

Driver, F. (2004). Imagining the tropics: views and visions of the tropical world. *Singapore Journal of Tropical Geography* 25(1): 1–17.

Elden, S. (2009). Reassessing Kant's geography. *Journal of Historical Geography* 35(1): 3–25.

Gould, S. J. (1981). *The Mismeasure of Man*. London & New York: Penguin.

Grierson, J., and Gale, D. (11 October 2021). Oxford College installs plaque calling Cecil Rhodes a 'committed colonialist', *Guardian* https://www.theguardian.com/education/2021/oct/11/oxford-college-installs-plaque-calling-cecil-rhodes-a-committed-colonialist

Hinsliff, G. (16 October 2021). Cream teas at dawn: inside the war for the National Trust, *The Guardian*, https://www.theguardian.com/uk-news/2021/oct/16/cream-teas-at-dawn-inside-the-war-for-the-national-trust

Huxtable, S.-A., Fowler, C., Kefalas, C., and Slocombe, E. (eds.) (2020). Interim report on the connections between colonialism and properties now in the care of the National Trust, including links with historic slavery, National Trust. https://nt.global.ssl.fastly.net/binaries/content/assets/website/national/pdf/colonialism-and-historic-slavery-report.pdf

Indigenous Peoples Speciality Group of Association of American Geographers. (2023). https://www.aag.org/groups/indigenous-peoples/

Inwood, J. F. J., Alderman, D. H., and Hanna S. P. (2020). Slavery and Empires. In *Sage Handbook of Historical Geography*, eds. M. Domosh, M. Heffernan, and C. W. J. Withers. London: Sage, 297–314.

Jackson, P. (1989). *Maps of Meaning*. London: Routledge.

Kobayashi, A. (2003). The Construction of Geographical Knowledge: Racialization, Spatialization. In *Handbook of Cultural Geography*, eds. K. Anderson, M. Domosh, S. Pile, and N. Thrift. London: Sage, 544–556.

Kosek, J. (2009). Race. In *Dictionary of Human Geography*, eds. D. Gregory, R. Johnson, G. Pratt, M. Watts, and S. Whatmore (5th edn.). Chichester: Wiley-Blackwell, 615–618.

Lester, A. (7 June 2021). Culture warriors' attack on the National Trust https://blogs.sussex.ac.uk/snapshotsofempire/2021/06/07/culture-warriors-attacks-on-the-national-trust/

Library of Congress. (2023). Curtis Collection. https://www.loc.gov/pictures/collection/ecur/

Livingstone, D. N. (1992). *The Geographical Tradition: Episodes in the History of a Contested Enterprise*. Oxford, UK & Cambridge, USA: Blackwell.

Malik, K. (2008). *Strange Fruit: Why Both Sides Are Wrong in the Race Debate*. Oxford: Oneworld.

Mangcu, X. (2017). Shattering the myth of a post-racial consensus in South African higher education: 'Rhodes must fall' and the struggle for transformation at the University of Cape Town. *Critical Philosophy of Race* 5(2): 243–266.

Mills, S. (1993). *Discourses of Difference: An Analysis of Women's Travel Writing and Colonialism*. London: Routledge.

Morin, K. M. (1998). British women travelers and constructions of racial difference across the nineteenth century American West. *Transactions of the Institute of British Geographers* 23(3): 311–330.

Morrissey, J. (2014). Imperialism and Empire. In *Key Concepts in Historical Geography*, eds. J. Morrissey, D. Nally, U. Strohmayer, and Y. Whelan. London: Sage, 17–35.

Motohashi, T. (1999). The Discourse of Cannibalism in Early Modern Travel Writing. In *Travel Writing and Empire: Postcolonial Theory in Transit*, ed. S. Clark. London: Zed Books, 83–99.

Muslim Hikers Network. (2022). https://muslimhikers.com/

Nash, C. (2012). Genetics, race, and relatedness: human mobility and human diversity in the Genographic Project. *Annals of the Association of American Geographers* 102: 1–18.

Nash, C. (2013). Genome geographies: mapping national ancestry and diversity in human population genetics. *Transactions of the IBG* 38: 193–206.

Nash, C. (2015). *Genetic Geographies: The Trouble with Ancestry*. Minnesota: Minnesota University Press.

Noxolo, P. (2017). Decolonial theory in a time of the re-colonisation of UK research. *Transactions of the Institute of British Geographers* 42: 342–344.

Parnell, N. S. (2020). Colonial and Postcolonial Landscapes. In *Sage Handbook of Historical Geography*, eds. M. Domosh, M. Heffernan, and C. W. J. Withers. London: Sage, 164–178.

Petronis, V. (2007). *Constructing Lithuania: Ethnic Mapping in Tsarist Russia, ca. 1800–1914*. Stockholm: Stockholm University.

Pollard, I. (1988). Pastoral Interlude. http://www.ingridpollard.com/pastoral-interlude.html

Pollard, I. (August 2022). It's all a story or clues, Tate video https://www.youtube.com/watch?v=EFGJOwVUGTA

Radcliffe, S. (2022). *Decolonising Geography*. Polity.

Ryan, J. (1998). *Picturing Empire: Photography and the Visualization of the British Empire*. Chicago: University of Chicago Press.

Said, E. (1978). *Orientalism*. Harmondsworth: Penguin.

Sharp, J. (2023). *Geographies of Postcolonialism* (2nd edn.). London and Thousand Oaks: Sage.

Siddique, H., and Skopeliti, C. (7 June 2020). BLM protesters topple statue of Bristol slave trader Edward Colston, *Guardian* https://www.theguardian.com/uk-news/2020/jun/07/blm-protesters-topple-statue-of-bristol-slave-trader-edward-colston

The Linnean Society of London. (2023). *Linnaeus and Race*. https://www.linnean.org/learning/who-was-linnaeus/linnaeus-and-race

Whelan, Y. (2014). Landscape and Iconography. In *Key Concepts in Historical Geography*, eds. J. Morrissey, D. Nally, U. Strohmayer, and Y. Whelan. London: Sage, 161–171.

Winlow, H. (2006). Mapping moral geographies: W.Z. Ripley's races of Europe and the U.S. *Annals of the American Association of Geographers* 96(1), 119–141.

Winlow, H. (2020). Mapping, Race and Ethnicity. In *International Encyclopedia of Human Geography*, ed. A. Kobayashi (2nd edn.). Volume 8, Elsevier, 309–321.

Wintle, M. (1999). Renaissance maps and the construction of the idea of Europe. *Journal of Historical Geography* 25(2): 137–165.

Online materials

- Appiah, K.A. Mistaken Identities: Colour, BBC Reith Lecture Podcast https://www.bbc.co.uk/sounds/play/b080t63w
- Curtis Collection, Library of Congress. (2023). http://www.loc.gov/pictures/collection/ecur/

- Huxtable, S.-A., Fowler, C., Kefalas, C., and Slocombe E. (eds.) (2020). Interim Report on the Connections between Colonialism and Properties now in the Care of the National Trust, including Links with Historic Slavery, National Trust. https://nt.global.ssl.fastly.net/binaries/content/assets/website/national/pdf/colonialism-and-historic-slavery-report.pdf
- Pollard, I. (2022). It's all a story or clues, Tate video https://www.youtube.com/watch?v=EFGJOwVUGTA

Further reading

Gilroy, P. (1993). *The Black Atlantic: Modernity and Double-Consciousness*. London: New York, Verso.
A classic text. A postmodern challenge to traditional categories of race and national identity. Gilroy argues that the Black Atlantic is defined by 'routes' not 'routes', whereby the movement of peoples and cultural traditions have resulted in a transatlantic Black diaspora.

Gould, S. J. (1981). *The Mismeasure of Man*. London & New York: Penguin.
Classic work outlining and critiquing the development of scientific racism.

Ryan, J. (1998). *Picturing Empire: Photography and the Visualization of the British Empire*. Chicago: University of Chicago Press.
Historical geographical account of how photography was used to support colonial perspectives on overseas peoples and environments.

Said, E. (1978). *Orientalism*. London: Penguin.
Classic postcolonial text introducing concept of *Orientalism*, based on analysis of European writings about the Orient.

Sharp, J. (2023). *Geographies of Postcolonialism* (2nd edn.). London and Thousand Oaks: Sage.
Introduces key themes relating to postcolonialism and explores postcolonialism through the geographies of imagination, knowledge and power.

Winlow, H. (2020). Mapping, Race and Ethnicity. In *International Encyclopedia of Human Geography*, ed. A. Kobayashi (2nd edn.). Volume 8, Amsterdam: Elsevier, 309–321.
Analysis of the ways in which cartography has reinforced ideas about racial division and how this developed historically.

PART THREE

THEMES

SECTION ONE

AREA GEOGRAPHIES

14 Knowing area geographies

Junxi Qian and Andrew Williams

Introduction: the scope of area geographies

One of the primary missions of geography is to investigate spatial variation and differentiation. Landscapes and socioeconomic activities are not evenly distributed geographically, and one of the most pronounced differentiations is between the urban and the rural – while the urban is characterised by the spatial **agglomerations** of non-agricultural activities, the rural is conventionally defined by low density of land use, agricultural production, and often a non-market-based subsistence economy. In parallel, we live in the world as a mosaic of regions demarcated by boundaries – some of the boundaries are legally or administratively codified, sometimes quite arbitrarily, while others, such as in the cases of cultural regions, bioregions, and language regions (see Chapter 21), are based on time-honoured perceptions and conventions. Depending on how boundaries are drawn, there are significant over-layering, overlaps, and intersections among different regions – for example, while state development policies may be formulated based on massive translocal regions such as the Bay Area in the US and the Greater Bay Area in China (Figure 14.1), for ordinary people the region that serves as the functional anchor of their everyday life may be quite small and at a relatively localised scale, occupying only a small portion of the larger region.

Collectively, human geography's interest in urban, rural, and regional geographies expresses an established geographical tradition that prioritises the analysis of specific spatial units. By examining the historical development of particular 'cells' and comparing them with others, geographers can reveal a diversity of differentiated and lived regional worlds and explore how spatial differentiations contribute to our situated 'sense of place' – namely, an amalgam of structural and institutional conditions, sensory perceptions, **embodied** experiences, and routinised practices. For instance, living in New York is phenomenologically different from living in London or Beijing, while lifestyles in cities are different from those in the countryside. In this introductory chapter to the section on Area Geographies, we engage with three sub-disciplines of human geography that most directly reflect this tradition – urban geography, rural geography, and regional geography. A brief definition of and introduction to each will be outlined below.

Firstly, urban geography can be quite straightforwardly defined as an enquiry investigating the sociospatial processes that contribute to the making and remaking of cities. Scott and Storper (2015) and Jonas et al. (2015) see cities as products of *urbanisation*, which refers to the spatial

DOI: 10.4324/9780429265853-18

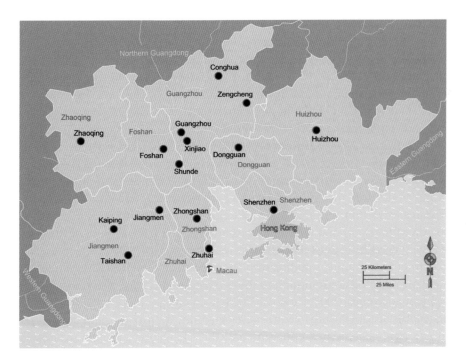

Figure 14.1
A map of the Greater Bay Area initiative traversing Hong Kong and Mainland China

Source: Wikimedia Commons

agglomeration of non-agricultural activities, the increasing density of population and land use, and a social heterogeneity of people and general anonymity among urban residents, as opposed to the closely knit social and kinship ties in rural areas. To put it in a more nuanced way, we experience cities in terms of the commodified access to agricultural products, the **capitalist** system of production and waged labour, market-based exchange and consumption, the quick expansion of the built environment, and the provision of **infrastructures** connecting cities to translocal networks, which feed into their global influence (Jonas et al., 2015). To unpack such landscapes and processes, Jonas et al. (2015) advocate an explicitly geographical approach within which urban social processes are shot through with an analysis of **space**, place, and scale, as well as the 'connections and similarities across regions or landscapes' (p. 6). This approach equips us to probe into a wide range of sociospatial phenomena, inter alia, (i) institutional and structural factors at different scales that shape urban changes, from global processes to grassroots actions at the neighbourhood scale; (ii) political economic processes, and the contingent alliance of state, society, and capital, that contribute to the production of urban spaces and urban forms; (iii) basic welfare essential to living in the city, such as housing, education, and medical care, as well as the variegated social geographies that ensue, including spatial concentration, homogenisation, segregation, and the emergence of **gated communities** and enclaves; and (iv) everyday experiences of living in the city, referring not only to the tastes, meanings, and identities that people invest in urban spaces and lifestyles but also the ways in which their selves and **subjectivities** are governed and engineered by those in power, through the introduction of development visions and projects (Hall and Barrett, 2015, Jonas et al., 2015).

Secondly, the Area Geographies section addresses the counterpart of urban geography, that is, rural geography. At first glimpse, rural geography looks at exactly the opposites of cities: rural areas with smaller populations, lower density of land use, and culturally more 'organic' and cohesive communities (Woods, 2005) – all these qualities are likely to conjure up imaginations of rurality as timeless, tranquil, and idyllic (Williams, 1973). However, in reality, rural areas are often no less dynamic and volatile than urban ones, especially in an era when many rural communities are implicated in global flows and linkages, leading to the formation of the global countryside (see Woods, 2007). Far from being encoded by stasis and quietude, rural areas are at the forefront of intersecting economic, social, political, and cultural forces. Testimonies to this point proliferate across different rural contexts, such as the commodification and **globalisation** of agricultural production, the boom and bust associated with commercial crop production and natural resource extraction, the relocation of employment opportunities to rural regions due to the progress of transport and telecommunication technologies, the rise of the consumption countryside with deepening **gentrification** of rural spaces (Figure 14.2), the resurgence of rural places as centres of community building through arts and cultural initiatives, and the revival of localised and organic food consumption to shorten food chains and reclaim social responsibility in rural economies (Woods, 2005, Yarwood, 2023).

Throughout the histories of urban and rural geographies, the **ontological** boundaries between the urban and rural have invited criticisms, and there have been emerging voices advocating that the two enquiries should be analysed in unity – there are rural activities that urbanisation

Figure 14.2
Wencun Village in Zhejiang Province, China, at the nexus of rural revival and lifestyle migration from the city

Source: Photo credit: Yanheng Lu

depends on and, vice versa, urban activities frequently penetrate the rural. Among theoretical provocations of this sort are Pahl's (1966) well-known notion of the rural-urban continuum and McGee's (1991) thesis on the desakota, referring to the hybridity of urban and rural functions and land uses. A more recent attempt revolves around the idea of planetary urbanisation (Brenner and Schmid, 2015), which does not see the urban in terms of a **territorial** unit or settlement type, but a pervasive, ever-emergent process without any non-urban outside. As such, *concentrated urbanisation*, which is traditionally the focus of urban geography, is co-constituted by *extended urbanisation*, in which 'places, territories and landscapes, often located far beyond the dense population centres' (Brenner and Schmid, 2015: 167) are co-opted to serve urban socio-economic dynamics. Urbanisation, therefore, is rethought as an uneven, differential process, which manifests as different sociospatial configurations across different space-times. It is reliant on a kaleidoscope of operational landscapes whose making is decentred and multi-dimensional. Of course, there is much to be criticised in the planetary urbanisation thesis. On the one hand, it seems to treat urbanisation as a homogenous process and does not sufficiently specify what urban processes are being 'planetised' in this planetary urban revolution. On the other hand, by reducing the countryside to merely the operational landscapes of urbanisation, it loses sight of the revival and celebration of rural identities and lifestyles around the world despite the expanding frontiers of cities. That said, the idea that it is now obsolete to speak of a rigid urban-rural divide warrants our serious consideration, which we revisit in the next part of the chapter.

Compared to urban and rural geographies, it is more difficult to define regional geography. The task is made more difficult given both regional and areal studies had longstanding association with Western imperialist projects to catalogue and control the '**other**' (Sidaway et al., 2016). On the one hand, however, all geographical research into a particular territorial unit can be seen as regional geography, from a local place to a **transnational** economic corridor such as the 'BE-SETO ecumenopolis' that stretches across East and Southeast Asia (Qian et al., 2021). Hence, at a general level, regional geography can be formulated, in a straightforward way, as an in-depth portrayal of a region – for example, the regional geography of China may refer to a detailed account of natural, social, economic, political, and cultural idiosyncrasies of China, taking into account its similarities with and differences from other regions in the world. At a more specific level, on the other hand, regional geography – and its close cousin regional studies – is often allied with theoretical concerns in economic geography that conceive the region, which often transgresses the urban-rural divide, as a functional unit and object of holistic economic planning and policy at a sub-national or local scale. In this line of work, the overarching question is how to achieve regional economic development vis-à-vis the competition from other regions. This question has been addressed in a long pedigree of regional development theories: from concerns with the absolute advantages and comparative advantages of regions (Adam Smith and David Ricardo); to the assumption that all regions would undergo a universal trajectory of modernisation that can be divided into a sequence of stages, eventually evening out regional disparities (Jeffrey Williamson and Walt Rostow); to the assertion that economic development actually depends on a small number of growth poles expressing the effect of cumulative causation rather than spatial convergence (Gunnar Myrdal and Albert Hirschman) which has heightened scholars' concern about persistent spatial imbalances and inequalities in economic development.

Since the 1980s and with the ascendancy of economic globalisation, the most influential theory in regional geography has questioned regional development as part of economic coordination and planning within the framework of the **nation-state**. In contrast, regional development has been both scaled up and scaled down. At a global level, economic resources and knowledge have become increasingly footloose, while regions need to sharpen a competitive edge to tap into and harness mobile resources. At a regional level, many scholars influenced by institutionalism and evolutionism in economics and Paul Krugman's New Trade Theory became interested in the positive externalities generated by traded and untraded dependencies (Storper, 1995) among firms and actors clustered in specific regional contexts, and the vibrant institutions of local learning and knowledge production based on territorially sticky interactions and 'buzz' (Storper and Venables, 2004). In sum, with the 'hollowing-out' of the nation-state, the region is no longer thought of as a clearly demarcated spatial entity with fixed resource endowments but as a relational construct at the nexus of global processes and local social, cultural, and economic institutions (Jessop, 2000; also see Chapter 20).

Summary

- Urban geography investigates sociospatial processes that contribute to the making and remaking of cities.
- Rural geography focuses on the dynamic forces that co-constitute rural places.
- The divide of urban/rural needs to be critically questioned.
- Regional geography often conceives of the region as a functional unit and object of holistic economic planning and policy at a sub-national or local scale.

Paradigmatic shifts in area geographies

All three sub-disciplines – urban, rural, and regional geographies – are highly established areas in human geography, and it is simply impossible to map the contours of their theoretical landscapes in an exhaustive manner. This section, therefore, only provides an outline of some of the most pivotal theoretical reorientations and paradigmatic shifts that have fundamentally reshaped these fields, but in doing so it will also hint at the rationales underlying the selection and organisation of chapters in the Area Geographies section.

For urban geography, a powerful and highly unsettling movement has, during the past decade, trenchantly questioned the fact that the orthodox theoretical models in urban geography and urban studies are predominantly based on Western urban contexts. When non-Western cities are brought into the purview of urban studies, they are either evaluated based on their position along spectrums of 'modern-tradition', 'development-underdevelopment', etc. (Robinson, 2004, 2006), or their compatibility with, or divergence from, Western urban paradigms (McFarlane, 2010). Western urban experiences – such as Chicago's exemplification of the era of industrialisation and Los Angeles' heralding of the advent of **postmodern** urbanism – are codified as archetypical or prototypical, with which non-Western cities (and scholars) are eventually anticipated to converge, often through the emulation of development models and policies (Brenner, 2003). As a result, the potential for taking stock of the distinctiveness, inventiveness, and creativity of urban experiences across different contexts is truncated (Robinson, 2006). In this context, urban theorists have made a vocal appeal for more truly comparative work in urban geography/studies. The starting point of this agenda is to view all cities in the world as sources of urban knowledge, and as Robinson succinctly states in *Ordinary Cities* (2006), all cities are 'dynamic and diverse, if conflicted, arenas for social and economic life' (p. 1). Comparative urbanism is passionate about, on the one hand, insights generated by comparisons between radically different, even seemingly incompatible urban contexts, and on the other hand, a thoroughly decentred and pluralised endeavour of urban theorisation, which can be initiated from anywhere (McFarlane, 2010, Robinson, 2011, 2016a). Its ultimate purpose is to foster the provincialisation of urban knowledge and the formation of an **epistemological** ecosystem in which the diversity of urban theories, each suited to particular urban contexts but not to others, is adequately appreciated (Leitner and Sheppard, 2016).

Although this does not entail discarding altogether the inventory of major concepts that we currently employ in building up urban analyses, it nonetheless means that the concepts need to be revised, enriched, and refashioned into 'a chorus of differently located meanings' (Qian and Lu, 2019: 694), in conjunction with systematic, sustained attempts at generating new concepts and theories (Robinson, 2016a, 2016b). Meanwhile, the comparative gesture refrains from seeing specific cities as 'variants' of larger processes such as globalisation and **neoliberalism**, but rather as social, economic, and political territorialisations grounded in local contexts that are nonetheless implicated in translocal connections and circulations (Robinson et al., 2022). This leads us to engage with relational comparison (Cook and Ward, 2012), or what Robinson (2016a) calls 'genetic' comparative tactics, to trace the connections between urban places and investigate how the circulations of policies, knowledge, resources, political power, etc. culminate in variegated urban outcomes. Alternatively, comparative study can be formulated in a 'generative' manner, for example, comparing between and across cases with shared features and revealing how they are derived from different constellations of situated processes, and in so doing develop new concepts and theories better suited to diverse urban contexts (Robinson, 2016a).

Similar debates can be found in rural geography – a sub-discipline that has wrestled with a functional concept of the rural and an approach that conceptualises the rural from the vantage points of cultural **representations**, identities, and lived experiences (Cloke, 2006). The former is premised on relatively fixed and clear-cut definitions of the rural to identify the extent to which specific areas can be categorised as rural. Most exemplary of this approach is the 'index of rurality' framework developed by Cloke (1977). With this approach, researchers use a combination of indicators related to population, household amenities, employment structure, commuting patterns, and distances to urban centres to calculate the varying ruralness of different places, which fall into one of five categories – extreme rural, intermediate rural, intermediate non-rural, extreme non-rural, and urban. Proponents of the second approach, in contrast, argue that framing rurality within objective indices runs the risk of positivism and neglects the socio-cultural meanings and values that people invest in rural spaces and the different ways in which people experience the rural (Cloke, 1997, 2006, Woods, 2005). Moving beyond a functional and territorial view of the rural also enables us to appreciate the non-local political and economic processes that intervene in the production of rurality, mediated by changes in meanings, identities, and experiences. For example, rural gentrification, which involves the migration of the urban middle class to rural places in the pursuit of environmental and cultural amenities, expresses the mutual translation between economic and symbolic capital and rests on notions of the idyllic rural that are not an objective given but 'constructed, negotiated, and experienced' (Bounce, 2005, Cloke, 2006: 21). Yet, the socio-cultural constructions of the rural idyll as a 'problem-free' place have a 'dark side'. Poverty, racism, homelessness, domestic violence, and hunger are all experiences that have been actively denied or simply rendered 'out of sight and out of mind' in many rural areas in the UK (Cloke, 2006), for instance. That said, changing socio-economic demography alongside growing ethnic and cultural diversity in rural areas is fragmenting any stereotype of a parochial, homogenous, and politically conservative countryside (Woods, 2018). More recently, the emphasis on cultural meanings and textual representations of rurality has been complemented by attention to the roles of **affects**, **embodiments**, material objects, and non-human organisms in the constitution of rurality, which further heightens the centrality of practice and experience in the conceptualisation of the rural (Halfacree, 2006). Within this, scholars have also developed relational understandings of rural space to analyse the ways representational, material, and lived dimensions of the rural are intertwined and constantly being re-made in hybrid and differentiated ways (see Heley and Jones, 2012). These discussions, however, are not to suggest that a functional definition of the rural is obsolete and no longer relevant. Despite political economic processes that produce and reproduce rurality at translocal, even global scales, there are still territorial units that are perceived to be more rural than others, and identities and meanings associated with the rural are not free plays at the **discursive** and **ideological** level, but at least partly tied to the material indicators such as land use, economic structures, and architectural styles. The question, rather, is how rural changes constantly problematise the narrow scope of rural worlds delimited by functional definitions, especially when it comes to dividing urban-rural. For one thing, rural transformations reveal the diverse ways in which rural areas become integral to the agenda of planetary urbanisation: not only is the rural addressing cultural malaise and **alienation** that have their roots in urbanisation (such as the counter-urbanising movements of rural gentrifiers seeking spiritual solace in rural areas) but also is becoming a new frontier of urban investment and capital. In addition to the urbanisation of the rural, the ruralisation of the urban is no less salient (Gillen et al., 2022) – for example, in China and Southeast Asia, many peri-urban villages are now engulfed by urbanising land use and exist in the interstices of large urban developments. They not only provide alternative bases of livelihoods and subsistence for people navigating the urban-rural interfaces (Kusno, 2019) but also embody people's continued attachment to the lifestyles, identities, and communal relations that are known or reputed as 'rural'. In this vein, the rural powerfully disrupts the ontological purity of the urban as we know it.

Although urban and rural geographies address different theoretical questions and empirical concerns, their explicit engagement with a relational perspective and a constructionist view of territoriality and settlement types is applicable to regional geography. The former emphasises that any locality is produced at the nexus of local processes and translocal linkages, while the latter asserts that a place's ontological properties are not fixed, but overdetermined by a wealth of discursive, economic, social, and political forces. In regional geography, the shift to this paradigm has been encapsulated by the term 'new regionalism' (see Chapter 20). The concept has predominantly been used by economic geographers studying the erosion of the nation-state as the principal regulator of economic development and the rediscovery of regions as drivers of economic growth in a competitive global economy. Overall, new regionalism is writ large in two theoretical reorientations.

On the one hand, regional identity is no longer seen as an a priori and primordial existence, but as a social construct borne out of specific practices and **discourses** that make a region intelligible and meaningful. The production of dominant narratives about regional identity is embedded in 'a wider network of cultural, political and economic processes and of divisions of labour' (Paasi, 2002: 804) and serves particular interests and power relations. Scholars, hence, must move beyond the 'objectivity' of regions and think of them as institutionalised entities that result from 'a perpetual struggle over the meanings' attached to specific territorial units (ibid: 805). The discursively inflected and contested nature of **regionalisation** is played out, for example, in the popularisation of cross-border regions as an economic strategy pursued by many state agencies (Perkmann and Sum, 2002). Cross-border regions refer to a unique form of economic collaboration that coordinates activities at different sides of state borders to foster an articulation among unevenly distributed comparative advantages and thus cultivate new frontiers of economic growth. While the relative advantages and resource endowments of each side of the border appear to be objective and given (for instance, in the Singapore-Malaysia-Indonesia Growth Triangle, Singapore is rich in capital and knowledge, while Malaysia and Indonesia have ample supply of land and labour; see, Sparke et al., 2004), in fact, discursive constructions and complex policy practices need to be invested to channel heterogeneous local histories and social relations into a unified vision of a regional future, so as to reimagine the region as an internally coherent unit for the implementation of economic strategies. At the Chinese-Burmese border, for example, the Chinese state is passionate about pursuing cross-border economic integration with Myanmar. To achieve this, it actively propagates a discourse about the long-term cultural affinity between the Chinese and Burmese people, while consigning into invisibility a long history of local political conflicts, including China's support of the Burmese Communist Party in the 1960s and 1970s. Besides, the Chinese state has made a lot of efforts to relocate manufacturing activities from the inland of China to the border city of Ruili to fulfil the vision of Myanmar and other Southeast Asian countries as markets in the making for Chinese industrial products (Qian and Tang, 2019).

On the other hand, as the imperative of economic development has been rescaled from the nation-state to the regional level, regional development is increasingly contingent on the relativisation of scale (Jessop, 2002). With the deepening of globalisation, nation-states have gradually lost the ability to manage economic planning and coordination within their boundaries and thus surrendered their superior position in shaping the structural coherence of economies (Jessop, 2000). In the meantime, 'the territoriality of globalization leads capital, people, institutions and technologies to be ever more intensely motivated by and stimulated through localised geographical agglomeration and spatial clustering' (MacLeod, 2001: 804–805). Indeed, the growing importance of spatial agglomerations in a small number of 'growth pole' regions heightens the question of where and how to cultivate these regions, as a key component of the state's accumulation strategies – what Jessop (1990) has called the strategic selectivity of the state. In tandem with this trend, state functions and capacities have also been reorganised and rescaled. The mission to foster flexibility, competitiveness, and a favourable business climate has been largely delegated to the local state in many countries. A key lens into this restructuring concerns institutional building and governance capacity at the scale of the local state, although local socio-political infrastructure continues to be shaped by the interests and priorities of the national state.

More broadly, recent work has sought to reflect on what regions are and their relevance for cultural, social, and political life. While theorising the **social construction** of regions, distinction can be made between a top-down view – such as the construction of regional identity for the implementation of economic strategies – and a bottom-up one. The latter refers to the ways in which a regional space is lived and experienced, serving as the organising framework of daily livelihoods and social relations. These regions – such as the Zomia and South Asia massif – are based on Indigenous cultural knowledge and transgress institutionalised boundaries, whether internal or international (Chapter 21). Alternatively, James Riding's (2018) account of the *Plenum Movement*, a radical experiment in non-institutional politics and horizontal democracy in post-conflict Bosnia, also illustrates the value of rethinking the assumptions of regional geography:

> alternative geographical writing of nascent socio-political movements is possible, which considers regions and their everyday processes and affects and the embodied practice of citizen-activists in regional landscapes. Through this alternative regional landscape geography an emancipatory struggle is physically placed in the region from which it emerged and a radical fracturing of space is represented on-the-ground. *pp. 22–23*

Summary

- Urban geography is subject to the influence of comparative urbanism.
- Rural geography has oscillated between a functional concept of the rural and various relational approaches that conceptualise the rural as a product of representational, material and lived processes that combine in hybrid and differentiated ways.
- Regional geography draws on relational and constructionist perspectives to understand the representational and scalar processes underlying regionalisation vis-a-vis the imperative of cultivating regional competitiveness.

Engaging area geographies: a journey into the section

Collectively, the seven chapters in the Area Geographies section provide a general outline of the key theoretical and conceptual developments in urban, rural, and regional geographies. As you can see from the three duoes of chapters – urban theory and comparative urbanism, ruralities and comparative ruralities, regions and lived regions – a comparative gesture and an urge to provincialise and decolonise knowledge production currently dominated by the West runs throughout this section. In Chapter 15 on urban theory, Regan Koch adroitly traces the intellectual trajectory of theoretical developments in urban geography, from Chicago School theories on industrial cities to neo-Marxist critiques of capitalism and social injustices in the city, to new research paradigms such as global cities and the focus on lived experiences, cultures, and differences, and finally, to the enthusiasm around comparative urbanism, global urbanism, and Southern cities. Special caution, however, is needed for the fact that these theories are almost all intrinsically 'Western' and based on the evolution of urban experiences in the West. Indeed, Ben Derudder's Chapter 16 on global cities and global urban networks notes the prominence of

Global and World Cities (GaWC) research in contemporary urban studies which can nonetheless be criticised as a dominantly and **hegemonically** Western enterprise. Yet, the theoretical value of this enterprise, and the fact that it has served as the backbone of so many urban analyses, is undisputable, because it vividly exemplifies the spatial logics of economic development that we mentioned earlier – as economic flows and connections are increasingly globalised, corporate branches that exert control over such flows tend to be concentrated in a select number of cities as the primary hubs and nodes in global economic networks. This thesis, undoubtedly, faces the risk of enshrining a singular, **teleological** model of urban development and implying that all cities should strive towards the global city status in order to be successful. Indeed, as Derudder reflects in his chapter, GaWC researchers are well aware of such critiques. Instead of dismissing any specific theoretical approach, it is more productive, as Koch points out in his chapter, to take more seriously the plurality of approaches and concepts, recognising that all theories are minor theories that explain certain aspects of urban processes but not others.

This is why the section includes a chapter that specifically addresses comparative urbanism. In Chapter 17, Jennifer Robinson suggests that comparison can be developed by tracing circulations among cities – be they financial practices, material resources, or mobile policies; alternatively, we can start from comparable phenomena located in different contexts or different cases that speak to similar theoretical questions, and reveal how they are contingent on situated factors and contexts, and how the same causal mechanisms operate through different processes and practices.

These three chapters on urban geographies are followed by two chapters on rural geographies. Menelaos Gkartzios' Chapter 18 on rurality points out the ambiguity and difficulty around defining rurality in functional terms, and unsurprisingly, scholars have turned towards an approach centred on representation, discourse, and lived experience, with questions of **power** and different claims to rurality underpinning much of the debate. The departure from any fixed definition of rurality also makes room to reconceptualise rurality in relational terms, for example, through the lens of mobility and extra-local connections. Ultimately, the definition of rurality is also closely tied to the politics of language, as vocabularies that describe rural experiences and places vary across different languages, contexts, and social groups. In response to this, this section deliberately includes Chapter 19 on 'comparative ruralities'. Comparative rural studies are not as established as their urban counterparts. Still, Li Yurui's chapter points out a series of issues that are central to rural communities in the Global South, or Majority World, but may not be equally salient in Western academic discourses – the survivability of smallholder agricultural production, the integration of poor rural peripheries into large-scale commercial agriculture, the ensuring environmental risks, and the political ramifications of neoliberal restructuring.

This section ends with two chapters on regions. Enrico Gualini's Chapter 20 offers a detailed elaboration on the rise of new regionalism in the **post-Fordist** global economy, and its challenge to the traditional principles of territorial governance based on the dominant role of the nation-state and administratively demarcated boundaries of regions. However, although the corpus of new regionalism has clearly articulated a view on the **socially constructed** nature of regions, the application of the thesis to empirical research is largely lopsided towards policy experiments geared towards regional economic growth. As such, these works largely conceal the situated and lived sense of region that people across many different contexts and cultures adhere to. The organising logic of those regions is not necessarily economic growth, but an Indigenous system of livelihoods and cosmological knowledge. In tandem with this, Andrew McGregor signposts a research agenda on the 'lived region', a term referring to those regions that 'emerge from the practices, beliefs, experiences, ecologies and relationships of people in places' (see Chapter 21). In contrast to world regions delineated by geopolitical interests and administrative regions whose boundaries are institutionalised by the state, lived regions express the cultural identities and symbolic meanings that people attach to territorial entities and/or their multi-faceted relationships with their biophysical milieus.

Discussion points

- Can you think of examples that illustrate the increasing blurring of the urban/rural divide?
- Why is it so important to adopt a comparative lens in the study of cities, rural places, and regions?
- Can you name examples that testify to regionalisation as a relational process and a social construction?
- What is the value, and the social, cultural, and political implications, of thinking about regions from a bottom-up perspective as opposed to a narrow focus on regional competitiveness and economic growth?

References

Bounce, M. (2005). *The Countryside Ideal*. London: Routledge.

Brenner, N. (2003). Stereotypes, archetypes, and prototypes: three uses of superlatives in contemporary urban studies. *City* 2(3): 205–216.

Brenner, N., and Schmid, C. (2015). Towards a new epistemology of the urban? *City* 19(2–3): 151–182.

Cloke, P. (1977). An index of rurality for England and Wales. *Regional Studies* 11(1): 31–46.

Cloke, P. (1997). Country backwater to virtual village? Rural studies and 'the cultural turn'. *Journal of Rural Studies* 13(4): 367–375.

Cloke, P. (2006). Conceptualizing Rurality. In *The Handbook of Rural Studies*, eds. P. Cloke, T. Marsden, and P. Mooney. London: Sage, 18–28.

Cheskin, A., and Jašina-Schäfer, A. (2022). Relational area studies: Russia and geographies of knowledge. *Transactions of the Institute of British Geographers* 47, 1044–1057.

Cook, I., and Ward, K. (2012). Relational comparisons: the assembling of Cleveland's waterfront plan. *Urban Geography* 33(6): 774–795.

Gillen, J., Bunnell, T., and Rigg, J. (2022). Geographies of ruralization. *Dialogues in Human Geography* 12(2): 186–203.

Halfacree, K. (2006). Rural Space: Constructing a Three-Fold Architecture. In *The Handbook of Rural Studies*, eds. P. Cloke, T. Marsden, and P. Mooney. London: Sage, 44–62.

Hall, T., and Barrett, H. (2015). *Urban Geography* (5th edn.). London: Routledge.

Heley, J., and Jones, L. (2012). Relational rurals: Some thoughts on relating things and theory in rural studies. *Journal of Rural Studies* 28(3), 208–217.

Jessop, B. (1990). *State Theory: Putting the Capitalist State in Its Place*. London: Polity.

Jessop, B. (2000). The crisis of the national spatio-temporal fix and the tendential ecological dominance of globalizing capitalism. *International Journal of Urban and Regional Research* 24(2): 323–360.

Jessop, B. (2002). The Political Economy of Scale. In *Globalization, Regionalization and Cross-Border Regions*, eds. M. Perkmann and N. Sum. London: Palgrave Macmillan, 25–49.

Jonas, A., McCann, E., and Thomas, M. (2015). *Urban Geography: A Critical Introduction*. Oxford: Wiley Blackwell.

Kusno, A. (2019). Provisional Notes on Semi-Urbanism. In *Routledge Handbook of Urbanization in Southeast Asia*, ed. R. Padawangi. London: Routledge, 75–89.

Leitner, H., and Sheppard, E. (2016). Provincializing critical urban theory: extending the ecosystem of possibilities. *International Journal of Urban and Regional Research* 40(1): 228–235.

MacLeod, G. (2001). New regionalism reconsidered: globalization and the remaking of political economic space. *International Journal of Urban and Regional Research* 25(4): 804–829.

McFarlane, C. (2010). The comparative city: knowledge, learning, urbanism. *International Journal of Urban and Regional Research* 34(4): 725–742.

McGee, T. (1991). The Emergence of Desakota Regions in Asia: Expanding a Hypothesis. In *The Extended Metropolis: Settlement Transition in Asia*, eds. N. Ginsburg, B. Koppel, and T. McGee. Hawaii: University of Hawaii Press, 3–25.

Paasi, A. (2002). Place and region: regional worlds and words. *Progress in Human Geography* 26(6): 802–811.

Perkmann, M., and Sum, N. (2002). Globalization, Regionalization and Cross-Border Regions: Scales, Discourses and Governance. In *Globalization, Regionalization and Cross-Border Regions*, eds. M. Perkmann and N. Sum. London: Palgrave Macmillan, 3–21.

Pahl, R. E. (1966). The rural-urban continuum. *Sociologia Ruralis* 6(3–4): 299–329.

Qian, J., Ling, J., and He, S. (2021). Making Cities and Regions in Globalizing East Asia. In *Companion to Urban and Regional Studies*, eds. A. Orum, J. Ruiz-Tagle, and V. Haddock. Chichester: Wiley Blackwell, 21–42.

Qian, J., and Lu, Y. (2019). On the trail of comparative urbanism: square dance and public space in China. *Transactions of the Institute of British Geographers* 44(4): 692–706.

Qian, J., and Tang, X. (2019). Theorising small city as ordinary city: rethinking development and urbanism from China's southwest frontier. *Urban Studies* 56(6): 1215–1233.

Riding, J. (2018). A new regional geography of a revolution: Bosnia's Plenum movement. *Territory, Politics, Governance* 6(1):16–41. https://doi.org/10.1080/21622671.2016.1260491

Robinson, J. (2004). In the tracks of comparative urbanism: difference, urban modernity and the primitive. *Urban Geography* 25(8): 709–723.

Robinson, J. (2006). *Ordinary Cities: Between Modernity and Development*. London: Routledge.

Robinson, J. (2011). Cities in a world of cities: the comparative gesture. *International Journal of Urban and Regional Research* 35(1): 1–23.

Robinson, J. (2016a). Thinking cities through elsewhere: comparative tactics for a more global urban studies. *Progress in Human Geography* 40(1): 3–29.

Robinson, J. (2016b). Comparative urbanism: new geographies and cultures of theorizing the urban. *International Journal of Urban and Regional Research* 40(1): 187–199.

Robinson, J., Wu, F., Harrison, P., and Wang, Z. (2022). Beyond variegation: the territorialisation of states, communities and developers in large-scale developments in Johannesburg, Shanghai and London. *Urban Studies* 59(8): 1715–1740.

Scott, A., and Storper, M. (2015). The nature of cities: the scope and limits of urban theory. *International Journal of Urban and Regional Research* 39(1): 1–15.

Sidaway, J. D., Ho, E. L., Rigg, J. D., and Woon, C. Y. (2016). Area studies and geography: trajectories and manifesto. *Environment and Planning D: Society and Space* 34(5): 777–790.

Sparke, M., Sidaway, J., Bunnell, T., and Grundy-Warr, C. (2004). Triangulating the borderless world: geographies of power in the Indonesia-Malaysia–Singapore Growth Triangle. *Transactions of the Institute of British Geographers* 29(4): 485–498.

Storper, M. (1995). The resurgence of regional economies, ten years later: the region as a nexus of untraded interdependencies. *European Urban and Regional Studies* 2(3): 191–221.

Storper, M., and Venables, A. J. (2004). Buzz: face-to-face contact and the urban economy. *Journal of Economic Geography* 4(4): 351–370.

Williams, R. (1973). *The Country and the City*. Oxford: Oxford University Press.

Woods, M. (2005). *Rural Geography: Processes, Responses and Experiences in Rural Restructuring*. London: Sage.

Woods, M. (2007). Engaging the global countryside: globalization, hybridity and the reconstitution of rural place. *Progress in Human Geography* 31(4): 485–507.

Woods, M. (2018). Precarious rural cosmopolitanism: negotiating globalization, migration and diversity in Irish small towns. *Journal of Rural Studies* 64: 164–176.

Yarwood, R. (2023). *Rural Geographies: People, Place and the Countryside*. London: Routledge.

Online materials

- Key journals in urban geography:
  Urban Geography: https://www.tandfonline.com/journals/rurb20
  Urban Studies: https://journals.sagepub.com/home/usj
  International Journal of Urban and Regional Research: https://onlinelibrary.wiley.com/journal/14682427
- Key journals in rural geography:
  Journal of Rural Studies: https://www.sciencedirect.com/journal/journal-of-rural-studies
  Sociologia Ruralis: https://onlinelibrary.wiley.com/journal/14679523
- Key journals in regional geography and regional studies:
  Regional Studies: https://www.tandfonline.com/journals/cres20
  Territory, Politics, and Governance: https://www.tandfonline.com/journals/rtep20

Further reading

Harding, A., and Blokland, T. (2014). *Urban Theory: A Critical Introduction to Power, Cities, and Urbanism in the 21st Century*. London: Sage.
A comprehensive introduction to different schools of urban theory.

Cloke, P., Marsden, T., and Mooney, P. (2006). *Handbook of Rural Studies*. London: Sage.
One of the most used reference books in rural geography and rural studies.

Börzel, T. A., and Risse, T. (2016). *The Oxford Handbook of Comparative Regionalism*. Oxford: Oxford University Press.
An edited volume that uses a comparative perspective to understand processes of regionalisation across the world.

15 Urban theory

Regan Koch

Introduction

Cities began to emerge around 10,000 years ago, pulling together people, goods, technologies and nature into concentrated locations. As sites of interaction and exchange, they were places where innovation flourished in response to human needs and desires. The longevity and durability of cities required the development of new systems for trade, administration, building and **infrastructure**. Successful urban settlements amassed great wealth and population. They became centres of political, economic, cultural and military power, further intensifying their productive capacities and reach. Urbanisation progressed in various regions of the world for millennia, albeit in a non-linear fashion – some cities grew, while others died out. In the late 18th and 19th centuries, however, urbanisation really took off. Driven by and central to the accelerating forces of industrial **capitalism**, cities exploded in number, population and size. They became key nodes in far-reaching processes of modernisation, **colonisation** and **globalisation**. Cities also became increasingly complex built environments, thick with institutions and practices for organising social and economic activity – divisions of labour and specialisation, laws and regulation, architectures, systems of care, education, policing and transportation, just to name just a few. City living fostered new and hybrid cultures that deeply unsettled more traditional ways of life. Urbanisation raised questions about society and the future of the planet that scholars are still grappling with today.

Urban theory refers to a collection of ideas and concepts for understanding cities and processes of urbanisation. Its origins can be traced to those dramatically expanding industrial cities of Europe and North America in the late 18th and 19th centuries, notably Berlin, Manchester, London, Paris, New York and especially Chicago, home to the first 'School' of urban sociology. Intellectuals at this time were becoming broadly concerned with '**modernity**' as a new era in human history; an emergent political, economic and cultural formation centred in cities and requiring new forms of enquiry in the 'social sciences'. Urban theory developed as scholars sought to explain why cities held such gravitational pull, and how the **agglomeration** of economic and social activities generated such powerful effects. Foremost, however, scholars sought to define and interpret the impacts of modern urban life on society. How do conditions of density, intensity and diversity impact human relationships? How do cities affect the way people behave, encouraging cooperation or conflict? They also questioned why some cities succeed, while others fail. Theories of urbanisation emerged as a varied set of approaches to these questions, and they were given urgency by the striking contrasts of wealth and poverty, opportunity and hardship that could be found in cities. Answers were developed through field studies, descriptive accounts, theoretical explanations, diagrams, categorical schema, concepts and experiments

DOI: 10.4324/9780429265853-19

Figure 15.1
Aerial view of Taipei, Taiwan

Source: Photo credit: Kanghee Han from Pixabay

with quantitative and qualitative research methods. These were often directed towards inner-city reformers, planners and policy makers concerned with social disorder and improving the welfare and material conditions of cities. The foundational ideas and approaches of urban theory were taught to generations of students and practitioners, and these ideas continue to hold a remarkable influence on how cities and urbanisation are understood today (Figure 15.1).

Today it is often said that the planet has fully entered an 'urban age' given the extraordinary concentration of population, economic productivity and wealth in urban environments. Cities spill beyond any historic walls or boundaries into networks of urban centres and peripheries, suburbs, exurbs and corridors that are home to roughly 70% of the world's population. Urban areas offer better standards of living for more people than at any point in history, and even the poorest urban residents have higher living standards than those in many rural areas. Cities and urban regions continue to be primary centres of economic, technological, and social innovation, although the astounding growth in their size and number has shifted substantially to the mega-cities and conurbations in East Asia and the Global South. There are intense concentrations of poverty, inadequate and unaffordable housing, insufficient access to basic life necessities, ethnic conflicts, social isolation, violence, crime and other social problems. Beyond the social benefits and deficits found in cities, climate change and other ecological problems are driven by the resource demands of urbanisation as developments sprawl onto ever more land, making them susceptible to shortages and climate-related disasters. Worldwide, there is unprecedented displacement of individuals and communities, resulting in global migration. The urgency of urban problems has been met with a proliferation of academic and policy-related research. Urban studies span the disciplines of sociology, geography, economics, anthropology, political science, history and more. Urban analysis also extends beyond the social sciences to include planning, design and policy studies, architecture and varied engagements with the arts and humanities, NGOs and activist groups.

Far from being a unified field, contemporary urban theory is best understood as a loose collection of intellectual resources – ideas, concepts, methods and key thinkers – that help to frame discussion and research. It has become avowedly critical in nature and is marked by many active debates, primarily centred on identifying and addressing the manifold social, economic and environmental inequalities prevalent in cities. Some see urban theory as offering generalisable ideas and concepts that can be readily put to work in making sense of life in cities and the expanding pace of urbanisation, albeit with the need for ongoing revisions to its perspectives, methods and areas of focus. Others have argued that imaginations rooted in twentieth-century ideas are inadequate, and that urban theory needs a radical rethinking. And finally, there are many who are sceptical of urban theory altogether, viewing it as a primarily intellectual pursuit removed from actual problems cities and their inhabitants face. This chapter combines these perspectives, sketching out some contours of urban theory as follows: an imaginative set of ideas and approaches for understanding cities and processes of urbanisation; a site of ongoing debate and critical re-assessment of the knowledge politics of urban studies; and a mode of thinking that tends to privilege theorisation, but which nonetheless can be oriented towards practical engagements with the challenges and potentials of cities and an increasingly urbanised world.

Summary

- Cities began to emerge around 10,000 years ago, bringing humans, things and technology into concentrated locations. They become centres of great wealth and power with influence that stretched far beyond their borders.
- Urbanisation greatly accelerated with the rise of industrial capitalism in the late 18th and 19th centuries. Cities grew vastly in number, population and overall size.
- It is often said that today we live in 'urban age', with more than 70% of the population now living in urban environments that include cities, but also sprawling suburbs, exurbs and satellite cities. Whereas modern industrial cities first concentrated in Europe and North America, urbanisation is now happening most rapidly in the mega-cities and conurbations of Asia and the Global South.
- Urban theory is a collection of tools for describing, explaining and further researching the power of cities and urbanisation as a social and economic force.

Urban imaginations and ongoing debates

Moral and cultural concerns about life in early industrial cities was a starting point for urban theory. Rapid urbanisation brought with it a profound sense of unsettling to many of the norms and routines of rural and village life. Cities of the late 18th and 19th centuries were also marked by social problems ranging from poor health and disease to congestion and crime, poverty and homelessness. Sociologists at the time, including Ferdinand Tönnies and Emile Durkheim, worried that the bonds of community and social cohesion were being eroded by conditions of density and diversity, as well as the pace of city life. The individualistic, impersonal nature of cities, they argued, was further compounded by the rise of city-states and market economies that increasingly replaced more traditional, collective forms of solidarity through which human needs were met. Fredrich Engels highlighted the dehumanising treatment and brutal conditions workers faced in industrial cities, exploited by capitalists who were physically close but morally distant. Georg Simmel (1903) influentially described the psychological effects of life among strangers whereby urban inhabitants developed cold, calculating rationalities and 'blasé attitudes' as relations between people became akin to financial transactions. Yet Simmel also argued that urban environments brought greater personal freedom, allowing people to cultivate the parts of them that traditional communities suppressed, thus making cities nodes of creativity and innovation.

The idea of cities as ecosystems with distinctive socio-cultural dynamics was further developed by the Chicago School of Urban Sociology. Founders Robert Park and Ernest Burgess (1925) imagined the city as a 'laboratory' for examining how humans adapted to new urban social and spatial conditions (Figure 15.2). Observation and **ethnographic** fieldwork were established as part of the methodological repertoire for analysing the distinctive 'social types' and 'sub-cultures'

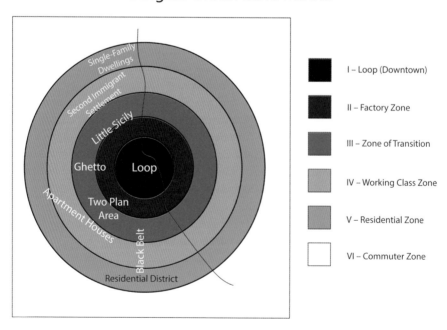

Figure 15.2
Burgess' concentric zone model of urban land use

Source: Figure credit: Nick Brennan

that emerge in cities. In early twentieth-century Chicago, this included studies of immigrant communities, political parties, the homeless, gangs, sex workers, taxi drivers, jazz musicians, and ethnic and racial **ghettos**. Among their contributions to urban theory is an understanding of cities as mosaics of socially differentiated neighbourhoods caught up in dynamics of ecological succession, with waves of change producing new forms of order and disorder, social norms and deviant behaviour. However, the School's most enduring legacy has been their representations of cities in the form of models and diagrams that sought to explain patterns of land use, phases of resident occupation, social segregation and zones of socio-economic transition. Most famous among these are Burgess' concentric zone model and Hoyt's sector model which are still frequently taught in universities today, albeit primarily as examples of oversimplification in trying to understand the complexities of urban environments.

Geographers became more focused on cities in the years following World War II, first by applying and then further advancing the styles of modelling and measurement initiated by the Chicago School. In contrast to sociological approaches, their initial aim was to establish a rigorous **spatial science** that harnessed new technologies of quantification, computing and mapping. The focus of urban theory in this case was the development of hypotheses that could be tested and verified in ways akin to the physical sciences. Urban geography was thus seen as 'useful' to the extent that it could accurately represent cities and predict their future via patterns of residential migration, settlement, land use and land value. Claims to objectivity and scientific rigour gave credibility to urban research that was readily adapted into planning and policymaking. Urban development projects became more ambitious in scope and scale, emboldened by the idea the complexity of cities could be accurately quantified.

By the 1960s, however, efforts to calculate and control urban processes started to come under critical scrutiny. Inner-city neighbourhoods and communities were being demolished in the spirit of rational planning for modernisation and growth via large-scale developments, infrastructure projects and new highways and tunnels leading to suburban neighbourhoods. Citizen-activist Jane Jacobs (1961) famously critiqued 'top-down' planning models for failing to understand the kind of complex problems cities present. She saw the diversity of city life as fundamental to economic growth and social wellbeing. Jacobs championed streets and sidewalks as the 'lifeblood' of cities; their regular use enabled people to feel safe to conduct their daily lives under the natural surveillance provided by a diversity of 'eyes on the street'. Around the same time, planning scholars such as Kevin Lynch (1960) brought renewed attention to the lived experience of cities, developing research into how humans think, feel and behave in urban environments by introducing methods such as mental maps, questionnaire surveys and photographic documentation to inform architecture and urban design.

A more radical shift in urban theory came in the late 1960s and 1970s from scholars determined to outline the fundamental structures of urban society and **space**. This was given urgency by the rise of social movements demanding improved civil rights, decolonialisation and environmental protection. Manuel Castells (1977) for example critiqued the Chicago School, quantitative geography and mainstream sociology for failing to recognise the dominance of capitalism as the driving force in urbanisation processes. Likewise, sociologist-philosopher Henri Lefebvre and geographers including David Harvey and Milton Santos led a critical turn in urban thinking that re-imagined cities as sites of **class** struggle in which land and property markets served as crucial mechanisms for the accumulation of wealth. New theories of 'the urban' sought to dismantle older orthodoxies in favour of avowedly critical frameworks rooted in **Marxist** thought.

Urban theory underwent a shift in focus from the social-cultural dynamics of cities towards an emphasis on their **political economy** and patterns of inequality and **uneven development**. These changes also brought more attention to urban political movements and the struggles of marginalised groups to claim urban space, resources and citizenship rights. Highly influential in this regard was Lefebvre's (1968) notion of 'the right to the city', an aspiration and slogan taken up by activists, grassroots organisations and researchers in their efforts to counter urban injustice and reclaim the city as a collective project.

Critical perspectives on urbanisation developed in parallel with periods of de-industrialisation in the 1970s and 1980s that led to high levels of unemployment, poverty, urban decay and civil unrest. Urban thinking rooted in political economy approaches gained influence as they helped to explain inherent fluctuations in capitalism that lead to cycles of overaccumulation, depression and '**creative destruction**'. These perspectives also helped to make sense of 'post-industrial urbanisation' as it unfolded in the decades that followed. Many cities became defined by increasing globalisation, new flows of human and financial capital and the growth of large multinational corporations. Scholars such as Saskia Sassen (2002) theorised the rise of a new international system based on hierarchies of 'city-regions' through which places like New York, London and Tokyo served as 'command and control centers' of a new global economy. Economic restructuring paralleled political changes in favour of market-driven, **neoliberal** policymaking that included governmental deregulation, cuts to social welfare spending, and public-private urban development projects. The impacts of these changes on city life came firmly into urban theory through a critical focus on the dynamics of urban regeneration and displacement. Processes of **gentrification** – first conceptualised by Ruth Glass (1964) in London – became widely observed in cities around the world. Geographers such as Mike Davis (1990) and Neil Smith (1996) developed powerful, widely read critiques of new urban developments in their analysis of how working class and racialised groups are spatially sorted and segregated in cities.

In the last decade of the twentieth century and well into the twenty-first, urban theory further developed through engagements with post-structuralist thinking. To some extent, this was led by a dissatisfaction with the dogmas of Marxism that privileged structure over **agency**. Geographers such as Nigel Thrift argued that structural accounts of capitalist urbanisation stripped cities bare of lived experience and cultural difference. There became a growing interest in expanding lines of enquiry and critique to bring about social and political change. **Feminist** scholars including Doreen Massey (1994) established analytical frameworks focusing on the **gendered** dimensions of urban life and the ways that cities and suburbs hardened and reproduced inequalities. Others revitalised longstanding concerns with **race** and **ethnicity** in cities, developing **intersectional** perspectives that were expanded to include class, sexuality, (dis)ability and age. Urban theory was in some cases tied to critical pedagogy as scholar-activists sought to challenge existing power structures 'from below' through engagements with marginalised and Indigenous groups. At the same time, efforts to rethink **power** in more dynamic terms – as not only vertical but also horizontal or rhizomatic – led to engagements with theorists such as Giles Deleuze and Felix Guattari, as well as **Actor-Network Theory** popularised by Bruno Latour. Renewed attention was thus given to non-humans, objects, nature, technologies and the diverse materialities and immaterialities that constitute urban experience (cf Amin and Thrift, 2002). Urban studies became re-animated by a range of descriptive accounts detailing the '**assemblage**' of urban life, depicting cities as never entirely static but rather open to possibility and surprise. These changes

Figure 15.3
Aerial view of Dhaka, Bangladesh

Source: Photo credit: M Rahman/Alamy

in approach have been met with scepticism by defenders of political economy who worry that in moving away from more structural, systematic analyses of urbanisation, urban theory is being stripped of its critical purchase.

Further developments in urban theory have come from **postcolonial** perspectives and their critiques of the **hegemony** of Western geographical imaginations. Their arguments have exposed blind spots in theoretical analysis and the perpetuation of developmentalist ideas about cities of the Global South (Figure 15.3). A compelling case has been made by geographers such as AbdouMaliq Simone (2004) and Ananya Roy (2009) who argue the need to produce new ideas and concepts rooted in the experiences and dynamics of a much wider range of urban environments. Relatedly, there have also been calls for more comparative forms of urban studies (Robinson, 2011) that view all cities as 'ordinary' and see differences between them as a source of insight and theory building (see Chapter 17). Urban theory has embraced relational perspectives that incorporate the mobility of people, policies, capital and more moving between cities as part of the distributed networks of power that shape how urban spaces are produced. Theorists of 'planetary urbanisation' (see Brenner, 2014) take the un-bounded nature of cities further, high-lighting how in the twenty-first century, distinctions between the urban and everything else have been blurred. The term 'city', they argue, only exists as an **ideological** framing that obscures the integrated, capitalist socio-economic networks shaping environments around the globe. Other scholars push back, emphasising that cities remain legible social-spatial formations comprising places such as downtown neighbourhoods, central business districts, industrial quarters, suburbs and so on (Storper and Scott, 2016). Cities continue to hold symbolic and analytic importance because they raise scale-specific questions of scientific, administrative and political importance. Still, others have called for a wholesale re-theorisation of the city, arguing that twentieth-century grammars of abstraction, modelling and grand theorisation fall woefully short of encapsulating and addressing the complexity of contemporary urban environments and processes.

Summary

- Theories of urbanisation can be traced to modern industrial cities where the apparent decline of community life and rise of social problems raised new questions about the social and moral effects of urbanisation on human society.
- Understanding cities as distinctive social-cultural ecosystems is a foundational idea in urban theory developed by the Chicago School of Urban Sociology. Its scholars pioneered the use of ethnographic fieldwork to understand diverse social groups and institutions. They also produced a range of highly influential diagrams and models that sought to explain patterns of urban change.
- Post-World War II geographers attempted to bring objectivity and scientific rigour to the study of cities by using computational methods and modelling to map and predict urban processes. Although widely adopted by planners and policy makers, they were also critiqued by activists and scholars for failing to truly understand and value the complexities and lived experiences of urban environments.
- Influenced by Marxism and focused on the political economy of urbanisation, urban theory developed more critical perspectives on capitalist urbanisation that emphasise structural dynamics, injustices and inequalities.
- Theories of cities and urbanisation have been further refined in response to global economic restructuring, changes in urban and national government and new forms of cultural politics and social theory – particularly post-structural theories, including feminism and postcolonialism. Urban theory today is a site of continuous debate over how cities should be understood and imagined.

Putting urban theory to work

The proliferation of ideas and debates about urbanisation has opened the study of cities to an extraordinarily wide range of topics and approaches. Research now includes a host of qualitative and quantitative methods, carried out in and between urban areas of varying sizes and geographical locations. Many, but certainly not all, of the conceptual and methodological approaches that shape such research are informed by urban theory. Yet the field is often characterised by highly specialised language and increasingly complex dialogue. This can be off-putting to some scholars and overwhelming for those new to urban research. Far too diverse in scope and detail to encapsulate in a brief entry, three areas of discussion give a sense of some of what currently animates the field. Drawing from these, the chapter concludes with some suggestions for engaging further with theories of cities and urban life.

First, there are continued debates about the origins and scope of urban theory. North American and European cities, and ideas formed by observing them, continue to be at the centre of many urban imaginations. However, postcolonial scholars have been resoundingly effective in calling for more **cosmopolitan** forms of theory that treat all cities as potential sources for developing enquiry as well as testing and revising concepts. Much new writing suggests that only the surface has been scratched in terms of the diversity of urban experiences around the world. More difficult questions abound regarding whether all cities should be understood in terms of their unique particularities, or whether such parochialism undermines efforts to develop more systematic explanations and theorisations of urbanisation processes. The disciplinary centre of gravity in urban research has also been dispersed well beyond geography, sociology and urban planning. Thinking and research on cities now incorporates an even broader set of fields spanning the natural and environmental sciences, engineering and design, arts and humanities, and medical sciences – although it remains to be seen how these fields will influence urban theory.

Second, some scholars see the plurality of approaches and concepts in urban studies as a problem of incoherence. The lack of a unified urban theory is viewed as a weakness by those who insist that urbanisation needs to be distinguished from other social processes – not everything that takes place in cities is necessarily a matter of urbanisation. Drawing out key features such as agglomeration and density, it is argued, enables a shared vocabulary for research dialogue and helps to better target policy interventions. Others are sceptical about the extent to which urban research can or should try to identify and agree upon essential characteristics of 'the urban' that are generalisable to a world of cities. Most at the forefront of urban theory resist any kind of one-model-fits-all style of theorising. Instead, they insist on the partiality of knowledge and embrace experimentalism and plurality, holding open space to approach cities from a range of perspectives. Running parallel to these debates are new forms of spatial science that draw on complexity theory, computational modelling and the tools of '**big data**' to illuminate fundamental features and processes of urbanisation (see Chapter 66). While ostensibly avoiding pitfalls of earlier generations, such approaches are often dismissed by critical urban scholars for eliding the complexities of lived experience.

Third, then, there are continued debates over how best to grasp the materialities of urban life. Tensions still exist between approaches rooted in qualitative versus quantitative research. There are also longstanding rifts between those committed to Marxist political economy and political ecology as opposed to post-structural perspectives which insist that not everything going on in cities can be understood in terms of the power of capital. Many researchers have become weary of the implicit assumption that to engage with cities and urban environments, one must first choose sides and get the theory right. Urban theory tends to implicitly privilege theorisation as a mode of engaging with urban problems. A relatively small number of thinkers are at the centre of current debates, and much research gets framed through them. This can leave the field sometimes feeling like an overly intellectual affair far removed from actual urban problems.

However, there are a range of different ways that urban theory can be put to work in making practical sense of cities and urban environments. A good starting point is to read widely from the diverse writings of people concerned with cities. Doing so reveals that urban life has been thought about, researched and intervened into from a variety of positions and perspectives (cf. Koch and Latham, 2017). Different academic disciplines have their histories and approaches, but there are also fundamental differences in styles of thinking that cut across disciplinary boundaries. This includes urban studies focused on providing rich descriptions of places or phenomenon as they are constructed, as well as scholarship concerned with developing critiques. The insights of urban theory can help draw attention to the myriad entanglements and relations that shape urban encounters and developments. They can also help to expose hidden and unacknowledged biases and power asymmetries – both in terms of the place or phenomenon being researched and the imaginations and ideas brought to look at them. The more immediate kinds of interventions into cities made by architects, artists, designers, engineers and planners are also a kind of urban thinking. If not always overtly theoretical, they are forms of action in which urban problems can be addressed, and they too can be a source of critical insight and inspiration.

Finally, it should be emphasised that much urban theory works in a minor register. That is to say, it does not seek to offer definitive models or explanations of how cities work. Rather, writing and research on cities offers a variety of tools and heuristics for framing urban problems in different ways, enabling dialogue, generating ideas for practice and politics and prompting further lines of enquiry. One example is the widespread attention given to infrastructure by urban theorists and others in recent years. Conceptualised as varied systems for the provision of human needs, infrastructure has come to be seen as at-once social, technical and legal. Infrastructure is crucial for the wellbeing of humans and the environment and is often seen as a pathway towards better urban futures. Thus, various theories and research programmes have sought to develop better understandings of how infrastructure is produced and maintained, and how it fails in different contexts. This includes tracing relationships between scales, structural formations and everyday practices. It involves locating human as well as **non-human agency** and the varied power dynamics between the two. Urban theory has helped to animate the study of infrastructure in several ways. Political economy and political ecology perspectives have provided one set of understandings; as have feminist, queer, postcolonial and other forms of post-structural thought. Theorisation and research have provided insights that help to think sceptically about claims made by developers, engineers or politicians, and they have prompted imaginative engagements with designers, architects, charities and NGOs. Theorising and thinking about infrastructure has also meant engaging with other urban-related concepts, including sustainability, materiality, social justice, **neoliberalism**, informality, governance and many more.

Putting urban theory to work often means dipping into different approaches and case studies to learn and gain perspective, before pragmatically selecting tools of thought that feel appropriate to a matter of concern. At the same time, it means acknowledging tensions between different theoretical traditions and negotiating among competing perspectives. Critical urban thinking means refusing to take things for granted. This includes questioning what different theories and concepts offer: what do they direct attention to? What complexities or particularities do they fail to capture? These are questions that make urban theory an area of ongoing debate over how cities and urbanisation are best understood.

Discussion points

- What do you think are some urgent issues or questions that urban theory should seek to address?
- Is it useful to think of cities as a kind of 'organism' or 'machine' as many urban theorists have done? Or, are there better metaphors that help grasp the complexity of urban life?

- Has the 'urban age' potentially hit its peak, given new developments in technology and remote working?
- What is the difference between 'the city' and 'the urban', and why might the distinction matter?

References

Amin, A., and Thrift, N. (2002). *Cities: Reimagining the Urban*. Malden: Polity Press.

Brenner, N. (ed.) (2014). *Implosions/Explosions: Towards a Study of Planetary Urbanization*. Berlin: Jovis.

Castells, M. (1977). *The Urban Question. A Marxist Approach*. London: Edward Arnold.

Davis, M. (1990). *City of Quartz: Excavating the Future in Los Angeles*. London: Verso.

Glass, R. (1964). Introduction: Aspects of Change. In *London: Aspects of Change*, ed. Centre for Urban Studies. London: MacKibbon and Kee, xiii–xlii.

Jacobs, J. (1961). *The Death and Life of Great American Cities*. New York: Random House.

Koch, R., and Latham, A. (eds.) (2017). *Key Thinkers on Cities*. London: SAGE.

Lefebvre, H. (1968). *La Droit a Le Ville*. Paris: Anthropos.

Lynch, K. (1960). *The Image of the City*. Cambridge, MA: MIT Press.

Massey, D. B. (1994). *Space, Place, and Gender*. Minneapolis: University of Minnesota Press.

Park, R. E., Burgess, E. W., and McKenzie, R. D. (1925). *The City*. Chicago: University Press.

Robinson, J. (2011). Cities in a world of cities: the comparative gesture. *International Journal of Urban and Regional Research* 35(1): 1–23.

Roy, A. (2009). The 21st-century metropolis: new geographies of theory. *Regional Studies* 43(6): 819–830.

Sassen, S. (2002). *Cities in a World Economy*. London: Sage.

Simmel, G. ([1903] 2010). The Metropolis and Mental Life. In *The Blackwell City Reader*, eds. G. Bridge and S. Watson. Oxford: Blackwell, 23–31.

Simone, A. (2004). *For The City Yet To Come: Changing African Life in Four Cities*. Durham: Duke University Press.

Smith, N. (1996). *The New Urban Frontier: Gentrification and the Revanchist City*. New York: Routledge.

Storper, M., and Scott, A. J. (2016). Current debates in urban theory: a critical assessment. *Urban Studies* 53(6): 1114–1136.

Online materials

- *City Lab*. Regular reports on cities and urban neighbourhoods around the world. https://www.bloomberg.com/citylab
- *The Atlantic Cities*. Innovative ideas and pressing issues in global cities and neighbourhoods. https://www.theatlantic.com/author/the-atlantic-cities

Further reading

For an introduction to foundational ideas and thinkers in urban studies, see the following:

Jonas, A. E. G., McCann, E., and Thomas, M. (2015). *Urban Geography: A Critical Introduction*. Oxford: Wiley-Blackwell.

Koch, R., and Latham, A. (eds.) (2017). *Key Thinkers on Cities*. London: SAGE.

Samples of highly influential writing on cities and urban life can be found in these collections:

Bridge, G., and Watson, S. (eds.) (2010). *The Blackwell City Reader* (2nd edn.). Oxford: Blackwell.
LeGates, R., and Stout, F. (eds.) (2020). *The City Reader* (7th edn.). London: Routledge.

To engage with debates currently animating the field, see the following:

Amin, A., and Lancione, M. (2022). *Grammars of the Urban Ground*. Durham and London: Duke University Press.
Jayne, M., and Ward, K. (eds.) (2017). *Urban Theory: New Critical Perspectives*. New York: Routledge.

16 Global cities

Ben Derudder

Introduction

On the surface, New York and London appear to be very different cities. They operate in different national contexts, went through specific historical developments, and their morphology has distinctive elements. For example, Manhattan's skyscrapers and regular street grids have no clear equivalent in London's city center. However, there has been a gradual convergence between contemporary New York and London: today, their economic basis and governing regimes are broadly comparable, evolutions in their labour and housing markets point to significant parallels, and they are among the most unequal and diverse places in their respective countries. New York's Broadway and London's West End run similar musicals, while events such as the *NY: LON Connect Global Music Summit* – a conference 'traveling' between New York and London and bringing together decision-makers in the music industry (musically.com) – accentuate the strategic and integrated nature of their cultural economies. According to Smith (2005: 173), it 'is a sign of our "global times" that London can be said to have more in common with New York than other UK cities (…) and vice-versa'.

There are many dimensions to the similarity and connectivity between New York and London. Nonetheless, there is a clear sense that their extensive integration comes on the back of the economic and financial knowledge flowing through and between them (Wójcik, 2013). Global cities research examines why cities such as New York and London have become so central in global-scale economic and financial processes and how this leads to new geographies of advantage and disadvantage within them. In human geography research, the global city concept is more generally used to highlight how London and New York, but increasingly also other major cities, including Hong Kong, Singapore, Dubai, Tokyo, Sao Paulo, Paris, Sydney, Shanghai, and Johannesburg, are now so strongly connected and alike that they constitute one of the major **territorial** frameworks of the world we inhabit. This chapter summarises the major foundations of global cities research and explores the consequences of global city-formation for people living and working in those cities. This is followed by an attempt to formally identify global cities by measuring cities' levels of global connectivity. The chapter concludes with a brief discussion of some of the critiques leveled at global cities research.

DOI: 10.4324/9780429265853-20

Summary

- Global cities research examines why cities such as New York and London have become so central in global-scale economic and financial processes…
- …and how this leads to new geographies of advantage and disadvantage within them.
- The global city concept is more generally used to highlight how and why certain cities across the world are now so strongly connected and alike.

Foundations

Global cities research does not focus on the demographic or economic size of cities. Rather, it emphasises cities' levels of *global connectivity* (Friedmann, 1995). Although New York and London are major cities by any conceivable size metric, their designation as global cities starts from a very different vantage point: their central role in the blizzard of interactions constituting the world economy. Geographical complexity of economic activities – for example, the increasingly global reach of corporate, financial, and logistical networks – goes hand in hand with geographical concentration of the organisation of and control over those economic activities: some locations become crucial sites for managing and overseeing these globalising corporate, financial, and logistical networks.

From this perspective, global cities are defined as locations from which **transnational** control over global networks is produced, projected, and exercised. In addition to London's and New York's position in global financial networks, obvious examples include Los Angeles' crucial role in the creation and dissemination of cultural and consumer identities and Geneva's strategic function in the networks of international humanitarian organisations. Centrality in global-scale networks is often facilitated by strong connectivity in world-spanning **infrastructure** networks, as well as policies that (often quite literally) allow capitalising on integration in global networks. For example, London-as-a-global-city is *inter alia* built on the back of London Heathrow being one of the world's most connected airports, while most global financial networks flowing through London do so via the 'square mile' of the City of London where banks can shelter themselves from the 'problem' of regulation and taxation.

Contemporary research on global cities has longstanding and diverse roots. One of the classical studies is 1966 Peter Hall's *The World Cities* in which he used the term as a shorthand for cities on the forefront of **modernity** and development. In John Friedmann's (1986) *World City Hypothesis*, global cities were redefined in a more critical vein: he identified global cities as central nodes in the then-emerging geographical expansion of production networks and multinational corporations. Friedmann's ideas were later complemented and extended in what arguably remains the landmark study on global cities: Saskia Sassen's (1991) *The Global City*. In this book, Sassen provides an in-depth analysis of the post-industrial transformation of New York, London, and Tokyo. She pointed to the attraction of firms – firms offering financial, legal, consultancy, advertising, accountancy, and ancillary services – to cities offering the most knowledge-rich, technology-enabled, and globally connected environments. These cities often also offer the kind of lifestyle that increasingly transnational elites and professionals are seeking (Ley, 2004). From the 1980s onward, many producer services firms started following their globalising clients and became important multinational corporations in their own right, operating from and through major cities. Based on this, Sassen argued that a key dimension of global city-formation is the production of *knowledge capabilities* for organising globalising production networks, financial markets, cultural economies, and logistics networks. For some types of economic and financial transactions, global cities have even become 'obligatory passing points' given their quasi-monopoly over certain types of knowledge and capabilities (Bassens and van Meeteren, 2015).

A visible manifestation of these processes is that the largest producer services firms have created office networks covering major cities across the world. Figure 16.1 captures Sassen's global city thesis in pictures taken at Amsterdam Schiphol Airport in April 2004. These pictures were part of a global advertisement campaign of Deloitte, a firm administering a vast network of offices around the world. Deloitte is headquartered in London and arguably the world's largest producer services network by revenue and number of professionals. The strategic location of the advertisement (a hub for global air traffic), its use of iconic buildings to refer to major cities (New York and Amsterdam), and the key message ('we are wherever global business needs us to be') jointly convey how firms such as Deloitte have become central to the world economy and how they use certain cities as key platforms for their engagements with the world economy. The location strategies of producer services firms such as Deloitte are both cause and consequence of global city-formation.

Figure 16.1
Deloitte advertisements at Amsterdam Schiphol Airport

Source: Photo credit: Ben Derudder

Summary

- Global cities research does not focus on the demographic or economic size of cities but highlights their levels of global connectivity.
- A more complex and integrated world economy implies centralised coordination and control exercised from global cities.
- A key element of global city-formation is the presence of knowledge capabilities for organising various global networks.
- These knowledge capabilities are often provided by producer services firms that have created office networks covering major cities across the world.
- Globalised producer services firms are therefore both cause and consequence of global city-formation.

Living and working in the global city

One of the most important themes in global cities research is the consequences of global city-formation for people living and working in those cities. Beaverstock (2004) and Wills et al. (2009) detailed a range of emerging geographies in London in the wake of the city's ascendance to 'Alpha global city' status from the mid-1980s onward. One of their observations is that the location strategies of globalised producer services firms, shown in Figure 16.1 and almost invariably involving an important office in London, often go hand in hand with the **expatriation** of professionals and managerial elites. Expatriation is a deliberate organisational strategy adopted by firms to harness, develop, manage, and circulate 'global knowledge' to boost profitability, build markets, and increase their share therein. This leads to highly skilled and well-paid migrants from all over the world flowing into London's financial district, complementing and extending the longstanding work of British professionals and elites who also capitalise on the expansion of the producer services sector. The labour of these national and international professionals and elites is indispensable for the (re)production of London-as-a-global-city, but so too is the often-invisible labour of vast numbers of poorly paid workers engaged in service industries catering to the privileged: office cleaners, building attendants, housekeepers for dual-career families, restaurant staff, etc. This expanding low wage economy is also increasingly taken up by migrant workers, albeit that these often come from different parts of the world. Global city-formation, therefore, entails an increasingly diverse and unequal London.

The above summary is, of course, stylised and even simplistic. However, it does help bring out why as an urban society London is gradually acquiring a specific profile:

1. London is in many ways the richest city in England, but it is also by far its most unequal city. London houses a significantly larger slice of the country's poorest *and* richest residents than anywhere else. According to a recent Trust for London publication (2022), in 2019/20 the net income ratio between those in the 90th percentile and those in 10th percentile was 10.5, while in the rest of England this net income ratio was 5.3. Furthermore, the level of this

net income inequality has risen steadily in London over the last 20 years, while it remained relatively stable in the rest of England.

2. This stark income inequality is related to the evolving nature of London's job market: there has been a gradual shedding of jobs in relatively stable and unionised sectors such as manufacturing and the public sector alongside a gradual creation of jobs in the services sector. Crucially, London's services sector is marked by stark inequalities in renumeration: for every well-paid position in the producer services sector, there are several poorly paid positions servicing the professionals and managerial elites working in it.

3. London is by far the most diverse place in England. Today, about 40% of London's population is foreign-born. The 2021 Census highlighted how those identifying as 'White British' accounted for 43.4% of London's population, compared with 78.4% for England as a whole. However, London's diversity is much more complex and vibrant than these mere numbers suggest. In the past, London's migration was strongly tied to the colonial legacy of the British Empire. Today's migration is **superdiverse** with many overlapping processes and patterns at play: there is a 'diversification of diversity' defined by a dynamic interplay of characteristics, including rising numbers of new, multiple-origin, transnationally connected, and legally stratified immigrants.

4. London's superdiversity is directly related to its socio-economic stratification. Expatriation implies that some of the most well-paid jobs in the producer services sector are no longer the exclusive playground of the Oxbridge community but involve international and sometimes hypermobile migrants. Data from 2016 show that almost one in every five workers in the City of London's financial industry originated from another European country, the highest figure since records began. At the same time, the day-to-day functioning of London is built on vast numbers of sometimes undocumented migrants who work in jobs that are sometimes paid below the living wage. It is estimated that more than half of London's low wage jobs are occupied by foreign-born workers, with the reliance on migrant workers even more significant in sectors such as cleaning. The constant influx of new migrants further polarises earnings by depressing wages among low-income workers.

5. London's inequality is both reflected in, and further fueled by, its housing and real estate market. Although median wages in London are often slightly higher than elsewhere in England, this is reversed after considering housing costs. London having the largest number of wealthy people per capita is directly related to its property price boom. It is the place to hide one's wealth in plain sight, with houses in some neighbourhoods above all representing financial investments of the global rich or sovereign wealth funds. Meanwhile, new groups of migrant professionals working in the City of London are often at the root of waves of **gentrification** as documented in the Inner London neighbourhood of Barnsbury. This gentrification goes hand in hand with the expulsion of the urban poor in the face of lagging investments in public housing. The Grenfell Tower fire, which claimed the lives of 72 people in June 2017, is a hallmark example of London's extreme polarisation in general and its housing market in particular: in close proximity to multi-million-dollar houses, there is sub-standard housing that is mainly inhabited by poor migrants (many of them undocumented), still expensive considering the residents' wage levels, and both overcrowded and under-regulated (see Chapter 55).

6. Importantly, each of these dimensions has a constantly evolving geographical component. The examples of Barnsbury and Grenfell Tower show that London's societal inequalities are manifested in and through socio-spatial inequalities: London itself is being geographically

differentiated by places' uneven relation to global city processes. Developments in Inner London's real estate market in particular have affected socio-spatial inequalities across the city: while Inner London historically had higher poverty rates than Outer London, global city-induced real estate prices, above all exploding in the former, have reversed this long-standing feature of London's urban geography. Note, however, that the shifting Inner London/Outer London geography is but an example of constantly changing patterns of socio-spatial inequality across London, which are both an **embodiment** and a further source of myriad socio-economic inequalities.

In short, there is a direct connection between London's global city status and its marked income polarisation, sizable and superdiverse migration, spiraling housing crises, and how these unevenly manifest themselves in space. Crucially, these and a range of related processes are **intersectional**: they overlap and reinforce each other and jointly lead to new and deeply interwoven geographies of advantage and disadvantage in London. Global cities researchers suggest that, despite a range of differences, broadly similar processes and patterns can be found in other cities around the world. The concept is accordingly used to understand urban change in very different parts of the world, hence its importance in human geography research. Inequality, diversity, and housing crises are increasingly present well beyond global cities. However, it is argued that the speed, complexity, and scope of these processes are much more marked in global cities, which is also why researchers often use the prefix 'super' – **super-diversity** (Vertovec, 2007) and **super-gentrification** (Butler and Lees, 2006), for example – to capture their palpable manifestation there.

Summary

- It is often argued that global cities such as London are developing a specific socio-economic profile.
- London's socio-economic profile is marked by spiraling income polarisation, diversity, and housing crises.
- These characteristics are intersectional: they overlap and reinforce each other, creating an increasingly unequal London.
- The global city thesis suggests that, notwithstanding a range of contextual differences, broadly similar processes and patterns are found across global cities.

Identifying global cities

Up to this point, this chapter adopted an intuitive approach to naming instances of global cities and largely focused on the obvious example of London. Researchers have tried to formally identify global cities based on their level of connectivity in global economic and financial networks. There are now myriad approaches to identifying global cities, but this chapter will focus on the methodology devised by the Globalization and World Cities Research Network (GaWC) that draws inspiration from the work of Sassen: it starts from the observation that it is a central position in business connections between cities, enacted by (people working in) globalised producer services firms, that can be used as a marker of global city-formation (Derudder and Taylor, 2020).

GaWC's identification of global cities in 2020 draws upon an investigation of the office locations of producer services firms. This is based on information that is readily available on firms' corporate websites where they describe their office network to impress potential clients as per Deloitte's advertisement in Figure 16.1. Drawing on data on the size and relative importance of firms' office presences, a matrix is created arraying 175 firms against 707 cities. The standardised measures in this matrix are called 'services value' sv_{ij}, which reflect the importance of the presence of firm j in city i. Based on the corporate websites of each of the 175 firms, for each of the 707 cities, information is gathered on the relative size of a firm's presence (e.g. number of offices it has in a city for accountancy/financial services firms, or areas of expertise for law firms) and/or extra-locational functions (e.g. headquarter functions). This standardisation involves assigning values to sv_{ij} ranging from 0 to 5, with a city housing a firm's headquarters scoring 5, a city with no office scoring 0, and in-between values assigned based on the relative size and functions of offices.

From this service value data matrix, estimates of knowledge flows (advice, direction, plans, strategies, etc.) between cities are generated by applying a network model. In this model, offices are treated as commercial assets of a city that are important because they enable flows of information, knowledge, instruction, ideas, innovations, personnel, etc. with offices in other cities. In other words, the network model converts the service value matrix so that it gives us insight in the interaction between any pair of cities a and b through the relative importance of their office presences for firm j. This measure is called city-dyad connectivity (CDC) and is calculated as follows:

$$CDC_{a-b,j} = sv_{aj} \cdot sv_{bj}$$

The rationale behind this approach is the assumption that the size and strategic nature of flows between two cities will be large if two cities both house a major office for a firm, smaller if one or both of these cities have a less important office for a firm, and non-existent if one or both of these cities have no office for a firm. Aggregating these city-dyad connectivities across all cities and across all firms gives insight into a city's overall connectivity. This measure is called global network connectivity (GNC) and is calculated as follows:

$$GNC_a = \sum_b CDC_{a-b} = \sum_{bj} SV_{aj}.SV_{bj} \quad a \neq b$$

As GNC depends on the size of V, it is commonly reported as a proportion of the maximum value, thus ranging from London as the most connected city (100%) to Pyongyang/Tehran as the least connected cities (0%). A series of related measures also allow an examination of where cities are connected (ranging from London being strongly connected with other major global cities to Cologne being primarily connected with other secondary European cities), and how this connectivity changes over time (Dubai and Shanghai gained a lot of connectivity over the last two decades).

This 2020 geography of global cities based on GNC is summarised in Figure 16.2. The cartogram shows all cities with a GNC >20%. In the cartogram, each city is given its own equal space in approximately its correct relative position, with darker shades reflecting stronger connectivities. Cities are indicated by intuitive two-letter codes, e.g. 'NY' for New York and 'JB' for

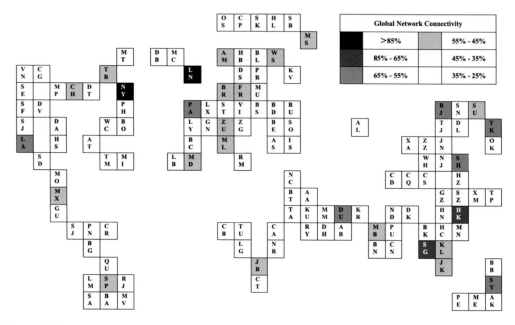

Figure 16.2
Basic geography of global network connectivity

Source: Drawing by Taylor and Derudder, 2016

Johannesburg. Overall, the results clearly capture show how global city-formation is above all confined to Northern America, Western Europe, and parts of Pacific Asia. Beyond these world-regions, there are no regions with major concentrations of highly connected cities. However, this does not imply that there are no global cities beyond these three regions, as shown by the sizable connectivity of Sao Paulo, Mumbai, Dubai, and Johannesburg.

Formally identifying the degree of global connectivity of cities allows making analytical connections to other dimensions of global city-formation. For example, connectivity measures can be used in analyses of how global cities are characterised by rising levels of inequality. Furthermore, these results can also be used as a starting point for in-depth analyses of the foundations of global connectivity. Lai (2012) explains how and why Beijing, Shanghai, and the Special Administrative Region of Hong Kong have come to take on a leading role in China's engagements with the world economy. Although the gradual 'opening up' of the Chinese economy entails that most if not all its cities increasingly engage with the world economy, these three cities stand out in Figure 16.2. There are now more than 100 Chinese cities with more than 1 million inhabitants, but there is a clear 'tri-primate' city pattern of global connectivity centered on Beijing, Shanghai, and Hong Kong. This pattern is the result of a number of interlocking processes: the sheer size of the Chinese market; Hong Kong still operating as a quasi-autonomous territory in financial and economic terms; boosterist visions of inter-city competition among Shanghai's powerful urban elites in light of its long-standing role as a gateway into China; and the Chinese political system imposing a context where producer services need to be near the centre of political decision-making in Beijing.

Until recently, global city researchers identified almost wholesale increases in global connectivity: with some notable exceptions, increasingly many cities from increasingly many geographical contexts appeared on the map of global cities, with London even further expanding its global remit (Taylor and Derudder, 2022). However, it is important to stress that there is nothing inevitable about global city-formation: it is an ongoing process rather than an end state. Trump's America First narrative, Brexit, and China's isolationist tendencies can, in fact, be seen as signs of stalling global integration that will also impact global city-formation. However, it is too soon to tell: future analyses of the evolution of global connectivity will identify if, where, and how the geographies of global cities change.

Summary

- Global cities can be formally identified based on their level of connectivity in transnational economic and financial networks.
- Global city-formation is above all confined to Northern America, Western Europe, and parts of Pacific Asia.
- There are also cities with sizable connectivity beyond these regions, including Sao Paulo, Mumbai, Dubai, and Johannesburg.
- Identifying global cities can inform other research agendas.
- Until recently, we have witnessed overall intensification of global connectivity, albeit geographically unevenly so with Dubai and Shanghai standing out.

Critiques of global cities research

Although global cities are now a commonly used concept in human geography, the research agenda is sometimes criticised. A first critique is that even among the most globally well-connected cities there is so much diversity that we should not over-emphasise the explanatory power of the global city concept. Two obvious examples are the much smaller role of migration in Tokyo (given stricter migration policies), and the somewhat less striking inequality in Paris (given a relatively stronger welfare state). More generally, the global city thesis is often argued to be over-simplifying urban complexities and trajectories.

A second critique is that we may be spending too much attention to global city processes/London compared to other processes/cities. Combining bibliometric, demographic, economic, and georeferenced data, Kanai et al. (2018) recently compared how much research attention cities receive. They identified a clear-cut research focus (albeit a somewhat declining one) on 'EuroAmerica' in general and on cities featuring prominently in Figure 16.2 more specifically. The prominence of global cities research is an obvious example of research attention not keeping pace with major economic/demographic trends in different parts of an urbanising world, and too much focus on global cities implies that many cities risk remaining 'off the map' (Robinson, 2002) of human geography research. The obvious solution here is to put global cities research in its place and see it as one of the many possible approaches to making sense of a world of cities (Ren and Keil, 2017).

A third critique directly builds on this second critique and is perhaps the most significant one. The uneven geographical coverage of research has much more profound consequences than producing an uneven empirical knowledge basis: it also impacts *how* we understand cities and urban change. Bunnell and Maringanti (2010) argued that the abundant attention paid in research and education to global city processes and their embodiment in a city such as London are an example of 'metrocentricity': the tendency to set up major cities in EuroAmerica and specific types of economic and financial processes within them as a *norm* against which other cities and processes are compared, even if implicitly so. Figure 16.2 can be seen as a case in point: the percentages in the cartogram can be read as an assessment of the extent to which cities live up to the London global city archetype. In the extreme case of putatively unconnected cities such as Pyongyang and Tehran, this implies that they are 'understood' as being totally unlike London. This may well be the case, but surely there must be more insightful, richer, and more nuanced ways to comprehend the complexities of both cities than saying they are not like London!

In other words, the uneven geographies of empirical attention identified by Kanai et al. (2018) are directly reflected in uneven geographies of theory-building (Roy, 2009). Sheppard et al. (2013) therefore argued that we need to 'provincialise' urban theory: creating a space from which to challenge urban theories such as the global city concept that tends to treat specific cities/processes as the norm, to incorporate the expertise and perspectives of urban majorities, and to imagine and enact alternative urban futures. Importantly, this does not imply that cities are 'beyond compare' (Peck, 2015). Rather, it implies recognising that there is no reason why, say, Algiers and Buenos Aires could not just as well be the starting for theorising about cities. There is now a vibrant literature in human geography on 'comparative urbanism' that explicitly considers the opportunities, challenges, and limitations involved in benchmarking, associating, and comparing cities and urban processes (see Chapter 17). Nonetheless, we should not throw out the baby with the bath water: global city processes are a key geographical feature of today's capitalist world economy and impact different aspects of our life, even for those not living in cities or living in cities that are 'off the map'.

A fourth and final critique is related to the concept's (ab)use in policy and corporate circles. As is hopefully clear from this chapter, global cities research has critical roots. It started out as an 'agenda for research and action' (Friedmann and Wolff, 1982), an attempt to critically analyse and act upon the mutable geographies of global **capitalism** and its baleful consequences at different scales and in different contexts. This critical spirit is still present in much of the research agenda, but it has to increasingly compete with a simplified version of 'the global city' circulating in policy and corporate circles that selectively draws upon global cities research. For example, exercises ranking cities according to their global connectivity as per Figure 16.2 have in some quarters morphed into popular 'league tables' (Acuto et al., 2021). In the process, the social consequences of London being the most globally connected city are often strategically overlooked. In addition, seeing global cities as a (desirable) norm ignores that many cities lack the material conditions to emulate the 'Alpha global cities' of this world. For example, London's contemporary position builds directly and indirectly on the United Kingdom's colonial past and the city's centrality in and for the colonial project. Assuming that global city London can serve as an example for, say, Jakarta or Durban, implies that the scope of possible urban policies is narrowed to options that are neither desirable nor viable. Such approaches imply that global city maps and rankings are stripped from their origins and context and paradoxically acquire an aspirational meaning: 'being a global city' becomes a utopian pursuit of an often-dystopian reality and replaces it as analytical category for examining questions of inequality, identity, and social and political responsibility (Massey, 2007). Even if global city researchers are not directly responsible for this, it does signal that as human geographers we need to take the (unintended) effects of our research into account (Acuto, 2022).

Summary

- Although global cities are now a commonly used concept in human geography, the research agenda is sometimes criticised.
- Even among the most globally connected cities, there is much diversity.
- Global cities research is but one of the many possible approaches to understanding a world of cities.
- The global cities concept has entered policy and corporate discourse, often carrying an aspirational dimension that is deeply problematic.

Discussion points

- Not unlike producer services firms, non-governmental organisations also arrange their global networks from and through major cities. Which cities do you think would be on/off this map?
- Shanghai differs from London in that it does not have large numbers of poorly paid foreign-born immigrants. Yet it can be argued that the intersectional processes described for London are also present in Shanghai, albeit under a different arrangement. What makes Shanghai different yet also similar to London in this respect?
- One reason why studying global cities is important is that what happens there impacts different aspects of our life, even if we are not living in a global city ourselves. Could you describe an example of such an impact?
- As geographers, we know New York is not the official capital city of the USA, and while the official capital city of the Netherlands is Amsterdam, the *de facto* capital and the country's seat of government is The Hague. Why then did Deloitte use this term in their advertisement? What does it tell us about how they look at the world?
- Why is there some irony in having a chapter on global cities in an introduction to human geography that emphasises the importance of diversity and difference in how we understand the world?

References

Acuto, M. (2022). *How to Build a Global City: Recognizing the Symbolic Power of a Global Urban Imagination*. New York: Cornell University Press.

Acuto, M., Pejic, D., and Briggs, J. (2021). Taking city rankings seriously: engaging with benchmarking practices in global urbanism. *International Journal of Urban and Regional Research* 45 (2): 363–377.

Bassens, D., and Van Meeteren, M. (2015). World cities under conditions of financialized globalization: towards an augmented world city hypothesis. *Progress in Human Geography* 39(6): 752–775.

Beaverstock, J. V. (2004). 'Managing across borders': knowledge management and expatriation in professional service legal firms. *Journal of Economic Geography* 4(2): 157–179.

Bunnell, T., and Maringanti, A. (2010). Practising urban and regional research beyond metrocentricity. *International Journal of Urban and Regional Research* 34(2): 415–420.

Butler, T., and Lees, L. (2006). Super-gentrification in Barnsbury, London: globalization and gentrifying global elites at the neighbourhood level. *Transactions of the Institute of British Geographers* 31(4): 467–487.

Derudder, B., and Taylor, P. J. (2020). Three globalizations shaping the twenty-first century: understanding the new world geography through its cities. *Annals of the American Association of Geographers* 110(6): 1831–1854.

Friedmann, J. (1995). The world city hypothesis. *World Cities in a World System*, 317–331.

Friedmann, J., and Wolff, G. (1982). World city formation: an agenda for research and action. *International Journal of Urban and Regional Research* 6(3): 309–344.

Kanai, J. M., Grant, R., and Jianu, R. (2018). Cities on and off the map: a bibliometric assessment of urban globalisation research. *Urban Studies* 55(12): 2569–2585.

Lai, K. (2012). Differentiated markets: Shanghai, Beijing and Hong Kong in China's financial centre network. *Urban Studies* 49(6): 1275–1296.

Ley, D. (2004). Transnational spaces and everyday lives. *Transactions of the Institute of British Geographers* 29(2): 151–164.

Massey, D. (2007). *World City*. Cambridge: Polity Press.

Peck, J. (2015). Cities beyond compare? *Regional Studies* 49(1): 160–182.

Ren, X., and Keil, R. (2017). *The Globalizing Cities Reader*. London: Routledge.

Robinson, J. (2002). Global and world cities: a view from off the map. *International Journal of Urban and Regional Research* 26(3): 531–554.

Roy, A. (2009). The 21st-century metropolis: new geographies of theory. *Regional Studies* 43(6): 819–830.

Sassen, S. (1991). *The Global City*. New York, London, Tokyo: Princeton University Press.

Sheppard, E., Leitner, H., and Maringanti, A. (2013). Provincializing global urbanism: a manifesto. *Urban Geography* 34(7): 893–900.

Smith, R. G. (2005). Networking the city. *Geography* 90(2): 172–176.

Taylor, P. J., and Derudder, B. (2022). NY-LON 2020: the changing relations between London and New York in corporate globalisation. *Transactions of the Institute of British Geographers* 47(1): 257–270.

Trust for London (2022). *Income Inequality*. https://www.trustforlondon.org.uk/data/income-inequality-over-time/

Vertovec, S. (2007). Super-diversity and its implications. *Ethnic and Racial Studies* 30(6): 1024–1054.

Wills, J., Datta K., Evans, Y., et al. (2009). *Global Cities at Work: New Migrant Divisions of Labour*. London/New York: Pluto Press.

Wójcik, D. (2013). The dark side of NY–LON: financial centres and the global financial crisis. *Urban Studies* 50(13): 2736–2752.

Online materials

- https://www.lboro.ac.uk/gawc/

  Created in the Geography Department at Loughborough University, the Globalization and World Cities (GaWC) Research Network focuses upon research into the external relations of global cities. Its website brings together a wide array of datasets, research bulletins, visualisations, and other online resources.

- https://www.kearney.com/global-cities/2021

  The uneven adoption of the global city terminology in policy and corporate circles has led to major consultancy firms producing and marketing their own 'league tables'. Kearney, for example, produces a yearly Global Cities Report, and it is useful to critically appraise the narrative underlying this report in light of this chapter's contents.

Further reading

Abu-Lughod, J. L. (1999). *New York, Chicago, Los Angeles: America's Global Cities*. Minneapolis: University of Minnesota Press.
An in-depth study that looks at how New York, Chicago, and Los Angeles became global cities and considers each city's unique history.

Acuto, M. (2022). *How to Build a Global City: Recognizing the Symbolic Power of a Global Urban Imagination*. New York: Cornell University Press.
Details the rise of global cities such as Singapore, Sydney, and Dubai, and analyses the power this concept has had in urban public policy practice.

Atkinson, R. (2021). *Alpha city: How London Was Captured by the Super-Rich*. London: Verso Books.
The most detailed account of how London's property boom economy is linked to its global city-formation, showing the impact of widening inequality on the urban landscape.

Clark, G. (2016). *Global Cities: A Short History*. Washington: Brookings Institution Press.
A concise introduction to how trade, migration, war, and technology have enabled some cities to emerge into global prominence.

Derudder, B., and Taylor, P. J. (2021). The GaWC Perspective on Global-Scale Urban Networks. In *Handbook of Cities and Networks*, eds. Z. P. Neal and C. Rozenblat. London: Elgar Publishing, 601–617.
A comprehensive overview of global cities research which focuses on both the external relations and internal structures of major cities.

Robinson, J. (2005). *Ordinary Cities: Between Modernity and Development*.London: Routledge.
One of the most forceful and comprehensive analyses of the limitations of the global city thesis.

Sassen, S. (2018). *Cities in a World Economy*. California: Pine Forgess Press.
An accessible and updated introduction to Sassen's global city thesis.

Sigler, T. J. (2016). After the 'world city' has globalised: four agendas towards a more nuanced framework for global urban research. *Geography Compass* 10(9): 389–398.
Spells out agendas for future human geography research on global cities.

Taylor, P. J., and Derudder, B. (2016). *World city Network: A Global Urban Analysis* (2nd edn.). London: Routledge.
A comprehensive and systematic analysis of the geographies of global cities as the 'skeleton' upon which contemporary globalisation has been built.

Wills, J., Datta, K., Evans, Y., et al. (2009). *Global Cities at Work: New Migrant Divisions of Labour*. London/New York: Pluto Press.
The most detailed study linking London's new **migrant division of labour** to its global city-formation.

17 Comparative urban studies

Jennifer Robinson

Introduction

Urban studies has developed in close relationship with its object of study. Over the last century, the urban world has changed profoundly and so, therefore, has its analysis. Where the focus had been on cities, tracing their expansion from the centre-out to their edges – suburbs, edge-cities, peripheries – attention is now drawn to the seemingly unstoppable sprawling and expansive nature of urbanisation which is leading to conurbations, metropolises, megalopolises, to city-regions or metropolitan regions and even 'urban galaxies'. We are increasingly aware of the impact of urbanisation on the planet – the footprints or operational landscapes of urban life (all that is needed to support living in concentrated urban areas) stretch into the remotest corners. And there is mounting evidence that urbanisation follows large-scale **infrastructure** investments or corridors, or emerges with new logistics activities associated with mining, commodity and agriculture-focussed developments in even quite peripheral regions. Scholars are searching for new terms and vocabularies to understand these processes (Brenner and Schmid, 2014).

Urban studies has also increasingly adopted a global perspective – partly in response to its changing object, but also as scholars have embraced a **post-colonial** critique of the field. By the late twentieth century, the insights and ideas which shaped urban studies had become focussed on a narrow range of urban experiences in the 'Global North', with even some individual cities becoming iconic of developments there – such as New York, Chicago or Los Angeles (Robinson, 2006, see also Chapter 15). The limits of this approach have become heightened as the dynamic sites of rapid urbanisation, the largest urban areas and the majority of the world's urban population have shifted to Asia and Africa (see Figure 17.1). Along with the great diversity of forms of urban settlement and the increasingly world-wide impacts of urbanisation processes, many urbanists propose a renewal, if not a fundamental transformation, of urban theory (Robinson, 2006, Roy, 2009, Bhan, 2019).

It is clear, though, that urbanisation processes and urban experiences are not the same across this urbanising planet. The physical form, social life, governmental configurations and economic dynamics of urban settlements vary in so many ways. Even within individual cities, a great variety of ways of life emerge, associated with social and spatial divisions, or arising from

224

DOI: 10.4324/9780429265853-21

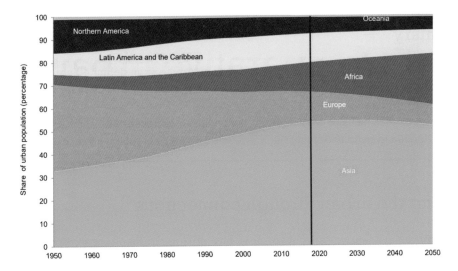

Figure 17.1
Share of urban population of the world by geographic region, 1950–2050

Source: United Nations, Department of Economic and Social Affairs, Population Division (2018a). *World Urbanization Prospects 2018*

the creative efforts of people to make a living (Peake, 2016, Simone, 2019). Also, the institutional arrangements shaping urban government are widely varied including, for example, democratic or authoritarian, centralised or devolved, as well as informal and traditional forms of government.

All this makes global urban studies a dynamic and interesting field – but also raises some challenges. How can concepts be reviewed, renovated, overthrown or invented across diverse urban outcomes? How can urban theory work effectively with different cases, thinking with the diversity of the urban world? In response to these challenges, all kinds of initiatives have emerged in urban studies, inspired by different empirical themes and a wide variety of theoretical perspectives to propose new thinking on the nature of the urban (Leitner et al. 2019).

One practical way in which to frame exploration of the nature of the global urban across a wide variety of different experiences is through a comparative imagination. Thinking with elsewhere, a key aspect of comparative practice, takes us beyond our ethno-centric perspectives, asking us to reflect on the diverse urban world. This can also support an ex-centric approach to urban studies more generally, encouraging urbanists to draw insights from scholars based in urban contexts which have been neglected in dominant understandings, including those places seen as part of the 'Global South' (Myers, 2020). More generally, comparative urbanism seeks to counter the ambitious scope of universalising analyses and rather proposes a more modest theoretical practice committed to the strong revisability of concepts and opening to a wider variety of voices (Robinson, 2022).

The next two sections outline some of the ways in which a comparative imagination has been used to globalise urban studies: tracing connections amongst different urban contexts; and generating insights through composing comparisons across difference.

Summary

- The geography of urbanisation has changed over time, from delimited areas like cities and suburbs, to sprawling, extensive, fragmented, dispersed and often far-flung urbanised **territories**.
- Urban studies has also responded to post-colonial critiques of northern-centrism and has looked to build understandings across the diversity of global urban experiences.

Thinking the urban through connections

Urban territories (which we can use to mean any urbanised/urbanising territory, rather than talking about cities, suburbs or peripheries) are partly produced through the wider circulations and relationships which shape them. Drawing on some classic geographical insights, such as Doreen Massey's idea of a 'global sense of place', we can see that the prolific flows and trajectories which link one place to another make (urban) 'places' (Massey, 2005). This has inspired many comparative experiments – 'relational comparisons' – which proceed by tracing the connections and relations amongst urban areas (Hart, 2003, Ward, 2010).

Many circulating phenomena (such as people, ideas or goods) shape urbanisation. For example, circulating or footloose capital, or more recently the 'wall of money' associated with **financialisation**, are seen as looking for opportunities to invest in urban areas, such as creating new enterprises, or building housing (Aalbers, 2016). But, if we are to include cities from the broad domains of the 'Global South' in theorisation, it is important to also pay attention to the role of international agencies, such as the World Bank, numerous donor organisations and powerful sovereign lenders, such as China, who are all investing in urban development (see Figure 17.2). 'Policy mobilities' are also crucial to understanding urban governance, notably the circulation of **neoliberal** ideas (McCann, 2011).

All these circulating phenomena are by no means uniform across **space** in their form and impact. So, tracing connections leads us to a comparative approach, as many urban places are linked together but the outcomes are different in each case. Practically, how can we design comparative experiments using these connections to explore a highly differentiated urban reality?

Firstly, we can draw on different cases to add up their experiences to help us understand the circuits themselves better. For example, by looking at many instances of financialised investment by international pension funds in rental housing or retail property in a number of cities, we might notice their consistent behaviour, as they seek to secure reliable and replicable arrangements to safeguard their returns on investment. In this way we can better understand the flows of money which shape urban development (Aalbers, 2016).

Alternatively, following connections could lead us to identify a range of different cases where the same processes have been important but the outcomes have been different. We could then use this to understand the variety of outcomes shaped by the circulating phenomenon. For example, many different cities are the focus of World Bank projects to promote urban resilience. Some World Bank projects will work out in ways that their policies hope – local governments might become better resourced, have more political autonomy, be 'bankable' (able to borrow

Top Chinese Source Province
1. Zhejiang
2. Shandong
3. Jiangsu
4. Beijing

Top African Destination Country
1. Nigeria
2. South Africa
3. Zambia
4. Ethiopia
5. Tanzania

Source: He and Zhu, 2017, based on Peking University data. Map Wall 2017

Figure 17.2
Value of Chinese Greenfield FDI into Africa: Source regions and destination countries (2003–2014)

Source: C He and S Zhu 'China's Foreign Direct Investment into Africa' in UN Habitat and IHS-Erasmus University Rotterdam (2018), The State of Africa Cities 2018, p. 116

money for projects), and capable of good governance. In these cases, local authorities can be supported to be more closely involved in shaping investments to protect citizens against the impacts of climate change, such as dangerous floods. But in other contexts, notably across many African countries, central government agencies dominate urban planning and development and have sought to control more of the flows of international money coming to the urban domain in the wake of the agreement to set an international Sustainable Development Goal (No. 11) focussed on urban settlements (Parnell, 2016). Different outcomes in each case therefore reflect different national political agendas, supportive or not of decentralising power to local government. In some cases, urban funds and projects might be diverted to address the personal or political interests of national leaders and their parties. We learn, then, from looking across a diversity of cases that 'urban' governance is not only about local government, but usually transcalar in nature, drawing in many different levels of government, and actors from community organisations to **transnational** agencies (Halbert and Rouanet, 2014). Such comparative analysis can be practically important, for example, to inform decisions about how to manage and direct investments to achieve greater environmental security for urban dwellers in the face of climate change.

A third possibility for relational comparative analysis is to consider how 'circuits' and different 'contexts' interact. In the example above we might expect that the World Bank would adjust its approach in new contexts based on earlier learning and experiences. Brenner et al. (2010) use the term 'variegation' to capture how circulations, or wider systemic processes, and different contextual outcomes mutually shape each other. They use this approach to understand 'urban neoliberalisation' – a powerful set of policy proposals prominent since the 1970s promoting pro-market governance and developments such as privatisation, public-private partnerships and a range of entrepreneurial urban policies promoting local economic growth (see Chapter 52). But each context shapes neoliberal policy differently, influenced by its own historical developments and specific political and social formations and contestations. Brenner et al. (2010) insist that each new example of urban neoliberalisation in turn shapes the wider systemic processes associated with circulating neoliberal ideas and practices. So, studies of different cases can help to trace the contours of how a wider process is produced, transformed and diversified.

A further possibility, though, is that comparisons could focus our attention more closely on the 'contingent' (as opposed to systemic) processes in each place which are shaping the 'variegations' of neoliberalisation. So, even if we start off by tracing circuits of neoliberalisation, we might find ourselves looking more closely at some other processes which are prominent in explaining individual 'contextual' outcomes.

In the post-hurricane Katrina reconstruction of New Orleans, for example, powerful actors and organisations lobbied strongly to achieve a pro-market development regime through neoliberal policies, a classic case of 'urban neoliberalisation' (Fox Gotham and Greenberg, 2008). But Ana Brand (2018) considers the post-Katrina reconstruction in New Orleans through the lens of W. B. Du Bois' idea of 'double consciousness' – that for African American people in the US, the white-dominant regime is only one aspect of urban experience. Instead of focussing on neoliberalisation, she identifies the post-Katrina redevelopment as a product of 'macro processes of racialization' (p. 14) in which Black residents have been further marginalised and excluded. She also considers the potential for alternative, **subaltern** visions of socially just development to emerge from communal spatial practices of Black New Orleans residents in historically Black neighbourhoods. The 'duality of space' speaks to the importance of paying attention to racialisation in any analysis of urban 'neoliberalisation' in the US and many other places; more broadly it suggests the need for much stronger attention to Black histories and experiences in urban studies (see also Chapter 70).

Pushing this further, comparative analysis might also reveal that in some situations neoliberalisation is not very relevant to understanding urban development and governance or might offer quite a different view of neoliberalisation. This also addresses the relative dominance of Global North experiences in urban studies. Bluntly put, what would we say urban neoliberalisation IS if we had started to build theorisations with cases from across the African continent? This would require, for example, an acknowledgement that in these contexts neoliberalisation was strongly organised around national institutions. Draconian **structural adjustment policies** implemented by international financial institutions since the 1980s in response to economic crises saw state institutions decimated, and services such as education and welfare vastly reduced. The urban impacts have been considerable but have not been to do with the neoliberalisation of urban governance – such policy initiatives have, in fact, often failed. Neoliberalisation has rather entailed the informalisation of much of the urban landscape: the slummification of urban living for many, the self-provisioning of nearly all services, the precarisation of formal employment and the restriction of the middle class. And an African account of neoliberalisation would also have to acknowledge that neoliberalisation has arguably led to some developmental outcomes, as extensive international humanitarian and developmental ambitions, including the Sustainable Development Goals, have mobilised international policy which often embeds a normalised neoliberal vocabulary (Parnell, 2016). In these contexts, scholars call for alternative global policy circulations to be the focus of attention, such as those concerned with practical state-building and developmental interventions (Parnell and Pieterse, 2016).

Expanding the range of connections considered matters more generally to creating a global perspective in urban studies. Lukasz Stanek (2020) draws attention to urban design and planning circuits which linked socialist architects from Eastern Europe to many post-colonial countries in Africa and some contexts in the Middle East and Asia, during the early post-independence period. As he argues, 'urban histories of twentieth century Baghdad and numerous other cities in the Global South cannot be understood without accounting for the exchanges with Eastern European and socialist countries elsewhere' (2020: 3). He argues that these encounters, which bypassed the Global North to some extent, could inspire more respectful and decentred comparative methods of equivalence.

Finally, we might consider comparing the connections themselves. Söderström (2014) conducted an experimental comparison which assessed how two urban areas (Hanoi, Vietnam and Ougadougou, Burkina Faso), which had been part of isolationist or 'autarkic' regimes, re-articulated with global processes in quite divergent ways. In Ougadougou this came about through diplomatic (geopolitical) circuits and city-to-city relations (like 'twinning'), policy learning and alliances; but in Hanoi, new global economic connections were fostered through close investment and trading relations with dynamic neighbouring Asian countries. Different connections were the important shapers of material, economic and political dynamics in each city, leading Söderström to invite scholars in urban studies to be specific about cities' 'multiple relations with elsewhere and what they produce' (p.152).

In different ways, working with connections and tracing the links amongst urban areas has the potential to expand the geographical scope and concerns of urban studies. And while comparisons might help to confirm our understandings of wider processes, by looking at many cases we might also be led to consider that our initial understanding was less valid – perhaps we need to think again! Each new case might also be 'analytically subtractive', taking away from existing theories and inviting us to revise our perspective.

Summary

- Following the many urban phenomena which are interconnected and repeated across different contexts is a key comparative tactic and opens up the possibility to think across a multiplicity of different urban contexts and learn from the diversity of the urban world.
- Tracing circuits of mobile policy, investment flows or material connections across many examples can help us to define a circuit or process better.
- Tracing connections also draws attention to differences and/or repetitions in outcomes and can inspire comparative reflections on the specific contexts and differences between them.
- And as each urban context is shaped by many different connections, it can be helpful to compare the circuits themselves and to expand the range of connections and processes which are considered analytically important to understanding contemporary urbanisation.

Starting from urban territories

While the urban is produced through widely shared processes or circulating phenomena, urban settings are also incredibly diverse – each urban context is distinctive. Why is this? Partly it is because particular combinations of flows and wider connections come together to shape how each individual urban context develops. In addition, over time quite specific ways of regulating developments (or urban governance) emerge in each urban context, and social groups and communities create distinctive ways of living. These influence future pathways of development ('path-dependency') shaped by wider processes. Taking a global view of urbanisation must face up to this distinctiveness of urban settlements.

On this basis, bringing different cases or contexts into comparison, or thinking with elsewhere, is based on the curiosity of the researcher rather than tracing connections (Robinson, 2022, Part 3). Comparisons might be inspired by analytical questions – such as, can we ever really know where a 'city' ends, or what exactly is 'urban'; they might be driven by practices of solidarity and collaboration with community groups to learn about the complex struggles over urban space and resources in other contexts; or they might embark on open processes of shared curiosity and exploration with researchers from other contexts. Comparative research can be designed to consider the widest variety of forms of a phenomenon to generate insights which could be useful across the global urban world. In comparing the governance of large-scale developments in Asia, for example, Gavin Shatkin (2017) selected contrasting cases which included centralised authoritarian, democratic and clientelistic forms of governance (respectively in China, India and Indonesia). Comparative imaginations can also be designed to inspire new learning from unexpected contexts. For example, Chinese or African experiences could be taken as the starting point for analysis of London, bringing to the fore the role of the state and community activism, rather than the global developers who dominate many accounts of London's urban development (Robinson, 2022, Chapter 8).

These kinds of comparisons are more dependent on the different perspectives of the scholars doing the research – both their chosen theoretical perspective and their individual **positionality**. Julie Ren (2020) has argued that as we turn to design comparative analyses, it is the 'theoretical case' which could define the urban phenomena we choose to understand through quite different contexts. She suggests that researchers set out with a 'theoretical case as a "case of something"' (p. 20). Often when designing research more generally, we ask each other – but what is this or that phenomenon a case of? In her book, she considers many different aspects of artists' activities in Berlin and Beijing and follows some international connections between these two artistic communities. For her, these rich urban worlds are 'cases of' what she calls 'art spaces' – the interaction between artists' practices and aspirations, and the urban contexts. In many places, including Berlin and Beijing, artists' practices have generated lively new cultural centres and transformed neighbourhoods or former industrial districts. In turn, city spaces have shaped artists practices – high rents or challenges of finding spaces to exhibit can limit their work.

More broadly, theoretical perspectives can play an important role in guiding how we select cases and compose comparisons. **Marxist**-inspired perspectives, for example, see urban outcomes as embedded in historically and geographically specific 'conjunctures' shaped by a range of wider and systemic processes such as **capitalism** or political ideologies (Leitner et al. 2019). This provides good reason to think about quite different cities which are part of the same historical moment, or conjuncture, but perhaps differently affected. For example, global processes of economic crisis in the 1970s and 1980s led to de-industrialisation in some places (US and Europe), devastating the economic base of many cities; at the same time, disciplining measures from international financial institutions led to severe cutbacks in national government funding for urban services across much of Africa; while in other parts of the world, notably in China, industrialisation and new forms of global economic development shaped massive processes of urbanisation (Wu, 2022). In this way we can build a more global analysis of the trends and tendencies in urbanisation.

In other perspectives, which start with each urban context or urban territory as distinctive, a comparative imagination can help us identify some of the shared causal processes of urban development, such as land use dynamics, migration processes and the processes shaping the spatial form of urban contexts including segregation (Scott and Storper, 2016). In each urban context, these 'causal mechanisms' operate in different ways, and generate different outcomes, which we can try to understand through comparative analysis. Empirical research by urban scholars starting with specific urban territories has helped to examine various socio-spatial configurations of 'urbanisation processes' shaping urban territories, with the hope that those identified in one context might also be relevant to explaining other urban situations (Schmid et al., 2018). Here, then, we can think comparatively about urbanisation processes, rather than needing to classify territories as 'urban' or compare 'cities'. In a world where it is very unclear what or where the urban is, such a shift in focus could be very productive.

Most famously, for example, the term '**gentrification**' describes an urbanisation process that arose in London in 1964. Based on her careful observations, Ruth Glass coined this term to describe physical and social change in the built environment associated with the return of the middle classes from the suburbs to the inner city. This led to new rounds of investment in the built environment and the displacement of often working class or racialised communities (see Chapter 55). This term has since circled the globe and seen many conceptual iterations. Alert to the post-colonial critique of too narrow a base for urban theorising, though, Schmid et al. (2018) insist that many other urbanisation processes can be identified across a diversity of urban contexts. They coin terms like 'plotting urbanism', for example, which refers to when urbanisation proceeds plot by plot but cumulatively amounts to large-scale transformation of the landscape. This is iconically visible in African contexts such as Lagos or Accra where traditional authorities or family-based institutions allocate individual plots of land to members of the group leading to incremental but extensive transformation of urban areas, and much contestation over land rights and developments (Gough and Yankson, 2000; see Figure 17.3). Or, drawing on South American conceptualisations, 'popular urbanisation' describes when communal and collective resources are mobilised in contexts of auto-construction (Caldeira, 2017). 'Bypass urbanism', which can be seen in many contexts in Asia, results from mostly private-sector investment in large-scale urban developments shaped by major new infrastructural projects as part of a wider 'scramble for infrastructure' (Kanai and Schindler, 2019). This generates urbanisation which potentially abandons, or bypasses, old urban centres with decaying infrastructure and highly informalised networks.

In contrast, in other theoretical perspectives, like those inspired by **actor network theory**, scholars see strong limits to the potential for concepts generated in one context to be of use in others. In their 'experimental comparison' Michele Lancione and Colin McFarlane (2016) consider the sanitation experiences of homeless people in Turin, and shack dwellers in Mumbai. They identify 'resonances' or shared grounds across their cases and make some 'generalisations' about sanitation experiences of poor people – continuous displacement, forceful negotiation, unavoidable exposure, which they link to 'ordinary affects of exhaustion, stress and shame' (p. 2417). But they are eager to restrict the learning to these two cases, rather than propose concepts that apply to other cases. They want to be respectful of heterogeneity and for

Figure 17.3
Notice to warn off potential fraudulent sales of traditional stool (family) land in Accra, Ghana.
Competing land claims are common in urban contexts with dual (traditional and formal titled) land
ownership

Source: Photo credit: Jennifer Robinson

their work to remain directly useful to addressing the challenges of sanitation for poor people in
these two contexts. Of course, as we have seen with gentrification, such a locally based concept
might nonetheless have potential for a wider reach.

As we respond to the urban as specific, we might consider designing much looser comparative experiments, perhaps as 'conversations', allowing insights from one context to reflect
back to another (Robinson, 2022, Chapter 10). In this vein, for example, social housing and
co-operative housing in wealthy contexts, and informal housing on traditional authority land in
many African urban situations, can all be seen as ways to take land and housing for the poor out
of the formal capitalist market economy, creating affordable options from Zurich to Accra (Potts,
2020). Opening up conversations from different starting points can stimulate new vocabularies,
and insights – thinking with the Chinese concept of urban-rural configurations (*Jiehebu*) rather
than suburbs can stimulate new lines of comparison which sidestep western narratives and experiences (Zhao, 2020). Thus, concepts emergent in particular contexts might be 'launched' into
wider conversations, transforming urban studies from places and positionalities which have
hitherto been treated as marginal to conceptualisation.

This section has demonstrated how urban studies now offers many opportunities to generate
new concepts while engaging with the diversity of urban life, globally. Composing comparisons
driven by researcher curiosity establishes a wide-open analytical agenda to learn from very divergent cases. But the active role of the researcher in designing or composing comparisons also

highlights that crucial to transforming urban studies is not only expanding the variety of cases and concepts but also expanding the voices and authors, or 'subjects', of urban theory: who compares, matters.

Summary

- In this section we have explored what might it mean to think from the urban as distinctive, starting with 'individual' outcomes to generate insights.
- By bringing in the most diverse of urban experiences, we can enrich understandings so that they might speak to a wider range of urban situations.
- How comparative experiments are designed is often strongly influenced by the theoretical perspective and positionality of the researcher.

Conclusion

The point of a reformatted comparative practice is to provoke new conceptualisations, starting anywhere, with a strong orientation to revising existing concepts. Comparative urbanism seeks to contribute to innovative conceptualisation, displacing inherited 'theories', by composing analytical reflections across diverse urban contexts, tracing connections across their differentiation in many urban contexts or launching concepts starting from anywhere. On this basis, global urban studies can be a field in which concepts are intrinsically highly revisable, where research is conducted in a modest authorial voice, and researchers are open to insights starting from anywhere.

As a manifesto to think the urban from anywhere, however, comparative urbanism throws a spotlight on the urgent need for institutional transformation in urban studies. Many scholars around the world are based in under-resourced institutions and may struggle to find time to write up their cutting-edge insights for 'international' journals. Institutional inequalities in academic research need to be addressed and new practices of learning, reading and writing about the global urban developed (see further resources below). Strategies might include: wider reading and citation of locally and regionally circulated publications; firm expectations of full acknowledgement (including co-authorship) of the contribution of scholars one has worked with and learned from in the course of research; changing what counts as excellent international research to recognise a variety of kinds of contributions (Parnell and Pieterse, 2016). For scholarly practices to support revisable theory and to learn from the insights and voices of scholars in different contexts, research also needs to be done collaboratively, both with other scholars and with urban dwellers.

Globalising urban studies can certainly be supported by reformatted comparative methods, such as those which have been discussed in this chapter. But who is producing this knowledge ('the subject of urban theory') also matters. This approach, then, can contribute to the **decolonisation** of established practices, agendas and voices, and the hopes of stimulating practices of thinking 'in-common' (Mbembe, 2017) which embrace the lively differences of the urban world and open to new ways of thinking and practicing urban life.

Discussion points

- Have you seen something identical from your own urban context in another city? This could be something as simple as a particular style of streetlights, street signs, markets or pavements, or something as complex as iconic buildings designed by famous international architects, or social housing designs. What are the circuits that led to these? For instance, colonial circuits saw 'shop houses' developed and spread across East Asia, including space for both trade and living. Or is there something very specific to a context you are familiar with? The pedestrian crossing signals in some parts of Berlin, for example, are a distinctive inheritance from the former socialist era German Democratic Republic.
- Should understandings or concepts of the urban be applicable in places beyond where they are developed? Can you think of a term you have come across in the literature (or this chapter) which you think is not relevant to your context?
- How can you practice learning from scholars in different parts of the world? What might be the difficulties in this? One suggestion is to search for interesting and relevant contributions on issues you are exploring in publications from different parts of the world. For example, *Urbanisation* draws from many Indian scholars, *Urban Forum* draws on Southern Africa. Also look for events organised by key centres of urban expertise in different regions, including African Centre for Cities, Indian Institute of Human Settlements or Beirut Urban Lab.

References

Aalbers, M. (2016). *The Financialization of Housing: A Political Economy Approach.* London: Routledge.

Bhan, G. (2019). Notes on a Southern urban practice. *Environment and Urbanization* 31(2): 639–654.

Brand, A. L. (2018). The duality of space: the built world of Du Bois' double-consciousness. *Environment and Planning D: Society and Space* 36(1): 3–22.

Brenner, N., Peck, J., and Theodore, N. (2010). Variegated neoliberalization: geographies, modalities, pathways. *Global Networks* 10(2): 182–222.

Brenner, N., and Schmid, C. (2014). The 'urban age' in question. *International Journal of Urban and Regional Research* 38(3): 731–755.

Caldeira, T. (2017). Peripheral urbanization: autoconstruction, transversal logics, and politics in cities of the global South. *Environment and Planning D, Society and Space* 35(1): 3–20.

Fox Gotham, K., and Greenberg, M. (2008). From 9/11 to 8/29: post-disaster response and recovery in New York and New Orleans. *Social Forces* 87(2), December 2008: 1–24.

Gough, K., and Yankson, P. W. K. (2000). Land markets in African cities: the case of peri-urban Accra, Ghana. *Urban Studies* 37(13): 2485–2500.

Halbert, L., and Rouanet, H. (2014). Filtering risk away: global finance capital, transcalar territorial networks and the (Un)making of city-regions: an analysis of business property development in Bangalore, India. *Regional Studies* 48(3): 471–484.

Hart, G. (2003). *Disabling Globalisation: Places of Power in Post-Apartheid South Africa.* Berkeley: University of California Press.

Kanai, J. M., and Schindler, S. (2019). Peri-urban promises of connectivity: linking project-led polycentrism to the infrastructure scramble. *Environment and Planning A: Economy and Space* 51(2): 302–322.

Lancione, M., and McFarlane, C. (2016). Life at the urban margins: sanitation infra-making and the potential of experimental comparison. *Environment and Planning A* 48(12): 2402–2421.

Leitner, H., Peck, J., and Sheppard, E. (eds). (2019). *Urban Studies Inside/Out: Theory, Practice and Method.* London and New York: Sage.

Massey, D. (2005). *For space.* London: Sage.

Mbembe, A. (2017). *Critique of Black Reason,* trans. Laurent DuBois. Durham: Duke University Press.

McCann, E. (2011). Urban policy mobilities and global circuits of knowledge: towards a research agenda. *Annals of the Association of American Geographers* 101(1): 107–130.

Myers, G. (2020). *Rethinking Urbanism: Lessons from Postcolonialism and the Global South.* Bristol: Policy Press.

Parnell, S. (2016). Defining a global urban development agenda. *World Development* 78: 529–554.

Parnell, S., and Pieterse, E. (2016). Translational global praxis: rethinking methods and modes of African urban research. *International Journal of Urban and Regional Research* 40(1): 236–246.

Peake, L. (2016). The twenty-first century quest for feminism and the global urban, *International Journal of Urban and Regional Research* 40(1): 219–227.

Potts, D. (2020). *Broken Cities: Inside the Global Housing Crisis.* London: Zed Books.

Ren, J. (2020). *Engaging Comparative Urbanism: Art Spaces in Beijing and Berlin.* Bristol: Bristol University Press.

Robinson, J. (2006). *Ordinary Cities: Between Modernity and Development.* London: Routledge.

Robinson, J. (2022). *Comparative Urbanism: Tactics for Global Urban Studies.* Oxford: Wiley-Blackwell.

Roy, A. (2009). The 21st century metropolis: new geographies of theory. *Regional Studies* 43(6): 819–830.

Schmid, C., Karaman, O., Hanakata, N., Kallenberger, P., Kockelkorn, A., Sawyer, L., Streule, M., and Wong, K. P. (2018). Towards new vocabularies of urbanization processes: a comparative approach. *Urban Studies* 55(1): 19–52.

Scott, A., and Storper, M. (2016). Current debates in urban theory: A critical assessment. *Urban Studies,* 53(6): 1114–1136.

Shatkin, G. (2017). *Cities for Profit: The Real Estate Turn in Asia's Urban Politics.* Ithaca: Cornell.

Simone, A. (2019). *Improvised Lives: Rhythms of Endurance in an Urban South.* Cambridge: Polity.

Söderström, O. (2014). *Cities in Relations: Trajectories of Urban Development in Hanoi and Ougadougou.* Oxford: Wiley-Blackwell.

Stanek, L. (2020). *Architecture in Global Socialism: Eastern Europe, West Africa, and the Middle East in the Cold War.* Princeton: Princeton University Press.

Ward, K. (2010). Towards a relational comparative approach to the study of cities. *Progress in Human Geography* 34(4): 471–487.

Wu, F. (2022). *Creating Chinese Urbanism: Urban Revolution and Governance Changes.* London: UCL Press.

Zhao, Y. (2020). *Jiehebu* or suburb? Towards a translational turn in urban studies. *Cambridge Journal of Regions, Economy and Society* 13(3): 527–542.

Online materials

- https://planetaryurbanisation.ethz.ch/assets/publications/hinterland-singapore-johor-riau-studio-report/TOPALOVIC_HINTERLAND_FULL-BOOK_reduced-file-size.pdf
  A report on the flows and connections that shape Singapore's urbanisation. Notice the extent to which urban life in Singapore depends on flows of materials (such as sand), people and money. Singapore in turn 'travels' as it has become a significant model of successful urban development. On the UN SDG website link below, you will find a discussion of how the Kigali 2050 Masterplan supports the SDGs, links to the masterplan and to the Singapore group who were the consultants working on it. https://sdgs.un.org/partnerships/kigali-city-masterplan-2050

- https://sdgs.un.org/goals/goal11
  A site maintained by the United Nations to monitor efforts through the Sustainable Development Goal 11: Make cities and human settlements inclusive, safe, resilient and sustainable.

- https://unhabitat.org/wcr/#downloads
  Download or access the Statistical Annex to this 2022 UN Habitat World Cities Report. Glance through Table A1, which tries to capture the percentage of each country which is declared urban. If you focus on Africa, you will see that many countries have quite low levels of urbanisation, but very high rates of population growth in urban areas (take a look at Malawi, for example). You could follow up with exploring some of the other indicators (e.g. water, slums).

- https://www.gfdrr.org/en/crp. World Bank City Resilience Programme: 'Enabling Cities to save lives, reduce losses and unlock economic and social potential'. Here you can read more about the goals of the World Bank initiative to promote resilience in urban areas across the world.

Further reading

Brenner, N. (ed.) (2013). *Implosions/Explosions: Towards a Study of Planetary Urbanisation*. Berlin: Jovis. If you want to read more about Planetary Urbanisation – a general term to indicate the new geographies of urbanisation emerging across and impacting the planet – you can browse this collection. Try Chapter 8 from Brazilian scholar Roberto Monte-Mór, inspired by the Brazilian experiences of urbanisation of remote forest and mining areas or Chapter 28 which presents some experiments in mapping and visualising contemporary extended urban developments.

Leitner, H., Peck, J., and Sheppard, E. (eds). (2019). *Urban Studies Inside/Out: Theory, Practice and Method*. London and New York: Sage.
This text reviews current methodological debates and approaches in global urban studies, from a broadly Marxist perspective. It is written in an accessible and student-friendly style and includes several essays on major comparative texts in urban studies, written by graduate students.

Parnell, S., and Pieterse, E. (2016). Translational global praxis: rethinking methods and modes of African urban research. *International Journal of Urban and Regional Research* 40(1): 236–246.
This short text reflects on how urban studies needs to change in order to accommodate a wider range of perspectives from scholars across the globe. It makes a bold statement about the importance and challenges of including contributions from African based scholars, and addressing themes that matter to this most rapidly urbanising continent.

Robinson, J. (2022). *Comparative Urbanism: Tactics for Global Urban Studies*. Oxford: Wiley-Blackwell.
This book expands on the themes in this chapter – tracing connections, composing comparisons and generating new concepts in the field are explored through many examples. Try Chapters 5 and 10 to get a flavour of the range of possibilities in comparative urban studies.

Wu, F. (2022). *Creating Chinese Urbanism: Urban Revolution and Governance Changes*. London: UCL Press.
Free download is available at: https://www.uclpress.co.uk/products/195093
Fulong Wu approaches trends in global urbanisation from the Chinese perspective. He traces the distinctive history of Chinese urban growth, governance and planning through the twentieth and twenty-first centuries and is a great example of building new understandings of global urbanisation, from different perspectives and situations.

18 Rurality

Menelaos Gkartzios

First encounters

Every year I ask my undergraduate students to 'define the rural'. The term *rurality* is not particularly meaningful to them, especially if English is not their first language. The responses vary, and at times are amusing and exciting, but always start with some speculation on population levels and densities, settlement sizes, types of housing, farming activities and so on. Once I was told that settlements could be defined as either urban or rural based on whether they have pavements or not. A few walks around global metropoles (Tokyo for example) would easily demonstrate this is not the case. This year a student told us that if you can't get a signal on your mobile phone, 'it is definitely rural' – they had a point, but still. The discussion usually moves on to land uses and services, agriculture and food production, natural resources, landscape features and topography. Finally, we arrive at issues of identity and **representation**, what they understand a person from the countryside to be like, and we also discuss what might have influenced their responses in the conversation, whether they grew up in the countryside and so on. Through this introductory question, we touch on most scholarly approaches and struggles associated with theorising ruralities in human geography: from negatively defined spaces (essentially what is non-urban) to numerical, functional or statistical definitions of rurality and more complex typologies; and from values we attach to rural places and rural identities (both positive and negative) to symbols, representations and **discourses** of the rural. This interaction with the students is engaging because they all know what the rural is, but to define it in absolute terms or even *on its own terms* (especially not in negative terms) remains a challenge. In the remainder of this chapter, I will introduce some of the most influential scholarship in human geography that has dealt with the concept of rurality, including some more recent developments, particularly around decoloniality, artistic practice and language politics.

From dualities to power dynamics

Most unequivocally, geographer Keith Halfacree (1993) has argued that the rural matters – and is therefore worth defining – because it is used and understood in everyday talk. The rural carries emotional connotations in people's biographies and life aspirations; it is an important element of one's identity rather than a marginal explanatory descriptor. In an early, but highly influential, effort to unpack it, Halfacree (1993) describes four main ways to define the rural, embracing both historical developments and interdisciplinary perspectives: descriptive definitions; socio-cultural

DOI: 10.4324/9780429265853-22

definitions; rural as distinctive locality; and rural as social representation. As such, he first distinguishes between the various definitions of rurality that are associated with specific and measurable variables (i.e. population density); these have also been used to develop a series of positivist rural typologies drawing on multiple variables (usually derived from census data), such as educational qualifications, income levels, distance from cities and taxation per capita (for an early example see Cloke, 1977; and more recently, Nelson et al., 2021). An inherent bias of many of these approaches is that policy makers and researchers were not necessarily interested in defining rurality *per se*, but rather urban spaces, with the rural constituting all space that was literally left out. This exemplifies a particular phenomenon whereby rural areas are defined either as spaces that are *not* urban or in relation to how those spaces are used, especially for farming and agriculture. As a consequence, our understandings of urban and rural spaces operate in a dynamic relationship: while they are inextricably connected in their conceptualisation, they are not exactly antithetical, and they are not opposite in equal terms (Gkartzios et al., 2020) (Figure 18.1).

Although these descriptive definitions vary greatly from one context to another, every country has developed such measurable definitions of rurality. The urban-rural cut-off point in England,

Figure 18.1
Syrrako village (of Vlach heritage) in Greece

Source: Photo credit: Menelaos Gkartzios

for example, is 10,000 people per settlement (UK Government Statistical Service, 2011), while it is set at only 1500 people just across the Irish Sea in the Republic of Ireland (CSO [Central Statistics Office], 2019). The OECD (2011) also uses a descriptive definition to distinguish between urban and rural areas by referring to the population density of small administrative units (i.e. rurality constitutes areas with less than 150 people per square kilometre, excluding Japan and South Korea in recognition of their contrasting higher density levels). Such context-specific definitions are helpful in policymaking, but they also further exacerbate urban-rural dichotomies, are arbitrary (particularly for further academic scrutiny and analysis) and add confusion to international discussions about rural policies (Woods, 2005). For this reason, the proposition of an **urban-rural continuum** (Pahl, 1966) has been more appealing in understanding the way rural and urban places operate as part of a networked settlement pattern particularly in less industrialised contexts, although in reality policy framing in many cases still suffers from an urban-rural binary imposition. This suggests that while we acknowledge the complexity of settlement patterns across multiple and overlapping layers of urbanity and rurality (embracing places, identities, networks, mobilities etc.), we tend to have very different priorities and policy aspirations for settlements we broadly understand and describe as either urban or rural (see also Gallent and Gkartzios, 2019).

Halfacree (1993) further acknowledges scholarly attempts to define rurality by observing unique socio-economic phenomena in rural spaces. These efforts were not successful, which led to calls to dismiss altogether the idea of the rural as a meaningful scale for policy implementation and to some extent as a field of geographical scholarship (Hoggart, 1990). Rather than marginalising the rural because of a scholarly inability to define it in absolute or unique terms, the cultural turn of the late 1980s gave rise to a new and exciting set of questions about the lived experience in rural places (Cloke, 2006), embracing discussions about power struggles in the countryside across identities of **gender**, **race**, **ethnicity** and sexuality. In that context, research on rurality has focused on the symbols, signs and images people think of as rural – *representations* of rurality. These developments not only invited critical questions about rural identity – beyond what Philo (1992) refers to as 'Mr Average' – but also grounded the idea of a contested rurality (e.g. Scott, 2006): a socio-political space infused with **power**, multiple meanings and representations (Woods, 2005). As a consequence, there have been a series of research projects that, instead of focusing on functional terminologies of the rural, have explored how actors define such ruralities – a 'post rural' in the context of earlier definitional attempts (Cloke, 2006) – and how such representations are used to frame and legitimise policies and interests in the countryside (e.g. Rye, 2006). It wasn't that earlier scholarship hadn't attempted to attach meaning and values to urban and rural places (see, for example, the works of Ferdinand Tönnies and Louis Wirth). What the cultural turn allowed was the exploration of such representations as not fixed in time and/or space but instead as constantly evolving, mirroring wider interests and power struggles in the countryside.

Although such representations are, of course, complex and dynamic, culturally and place contingent, two narratives frame the way in which the rural is usually discussed and captured across policy, political and media discourses of the rural (Woods, 2005). These have been conceptualised by Murdoch et al. (2003) as another binary, between *pastoralism* and **modernism**. The pastoral, pre-industrial and romantic view of the countryside is commonly referred to as the 'rural idyll' (Bell, 2006) and has frequently been used to encapsulate middle-class interests in the countryside. By contrast, modernism frames a backward version of the countryside, lagging behind culturally and technologically – a narrative that is often used to support development in the countryside. In many cases, these two narratives operate almost in parallel, each evidencing the existence of the other. Of course, rural areas demonstrate far more complex narratives than these two **hegemonic** discourses (da Silva et al., 2016), both progressive and parochial, both privileged and forgotten, and the analysis of those has also embraced multidisciplinary and geo-humanity perspectives.

Although the rural still needs to be defined in some descriptive ways for policy intervention, these contributions have analysed which social groups frame understandings of selective ruralities, how and to what purpose, embracing also questions of **power** and **agency** in the debate of rurality. Such explorations are central to a highly influential proposition about rural geographies: the 'differentiated countryside' (Murdoch et al., 2003), a critical lens through which to understand shifting politics and power relations in the contemporary countryside. Acknowledging great diversity *amongst* rural areas (and thus moving beyond the urban-rural dichotomy), the differentiated countryside introduced a more nuanced typology of rural areas based on the contrasting interests and power dynamics across various agents in the countryside. Ranging from agriculture-dominated areas based on state support to areas of increasing conflict between economic development and environmental conservation interests, the differentiated countryside has made a profound contribution to proposing a place-specific approach to understanding rural areas. This has revealed complex power hierarchies that are central to the development of rural areas. The 'ideal' types that have been proposed by its authors (drawing on English cases) are: the 'preserved countryside', characterised by the dominance of conservation and anti-development interests; the 'contested countryside', implying contested rationalities across rural development interests; the 'paternalistic countryside', highlighting the role of large landowners monopolising development opportunities; and the 'clientist countryside' whereby state agencies, as institutional landowners, are the crucial actors framing opportunities for rural development.

Summary

- There is no single way to define the rural, although certain aspects of rurality can be more dominant than others (e.g. association with agriculture).
- Rurality encompasses material and symbolic characteristics.
- The notion of a 'differentiated countryside' implies the heterogeneity of rural areas as well as power struggles regarding their rural development trajectories.

Mobilities and relationality

The debates around rurality, of course, did not stop with the cultural turn and various scholarly influences (for example the turns to mobility, the spatial and the **performative**) have given rise to more nuanced understandings of rurality, freeing on the one hand the rural from the conceptual boundaries of population density and proximity to the city, while on the other hand also seeking to re-materialise rurality and its farming/agricultural preoccupations (e.g. Zhang, 2022). Such understandings are evident in relational and more-than-representational approaches to rurality (e.g. Heley and Jones, 2012, Phillips, 2014). Askins (2009), for example, introduces a 'transrural' approach which extends to scales of experiencing rurality *beyond* the countryside – for example through mobilities and desire from/to rural spaces/places. A significant contribution in aligning the **social construction** of rural places with material processes of change has been Halfacree's (2006) three-fold conceptualisation of rurality, drawing on Henri Lefebvre, which consists of *rural localities* associated with production or consumption actions of rurality, formal *representations of space* as articulated by professional experts including planners, and *everyday lives of the rural*, for example personal experiences of rurality (for an application in the Chinese context see Chung, 2013).

Mobilities have been central in understanding the rural, because of the multiple ways mobilities shift rural meanings and practices, evoking new politics and conflicts (Milbourne and Kitchen, 2014). The most significant driver of rural social change has been counterurbanisation, broadly defined here as a move towards a more rural residential environment (Figure 18.2). Counterurbanisation has indeed been one of the most discussed topics in rural geography for over five decades, and although originally describing a Global North or western social phenomenon, it is now commonly discussed across globally differentiated contexts; see for example

Figure 18.2
Art wall and new housing in Puli, Taiwan

Source: Photo credit: Menelaos Gkartzios

scholarly contributions in Africa (Geyer and Geyer, 2017, Crankshaw and Borel-Saladin, 2019), Asia (Jain and Korzhenevych, 2019, Klien, 2020) and Latin America (García-Ayllón, 2016).

The complexity of counterurbanisation as a concept mirrors the difficulty of defining mutually exclusive urban and rural spaces, especially across complex and differentiated histories of industrialisation around the globe (Gkartzios, 2013). It also invites multiple reasons in explaining why people move (or return) to the countryside, from economic rationality to wellbeing perceptions attached to the social construction of the countryside, across various social groups (e.g. from middle-class urban-based families moving in peri-urban rural areas to more radical and counter-cultural moves towards marginal and remote rural areas) (see a suggested typology by Mitchell, 2004). More critically, counterurbanisation demonstrates why scholarly interest in rurality still matters: new agents are entering the countryside, bringing new skills, networks and values in relation to rural life which shift development trajectories and create conflicts with other groups that are positioned as 'local' or 'authentic'. For example, a particular aspect of counterurbanisation is the colonisation of the countryside by more middle-class groups, leading to the **gentrification** of rural space, and ultimately issues of displacement, housing unaffordability and exclusion (Gkartzios and Ziebarth, 2016). However, the experience of counterurbanisation is not necessarily attached to processes of gentrification (Phillips, 2010) and, in certain contexts, counterurbanisation presents an opportunity to develop the countryside (Dilley et al., 2022). Furthermore, the discourse around mobility has opened the debate for explorations beyond counterurbanisation, including rural-to-rural migration, ephemeral and open-ended mobilities (e.g. Halfacree and Rivera, 2012), leading to the proposition of 'messy mobilities' by Stockdale (2016): that rural mobilities indeed are complex, multi-directional and beyond dichotomous explanations and typologies.

Aside from the tendency to focus on mobility, understandings of rurality as part of a networked – and therefore interrelated – world gave rise to the notion of a 'global countryside' (Woods, 2007), acknowledging that rural areas are part of interconnected and interdependent global systems and processes and that in many instances rural areas constitute important localities in which to address global challenges (Gkartzios et al., 2022). The positionality of rural areas in a globalised world suggests that their future development trajectories are heavily contested, but in essence they constitute a new politics of place, introduced as the 'the politics of the rural' by Woods (2006), whereby the meaning and regulation of rurality underpins conflicts and dictates development trajectories. Such processes of **globalisation** and the development of networked economies in the countryside have also been discussed as 'hybrid ruralities' (Lin et al., 2016): on one hand, technological and scientific advancements have radically transformed rural places and allowed them to be part of a globalised world; and, on the other hand, the same processes have resulted in **alienation**, resistance and rejection of modernisation.

Another way to discuss relationality in the conceptualisation of rurality is to explore approaches that are not specifically preoccupied with what the countryside *is* but, instead, aim to understand *how* it functions. This implies an understanding of how to support bottom-up and place-based policy interventions that result in more socially just, sustainable and inclusive countrysides; governance relationships and actions which are usually recognised under the umbrella of neo-endogenous (or networked) rural development. The approach of seeing what rural areas are *made of* has given rise to various capital framings which aim to articulate and valorise the place-based assets or resources – both material and immaterial – that constitute the countryside and ultimately can underpin local and sustainable development pathways. Prominent propositions have been the *Sustainable Livelihoods Framework* (Scoones, 1998) and the *Community Capital*

Framework (Flora et al., 2004), which acknowledge interrelated forms of capital specific to the rural context. Similar approaches have been proposed by various other scholars of rurality who emphasise how these capitals work and interact towards desired policy actions (e.g. Gkartzios et al., 2022, Natarajan et al., 2022).

Summary

- Mobilities frame an important aspect to understand and research the shifting nature of rurality.
- Counterurbanisation commonly refers to urban relocations in rural areas (or areas per-ceived to be 'more rural') pointing to new and contested understandings and represen-tations of rurality.
- The 'politics of the rural' is a framework to understand conflict and change in the coun-tryside, particularly within a globalised and networked world.

New ruralities: decoloniality, language and art

Scholarship about rurality has evolved within particular socio-cultural contexts, disciplinary knowledge silos, natural languages – and the politics that all these entail. Indeed, following the cultural turn, rural geography in Britain not only dominated other disciplinary approaches within the broader framing of rural studies but also enjoyed a more critical position compared to that adopted in other countries (Bell, 2007). A direct result of such asymmetries, coupled with the fact that English emerged as the *lingua franca* of academic scholarship after the second half of the twentieth century (de Swaan, 2001), has meant that many social phenomena related to rurality have been conceptualised through the English language and, more widely, within anglo-phone contexts (as demonstrated also by the language of this global book). The proliferation of anglophone scholarship in rural studies has resulted in critical questions about whose knowledge and experience matters in the production of academic discourse about rurality:

> As all knowledge is produced in specific geographical and cultural contexts, a frank recogni-tion and examination of the social bases of knowledge is required. That is not only necessary for the pursuit of objectivity. It is also important to appreciate the limits of knowledge in con-sidering its relevance or applicability. Otherwise, we risk building a globalised knowledge (say, an international rural sociology) on the false assumption that we all speak the same language. Yet, even when we do speak the same language, we do not always share the same meaning.
>
> *Lowe, 2012: 35*

The influence of the anglosphere in rural scholarship is particularly evident in the research on the social construction of idyllic ruralities (Vepsalainen and Pitkanen, 2010), on counterurbani-sation research (Grimsrud, 2011) and also in the deployment of the 'differentiated countryside' as a frame of analysis in rural studies globally (e.g. Brunori and Rossi, 2007) in spite of the fact that it draws on the unique spatial rural realities of England (Gkartzios and Remoundou, 2018). This suggests that knowledge production about rurality has its own politics and exclusions and that we need to engage with scholarship and authors that mirror the rural experience across the world (see also Chapter 19 on 'Comparative Ruralities'). In that regard, and in the context of wider efforts to decolonise the academy, recent works have drawn, first, on rurality struggles in the Global South (e.g. Gillen et al., 2022) researching, in particular, Indigenous rural community conflicts, discussed sometimes as 'indigenous ruralities' (Majer, 2019). Second, recent work aims also to reconsider language **performativity** and translation politics in the research process and subsequent anglophone dissemination (e.g. Gkartzios et al., 2020, Wang, 2022), especially because meanings and identities of rurality are so diversified and complex globally, intersected with Indigenous languages and vernacular cultures, ranging from discriminatory and derogative connotations to bourgeois lifestyles and aspirations. The point of these debates is not to abandon research on rurality or even abandon the term rurality itself (as Hoggart suggested much earlier) but to critically interrogate other power struggles in the production of rural knowledge beyond the experience of European and North American contexts (Figure 18.3).

Figure 18.3
Co-op café and library in Gödence, Turkey

Source: Photo credit: Menelaos Gkartzios

These debates inherently acknowledge a much older proposition of course (Jones, 1995, Halfacree, 2006): that many different agents produce discourse about rurality, and they are not all the usual suspects, such as rural residents, policy makers, farmers and rural scholars. While much work focuses on lay, policy, media and academic discourses of rurality, other actors play significant roles as well. Indeed, in recent years, there appears to be significant excitement about the countryside, evident, *inter alia*, in the capture of rurality in cultural production and specifically within the global circuits of the 'art world'. In New York for example, the Guggenheim Museum hosted an exhibition on the 'Countryside, The Future' exploring 'radical changes in the rural, remote, and wild territories collectively identified here as "countryside", or the 98% of the Earth's surface not occupied by cities [...]' (Guggenheim, 2020; see also online materials at the end of the chapter). Furthermore, the Chinese entry at the 2018 Venice Architecture Biennale, aimed to 'build a future countryside', rooted in 'forgotten values and overlooked possibilities' (La Biennale di Venezia, 2018).

Aside from these large-scale events, creative arts practice in and about rurality abounds globally (e.g. Leung and Thorsen, 2022) and can be seen also in the growth of artist residency programmes in rural areas (Gkartzios and Crawshaw, 2019). The work here includes not just creative arts practice positioned in or transferred physically to the countryside, but, more critically perhaps, creative arts practice that is *about* the countryside, artistic practice that reflects, challenges and researches rural futures and rural livelihoods. Such contributions have offered new explorations and imaginations about struggles in rural places. Work in this area is inherently inter- and trans-disciplinary and extends beyond the recognition of the 'creative countryside' and development opportunities associated with place-based cultural assets in rural areas (see for example Bell and Jayne, 2010); indeed, the artistic experience can offer sensory ways of reading and understanding communities and rural places (Crawshaw and Gkartzios, 2016). But more importantly, there appears to be a new wave of artists, scholars and rural/urban residents interested in artistic expression and experiences in the countryside, adding to the continuously evolving discourse of rurality (Argent, 2018) and giving rise to new research approaches, methods and knowledges in researching the countryside (Crawshaw, 2022).

Summary

- Knowledge production about rural places has its own politics and power struggles, framed also by **colonialism**.
- All knowledge and discourse about rural places are important, especially beyond scholarly contributions.

Rurality in the twenty-first century

Irrespective of the definitions or approaches used, rurality encompasses both material features and abstract social characteristics. The consensus is that rural areas are heavily differentiated and contested places, characterised by significant transformations and emerging politics of place. This is also evident in the numerous expressions that encapsulate rural change, such as the '**post-productivist transition**', the '**consumptive countryside**', '**rural restructuring**' and the '**multifunctional countryside**' (Figure 18.4; see also the discussion in Chapter 19). At the heart of all such concepts is an appreciation that change (environmental, demographic, economic, cultural, built etc.) has been a fundamental aspect of rural realities.

Rural areas have been at the forefront of debates around climate change mitigation and adaptation. It is not difficult to understand why: the vast majority of the Earth's surface is rural; food and fibre are largely produced in rural areas; many rural areas are associated with natural resource extraction. But rural areas matter not only in the context of the climate emergency – they have been critical spaces for attention through various crises. For example, the global coronavirus pandemic demonstrated that rural places have suffered disproportionately due to their unique socio-spatial characteristics, while, in other cases, crises have offered unique opportunities for new forms of resilience to be explored (Gkartzios and Scott, 2015). Rural areas also form politically important constituencies; sometimes they are discussed as bastions of populism and associated with the growth of right-wing politics (see Edelman, 2021, Mamonova and

Figure 18.4
Agriculture in front of Teshima Art Museum in Teshima Island, Japan

Source: Photo credit: Menelaos Gkartzios

Franquesa, 2020), while at the same time some offer resistant alternatives to **neoliberalism** (e.g. Shucksmith and Rønningen, 2011), embedded within emergent queer politics and progressive post-capitalist visions (e.g. Gray et al., 2016).

The dynamic of all these changes signals that there is a need to articulate better rural futures, as expressed by Shucksmith's (2018) concept of 'the good countryside'. Visions of what constitutes a good countryside, of course, abound and are conflicted – we must accept that it is that *plurality* that legitimises the ambition of more sustainable, socially just and resilient rural areas (Bell, 2007). However, while the imagination of a better countryside remains open and flexible, the route to get there rests upon the realisation of new development pathways that are critically embedded in and committed to rural places. This suggests an understanding of rurality as part of an interconnected planetary system in which the urban-rural distinction serves as one of its boundaries that we need to tackle, while demonstrating care for a rural place and valuing its material and immaterial resources (Gkartzios et al., 2022).

Calls to recognise the importance of rurality are regularly made in scholarly and policy literature (see for example a blog published in Planetizen, by Hibbard and Frank [2022]). At the same time, our collective and institutional understandings of urbanity and rurality are not without biases. While scholarly engagement with the rural requires the articulation of parallels with related social phenomena in the metropolis, the opposite is hardly ever the case. It is interesting to note that the urban-rural divide is also mirrored in academic boundaries between urban and rural studies, each having its own fora, learning communities and academic journals. The point of this chapter is to contribute to understandings of the rural as a place identity of contrasting yet numerous values and imaginations. Drawing on Halfacree (2006), rurality is not simply the antithesis of urbanity; like any other place, rurality is experienced, lived, negotiated and contested. It is, however, equally important to appreciate rurality as a body of knowledge – both vernacular and scholarly – with its own politics and power dynamics, and support increased demands to value knowledge about rurality produced not only outside white, western and Global North contexts but also outside the academy itself.

This chapter is dedicated to the memory of Professor Paul Cloke whose contributions in the development of rural scholarship remain unparalleled.

Discussion points

- How would you define the rural?
- What values and beliefs do we hold for rural places? Where do they come from? Are they consistent across various social groups? How do such values find their ways in policymaking?
- What kind of conflicts are observed in the contemporary countryside? What is their global diversity and relevance to sustainability agendas?
- How should we approach rural places in policymaking?

References

Argent, N. (2018). Rural geography III: marketing, mobilities, measurement and metanarratives, *Progress in Human Geography* 43(4): 758–766.

Askins, K. (2009). Crossing divides: ethnicity and rurality, *Journal of Rural Studies* 25(4): 365–375.

Bell, D. (2006). Variations on the Rural Idyll. In *The Handbook of Rural Studies*, eds. P. Cloke, T. Marsden, and P. Mooney. London: Sage, 149–160.

Bell, D., and Jayne, M. (2010). The creative countryside: policy and practice in the UK rural cultural economy. *Journal of Rural Studies* 26(3): 209–218.

Bell, M. M. (2007). The two-ness of rural life and the ends of rural scholarship. *Journal of Rural Studies* 23(4): 402–415.

Brunori, G., and Rossi, A. (2007). Differentiating countryside: social representations and governance patterns in rural areas with high social density: the case of Chianti, Italy. *Journal of Rural Studies* 23(2): 183–205.

Chung, H. (2013). Rural transformation and the persistence of rurality in China. *Eurasian Geography and Economics* 54(5–6): 594–610.

CSO (Central Statistics Office). (2019). Urban and Rural Life in Ireland, 2019. https://www.cso.ie/en/releasesandpublications/ep/p-urli/urbanandrurallifeinireland2019/introduction/#d.en.211130

Cloke, P. (1977). An index of rurality for England and Wales. *Regional Studies* 11(1): 31–46.

Cloke, P. (2006). Conceptualizing Rurality. In *Handbook of Rural Studies*, eds. P. Cloke, T. Marsden, and P. Mooney. London: Sage, 18–28.

Crawshaw, J. (2022). *Art Worlding: Planning Relations*. London: Routledge.

Crawshaw, J. and Gkartzios, M. (2016). Getting to know the island: artistic experiments in rural community development. *Journal of Rural Studies* 43: 134–144.

Crankshaw, O. and Borel-Saladin, J. (2019). Causes of urbanisation and counter-urbanisation in Zambia: natural population increase or migration? *Urban Studies* 56(10): 2005–2020.

da Silva, D. S., Figueiredo, E., Eusébio, C., and Carneiro, J. (2016). The countryside is worth a thousand words – Portuguese representations on rural areas. *Journal of Rural Studies* 44: 77–88.

de Swaan, A. (2001). English in the Social Sciences. In *The Dominance of English as a Language of Science: Effects on Other Languages and Language Communities*, ed. U. Ammon. Berlin: Mouton de Gruyter, 71–84.

Dilley, L., Gkartzios, M., and Odagiri, T. (2022). Developing counterurbanisation: making sense of rural mobility and governance in Japan. *Habitat International* 125: 102595.

Edelman, M. (2021). 'Hollowed out Heartland, USA: How capital sacrificed communities and paved the way for authoritarian populism. *Journal of Rural Studies* 82: 505–517.

Flora, C. B., Flora, J. L., and Fey, S. (2004). *Rural Communities: Legacy and Change*. Boulder: Westview Press.

Gallent, N., and Gkartzios, M. (2019). Defining Rurality and the Scope of Rural Planning. In *The Routledge Companion to Rural Planning*, eds. M. Scott, N. Gallent, and M. Gkartzios. London: Routledge, 17–27.

García-Ayllón, S. (2016). Rapid development as a factor of imbalance in urban growth of cities in Latin America: a perspective based on territorial indicators. *Habitat International*, 58: 127–142.

Geyer, N. P., and Geyer, H. S. (2017). Counterurbanisation: South Africa in wider context. *Environment and Planning A* 49(7): 1575–1593.

Gillen, J., Bunnell, T., and Rigg, J. (2022). Geographies of ruralization. *Dialogues in Human Geography*, DOI: 10.1177/20438206221075818

Gkartzios, M. (2013). 'Leaving Athens': narratives of counterurbanisation in times of crisis. *Journal of Rural Studies* 32: 158–167.

Gkartzios, M., and Crawshaw, J. (2019). Researching rural housing: with an artist in residence. *Sociologia Ruralis* 59(4): 589–611.

Gkartzios, M., Gallent, N., and Scott, M. (2022). *Rural Places and Planning: Stories from the Global Countryside*. Bristol: Policy Press.

Gkartzios, M., and Remoundou, K. (2018). Language struggles: representations of the countryside and the city in an era of mobilities. *Geoforum* 93: 1–10.

Gkartzios, M., and Scott, K. (2015). A Cultural Panic in the Province? Counterurban Mobilities, Creativity, and Crisis in Greece. *Population, Space and Place* 21: 843–855.

Gkartzios, M., Toishi, N., and Woods, M. (2020). The language of rural: reflections towards an inclusive rural social science. *Journal of Rural Studies* 78: 325–332.

Gkartzios, M., and Ziebarth, A. (2016). Housing: A Lens to Rural Inequalities. In *International Handbook of Rural Studies*, eds. M. Shucksmith and D. Brown. London: Routledge, 495–508.

Gray, M. L., Johnson, C. R., and Gilley, B. J. (2016). *Queering the Countryside: New Frontiers in Rural Queer Studies*. New York: New York University Press.

Grimsrud, G. M. (2011). How well does the 'counter-urbanisation story' travel to other countries? The case of Norway. *Population Space Place* 17: 642–655.

Guggenheim. (2020). Countryside, The Future, https://www.guggenheim.org/exhibition/countryside

Halfacree, K. (1993). Locality and social representation: space, discourse and alternative definitions of the rural. *Journal of Rural Studies* 9: 1–15.

Halfacree, K. (2006). Rural Space: Constructing a Three-Fold Architecture. In *Handbook of Rural Studies*, eds. P. Cloke, T. Marsden, and P. Mooney. London: Sage, 44–62.

Halfacree, K., and Rivera, M. J. (2012). Moving to the countryside … and staying: lives beyond representations. *Sociologia Ruralis* 52(1): 92–114.

Heley, J., and Jones, L. (2012). Relational rurals: some thoughts on relating things and theory in rural studies. *Journal of Rural Studies* 28(3): 208–217.

Hibbard, M., and Frank, K. I. (2022). Bringing Rurality Back to Planning Culture. https://www.planetizen.com/blogs/116295-bringing-rurality-back-planning-culture

Hoggart, K. (1990). Let's do away with rural. *Journal of Rural Studies* 6(3): 245–257.

Jain, M., and Korzhenevych, A. (2019). Counter–Urbanisation as the growth of small towns: is the capital region of India prepared? *Tijdschrift voor Economische en Sociale Geografie* 110(2): 156–172.

Jones, O. (1995). Lay discourses of the rural: developments and implications for rural studies. *Journal of Rural Studies* 11: 35–49.

Klien, S. (2020). *Urban Migrants in Rural Japan: Between Agency and Anomie in a Post-Growth Society*. New York: Sunny Press.

La Biennale di Venezia. (2018). China (People's Republic of): Building A Future Countryside. https://www.labiennale.org/en/architecture/2018/national-participations/china-people%E2%80%99s-republic

Leung, K. Y., and Thorsen, L. M. (2022). Experiencing art from a field of rice: how farmers relate to rural revitalisation and art at Japan's Echigo-Tsumari Art Festival. *Sociologia Ruralis*, DOI: 10.1111/soru.12379.

Lin, G., Xie, X., and Lv, Z. (2016). Taobao practices, everyday life and emerging hybrid rurality in contemporary China. *Journal of Rural Studies* 47: 514–523.

Lowe, P. (2012). The Agency of Rural Research in Comparative Context. In *Rural Transformations and Rural Policies in the US and UK*, eds. M. Shucksmith, D. L. Brown, S. Shortall, J. Vergunst, and M. E. Warner. New York: Routledge, 18–38.

Majer, R. (2019). Pragmatic community resistance within new indigenous ruralities: lessons from a failed hydropower dam in Chile. *Journal of Rural Studies*, 68: 63–74.

Mamonova, N., and Franquesa, J. (2020). Populism, neoliberalism and agrarian movements in Europe. Understanding rural support for right-wing politics and looking for progressive solutions. *Sociologia Ruralis* 60(4): 710–731.

Milbourne, P., and Kitchen, L. (2014). Rural mobilities: connecting movement and fixity in rural places. *Journal of Rural Studies* 34: 326–336.

Mitchell, C. J. A. (2004). Making sense of counterurbanization. *Journal of Rural Studies* 20: 15–34.

Murdoch, J., Lowe, P., Ward, N., and Marsden, T. (2003). *The Differentiated Countryside*. London: Routledge.

Natarajan, N., Newsham, A., Rigg, J., and Suhardiman, D. (2022). A sustainable livelihoods framework for the 21st century. *World Development* 155: 105898.

Nelson, K. S., Nguyen, T. D., Brownstein, N. A., Garcia, D., Walker, H. C., Watson, J. T., and Xin, A. (2021). Definitions, measures, and uses of rurality: a systematic review of the empirical and quantitative literature. *Journal of Rural Studies* 82: 351–365.

OECD Regional Typology. (2011). https://www.oecd.org/cfe/regionaldevelopment/OECD_regional_typology_Nov2012.pdf

Pahl, R. E. (1966). The rural-urban continuum. *Sociologia Ruralis* 6(3): 299–329.

Philo, C. (1992). Neglected rural geographies: a review. *Journal of Rural Studies* 8: 193–207.

Phillips, M. (2010). Counterurbanisation and rural gentrification: an exploration of the terms. *Population Space and Place* 16(6): 539–558.

Phillips, M. (2014). Baroque rurality in an English village. *Journal of Rural Studies* 33: 56–70.

Rye, J. F. (2006). Rural youths' images of the rural. *Journal of Rural Studies* 22(4): 409–421.

Scoones, I. (1998). Sustainable Rural Livelihoods: A Framework for Analysis. In *IDS Working Paper No 72*. Sussex: Institute of Development Studies.

Scott, M. (2006). Strategic spatial planning and contested ruralities: insights from the Republic of Ireland. *European Planning Studies* 14(6): 811–829.

Shucksmith, M. (2018). Re-imagining the rural: from rural idyll to good countryside. *Journal of Rural Studies*, 59: 163–172.

Shucksmith, M., and Rønningen, K. (2011). The uplands after neoliberalism? The role of the small farm in rural sustainability. *Journal of Rural Studies* 27(3): 275–287.

Stockdale, A. (2016). Contemporary and 'Messy' rural in-migration processes: comparing counterurban and lateral rural migration. *Population, Space and Place* 22(6): 599–616.

UK Government Statistical Service. (2011). The 2011 Rural-Urban Classification for Output Areas in England. https://assets.publishing.service.gov.uk/government/uploads/system/uploads/attachment_data/file/1009128/RUCOA_leaflet_Jan2017.pdf

Vepsalainen, M., and Pitkanen, K. (2010). Second home countryside. Representations of the rural in Finnish popular discourses. *Journal of Rural Studies* 26(2): 194–204.

Wang, C. M. (2022). Performing rurality and urbanity: language performations, materials and land-use politics, *Journal of Rural Studies*, DOI: 10.1016/j.jrurstud.2022.03.016

Woods, M. (2005). *Rural Geography*. London: Sage.

Woods, M. (2006). Redefining the rural 'question': the new 'politics of the rural' and social policy. *Social Policy and Administration* 40(6): 579–595.

Woods, M. (2007). Engaging the global countryside: globalization, hybridity and the reconstitution of rural place. *Progress in Human Geography* 31(4): 485–507.

Zhang, Q. F. (2022). Building productivism in rural China: the case of residential restructuring in Chengdu. *Geoforum* 128: 103–114.

Online materials

- https://unhabitat.org/topic/urban-rural-linkages
- https://www.guggenheim.org/teaching-materials/countryside-the-future
- https://www.oecd.org/regional/rural-development/
- https://europeanruralparliament.com

Further reading

Gkartzios, M., Gallent, N., and Scott, M. (2022). *Rural Places and Planning: Stories from the Global Countryside*. Bristol: Policy Press.
A recent textbook on the relationship between planning and rural places drawing on 12 global case studies.

Murdoch, J., Lowe, P., Ward, N., and Marsden, T. (2003). *The Differentiated Countryside*. London: Routledge.
A classic text developing the notion of 'differentiation' in rural areas drawing on the English context.

Rodriguez Castro, L. (2021). *Decolonial Feminisms, Power and Place: Sentipensando with Rural Women in Colombia*. Cham: Palgrave.
A recent critical text on the intersection of feminist, decolonial and rurality scholarship.

Woods, M. (2011). *Rural*. Oxon: Routledge.
A classic textbook in human geography discussing all aspects of rurality (functional, imagined, economic, performative etc.).

19 Comparative ruralities

Yurui Li

Introduction

Under the rising sun in the east, Chinese farmers in the middle-lower Yangtze Plain are seen busy across rice paddies. Although mechanisation has largely increased production efficiency in peasant agriculture, limited by budget and field size, peasant agriculture still relies heavily on human labour in land preparation, seedling cultivation and transplantation. A piece of farmland, carefully attended and loved, tells the life story of an aged Chinese farmer.

In contrast to such self-sufficiency, peasant agriculture with hired farm labour in Latin American countries conjures up a striking image of inequalities in agriculture. In Latin America and the Caribbean, nearly 41% of the population in extreme poverty live in the countryside, inhabiting dilapidated shelters made of wood, mud, and plastic. Ironically, those struggling to survive produce the most expensive coffee served at upscale cafés and restaurants around the world.

However, stereotypes aside, the countryside in developing countries is far more variegated. With the increasing involvement of large and multi-national corporations, more giant machines have begun to replace scattered human farmers on boundless farmlands. Sights of mechanised farming familiar in the US or Canada—large-scale, innovative, and professional—can now also be observed in many rural regions of China, Brazil, and India.

The rural is idyllic and poetic for many people for various reasons. The passion for country living reveals urban dwellers' continued desire for rural retreats, as well as a **topophilia** felt by those from the countryside. For Mo Yan, a Nobel Prize-winning Chinese novelist whose works are reputed to be 'grounded in the soil', a major motif in his *Red Sorghum*, homeland nostalgia is the bright-red sorghum fields that rustle in the wind. The picturesque imagery of such rural landscapes is well established in society and culture, and in this way, the countryside is redefined to extend beyond its spatial borders. Rural areas, in today's consumerist society, are heavily commodified and commercialised, turning into a multi-faceted space exhibiting economic, social, **ecological**, and cultural values.

As we saw in Chapter 18, the theorisation of ruralities within human geography continues to evolve. This is partly because the multi-dimensional nature of rural spaces shows a high geographical heterogeneity in terms of economic, social, cultural, and environmental forms, which helps to shape very different comparative ruralities in different parts of the world. This high level of geographical heterogeneity presents as many opportunities as challenges for rural renaissance, conservation, and sustainability. Given this background, it is important to explore rurality from

252

DOI: 10.4324/9780429265853-23

a comparative perspective to better understand the essence of sustainable rural development. 'Comparative' here refers to a broad research perspective rather than a specific research method. When you treat any particular rural reality as 1 of 10,000 possibilities, you develop a 'comparative vision'. Comparative rurality is indeed the process of contrasting visible rural reality with invisible rural possibilities.

Peasant economy: the normality of rural production

In many parts of the world, rural production still features a peasant economy. Such peasant economies are crucial in identifying and defining the rurality of a community and, especially in developing countries, significantly influence agricultural production, peasant livelihoods, and rural development. The term smallholding commonly refers to farms less than two hectares in size, characterised by small-scale and decentralised management. Based on FAO (Food and Agriculture Organization of the United Nations [UN]) statistics, smallholdings make up over 80% of the agricultural farms globally and are the backbone of global food security, producing crops, cocoa, coffee, tea, rubber, and palm products (FAO, 2019). They also account for 65% of global rice production.

Smallholding-oriented farming contributes to the stability of rural societies by minimising conflicts due to the unequal distribution of resources and preventing the forced migration of peasants to cities due to land loss and/or scarce employment. As a result, many countries, by direct or indirect means, limit the size of large and consolidated farms: Chile, Ethiopia, India, Korea, Pakistan, Peru, and the Philippines limit the maximum size of farms; Zimbabwe, Pakistan, Brazil, and Namibia impose differential taxes based on the size of individual farms, pitching higher taxes on larger farm holdings; Kenya, Malawi, Tanzania, and Zambia only offer government subsidies to smallholdings to regulate farm size (Adamopoulos and Restuccia, 2014).

On the other hand, however, traditional smallholding agriculture may hinder rural development, counteracting the much-needed increases in production efficiency and household income. Small and decentralised agricultural activities are adverse to the adoption and popularisation of new technologies and consequently cause higher costs and lower production and productivity. According to the US Census of Agriculture, the productivity per capita of the smallest farm only makes 1/16 of its largest counterpart. Countries such as Ghana, Peru, and Bangladesh also observe similar phenomena (Nguyen and Warr, 2020). Despite differences in geographical conditions, agricultural structure, and land scarcity, this pattern is recognised across national contexts.

Also, smallholders are comparatively less adept at negotiating with downstream buyers. Agricultural products are price-suppressed, further stressing smallholders under the tremendous impact of **globalisation**. In a global trading network, the change in demand by one country can easily jeopardise the agricultural production of another. Under globalisation, cropping systems favour larger scale, more incorporated, and industrialised production models with limited room left for smallholders. Smallholders are greatly disadvantaged in terms of market information, technological innovation, and production efficiency, thereby lacking competitiveness. For instance, in Indonesia, although a more direct distribution channel was established between coffee roasters and smallholders and the coffee sold straight to customers saw an upgrade in value, the profit generated by such an upgrade was not fairly distributed between smallholders but instead retained largely by coffee roasters and the more prominent farmers (Vicol et al., 2018).

Table 19.1 Comparison of farm size and poverty headcount ratio in various countries

Countries	Average farm size (ha)	Percentage of smallholder farms (%)	Poverty headcount ratio at $1.90/day (%)	Poverty headcount ratio at $3.20/day (%)
New Zealand	223.4	0.0	0	0
Australia	3243.2	0.0	0.2	0.3
United States	178.4	0.0	0.4	0.5
Argentina	582.5	0.0	0.9	3.5
Denmark	49.8	1.7	0.2	0.2
Ireland	33.3	2.2	0.1	0.1
Canada	273.4	2.5	0.2	0.3
Germany	40.5	8.0	0.2	0.3
The Netherlands	22.1	15.9	0.2	0.3
France	45.0	16.8	0.1	0.2
Brazil	72.8	20.3	3.9	10.6
Chile	83.7	24.8	0	0.2
Colombia	25.1	31.6	4.7	13.7
Myanmar	2.5	56.9	0.6	9.7
The Philippines	2.0	68.1	6.2	26.8
Rwanda	0.9	80.0	45.2	72.4
India	1.3	81.8	6.2	37.2
Ethiopia	1.0	87.1	23.3	56.8
Malawi	0.7	94.9	73.0	90.1

Notes: Smallholder farms refer to farms less than two hectares. The table is sorted by percentage of smallholder farms from smallest to largest. Data on farm size are from https://ourworldindata.org/; Data on poverty headcount ratio are from https://data.un.org/.

Therefore, smallholders in developing countries often find themselves in a vicious circle: low income—low investment—low productivity—low income (Table 19.1). In Malawi and Rwanda, peasants account for the majority of the population, and most are smallholders (de Janvry and Sadoulet, 2020). In 2021, the poverty rate was 90.1% in Malawi and 72.4% in Rwanda, measured at earnings of $3.2 a day. Countries in similar situations have chosen to financially support smallholding-led agricultural structures to boost production and alleviate poverty. In such scenarios, developing the agricultural product processing industry, the service industry, and other industries related to agricultural activities can be a way out. This is very different from the labour-intensive industrialisation structure proposed in W. Arthur Lewis's dual economy model, which posited taking the peasants out of agriculture and into an urban-industrial environment (de Janvry and Sadoulet, 2020).

Summary

- Globally, smallholding is common in rural production, characterised by small-scale and decentralised management.
- In many countries, smallholding is crucial in defining rurality and often preferred by policymakers for its contribution to social equality and stability.
- Smallholding faces major challenges, including low production efficiency and low income, intensified by globalisation. Notably, smallholding-led agricultural countries are often struck by poverty and need an industrial development strategy different from the dual economy model.

Large-scale modernised production: to be or not to be?

Across the vast European and North American plains, the use of modern machinery in agriculture has boosted productivity and liberated human labour, playing a very different role in the shaping of rurality from that of the peasant economy. Major agricultural powers such as the US, Canada, Germany, France, and Australia have mechanised agricultural practices for much higher efficiency and productivity that give them an advantage in the **global value chain**. Such stories of success, coupled with **productivist** objectives, convince more and more countries to prioritise production and implement modern agricultural techniques.

Large-scale modernised production, nonetheless, is not a universal solution as, for example, mountainous regions are unsuited to mechanised production. Larger scale operations do not necessarily guarantee higher productivity. In countries with a less sophisticated market and credit system and a less skilled labour force, expanding the scale of agricultural production alone cannot meet expected production or productivity targets. Southeast Asia in the 1960s, Latin America in the 1990s, and Sub-Saharan Africa presently have all witnessed larger scale but poorer production performance (Garzón Delvaux et al., 2020).

The flipside of large-scale industrialised production has also come to public attention, largely in the form of ecological and socio-political risks (Foley et al., 2005, Tscharntke et al., 2012, Hendershot et al., 2020, Leakey, 2020). Ecological risks include environmental damages that cause soil erosion and biodiversity loss and are commonly faced in regions where large-scale modernised production has occurred. Modernised agricultural production relies on chemical pesticides and fertilisers that can pollute soil and water. Land degradation forces more extensive use of chemical pesticides and fertilisers to meet production goals, and farmers are once again trapped in a vicious circle. Large-scale modernised production and monoculture also threaten global biodiversity. Pest attacks are one of the major consequences of biodiversity reduction and are difficult to manage. These ecological issues are commonly seen in the rural areas of developed economies and modernised agricultural systems across the world, and in some places have led to new collaborations between farmers, environmental protection and animal welfare groups (see Figure 19.1).

Figure 19.1
'No farmers, no food, no future'. On the 18th of January 2020, German farmers drove 5000 tractors through the streets, and tens of thousands of people gathered in the capital to demonstrate against corporate agribusiness, intensive agriculture, and biodiversity loss. The protest coincided with 'International Green Week', the world's largest fair for food, agriculture and horticulture, which takes place in Berlin each year

Source: Photo credit: Agencja Fotograficzna Caro/Alamy Stock Photo

Large-scale modernisation is often accompanied by political change as a result of **neoliberal** agricultural policies in the growing economies of Africa, South Asia, and Latin America (Moseley et al., 2010). Neoliberalism promises less government intervention, embraces foreign investment and competition, and makes it possible for agricultural monopolies to wield enormous control over global agriculture and food production (see Chapter 52). Businesses often prioritise profitability at the expense of ecological integrity, farmer well-being, and sustainable development. Argentina, for example, underwent neoliberal reforms in the 1970s. These reforms promoted foreign agricultural imports, reduced subsidies on domestic production, and replaced domestic production with foreign imports. As a consequence, Argentine smallholders found themselves at a disadvantage in competition with foreign alternatives and overwhelmed by the dominance of professionalised, large-scale farms. Since then, the country's economy has become dependent on foreign capital and corporate agribusiness, compromising its food sovereignty and giving rise to the alleged 'paradox' of hunger and malnutrition in one of the world's largest food exporting countries (Baldock 2002). In 2021, neoliberal reforms that sought to deregulate the Indian agri-food system were successfully repealed following a year of protests by farmers who argued the legislation would advantage large companies and threaten the land ownership and livelihoods of peasant farmers (Kumar 2022).

Productivism is frequently criticised for unthinkingly expanding production regardless of the ecological, political, and economic uncertainties that often result. But what are the ultimate goals of agricultural and rural development, and how might these be achieved? We must always bear these questions in mind.

Summary

- Under the influence of productivism and globalism, modernised production, characterised by high productivity and profit, took off in popularity.
- Differences in geography and resources led to localised responses to agricultural modernisation.
- However, large-scale intensive farming breeds ecological risks, including environmental damage, water and soil pollution, and biodiversity reduction.
- Large-scale modernised production allows foreign intervention into the rural economy, producing consequences such as poverty and hunger, and threatening the food sovereignty of many rural areas in developing countries.

Multifunctional rural development: another option

The paradigm of modernised agriculture seems to have exhausted its theoretical and explanatory value vis-à-vis the diversification of rural experiences. Large-scale production, centralisation, professionalisation, and industrialisation are all consequences of a modernised agricultural system. Traditional peasants become farmworkers and lose many of the advantages of their previous roles. They are now nothing but rational economic agents who only pursue their own best interests and drain the vitality from rural communities as part of their transformation. In response to this, new policies concerning rural development have been proposed. Since the late 1980s, multifunctionality has been extensively studied in rural research across Japan, Korea, the US, and the EU. From **multifunctional agriculture** to the **multifunctional countryside**, the concept of multifunctionality has been widely recognised and applied, first to agriculture and then to rural resource utilisation more broadly (Wilson, 2010).

Initially proposed in the EU's revolutionary *The Future of Rural Society* initiative, multifunctional agriculture was promoted as a new reason for the EU to justify its continued support and subsidiarity to farmers in global trade negotiation with the US (Potter and Tilzey, 2005). Multifunctional agriculture provides both **commodity** outputs (e.g. food and fibre) and non-commodity outputs such as landscape enhancement, flood protection, biodiversity preservation, and food security. In the mid-1990s, in an effort to usher in a post-productivist future, the UK initiated a series of white papers to encourage farmers to develop tourism and environmental services as an additional market through providing a unique countryside experience (Lowe and Ward, 2001). The Australian government also formulated regulations and incentives to promote environmental management (Marsden, 1998). In France, farms have diversified to create employment opportunities and improve land management (Hervieu, 2002). China, in its Rural Revitalization Promotion Law, defines rural as a territorial-production complex composed of natural, social, and economic components and integrated across production, life, ecology, and socio-culture.

The idea of the multifunctional countryside reflects a deepened exploration of multifunctional agriculture. Urban interests and needs contribute to the formation of a multifunctional countryside that shifts from agricultural productivism to consumerism. Rural lands experience agricultural change in a non-productivist way, witnessing diversification in terms of functionality. The new countryside is a multifunctional space where values of traditional culture and natural resources are preserved. Not only does it enable agricultural production, but it also accommodates tourist activities and environmental protection and preserves ruralities, traditions, memories, and heritages (Brouwer and Heide, 2009).

The multifunctional development of the countryside has been necessitated in mountain areas in developed countries, and in regions with low agricultural capacities where non-productive alternatives are limited. The rural-urban fringe enjoys more potential; its proximity to markets, innovations, and diversified urban needs connect farmers to new opportunities beyond agricultural production. Farmers have found employment outside the farm as the rural attracts various interest groups with its environmental and economic capital, converting tourism into a principal driver of multi-faceted growth (Long et al., 2022). For example, farms in Norway and Finland are historically multifunctional. The integration of agriculture, forestry, fishery, and hunting compensates for low productivity on less fertile lands. France and Italy exercise a very inclusive and diverse rural tradition that has long fostered the integrated management of farms.

Unfortunately, multifunctional rural development can also be confronted by economic and environmental challenges (Potter and Tilzey, 2007). It requires a lot of financial and material support that rural society is comparatively less able to provide. The low availability of financial resources impedes multifunctional development and makes loan qualification difficult amongst rural entrepreneurs. Multifunctional rural development must also consider how to move smallholder farmers into commercial markets. Moreover, multifunctional agriculture is regarded as a much broader socio-political **ideology** that suffers from a lack of agreement on its composition and definition among WTO member countries (Moon, 2015). The demand for various components of multifunctionality differs across countries and even between villages. It is sometimes challenging to avoid conflicts between various functions, and multifunctional rural development will also ultimately need to coordinate the social, economic, ecological, and cultural development of rural areas in order to fully realise their unique value (McCarthy, 2005).

Summary

- Multifunctional agriculture was initially proposed to support smallholder farmers in neoliberal trade negotiations, focusing on the joint production of commodity and non-commodity goods.
- The multifunctional countryside derives from the implementation of multifunctional agriculture.
- The countryside is evolving from an agricultural to a broader commercial use, and its functionality is further diversified.
- Multifunctional rural development is a favourable choice in mountain areas in developed regions with low agricultural capacities.
- However, this approach needs a lot of investment and corresponding capital management capacity, which is difficult for rural areas.

Poverty alleviation and sustainable development in rural areas

The UN adopted the Sustainable Development Goals (SDGs) in 2015 as a universal call to bolster global development over the period from 2015 to 2030 (see Chapter 42). A brief review of the 17 SDGs and their targets shows that many of them are highly related to rural development (Table 19.2). So far, endemic poverty has meant that rural areas have been comparatively disadvantaged in global development, and thus poverty eradication is of primary importance for achieving the SDGs.

Poverty results from a complex intersection of political, social, and economic marginalisation. Broad issues such as geopolitical tensions and struggles, geographical isolation, conflict and unrest, and local problems such as resource scarcity, food shortages, and a lack of employment opportunities and **infrastructure** all contribute to rural poverty (Woods, 2007, Markey et al., 2008, Wood, 2008, Carr and Kefalas, 2010). Many countries around the world are working hard to eradicate poverty. For example, in India, where the rural poor often migrate to the cities, the Indian government has made great efforts to improve the educational literacy of the rural population, but the situation remains dire (Tilak, 2007). The UN and the World Bank have called for attention to the deep rural poverty in sub-Saharan Africa, South Asia, East Asia, and other regions and increased investment in education, health care, and social welfare. As of now, more efforts are still required to eliminate absolute rural poverty by 2030.

Rural poverty eradication and rural sustainable development are long-term and systematic endeavours. Present policies target economy, resources, infrastructure, health care, education, social justice, and welfare on local, national, regional, and global levels, respectively, but due to its multi-dimensional nature, poverty eradication in the form of rural development needs comprehensive solutions.

Since 2013, China's Targeted Poverty Alleviation programme has brought a new perspective to this agenda. The programme has lifted millions of people out of poverty and has contributed to global poverty alleviation over the last ten years, which is indisputable. Traditional poverty eradication policies tend to support poverty-stricken areas in a blanket fashion, resulting in high cost, low efficiency, and little difference. With a lowered poverty rate, poverty hotspots become increasingly scattered and the issue more stubborn, forming isolated islands of rural poverty (Liu et al., 2017). China has embarked on a distinctive path. Development-oriented, it values precision in policy implementation and administration, guaranteeing that every impoverished family receives timely, individualised support (Yang and Liu, 2021). Although China has eliminated absolute poverty as of 2020, it is still working to keep all its population out of poverty (Figure 19.2). As a preventative measure in the context of poverty eradication, rural vitalisation has been adopted to tackle socio-economic development issues. In the post-targeted-poverty-alleviation era, rural vitalisation symbolises the further exploration of China's rural sustainable development that aims to remedy urban-rural inequality and rural insufficient development and modernise agriculture and rural areas.

We must gather together these different experiences to learn from both the successes and failures in different parts of the world, enabling us to adopt a targeted approach to counteract the challenges brought by the geographical heterogeneity of poverty. In this way, we can better promote human equality and achieve global sustainable development; but, to do so, cross-national, inter-disciplinary and long-term efforts will be needed to end rural poverty and achieve the goals of the 17 SDGs.

Table 19.2 SDGs and their status in rural areas

SDGs	Overview	Status in rural areas
1. No poverty	End poverty in all its forms everywhere	In developing countries, the incidence of poverty is comparatively more severe in rural areas
2. Zero hunger	Zero hunger	In developing countries, people in rural areas experienced deeper struggles with hunger compared to those in urban areas
3. Good health and well-being	Ensure healthy lives and promote well-being for all at all ages	In developing countries, people living in rural areas often have worse health and well-being outcomes compared to those in urban areas
4. Quality education	Ensure equal access to quality education for all and promote lifelong learning opportunities	Rural communities tend to have poorer access to and quality of education
5. Gender equality	Achieve gender equality and empower all women and girls	In developing countries, gender inequality is still prevalent in rural areas
6. Clean water and sanitation	Ensure access to water and sanitation for all	Rural areas are even more lacking in reliable water supply and basic sanitation services
7. Affordable and clean energy	Ensure access to affordable, reliable, sustainable, and modern energy	Many rural areas remain in a state of energy poverty, in the lack of access to sustainable modern energy services and products
8. Decent work and economic growth	Promote inclusive and sustainable economic growth, employment, and decent work for all	Although the rural economy makes up a large share of jobs in many developing and emerging countries, decent work deficits are typically severe
9. Industry, innovation, and infrastructure	Build resilient infrastructure, promote sustainable industrialisation, and foster innovation	In rural areas, innovation and infrastructure are more limited and in many cases highly inadequate
10. Reduced inequalities	Reduce inequality within and among countries	The disparity between urban and rural areas, or, within rural areas, is pronounced
11. Sustainable cities and communities	Make cities inclusive, safe, resilient, and sustainable	Rural communities should also be more inclusive, safe, resilient, and sustainable

Continued

Table 19.2 *continued*

SDGs	Overview	Status in rural areas
12. Responsible consumption and production	Ensure sustainable consumption and production patterns	To feed the world sustainably, agricultural producers need to grow more food, and consumers must reduce their environmental footprint
13. Climate action	Take urgent action to combat climate change and its impacts	Rural areas inherently vulnerable to climate change
14. Life below water	Conserve and sustainably use the oceans, seas, and marine resources	Coastal villages are in the face of fisheries development and resource-usage conflict
15. Life on land	Sustainably manage forests, combat desertification, halt and reverse land degradation, halt biodiversity loss	Most of these regions are rural
16. Peace, justice, and strong institutions	Promote just, peaceful, and inclusive societies	Social injustice is also common in rural areas, which remains one of the most significant barriers to inclusive governance
17. Partnerships for the goals	Revitalise the global partnership for sustainable development	Collective actions for sustainable rural development are urgently needed

Figure 19.2
Seedling sheds at a poverty alleviation point, Songxian County, Henan Province, China

Source: Photo credit: Tuchong/Alamy

Summary

- Rural areas and populations are often left behind in global sustainable development.
- Poverty is the most prominent barrier to rural development and the greatest challenge to global sustainable development.
- Poverty is multi-dimensional, a complex result of political, cultural, and social factors and is subject to the influence of wider geopolitical and environmental tensions and conflicts.
- Marginalised areas and populations are more prone to poverty vulnerability.
- China has contributed to global poverty alleviation through its Targeted Poverty Alleviation programme, which provides impoverished families with timely and individualised assistance.

Conclusion: exploring a more systematic and sustainable path for rural transformation

Based on a comparative analysis of ruralities, we find that: (i) rural economies and societies are complex in their formation—they are multi-layered and multi-dimensional and shaped by the coupling of human and environmental factors; (ii) rural areas are diverse in their functionality—their variegated landscapes allow for high versatility, flexibility, and diversity. According to their economic and social characteristics, rural areas are often categorised as smallholding-led, large-scale production-led, or multi-functional; (iii) rural areas are dynamic in their transformation—they are subject to constant and continuous change driven by various external and internal factors; and (iv) rural areas are fragile in their resilience—each type of rural area has its own limits and weaknesses. Smallholding-led rural areas are often challenged by high labour costs and consequently plagued by poverty; large-scale production areas are more prone to the impact of foreign capital and inundated with ecological and food security problems; multi-functional rural areas need more financial investment and face homogenisation and environmental destruction. Against the backdrop of global climate change, rural areas in general are also less likely to withstand natural disasters.

More responsible production practices must be adopted to better revive rural communities and achieve the SDGs set up by the UN. Rural development, therefore, is expected to incorporate strategies that target commercialisation and conservation, always taking account of the unique conditions of different rural environments. In most rural areas, rural transformation should attach increasing importance to urban-rural interactions, regional interactions, and human-nature interactions (Liu, 2021). Numerous cases show that rural development can be seen as the continuous unfolding of rural networks and webs (van der Ploeg and Marsden, 2008), a process that requires the organisation, coordination, cooperation, co-management, and collective actions of various subjects (Li et al., 2019). The way this unfolding takes place differently in different countries will mean that comparative ruralities will continue to be a vibrant topic for human geographers to investigate.

Discussion points

- What strategies should smallholder farmers adopt to cope with the wave of globalisation?
- Why is it important to critique productivism?
- Discuss, with examples, what characteristics make a country suitable for the development of smallholder farmers, and what characteristics make a country suitable for the development of large-scale modernised production?
- Is there a better path to rural development than through the idea of the multifunctional countryside?
- How do you think Targeted Poverty Alleviation can be better realised?

References

Adamopoulos, T., and Restuccia, D. (2014). The size distribution of farms and international productivity differences. *American Economic Review* 104(6): 1667–1697.

Baldock, H. (2002). Child hunger deaths shock Argentina. *The Guardian* 25th November. https://www.theguardian.com/world/2002/nov/25/famine.argentina

Brouwer, F., and Heide, C. (2009). *Multifunctional Rural Land Management: Economics and Policies*. London, Sterling: Earthscan.

Carr, P. J., and Kefalas, M. J. (2010). Hollowing out the middle: the rural brain drain and what it means for America. *Journal of Rural Social Sciences* 291(14): 30–34.

De Janvry, A., and Sadoulet, E. (2020). Using agriculture for development: supply- and demand-side approaches. *World Development* 133: 105003.

FAO (Food and Agriculture Organization of the United Nations [UN]) (2019). *Farms, family farms, farmland distribution and farm labour: What do we know today?* FAO Agricultural Development Economics Working Paper 19-08.

Foley, J. A., DeFries, R., Asner, G. P., Barford, C., Bonan, G., Carpenter, S. R., ... and Snyder, P. K. (2005). Global consequences of land use. *Science* 309(5734): 570–574.

Garzón Delvaux, P. A., Riesgo, L., and Gomez y Paloma, S. (2020). Are small farms more performant than larger ones in developing countries? *Science Advances* 6(41): 1–12.

Hendershot, J. N., Smith, J. R., Anderson, C. B., Letten, A. D., Frishkoff, L. O., Zook, J. R., Fukami, T., and Daily, G. C. (2020). Intensive farming drives long-term shifts in avian community composition. *Nature* 579(7799): 393–396.

Hervieu, B. (2002). La multifonctionnalité de l'agriculture: genèse et fondements d'une nouvelle approche conceptuelle de l'activité agricole. *Cahiers Agricultures* 11(6): 1–6.

Kumar, S. (2022). New Farm Bills and Farmers' Resistance to Neoliberalism. *Sociological Bulletin* 71(4): 483–494. https://doi.org/10.1177/00380229221116994

Leakey, R. R. B. (2020). A re-boot of tropical agriculture benefits food production, rural economies, health, social justice and the environment. *Nature Food* 1(5): 260–265.

Li, Y., Fan, P., and Liu, Y. (2019). What makes better village development in traditional agricultural areas of China? Evidence from long-term observation of typical villages. *Habitat International* 83: 111–124.

Liu, Y. (2021). *Urban-Rural Transformation Geography*. Singapore: Springer.

Liu, Y., Liu, J., and Zhou, Y. (2017). Spatio-temporal patterns of rural poverty in China and targeted poverty alleviation strategies. *Journal of Rural Studies* 52: 66–75.

Long, H., Ma, L., Zhang, Y., and Qu, L. L. (2022). Multifunctional rural development in China: pattern, process and mechanism. *Habitat International* 121: 102530.

Lowe, P., and Ward, N. (2001). New labour, new rural vision? Labour's rural white paper. *Political Quarterly* 72(3): 386–390.

Markey, S., Halseth, G., and Manson, D. (2008). Challenging the inevitability of rural decline: advancing the policy of place in Northern British Columbia. *Journal of Rural Studies* 24(4): 409–421.

Marsden, T. (1998). Agriculture beyond the treadmill? Issues for policy, theory and research practice. *Progress in Human Geography* 22(2): 265–275.

McCarthy, J. (2005). Rural geography: multifunctional rural geographies – reactionary or radical? *Progress in Human Geography* 29(6): 773–782.

Moon, W. (2015). Conceptualising multifunctional agriculture from a global perspective: implications for governing agricultural trade in the post-Doha round era. *Land Use Policy* 49: 252–263.

Moseley, W. G., Carney, J., and Becker, L. (2010). Neoliberal policy, rural livelihoods, and urban food security in West Africa: a comparative study of The Gambia, Côte d'Ivoire, and Mali. *Proceedings of the National Academy of Sciences of the United States of America* 107(13): 5774–5779.

Nguyen, H. Q., and Warr, P. (2020). Land consolidation as technical change: economic impacts in rural Vietnam. *World Development* 127: 104750.

Potter, C., and Tilzey, M. (2005). Agricultural policy discourses in the European post-Fordist transition: neoliberalism, neomercantilism and multifunctionality. *Progress in Human Geography* 29(5), 581–600.

Potter, C., and Tilzey, M. (2007). Agricultural multifunctionality, environmental sustainability and the WTO: resistance or accommodation to the neoliberal project for agriculture? *Geoforum* 38(6): 1290–1303.

Tilak, J. (2007). Post-elementary education, poverty and development in India. *International Journal of Educational Development* 27(4): 435–445.

Tscharntke, T., Clough, Y., Wanger, T. C., Jackson, L., Motzke, I., Perfecto, I., Vandermeer, J., and Whitbread, A. (2012). Global food security, biodiversity conservation and the future of agricultural intensification. *Biological Conservation* 151(1): 53–59.

Van der Ploeg, J. D., and Marsden, T. K. (2008). *Unfolding Webs: The Dynamics of Regional Rural Development*. Assen: Van Gorcum.

Vicol, M., Neilson, J., Hartatri, D. F. S., and Cooper, P. (2018). Upgrading for whom? Relationship coffee, value chain interventions and rural development in Indonesia. *World Development* 110: 26–37.

Wilson, G. (2010). Multifunctional 'quality' and rural community resilience. *Transactions of the Institute of British Geographers* 35(3): 364–381.

Wood, R. E. (2008). *Survival of Rural America: Small Victories and Bitter Harvests*. Lawrence: University Press of Kansas.

Woods, M. (2007). Engaging the global countryside: Globalization, hybridity and the reconstitution of rural place. *Progress in Human Geography* 31(4): 485–507.

Yang, Y., and Liu, Y. (2021). The code of targeted poverty alleviation in China: a geography perspective. *Geography and Sustainability* 2(4): 243–253.

Online materials

- The UN's Sustainable Development Goals outline a global roadmap for ending poverty, protecting the planet, and tackling inequalities: https://www.un.org/sustainabledevelopment/
- The Smallholder Farmers' Dataportrait is a comprehensive data set on the profile of smallholder farmers across the world: https://www.fao.org/fileadmin/templates/esa/smallholders/Concept_Smallholder_Dataportrait_web.pdf
- A good resource on data, visualisations and commentary on farm size and productivity: https://ourworldindata.org/farm-size
- Latin American Center for Rural Development (RIMISP) is broad and diverse network of partners and allies, which since 1986 has contributed to understanding rural transformations and

formulating better strategies to achieve equitable territorial development in Latin America: https://www.rimisp.org/dtr

- For further details about China's Poverty Alleviation plan: http://language.chinadaily.com.cn/a/202104/06/WS606bffe7a31024ad0bab3c43_1.html

Further reading

Cloke, P., Marsden, T., and Mooney, P. (eds.) (2006). *Handbook of Rural Studies*. London: Sage.
A comprehensive review of theory, research, and the study of rural questions; it shows how political economy and the 'cultural turn' redefine rurality.

Payne, R. K. (2005). A Framework for Understanding Poverty. AHA Process.
A conceptual discourse on the countryside, class, and poverty.

Liu, Y. (2021). *Urban-Rural Transformation Geography*. Singapore: Springer
A more advanced and conceptual text on urban-rural transformation.

Long, H. (2020). *Land Use Transitions and Rural Restructuring in China*. Singapore: Springer.
A more advanced text on Rural Restructuring. Comprises numerous short essays on landscape empirical studies in China.

Lele, U. (1981). Rural Africa: modernization, equity, and long-term development. *Science* 211(4482), 547–553.
A classic essay on rural modernisation in developing countries.

Wood, R. E. (2008). *Survival of Rural America: Small Victories and Bitter Harvests*. Lawrence: University Press of Kansas.
A reflection on the Recession of rural American and Prospects for the Future.

Wilson, G. (2010). Multifunctional 'quality' and rural community resilience. *Transactions of the Institute of British Geographers* 35(3): 364–381.
A paper aims to contribute towards emergent debates on the 'quality' of multifunctional trajectories in rural development.

Woods. M. (2011). *Rural*. Abingdon: Routledge.
A textbook that depicts the imagined, economic, political, and social characteristics of rural societies in vivid detail.

Li, Y., Long, H., and Liu, Y. (2015). Spatio-temporal pattern of China's rural development: a rurality index perspective. *Journal of Rural Studies* 38: 12–26.
My publication of establishing a comprehensive index system to measure rurality in China at the county level.

Nelson, K. S., Nguyen, T. D., Brownstein, N. A., Garcia, D., Walker, H. C., Watson, J. T., and Xin, A. (2021). Definitions, measures, and uses of rurality: a systematic review of the empirical and quantitative literature. *Journal of Rural Studies* 82(February): 351–365.
A useful article with instructional value on the measurement and application of rurality.

20 Region

Enrico Gualini

Introduction

The 'region' in human geography – reassessment and extension of a concept

As Michael Keating pointed out many years ago, '[t]he very word "region" has a multiplicity of meanings in the various social science disciplines and the historical traditions of European countries': as a concept, it is 'politically loaded and sensitive because the very definition of a region as a framework and a system of action has implications for the distribution of political power and the content of public policy' (Keating, 1997: 383).

This chapter moves from this observation to discuss the 'region' as a key concept of human geography and traces the theoretical developments as well as the political-institutional practices which have contributed to redefining and expanding its meaning. Against the background of the epochal transformations experienced by the **territorial** sovereignty and **political economy** of **nation-states** since the last decades of the last century, the complex features taken by the 'invention of regions' (Keating, 1997) as well as by the 'paradox(es) of the region' (Trigilia, 1991) require a multidimensional perspective which examines political-economic, institutional and cultural factors.

Reference to the European Union is chosen as a paradigmatic case for understanding the complexity of the processes involved. While the variegated articulation of **regionalisms** and **regionalisation** processes is a global phenomenon and, as such, highly connected to geopolitical developments at global macro-regional and **transnational** scales, the European integration process offers a prism through which to read recent and, possibly, even future trajectories of the 'region'.

The 'region' in the 'global': regions and regionalism in post-Fordist capitalism

As Anderson and O'Dowd (1999: 595) remind us, 'the drawing of any given state border represents an arbitration, and a simplification, of complex geo-political, political and social struggles. [...] It seldom, if ever, offers a coincidence of economy, polity and culture, but instead represents and often reifies a particular relationship between them that may prove either transitory or durable'.

DOI: 10.4324/9780429265853-24

Critical debates on **post-Fordism** and **globalisation** have been crucial in challenging a rei-fied assumption of spatial concepts in economic, political and social geography, and in promot-ing a critical revision of geographical concepts addressing the nature and logic of state agency. The resulting elaborations have highlighted the contingency of received understandings while opening the way for a complex redefinition of their meaning. Along these lines, the concept of the 'region' has been affected by a revision of its traditionally dominant semantic connection to the territorial articulation of the nation-state.

Regions have been long understood and identified as internal jurisdictional subdivisions of the territorial state. According to the historical process referred to as the so-called Westphalian model of nation-state building, modern statehood developed in western European countries since the seventeenth century following a path defined by the consolidation of state sovereignty through the fixation of state boundaries. Modern nation-state formation accordingly has been characterised (both institutionally and ideologically) by two complementary processes: external differentiation (through the definition and control of strict boundaries and the identification of state sovereignty with the spatial domain of the national territory) and internal homogeni-sation (as a condition for the cohesion and welfare of the national citizenry and of the legit-imation of state power). One important feature of this is the idea of nation-state sovereignty as being 'fixed' and defined – in both political-institutional and political-economic terms – in the form of stable 'nested' and hierarchical territorial articulations. In this territorialist con-ception, nation-state sovereignty is articulated hierarchically along regional and local levels of state jurisdiction, which grants the pursuit of policies of equalisation of living conditions in line with principles of national welfare economy as well as the pursuit of aggregate perfor-mance of the national economy. Regionalism, within this state-centred paradigm, was iden-tifiable with the struggle for the most effective political-institutional and political-economic articulation of the nation-state's capacity to act and exert its sovereignty through its hierarchy of territorial jurisdictions.

While this model of statehood has been determinant for historical developments throughout the twentieth century (including geopolitical conflicts, colonial rule and post-colonial struggles) and has long even dominated conceptions of transnational forms of government (as in the case of European integration), geopolitical and socioeconomic transformations at the turn of the last century have concurred in radically changing this understanding.

A key aspect in the redefinition of the meaning of regions as policy objects of post-Fordism refers to the reassessment and reframing of the role of territoriality in economic processes. This aspect may appear paradoxical, in the light of the apparent volatile and 'despatialised' nature of globalised economies and of the loss in the meaning of 'bounded' forms of territoriality (see Chapter 47). The inability of traditional forms of state regulation to cope with the economic dynamics of globalised post-Fordist **capitalism** – and its 'inconstant geography' (Storper and Walker, 1989) – have been recognised by critical geographers such as Harvey (1985) and Cox (1998) as a constitutive spatial challenge to the effectiveness and integrity of nation-states. A key aspect of their critique addressed the fallacy of assumptions about the 'despatialisation' of capitalist economies and pointed to the involvement of state policies in redefining spatial con-ditions for capital accumulation. Of particular importance here is a critique of received under-standings of the territorial nature of the state and of its scalar 'fixity'. This aspect was further addressed by regulationist interpretations of the changing political geography of capitalism as part of broader processes of making and unmaking of regulatory systems at different spatial scales (Jessop, 2002, Brenner, 2004).

With the development of post-Fordist economies and increasingly globalised competition, the nature and role of territories have changed. The emergence of new globally competitive regional economies, the decline of traditional regional structures of national economies and the crisis of the capacity to govern territorial transformations at the nation-state level have underscored a view of the nation-state as a historically contingent construct (Ruggie, 1993, Jessop, 2002, Brenner, 2004). Processes of restructuration of the state as a key site of regulation have emerged in three correlated forms (Jessop, 2002):

- the 'denationalisation' of the state, i.e. 'the territorial dispersion of national state's activities' (199), manifested in 'the "hollowing out" of the nation-state apparatus with old and new state capacities being reorganised territorially and functionally on supranational, national, subnational and translocal levels as attempts are made by state managers on different territorial scales to enhance their respective operational autonomies and strategic capacities' (195);
- the 'destatisation' of political systems, i.e. 'redrawing the public-private divide, reallocating tasks, and rearticulating the relationship between organisations and tasks across this divide on whatever territorial scale(s) the state in question acts' (199);
- the 'internationalisation' of policy regimes, i.e. the development of supra- or transnational metagovernance institutions in crucial areas of economic and social policy.

As this reading makes apparent, these processes have affected nation-state sovereignty not only at its external margins, in terms of an increasing involvement in and dependence on supra- and transnational policy arrangement, but also in terms of challenging received understanding of territorial sovereignty and of its internal articulation.

Regionalism must be hence interpreted against this background as the result of converging processes of functional restructuring, political mobilisation and institutional restructuring – that is, as a mixture of processes 'from above' and 'from below' – in coping with emergent spatial challenges. Regionalisation initiatives, in turn, express the complex and not always linear struggle for finding a political-institutional functional and territorial coherence – or 'spatial fix' – between these different dimensions. Let us now review these challenges in more detail.

Summary

- Region was once understood as a rigid administrative division of a territorial state.
- In the post-Fordist context, and against the backdrop of an allegedly 'despatialised' global economy, the governance of the region has moved beyond rigid and fixed territorial frameworks and scalar relations.
- It is important to consider denationalisation, destatisation and internationalisation as key factors that shape regional development.

Shifts in framing 'regions': the (contested) rise of 'new regionalism'

The erosion of territorially bound sovereignty in terms of the capacity to effectively regulate conditions for economic development and social welfare has thus defined a new challenging condition for post-Westphalian nation-states: one in which the blurring of external differentiation calls for an increasing internal differentiation as a condition for policy effectiveness and legitimacy.

Part of this challenge – which has significantly affected understandings of geographical notions such as 'region', 'territory' and 'scale' – has been the need to revise the dependence of state policy and governance on traditional territorialist principles of jurisdictional demarcation and autonomy. For regional policy specifically, the challenges this represents are threefold.

The first challenge relates to *changes in the functional role of territories*. Processes of the internationalisation and globalisation of a post-Fordist, knowledge- and information-based economy have challenged the capacity of nation-states to steer economic processes within their territorial domain (Jessop, 2002). The result has been a twofold and contradictory spatial feature of volatile, 'globalised' economies. On the one hand, production and accumulation processes are no longer subject to effective regulation at the level of national policies, and this is expressed in their increasing 'de-spatialisation'. On the other hand, production and accumulation processes require new, less institutionalised forms of 're-territorialisation', as the regional embeddedness of economies is sought as a condition for securing important competitiveness factors, such as specific, high-level skills and place-bound 'tacit' forms of knowledge (Storper, 1997).

The second challenge relates to *emerging processes of political mobilisation*, as regional actors and economic networks react (with increasing salience since the 1990s, particularly in Europe: Harvie, 1994, Keating, 1997, Le Galès and Lequesne, 1998) – by attempts at re-positioning the region with regard to new scales of economic competition and with regard to economic policies. Political regionalist movements are hence backed by political claims for the acknowledgement of regional identity as a factor for economic competitiveness and for more involvement and autonomy in devising development policies.

The third challenge amounts to a combination of these phenomena, resulting in a *need for institutional restructuring* with the effect of introducing a paradigm shift in approaches to the political-economic and administrative rationale of regional policy at both the nation-state and (as we will see) the supra- and transnational level. Regionalism and regionalisation become increasingly targeted at actively promoting capacities for local-regional cooperation and economic mobilisation at a variety of scales – well beyond the traditional jurisdictional level of political-administrative 'regions' (Keating and Loughlin, 1997).

Against the background of these challenges to the territorial sovereignty of nation-states, regions gained new meanings and new dimensions, beyond a territorialist understanding of regions as 'bounded' and institutionalised spatial entities. Regionalism and regionalisation as policy concepts have extended since the 1990s – a symbolic threshold in many respects, as we will see – beyond mere issues of uneven territorial development and territorial equalisation, typically dealt with in the domain of sovereign nation-state policies and their political-institutional articulations. In policy practice, regions have turned into arenas of experimentation, opportunities for mobilisation and sites of increased political-institutional complexity. Regionalism and regionalisation have thus developed into a significant terrain for the reconstruction of a 'spatial fix' for recovering state governance and regulation capacity in dealing with the transformation of conditions for economic development in a globalised **neoliberal** capitalism (Jessop, 2002).

What these developments highlight is that regions are anything but natural entities: they are, at the same time, institutional, political-economic and socio-cultural spaces. Their territorial identification, if any, is the result of institutional compromises between the contrasting claims emerging from these dimensions.

This shift in understanding has been foundational, in particular for the rise of 'new economic geography', developing into what – despite its variegated contents and contributions – has at its heart the 'new regionalism', intended as a paradigmatic normative re-orientation of applied regional studies (Bagnasco, 1977, Sabel, 1989, Scott and Storper, 1992, Florida, 1995, Storper, 1995, Scott, 1996, Morgan, 1997, Cooke and Morgan, 1998).

Spatial theories have backed this shift in understanding by focusing on a **performative** concept of region. Central to it is a relational conception of 'regionalisation' – intended as the spatial pattern taken by specific, contingent and recursive localised interactions (Giddens, 1984) – which underlines its social-constructive dimension (Allen et al., 1998). From this relational, performative and social-constructivist perspective, the changing position of regions and localities in a 'globalised' political economy can be seen as originating from a multiplicity of context-specific forms of social and political regionalism. Next to 'old' forms of regionalism – related to traditional approaches to state modernisation via decentralisation or **devolution** – 'new regionalist' forms emerge that rather refer to regionalisation as either a 'bottom up' mobilisation process or as an institutionally promoted governance arena: either way, the aim is that of constituting a collective political-economic acting capacity at a regional scale. Their central tenet is the constitution of a sense of collective commitment towards regional development goals among public and private governance actors. It is the capacity of regional actors to become actively involved in regional policy arenas – intended performatively as 'action spaces' rather than institutionally as 'action units' – that is seen as conferring identity to a region, rather than its identification with a formal territorial jurisdiction (Amin and Thrift, 1995, Amin, 1999, Schmitt-Egner, 2002).

Geographers have hence been sensitised to the multidimensional socio-cultural implications involved in the 'institutionalisation of regions' and in building regional identity (Paasi, 1986, 2001). Far from becoming irrelevant in a 'globalised' economy, the embeddedness of economies in regional contexts emerges as an important factor for capitalising on localised knowledge and skills. Regions are seen as a nexus of 'untraded interdependencies' (Storper, 1995) that represent key factors for competitiveness and, as such, pose limits to the 'hypermobility' of productive capital. They can, however, only to a limited extent be produced by institutional design: they require building institutional capacities for mutual exchange and reflexivity.

'New regionalist' policies aimed at constituting new spatial fixes for economic processes have been therefore directed at enhancing the 'institutional thickness' of regional economic complexes – that is, the development of a social **infrastructure** sustaining institutionalised capacities to learn and innovate (Cooke and Morgan, 1995, Amin and Thrift, 1995, Amin, 1999). As critical geographers have considered, however, the 'region' as a social and political construct also lends itself to becoming a stake in the discursive constitution of politics: accordingly, political **discourses** defining regions as 'imagined units of competition' have been seen as legitimising devices for one-sided economic competitiveness strategies and, thus, as supportive of the **hegemony** of 'neoliberal' market-led imperatives of 'entrepreneurial' territorial valorisation over more balanced welfare-oriented goals of territorial equalisation (Lovering, 1999, Swyngedouw, 2000, 2005). Indeed, emergent forms of regionalisation as promoted by the 'new regionalism' are anything but uncontested: they constitute arenas for playing out interests and power relations, and, as such, they raise important issues of democratic accountability within a broader process of transformation of 'state power' (Jessop, 2008).

Summary

- The era in which state policy and governance depended on fixed jurisdictional demarcation and autonomy is now bygone.
- Now, the understanding of region needs to confront three major challenges: changes in the functional role of territories; emerging processes of political mobilisation; and a need for institutional restructuring.
- New economic geography and new regionalism examine the region from a relational, performative and social-constructivist perspective, highlighting the institutionalisation of regions.

The European Union as a case-in-point: European integration as 'experimental regionalism'?

The redefinition of regions as relational constructs along institutional, political-economic, and socio-cultural lines is strikingly exemplified by the way it has imprinted political-institutional projects like the European Union and the European integration process. The European integration process can, in fact, be seen as paradigmatic of the convergence of the abovementioned shifts into a new orientation of territorial development policies 'beyond' nation-states. In this process, reference to a renewed and extended understanding of regions has played a significant role.

Between the 1980s and the 1990s, the dynamics of regionalisms in Europe have been significantly backed by policies of the EU promoting structural changes towards a 'Europe of the regions'. Far from reducing regions to a deterministic side-effect of the relativisation of nation-state borders and of 'the creation of an area without internal frontiers' (Treaty on EU, Article 2), European integration has underscored the role of regions as new 'units of competition', highlighting regional innovation, cooperation and synergy as conditions for ensuring European economic performance. This attitude, inspired by the 'resurgence of the regions' (Storper, 1995) heralded by 'new economic geography', was crucially backed by a perception of the (relative) retreat of nation-state-based economies in the context of European economic integration: Jacques Delors' idea of the regions as *forces vives*, as the 'living forces' of Europe, highlighted the European Commission's commitment to promoting the economic potential lying within regional economic complexes.

Indeed, since the 1980s, EU involvement in regional policy – traditionally an expression of nation-state sovereignty – has contributed to developing a 'regionalised' European multi-level polity as well as to introducing innovations in regional development processes. EU policy has contributed to strengthening regions in Europe not only in terms of a 'Europeanisation' of regional policy but also by fostering a cultural shift in the geographical notion of 'region', as represented by the 'new regionalism' that has emerged in economic geography and spatial planning literature over recent years.

As a major policy field of the EU, Cohesion Policy has influenced the nature of regional policies along three dimensions:

- the promotion of integrated approaches to regional development based on activating endogenous potentials and mobilising regional development coalitions;
- the strengthening of regional authorities – including their institutionalised representation in Bruxelles through the Committee of the Regions;
- the 'invention' of regions as new spaces and arenas for cooperation at the cross-border and transnational level, through 'experimental' programmes like the Community Initiative Interreg (Anderson and O'Dowd, 1999, Scott, 2001, Perkmann and Sum 2002, Gualini 2003).

A key factor for this was that EU cohesion policy opened up community processes to the active participation of subnational actors. The arena of regional programming was no longer defined by bargaining on national priorities – as in traditional intergovernmental policy-making – but by multi-level negotiations systematically involving subnational governments and actors.

The concept 'multi-level governance' has been advanced precisely to capture the emergence of this new dimension beyond 'state centric' interpretations of European integration: it contends that 'European integration is a polity creating process in which authority and policy-making influence are shared across multiple levels of government subnational, national, and supranational' (Marks et al., 1996: 342). Its assumptions on the nature of EU policy-making in areas like cohesion policy are threefold:

- subnational governments are seen emerging as governmental levels of their own importance next to national and European levels;
- subnational empowerment is seen as a process that is not replacing nation-states: it is rather seen as a dynamic within a broader process of 'power dispersion [...] in which political control has spun away to strengthen European institutions, *and* in which national states institutions have retained significant control over resources' (Hooghe, 1996: 18);
- supra-national institutions, moreover, are seen as changing roles from that of 'authoritative allocation and regulation 'from above' to the role of partner and mediator' (Kohler-Koch, 1996: 371) of multi-level negotiations.

Multi-level governance redefines the nature of processes by which Europe affects nation-states and their subnational polities: the mobilisation and empowerment of subnational governments and the increasing independent influence of supranational institutions are interpreted as part of a dynamics of 'power dispersion' in the European Union, involving a relative shift in regulatory power towards the supranational level and in decision-making and operational capacity to the subnational level (see Figures 20.1 and 20.2 for two contrasting representations of European regions).

Moreover, EU cohesion policy has been instrumental in diffusing a competitive 'frame' of regional development policy oriented towards achieving economic competitiveness on a territorial basis and has provided new 'opportunity structures' for actors to define policies and to

NUTS 3

NUTS 2

NUTS 1

Country

Figure 20.1
The 'nested' administrative logic of regions in the European Union (as exemplified by the systematics of NUTS level, the geographical units of EU statistics based on administrative regions)

Source: EUROSTAT

actively engage in shaping new regional arenas. In general terms, EU cohesion policy has played an important role in mediating between 'regionalisation', seen as a process 'from above', and 'regionalism' as a process 'from below', favouring the building of new institutional capacities as well as of interest coalitions and collective commitments for regional development: in short, by contributing to the emergence of truly regional policy arenas. European regions have developed as systems of action in and through which 'territory is being reinvented, as the European state restructures, collective identities are reforged, and new systems of collective action emerge in state and civil society' (Keating, 1997: 395).

For most member states, EU cohesion policy has become a major factor in reframing domestic interventionist policies in support of regional economies. This explains why during the 1990s, in the

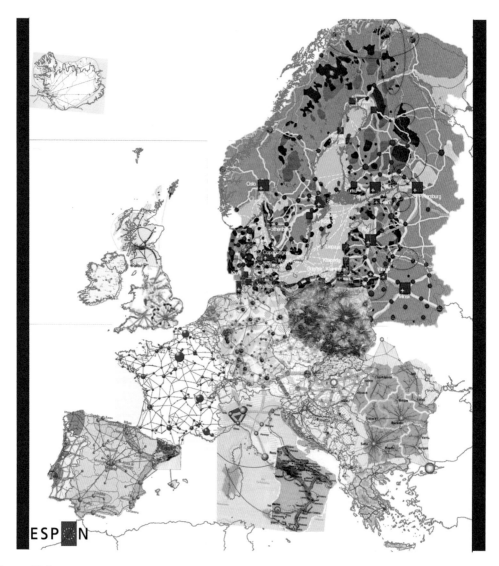

Figure 20.2
The dynamics of regionalisation expressed by the 'multispatial metagovernance' (Jessop 2016) of
European territories (as exemplified by 'Territorial Visions and plans' collated by the ESPON study
'ET2050 Territorial Scenarios and Visions for Europe', 2014)

Source: ESPON

framework of a competition-oriented European integration process, many European countries have
been 'forced' to adapt their regional policies to EU rationales. EU cohesion policy has thus offered
a frame of reference in which a growing attention to regional development issues could be turned
into practice. Meanwhile, it offered the Commission a terrain for developing community policies of
'positive integration', not relying on pure market-based convergence mechanisms (Scharpf, 1999).
During the 1990s, cohesion policy has grown to become financially the second-largest policy field
of the EU and accordingly a key field for experimentation and policy innovation.

In this respect, its impact has been, of course, highly diverse but nonetheless significant. In more resource-dependent countries, the Europeanisation of regional policy has promoted patterns of intergovernmental cooperation that have enhanced institutional capacity building at the regional level (Italy, Spain) and even induced processes of regional formation (Ireland, UK, and less successfully elsewhere). In France, it has led the *Régions* to gain a role in regional programming which largely exceeds their statutory competencies, even supporting the emergence of new regional constituencies on the national political scene. In Italy, it has contributed to a radical revision of state-centred policies towards a more demand-oriented and society-based view of development. In less resource-dependent countries, like Germany, it has likewise opened opportunities for original interpretations in a pluralist and highly competitive field, facilitating the introduction of policy innovations at different levels (for an extended discussion, see: Gualini, 2004a, 2004b, 2016). In general, it has led to a revision of domestic intergovernmental relationships towards more subsidiary and negotiated patterns, as well as to an acknowledgement of regions as key intermediary arenas for promoting endogenous trajectories of development. In many of these countries, moreover, the combination between competition-oriented, 'new-regionalist' policy frames and requirements for territorially based forms of partnership has led to experimenting with modes of representation and cooperation based on institutionally promoted and facilitated forms of 'bottom-up' regionalism.

However, Europe has also experienced a variety of regionalisation initiatives targeted at exploring the new regional dimension of economic processes and at experimenting with new policy approaches, often in connection to concrete opportunities. These initiatives in regionalisation, often originated 'from below', and, characterised by highly different degrees of formalisation, are hardly understandable if we adopt a traditional state-centred institutional perspective on regionalisation. Instead, they invite us to shift from a 'governmental' to a 'governance' perspective in understanding what a 'region' is.

Since the 1980s Europe has experienced a significant 'recomposition of political space', of which the emergence of regions as new political arenas has been an important part. Regions have emerged on the European arena as collective actors dealing with political, social and economic issues of local interest – most notably, regional economic development.

In this respect, the idea of a 'Europe of the regions' has been an inspiring but simplistic paradigmatic reference. By its primary reference to regions as intermediate governmental jurisdictions, it has been instrumental to important policy reforms – the regionalisation of the Structural Funds, the institutionalisation of regional representation in the EU and several domestic constitutional reforms – and to a first stage of operationalisation of the subsidiarity principle, but it does not exhaust the nature of regionalisation processes. In other words, there is, in fact, a reality we could call a 'Europe *with* the regions' (Hooghe, 1996, Bache, 1998, Le Galès and Lequesne, 1998), in which regions are structurally involved at both the European and national levels of policy-making. But rather than as a new institutional order, the regional dimension of Europe should be seen as the emergence of institutional and policy innovations at a plurality of intermediate territorial levels (Le Galès, 1998).

This has favoured policy-driven institutional innovations to emerge below the threshold of constitutional interventions (Kohler-Koch and Eising, 1999, Héritier, 1999). In fact, next to multi-level dynamics of 'upwards' and 'downwards' movements of 'power dispersion' across governmental jurisdictions, a dynamic has developed of 'sideways' processes leading to the constitution of new scales of territorial governance. These take the highly diverse forms of 'informal governance' arenas, characterised by flexible, ad-hoc, non-exclusive and sometimes overlapping arrangements, extending to transnational cooperations (Hooghe and Marks, 2001, 2003, Christiansen and Piattoni, 2003) – with often problematic relationships with existing territorial general-interest jurisdictions and with requirements of democratic legitimacy and accountability of policy agendas and choices – that can be interpreted as constituting an emerging geography of 'multispatial metagovernance' articulated at different scales (Jessop, 2016), in which EU policies and nation-state policies play an important meta-governance role (see Figure 20.2).

Summary

- In the EU, the region is imagined as a primary unit for cultivating competitiveness and a fertile ground for experimenting with policies and institutions.
- The participation of subnational actors has been encouraged.
- Multi-level governance has been fostered to replace state-centric approaches towards regional development.

Conclusion

As processes developing along complex lines have contributed to what Keating (1997) defined as 'the invention of regions', our understanding of 'regions' has embraced a more fluid domain of meanings, rather than a singular association with territorialised state power. As a result, referring to 'regions' does not only call for referential consistency but also for an understanding of the complex interdependencies that may be in place in defining 'regions' as action spaces and policy objects.

For one, the re-making of regions can be understood as partaking in practices of de-territorialisation and re-territorialisation and in more general processes of redefinition of scale (see Jessop, 2002, Brenner, 2004, Elden, 2006), expressing a struggle for constituting 'new state spaces' of action in globalised, neoliberal post-Fordist capitalist economies. In that, the promotion of experimental governance practices intimately connects with the quest for new ways by which statehood and 'state power' can be expressed spatially. Moreover, new approaches to regionalism and regionalisation open up a variety of directions by which 'regions' are redefined as policy objects, of which only a few – such as 'learning regions', 'innovation regions', 'smart regions' and others – can be even hinted at here. And in the process, 'new regionalist' takes on governance involve a redefinition of relationships between state and non-state actors, in which even the mobilisation of alleged 'regional identities' may be at stake.

In this perspective, what Trigilia (1991) referred to long ago as the 'paradox(es) of the region' might as well become even more salient. In fact, the relativisation of regions as formal-institutional territorial jurisdictions of the state – even when backed by more regional political autonomy – is complementary to the rise of new dimensions of 'state power', premised on the mobilisation of 'regional societies' and 'regional interests', often grounded in historical and socio-cultural identities – possibly 'invented' or manipulated – which highlight in new forms the challenges facing the regional as an effective scale of democratic political representation.

Discussion points

- How far has the diffusion of 'new regionalism' affected the nature of the state, especially with regard to democratic involvement, representation and empowerment of regional communities?
- To what extent is 'new regionalism' primarily an expression of a neoliberal policy biased by imperatives of economic competitiveness?
- To what degrees do regionalism and regionalisation promote new forms of **uneven development** across territories?
- What are the challenges associated with forms of regionalism and regionalisation based on networks in loosely institutionalised governance arrangements?
- What differences can be found in nation-state responses to regionalist challenges? What are the most significant path-dependencies in facing regional change? What are the most promising lines of innovation?

References

Allen, J., Massey, D., and Cochrane, A. (1998). *Rethinking the Region*. London: Routledge.

Amin, A. (1999). An institutionalist perspective on regional economic development. *International Journal of Urban and Regional Research* 23: 365–378.

Amin A., and Thrift, N. (1995). Institutional issues for European regions: from markets and plans to socioeconomics and powers of association. *Economy and Society* 24(1): 41–66.

Anderson, J., and O'Dowd, L. (1999). Borders, border regions and territoriality: contradictory meanings, changing significance. *Regional Studies* 33(7): 593–604.

Bache, I. (1998). *The Politics of European Union Regional Policy*. Sheffield: Sheffield Academic Press.

Bagnasco, A. (1977). *Tre Italie: la problematica territoriale dello sviluppo italiano*. Bologna: Il Mulino.

Brenner, N. (2004). *New State Spaces: Urban Governance and the Rescaling of Statehood*. Oxford: Oxford University Press.

Christiansen, T., and Piattoni, S. (eds.) (2003). *Informal Governance in the European Union*. Cheltenham: Edward Elgar.

Cooke, P., and Morgan, K. (1998). *The Associational Economy: Firms, Regions, and Innovation*. Oxford: Oxford University Press.

Cox, K. R. (1998). Spaces of dependence, spaces of engagement and the politics of scale or: looking for local politics. *Political Geography* 17(1): 1–23.

Elden, S. (2006). The state of territory under globalization: empire and the politics of reterritorialization. *Thamyris/Intersecting* 12: 47–66.

Florida, R. (1995). Towards the learning region. *Futures* 27(5): 527–536.

Giddens, A. (1984). *The Constitution of Society*. Cambridge: Polity Press.

Gualini, E. (2003). Cross-border governance: inventing regions in a trans-national multi-level polity. *DISP* 39(152): 43–52.

Gualini, E. (2004a). *Multi-Level Governance and Institutional Change: The Europeanization of Regional Policy in Italy*. Aldershot: Ashgate.

Gualini, E. (2004b). Regionalization as 'Experimental Regionalism': the rescaling of territorial policy-making in Germany. *International Journal of Urban and Regional Research* 28(2): 329–353.

Gualini, E. (2016). Multilevel Governance and Multiscalar Forms of Territorialization. In *Handbook on Cohesion Policy in the EU*, eds. S. Piattoni and L. Polverari. Cheltenham: Edward Elgar, 506–523.

Harvey, D. (1985). The Geopolitics of Capitalism. In *Social Relations and Spatial Structures*, eds. D. Gregory and J. Urry. London: MacMillan, 128–163.

Harvie, C. (1994). *The Rise of Regional Europe*. London: Routledge.

Héritier, A. (1999). *Policy-Making and Diversity in Europe: Escaping Deadlock*. Cambridge: Cambridge University Press.

Hooghe, L. (1996). Introduction: Reconciling EU-Wide Policy and National Diversity. In *Cohesion Policy and European Integration: Building Multi-Level Governance*, ed. L. Hooghe. Oxford: Clarendon Press, 1–24.

Hooghe, L., and Marks, G. (2001). *Multi-Level Governance and European Integration*. Lanham: Rowman and Littlefield.

Hooghe, L., and Marks, G. (2003). Unraveling the central state, but how? Types of multi-level governance. *American Political Science Review* 97(2): 233–243.

Jessop, B. (2002). *The Future of the Capitalist State*. Cambridge: Polity Press.

Jessop, B. (2008). *State Power*. Cambridge: Polity Press.

Jessop, B. (2016). Territory, politics, governance and multispatial metagovernance. *Territory, Politics, Governance* 4(1): 8–32.

Keating, M. (1997). The invention of regions: political restructuring and territorial government in Western Europe. *Environment and Planning C* 15(4): 383–398.

Keating, M., and Loughlin, J. (eds.) (1997). *The Political Economy of Regionalism*. London: Frank Cass.

Kohler-Koch, B. (1996). Catching up with change: the transformation of governance in the European Union. *Journal of European Public Policy* 3(3): 359–380.

Kohler-Koch, B., and Eising, R. (eds.) (1999). *The Transformation of Governance in the European Union*. London: Routledge.

Le Galès, P. (1998). Regulation and governance in European cities. *International Journal of Urban and Regional Research* 22(3): 482–506.

Le Galès, P., and Lequesne, C. (eds.) (1998). *Regions in Europe*. London: Routledge.

Lovering J. (1999). Theory led by policy: the inadequacies of the 'New Regionalism' (Illustrated from the case of Wales). *International Journal of Urban and Regional Research* 23: 379–396.

Morgan, K. (1997). The learning region: institutions, innovation and regional renewal. *Regional Studies* 31(5): 491–503.

Paasi, A. (1986). The institutionalisation of regions: a theoretical framework for understanding the emergence of regions and the constitution of regional identity. *Fennia* 164: 105–146.

Paasi, A. (2001). Europe as a social process and discourse: considerations of place, boundaries and identity. *European Urban and Regional Studies* 8(1): 7–28.

Perkmann, M., and Sum, N. L. (eds.) (2002). *Globalization, Regionalization and Cross-Border Regions*. Hampshire: Palgrave.

Ruggie, J. G. (1993). Territoriality and beyond: problematizing modernity in international relations. *International Organization* 47(1): 139–174.

Sabel, C. F. (1989). Flexible Specialization and the Reemergence of Regional Economies. In *Reversing Industrial Declines*, eds. P. Hirst and J. Zeitlin. New York: St. Martin's Press, 17–70.

Scharpf, F. W. (1999). *Governing in Europe: Effective and Democratic?* Oxford and New York: Oxford University Press.

Schmitt-Egner, P. (2002). The concept of 'Region': theoretical and methodological notes on its reconstruction. *European Integration* 24(3): 179–200.

Scott, A. J. (1996). Regional motors of the global economy. *Futures* 28: 391–411.

Scott, J. W. (2001). Euroregions, governance and transborder cooperation in the EU. *European Research in Regional Science* 10(1): 104–115.

Scott A. J., and Storper, M. (1992). Regional Development Reconsidered. In *Regional Development and Contemporary Industrial Response: Extending Flexible Specialization*, eds. H. Ernste and V. Martin. London: Belhaven Press, 1–24.

Storper, M. (1995). The resurgence of regional economies, ten years later: the region as a nexus of untraded interdependencies. *European Urban and Regional Studies* 2: 191–221.

Storper, M. (1997). *The Regional World: Territorial Development in a Global Economy*. New York: Guilford.

Storper, M., and Walker, R. (1989). *The Capitalist Imperative*. Oxford: Blackwell.

Swyngedouw, E. (2000). Authoritarian governance, power, and the politics of rescaling. *Environment and Planning D: Society and Space* 18: 63–76.

Swyngedouw, E. (2005). Governance innovation and the citizen: the Janus face of governance-beyond-the-state. *Urban Studies* 42(11): 1991–2006.

Trigilia, C. (1991).The paradox of the region: economic regulation and the representation of interests. *Economy and Society* 20(3): 306–327.

Online materials

- EU Directorate-General Regional and Urban Policy
  https://commission.europa.eu/about-european-commission/departments-and-executive-agencies/regional-and-urban-policy_en
- European Committee of the Regions
  https://cor.europa.eu/en/
- Regional Studies Association
  https://www.regionalstudies.org/

Further reading

Allen, J., Massey, D., and Cochrane, A. (1998). *Rethinking the Region*. London: Routledge.
A milestone in the critical reassessment of the notion of 'regions' in geography.

Brenner, N. (2004). *New State Spaces: Urban Governance and the Rescaling of Statehood*. Oxford: Oxford University Press.
Jessop, B. (2002). *The Future of the Capitalist State*. Cambridge: Polity Press.
Two reference texts for a critique and reformulation of geographical notions in relationship to transformation of the state in globalised post-Fordist capitalism.

Elden, S. (2006). The state of territory under globalization: empire and the politics of reterritorialization. *Thamyris/Intersecting* 12: 47–66.
An essay contributing to understanding the redefinition of the meaning of regions against the background of a theoretical discussions of the geographical notions of 'territory'.

Keating, M. (1997). The invention of regions: political restructuring and territorial government in Western Europe. *Environment and Planning C* 15(4): 383–398.
A classic and still relevant contribution to a multi-dimensional understanding of 'regions' and of dynamics of change in regionalist movements and regionalisation practices.

Paasi, A. (2001). Europe as a social process and discourse: considerations of place, boundaries and identity. *European Urban and Regional Studies* 8(1): 7–28.
A reference text for discussing the socio-political and cultural dimensions of regional identity formation in the context of European integration.

Storper, M. (1995). The resurgence of regional economies, ten years later: the region as a nexus of untraded interdependencies. *European Urban and Regional Studies* 2: 191–221.
A milestone and among the most effective accounts of the contribution of 'new economic geography' to rethinking regions.

21 Lived regions

Andrew McGregor

Introduction

I am writing this chapter from Dharug (or Darug) Ngurra (Dharug Country). I acknowledge the traditional custodians of the land and pay my respects to the Elders past, present and future of the Wallumattagal and Cammeraygal clans on whose unceded lands I work and live, and who have nurtured, and continue to nurture, Dharug Ngurra, since the Dreamtime. You probably haven't heard of these people and regions, unless you come from around here, and yet they have existed for far longer than any modern city, or even any modern state. Aboriginal people have been present in Dharug Ngurra at least 20,000 years prior to European invasions, and 80,000 years earlier in other places. Dharug Ngurra has its own language, culture, social structures, **ecologies**, lands, knowledges and ways of being that have evolved over generations.

Dharug Ngurra, like all the Aboriginal nations across Australia, is an example of what this chapter will refer to as a 'lived region'. The lived region concept is under-developed academically but used here to indicate a region that is bound together through the ongoing shared practices, cultures, relations, politics, materialities and identities of the people that live within them. Lived regions are socially and culturally, rather than purely politically or economically, determined. Sometimes they map well with formal political and administrative jurisdictions, while at other times they may cross borders or bubble along largely unseen or actively repressed by governing authorities. Dharug Ngurra, for example, coexists with the settler-colonial state of Australia, in the northern suburbs of the city of Sydney. I'm sure most of you have heard of Sydney, but it's likely you, and most settler-colonial Australians like me, have not heard of Dharug Ngurra.

In this chapter we explore lived regions as ways of understanding how places gain identities and meanings. By researching lived regions, they become more visible, inviting alternative ways of being within and imagining the world. For example, you can explore an Aboriginal language map of Australia here: https://aiatsis.gov.au/explore/map-indigenous-australia. Such maps invite engagement with Aboriginal and colonial histories and identities, and different ways of engaging with and understanding place. We will explore different approaches to lived regions, like those of Aboriginal Australia, by initially discussing how human geography and area studies have approached regions. We then consider two approaches for recognising lived regions, one based on culture and the other on the biophysical characteristics of place. Finally, we introduce Zomia, one of the most famous and controversial examples of a lived region, stretching across the highland areas of Southeast and East Asia.

DOI: 10.4324/9780429265853-25

From regional geography to area studies to lived regions

Geographers have long been fascinated by diversity in the world. Indeed, geography is often portrayed as a world or global discipline, with expertise in the physical and cultural unique-ness of places. The growing National Geographic media empire depicts geographers as intrepid explorers, attracted to distant, exotic, often risky locations. To some extent, such depictions echo older disciplinary approaches when geography was associated with attempts to describe diversity in the world. Unfortunately, this was often done from a Eurocentric perspective, focusing on regional traits to highlight, and often stereotype and criticise, how other places differed from Europe. Jonas (2012: 265) explains, 'the main task of the geographer was to draw boundaries around those territories of interest to colonialist and imperialist ventures'. There was an empha-sis on mapping difference and explaining those differences in simplistic ways that reflected as much about the interests of imperial powers as the place being mapped.

By the 1950s, as colonial empires crumbled in the post-war period, geographers became aware of the ethical and theoretical weaknesses of descriptive approaches. The discipline pivoted from a focus on regional traits to a focus on spatial processes, from description of places to analysing spatial connections and flows that shaped places. Regional knowledges and distinctions became less important, particularly as the world was expected to become more homogenous through processes of **globalisation**. Today, geographers specialise in cul-tural, social, economic, political, development, environmental or physical geography rather than say Southeast Asian, Oceanic, sub-Saharan African, European or North American geog-raphies. However, regional research, while less visible, has not disappeared. Instead, most geographic research focuses on Western countries, deepening understandings of the West at the expense of other regions. Non-Western research is often referred to as 'development geography', which groups a huge diversity of regional contexts and research agendas together into a single label. The outcome, somewhat ironically, is the perpetuation of a Western way of seeing and understanding the world, exactly what the shift away from regional geography was supposed to avoid.

As regional geographies fell from favour, the multidisciplinary subject of area studies emerged in the United States to become the primary lens for understanding regions. Area studies sought to generate insights into 'foreign places', often through fieldwork and lan-guage training, to deepen understandings and cultivate knowledge about foreign areas. It has attracted similar criticisms to earlier forms of regional geography for being overly descrip-tive and focused on difference. Critics argue that **representations** of non-Western places often reflected and perpetuated Western imaginations rather than lived experiences of those being studied. A related criticism is that area studies has been heavily shaped either directly or indirectly by Western geopolitical interests. Southeast Asian funding, for example, peaked before rapidly dropping off after the Vietnam-American War (Lewis and Wigen, 1999). In other words, knowledge production in area studies has responded to the shifting geopolitical needs of Western institutions.

Such critiques simplify a complex and diverse multidisciplinary field, much of which doesn't fit or has moved on from such depictions. Sharp (2018), for example, describes a much more critical and diverse area studies that has been informed by **post-colonial** critiques since at least the 1980s. New forms of regional geography have also emerged as geographers have become concerned about the Anglo-American focus of the discipline and the need to diversify where and how knowledge is produced. The globalisation of higher education has accentuated this need as academics emerge from across the world, contributing their own regional perspectives about geographic issues. Several researchers have argued for a closer relationship between contemporary area studies and new forms of regional geography that are informed by post-colonial, **feminist** and other theories. Core to these discussions is an appreciation of knowledge produced in and from regional areas, not in the sense of 'testing' Anglo-American theory in new places, but instead, as Sharp (2018) suggests, in the refraction of geographical knowledge, whereby geographical concepts and ideas emerge from and travel between places, developing, changing and evolving as they do.

A key step in recognising more diverse and inclusive regional perspectives is to recognise that regions are **socially constructed** rather than given. The regions we are familiar with are outcomes of politics and **power**, with actors striving to influence what will be recognised as a region, its **territorial** reach, and how it will be represented. Well-known world regions, for example, East Asia, Southeast Asia, South Asia, the Middle East, sub-Saharan Africa, Latin America, North America, Russia and Eastern Europe, Western Europe and Oceania, were formed through debates by predominantly US scholars in area studies (Lewis and Wigen, 1999). These classifications sought to make the world legible for geopolitical strategies by highlighting the similarities and distinctiveness of those regions. However, in doing so they simultaneously concealed similarities between regions and differences within regions. Drawing similarities between the physical or cultural characteristics of mountainous Kachin communities in northern Myanmar, gated urban communities in Singapore and Filipino fishing communities from the Sulu Archipelago, all within the world region of Southeast Asia, is not an easy task. However, recognising that regions are socially constructed is not the same as saying that regional differences don't exist. As Agnew (1999) succinctly states, 'Regions both reflect differences in the world and ideas about differences. They cannot be reduced to one or the other'. North America is different to East Asia, just as Dharug Ngurra differs from Pitjantjatjara Country in central Australia, both in peoples' minds and in their social and physical characteristics.

Lived regions are also socially constructed. Unlike world regions, though, or the administrative regions used by governments, lived regions emerge from the practices, beliefs, experiences, ecologies and relationships of people in places. They form when people self-identify with regional identities and share a sense of place and associated practices, values or beliefs that distinguish their region from others. In Australia, lived regions are evident when Aboriginal peoples self-identify with the lands of their ancestors and the values, cultures, beliefs, practices, politics and ecologies associated with that. In Aotearoa New Zealand, Māori peoples or iwi similarly identify with ancestral regions, while broader regional identities have formed for north and south islanders, despite there being no formal governing bodies at this scale. As Paasi (2002: 138) notes, 'regional consciousness has no necessary relation to administrative lines drawn by governments'. However administrative boundaries sometimes recognise, and are based on, pre-existing lived regions; and regional identities can grow from, or be influenced by, administrative boundaries. The driving force for lived regions, though, is the everyday lives, practices and values of people living there. Recognising lived regions and creating opportunities for those regions to be represented in planning and decision-making is an important step towards more inclusive and just societies.

Summary

- Lived regions refer to areas that are bound together through the shared practices, cultures, relations, materialities and identities of the people that live within them.
- Regional geography and area studies have shifted from describing regional traits and differences to focusing on how regions form, interact and influence people living there.
- World regions were originally shaped by geopolitical interests, revealing as much about those who identified the regions as much as the regions themselves.
- Lived regions emerge through cultural practices and ecologies of place and are often maintained irrespective of administrative recognition.

Identifying lived regions

Two ways in which researchers have sought to identify lived regions are through culture and ecology. In what follows we explore cultural regions and bioregions, and some of the strengths and weaknesses of each.

Cultural regions

Cultural regions are places associated with cultural values and practices that distinguish them from other places. For example, people may be united through shared religious beliefs, languages, histories, food, rituals, stories, customs, community economies or behaviours. In most cases cultural regions are spatially defined, although there has been work exploring cultural regions that exist in online spaces. They can differ wildly in scale, from world cultural regions, such as North America, the Middle East or Oceania, through to sub-national cultural regions, distinguishing, for example, between the culture of the deep south of the United States with the east coast or the west coast. While some cultural regions are named and gain recognition, many cultural regions persist primarily in people's imaginations and practices rather than in official documents, such as the differing cultural regions in northern and southern England.

As this brief survey shows, the concept of a cultural region can be used quite loosely and at multiple scales. To provide a little more shape Paasi (2002) suggests a cultural region has:

1. A territorial shape – the boundaries that are associated with the region and distinguish it from other places;
2. A symbolic shape – including the name, symbols and practices associated with the region;
3. Institutions – that promote and maintain the territorial and symbolic shapes, creating 'us' and 'them' distinctions;
4. A regional identity – exhibited in social practices and consciousness that people associate with the region and can be a source of pride or meaning.

As cultural regions are often not formally recognised, they must be continually reproduced through practices, narratives and institutions, shifting over time and **space**. Some cultural regions are recognised and promoted to raise the profile of places, such as food and wine regions advertised in regional tourism strategies. However, Paasi cautions that there are *ideal* and *factual* regional identities, where ideal refers to official regional identities promoted in tourist brochures and factual regional identities derive from the narratives of institutions within the region. Factual regional identities are more likely to reflect the lived experiences of those within the region, often diverting from and fracturing more official narratives.

In some cases, states may seek to repress cultural regions as they are perceived as a threat to their power and stability. People in the cultural region of West Papua, currently part of Indonesia, for example, are often associated with a broader Melanesian cultural region incorporating Papua New Guinea, the Solomon Islands, Vanuatu, Fiji and nearby islands, rather than Indonesia (Lawson, 2016). The Indonesian state has actively attempted to weaken this cultural identity through ongoing military repression and the prevention of cultural expression, such as the flying of the West Papuan Morning Star flag, now associated with independence (Figure 21.1). A less obvious form of repression has been through the transmigration of Indonesians into the province, diluting regional identities. In contrast, while many factors contributed to cessation of hostilities in the long running secessionist conflict in the Indonesian province of Aceh, one of the most significant was the granting of special autonomy laws that protect Aceh's traditional Islamic identity.

In other cases, the cultural region itself may be a source of tension for people living within the region who do not identify with it. There is a risk that cultural regions can erase diversity and difference and perpetuate stereotypes, becoming static depictions that do not reflect changing cultures and increasing mobility. Those who do not 'fit' the supposed culture of the region may become targets for violence and harassment, for diluting the 'purity' of the regional identity. One response to minimise this risk is to emphasise the importance of multiculturalism and diversity as part of the culture of a region, something that has been attempted, with varying degrees of

Figure 21.1
West Papuan Morning Star flag

Source: Photo credit: Georg Berg/Alamy

success, in my home city of Sydney. Another tactic is to engage in countermapping practices that provide ways of highlighting alternative cultural regions that differ from official accounts. Mapping Aboriginal lands in Australia, for example, is a practice of counter mapping. Such maps emphasise the multiple Aboriginal nations that pre-existed **colonialism**, and continue today, but are insufficiently recognised and embedded into national **discourse** and policy.

Bioregions

In contrast to cultural regions which are united by a shared sense of identity, bioregions are held together and delineated by biophysical characteristics. For example, a watershed, a desert, a forest, an island or an ecosystem that hosts similar forms of animal and plant life may form the basis for a bioregion. What unites people is not culture per se, although people living within a bioregion may share similar cultures, but the shared physical environment in which people live. Kirkpatrick Sale (2001) argued for 'regions defined by nature, not by legislature' and for societies 'living by ecological principles of sustainability dictated by the limits of the land itself' (p. 41). Such principles include co-operation rather than competition, decentralisation, and symbiosis, in pursuit of small societies living in harmony with local ecologies and the different rhythms and challenges of bioregional life. While admitting such views may sound utopian, Sale argues that humans have long lived in small bioregional units, evidencing Indigenous peoples prior to settled agriculture, and framing many secessionist conflicts today as bioregional conflicts, with people seeking autonomy at a bioregional scale (Figure 21.2).

Figure 21.2
Spreewald, Germany. Biosphere reserve

Source: Photo credit: Berndt Güntzel-Lingner/Pixabay

Despite its ecological appeal bioregionalism has never really taken off. Instead of fracturing into smaller, more self-sufficient bioregional units, most places have become more incorporated and reliant upon national and international flows of goods and services through processes of globalisation. Bioregions are recognised for natural resource management purposes, with institutions set up to govern rivers and watersheds for example; however, it is rare for people to strongly identify with those bioregions, and rarer still for people to intentionally shape their social and political processes to reflect those ecologies. Perhaps the most similar officially recognised governance structures are the UNESCO Biosphere Reserves which are nominated by national governments for conservation and sustainable forms of development. There are over 700 biosphere reserves around the world where conservation of the environment and biodiversity play a prominent role in decision-making. Even in these places, however, cultural attachment to the biosphere reserves can be weak, and the biosphere reserve may run across multiple bioregional boundaries. Nevertheless, bioregionalism retains some appeal as a way of rethinking society, with regions like Cascadia in the United States, gaining some academic and activist traction (see McKendry and Janos, 2021), while concepts like watersheds remain critical to environmental management.

Summary

- Cultural regions and bioregions provide two ways of approaching and identifying lived regions.
- Cultural regions are places associated with cultural values and practices that distinguish them from other places.
- *Ideal* regional identities are officially promoted versions of a cultural region, whereas *factual* regional identities are those that are expressed by local institutions and are likely to be more reflective of lived experiences.
- Cultural regions can be repressed by states concerned about their authority, and cultural regions can be repressive if they are not accepting of difference.
- Bioregions are places whose spatial extent and political principles are shaped by biophysical characteristics and ecological processes.

Zomia as a lived region

In this final section we look at an example of a lived region that includes elements of both cultural regions and bioregions, without quite fitting either of them. Zomia shows how the practice of identifying lived regions can change how and where knowledge is produced.

Zomia

Most people have not heard of Zomia, including Zomians. The term was originally proposed by the academic Willem van Schendel (2002) and has since been taken up by mostly foreign researchers.

Van Schendel argued that area studies had created regions that did not fit with people's lived experiences and were too focused on what he called 'heartland', or mainstream, cultures. The outcome was expertise in majority areas but little understanding about the flows and exchanges that took place across borders or between regions, or the experiences of minority cultures who lived at the fringes. The problems derived from the way world regions had been divided up and the lack of interaction between regional experts, creating gaps in knowledge about people who lived at the borders of world regions. Van Schendel notes this absence is reflected in cartography, '…anyone interested in finding fairly detailed modern maps showing the region covering Burma, Northeast India, Bangladesh, and neighbouring parts of China knows that these do not exist' (Van Schendel, 2012: 652). He gives the example of four highland settlements within 50 km of one another in the Eastern Himalayas that are allocated to four different world regions East Asia, Southeast Asia, South Asia and Central Asia. The lived experiences of those in the settlements are much more connected to one another than to the world regions they are contained within, but each seems insignificant to those broader regions and so attracts little research interest.

Van Schendel proposed the term Zomia, building on the word *Zomi* which means highlander in several local languages, to refer to the highland areas across ten countries in northern Southeast Asia, eastern South Asia, southern Central Asia and southwestern East Asia (see Figure 21.3). In naming this region van Schendel wanted to encourage a different form of scholarship that recognised the shared experiences of highlander people, who till then were generally seen as small

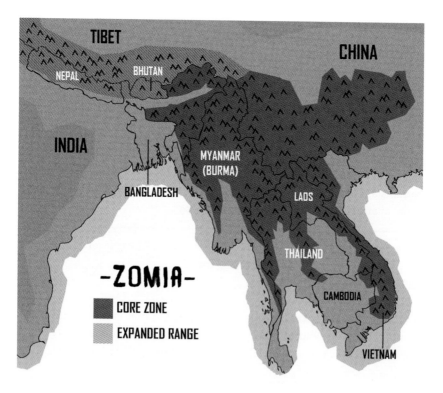

Figure 21.3
Map of Zomia

Source: Adapted from van Schendel (2002)

Figure 21.4
Hmong Cultural Dress

Source: Photo credit: Phoua Vang/Pixabay

and not particularly significant minority groups within state boundaries (Figure 21.4). The visibility of Zomia received a boost with the subsequent publication of a book by James Scott (2009) entitled *The Art of Not Being Governed: An Anarchist History of Upland Southeast Asia* in which he argued that Zomia represented one of the last world regions outside state control, where people had fled, sought refuge and resisted lowland pre-colonial, colonial and post-colonial authorities. It is this resistance and avoidance of lowland states – a resistance that is enabled through mountainous terrains and altitudes, rather than a singular culture or bioregion – that Scott believes provides a rationale for claiming Zomia as a lived region. Scott estimates that 80–100 million people live in Zomia who share 'comparable patterns of diverse hill agriculture, dispersal and mobility, and rough egalitarianism, which, not incidentally, includes a relatively higher status for women than in the valleys' (ibid: 19).

Not everyone agrees that Zomia is a lived region. The boundaries are fluid, with van Schendel's Zomia being larger than Scott's Zomia, both of which differ from the Southeast Asian Massif and the Hindu Kush Himalaya, two pre-existing regional concepts referring to similar high-altitude populations (Michaud, 2018). Nor is it a politically or culturally united region, indeed '[v]ariety, more than uniformity is its trademark. In the space of a hundred kilometers in the hills one can find more cultural variation – in language, dress, settlement pattern, ethnic identification, economic activity, and religious practices – than one would ever find in the lowland river valleys' (Scott, 2009: 16). Nor is the singular characteristic Scott uses to define Zomia, opposition to lowland states, necessarily common across this diversity, at least not anymore. Qian and Tang (2017) have shown how highland ethnic minorities crossing the borderlands of China and Vietnam, as well as China and Myanmar, do identify with lowland states to varying degrees and may use state borders to stress intra-ethnic differences and associations with more modern regional identities.

Despite such concerns Jean Michaud (2018: 80) maintains that '[c]areful inquiries on the ground throughout the Massif show that these peoples actually share a sense of being different from the majorities, a sense of geographical remoteness, and a state of marginality that is connected to political and economic distance from regional seats of power'. Naming this distinctiveness and identifying them as a lived region has been enough to bring the people of Zomia into view, directing attention away from state and world regional boundaries, towards the lived regions made up of highlands, borderlands, migrations, minorities and flows.

Summary

- Zomia has been proposed as a lived region incorporating a diverse range of highland communities spread across four different world regions. Zomians share similarities in agriculture, mobility, egalitarianism, opposition to the state and sense of marginality.
- Some question the concept of Zomia as being too culturally and politically diverse to be a lived region, recognising diversity in relation to lowland states.
- Recognising Zomia as a lived region has made the lives of 80–100 million people more visible and central to research agendas.

Conclusion

Lived regions are the places where we live and the places from which we came. They bring meaning to our lives and a sense of belonging, influencing who we are. They are imagined, but also real, often having blurry boundaries. They coexist across different layers and scales. Sometimes lived regions match well with administrative boundaries, while at other times they challenge those boundaries and are a source of tension. Their longevity may be threatened by globalisation and the increasing mobility of people and capital, as well as repression if state authority feels threatened. And yet, somehow, despite all this, lived regions survive. Some are largely out of public sight, contained within the daily lives of cultural groups, whereas others are much more visible, being the focus of public campaigns or research agendas pursuing greater social and political recognition. Regions like Zomia contest accepted boundaries and are providing ways for reimagining the world from the experiences of people rather than power. We can similarly imagine other socio-ecologies, located in forests, deserts, mountains, seas and rivers, as potential sites where lived regions might also be found that recentre the margins and contest existing boundaries.

In Australia, the lived regions of Aboriginal peoples are finally gaining public and official recognition after long histories of repression and neglect. Since beginning to write this chapter, my own campus has been renamed Wallumattagal campus, in recognition of the Dharug clan on whose unceded land the University is situated. It is a small step, and there is a long way to go in the pursuit of justice. Some of my colleagues are working hard to not only advance recognition for Dharug Ngurra as a lived region but also work with all the human and non-human lives and relations that make up this place, to work with the region, what we call Country, to bring about new ways of understanding and interacting with the world (Darug Ngurra et al., 2021; see also Bawaka Country et al., 2015). Far from being erased by globalisation, lived regions are proving resilient and insightful, providing exciting opportunities for geographers to learn from, work with and support regional communities. In doing so geographers can help widen knowledge about lived cultures and contribute to efforts to have regional voices and perspectives inform broader debates about how to live well in this dynamic world.

Discussion points

- What lived regions do you live in or are nearby? What are their characteristics and how did they form?
- How and why have regional geography and area studies moved away from describing regional traits?
- Discuss, with examples, how a cultural region can be repressed, and how it can be repressive.
- Are cultural regions and bioregions likely to overlap? Discuss why or why not.
- How does Zomia change the way in which people in highland areas of Southeast Asia are understood?
- Why is it important to recognise Indigenous lived regions like Dharug Ngurra? What does recognition enable?

References

Agnew, J. (1999). Regions on the mind does not equal regions of the mind. *Progress in Human Geography* 23: 91–96.

Bawaka Country, Wright, S., Suchet-Pearson, S., Lloyd, K., Burarrwanga, L., Ganambarr, R., Ganambarr-Stubbs, M., Ganambarr, G., Djawundi, D., and Sweeney, J. (2015). Co-becoming Bawaka: towards a relational understanding of place/space. *Progress in Human Geography* 40(4): 455–475.

Jonas, A. (2012). Region and place: regionalism in question. *Progress in Human Geography* 36: 263–272.

Lawson, S. (2016). West Papua, Indonesia and the Melanesian Spearhead Group: competing logics in regional and international politics. *Australian Journal of International Affairs* 70: 506–524.

Lewis, M. W., and Wigen, K. (1999). A maritime response to the crisis in area studies. *Geographical Review* 89: 161–168.

McKendry, C., and Janos, N. (eds.) (2021). *Urban Cascadia and the Pursuit of Environmental Justice.* Washington: University of Washington Press.

Michaud, J. (2018). Zomia and Beyond. In *Routledge Handbook of Asian Borderlands*, eds. A. Horstmann, M. Saxer, and A. Rippa. London: Routledge, 73–88.

Darug Ngurra, Dadd, L., Norman-Dadd, C., Graham, M., Suchet-Pearson, S., Glass, P., Scott, R., Narwal, H., and Lemire, J. (2021). Buran Nalgarra: an Indigenous-led model for walking with good spirit and learning together on Darug Ngurra. *AlterNative: An International Journal of Indigenous Peoples* 17: 357–367.

Paasi, A. (2002). Bounded spaces in the mobile world: deconstructing 'regional identity'. *Tijdschrift voor Economische en Sociale Geografie* 93: 137–148.

Qian, J., and Tang, X. (2017). Dilemma of modernity: interrogating cross-border ethnic identities at China's southwest frontier. *Area* 49: 52–59.

Sale, K. (2001). There's no place like home. *The Ecologist* 31: 40–43.

Scott, J. (2009). *The Art of Not Being Governed: An Anarchist History of Upland Southeast Asia.* New Haven and London: Yale University Press.

Sharp, D. (2018). Difference as practice: diffracting geography and the area studies turn. *Progress in Human Geography* 43: 835–852.

Van Schendel, W. (2002). Geographies of knowing, geographies of ignorance: jumping scale in Southeast Asia. *Environment and Planning D: Society and Space* 20: 647–668.

Online materials

- https://bawakacollective.com/

  The Bawaka Collective is an Indigenous and non-Indigenous, human-more-than-human research collective that conducts research from and involving Bawaka Country. It is an example of some of the novel and innovative ways in which the relations that make up lived regions are being recognised and expressed (see Chapter 43).

- https://cascadiabioregion.org/a-cascadia-primer

  A website devoted to building recognition for the bioregion of Cascadia in the Pacific Northwest of the United States.

- https://aiatsis.gov.au/explore/map-indigenous-australia

  A map of Indigenous Australia, helping make lived regions more visible.

Further reading

Agnew, J. (1999). Regions on the mind does not equal regions of the mind. *Progress in Human Geography* 23: 91–96.

A classic essay that examines how regions are both real and imagined.

Lewis, M. W., and Wigen, K. (1999). A maritime response to the crisis in area studies. *Geographical Review* 89: 161–168.

Explains how area studies contributed to the formation of world regions and efforts to rethink regions that better fit lived experiences.

Darug Ngurra, Dadd, L., Norman-Dadd, C., Graham, M., Suchet-Pearson, S., Glass, P., Scott, R., Narwal, H., and Lemire, J. (2021). Buran Nalgarra: an Indigenous-led model for walking with good spirit and learning together on Darug Ngurra. *AlterNative: An International Journal of Indigenous Peoples* 17: 357–367.

An introduction to the lived region of Darug Ngurra, reflecting Darug ways of understanding and interacting with the world.

Paasi, A. (2002). Bounded spaces in the mobile world: deconstructing 'regional identity'. *Tijdschrift voor Economische en Sociale Geografie* 93: 137–148.

A comprehensive introduction to cultural regions and regional identity in the context of increasing mobility and globalisation.

Sale, K. (2001). There's no place like home. *The Ecologist* 31: 40–43.

A short easily accessible introduction to bioregions by one of its most prominent advocates.

Scott, J. (2009). *The Art of Not Being Governed: An Anarchist History of Upland Southeast Asia.* New Haven
    and London: Yale University Press.
Chapter one lays out Scott's argument that Zomia is a lived region that shares an opposition to lowland Asian states.

Van Schendel, W. (2002). Geographies of knowing, geographies of ignorance: jumping scale in
    Southeast Asia. *Environment and Planning D: Society and Space* 20: 647–668.
Classic paper setting out the case for recognising the lived region of Zomia.

SECTION TWO

CULTURAL GEOGRAPHIES

22 Knowing cultural geographies

Junxi Qian and Andrew Williams

Introduction: the development and evolution of cultural geography

Cultural geography investigates the relationships between **cultures** and the world's geographical constituents (**space**, place, landscape, etc.) and processes (mobilities, connections, distribution, spatial variation, etc.). This appears to be a straightforward and simple statement. But the definition of culture is contested and volatile and its relationships to geography are also subject to radically different theorisations and interpretations. In this section introduction, we give a brief overview of the trajectory along which this subdiscipline has evolved over a period of more than two centuries.

Early forms of cultural geography can be traced to scholarly interest in the relations between human cultures and the environments in which they were situated. During the geographical explorations of the 18th and 19th centuries, Western geographers were already busy mapping cultures of 'exotic' lands and peoples, and geographic knowledge consolidated the power of colonial administration (Driver, 2000, see also Chapters 10 and 13). This theoretical enquiry later became associated with the tradition of environmental determinism (see Chapter 39), which asserted that 'cultures were produced due to the overwhelming influence of the natural conditions they developed in' (Anderson, 2021: 25). In a slightly more open-ended variation, environmental possibilism suggested that the possibilities of human cultures and lives were conditioned by the environment but not unilinearly determined by it – in other words, humans were seen as active agents in response to their environmental conditions. So, how was culture conceptualised in these traditions? A good illustration came from Vidal de Blanche's thesis on the relationship between people's milieu and *genre de vie* (way of life). Broadly conceived, *genre de vie* comprised routine material practices on which people drew their substance and eked out livelihoods, the particular landscapes that embodied these ways of life, and human practices articulated at the **ideological**, symbolic, and spiritual levels (Crang, 1998, Benko and Desbiens, 2009). These approaches, however, were later criticised for their crude empiricism and the inability to establish rigorous causal explanations.

With the ascendancy of scientific and quantitative revolution in geography during the 1950s and 1960s, cultural geographers made efforts to construct more 'systematic' and 'scientific' models to explain the geographical dimensions of cultural formation and transformation. Terry

DOI: 10.4324/9780429265853-27

Jordan (1976), for example, categorised five themes for the study of cultural geography: cultural region, cultural diffusion, cultural ecology, cultural integration, and cultural landscape. The mission underlying this framework was to understand how cultures were geographically distributed, and how cultures diffused and merged with others through geographical processes and relations. This approach, however, faced a series of difficulties, both conceptual and **epistemological**. First, it did not theorise the notion of culture per se but took cultures as given without questioning how cultures were constituted in the first place. Second, it developed a sophisticated spatial typology without explaining it, failing to reveal the political, social, and economic dynamics underlying spatial processes such as distribution and diffusion. Third, its theorisation of cultural diffusion and integration was relatively abstract and mechanical, without thinking about the meanings, practices, and contestations unfolding on the ground.

In a different vein, the Berkeley School of cultural geography (active in the United States from the 1950s to the 1970s), whose representative figures included prominent geographers such as Carl Sauer, Wilber Zelinsky, Philip Wagner, Marvin Mikesell, developed a more explicit conceptualisation of culture (see also Chapter 39). In the works of Sauer (1925) and Zelinsky (1973), each cultural region was defined by a super-organic mechanism, that is, culture, which coincided with regional boundaries. For these scholars, the region was an ensemble of cultural landscapes that collectively expressed the operation of a local culture, something that was so all-encompassing that all livelihoods, tactics, materials objects, and knowledge systems within the region could be brought to bear on a cultural interpretation, in tandem with a particular identity of the region (Crang, 1998). In this vein, the Berkeley School saw culture as an **ontological** entity with its own logics of existence, which could explain local cultural practices and landscapes *causally*. But exactly what was *the* culture like at a specific regional scale? To address this question required scholars to name certain labels for a regional culture. For example, American culture was defined by individualism, liberal democracy, and market superiority (Zelinsky, 1973); English culture by a deep love for rural pastoralism; and Chinese culture by Confucianism, paternalism, and collectivism.

The thesis of superorganism suffered from many theoretical flaws. According to Jackson (1989), it firstly reduced the **agency** of humans to that of accepting the guidance of a pre-existing 'culture', rather than to their active role in constructing and transforming it. Secondly, for the Berkeley School, culture was homogenous and monolithic rather than heterogenous and plural (see also Mitchell, 2000). Culture was largely equated to traditions and customs fixed in the past and rural areas, while the thesis exhibited discernible anti-modern, anti-urban connotations. Finally, it was biased towards cultural landscapes, at the expense of other cultural elements such as practices, meanings, values, and ideologies.

Jackson's book, together with various other texts, marked the beginning of what is termed the 'cultural turn' in cultural geography, a movement turning away from the idea of culture as 'a force larger than and relatively independent of the lives of human themselves' (Mitchell, 2000: 30) into which people are automatically assimilated (Naylor et al., 2000). Instead, the cultural turn moves **human agency** centre stage and aligns itself with a kind of cultural materialism, exemplary of which are the works of British cultural theorists Raymond Williams and Stuart Hall (Jackson, 1989, Mitchell, 1995). In their formulations, culture is an ensemble of symbols, meanings, values, and ideologies that different social groups create in response to structural and social contexts. 'Culture' was 'not a residual category...it is the very medium through which social change is experienced, contested and constituted' (Cosgrove and Jackson, 1987: 95). Cultures not only help people adapt to prevalent conditions but also resist and rework dominant social and political relations – in other words, culture can be polemic and resistant. Culture is hence 'overdetermined', in the sense that it is simultaneously determined by many things: by social conditions but it also expresses the capabilities of people in making their own histories. These collective experiences make up a '**structure of feeling**' that is historically contingent (Williams, 1977). Given the socialised and dynamic nature of cultures, they are also inherently negotiated, plural, power-laden, and contested, implicated in cultural wars and social struggles (Jackson, 1989).

Running parallel to the cultural turn, another set of geographical theories was that of **humanistic geography**. Humanistic geographers see place and space not so much as a bundle of social relations but a phenomenological process. Among the series of theoretical assertions advocated by the school of humanistic geography, three are highlighted here: (i) this paradigm prioritises the role of experience in the making of space and place, emphasising the emotional binding and attachment that connect humans with their milieus; (ii) it dedicates a lot of analysis to the *practices* through which people encounter and know spaces and places, which culminates in **embodied** skills and knowledge; and (iii) it singles out everyday movement and mundane routine as a crucial lens to interrogate how a spatialised self is made (Ley and Samuels, 1978, Cresswell, 2015). While humanistic geography is **epistemologically** divergent from cultural turn's view of culture as a social product, many of its insights have later been absorbed into new and emerging cultural geographies of practice, emotion, **affect**, and embodiment.

Over the last three decades, some scholars have argued that the cultural turn emphasised too much the discursive articulation of culture and how it is contingent on structural contexts and social relations but dedicated limited attention to the mediating effects of emotions, bodies, material things, everyday practices, non-human elements (see Chapters 8 and 24). Nevertheless, the cultural turn casts light on at least three qualities of culture that resonate closely even with the latest scholarships in cultural geography: (i) culture is **socially constructed**; (ii) culture is not fixed but dynamic; and finally, (iii) culture expresses power relations and is contested. The next section, which reviews major topics of research in cultural geography, will further cast light on these points.

Summary

- Earlier approaches in cultural geographies were interested in theorising the relations between cultures and the environments that people lived in.
- Later and more systematic approaches investigated the spatial dynamics of cultural changes or conceptualised culture as a super-organic entity.
- With the cultural turn and subsequent theoretical re-orientations in the field, cultural geographers have been working with socially constructed, embodied, **performative**, and material conceptions of culture.

What does cultural geography study?

Since the cultural turn, the concept of culture has been continuously updated and enriched through the field's ongoing engagements with **postmodern**, poststructural, **feminist**, **Marxist**, post-colonial, and posthumanist thinking in social sciences. This endeavour has also benefited from the diversity of topics in cultural geography and its close relationships with other subdisciplines – especially social, political, economic, and historical geography. There is hardly any social process that does not unfold with a dimension of meanings, values, ideologies, and identities. Culture is pervasive and diffused in the fabric of everyday social, political, and economic life. As such, cultural geographies are often studied at the interfaces shared with other subdisciplines of human geography – area geographies, economic geographies, political geographies, environmental geographies, social geographies, and more, which are introduced separately in this book. It is thus safe to say that culture is a theme that runs throughout the book, rather than confined to this section per se.

For example, cross-disciplinary engagement between cultural and economic geographies has nurtured a vibrant enquiry into 'cultural economies'. The 'economy', according to Smith et al. (2010: 20), is 'constituted through a myriad of social, emotional, political, material, and symbolic activities and arrangements – events and relationships that are not "additional to" economic affairs but inherent within them' (see Chapter 30). Speaking about the chapters in Section Three (Economic geographies), for instance, it is widely concurred that financial practices are not only regulated by market and profit but also ethical sensibilities (such as in Islamic finance, e.g. Bassens et al., 2011, Pollard and Samers, 2013) or the aspiration of using financial instruments to contribute to social goods (Berndt and Wirth, 2019). Consumption, to take another example, has long been analysed by geographers as a practice through which people accumulate social and symbolic capital – an association that is vividly played out in the processes of urban and rural **gentrification** (e.g. Ley, 2003, see also Chapter 32). It is also an important mechanism that contributes to the reproduction or destabilisation of cultural beliefs and norms at different scales. Take, for example, **gendered** practices of shopping and its relation to **social constructions** of 'motherhood' and 'family' (McDowell et al., 2005), or, for example, the growth of *alternative* consumption practices such as fair trade, moral consumption, and sustainable consumption (see Chapter 64). Besides, work – whether formal or informal – is shaped by cultural conventions and norms based on gender, **ethnicity**, religion, etc., as was the case in Thompson's (1963) investigation of the English working class, or the focus of informal economy literatures on negotiated collective identities and grassroots routines of collaboration (see Chapters 33 and 34).

As to environmental geographies, it has widely been documented that many Indigenous peoples have a sophisticated system of cultural knowledge and practices that situate people and nature within an integrated cosmological universe, and their understandings of, and responses to, global environmental crises such as climate change, pollution, and disasters draw justification and rationale from such cultural and symbolic relations (see Chapters 39 and 45). Moreover, **Anthropocene** theorists have argued that human society's transition towards sustainability is premised upon cultural reinventions at different scales, set in motion by interventions that prompt people to recognise the **sovereignties** and **subjectivities** of nature and develop new conventions of consumption. These conventions fundamentally depart from the norms of conspicuous consumption that easily result in excessive and wasteful use of resources (see Chapter 62; also see Castree 2014a, 2014b for critical review). Dialogues can also be effortlessly and productively established with the chapters in the area geographies, political geographies, social geographies, and emerging collaborations sections. Lived regions, **nation-states**, borders, identity, and so on are, after all, cultural constructs, reflecting how people use meanings, symbols, and ideologies to construct a sense of self and bring the latter to bear on the construction of space, place, region, and borderline (Chapters 21, 48, 50, and 58). Moreover, both geographies of care (Chapter 61) and postsecularity (Chapter 73) highlight the negotiation of moralities and ethics vis-à-vis new landscapes of global economy and social welfare.

The seven chapters in the Cultural Geographies section represent some typical topics to which cultural geographers conventionally lay a claim. By way of a journey through these chapters, we highlight some of the fundamental theoretical concerns in contemporary cultural geography, which are relevant but not restricted to these same chapters.

First, cultural geography puts a great emphasis on **representation** and **discourse**, namely how the world is represented and narrated through a sophisticated array of symbols, signs, texts, images, statements, arts, etc. The basic conviction here is that our access to the world is not in the form of encountering a 'given' reality but rather mediated by representational schemes. More importantly, representations and discourses are social constructs, since they are deeply implicated in the complex ways in which people formulate, negotiate, and resist social and structural relations. As such, representations and discourses are constitutive of the relations of power, as claims to truth feed into the production of political authority – a nexus of **power** and knowledge that Foucault (1972) famously dissected (Cosgrove, 1989, Anderson, 2019). Anderson (2017) summarises how cultural politics has been largely focused on:

> discerning systems of representation, particularly how power works through forms of **othering**; to disclose and critique the symbolic and material violences that are enacted through them or that they enable; and to give attention to, cultivate and sometimes create representations that may break with existing formations and enable resistances or alternatives.
>
> *Anderson, 2017: 502*

This concern with representation is most evident in Ning An's chapter on **imaginative geographies**, which reveals that our understanding of the world is as much a subjective construction as an objective description, and the former is played out most often through representational forms: (Chapter 23). Geographical imaginations, subsequently, feed into the structuring of sociopolitical relations at multiple scales: from colonial domination and geopolitics (exemplified by Edward Said's theses on **Orientalism** and cultural **imperialism**) (Figure 22.1), to the making of centre-periphery hierarchies in a nation-state; and to the politics of encounter and difference at the scale of neighbourhoods and communities in cities (Wilson, 2017).

Secondly, culture is placed and simultaneously on the move (Matless, 1996). Although Sauer can be criticised for promulgating an overly static, epistemologically closed conceptualisation of culture, his view that culture shapes and is shaped by a regional identity is not invalid. This is because social and economic practices that condition the possibilities of cultural production and reproduction are inherently situated and localised, depending on material **infrastructures**, institutional conditions, and webs of social relations at the local scale. As a result, all cultural practices are closely tied to people's sense of place (Cresswell, 2015), or in the words of Matless (1997), a geographical self. However, culture is often on the move as well, reflected in cultural geography's long-time engagements with the issues of travel, migration, tourism, etc. These place-crossing practices not only create a sequence of contact zones along the routes, in which different cultures encounter and hybridise with each other. More importantly, movement is more than a functional practice that brings people from Point A to Point B, but itself generative of rich cultural experiences and practices that are representational or **non-representational**,

Figure 22.1
Odalisque/Odalisca 1889 by Francesc Masriera i Manovens (1842–1902) Catalonian figure painter
influenced by Orientalism

Source: Photo credit: Peter Horree/Alamy

in tandem with the material forms they take and social contexts that they traverse (Blunt, 2007).
Indeed, cultural geographical works have responded to a broader 'new mobilities paradigm' in
social sciences, which accumulated much momentum during the past two decades (Urry, 2000).
The placed and mobile nature of culture is explicitly or implicitly articulated in many chapters
throughout this section, and indeed the whole book. Religion, as Orlando Woods elaborates
in his chapter (Chapter 28), demands significant labour of sacralising space/place. For Julian
Holloway's chapter on spectral geography (Chapter 29), while much ink has been spilled on the
ephemerality of affects, feelings, ambiences, and bodily **encounters**, the placed dimension of
spectrality is also evident because the past disrupts the present and future precisely by folding

Figure 22.2
Children dance at the annual celebration of Confederate settlers in Santa Barbara d'Oeste, Brazil, Sunday, April 26, 2015. Following defeat in the American Civil War (1861–1865), up to 20,000 Confederates from the Southern Slave States emigrated to Brazil where slavery was not yet abolished

Source: Photo credit: Andre Penner, Associated Press/Alamy

into specific locations and places. In their chapter on travel and tourism (Chapter 27), JJ Zhang and TC Chang elaborate on a dialectic between place and travel – in essence, tourism involves a series of place-making processes at different scales, which are fraught with political connotations and contestations.

Thirdly, in addition to representations that mediate our knowing of the world, there are more direct means through practices, bodily experiences, affective processes, and performativities (Figure 22.2). In particular, the concept of performativity, inspired principally by the works of feminist scholar Judith Butler, refers to the notion that meanings and identities are neither pregiven nor fixed. It is the routinisation and repetition of practices, often at the everyday and bodily levels, that render them concrete and intelligible. As Nash (2000) suggests, 'the concept of performativity is an attempt to find a more embodied way of rethinking the relationships between determining social structures and personal agency' (p. 654). In other words, codifying cultural norms, meanings, and identities is impossible without habitual, often unreflexive, processes of doing. Without the intermediary of texts or images, people use their practices, bodies, senses, and inner selves to encounter space and navigate the world creatively with situatedly produced meanings, identities and affects, which are never stable but always in flux. Such elasticity and fluidity enable people to resist dominant social orders in some cases while reproducing, even consolidating them in others.

In parallel, since the 2000s cultural geography has witnessed the emergence of a variety of more-than-representational theories (Chapter 8), the area first systematically introduced to geography by the British geographer Nigel Thrift (2007). Collectively, these different lines of research question the use of representations as the primary vehicle by which knowledge is produced and advocate that not only should we study cognitive processes based on meaning-making but also those that are precognitive or non-cognitive. The epistemological turn to decentred, relational, and expressive body-subjects has kindled geographers' interest in research topics such diverse as everyday life, prosaic practice, embodiment, affect, emotion, and materiality (Nash, 2000, Lorimer, 2005). In Chapter 24 on affect and emotion, Ben Anderson emphasises the pervasive existence of emotions in all geographies and their significance beyond the personal level, given that they express rich linkages among people, things, and places, as well as how emotions shape the ways that people live through major socioeconomic transformations. Different from emotion, which points to our psychological feelings and resonances, the term affect refers to the largely unreflexive and unconscious elements of everyday life that nonetheless fit us into particular contexts and activities. Emotion and affect play crucial roles in the construction of spaces and spatial relations – from the careful engineering of the **atmospheres** in shopping malls to the ways that **transnational** investments are experienced locally. Amanda Rogers and Charlotte Veal's chapter (Chapter 25) investigates the issues of embodiment and performativity through the lens of performing arts. Highlighting key qualities of performing arts – placed, political, and expressive, the chapter offers a rich analysis of how performing arts draw upon specific placed contexts but simultaneously problematise and resist them, and how they enable us to negotiate and problematise the representational codes of difference and identity, as well as the prevalent social and cultural norms. Embodiment and affect are equally important to everyday religiosities (Chapter 28), given that much attention from academics has been paid to the embodied and affective dimensions of lived religion and how emotions serve as the cohesive that builds up religious communities.

Finally, it is important to pay attention to the material conditions and practices through which cultures are produced and negotiated. Cultures may appear to be quite amorphous, and we imagine them as existing nowhere, but in our minds and spiritual worlds. In reality, however, culture is co-constituted by the polyvalent relationships between humans and the material worlds. Two key theoretical perspectives in social sciences are highlighted here to elucidate this assertion. Scholars, mainly from the field of cultural studies, have developed an agenda interrogating the social lives of things and how material objects are thoroughly implicated in the constitution of social orders and relations (Miller, 2008). The 'material turn' in human geography has drawn heavily from the **actor-network theory** (ANT) developed by academics such as Bruno Latour, Michel Callon, Annemarie Mol, amongst others, and also drawing from feminist scholars such as Donna Haraway and the **assemblage** thinking typical of which are the works of Gilles Deleuze and Félix Guattari. Despite highly noticeable divergences between the two paradigms – for example, ANT emphasises more the conferment of agency to non-human actors in social scientific analyses, while assemblage thinking is focused more on theorising the profligacy of the generative possibilities borne out of the promiscuous associations among humans and non-humans – they both alert us to the importance of tracing the biographies of things, and how their implications in relational networks may effectuate sociocultural changes and indeed extend the boundaries of human ontologies and agencies (Kirsch, 2013, Tolia-Kelly, 2013). Chapter 26 by Joseph Pierce addresses these points by looking at the mutually constitutive relationships between the tangible and intangible elements of culture. After tracing how materialism was critiqued but later revived in human geography, the chapter then dwells at length on a key point – how the control of people and the engineering of behaviours in cities are reliant on specific material infrastructures.

Summary

- Cultural geography examines a wide variety of topics and has rich intersections with other subdisciplines in geography.
- Cultural geography pays particular attention to such issues as: representation and discourse; place and movement; practices, bodily experiences, affective processes, and performativities; and material conditions and practices.

Conclusion: challenging the future of cultural geography

Cultural geography remains a popular subdiscipline and its theoretical and empirical concerns continue to diversify and evolve. This, however, does not mean that the area does not face significant challenges, even setbacks. One of these is that cultural geography has been criticised for a lack of political relevance and policy engagement (Martin, 2001, Ward, 2005, Rose-Redwood et al., 2018). Yet, cultural geographers have long been concerned about power relations, particularly the ways that they are arranged and produced through cultural practices, discourses, and representations. Equally, cultural practices and representations can be used to challenge or resist dominant power relations and create alternative forms of social and political organisation. Ben Anderson (2017, see also Chapter 24), for example, reviews some of the key contributions that cultural geographers are making to understanding precarity, dispossession, the state, and anti-Black violence. There are also important questions to ask about the contested and changing cultural geographies underlying global economic integration, transnational **capitalism**, geopolitical competition (especially between the US and a globalising China), global environmental changes, and resource scarcity. Cultural geographers have much to offer examining the online and offline **spatialities** of the 'Alt-right' and fascist sensibilities, how they are produced and sustained, and countered effectively (Ince, 2019, Luger, 2022), for example. Cultural geographers have also mainstreamed the use of creative practice – sculpture, dance, painting, poetry, drawing, sound, theatre-making – as a legitimate geographical research method, as a means to engage diverse 'publics', and as a medium of knowing the world itself (Hawkins, 2021). Cultural geographers have explored incidental and engineered social encounters that tackle prejudice and conflictual cultural values (Mayblin et al., 2015) and have used participatory action research concentrating on community, care, and welfare provision against the backdrop of urban **neoliberalism** and austerity (Mason, 2015), to name just two examples.

The politics and public relevance of cultural geography are as pertinent as ever. A new and volatile cultural landscape has emerged in many cities and societies across the world. Authoritarian populism (Featherstone, 2022) is increasingly marshalling a 'culture war' understood as 'a political technique for gathering a disparate group of people with conflicting, even contradictory, interests into your camp' (Trilling, 2021, cited in Featherstone, 2022: 23). From threats to sexual, gender, and reproductive rights (Calkin et al., 2022), to conflicts over heritage and memory in schools and public spaces (Hall, 2018, Philogene Heron, 2022), conflicts over 'culture', identity, and place underline the importance of cultural geography (Figure 22.3). While there is now a heightened awareness of the imprints of **colonialism** and cultural oppressions engraved

Figure 22.3
Black Lives Matter protesters throw the statue of Edward Colston (1636–1721) into Bristol harbour, UK. The statue was erected in 1895 as a memorial to his philanthropic works – financed by wealth Colston acquired as member of the Royal African Company (RAC) that had the monopoly on the West African slave trade

Source: Photo credit: Ben Birchall, AP/Alamy

in spaces in and beyond the West, the task for geographers is to develop effective ways of sustaining and implementing a politics of recognition alongside a politics of redistribution – doing so in a self-conscious, pluralist, and spatially sensitive manner. The documentation of injustice – its durabilities, unevenness, and ongoing iterations – only goes so far. This is more than a clarion call for more, 'better', public or policy engagement. Rather, it is to re-envision and explore a new politics and **poetics** of living together – between humans and non-humans – and of developing ethical sensibilities among those privileged by prevailing hierarchies, to be willing to go beyond gestures or lukewarm commitments to societal transformation, even if it comes at a cost (see, for example, the debate that followed Ta-Nehisi Coates' classic essay *The Case for Reparations*, 2014).

Secondly, we would like to highlight the need for comparative research in cultural geographies across different contexts, so that we can better appreciate the situated nature of theory and refuse the temptation of fitting a diversity of local contexts into frameworks of interpretation and explanation based on Western worldviews and experiences. For example, since 2003, the journal *Social & Cultural Geography* published a series of *Country Reports*, summarising the development of cultural geographical research in Western countries outside the Anglophone core (such as Italy and Portugal), as well as non-Western countries. From the reports, it is obvious that cultural geographies in different contexts demonstrate: (i) different intellectual lineages and theoretical traditions; (ii) different empirical foci based on their local contexts; and (iii) even different normative and ethical principles – for example, when it comes to the relationships between state, society, and knowledge production. However, so far there is little sign that the Anglophone **hegemony** in (cultural) geography is being destabilised, despite the repeated appeals from scholars. By all measures – the provenance of publishing authors and institutions, the contexts studied, the theoretical perspectives employed, the composition of editors possessing decision-making power, etc. – this hegemonic position has remained largely intact, if not further consolidated. Although more and more authors from non-Anglophone or non-Western regions have made their research to the pages of leading and mainstream Anglophone journals, it is more often that they need to squeeze their studies into a framework based on a review of mainstream Anglophone scholarship, rather than vice versa, namely, to deploy non-Anglophone scholarship for an endeavour of theorising from elsewhere or anywhere, as Robinson suggests in Chapter 17. It is probably beyond the scope of this book to envision an effective solution to this challenge, but it certainly warrants the attention and vigilance of the younger generation of human geographers.

Discussion points

- What are the merits and disadvantages of the various approaches to cultural geography that have developed over a long history?
- In your view, what is still missing in the account of cultural geography developed so far?
- Using a mind-map, make a list of examples where culture and politics are interconnected. Consider how these relationships are produced, sustained or contested across different spaces or scales.
- Why is it important to foster comparative insights in cultural geography?

References

Anderson, B. (2017). Cultural geography 1: intensities and forms of power. *Progress in Human Geography* 41(4): 501–511.

Anderson, B. (2019). Cultural geography II: the force of representations. *Progress in Human Geography* 43(6): 1120–1132.

Anderson, J. (2021). *Understanding Cultural Geography: Places and Traces*. London: Routledge.

Bassens, D., Derudder, B., and Witlox, F. (2011). Setting Shari'a standards: on the role, power and spatialities of interlocking Shari'a boards in Islamic financial services. *Geoforum* 42(1): 94–103.

Benko, G., and Desbiens, C. (2009). Francophone Geography. In *International Encyclopedia of Human Geography*, eds. R. Kitchin and N. Thrift. Amsterdam: Elsevier, 271–276.

Berndt, C., and Wirth, M. (2019). Struggling for the moral market: economic knowledge, diverse markets, and market borders. *Economic Geography* 95(3): 288–309.

Blunt, A. (2007). Cultural geographies of migration: mobility, transnationality and diaspora. *Progress in Human Geography* 31(5): 684–694.

Calkin, S., Freeman, C., and Moore, F. (2022). The geography of abortion: discourse, spatiality and mobility. *Progress in Human Geography* 46(6): 1413–1430.

Castree, N. (2014a). The Anthropocene and geography I: the back story. *Geography Compass* 8(7): 436–449.

Castree, N. (2014b). Geography and the Anthropocene II: current contributions. *Geography Compass* 8(7): 450–463.

Coates, T. N. (2014). The Case for Reparations. The Atlantic (June 2014).

Cosgrove, D. (1989). A terrain of metaphor: cultural geography 1988-89. *Progress in Human Geography* 13(4): 566–575.

Cosgrove, D., and Jackson, P. (1987). New directions in cultural geography. *Area* 19: 95–101.

Crang, M. (1998). *Cultural Geography*. London: Routledge.

Cresswell, T. (2015). *Place: A Short Introduction* (2nd edn.). Chichester: Wiley Blackwell.

Driver, F. (2000). *Geography Militant: Cultures of Exploration and Empire*. Oxford: Blackwell.

Featherstone, D. (2022). Culture wars and the making of authoritarian populism: articulations of spatial division and popular consent. *Soundings* 81(81): 23–42.

Foucault, M. (1972). *The Archaeology of Knowledge*. London: Tavistock.

Hall, C. (2018). Doing reparatory history. *Race and Class* 60(1): 3–21.

Hawkins, H. (2021). Cultural geography I: mediums. *Progress in Human Geography* 45(6): 1709–1720. https://doi.org/10.1177/03091325211000827

Ince, A. (2019). Fragments of an anti-fascist geography: interrogating racism, nationalism, and state power. *Geography Compass* 13(3): e12420.

Jackson, P. (1989). *Maps of Meaning: An Introduction to Cultural Geography*. London: Routledge.

Jordan, T. (1976). *The Human Mosaic: A Thematic Introduction to Cultural Geography*. San Francisco: Canfield Press.

Kirsch, S. (2013). Cultural geography I: materialist turns. *Progress in Human Geography* 37(3): 433–441.

Ley, D. (2003). Artists, aestheticisation and the field of gentrification. *Urban Studies* 40(12): 2527–2544.

Ley, D., and Samuels, M. (eds.) (1978). *Humanistic Geography: Problems and Prospects*. London: Routledge.

Lorimer, H. (2005). Cultural geography: the busyness of being 'more-than-representational'. *Progress in Human Geography* 29(1): 83–94.

Luger, J. (2022). Celebrations, exaltations and alpha lands: everyday geographies of the far-right. *Political Geography* 96: 102604.

Martin, R. (2001). Geography and public policy: the case of the missing agenda. *Progress in Human Geography* 25(2): 189–210.

Mason, K. (2015). Participatory action research: coproduction, governance and care. *Geography Compass* 9(9): 497–507.

Matless, D. (1996). New material? Work in cultural and social geography, 1995. *Progress in Human Geography* 20(3): 379–391.

Matless, D. (1997). The geographical self, the nature of the social and geoaesthetics: work in social and cultural geography, 1996. *Progress in Human Geography* 21(3): 393–405.

Mayblin, L., Valentine, G., Kossak, F., and Schneider, T. (2015). Experimenting with spaces of encounter: creative interventions to develop meaningful contact. *Geoforum* 63: 67–80.

McDowell, L., Ray, K., Perrons, D., Fagan, C., and Ward, K. (2005). Women's paid work and moral economies of care. *Social & Cultural Geography* 6(2): 219–235, https://doi.org/10.1080/14649360500074642

Miller, D. (2008). *The Comfort of Things*. London: Polity.

Mitchell, D. (1995). There's no such thing as culture: towards a reconceptualization of the idea of culture in geography. *Transactions of the Institute of British Geographers* 20(1): 102–116.

Mitchell, D. (2000). *Cultural Geography: A Critical Introduction*. Oxford: Blackwell.

Nash, C. (2000). Performativity in practice: some recent work in cultural geography. *Progress in Human Geography* 24(4): 653–664.

Naylor, S., Ryan, J., Cook, I., and Crouch, D. (eds.) (2000). *Cultural Turns/Geographical Turns: Perspectives on Cultural Geography*. London: Routledge.

Philogene Heron, A. (2022). Goodnight Colston. *Antipode* 54(4): 1251–1276.

Pollard, J., and Samers, M. (2013). Governing Islamic finance: territory, agency, and the making of cosmopolitan financial geographies. *Annals of the Association of American Geographers* 103(3): 710–726.

Rose-Redwood, R., Kitchin, R., Rickards, L., Rossi, U., Datta, A., and Crampton, J. (2018). The possibilities and limits to dialogue. *Dialogues in Human Geography* 8(2): 109–123.

Sauer, C. (1925). The morphology of landscape. *University of California Publications in Geography* 2: 19–54.

Smith, S. J., Marston, S. A., Pain, R., and Jones, J. P. (2010). *The SAGE Handbook of Social Geographies.* London: Sage, 1–632.

Thompson, E. P. (1963). *The Making of the English Working Class.* London: Victor Gollancz Ltd.

Thrift, N. (2007). *Non-Representational Theory: Space, Politics, Affect.* London: Routledge.

Tolia-Kelly, D. P. (2013). The geographies of cultural geography III: material geographies, vibrant matters and risking surface geographies. *Progress in Human Geography* 37(1): 153–160.

Trilling, D. (2021). Attacking lifeboats may seem like a new low, but the right craves a 'migrant crisis'. *Guardian*, 3 August 2021.

Urry, J. (2000). *Sociology Beyond Society: Mobilities for the 21st Century.* London: Routledge.

Ward, K. (2005). Geography and public policy: a recent history of 'policy relevance'. *Progress in Human Geography* 29(3): 310–319.

Williams, R. (1977). *Marxism and Literature.* Oxford: Oxford University Press.

Wilson, H. (2017). On geography and encounter: bodies, borders, and difference. *Progress in Human Geography* 41(4) 451–471.

Zelinsky, W. (1973). *The Cultural Geography of the United States.* Englewood Cliffs: Prentice Hall.

Online materials

- *Cultural Geographies*, https://journals.sagepub.com/home/CGJ

  This is one of flagship journals in cultural geographies that has heralded many important theoretical debates in the field.

- *Social & Cultural Geography*, https://www.tandfonline.com/journals/rscg20

  A key journal in social and cultural geography that publishes a broad range of theoretically informed and empirically rich studies.

- *Gender, Place and Culture*, https://www.tandfonline.com/journals/cgpc20

  A long-established journal of feminist geography and women's studies, with a focus on feminist geographies of difference, resistance and marginality.

Further reading

Anderson, J. (2021). *Understanding Cultural Geography: Places and Traces* (3rd edn.). London: Routledge. This is an accessible and comprehensive introduction to the subdiscipline, its evolving history, and substantive sections on place and power; culture and identity; and the more than human, amongst others.

Kong, L., and Qian, J. (2021). Cultural geography. *Oxford Online Bibliographies*. https://www. oxfordbibliographies.com/display/document/obo-9780199874002/obo-9780199874002-0003.xml A comprehensive list and a summary of key readings in cultural geography according to different themes and approaches. An excellent resource for students and academics alike who want to get an overview of a topic.

Naylor, S., Ryan, J., Cook, I., and Crouch, D. (eds.) (2000). *Cultural Turns/Geographical Turns: Perspectives on Cultural Geography*. Abingdon: Routledge. This edited collection considers the impact, significance, and characteristics of the 'cultural turn' in human geography and adjacent disciplines.

Rose, M. (2021). The question of culture in cultural geography: latent legacies and potential futures. *Progress in Human Geography* 45(5): 951–971.
A slightly more advanced paper that provides a detailed review of the development of cultural geography and the different theoretical schools emerging throughout this history.

The following are several key textbooks in cultural geography that are not cited in References:
Anderson, K., Domosh, M., Pile, S., and Thrift, N. (eds.) (2003). *Handbook of Cultural Geography*. London: Sage.
Horton, J., and Kraftl, P. (2014). *Cultural Geographies: An Introduction*. London: Routledge.
Johnson, N., Schein, R., and Winders, J. (eds.) (2013). *The Wiley-Blackwell Companion to Cultural Geography*. Chichester: Wiley Blackwell.
Oakes, T., and Price, P. (2008). *The Cultural Geography Reader*. London: Routledge.

23 Imaginative geographies

Ning An

Introduction

In the long history of geography as a discipline, most geographers have talked about the material world and used the materiality of the world as an essential approach in their academic career or to interpret their environment. However, this history does not mean that geographical debates are limited to the physical world and ignore virtual, fictional, and imaginary worlds. In fact, a few human geographers have expressed interest in observing and studying images of places and spaces that are invisible to the naked eye, impalpable to our touch, and that mainly exist in our minds, such as the nostalgia for a particular place triggered by old photographs (e.g. Datta, 2008), the sketches of a city that we keep in our minds (e.g. Zhu et al., 2011), or the fiction of interstate geopolitical relations in films (e.g. the portraits of international relations in post-9/11 anti-terrorism films, see Carter and Dodds, 2011). The images of places and spaces in these geographic vignettes are not necessarily related to the material world, but they are of great significance for us to understand the environment in which we live. The purpose of this chapter is to introduce an important field in human geography that is closely related to these vignettes—imaginative geographies—and the core debates that this field brings.

This chapter consists of three main parts. Part One describes what imaginative geographies are and why they matter in human geography, including a brief introduction to the definition of imaginative geographies and how this concept has been applied in human geography. Part Two describes imaginative geographies at multiple scales, including their various manifestations in different **territorial** units such as regions, countries, cities, and communities. Part Three addresses the political nature of imaginative geographies, emphasising that imaginative geographies are processes or outcomes of knowledge production that essentially reflect how **power** works in the everyday realm; a brief conclusion follows.

Imaginative geographies and why they matter

In the disciplinary history of geography, the term imaginative geographies has emerged as an **ontologically** and **epistemologically** revolutionary concept. From the disciplinary

DOI: 10.4324/9780429265853-28

tradition, geography has always been regarded as a basic discipline to describe the Earth's surface system, and the objects to be described are usually a series of objective geographical realities, such as location, topography, or natural resources. However, human geographers have gradually realised that when we need to explain the meaning of a space/place to others, we may resort to some tools or mediums, such as globes, maps, books, travel journals, magazines, pictures, TV, or photographs (Barnes and Duncan, 1992). In this process, the **subjectivity** of humanity may have a significant impact on the understanding of spatial meaning. From this point of view, the meaning of space/place has the possibility of being subjectively 'graph-ed', while we can therefore believe that the research objects of geography are not entirely the geographical realities waiting to be discovered. Based on this **ontological** and **epistemological** innovation, this chapter defines the term imaginative geographies as a mental process by which the information of known or unknown, visited or unvisited place/space is (re)processed to shape new images and imaginations. This concept is widely used in discussions of **postcolonialism**, geopolitics, cultural geography, everyday geography, and other fields in and out of the geography discipline.

From the definition, we can see that the essence of imaginative geographies is to explore how space/place is given meaning in a series of subjective ways. Obviously, the subjectivity here mainly refers to the divergences between people and between groups. For example, people are born in different regions, whether urban or rural, or mansions or slums; and people also experience different cultural **atmospheres** and religious environments, hold different **ideological** positions, obtain various degrees, and receive different types of education. All these factors determine the different ways in which they experience and understand the world. This uniqueness makes imaginative geographies a highly subjective process of **social construction**.

In terms of the different paths through which space/place meanings are socially constructed, imaginative geographies can be divided into two categories: one is the imaginative geographies of authors and the other is about the imaginative geographies of audiences. First, when people process information about place or space as authors, their subjectivity has an impact on how they organise the information and tell stories. A typical example of this process occurs when a person's personal experience or identity impacts the ways how he/she writes about place. For example, in the early days of the Cold War, George Kennan and his historical and geographic accounts of the Soviet Union, such as his 8,000-word 'Long Telegram' and his 'Mr. X' paper on Foreign Affairs, played a key role in promoting the changes in the US geopolitical strategy towards the Soviet Union (Ó Tuathail and Agnew, 1992). George Kennan's personal experience in the Soviet Union as a diplomat as well as his own political standpoint helped shape much wider geopolitical imaginations about the Soviet Union (Ó Tuathail and Agnew, 1992). Second, when people attempt to interpret information about place and space as the audience, their subjectivity also shapes their understanding of these places and spaces. It is their unique backgrounds, including their systems of knowledge and other sociocultural contexts like nation, language, **class**, politics, religion, and ways of life, that determine how the target information helps them construct their perceptions of places and spaces, rather than a linear flow of information from the author to them. Here, a typical example would be Woon's (2014) study on how the Filipinos look at their official newspaper's portrayals of Mindanao (an island in the Philippines), by which he concluded that the readers' imaginative geographies about particular place (e.g. the Mindanao Island) through the reading were still intricately linked with their personal positionalities and experiences.

Turning to how the imagination about place and space develops within imaginative geographies, human geographers realise that such imagination is neither merely a purely individual-based psychological process nor an unseen and intangible illusion that is absolutely opposed to the real world. According to the different means by which the imagination of space/place is **socially constructed**, human geographers have identified two ways how imaginative geographies are usually formed: (i) **representation** and (ii) **embodied** practice. As the etymology of the term shows, representation is kind of cultural practices and forms whereby people can use symbolic and semantic systems such as language, texts, pictures, literature, or art to interpret, portray, and 're-represent' the world around them to others (Hall, 1997). Here, representation relies highly on the shared meaning of communication, usually via the common-sense meaning systems like mass media or popular culture, through which symbols spread the meanings of certain space/place among the target people, thereby shaping their perceptions of these spaces and places. The different communication means that have existed through history have also had different effects on the transmission of meanings. Before the advent of the internet, television and print media had the greatest influence; however, with the rise of the internet in the late twentieth century, the impact of social media, represented by Facebook and Twitter, has become more prominent. In this regard, it is also important to discuss the formation of imaginative geographies in terms of differences within the various representational systems.

In addition to representation, people's embodied practices also influence the construction of images about place and space. We may opt to use symbols to understand the **culture** of a place and its people, as well as what they wear, or how they eat and socialise. However, these symbols perhaps do not make as strong an impression on us as an embodied experience, which means that humans' embodied practices may constitute more effective and intuitive ways to transmit culture. A typical example would be An et al.'s (2023a) study on Zimbabwe's imaginative geographies of China. From this study, they found that TV and newspapers were not so dominant any more in the field of forming social **ideology**, like what they were used to be in the end of last century in Zimbabwe, while the increasing presence of the Chinese immigrants as well as their embodied practices here has obviously played a more important role in reshaping China's imaginative geographies. As a more intuitive example, An et al.'s (2023a) study found that *Love in Africa*, a female Chinese charitable network in Zimbabwe, played a vital role in maintaining China's imaginative geographies here (Figure 23.1). Furthermore, throughout history, people's embodied practices have been limited by mobility. Nevertheless, human mobility has been largely improved alongside with **globalisation** through great progress in transportation technology, which has given people more opportunities to move and to participate in cultural exchanges on a global scale, thereby giving people more opportunities to use these embodied practices as powerful tools to (re)shape images of certain spaces and places.

Figure 23.1
A member of *Love in Africa* is participating in an event at Hossana Primary School, Zimbabwe

Source: Photo credit: Ning An

Summary

- Imaginative geographies refer to a mental process by which the information of known or unknown, visited or unvisited, places and spaces is (re)processed to shape new images.
- Imaginative geographies involve a highly subjective process of social construction by which the subjectivities of both 'authors' and 'audiences' impact their spatial perceptions.
- Imaginative geographies are neither simple individual psychological processes, nor are they unseen and intangible wonders in conflict with the real world. Imaginative geographies rely on the real world through which they are achieved via symbols and social practices.

Imaginative geographies at multiple scales

Imaginative geographies have been applied to a wide range of fields in human geography and adopted as a theoretical-conceptual tool to rethink research themes that have long been the focus of geographers. For example, political geographers have discussed interstate geopolitical imaginations, urban geographers have explored city images or community perception, social and cultural geographers have researched the construction of place culture, and tourism geographers have focused on how tourist destinations are packaged through imagery. Hence, imaginative geographies are not limited to any specific subfield within human geography but are a theoretical-conceptual path that is commonly shared across human geography subfields, as well as other social sciences beyond it. This broad application is reflected in the ways imaginative geographies can be applied to various territorial units at multiple scales.

First, on the global or international scales, imaginative geographies constitute an effective way to build or interpret interstate geopolitical imaginations. A classic example of this approach of research can be seen in the ways in which the Chinese population has developed spatial perceptions about African countries. In Chinese society, most people do not have actual experience living, working, or travelling in or to Africa. Therefore, many people rely on travelogues to learn about African countries. Even in today's internet age, the role of travelogues has not altered fundamentally. As a renowned Mandarin online tourist forum, Mafengwo (https://www.mafengwo.cn) has a long-standing reputation for allowing people to write, read, and share travel notes with the world. Through a discourse analysis of nearly 3,000 travelogues about African countries on Mafengwo, An et al. (2023b) found that these travel notes described images of African countries in ways that made them seem exotic, backwards, wild, supported by Chinese aid, and rich in Western cultural characteristics. This vision of African countries is certainly similar to that in Said's (1978) *Orientalism*, although not identical. This image that Chinese people have of Africa certainly includes certain **orientalist** descriptions. Compared to China's local cultures and rapid economic successes, Africa is described as exotic and backward, and its wilderness is opposed to China's **modernity**, thereby establishing a hierarchical relationship between China and Africa. However, this image also describes the complex entanglements that exist between African and Western countries, also illustrating how imaginative geographies are embedded into and made through complex global geopolitical patterns.

Figure 23.2 shows an example of imaginative geographies on a small geographical scale. It reflects how tourism activities have shaped Lugu Lake—a place with beautiful natural landscapes and a distinctive minority (marriage) culture—into a romantic place. Lugu Lake, which is located on the border between the Sichuan and Yunnan Provinces in China, boasts a magnificent natural landscape, with a small island in the centre of the lake that can be reached by canoe. From the centre of the lake, people can see a gem of a lake, surrounded by aquatic plants, sandy beaches, or aspen trees. Enclaved in the northwest corner of the lake, a natural peninsula appears to be holding this gem. More attractive than the natural scenery are the people of Lugu Lake and their customs. Specifically, Lugu Lake is one of the few areas in China (perhaps globally) that maintains a matrilineal social structure based on clanship, which means that lineages pass on through the blood lineage of the women. This unique social structure and marriage customs cast a mysterious veil on the already magnificent Lugu Lake. When Lugu Lake became a popular tourist destination, the local (marriage custom) culture became an important element for both tourism developers and local communities who built an image of the place. Figure 23.2 shows a young Mosuo man performing a local marriage custom that tells tourists how Mosuo men fall in love and form families in a female-dominated society. Qian et al.'s (2012) study discussed how the unique imaginative geographies of Lugu Lake have reshaped the encounters between incoming tourists and local people in the context of tourism development. Their central argument was that the **gendered** encounters between the local and the tourists are conditioned by the mystified and **romanticised** imaginative geographies of the Mosuo sexual practices. However, the

313

Figure 23.2
A Mosuo (local minority) man performs the local wedding custom for tourists at Lugu Lake, a border area between Sichuan and Yunnan, China

Source: Photo credit: Ning An

tourism encounter in tourism between visitors and locals also accommodates the renegotiation of social relations and complex identities.

Figure 23.3 shows a street in Guangzhou, China, where thousands of traders from African countries (mainly from Nigeria, Mali, Guinea, Cameroon, Benin, Liberia, and the Democratic Republic of Congo) live. For this reason, this community has been called 'Chocolate City', and Guangzhou has been seen as the capital of developing countries. Guangzhou has long been a

Figure 23.3
Xiaobei Street, a city street in Guangzhou, China, also known as 'Chocolate City'

Source: Photo credit: Ning An

commercial city that plays a vital role in the global trade chain. In this city, wholesale markets can be seen everywhere; the exhibition industry is highly developed, and any **commodity** can be found or produced. All these factors provide excellent opportunities for global traders to develop their business, especially those from developing countries. Xiaobei is a typical commercial street in Guangzhou; it is lined with many wholesale markets and enjoys a convenient location within the city. Rents on Xiaobei street are relatively cheap, which makes it attractive for global merchants and entrepreneurs, especially those from African countries. The symbolic representations and social practices that come with this kind of grouping, such as specific clothing, language, and even eating habits, have rapidly reshaped the image of this street as an ethnic community, i.e. as a 'Chocolate City' (Li et al., 2012). As this population and related media attention have grown, Guangzhou has been increasingly imagined as an inclusive city with **cosmopolitan** features. This kind of community and urban imagination is not static; they change as the social context changes. At first, due to cultural differences and conflicts, this urban imagination was accompanied by stigma. Indeed, Xiaobei was imagined by citizens and visitors as a dangerous place. Such imaginative geographies even resulted in tangible conflicts. However, with the interventions of the municipal administration and state and interstate forces, these imaginative geographies have begun to be renegotiated.

These examples illustrate that imaginative geographies are theoretical and multiscale and cross-scale conceptual tools of interest across many subfields of human geography and beyond, including, but not limited to, political geography, tourism geography, urban geography, and social and cultural geography.

Summary

- Within and beyond human geography, a wide range of subfields find interest in imaginative geographies, including, but not limited to, political geography, tourism geography, urban geography, and social and cultural geography.
- Imaginative geographies intervene in various geographic units at different scales.
- The subjects involved in imaginative geographies, particularly in spatial information processing, are unequal in the face of information accessibility, operability, and dissemination, which determine the entanglement of imaginative geographies with power dynamics.

The political nature of imaginative geographies

Imaginative geographies pertain to human geography and feature power entanglements. Although those imaginative geographies emphasise the role of human subjectivity in processing spatial information, the individuals processing this spatial information clearly do not fairly control the accessibility, operability, and dissemination of this information. Therefore, when we understand imaginative geographies, we should focus not only on how an image about a space is constructed but also on the power relationships behind the uneven processing of spatial information. This claim implicates Foucault's (1980) philosophical idea about the nexus between power and knowledge. Thus, we can say that imaginative geographies, as a means of knowledge production, result from power relations. The political nature of imaginative geographies is mainly reflected in its wide application and popularity in **postcolonial** geographies.

Imaginative geographies in postcolonial geography

The origin of the concept of imaginative geographies is inherently embedded in postcolonial observations. It was first proposed by Said (1978) in his well-known book *Orientalism*, in which he unveiled the Eurocentric **discourse** through which literary works, paintings, travel notes, and photos from Oriental countries (mainly in North Africa and the Middle East) are depicted in Western countries as backwards, barbaric, and undeveloped, contrasting an image of this **'Other'** with self-depictions of the West as advanced, civilised, and developed. For Said, the so-called Oriental countries, or third world countries, are indeed geographically separated from the Western world. However, for him, the term 'Oriental' does not refer to as geographical location; rather, it has profound political and cultural connotations. For Said, the Eurocentric discourse system constructs an image of Oriental countries as part of imaginative geographies, which have been highlighted in numerous subsequent studies as postcolonial cultural and discursive strategies intended to maintain and legitimise the political and economic interests of the West in the East. This approach can be critiqued through some of the most common discourses of daily othering, for example through the use of terms such as **'modernity'**, 'development', and 'democracy'. What kind of lifestyle is 'modern'? Why do Eastern countries need a **'modern'** lifestyle? What is the purpose of 'development' in a given region or country? Why must Eastern countries follow the 'development' model used in Western countries? How can the democratic political system be defined? Why do Eastern countries necessarily need to choose such a political system, even at the expense of trading it for war?

Said has been a key figure in postcolonial studies and serves as a model for the study of imaginative geographies. His main object of analysis was literary works, and his geographical area of predilection was comprised the so-called Oriental countries, i.e. mainly places in the Middle East and North Africa where he had lived. However, in subsequent studies, human geographers and other interdisciplinary scholars have found that the discourse system that perpetuates Eurocentric postcolonial imaginary geographies has become increasingly diverse, going far beyond Said's scope. Some of the most popular cultural media have also played a role in these imaginary geographies, including television, movies, comics, and music. Moreover, in line with Said, contemporary studies focusing on the mapping of imaginative geographies to show postcolonial intentions have also extended far beyond North Africa and the Middle East. These scholars have focused on Asian countries and those that have been globally marginalised and made into enemies of the West. In addition, the knowledge/power nexus involved in these imaginative geographies has also become increasingly hidden. This nexus is not limited to the maintenance of postcolonial relations but involves more complex geopolitical endeavours, such as the shift in the contradictions that emerge out of production relations or in electoral objectives. A classic example of these extensions in postcolonial imaginative geographies is the popularity of a fictional Chinese character—Fu Manchu—and the profound social impact this character has had on Western societies' geographical imaginations of China (Mawdsley, 2008). This figure was first created in British literature bearing the characteristics of the Chinese Qing Dynasty; he was hideous, had a dark heart, and was obsessed with engaging in terrorist activities to gain political influence. This image later appeared in many Western pop cultures, including the Marvel movies *Iron Man 3* and *Shang-Chi,* and became an important source for people in Western societies to build their image of China. When Trump was in power in the United States, his nationalistic policy orientation led society at large to use these imaginative geographies to engage in hate crimes against Asians.

These examples illustrate that imaginative geographies are political in nature. Knowledge production about place and space usually occurs within sweeping and significant geopolitical turbulences.

The politics of imaginative geographies in other areas of research

The previous section emphasised that imaginative geographies are manifested in various ways at different geographical scales. The diverse and multiscalar nature of imaginative geographies has also highlighted that their political nature is not always linked to postcolonial geopolitical strategies; they also appear in the unpacking of the power relations that shape the subjectivities of geographical knowledge production. The case of Lugu Lake shows how the (re)shaping of imaginative geographies implicates many subjectivities by which complex political relations become entangled (Qian et al., 2012). On one hand, the actors of tourism development are satisfied with the emergence of an image of Lugu Lake that shows the lake to be a place of sexual freedom and romance, as this image will attract more tourists and increase economic revenue. On the other hand, the Mosuo locals insist that the tourists' romantic imaginative geographies of Lugu Lake do not respect their ethnic culture. Therefore, a clash emerges between the different cultural identities.

These examples, once again, show that imaginative geographies are essentially representative of Foucauldian politics. Regardless of the ways in which the imagined subjects change, where they are located on the map, or how complex the medium that carries imaginative geographies is, the process of knowledge production is always inseparable from the intricacies of power relations.

Summary

- Imaginative geographies are political in nature and involve a Foucauldian nexus between power and knowledge production.
- The concept of imaginative geographies is inherently embedded in postcolonial observations, within which the Eurocentric discourse system has attempted to establish a binary discourse based on othering that constructs images of Oriental countries as backward, barbaric, and uncivilised to serve Western interests.

Conclusion

Most geographers prefer discussing the material world. This chapter introduces the debate around imaginative geographies that has taken place among a significant community of human geographers. By definition, the term 'imaginative geographies' refers to a psychological process by which the information of known or unknown, visited or unvisited places and spaces is (re)processed to shape new images people have of them. This reshaping is usually socially constructed through symbolic representations or social practices. In terms of the various paths whereby space/place meanings are socially constructed, imaginative geographies can be divided into two categories: the imaginative geographies of authors and the imaginative geographies of audiences. From the application of this concept in the discipline of geography, it can be seen that imaginative geographies influence geography broadly and manifest themselves at multiple scales, from macroscale to microscale observations, from political geography, urban geography, social and cultural geography, to tourism geography. Moreover, as imaginative geographies emphasise subjectivity in spatial knowledge production and dissemination, the term and the scholarship that uses it have also widely contributed to unpacking their political nature, for example through an understanding of their situatedness in postcolonial observations. In this regard, although imaginative geographies appear to focus on the virtual, fictional, mental, and intangible world when observing objects, they also play a vital role in helping us to understand the material environment in which we live, due to their wide application in the field of human geography and its politicised nature. From these perspectives, imaginative geographies can be seen as a very typical thought of **humanistic geography** that will be of great help for young scholars or students in the discipline of geography or beyond to understand how spaces and places inhabited by humans are given social, political, and cultural meaning.

Discussion points

- What are imaginative geographies and why do they matter?
- How are imaginative geographies generated and manifested at different geographical scales?
- How do different subfields within human geography discuss imaginative geographies?
- What kinds of implications could Said's *Orientalism* offer to the discussion on imaginative geographies? Does Orientalism still make sense in the twenty-first century?
- Can you share stories about imaginative geographies and their entanglements with power relations?

References

An, N., Wang, M., and Zhu, H. (2023a). The geopolitics of a female Chinese migrant charity network in Zimbabwe: insights from *Love in Africa*. *Social & Cultural Geography* 24(7): 1262–1280.

An, N., Zhang, J., and Wang, M. (2023b). The everyday Chinese framing of Africa: a perspective of tourism-geopolitical encounter. *Geopolitics* 28(4): 1422–1441.

Barnes, T., and Duncan, J. (1992). *Writing Worlds: Discourse, Text & Metaphor in the Representation of Landscape*. London: Routledge.

Carter, S., and Dodds, K. (2011). Hollywood and the 'war on terror': genre-geopolitics and 'Jacksonianism' in the Kingdom. *Environment and Planning D: Society and Space* 29(1): 98–113.

Datta, A. (2008). Building differences: material geographies of home(s) among Polish builders in London. *Transactions of the Institute of British Geographers* 33(4): 518–531.

Foucault, M. (1980). *Power/Knowledge*. New York: Vintage.

Hall, S. (1997). *Representation: Cultural Representations and Signifying Practices*. London: Sage.

Li, Z., Lyons, M., and Brown, A. (2012). China's 'Chocolate City': an ethnic enclave in a changing landscape, *African Diaspora* 5(1): 51–72.

Mawdsley, E. (2008). Fu Manchu versus Dr Livingstone in the dark continent? Representing China, Africa and the West in British broadsheet newspapers. *Political Geography* 27(5): 509–529.

Ó Tuathail, G., and Agnew, J. (1992). Geopolitics and discourse: practical geopolitical reasoning in American foreign policy. *Political Geography* 11(2): 190–204.

Qian, J., Wei, L., and Zhu, H. (2012). Consuming the tourist gaze: imaginative geographies and the reproduction of sexuality in Lugu Lake. *Geografiska Annaler: Series B, Human Geography* 94(2): 107–124.

Said, E. (1978). *Orientalism*. New York: Vintage.

Woon, C. Y. (2014). Popular geopolitics, audiences and identities: reading the 'War on Terror' in the Philippines. *Geopolitics* 19(3): 656–683.

Zhu, H., Qian, J., and Gao, Y. (2011). Globalization and the production of city image in Guangzhou's metro station advertisements. *Cities* 28: 221–229.

Online materials

- https://geographicalimaginations.com/about/

  The personal blog of the leading scholar on geographical imaginations, Derek Gregory.

- https://www.mafengwo.cn

  If you read Chinese, Mafengwo, an online tourist forum for exchanging tourism experiences and travelogues, will be a very interesting place to start for understanding the subjective construction of place and space.

Further reading

Lefebvre, H. (1991). *The Production of Space*. Oxford: Blackwell.
This is a classic work that heavily theorises the imagined and perceptive nature of space and opens a window to understand the geographical world where we are living from the perspective of imaginative geographies.

Gregory, D. (1994). *Geographical Imaginations*. Oxford: Blackwell.
The classic work that first systematically introduces the concept of imaginative geographies and discusses the possibility and potential of integrating this concept into modern human geography.

Gregory, D. (2004). *The Colonial Present: Afghanistan, Palestine, Iraq*. Oxford: Blackwell.
A classic empirical work that traces the imaginative geographies of the United States and other Western countries' military intervention in the Middle East into the colonial present.

Cosgrove, D. (2008). *Geography and Vision: Seeing, Imaging and Representing the World*. London: I.B. Tauris.
An evocative set of essays from an influential cultural geographer that illustrates how geographical description has attempted to present its audience with rich visual images.

24 Affect and emotion

Ben Anderson

Introduction

Scene one: 'Make America Great Again'

Donald J Trump's political rallies regularly involve the repetition of a chant: 'make America great again'. In rambling, apparently chaotic, speeches mixing humour with bellicosity, Trump offers a form of hope to his mostly white audience – the hope of the future as a return to a supposedly better past where America was 'great'. A hope that mixes with anger-infused resentment at immigrants, 'the elite' and various other groups constructed as enemies of 'the people'. For attendees at the rallies (Figure 24.1), what might it have felt like to chant and be part of the crowd? How are clips of the rally and Trump's speeches encountered as they circulate through social media – indifference, anger, laugher, outrage?

Scene two: becoming energised

Protestors march, then sit down blocking a road in a UK city. They hold placards that warn of imminent extinction and demand those in authority tell the truth. The mood is defiant, desperate, joyful. Part of the new wave of climate activism and linked to the protest movement Extinction Rebellion (Figure 24.2), they inhabit a present moment full of talk of emergency and crisis as the threat of climate change looms, and climate impacts begin to be unevenly felt globally. Urgency, and the sense of time running out, animates the protestors as they block the normal circulations that make up urban life. Passersby and motorists respond to them in all kinds of ways; support that momentarily cuts through indifference, annoyance, and frustrations as daily rhythms are disrupted, anger, patience.

Scene three: becoming bored

You are sitting and trying to listen to a first-year lecture in a compulsory module. Interest begins to wane. A lecturer attempts to hold your attention as you sit in lines in a tiered lecture theatre with other students, some making notes on laptops, some not. You switch off. Something like boredom seems to infuse the room: a stilling and slowing of life that interrupts the demand to always be interested (Figure 24.3). Distractedly, you look around the room. You daydream. Before you notice it, you reach for your phone, scrolling to exit the boredom. Occasionally, your interest returns, piqued by a word, an image.

DOI: 10.4324/9780429265853-29

Figure 24.1
Trump supporter holding up a sign at a Trump Rally

Source: Photo credit: El Sun/Pixabay

Figure 24.2
Extinction Rebellion Protest, October 2022, London, UK

Source: Photo credit: Guy Bell/Alamy

Hope mixing with anger in a rally, the energies of protest amid the threat of extinction, boredom in a lecture theatre: this chapter discusses why geographers should consider these and other experiences. It does so by introducing geographical work on the topic of **affect** and emotion. Emotion as an everyday word will, of course, be familiar to you. By contrast, the term 'affect' is likely to be new to you. Affect is not generally a part of our ordinary vocabularies. Whilst we will look in more detail at definitions below, to start with we can understand 'affect' and 'emotion' in straightforward terms: both orientate us to the experience of life as it is lived. We can get a sense of what is meant by this by looking at the example of protest. One of the things that might be shared at a protest is an *affect of participation and accompanying emotions of excitement, trepidation, anger, and so on.* And the temporary space of the protest, in the above scene a road in a city, is in part constituted through those shared affects and emotions; affects and emotions that change as the protest marches and sits. The starting point of recent work on affect and emotion is that neither is unique to intensified spaces such as protests: any and all spaces are spaces of affect and emotion. There are no geographies without affect and emotion.

Beginning from this insight, a wide range of work has developed on what Pile (2010) named 'affectual geographies' and 'emotional geographies'. As with all other social science and humanities disciplines, over the last 20 years, human geography has witnessed an 'emotional' or 'affective' turn. The first section introduces and summarises some of the different ways in which the terms 'affect' and 'emotion' are being used in contemporary human geography. There are no stable definitions of either, but there are nevertheless a number of commonalities across different theorisations. The second section considers some of the different 'spaces of affect and emotion' that research has focused on to develop the starting principle that understanding affect and emotion matter profoundly to human geography. By way of a conclusion, I will briefly reflect on some of the issues around affect or emotion-based research.

Figure 24.3
Students in a lecture hall

Source: Photo credit: Yan Krukau/Pexels

Understanding affect and emotion

The terms affect and emotion have been used by geographers to describe a wide range of quite different phenomena; background moods such as depression, moments of intense, and focused involvement such as euphoria, immediate visceral responses of shame or hate, shared **atmospheres** of hope or panic, eruptions of passion, livelong dedications of love, fleeting feelings of boredom, societal moods such as anxiety or fear, neurological bodily transitions such as a feeling of aliveness, waves of feeling, anaesthetic bodily states … amongst much else. In human geography alone there have been a wonderfully diverse range of 'emotional geographies' and 'affective geographies'; food banks (Strong, 2021), weapons (Ruppert, 2022), gig economy work (Bissell, 2022), landscape relations (Wylie, 2009), new forms of work (Cockayne, 2016); **race** and racism (Lim, 2010), obesity (Evans, 2009), austerity (Raynor, 2017), queer and **feminist** space (Bettocchi, 2022), climate change (Boyd et al., 2023), transgender geographies (Brice, 2020), and animals and other non-humans (Greenhough and Roe, 2011), to name but some.

The principle animating this work is a simple one – all geographies are affective or emotional geographies. If emotions, in particular, were once downplayed marginalised or trivialised in geography (Bondi et al., 2005), there is no longer anything controversial about taking affect or emotion seriously. Across this varied work, you will find that the terms 'affect' and 'emotion' are used in multiple ways. Sometimes this can be confusing. Not only is there no consensus about what is or is not included within the categories, but something about the type of experience being described appears to be difficult to fully capture in a definition. Nevertheless, we can identify some key uses of the terms. These uses are not mutually exclusive, but they do have different consequences for how geographers understand and make sense of affective-emotional life.

Use of the term 'emotion' in human geography is indebted to the work of humanistic and especially feminist geographers (see, for example, Tuan, 1977, Rose, 1993). In different ways, both approaches argued that geographers should engage with the emotional dimensions of life, and both practice styles of research practice and theory that value emotional knowledges. Emotion is rarely defined explicitly in these literatures, with much work resting on taken-for-granted uses of emotion, whilst drawing on a heterogeneous range of theories – psychoanalysis, phenomenology, existentialism, social psychology, amongst much more. As a consequence, 'emotion' is typically taken to be equivalent to the expressed feeling of a person. When a definition is offered, emphasis is placed on how 'emotions' are produced. So the foundational claim is that emotions are relations and are produced in, by, and through relations (see, for example, Bondi, 2005).

This claim is disruptive, in particular when articulated through feminist geographies. We tend to think of feelings as our own and, as such, as private and idiosyncratic. This is a view of emotional life with its origins in a masculine distinction between the rational and emotional and an assumption of individuality. Feminist and queer theory research on emotions has done much to critique this divide, showing the negative consequences of implicitly or explicitly identifying reason as masculine and emotion as feminine (for foundational work see Rose, 1993, Pain, 1997, Bondi, 2005). Likewise, psychoanalytical approaches have tied the supposedly 'inner' workings of the mind, including 'unconscious' processes as well as expressed emotions, to various 'outside' geographies (Pile, 2021). As a consequence, one of the main claims of research on emotional life is that emotions are never simply personal. We find that our experience always connects us to people or things or places beyond ourselves (an emphasis on relations shared with work from

Black studies and **decolonial** approaches [McKittrick, 2021, Yao, 2021]). There is something of a paradox here: what appears to be most personal, most unquestionably ours, is an index of our participation in wider processes. For one example of how emotional experience connects us to processes beyond ourselves, consider work on 'austerity'. A range of feminist work has demonstrated how the processes of economic-political restructuring associated with austerity are lived through ordinary emotions of worry, loss, and anxiety and play out through intimate relationships of family and friendship (e.g. Hall, 2019).

The term affect is a little different, not being part of ordinary ways of talking about and articulating experience. For this reason, it has been more subject to elaboration and contestation. In the main, the uses of the term affect emerge from the introduction of **non-representational theory** into human geography (Thrift, 2008, Anderson and Harrison, 2010). Typically, the term affect is used to describe a body's capacities to affect and be affected that may subsequently be expressed in emotions or feelings. A study of such capacities orientates enquiry to two things. First, emphasis is placed on what a body can do, i.e. on a body's capacities rather than its properties. Second, capacities to affect and be affected are two sided. As bodies do things, as they act, they open themselves up to being affected by things outside of themselves. Consider what it feels like to play a video game. Ash's (2010) research shows how the careful designing of an 'environment' in games conditions a specific feeling of immersion in game play. This immersion is not necessarily consciously reflected upon by the game player; it acts more as a taken-for-granted background that enables her/him to play the game. It is this sense of the taken-for-granted background of life that research on affect has focused on. Similarly, Hitchen (2021) thinks with the concept of affect to understand the specific forms of paranoia that exist in the background to public sector organisations, in the case of her research libraries, as they go through rounds of austerity-induced restructuring. Sometimes this work has involved a claim that the lived present of experience is *partly* **non-conscious**, in the sense that something about experiences such as playing games, or working under the threat of unemployment, is at least partially below the threshold of conscious reflection and deliberation. Normally this use involves invoking an analytic distinction between affect and emotion: emotion being used to refer to the ways in which that non-conscious background is named, interpreted, and reflected on by people. By contrast, affect refers to the felt quality of an experience: a quality that provides something close to the background sense of an event or practice or space.

Debate rages about whether a distinction between affect and emotion is possible or useful – does a distinction help us notice something important about experience? Part of this debate has been questions of how geographers should relate affective-emotional life to race, **class**, and other forms of social difference. Should we, for example, try to integrate an understanding of neurochemical processes into our understanding of the unequal patterning of affective-emotional life, even though this may risk a form of biological reductionism (Papoulias and Callard, 2010, Brigstocke et al., 2023)? Might we think with the insights of corporeal feminism and begin with the forces that form and are formed by bodily differences (Ahmed, 2004, Colls, 2012)? How could decolonial thought and work from Black studies help us understand how affects and emotions emerge from fractured, broken, or lost relations and relate to types of violence and loss (Yao, 2021)?

Recently, the lines between affect and emotion have been blurred in work that orientates a little more to collective affective-emotional experiences. One example would be the idea that a space has a characteristic atmosphere. Whether it is a 'cosy' room, 'uplifting' building, or 'romantic' setting, atmospheres are strange things for geographers to try and research (McCormack, 2018, Bille and Simonsen, 2021). Even though the quality of an atmosphere can be named, they are still vague. It is unclear where the atmosphere is located or what its boundaries are. Like a gas or air, an atmosphere might appear to infuse a whole space without being definitely locatable anywhere. Closs-Stephens (2022) captures this in her careful description of the atmospheres of nationalism that envelope particular places and make them therapeutic. She shows how major political events in UK life – the death of a politician like Margaret Thatcher or events like Brexit – are felt in specific ordinary sites and scenes that come to have particular atmospheres. Collective affects/emotions are not only linked to specific sites, however. We might try and apprehend the distinctive **structure of feeling** that characterises a particular society or culture. One example would be the claim that in the midst of intensified uncertainty as enacted in claims of crisis or emergency, contemporary liberal democracies are defined by 'precarity' (Harris, 2020).

Closely linked, affect/emotion has been used by work influenced by queer theory to identify how people's attachments happen and are organised (Anderson, 2023). Very often this involves carefully mapping how affective attachments relate to the ongoing (re)production of race, class, and other forms of social difference. For example, Berlant (2011) describes the 'cruel optimism' that infuses the lived experience of particular segments of the lower middle class in the United States as they attempt to hold onto fraying attachments in times of ongoing, structural crisis. 'Cruel optimism' names a relation of attachment where 'something you desire is actually an obstacle to your flourishing' (Berlant, 2011: 1). Their examples range widely as they move from 'affect' as the name for a structure of relations to 'emotion' as the **embodied** feeling of that relation, including the promise of particular types of family relations, participation in forms of secure work, or the hope for a career.

We can identify a vital commonality across these different uses of the terms affect and emotion, even as the range of influences have broadened over the past 20 years, and some of the intense debate and contestation has faded. All presume that affects and emotions are part of other geographies. There is no such thing as a circumscribed realm of 'affective geographies' or 'emotional geographies' that sits separately from other more familiar geographies. Rather, affects/emotions are a part of any and all geographies. We might, for example, think of how the geographies of racism and white supremacy are inseparable from resentment, hatred, pride or anxiety; or how the climate crisis is inseparable from eco-anxiety, urgency, and indifference. This starting point connects to another – that affect and emotion matter profoundly to how all spaces are organised, inhabited, and lived.

Summary

- All geographies are geographies of affect and emotion. There are multiple definitions of 'affect' and 'emotion' and understanding either term also involves considering the meaning and use of terms such as atmosphere and structures of feeling.
- Although the terms are used in different ways, affectual and emotional geographies share an emphasis on relations and relationality.

- The relation between affect and emotion has been subject to considerable discussion and debate, especially how conscious and non- or pre-conscious processes interact.
- Recently, work has explored shared experiences – such as atmospheres or structures of feeling – in ways that blur and undermine any distinction between affect and emotion.

Spaces of affect and emotion

Boredom, fear, joy, and other named affects and emotions are not timeless, ageographical, experiences. Even if they feel natural, or idiosyncratic and individual, all are part of how spaces are organised. Emotions and affects are formed and emerge through particular geographies. Let us look, then, at some examples of how recent affect- and emotion-based research have attempted to attune to and understand some different geographies – all of which begin from the starting point, introduced above, that affects and emotions are always made in, by, and through relations (including relations that are fractured, disrupted, or lost).

Work on affective and emotional life often starts by paying close attention to how particular affects and emotions emerge through **encounters** and interactions between people or between people and sites. We can get a sense of what is meant by this through an example of **ethnographic** research on what it feels like to live in a multicultural town (Swanton, 2010). What Swanton does is focus on specific, situated, occasions where different people and groups encounter one another in Keighley, a former mill town in Northern England. What he shows is that affects such as suspicion or fear form in, and give shape to, mundane moments of intercultural contact in spaces such as cafes, pubs, bookmakers, and back streets. Alongside the tolerances and indifferences that condition many ordinary encounters, occasionally hatreds will intensify. In the event of a terror alert, for example, ordinary encounters become charged with different affects as particular Muslim men become the object of suspicion and subject to forms of everyday racism from some white residents. To give another example, one which uses the language of emotions a little more, Waite et al. (2014) show how shared feelings of insecurity not only link together but also divide different populations. Focusing on relations between people claiming asylum and other residents in a city in the UK, they demonstrate how shared, but differently lived and felt insecurity can lead to intensified racialised forms of hatred and mistrust.

Encounters and interactions might be between two or more individuals or groups; but they also might be between an individual and a particular set of things, a place or environment, an event, a valued identity, or just about anything else. Consider, for example, Worth's (2016) work on millennial women and work. She shows how a feeling of millennial insecurity emerges from experiences of and expectations surrounding work but is also dampened and intensified by interactions with parents, partners, and friends. By contrast, in her ethnography of children's use of objects that are or become toys, Woodyer (2008) shows how encounters with things create the affective worlds of childhood. Encounters and interactions might also be between an individual and that which might be present in and through absence, most notably in work on grief, mourning, and haunting (Maddrell, 2020).

It is not enough, however, to only focus on spaces of encounter or interaction. One criticism of work on affect and emotion has been that it is primarily concerned only with small-scale interactions, ignoring or forgetting wider geographies of connection and disconnection. To address this criticism, recent work has focused on the extended, translocal, geographies of (dis)connection and attachment/detachment through which ordinary affective-emotional lives are constituted. So we should note that encounters and interactions always involve connections to other spaces and times. For example, Swanton's example of the terror alert shows how something that might seem far away – terrorist events in New York – conditions an encounter in a place like Keighley. What seems to be far away becomes part of encounters. Let's develop this point with another example – this time of anxiety and fear in Myanmar in relation to China's Belt and Road initiative. Mosafanezhad et al. (2023) focus on how specific infrastructural materialities – roads, drains, and pipelines – generate particular practices of affect and emotion. Specifically, they argue that a 'sovereign anxiety' exists in Myanmar – unease over the status of a political community in the context of China's infrastructural geopolitics. Emergent from specific interactions and encounters with **infrastructure**, 'sovereign anxiety' is also a product of China's investments and their wider geopolitical role in the region. Leaving aside the details of Mosafanezhad, Farnan and Loong's argument, why this kind of approach matters is that it helps us understand that whilst affects and emotions emerge from encounters, they are also determined by the ways in which those encounters are entangled with wider economic, political, social, and other forces. This means that the geographies of affect and emotion are always transpersonal and translocal: they extend beyond a specific site or person. Bringing together an emphasis on global-local (dis)connections with an attunement to encounters and interaction, Pain (2021), for example, shows the multiple ways in which different traumas are 'placed' as violence lives on, in, and through place.

So, spaces of affect and emotion extend beyond specific sites to wider geographies of connection and disconnection, attachment and detachment. At the same time, we should remember that specific spaces provide what Thrift (2008: 236) terms 'a series of conditioning environments that both prime and "cook" affect' [and emotion]. Through a case study of Singapore airport during the COVID-19 pandemic, Lin (2022) carefully details how the state and airport management deliberately advocate and attempt to create positive atmospheres that would facilitate the adoption of forms of automation, such as proximity touch screens. How airport workers capitulated to, abandoned, and desired to collaborate with processes of automation were conditioned by a range of affective atmospheres.

Likewise, the 'atmosphere' of a retail space such as a mall or shopping centre might be carefully designed to appeal to unconscious consumer experience. Lighting, shop window display, and music might all be crafted to generate a particular 'atmospherics' designed to facilitate the activity of shopping. Of course, people actually experience these designed environments in ways that do not correspond to the designer's intentions. It is not, then, that affective-emotional life is simply manipulated, which would be to presume that people respond automatically to efforts to shape conduct. Instead, efforts are made to shape the conditions of affective-emotional life. Developing this emphasis on how affective life is shaped, recent work has argued that the modulation of affect is a key site for the operation of contemporary forms of **power** (Anderson, 2014). Examples include the use of a new 'spatial science of emotion' in UK public policy organised around the promotion of individualised 'happiness' (Pykett, 2022), or the justification of austerity measures through recourse to a language of sacrifice (Hitchen, 2021).

It would be a mistake, then, to think that researching ordinary affects and emotions is only a way of talking about individual people and what and how they feel. Instead, the primary task of research on affective-emotional life is to offer careful, nuanced, descriptions of life as it is lived that connects affective-emotional life to the range of forces and events that shape and condition it.

Summary

- Affects and emotions such as hope, fear, anxiety, cruel optimism, and apathy are not 'natural' phenomena but the point at which individual lives are connected to spatial processes and practices.
- Affect and emotions are formed in encounters and interactions.
- Encounters and interactions are always entangled in transpersonal and translocal geographies of connection and disconnection, attachment and detachment.
- There are multiple relations between affective-emotional life and forms of power, including but not restricted to intentional manipulation.

Conclusion

Engaging with spaces of affect and emotion is necessary if Human Geography is to understand how ordinary life is lived and connected to wider processes. For this reason, the concepts have opened up new and novel directions for thinking and research; chiefly a focus on how life happens in specific encounters and interactions and on the ordinary affects and emotions of 'big', seemingly abstract, socio-spatial processes. The starting point for contemporary work is not only that affect and emotion matter to any and all geographers, but they are indispensable for any account of how experience is organised, and specific spaces come to feel.

Researching and understanding how emotional and affective life takes place poses particular methodological challenges to human geography. For how do you research experiences such as participation in protest or being bored that might seem to be fleeting, ephemeral? And how do you then analyse and represent that experience, if that is the aim? Returning to the scenes of hope-hate, participation, and boredom at the start of the chapter, did my combination of words evoke something of the experience? Perhaps not; and perhaps that failure is endemic to any attempt to represent affective or emotional life. Responding to the problem of how to research and represent affect and emotion, some Geographers have recast qualitative methods such as interviews, using them as a means of eliciting reflection on background affects and emotional experience. Often interviews are 'enriched' by supplementing spoken words with other materials, such as photos or interviews, designed to allow participant attunement to emotional or affectual worlds (Dowling et al., 2017). Other geographers have experimented with methods that draw on the creative arts and expand what counts as data or research material, including theatre, drawing, and poetry (Hawkins, 2020). There has also been a flourishing of interest in the possibilities of story and story-telling. These creative methods aim to participate in affective life, create encounters, and then evoke specific affects or emotions (see Boyd and Edwardes, 2019). However, should the task of a geographical analysis of affect or emotion be to evoke experience? Perhaps geographical work on affect and emotion should, instead, aim to explain the conditions of affective or emotional life, or critique the ways in which ordinary affects and emotions are structured (Ahmed, 2004)? Perhaps, affect- and emotion-based research should continue to learn from the insights of **participatory geographies** and work with people to co-produce knowledge (e.g. Barron, 2021).

These questions of how to research affect and emotion matter profoundly because of the key proposition of this chapter – that any and all spaces, from the intimate to the global, are always-already 'emotional geographies' and 'affective geographies'. There are no geographies without affect or emotion.

Discussion points

- Evaluate what a focus on affect and emotion contributes to geographical research and thought.
- Consider the reasons why affect and emotion have emerged as part of human geography research across the social sciences and humanities.
- What are the main points of difference between theories of affect and emotion?
- Using an example of a particular site, such as an airport or shopping mall, explore how different approaches to affect or emotion help us understand specific experiential geographies.
- What methodological challenges does researching affect and emotion pose to human geography and how have geographers responded to those challenges?
- What does a focus on affect and emotion have to offer analyses of spatial processes and forms such as **neoliberalism**, racism, or **capitalism**?

References

Ahmed, S. (2004). *A Cultural Politics of Emotion*. London: Routledge

Anderson, B. (2014). *Encountering Affect: Capacities, Apparatuses, Conditions*. London: Routledge.

Anderson, B. (2023). Forms and scenes of attachment: a cultural geography of promises. *Dialogues in Human Geography* 13(3), 392–409.

Anderson, B., and Harrison, P. (2010). The Promise of Non-Representational Theories. In *Taking-Place: Non-Representational Theories and Geography*, eds. B. Anderson and P. Harrison. Aldershot: Ashgate, 1–36.

Ash, J. (2010). Architectures of affect: anticipating and manipulating the event in practices of videogame design and testing. *Environment and Planning D: Society and Space* 28(4): 653–671.

Barron, A. (2021). More-than-representational approaches to the life-course. *Social & Cultural Geography* 22(5): 603–626.

Berlant, L. (2011). *Cruel Optimism*. London: Duke University Press.

Bettocchi, M. (2022). Affect, infrastructure and activism: the house of brag's London queer social centre in Brixton, South London. *Emotion, Space and Society* 42: 100849.

Bille, M., and Simonsen, K. (2021). Atmospheric practices: On affecting and being affected. *Space and Culture* 24(2): 295–309.

Bissell, D. (2022). The anaesthetic politics of being unaffected: embodying insecure digital platform labour. *Antipode* 54(1): 85–105.

Bondi, L. (2005). Making connections and thinking through emotions: between geography and psychotherapy. *Transactions of the Institute of British Geographers* 30(4): 433–448.

Boyd, C., and Edwardes, C. (eds.) (2019). *Non-Representational Theory and the Creative Arts*. London: Springer.

Boyd, C., Parr, H., and Philo, C. (2023). Climate anxiety as posthuman knowledge. *Wellbeing, Space and Society* 4: 10012. https://doi.org/10.1016/j.wss.2022.100120

Brice, S. (2020). Geographies of vulnerability: mapping transindividual geometries of identity and resistance. *Transactions of the Institute of British Geographers* 45(3): 664–677.

Brigstocke, J., Froes, M., Cabral, C., Malanquini, L., and Baptista, G. (2023). Biosocial borders: affective debilitation and resilience among women living in a violently bordered favela. *Transaction of the Institute of British Geographers* 48(3): 587–602.

Closs-Stephens, A. (2022). *National Affects*. London: Bloomsbury.

Cockayne, D. (2016). Entrepreneurial affect: attachment to work practice in San Francisco's digital media sector. *Environment and Planning D: Society and Space* 34(3): 456–473.

Colls, R. (2012). Feminism, bodily difference and non-representational geographies. *Transactions of the Institute of British Geographers* 37(3): 430–445.

Dowling, R., Lloyd, K., and Suchet-Pearson, S. (2017). Qualitative methods II: 'More-than-human' methodologies and/in praxis. *Progress in Human Geography*, 41(6): 823–831.

Evans, B. (2009). Anticipating fatness: childhood, affect and the pre-emptive 'war on obesity'. *Transactions of the Institute of British Geographers* 35: 21–38.

Greenhough, B., and Roe, E. (2011). Ethics, space and somatic sensibilities: comparing relationships between scientific researchers and their human and animal experimental subjects. *Environment and Planning D: Society and Space* 29(1): 47–66.

Hall, S. (2019). *Everyday Life in Austerity: Family, Friends and Intimate Relations*. London: Palgrave.

Harris, E. (2020). *Re-Branding Precarity: Pop-up Culture as the Seductive New Normal*. London: Zed Books.

Hawkins, H. (2020). *Geography, Art, Research: Artistic Research in the Geohumanities*. London: Routledge.

Hitchen, E. (2021). The affective life of austerity: uncanny atmospheres and paranoid temporalities. *Social & Cultural Geography* 22(3): 295–318.

Lin, W. (2022). Atmospheric conditioning: Airport automation, labour and the COVID-19 pandemic. *Transactions of the Institute of British Geographers* 47(1): 214–228.

Lim, J. (2010). Immanent politics: thinking race and ethnicity through affect and machinism. *Environment and Planning A* 42: 2393–2409.

Maddrell, A. (2020). Bereavement, grief and consolation: emotional-affective geographies of loss during COVID-19. *Dialogues in Human Geography* 10(2): 110–117.

McCormack, D. (2018). *Atmospheric Things*. London: Duke University Press.

McKittrick, K. (2021). *Dear Science and Other Stories*. London: Duke University Press.

Mosafanezhad, M., Farnan, R., and Loong, S. (2023). Sovereign anxiety in Myanmar: an emotional geopolitics of China's belt and road initiative. *Transactions of the Institute of British Geographers* 48(1): 132–148.

Pain, R. (1997). Social geographies of women's fear of crime. *Transactions of the Institute of British Geographers* 22: 231–244.

Pain, R. (2021). Geotrauma: violence, place and repossession. *Progress in Human Geography* 45(5): 972–989.

Papoulias, C., and Callard, F. (2010). Biology's gift: interrogating the turn to affect. *Body and Society* 16(1): 29–56.

Pile, S. (2010). Emotions and affect in recent human geography. *Transactions of the Institute of British Geographers* 35(1): 5–20.

Pile, S. (2021). *Bodies, Affects, Politics: The Clash of Bodily Regimes*. London: Blackwell.

Pykett, J. (2022). Spatialising happiness economics: Global metrics, urban politics, and embodied technologies. *Transactions of the Institute of British Geographers* 47(3): 635–650.

Raynor, R. (2017). Dramatising austerity: holding a story together (and why it falls apart …). *Cultural Geographies* 24(2): 193–212.

Rose, G. (1993). *Feminism and Geography: The Limits of Geographical Knowledge*. London: Polity.

Ruppert, L. (2022). Affective atmospheres of weapons technologies: the case of battle drones, combat fighters and bodies in contemporary German geopolitics. *Emotion, Space and Society* 45: 100909.

Strong, S. (2021). Towards a geographical account of shame: foodbanks, austerity, and the spaces of austere affective governmentality. *Transactions of the Institute of British Geographers* 46(1): 73–86.

Swanton, D. (2010). Sorting bodies: race, affect, and everyday multiculture in a mill town in northern England. *Environment and Planning A* 42(10): 2332–2350.

Thrift, N. (2008). *Non-Representational Theory. Space, Politics, Affect.* London: Routledge.

Tuan, Y-F. (1977). *Space and Place: The Perspective of Experience.* Minnesota: University of Minnesota Press.

Waite, L., Lewis, H., and Valentine, G. (2014). Multiply vulnerable populations: mobilising a politics of compassion from the 'capacity to hurt'. *Social & Cultural Geography* 15(3): 313–331.

Woodyer, T. (2008). The body as research tool: embodied practice and children's geographies. *Children's Geographies* 6(4): 349–362.

Worth, N. (2016). Feeling precarious: millennial women and work. *Environment and Planning D: Society and Space* 34(4): 601–616.

Wylie, J. (2009). Landscape, absence and the geographies of love. *Transactions of the Institute of British Geographers* 34(3): 275–289.

Yao, X. (2021). *Disaffected: The Cultural Politics of Unfeeling in Nineteenth Century America.* London: Duke University Press.

Online materials

- https://www.sciencedirect.com/journal/emotion-space-and-society

  The post-disciplinary journal *Emotion, Space and Society* was set up in 2008 and contains articles on affect and emotion from a wide range of theoretical perspectives in relation to a variety of empirical topics.

- https://capaciousjournal.com/

  Online journal that has been central to providing a platform for new decolonial, Black studies, and queer theory work on affect.

Further reading

Ahmed, S. (2004). *A Cultural Politics of Emotion.* London: Routledge.
A classic work on emotions and social life, drawing on feminist and anti-racist scholarship to show why and how emotions matter to political life.

Anderson, B. (2014). *Encountering Affect: Capacities, Apparatuses, Conditions.* London: Routledge.
Author's overview of different theories of affect and emotion, with a theory of affective life developed through case studies of precarity, emergency, morale, and other experiences.

Bondi, L., Davidson, J., and Smith, M. (2005). *Emotional Geographies.* London: Ashgate.
First edited collection on emotional geographies, gathering together a wide range of contributors showing the importance of emotions to various geographies.

Pain, R. (2021). Geotrauma: violence, place and repossession progress. *Human Geography* 45(5): 972–989.
Important account of the relations between trauma and place that draws on feminist theories and participatory research.

Pile, S. (2010). Emotions and affect in recent human geography. *Transactions of the Institute of British Geographers* 35(1): 5–20.
A critical overview of work on affect and emotion in Human Geography. Responses to Pile's paper can be found in Volume 36, Issue 4 of *Transactions of the Institute of British Geographers*. You should read the responses alongside Pile's paper.

Stewart, K. (2007). *Ordinary Affects*. Durham and London: Duke University Press.
An inventive attempt to understand the everyday dynamics of affective-emotional life.

Yao, X. (2021). *Disaffected: The Cultural Politics of Unfeeling in Nineteenth Century America*. London: Duke University Press.
Example of recent work outside of geography that brings theories of race and decolonial thought to the study of affect and emotion, focusing on forms of disaffection.

25 Performance and the performing arts

Amanda Rogers and Charlotte Veal

Introduction

Geographers' interest in **performance** is both theoretical and empirical. Theoretically, ideas of performance challenge approaches that try to quantitatively capture a supposedly 'objective world' or that attempt to explain social and cultural phenomena through underlying structures or relations. In contrast, performance helps us to think about geographical worlds in the making – worlds that are processual and always changing, being made and remade through bodily practices. Empirically, it moves us away from forms of knowledge that foreground statistics to instead make space for other ways of knowing, doing, and being. This has value for opening geographers up to alternative narratives and scales of thinking and for engaging with multi-sensual, **affective**, and **embodied** realms. These theoretical and empirical transformations have informed a growing interest in performing-arts-led methods (including dance, theatre, and sound), enlivening geographers' research toolkits (see McCormack, 2014, Sachs Olsen and Hawkins, 2016, Veal, 2016, Raynor, 2019).

There are many lineages of, and ideas surrounding, performance within geography (for detailed overviews see Nash, 2000, Thrift, 2000). In the 1970s, for example, humanistic and time geographers examined the ordinary repeated tasks that make and 'choreograph' place (Hägerstrand, 1976, Seamon, 1980. See also Chapter 4). Geographers have also drawn on the writings of Erving Goffman (1956) who examined how theatre was a metaphor for social life, reflecting on how we act, or perform, in different social settings (Crang, 1994). In the 1990s, Judith Butler (1993) developed an alternative perspective on identity formation and social interaction through her conceptualisation of **performativity**. She defines performativity as 'discursive practices [that] produce that which it names (e.g., to "throw like a girl")' (1993: 13) – that is to say, social expectations normalise our understanding of identity and regulate how it is enacted. Theoretically, accounts of performance highlight how we create and re-create our identity through everyday 'doings' such as habits, gestures, rituals, routines, and tasks, for example, how acts of worship constitute religious identity (Mills, 2012).

As a result, identities are constructed and fluid – they are not something natural that we all inherently 'have' and simply express. Rather, they are constantly in formation. More recently, ideas of performance gained momentum within human geography through the work of **non-representational theory** (Thrift, 2008, see Cadman, 2009, Boyd and Edwardes, 2019,

DOI: 10.4324/9780429265853-30

see Chapter 6). Here, performance and the performing arts have been central concepts because they shift scholars away from textual forms of knowing, and towards events and **encounters** that draw attention to spontaneous, lived, and felt experiences. It is important to recognise the many lineages and traditions of performing arts practice from across the world and to consider the range of expertise involved, from the professional to the amateur, across the disciplines of theatre, dance, music, and performance art.

This body of work has been an influential part of the wider creative turn across geography (Hawkins, 2019). Rather than addressing a series of core questions, performance is a slippery concept that geographers have explored in different ways across multiple sub-disciplinary fields. Arguably, social and cultural geographers have sustained the most interest in performance, with work examining its different forms and forces (e.g. performance as embodied feeling such as mourning, as a mode of statecraft and the legal instruments of power, or as the **temporalities**, **spatialities**, and rhythms of action). These are often focused on the embodied spaces of doing and making, which, whilst present in all our everyday actions, has also been emphasised by examining the performing arts specifically. Our chapter takes such a focus because for us, the performing arts make and are made by geographical phenomena. Yet the performing arts also raise two critical questions that underpin this chapter: who is performance *for*? And what might performance *do*?

Human geography and the performing arts

First, the performing arts appear in specific places, whether it is a conventional theatre or some-where 'site-specific', a public square, train station, or shopping centre. All places have distinctive identities, and while various social, economic, cultural, or political challenges may be common to other places, they are always experienced differently. In such contexts, performances, and their embodied manifestations, have helped make visible and call into question place-based political issues as they impact specific people. Often this work has connected with writings on the right to public space and the city. Combining a focus on the performing arts with ques-tions of rights and justice, geographers have illustrated how the appearance of bodies moving (choreographed or improvised; highly skilled or amateur; dramatised or subtle; individually or collectively) in space *do* political work: they animate, disrupt, intervene, challenge, and frustrate the social, economic, or political order of that space (see Houston and Pulido, 2002, Simpson, 2011, Keegan, 2022). Protest marches, live music, dance, and performance installations, carefully choreographed within chosen space-times, can assert the right of participants to be present or to contribute to decisions about the future of that space (Figure 25.1).

This leads to our second point. The performing arts can produce political space (Gregson and Rose, 2000) and geographers have followed performance scholars in arguing for its radical potential. As Derek McCormack (2008: 1822) has articulated, bodies move in multiple ways – spatio-temporally, kinaesthetically, affectively – 'and this movement is potentially generative of different kinds of spaces'. In their experimental and improvisational process and staging, the performing arts have the *potential* to advocate for new socio-political realities. This includes the capacity to act as a forum for sharing political ideas (to follow performance theorist Bertolt Brecht); to present a utopian vision of the future and expose that which is impossible to reveal

Figure 25.1
21 January 2017 – the Women's March on Washington drew an estimated half-million people to protest
President Donald Trump, Washington, DC, USA

Source: Photo credit: Jim West/Alamy

(Dolan, 2006) or alter the thoughts and behaviours of an audience (Kershaw, 2013). The implication is that something so fleeting as a recital or dance might threaten normative **discourse**, if
only temporarily. Crosscutting the literature is a recognition of the critical and creative possibilities of performance to explain how **power** operates *and* how it might be resisted.

Third, in considering what performance and the performing arts might do, scholars working
at the intersection of geography and the performing arts have interrogated the specificities of

how or through what *form* the performances they produce or reflect upon deliver their conceptual or methodological objectives. For many, this is about disentangling the unique contributions of artistic genres and their various forms. Practices of performance, including dance techniques and sonic worlds, have allowed geographers to analyse embodied feelings and their politics (Smith, 2000). While Western formats such as ballet and contemporary (Narbed, 2016, Veal, 2017) have dominated research, 'traditional' dance forms have also received significant attention as part of an effort to situate movement narratives within their wider socio-cultural and political contexts (Rogers, 2020). This extends to particular steps or micro-mobilities being deemed 'deviant' (Cresswell, 2006). Furthermore, the performing arts are useful in illustrating global flows as they travel unevenly and unequally as a result of (geo)political histories and practices (slavery, **imperialism**, cultural tourism, post-conflict democracy). As geographers, these performance practices can narrate alternative historical geographies of place, including pervading values around **gender** roles, the body, and morality, in addition to political aspirations such as multiculturalism (Gilbert and Lo, 2007).

In asking how performance delivers on its socio-political ambitions, others have turned to focus on the performing arts as a process, asking who engages with these processes, why, and what benefits (if any) are attributed to such participation. Central to this body of literature are the experiences of individuals and communities (professional, semi-professional, amateurs) throughout the creative process as they explore a particular issue. Creative processes are lauded as capable of facilitating difficult conversations. Theatre, dance, and sound each in their own ways incorporate non-verbal modes of communication that allow people to connect on a different level that might be more empathetic, affective, embodied or sensorial; qualities that are important when addressing violence and trauma. Others contend that in foregrounding experimentation, the performance process promotes pre-cognitive forms of doing, thus prioritising other ways of knowing (Thrift, 2000). While there is a danger of romanticising performance as capable of flattening hierarchies of power, engaging in performance-led processes has been shown to nurture individual and community transformation (Veal, 2017).

Finally, performance has been explored as a creative output. Research has analysed theatre productions, dances, soundwalks, arts festivals, and installations to gather insights into how they illuminate and rework geographies – from the micro-practices of the body to individual or community expression, to the broader social, economic, and political processes in which our daily lives are embroiled (see Lea et al., 2015 on learning yoga). Geographers have also observed, co-produced, and commissioned performing artists to create choreographies, compositions, and plays. Through these creative products, it has been possible to consolidate ideas on a socio-political issue as defined and experienced by that community or to amalgamate key findings on a predefined socio-political topic. In beginning to answer 'who performance is for', some geographers have enlisted creative outputs as a medium for research dissemination to public and academic audiences. Creative outputs question *how* research is told – sharing research in alternative ways, which in their affective liveness, can be powerful modes of knowledge transmission and knowledge transformation. For others, creative products are about *what* research is told – telling everyday stories that are lived, felt and experienced, stories that matter to ordinary people, and stories that are crucially curated with those individuals and/or communities at each step of the research process.

Summary

- Geographers have a longstanding interest in performance and the performing arts, with these now regarded as a way to access embodied and multi-sensual spaces.
- We offer five lenses through which geographers are currently engaging with performance: performance appears in place, performance produces space, performance as practice, performance processes, and performance as output.
- Two key questions underpin these approaches: who is performance for?; and what might performance do?

Place and (geo)politics

That politics is performative, and performance is political, has long interested geographers. Recent work in social and cultural geography has underscored the radical potential of the performing arts – both to support political agendas (i.e. as soft power) and to call them into question. In this section, we begin to respond to our opening question, what might performance do, by offering three scales through which the intersection between performance politics and place has furthered geographical knowledge on political contexts and political relationships: the intimate, the city, and the international.

Over the last three decades, the intimate scale, including the body, the home, and everyday spaces, has received mounting attention. Such a move responds to the corporeal turn in geography (1990s) and more sustained work of **feminist** geographers on bodies and embodiment. Geographers writing on and co-producing the performing arts have enlisted the performing body to draw attention to intimate struggles and embodied violence. Foremost in this is the work of Ruth Raynor (2017) on austerity. Using drama to tell stories of the slow violence of austerity, Raynor co-produced a fictional play with a group of women in the Northeast of England. Engaging with women's nuanced relations with various cuts and reforms of austerity, Raynor compellingly draws attention to austerity's effectiveness as a divisive force.

Another noteworthy work on theatre is Cree's (2019) exploration of everyday encounters with military power and of the corporeal and affective materialities of militarism. She argues that the **aesthetic** power of theatre lies in how it alters frames of perception and calls into question assumed knowledge. In particular, Butler (2006) discusses recorded testimonies from people who once lived and worked where a motorway now runs to provide listeners with evocative experiences from the past. And yet in producing plays and performances (about violence, urban planning, austerity), geographers working in these fields have had to engage productively with the ethics and care of participants and audiences, interrogate how the performing arts might stage violence or dramatise inequities, and are aware that performance can re-traumatise (see Veal, 2020). Nonetheless, we also contend that the performing arts have a vital role to play in the process of creating more inclusive, just societies. What these works have begun to open up therefore is the ethical possibilities for how we might do geographical scholarship differently.

Performance, place, and politics have been explored in the context of cities, building in part on geographers' long interest in urban rights and justice. On the one hand, performance's creative and dramatic force has helped spotlight urban inequalities such as policing or **gentrification**. On the other hand, performing arts projects have been mobilised by city governments as part of the wider creative cities' ethos. This complex and contentious relationship is explored in Charlotte's case study (2017) on Vancouver and the city's legislative efforts to cultivate 'A Healthy City for All' (Box 25.1).

BOX 25.1
CONTESTATION IN PERFORMANCE

In 2013 Charlotte worked with the Karen Jamieson Dance Company and the Carnegie Dance Troupe of Vancouver's Downtown Eastside. The collaboration saw community participants engage in dance training, dance workshops, and a dance performance in the streets of the Downtown Eastside. The final choreography, entitled *Connect*, explored changes to the urban fabric as a result of gentrification, privatisation, disinvestment, targeted policing, and a loss of low-income housing. Charlotte argues that in the lead-up to the 2010 Winter Olympics, city government rolled out, under the banner of Vancouver's Healthy City Strategy, a swathe of 'wellbeing' initiatives and policies that endeavoured to cultivate and manage healthy people, healthy communities, and healthy environments. Such measures were socially and spatially targeted to those communities and individuals deemed 'failing'. What is potentially unusual about this mode of governance is the novel legislative alliance cultivated between health and wellbeing and the performing arts industries.

Connect was staged during the neighbourhood-run *In the Heart of the City Festival*. Approximately 30 minutes in length, the choreography journeyed through the neighbourhood, stopping at various landmarks of personal and political significance to participants. In many respects, *Connect* embodies Vancouver's tri-level 'health and wellbeing' legislative ambitions. Charlotte traces how community participants were co-opted into endorsing this political initiative through engaging in an individualised healthy-body practice (healthy people) and community-arts-led workshops that endeavoured to build 'community connections' and foster a sense of 'belonging' in a community stigmatised in policy and media discourse as 'at risk' (healthy communities). Yet, she also illustrates how through performance, participants confronted Vancouver's urban health agenda (healthy environments). Dancing at sites of struggle, participants exposed the contradictions behind the healthy city legislation and the impacts of gentrification, urban policing, and disinvestment that prevented them from living in 'a healthy city for all'.

In a similar vein, Casquilho et al. (2021) have examined sonic urban branding strategies. Music in urban public spaces can not only conjure **atmospheres** that are 'hip' but also orchestrate conflicts between, for example, music promoters and those who have other claims on the space (residents, business owners; see Simpson, 2011 on sonic regulation). Sound and territory, the authors suggest, co-constitute each other in immersive and affective ways.

A final scale for thinking performance, politics and place has been at the international or geopolitical. Of course, there is much work on the performance and spectacle of nationalism and statecraft (see below), but the performing arts have allowed geographers to make critical interventions into the intimate and embodied workings of international and geopolitical *relations*. In their early research, Johnston and Pratt (2010) staged *Nanay*; a play expanded and reworked over the course of a decade exploring the complexities of **transnational** flows of care giving and those persons networked into the labour market. Reflecting on *Nanay's* staging in Canada and the Philippines, Pratt et al. (2017) discuss how the meaning and constitution of trauma change according to context. Some trauma narratives gain new interpretations or fresh perspectives in different locations, whilst others may stimulate the sharing of new experiences, creating a networked web of interrelated stories. As such, theatre can facilitate dialogues between places, raising questions about the politics of care, the ethics of doing research and sharing stories in different settings.

Performance has also illustrated how geopolitical knowledge is communicated. With the emergence of a creative geopolitical agenda, sonic geographers of performance including Kirby (2019) have analysed how, during periods of international conflict, instrumental film scores can circulate profound affective forces that can advance geopolitical visions, including of the nation and moral bifurcations between good and evil. At the other end of the spectrum, the performing arts can deliver counter messages to national or state-sponsored propaganda. Morley and Somdahl-Sands (2011), for example, reflect on the performance space of U2 tours where themes relating to trans/nationalism, tolerance, and social justice, were constituted in response to geopolitical events including 9/11 and the War in Iraq. And the performing arts have facilitated geographers in developing new critical lenses through which to understand transnational geopolitical *processes*. Amanda's *Performing Asian Transnationalisms* is a useful example here (Figure 25.2). Whether via people, scripts, performances, or imagination, Amanda illustrates how the performing arts are embedded in all manner of cultural flows and circulations that produce creative praxis (including political alliances, working practices, and creative opportunities). But what is also useful is her careful reading of ethnic minority theatre as embedded into global as much as national cultural and creative worlds.

Summary

- Politics are performative, and performance is political. Geographers have examined the radical potential of the performing arts at multiple scales.
- The performing arts allow geographers to tell everyday stories of slow violence and foreground the intimate workings of politics.
- Governments have mobilised the arts in urban governance agendas. Such alliances have been variously supported and contested.
- Geographers have examined how the performing arts explain global relations, illustrated how geopolitical imaginaries are communicated, and traced the processes of transnational relations.

Figure 25.2
A photo taken by Rogers of Choung Veasna and Chamroeun Dara performing Choung Veasna's Dark in Phnom Penh in 2022. The piece explores overcoming discrimination, but aesthetically it embodies a contemporary dance style that combines Cambodian and Euro-American forms of movement

Source: Photo credit: Amanda Rogers

Identity and difference

In highlighting cultural flow, the work above begins to draw our attention to questions of cultural interaction and identity – to who performance is for, who it represents, and who it might involve. First, geographers have explored how performing arts cultures stem from cross-cultural fertilisation and exchange, that is, from intercultural interaction. Noxolo (2016), for example, has examined how the Caribbean dancing body crosses multiple cultural contexts and, in so doing, expresses its complex and traumatic **postcolonial** histories. Thinking through the geographies of these encounters at both the micro-scale of the performing body and within broader networks of regional or global cultural flows highlights how performance expresses complex postcolonial relationships (Narbed, 2016). The move to decolonise geographical knowledge by challenging institutional silences and considering the contribution of marginalised voices and experiences has been important in work on performance. Niaah's (2008, 2010) theorisation of performance, for example, centres on blackness, arguing that performance geographies constitute the ability to (re)construct a sense of self in the context of violence and rupture. By considering the space of the Black Atlantic, she draws attention to inequality and power in the performing arts.

This work emphasises the potential of embodied performances to create resistance. If identities are partly formed through our actions, then there is a political potential for the performing arts that can challenge existing **representations** and expectations of identity. This draws attention to our second focus which is the politics of representation in performance (see Box 25.2). Here, theatre and dance can be important spaces of self and community expression (see Gembus, 2018 on the creation of theatre pieces by second-generation British Somalis). However, the performing arts also draw attention to questions of cultural ownership and the politics of identity. Arun Saldanha's (2005, 2007) research on Goa's rave scene, for example, explores how **race** emerges through a complex **assemblage** of bodies (skilled dancing and talking bodies), affective forces (the time of day, the weather, sounds, music), and things (drugs, drink). However, whilst

BOX 25.2
REPRESENTATION IN PERFORMANCE

Amanda's research (Rogers, 2010, 2012, 2014) has examined how theatre can create alternative imaginations of Asian American and British East Asian **subjectivity**. By creating emotionally complex characters and telling stories about the experiences of these communities, theatre can challenge two-dimensional stereotypes of Asian minorities as geeks, gangsters, and prostitutes. However, this co-exists with an ambivalence that such work is often based on normative forms and modes of performance practice that can reinforce the status quo. In deploying specific techniques of acting, directing, and staging, productions constantly navigate the possibility that Asian American bodies are being 'whitewashed', working against the desire to explicitly recognise and raise the profile of such bodies and their racialisation.

There is, therefore, an ambivalence around the fluidity of identity in performance. In analysing debates around casting practice, particularly in *The Orphan of Zhao* controversy at the Royal Shakespeare Company (Rogers and Thorpe, 2014), the unequal power relationships between differently raced bodies in performance were starkly realised. In this production, only three British East Asian actors were cast in ethnically Chinese roles out of a potential 18 parts. With largely white actors performing as Chinese, the performance was widely condemned as a form of racialised minstrelsy or 'yellowface'. Examining the production highlighted that the fluidity of identity only operated in particular directions: white actors could play Chinese roles, but the reverse was not necessarily the case. The casting prised open wider debates around cultural ownership, the politics of representation, the problems and inequalities of 'authentic' racial casting, and the lack of opportunities afforded to East and South East Asian minorities in British theatre and entertainment.

Figure 25.3
BalletBoyz collaboration with Adugna Dance Company

Source: Photo credit: Charlotte Veal

race is theorised as a fluid construct, such fluidity also produces divisions between differently raced and empowered bodies.

In a similar vein, research on disability and the performing arts in geography has challenged ideas of what bodies can do or are capable of through a focus on micro-bodily practice. Charlotte's work on a contact improvisation/dance collaboration between BalletBoyz and Adugna Potentials of Addis Ababa entitled *Lost in Perfection* problematises what constitutes the image of the 'perfectly able body' (Figure 25.3). Using a multi-sensual **ethnographic** approach illustrates how working with disabled dancers and integrating their movements into the piece exceeded able-bodied imaginations and practices of mobility (see Veal 2018). Similarly, Amanda's work on contemporary dance experiments in Cambodia with differently abled bodies explored how these both implicitly and explicitly challenged the physicality of the 'ideal' Cambodian dancer (Rogers 2020). Given the prominence of dance to the Cambodian national imaginary, such experiments stake a claim for greater inclusion whilst also attending to what movement means, what cultures movements represent, and which bodies are able – or allowed – to enact specific types of movement.

These examples collectively illustrate the way in which geographers have used the performing arts as a way to open up a consideration of how we might be and belong together. The nation is the common space for articulating this sense of community and for thinking through who gets to be included and excluded within it. There has been extensive geographical research on how lyrics and music represent national identities, not least through national anthems. Wood (2012) foregrounds how the emotive experience of listening to and watching music is also part of representational expression leading to claims of (in this instance) 'Scottishness'. Similarly, Devadoss (2017) examines how soundscapes of music and language can be used to perform Tamil identities that distinguish themselves from wider national identities. The contradictory feelings that can accompany nationality and national events have been explored by Angharad Closs Stephens (2019). In a paper called 'Feeling Brexit', she examines how feelings of shame, hostility, and resentment associated with Brexit were explored through dance. The movement here opened up hopeful avenues of how we might live together in new ways and challenge easy, populist narratives of nationalism.

Whether through cross-cultural interaction, the politics of representation, or how we work to belong together, each of these accounts highlights the creative possibilities of the performing arts and how they can rework socio-economic relationships or change public perceptions. However, there are limits to the performance's revolutionary potential, particularly as decisions have to be made over whose stories to tell. Mattingly's (2001: 447) research on a community theatre project in San Diego discusses these issues of 'narrative authority'. She describes how choices were made to represent the neighbourhood of City Heights through a safe image of multicultural harmony, rather than by addressing the real problems that teenagers face. This representation was promoted because the theatre performance was part of a wider strategy of urban regeneration that attempted to improve the image of City Heights in order to make it more attractive for investment. However, residents contested this sanitised image of their neighbourhood and teenagers challenged expectations around why they should be involved. Such research demonstrates the careful consideration of the ambivalent, power-laden politics of performance in relation to identity. Choices around whose voices are heard, the style of work created, and the locations in which performances are enacted and made can celebrate marginalised communities and place them 'centre stage', but new forms of erasure, difference and discrimination can also emerge in the process.

Summary

- The performing arts both create and express identity.
- Geographical work draws attention to processes of cross-fertilisation and cross-cultural interaction.
- The performing arts can be used to 'give space' for the expression of marginal identities, challenging dominant representations and expectations.
- Such work draws attention to how we can live together across the differences and divisions.
- It also enables reflection on whose stories are told and the politics that surround creative choices in representation and expression.

For the performing arts

In this chapter, we have outlined a series of perspectives and thematics relating to geography and the performing arts. In bringing the chapter to a close, we want to return to the two key questions we opened with; who is performance for, and what does performance do?

The performing arts have allowed geographers to engage with diverse and under-represented communities in more accessible ways. However, these collaborations have often been many years in the making in order to build trust, allow participants to voice what really matters to them, and articulate concerns in their own language. Much of this work has been in spaces of individual and collective choosing, meaning that the geographical stories told are situated in real places and in response to relevant issues to produce highly contextual work. However, in saying this, we are mindful of the need to be sensitive to issues of 'narrative authority' (Mattingly, 2001) and how performing arts projects can be co-opted (by the state, military, local government, institutions, individuals) for ends other than those originally intended. For academics, creating and researching the performing arts has also allowed for a radical transformation in valuing different types of knowledge – particularly within the Western academy. In particular, the performing arts force a greater consideration of embodied, material, multi-sensual worlds, and the kinds of feelings and experiences they create. In turn, this has implications for questioning what constitutes geographical scholarship and how it matters in our everyday world.

In developing these ideas and answering our second question, what might performance do, we recognise that performance is an ambiguous force. Its potential is multiple. On the one hand, performance can evoke embodied feelings and responses that can motivate people to act for progressive forms of change, give marginalised groups a space for expression against dominant forces, represent the grounded complexities of issues, and stimulate a move for social justice and the desire for alternative futures. Such possibilities are partly why social and cultural geographers have gravitated towards the performing arts. However, on the other hand, the performing arts can also be harnessed in the service of dominant forces that seek to maintain the status quo. In recognising that the performing arts are political tools, it is vital that geographers maintain critical attention to the claims made about performances, their embodied manifestations and their purpose.

Discussion points

- Why are geographers interested in performance and the performing arts?
- What spaces have geographers explored through the performing arts?
- How might performance and embodiment be used as part of research data collection?
- How might everyday performances be used to resist dominant forms of power? Can you think of any examples?
- Do you have any experience of performance? Can you apply a geographical lens to them?
- Consider a space before a performance, during a performance and after a performance. How might these states differ?

References

Boyd, C. P., and Edwardes, C. (eds.) (2019). *Non-Representational Theory and the Creative Arts*. London: Palgrave Macmillan.

Butler, J. (1993). *Bodies That Matter: On the Discursive Limits of 'sex'*. London: Routledge.

Butler, T. (2006). A walk of art: the potential of the sound walk as practice in cultural geography. *Social & Cultural Geography* 7: 889–908.

Cadman, L. (2009). Nonrepresentational Theory/Nonrepresentational Geographies. In *International Encyclopaedia of Human Geography*, eds. R. Kitchen and N. Thrift (1st edn.). Oxford: Elsevier, 456–463.

Casquilho, C., Gonçalves, P., Mourão, C., Nunes, P., and Paiva, D. (2021). 7 In *Territories, Environments, Politics*, eds. A. M. Brighenti and M. Kärrholm. London: Routledge, 174–187.

Closs Stephens, A. (2019). Feeling 'Brexit': nationalism and the affective politics of movement. *GeoHumanities* 5(2): 405–423.

Crang, P. (1994). 'It's showtime!': on the workplace geographies of display in a restaurant in southeast England. *Environment and Planning D: Society and Space* 12: 675–704.

Cree, A. (2019). Encountering the 'lively' in military theatre. In *A Research Agenda for Military Geographies*, ed. R. Woodward. Cheltenham: Edward Elgar Publishing, 162–173.

Cresswell, T. (2006). 'You cannot shake that shimmie here': producing mobility on the dance floor. *Cultural Geographies* 13(1): 55–77.

Devadoss, C. (2017). Sound and identity explored through the Indian Tamil diaspora and Tamil Nadu. *Journal of Cultural Geography* 34(1): 70–92.

Dolan, J. (2006). Utopia in performance. *Theatre Research International* 31(2): 163–173.

Gembus, M. P. (2018). The sage spaces 'in-between' – plays, performance and identity amount young 'second generation' Somalis in London. *Children's Geographies* 16(4): 432–443.

Gilbert, H., and Lo, J. (2007). *Performance and Cosmopolitics: Cross-cultural Transactions in Australasia*. London: Palgrave.

Goffman, E. (1956). *The Presentation of Self in Everyday Life*. London: Penguin.

Gregson, N., and Rose, G. (2000). Taking Butler elsewhere: performativities, spatialities and subjectivities. *Environment and Planning D: Society and Space* 18(4): 433–452.

Hägerstrand, T. (1976). Geography and the study of interaction between nature and society. *Geoforum* 7(5–6): 329–334.

Hawkins, H. (2019). Geography's creative (re) turn: toward a critical framework. *Progress in Human Geography* 43(6): 963–984.

Houston, D., and Pulido, L. (2002). The work of performativity: staging social justice at the University of Southern California. *Environment and Planning D: Society and Space* 20(4): 401–424.

Johnston, C., and Pratt, G. (2010). Nanay (mother): a testimonial play. *Cultural Geographies* 17(1): 123–133.

Keegan, C. (2022). A minor theory of direct action politics and performance in New Orleans' economic justice movement. *Environment and Planning D: Society and Space* 40(1): 158–174.

Kershaw, B. (2013). *The Radical in Performance: Between Brecht and Baudrillard*. Abingdon: Routledge.

Kirby, P. (2019). Sound and fury? Film score and the geopolitics of instrumental music. *Political Geography* 75: 102054.

Lea, J., Philo, C., and Cadman, L. (2015). 'It's a fine line between self discipline, devotion and dedication': negotiating authority in the teaching and learning of Ashtanga yoga. *Cultural Geographies* 23(1): 69–85.

Mattingly, D. (2001). Place, teenagers and representations: lessons from a community theatre project. *Social & Cultural Geography* 2: 445–459.

McCormack, D. P. (2008). Geographies for moving bodies: thinking, dancing, spaces. *Geography Compass* 2(6): 1822–1836.

McCormack, D. P. (2014). *Refrains for Moving Bodies: Experience and Experiment in Affective Spaces*. London: Duke University Press.

Mills, S. (2012). Duty to God/my Dharma/Allah/Waheguru: diverse youthful religiosities and the politics and performance of informal workshop. *Social & Cultural Geography* 13: 481–499.

Morley, V., and Somdahl-Sands, K. (2011). Music with a message. *Aether*, 58.

Narbed, S. (2016). Creativity and the Dancing Body. In *Creativity: Live, Work, Create*, ed. H. Hawkins. Abingdon: Routledge, 41–45.

Nash, C. (2000). Performativity in practice: some recent work in cultural geography. *Progress in Human Geography* 24(4): 653–664.

Niaah, S. S. (2010). *DanceHall: From Slave Ship to Ghetto*. Ottawa: University of Ottawa Press.

Noxolo, P. (2016). Dancing maps: Thinking through the in/secure space of the black dancing body. ACME Lecture at the Royal Geographical Society-Institute of British Geographers Annual Conference, 2 September 2016.

Pratt, G., Johnston, C., and Banta, V. (2017). Filipino migrant stories and trauma in the transnational field. *Emotion, Space and Society* 24: 83–92.

Raynor, R. (2017). Dramatising austerity: holding a story together (and why it falls apart…). *Cultural Geographies* 24(2): 193–212.

Raynor, R. (2019). Speaking, feeling, mattering: theatre as method and model for practice-based, collaborative, research. *Progress in Human Geography* 43(4): 691–710.

Rogers, A. (2010). The geographies of performing scripted language. *Cultural Geographies* 17: 353–375.

Rogers, A. (2012). Emotional geographies of method acting in Asian American theater. *Annals of the Association of American Geographers* 102: 423–442.

Rogers, A. (2014). *Performing Asian Transnationalisms: Theatre, Identity and the Geographies of Performance*. Routledge.

Rogers, A. (2018). Advancing the geographies of the performing arts: intercultural Aesthetics, migratory mobility and geopolitics. *Progress in Human Geography* 42(4): 549–568.

Rogers, A. (2020). Transforming the national body: choreopolitics and disability in contemporary Cambodian dance. *Cultural Geographies* 27(4): 527–543.

Rogers, A., and Thorpe, A. (2014). A controversial company: debating the casting of the RSC's the orphan of Zhao. *Contemporary Theatre Review* 24(4): 428–435.

Sachs Olsen, C., and Hawkins, H. (2016). Archiving and urban exploration – Mr Nice Guy, cooking oil drums, sterile blisher packs and uncanny bikinis. *Cultural Geographies* 23(3): 531–543.

Saldanha, A. (2005). Trance and visibility at dawn: racial dynamics in Goa's rave scene. *Social & Cultural Geography* 6: 707–721.

Saldanha, A. (2007). *Psychedelic White: Goa Trance and the Viscosity of Race*. Minneapolis: University of Minnesota Press.

Seamon, D. (1980). Body-Subject, Time-Space Routines, and Place Ballets. In *The Human Experience of Space and Place*, eds. A. Buttimer and D. Seamon. London: Croom Helm, 148–165.

Simpson, P. (2011). Street performance and the city: public space, sociality, and intervening in the everyday. *Space and Culture* 14(4): 415–430.

Smith, S. J. (2000). Performing the (sound) world. *Environment and Planning D: Society and Space* 18(5): 615–637.

Thrift, N. (2000). Afterwords. *Environment and Planning D: Society and Space* 18(2): 213–255.

Thrift, N. (2008). *Non-Representational Theory: Space, Politics, Affect*. Abingdon: Routledge.

Veal, C. (2016). A choreographic notebook: methodological developments in qualitative geographical research. *Cultural Geographies* 23(2): 221–245.

Veal, C. (2017). Dance and wellbeing in Vancouver's 'A Healthy City for All'. *Geoforum* 81: 11–21.

Veal, C. (2018). Micro-bodily mobilities: choreographing geographies and mobilities of dance and disability. *Area* 50(3), 306–313.

Veal, C. (2020). Thinking intimate geopolitics creatively: choreographing spaces of performance, testimony, and law. *GeoHumanities* 6(1): 65–88.

Wood, N. (2012). Playing with 'Scottishness': musical performance, non-representational thinking and the 'doings' of national identity. *Cultural Geographies* 19(2): 195–215.

Online materials

- BalletBoyz. (2011). *BalletBoyz Next Generation*. https://www.imdb.com/title/tt6336668/ The film features the initiation of an all-male dance company and their collaboration with Addis Ababa's Adugna Dance Company.

- Cambodian Living Arts YouTube page https://www.youtube.com/c/CambodianLivingArts/videos
  One of Cambodia's leading arts NGOs, who have worked extensively in preserving traditional arts in the aftermath of war and in developing works exploring contemporary issues.

- Karen Jamieson Dance. (2022). *Karen Jamieson Dance: Works: Connect.* https://www.kjdance.ca/works/connect
  The website provides an introduction to the work of Karen Jamieson and the Carnegie Dance Troupe of the Downtown Eastside. It includes photographs and video footage from the 2012 work in progress and 2013 production of the street-procession-come-performance.

- *Nanay: A testimonial play.* https://vimeo.com/1569921
  An introductory video to Nanay. The snippet provides some of the key discussion points about the international relationships between Canada and the Philippines with regards to care.

Further reading

Johnston, C., and Pratt, G. (2010). Nanay (mother): a testimonial play. *Cultural Geographies* 17(1): 123–133.
The authors offer extracts from a co-produced testimonial play entitled *Nanay* about Filipino migration and Canada's Live-in Caregiver Program.

Nash, C. (2000). Performativity in practice: some recent work in cultural geography. *Progress in Human Geography* 24(4): 653–664.
A synthesis of debates around representation and performance in relation to the non-representational turn.

Raynor, R. (2017). Dramatising austerity: holding a story together (and why it falls apart…). *Cultural Geographies* 24(2): 193–212.
Raynor's paper shares stories of austerity that offer insight into the different and divergent experiences of the slow violence of sweeping waves of closures and cuts.

Rogers, A. (2018). Advancing the geographies of the performing arts: intercultural aesthetics, migratory mobility and geopolitics. *Progress in Human Geography* 42(4): 549–568.
This paper explores recent thematic debates in research on geographies of performance in detail.

Thrift, N. (2000). Afterwords. *Environment and Planning D: Society and Space* 18(2): 213–255.
Nigel Thrift's exposition of a non-representationalist style of thinking, outlining its theoretical bases and the multiple lineages of performance related work within geography.

Veal, C. (2016). A choreographic notebook: methodological developments in qualitative geographical research. *Cultural Geographies* 23(2): 221–245.
This paper explores the promises and possibilities of dance-led methods for geographical research and embodied thinking.

26 Materialities

Joseph Pierce

Introduction

In order to understand 'materialities' as a movement within human geography, it helps to trace how the relationship between the physical world and human experience has been theorised over time in geographical scholarship. Human geographers study individual experiences, shared narratives and myths, social and political institutions, and material **embodiment** to understand how people give meaning to places and landscapes as they make them together. Though it had effects well beyond the study of **culture**, the theoretical project of materialities in geography grew as a response to what was called 'the cultural turn' in the 1980s and 1990s, when some human geographers worked to assert the importance of **affect** and experience. This chapter traces a number of reactions to these efforts, culminating in contemporary theory about materialities.

An example of the relationship between the immaterial and material can be found in the relationships between religious faith, sacred architecture, and urban morphology. Religious communities have divergent beliefs about the spiritual world and humans' place in it. These deeply held beliefs both shape and are shaped by bodily practices and the physical contexts of religious practice. For example, many religions instruct adherents to pray in a particular direction: Muslims towards Mecca, Jews towards Jerusalem, and early Christians towards the east and thus the rising sun. These theologically driven directions for prayer shape buildings of worship as the faithful seek to build holy sites that facilitate a natural orientation in worshippers' preferred directions. In religious communities where direction of prayer is not specifically directed, religious architecture is freer to respond to the local landscape, perhaps emphasising dramatic views from within a chapel or a position of powerful visibility to the surrounding community.

These choices about location and spatial orientation can, in turn, iteratively shape the beliefs of the faithful. For example, by orienting churches to the east, historic Christian buildings of worship unconsciously emphasised the visceral experience of observing sunrise or sunset in their daily and weekly rituals. Furthermore, the location and orientation of buildings of worship shapes the towns and cities that grow around them, dictating street patterns and the direction of local traffic at sites throughout the world (see Figure 26.1). Thus, abstract beliefs about how best to demonstrate faith can also have long-lasting and systematic repercussions in the secular built environment at a large scale. Beliefs are reified in the cultural landscape.

Is religious culture something affective, defined by the shared experiences of humans? Or is it instead something material, reflected in the (sometimes epic) objects humans make and revere in the world? The answer for most human geographers today would be the following: it is both.

DOI: 10.4324/9780429265853-31

Figure 26.1
The Grand Mosque complex at Mecca in Saudi Arabia, dominating the layout of the city

Source: Photo credit: UPI/Alamy

Religious culture is a combination of norms and beliefs shared among a community of people at any scale; it is characterised by a sense of meaning, the shared values that come from shared practices. But culture is not only ephemeral or experiential: it is more than the sum of what is imagined, believed, or understood. In the illustration above, religious culture plays out in the material products of shared practices as well: we see this interplay in a wide array of human geographical phenomena.

Inevitably, there are moments when the collective attention of human geographers leans more strongly towards the material world on one hand or the ephemerally experienced/imagined world on the other. Research agendas are shaped by recent news events, technological change, or an existing line of compelling scholarship that draws colleagues into energetic responses. This chapter traces that give-and-take, beginning with what was labelled the cultural turn, and how the analytic of materialities emerges in the discipline.

The cultural turn and the limits of the material

In the 1980s and 1990s some scholars hailed a cultural turn in geography. They called for more attention to affect, experience, and emotion, and (sometimes implicitly) concomitantly less attention to that which could be mechanically measured and quantified (Jackson, 1997, Barnett, 1998). The cultural turn was associated with contemporaneous trends in the wider social sciences, rooted in poststructural theory (Valentine, 2001).

Scholars promoting a cultural turn for geography were critical of a rigid empiricism proposing that the only things that matter are the materials, objects and processes that can be observed physically. Two related but distinct lines of criticism emerged here. The first line is simpler: there are geographical phenomena that matter to people but aren't physically measurable. Affect,

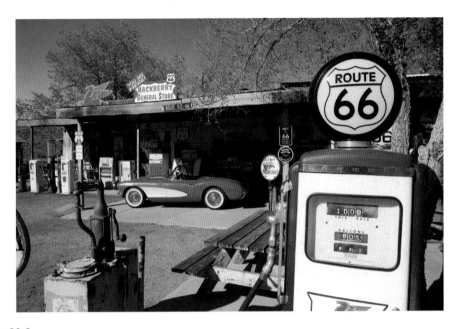

Figure 26.2
Route 66, the 'essence' of the USA?

Source: Photo credit: Michael Robertson/Alamy

identity, meaning: these are matters of human experience and are resistant to direct representation in the physical environment but are important objects of study. This chapter opened with an example of religious architecture, but meaning-making as a spatial practice is everywhere. When people assign the highest importance to those working on the top floor of a skyscraper; when they valorise US Route 66, a disused early generation highway, as the essence of America (see Figure 26.2); or when they trust a bank more because of its oversized classical columns, they are *assigning* meaning to their environments, not merely discovering their intrinsic physical values.

The second criticism of a vulgar physical empiricism is trickier: that the very terms of measurement are actually also contingent, wrapped up in the search for human meaning. Here, for example, consider the conditions of 'alive' and 'dead', which on their face are clear and distinct. Yet many doctors, when probed in their own time, struggle with these definitions. Brain activity or heart activity, the statistical likelihood of revival, and core body temperature can all be important factors. Yet outlier cases of supposedly dead people sitting up gasping for air hours later are documented; the analytical problem is not which category a person falls into, but rather that the categories themselves are **socially constructed** and defined, in order to solve a social problem. Most times and for most people, the two categories are sufficient; occasionally, however, they are revealed as insufficient to capture the real world in its fullness.

What has this to do with materiality and geography? Well, geographers of the cultural turn emphasised these two critiques (the importance of affective experience and the **discursive** limitations of categorisation/measurement) to push geographers towards studies of experiences. They called for a focus on text, on meaning-making, and on systems of beliefs, faiths, and norms. This was labelled as the 'cultural turn' in geography.

Summary

- Cultural geography studies both the immaterial – people's thoughts, feelings, emotions – and the material – the objects, buildings, and landscapes that surround us all.
- The cultural turn emphasised the immaterial, as criticism grew of work which looked solely at the material.

Re-materialising geography

In some ways, the cultural turn revived a longer history of a more phenomenological geography, which became popular in the 1970s and 1980s (Tuan, 1977, Thrift, 2007, Cresswell, 2012). Yet some geographers chafed at this movement in the scholarly conversation. Affect and experience are important subjects for geographical enquiry, but some worried that the direction of this work moved away from the strengths of geography as a discipline, with its focus on the interactions between humans and their physical environments. These scholars worried that this theoretical focus on things that cannot be 'rigorously' observed limited human geography's explanatory power and its relevance to wider scholarly conversations. In other words, they feared that geography would lose power by wandering away from attention to the real.

In addition to this negative argument, Philo (2000: 33) wrote that 'in the rush to elevate such spaces in our human geographical studies, we have ended up becoming less attentive to the more "thingy", bump-into-able, stubbornly there-in-the-world kinds of "matter" (the material) with which earlier geographers tended to be more familiar'. Philo and other geographers (Jackson, 2000, Lees, 2002) insisted that the material world is important. Even if immaterial experience is *also* important, these scholars insisted that the physical bases and traces of human experience are crucial and should be foregrounded by human geographers.

This 're-materialisation' is not a call to return to an atheoretical **spatial science**, but rather a demand for a richer understanding of the material world. To this point, then, the material turn is a story of a pendulum swinging back and forth between more experiential and more material approaches to human geography. For instance, Kaika (2006) examines the relationship between meaning and the material in the grand environmental engineering of dam-building, and Jeffrey (2019) traces materialities of the courtroom as a space engineered to engender particular ways of practising justice. In short, materiality-oriented scholars are interested in how meaning is invested in the physical.

A plurality of 'materialities'

Yet the title of this chapter is not 'material geography' but 'materialities'; this *plurality* of the material subjects of geography is still to be addressed. Lorimer (2013: 32) argues that the difference between emphasising materiality and materialities is not minor; he writes: 'What is at stake when the term "materialities" is employed is nothing less than the geographical authority to describe the nature of the lived world'. The emphasis in pluralising materialities is the statement that there are different ways of 'being material', and there are also social and political implications if we erase the differences between these modes.

Take as an example the so-called smart city. There are many different registers of the material that are important in the smart city: the material properties of the digital surveillance **infrastructure** being built out; the tactile properties of pavement surfaces that enable or disable active transport; the resilience of the built form to climate change; the resilience of that same built form to economic catastrophe or reconfiguration through political revolution. These, argue proponents of a materialities approach, are very different modes of materiality. The centring of one or another of these materialities is often a deliberate choice that carries with it different types of politics.

For example, the mobility infrastructure of townships around Johannesburg in South Africa were intentionally designed to enable military control during the Apartheid era. Urban neighbourhoods and subdivisions were linked (but also isolated from each other) using natural barricades, buffer zones, and traffic choke points, which made it easier to control non-white populations (see Lemon, 1991). Paris was famously rebuilt in the 1800s, with new wide boulevards constructed throughout the city, designed by Haussmann to enable, among other things, military deployment in response to civil unrest in the city (see Harvey, 2005). This long history of surveillance and control in urban environments is certainly material: it is a set of values baked into the built environment, shaping social, political, economic, and cultural experiences of the urban. The materiality of Haussmann's projection of power via the Paris boulevards has much in common with that of Apartheid-era townships, despite their distinct **aesthetics**.

In contrast, the emerging materialities of smart city surveillance are very different in kind. There may be genuine public benefits that come from a widespread network of microphones, CCTV cameras, temperature and proximity sensors, and more baked into the fabric of public and private spaces alike (see Figure 26.3). However, widespread use of ambient sensors can remake

Figure 26.3
CCTV cameras in Singapore

Source: Photo credit: Carpe Diem/Alamy

core concepts of privacy and the public sphere. Spaces that were publicly (or even privately) owned but practically anonymous, like streets and park benches, for example, are transformed into spaces of identification and tracking. It may be that in a smart city, privacy becomes a thing that can only exist in domestic spaces, even for people whose public actions are of no public interest.

The materiality of historic urban power-projection, as in Paris, plays out in a register of mass control, restricting and directing crowds but without attention to individuals. The materiality of the smart city, in contrast, observes both crowds and individuals. It shapes behaviour at a much more intimate and granular level. These two very different registers of urban materiality are both relevant to affective experiences of the urban in very different ways. In Johannesburg, the infrastructure of mobility is designed in a way that subverts urban interconnectedness and dynamism. It is echoed in the form of North American suburban cul-de-sacs and **gated communities** designed explicitly to enable the spatial exclusion of low-income and racialised populations. (Massey and Denton, 1998).

Despite also being conceptually related to urban visibility and control, the materiality of smart cities interrupts classic ideas about urban anonymity and the nature of social relations in crowded streetscapes. Going back to the late 19th and early 20th centuries, urban scholars noticed – sometimes lamenting, sometimes honouring – how cities were sites of a very different mode of social and cultural exchange, where people's everyday lives played out in public but without systematic observation. The shift to systematic algorithmic observation is, in some ways, a kind of return to small-town cultural dynamics in big-city concepts, unmaking urban invisibility, for better or worse.

As in the case of worship at this chapter's outset, these kinds of choices about material urban design, technology, and social control contribute to cultural domains as well. In Apartheid-era South Africa, racist beliefs about the 'natural' separation of racialised groups were reinforced by the deep divisions engraved in the landscape. In emerging 'smart' landscapes of widespread passive observation, beliefs about what kinds of actions should be kept strictly private or secret are likely to evolve. The shared community values that emerge from dwelling in different material environments inevitably respond to these socio-physical constraints. In the South African instance, the deep separation between communities at the city-scale is repeated in a discounting of the need for public parks and a normative expectation of strongly delineated public and private spaces. At the scale of the individual home, for example, electric fences and razor wire topped walls have become the normal and expected way to surround middle-class lawns in historically white neighbourhoods of Johannesburg (Jürgens and Gnad, 2002).

Advocates for a 'materialities turn' (i.e. beyond a singular materiality) see the material world through a pluralist lens. For these scholars, materiality is not an excuse to relegate the affective or experiential to second-tier status. In a certain sense, recent scholarship in materialities seeks to synthesise the 'thing-ness' of geography with the critiques of the cultural turn (Lorimer, 2013). The plurality that Lorimer highlights is not just **ontological** (that there are different kinds of spatial or material 'things') but also **epistemological**. Lorimer argues that we see different modes or registers of the material from different perspectives. Distinctive politics or agendas highlight specific ways of being material. Thus, the relationship between human perspective and the physical world is a reciprocal (or even perhaps **dialectical**) one (Kaika, 2006, Bumpus, 2011).

Summary

- Following the cultural turn, geographers were keen to 're-materialise' their cultural research by emphasising the importance of the material world.
- There was a plurality of research as a result, investigating different elements and aspects of the material.
- Eventually studies looked at the relationship between the material and the immaterial, rather than stressing one or the other.

Conclusion

If the call for study of materiality was a corrective, the move towards materialities is about an explicit expansion of the perspectives that fall under the rubric of materiality. One way of noticing the success of this project is that many scholars who are not focused on materiality/ies *per se* are nonetheless addressing questions of the relationship between meaning-making and the material. Attention to the relationship between registers of the material, meaning, and politics are increasingly centred within the discipline.

For example, scholars in the Black geographies tradition explicitly trace how Black culture emerges in relationship with material landscapes (McKittrick and Woods, 2007, Ogundiran and Saunders, 2014, Bledsoe et al., 2017), while geographers focused on Indigenous epistemologies increasingly discuss alternative materialities to those foregrounded by settler-colonial **modernity** (Larsen, 2016, Radcliffe, 2018). Scholars in these subdisciplines emphasise how shared cultural experiences lead to both distinctive kinds of meaning-making within the landscape and distinct relations of power. Black geographers, for example, note how meaning-making is a strategy of resistance for communities without the power to shape the physical landscape directly (Allen et al., 2019). Geographers focused on Indigenous knowledge, in contrast, often highlight how the material world can be credited with more agentic power than in classic settler-colonial approaches to geography, reframing human action and meaning-making as more reactive to the 'actions' of physical landscapes (Gordillo, 2021).

While this chapter has focused on illustrations of the materialities agenda in cities, geographers have taken on a wide array of topics through this lens. Those who study place and place-making increasingly take a pluralist view of the registers of materiality, insisting that what matters about the material is the different meanings that different constituencies make of it (Martin and Pierce, 2023). Studies of topics including nationhood (Merriman and Jones, 2017), the urban (Latham and McCormack, 2004), maritime regions (Steinberg, 2013), human-animal relations and post-humanism (Whatmore, 2006), theatre performance (Rogers, 2017), and energy economies (Forget and Bos, 2022) have been framed through a materialities lens. The relationships between affective experience and the material in human geography are increasingly explicitly addressed in geographical scholarship.

Thinking of materialities as registers, practices, or perspectives rather than somehow different kinds of physical objects emphasises the approach of this body of work. Physical things matter, but they matter in relation with ongoing processes of observation and meaning-making.

Scholars of materialities attend to both the material and the socio-cultural processes that produce meaning. In doing so, they draw attention to how the material world is also an interpretive one.

Discussion points

- Why do you think re-materialising cultural geography was a concern for scholars at the end of the 1990s?
- Why do you think it is important to speak of materialities rather than materiality?
- Aside from urban infrastructure, can you think of other forms of contemporary materialities which are important for the cultural geographer to study?
- Can you think of some examples of the ways in which material and immaterial elements combine to produce an understanding of particular cultural practices?

References

Allen, D., Lawhon, M., and Pierce, J. (2019). Placing race: on the resonance of place with black geographies. *Progress in Human Geography* 43(6): 1001–1019.

Barnett, C. (1998). The cultural turn: fashion or progress in human geography? *Antipode* 30(4): 379–394.

Bledsoe, A., Eaves, L. E., and Williams, B. (2017). Introduction: black geographies in and of the United States South. *Southeastern Geographer* 57(1): 6–11.

Bumpus, A. G. (2011). The matter of carbon: understanding the materiality of tCO_2e in carbon offsets. *Antipode* 43(3): 612–638.

Cresswell, T. (2012). *Geographic Thought: A Critical Introduction*. Chichester: Wiley.

Forget, M., and Bos, V. (2022). Harvesting lithium and sun in the Andes: exploring energy justice and the new materialities of energy transitions. *Energy Research & Social Science* 87: 102477.

Gordillo, G. (2021). The power of terrain: the affective materiality of planet Earth in the age of revolution. *Dialogues in Human Geography* 11(2): 190–194.

Harvey, D. (2005). *Paris, Capital of Modernity*. London: Routledge.

Jackson, P. (1997). Geography and the cultural turn. *Scottish Geographical Magazine* 113(3): 186–188.

Jackson, P. (2000). Rematerializing social and cultural geography. *Social & Cultural Geography* 1(1): 9–14.

Jeffrey, A. (2019). Legal geography 1: court materiality. *Progress in Human Geography* 43(3): 565–573.

Jürgens, U., and Gnad, M. (2002). Gated communities in South Africa: experiences from Johannesburg. *Environment and Planning B: Planning and Design* 29(3): 337–353.

Kaika, M. (2006). Dams as symbols of modernization: the urbanization of nature between geographical imagination and materiality. *Annals of the Association of American Geographers* 96(2): 276–301.

Larsen, S. C. (2016). Regions of care: a political ecology of reciprocal materialities. *Journal of Political Ecology* 23(1): 159–166.

Latham, A., and McCormack, D. P. (2004). Moving cities: rethinking the materialities of urban geographies. *Progress in Human Geography* 28(6): 701–724.

Lees, L. (2002). Rematerializing geography: the 'new' urban geography. *Progress in Human Geography* 26(1): 101–112.

Lemon, A. (1991). Chapter 1: The Apartheid City. In *Homes Apart: South Africa's Segregated Cities*, ed. A. Lemon. Bloomington: Indiana University Press, 1–25.

Lorimer, H. (2013). Chapter 5: Materialities. In *The Wiley-Blackwell Companion to Cultural Geography* (1st edn.), eds. N. C. Johnson, R. H. Schein, and J. Winders. Chichester: John Wiley & Sons, Ltd., 32–34.

Martin, D. G., and Pierce, J. (2023). *How to Think About Cities*. Cambridge: Polity Books.

Massey, D., and Denton, N. (1998). *American Apartheid*. Cambridge, MA: Harvard University Press.

McKittrick, K., and Woods, C. (eds.) (2007). *Black Geographies and the Politics of Place*. Toronto: University of Toronto Press.

Merriman, P., and Jones, R. (2017). Nations, materialities and affects. *Progress in Human Geography* 41(5): 600–617.

Ogundiran, A., and Saunders, P. (2014). On the materiality of black Atlantic rituals. *Materialities of ritual in the Black Atlantic*, 1–27.

Philo, C. (2000). More Words, More Worlds: Reflections on the Cultural Turn and Human Geography. In *Cultural Turns/Geographical Turns: Perspectives on Cultural Geography*, eds. I. Cook, D. Crouch, S. Naylor, and J. Ryan. Harlow: Prentice-Hall, 26–53.

Radcliffe, S. A. (2018). Geography and indigeneity II: critical geographies of indigenous bodily politics. *Progress in Human Geography* 42(3): 436–445.

Rogers, A. (2017). Material migrations of performance. *Area* 49(4): 495–502.

Steinberg, P. E. (2013). Of other seas: metaphors and materialities in maritime regions. *Atlantic Studies* 10(2): 156–169.

Thrift, N. (2007). *Non-Representational Theory: Space, Politics, Affect*. London: Routledge.

Tuan, Y. (1977). *Space and Place*. Minneapolis: University of Minnesota Press.

Valentine, G. (2001). Whatever happened to the social? Reflections on the 'cultural turn' in British human geography. *Norsk Geografisk Tidsskrift-Norwegian Journal of Geography* 55(3): 166–172.

Whatmore, S. (2006). Materialist returns: practising cultural geography in and for a more-than-human world. *Cultural Geographies* 2006(13): 600–609.

Online materials

- For a discussion on the continuing legacies of apartheid urban infrastructure in Johannesburg, https://urbanage.lsecities.net/essays/johannesburg-mobility-and-transport
- The wider LSE Cities web site contains many more examples of the materiality of urban planning. See https://www.lse.ac.uk/Cities

Further reading

For a set of readings which argued for a return of materiality to cultural geography, see the following:

Jackson, P. (2000). Rematerializing social and cultural geography. *Social & Cultural Geography* 1(1): 9–14.

Lees, L. (2002). Rematerializing geography: the 'new' urban geography. *Progress in Human Geography* 26(1): 101–112.

Philo, C. (2000). More Words, More Worlds: Reflections on the Cultural Turn and Human Geography. In *Cultural Turns/Geographical Turns: Perspectives on Cultural Geography*, eds. I. Cook, D. Crouch, S. Naylor, and J. Ryan. Harlow: Prentice-Hall, 26–53.

27 Travel and tourism

J.J. Zhang and T.C. Chang

Introduction

Tourism is arguably one of the world's largest industries in terms of revenues generated and people employed. It is an economic development option sought by many countries, particularly in the Global South. Tourism is also an inherently geographical phenomenon in the way it 'makes places' across multiple geographic scales. 'Place making' refers to the process by which spaces are endowed with meaning, value and identity by different people. In the tourism context, the development of unremarkable spaces into tourist-friendly sites with amenities, **infrastructure** and attractions is an example of place making. We will be looking at the different actors, geographic scales and outcomes of tourism place making in this chapter.

A foundational concept in human geography is 'place' (Tuan 1977, and see Chapter 5). As evident in various chapters in this book, places have different meanings for different groups of people and are regarded as highly personal and experiential (Chapter 7). There are a variety of ways in which spaces are converted into meaningful places through subjective experiences – be it through human emotions (Chapter 24), consumption (Chapter 32), work (Chapter 33) or even social movements and activism (Chapter 53). Travel and tourism present another means through which places are developed, with a specific focus on leisure experiences, personal consumption and the provision of services. This chapter uses tourism and travel as a lens to explore place making in two distinct yet interconnected ways: by different *people* and across different *scales*.

Firstly, different people are involved in place making. According to Gillian Rose (1995: 88), 'place is something created by people, both individuals and in groups'. In tourism, the most obvious place makers are powerful groups such as government authorities, property developers and business operators who make places by transforming landscapes and developing infrastructure for commercial purposes. Apart from them, individuals are also able to engage in place making through their emotional attachments or positive connections to spaces. Rose explains this connection using the concept of 'identity'. She argues that the 'meanings given to a place may be so strong that they become a central part of the people experiencing them' (Rose 1995: 88). Hence, for example, through active participation and on-site experiences, individual tourists may acquire strong impressions of a place they visit, transforming the formerly alien site into a locale of highly personal encounters and memories.

Secondly, tourism place making occurs across different geographic scales from local to national to global. Tourists and residents most often witness tourism at the local scale, for example in the

DOI: 10.4324/9780429265853-32

way amenities are created in particular locales for them or when problems emerge at specific sites. Tourism development also occurs at the city level. The development of historic precincts and neighbourhoods like Chinatowns as urban attractions are examples. Developments occur at the national scale too, particularly when tourism projects impact entire countries and regions. An example is the development of transportation networks that connect people across a nation. Finally, at the global level, we often think of tourism as operating across national borders when countries collaborate to develop or market a trans-national project (for example, a national park shared by several countries).

This chapter begins by looking at tourism and place making. We identify five ways in which tourism contributes to place making at the local and urban scales. It is important to note that different actors engage in place making, although it is often assumed that government planners and the private sector are most dominant. The second section looks at the politics and power relations inherent in tourism particularly at the national and trans-national scales. How places and spaces are shaped by tourism is a highly politicised process depending on the power relations between different stakeholders. The chapter ends on a more hopeful note as we contemplate how tourism knowledge may be 'put to work' in the pursuit of responsible consumption, social transformation and a more sustainable future.

Tourism and place making

As a planning concept, the term 'place making' first emerged as an urban development strategy in the 1990s, aimed at improving the quality of city design through feedback from people who live, work, and visit cities (Friedmann 2010). In tourism, place making has been embraced in destination planning, management and marketing, as a way to connect people with places, and to ensure repeat visitation. We identify five ways in which tourism contributes to place making:

- Placemaking
- Place-making
- Place making using tangible and intangible elements
- Creative placemaking
- Place making and marketing

Tourism geographer Alan Lew (2017) provides a key distinction between 'placemaking' and 'place-making'. While the former refers to large-scale, often costly, intentional planning of tourist destinations by governments and private enterprises (e.g. development of airports and mega attractions), the latter includes organic, bottom-up development by the lay-person (e.g. setting up an eatery, organising an event or outdoor market as a way to attract visitors). Placemaking creates 'safe, known, predictable, familiar' spaces catering to mass tourists, whereas place-making promises a sense of 'risk, uncertainty, surprise, escape' appealing to alternative travellers (Lew 2017: 451). Very often, however, most tourist destinations offer a combination of both forms of place making.

Examples of tourism placemaking and place-making abound each Christmas in Singapore. Every year, the Singapore Tourism Board works with the Orchard Road Business Association

Figure 27.1
Christmas at Orchard Road, Singapore. Note the decorative buntings and Christmas motifs, along with blooming landscape of trees and flowers, all of which are part of the tourism placemaking of Orchard Road

Source: Photo credit: T.C. Chang

to organise a Christmas light-up event in the Orchard Road retail strip (Figure 27.1). In 2021, the event was called 'Christmas on a Great Street' and lasted from November 2021 to early January 2022. Multi-coloured lights, baubles and decorations festoon public walkways, street furniture and roadside trees; privately owned buildings are also decorated to add to the festive atmosphere. Each Christmas event takes months to prepare, and private enterprises are tapped for sponsorships. The highly planned and well-funded annual event is a classic case of tourism placemaking – catering to mass markets and showcasing Singapore as a **cosmopolitan** destination. By contrast, neighbourhood illuminations may be regarded as counter examples of place-making. In suburban neighbourhoods where the majority of Singaporeans reside, a few resident committees and private individuals have started their own light-up events catering to children and families. Despite the lack of publicity and modest funds, these events have also earned praise for injecting festivity to suburban environments.

Tourism also contributes to place making through 'tangible' and 'intangible' means. By 'tangible', we refer to planning efforts that leverage the material components of place such as buildings, street furniture and amenities (what is often called 'hardware'). On the other hand, intangible elements include non-material dimensions such as events, street life, histories and cultures ('software'). While developing infrastructural hardware will not necessarily inject life and soul to a place, introducing software alone cannot overcome tangible shortcomings. Both tangible and intangible elements must be harnessed to attract tourists and tourism investments. The most successful tourist sites often combine both.

Let us take the example of the Taj Mahal. As a site visited by some 7–8 million visitors annually, the Taj Mahal's appeal lies in its mix of tangible elements of architecture and sumptuous gardens as well as its intangible histories and legends. Built by the first Mughal Emperor in the seventeenth century in memory of his wife, the monument of love is famous for its gleaming Makrana white marble and the legends surrounding its construction, royal romance and the 'hidden' burial sites of the emperor and empress. The place making of Taj Mahal is therefore a comingling of tangible and intangible elements, producing one of the world's foremost tourist attractions.

The relationship between tourism and local cultures brings us to 'creative placemaking'. The term creative placemaking was coined by the U.S. National Endowment for the Arts in a 2010 report encouraging arts and culture as a means to develop places and communities (Markusen and Gadwa, 2010). It is defined as a planning practice that unites the public, private, non-profit sectors and local community to shape the character of a place through arts and cultural activities. There are two spatial manifestations of creative tourism placemaking. The first involves the development of creative zones. In China, for example, creative clusters like Beijing's 798 Zone, Shanghai's M50 (Figure 27.2) and Guangzhou's 1850 Creativity Zone have been populated by non-mainstream artists since the 2000s and are extremely popular with visitors (Ning and Chang, 2022). Originally a process of place-making where artists informally occupy defunct factory spaces and disused industrial sites, many zones are today managed and marketed by property developers with links to the municipal government. Their popularity with young trendy tourists interested in arts and lifestyle has soared over time.

A second dimension in creative placemaking turns the focus on the tourist. Here, the emphasis is not so much on governments, private sector or cultural enterprises creating places, but on travellers taking charge of their own activities and cultural experiences (Richards, 2020). By enrolling themselves in a painting or culinary class, or talking to a museum curator, tourists are able to make places through pro-active immersions. Richards (2020: 4) explains the nexus between creativity, place-making and co-creation in the following way: 'A placemaking perspective on creative development has important implications for tourism. Tourists become essential actors in the co-creation of place, re-negotiating meanings of place that attract them'. By seeking

Figure 27.2
Shanghai's M50 district, Shanghai, China

Source: Luciano Mortula/Alamy

immersive participation in a place, the individual traveller establishes meaningful contact with the local community thereby enhancing their affinity with a place.

The emphasis on individual travellers casts the spotlight on the agentic powers of tourists. Place making is not just the domain of planners, enterprises and local service providers no matter how impactful they might be but also within the control of individuals. Seen in this light, place making can be understood as a personalised process in which travellers negotiate physical environments wherever they might be, to create meaningful experiences for themselves. Indeed 'people never simply visit places but are always actively shaping and making these places'; tourists are more than just 'viewing subjects' but also 'doing subjects' (Thurlow and Jaworski, 2014: 459). Through action and bodily movements – taking photographs, talking to a shopkeeper, sampling a local delicacy – spaces are invested with meaning and personal memories.

A final link between tourism and place making revolves around marketing and media **representations**. Even before one visits a city or country, a place might already be 'made' in a person's mind. Popular marketing campaigns like '100% Pure New Zealand' and 'Malaysia Truly Asia' or city-specific slogans like 'Let's Do London' are more than just publicity statements. In many ways, tourism marketing is suggestive of a place and its people and invites prospective travellers to 'buy into' the promises of the destination (Lew, 2012). A two-way place making process is at work here; while marketers 'make places' through conjuring images of fun, beauty and vibrancy, individuals 'place make' through their own powers of projection and imagination. As much as place making is in the hands of planners and marketers, it also resides in the hearts and minds of travellers who can endorse or reject these marketing claims. Acknowledging the dual-nature of place making yields a more holistic perspective on tourism development and traveller experiences.

Summary

- Geographers are well placed to study how 'empty spaces' become 'places of meaning and identity' through tourism. The essence of tourism development is place making.
- There are different ways in which tourism and place making intersect. Five are identified here, including 'placemaking', 'place-making', the use of tangible and intangible elements, 'creative placemaking' and 'tourism marketing'.
- While government planners and the private sector are often regarded as key actors in tourism placemaking, the power of individual actors (tourists) should not be underestimated. Travellers 'make or break' places through their activities, experiences and perceptions of destination areas. Having positive experiences in a location transforms a meaningless space into a site of memory and identification.

Political dimensions of travel and tourism

While the previous section sets the stage of us to understand how tourism landscapes are formed via place making processes involving multiple stakeholders, it also alludes to the fact that these processes are never neutral. Tourism is, after all, inherently political. Consider these questions for a start: Who has the **power** to decide how to develop a particular destination? For whom is a tourist destination developed? Who has the ability to travel, and why? To what extent do locals benefit from travel and tourism? Why does host-guest relationship turn sour at times? To address these critical questions and make constructive contributions to existing debates, we need to interrogate the political dimensions of the subject matter. In this section, we look broadly at two aspects: macro- and micro-politics.

Despite the proliferation of tourism research in the 1980s and 1990s, the political dimensions of travel and tourism were not widely recognised. Linda Richter and Michael Hall were among the first tourism scholars to advocate for a serious treatment of tourism studies and, more specifically, of the intrinsic political nature of tourism. In particular, Hall (1994: 4) laments that due to the perception of tourism as a frivolous affair, the political aspects of tourism are 'not willingly acknowledged by individuals or institutions involved in the decision-and policy-making process'.

Early works on the political dimensions of travel and tourism focus on the macro aspects of politics. For example, in her book *The Politics of Tourism in Asia*, Richter (1989: 3), argues for 'immediate attention' to the international political and policy implications of tourism. She discusses the effect of political dimensions of tourism on national policies in various Asian countries and is optimistic about the political potential of tourism in advocating for policies on environmental cooperation and peace initiatives. Citing examples from the opening of the People's Republic of China (PRC), Cuba and Vietnam to Western tourism, Richter (1989: 2) attests that '[t]ourist flows in general can be seen as a crude but reliable barometer of international relations among tourist-generating and tourist-receiving countries'.

Building on the empirical evidence to Richter's claim, Hall (1994) analyses international tourism policies of destinations like Australia, New Zealand, Japan, Taiwan, South Korea, China and the Philippines, shedding light on issues ranging from foreign diplomacy and trade, restrictions and restraints, to international recognition and political stability. Similarly, according to Robinson and Smith (2006: 2),

> Each nation, no matter what their position in any notional global political league table, promotes tourism as an actual and potential source of external revenue, a marker of political status that draws upon cultural capital, and as a means to legitimise itself as a **territorial** entity.

As such, tourism is not only an economically important industry but also a geopolitically useful tool in promoting state ideologies and gaining publicity and recognition in the global arena.

Diplomatic ties between countries involved in tourism exchanges can also be linked to local politics. Thirumaran (2007) provides an interesting example to justify his argument that tourism 'is embedded with power dimensions within the local and between the local and global forces' (p. 194). He relates the Malaysian cabinet's move to open the Zheng He Gallery in Malacca within a two-week notice, to coincide with the visit of a deputy minister for culture from China. Zheng He, also known as Cheng Ho, was a Chinese admiral of Muslim descent, born in 1371 in Yunnan, China. He was an ocean navigator famous for his diplomatic voyages between 1405 and 1433 to port cities, including Malacca, Malaysia. Such an unprecedented episode prompted Thirumaran to conclude that 'the extent to which the [Chinese] ethnic minorities are included in the national tourism landscape is dependent on domestic Malay politics and the economic importance of China' (2007: 206).

Macro-political dimensions of tourism are but one side of the coin. There is a need to understand the politics of tourism 'from below', 'which involves documenting everyday micro-situations and situated social practices' (Bramwell, 2006: 959). Such 'bottom-up' or post-structural analysis, which takes into consideration the power relations amongst different stakeholders, as well as the resultant impacts on the tourism landscape, can be said to constitute the micro-politics of tourism.

Conflict between the tourism authority and locals over the representation of their **ethnicity** or culture is one of the ways in which micro-politics is played out. A good example of this power relation is provided by D'Arcus' (2000) discussion of the conflicts over ethnic tourism in Gallup, New Mexico, in the late 1960s and early 1970s. The American Southwest of Gallup was marketed as a 'Land of Enchantment' by the tourism authority, in a bid to create a National Indian Memorial Park. Such an attempt to create an enchanted landscape for tourists was resisted by a group of young Navajo activists - Indians Against Exploitation - who claimed that they had been objectified by tourism planners and that the touristic portrayal was not reflective of their disadvantaged socio-economic situation. Resistance was manifested through various material and representational efforts by the group: ranging from distributing leaflets at staged Indian ceremonial events questioning their 'authenticity', to organising boycotts and setting up alternative Indian arts and crafts markets and dance performances for tourists. As much as travellers possess agentic powers in place making processes (as earlier discussed), locals are also not passive actors at the losing end of cultural commodification. In Gallup, we clearly see locals as active performers and reflexive tourism subjects who were able to make use of tourism to construct and re-construct their identities.

Relationships between hosts and guests are not always cordial. According to Ashworth and Tunbridge (1990), urban tourist landscapes serve multiple functions such as entertainment, commercial and residential. For this reason, 'the power relations between various stakeholders provide an opportunity to look at cities as shared spaces' (Chang, 2000: 347), and a 'function of conflict and compromise' (Short, 1996: 168). Zhang and Kwong (2017) capture such interplay of micro-political forces in Sheung Shui, a Hong Kong border town and shopping haven popular amongst day-trippers from neighbouring cities in mainland China (Figure 27.3). The mainland Chinese travellers often take advantage of the stronger Yuan and cheaper prices to bulk purchase items like infant milk formula, diapers, supplements and other food items. Residents blame travellers for overcrowding, shortage of daily necessities and rental hikes. Angry protests were staged to show their hostility towards the Chinese shoppers. Interestingly, counter protests were also organised by some locals who alleged that protestors were simply 'naïve troublemakers' harbouring ill intentions that would 'sabotage Sheung Shui's development'. Indeed, while this example illustrates the 'exceeded social carrying capacity' of the border town, residents' actions are 'excellent examples of **embodied** geopolitics in tourism encounters' that should be read alongside anti-Chinese sentiments in Hong Kong (Zhang and Kwong, 2017: 197). Similar to the Gallup example, forays into the **performative** geographies of tourism and its stakeholders contribute to the literature on the politics of tourism by demonstrating the potential of individuals as unique political entities in the negotiation of their everyday identities.

Power relations among tourism stakeholders do not merely comprise opposing forces; there remain practices that elude rather than subvert or confront power. A limited but nevertheless important strand of research on state-trained tour guides serves as a good example. Instead of

Figure 27.3
Luggage and shopping belonging to mainland Chinese day-trippers outside a restaurant in the border town of Sheung Shui. Residents often complained about overcrowdedness, and overconsumption caused by the visitors

Source: Photo credit: J.J. Zhang

emphasising state's **hegemony** in tour guide training, writings informed by micro-political optics focus on the **agency** of the tour guides. A vivid case of negotiation by tour guides is discussed in Salazar's (2006) study of Tanzanian tour guides in the city of Arusha. During their training, tour guides 'are instructed, both implicitly and explicitly [on] how to use global **discourses** to represent and sell their natural and cultural heritage as authentically local' (p. 833). However, in reality, they do not follow the script strictly but creatively retell stories that subtly challenge the official narratives.

An important contribution of such an analysis of tourism politics is that it transcends taken-for-granted notions of state dominance in tourism policy-making (as adopted by a structural view), and the necessarily conflicting relationship between structure and agency (as often assumed by post-structural analysis). In contrast, it portrays the real politics behind the construction of discourses and knowledge by different actors in the alignment and negotiation of their interest with tourism policies. Such recognition of the complex power relations amongst tourism stakeholders is useful for a more nuanced understanding of tourism politics.

Beyond humans, things related to tourism are increasingly accorded 'actor status' (van der Duim, 2011) in emerging studies that argue that tourism objects are not merely representations of social and cultural meaning and can actively participate in tourism politics. More specifically, scholars contributing to this genre of work often analyse the sensorial and **affective** experiences mediated by the materialities of things associated with travel and tourism.

365

Take the Taiwanese island of Kinmen for example. Once a military outpost of the Kuomintang's (KMT) Nationalist Army after its forces retreated from mainland China in 1949 during the civil war with the Chinese Communist Party's People's Liberation Army (PLA), the island's defunct military infrastructures have become a valuable tourism resource. Battlefield heritage 'stuff' proves to be popular among tourists from mainland China who are now free to travel to the island. In exploring Kinmen's post-war material culture, Zhang and Crang (2016) go beyond conventional visual-centric analysis to experiment with what they call 'sensuous material-ism'. Specifically they elucidate how touristic things like household knives made from artillery shell cases, and an annual music festival advocating for peaceful cross-strait relations held in a defunct military tunnel carved out of granite, help to commemorate the island's battlefield past. Discussion shows that these things are 'full of life and energy in their ability to animate the object–human relationship' through interactions with tourists' senses and perceptions of peaceful cross-strait relations (Zhang and Crang, 2016: 421). By unpacking the 'political' from the vantage points of nations, individuals and things, we get a better sense of what tourism is and what it can do for humanity.

Summary

- Tourism is inherently political.
- The political dimensions of travel and tourism are often a complex interplay of macro- and micro-politics.
- Tourism is not only an economically important industry but also a geopolitically useful tool in promoting state ideologies and gaining publicity and recognition in the global arena.
- Embodied geopolitics in tourism encounters treat tourists and locals as unique political entities in the negotiation of their everyday identities.
- Tourism objects are not merely representations of social and cultural meaning and can actively participate in the tourism process.

Conclusion

In this chapter, we have demonstrated that tourism and travel provide windows for inter-preting a range of social, cultural, economic, political and spatial issues across different scales. It is apparent that tourism development is a double-edged sword. However, we want to end this discussion on a more positive note. Rather than merely analysing how various stakeholders or actors contribute to shaping the tourism landscape, it is important to con-sider what tourism knowledge can do for us. In other words, beyond asking what tourism is/means, we should also contemplate what it does/can do. We point to three possibilities by way of conclusion.

Firstly, social transformation. Recently, in an effort to move analysis away from those that investigate solely the negative impacts of tourism, scholars are beginning to refocus on the moral value of tourism and the benefits of travel for travellers themselves. Issues explored include tourism poverty among school children in affluent societies (Sedgley et al., 2012), the effect of tourism on travellers with autism (Sedgley et al., 2017) or visual impairment (Richards et al., 2010) as well as social tourism and well-being in later life (Morgan et al., 2015). Such studies ponder questions like the following: What can tourism do for people who are disadvantaged or marginalised? How can tourism lead to a more inclusive and compassionate society? Such research celebrates the moral worth of tourism and can potentially lead to positive social transformations.

Secondly, responsible consumption. Besides academics, tourism operators and non-government organisations have increasingly embraced the concept of responsible tourism. This form of tourism does not shy away from ethical questions pertaining to travel and tourism; instead, it confronts them. Proponents seek to educate tourists while at the same time support local communities and the natural environment. Take the Mumbai Slum Tours organised by Reality Tours and Travel (http://realitytoursandtravel.com/slum-tour.php), for example. The organisation runs educational tours with a maximum of six people at any one time and conforms to a no camera policy. Overall, 80 per cent of its profit is invested back into the community. Such tours aim to raise awareness and give something back to the community in which it works. In 2012, it was awarded a Responsible Tourism Award by Responsible Travel (https://www.responsibletravel.com/).

Finally, a more sustainable future. The issue of sustainability has been a mainstay in tourism research, especially those related to negative environmental impacts. The COVID-19 pandemic is said to have contributed to a 'reset' of the global tourism industry as destinations 'suffering' from overtourism and environmental damage were able to 'catch a breather'. With regard to nature, the simple solution is to keep tourists away from vulnerable environments. However, as Franklin (2011: 146) argues, keeping humans away 'may serve to reduce the personal connection to, or bonds with, these spaces and natures and thus their ultimate source of an effective political base that could preserve them against destruction'. So, how can tourism contribute to a more sustainable future? We propose that instead of leaving tourism out of the equation, we should come up with creative ways in which tourism can be part of a solution. A good place to start is a couple of questions we often ask students in our respective tourism classes: How can tourism contribute to each of the 17 Sustainable Development Goals (SDGs) set out by the United Nations? In what ways can we as travellers and consumers assist with these endeavours? So, perhaps we should be thinking more in plurality and endeavour to conceive creative, sustainable futures through a more kindred spirit of experimentation with tourism, rather than a fear of it (Franklin, 2011).

In all, as a response to the call for promoting an 'academy of hope in tourism enquiry' (Ateljevic et al., 2011), it is hoped that this chapter contributes in a small way in encouraging budding tourism geographers to work towards imagining hopeful futures of and for tourism. This important endeavour is itself a process of becoming and a project of humanity in the making.

Discussion points

- What do you consider to be the key geographical characteristics of tourism and travel?
- How does tourism contribute to 'place making' across different geographic scales?
- Who are the key actors involved in place making and tourism?
- Choose an example of a tourist destination in your home country or abroad. Introduce it to your peers and try to think of how power and politics may be manifested in the development and maintenance of the destination.

- In what ways can the concept of 'responsible tourism' contribute to a more sustainable future?
- Refer to the 17 Sustainable Development Goals (SDGs) set out by the United Nations (https://sdgs.un.org/goals). How can tourism contribute to each of these goals?

References

Ashworth, G. J., and Tunbridge, J. E. (1990). *The Tourist-Historic City*. London: Belhaven Press.

Ateljevic, I., Morgan, N., and Pritchard, A. (2011). Editors' Introduction: Promoting an Academy of Hope in Tourism Enquiry. In *The Critical Turn in Tourism Studies: Innovative Research Methodologies*, eds. I. Ateljevic, A. Pritchard, and N. Morgan. New York: Routledge, 1–8.

Bramwell, B. (2006). Actors, power, and discourses of growth limits. *Annals of Tourism Research* 33(4): 957–978.

Chang, T. C. (2000). Singapore's Little India: a tourist attraction as a contested landscape, *Urban Studies* 37: 343–366.

D'Arcus, B. (2000). The 'eager gaze of the tourist' meets 'our grandfathers' guns': producing and contesting the land of enchantment in Gallup, New Mexico. *Environment and Planning D: Society and Space* 18: 693–714.

Franklin, A. (2011). The Problem With Tourism Theory. In *The Critical Turn in Tourism Studies: Innovative Research Methodologies*, eds. I. Ateljevic, A. Pritchard, and N. Morgan. New York: Routledge, 131–148.

Friedmann, J. (2010). Place and place-making in cities: a global perspective. *Planning Theory and Practice* 11(2): 149–165.

Hall, C. M. (1994). *Tourism and Politics: Policy, Power and Place*. Chichester, New York: Wiley.

Lew, A. (2012). Geography and the Marketing of Tourism Destinations. In *The Routledge Handbook of Tourism Geographies*, ed. J. Wilson. London and New York: Routledge, 181–186.

Lew, A. (2017). Tourism planning and place making: place-making or placemaking? *Tourism Geographies* 19(3): 448–466.

Markusen, A., and Gadwa, A. (2010). *Creative Placemaking*. Washington: National Endowment for the Arts. https://www.arts.gov/sites/default/files/CreativePlacemaking-Paper.pdf

Morgan, N., Pritchard, A., and Sedgley, D. (2015). Social tourism and well-being in later life. *Annals of Tourism Research* 52: 1–15.

Ning, Y., and Chang, T. C. (2022). Production and consumption of gentrification aesthetics in Shanghai's M50. *Transactions of the Institute of British Geographers* 47(1): 184–199.

Richards, G. (2020). Designing creative places: the role of creative tourism. *Annals of Tourism Research* 39(2): 102922. https://doi.org/10.1016/j.annals.2020.102922

Richards, V., Pritchard, A., and Morgan, N. (2010). (Re)envisioning tourism and visual impairment. *Annals of Tourism Research* 37(4): 1097–1116.

Richter, L. K. (1989). *The Politics of Tourism in Asia*. Honolulu: University of Hawaii Press.

Robinson, M., and Smith, M. (2006). Politics, Power and Play: The Shifting Contexts of Cultural Tourism. In *Cultural Tourism in a Changing World: Politics, Participation and (Re)presentation*, eds. M. Smith and M. Robinson. Buffalo, NY: Channel View Publications, 1–18.

Rose, G. (1995). Place and Identity: A Sense of Place. In *A Place in the World? Places, Cultures and Globalization*, eds. D. Massey and P. Jess. Milton Keynes: Open University/Oxford University Press, 88–106.

Salazar, N. B. (2006). Touristifying Tanzania: local guides, global discourse. *Annals of Tourism Research* 33(3): 833–852.

Sedgley, D., Pritchard, A., and Morgan, N. (2012). Tourism poverty in affluent societies: voices from inner-city London. *Tourism Management* 33: 951–960.

Sedgley, D., Pritchard, A., Morgan, N., and Hanna, P. (2017). Tourism and autism: journeys of mixed emotions. *Annals of Tourism Research* 66: 14–25.

Short, J. (1996). *The Urban Order: An Introduction to Cities, Culture and Power*. Cambridge: Blackwell Publishers.

Thirumaran, K. (2007). The Politics of Tourism: Ethnic Chinese Spaces in Malaysia. In *Tourism and Politics: Global Frameworks and Local Realities*, eds. P. M. Burns and M. Novelli. Oxford: Butterworth-Heinemann, 193–210.

Thurlow, C., and Jaworski, A. (2014). 'Two hundred ninety-four': remediation and multimodal performance in tourist placemaking. *Journal of Sociolinguistics* 18(4): 459–494.

Tuan, Y. F. (1977). *Place and Space: The Perspective of Experience*. Minneapolis: University of Minnesota Press.

Van der Duim, V. R. (2011). Tourism, Materiality and Space. In *The Critical Turn in Tourism Studies: Innovative Research Methodologies*, eds. I. Ateljevic, A. Pritchard, and N. Morgan. New York: Routledge, 149–163.

Zhang, J. J., and Crang, M. (2016). Making material memories: Kinmen's bridging objects and fractured places between China and Taiwan. *Cultural Geographies* 23(3): 421–439.

Zhang, J. J., and Kwong, Y. M. (2017). Reconceptualising host-guest relations at border towns. *Annals of Tourism Research* 66: 196–199.

Online materials

- Place making projects in the U.S.A. by 'Projects for Public Spaces' (PPS) https://www.pps.org/
- Tourism and place making in Singapore occurs in two particular sites: cultural precincts and lifestyle precincts https://www.stb.gov.sg/content/stb/en/about-stb/what-we-do/placemaking.html
- Archive of publications by Tourism Concern, a British NGO that campaigned for ethical tourism development from 1988 to 2018 https://travindy.com/2019/02/the-tourism-concern-archive/
- A collection of stories, videos and podcasts by *The Straits Times* about marginalised and forgotten communities in Asia https://www.straitstimes.com/asia/weve-always-lived-here-yet-we-dont-belong

Further reading

Ateljevic, I., Pritchard, A., and Morgan, N. (eds.) (2011). *The Critical Turn in Tourism Studies: Innovative Research Methodologies*. New York: Routledge.
A more advanced but still accessible collection of essays offering insights into new approaches to the study of tourism.

Friedmann, J. (2010). Place and place-making in cities: a global perspective. *Planning Theory and Practice* 11(2): 149–165.
A classic essay that explores the terms 'place' and 'place-making' in the urban context, offering a range of examples from across the globe.

Lew, A. (2017). Tourism planning and place making: place-making or placemaking? *Tourism Geographies* 19(3): 448–466.
An introductory essay outlining the different ways in which tourism development and place making intersect.

Richards, G. (2020). Designing creative places: the role of creative tourism. *Annals of Tourism Research* 39(2): 102922.
An essay offering insights on what creative tourism entails and how creative attractions might be developed.

Richter, L. K. (1989). *The Politics of Tourism in Asia*. Honolulu: University of Hawaii Press.
A classic text arguing that tourism is inherently political, offering a range of examples across Asia.

Woon, C. Y., and Zhang, J. J. (2021). Subterranean geopolitics, affective atmosphere and peace: negotiating China-Taiwan relations in the Zhaishan Tunnel. *Geoforum* 127: 390–400.
An account of how elemental materialities and embodied geopolitics play a part in the reincarnation of a former military tunnel.

28 Religion

Orlando Woods

Introduction

Whilst geographical explorations of religion go back many years, the past three decades or so have witnessed a significant expansion in its scope. Alongside this expansion has been a forging of a uniquely geographical voice to issues that intersect with the domain of 'religion' or the supernatural world more generally. In many respects, this voice has been shaped by, and has thus come to reflect, broader shifts within geography and the social sciences that started to take root from the 1980s onwards. In terms of geography, the cultural turn represented a point of departure from earlier, Cartesian-inspired approaches to understanding the mapping of phenomena across **space**. With it there has been a more sustained engagement with the politics, **poetics**, and **power** that is embedded within 'the cultural'. In terms of the social sciences, the influence of prominent French social theorists like Michel Foucault, Henri Lefebvre, and Michel de Certeau saw more sustained theoretical engagement with the idea of 'space', particularly how exploring its (re)production might offer a subtle and more nuanced way in which social life might be analysed and understood. Engagements of this kind underpin the poststructural turn in social sciences, and with it the destabilisation of any pregiven, stable, or coherent categorisation of the world in favour of more open-ended, processual, and potentially ambiguous understandings instead (see Foucault, 1980). The emergence and expansion of the geographies of religion as a distinct subfield within the broader geographical enterprise is very much located at the nexus of these broader **epistemological** shifts. Indeed, as much as the evolution of the subdiscipline has been prompted by developments that might not, at first blush, have much to do with 'religion', so too have geographers increasingly adopted a more outward-looking orientation by engaging with debates from cognate disciplines.

These engagements reflect the ongoing maturation of the geographies of religion. Since the 1990s, there has been a perceptible move *away* from the areal mapping of religion in space, and an embrace of the religious reproduction of space by institutions, organisations, and individuals (after Kong, 1990). With this embrace, so too has scholarship looked to understand not just 'official' expressions of religion and religiosity but more discrete, 'unofficial' expressions as well. These are expressions that are inflected by, and often mutually constitutive of, the secular world. They might not, in other words, appear to have much to do with religion at first. And just as the analytical (in)distinctions between the 'religious' and the 'secular' have been blurred, so too has the role of each in the formation of individual subjects, citizens, and identities been reified anew. Indeed, how geographers have engaged with religion as an aspect of individual identity has undergone a dramatic transformation: from essentially ignoring it, to including it in the roster of

DOI: 10.4324/9780429265853-33

other identity categories (like **ethnicity**, **class**, age, nationality, and so on), to embracing how religion might wax and wane in response to its intersectional validity and negotiations throughout the spaces and places of daily life (Kong, 2001). Extending this line of thinking even further, some of the most progressive geographical scholarship of recent years has tried to explore and understand the (re)enchantment of society through materialist, **affective**, and non-/post-/**more-than-human** lenses (see also Chapter 7). I return to these shifts in the second section that follows. Before that, it is important to consider some of the key theoretical contributions of the geographies of religion to debates concerning the **social construction** of religion, secularity, and postsecularity (see also Chapter 73).

The social construction of religion, secularity, and postsecularity

Arguably one of the most distinguishing features of the geographies of religion is to view a variety of religious or supernatural phenomena through the theoretical lenses of space and place. Engaging Mircea Eliade's (1959) foundational distinction between sacred and profane space – whereby the sacred has certain innate qualities that manifest in the world as 'hierophanies' – geographers have sought instead to understand 'how place is sacralized' (Kong, 2001: 213). This in turn has led to sacred spaces – and the religious places that they tend to be associated with – to be seen not as distinct from the profane or secular spaces around them, but rather as relational spaces that are indexed to the sacralising qualities of the people, organisations, symbols, rituals, and other things and practices that are associated with them. In many cases, these associations have become to underpin the formation of 'officially' sacred places that are associated with a formalised presence and hierarchical forms of religious authority. In other cases, however, a more informal religious presence – such as the use of schools or hotel function rooms for the purposes of worship, for instance (Woods, 2019a; see Figure 28.1); or connecting to the spirit world through the séance (Holloway, 2006; Chapter 29) – might be seen to challenge or subvert these hierarchies, giving rise to spatial politics. These politics mostly arise from competition for resources – people (adherents), funding, space, symbolic meanings, and more – and how the outcomes of competition might both reveal, reify, or challenge majority versus minority group dynamics (Chidester and Linenthal, 1995, Kong and Woods, 2016). To manage these politics, the state sometimes plays a mediatory role; other times, it is civil society or politically motivated groups that intervene.

Whilst much empirical work has helped to explore the nuanced interactions, negotiations, and outcomes that emerge from the politics and poetics of sacred (and/or religion *in*) space, so too has it spurred a more theoretical shift in the geographies of religion. This shift has occurred over the past ten years or so and has resulted in critical interrogation of the assumptions that underpin any predetermined notion of what the 'religious' or the 'secular' might entail. In many respects, these shifts aim to get to the heart of how religion, secularity, and postsecularity are **socially constructed**, and what these constructions might tell us about the contemporary world. Typically, geographical contributions have explored the interdependent relationship between the categorical construct and the spatial construct through which it is brought to life. Offering a category-first perspective, Ivakhiv (2006: 169) points out that both the religious and the secular have been deployed as 'categories distinguishing certain things from others' and that

Figure 28.1
A church meeting in an informal space, Manila

Source: Photo credit: Roddy Mackay/Alamy Stock Photo

they should, therefore, by 'studied by geographers as ways of distributing particular kinds of significance across geographic space'. Reversing this logic and offering a space-first perspective, Knott (2005: 3, original emphasis) draws on the spatial theorisations of Henri Lefebvre (1991) to argue that space should be analysed as 'a *medium*, a *method*, and an *outcome*' of religious **reifica-tion**. Both perspectives, although distinct, have attuned geographical discourses to the vibrant theoretical potential that exists from bringing social constructs into conversation with spatial constructs.

Since then, work has helped to bring geographical understandings of space into mutually enriching conversation with bigger debates that have been animating the social scientific and humanistic study of religion. Notably, Wilford (2010, 2012) draws attention to the scalar con-tingencies of secularisation, arguing that its differentiating effects – a theoretical mainstay of the secularisation thesis (Chapter 71) – can create both opportunities and challenges for religious vitality when understood through a scalar lens. Drawing on Berger's (1967) notion of the sacred canopy, Wilford (2010: 339) instead offers a more fine-grained and spatially nuanced way of understanding how religious organisations have evolved from working under broad-based reli-gious authority (the sacred canopy) to 'working under countless sacred umbrellas in countless sacred archipelagos' according to the 'particular geographic scale and social level in question'. Subsequently, these ideas have been further developed by Tse's (2014: 202, original emphases) notion of 'grounded theologies', which are said to be

> **performative** practices of place-making informed by understandings of the transcendent. They remain *theologies* because they involve some view of the transcendent, including some that take a negative view towards its very existence or relevance to spatial practices; they are

grounded insofar as they inform immanent processes of cultural place-making, the negotiation of social identities, and the formations of political boundaries, including in geographies where theological analyses do not seem relevant.

What Tse (2014) argues here is that even the secular can be understood as a theological construct when interpreted through the grounded schema of theology. In his view, the transcendent is the lowest common denominator of humanity and is therefore the basic, place-based building block upon which any social construction of religiosity or secularity might unfold. Whilst it is undoubtedly a theoretically bold move to argue that the 'secular' is borne of the 'religious' (or the theological, or transcendent), others have pursued a more balanced approach to understanding how the secular and the religious interact and come to be mutually constitutive of each other across space and time. Notable in this regard has been della Dora's (2018) notion of 'infrasecular geographies', which revisits the idea of sacred space – the bedrock of the geographies of religion – and considers the traces of the secular that come to permeate sacredness over time. In her words, the notion of 'infrasecular geographies' is a 'spatial paradigm able to capture the complexity and materialities of multi-layered coexistences' and has therefore come to be 'characterized by the contemporaneous co-habitation and competition between multiple forms of belief and non-belief, as well as by hidden layers of collective religious subconsciousness which underpin contemporary Western European societies' (della Dora, 2018: 44). Infrasecular geographies embrace the idea that there might be multiple, overlapping, sometimes convergent, other times divergent, pathways that contribute to the social construction of phenomenon that might be understood as either religious or secular, and that our task as geographers is to be alive to the sedimented nature of spatial becoming.

A parallel seam of work has evolved alongside and in conversation with these theoretical innovations and has considered the spatial framing and extent of the idea of the 'postsecular' (see Chapter 73). Beyond generalising narratives of the resurgence of religion in ostensibly 'secular' public spheres, geographers have focussed on the specific spaces, practices, and **subjectivities** through which relationships between the 'religious' and the 'secular' are being worked out. Located primarily at the spatial scale of the city (Molendijk et al., 2010, Beaumont and Baker, 2011), geographers have drawn attention to the important role of faith-based organisations in offering care, welfare, and socio-spatial justice to the most marginal sections of society. Perhaps one of the defining themes in this body of work has been consideration of the negotiations and outcomes that emerge when religion comes into contact with other religious and secular actors. Theorised as 'postsecular rapprochement' (Cloke and Beaumont, 2012), the importance of unifying narratives to overcome religious-secular distinctions in the pursuit of ethical ideals and practical, material needs has been foregrounded. Through this, the contributions of geographers have problematised the assumption that many Western societies and cities are shifting from a secular to a postsecular modality and emphasised instead the spatial contingencies of when and where the religious and secular are co-produced and thus give rise to 'postsecular' formations (Williams, 2015, Gao et al., 2018, Cloke et al., 2019). To this end, research has focussed thematically on socio-spatially distinct and pressing issues concerning poverty, homelessness, drug and alcohol rehabilitation, and more (Williams et al., 2012). Within this, critical attention has also been given to the ethics of care and the experience of 'service-users' in faith-based welfare provision, with geographers contributing spatial perspectives to the ethics and politics of religious conversion (Woods, 2012, Jayne and Williams, 2020).

Much of the theoretical developments that have come to define the geographies of religion have been illustrated empirically through the study of how religion manifests in urban environments (see Chapter 26). In many respects, the study of religion in/and cities brings to light the social constructions of religion, the secular, and the postsecular most clearly. In Singapore, for example, Woods (2019a) has explored how the **neoliberal** inflections of urban space, coupled with an interventionist state, cause fast-growing Christian groups to embrace the market and to operate less as churches and more as businesses in order to secure access to space. Qian and Kong (2018a: 159) explore how a Buddhist monastery in Hong Kong is able to 'refashion' and 're-invent' itself by 'appropriating rationalities, values and logics normatively defined as "secular"' into its operating ethos. In many respects, work like this foregrounds the role of the state in determining the norms of religious engagement with society, and in some cases forcing religion to compete with ostensibly secular forces. These norms are wide-reaching and have, for example, been shown to extend to the subdomains of religion, such as schools (Kong, 2005, Qian and Kong, 2018b) and cemeteries (Gao et al., 2021). Uniting this work is a focus on Asian contexts, which, whilst being embraced with growing regularity by geographers, remains peripheral to the mainstream geographical enterprise. Continuing this trajectory in the years to come is, however, important if the full theoretical and empirical potential of geographic scholarship is to be achieved.

Summary

- Religion, secularity, and postsecularity are social constructs.
- Place is sacralised by people, objects, and organisations.
- Spatial politics emerge from competing or alternative methods of sacralisation.
- The state can determine the extent to which religion engages with society.

The embodied and affective dimensions of everyday religiosity and spirituality

Whilst the theoretical developments outlined above are wide-ranging in their impacts, a parallel trend has been to embrace the religious subject as the focus of analysis. Doing so has yielded a vibrant, and fast-growing, body of scholarship on the **embodied** and affective dimensions of everyday religiosity and spirituality. This scholarship can, in many respects, be seen as a response to Olson et al.'s (2013: 7; after Kong, 2010) lament that 'the implications of plurality and diversity of religious subjects are not always recognized within geographical work... Lived religion, public piety, and religious embodiment complicate our analyses, for they request a disassemblage of meta-religious categories and their assumptions'. Whilst this provocation has yielded various responses, notable is Sutherland's (2017) theoretical exposition of the religious subject, which is captured in his notion of 'theography'. Emphasising the reflexive, and thus contextually contingent, nature of religious belief and praxis, theography is a call for research to focus on how individuals face 'struggles over the content of theology, its effects on their spatial imagination, and their praxis' (p. 321). Foregrounding these struggles and effects can problematise pre-defined categories of distinction – the Christian as opposed to the Muslim, for example, or the Muslim/ private self as opposed to the secular/public self – and helps to flesh out the competing and often contradictory forces that contribute to religious meaning-making. In this vein, theography can be understood as a 'technique of the self that enables the subject to both dissent from and conform to religious hegemonies' (Sutherland, 2017: 322). By challenging hierarchies of religious or doctrinal authority, by destabilising categories of distinction, and by emphasising the messy realities of *lived* religion, a more accurate understanding of the religious subject can be forged.

These ideas have found most meaning and relevance in relation to Muslims navigating ostensibly secular public spheres. Recent decades have witnessed significant numbers of Muslims migrating to Australia, Europe, and North America, which in turn has contributed to the emergence of greater social complexity and the politicisation of (in particular, ethno-religious) identity. Some of the earlier work in this regard explored how Muslim women of South Asian descent living in the UK forge a British-Islamic identity that reflects the fact that they are caught between two cultures (Dwyer, 1999). The importance of this contribution is that it reveals how Islamic clothing – notably the veil – might be a 'powerful and overdetermined marker of difference' for young British Muslim women, for whom the embodiment of *both* Britishness and Islamicness can contribute to the 'reworkings of meanings' (Dwyer, 1999: 5) in the ever-shifting socio-cultural context of contemporary Britain. Building on this work, research has tended to focus on exploring minority Muslim groups, and how

> …piety and secularism, in particular, contain a spectrum of practices. In every case, identity categories are contingent on the meanings produced through local place. Studies of religion and identity in predominantly Muslim societies also involve studies of minority ethnic/religious identities in those places (whether of non-Muslim minorities or Muslim minorities within larger Muslim groups), something that is not a major strand of research in Anglophone geography.
>
> *Mills and Gökariksel, 2014: 906*

For minority Muslim groups, the **intersectionality** of their embodied identities is brought into stark relief through the negotiation of sometimes hostile public spheres. Within these spheres, they are forced to negotiate normative understandings of **gender**, **race**, and racism. In terms of gender, Gökariksel and Secor (2015) have explored the fluidity of gendered Muslim subject positions in relation to the evolution of the secular state. Drawing on research conducted in Istanbul, Turkey, they demonstrate how the evolution of a postsecular public sphere creates a 'gendered moral order of public space that positions devout headscarf-wearing women in a particular way within diverse city spaces where others may be consuming alcohol or wearing revealing clothing' (Gökariksel and Secor, 2015: 21). How Muslims negotiate alternative understandings of Muslimness can, in turn, provide insight into the 'integration of religious ways of being within a public arena shared by others who may practice different faiths, practice the same faith differently, or be non-religious in outlook' (ibid). In terms of race and racism, notable is Hopkins' (2020) work on Islamophobia in Britain, and how the suspicion of Muslims intersects with other forms of societal unease. The complexity of measuring, monitoring, and even studying Islamophobia rests on the fact that it is so often 'intertwined with debates about immigration and asylum, citizenship and belonging, and security and borders' (Hopkins, 2020: 584). This

Figure 28.2
A Tang-ki, or Taoist spirit medium, in a trance as she hosts a deity from the Taoist pantheon, Singapore

Source: Photo credit: Terence Heng

intersectional complexity means that religious identity can rarely be seen as separate from the corporeality of the individual to which it is attributed. Accordingly, religious identity becomes a relational construct that is asserted and retracted in close conversation with the space-times of everyday life.

Building on the idea that embodied ways of being can foreground the (re)negotiation of power in and through social life, research has, over the past 15 years or so, embraced the role of affect (see Chapter 24) in triggering and shaping the experience of sacredness (see Figure 28.2). Very much a response to Holloway's (2006) lament that geographies have hitherto overlooked the affective underpinnings of sacred experience, geographers have explored, for example, how the construction of sacred space can determine the extent of their 'affective capacity' (Finlayson, 2012: 1764), or how the affective underpinnings of religious belonging and **performances** might foreground the formation of (therapeutic) communities (Brace et al., 2006, Williams, 2016). Going further, affect has also been shown to trigger new forms of spiritual connection that push the boundaries of how 'religion' might manifest in space (Bartolini et al., 2017). In this vein, Woods (2019b), for example, considers how the sonic spaces that are created by roots reggae soundsystems can cause the locus of spirituality to emerge from within, thus causing the body to become more spiritually attuned, and spiritually aware, irrespective of the prescriptive matrix of religious doctrine or belief. As we can begin to see, affect has been studied as a resolutely spatial phenomenon with wide-ranging implications for our understandings of individual and collective religious subjectivities, and the theoretical parameters of the role and place of religion in the contemporary world.

Finally, some of the most progressive scholarship on the embodied and affective dimensions of everyday religiosity and spirituality has sought to destabilise the centrality of the human.

Drawing on the 'more-than-human' and 'post-human' turns in geography, and the associated search for more generative ways in which a religious or spiritual orientation might manifest in and to the world (Gergan, 2015, Wright, 2015), research has sought to move beyond 'religion' per se and instead explore more metaphysical, supernatural, and even superstitious forms of belief and experience. Notable in this regard is Holloway and Kneale's (2008) work on spectral geographies, and associated attempts to 'represent the unrepresentable'. Through an explicit focus on ghost-hunting, and **representations** of hauntings thereof, their work highlights the textual and material cues through which the supernatural might manifest. This emphasis on materiality can be seen to ground the ineffable in place, rendering it something that can be observed, analysed, and interpreted (see Chapter 29). Going further, Holloway (2010) draws on an empirical exploration of ghost tourism in the UK to demonstrate how the overlapping of **discursive**, affective, and material cues can lead to the creation of a sense of supernatural *possibility* that can 'momentarily transform space into something charged with the strange and anomalous' (p. 618). More than anything else, Holloway's work can be seen to draw attention to the paradoxes and limits of postsecularity by revealing the profound sense of artifice that under-pins **modern** enchantment. More hopeful is Gergan's (2015: 262) call for research to 'take seri-ously the **agency** of gods, spirits, and deities' if the more-than/post-human turn is to achieve its full epistemological potential. Calls like this, which develop from the premise that the sacred can be indexed to any form of 'space, place, object, human or nonhuman' (Gergan, 2015: 263), provide a suitable starting point from which a truly open-ended and post-humanist geography of religion might unfold.

Summary

- There are multiple and sometimes divergent understandings of the religious subject.
- Affect can trigger and shape the experience of sacredness.
- More-than-human and post-human understandings of religion seek to decentre the human in the analysis of religion.

Conclusion

More than anything else, this chapter has demonstrated how fluid the geographies of religion are, and how responsive they have been to shifts in geography, in cognate disciplines, and within the social worlds that they speak from and to. The ongoing viability of the geographies of religion is often indexed to the extent to which they can contribute to debates that might, at first blush, have little to do with 'religion' per se, but which speak to more generalisable concerns about space, place, community, identity, and, increasingly, the environment as well. Accordingly, as much as this entry has focussed on just two directions – theoretical and embodied – in which the geographies of religion have evolved, there are many more to consider as well. How the inter-sections of religion, space, and secularity continue to evolve in response to the **Anthropocene**, digital transformations, migration, and indeed public health crises like COVID-19 provide important indications of where the subdiscipline might – and indeed should – be heading.

Discussion points

- From your experience, what does a religious and/or sacred space look, feel, smell, and sound like?
- How might these characteristics change across 'officially' and 'unofficially' sacred spaces?
- What about religious and non-religious or secular spaces?
- What about public and private spaces?
- What might be the relationship between space and the religious body?
- How might being 'religious' complicate your understanding of yourself, or your identity?
- Why do you think the city is such an important analytic lens to understand the role of religion in the contemporary world?
- What about the digital?
- How might ideas of spirituality, the supernatural, or the superstitious manifest, or make themselves known to you, throughout your everyday life?

References

Bartolini, N., Chris, R., MacKian, S., and Pile, S. (2017). The place of spirit: modernity and the geographies of spirituality. *Progress in Human Geography* 41(3): 338–354.

Beaumont, J., and Baker, C. (eds.) (2011). *Postsecular Cities: Space, Theory and Practice*. London: Bloomsbury.

Berger, P. (1967). *The Sacred Canopy: Elements of a Sociological Theory of Religion*. New York: Doubleday.

Brace, C., Bailey, A., and Harvey, D. (2006). Religion, place and space: a framework for investigating historical geographies of religious identities and communities. *Progress in Human Geography* 30(1): 28–43.

Chidester, D., and Linenthal, E. (eds.) (1995). *American Sacred Space*. Bloomington: Indiana University Press.

Cloke, P., Baker, C., Sutherland, C., and Williams, A. (2019). *Geographies of Postsecularity: Re-Envisioning Politics, Subjectivity and Ethics*. London: Routledge.

Cloke, P., and Beaumont, J. (2012). Geographies of postsecular rapprochement in the city. *Progress in Human Geography* 37(1): 27–51.

della Dora, V. (2018). Infrasecular geographies: making, unmaking and remaking sacred space. *Progress in Human Geography* 42(1): 44–71.

Dwyer, C. (1999). Veiled meanings: young British Muslim women and the negotiation of differences. *Gender, Place and Culture* 6(1): 5–26.

Eliade, M. (1959). *The Sacred and the Profane: The Nature of Religion*. New York: Harcourt, Brace & World.

Finlayson, C. (2012). Spaces of faith: incorporating emotion and spirituality in geographic studies. *Environment and Planning A* 44: 1763–1778.

Foucault, M. (1980). *Power/Knowledge: Selected Interviews and Other Writings, 1972–1977*. New York: Pantheon.

Gao, Q., Qian, J., and Yuan, Z. (2018). Multi-scaled secularization or postsecular present? Christianity and migrant workers in Shenzhen, China. *Cultural Geographies* 25(4): 553–570.

Gao, Q., Woods, O., and Kong, L. (2021). The political ecology of death: Chinese religion and the affective tensions of secularised burial rituals in Singapore. *Environment and Planning E: Nature and Space*. DOI: 10.1177/25148486211068475.

Gergan, M. (2015). Animating the sacred, sentient and spiritual in post-humanist and material geographies. *Geography Compass* 9(5): 262–275.

Gökariksel, B., and Secor, A. (2015). Post-secular geographies and the problem of pluralism: religion and everyday life in Istanbul, Turkey. *Political Geography* 46: 21–30.

Holloway, J. (2006). Enchanted spaces: the séance, affect, and geographies of religion. *Annals of the Association of American Geographers* 96: 182–187.

Holloway, J. (2010). Legend-tripping in spooky spaces: ghost tourism and infrastructures of enchantment. *Environment and Planning D: Society and Space* 28(4): 618–637.

Holloway, J., and Kneale, J. (2008). Locating haunting: a ghost-hunter's guide. *Cultural Geographies* 15(3): 297–312.

Hopkins, P. (2020). Social geography II: islamophobia, transphobia, and sizism. *Progress in Human Geography* 44(3): 583–594.

Ivakhiv, A. (2006). Toward a geography of 'Religion': mapping the distribution of an unstable signifier. *Annals of the Association of American Geographers* 96(1): 169–175.

Jayne, M., and Williams, A. (2020). Faith-based alcohol treatment in England and Wales: new evidence for policy and practice. *Health & Place* 66: 102457.

Knott, K. (2005). *The Location of Religion: A Spatial Analysis*. London: Taylor and Francis.

Kong, L. (1990). Geography and religion – trends and prospects. *Progress in Human Geography* 14: 355–371.

Kong, L. (2001). Mapping 'new' geographies of religion: politics and poetics in modernity. *Progress in Human Geography* 25: 211–233.

Kong, L. (2005). Religious schools: for spirit, (f)or nation. *Environment and Planning D: Society and Space* 23(4): 615–631.

Kong, L. (2010). Global shifts, theoretical shifts: changing geographies of religion. *Progress in Human Geography* 34(6): 755–776.

Kong, L., and Woods, O. (2016). *Religion and Space: Competition, Conflict and Violence in the Contemporary World*. London: Bloomsbury.

Lefebvre, H. (1991). *The Production of Space*. Oxford: Blackwell.

Mills, A., and Gökariksel, B. (2014). Provincializing geographies of religion: Muslim identities beyond the 'West'. *Geography Compass* 8(12): 902–914.

Molendijk, A., Beaumont, J., and Jedan, C. (eds.) (2010). *Exploring the Postsecular: The Religious, the Political and the Urban*. Leiden: Brill.

Olson, E., Hopkins, P., and Kong, L. (2013). Chapter 1: Introduction – Religion and Place: Landscape, Politics, and Piety. In *Religion and Place: Landscape, Politics and Piety*, eds. P. Hopkins, L. Kong, and E. Olson. Dordrecht; Heidelberg; New York; London: Springer, 1–20.

Qian, J., and Kong, L. (2018a). Buddhism Co. Ltd? Epistemology of religiosity, and the re-invention of a Buddhist monastery in Hong Kong. *Environment and Planning D: Society and Space* 36(1): 159–177.

Qian, J., and Kong, L. (2018b). When secular universalism meets pluralism: religious schools and the politics of school-based management in Hong Kong. *Annals of the American Association of Geographers* 108(3): 794–810.

Sutherland, C. (2017). Theography: subject, theology, and praxis in geographies of religion. *Progress in Human Geography* 41(3): 321–337.

Tse, J. (2014). Grounded theologies: 'Religion' and the 'secular' in human geography. *Progress in Human Geography* 38(2): 201–220.

Wilford, J. (2010). Sacred archipelagos: geographies of secularization. *Progress in Human Geography* 34: 328–348.

Wilford, J. (2012). *Sacred Subdivisions: The Postsuburban Transformation of American Evangelicalism*. New York: NYU Press.

Williams, A. (2015). Postsecular geographies: theo-ethics, rapprochement and neoliberal governance in a faith-based drug programme. *Transactions of the Institute of British Geographers* 40 (2): 192–208.

Williams, A. (2016). Spiritual landscapes of Pentecostal worship, belief, and embodiment in a therapeutic community: new critical perspectives. *Emotion, Space and Society* 19: 45–55.

Williams, A., Cloke, P., and Thomas, S. (2012). Co-constituting neoliberalism: faith-based organisations, co-option, and resistance in the UK. *Environment and Planning A* 44(6): 1479–1501.

Woods, O. (2012). The geographies of religious conversion. *Progress in Human Geography* 36(4): 440–456.

Woods, O. (2019a). Religious urbanism in Singapore: competition, commercialism and compromise in
the search for space. *Social Compass* 66(1): 24–34.

Woods, O. (2019b). Sonic spaces, spiritual bodies: the affective experience of the roots reggae soundsys-
tem. *Transactions of the Institute of British Geographers* 44(1): 181–194.

Wright, S. (2015). More-than-human, emergent belongings: a weak theory approach. *Progress in Human
Geography* 39(4): 391–411.

Online materials

- The Religion in Place project site: https://web.archive.org/web/20230930135121/https://
religioninplace.org/blog/
- The Making Suburban Faith project site: https://makingsuburbanfaith.wordpress.com/
- The Sacred Sites in Contested Regions site: http://sacredplaces.huji.ac.il/
- The Immanent Frame: https://tif.ssrc.org/

Further reading

della Dora, V. (2018). Infrasecular geographies: making, unmaking and remaking sacred space. *Progress
in Human Geography* 42(1): 44–71.
A key text on the over-layering of sacralisation and desacralisation in the production of religious
spaces.

Kong, L. (2001). Mapping 'new' geographies of religion: politics and poetics in modernity. *Progress in
Human Geography* 25: 211–233.
A pioneering work on the new theoretical approaches towards religion, focusing on the making of
politics and poetics.

Kong, L. (2010). Global shifts, theoretical shifts: changing geographies of religion. *Progress in Human
Geography* 34(6): 755–776.
A more recent report on the development of geographies of religion against the backdrop of major
socio-spatial shifts.

Tse, J. (2014). Grounded theologies: 'Religion' and the 'secular' in human geography'. *Progress in Human
Geography* 38(2): 201–220.
A provocative essay arguing that the era of secularisation is always-already sacred. It uses the idea of
'grounded theologies' to investigate contemporary geographies of religion in a secular age.

Wilford, J. (2010). Sacred archipelagos: geographies of secularization. *Progress in Human Geography* 34:
328–348.
Unpacking the relationships between space and secularisation by highlighting scale as a key perspective.

29 Spectral geography

Julian Holloway

Introduction

In 1971, two young boys, Leslie and Colin Robson, were digging in the garden of their council house on Rede Avenue in the market town of Hexham in the northeast of England. They dug up two small stones, about 6 cm in diameter, with roughly carved faces on them (see Figure 29.1). Intrigued by what they believed to be ancient artefacts, they brought them inside the house with the intention of sending them to an expert. Then things started to get weird: the 'heads' seemed to move of their own accord and faced different ways to which they were left; glass objects in the house were smashed against the walls of the home; and one of the boys of the Dodd family next door has his hair pulled in the middle of the night by some unknown assailant. That night his mother witnessed the terrifying sight of a monstrous creature – half human and half sheep and standing on two legs – escaping from the house. The heads were sent to Dr. Anne Ross at the University of Southampton, an expert on Celtic artefacts. She left the stone heads in her home. Within the week she and her children were horrified by the visit of a weird cryptid – a humanoid biped with the muzzle of a dog or wolf.

The previous occupant of the Robson's house, Des Craigie, who worked for a concrete processing firm, stepped forward to claim he made the heads for his daughter. He fashioned something similar on the invitation of Dr. Ross. Were they Craigie's daughter's playthings? Some claim that they were concrete, whilst others claim they were made of local sandstone. It is alleged that Dr Ross told the Robson family that they were the products of a Romano-British shrine or burial ground upon which the house was built. The house was also very near a slaughterhouse which led some to speculate that the monsters witnessed were weird psychological projections resulting from the proximity of living to a place of death. Or, as one local claimed, Mrs Dodd had seen an inebriated reveller who had somehow broken into the slaughterhouse and dressed themselves with dead sheep parts. Others argued the were-sheep and were-wolf were cursed creatures summoned by the stones. Speculation as to the origin of the heads, the supernatural encounters, and the location of the house on Rede Avenue continued (in fact, to this day). After seemingly moving from place to place, the last known location of the heads was a council office in Hexham. Yet this has never been confirmed. It seems the heads are lost (see Screeton, 2012 for more).

In the world of paranormal investigation, this tale is very well-known and very much resides in the 'unexplained' file. Yet, what does this story have to do with geography and what questions does it raise? Monsters, cursed stones, poltergeist activity, the **agency** of ancient burial

DOI: 10.4324/9780429265853-34

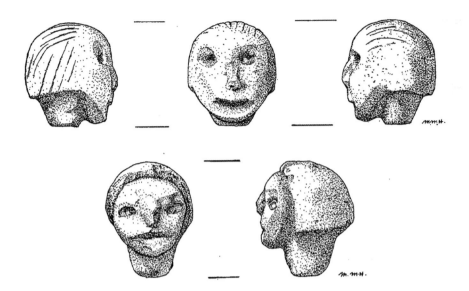

Figure 29.1
The stone heads from Hexham

Source: Ross, A. (1973). Some new thoughts on old heads. *Archaeologia Aeliana* 5(1): 5

grounds – surely this is beyond the scope of human geography? Well, some human geographers would disagree. First, this story tells us that the very stuff – the materiality – that makes up a place can affect us, as well as revealing that the meanings and emotions that material objects evoke are not always unambiguous – or even fully decipherable. Indeed, does the story hint at other alternative, stranger, sometimes more disturbing, meanings of place? Moreover, can an object or a place evoke, or even retain, memories and meanings that can be reanimated or re-emerge many years later?

Second, the histories of a place – often central to our experience of a place – can become forgotten, obscured, written over, or lost. Can these hidden histories of place suddenly appear in the present – for example, a forgotten Romano-British ritual site under a council house? Can they be revived and brought back into the present, through for example, a material object? Indeed, are the histories of a place, and the memories associated with it, always clearly remembered, and recorded, if at all? Or are these histories sometimes only vaguely there in our experience of a place – half-remembered and hazy recalls of what a place means but still acting in some way on the present?

Third, this story tells us of strange creatures and monstrous entities that certainly exist for those who witness them and often trouble investigators to find 'rational' and 'natural' explanations for them. These supranormal beings also point to wider concerns about, and importantly the fascination with, the very existence of animals, both recorded and seemingly imagined, that circulate through both popular culture and, as we shall see, science. Overall, then, the Hexham Heads story points towards the potential for different, disturbing, ambiguous, and even supernatural geographies and senses of place. It is but one example of the possible shadow-side to the things, spaces, and places we make our lives through. What might these weird and occluded

BOX 29.1
SPECTRAL GEOGRAPHY

A spectral geography is a place or space that is produced by something that is both there (present) but also not there (absent). Geographers have become increasingly interested in how time – the present, past, and future – can be folded into space and place, and how this folding disturbs and *haunts* what we take as settled and given in space and place. Hence geographers have analysed how geography is haunted such that place and space becomes disturbingly less stable, less fully here and now (by memories and past events, for example). Yet, geographers are also interested in the social and cultural geographies of ghosts, the paranormal, and those who enjoy or believe in the supernatural (for example, in popular culture or through spirituality). Both approaches can be deemed part of spectral geography.

events and phenomena do to our sense of **space** and place – and indeed, the analyses of human geography itself? If we were to write a full-blown geographical account of the Hexham Heads story and seek to build conceptual analyses in answer to the multiple questions it raises, it would be labelled part of spectral geographies (see Box 29.1).

Spectral geographies: an overview

The aim of this chapter is to explore how human geographers have sought to answer and explore the sorts of questions the Hexham Heads story raises. So, what do you think of when you hear the word spectre or ghost? A ghost is something seemingly insubstantial, less than solid – a bump in the night, a blurred figure or vision, a strange sensation, something glimpsed out of the corner of your eye, or something only partially heard – but when it appears it affects you in some way – it scares, disturbs, challenges, intrigues, or makes you wonder (was it a trick of the light? An over-active imagination?) In short, ghosts and spectres *haunt* us. Human geographers have used the figure of the ghost and the process of haunting to (re)think how we make sense of and experience space and place. Theoretically, geographers and other social scientists talk of ghosts in terms of *presence* – something that is there – and *absence* – something that is not there. And this is where many argue that ghosts and haunting have their analytical value and power. The ghost or the spectre is something that is there but not there at the same time: it is substantial enough to affect us and our emotions, but never substantial enough to be fully grasped, captured, or trapped (unless you count those devices used in the movie Ghostbusters, of course). Therefore, the ghost is a figure of presence *and* absence at the same time. Think about it this way: are places fully here and now? Is what you hear, see, touch, or smell in a place all there is to a place or space? Or are they formed through vestiges, what we might call traces, of something that has gone before. What is present in a place is always accompanied – one could say haunted – by what is not there or possibly what has been forgotten. In this way, the presence of place is always made through it's absences – what is missing, what has been overlooked – and these absences form the presence and present of place and space.

The ghost therefore does something to the presence and present of a place through haunting. Thus, ghosts and haunting do something to the *time* or **temporality** of a place. The ghost that haunts folds time in on itself: the past haunts the present, and even the future. Yet there is something specific, even peculiar, about the ghost that haunts space and place. You might be thinking that all places and spaces have their histories and memories folded back into them as we experience them in the present. And you'd be right. Think of the statues that stand seemingly proud in most urban centres, silently speaking to the history of a city or nation's great achievements. Are these ghosts? Do they haunt the present through their material presence when we know clearly who they are and what they did? The answer to this question would probably be no they are not ghosts. For a place to become haunted, these statues would have to disturb or unsettle the present in some way. Or, what these figures did in the past needs to have been obscured or forgotten. Or, as is often the case in recent years, their history would be made present today as an injustice from the past.

Take for example, the pulling down of the statue of Edward Colston in Bristol in 2020 by Black Lives Matter (BLM) protestors in the UK (Figure 29.2). For these protestors Colston

Figure 29.2
The empty plinth where the statue of Edward Colston once stood in Bristol

Source: Photo credit: Ben Birchall/Alamy

was a presence in the material memorialisation of the city's past that had made absent his involvement in the slave trade; his history and the social and colonial injustices he performed haunted the present. For the BLM protestors his ghost needed to be banished – a banishment that simultaneously brought to the present the forgotten histories of Bristol's part in the slave trade that should not be carried forth into the future. Colston then haunted and disturbed Bristol's past, present, and future. Those who decried his statue's unceremonious dumping in the harbour as vandalism argued that this past was irrelevant, a thing of the past, or not even remembered – as if the ghost never existed and the place was not haunted. Yet in their complaints, we could say they were as haunted by these ghosts as the protestors, but they sought to deal with the ghost in a different way – by trying to ignore it or even claiming it did not exist.

One could say *before* this protest, Colston's presence and actions presented in material form – and this is arguably the same for many such statues – were only a vaguely remembered, if not forgotten and ignored. Hence, his presence was not a fully substantial memory of place for the many people who passed him going about their daily lives. Yet crucially, as De Certeau (1984: 108) puts it, 'haunted places are the only ones people can live in'. For some this ghost became an issue to deal with – for them, a spectre haunted the past and future of Bristol's place identity. Through the emergence of a global protest movement concerned with racial injustice, the simultaneous absence *and* presence of this statue impacted on their lives and required action. Therefore, the power of ghosts to disturb and unsettle, and to make unfamiliar, requires we relate to them in some way (see Frers, 2013). Ghosts emerge and enact their power when we get a feeling that something else is going on here and that this 'here' is not all it seems to be. One could even say that these spectral geographies are composed through an **atmosphere** – a pervading sense or mood that something is wrong, out of joint, forgotten, troubled, or only vaguely *there*, in a place. An atmosphere of haunting circulates in a spectral place, affecting the dispositions, the emotions, the sensations of those who experience and move through it. And again, this is an atmosphere that suffuses, moves, and affects our selves and identities with a sense of being that is unsettled and disturbed. Is it any wonder then that concert venues, schools, and pubs in Bristol dropped the name Colston after the protest? The atmosphere of Bristol had become haunted by the presence of a ghost which affected many people such that it demanded action in the present. Thus, spectres, revenants, and ghosts ask us to heed their (often political) calls.

Summary

- Human geographers have thought about space and place as haunted by traces of the past.
- These traces can be understood as ghosts – something that is both material and immaterial at the same time, which disturbs our taken-for-granted understanding of space and place.
- Human geographers have sought to analyse the political importance of ghosts and how they require action in the present.

Spectral geographies: some examples

Haunting can pervade a place as an atmosphere and produces **affects** and emotions in those who experience this **spectrality**. And if this ghost demands our attention – whether we fully understand what it is trying to say or whether that calling is ambiguous or a source of conflict – we are often called to action to make sense of or even appease the ghost. One way in which this topic has been discussed in human geography is through the lens of **post-colonial** critiques. Here the traces and vestiges of **colonialism** and **imperialism** haunt contemporary geographies – in the sense they are (always) an absent-presence. These ghosts make a claim not to be forgotten or excluded or demand justice in the present due to traumatic histories or instances of unresolved social violence in the past. For example, Best and Ramírez (2021) examine performance art to explore the racial banishment of Black women from US cities in the past and how this art troubles and haunts how we think about racial eviction, possession, and property in the urban today and in the future. Coddington (2011) uses the idea of haunting to explore how Native Alaskan claims for state recognition are haunted by colonial practices from the past that continue to form the present (see also McEwan, 2008, Fortier, 2021). Many of these geographers have been influenced by the sociologist Avery Gordon (1997: 8) who argues ghosts are like 'a seething presence, acting on and often meddling with taken-for-granted realities' and thus haunting becomes political through a process of 'transformative recognition'. The colonial past thus presses on, calls to, or *haunts* the present and the future with its ghosts destabilising and sometimes transforming space and place.

Often ghosts can be very mundane and everyday phenomena – as with the unsettling presence of silent statues in urban landscapes. For example, Edensor (2008: 315) has examined how the city is littered with places of everyday haunting through the leftovers of 'previous material forms, cultural practices, inhabitants, politics, ways of thinking and being, and modes of experience'. Edensor explores how these everyday ghosts speak to the erasure of, especially working class, cultures and histories through **neoliberal** strategies of urban regeneration and place promotion. He argues that such ghosts haunt these strategies by disrupting unified 'visions' for or of the city. Indeed, when it comes to cities, as Pile (2005: 143) argues, 'what is distinctive about urban haunting – or haunting the city – is the sheer quantity, heterogeneity and density of ghosts'. Not only can these ghosts disrupt, they can also make us wonder about the city: they can allow urbanites to imagine other urban 'realities' that are elusive, vague, and inscrutable – for example, through 'leftover' and seemingly unused spaces and objects that do not quite fit the practices of the neoliberal, entrepreneurial, or cosmopolitan city.

The mundanity of ghosts can also be traced in other everyday settings, such as the domestic garden. For example, as Ginn (2014) reveals, absence haunts many gardens through the work of previous owners, or the memory of loved ones now passed who enjoyed or tended to the space. Suffused with such traces and memories, gardeners in the present work with the nature and materiality of the space to honour or remember these absences via a form of therapeutic appeasement of the garden's ghosts – through memorial plants, paths, particular spots in the garden, or things like spades passed through the generations. Here ghosts, their demands, and the spectral geographies generated can comfort as much as they can scare and frighten (see also Draus et al., 2019).

The idea of the spectral has also appeared – or materialised – in human geography writing on conservation work and debates around species extinction. Through the violence wrought on the biosphere through, for example, habitat destruction, many animals, and other species are argued to be extinct or about to be made extinct. Yet this absence or potential absence of species is often challenged by the continuing, often uncertain, and vague, traces of presence of the species in the landscape. In other words, these species *haunt* the landscape through sightings or other evidence such that they become ghost species – neither definitively there/here nor definitively not there/here. As McCorristine and Adams (2020: 103) argue, conservation efforts 'involve engagements with beings that are liminal and spectral in the imagination, inhabiting a borderland between visibility and invisibility'. And, of course, these spectral species, in their absent-presence, become calls for action for conservation either to lay their ambiguous status to rest – they are there, or they are gone, forever – or through practices such as re-wilding or the reintroduction of the species. Once again, the ghost, this time felt and seen through the process of extinction, affects us, as the past, present, and the potential future (especially of 'at risk' species), is made ambiguous, and once again the call of the spectral becomes an imperative to do something (see also Garlick, 2019, Searle, 2021).

Summary

- The ideas of haunting and spectrality have been used in many different areas of human geography.
- Key areas of human geography where spectral histories have been analysed are post-colonial geographies and the geographies of conservation and species extinction.
- Human geographers have also explored how ghost can haunt more everyday spaces such as cities or the domestic garden.

Ghosts as ghosts? Exploring supernatural geographies

The ghost as it has been explained in this chapter so far is a disruptive figure that needs appeasement or honouring. In other words, human geographers have been keen to stress the political import of ghosts and the need to do something about them – to exorcise them in some form or other. Yet there is something else going on here if you have been reading carefully. Arguably in a lot of the spectral geographies' literature, the ghost has become a metaphor. Ghosts stand in for or replace something else; the not fully decipherable absent-presence of ghosts becomes allegorical of other processes and issues. This 'something else' might be a forgotten or obscured colonial past, a working-class culture eradicated from the regenerated city, a memory of a loved one in a garden, or a nearly or supposedly extinct species. For sure, the ghostly and the spectral has much analytical power when used in this way, as the examples above prove. Yet what if, and this might be a dangerous question in a social *science* such as human geography, ghosts actually exist? Can we approach the topic of spectral geographies in such a way as to allow these barely tangible absent-presences *not* to be explained away by making them metaphors, allegories, and symbols? In short, what if we took ghosts seriously? Or if this is a somewhat ridiculous proposition (I mean, ghosts are made up, right?), what happens if we take the *belief* in ghosts seriously and explore them through a geographical lens? In this final section, I want to discuss some of the ways human geographers have examined ghosts as supernatural 'real' phenomena. Or at the very least, the belief in ghosts as real. In other words, I want to look at those who have attempted *not* to eradicate ghosts completely through our analytical use or treatment of them (see Stevens and Tolbert, 2018).

Perhaps one of the reasons why human geographers and other social scientists have used the metaphorical ghost is because we often see ourselves as rational investigators searching for logical explanations to things. As Meier et al. (2013: 423) argue the 'social sciences and the humanities are mostly concerned with what is present, observable, tangible and measurable'. Perhaps this is because a discipline such as human geography often sees itself as thoroughly secularised – i.e. having no truck with the 'reality' of the supernatural or the paranormal, or even faith, religion, or spirituality (although see Dewsbury and Cloke, 2009). Arguably here the discipline is at odds with wider society and culture where the supernatural and the paranormal, as well as the divine and the sacred, continue to be very important in many people's lives. As Bartolini et al. (2017: 346) put it:

> ... different occult, divine, otherworldly, superstitious, supernatural, paranormal and spiritual (etc.) ideas (from whatever source) continue to thrive and weave through **modernity** [...] vampires, werewolves, wizards, witches, faeries, zombies, super-humans, ghosts, demons, demi-gods, and gods are seemingly unavoidable in today's (most) popular movies and books.

Admittedly one could argue that for many people settling to watch a good vampire movie on Netflix or the unfolding of a zombie apocalypse on Amazon Prime is merely for entertainment and pleasure. Yet, should we dismiss fans of occulture as 'merely' seeking entertainment? Should we ignore the affective and emotional impression that comes from being spooked by a ghost story or horrified by a hoard of groaning zombies?

One thing these forms of popular culture do is to generate a sense of possibility and specu-lation in the spaces and places we inhabit. Have you ever watched a horror film and then felt a shiver of fear going upstairs to bed in a dark house? Have you ever felt a shudder of apprehension and unease walking through a graveyard at night? Examining the 'reality' of ghosts, monsters, vampires and werewolves and the like, is to explore the possibility of the otherworldly in the places and spaces we make our lives through, and in. One popular practice that does just that is ghost tourism. In many cities throughout the world, guides take participants on walking tours to learn about the darker and paranormal histories of spaces and places. These 'dark heritage' tours reveal the hidden histories – often macabre – of space and place and build alternative narratives or 'realities' of localities. In this sense, they align with the more political idea of spectrality we discussed above to reveal and heed the call of haunted spaces where some form of injustice has been performed and has subsequently been forgotten or occluded. Yet ghost tours, like hor-ror films, also allow us to *imagine* and *experience* the supernatural and ghostly geographies that surround us. As such, they allow the unknown and 'what if?' to potentially alter our everyday geographies. Indeed, ghost tourism generates this speculative transformation through weaving atmospheres that allow the potentialities of space and place to flourish; as participants, we feel the tremor of possibility that a ghost might manifest as the guide's storytelling (as well as the architecture, the sounds, sights, and sometimes the smells of the place) generates a spooky atmo-sphere. Central to this atmosphere is the undecidable and the insubstantial – thus, the spectral. As Kolk (2020: 135) in his research on dark heritage tours of St. Louis states, this form of tourism 'generally resist providing a rationalist framework, or indeed a unifying narrative (beyond the kind that emerges through attention to broader themes of local history) that would make sense of them' (see also Holloway, 2010). Ghost tourism makes places spectral (and thus never fully there, here, or fixed) through practices of imagination and speculation.

As human geographers we do not need to believe in ghosts to examine supernatural and para-normal geographies. What is important is that we do not *always* make the ghost into something else, like a metaphor, or always seek out the overriding cause of these phenomena – the psychological, physical, visual, the neoliberal, the post-colonial, etc. (see Holloway and Kneale, 2008). Instead, we take the fascination, the imaginative pleasure, and the outright frights performed by the ghost *seriously*. Also, and importantly, by doing this we respect those cultures throughout the world and through history that *do* believe in ghosts and spirits, as well as monsters, demons, and faeries (such as many Indigenous cultures). There are quite a few examples of this respectful, serious approach to the supernatural in human geography. For example, Heng (2021) examines the Hungry Ghost Festival in Singapore, a period in Chinese religion (comprising Taoist, Buddhist, and folk religion) where the spirits of ancestors and the dead travel from the netherworld to wander amongst the living. These spirits require appeasement and offerings and Heng uses photography as a way of visualising how these rituals make the absent and intangible spirits present and tangible (see also Tong and Kong, 2000). Another example would be Pile's (2006) argument that magic and the occult, instead of being something eradicated from the 'rational' and 'modern' West, are very much still part of it. Pile (2006: 316) traces the flows of practices such as West African witchcraft or the ritual magic of the Hermetic Order of the Golden Dawn to cities such as London to argue that far 'from magic dying out in the modern Western city, magic is thriving'. Here, Pile examines the very real social, political, and cultural impacts of these phenomena and practices on how we understand Western urbanism and modernity. Similarly, I have explored nineteenth-century Spiritualism to understand the affective and **embodied** relations of the séance, a space where the spirits of the dead were and continue to be contacted (see Holloway, 2006; also Bartolini et al., 2019). And it is not just witchcraft, the occult, and spirits that human geographers have examined: they have also investigated monsters – as something both fearful and fascinating, both horrific and inspiring awe – to explore their potential for rethinking geographies (see Dixon and Ruddick, 2013, Holloway, 2017).

Summary

- In human geography ghosts are often analysed as representative of something else and thus allegorical figures that 'stand for' other geographical processes.
- Other human geographers have taken the belief in, and even the very existence of, ghosts and haunting as something to analyse and explore.
- Ghosts have the potential to make us wonder, speculate, and think differently about space and place, and human geographers have sought to explore how this can transform or enchant our geographies.

Conclusion

Spectral geographies are spaces and places made up of materialities, processes, and practices that are never fully present and never fully fixed and are haunted by absent yet present disruptive forces that make them insubstantial, undecidable, unpredictable, and unsettling. The recognition of spectrality in human geography is therefore, as Maddern and Adey (2008: 292) argue, 'a concern for the just perceptible, the barely there, the nagging presence of an absence in a variety of spaces'. In this chapter, we have seen that human geographers have utilised the figure of the ghost to explore the ways in which then hidden or forgotten memories and histories of space and place can erupt or materialise in the present and influence the future. These processes and figures – the haunting and ghosts of space and place – demand action and ask us to heed their call, often through their re-emergent political demands. Yet we have also seen how the spectral and the ghostly are sources of wonder, intrigue, imagination, and speculation. Ghosts, then, not only demand us to act on the injustices and wrongs they suffered in a previous time, but they also allow us to think about how space and place might be perceived and experienced differently. In short, ghosts are and can be both political *and* enchanting – 'to be struck and shaken by the extraordinary that lives amid the familiar and the everyday', as Bennett (2001: 4–5) defines it.

Hopefully, you have a better idea of what a spectral geography is or might be after reading this chapter. Moreover, I hope you have taken ghosts, spirits, and even monsters a little bit more seriously after reading it. What I mean by taking something more seriously is to allow the ghost, and certainly the belief in ghosts, to exist and be real in our human geographical work. But can ghosts ever be (fully) banished? Is Bristol now free from its haunting colonial past after the toppling of the Colston statue? Does the story of the Hexham Heads still make us wonder and intrigue us? As many have argued, the power of the ghost and spectral lies in their undecidability. So, take a listen to the podcast 'Unexplained'. Whilst not all episodes deal directly with ghosts – although many do – the power and popularity of this pod (with over 50 million downloads) is that no answers, no causes, are given to the mysteries, the hauntings, and the eerie events it documents. The stories are left *unexplained*. Or read the marvellous paper by Thurgill's (2018) on the literary geographies M.R. James' ghost stories. Here Thurgill visits and explores the 'real' world places and spaces on the East Anglian coastline in which James' stories are set and unfold. The power of the ghost – its affective force – is very real here as he searches for these sites and is haunted by both the presence and absence of the characters and the places in which James set his tales. In Thurgill's research, the ghost is very powerful because it is never reduced to a symptom of something else or a metaphor. Instead, the ghost is *allowed* to haunt in his analysis.

So, if you are digging in your garden and you come across two small carved stone heads...

Discission points

- How and in what way is your everyday geography *haunted*?
- How can a ghost be political such that we need to heed its call? Use an example to justify your answer.
- Think of some examples of ghosts and supernatural in popular culture. What do they tell us about space and place?
- Listen to an episode of 'Unexplained' (for example, Season 6, Episode 7). How is the story performed and told? What sort of affective and emotional impact does it have on you? Does it make you think differently about space and place?
- What would be the consequences of taking ghosts seriously or even 'real' for the discipline of human geography?

References

Bartolini, N., Chris, R., MacKian, S., and Pile, S. (2017). The place of spirit: modernity and the geographies of spirituality. *Progress in Human Geography* 41(3): 338–354.

Bartolini, N., MacKian, S., and Pile, S. (2019). Spirit knows: materiality, memory and the recovery of Spiritualist places and practices in Stoke-on-Trent. *Social & Cultural Geography* 20(8): 1114–1137.

Bennett, J. (2001). *The Enchantment of Modern Life: Attachments, Crossings and Ethics*. Princeton: Princeton University Press.

Best, A., and Ramírez, M. M. (2021). Urban specters. *Environment and Planning D: Society and Space*. https://doi.org/10.1177/02637758211030286

Coddington, K. S. (2011). Spectral geographies: haunting and everyday state practices in colonial and present-day Alaska. *Social & Cultural Geography* 12(7): 743–756.

de Certeau, M. (1984). *The Practice of Everyday Life*. Berkeley: University of California Press.

Dewsbury, J. D., and Cloke, P. (2009). Spiritual landscapes: existence, performance, and immanence. *Social & Cultural Geography* 10(6): 695–711.

Dixon, D., and Ruddick, S. (2013). Monsters, monstrousness, and monstrous nature/s. *Geoforum* 48: 237–238.

Draus, P., Haase, D., Napieralski, J., Roddy, J., and Qureshi, S. (2019). Wounds, ghosts and gardens: historical trauma and green reparations in Berlin and Detroit. *Cities* 93: 153–163.

Edensor, T. (2008). Mundane hauntings: commuting through the phantasmagoric working-class spaces of Manchester, England. *Cultural Geographies* 15(3): 313–333.

Fortier, C. (2021). The Humber is a haunting: settler deathscapes, Indigenous spectres, and the memorialisation of a Canadian heritage river. *Antipode* 54(1): 259–283.

Frers, L. (2013). The matter of absence. *Cultural Geographies* 20(4): 431–445.

Garlick, B. (2019). Cultural geographies of extinction: animal culture among Scottish ospreys. *Transactions of the Institute of British Geographers* 44(2): 226–241.

Ginn, F. (2014). Death, absence and afterlife in the garden. *Cultural Geographies* 21(2): 229–245.

Gordon, A. (1997). *Ghostly Matters: Haunting and the Sociological Imagination*. Minneapolis: University of Minneapolis Press.

Heng, T. (2021). Photographing absence in deathscapes. *Area* 53(2): 219–228.

Holloway, J. (2006). Enchanted spaces: the seance, affect, and geographies of religion. *Annals of the Association of American Geographers* 96(1): 182–187.

Holloway, J. (2010). Legend-tripping in spooky spaces: ghost tourism and infrastructures of enchantment. *Environment and Planning D: Society and Space* 28: 618–637.

Holloway, J. (2017). On the spaces and movement of monsters: the itinerant crossings of Gef the talking mongoose. *Cultural Geographies* 24(1): 21–41.

Holloway, J., and Kneale, J. (2008). Locating haunting: a ghost-hunter's guide. *Cultural Geographies* 15(3): 297–312.

Kolk, H. A. (2020). Negative heritage: the material-cultural politics of the American haunted history tour. *Journal of Cultural Geography* 37(2): 117–156.

Maddern, J. F., and Adey, P. (2008). Editorial: spectro-geographies. *Cultural Geographies* 15(3): 291–295.

McCorristine, S., and Adams, W. M. (2020). Ghost species: spectral geographies of biodiversity conservation. *Cultural Geographies* 27(1): 101–115.

McEwan, C. (2008). 'A very modern ghost': postcolonialism and the politics of enchantment. *Environment and Planning D: Society and Space* 26: 29–46.

Meier, L., Frers, L., and Sigvardsdotter, E. (2013). The importance of absence in the present: practices of remembrance and the contestation of absences. *Cultural Geographies* 20(4): 423–430.

Pile, S. (2005). *Real Cities*. London: Sage.

Pile, S. (2006). The strange case of western cities: occult globalisations and the making of urban modernity. *Urban Studies* 43(2): 305–318.

Screeton, P. (2012). *Quest for the Hexham Heads*. Bideford, UK: Fortean Words

Searle, A. (2021). Hunting ghosts: on spectacles of spectrality and the trophy animal. *Cultural Geographies* 28(3): 513–530.

Stevens, V., and Tolbert, J. A. (2018). Beyond metaphorical spectrality: for new paranormal geographies. *New Directions in Folklore* 16(1): 27–57.

Thurgill, J. (2018). Extra-textual encounters: locating place in the text-as-event: an experiential reading of M. R. James' 'A Warning to the Curious'. *Literary Geographies* 4(2): 221–244.

Tong, C. K., and Kong, L. (2000). Religion and modernity: ritual transformations and the reconstruction of space and time. *Social & Cultural Geography* 1: 29–44.

Online materials

- 'Uncanny Podcast' – an incredibly popular BBC podcast that has spawned a television series and a theatre show: https://www.bbc.co.uk/sounds/brand/m0010x7c
- The BBC's version of M.R. James 'A Warning to the Curious' (Gordon Clark, 1972): https://www.youtube.com/watch?v=w7xJSQY8Ssw
- 'Hellier' (2019) – a recent TV show that has proved influential on 'real life' ghost hunting and paranormal investigation: https://www.amazon.co.uk/gp/video/detail/amzn1.dv.gti.2cb74319-81f1-8235-694c-f75e379715f4?autoplay=1&ref_=atv_cf_strg_wb
- 'Unexplained' podcast: http://www.unexplainedpodcast.com/
- 'Lore' podcast – another popular podcast that documents strange and eerie folklore and legends: https://www.lorepodcast.com/
- 'Dark Histories' podcast – a fascinating telling of the stranger side of history and geography: https://www.darkhistories.com/

Further reading

Holloway, J., and Kneale, J. (2008). Locating haunting: a ghost-hunter's guide. *Cultural Geographies* 15(3): 297–312.
An article in which the authors, through two case studies, argue that ghosts and spirits should be understood as more than metaphorical or allegorical.

Maddern, J. F., and Adey, P. (2008). Editorial: spectro-geographies. *Cultural Geographies* 15(3): 291–295.
An important editorial giving an overview of the area of spectral geography. See also the papers contained in this special issue.

McEwan, C. (2008). 'A very modern ghost': postcolonialism and the politics of enchantment. *Environment and Planning D: Society and Space* 26: 29–46.
An article which explores the political importance of ghosts in the present.

Pile, S. (2005). *Real Cities*. London: Sage.
A book which argues for the importance of a variety of supernatural forms in our experience of the city.

Thurgill, J. (2018). Extra-textual encounters: locating place in the text-as-event: an experiential reading of M.R. James' 'A Warning to the Curious'. *Literary Geographies* 4(2): 221–244.
An excellent paper dealing with how our experiences of place can become haunted.

SECTION THREE

ECONOMIC GEOGRAPHIES

30 Knowing economies

Mark Goodwin and Kelly Dombroski

Introduction

When you think of 'the economy', what do you think of? How do we know about economies, and how might our knowledge change when we take a geographical perspective? This chapter introduces you to Section Three. It does so by taking a look at how we come to know economies and know about economies, before looking at the development of the sub-discipline of economic geography as one approach to knowing economies. We then set out the ways in which contemporary human geography seeks to analyse and even transform the economic world. It finishes by presenting an outline of each of the chapters in this section, and by looking at the ground that they cover collectively, so that you can situate the material we present here within the broader context of economic geography more generally.

We all know something about the economy, and we all participate in the economy in some way – even in multiple economies! You might hear the word 'economy' being thrown around a lot these days, including phrases such as 'economic downturn', 'circular economies', 'bioeconomy', 'economic growth (or degrowth)' and 'postcarbon economies'. You might also hear 'economy' with reference to something that is efficient or resource saving (like the economy cycle on a washing machine or dishwasher). When some of us were young, the classes at school where you learned how to cook were known as 'home economics', teaching among other skills the efficient use of home resources. This is actually pretty close to the original understanding of the Greek word *oikos* which the English word 'economy' (and ecology) has emerged from. *Oikos* referred to the management of a household (Waring, 2018) and, for a long time, the word 'economy' was mainly used to refer to ideas of frugality. The word then expanded in meaning to cover the management and use of resources at a much larger scale – the **political economy** of the **nation-state**, or even what we sometimes refer to as 'the global economy'. What we mean by 'the economy' can therefore differ depending on the perspective we are coming from.

In the field of economic geography, there are also different ways of thinking about and studying economies and their interaction with geography, place and **space**. Geographers emphasise the role of place, space and environment in economic activity and thus the shape of particular economies – for example, the presence of forests of hardwood trees depends on certain climate, soil and geographical characteristics, which enable and affect the kinds of economy that might be possible in such a place. But the reverse is also true: the geographies of a place are shaped by the economic processes that come to bear on it – for example, the rise of multinational corporations has changed the nature of urban spaces in the cities where their headquarters have come to be clustered, and the environments of the places where resources are intensely extracted to

DOI: 10.4324/9780429265853-36

BOX 30.1
WHAT IS ECONOMIC GEOGRAPHY?

'What economic geography is definitely not is an unyielding insistence on explaining everything about the economic world in geographical terms or as a function *of* geography. Rather, economic geographic scholarship *emphasizes* geographical factors in its explanation, while not neglecting other factors… This notion of the "materiality of geography" is what we refer to as the *implication* of space, place, scale, landscape, and environment in economic processes. By "implicated" we mean that the geographies in question *affect* the processes in question. Whether it is inflation, globalization, raw material extraction, industrial waste disposal, or whatever else, geography is integral rather than peripheral or incidental to the form and outcomes of the process… the effects of the geographic are not trivial or marginal. They are significant to the degree of being necessary to explanation. Or, to look at things from an alternative perspective, one might say that the forms and outcomes of economic processes in which space and other factors are *substantively* implicated would be significantly different were it *not* for those factors. Geography makes a (big) difference. As such, meaningful understanding and explanation of such processes requires explicit attention to and consideration of their geographical dimensions'.

Barnes and Christophers, 2018: 36–37

support globalised manufacturing bear that imprint. As such, the link between geography and economic activity works both ways – as Lee and Wills put it 'while attempts to understand the economy are enhanced by … a geographical approach, so too the geographical discipline is augmented by careful attention to the economic' (2014: 357). In Box 30.1 we present one view of how to approach this two-way relationship between geography and economic activity.

What we find helpful about this approach is that it is non-exclusive and non-limiting. It does not specify in advance what the object of study of economic geography should be, and it does not identify any particular elements of economic activity as being more worthy of geographical attention than others. Instead, it is an approach based on seeking the materiality of geography, wherever it is found and in whichever economic practices. And why this is important, as Barnes and Christophers point out, is because 'the "economic" and the "economy" are **socially constructed**' (2018: 29). Or as Massey puts it in her chapter in the Lee and Wills collection, 'What we think of as "the economic" is itself expressive of other aspects of our culture/society' (1997: 35). And why this, in turn, is important is because socially constructed and accepted definitions of 'the economy' have tended to be partial and limited to formal, measurable and taxable elements of economic activity. The economy is also often framed as something much bigger than us, and to which we are subject – a bit like the weather. Thus, in formal economic measures, paid-for childcare is accepted as part of economic activity, while the same amount of time spent by a parent looking after a child is not, and driving or taking public transport to work is included as part of economic activity, while cycling or walking to work is not. But if we go back to the meaning of economy emerging from *oikos*, we can see that all these activities are economic, and indeed, all are influenced by broader cultural norms about what 'counts' as 'real' economic activity (Waring, 2018). From a broader perspective, as Mitchell points out, across the globe 'even today, a century or more after the global consolidation of the **capitalist** order…, a majority of people live hybrid lives, neither market nor subsistence, neither capital nor labour, neither within the national economy nor quite outside it, escaping the fixed categories of economic discourse' (1998: 99–100). As we shall see in the next two sections of the chapter, for much of its history, economic geography has tended to limit its concerns to these 'fixed categories of economic discourse' and consequently has missed the richness and diversity that makes up the full spectrum of economic activity.

Geography and the economy: differing approaches to economic geography

Lee and Wills conclude that 'understanding the human landscape is impossible without unpacking the processes of economic activity in all their diversity' (2014: 357). The crucial point about this is that geographers have taken different stances towards such 'unpacking' and have deployed different definitions of 'economic activity', which have led as a result to different types of economic geography. For a long while, economic geographers didn't really think too hard about these definitional questions; they simply described, in their terms, what was out there in the world in front of them, often in the late nineteenth and early twentieth centuries in the service of colonial and imperial expansion (Buchanan, 1935a). Barnes and Christophers conclude that 'economic geography did not simply describe the late nineteenth-century imperialist world in which it arose, but was complicit with it, contributing to its maintenance and expansion' (2018: 58). Figure 30.1 is a map of India taken from the first edition of Chisholm's *Handbook of Commercial Geography*, first published in 1889 (but republished in 20 editions, with the last as recently as 2011!). As Barnes and Christophers explain, once the 'subcontinent was laid out on a piece of paper, its spaces could then be literally written on by the British colonial project: tea in the Northeast, opium in the Northwest, coffee in the Southwest, and wheat, millet, cotton and oil seeds in the center' (2018: 54). In this vein, the earliest economic geography produced factual descriptive accounts of industries and resources – whether in individual countries or regions, such as agriculture in New Zealand (Buchanan, 1935b) or within compendiums such as Chisholm's handbook. It was only after World War II that a more systematic 'unpacking' of the processes of economic activity began to emerge, and following Coe et al. (2020), we can discern three broad approaches to analysing the 'materiality of geography' over the past 75 years or so.

The first of these more systematic 'unpackings' took place within the framework of **spatial science**. As we set out in Chapter 1, spatial science is the generic description given to an approach to human geography that sought to identify universal spatial laws about why geographical objects are located where they are and how they relate to each other. In the case of economic geography, this led to the use of quantitative data, statistical techniques and mathematical models to identify patterns of industrial location and regional growth. In this approach, 'unpacking' the processes of economic activity took place via punch cards, calculators and computers, along with a set of abstract laws borrowed from physics and economics. Returning to

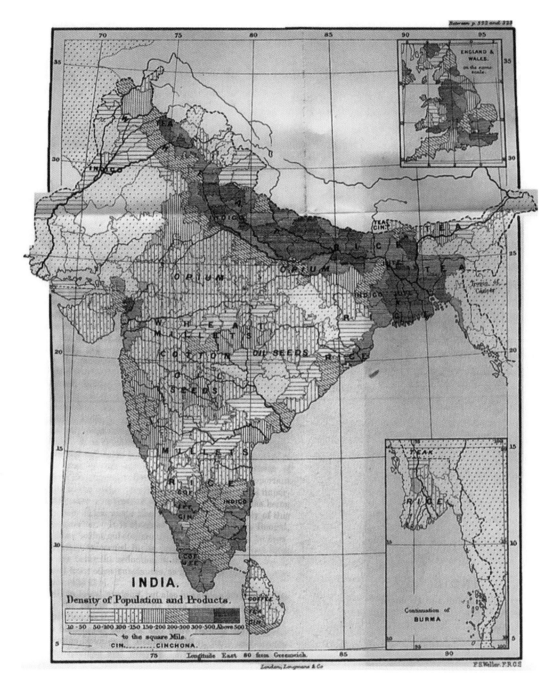

Figure 30.1
Chisholm's Map of India, taken from Barnes, and Christophers (2018). *Economic Geography: A Critical Introduction*, 55

Source: Originally from Chisholm, 1889, between pages 322 and 323

Barnes and Christophers, economic geography now 'concerned itself with finding causes and explanations, and not simply with classification; and it was not content with written descriptions of the unique, but focused on the logical and numerical analysis of the general... as economic geographic **discourses** and practices were reinvented, an entirely different economic geographic world emerged. It was defined by Euclidian and non-Euclidian space, geometrical axioms, Greek symbols and regression lines' (2018: 62).

One prominent example of this search for general laws was Weber's industrial location theory, which sought to account for the location of industry in terms of transportation costs, distance from raw materials and markets, and the weight of materials. Other universal laws were developed to account for the trajectory of urban economies and regional development, and for land use patterns (see Barnes and Christophers [2018] and Coe et al. [2020] for more detailed reviews). They shared a belief that the economic world could be understood through quantitative measurement, and that the phenomena being measured displayed a consistency across time and space, allowing the formulation and testing of general principles and laws. However, from the late 1960s and early 1970s, these beliefs came under increasing challenge from those who argued that an abstract spatial science, based on the laws of physical science such as gravity models, could not account for changes in the social world. Box 30.2 sets out how economic geography was influenced by these wider social changes.

In their search for the underlying structural processes that lay behind the uneven geographies of economic activity, economic geographers increasingly turned to a set of concepts and theories drawn from **Marxist** political economy to uncover the materiality of geography to economic activity. Using these, they showed that economic, social and spatial inequalities were not accidental, and therefore short-lived, but were instead built into the very fabric of **capitalism**, and they argued that economic production necessarily entails the exploitation of whole sections of society by those with political and economic power. This work proved tremendously

---

BOX 30.2
STRUCTURAL CAUSES OF ECONOMIC PHENOMENA

'While quantitative geography and locational analysis emerged to address the needs of growing post-war national economies in the mid twentieth century, various social movements took hold in the late 1960s and economic growth began to slow down in the early 1970s. In the United States in particular, civil rights protests, **feminist** and environmental movements, and the anti-Vietnam War campaign all gave rise to alternative and anti-establishment thinking. In Economic Geography, the scientific certainties of the quantitative approach seemed less capable of addressing the clear social problems that these movements highlighted. In North America and Western Europe, urban poverty and segregation, **gender** inequalities, uneven international development, and deindustrialisation were all pressing issues. They demanded an understanding of the structural processes that underpinned observable economic phenomena, and a political agenda to change them'.

Coe et al., 2020: 497

influential, and as Coe et al. state, 'our ability to think about the structural logics of capitalism, to identify **class**-based power relations in economic processes, and to conceptualise **uneven development** are all dependent on the legacies of Marxist theory in the field of Geography' (2020: 498). Much of this work on Marxism within human geography was being carried out in the sub-discipline of economic geography, and the five human geographers whose work grew the most in terms of citations across the 1980s – Alan Scott, Doreen Massey, David Harvey, Gordon Clark and Neil Smith – were all researching economic activity and uneven development from a broadly Marxist perspective (Bodman, 1992).

Given this influence it is not surprising that across the 1980s and 1990s, economic geography witnessed a huge flowering of work inspired by Marxist political economy. This covered, amongst other topics, local studies of industrial closures and restructuring, analyses of labour markets and geographies of labour, work on gendered divisions of labour and the role of women in the economy, and studies of multinational companies and global production networks. One especially influential strand of analysis was built around regulation theory, which looked at how a crisis-prone economic system has managed to avert crisis through political and institutional regulation, as witnessed in the shift from a Fordist to a **post-Fordist** mode of regulation. (Again, see Barnes and Christophers [2018] and Coe et al. [2020] for further details of this Marxist work within economic geography.) What all these studies shared was an approach which sought to understand the geography of economic activity through an uncovering of the underlying structures of power and control.

Around the turn of the century, an alternative approach began to gain a foothold in economic geography. We can loosely group this under the banner of 'poststructuralism', although it has many different components. While spatial science sought to reach the scientific truth through observable facts, and Marxist political economy sought it by uncovering underlying structures, poststructuralism understands reality to be overdetermined – that is, determined by a wide range of factors that might include structures and observations, but one that is also shaped by the particular perspectives and experiences of the observer. As such, there is not a single 'true' reality that research uncovers – research instead is thought to participate in the making and unmaking of multiple realities. In economic geography, a key text in the poststructuralist approach was the book *The End of Capitalism (As We Knew It): A Feminist Critique of Political Economy*, first published in 1996 by J-K Gibson-Graham. Box 30.3 shows how the work of Gibson-Graham in Geography, and indeed poststructuralism more broadly, opened up new possibilities of thought and action.

What is significant about the work of Gibson-Graham is not just that it represents another way of 'unpacking' the processes of economic activity – it also questions what those processes of economic activity actually are. To a certain extent, economic geographers within spatial science and Marxist political economy were looking at the same object of study – broadly defined as the formal capitalist economy, with an emphasis on the industrial and manufacturing sectors of the Global North – even if they approached it from totally different starting (and finishing) points. In contrast Gibson-Graham emphasised that these kinds of economic activities are only the (capitalist) tip of a much bigger economic iceberg. For her, a lot of different kinds of economic activity are generally invisible in academic analysis, and indeed in political and ethical discourse. The 'underwater' part of the economy is made up of a myriad of diverse relations and processes, some of which are as much social and cultural as they are economic – although all contribute to economic life and economic activity. This opens up whole new areas

BOX 30.3
POSTSTRUCTURALIST ECONOMIC POSSIBILITIES

'Poststructuralism provided a means to rethink the nature of capitalism so that it was no longer as intimidating and unchallengeable. That was the significance of Gibson-Graham's 1996 book title *The End of Capitalism (As We Knew It)* (Figure 30.2). To change capitalism, to end it, we must learn to know it in another way. Poststructuralism enabled that new kind of knowing. It undid capitalocentrism. Instead of representing capitalism as a single essential force, determining everything else, it was portrayed as varied and diverse, constructed by joining different elements, many of which were not traditionally economic at all.

Figure 30.2
Cover of the Turkish translation of *The End of Capitalism (As We Knew It)*. It shows Julie Graham and Katherine Gibson (who published under the pseudonym JK Gibson-Graham) fighting the 'monster' of capitalism

Source: Photo credit: Asya Saydam

Rather, many were cultural, and the turn to poststructuralism in economic geography thus overlapped with a larger "cultural turn" in the discipline to take more seriously the cultural specificity and "embeddedness" of all economies. In any event, Gibson-Graham contended that poststructuralism allowed one to move away from the iron cage of capitalocentrism, and instead to conceive the economy as piecemeal, varied, fragile, and vulnerable. Once capitalism was thought about in those terms, it was less powerful and scary. It could be chipped away, resisted bit by bit'.

Barnes and Christophers, 2018:70

of study for economic geography – including the role of cultural and social identities in the workplace and the firm, the informal economic activities which are interconnected with formal economic activities (see Chapter 34), the home as a workplace (see Chapters 33 and 36), Indigenous and **postcolonial** economies of the Global South or Majority World (see Chapter 38) and the role of **representations** and discourses in helping shape our understanding of economic activity. According to Barnes and Christophers (2018: 35) 'in the work of (post-colonial) scholars … and Gibson-Graham, the "economic" in economic geography is being given perhaps its most substantial and significant makeover in several decades'.

Summary

- Geographers have different approaches to economic geography, leading to diverse definitions of 'economic activity' and resulting in various types of economic geography.
- The development of economic geography involved a shift from descriptive accounts of industries and resources to the systematic analysis of the processes of economic activity using quantitative data and mathematical models. Later, Marxist political economy and poststructuralism emerged as influential frameworks in economic geography, focusing on uncovering underlying structures of power and understanding multiple realities, respectively.

The challenge of diverse economies

Once the challenge of diverse economies had been made, the project encompassed a number of different directions. One direction was the ongoing project of 'inventorying as ethical action', that is documenting and making an inventory of the diversity of economic geographies and place-based economies out there in the world, as detailed by Gibson-Graham and Dombroski in the introduction to *The Handbook of Diverse Economies*. Another direction was the development of a new, more normative project that tried to imagine and experiment with different forms of economies and economic geographies in specific places and through specific action research projects. This is best exemplified in the work of Gibson-Graham, Cameron and Healy in their popular book *Take Back the Economy* (Gibson-Graham et al., 2013), as well as by the book *A Postcapitalist Politics* which developed the theory behind the work seeking to produce a different kind of economic future (Gibson-Graham, 2006). The first direction, that of inventorying, is often referred to as 'diverse economies'. The second area, of action research and imagining new economies, is often referred to as 'community economies'. Both these areas of research have multiplied into a range of challenges that constitute the 'makeover' to economic geography noted by Barnes and Christophers, and they have gone on to influence other kinds of postcapitalist geographies (see Chapter 64).

In the area of diverse economies, this makeover has acted as the invitation for all kinds of geographers to participate in the work of promoting alternative economic geographies in particular places (Gibson-Graham, 2008). It also constitutes a makeover of the object of study that we call 'the economy'. The economy, for Gibson-Graham and others in the diverse economies tradition, is an overdetermined **assemblage** of culture, history, politics and more. Gibson-Graham and the diverse economies tradition reject structuralist accounts of the economy that see it as made up of essential laws that play out in much the same way as Newton's laws of gravity might in the discipline of physics. Instead, diverse economies theory holds that while there are certain patterns of economic activity strongly influenced by power dynamics, they are not laws. They thus preserve and emphasise the **agency** of collectives and communities to make economic decisions based on rationalities other than the self-interested 'rational economic man' (Dombroski, 2020). For diverse economies scholars, economic geography is thus thrown wide open to a different kind of analysis, where the goal is not to develop theories or laws of economic change but to challenge and shape economic change through documenting and inventorying the diversity of economic activities already present (such as those economic activities that are 'underwater' in the economic iceberg diagram Figure 30.3). This project has had some critiques. Firstly, critics argue that this project of documenting and inventorying does not adequately account for the power dynamics at play that push economic actors to act in certain ways. Secondly, critics argue that this project does not have a meaningful endpoint or alternative in sight, so risks proliferating studies of small-scale economic projects without putting them together into a coherent alternative to the capitalist economy. Gibson-Graham and diverse economies scholars have recognised these limitations and have moved to a second step in the economic geography of diverse economies, one which theorises the transition to postcapitalist economies.

Transitioning to postcapitalist economies is a project with a wide mandate during these times of climate and planetary crisis. There is a role for economic geographers to participate in imagining and proposing economic transitions based on their knowledge and understanding of economies in place. For Gibson-Graham and others in the Community Economies Collective, transitions to postcapitalist economies are envisioned as a process that happens in many places in diverse ways with many unrelated actors. Gibson-Graham took inspiration from the feminist movement, which resulted in widespread change across the globe without a central organising committee or even a shared vision of what the transformation would be. The slogan 'the personal is political' meant that feminists and allies worked on different place-based struggles, in solidarity with each other but without a specific vision of what women's equality might look like. To this day, gender-based activism continues in a variety of places with a

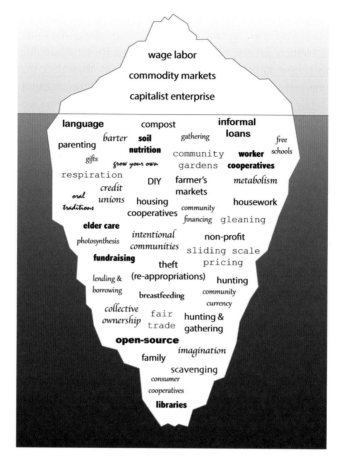

Figure 30.3
Diverse Economies Iceberg, showing that capitalist economic activities are just the tip of a larger and more diverse economic iceberg

Source: Community Economies Collective (licenced under a Creative Commons Attribution-ShareAlike 4.0 International License)

variety of different justice-seeking goals. This solidarity in diversity is part of its strength. In *A Postcapitalist Politics*, Gibson-Graham laid down a challenge for a similar politics of justice-seeking in the economic sphere of life – which, as we have seen already, for them includes things that might be seen by some as 'social' or 'cultural', such as domestic work and environmental care (see also Chapter 64).

Gibson-Graham's specific vision and activism for change has been developed through the concept of community economies, where community here does not mean a specific place-based or social identity, but is left as an open and invitational space for collaboration. The kinds of collaborations that have developed through community economies research include many different kinds of action research projects where the economic geographer gets *involved* in research with these communities. These range from independent cooperative renewable energy trusts supplying power to communities seeking to divest from coal (Hicks, 2020) and locally owned social enterprises transforming rural economies in Fiji (Vunibola et al., 2022) to developing educational, art and healthcare programs in partnership with states in both the Majority and Minority Worlds (Carnegie et al., 2012, McKinnon, 2022). Alongside these experiments with trying to do things differently, community economies scholars write and publish critical reflections on such experimental interventions, sharing knowledges about transformative practices that may, or may not, have worked – without waiting for a fully fledged alternative economy to be implemented from 'above' (Bargh, 2011, McKinnon et al., 2019, McLean, 2022).

This is considered a significant makeover of economic geography because it encourages both new forms of creative and interdisciplinary experiments with place-based economies and a theory of economic change that adds a hopeful and nuanced challenge to researchers and communities alike (Cameron, 2009). It invites economic geographers to take a shift in their stance, from a detached observer searching for patterns and laws to an active political and economic actor intervening and experimenting with change (Gibson-Graham, 2005). In contemporary times, economic geography still includes both spatial science and structuralist perspectives, but with a much wider recognition of the role of research in producing the economy it purports to merely describe (Mitchell, 2005, Muniesa, 2014). Similarly, social economy, solidarity economy, Indigenous economies and Black economies are all important contributions to thinking about the economic geographies of a range of social groups, with racial capitalism as a more recent concept inviting reflection on the power structures that embed exploitative practices into economies (Hossein and Christabell, 2022). In contemporary economic geography, then, there is less desire for all-encompassing explanatory laws, and more attention paid to the nuances of power, identity, space, place and possibility that particular assemblages of economy bring together and reproduce. It still remains to be seen, however, if economic geography can answer the call to 'attend to ethical economic actions that make other worlds possible' (Gibson-Graham et al., 2019).

Summary

- The challenge of diverse economies has led to two main directions in research: inventorying and documenting the diversity of economic geographies and place-based economies, and imagining and experimenting with new forms of economies through action research projects.
- The concept of diverse economies challenges the traditional understanding of the economy as an overdetermined assemblage influenced by culture, history and politics, emphasising the agency of collectives and communities in making economic decisions.

A journey through the section

The section begins with a chapter by Sarah Hall, looking at the notion of money and finance. She shows how money, although highly mobile and transferable across the globe in milliseconds, has a very particular geography. A small number of world financial centres, which are the major source of capital for investment, form a very tight core within the global finance industry. She then shows how this global situation is mirrored at the national level, where financial services tend, again, to be concentrated and how this leads to increased 'financial exclusion' when large segments of the community are denied access to these services. By contrast, in Chapter 32, Juliana Mansvelt discusses the more pervasive nature of consumption and seeks to understand the ways in which consumption connects people, places and things. She shows how consumption both requires and makes particular geographies, which may extend from the individual to the global. In Chapter 33, Katharine Mckinnon and Kelly Dombroski draw on diverse economies to problematise the notion of work by investigating many different types of work: waged and unwaged and alternatively compensated, in public spaces, commercial spaces and at home, and mixed in with many other activities. They discuss workplaces during the COVID-19 pandemic, before finishing with a discussion about the future of work.

In Chapter 34, on informal economies, Gengzhi Huang also explores the economy beyond the formal waged sector. He looks at different theoretical perspectives on the informal economy, before discussing the heterogeneity of informal economies, including those tied into the global capitalist economy. Gengzhi finishes by looking at the spaces of the informal economy, including those in the home and on the street, and shows how platform technologies have led to new spaces of informal work. In Chapter 35 Jana Kleibert explores the processes of economic **globalisation** and shows how globalisation has been made and remade over several centuries. She then looks at the components of globalisation, including those driven by **transnational** corporations. Jana then looks at the networks and value chains which tie the global economy together, before finishing with a consideration of the likely future state of economic globalisation.

In Chapter 36, Gianne Sheena Sabio and Rhacel Salazar Parreñas examine the significant geographical flows involved in the global economies of care. They use the concept of the '**international division of reproductive labour**' to show how the global care economy shapes and is shaped by, both global capitalism and gender inequality, before exploring the different types of international and national migrations that underpin this type of work. They finish by examining the **infrastructures** and supports which purposefully shape these migration patterns and thereby fuel the global care sector. Chapter 37, by Elise Klein, explores the new economic geographies of development, looking at how cooperation between countries in the Global South is reshaping the practices and geographies of aid and development. The chapter looks at the links between **colonisation** and development, and at those between capitalism and racism, before concluding with a consideration of the concept of '**postdevelopment**'.

Chapter 38 by Suliasi Vunibola and Steven Ratuva draws on a diverse economies perspective to examine the ideas and practices of Indigenous innovation. Using case studies drawn from Fiji, they contrast Indigenous innovation with more typical forms of 'Western' innovation and explore the social, cultural and ecological practices which underpin the former. In doing so they remind us that economic activities are never just economic – and that the form they take will inevitably vary from place to place. We saw earlier in this chapter how economic geography has evolved over the past 75 years or so, and how the materiality of geography to the economy has been explored from a number of different perspectives using different theoretical and conceptual approaches. Taken together, these eight chapters use the latest perspectives to explore a number of different elements and components within the contemporary economy. They show how the materiality of geography continues to be crucial to how economic life unfolds and reveal how this is not a simple mapping of economic activities onto an already differentiated space – these spaces and geographies are themselves constitutive of their economies.

Discussion points

- When you think about the economy, what do you think about? How about when you think about economic geography?
- What does economic geography add to our understanding of economies that the discipline of economics might not usually address?
- Which of the chapters piques your interest? Why do you think you are drawn to some over others?
- This book does not have a separate section on 'development studies' or 'development geography', because we think economic geography should also encompass critical and Majority World perspectives. What do you think we missed in taking this approach? What might we gain?

References

Bargh, M. (2011). The triumph of Maori entrepreneurs or diverse economies? *Aboriginal Policy Studies* 1(3): 53–69.

Barnes, T., and Christophers, B. (2018). *Economic Geography: A Critical Introduction*. Oxford: Wiley.

Bodman, A. (1992). Holes in the fabric: more on the master weavers in human geography. *Transactions of the Institute of British Geographers* 17: 108–109.

Buchanan, R. (1935a). *Economic Geography of the British Empire*. London: University of London Press.

Buchanan, R. (1935b). *The Pastoral Industries of New Zealand: A Study in Economic Geography. Institute of British Geographers Publications Number 2*. London: Philip and Son.

Cameron, J. (2009). Experimenting with Economic Possibilities: Ethical Economic Decision-Making in Two Australian Community Enterprises. In *The Social Economy: International Perspectives on Economic Solidarity*, ed. A. Amin. London: Zed Press, 92–115.

Carnegie, M., Rowland, C., Gibson, K., McKinnon, K., Crawford, J., and Slatter, C. (2012). Gender and economy in Melanesian communities: a manual of indicators and tools to track change. University of Western Sydney, Macquarie University and International Women's Development Agency.

Chishom, G. (1889). *Handbook of Commercial Geography*. London: Longman.

Coe, N., Kelly, P., and Yeung, H. (2020). *Economic Geography: A Contemporary Introduction*. Oxford: Wiley.

Dombroski, K. (2020). Caring Labour: Redistributing Care Work. In *The Handbook of Diverse Economies*, eds. J. K. Gibson-Graham and K. Dombroski. Cheltenham: Edward Elgar Publishing, 154–160.

Gibson-Graham, J. (2008). Diverse economies: performative practices for other worlds. *Progress in Human Geography* 32(5): 613–632.

Gibson-Graham, J. K. (2006). *A Postcapitalist Politics*. Minneapolis: University of Minnesota Press.

Gibson-Graham, J. K. (2005). Surplus possibilities: postdevelopment and community economies. *Singapore Journal of Tropical Geography* 26(1): 4–26.

Gibson-Graham, J. K. (1996). *The End of Capitalism (As We Knew It): A Feminist Critique of Political Economy*. Oxford: Blackwell

Gibson-Graham, J. K., Cameron, J., and Healy, S. (2013). *Take Back the Economy: An Ethical Guide for Transforming Our Communities*. Minneapolis: University of Minnesota Press.

Gibson-Graham, J. K., Cameron, J., Healy, S., and McNeill, J. (2019). Roepke lecture in economic geography—economic geography, manufacturing, and ethical action in the Anthropocene. *Economic Geography* 95(1): 1–21. https://doi.org/10.1080/00130095.2018.1538697

Gibson-Graham, J. K., and Dombroski, K. (2020). *The Handbook of Diverse Economies*. Cheltenham: Edward Elgar.

Hicks, J. (2020). Community Finance: Marshalling Investments for Community-Owned Renewable Energy Enterprises. In *The Handbook of Diverse Economies*, eds. J. K. Gibson-Graham and K. Dombroski. Cheltenham: Edward Elgar, 370–378.

Hossein, C. S., and Christabell, P. (2022). *Community Economies in the Global South: Case Studies of Rotating Savings and Credit Associations and Economic Cooperation*. Oxford: Oxford University Press.

Lee, R., and Wills, J. (2014). *Geographies and Economies*. London: Routledge.

Massey, D. (1997). Economic/Non-Economic. In *Geographies and Economies*, eds. R. Lee and J. Wills. London: Routledge, 27–36.

McKinnon, K. (2022). Positioning kindness and care at the centre of health services: a case study of an informal health and development programme oriented to surviving well collectively. *Asia Pacific Viewpoint* 63(1): 138–150. https://doi.org/10.1111/apv.12336

McKinnon, K., Healy, S., and Dombroski, K. (2019). Surviving Well Together: Postdevelopment, Maternity Care, and the Politics of Ontological Pluralism. In *Postdevelopment in Practice: Alternatives, Economies, Ontologies*, eds. E. Klein and C. E. Morreo. London: Routledge, 190–202.

McLean, H. (2022). Creative arts-based geographies: some cautionary and hopeful reflections. *ACME: An International Journal for Critical Geographies* 21(3): 311–326. https://acme-journal.org/index.php/acme/article/view/2195

Mitchell, T. (1998). Fixing the economy. *Cultural Studies* 12(1): 82–101.

Mitchell, T. (2005). The work of economics: how a discipline makes its world. *European Journal of Sociology/Archives Européennes de Sociologie* 46(2): 297–320.

Muniesa, F. (2014). *The Provoked Economy: Economic Reality and the Performative Turn*. London: Routledge.

Vunibola, S., Steven, H., and Scobie, M. (2022). Indigenous enterprise on customary lands: diverse economies of surplus. *Asia Pacific Viewpoint* 63(1): 40–52. https://doi.org/10.1111/apv.12326

Waring, M. (2018). *Still Counting: Wellbeing, Women's Work and Policy-Making* (Vol. 73). Wellington: Bridget Williams Books.

Online materials

- Economic Geography, the journal: https://www.tandfonline.com/journals/recg20

  Access the journal and past editions here. You might have to log in to your university library to see articles that are not open access.

- World Development, the journal: https://www.sciencedirect.com/journal/world-development

  Access the journal and past editions here. This journal is a multi-disciplinary development studies journal, but there are many others. Again, you may need to log in to your university library to access.

- Community Economies Institute: www.communityeconomies.org

  Find out more about the work of diverse economies and community economies scholars on this website. It has news, opportunities for further study and networking, and free papers and teaching resources.

Further reading

Two excellent textbooks which cover the full range of approaches introduced in this chapter are

Barnes, T., and Christophers, B. (2018). *Economic Geography: A Critical Introduction* Oxford: Wiley.

Coe, N., Kelly, P., and Yeung, H. (2020). *Economic Geography: A Contemporary Introduction.* Oxford: Wiley.

For an up-to-date introduction to diverse economies, see

Gibson-Graham, J. K., and Dombroski, K. (2020). *The Handbook of Diverse Economies.* Cheltenham: Edward Elgar.

For the book which stimulated the diverse economies approach, see

Gibson-Graham, J. K. (1996). *The End of Capitalism (As We Knew It): A Feminist Critique of Political Economy*, Oxford: Blackwell.

For recent work led by diverse economies scholars in Asia Pacific, see the 2022 special issue in the journal Asia Pacific Viewpoint *Surviving well: from diverse economies to community economies in Asia Pacific.*

31 Money and finance

Sarah Hall

Introduction

The international financial system plays an increasingly important role in shaping the everyday economic activities of households, firms and **nation-states**. For example, high street banks and building societies that sell us the financial products we use on a daily basis, such as personal loans, credit cards and savings accounts, rely on the activities of financiers working in **international financial centres** such as London and New York for the production of these financial products. Firms operating in sectors seemingly far removed from the glistening towers of Canary Wharf and Wall Street, such as manufacturing and food production, are tied into the international financial system as they face growing pressures to meet the financial targets expected of them by their shareholders, and they rely on global financial markets to access the capital they need to invest in new machinery and technology. Finally, in several advanced Western economies, banking, accountancy and financial markets – collectively known as the financial services industry – make a highly significant contribution to national economic growth and employment. This trend is particularly marked in the UK. Here, over 1 million people were employed in financial services in 2021, 3% of all jobs (Commons Library, 2022a).

Economic geographers, together with other social scientists, term the process by which these everyday economic activities of individuals, households and firms increasingly rely upon the international financial system, **financialisation**. During the 2000s, this process went largely unnoticed by academics, politicians and the media as the global economy enjoyed a period of significant expansion and households saw their standard of living and purchasing power increase, fuelled to a significant extent by relatively easy access to cheap credit. However, what Mervyn King, the Governor of the Bank of England, termed the NICE decade (no inflation, constant expansion) of the 2000s ended with the 'global' financial crisis dating back to late summer 2008. This crisis saw the collapse of several of the financial firms that had played a vital role in facilitating the process of financialisation, notably the investment bank Lehman Brothers, and the bailing out of a number of others including the multinational insurance company AIG. These events placed the relationship between ordinary households, firms and national economies, on the one hand, and the international financial system, on the other, in the political, media and academic spotlight.

Immediately following this financial crisis, it appeared as though the power of finance in shaping economic geography may be diminished. This has not turned out to be the case. Finance has reasserted itself in a number of ways in the intervening years. For example, there has been a significant digitisation of finance through fintech companies. These firms, including buy now

DOI: 10.4324/9780429265853-37

pay later lending companies such as Klarna as well as new digital banks such as Monzo, have become increasingly integrated into the international financial system and, in so doing, have shaped its development (Lai and Samers, 2021). Finance has also been increasingly implicated in other major transitions, notably in relation to responding to climate change.

These developments reveal the importance of thinking geographically about financialisation and money, and about finance more generally. In this chapter, I show how recent research on the geography of money and finance reveals how geography matters to both the operation of the international financial system, our own economic practices and the links between the two. In particular, I argue that understanding the cultural and social dimensions of money and finance is vital to revealing how these geographies are produced and their uneven effects on everyday economic life.

Placing and spacing the international financial system

Despite the importance of money and finance to the global economy, economic geographers only began to focus on money as a substantive research concern from the late 1970s onwards. David Harvey's detailed examination of the role of money and finance in shaping urban environments through investment strategies marks one of the most significant contributions to this early research on the geographies of money and finance (Harvey, 1982). This work provided the basis for the emergence of a sub-field of economic geography, focusing on money and finance, that developed most significantly from the early 1990s onwards. Research at this time continued to adopt the critical approach to the (il)logics of the international financial system that had been initiated by Harvey. For example, following economic geography's broader interests in macro-scale socio-economic transformation associated with the intensification of **globalisation** processes, research focused on the changing geo-politics of the international financial system. This work examines how geographically specific financial regulations and working cultures combined to produce an international financial system that was anchored in a small number of international financial centres (notably London and New York) and offshore financial centres which have attractive regulatory environments for financial firms (Martin, 1999).

By pointing to the continued importance of a relatively small number of places within the international financial system, this research refutes claims that the deepening integration of financial markets driven by technological innovation and deregulation would herald the demise of geography as a key determinant of the location of financial services activity. For example, O'Brien (1991) in his 'end of geography' thesis argued that greater use of technology and virtual forms of communication would mean that financial firms would no longer have to co-locate within financial districts in order to conduct business. However, echoing geographical work on money and finance, the business pages of newspapers and the financial news on television and radio clearly show how financial services activities remain concentrated in a small number of international financial centres.

This clustering of financial services activity is not new. For example, London's financial services cluster began to develop from the 1700s onwards, supporting the rise of Britain as an imperial power (Cain and Hopkins, 1986). However, the clustering of financial services activity intensified throughout the twentieth century, giving rise to a distinct hierarchy of international financial centres (see Table 31.1). The relative importance of different financial centres can be partly explained by the geographical reach of the markets they service (Beaverstock et al., 1999).

Table 31.1 Ranking of top 20 international financial centres

Financial centre	2022 Rank	2021 Rank	Change
New York	1	1	–
London	2	2	–
Singapore	3	6	+3
Hong Kong	4	3	−1
San Francisco	5	7	+2
Shanghai	6	4	−2
Los Angeles	7	5	−2
Beijing	8	8	–
Shenzhen	9	10	+1
Paris	10	11	+1
Seoul	11	12	+1
Chicago	12	13	+1
Sydney	13	23	+10
Boston	14	14	–
Washington, DC	15	15	−1
Tokyo	16	9	−7
Dubai	17	17	–
Frankfurt	18	16	−2
Amsterdam	19	19	–
Geneva	20	25	+5

Source: Adapted from Z/Yen (2022)

At the top of the hierarchy sit London and New York (see Figure 31.1). These alpha world cities offer the full range of financial services to global clients (including investment banking, insurance, trading of financial products on stock exchanges and new services such as those associated with Islamic finance). Following these two centres are secondary, or beta centres such as Hong Kong and Singapore, that service pan-regional markets. Below these sit sub-regional, or gamma, centres such as Chicago and Zurich that offer more geographically and organisationally specialist services. However, whilst London and New York have dominated this hierarchy for at least 50 years, a number of smaller centres have grown rapidly in recent years. For example, Singapore and Hong Kong have developed from regional centres into established financial centres in their own right. Meanwhile, alongside these two, Shanghai, Beijing and Shenzhen also currently feature in the top 10 financial centres, reflecting the growing importance of South East Asia in the international financial system.

Beyond the size of the markets that different financial centres service, geography is also important in explaining the dominance of a small number of financial clusters in other ways. For

Figure 31.1
New York Stock Exchange on Wall Street

Source: Photo credit: Pacifica/Alamy

example, the continued dominance of London and New York reflects their historic importance as trading centres more generally, as this gave them a competitive advantage over other cities as the international financial system developed. Their location in different time zones is also an important factor as this allows financial firms to trade around the clock if they have offices in both London and New York. Moreover, the nature of financial services work itself is an important factor in driving the continued concentration of financial markets in particular cities. Three **agglomeration** benefits are particularly significant in this respect. First, financial clusters facilitate liquid financial markets. This means that already existing financial markets attract more buyers and sellers of financial products because they are most likely to find customers for their own products there. Second, the clustering of financial firms within financial centres gives rise to 'buzz' between financiers (Bathelt et al., 2004). This buzz, built around dense inter-personal and inter-firm relations, facilitates processes of innovation and the production of new financial products because financiers can learn about the specific demands of their clients and gather information on their competitors' activities. Third, once a financial centre becomes established, it continues to attract the highly skilled labour force that is necessary for the production of bespoke financial products.

This interest in the nature of financial services work, and its role in shaping the geographies of the international financial system has been the focus of much of the research conducted by economic geographers from the late 1990s onwards. This work is significant because it marks an expansion in the theoretical toolkit used by geographers interested in money and finance beyond its earlier focus on the geo-politics of finance. Instead, this more recent work examines how the social and cultural dimensions of money and finance are also important factors in explaining the continued dominance of a small number of financial centres. A focus on the financiers working within international financial centres is particularly important in this respect since by understanding their activities, it is possible to enhance our understanding of the uneven geography of the international financial system more generally.

This work focuses on the routinised, formal and informal actions of individual financiers. This includes studies of their daily working practices and their out-of-work networking in social spaces such as bars and restaurants within financial centres, airport departure lounges and **expatriate** clubs, echoing the global nature of financial careers (see, for example, Beaverstock, 2002). In so doing, sophisticated accounts of the ways in which working practices associated with the information-rich nature of financial services are crucial in shaping the continued importance of a small number of international financial centres have developed.

Three aspects of this work are particularly important. First, research has revealed how establishing inter-personal relations within and between financial centres is vital for financiers to produce and circulate technical knowledge about financial products and the demands of customers (Clark and O'Connor, 1997). Indeed, the importance of these networks gives rise to frequent travel between financial centres, either for specific meetings or for longer term secondments as financial firms seek to disseminate their corporate knowledges between financial centres. Second, research has examined how financial services work also involves a more **embodied** and emotive set of knowledges that are played out through bodily **performances**. In this respect, individuals gain access to the personal networks that are important for their daily work by dressing and acting in similar ways to their peers in order that the trust necessary for building such networks might be fostered (Thrift, 1994). Moreover, McDowell (1997) has demonstrated how such bodily performances are **gendered** such that women working in financial services often adopt similar bodily comportment to their male counterparts in order to gain acceptance and recognition within elite financial labour markets. Third, whilst educational background has been well documented as an important element in securing access to these networks, recent research has demonstrated how ongoing training and education within financial workplaces through schemes such as graduate training courses within investment banks and MBA degrees from leading business schools are also important activities through which individuals learn how to act as an international financier and gain access into the personal networks within financial centres that are crucial for their own career success.

Summary

- Despite processes of technological innovation and regulatory reform, global finance remains concentrated in a small number of international financial centres.
- There is a dynamic hierarchy of international financial centres that reflects their relative importance as command and control points within global finance.
- This hierarchy reflects changes in the nature of finance itself. For example, the increasing importance of San Francisco reflects the growing links between tech firms and financial services.
- In order to explain the continued importance of international financial centres, research needs to consider money and finance as social and cultural practices as well as sets of economic and political relations.

Geographies of everyday financialised lives

The geographies of the international financial system and the continued importance of international financial centres within it are not only important for the working practices of financial elites. Our own everyday lives are increasingly tied into this financial system through our consumption of financial products and here too, geography matters. In this respect, economic geographers have well-established research interests in retail finance – that is, financial services offered to households through high street banks and building societies and internet providers. Indeed, early research on mortgage finance, negative equity (meaning home-owners who owe their mortgage provider more than the current value of their home) and financial exclusion provided an important impetus for the development of a sub-field of geographical work on money and finance in the 1990s (Leyshon, 1995).

These research topics re-emerged in the 2010s, driven by the ways in which personal finance was central to the 'global' financial crisis of 2008. Again, issues of mortgage finance have been placed centre stage as the inability of sub-prime (higher risk) borrowers in certain parts of the US to meet their mortgage payments was a critical factor in triggering the crisis as mortgage lenders had to react to the fact that the loans they had made might not be paid back. Moreover, in the wake of the crisis, personal finance has been affected significantly with continued stock market falls impacting negatively on pension fund performance and home loans still being highly limited as lenders seek to minimise their exposure to risk. Echoing research on the international financial system, this more recent interest in personal and retail finance has adopted a more socially and culturally sensitive mode of analysis as compared to earlier work, focusing in particular on questions of financial inclusion, exclusion and their uneven geographies.

Financial exclusion refers to 'those processes by which individuals and households face difficulties in accessing financial services' (Leyshon et al., 2008: 447). Two processes have increased the extent of financial exclusion during the 2000s. First, de-regulatory reforms of the financial services industry in advanced **capitalist** economies have allowed financial firms to develop new financial products that reflect the fact that individuals and households, rather than the state, are increasingly responsible for their own future financial security. This process is particularly marked in terms of pension provision as individuals are tied into the international financial system through the decline of defined benefit pension provision in which individuals were guaranteed a level of retirement income. Instead, individuals are reliant upon becoming active managers of their retirement income through using a range of investments in international financial markets (Clark, 2003). In this way, individuals are expected to act as responsible financial consumers who, through suitable education from financial literacy schemes, manage and take risks in order to manage their own financial futures (Langley 2008). However, these products are often targeted at the most profitable individuals and hence other individuals, especially those not able to engage with financial literacy, are marginalised from these financial products. Second, technological innovation and the development of new financial products, particularly those linked to the international financial system through processes of securitisation, have led to a number of new channels for financial services being developed that increasingly use virtual forms of communication, particularly through activities like internet banking (Leyshon and Pollard, 2000).

Two consequences of the intensification of these financial exclusion processes are particularly significant, both of which are inherently geographical. First, research has demonstrated how the

415

growing focus on profitable financial customers has given rise to a highly uneven geography of financial services withdrawal. This is most marked in terms of bank and building society branch closures, which have meant that the number of branches in the UK has shrunk by about two thirds between 1986 and 2021 (Commons Library, 2022b). These closures have been driven by social and technological change, and accelerated by the pandemic, but geographers have played a vital role in demonstrating the importance of space and place to such processes. In this respect, the physical **infrastructure** of bank and building society branches has been conceptualised as a network, the scope and density of which can be measured, both by region, but also, and more significantly, along socio-economic lines. By adopting the latter approach, Leyshon et al. (2008) demonstrated the disproportionate impact of service withdrawal in socio-economically deprived wards in the UK. This focus on the geographies of processes of financial exclusion was developed further through the identification of different forms of retail financial ecologies (Leyshon et al., 2004). This metaphor is used to demonstrate how the working practices of financial service providers, particularly in terms of their assessment of potential customers 'at a distance' using a range of credit scoring techniques, is co-constitutive of financial landscapes. This approach has identified two contrasting idealised types of ecology: first, the middle-class ecology in which highly financially literate customers use a range of distribution channels to access financial services and hence maintain a strong physical and virtual bank and building society branch network; and second 'relic' ecologies in which socio-economically deprived groups suffer both the demise of mainstream financial provision on the basis of their lack of profitability and are instead subjected to a range of more exploitative forms of financial provision such as credit offered by door-to-door lenders. This is manifested in the built environment through the greater branch closure rates in more economically deprived neighbourhoods (see Figure 31.2).

Figure 31.2
Closed branch of the bank Santander, London, UK

Source: Photo credit: Troika/Alamy

The relationship between space, socio-economically deprived financial subjects and retail financial services provision has also been examined through work that looked at access to credit, notably sub-prime mortgage finance (Aalbers, 2005, 2008). This work demonstrated how high street financial firms accessed credit via commercial banks within the international financial system in order to increase lending in the 2000s. However, access to such credit was highly uneven, with **race** and **class** acting as important factors when lenders were making decisions concerning which potential customers were deemed credit-worthy and how favourable (or otherwise) the terms of any home loan would be. In addition to revealing the different ways in which individuals and households have experienced the fall-out from the financial crisis, this work also points to the relationship between elite and 'everyday' financial systems that were fostered through processes of financialisation.

Economic geographers have also increasingly sought to understand how changes in financial services associated with the growing use of digital technology have their own economic geographies. This work centres on the fintech sector. Fintech is a broad category that relates to forms of payment, banking and insurance. It can be defined as operating 'at the intersections of the finance and technology sectors where technology-focused start-ups and new market entrants are creating new platforms, products, and services beyond those currently provided by the traditional finance industry [that are] changing how businesses and consumers make payments, lend, borrow, and invest' (Lai and Samers, 2021: 720). Work in economic geography has explored the geographies of the new fintech firms themselves, the changing nature of money associated with the development of crypto, or essentially online, currencies and the regulation of fintech. It is clear that the fintech sector is beginning to shape the mainstream financial services sector through, for example, cities with large fintech clusters climbing up the rankings of financial centres as shown in Table 31.1. As the sector continues to grow and become more closely linked to mainstream finance, it is likely to be a key future area of work for economic geographers.

Summary

- Individual households are increasingly tied into the international financial system through investment products, most notably mortgage finance and pension funds.
- This process is termed financialisation but has led to financial exclusion as certain groups are unable to access financial services.
- Financial exclusion disproportionately affects minority and lower socio-economic groups. This was particularly noticeable following the 'global' financial crisis that began in 2008.
- Economic geographers are increasingly studying new forms of technologically mediated finance, notably fintech.

Conclusion

Economic geographical research into both the international financial system and the everyday financial geographies of households has developed rapidly since being framed as central research issues for geographers from the 1990s onwards. Whilst the rise of virtual forms of communication, technological innovation and deregulation might appear to lead to a decline in the importance of space and place to these economic activities, the research presented in this chapter clearly demonstrates that conceptualising money and finance geographically is vitally important in order to understand the uneven production and consequences of both the international financial system and its links to household economies. In order to understand these geographies fully, recent research has revealed the importance of considering finance as a cultural and social practice, as well as a set of economic and political relations. In particular, the value of this approach lies in documenting how the activities of financial elites working in a select number of international financial centres are linked to the financial products that individuals and households increasingly rely upon for their own financial futures, particularly pension funds and mortgages.

However, the research discussed above on these processes of financialisation and on new developments such as fintech also has its own, partial geography in that the vast majority of research has been conducted within the heartlands of the international financial system, particularly the US and Western Europe. This selectivity in research sites is important because it means that the accounts generated of money and finance are themselves partial. This partiality was revealed most clearly by the aftermath of the so-called global financial crisis of 2008, which was actually experienced rather differently beyond the US and Europe. It is important that future research into the geographies of money and finance expands its own geographical horizons to develop more fully accounts of financial geographies in emerging economies. Within this emerging research agenda, the cases of South East Asia and the BRIC economies (Brazil, Russia, India and China) are particularly important since these are home to both rapidly growing international financial centres such as Singapore and Shanghai as well as vast domestic markets for everyday financial products. Understanding these emerging geographies of money and finance will be vitally important if economic geographers are to continue to understand the dynamic and uneven geographies of international finance and the consequences of this for individuals and households.

Acknowledgement

I am grateful for the support of the ESRC (ES/T000821/1) that has allowed me to develop the ideas presented in this chapter.

Discussion points

- The majority of research into the geographies of money and finance has been conducted in the US and Western Europe. What are the limitations of this approach and why are they important?
- What is the value of understanding money and finance as social and cultural practices?
- In what ways are the geographies of the international financial system linked to household economies and why do these linkages, known as processes of financialisation, matter?
- How is your daily life tied into the international financial system and how is this changing with the growth of fintech?

References

Aalbers, M. (2005). Place based social exclusion: redlining in the Netherlands. *Area* 37: 100–109.

Aalbers, M. (2008). The finanicialization of home and the mortgage market crisis. *Competition and Change* 12: 148–166.

Bathelt, H., Malmberg, A., and Maskell, P. (2004). Clusters and knowledge: local buzz, global pipelines and the process of knowledge creation. *Progress in Human Geography* 28: 31–56.

Beaverstock, J. V. (2002). Transnational elites in global cities: British expatriates in Singapore's financial district. *Geoforum* 33(4): 525–538.

Beaverstock, J. V., Smith, R. G., and Taylor, P. J. (1999). A roster of world cities. *Cities* 16(6): 445–458.

Cain, P. J., and Hopkins, A. G. (1986). Gentlemanly capitalism and British expansion overseas I. The colonial system 1688–1850. *Economic History Review* 39(4): 501–525.

Clark, G. L. (2003). *European Pensions and Global Finance*. Oxford: Oxford University Press.

Clark, G., and O'Connor, K. (1997). The Informational Content of Financial Products and the Spatial Structure of the Global Finance Industry. In *Spaces of Globalization: Reasserting the Power of the Local*, ed. K. Cox. New York: Guildford, 89–114.

Commons Library. (2022a). Financial services: contribution to the UK economy available from https://commonslibrary.parliament.uk/research-briefings/sn06193/

Commons Library. (2022b). The future of local banking services and access to cash available from https://researchbriefings.files.parliament.uk/documents/CBP-9453/CBP-9453.pdf

Harvey, D. (1982). *The Limits to Capital*. Oxford: Blackwell.

Lai, K. P. Y., and Samers, M. (2021). Towards an economic geography of FinTech. *Progress in Human Geography* 45(4): 720–739. Available at https://doi.org/10.1177/0309132520938461

Langley, P. (2008). *The Everyday Life of Global Finance: Saving and Borrowing in Anglo-America*. Oxford: Oxford University Press.

Leyshon, A. (1995). Geographies of money and finance I. *Progress in Human Geography* 19: 531–543.

Leyshon, A., Burton, D., Knights, D., Alferoff, C., and Signoretta, P. (2004). Towards an ecology of retail financial services: understanding the persistence of door-to-door credit and insurance providers. *Environment and Planning A* 36: 625–646.

Leyshon, A., French, S., and Signoretta, P. (2008). Financial exclusion and the geography of bank and building society closure in Britain. *Transactions of the Institute of British Geographers* 33: 447–465.

Leyshon, A., and Pollard, J. (2000). Geographies of industrial convergence: the case of retail banking. *Transactions of the Institute of British Geographers* 25: 203–220.

Martin, R. (ed.) (1999). *Money and the Space Economy*. Oxford: Wiley.

McDowell, L. (1997). *Capital Culture*, Oxford: Blackwell.

O'Brien, R. (1991). *Global Financial Integration: The End of Geography*. London: Pinter.

Thrift, N. (1994). On the Social and Cultural Determinants of International Financial Centres: The Case of the City of London. In *Money, Power and Space*, eds. N. Thrift, S. Corbridge, and R. Martin. Oxford: Blackwell, 327–355.

Z/Yen. (2022). *The Global Financial Centre Index 32*. London: Z/Yen.

Online materials

- Talking Politics podcast 113, Crashed.

  Available at https://www.talkingpoliticspodcast.com/blog/2018/113-crashed. In this podcast, two Cambridge researchers, David Runciman and Helen Thomson, along with the historian Adam Tooze, discuss the financial crisis.

Further reading

The following texts introduce the broad field of economic geographical research into money and finance and the value of a socially and culturally sensitive approach:

Leyshon, A., and Thrift, N. J. (1997). *Money/Space*. London: Routledge

Martin, R. (ed.) (1998). *Money and the Space Economy*. Chichester: John Wiley.

Hall, S. (2017). *Global Finance: Places, Spaces and People*. London: Sage.

Knorr Cetina, K., and Preda, A. (eds.) (2004). *The Sociology of Financial Markets*. Oxford: Oxford University Press.

The following are more specialist texts that deal with the gendered nature of financial services work and the links between everyday and international finance respectively.

McDowell, L. (1997). *Capital Culture*. Oxford: Oxford University Press.

Langley, P. (2008). *The Everyday Life of Global Finance: Saving and Borrowing in Anglo-America*. Oxford: Oxford University Press.

A number of academic journals regularly publish papers reporting research into the geographies of money and finance. The following journals are particularly important, several of which have published special issues on the topic: *Journal of Economic Geography, Economic Geography, Environment and Planning A, Geoforum, Transactions of the Institute of British Geographers.*

32 Consumption

Juliana Mansvelt

Introducing consumption

In March of 2022, news articles reported that a 20-year-old New Zealander Stephen van Blerk had made $103 million (US $70 million) in 10 minutes for selling digital artworks in an online auction for his fantasy cyberworld called Pixelmon (Church, 2022). The story of a relatively young New Zealander making 'it big' internationally is a familiar media motif, but what drew my attention to this story was not this narrative but the fact that his Pixelmon scheme provoked outrage from purchasers. It seems that van Blerk had presold his Pixelmon NFTs (non-fungible tokens) on an online auction site and the promised digital artwork was not of expected quality.

NFTs are a form of **commodity** – a good, experience or service bought or sold in a market. NFTs are unique and irreplaceable. A purchaser of an NFT uses cryptocurrency to acquire a unique piece of digital code. It is not uncommon for buyers to purchase code for digital art based on promised designs and Van Blerk had provided a mock-up of the digital creatures he was selling. The presold Pixelmons fetched a substantial price of 3 Etherums (approximately $NZ 4800) each, but purchasers were disappointed with the final product. One purchaser noted that when the 'egg' holding his character hatched, 'It literally looked like something from Microsoft Paint. It was so comically bad that anyone in their right mind would look at that and say that you can't release that' (Church, 2022, https://www.1news.co.nz/2022/03/03/comically-bad-nz-made-nft-scheme-pixelmon-sparks-outrage/).

The dashed expectations and subsequent anger of those NFT consumers reveal why consumption involves so much more than a singular moment of purchase or economic exchange. Whether we acquire commodities in online sites or in bricks and mortar stores, the emotions, practices and consequences of our consumption have real effects. In this chapter, we will consider what consumption involves and why it matters for our social and spatial relationships with people, things and places.

Consumption moments, practices and places

Consumption can be defined as a set of social relations, practices and **discourses** which centre on the acquisition, use and disposal of commodities (Mansvelt, 2005). In contemporary society, consumption is often caught up in consumerism, which involves the individual and collective pursuit of commodities, and the ubiquitous cultural expression of consumption in everyday life (Miles, 1998). David Evans (2019), in extending the work of sociologist Alan Warde (2014), suggests there are six moments (three As and three Ds) associated with consumption.

DOI: 10.4324/9780429265853-38

Acquisition, appropriation and appreciation

According to Evans (2019), acquisition involves the set of processes concerning how people acquire and obtain experiences, goods and services. Acquisition may involve purchase of commodities in a market (whether digitally or face to face) but also incorporates other ways people access the goods, services and experiences they consume (e.g. through gifting or passing on). For those who have sufficient money to buy commodities, acquisition may seem like a straightforward or even taken for granted process; however, access to and an ability to acquire items may be uneven. Commodity choices available to individuals and households can vary considerably because of political, social, economic and cultural processes and networks operating across multiple scales. Commodity supply and availability, personal or geographical accessibility, affordability and social or spatial exclusion can impact acquisition (see, for example, Sarah Hall's [2019] work on austerity). Government-imposed COVID-19 lockdowns experienced in many parts of the world during 2020 and 2021 also demonstrate the diversity of Covid-related impacts on acquisition (Chung et al., 2020). Box 32.1 describes my own experience of lockdown in New Zealand.

Consumption is nevertheless more than acquisition. Those who market and sell commodities are keen to offer consumers intended meanings, uses, expectations, sensations and feelings. Humans do things with the goods and services they purchase, investing meaning in them, using them and valuing them outside of their economic cost. The properties of goods, services and experiences (NFTS included!) also affect people, impacting our senses and emotions and influencing behaviours. These elements of consumption speak to processes of appropriation and appreciation, which involve the attribution of social, cultural and symbolic values to goods and services.

Appropriation comprises the process by which commodities become possessions and are given meaning and value outside of spaces of commodity exchange (Kopytoff, 1986). Goods and services lose their commodity status as we integrate them into our lives, practices and spaces. Appropriation may involve acceptance or rejection of the commodity meanings offered to us by marketers and retailers. Appropriation occurs through a range of practices, such as wearing, preparing, assembling, using up, displaying and sharing. Acts of appropriation also apply to digital commodities, for example wielding or displaying digital artefacts in online worlds or curating collections of favourite digital music.

Appreciation is a corollary to appropriation, contributing further to how we give/add value to the things we consume. It involves how people derive satisfaction or pleasure from goods, services and experiences. For example, savouring the taste and texture of food while eating may be an **affective** and joyful experience influenced by broader cultural tastes (Bourdieu, 2010). Repeated acts of appropriation and appreciation are also significant in the social reproduction of gendered, sexed, ethnic and aged relations of families, organisations and social groups. Consider, for example, how meal routines and practices might shape the culture of families, generations or households and, in turn, be influenced by these.

Like acquisition, processes of appropriation and appreciation are formed in relation to other people and things, for example, an individual commenting favourably on an item you have acquired might enhance your appreciation of it. Places matter too – the enjoyment of delicious food may be increased through socialising with others in a café or restaurant or because of the ambience and experience of being in these places.

BOX 32.1
COVID-19: CHANGING SPACES AND EXPERIENCES OF ACQUISITION

The altered networks and flows which impacted consumption following the outbreak of COVID-19 were not just felt at international, national or regional scales but also impacted personal geographies. New Zealand entered its first lockdown on 25 March 2020, and households went into complete isolation. I was grateful to continue my employment from home, aware that lockdowns were dramatically affecting livelihoods globally, particularly in nations without social provision for lost income. I had access to the internet and was one of many shoppers who began to purchase more of their goods and services online (Tymkiw, 2022). Only essential businesses remained open in New Zealand for face-to-face transactions (primarily grocery stores, health providers and petrol stations). Encouraged by supermarkets to save online delivery slots for the immune-compromised, I was the member of our household nominated to shop in-store. Here is a diary excerpt regarding my first foray into a small supermarket, a familiar space, now made foreign by the impact of the virus:

Sunday 29th March. Day 4 of NZ's lockdown 65 Covid cases today, and NZ's first death.

I ventured out just before 9 am to get some milk and vegetables from our local Four-Square (superette) in Shannon. It felt really weird to leave home - hardly any cars on the road, only another customer in the shop. The attendant was behind a Perspex screen and there were signs on the floor indicating we must stand 2 metres apart. There were also instructions to get in and out of the store as quickly as possible and not stock-up. Taking only what I needed wasn't difficult - all I could buy had to be carried in my hands as the shopping baskets had been taken away! The fruit and vegetables were all wrapped in plastic; this seemed really strange given the banning of single-use plastic bags in New Zealand and efforts to reduce plastic packaging. I grabbed 4 litres of milk, broccoli, pears and nectarines. There were no bananas or apples - the fruits we normally have. There was no Paywave, so I felt conscious of touching the keypad on the EFTPOS (electronic point of sale machine), something I had never thought about before. Back at the car I used the hand-sanitiser before I touched my key. Once home the bags were left in the garage, and the milk bottles and plastic bags swabbed down in dilute bleach. So strange to be treating everyday objects like some contagion.

This excerpt illustrates how moments of consumption reverberate in our lives, influencing our sense of self, our relations with others and how we feel about places. When everyday practices are disrupted, structures, networks, flows and processes that make consumption possible can become visible. I felt shocked to see empty shelves, a reminder of **globalisation** and the failure of the supply chains which brought imported goods into New Zealand – yet empty shelves are much more a normal part of daily lives for those in countries with civil unrest/war famine. Restrictions on purchase, movement and physical distancing became a reminder of the relative freedoms I usually associated with acquisition (see Figure 32.1).

Figure 32.1
Covid restrictions in many places changed the ways in which consumption practices have been manifested and experienced, such as using hand sanitiser before touching shared objects (32.1a). Social distancing restrictions became part of a new norm while shopping (32.1b)

Source: Photo credit: Inge Flinte

Earlier in the pandemic, limited understanding of COVID-19 transmission (e.g. surface contact versus aerosols) and a fear of contagion made me acutely aware of the materiality of touch in the shop. Wiping and sanitising became part of my acquisition practices, helping overcome my anxieties and enabled me to reassert some **agency** over the commodities that came into my household.

Devaluation, divestment and disposal

Over time, however, our attitudes to our use of services and the things we possess may change. Objects of consumption may wear, break, or lose their utility and meaning. Practices, places and relationships previously associated with commodities can be undone. Evans (2019) suggests there are three moments at work here – devaluation, divestment and disposal. Such moments are important, not just because they may lead to wasting and negative environmental impacts, but because devaluation and the removal of goods and services from our lives can provide a stimulus for, and an intersection with, further cycles of first-hand or second-hand consumption.

Devaluation is the opposite of appreciation, comprising the process whereby we lose our affinity with, and/or the pleasure derived from goods, services and experiences. A worn item of clothing, for example, may no longer bring enjoyment it once did to the wearer – it may lose its status and meaning as a cool, fashionable or comfortable item, or when worn, it may not invoke the same material feel, emotions or aesthetic as it once did (see Box 32.2).

BOX 32.2
DEVALUATION AND DIVESTMENT IN CLOTHING PRACTICE

Elyse Stanes (2019, 2021) work on the microgeographies of clothing provides insight into the complexity of consumption practices beyond acquisition. Stanes' **ethnographic** research into the clothing practices of 23 young Australians revealed the ways in which the haptic (senses and feelings based on material touch) influences the valuation and devaluation of clothing. Her focus on polyester clothing demonstrates how the material properties of this human-made fibre impact how long it lasts, as well as the subsequent practices of devaluation, divestment and ultimately disposal. Though polyester material sheds plastic fibres through pilling and washing, it lasts longer relative to naturally derived fabrics which wear and tear more easily. The persistence of polyester clothing meant Stanes' participants found it more difficult to divest and dispose of this apparel and devalued items often lingered in wardrobes

Figure 32.2
Worn, but not 'worn out': A difficult to divest polyester garment 'stuck' in a wardrobe

Source: Photo credit: Elyse Stanes

and storage spaces (see Figure 32.2). Studying the everyday microgeographies of touch and feel, Stanes sheds light into the journeys of clothing from acquisition to divestment or wasting, connecting individual practices, such as wearing, washing and ridding, to the materiality of polyester fabrics, to wider geographies and to further circuits of second-hand clothing/ fabric consumption (for a fascinating study of these circuits, see the work of geographer Andrew Brooks, 2019).

Divestment often accompanies devaluation as goods, services and experiences lose their utility and social value for the user, and their status as items of personal or social attachment may be severed. The removal of such attachments may be sudden (as with the failure of appliances or devices that cannot be repaired) or more gradual (the losing of attachments to family photos over generations for example). Such detachments are easier to see with material goods – the leftover food which lingers at the back of the fridge or the pair of shoes which once a favourite are now rarely worn. However, services and digital goods can also be subject to devaluation and divestment – for example, I feel somewhat guilty about my paid online fitness app that has remained unopened on my phone for a couple of months!

The cancellation of payment for my fitness app and its deletion would be the final stage in my ridding of this good from my life and speaks to the third of the 'Ds', Disposal. When we think of disposal, we often think of wasting, but there are numerous other conduits by which things can be removed from our lives. Re-gifting, passing on, recycling, repair, composting, reusing and re-purposing are practices that can divert material from waste streams. Hetherington (2004) argues wasting is also an act of placing, with waste continuing to have a material presence even as it is transformed into other states (the environmental effects of microplastics in waterways is a good example of this; see Woodward et al., 2020).

The moments which comprise consumption are not necessarily mutually exclusive. For example, the sudden failure of an appliance may result in processes of devaluation, depreciation and disposal, which occur almost simultaneously. Devalued and divested items may be re-valued and reappropriated – an unused item of clothing may be appreciated as an item of nostalgia or reappropriated as it becomes useful in a new work or leisure context. Consequently, a focus on these moments of consumption illuminates both the complexity and the connectivity of consumption practices in and across places.

Summary

- Consumption is a set of social relations, practices and discourses, which centre on the acquisition, use and disposal of commodities. Consumption is enabled and expressed through digital and physical spaces and practices.
- There are six moments which underpin processes of consumption: acquisition, appropriation, appreciation, devaluation, divestment and disposal.
- Studying these moments, the practices which comprise them and the places in which they occur can enable us to understand why consumption matters to individuals, societies, and environments.

Bringing it all together: why geographical connections matter

Consumption, like production, involves political, cultural and economic processes which are integral to creating meaningful places and maintaining everyday life. Geographical research has centred on the spatial form of consumption networks and flows and the contexts in and across which consumption is constituted and expressed (**spatialities**). It has also focussed on the **socialities** or social relationships which centre on moments and practices of consumption (including relationships between human and non-human entities). A third focus has been on the formation of **subjectivities**, that is, identity and subject positions and the moral and material outcomes that stem from their construction and reproduction in place.

Spatialities

Much of late twentieth century geographical research on consumption focussed on spaces of consumption and consumer culture, initially shopping malls, theme parks and fairs (e.g. Goss, 1999), and then onto less spectacular spaces, markets, high streets, homes (e.g. Cox, 2013) and second-hand spaces of consumption (e.g. Gregson and Crewe, 2003). The growth of the internet and platform economies as a site of consumption have seen a growing body of research on practices of digital consumption (Bissell, 2020, Rao, 2020). Increasingly, scholars have come to recognise that online and physical spaces and the consumption practices associated with them are entangled, connected by financial, cultural and political flows and networks.

Ethnographic studies of consumption have revealed the complexity of consumption practice beyond acquisition and have primarily focused on individuals and households as final consumers (Lane and Gorman-Murray, 2011). More recent research has centred on the intersection of home with wider flows, **infrastructures** and networks (e.g. Foden et al., 2019 on consumption at home and the nexus between water, energy and food practices and policies). Geographers have highlighted the production of consumption – the work, skill and knowledge necessary to acquire, appropriate and appreciate, maintain, keep, value and dispose of commodities (Bell, 2019) and the ways in which emotion and affect operate to influence consumption in place. Miller's (2015) research in Abasto Shopping Mall, Buenos Aires, for example, demonstrates that visitors relate to the mall differently in terms of their affective and emotional relationships. He also highlights how visitors' experiences are not produced exclusively through practices and moments of consumption but are shaped through the exercise of other forms of **power** (such as the reproduction of racism and hetero-normativity). Accordingly, understanding why, where and how places of consumption enable certain practices and experiences, while constraining or obscuring others, is important too. Research on night-life and night cultures, for example, has examined the consumption of drugs and alcohol, noting how people, environments and objects are entities/agents which come together as an **assemblage** to influence how consumption is practiced, **embodied**, felt and experienced in place (Duff and Moore, 2015, Wilkinson, 2017).

Space and place are not just produced through consumption; they are also consumed through production and social reproduction (Goodman et al., 2010). Resources may be used up, land, sea or air may become commodified and existing uses of space may be reconfigured (e.g. for new factories, housing, leisure pursuits or schools). Place and commodity meanings can be altered or displaced as a consequence. Research by Gregson and Crang (2015) on waste economies broadened research beyond individual consumption and household practices to consider firms, organisations and the politics and flows of waste networks as they impact local, regional and global scales. Scholarship on commodity chains/networks and circular economies has provided geographers with a way of making sense of connections between production and consumption (see Box 32.3).

BOX 32.3
MAKING CONNECTIONS BETWEEN CONSUMPTION AND PRODUCTION: COMMODITY CHAINS AND CIRCULAR ECONOMIES

For many years, geographers have studied commodity chains which comprise the connections between aspects of production and the production of a commodity for final consumption (see Figure 32.3). Initial scholarship (e.g. Gereffi and Korzeniewicz, 1994) emphasised linear global commodity chains which focussed on the role of lead firms in determining economic activities as they were spread across spaces and scales.

Over time, the metaphor was extended to reflect the development of more complex production networks and the way commodity value is created. This research centred on the range of related activities that firms and workers performed to create or bring a product from conception to end use for consumers, through processes such as research and development (R&D), design, production, marketing and distribution (Gereffi, 2018: 306). Though work on commodity and value chains has been criticised in recent years for its narrow conceptual focus on firm activity and for lack of focus on inequalities (Argent, 2017), commodity chain research has been significant in highlighting the connections between production and acquisition, interrogating where and how value is created and for thinking about why particular activities within the chain touch down in particular places. It has provided a starting point for scholars to follow the social and spatial lives of 'things', enabling geographers to consider how firms have organised their various activities across space, and

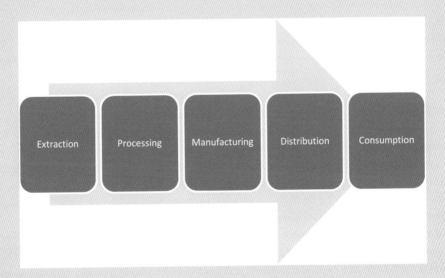

Figure 32.3
A simplified commodity chain
Source: Figure credit: Juliana Mansvelt

Figure 32.4
Simplified representation of a circular economy

Source: Figure credit: Hannah Wedlock, adapted from Figure 1, Attribution 4.0 International (CC BY 4.0) in Barbaritano, M., Bravi, L., and Savelli, E. (2019). Sustainability and quality management in the Italian luxury furniture sector: a circular economy perspective. *Sustainability* 11: 3089. https://doi.org/10.3390/su11113089

allowing NGOs and consumer activists to invoke and morally frame the actions of producers, consumers and governments (Jackson et al., 2009). However, commodity chain research has not accounted well for consumption beyond acquisition or those aspects of consumption (e.g. resource and energy use, disposal and wasting) that may be part of production (Hobson, 2016, Pollard et al., 2016). Circular economy models (see Figure 32.4 for an idealised representation) redress this by highlighting the consumption which occurs at all parts of the production and use of commodities.

Circular economy models draw attention to how consumption by a range of actors (growers, manufacturers, distributors, retailers and consumers) in commodity networks can influence further cycles of production and consumption. Examining consumption that occurs throughout a production-consumption network is intended to encourage better resource use, energy conservation, recycling, reuse and waste through all parts of a commodity network (The Ellen Macarthur Foundation, https://ellenmacarthurfoundation.org/).

Both commodity chain and circular economy approaches have limitations in accounting for the complex networks and flows which characterise production and consumption relationships. Focusing on firm and consumption activities may obscure wider structural **political-economic** relations (including those associated with **colonialism**, **neoliberalism** and **gender**) in which producer-consumer connections are formed (Patchett and Williams, 2021) and the ways in which the non-human world (e.g. the nature of 'objects' of consumption, the agency of plants, animals and 'natural' processes or the material features of digital and physical places) may impact human thought and practice. Nevertheless, these approaches have drawn attention to the human and environmental impacts of production and consumption relationships. Concerns about environmental degradation and resource use, for example, have encouraged geographers to consider how wasting might be circumvented at multiple scales from the individual, households, municipal authorities to governments (e.g. Dominish et al. [2018] on metal recovery and circular economies) and through multi-lateral agreements such as the Basel Convention on the movement of electronic waste.

Socialities

Acquisition, possession and disposal of commodities also have a social function, symbolising both connection and difference to others who may be proximate or distant. Consumption is consequently a moral and political practice connected with geographies and power relationships. Cultural, political and economic regulations, discourses and norms can place additional demands and responsibilities on consumers. Geographers have been instrumental in highlighting the ways in which **race**, gender and income, for example, may foreclose some choices while promoting others (Slocum and Saldanha, 2013). Consequently, consumption is not only a significant place-making activity but a powerful one which involves the social reproduction of cultural and economic systems. Recent work on material geographies has also drawn attention to the ways in which the non-human world (e.g. animals, plants, things and technologies) act on humans, provoking and compelling forms of haptic practices and affect, and effecting relationships and practices (see, for example, Barry's [2017] work on backpackers and their bags).

The outcomes of climate change in its various incarnations (intensified weather patterns, storms, fires, floods etc.) may prompt human responses to efforts to mitigate its effects. The impact of climate change is also beginning to provoke shifts in the organisation, regulation and management of consumption by supra-national bodies, governments, civil society organisations and by consumers and the producers of commodities. Consequently, there is a growing awareness in academia and beyond, of the need to examine consumption practices and the relational nature of human-non-human interactions in order to attend to some of the world's 'wicked' problems.

Subjectivities

Thinking about consumption in terms of subjectivities helps us consider the ways in which consumption provides a medium through which our identities are produced and positioned materially and discursively across time and place. Historian Frank Trentmann (2016) argues that consumer identity has become a dominant subject position in the last couple of centuries as part of economic, cultural and political discourse and practice. Consumer identities and various subject positions (such as the good parent, the contributing citizen, the attractive individual, the altruistic giver) may be promoted by various organisations, including retailers, marketers, States and the media (Ruvio and Belk, 2013).

Advertising and marketing industries are aware of the social, sensory and identity affects of consuming and appeal to us to acquire commodities by promoting the necessity and desirability of purchasing and using goods and service. Such appeals do not simply focus on the material properties of goods but on the role of commodities and consumer spaces in 'fashioning' personal and social identity. Though geographers have shown that much of our daily consumption practice is concerned with notions of sociality rather than individual, anxiety-ridden identity production, our subjectivities are shaped in part through practices of consumption. Indeed, consumption of everyday and exceptional physical or digital commodities, whether occurring conspicuously in 'public spaces' or relatively unseen, provide a way of communicating our 'selves' and can symbolise our belonging and difference to others (Noble, 2008).

Identities are not simply individual, self-selected or chosen (as much as advertisers of products would have us believe) but are formed in relation to discourses, which may define appropriate actions, ways of being and responsibilities. The objects of our consumption and the kinds of practices we engage in also form a basis for the moral ascriptions of others (both human and non-human) whether we intend this or not. Others may read our identities from what we possess (or do not possess); the spaces in which we live, work and recreate; and our social/cultural tastes. The norms and expectations which derive from consumer discourses may also influence everyday practices and the ways in which we relate to others creating inclusion and exclusion in groups and spaces. Psychologist Rebekah Graham, for example, noted the stigma experienced by New Zealanders suffering from food insecurity. Those in food poverty often felt judged by others for receiving charity from foodbanks and for the appropriateness of their food purchases, including what was/wasn't present in their supermarket trolleys (Graham et al., 2018).

Geographers have highlighted how aspects of identity matter to how consumption is experienced in place, for example, the censure experienced by fat people as they travel (Evans et al., 2021), the exclusion of older people who are unable to use or access information and communication technologies (Mansvelt et al., 2020) and how the differential and diverse commodification of sexuality in cities can create social and spatial inclusions and exclusions (Hubbard et al., 2017). Aspects of identity are also **intersectional**, whereby different dimensions of identity (e.g. age, socio-economic status, gender, **ethnicity**, religion and sexuality) can combine to exacerbate consumption inequalities.

Summary

- Consumption is essential, not simply because it is necessary for material survival but because it has an important role in shaping social relationships, emotions, environments and the identities of people, groups and non-human things.
- Consumption involves particular arrangements of spaces which connect people, places and things. These spatialities may be expressed across multiple scales from the body to the global.
- Spaces, practices and discourses of consumption play an important role in shaping socialities, the ways in which we relate to other people and things.

- Subjectivities are also shaped through practices and discourses associated with consumption, with the norms, rules and expectations arising from these contributing to the (re)production of identity and moralised subject positions which can be experienced as social and spatial inclusions, exclusions and inequalities.
- Understanding the moments which comprise consumption can help address the social and environmental impacts of consumption.

Conclusion

Consumption practices are something we all engage in, to a greater or lesser extent, in the places we inhabit. Experiences and the impacts of consuming have real and material affects and effects, whether we engage in consumption in online or physical spaces. While products, places and practices of consumption seem to penetrate almost every aspect of everyday life, these are experienced unevenly. Access to consumer services, goods and spaces, and the outcomes of the aquisition, use and disposal of commodities for people, non-human things and environments may be vastly different. An understanding of how and why consumption takes (and makes) place can highlight what is consumed where, and the equity, ethics and sustainability of consumption practices and outcomes in a changing world. These are issues geographers are well positioned to speak to and research on the geographies of consumption looks set to expand.

Discussion points

- Why is it important for geographers to consider practices beyond acquisition as part of consumption?
- Think of your last purchase of clothing. Can you reflect on how your last purchase accrued different types of economic, social, material, symbolic and emotional value for you (The 3As) and how your chosen item might lose these values (the 3Ds)? What spaces, networks and flows might be associated with each of these moments?
- Again reflecting on the consumption of particular commodity (food, music or technology, for example) identify some socialities, subjectivities and spatialities which might emerge in relation to aspects of social difference, e.g. age, gender, class, ethnicity and sexuality.
- What moral or ethical demands and responsibilities are placed on you as a consumer? From where (and whom) do these derive? Do these influence your consumption practice and why or why not?

References

Argent, N. (2017). Rural geography I: resource peripheries and the creation of new global commodity chains. *Progress in Human Geography* 41(6): 803–812.

Barry, K. (2017). *Everyday Practices of Tourism Mobilities: Packing a Bag*. London: Routledge.

Bell, L. (2019). Place, people and processes in waste theory: a global South critique. *Cultural Studies* 33(1): 98–121.

Bissell, D. (2020). Affective platform urbanism: changing habits of digital on-demand consumption. *Geoforum* 115: 102–110.

Bourdieu, P. (2010) [1979]. *Distinction: A Social Critique of the Judgement of Taste*. London: Routledge.

Brooks, A. (2019). *Clothing Poverty: The Hidden World of Fast Fashion and Second-Hand Clothes*. London: Bloomsbury Publishing.

Chung, C. K. L., Xu, J., and Zhang, M. (2020). Geographies of COVID-19: how space and virus shape each other. *Asian Geographer* 37(2): 99–116. https://doi.org/10.1080/10225706.2020.1767423

Church, L. (2022). 'Comically bad' NZ-made NFT scheme 'Pixelmon' sparks outrage. https://www.1news.co.nz/2022/03/03/comically-bad-nz-made-nft-scheme-pixelmon-sparks-outrage/

Cox, R. (2013). House/work: home as a space of work and consumption. *Geography Compass* 7(12): 821–831.

Dominish, E., Retamal, M., Sharpe, S., Lane, R., Rhamdhani, M. A., Corder, G., Giurco, D., and Florin, N. (2018). 'Slowing' and 'narrowing' the flow of metals for consumer goods: evaluating opportunities and barriers. *Sustainability* 10(4): 1096.

Duff, C., and Moore, D. (2015). Going out, getting about: atmospheres of mobility in Melbourne's night-time economy. *Social & Cultural Geography* 16(3): 299–314.

Evans, D. M. (2019). What is consumption, where has it been going, and does it still matter? *The Sociological Review* 67(3): 499–517.

Evans, B., Bias, S., and Colls, R. (2021). The dys-appearing fat body: bodily intensities and fatphobic sociomaterialities when flying while fat. *Annals of the American Association of Geographers* 111(6): 1816–1832. https://doi.org/10.1080/24694452.2020.1866485

Foden, M., Browne, A. L., Evans, D. M., Sharp, L., and Watson, M. (2019). The water–energy–food nexus at home: new opportunities for policy interventions in household sustainability. *The Geographical Journal* 185(4): 406–418. https://doi.org/10.1111/geoj.12257

Gereffi, G. (2018). *Global Value Chains and Development: Redefining the Contours of 21st Century Capitalism*. Cambridge University Press. https://doi.org/DOI:10.1017/9781108559423

Gereffi, G., and Korzeniewicz, M. (1994). *Commodity Chains and Global Capitalism*. Westport: Praeger.

Goodman, M. K., Goodman, D., and Redclift, M. (2010). *Consuming Space. Placing Consumption in Perspective*. Farnham and Burlington: Ashgate.

Goss, J. (1999). Once-upon-a-time in the commodity world: an unofficial guide to mall of America. *Annals of the Association of American Geographers* 89(1): 45–75.

Graham, R., Hodgetts, D., Chamberlain, K., and Stolte, O. (2018). Hiding in plain sight: experiences of food insecurity and rationing in New Zealand [article]. *Food, Culture and Society* 21(3): 384–401. https://doi.org/10.1080/15528014.2018.1451043

Gregson, N., and Crang, M. (2015). From waste to resource: the trade in wastes and global recycling economies. *Annual Review of Environment and Resources* 40(1): 151–176. https://doi.org/10.1146/annurev-environ-102014-021105

Gregson, N., and Crewe, L. (2003). *Second-Hand Cultures*. Oxford: Berg.

Hall, S. M. (2019). *Everyday Life in Austerity: Family, Friends and Intimate Relations*. London: Palgrave Macmillan.

Hetherington, K. (2004). Secondhandedness: consumption, disposal and absent presence. *Environment and Planning D: Society and Space* 22(1): 157–173.

Hobson, K. (2016). Closing the loop or squaring the circle? Locating generative spaces for the circular economy. *Progress in Human Geography* 40(1): 88–104. https://doi.org/10.1177/0309132514566342

Hubbard, P., Collins, A., and Gorman-Murray, A. (2017). Introduction: sex, consumption and commerce in the contemporary city. *Urban Studies* 54(3): 567–581.

Jackson, P., Ward, N., and Russell, P. (2009). Moral economies of food and geographies of responsibility. *Transactions of the Institute of British Geographers* 34(1): 12–24.

Kopytoff, I. (1986). The Cultural Biography of Things: Commoditisation as Process. In *The Social Life of Things: Commodities in Cultural Perspective*, ed. A. Appadurai. Cambridge: Cambridge University Press, 64–91.

Lane, R., and Gorman-Murray, A. (eds.) (2011). *Material Geographies of Household Sustainability*. Farnham: Ashgate.

Mansvelt, J. (2005). *Geographies of Consumption*. London: Sage.

Mansvelt, J., Elms, J., and Dodds, S. (2020). Connecting meanings of ageing, consumption, and information and communication technologies through practice. *Geographical Research* 58(3): 289–299. https://doi.org/10.1111/1745-5871.12392

Miles, S. (1998). *Consumerism: As a Way of Life*. London: Sage.

Miller, J. C. (2015). The critical intimacies of walking in the Abasto Shopping mall, Buenos Aires, Argentina. *Social & Cultural Geography* 16(8): 869–887. https://doi.org/10.1080/14649365.2015.1026928

Noble, G. (2008). Living with Things: Consumption, Material Culture and Everyday Life. In *Cultural Theory in Everyday Practice*, eds. N. Anderson and K. Schlunke. Melbourne: Oxford University Press, 98–113.

Patchett, M., and Williams, N. (2021). Geographies of fashion and style: setting the scene. *GeoHumanities* 7(1): 198–216. https://doi.org/10.1080/2373566X.2021.1925138

Pollard, S., Turney, A., Charnley, F., and Webster, K. (2016). The circular economy – a reappraisal of the 'stuff' we love. *Geography* 101(1): 17–27.

Rao, F. (2020). Unravelling material/digital shopping space: an assemblage approach. *Geography Compass* 14(11): e12539.

Ruvio, A. A., and Belk, R. W. (2013). *The Routledge Companion to Identity and Consumption*. London: Taylor & Francis. https://books.google.co.nz/books?id=rVJCjkLnjOkC

Slocum, R., and Saldanha, A. (eds.) (2013). *Geographies of Race and Food: Fields, Bodies, Markets*. Ashgate: Farnham.

Stanes, E. (2019). Clothes-in-process: touch, texture, time. *Textile* 17(3): 224–245.

Stanes, E. (2021). Dressed in Plastic The Persistence of Polyester Clothes. In *Plastic Legacies*, eds. T. Farrelly, S. Taffel, and I. Shaw. Athabasca: Athabasca University Press, 117–137.

Trentmann, F. (2016). *Empire of Things: How We Became a World of Consumers, from the Fifteenth Century to the Twenty-First*. London: Penguin.

Tymkiw, C. (2022). How shopping habits changed due to COVID-19. *Investopedia*, 15th April. https://www.investopedia.com/how-shopping-habits-changed-due-to-covid-5186278

Warde, A. (2014). After taste: culture, consumption and theories of practice. *Journal of Consumer Culture* 14(3): 279–303. https://doi.org/10.1177/1469540514547828

Wilkinson, S. (2017). Drinking in the dark: shedding light on young people's alcohol consumption experiences. *Social & Cultural Geography* 18(6): 739–757. https://doi.org/10.1080/14649365.2016.1227872

Woodward, J., Rothwell, J. J., Hurley, R., Li, J., and Ridley, M. (2020). Microplastics in rivers. *Environmental Scientist* 29(1): 36–43.

Online materials

- Followthethings.com

  A site initiated by British geographer Ian Cook and other researchers/students, which provides research, news, empirical case studies and links to videos which enable viewers to explore relationships of connection between production and consumption through various objects and commodities. http://www.followthethings.com/

- The Story of Stuff Project

  A website initially based on the 2007 documentary created by Annie Leonard. It contains links to videos and projects which draw attention to matters of (over)consumption and commodity chains, encouraging encourage viewers to think about the connections between production and consumption and the ways in which these relationships might be shaped more sustainably. https://www.storyofstuff.org/

- Ellen Macarthur Foundation

  Contains information about the concept of the circular economy as well as a number of case studies of the circular economy in practice. Links to both videos and resources are available on the website. https://ellenmacarthurfoundation.org/topics/circular-economy-introduction/overview

- Bored Ape Yacht Club

  A collection of 10,000 unique Bored Ape Non Fungible Tokens. Collectors of Board Ape NFTs have access to exclusive face to face events and a private online club. These NFTS have been purchased by a number of international celebrities and have become something of a status symbol. https://boredapeyachtclub.com/#/

- Statista

  A site which contains a raft of e-commerce statistics – including stats which document how online shopping has altered with the COVID-19 Pandemic. https://www.statista.com/topics/871/online-shopping/#editorialPicks

Further reading

Evans, D. M. (2019). What is consumption, where has it been going, and does it still matter? *The Sociological Review* 67(3): 499–517.

Goodman, M. K., Goodman, D., and Redclift, M. (eds.) (2010). *Consuming Space. Placing Consumption in Perspective*. Farnham and Burlington: Ashgate.

Mansvelt, J. (2013, updated 2022). Geographies of consumption. *Oxford Bibliographies*. https://www.oxfordbibliographies.com/view/document/obo-9780199874002/obo-9780199874002-0054.xml

Shove, E., Trentmann, F., and Wilk, R. (eds.) (2020). *Time, Consumption and Everyday Life: Practice, Materiality and Culture*. London: Routledge.

33 Work

Katharine McKinnon and Kelly Dombroski

Introduction

We begin our discussion of work with two stories from two different parts of the world. James and Emi are fictional but are composite characters drawing on interviews and discussions with real people in our research in different countries around the Asia-Pacific region (see McKinnon, 2020). Their daily activities have continuities and discontinuities with each other, with us and with you, the reader. As you read through their daily account, think about which of these activities you might count as 'work'.

James

It's a normal Tuesday morning. James gets up wearily out of bed. He prepares breakfast and school lunches for three children, cajoles them into their school uniforms and herds them out into the car. He leaves them at the school gate with a hug and kiss each and continues on to the train station. On the train he catches up with his neighbours, tries to read a document and conducts an interview with a local radio station that is interested in the outcomes of his recent research on the cooling effects of trees on suburban streets. Arriving in the city he dashes to his office, deals with a swathe of incoming emails, has a meeting with his research team, takes a working lunch with a colleague during which they talk through recent tension in the office around the move to a new building on campus. Back in his office he does some last-minute preparation for his lecture, then he heads out to teach class for 2 hours. After class he runs for the next train home. At home his partner is already there having picked up the kids, and while he helps with final dinner preparations, he talks through his day, discussing an aspect of his teaching that didn't go so well and getting ideas on how to work through it, while listening to his family's stories from the day, sharing the triumphs and disappointments. Once the children are in bed, he settles next to his partner on the couch, both of them on laptops catching up on tasks left undone during the working day while commiserating with one another about how nice it would be to relax by watching TV. They plan a picnic outing for the weekend around the obligation to contribute to a working bee at the school.

Emi

The day begins for Emi before the sun comes up. Everyone else sleeps on while she starts a fire in the hearth and sets the rice to cook. While it cooks, she fetches water from one of the two

DOI: 10.4324/9780429265853-39

communal taps in the village. As she prepares breakfast, her five children, husband and parents-in-law wake and begin to get ready for the day. She sets her eldest daughter to feed the chickens, her son to water the small plot of vegetables next to the house, while the younger children finish their homework. Once everyone has eaten she sends her older children to walk to school and quickly washes the clothes in the tub by the back door, deposits her youngest child in the care of a neighbour and sets off with her husband to walk half an hour to the fields. Today, they will work together to clear the weeds from under the cashew nut trees, clearing the ground in preparation for the upcoming harvest. When the sun is at its highest, the couple return home for lunch, and, while her husband rests, Emi sets up her loom and continues to work on a weaving she hopes will fetch a good price at market when it is completed. As she works, she watches over her youngest who has returned home and chats with the neighbour who has come over to socialise. Later she will tend the vegetable plot, feed the pigs and start to prepare the evening meal. After dinner she will take a walk to visit a friend, and together they will go to attend a meeting with others in the sellers' cooperative to discuss plans for the upcoming harvest and the proposal that families should consider processing a proportion of the crop in order to try to get a better price.

Emi and James are involved in very different kinds of working day, but both are balancing a range of work activities, some of which will earn money, some produce food for the family, and some are delivering care for family members and the wider community. In our research and teaching, we sometimes use a 24-hour clock to get a sense of what people do in a normal day. We might ask them to tell us about the day before, or a typical day, or a weekday and a week-end. We might ask them to add up how many hours are spent in work. This usually gets into a discussion of what we mean by work, and what counts as work – and what counts as leisure. If you mapped James and Emi's activities on a 24-hour clock, how much leisure time would there be? How much work time? How much sleep? Are there other nuances we might consider? Figure 33.1 shows our attempt to map their activities on such a clock – do you agree with our mapping, or did you reach a different conclusion as to what counts as work and what doesn't?

What counts as work will vary depending on your cultural and social background, the type of economy you are engaged in, and where you are in the world. As we saw in the introduction to this section, for much of its history, the subdiscipline of economic geography has been largely focused on studying the formal waged economy, often neglecting the informal economy and the social economy (sometimes termed 'reproductive' economy). As a result, the many different kinds of work people do to sustain life have not been given recognition (Cameron and Gibson-Graham, 2003). Indeed, little attention has been paid to the way in which some leisure activities might also be forms of work – volunteering, provisioning food through gardening or preserving, provisioning clothing through knitting or sewing or shopping. In addition, it is only very recently that geographers have started to acknowledge the work that other species do – human lives and livelihoods are reliant upon the work done by myriad plants and animals to sustain their own lives and ours (Barron and Hess, 2020).

As we also noted in Chapter 30, in order to bring recognition to diverse economic activities not usually recognised in economic studies, the Community Economies Collective produced an image of an iceberg (see Figure 30.3). Figure 33.2 shows a similar image of a floating coconut, which was created to reflect the diverse economies of communities in the Pacific (Carnegie et al., 2012). Based on JK Gibson-Graham's thinking in their 1996 book *The End of Capitalism (as we knew it)*, these images illustrate the ways in which some economic activities are often more visible in economic scholarship and commentary (usually monetary transactions and wage labour for a **capitalist** firm).

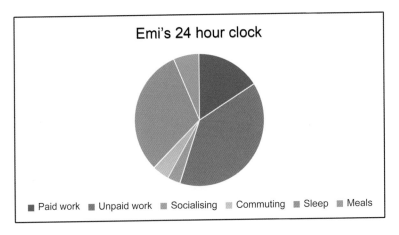

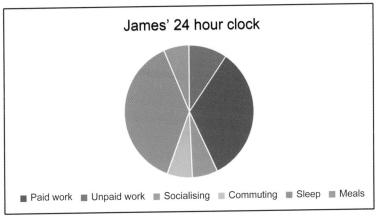

Figure 33.1
James (a) and Emi's (b) 24-hour clock representing hours spent on work, rest and recreation

Source: Figure credit: Inge Flinte

In the 'underwater' part of the floating coconut, we are invited to consider all the other kinds of economic activities that help us get what we need to sustain life and to reflect on the processes which prevent us from seeing and valuing them as part of our economies. Recent scholarship in diverse economies (Gibson-Graham and Dombroski, 2020a) and **feminist** studies on 'life's work' (Mitchell et al., 2004, Meehan and Strauss, 2015) asks us to challenge the idea that 'the economy' is something big and far away that we have no power over (Gibson-Graham et al., 2013, see also Chapter 64 Postcapitalist Geographies). Through the different kinds of work, recognised below the waterline on the floating coconut, we all participate daily in the economy, including the everyday 'underwater' activities undertaken in households and communities around the world.

Different kinds of work

Many scholars have studied work and tried to divide it up into different kinds of work as a way of explaining how societies and economies function. Karl Marx was a scholar and activist who,

Figure 33.2
Floating coconut economy

Source: Figure credit: Imogen Dombroski, adapted from Carnegie et al. (2019)

along with his contemporaries, was concerned about the rise of industrial **capitalism** in Europe in the nineteenth century. He wrote about how peasant labourers in Europe were pushed off the land and absorbed into new exploitative relationships – this time with the capital-owning **class** of industrial business owners. He wrote about how the capital-owning class of industrialists (capitalists) used their economic power to exploit workers, who were drawn into long working days where they often produced many times the value of what they were paid. Marx's economic analyses showed how capitalists were able to secure workers' labour for a minimum wage, while selling the product of their labours at a very high-profit margin. In this way, those with capital, and thus the financial ability to own the 'means of production', were able to accumulate more and more wealth, often at the expense of workers' health and well-being. In *The Communist Manifesto* (2017 [1848]), Marx and Engels call for workers to unite and struggle for a different kind of social and economic order, where they could own the means of their own production and distribute the surplus produced by their own labour. In Marx's understanding of work then, the important divisions were between the bourgeoisie and the proletariat. The bourgeoisie being the capitalist and professional classes whose social concerns are mainly about preserving property ownership, and the proletariat being the working class whose social concerns are mainly about earning a living.

Yet as we have seen represented in the diverse economies iceberg and coconut, there are also many other kinds of work carried out, under a variety of different arrangements, including other kinds of exploitation and also independent and communal work. One important division in the way work is understood by geographers is the division between waged and unwaged work. Feminist economic geographers have extended and critiqued Marx's analysis to come up with the concept of 'social reproduction'. This is often understood as all the unpaid work required to get the worker to the factory gates each morning ready to spend the day working for wages (Mitchell et al., 2004). In Marx's time, this work was usually performed by women and it included provisioning food and cooking, washing and cleaning, bearing and caring for children (the next generation of workers) and the elderly and others unable to work, attending to the social relations on which we all rely. (Even today, as Figure 33.3 shows, more of this work is done by women than men in the majority of countries.) Feminist economic geographers influenced by **Marxism** thus understand that women's unpaid work is not necessarily *men* exploiting women as part of the system of **patriarchy**, but as an extension of *capitalist* exploitation – since the capitalist relies on this work being done on an unpaid basis. More recently, feminist researchers have paid attention to the kinds of unpaid emotional labour that people in the workplace engage in that ensures the smooth running of the work environment. For example, cleaning up in the office tearoom, undertaking roles and responsibilities outside official contractual obligation (serving on a committee, organising social events), or the **performance** of particular emotions (friendliness, enthusiasm, sympathy) in the workplace. This work is also **gendered** and racialised depending on the social expectations on what 'normal' behaviour of different social groups looks like (Kobayashi and Peake, 1994). In feminist economic geographies then, important divisions have been drawn between paid and unpaid labour, with particular attention to their gendered nature.

Another important division is studied in other kinds of economic geography focusing on the **Majority World** (such as development studies). In these analyses, scholars distinguish between *formal* and *informal* work – you can see this running through James' and Emi's stories, and it is represented on Figure 33.1. Formal work is usually a paid job, protected by employment law, with formal tax and welfare arrangements. Informal work is also usually paid, but it may not involve contracts or tax payments, and workers may be unprotected by law (see also Chapter 34 on Informal Economies). In the Pacific economies represented by the floating coconut image, this includes the work involved in producing and selling goods at a local market (such as Emi's weaving), running small unregistered businesses such as a village canteen, or working as a labourer. In other parts of the world, the informal economy works differently – in China, for instance, many Tibetan migrant workers do not trust contracts written in Chinese and work informally as construction workers for Han Chinese bosses outside the formal economy (Duojie, 2022). While this might sometimes be a good way of avoiding too much attention, it can also go very wrong if wages are not paid on time, meaning that workers might not receive their pay for months, if at all. Other kinds of informal work in places like Australia might be babysitting someone's children or cleaning someone's house for cash (often below formal minimum wage), trading second-hand goods on e-bay or Facebook marketplace or contributing to a school working bee as in James's story earlier. There are levels of (in)formality, and some places might have more informal work as part of their local economy than other places (see Chapter 34 on Informal Economies for further details).

In the floating coconut, further categories have been added to recognise the contributions that unpaid work makes to the economy. The types of work included here include unpaid work in the home, recognised by feminist economic geographers as part of the reproductive economy, such as doing housework, taking care of children or washing clothes. And it also takes into account volunteer work in the community (such as James' contribution to the school working bee) or

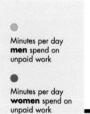

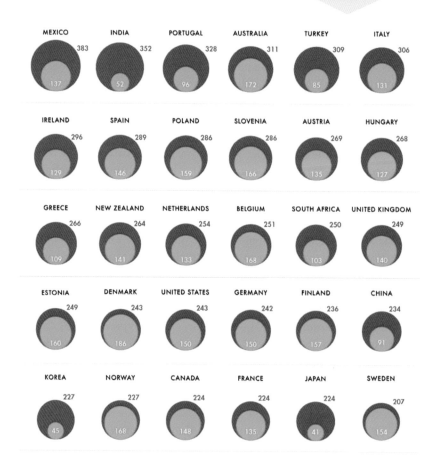

Figure 33.3
Minutes spent on unpaid work

Source: Figure credit: OECD

Note: Unpaid work includes routine household shopping, care for household members, volunteering, travel related to household activities work provided for neighbours (such as Emi's neighbour watching her children for a morning). While these forms of work do not earn a cash income, they are not without compensation.

Diverse economies scholarship recognises that work is not always strictly paid or unpaid, formal or informal. It also recognises that people who do work cannot always fit easily into the distinction between worker and capitalist. In the framing developed by JK Gibson-Graham, the important idea is about the relationship between work and the compensation or remuneration that workers receive (which may not be adequate for surviving well). This acknowledges that work may involve some kind of compensation outside of wages, as well as unpaid or unremunerated work, and it may involve forms of compensation that are not liveable or ethical (for example, slavery), or that *are* liveable even if they are not formal (for example, self-provisioning or reciprocal labour). It can also involve other kinds of partial compensation, for example, a parent may coach a sports team voluntarily and as a result their child can join the team for free. In Table 33.1, you can see some of this diversity both in types of labour and forms of remuneration (Gibson-Graham and Dombroski, 2020b). It acknowledges both formal and informal kinds of work and compensation.

Workplaces

While prior to industrialisation and the advent of factories and large commercial offices, many people worked from home or around their homes, in the 19th and 20th centuries in Western societies, work came to be also understood as a place. We might say 'I'm going to work now!' as we leave the house in the morning. This led to clearer boundaries between home and work, and unpaid and paid work too. Yet in many parts of the world, home and work do not have clear divisions. In Emi's story, work included work in her home and in her garden, in community areas, and in public. In the informal 'slum' settlements of Dhaka, Bangladesh,

> both domestic and income-generating activities were simultaneously performed in most of the slum spaces. The blending of private (e.g., living quarters) and public spaces (e.g., retail or recreational activities) makes it difficult to distinguish between 'mine' and 'ours'.
>
> *Waliuzzaman and Alam, 2022: 103*

In these settlements, people sort recycling for resale, sew garments for sale while caring for children, store lumber in their homes for sale and run small eateries or takeaway food stalls. This kind of mixing of workplace and home continues to this day and is not unusual in the Majority World (see also Chapter 9 on Majority and Minority Worlds).

For many people in the **Minority World** (which includes the wealthier echelons of society around the world), the COVID-19 pandemic forced people who previously worked in an office or other workplace to shift their work home. This mainly applied to the professional classes, those with office jobs whose work was conducted on computers, or those providing professional services that could be offered online (such as university courses, school education, some kinds of medical consulting, music lessons and counselling). The shift to working from home during COVID-19 lockdowns has resulted in a major shift in the way such forms of professional work are done, with many industries now allowing or even encouraging people to work from home. For example, Spotify's Work from Anywhere programme has the tagline: 'Work isn't somewhere

Table 33.1 Diverse forms of labour and remuneration

Labour	Form of remuneration
Unpaid	
Earth Others	Nonmonetary or none
Housework	Nonmonetary or none
Family care	Nonmonetary or none
Emotional labour	Nonmonetary or none
Neighbourhood work	Nonmonetary or none
Volunteering	Nonmonetary or none
Slave labour	Food and lodging
Waged	
Salaried	Negotiated salary + benefits
Unionised	Protected wage + benefits
Non-unionised	Unprotected wage
Part time	Un/Protected wage
Temporary	Unprotected wage
Seasonal	Unprotected wage
Familial	Personally set wage
Otherly remunerated	
Self-employed labour	Living expenses + savings
Self-provisioning labour	Food and other goods
Cooperative labour	Cooperative wage + share
Indentured labour	Food, lodging and stipend
Feudal labour	A portion of the harvest
Reciprocal labour	Reciprocated labour
Bartered labour	In-kind payment
Work for welfare	Dole payment
Intern labour	Job experience + stipend

Source: From Gibson-Graham and Dombroski (2020b: 13)

you go, it's something you do. We give our people the freedom to work where they work best, wherever that may be'.

The flipside of the shift toward flexible workplace arrangements is that workers cannot really work from *anywhere* – they need to have access to spaces appropriate to their work along with high-speed internet, and sometimes need to supply their own computer, headphones and other required equipment. In this change in work norms, the 'means of production' that Marx was speaking of refers mainly to the online platform and business credentials of the company, while the actual tools of work – computers, internet, chairs, electricity – may be owned by the worker themselves. Some people may experience this as 'freedom', while others may find this an additional burden, especially if their home environment is not conducive to work. These workers may work in co-working spaces, with other creatives doing similar gig economy work, sometimes paying their own way, while in other cases employers may cover these costs.

While Spotify still offers full-time jobs with some protections, offices and office equipment for those who want it, other jobs in the digital economy do not. Some economic geographers have analysed this 'gig economy', where workers go from insecure 'gig' (or contract) to insecure gig, usually without long-term job protections (Woodcock and Graham, 2019). For business owners, this means that they can respond relatively quickly to changes in demand, and if profits start to dip due to changes in the market, workers do not have to be made redundant (which means that employers have to pay redundancy packages). Instead, contracts are just not renewed. This 'lean' model of business and work has been at the heart of **neoliberal** transformations in the 'gig' economy and is most clearly seen in areas of the economy closely linked to new platform technologies, such as Amazon, Uber and Deliveroo. Job insecurity is not just something in the digital economy, however, but can be increasingly found in professional work as well. You are probably familiar with the notion of actors only being employed if they are successful in auditions – if they pass the audition, they get the part and are employed, if they don't, they remain unemployed until their next successful audition. This model of the competitive economy and precarious employment has now spread, and as Jodie Dean writes:

> Academics, writers, architects, designers and even programmers and consultants feel fortunate to get work, to get hired, to get paid. The logic of the contest structures ever more tasks and projects as competitions, which means that those doing the work are not paid unless they win. They work but only for a chance at pay.
>
> *Dean, 2017: 17*

The process of bidding for work has become widespread in the professions. Architects and consultants have long entered competitions to be awarded contracts, and research staff in universities have typically only been employed for as long as the research project they are working on is funded. But now even large corporations are increasingly moving to employ staff on a temporary basis to undertake particular tasks. Broadcasting companies, for instance, used to employ thousands of production technicians, presenters, writers and producers on long-term, permanent contracts to make programmes for TV and radio – now they source programmes from independent companies, whose employees have to bid to make the programme: again, if they win the bid, they get the work, if they don't win the bid, they remain unemployed (Graeber, 2019). Even those who are employed permanently may be expected to carry out additional tasks at home with their own equipment. In Australia, for example, it is common that universities require a personal mobile phone in order to sign into the IT system, even when at the workplace. Other universities in the United States expect employees to travel for work using their own money and be reimbursed sometimes months later. All these kinds of expectations demonstrate the increased blurring of boundaries between work and home in some industries.

The COVID-19 pandemic hit other workplaces differently. For work where in-person service was required, things were more complicated. 'Essential services workers' included those who worked in food production, distribution and waste management services, as well as healthcare and transport. These essential services workers were not able to do their jobs from home, and indeed, the rest of society was relying on them for their own survival. Other 'in-person' jobs such as retail and hospitality were also unable to shift to at-home work. In some parts of the world (including New Zealand and Australia, where we write from), people received payments from their governments to support them in these circumstances. But in other parts of the world, people were unable to leave their homes to make a living, and people faced very difficult times, lacking food and essential supplies. In Indonesia, for example, informal workers were particularly vulnerable, because people needed to work in order to earn and eat and had to continue to use public transport and public places thus increasing their risks of infection (Pitoyo et al., 2020).

The COVID-19 pandemic has also prompted a cultural shift in attitudes to work, now noticed in many Minority World settings around the world. In the United States, Britain and Australia, for example, commentators, journalists and researchers have been discussing the 'Great Resignation' – an apparent increase in the number of voluntary resignations from professional workplaces prompted by the pandemic. It is suggested that the pandemic has prompted many to re-assess the personal costs of participating in paid employment, and that in great numbers than ever before people are choosing to resign because their jobs take too great a toll on their personal health and well-being.

The future of work

As workplaces are restructured, and we come to pay more attention to the necessity and value of 'under-the-waterline' work in our societies, there is increasing interest in rethinking what work is and how work is compensated. One intriguing line of enquiry is the scholarship of 'post-work' which explores what work might look like if we stopped assuming that paid employment is the best, or indeed the only, type of work that really matters (Weeks, 2011). Post-work scholars argue that the valorisation of wage work and employment can have damaging effects, for example, those who cannot obtain 'gainful employment' are punished and stigmatised, and subject to surveillance by the state (if they seek access to social welfare), and experience social isolation (MacLeavy and Lapworth, 2020). These scholars argue that the injustices and brutality of the work society that we live in are well understood and well documented, resulting in chronic overwork alongside unemployment, marginalisation and poverty, with devastating effects on health and well-being, environmentally destructive patterns of production and consumption, and a catastrophic and pervasive anthropocentrism – the insistence of many governments around the world that what is needed to improve living conditions is *more* productive workers can only exacerbate these conditions (Graeber, 2019).

The broader understanding by geographers of what productive work actually is anticipates a future in which the definition of work is widely understood to include all the things people do to support our livelihoods and the means by which we secure the necessities of life and maintain our households and communities. As the diverse economy scholarship shows, the most prevalent form of work globally, over any other kind of work, is 'the unpaid work that is conducted in the household, the family and the neighbourhood, or the wider community' (Gibson-Graham, 2006: 62). The future of work could, and should, involve a shift away from the sense that there is only one way to ensure our prosperity, but this requires us to think more imaginatively, and more ethically, about what kind of a society we want to live in. There are indications that such a shift is underway, as people reshape their working lives through alternative enterprises, act collectively through formal and informal groups and cooperatives and refuse to participate in the work-society as demonstrated by the 'Great Resignation' post-COVID. It remains to be seen how far this shift progresses, and what geographies of work result from it.

Discussion points

- If you were to do your own 24-hour clock, how much leisure, work and rest would you see? What difficulties do you face in distinguishing between these categories in your own life? How might this compare to other people's lives elsewhere in the globe?
- Think about your own family background, and the types of work your family members, and yourself, have done. How might this work have changed recently, and how has this affected your own attitude to work as well as your time at university?
- What unpaid work do you do each day? How does this compare to people of other genders in your household or social circles? Are there different kinds of unpaid work performed? Do you think you do more or less than others? Is it valued in your social group? How does this compare to your parent's generation?
- What are your dreams for a different kind of work society? What actions could you take to help get there? What pushes back against those actions?

References

Barron, E. S., and Hess, J. (2020). Non-Human 'Labour': The Work of Earth Others. In *The Handbook of Diverse Economies*, eds. J. K. Gibson-Graham and K. Dombroski. Cheltenham: Edward Elgar, 163–169.

Cameron, J., and Gibson-Graham, J. K. (2003). Feminising the economy: metaphors, strategies, politics. *Gender, Place and Culture: A Journal of Feminist Geography* 10: 145–157.

Carnegie, M., McKinnon, K., and Gibson, K. (2019). Creating community-based indicators of gender equity: A methodology. *Asia Pacific Viewpoint* 60(3): 252–266.

Carnegie, M., Rowland, C., Gibson, K., McKinnon, K., Crawford, J., and Slatter, C. (2012). *Gender and Economy in Melanesian Communities: A Manual of Indicators and Tools to Track Change*. University of Western Sydney, Macquarie University and International Women's Development Agency.

Dean, J. (2017). Introductory Essay: The Manifesto of the Communist Party for Us. In *The Communist Manifesto*. London: Pluto Press, 1–46.

Duojie, C. (2022). Beyond sustainable livelihoods: a diverse economies approach to rural peasant livelihoods in China's Qinghai Province. *Asia Pacific Viewpoint* 63: 12–24.

Gibson-Graham, J. K. (1996). *The End of Capitalism (As We Knew It)*. Minneapolis: University of Minnesota Press.

Gibson-Graham, J. K. (2006). *A Postcapitalist Politics*. Minneapolis and London: University of Minnesota Press.

Gibson-Graham, J. K., Cameron, J., and Healy, S. (2013). *Take Back the Economy: An Ethical Guide for Transforming Our Communities*. Minneapolis: University of Minnesota Press.

Gibson-Graham, J. K., and Dombroski, K. (2020a). *The Handbook of Diverse Economies*. Cheltenham: Edward Elgar.

Gibson-Graham, J. K., and Dombroski, K. (2020b). Introduction to the Handbook of Diverse Economies: Inventorying as Ethical Intervention. In *The Handbook of Diverse Economies*, eds. J. K. Gibson-Graham and K. Dombroski. Cheltenham: Edward Elgar, 1–25.

Graeber, D. (2019). *Bullshit Jobs: A Theory*. London: Penguin.

Kobayashi, A., and Peake, L. (1994). Unnatural discourse. 'Race' and gender in geography. *Gender, Place & Culture* 1: 225–243.

Marx, K., and Engels, F. (2017) [1848]. *The Communist Manifesto*. London: Pluto Press.

McKinnon, K. (2020). Framing Essay: The Diversity of Labour. In *The Handbook of Diverse Economies*, eds. J. K. Gibson-Graham and K. Dombroski. Cheltenham: Edward Elgar, 116–128.

Meehan, K., and Strauss, K. (2015). *Precarious Worlds: Contested Geographies of Social Reproduction*. Athens, GA: University of Georgia Press.

Mitchell, K., Marston, S. A., and Katz, C. (2004). *Life's Work: Geographies of Social Reproduction*. Maldon: Wiley-Blackwell.

Pitoyo, A. J., Aditya, B., and Amri, I. (2020). The impacts of COVID-19 pandemic to informal economic sector in Indonesia: theoretical and empirical comparison. *E3S Web of Conferences* 200: 03014.

Waliuzzaman, S. M., and Alam, A. (2022). Commoning the city for survival in urban informal settlements. *Asia Pacific Viewpoint* 63: 97–112.

Woodcock, J., and Graham, M. (2019). *The Gig Economy: A Critical Introduction*. Cambridge: Polity.

Online materials

- The 'Take back the economy' website has downloadable tools and exercises for exploring our relationship to work in the context of both people and planet. https://www.communityeconomies.org/take-back-economy

Further reading

Gibson-Graham, J., Cameron, J., and Healy, S. (2013). *Take Back the Economy: An Ethical Guide for Transforming Our Communities*. Minneapolis: University of Minnesota Press.
This easy-to-read book is aimed at transforming our economies from the ground up. It has lots of exercises and activities you might try out with small groups. The chapter on 'Work' is particularly relevant.

Marx, K., and Engels, F. (2017 [1848]). *The Communist Manifesto*. London: Pluto Press.
In this version of *The Communist Manifesto*, there is also an introductory essay by Jodie Dean, explaining the context of its writing, and applying Marx's thinking to the digital economy. It is available as a digital book.

McKinnon, K., Carnegie, M., Gibson, K., and Rowland, C. (2016). Gender equality and economic empowerment in the Solomon Islands and Fiji: a place-based approach. *Gender, Place & Culture* 23: 1376–1391.
This article uses a place-based approach to think about what gender-equal work might look like in the Pacific Islands. This is the project team that developed the 'coconut economy' diagram used in this chapter.

Mitchell, K., Marston, S. A., and Katz, C. (2003). Life's work: an introduction, review and critique. *Antipode* 35(3): 415–442.
In this classic collection of articles in the radical journal *Antipode*, three feminist geographers explain the concept of social reproduction and life's work.

34 Informal economies

Gengzhi Huang

Introduction

The term 'informal sector' was initially coined by Keith Hart to conceptualise the **urban sub-proletariat's** income-generating activities in Accra in the early 1970s (Hart, 1973). Since then, the International Labour Organization (ILO) has popularised the term and contributed to the thriving study of informal economies for the past several decades. The informal economy is generally defined as income-generating activities that are legal (or non-criminal) but are either not covered or insufficiently covered by the regulatory system in which similar activities are regulated (Chen, 2006). Informal economies are diverse and dynamic within the changing global economy, encompassing a wide range of economic activities from street vending as a traditional retailing economy, to the home-based work embedded in **global value chains**, to the emerging jobs intermediated by digital platforms. While the informal economy was coined to describe a widespread phenomenon in the Global South, the informal sector is now on the rise in the Global North. It is estimated that 2 billion people in the world or more than 60 per cent of the global workforce make their living in the informal economy (ILO, 2018). The informal economy has been identified as a major challenge to inclusive economic growth and decent standards of work by the UN in the 2030 Sustainable Development Goals.

There has been a significant change to our understanding of the informal economy in the past decade, which has brought about a renewed interest in the concept across the world. In brief, the informal economy is now seen as a constituent part of **capitalist** economies, rather than as a transitory phenomenon that will decline and disappear with economic development (see also Chapter 37). In parallel with this new thinking, old forms of informal employment have persisted, and new forms emerged, in both the Global South and North. The informalisation process has reshaped both labour markets and spaces of work and employment, as well as generated new challenges to the global development agenda on decent work, poverty and inequality. This chapter examines the nature and forms of the informal economy, highlighting its connection with current economic, political and social processes. It starts with an overview of dominant theoretical perspectives on the informal economy. The second section examines the multiple dynamics of informalisation to develop a new vision of the informal economy. The third section analyses the heterogeneity of informal economies, followed by an examination of spaces of informal work in the fourth section. The final section summarises the nature of the informal economy and opens some key questions for future studies.

DOI: 10.4324/9780429265853-40

Theories of informal economies

Four dominant theoretical perspectives can be identified in the understanding of informal economies: dualist, structuralist, legalist and voluntarist. The dualist perspective sees the informal sector resulting from the formal sector's inability to create sufficient jobs for the growing urban labour forces in the context of the large-scale rural-to-urban migration and insufficient industrial development witnessed in many developing countries (Tokman, 1978). The informal sector is seen as both a safety net in times of crisis and a problem of poverty, unemployment and underdevelopment. The dualists argue that the informal sector is separated from the formal sector, and distinct from it in terms of economic size (small scale), the form of employment (self-employment), production organisation (low input, low technology) and economic outcomes (low productivity, low income) (Rakowski, 1994). It is believed that the informal sector is a transitory problem that will ultimately disappear with sufficient economic development.

The structuralist perspective sees the informal economy as a by-product of contemporary capitalist restructuring and a way of capital accumulation for formal enterprises to cut costs and improve competitiveness (Castells and Portes, 1989). The informal economy is not separated from, but structurally linked with, the formal economy. As informal economic activities also exist in the formal sector, the notion of the 'informal economy' replaced the idea of the 'informal sector' and became widely used. The informal economy is not necessarily linked to poverty but is rather a particular form of production relationship, and workers in the informal economy are poor and precarious because the production relationship in its current form is exploitative and dominated by capital. Informalisation is a process of capitalist restructuring facilitated by **neoliberal** regimes that empowers capital while weakening state regulation and union power. The structuralists argue that informal economies, as a mechanism of capital accumulation, will tend to grow rather than decline with the expansion of the neoliberal capitalist economy (Portes, 1997).

The legalist perspective initiated by de Soto (1989) is concerned with the influences of state regulation on the development of economies. Legality/formality is considered to be a privilege of those with economic and political power, with the disadvantaged being forced into extra-legality/informality to earn a living. Informal economies are thus people's spontaneous responses to excessive state regulations that exclude them from formal economies. They represent the power of the free market from the bottom. The legalists, therefore, highlighted people's **agency** and entrepreneurial spirit in informal economies, advocating policies of deregulation to stimulate the development of market economies.

The voluntarist perspective sees the informal economy as the choice of workers who make a decision based on weighing the costs and benefits of informality and formality (Maloney, 2004). Such workers pursue the advantages of informality such as flexibility, autonomy and freedom so that they can balance their income earning and non-work responsibilities (Perry et al., 2007). Unlike the legalists who argue that workers are forced into informality due to excessive state regulations, the voluntarists highlight the voluntariness of the choice as informal workers enjoy advantages of informality which are often absent in the field of formality. However, the willingness of informal workers to earn their living in this manner does not necessarily mean that they are not living in poverty – it just means that the formal employment available to them would not be a better option. Given their range of preferences and constraints, working in the informal economy may be the best decision.

Despite the divergence within these theories, there are some emerging common understandings of the nature of the informal economy. The first and most important point is that the informal economy is no longer regarded as a time-bound problem and a transitory phenomenon that will inevitably disappear with economic development. It is viewed as a constituent part and an internal feature of the restructuring processes of the global capitalist economy. Second, the informal economy is acknowledged as heterogeneous and complex, existing in both formal and informal sectors, which, whether accessed out of choice or of necessity by different segments of the population, varies considerably across time and **space**. Third, despite no necessary linkage to poverty, informal workers in the current conditions of capitalist economies are poor and deprived of the right to social protection.

Summary

- The dualist perspective sees the informal sector as the result of the formal sector's inability to create sufficient jobs for the growing urban labour forces. It argues that the informal sector is a transitory problem that will ultimately disappear with economic development.
- The structuralist perspective sees the informal economy as a by-product of contemporary capitalist restructuring and a way of capital accumulation for formal enterprises by cutting costs and improving competitiveness.
- The legalist perspectives see the informal economy as people's spontaneous responses to the excessive state regulations that exclude them from formal economies.
- The voluntarist perspective views the informal economy as the choice of workers who pursue advantages of informality which are often absent in the formal economy.

A new vision of informal economies

A classical view of economic development, based on the historical experience of advanced capitalist countries, is that labour moves from agriculture into industrial and service sectors and at the same time into a waged employment relationship which in turn becomes increasingly regulated and formalised (Heintz, 2020). Formalisation was considered as the norm and the predominant historical tendency within the employment system. However, this view of the development trajectory has been increasingly undermined by the rapid spread of 'informal' or 'precarious' labour in the Global North. Breman and van der Linden (2014) contend that the real norm in global capitalism is informality and insecurity, and that formal employment, known as the standard employment relationship, is a historical phenomenon which took place in a small part of the world for a short period of time. They argue that the historical phenomenon of capitalism with relatively full formalised employment, which was experienced in the Global North after World War II, will not necessarily be copied elsewhere but was rather a specific system bolstered by flows of raw material and labour from the Global

South and the political need to fight against communism in the Cold War era. In fact, the economic crisis experienced by Western capitalism in the early to mid-1970s and the collapse of the Soviet Union in 1989 have together undermined the economic and political foundation of full formal employment. The argument goes that since the 1970s, informality has become the organising principle of both economic production and employment practices. Protected wage employment declined and was informalised, with the rapid growth of temporary and part-time work and self-employment in Western countries (Rani, 2020). Arguably, the dominant trajectory has become one in which not all economies in the Global South are on a path to the formalisation of employment. Rather, the advanced capitalist economies are now experiencing the informalisation process which has always been the dominant mode of employment in the Global South.

Structural economic, political and social changes since the 1970s have combined to fuel the expansion of informal economies across the globe. First, the reorganisation of production systems from Fordist mass production towards flexible specialisation has activated the linkages between formal and informal economies (Chen, 2006). To reduce costs and retain global competitiveness, firms not only hire workers on an informal basis but also outsource production and services to small firms, often elsewhere in the world, through outsourcing and subcontracting systems. As Theodore (2007) argues, economic informalisation reconstructs employment relationships and offers new opportunities for firms to achieve competitiveness through sweating labour and other cost-containment strategies. The process leads to an increase in unregulated, temporary, part-time and contract jobs accompanied by outsourcing. In the Global North, this process is facilitated by the decline of trade union power which was weakened by neoliberal policies (see Chapter 52). Moreover, this process is in turn undermining the traditional unionisation of the working class based on the standard employment relationship. This has caused many scholars to question the concept of the 'working class' along with the traditional ways it protects its interests (Breman and van der Linden, 2014). Linked to this, Standing (2011) coined the term 'precariat' by welding together elements of the words 'precarious' and 'proletariat' to conceptualise the new working class that seems to be growing in European countries. In turn, the term precarity has now become an analogy for informality and is used to describe the temporary, insecure and uncertain condition of work and employment for many in the contemporary Global North, especially in European countries.

The second major factor in boosting such precarity is the new wave of technology-driven capitalism characterised by the rise of services and platform economies. Internet technology companies, which previously used permanent workers to perform most tasks, now choose to outsource work to crowd-work platforms and use global labour resources to complete tasks. Many have identified this as a new business model – known as the new Taylorist production process – that is catching on globally as it reduces transaction costs, increases productivity and enables the hiring of the best global workforce by breaking time and space constraints (Rani, 2020). The wide application of **artificial intelligence** and **big data** has accelerated the platform economy, resulting in the significant growth of digital platform workers, such as Uber drivers and food delivery staff. The rise of such platforms relies heavily on ambiguous labour relations (Webster and Zhang, 2021), and platform companies have sought to dilute their responsibility as employers through implementing 'invisible' digital control, while shifting labour conflicts to those between, say, passengers and drivers. Various legal disputes around the employment status of platform workers have emerged as a result. Taking Uber drivers in Western Europe as one example, in France, the court ruled on Uber drivers as employees (salarié). In Belgium, Uber drivers are classified as 'self-employed', rendering most employment laws inapplicable, while in the UK, the court judged that Uber drivers are 'workers', which is neither the same as 'employees', nor the 'self-employed' that Uber had been claiming. Perhaps finding a way beyond the employee-self-employed dualism is required to establish the legal status of platform workers (Ratti, 2017). Another factor leading to weak labour protection in platform economies is the difficulty in unionising platform workers as they are engaged in temporary, flexible and fragmented jobs in atomised ways. As a result, platform workers face worse working conditions, algorithm-based control and more precarious incomes.

Another factor catalysing the informalisation process is related to the change of labour supply characterised by the increase in migration and female workforces. It is argued that the growth of immigration induces the expansion of the informal economy across migrant-receiving societies (Visser and Guarnizo, 2017, Huang et al., 2020). As most of the international and internal migrants, particularly those who are illegal, have no full citizenship in receiving societies, they are more likely to end up working informally and become cheap labour for global capitalism. Migrants fill the gap between the shortage of Indigenous labour in taking low-end jobs and the growing demand of employers for low-end flexible labour in the context of growing cost competition (Peck and Theodore, 2012). Migration is thought by some to boost local informalisation as the persistence of migrant workers in the informal economy diminishes the bargaining power of domestic labour supplies and may push locally born workers into informal work themselves (Bohn, 2010). These arguments have led scholars to call for attention to be paid to the connection between immigration, informality, and social deterioration and its geographical complexities across the globe (Visser and Guarnizo, 2017).

The increase in women's participation in the labour market is also said to contribute to the expansion of informal economies. The International Labour Organization has indicated that the higher the participation rate of women in the labour market, the higher the share of informal employment in total women's employment (ILO, 2018). Although informal employment at a global level presents a greater source of employment for men than for women, more than 55 per cent of countries have a higher proportion of women in informal employment than men, especially in low and lower middle income countries (ibid). In Africa, for example, 89.7 per cent of employed women are in informal employment, compared to 82.7 per cent of men (ibid). In understanding the greater likelihood of women working informally, three factors might stand out: the existence of **gender** discrimination in labour markets, the demand for women to fill feminised work, such as domestic service and care (see Chapter 36), and the need to balance work and family responsibilities (Huang et al., 2018). The third factor means that women often work informally to enjoy the flexibility that enables them to look after their families while earning a living, in the absence of better formal jobs suitable for them (Figure 34.1). Female informal workers are more often found in employment sectors such as domestic work, home-based work or contributing to family work (Chen, 2016). The feminisation of informal employment and the informalisation of women's employment focus attention on the interrelation of informality, poverty and gender inequality, which has become a key concern of the global organisation WIEGO (Women in Informal Employment: Globalizing and Organizing).

Figure 34.1
A vendor making pancakes with a baby on her back in front of Pazhou Exhibition Centre, Guangzhou, China

Source: Photo credit: Gengzhi Huang

Summary

- The informal economy is a part and parcel of the restructuring processes of the global capitalist economy, rather than a transitory phenomenon that will disappear with economic development.
- The reorganisation of production systems from Fordist mass production towards flexible specialisation has led to the growth of informal economies. Informalisation is a strategy firms use to cut costs and weaken union power.
- The technology-driven capitalist economy characterised by the rise of services and platform technologies has accelerated the informalisation of economies by involving increasing labour in temporary, flexible and fragmented jobs.
- The increase in migrant and female workforces has contributed to the expansion of the informal economy. Scholars have called for attention to be paid to the connections between informality and immigration, gender inequality, social deterioration and poverty.

Heterogeneity of informal economies

Informal economies across the world are complex and vary across time and place. The landscape of informal work in any particular place is best viewed as the result of the geographical coupling of local economic, political, social and cultural systems under specific historical circumstances. This local economic system and its subsequent interactions with the global economy then largely determine the structure and forms of informal economies. The significant difference between the proportions of informal employment in developed countries, and in developing and emerging countries, indicates a correlation between the levels of economic development and informal economies (ILO, 2018). The political system tends to set the framework and context for the possibility of informality and shapes its patterns and paths of development by determining what is informal and what is not, and which forms of informality will thrive and which will decline (Roy, 2005). But this relation is not fixed. In times of economic crisis, a political system that used to outlaw certain informal economies may turn to a toleration and authorisation of them, in order to address problems of unemployment (Xue and Huang, 2015). In the post-pandemic context, for instance, the Chinese government lifted the ban on informal street vending to mitigate unemployment problems. Additionally, social and cultural parameters such as the supply of migrant labour, the nature of racial and ethnic hierarchies and a social bias against women's work also contribute to the geographical differentiation of local informal economies. Given the interaction of these contingent local factors, the scale, structure and types of informal economies in different parts of the world can differ significantly.

Recognising the diversity of the informal economy, scholars have attempted to develop models for analysing its composition. A general approach divides informal employment into self-employment and wage employment, which can be subdivided into several sub-categories according to employment status (Chen, 2016). Self-employment includes employers in informal enterprises, workers in informal enterprises, contributing family workers, and members of informal producers' cooperatives. Self-employment has grown with the transition from industrialism to post-industrialism in developed countries and is advocated in these countries as an entrepreneurial rational behaviour. Informal wage employment refers to employees who are hired without access to social protection by formal or informal firms or as paid domestic workers by households. They include employees of informal enterprises, casual labourers (see Figure 34.2), temporary or part-time workers, paid domestic workers, contract workers and industrial outworkers/homeworkers. The recent flexible turn of capital accumulation has led to an increase in informal waged employment, which in the context of developed countries has replaced permanent and full-time employment.

A more refined approach is the multi-segmented model developed by the global research network WIEGO, which disaggregates informal employment into six categories according to status in employment, gender, average earnings and poverty risk (Chen, 2016). These categories include employers in informal enterprises, regular informal wage workers, own account operators, casual informal wage workers, industrial outworkers/homeworkers and contributing family workers (see Figure 34.3). This model is founded on the links between informality, gender and poverty and highlights the heterogeneous nature of informal employment, especially in terms of economic income and risks. As illustrated in Figure 34.3, the risk of being from poor households goes up and average earnings go down when workers move down in employment status.

Figure 34.2
Workers waiting for casual labour contracts in an industrial zone of Shenzhen, China

Source: Photo credit: Gengzhi Huang

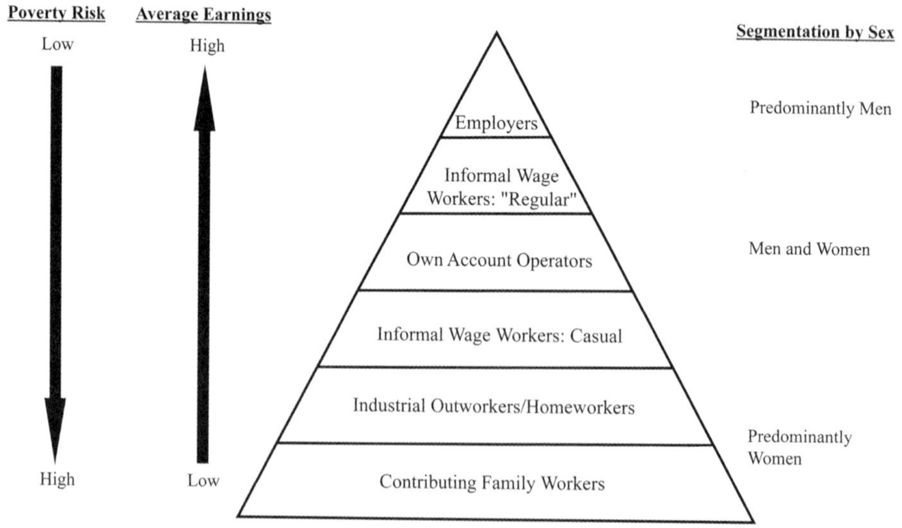

Figure 34.3
WIEGO's multi-segmented model of informal employment

Source: Chen 2016, redrawn by Gengzhi Huang

Men are more likely to be employers in the very top segment, while women are more likely to be homeworkers and unpaid contributing family workers in the bottom segment. Hence, while informality is generally associated with poor income, attention should also be paid to internal inequality in terms of the significant income gaps which exist between informal workers. The WIEGO model provides a useful approach for examining the internal inequality of informality and the complex association between informality, gender and poverty. The heterogeneity implies that policy support needs to be differentiated to take into account a consideration of the segmentation of informal workforces in the economy.

Summary

- The landscape of informal work varies across places. It is better seen as a 'cocktail' of the interaction of local economic, political, social and cultural factors in specific historical circumstances.
- The informal economy is internally heterogeneous in terms of its forms. Informal employment can be disaggregated into six categories according to status in employment, gender, average earnings and poverty risk, including employers in informal enterprises, regular informal wage workers, own account operators, casual informal wage workers, industrial outworkers/homeworkers and contributing family workers.

Spaces of informal work

The expansion of informal economies has reshaped spaces of work and employment. Generally, places of work in the formal/standard employment system belong to the employer, with all workers concentrated in organised and ordered working spaces. By contrast, workplaces of informal work are more diversified, decentred and unorganised. They do not necessarily belong to an employer, and informal work can take place in private and public spaces. Actually, given the particular traits of workplaces for informal work, the 'place of work' has been considered a key indicator for identifying and classifying informal workers (Chen, 2020). However, spaces of informal work are by no means independent and isolated from the formal economic system and its geographies but instead are linked to that in various ways, depending on the types of work being discussed. Three case studies make this clearer.

The first example is the emerging working space of home-based workers, who produce goods and services in their own homes (Figure 34.4). Home-based workers are largely invisible from official employment statistics, though they account for a large proportion of urban employment in many developing countries within Asia, Africa and Latin America (Chen and Sinha, 2016). There are two types of home-based workers: the self-employed who work on their own and subcontracted workers who work for others. While most self-employed work for local markets, subcontracted workers are embedded in global and domestic value chains (ibid – see also Chapter 35). The subcontracted home-based workers often have little bargaining power and bear the majority of the costs and risk shifted down from larger firms and suppliers. Plenty of home-based

Figure 34.4
A home-based worker is sewing in an urban village of Guangzhou, China

Source: Photo credit: Gengzhi Huang

workers live and work in informal settlements with little or no basic **infrastructure**, includ-ing water, sanitation and electricity (ibid). In China, for instance, many home-based workers are rural migrants who live in villages-in-the-city (*chengzhongcun*), which are dark and crowded but with cheap and less regulated housing. Informal settlements, such as *chengzhongcun*, have been the favourable location for flexible capital accumulation as they provide low-cost spaces for production and social reproduction with low-price housing and minimum infrastructure ser-vices. Viewed from this position, informal settlements are partly the spatial outcome of the link between informal and formal capitalist production.

New spaces of informal work are emerging with the growth of platform economies. Platforms have gradually penetrated most sectors of the economy and fall into three categories: those that provide services and products to individual users, such as social media; those that facilitate the exchange of goods and services, such as e-commerce platforms; and those that coordinate the exchange of labour between service providers and users, including digital labour platforms such as Uber (Pollio, 2021). The platform economy is a 'centre-periphery' mode of production, with a combination of highly skilled workers and knowledge-based means of production at the centre, and **subaltern** workers who work directly for consumers at the periphery, mostly in informal, flexible and fragmented jobs. Spaces of informal work in platform economies are scat-tered, atomised and mobile. Taking food delivery staff as an example, they shuttle back and forth

Figure 34.5
Food delivery men waiting for takeaway orders from the Meituan platform at the Huacheng Plaza in Guangzhou, China

Source: Photo credit: Gengzhi Huang

through city streets to complete the tasks assigned by the platform based on certain algorithms (see Figure 34.5). This is entirely different from working spaces in factories, offices, shops or restaurants which are spatially bounded and regulated by employers. There is an urgent need to understand the organisation and regulation of working spaces of platform-based informal work and its impacts on workers' life.

A third type of space for informal work is exemplified by street vending, which is a major part of informal economies in many countries of the Global South. The livelihood of street vendors relies on the appropriation of public spaces, particularly the prime city spaces and historic centres which are more profitable for vending. However, in many cities, public spaces are beautified and secured by city authorities to create a modern and world-class city image attractive to global investors and tourists. This contradictory definition and use of public spaces often leads to the illegalisation of street vending and to a conflict between the state and street vendors. In Latin American countries, street vendors have organised to collectively defend their working spaces. But in other countries such as China, unorganised street vendors can only use the tactics of constantly moving in individual ways to fight against the state's increasing regulation of space. Spaces of informal work are, in the case of street vending, spaces of conflict, resistance and violence, leading scholars to question the rationality of modern urban planning. Street vending and the questions it raises about the use and control of public space have been a particular object of concern for the ILO and the WIEGO.

Summary

- Workplaces of informal work are relatively more diversified, decentred and unorganised than those of formal work. They tend not to belong to the employer and can take place in private and public spaces.
- Spaces of informal work are linked in various ways to formal economic and spatial systems, depending on which type of work is being considered.
- Spaces of informal work are often unprotected and insecure. They are subject to regulation and harassment by the state and might become spaces of resistance and conflict.

Conclusion

Today, the informal economy is part and parcel of globalised and neoliberal economies. Increasing evidence suggests that the informal economy is not a transitory phenomenon that will disappear with economic development but a constituent part of capitalist economies. It expands with the processes of **globalisation**, deregulation and flexibilisation of the economy, which are politically underpinned by neoliberal policies (see Chapter 52). Technological change contributes to the production of new forms of informal work to enable the use of global labour resources by capital in more flexible ways. The growth of migration and female workforces maintains the supply of cheap and unprotected labour for the informalisation of economies. The nature of the informal economy can best be understood by connecting the relations between these economic, political, technological and social dynamics in various ways in different historical and geographical contexts. The prevalence of informalisation calls into question the presupposition of formalisation as the normal and dominant tendency of employment, and exposes the need to make space for informality in any theorisation of work and employment within global capitalism.

Above all, the informal economy is heterogeneous, and research should be concerned with the complexity and diversity of its dynamics, forms and impacts in different contexts. The growth of informal economies is determined by local political, economic and social factors and their connections with more formal global processes. Attention should be paid to the questions of how these multiple factors combine to produce the conditions for the informal economy, what new forms of informality are created and what new spaces of informal work are produced. The connections between technological change (e.g. platform economies) and informality, migration and informality, and gendered employment and informality provide three lines of enquiry for such questions. Moreover, attention should be paid to the multiple impacts of informalisation. While the informal economy provides job opportunities for people, it results in the erosion of working conditions, incomes and social benefits and the weakening of workers' bargaining power. In what ways, and in what conditions, informality, poverty, insecurity and inequality interrelate, and how informal workers can be organised and empowered, are important questions to examine if we want to reverse the current trend towards extreme inequality and open up the possibilities of decent employment and inclusive economic growth.

Discussion points

- How is the informal economy understood as part and parcel of the capitalist economy? Would you agree with the argument that informality is now the norm for employment under contemporary capitalism?
- How can we explain the differences in the informal economy of different countries?
- How is the informal economy linked to the formal economy? Can you give some examples?
- How is immigration connected to the growth of the informal economy?
- How might the participation in informal work affect women's work and life?
- Now that informality is becoming the norm within current capitalist economies, how is it possible to reverse the erosion of working conditions and social benefits caused by informalisation?
- Can you give some examples of the local organisation of the informal economy close to where you live or study?

References

Bohn, S. (2010). The quantity and quality of new immigrants to the US. *Review of Economics of the Household* 8(29): 29–51.

Breman, J., and van der Linden, M. (2014). Informalizing the economy: the return of the social question at a global level. *Development and Change* 45(5): 920–940.

Castells, M., and Portes, A. (1989). World Underneath: The Origins, Dynamics and Effects of the Informal Economy. In *The Informal Economy. Studies in Advanced and Less Developed Countries*, eds. A. Portes, M. Castells, and L. A. Benton. Baltimore: Johns Hopkins University Press.

Chen, M. A. (2006). Rethinking the Informal Economy: Linkages with the Formal Economy and the Formal Regulatory Environment. In *Linking the Formal and Informal Economy. Concepts and Policies*, ed. R. K. A. E. Basudeb Guha-Khasnobis. Oxford: Oxford University Press, 75–92.

Chen, M. A. (2016). The informal economy: recent trends, future directions, *New Solutions. A Journal of Environmental and Occupational Health Policy* 26(2): 155–172.

Chen, M. A. (2020). WIEGO Research on Informal Employment: Key Methods, Variables and Findings. In *The Informal Economy Revisited. Examining the Past, Envisioning the Future*, eds. M. A. Chen and C. Francoise. London and New York: Routledge, 67–75.

Chen, M. A., and Sinha, S. (2016). Home-based workers and cities. *Environment and Urbanization* 28(2): 343–358.

de Soto, H. (1989). *The Other Path. The Invisible Revolution in the Third World*. New York: Harper & Row.

Hart, K. (1973). Informal income opportunities and urban employment in Ghana. *Journal of Modern African Studies* 11(1): 61–89.

Heintz, J. (2020). Informality and the Dynamics of the Structure of Employment. In *The Informal Economy Revisited. Examining the Past, Envisioning the Future*, eds. M. A. Chen and C. Francoise. London and New York: Routledge, 84–87.

Huang, G., Xue, D., Guo, Y., and Wang, C. (2020). Constrained voluntary informalisation: analysing motivations of self-employed migrant workers in an urban village, Guangzhou. *Cities* 105: 102760.

Huang, G., Zhang, H., and Xue, D. (2018). Beyond unemployment: informal employment and heterogeneous motivations for participating in street vending in present-day China. *Urban Studies* 55(12): 2743–2761.

ILO. (2018). *Women and Men in the Informal Economy. A Statistical Picture* (3rd edn.). Geneva: International Labour Office.

Maloney, W. F. (2004). Informality revisited. *World Development* 32(7): 1159–1178.

Peck, J., and Theodore, N. (2012). Politicizing contingent work: countering neoliberal labor market regulation... from the bottom up? *South Atlantic Quarterly* 111(4): 741–761.

Perry, G. E., Maloney, F. M., Arias, O. S., et al. (2007). *Informality. Exit and Exclusion*. Washington: World Bank.

Pollio, A. (2021). Uber, airports, and labour at the infrastructural interfaces of platform urbanism. *Geoforum* 118: 47–55.

Portes, A. (1997). Neoliberalism and the sociology of development: emerging trends and unanticipated facts. *Population and Development Review* 23(2): 229–259.

Rakowski, C. A. (1994). Convergence and divergence in the informal sector debate: a focus on Latin America, 1984–1992. *World Development* 22(4): 501–516.

Rani, U. (2020). Old and New Forms of Informal Employment. In *The Informal Economy Revisited. Examining the Past, Envisioning the Future*, eds. M. A. Chen and C. Francoise. London: Routledge, 88–91.

Ratti, L. (2017). Online platforms and crowdwork in Europe: a two-step approach to expanding agency work provisions? *Comparative Labor Law & Policy Journal* 38(3): 477–512.

Roy, A. (2005). Urban informality: toward an epistemology of planning. *Journal of the American Planning Association* 71(2): 147–158.

Standing, G. (2011). *The Precariat. The New Dangerous Class*. London: Bloomsbury.

Theodore, N. (2007). Closed Borders, Open Markets: Immigrant Day laborers' Struggle for Economic Rights. In *Contesting Neoliberalism. Urban Frontiers*, eds. H. Leitner, J. Peck, and E. Sheppard. New York: Guilford Press, 250–265.

Tokman, V. E. (1978). An exploration into the nature of informal-formal sector relationships. *World Development* 6(9–10): 1065–1075.

Visser, M. A., and Guarnizo, L. E. (2017). Room for manoeuvre: rethinking the intersections between migration and the informal economy in post-industrial economies. *Population Space & Place* 23(7): e2085.

Webster, N. A., and Zhang, Q. (2021). Centering social-technical relations in studying platform urbanism: intersectionality for just futures in European cities. *Urban Transformations* 3(1): 1–7.

Xue, D., and Huang, G. (2015). Informality and the state's ambivalence in the regulation of street vending in Guangzhou, China. *Geoforum* 62: 156–165.

Online materials

- https://www.ilo.org/topics links to a series of ILO (International Labour Organization) reports on the informal economy and informal employment over the world.
- https://www.wiego.org/ links to a range of information on the informal economy from the global research network WIEGO (Women in Informal Employment: Globalizing and Organizing), including reports, working papers and publications.
- https://www.ted.com/talks/robert_neuwirth_the_power_of_the_informal_economy links to a video about the power of the informal economy.

Further reading

Breman, J., and van der Linden, M. (2014). Informalizing the economy: the return of the social question at a global level. *Development and Change* 45(5): 920–940.

A classic essay on the theoretical reflection on the view of the informal economy as a transitory phenomenon. It contends that informalisation is the norm and tendency of the capitalist development, while formalisation was a historical exception.

Chen, M. A., and Francoise, C. (eds.) (2020). *The Informal Economy Revisited. Examining the Past, Envisioning the Future*. London and New York: Routledge.
A classic book of cross-disciplinary and multi-regional studies on both the theoretical evolution and policy practices of the informal economy.

Hart, K. (1973). Informal income opportunities and urban employment in Ghana. *Journal of Modern African Studies* 11(1): 61–89.
A pioneering essay on the conceptualisation of the informal sector.

Maloney, W. F. (2004). Informality revisited. *World Development* 32(7): 1159–1178.
An important essay on 'informality as a voluntary choice of workers'.

Portes, A., Castells, M., and Benton, L. A. (eds.) (1989). *The Informal Economy: Studies in Advanced and Less Developed Countries*. Baltimore: Johns Hopkins University Press.
A classic book on the exploration of the informal economy as a structural production of the restructuring of capitalist economies.

Roy, A., and AlSayyad, N. (eds.) (2004). *Urban Informality: Transnational Perspectives from the Middle East, Latin America and South Asia*. Oxford: Lexington Books.
Another classic book on theorising the connection of informalities with the processes of liberalisation, globalisation and urbanisation.

Waibel, M., and McFarlane, C. (eds.) (2016). *Urban Informalities: Reflections on the Formal and Informal*. London and New York: Routledge.
An interdisciplinary book reflecting on the notion of the formal-informal divide.

35 Economic globalisation

Jana Kleibert

Introduction

Where does your T-shirt come from? This seemingly simple question is actually not an easy one to answer, especially if you aim to go beyond the name of the retail shop you bought it from. The label 'Made in …' might give you some indication as to where the final product was sown together and assembled (e.g. China, Bangladesh or Vietnam) but does not reveal where the cotton was harvested, where the fabric was dyed (with all its ecological consequences), where it was designed or its brand image devised. In today's globalised economy, it is increasingly common for the things we consume on a daily basis to have crossed multiple national borders in their production process before they reach us. In this chapter, we aim to understand how this system of globalised production came into being and how it operates.

Globalisation is a process of increasing interconnectedness and interdependence of places and actors on a global scale. In this broad sense, globalisation encompasses economic, political, cultural and ecological dimensions. In this chapter, we focus on the economic dimension of globalisation.

The next section discusses how the global economy has come about and explains how contemporary economic globalisation differs qualitatively from earlier forms. The third section discusses the key role of transnational corporations (TNCs) in the global economy. We then turn our attention to approaches that are frequently used by geographers to analyse the geographies of the global economy, before the concluding section considers the extent to which globalisation has slowed down or come to a halt in recent times.

The making of the global economy

The history of globalisation is long, and there are many debates as to when exactly it started. Some date the beginning of globalisation to the emergence of international trade routes. If you lived during the Middle Ages, the precursor of your T-shirt would have most likely been made from materials found in the vicinity of your residence and been spun, dyed and knitted in the same place – unless you belonged to the nobility and could afford the import of silk from the Chinese Empire. Early trade across the Silk Road occurred as far back as 130 BCE and enabled the exchange of goods between Europe and Asia (Frankopan, 2015).

DOI: 10.4324/9780429265853-41

More commonly, the starting point of globalisation is set in 1492. In this year, Christopher Columbus' 'discovery' of America marks the beginning of **colonialism** and the exploitation of colonies by colonial European empires. Under colonialism, the international trade of commodities between the colonies and colonising countries was very uneven. In this exploitative form of trade, not only were goods transported across the oceans, but slaves were also shipped to the colonies to work on plantations. The cotton industry in the United States, for instance, was based on the forced labour of slaves harvesting cotton. So, while in the 1800s your clothes may still have been produced in the United States, the cotton economy was clearly linked to the global slave trade. Increasingly, uneven international trade in raw materials and finished goods occurred between countries, creating an international division of labour that linked places in a **capitalist** world-system. Through this, exploitation of the colonies continued in various forms (see also Chapters 37 and 49).

Global trade increased rapidly after the Second World War. Political decisions to dismantle trade barriers were taken, and formalised, for instance, under the General Agreement on Tariffs and Trade, which was a precursor to the World Trade Organisation. Advances in technology and the standardisations in container-shipping further reduced transportation costs, leading to ever larger volumes of internationally traded goods.

Since then, we have witnessed a *qualitative* transformation of the world economy. Rather than **commodity** trade between individual national economies, we now see deeply integrated global interdependencies in a fragmented and globalised production process. We can now speak of a **new international division of labour** (in contrast to the colonial international division of labour), which comes into existence as firms decide to relocate parts of the production process for reasons of labour arbitrage (taking advantage of relatively lower labour costs in other places of the world). The clothing industry is labour intensive and was among the first to take on this trend. Firms started to offshore production to countries with lower labour costs. This shift has been characterised by a strong growth of **foreign direct investment** (see Figure 35.1), the rise of TNCs and **global value chains**.

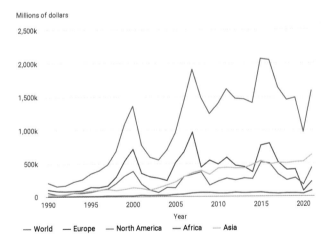

Figure 35.1
Foreign Direct Investment Flows, 1990–2021

Source: From Global foreign direct investment flows over the last 30 years, available at https://unctad.org/data-visualization/global-foreign-direct-investment-flows-over-last-30-years (downloaded 23/6/2023). ©(2022) United Nations. Reprinted with the permission of the United Nations

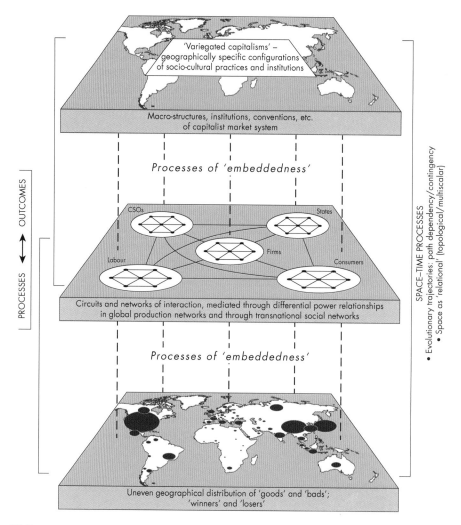

Figure 35.2
A simplified analytical framework of the global economy

Source: Image source: Dicken (2015: 51)

Foreign direct investment enables firms to establish control over production facilities abroad, either through the acquisition of existing production facilities (through mergers and acquisitions) or the establishment of new facilities. The flows of foreign direct investment have risen dramatically but also fluctuate considerably as can be seen in Figure 35.1. The graph shows the past 30 years of global FDI flows, with dents in periods of recessions, for instance following the attack on the World Trade Centre 2001, the financial crisis starting in 2008 and the outbreak of the COVID-19 pandemic in 2020.

Figure 35.1 also shows that the geographies of foreign direct investment have shifted considerably over time. The origin of FDI flows has traditionally been from North America and Europe. Japanese FDI has risen since the 1970s, followed by other Asian economies, for instance South Korea and Singapore. During the last 30 years, we can see how Asian FDI has continuously risen and flows today exceed those from Europe and North America. FDI flows from African countries remain on a very low level. The increase of FDI flows has also led to a rise of intra-firm trade, occurring within different arms of the same TNC. These FDI flows have helped to produce the differential 'embeddedness' – of labour, firms and consumers – captured in Figure 35.2, which presents the complex processes shaping and re-shaping the global economy in a simplified analytical form.

Summary

- Economic globalisation refers to a process of increasing economic interdependence and interconnectedness on a global scale.
- Economic globalisation has a long history. Since the 1970s we see a qualitative transformation towards a new international division of labour that is characterised by a rise in foreign direct investment.
- The contemporary global economy can best be depicted as a complex system that comprises a range of actors and inter-relationships, which together lead to an uneven geographical distributions of 'winners' and 'losers'.

Transnational corporations as key actors

The global economy is produced by many different actors, including states, firms, workers and consumers. Paradigmatic actors in contemporary global capitalism are TNCs. These firms are active across multiple geographies and operate international subsidiaries. TNCs have risen in number and are now a vital backbone of the global economy. About 80% of trade is organised by TNCs and their networks (UNCTAD, 2013). TNCs organise the globalised production and distribution of goods and services, even if they do not necessarily own all the production facilities. In the global clothing industry, for instance, TNCs are often retailers who are responsible for branding but have outsourced all production to supplier firms. An example is the Spanish TNC Inditex.

CASE STUDY
INDITEX, A TRANSNATIONAL CORPORATION

Inditex is a Spanish TNC active in fast-fashion. The company includes brands such as Zara, Bershka, Massimo Dutti and Pull&Bear. In 2022, it operated 6,477 stores (1,064 of which were franchised) across 60 different markets, and it employed 165,000 people with a total of 177 nationalities (Inditex, 2022). The actual production of T-shirts and other garments is not done by Inditex and its employees, but is outsourced to supplier firms. The 565,000 million tonnes of clothing placed on the market by Inditex in 2021 were produced by 1,790 direct suppliers with a total of 8,756 factories in 44 countries. Together these suppliers employ over 3 million workers, 18 times more than the staff directly employed by Inditex (Inditex, 2022).

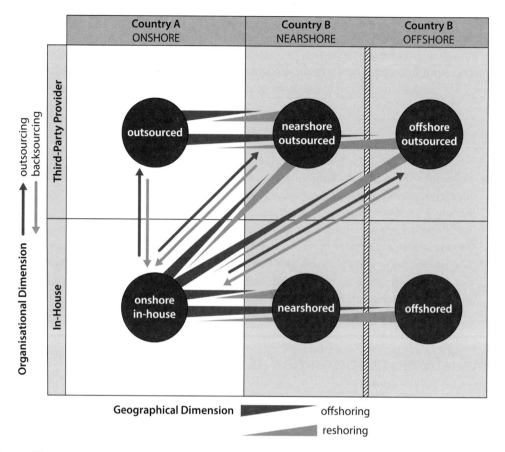

Figure 35.3
Distinguishing offshoring and outsourcing: organisational and geographical dimensions

Source: Figure credit: Jana Kleibert

Whereas outsourcing denotes the shift of activities previously conducted by the firm to another firm (either in the same country or abroad), offshoring denotes the geographical relocation of activities across national borders. Both processes can occur simultaneously, if a firm decides to transfer its activities towards a supplier in a foreign country. If the geographic distance between the two countries is relatively small, the term nearshoring may be used (see Figure 35.3).

Decisions by companies to offshore are traditionally understood as either market-seeking or asset-seeking. The latter involves not only access to natural resources but more commonly labour and knowledge. Offshoring and outsourcing both enable an organisational or geographic distancing between a firm's headquarters, places of consumption and some of the darker sides of the value chain (for instance poor working conditions and employment practices). The complexity of global value chains moreover makes it difficult to attribute responsibility. Activists in the clothing industry are now placing pressure on fashion brands and retailers to be more transparent and provide information about their supplier networks (Fashion Revolution, 2022).

CASE STUDY
SERVICES OFFSHORING

The relocation of production activities to countries with lower labour costs has occurred in many labour-intensive industries, such as clothing or consumer electronics. With advances in telecommunications and information and communication technology (ICT), it has also become possible to unbundle production tasks and relocate a number of office jobs across national borders. This has led to the creation of an entire corporate industry, the 'outsourcing complex' (Peck, 2017). Nowadays, call centre agents assist customers, and workers process forms, transcribe medical records or offer financial back-office activities from cities in the Global South. In fact, the Metro area of Manila in the Philippines has become the centre of business process outsourcing activities, with more than 1 million predominantly young workers servicing clients in the Global North (see Figure 35.4). Offshored work often includes routinised and/or emotionally draining work, such as content moderation on social media platforms.

Figure 35.4
The Philippine business district Makati with high-rise buildings that host business process outsourcing firms. Manila, the Philippines

Source: Photo credit: AGD Productions/Pixabay

A different, yet related, aspect of offshoring is the use of so-called offshore tax havens. TNCs, including fashion firms like Inditex, can set up complex subsidiary structures with the aim of evading taxes by shifting profits through different jurisdictions with lower corporate tax rates, including the Netherlands, Ireland and Switzerland. These contentious practices of the offshore finance industry are often legal in strictly technical terms but drain states of important tax revenue. Investigative journalists have exposed these techniques through using the Panama Papers and related reports. The complex subsidiary structures of TNCs that enable the shift of value from one place to another are opaque by design. However, as we shall see in the next section, economic geographers have devoted considerable attention to understanding the rise and configuration of these value chains, as well as to explaining the geographically **uneven development** which results.

Summary

- TNCs are key actors in contemporary globalisation, organising globalised production through offshoring and outsourcing.
- The fragmentation of production processes within firms through outsourcing and the stretching of production relations geographically through offshoring have led to the rise of global value chains.

Researching economic globalisation: chains and networks

Global value chains are so pervasive that they can be thought of as 'the world economy's backbone and central nervous system' (Cattaneo et al., 2010: 7). The making of a contemporary commodity, like a simple T-shirt, requires the transformation of inputs into an output that can be conceived as the following chain:

Raw materials → Processing → Assembly → Logistics → Sales, or in this case,
Cotton → Processing into fabric → Sewing into clothes → Distribution → Retailing

This transformation from raw materials to final product is often referred to as a supply or value chain and requires not just the core activities of manufacturing, marketing and logistics but also a number of support activities, including information technology, finance and human resources. When we try to understand the actors involved in the production of a 'simple' commodity, the neat logic of a sequential chain becomes very messy, as multiple actors in different locations are involved across the length of the production and distribution process.

Global commodity chains, global value chains and global production networks are related analytical perspectives that economic geographers use to investigate globalised production and its outcomes. A global commodity chain was first defined as 'a network of labour and production processes whose end result is a finished commodity' (Hopkins and Wallerstein, 1986: 159). The concept was developed by sociologists and has its origin in world-systems theory, and aims to explain uneven development in the capitalist world economy based on four interrelated dimensions: the input-output structure, **territoriality**, governance and the institutional context (Gereffi, 1994). Of these, the governance dimension has become the most important one to explain uneven outcomes. Asking the question of governance is asking about **power** in the commodity chain: who is able to control which part of the chain and thus able to reap value from it?

A key analytical distinction is made between *producer-driven* and *buyer-driven* global commodity chains (Gereffi, 1994). Producer-driven chains are capital and technology-intensive, meaning that producers are those with the ability to control the chain. Examples of producer-driven chains are found in the automotive industry, where innovation takes place in the production process. Buyer-driven chains, in contrast, exist in sectors where entry barriers exist in design and marketing but not in the manufacturing process. Global retailers in the clothing industry are a prime example of buyer-driven chains. Retailers, such as Inditex, orchestrate the chain and are able to exert pressure on suppliers, who are responsible for manufacturing. The largest profits tend to accrue not in the labour-intensive production process, most often located in the Global South, but instead are in the fields controlled by the retailers as buyers of contractually manufactured commodities. The global commodity chain approach (also more recently labelled the global value chain approach) focuses on understanding the governance mechanisms and the potential for firms to change their position within the chain and 'upgrade' into higher value-generating fields.

CASE STUDY
THE TRAVELS OF A DRESS

Tracing a final product from the shelf of a retailer all the way back to its origins tends to be no straightforward task, given the large volume of contract manufacturers and suppliers in clothing value chains and the general lack of transparency in the industry. In the case of a Zara dress, by the Spanish Inditex corporation we encountered above, the BBC journalist Katie Hope (2017) was able to trace its travels (see Figure 35.5). The lyocell fibres are sourced from

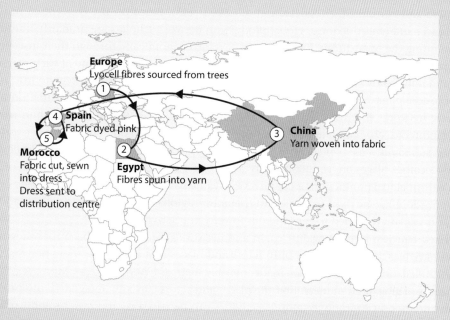

Figure 35.5
The travels of a dress

trees in Europe and transported to Egypt, where they are spun into yarn. The yarn was sent to China where it was woven into a fabric. After this, the fabric was sent to Spain to be dyed. The coloured fabric was shipped to Morocco to be cut and sewn into a dress. From Morocco it was shipped back to the distribution centre in Spain, from where it is transported to any of the Zara retail shops in Europe, North America or Asia.

Interestingly, by industry standards, this is an example of a value chain that is characterised by production in relatively close geographical proximity to the firm's headquarters. In the fast-fashion industry, time is a critical resource. By reducing shipping times through the use of near-shore suppliers (e.g. in Morocco, Turkey) rather than manufacturing contractors in China or Bangladesh, Inditex has been able to speed up the production cycle. It reduced the time required from design to shelf from several months to six weeks, enabling the fast-fashion firm to increase sales by producing more collections in a year.

A related analytical perspective on globalised production was developed by a team of economic geographers, namely the *Global Production Networks* approach (see Coe et al., 2008). The approach uses the term production rather than commodity to encompass broader economic activities, including services. More importantly, it exchanges the notion of a 'chain' with that of a network, as the authors critique the linearity and sequentiality that is associated with the metaphor of the chain. Global production networks are defined as 'the nexus of interconnected functions, operations and transactions through which a specific product or service is produced, distributed and consumed' (Henderson et al., 2002: 445). Based on the conceptual notions of value, power and embeddedness, global production network scholars are primarily interested in understanding the opportunity for regions to develop economically through their insertion into **transnational** production networks. In a globalised economy, the fortune of each region is no longer determined by endogenous factors but depends on the ability to integrate into international economic networks and flows. Regions are believed to benefit from participation in these economic networks through a process of 'strategically coupling' their assets (such as resources, skilled labour or technology) to the demands of lead firms, which orchestrate the networks. This coupling supposedly enables local value capture, and thus, regional economic development. However, not all places are simultaneously able to upgrade their position into more profitable niches within global production or capture more value based on advantageous strategic coupling by simply adopting the right strategies. In the uneven global economy, some regions and actors necessarily remain relegated to carrying out lower value activities.

A linked criticism levelled against chain and network approaches has been that they have an 'inclusionary bias' by investigating only actors and places that are part of these networks, while those excluded, or divested from, are made invisible (Bair and Werner, 2011). Moreover, the shifting patterns of globalisation mean that the places and actors currently integrated into production processes are not set in stone. Economic activities can be relocated and regions and workers can face disinvestment and devaluation. Understanding the production and reproduction of uneven development operating through global value chains and unveiling the differential ability of actors to create and capture value within global production remains an important task for geographers.

Summary

- Geographers have used global chain and global network perspectives to guide their empirical explorations of economic production across a wide range of sectors, including agricultural products, electronics, clothing and logistics.
- A key question for geographers is how global production networks relate to (regional) economic development and who is able to reap the benefits from participation within these networks.
- Successive evolutions of these guiding frameworks have led geographers to focus on different elements of these chains and networks.

Conclusion: the end of economic globalisation?

Today, globalisation has become hotly debated again. Some commentators have argued that we are, in fact, witnessing the 'end of globalisation' given the multiple challenges and pressures on the global economy. Alongside the ever-present problem of climate change, the current war in Ukraine and the COVID-19 pandemic have also disrupted established patterns of economic globalisation. Indeed, a rise in protectionist trade policies and disruptions to global trade as a result of the COVID-19 pandemic means that we are likely to see a considerable reorganisation of value chains.

The idea of globalisation being an inevitable and unidirectional process, proceeding towards an end state of pure globalisation, has always been flawed. Capitalism is crisis-prone, and as we saw in Figure 35.1, empirical data show that crises tend to be followed by reductions of foreign direct investments. The recent COVID-19 pandemic is no exception to this: In 2020, the global flows of foreign direct investments shrunk by a third to $US 1 trillion (UNCTAD, 2021). However, in 2021 these numbers picked up again to $US 1.6 trillion, exceeding pre-2020 levels.

We can also see how some of this reorganisation is driven by political as well as economic factors, and by changing attitudes to **neoliberal** globalisation. Whereas criticism of the effects of globalisation used to be primarily a concern of the political left and the Global South, we have recently seen a 'big switch' in which the backlash against globalisation stems from the political right in the Global North (Horner et al. 2018). Protectionist measures have become central elements in the trade policies of states that have long heralded neoliberal trade. The trade tariffs introduced on aluminium, steel, washing machines or solar panels in the United States are a key example.

The question of where your T-shirt will come from in the future is an open one. It is possible that with heightened risks of disruptions in global value chains, we will see the formation of more regional value chains and even the re-shoring of production in certain sensitive industries. Heightened transportation costs due to more costly energy may make extensively stretched production processes pricier, and these could also exert pressure on overseas production activities. This may make production sites that are closer to the places of final consumption strategically better placed.

It is however highly unlikely that the T-shirt you will be buying in the future, and all its materials, will be produced with your home region or country. Full re-shoring of production and the disentanglement of economic relations beyond the **nation-state** is hard to imagine. The geographies of globalisation will continue to shift in response to political, economic and environmental crises, leading to the re-configuration of global value chains, but the division of labour is, for the foreseeable future, likely to remain a global – and uneven – one.

Discussion points

- Does globalisation have a start and an end point?
- How have the geographies of the global clothing industry changed over time? Who profits and who loses in the current production arrangements?
- How is (uneven) development explained through using the concept of global value chains or production networks?
- What do you expect the future geographies of economic globalisation to look like?

References

Bair, J., and Werner, M. (2011). Commodity chains and the uneven geographies of global capitalism: a disarticulations perspective. *Environment and Planning A* 43: 988–997.

Cattaneo, O., Gereffi, G., and Staritz, C. (eds.) (2010). *Global Value Chains in a Postcrisis World: a Development Perspective*. Washington, D.C.: World Bank Publications.

Coe, N., Dicken, P., and Hess, M. (2008). Global production networks: realising the potential. *Journal of Economic Geography* 8: 271–295.

Dicken, P. (2015). *Global Shift: Mapping the Changing Contours of the Global Economy*. London: Sage.

Fashion Revolution. (2022). https://www.fashionrevolution.org/about/transparency/

Frankopan, P. (2015). *The Silk Roads*. London: Bloomsbury.

Gereffi, G. (1994). The Organization of Buyer-Driven Global Commodity Chains: How U.S. Retailers Shape Overseas Production Networks. In *Commodity Chains and Global Capitalism*, eds. G. Gereffi and M. Korzeniewicz. Westport: Praeger, 95–122.

Henderson, J., Dicken, P., Hess, M., Coe, N., and Yeung, H. W. C. (2002). Global production networks and the analysis of economic development. *Review of International Political Economy* 9(3): 436–464.

Hope, K. (2017). Has This Dress Been to More Countries than You? *BBC News*. https://www.bbc.com/news/business-39337204

Hopkins, T. K., and Wallerstein, I. (1986). Commodity chains in the world-economy prior to 1800. *Review* 10(1): 157–170.

Horner, R., Schindler, S., Haberly, D., and Aoyama, Y. (2018). Globalisation, uneven development and the North–South 'big switch'. *Cambridge Journal of Regions, Economy and Society* 11: 17–33.

Inditex. (2022). Inditex Annual Report 2021. https://static.inditex.com/annual_report_2021/en/documents/annual_report_2021.pdf

Peck, J. (2017). *Offshore: Exploring the Worlds of Global Outsourcing*. Oxford: Oxford University Press.

UNCTAD. (2013). Global Value Chains and Development. https://unctad.org/system/files/official-document/diae2013d1_en.pdf

UNCTAD. (2021). World Investment Report: Investing in Sustainable Recovery. https://investmentpolicy.unctad.org/publications/1249/world-investment-report-2021---investing-in-sustainable-recovery

Online materials

- https://slate.com/news-and-politics/2021/09/atlantic-slave-trade-history-animated-interactive.html
  A gripping visualisation of the Atlantic slave trade through a depiction of more than 20,000 slave ship voyages in a two-minute animation.

- https://storymaps.arcgis.com/stories/20f488863e4a41a892f0dd7a346180c0

    An interactive map with extensive resources on the global cotton commodity chain.
- http://www.followthethings.com

    A geographer's website with information on where the things we buy come from, who made them and under what conditions.
- https://www.somo.nl/

    SOMO is a non-governmental organisation that critically investigates and publishes reports on the activities of TNCs.
- https://atlas.cid.harvard.edu/

    You can build your own data visualisations of global trade flows using the data visualisation tool on this website by the Harvard Growth Lab!

Further reading

Barnes, T. J., and Christophers, B. (2018). *Economic Geography: A Critical Introduction*. Oxford: Wiley Blackwell.

Chapter 8 'Globalization and Uneven Development' in this advanced textbook offers a concise discussion of globalisation from a critical economic geographic perspective.

Coe, N. M., Kelly, P., and Yeung, W. C. (2020). *Economic Geography: A Contemporary Introduction* (3rd edn.). Oxford: Wiley.

Chapter 4 'Networks' provides a more detailed introduction to the concept of global production networks and shows how these networks interconnect producers and consumers in the global economy.

Dicken, P. (2015). *Global Shift: Mapping the Changing Contours of the Global Economy* (7th edn.). London: Sage.

For 30 years, this has been a key textbook on globalisation and change in the world economy. It presents key issues in a very accessible way and empirically discusses changes in different sectors of the economy.

MacKinnon, D., and Cumbers, A. (2019). *An Introduction to Economic Geography: Globalization, Uneven Development and Place* (3rd edn.). London: Routledge.

Globalisation is one of three key themes that runs through this economic geography textbook, showing how central the subject is to the sub-discipline.

Parnreiter, C., and Bernhold, C. (2020). Global Commodity Chains. In *International Encyclopedia of Human Geography*, ed. A. Kobayashi. Oxford: Elsevier, 169–176.

A very useful review of the genealogy of the concept of global commodity chains and its link to uneven development.

Sheppard, E. (2016). *Limits to Globalization: Disruptive Geographies of Capitalist Development*. Oxford: Oxford University Press.

A more advanced text by a key thinker in economic geography that offers a geographical **political economy** reading of globalising capitalism.

Werner, M. (2016). *Global Displacements. The Making of Uneven Development in the Caribbean*. Oxford: Wiley Blackwell.

A fascinating **ethnography** on industrial restructuring and disinvestment of the apparel industry in the Caribbean that shows how **coloniality** and the production of racial and **gender** difference are central to globalised production.

Global economies of care

Gianne Sheena Sabio
and Rhacel Salazar Parreñas

Introduction

Globalisation has brought forth significant changes in the relationship between productive and reproductive labour. For one, greater labour market participation of women in wealthier countries has created the demand for women from poorer countries to take over the former's reproductive labour such as the care of children, elderly, and other dependents, the cleaning of homes, and the overall daily maintenance of households (Parreñas, 2000, Oishi, 2005). This demand has prompted the formation of geographical flows of women workers from poorer to wealthier countries across the globe (see Figure 36.1). They include the regional flow of women care workers within Africa, Asia, Europe and Latin America, as we see, for example, in the case of Zimbabwean women going to South Africa, Filipino women migrating to Hong Kong or Singapore, Polish women relocating to Germany, and Nicaraguan women working in Costa Rica. These flows also include women's migration from the Global South to the Global North as we see with the presence of Peruvian and Filipino women in Italy (Parreñas, [2001] 2015). While the geographical flows of women care workers are disparate and diverse, they are concentrated within and from certain regions, and the largest single constituency of domestic workers can be found in the Arab Gulf region, with most coming from Southeast Asia, particularly Indonesia and the Philippines (International Labour Organization [ILO], 2015).

Across the globe, there are an estimated 11.5 million migrant domestic workers performing 'work for or in a household or households' with 80 per cent of them being women (ILO, 2015). It is not only in the home that women perform reproductive labour. In non-domestic institutional settings, this is also the type of work that is dominated by women. For example, about 90 per cent of nursing and midwifery health workers are women (ILO, 2020). Many of these women are migrant workers, specifically nurses who have responded to the labour shortage of health professionals in a wide range of countries that include Germany, Great Britain, the United States, Singapore, Oman, Saudi Arabia, and the United Arab Emirates (see Figure 36.2). In the healthcare sector, labour migration has grown by 60 per cent in the past decade and is projected to continue to rise as populations age (World Health Organization, 2021). The Philippines and India are the two biggest source countries for nurses in particular (ibid).

DOI: 10.4324/9780429265853-42

Figure 36.1
Employment agency for foreign domestic workers and maids in Singapore

Source: Photo credit: Julio Etchart/Alamy

The global outflow of women workers is why any consideration of the economies of care needs to be situated within a global system of migration. Put simply, these geographical flows of female labour enable the global economy of care to function. How do global economies of care operate and what is the positioning of care workers within these economies? We aim to address these questions in this chapter. First, we unpack 'care' as a concept to examine the global economy. Next, we take a closer look at two concrete examples of care work, namely, domestic work and nursing. Finally, we draw attention to the different institutions that create, sustain, and direct the movements of workers across the globe.

Globalisation and care work

This section revisits existing conceptualisations of care work and frameworks that allow us to situate it within the broader global economic system. We introduce the concept of 'care work'

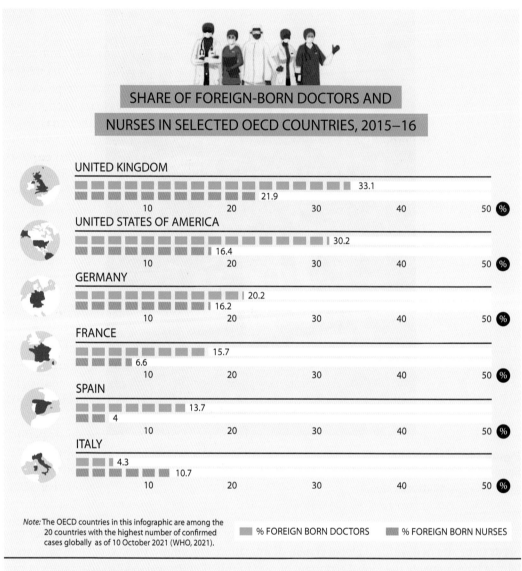

SHARE OF FOREIGN-BORN DOCTORS AND NURSES IN SELECTED OECD COUNTRIES, 2015–16

UNITED KINGDOM — 33.1 / 21.9

UNITED STATES OF AMERICA — 30.2 / 16.4

GERMANY — 20.2 / 16.2

FRANCE — 15.7 / 6.6

SPAIN — 13.7 / 4

ITALY — 4.3 / 10.7

Note: The OECD countries in this infographic are among the 20 countries with the highest number of confirmed cases globally as of 10 October 2021 (WHO, 2021).

■ % FOREIGN BORN DOCTORS   ▨ % FOREIGN BORN NURSES

Sources: OECD, *Recent trends in International Migration of Doctors, Nurses and Medical Students* (Paris, 2019).
OECD, *Contribution of Migrant Doctors and Nurses to Tackling COVID-19 Crisis in OECD Countries* (Paris, 2020).

© IOM GMDAC 2021
www.migrationdataportal.org

Figure 36.2
United Kingdom, United States of America, and Germany have the largest share of foreign-born nurses
Sources: OECD (2019, 2020)

and how this contrasts with 'reproductive labour'. Building on this distinction, we explain the key theoretical conception for understanding the global economy of care, which is the '**international division of reproductive labour**', or the care chain. We then juxtapose this key conception to other macro theoretical frameworks, specifically the 'care diamond' and 'care circulation'.

Key definitions and frameworks

In globalisation, production activities in one area cannot be understood solely from a uni-local perspective but must be situated in circuits of labour, goods, and capital across nations (see Chapter 35). In a similar vein, the concept of the international division of reproductive labour establishes the idea that reproduction activities, especially as they have been increasingly commodified, must be situated in the context of a global economy (Parreñas, 2000, Yeates, 2012). Like production activities, reproduction activities in one area are connected to reproduction activities in another. With the feminisation of wage labour, global **capitalism** is creating links among distinct systems of **gender** inequality. Women's labour market participation has not significantly decreased their housework, forcing many to outsource this labour and what makes this outsourcing affordable is the low-wage work of migrant women. In this sense, the migration of women connects systems of gender inequality in both sending and receiving nations to global capitalism. All these processes occur in the formation of the international division of reproductive labour, or what is also known as the 'care chain'.

The international division of reproductive labour is a **transnational** division of labour that is shaped simultaneously by global capitalism and systems of gender inequality in both the sending and receiving countries of the migrant labour. This division of labour applies to different geopolitical scales of migration, including regional migration, linking, for instance households in Hong Kong and the Philippines; south-to-south migration, tying families in Kuwait and the Philippines; and lastly south-to-north or global migration, connecting women, households, and families between, say, the Philippines and various nations in the Global North.

Under the international division of reproductive labour, migrant domestic workers perform the reproductive labour of class-privileged women in industrialised, or richer, countries, while they leave their own dependents to be cared for mostly by other women in the country of origin. This international division of labour refers to a three-tier transfer of reproductive labour among women in two **nation-states**: middle- and upper class women in receiving countries, migrant domestic workers, and domestic workers in the country of origin who are often too poor to migrate.

CASE STUDY
INTERNATIONAL DIVISION OF REPRODUCTIVE LABOUR

Carmen from the Philippines is both an employee and employer of domestic work. In Italy, she works for an architect who pays her more than 1000 euros a month to look after her children and help manage her household. At the same time, Carmen can only do this work if she employs a domestic worker of her own, one who stays in the Philippines, to care for her children. Carmen pays her domestic worker less than 100 euros a month to do the same work that she is doing in Italy for more than 1000 euros.

While the concept of the 'care chain' has been used interchangeably with the earlier concept of the 'international division of reproductive labour', it is important to note that they have substantial divergences. Care work, according to Paula England and her co-authors (2002), entails face-to-face contact and refers to the provision of a service that develops the human capabilities of the recipient. In contrast, reproductive labour encompasses the 'array of activities and relationships involved in maintaining people both on a daily basis and intergenerationally' (Glenn, 1992). Reproductive labour is a more expansive concept than care work, as it entails the work of sustaining a population instead of just one person. As such, reproductive labour entails a wider array of activities than care work does; it includes purchasing household goods, preparing food, laundering clothes, dusting furniture, sweeping floors, maintaining community ties, caring for adults and children, socialising children, and providing emotional support. Furthermore, much of the work done by migrant women is actually non-relational and would therefore not fit the traditional definition of 'care work'. As Mignon Duffy observes, 'A theoretical focus on [care] privileges the experiences of white women and excludes large numbers of very-low-wage workers' (2005: 79).

The concept of reproductive labour also enables us to account for racial inequalities among care providers and care recipients. For one, we can more fully account for the range of tasks performed by migrant domestic workers and the division of labour in the social reproduction of the population, allowing us to take note of who does menial and non-menial labour and nurturant and non-nurturant work in caring institutions, including households, hospitals, long-term care facilities, and schools (Duffy, 2005). In domestic work, 'spiritual' labour like reading books and providing emotional support is mostly done by the employers (Roberts, 1997); menial work, including nurturant (such as cleaning soiled clothes) and non-nurturant tasks (such as sweeping the floor), is mostly done by migrant women and women of colour (Glenn, 1992, Romero, 2002, Duffy, 2005).

As a concept, the international division of reproductive labour builds from the seminal formulation of the 'racial division of reproductive labour' (Glenn, 1992). Although reproductive labour has been historically relegated to women, Glenn argues that there is a hierarchical and interdependent relationship, one that interlocks the **race** and **class** status of women within both formal and informal labour markets. According to Glenn (1992: 30), class-privileged women free themselves of the 'mental, emotional and manual labour' needed for 'the creation and recreation of people as cultural and social, as well as physical beings' by hiring low-paid women of colour. This form of low-wage labour encompasses a wide array of jobs, including food-service production, hotel housekeeping, and nursing aide. In the commodification of reproductive labour, women are linked by gender and differentiated by race and class.

The concept of the 'international division of reproductive labour' extends Glenn's theory by placing it in an international context. It thus accounts for the costs of migrant reproductive labour to families and communities in countries of origin and juxtaposes such costs to the gains made by the employers' households in the host countries. The research informs us that such work concerns not just local but also transnational inequalities, and that service work also shapes political-economic ties between nations. This disrupts the assumption that the manufacturing of goods is the only relevant labour that links nations to each other. It shows that reproductive labour is a transnational division of labour simultaneously shaped by, and shaping, global capitalism and gender inequality in both sending and receiving states of migration.

Other approaches to global economies of care

Seeking to extend the international division of labour and care chain frameworks, other scholars have offered the concepts of 'care diamond' (Razavi, 2007) and 'care circulation' (Baldassar and Merla, 2013). The care diamond model argues that analysis must exceed households as the site for care and draws attention to other institutions (the state, community, and markets) that make up the care provision **infrastructure**. The care circulation perspective criticises the care chain analysis for the unidirectional image of care transfer that it portrays. It underscores the need to account for various directions and forms of care exchange, as well as the multiplicity of relationships (beyond mother-child relations) involved in these exchanges. Applying the care chain to the sphere of healthcare, Yeates (2009) offers the notion of the 'global nursing care chain', describing how nursing labour is extracted from nations at the bottom of the global chain for those at the top.

These alternative formulations have their own limitations. For instance, the care diamond's placed-based approach tends to contain its analysis within a nation-state, thereby downplaying the role of migration regimes that link providers and recipients of care across countries (Parreñas, 2012). It cannot account for the geographical dimensions of the global care economy. Likewise, care circulation's emphasis on the multidirectionality of care exchanges and 'disembodied' forms of care (arguing that care does not necessarily entail physical proximity) may inadvertently understate inequalities—in particular, access asymmetries to certain forms of care as a function of one's social positioning in global and local hierarchies. For instance, it cannot account for the different monetary valuation of care across different geographies.

Summary

- Researchers use a variety of key theoretical concepts for understanding the geographies of care economies, for example international division of reproductive labour or care chain, care diamond, and care circulation.
- The international division of reproductive labour allows an understanding of the global economy of care and the inequalities constituted in the geographic flows of care workers.

Pathways of care migration

As discussed earlier, economies of care or reproductive labour are deeply entwined with the global system of migration. Drawing on studies that appropriate what we refer to as the 'migration pathways approach', this section teases out how the global economies of care operate.

To describe the migration flow of care workers, we tackle three themes that the pathways approach emphasises: directions, intersections, and exclusions. With respect to directions, we look at how the migration pathways of care workers often involve multiple stops, as opposed to the 'single origin'-'single destination' image of migration portrayed in integration models. For intersections, we unpack the relationship between spatial and social mobilities of migrants. We discuss how the more global perspective of migration pathways enables a fuller examination of the non-linear and sometimes contradictory relationship between migration and social mobility. Finally with respect to exclusions, we show that multinational analysis can shed light on how regimes of exclusion are structurally and transnationally constituted.

Multinational migrations

First, central to the pathways approach is the argument that migration is not always geared towards a single site of incorporation but often involves multiple migrations. This is because of the temporary status of most migrant workers (Parreñas et al., 2019). This pattern is exemplified in the various typologies documented in studies of migration in the Global South. Migration scholars Paul and Yeoh propose 'multinational migrations' as an umbrella concept for capturing the multiplicity of flows or 'the varied movements of international migrants across more than one overseas destination with significant time in each country' (2021: 3). In her earlier piece on Filipino domestic workers in the Philippines, Hong Kong, and Singapore, Paul (2011) offers the concept of 'stepwise migration' to capture iterative multi-country migration, beginning with a lower cost destination and eventually a move to a more desirable higher tiered country in the West (see Figure 36.3).

Figure 36.3
A sign at an employment agency in Manila, the Philippines, advertising for domestic helpers to go to Hong Kong

Source: Photo credit: Betty Johnson/Alamy

Focusing on the migration of nurses from Asia, Walton-Roberts (2021) finds that in addition to direct migration, two other pathways are multi-stage migration (e.g. the study-work pathway from India to Canada), and multinational 'bus stop' migration (e.g. from the Philippines to Singapore, then to higher tier countries).

In contrast to this 'linear, progressivist trajectory' that stepwise international migration connotes, Parreñas and colleagues' (2019) study of Filipino and Indonesian domestic workers reveal a non-progressive, itinerant pattern of 'serial migration'. They show how this form of migration connects with various forms of precarities that preclude mobility. This non-progressive trajectory is similarly reflected in 'staggered migration' (Robertson, 2019, Parreñas, 2021b), 'return migration' (Parreñas, 2021b), and 'circular migration' (Hugo, 1982, Parreñas, 2010) among temporary migrant labourers. Robertson defines staggered migration as 'contingent, multi-directional and multi-stage mobility pathways' characterised by 'blurry and mutable boundaries between temporariness and permanence' (Robertson, 2019: 170). Return migrants in Parreñas' (2021b) study are those who terminate their temporary labour migration and go back to their country of origin (for instance, due to deportation or other reasons that have legal repercussions). Hugo uses circular migration to describe the repetitive or cyclical movements of temporary seasonal workers in Indonesia. Parreñas (2010) similarly uses circular migration to describe migrant entertainers' cyclical migration between Japan and the Philippines.

CASE STUDY
SERIAL LABOUR MIGRATION

Neneng is a 38-year-old domestic worker in the United Arab Emirates. A mother of two, she has been working outside the Philippines for more than two decades. She initially worked in the United Arab Emirates for three different employers from 1996 to 2003. Conflicts with her third employer led to her deportation back to the Philippines. She could not stay too long because of her lack of income. For this reason, she sought migration once again and landed in Saudi Arabia where she worked from 2003 to 2011. After accumulating sufficient savings to open a small eatery in the Philippines, she decided to return home. Yet, her business folded after two years. For this reason, she decided that she had to migrate once again, which is how she ended up in the United Arab Emirates for a second time.

Dora is a 45-year-old domestic worker in the United Arab Emirates, where she has been working since 2007. Yet, this was not her first migrant destination. Prior to the United Arab Emirates, Dora had worked in Malaysia, where she stayed for two years, and Taiwan, where she stayed for three years. Dora only completed single contracts in either Malaysia or Taiwan, because in the former she did not have a good experience with her employers as they refused to give her a day off and in the latter migrant domestic workers are subjected to a residency cap which at the time of her migration had only been three years.

Socio-spatial intersections

A second aspect of care migration flows that the pathways approach draws attention to is the way multinational migrations complicate the intersection between social mobility and migration. How spatial mobility connects with social mobility has long been a topic of interest in the social sciences (Savage, 1988, Faist, 2013). The concept of 'social mobility' is used to describe movement within a stratum in the social stratification system (i.e. horizontal social mobility, such as when moving across occupational positions that are more or less within the same stratum) or across different strata in society (i.e. vertical social mobility), whereas 'spatial mobility' pertains to geographic movement within and across national borders (Faist, 2013). Migration studies have shown how these two 'mobilities' are closely entwined. For instance, some literature points to how spatial mobility in itself has been seen as a marker of upward social mobility (Kelly and Lusis, 2006, Kelly, 2012, Faist, 2013). In contrast, some migrant workers are said to experience downward occupational mobility or social demotion upon shifting to a lower status occupation in their destination when they migrate (Umel, 2006, Pajo, 2008, Ghandnoosh, 2010, Guevarra and Lledo, 2013). Parreñas ([2001] 2015) offers the concept of 'contradictory class mobility' to describe how migrant domestic workers simultaneously gain upward economic mobility (through higher earnings) and downward occupational mobility.

The relationship between the spatial and social mobilities of migrant care workers is not always a positive progression. One illustration is Parreñas' (2021b) recent piece that explores the serial, staggered, and return migration pathways of migrant domestic workers. She argues that each of these pathways demonstrates 'how the socio-economic mobility of migrant domestic workers often exceeds one host society, questioning the applicability of straightforward integration or assimilation narratives to the full understanding of their experiences' (Parreñas, 2021b: 5). The precarities embodied in these three migration pathways refute the presupposition 'that the spatial mobility that is migration opens the door to social-economic mobility' (Parreñas, 2021b: 5).

The pathways approach to migration thus advances our understanding of the relationship between spatial and social mobilities in several ways. By allowing for a more complete account of the migration journey, it adds another analytic plane—a 'temporal' dimension—to the intersections of the 'social' and the 'spatial'. Current im/mobilities are importantly linked to migrants' imagined (or future) mobilities. The social mobility 'outcomes' then that result from migration—including the seemingly 'contradictory' ones—need to be understood in relation to the future pathways migrants aspire to, as well as their previous positionings in the migration journey.

Exclusionary structures

Finally, it is equally important to look at the broader exclusionary structures that impact migrant care workers' experiences. Studies have for instance explored the ways through which migrant women attempt to work around their 'constrained transnational mobility' as a result of gendered border regimes (Hwang, 2018). Parreñas (2021b) accentuates how serial, staggered, and returned migrations represent ways through which temporary labour workers attempt to circumvent exclusionary conditions in receiving countries.

The 'multi-scalar' research approach is increasingly gaining popularity among migration scholars. This type of analysis seeks to understand the different structures shaping migration processes at various levels. Multi-scalar analysis regards the local, regional, national, pan-re-gional, and global not as separate levels of analysis but as 'part of mutually constituting institu-tional and personal networks of unequal power within which people, both with and without migrant histories, live their lives' (Schiller, 2015).

Summary

- Migrant care workers are unlikely to only migrate to one destination.
- Scholars have developed different frameworks to capture the multi-country and multi-stage migration of care workers.
- In particular, they have looked at the directions, the intersections, and the exclusions of different migration pathways.

Migration infrastructure shaping global economies of care

How do various institutions direct care migration flows? The concept of 'migration infrastruc-ture' describes how migration is intensively mediated by 'systematically interlinked technolo-gies, institutions and actors that facilitate and condition mobility' (Xiang and Lindquist, 2014: 122). As a unifying concept, migration infrastructure covers an array of commercial (recruit-ment intermediaries), regulatory (state apparatus and procedures for documentation, licensing, training, and other purposes), technological (communication and transport), humanitarian (NGOs and international organisations), and social (migrant networks) actors and institutions (Xiang and Lindquist, 2014). In this section, we draw attention to two institutions that have been particularly influential in shaping the global economies of care, namely, the state and education.

State management of care migration

The transformations brought about by globalisation processes have made the role of the state more salient in promulgating development policies and managing labour migration. First, the state's role in legitimising and redefining economic opportunities is emphasised in studies of labour migration of women from the Global South. This typically involves deploying both mate-rial (policies and programmes) and **discursive** strategies, and scholars have identified the role of the 'labour brokerage state' in promoting the 'commodification of ideal labour' through state regulatory policies and reconfigured meanings of citizenship (Guevarra, 2009, Rodriguez, 2010). Rodriguez notes how other countries tap Philippine migration officials and bureaucrats' expertise in developing their labour export policies. She argues that the country's niche in the **neoliberal** global order is propelled by its labour brokerage state apparatus, which is geared towards mobil-ising, exporting, and managing migrants and consists of both institutional (e.g. embassies and consular offices) and **discursive** elements which promote reconfigured notions of citizenship that laud migrant workers as 'new heroes' (see Figure 36.4).

Figure 36.4
The notion of Filipino nurses as heroes, expressed by the nurses themselves at the London Pride event, 2015

Source: Photo credit: Zefrog/Alamy

Local and international labour markets are importantly intertwined and the redirecting strategies employed by the state sometimes involve repackaging international opportunities into local ones and vice versa. In Ortiga's (2021) article on 'shifting employabilities', she looks at how state institutions use certain **discourses** of skill to deal with an oversupply of employable nurses who could not fulfil their aspirations to migrate. The state constructs new 'employabilities' that reframe nursing as valuable labour beyond the context of foreign hospitals. These new employabilities include as follows: deploying nursing graduates to rural health centres; redirecting them sideways to the business process outsourcing industry or call centres while highlighting the 'health' aspects of the job (hence the rise of 'healthcare information'); and encouraging them to invest in more training and certification. These reconstructions of skill are couched in the promise that the work and training experiences they acquire will still count towards their future overseas employability.

Second, the state promotes care work migration by employing labour management strategies that appropriate the language of 'protection' or 'care'. Parreñas' (2021a) theorisation of state discipline provides a useful lens for unpacking this 'caring' strategy of the state. Parreñas identifies two forms of labour migration management that the state simultaneously engages in. Building on Foucault, she argues that on the one hand, the state exercises '**bio-power**' to create competitive yet docile workers; at the same time, it exercises 'pastoral power' by putting into place labour standards and other policies to ensure the care of its subjects. Parreñas further notes that 'pastoral power is a legitimating force in bio-power' (2021a: 1061). The state thus promotes labour migration through management strategies that couple control with benevolent care.

Export-oriented education

Particularly in the case of nursing, previous research has documented how state-regulated educational institutions play a key role in sustaining the supply of globally competitive nurses. Universities and colleges in source countries deploy strategies to constantly adjust to changing foreign labour demands. Examining the case of the Philippines, Ortiga (2017) uses the term 'flexible university' to describe how institutions constantly adjust their staffing composition and restructure units and reallocate space to respond to fluctuating demands; she likens them to Third World factories that strive towards maintaining 'just-in-time production of graduates' for foreign markets. Nurse training in India represents a parallel case of education that has been increasingly embedded in global labour markets (Walton-Roberts, 2015).

The goal of producing nurses for foreign markets poses the challenge of training students to practice 'first world' nursing in 'third world' health facilities (Ortiga, 2014). In their study of nursing schools in the Philippines, Ortiga and Rivero (2019) show that public hospitals in these less developed contexts actually provide an accessible training ground, with the abundance of sick, passive, and compliant bodies providing aspiring migrant nurses with plentiful opportunities to hone their skills. These patients are typically submissive given their limited economic means and lack of access to better treatment. Thus, global inequalities are inherent in the production of the nursing labour force itself; skilling requires practicing on poor bodies in countries positioned at the bottom of global hierarchies to provide better care for privileged bodies in more developed nations (Ortiga and Rivero, 2019).

These inequalities characterising the global economies of care have brought forth concerns about a brain (or care) drain or loss of skilled labour in less developed regions. Ortiga (2018) alternatively argues that export-oriented nursing education is more likely to produce a problem of 'brain waste' rather than brain drain. Looking at the case of the Philippines, she notes how unemployment and underemployment are exacerbated as the country produces a large supply of nursing graduates who face the dilemmas of a 'migration trap' (inability to leave due to volatile and fleeting overseas opportunities) and 'opportunity trap' (perpetual need to collect credentials to gain positional job market advantage).

Summary

- Domestic worker migration is often underpinned by the state, which institutionalises the global migration of care workers.
- There are three ways through which the state promotes care work migration: creating and reconfiguring ideal work opportunities; managing labour and labour conditions in a way that appropriates discourses of 'care' or 'protection;' and co-opting other institutions or actors, especially in the education sector.

Conclusion

This chapter draws from an extensive literature to examine how economies of care are embedded within and reproduced through a global system of migration. Reproductive labour, as opposed to care work, enables us to better understand the global and local hierarchies and relations of power that sit at the core of these economies. Neoliberal economic restructuring has transformed the ways through which women, in particular, engage in productive and reproductive labour. We have demonstrated how global economies of care operate by focusing on the highly feminised sectors of nursing and domestic work. Appropriating the migration pathways approach, we looked at the multiplicity of steps, decisions, and precarities that characterise the migration sojourns of nurses and domestic workers. We have demonstrated how this analytic approach provides a lens through which experiences of temporary migrants can be better examined and provide an instructive model for incorporating a multi-scalar approach. Migration studies of nurses and domestic workers from the Global South demonstrate that the state and state-regulated educational institutions play a key role in promoting labour migration. Rather than empowering women, these transformations tend to reinforce prevailing gender roles and expectations. With population ageing and intensification of migration, economies of care are bound to have increasing significance in societies across the globe, and future research will need to focus on emerging trends such as the ageing of migrant domestic workers and the medicalisation of reproductive labour. Within this research, the uneven global geographies of care and care work will continue to be critical.

Discussion points

- What is the international division of reproductive labour?
- What is the difference between the care chain, care diamond, and care circulation?
- What is the difference between care work and reproductive labour?
- What is the utility of focusing on migration pathways?
- How do sending states manage migration?

References

Baldassar, L., and Merla, L. (2013). Introduction: Transnational Family Caregiving Through the Lens of Circulation. In *Transnational Families, Migration and the Circulation of Care*. London: Routledge, 3–24.

Duffy, M. (2005). Reproducing labor inequalities: challenges for feminists conceptualizing care at the intersections of gender, race, and class. *Gender & Society* 19(1): 66–82.

England, P., Budig, M., and Folbre, N. (2002). Wages of virtue: the relative pay of care work. *Social Problems* 49(4): 455–473.

Faist, T. (2013). The mobility turn: a new paradigm for the social sciences? *Ethnic and Racial Studies* 36(11): 1637–1646.

Ghandnoosh, N. (2010). Organizing Workers along Ethnic Lines: The Pilipino Workers' Center. In *Working for Justice: The L.A. Model of Organizing and Advocacy*, eds. R. Milkman, J. Bloom, and V. Narro. Ithaca and London: ILR Press – Cornell University Press, 49–70.

Glenn, E. N. (1992). From servitude to service work: historical continuities in the racial division of paid reproductive labor. *Signs: Journal of Women in Culture and Society* 18(1): 1–43.

Guevarra, A. R. (2009). *Marketing Dreams, Manufacturing Heroes: The Transnational Labor Brokering of Filipino Workers*. New Brunswick: Rutgers University Press.

Guevarra, A. R., and Lledo, L. A. (2013). Formalizing the Informal: Highly Skilled Filipina Caregivers and the Pilipino Workers Center. In *Immigrant Women Workers in the Neoliberal Age*, eds. N. Flores-González, A. R. Guevarra, M. Toro-Morn, and G. Chang. Urbana: University of Illinois Press, 247–261.

Hugo, G. J. (1982). Circular migration in Indonesia. *Population and Development Review* 8(1): 59–83.

Hwang, M. C. (2018). Gendered border regimes and displacements: the case of Filipina sex workers in Asia. *Signs* 43(3): 515–537.

International Labour Organization (ILO). (2015). *ILO Global Estimates on Migrant Workers: Results and Methodology*. Geneva: ILO.

International Labour Organization (ILO). (2020). *Improving Nurses' and Midwives' Working Conditions: An Investment in Resilience for All*. Retrieved June 1, 2022 (https://www.ilo.org/resource/news/improving-nurses-and-midwives-working-conditions-investment-resilience-all).

Kelly, P. (2012). Migration, transnationalism, and the spaces of class identity. *Philippine Studies: Historical and Ethnographic Viewpoints* 60(2): 153–185.

Kelly, P., and Lusis, T. (2006). Migration and the transnational habitus: evidence from Canada and the Philippines. *Environment and Planning A* 38: 831–847.

OECD. (2019). *Recent Trends in International Migration of Doctors, Nurses and Medical Students*. Paris: OECD Publishing. Available at https://doi.org/10.1787/5571ef48-en.

OECD. (2020). Contribution of Migrant Doctors and Nurses to Tackling COVID-19 Crisis in OECD Countries. Paris: OECD Publishing. Available at https://www.oecd.org/coronavirus/policy-responses/contribution-of-migrant-doctors-and-nurses-to-tackling-covid-19-crisis-in-oecd-countries-2f7bace2/.

Oishi, N. (2005). *Women in Motion: Globalization, State Policies, and Labor Migration in Asia*. Standford: Stanford University Press.

Ortiga, Y. Y. (2014). Professional problems: the burden of producing the 'Global' Filipino nurse'. *Social Science & Medicine* 115: 64–71.

Ortiga, Y. Y. (2017). The flexible university: higher education and the global production of migrant labor. *British Journal of Sociology of Education* 38(4): 485–499.

Ortiga, Y. Y. (2018). Learning to fill the labor niche: Filipino nursing graduates and the risk of the migration trap. *The Russell Sage Foundation Journal of the Social Sciences* 4(1): 172–187.

Ortiga, Y. Y. (2021). Shifting employabilities: skilling migrants in the nation of emigration. *Journal of Ethnic and Migration Studies* 47(10): 2270–2287.

Ortiga, Y. Y., and Rivero, J. A. (2019). Bodies of work: skilling at the Bottom of the global nursing care chain. *Globalizations* 16(7): 1184–1197.

Pajo, E. (2008). *International Migration, Social Demotion, and Imagined Advancement: An Ethnography of Socioglobal Mobility*. New York: Springer.

Parreñas, R. S. (2000). Migrant Filipina domestic workers and the international division of reproductive labor. *Gender & Society* 14(4): 560–580.

Parreñas, R. S. ([2001] 2015). *Servants of Globalization: Migration and Domestic Work* (2nd edn.). Stanford: Stanford University Press.

Parreñas, R. S. (2010). Homeward bound: the circular migration of entertainers between Japan and the Philippines. *Global Networks* 10(3): 301–323.

Parreñas, R. S. (2012). The reproductive labour of migrant workers. *Global Networks* 12(2): 269–275.

Parreñas, R. S. (2021a). Discipline and empower: the state governance of migrant domestic workers. *American Sociological Review* 86(6): 1043–1065.

Parreñas, R. S. (2021b). The mobility pathways of migrant domestic workers. *Journal of Ethnic and Migration Studies* 47(1): 3–24.

Parreñas, R. S., Silvey, R., Hwang, M. C., and Choi, C. (2019). Serial labor migration: precarity and itinerancy among Filipino and Indonesian domestic workers. *International Migration Review* 53(4): 1230–1258.

Paul, A. M. (2011). Stepwise international migration: a multistage migration pattern for the aspiring migrant. *American Journal of Sociology* 116(6): 1842–1886.

Paul, A. M., and Yeoh, B. (2021). Studying multinational migrations, speaking back to migration theory. *Global Networks* 21(1): 3–17.

Razavi, S. (2007). The Political and Social Economy of Care in a Development Context: Conceptual Issues, Research Questions and Policy Options. In *Gender and Development Programme Paper 3*, United Nations Research Institute for Social Development. Geneva: United Nations.

Roberts, D. (1997). *Killing the Black Body: Race, Reproduction, and the Meaning of Liberty*. New York: Vintage Books.

Robertson, S. (2019). Migrant, interrupted: the temporalities of 'staggered' migration from Asia to Australia. *Current Sociology Monograph* 67(2): 169–185.

Rodriguez, R. M. (2010). *Migrants for Export: How the Philippine State Brokers Labor to the World*. Minneapolis: University of Minnesota Press.

Romero, M. (2002). *Maid in the U.S.A.* London: Routledge.

Savage, M. (1988). The missing link? The relationship between spatial mobility and social mobility. *The British Journal of Sociology* 39(4): 554–577.

Schiller, N. G. (2015). Explanatory frameworks in transnational migration studies: the missing multi-scalar global Perspective. *Ethnic and Racial Studies* 38(13): 2275–2282.

Umel, I. S. (2006). Cultivating strength: the role of the Filipino Workers' center COURAGE campaign in addressing labor violations committed against Filipinos in the Los Angeles private home care industry. *Asian Pacific American Law Journal* 12(1): 35–68.

Walton-Roberts, M. (2015). International migration of health professionals and the marketization and privatization of health education in India: from push-pull to global political economy. *Social Science & Medicine* 124: 374–382.

Walton-Roberts, M. (2021). Bus stops, triple wins and two steps: nurse migration in and out of Asia. *Global Networks* 21(1): 84–107.

World Health Organization. (2021). Health Workforce – Migration. *WHO*. Retrieved March 16, 2021 (https://www.who.int/teams/health-workforce/migration).

Xiang, B., and Lindquist, J. (2014). Migration infrastructure. *International Migration Review* 48(1): 122–148.

Yeates, N. (2009). Production for export: the role of the state in the development and operation of global care chains. *Population, Space and Place* 15: 175–187.

Yeates, N. (2012). Global care chains: a state-of-the-art review and future directions in care transnationalization research. *Global Networks* 12(2): 135–154.

Online materials

- https://www.kcrw.com/culture/shows/unfictional/the-rescue (KCRW, UnFictional: 'The Rescue'—a podcast episode on Fedelina Lugasan, a migrant domestic worker in the United States who was a victim of human trafficking and was enslaved for 65 years)
- https://www.theatlantic.com/podcasts/archive/2021/02/nurses/618110/ (The Atlantic, The Experiment Podcast: '4 Percent of Nurses, 31.5 Percent of Deaths: Why Filipino nurses have been disproportionately affected by the coronavirus pandemic')

Further reading

All of the following articles provide excellent empirical studies of nurse and domestic worker migration:

Ortiga, Y. (2018). Learning to fill the labor niche: Filipino nursing graduates and the risk of the migra-
    tion trap. *The Russell Sage Foundation Journal of the Social Sciences* 4(1): 172–187.
Parreñas, R. S. (2000). Migrant Filipina domestic workers and the international division of reproduc-
    tive labor. *Gender & Society* 14(4): 560–580.
Parreñas, R. S. (2021). The mobility pathways of migrant domestic workers. *Journal of Ethnic and
    Migration Studies* 47(1): 3–24.
Paul, A. M. (2011). Stepwise international migration: a multistage migration pattern for the aspiring
    migrant. *American Journal of Sociology* 116(6): 1842–1886.
Xiang, B., and Lindquist, J. (2014). Migration infrastructure. *International Migration Review* 48(1):
    122–148.

37 New economic geographies of development

Elise Klein

Introduction

This chapter traces key changes in the economic geographies of development. For the past two centuries, we have lived with a global economy that has been dominated by powerful Western economies, often underpinned by a geographical expansion that was itself built on **colonialism** and **imperialism**. However, recent years have witnessed the rise of China and India as significant economic powers, and attempts by those in the Majority World to consciously decouple their economies from Western authority. This chapter explores how these trends have resulted in new economic geographies emerging at a global level, and how 'south-south' cooperation is reshaping the practices and geographies of aid and development.

In the chapter, I use the terms Global North and Global South to depict an imprecise distinction between populations that have directed and benefited from global development, dispossession, **colonisation** and slavery, and those **postcolonial** and **subaltern** populations that have been the targets of such processes (Reuveny and Thompson, 2007, Müller, 2020). In some instances, the Global North and South terminology has been used to correspond with geographical North and South locations (see Chapter 9). However, the reality is a much messier picture than mere geographical descriptors – one of labour insecurity defined by the colour line, colonialism and slavery, but also by a **gendered** division of labour and other forms of exclusion. Also, there are many Global South populations within the Global North – for example Indigenous populations under settler colonial regimes – and some global elites living and working in the Global South. Whilst an increasing literature rightly points to the Global North and South terminology as imprecise and often problematic, I will purposefully continue with this terminology because the term 'Global South' is also used to signify an **epistemological** approach and is 'part and parcel of the postcolonial project of making the subaltern speak' (Müller, 2020: 735).

DOI: 10.4324/9780429265853-43

Colonisation: past and present

It is critical to note that before the set of European invasions, the Global South contained sophisticated, rich and longstanding economies and societies which were looted, oppressed and destabilised through European colonialism. Through these invasions and subsequent colonisation, the peoples of the Third World were set back in their development, sometimes for centuries. Scholars have long identified how the economic development of the Global North has been made possible through the expropriation of land, resources and lives in the Global South. The Trinidadian historian Eric Williams and other scholars have shown clearly how slavery and colonisation were fundamental to the industrial revolution in Europe and the unleashing of global **capitalism**. Essentially, they have argued that there is no capitalism without the triangular trade that stole and sold the lives of over 50 million people into slavery, or the colonisation that disrupted whole societies and economies across Africa, Asia and the Americas (Williams, 1944). So, whilst the industrial revolution of the eighteenth century is largely portrayed as a wonderful triumph of *man's* productive power, launching capitalism as the enduring global economic system, it was the 'triumph' of some at the expense of many. Marx made this point clear in Volume 1 of *Capital*: the rich didn't become so from being 'diligent, intelligent and above all frugal' (Marx, 1976: 873), while everyone else was busy being lazy. No, Marx states that 'in actual history it is notorious that conquest, enslavement, robbery, murder, briefly force, play the great part' (Marx, 1976: 874).

Colonial processes of dispossession and oppression were different depending on the empire, time-period and **territory** invaded, and as a result, populations around the world had different experiences of colonialism. For example, depending on the way in which the Europeans racialised and categorised populations, they were either deemed appropriate to be proletarianised where their labour would be exploited for profits of the empire, or people were marked for extermination – as the colonisers had no need for the populations, and they only wanted access to their land. The latter was particularly true in settler colonies where Europeans attempted to eliminate Indigenous populations in order to take their land for the establishment of European colonies (Wolfe, 2006, 2016).

Summary

- Before European invasion, the world was full of sophisticated, rich and longstanding economies and societies which were looted, oppressed and destabilised through European colonialism.
- Economic development of the Global North has been accomplished through the expropriation of land, resources and lives in the Global South.

Intervention and development

Whilst independence was eventually achieved by many Global South populations, the old European empires and the United States maintained economic, social and cultural ties with their former colonies. The exceptions are settler colonies, such as Australia, the United States, Canada and Aotearoa New Zealand, where the independence of Indigenous populations was never achieved, the settlers stayed and settler colonisation remains ongoing to this day.

Development interventions by European powers have continued to the current day, through the processes of what has been labelled as '**coloniality**'. So, while the formal colonial period has all but ceased, and many countries gained their legal independence from the colonial powers in the post-war period, the patterns of dispossession and the structures set up through the colonial period have continued through the process of coloniality, which has continued to define a set of cultures, labour relations, intersubjective relations and knowledge production well beyond the limits of formal colonial administrations (Quijano, 2000, Mignolo, 2021). Coloniality is an ongoing process of ordering relations based on perceived racial differences, stemming from the colonial period. Coloniality also involves constituting the structure and control of labour, resources and modes of production, ultimately upholding Western **hegemony** (Quijano, 2000).

Coloniality has long underpinned global processes of development as it codifies the relations underpinning those targeted as needing to be 'improved', and 'developed'. Specifically, since independence, the logic of Western interventions changed from direct oppression and exploitation towards one of 'modernisation' and 'improvement'. Subsequently, modernisation has involved the promotion and exportation of specific building blocks of Western progress to the Global South as part of a process of 'development'. In broad terms, Western development has had a focus not only on **infrastructure** and technology to promote capitalist integration, and liberal democracy to instil Western notions of security and peace, but has also included the modernisation of people themselves, through the shaping of their **subjectivities**, their worldviews, their aspirations and behaviour. The latter point became particularly important during the Cold War period, as the West was engaged in an **ideological** war with Russia where both superpowers were trying to win the geopolitical struggle for global influence. Both used proxy wars and development within the Global South, to exert influence and strategic advantage. As we shall see, a similar struggle could be said to be going on today, as China uses its Belt and Road initiative to challenge the power of the West across the Global South.

Global South populations reacted to the effects of colonialism in many ways, including formally launching the Non-Aligned movement. This was codified at the Bandung Conference, held in Indonesia in 1955, where five principles of peaceful co-existence were adopted, including 'respect for sovereignty, non-interference in the internal affairs of other nations, economic and technical cooperation, mutual benefit, the needs and rights of developing nations (including investment and the stabilisation of primary product prices), as well as peaceful co-existence' (Mawdsley, 2007: 408). The Bandung Conference is often viewed as a critical moment in the development of South-South cooperation (see Figure 37.1).

Figure 37.1
Delegations held a plenary meeting of the economic section during the Bandung Conference,
Indonesia, April 1955

Source: Photo credit: Government of Indonesia

Summary

- Whilst independence was achieved by many Global South populations, the old European empires and the United States maintained links with former colonies through processes of economic intervention and 'coloniality'.
- Global South populations and governments reacted by forging their own alliances.

Development as economic growth

Global South populations and their governments were also under direct influence from the West through international economic institutions, especially the so-called Bretton Woods institutions. The Bretton Woods institutions included the International Monetary Fund (IMF) and the International Bank for Reconstruction and Development, which later became the World Bank. Importantly, both of these institutions were designed to play a major role in governing the international economic order among states around the world, including monetary relations and regulations. Both institutions have upheld an economic hegemony that has supported specific modes of economic development which have overwhelmingly benefited the West. For example, **Structural Adjustment Programmes** (SAPs) were a suite of **neoliberal** policies designed by the World Bank and the IMF in the 1980s (see also Chapters 17 and 52). SAPs were imposed on countries across Africa, South America and parts of Asia and included a range of policies which Global South governments had to implement in order to receive aid to service their debts (Herbst, 1990). These policies differed from country to country but focused largely on fiscal deficit, monetary policy, privatisation of state assets and trade liberalisation. Their effect was to destabilise many local industries, as well as to limit social investment, all furthering economic insecurity and inequality. Structural Adjustment continued to deepen countries' economic dependence on former colonial powers and current hegemons.

Through such processes, the idea and practice of 'development' has provided a useful cover for dispossession in the Global South. Global South populations have been tied into an economic system that often benefits the Global North – through dependency, unequal terms of trade and value, and structural adjustment. This dependence has largely benefitted the Global North, as these industrial countries and their corporations have invested in the production and export of raw materials from developing countries, influencing terms of trade in their favour and perpetuating an unequal international division of labour.

Summary

- Global South populations and their governments have been under direct influence from the West through the Bretton Woods institutions.
- **Structural Adjustment Policies** of the IMF and World Bank destabilised many local industries, as well limiting social investment, furthering economic insecurity and inequality.
- Development has provided a useful cover for dispossession in the Global South through economic policies which have promoted dependency, unequal terms of trade and value, and structural adjustment.

Moving beyond the West's influence

Whilst the dominance of the Global North has debilitated many states and their economies around the world over a sustained period of time, some countries have bucked this trend by expanding their economies despite the West's dominance, including the economic development of China, Brazil, India, Indonesia, South Africa, Nigeria and Mexico. Specifically, China's rate of growth has rivalled, and often outpaced, the United States since the turn of the twenty-first century, but interestingly economic growth in China has also involved undertaking various initiatives to promote international dominance through development initiatives of their own. In doing so, China maintains this is providing an alternative to Western intervention, by making funds available for development projects without interference in domestic issues. However, it should be noted that some countries have withdrawn from economic agreements with China precisely because of such interference. The Chinese Belt and Road Initiative, launched in 2013 by China's

Figure 37.2
One (land) belt and one (maritime) road

Source: Figure credit: Aleksei Egorov/Alamy Stock Vector

President Xi Jinping, is perhaps China's major development initiative (see Figure 37.2). This aims to re-establish Chinese economic influence along the Silk Road which was a major trading route before European colonisation, as well as via a maritime route linking up Eurasia, Oceania and Africa (Oakes, 2021). The Belt and Road Initiative claims 'win-win cooperation' through common development and prosperity for Global South countries, although many instances have seen this relation work to Chinese advantage.

Other countries have also provided funds to underwrite development projects across the Global South, and this process is often called South-South Cooperation. South-South Cooperation is a term that 'refers to the transfer and exchange of resources, technology and knowledge, set within claims to shared colonial and post-colonial experiences and identities, and anchored within a wider framework of promoting the collective strength and development of the Global South' (Mawdsley, 2019: 259). However, whilst South-South Cooperation is seen by some as a major example of the shifts of Western dominance in global economic relations, there remain unresolved issues centred around who really does benefit. Specifically, whilst rates of economic growth measured in Gross Domestic Product (GDP) may have increased in these economies, mixed distributional outcomes are also evident. Questions remain as to whether this growth has translated into structural and sustainable transformation or just into new forms of inequality, insecurity and dispossession within particular countries of the Global South.

CASE STUDY
THE NEW INTERNATIONAL ECONOMIC ORDER

The New International Economic Order (NIEO) was a set of international economic proposals advocated by anti-colonial heads of state in newly independent countries. They aimed to end 'economic colonialism' – a term used to describe how the international economy set up under colonial rule was largely still in place through unfair trade rules, debt and continued economic exploitation, despite countries being given political independence. The NIEO sought to rework a global economy set up by the West, for the West. Despite their efforts, the NIEO ended in the era of structural adjustment which further destabilised Global South economies (To read more on the NIEO see Getachew, 2019).

Summary

- Some states have expanded their economies despite the West's dominance, including the economic development of China, Brazil, India, Indonesia, South Africa, Nigeria and Mexico.
- Countries beyond the Western powers have also provided funds to underwrite development projects across the Global South, and this process is often called South-South Cooperation.
- Questions remain as to whether this growth has translated into structural and sustainable transformation or just into new forms of inequality, insecurity and dispossession.

Inequality and economic insecurity

Whilst Western hegemony in global economic relations has been increasingly challenged by rival economies, logics of economic development continue to be reproduced in global economic relations. This is partly because capitalism continues to exploit and expropriate workers within the Global South because it needs to accumulate, either by keeping costs of production down (cheap or expropriated resources and labour) or by gaining higher market prices. The means through which land, resources and labour are still acquired is often through dispossession, or what David Harvey has called accumulation by dispossession (Harvey, 2003). So, while governments maintain that their economies support progress and development, this protection is often only for a lucky few. Capitalism can also be exploitative, cruel and ecologically destructive for many (often non-white) others (Hall, 2013, Fraser, 2018).

CASE STUDY
CLIMATE CHANGE AS DISPOSSESSION

One key part of capitalism is that it needs natural resources to turn into commodities, which are in turn sold to generate profits. In the production process of making commodities, as well as using them, waste is excreted into our ecosystems causing pollution, damage and dispossession. We see this most through the climate crisis where capitalist fuelled growth extracts fossil fuels from the ground, and through the production process as well as through their use, excretes CO_2 into the atmosphere. Indeed, the dispossession of life and livelihoods is a common feature of global capital accumulation. Often, the extraction of resources dispossesses populations from their land, particularly Indigenous people, and atmospheric and ecosystem pollution has had dramatic and long-term impacts. We know that climate change is dispossessing communities all around the world – particularly Global South communities. For example, in 2014, the then-Prime Minister of Kiribati, Anote Tong (Figure 37.3), purchased a 22 km sq parcel of land in Fiji as a potential new home for Kiribati people soon to be displaced by rising sea levels.

Figure 37.3
Anote Tong, former prime minister of Kiribati
Source: Photo credit: Angela Weiss/Getty

Indeed, much of the wealth accumulated by advanced economies rests on inequalities elsewhere. We have a global economy that is more like a global factory in that the formal economy often relies on the informal economy where the majority of the world works without labour protection and without economic security. In considering how the formal economy relies on the informal economy, think about the global supply chains of most of the things consumed by advanced economies – most of these items are made or produced by people working in poor conditions and paid far less than most would think reasonable. Thinking globally about the world of labour leads us to appreciate that many informal workers still predominantly produce for the global market, while finding it difficult to care for themselves and their families (Federici, 2012, see also Chapters 34 and 35).

It is a common misconception of traditional development policy to see the informal sector as being in a process of transition to what is called the formal economy – work regulated by political and judicial processes to ensure a certain level of labour standards (Mead and Morrisson, 2004, Munck, 2013, Bernards, 2017). This approach to framing conditions of labour in the Global South has been adopted in various ways by the international development industry, governments, the World Bank and the IMF. These institutions attempt to promote the transformation of informal labour into formal labour either through championing entrepreneurial acumen and skill development, as is the case with the World Bank, or through policies that encourage inclusive governance and social protection, as is the case with the International Labour Organisation (Bernards, 2017). Bernards (2017) contends that 'policy responses to informality often swing between "formalising" and "celebrating" informal work, with neither alternative actually doing much to address the root causes of poverty' (p. 1833). Scholars have cautioned against engaging in the language of micro-entrepreneurs, self-employed businesswomen and businessmen, or a reservoir of potential job creation as a way to think about informal workers (Ferguson, 2015). For the majority, the need to improvise is a function of immense economic insecurity and precarity where people are trying to make a subsistence living from limited resources and often in oppressive conditions (Rizzo, 2011, Ferguson, 2015). In this sense the 'development' of parts of the Global South often bypasses many of its populations.

Both the entrepreneurial approach and inclusive development and social protection policies underappreciate the enduring connection between labour insecurity and global capitalism (Munck, 2013, Bernards, 2017). Not only does the informal economy provide relative surplus labour to drive down formal labour costs, it also delivers sources of cheap labour, resources and commodities (Harris-White, 2006). The process of development also displaces and expropriates populations' land and labour in the process of accumulation by dispossession. For example, in India and China, the dispossession and displacement of rural communities from their land by national and international capital in the name of development is integral to economic production for the national and global economy (D'Costa, 2014). Whilst some formal employment has been created through this process, it is nowhere near the rate needed to absorb the people being dispossessed (D'Costa, 2014).

Processes of accumulation by dispossession inherent in development (D'Costa, 2014) generate large numbers of people with no access to land or a living wage (Li, 2010, Ferguson, 2015). Li (2010) points to the scale of structural labour insecurity, describing how the process of accumulation by dispossession of companies, aided by governments, generates large numbers of people with no access to land or a living wage. She argues that their existence has moved beyond forming a supply of relative surplus labour for the labour market at times of economic expansion, concluding that they are *surplus* to the whole capitalist system of production (Li, 2010).

Scholars point to the effects of dehumanisation that are inherent in processes of development in order to render populations available for dispossession (Wilson, 2012). The term racial capitalism refers to how accumulation can only accrue 'by producing and moving through relations of severe inequality among human groups—capitalists with the means of production/workers without the means of subsistence, creditors/debtors, conquerors of land made property/the dispossessed and removed. These antinomies of accumulation require loss, disposability, and the unequal differentiation of human value, and racism enshrines the inequalities that capitalism requires' (Melamed, 2015: 77). In this sense, although racisms predate capitalism, capitalism has used racial inequalities and segregation to 'adapt to the political and material exigencies of the moment' (Robinson, 2000: 66). Put in a different way, 'Racial difference… creates a variegated landscape that cultures and capital can exploit to create enhanced power and profits' (Fluri et al., 2020: 239).

CASE STUDY
RACIAL DIFFERENCE AS A FUNCTION OF CAPITALISM

Have you ever wondered why labour conditions for some people in the world are far, far worse than others? For example, the sweat shop conditions of many labourers in the Global South generally would not be tolerated in much of the Global North. These low-paid, and largely unregulated, sectors are essential for global capital accumulation – keeping costs low helps profit making. A big part of the reason for this is because there is a process of dehumanisation and racialisation of Global South people by the mainly 'white' Global North. The kind of thinking that says 'oh well, at least they have some work', or, 'if they work hard, things will get better' – this is an implicit acceptance that their dehumanisation justifies harsh labour conditions. We see this in parts of the Global North too, where migrant labourers, Indigenous and Black communities often face exploitative working conditions that the largely white population would not accept themselves.

This dynamic of capitalism and racism is significant because whilst clear examples of racial capitalism include historic processes of slavery, colonialism and genocide, it also includes contemporary forms of incarceration regimes, Indigenous dispossession, exploitation of informal workers and racial warfare (Melamed, 2015). It is for these reasons that while Western influence may be reducing, and new economic actors are influencing the global economic landscape, we must be cognisant of the ongoing functions of economic relations that underpin continued and expanding economic inequalities.

Summary

- Whilst Western hegemony in global economic relations may be challenged by the rise of rival advanced economies, logics of economic development continue to be reproduced in global economic relations.
- Processes of accumulation by dispossession are inherent in development and generate large numbers of people with no access to land or a living wage.
- Functions of dehumanisation and racism are inherent in processes of development in order to render populations available for dispossession.

Towards postdevelopment futures?

Postdevelopment is a set of ideas that cause us to question the apparatus of global capitalist development as a hegemonic principle organising social life (Esteva and Escobar, 2017). The Colombian scholar Arturo Escobar, a major contributor to the debates on postdevelopment, argued over two decades ago that '[w]e are not looking for development alternatives but alternatives to development' (1995: 215). For Escobar, postdevelopment critically examines a set of key principles: the support of pluralistic grassroots movements while tempering localised relations of power, and upholding a critical stance towards established capitalist notions of development. Postdevelopment encompasses the promotion of different conceptions of economy, taking into account solidarity, reciprocity and other forms of valuation as opposed to capitalism. Therefore, the concept of postdevelopment not only references alternatives to development but also works to overcome many of the dualisms which have hidden the ongoing and contemporary construction of unequal global economies.

Today, postdevelopment is not only concerned with the Global South but equally addresses issues of development in the Global North (Bendix et al., 2019) and has sought to displace the universalisation and **globalisation** of capitalism, insisting instead on the need for what Gustavo Esteva has described as 'a world in which many worlds can be embraced' (Esteva and Escobar, 2017: 4). Whilst development has long classified many populations, and non-capitalist practices and ways of being, around the world as subordinate and inferior, postdevelopment centres the '**pluriversality**' of diverse **ontologies** and ecologies of knowledge, economies and life words as valid pathways forward (Escobar, 2011, Kothari et al., 2019 – see also Chapter 38).

Practices of postdevelopment are well underway (Klein and Morreo, 2019, Kothari et al., 2019) in countless urban and rural communities around the world, especially in grassroots organisations and movements, and new social structures are in the making which can be described as being postdevelopmental in the sense that they are a reaction to, or a reflection of, the failure of 'development'. These alternatives are based on reclaiming the economy from the market (Gibson-Graham, 2006), reclaiming politics from the state and reclaiming knowledge from a strictly Western view of 'science' (see also Chapters 38 and 64).

Summary

- The work of postdevelopment has sought to displace the universalisation and global-isation of capitalism, insisting instead on the need for what Esteva and Escobar have described as 'a world in which many worlds can be embraced' (2017: 4).
- In the words of Escobar, practices of postdevelopment are based on the notion that we 'are not looking for development alternatives but alternatives to development' (1995: 215).

Conclusion

This chapter has mapped some of the key changes in the economic geographies of develop-ment. The global economy has long been dominated by powerful Global North economies, underpinned by an expansion of colonialism and imperialism. In recent years, there has been the rise of some Global South economies to significant economic power, such as China. Other movements and governments have sought better and fairer economic conditions through initia-tives such as the NIEO and the Bandung Conference. However, although global inequalities of development continue, often based on **race** and **ethnicity**, the ideas and practices of postde-velopment are identifying and pursuing alternative economic possibilities.

Discussion points

- How has colonisation shaped economies across the world, and how does it continue to shape them today?
- Why might we challenge economic development policy that assumes the informal economy is in transition to the formal economy?
- What was the significance of the Bandung conference?
- Why do scholars say that all capitalism is racial capitalism?
- What are some examples of South-South cooperation and how is it different to North-South development assistance?

References

Bendix, D., Muller, F., and Ziai, A. (2019). Postdevelopment Alternatives in the North. In *Postdevelopment in Practice: Alternatives, Economies, Ontologies*, eds. E. Klein and C. E. Morreo. London: Routledge, 133–148.

Bernards, N. (2017). The global governance of informal economies: the international labour organiza-tion in East Africa. *Third World Quarterly* 38(8): 1831–1846.

D'Costa, A. (2014). Compressed capitalism and development: primitive accumulation, petty commod-ity production, and capitalist maturity in India and China. *Critical Asian Studies* 46(2): 317–344.

Escobar, A. (1995). *Encountering Development: The Making and Unmaking of the Third World*. Princeton: Princeton University Press.

Escobar, A. (2011). Sustainability: design for the pluriverse. *Development* 54(2): 137–140.

Esteva, G., and Escobar, A. (2017). Post-development @ 25: on 'being stuck' and moving forward, sideways, backward and otherwise. *Third World Quarterly* 38(23): 1–14.

Federici, S. (2012). *Revolution at Point Zero: Housework, Reproduction, and Feminist Struggle*. Oakland: PM Press.

Ferguson, J. (2015). *Give a Man a Fish: New Politics of Distribution*. Durham: Duke University Press.

Fluri, J. L., Hickcox, A., Frydenlund, S., and Zackary, R. (2020). Accessing racial privilege through property: geographies of racial capitalism. *Geoforum* 132(4): 238–246.

Fraser, N. (2018). Roepke lecture in economic geography – from exploitation to expropriation: historic geographies of racialized Capitalism. *Economic Geography* 94(1): 1–17.

Getachew, A. (2019). *Worldmaking after Empire: The Rise and Fall of Self-Determination*. Princeton: Princeton University Press.

Gibson-Graham, J. K. (2006). *A Postcapitalist Politics*. Chicago: University of Minnesota Press.

Hall, D. (2013). Primitive accumulation, accumulation by dispossession and the global land grab. *Third World Quarterly* 34(9): 1582–1604.

Harriss-White, B. (2006). Poverty and capitalism. *Economic and Political Weekly* 41(13): 1241–1246.

Harvey, D. (2003). *The New Imperialism*. Oxford: Oxford University Press.

Herbst, J. (1990). The structural adjustment of politics in Africa. *World Development* 18(7): 949–958.

Klein, E., and Morreo, C. E. (2019). *Postdevelopment in Practice: Alternatives, Economies, Ontologies*. Abington: Routledge.

Kothari, A., Salleh, A., Escobar, A., Demaria, F., and Acosta, A. (eds.) (2019). *Pluriverse: A Post-Development Dictionary*. Delhi: Tulika Books and Authorsupfront.

Li, T. (2010). To make live or let die? Rural dispossession and the protection of surplus populations. *Antipode* 41: 66–93.

Marx, K. (1976). *Capital: Volume 1* (trans. B. Fowkes). Harmondsworth: Penguin.

Mawdsley, E. (2007). China and Africa: emerging challenges to the geographies of power. *Geography Compass* 1(3): 405–421.

Mawdsley, E. (2019). South–South cooperation 3.0? Managing the consequences of success in the decade ahead. *Oxford Development Studies* 47(3): 259–274.

Mead, D. C., and Morrisson, C. (2004). The informal sector elephant. *World Development* 24(10): 1611–1619.

Melamed, J. (2015). Racial capitalism. *Critical Ethnic Studies* 1: 76–85. https://doi.org/10.5749/jcritethnstud.1.1.0076

Mignolo, W. (2021). Coloniality and globalization: a decolonial take. *Globalizations* 18(5): 720–737. DOI: 10.1080/14747731.2020.1842094

Müller, M. (2020). In search of the global east: thinking between north and south. *Geopolitics* 25(3): 734–755.

Munck, R. (2013). The precariat: a view from the South, *Third World Quarterly* 34(5): 747–762.

Oakes, T. (2021). The belt and road as method: geopolitics, technopolitics and power through an infrastructure Lens. *Asia Pacific Viewpoint* 62(3): 281–285.

Quijano, A. (2000). Coloniality of power and eurocentrism in Latin America. *International Sociology* 15(2): 215–232.

Reuveny, R. X., and Thompson, W. R. (2007). The North–South divide and international studies: a symposium. *International Studies Review* 9(4): 556–564.

Rizzo, M. (2011). 'Life is War': informal transport workers and neoliberalism in Tanzania 1998–2009. *Development and Change* 42(5): 1179–1206.

Robinson, C. J. (2000). *Black Marxism: The Making of the Black Radical Tradition*. Chapel Hill: University of North Carolina Press.

Williams, E. (1944). *Capitalism and Slavery*. Chapel Hill: University of North Carolina Press.

Wilson, K. (2012). *Race, Racism and Development: Interrogating History, Discourse and Practice*. London: Zed Books.

Wolfe, P. (2006). Settler colonialism and the elimination of the native. *Journal of Genocide Research* 8(4): 387–409.

Wolfe, P. (2016). *Traces of History: Elementary Structures of Race*. London: Verso Books.

Online materials

- www.developmentgateway.org

  Development Gateway provides a range of development information focussing on the use of data in the areas of agriculture, aid, education, health, extractive industries and information management.

- www.eldis.org

  This website is hosted by the Institute of Development Studies, at the University of Sussex, and provides free and open access to a range of research on global development matters.

- www.chathamhouse.org/topics

  This website contains a large amount of information on global topics, including a section on economics and trade, covering, amongst other things, China's Belt and Road Initiative, the International Monetary Fund and the World Trade organisation. This includes podcasts and audio discussions, as well as factual information and research reports.

Further reading

Any of the following will allow you to explore the issued raised in the chapter in a deeper way:

Getachew, A. (2019). *Worldmaking after Empire: The Rise and Fall of Self-Determination*. Princeton: Princeton University Press.

Harvey, D. (2003). *The New Imperialism*. Oxford: Oxford University Press.

Kothari, A., Salleh, A., Escobar, A., Demaria, F., and Acosta, A. (eds.) (2019). *Pluriverse: A Post-Development Dictionary*. Delhi: Tulika Books and Authorsupfront.

Mignolo, W. (2021). Coloniality and globalization: a decolonial take. *Globalizations* 18(5): 720–737.

Robinson, C. J. (2000). *Black Marxism: The Making of the Black Radical Tradition*. Chapel Hill: University of North Carolina Press.

38 Innovation for the pluriverse

Suliasi Vunibola and Steven Ratuva

Introduction

There are different kinds of innovative systems in the world, although Western **capitalist** innovation systems constitute the dominant forms. Capitalist innovation is centred on technological progress and providing novel high-tech digital design and engineering solutions to solve economic and technological problems globally. It often aims to provide these solutions for global consumers, which results in massive wealth inequality between countries of the Global North and the Global South. While technological innovation within the market may generate profit for some, it does not necessarily address global economic disparity, nor does it improve the collective well-being of marginalised groups (Dahms, 1995). Questions over the distribution of the benefits of innovation and the impact of the commercial use of technological innovation on the environment are major challenges today. Increases in poverty and inequality, the effects of climate change, and other negative social issues have prompted a rethink about alternative ways of framing and implementing innovation. Thus, rather than serving the interests of large corporations and the richest segments of society, it is important to think about how innovation can deal directly with people and their capacity to survive, support their resilience, and build their adaptation mechanisms to global issues, as in the case of the climate crisis. Amongst the alternative systems of innovation are Indigenous ways of knowing and living.

Indigenous communities worldwide have long been using alternative forms of innovation to support their well-being, but in times of global crisis like the COVID-19 pandemic and the crash of economies across most of the Western world, people in the Global South have increasingly returned to alternative and Indigenous innovation systems to support their livelihoods (Ratuva, 2021). Indigenous innovation is place-based and focuses on human agencies, whereas Western innovation is largely aimed at capital accumulation and power dynamics in an attempt to influence lives globally. Indigenous innovation is thus a way of voicing the political struggles of Indigenous peoples, peasants, and marginalised groups in defending their **territories** and their entire ways of being against the encroachment of technocentric innovation and development (Escobar, 2018).

DOI: 10.4324/9780429265853-44

This chapter contributes to such a reimagining, exploring alternatives to technocentric and capitalist innovation. Such alternatives can further economic development practices and worldviews that better align with system and socio-ecological transformation, and they offer support to those who express opposition to the notion of one world order and one way of thinking about innovation. The chapter covers new visions of the economy which build on place-based practices (Gibson-Graham, 2008), including Indigenous connections (Diprose et al., 2017). It takes the notion of a **'pluriverse'** seriously, which counters the idea of a single, dominant universal approach to economic development (Kothari et al., 2019). In contrast, pluriversal approaches deepen and widen research, dialogue, and action agendas for activists, policymakers, and scholars with a variety of worldviews and practices which relate to the mutual search for an ecologically wise and socially just world. Such approaches make space for Indigenous conceptualisations of innovation, deeply engaged in place.

The chapter will first define how innovation is understood within capitalist domains and how this has fed through to dominant perceptions of economic innovation in human geography. It will then unpack some of the concerns around that notion of innovation, before discussing Indigenous innovation with case studies of Nayarabale Youth Farm in Fiji. The chapter concludes with discussions of how Indigenous innovation might contribute to system transition, socio-ecological transformation, and social and economic justice.

Framing Western innovation

Innovation was popularised as a separate research field in the 1960s, with, for instance, the establishment of the Science Policy Research Unit (SPRU) at the University of Sussex, which studied innovation purely within 'science studies' or 'science policy studies' (Fagerberg et al., 2005). Rosenberg and Frischtak (1984) stated that innovation refers to the development of new products, which may include new production processes and newly developed functions to reduce costs. However, others have drawn a distinction between invention and innovation, and Diamond (1996) proposed that invention is the first occurrence of a new idea aimed at a new product or process, whereas innovation is the original commercialisation of the idea. For instance, inventions may well be developed at universities, whereas innovation is facilitated through the commercial domain, within which the production of ideas is turned into consumer products at an industrial level, aimed at the market.

Economist Joseph Schumpeter linked innovation to the concept of **creative destruction**, by which new production units replace obsolete ones. Schumpeter acknowledged innovation as a significant feature of economic change, and his theory characterised five categories of innovation: (i) new production processes, (ii) new products, (iii) new materials or resources, (iv) new markets, as well as (v) new forms of organisations (Schumpeter, 1934: 66). Schumpeter identified the spatial diffusion of innovation as key, or the process of recognition, acceptance, and absorption of innovation within an economic system over time. In his view there is a symbiotic relationship between diffusion and innovation; without diffusion, an innovation remains isolated, and unable to gain a commercial foothold (Bauer, 1997). For example, it is through the diffusion of innovation that plastic is used globally, after Alexander Parkes patented the material in 1862 and then Leo Baekeland later pioneered synthetic plastic at the mass production level (Science

Museum, 2019). David Harvey has pointed out how such 'creative destruction' necessarily takes place over space as well as through time (Harvey, 2001, 2010), and Schumpeter himself noted how the endless evolution of production systems through new ideas results in even more resource exploitation (Schumpeter, 2003), as a result of imperialist and colonial resource extraction.

Summary

- The idea of innovation has a dominant legacy in the Western world, where it is linked to commercial expansion and capital accumulation.
- Recently, this dominant idea has been challenged by notions of Indigenous innovation, which stress place-based practices, leading to social and ecological transformation.

Economic innovation and geography

Economic geographers have studied the diffusion of innovation, and also the concentration of innovation in particular geographic locations. Emblematic 'innovation districts' include Route 128, around Boston in Massachusetts; Silicon Valley in California; Shenzhen, and the Greater Bay Area in China; SpaceX exploration in Hawthorne, California; or the 'miracle on the Han River' economic revolution in South Korea. All these examples occur in specific geographical spaces with particular norms, defined traits, and specific characteristics (see Figure 38.1).

Figure 38.1
A typical Western Innovation District: Google Campus, Mountain View, California

Source: Photo credit: Austin McKinley

CASE STUDY
THE GEOGRAPHICAL DIFFUSION OF INNOVATION

Gertler (2007) identified that the geographical diffusion of innovation occurs through well-established business networks accommodating knowledge sharing and skills (Gertler, 2003) between geographical spaces. A large engineering firm producing specialised machinery and industrial automation in Germany employed over 300 workers, with each production system designed according to customers' production requirements. Two identical flexible manufacturing systems were manufactured and tested before disassembling and transported to two firms to be reassembled. The parent firm in Germany was now establishing two new firms within its network, one in Germany and the other in the United States, to serve their geographical markets. Engineers of different levels travelled between the two firms crossing many borders to share tacit knowledge and skills, and the American counterparts had a three-month immersion in German language alongside with eight months of training to ease the diffusion of innovation and tacit knowledge exchange for both new plants. A year later, there was a six-month frequent exchange of engineers between the parent company and the two new manufacturing units, to ease sharing of information and to create an inter-plant and international community of practice in engineering and problem-solving. The process was repeated until the new plants were up to full capacity and with manageable but less frequent disruptions (Gertler, 2003). This example shows how the innovation process was facilitated through creating industrial learning regions for diffusing knowledge and skills, so consumers would be able to access the same product in different geographical market niches.

Innovation of this kind usually occurs within the world's largest economies, exclusively in the Global North. Acemoglu and Robinson (2013) also claimed that spatial and geographical aspects of innovation are crucial, serving to promote the diffusion of products or commodities to reach more markets globally, and they also note that this form of innovation usually happens in Global North countries with economic and political institutions that encourage private wealth and provide finance and resources for innovations and new entry businesses. Encaoua et al. (2013) point to the critical role of financial incentives and expertise accessible in modern economies to support innovation processes, from the initial idea to industrial mass production for the market, and the various papers in the collection edited by Warf (2017) also point to the essential connections between innovation and geography, highlighting how technological innovation intersects and works best within specific economies and particular social and political contexts. Given the focus of this work, it is no surprise that Acemoglu and Robinson (2013) stated that this form of innovation occurs in North America, rather than in any South American countries; in South Korea, and not in North Korea; and is generally not considered to have happened in South Africa, or indeed in most countries of the Global South.

This raises serious questions for human geographers looking at the kind of innovation that focuses on **human agency**, rather than on the market, especially as many communities depend on other forms of innovation through the collective sharing of resources in geographical areas where scientific and capital resources may be unavailable or unaffordable.

509

Concerns with market-orientated innovation

Scholars have identified several issues with market-oriented, technocentric, and capitalistic forms of innovation. Firstly, classical economic thinkers like Schumpeter tended to view innovation as the core of entrepreneurship, as a process influencing the outcome of competition in a global market economy, where there are inevitably winners and losers (Brouwer, 2000). Notably, this notion of innovation is based on capitalist Western economies, which disadvantage **subaltern** post-colonial communities in the Global South, and raises an intriguing question about the role of innovation in supporting collective well-being and equity. For Indigenous peoples, well-being is not bound by the market economy but bounded by their place, and by practices entailing traditional rights of access to natural resources, Indigenous governance systems, socio-cultural reproductions, redistribution and reciprocity, and community networks. In such societies, innovation will be governed by Indigenous knowledge systems (Gudeman, 2001), rather than the rules of a market economy.

Secondly, scholars from the Global South and Indigenous scholars have pointed out that the capitalist economy continues to expand and can drastically impact Indigenous peoples. The global market demands private ownership; in contrast, Indigenous peoples share customary resources to support their collective well-being. People can be displaced from their land, resources, and ways of being in the name of innovation via economic development (Kadirov, 2018). Western innovation emphasises the conventional disruptive entrepreneurial narrative, with an individual hero at the story's centre, such as Jeff Bezos or Elon Musk. But these entrepreneurs and innovators are merely the tip of the iceberg. Fixating on these only reveals what is above the surface and obscures the majority of innovations happening elsewhere.

Moreover, although issues emerging from the climate crisis are global, the debate over climate justice points to the historical responsibility of some countries in causing climate change. Modern Global North countries, including the United States, Canada, Japan, and much of Western Europe, account for just 12 per cent of the global population today but are responsible for 50 per cent of all the planet-warming greenhouse gases released from fossil fuels since the industrial revolution over the past 170 years (Carbon Brief, 2021). Studies show that Indigenous peoples globally, including the Pacific, have a higher probability of being disproportionately devastated by the severities of extreme weather (Bryant-Tokalau, 2018). While these innovation-driven places in the Global North might be leaders in global technology and development diffusion, the devastating results of their systems point to the need to change our practices of innovation to focus on reimagining human societies into ones that care more for others.

Lastly, **feminist** geographers have been critically questioning the dominant economic market system as the core of innovation (Waring, 2003, Dombroski et al., 2018). These evaluations have drawn attention to the vulnerabilities caused by Western modes of abstract reasoning (including 'rational economic man'), innovation, capitalist production, individualism, and the separation of self and nature (Smith and Wesley, 2017). The COVID-19 pandemic has also exposed the fragility of the modern economy, and feminist leaders, researchers, and activists in the Global South have been demanding alternative production systems to **extractive capitalism** (Tronto, 2017). This leads us to look at Indigenous innovation and consider the transition to a more holistic and sustainable form of innovation that is able to contribute to community resilience and well-being.

Summary

- Economic geographers have tended to focus on the rise of Western innovation districts and stress the importance of geographical proximity to the emergence of specific sets of knowledges and skills.
- Indigenous scholars have more recently questioned the assumptions which lay behind this particular definition of innovation.

Searching for alternatives: Indigenous innovation

Given the concerns outlined above by various human geography researchers, is there any way to rescue this concept of innovation and make it less flawed? Recent work from the Global South has argued that Indigenous innovation has quite different characteristics to the technocentric and capital-centred innovation found elsewhere (Vunibola and Scobie, 2022). For Howaldt and Schwarz (2017), innovation paradigms face three challenges: (i) Are they orientated towards societal challenges, finding practical expression in a mission-oriented innovation policy?; (ii) are they able to appreciate non-technological innovations geared at adjusting social practices?; and (iii) do they allow innovation processes to be opened up to society more widely? In meeting such challenges, there is a need for clear directions and innovative bottom-up solutions, such as social and Indigenous innovation (Howaldt and Kopp, 2012).

In the mainstream approach, innovation is often reduced to individuals innovating within the mainstream economy for profit. In contrast, Indigenous innovation can be considered a shared endeavour towards autonomy. Indigenous peoples have always been innovators, but colonial interests have obscured this innovation, and climate science and policy are no exception. Eurocentric **representations** of Indigenous peoples as backward and uncivilised have been dominant since European imperial expansion (Fry, 2019). This also applies to the concept of 'innovation', with the technologies introduced by colonists often put forward to justify **colonialism** and erase and replace the existing innovations in place that Indigenous peoples had developed across generations. At best, this represents a profound inability to recognise and understand innovation essential for sustaining Indigenous livelihoods and interests (Vunibola and Scobie, 2022).

Within the literature, three elements of Indigenous innovation are broadly recognised. An interdisciplinary body of literature has systematically documented Indigenous innovation (Alexiuk, 2013, Peredo et al., 2019). A second component explores concepts connected to Indigenous innovation, such as entrepreneurship, and tribal and community economies (Bargh, 2012, Vunibola and Scheyvens, 2019). A third strand focuses on the role of innovation broadly in pursuit of resilience and self-determination (Corntassel, 2012, Finau and Scobie, 2022). These multiple features have uncovered the complex nature of Indigenous innovation in colonial contexts, where innovation might not necessarily be directly related to progressing beyond the status quo but is also about furthering Indigenous interests within and under it.

Vunibola and Scobie (2022) maintain that Indigenous innovation is about bringing the margins of innovation to the centre and valuing what is not valued in capitalist production and ideologies of innovation. It is also about transforming the processes of innovation in response to the limitations of the conventional development model, moving away from an individual and privatised approach to a more collective operation and collective forms of organisation (Vunibola and Scobie, 2022). This transformation requires the typical innovation characteristics of an entrepreneurial spirit, leadership, and risk-taking but is informed by Indigenous knowledge and embedded into a broader set of obligations to people and place.

CASE STUDY
EXEMPLIFYING SYSTEMS OF INDIGENOUS INNOVATION

Nayarabale Youth Farm

This innovation mechanism is centred on placed-based social innovation, alongside a form of social protection, including 'solesolevaki', which supports people's resilience. Youths who drop out of the formal education system are engaged in the solesolevaki programme, which allows them to contribute to their community and family and build personal resilience and vision. During the pandemic, tribe members who lost their jobs moved back to Nayarabale village and were re-embedded within their culture and people. They were able to stay with their families without paying any bills and have a better opportunity to stabilise their family through traditional farming as an economic activity and being.

Nayarabale Youth Farm is located in an out-of-grid village in the interior of Vanua Levu, Fiji. It has been showcased in the media as an example of a million-dollar farm project that achieved success without government intervention, financial assistance, or mechanised systems. Most of the farm's activities are traditional and based on Indigenous innovations, especially in Indigenous Agricultural Knowledge (IAK), and people who work in a group become critical factors of their success. The farm involves cultivation of crops such as kava (piper methisticum), taro (calocasia esculanta), yam (diascorea alata), and cassava.

Looking within to innovate

There were two ongoing concerns for the Nayarabale village, one involved villagers who were attracted to the towns and nearby sugarcane farms to work as labourers to support their livelihood. The other included the inability of some tribal members to contribute to the itavi (socio-cultural responsibilities), which is usually in terms of money, food, or artefacts like tapa and mats. The itavi comprises three components: *vanua* – ceremonies and obligations like funerals and chiefly meetings, *lotu* – for church levies and church-related gatherings, and village development initiatives like building village halls and supporting education. In response, members of the community had meetings concerning developing a form of economic engagement to facilitate socio-cultural aims. The youth farm was initially planted on a sub-clan's land, and it was a way to attract the members back to their village and pursue *bula sautu* (collective well-being). The farm's members also worked with familiar crops which used to be cultivated by their ancestors and used their IAK and traditional tools to cultivate the crops. Although members have access to their customary land, they are unable to use that as collateral for raising capital to fund more westernised forms of innovation.

Solesolevaki, where people work together, is part of the itaukei (Indigenous Fijian) social protection system that Nayarabale used to venture into business, capitalising on the essential resources of customary land and *veiwekani* (kinship relations). In 2007, the land was cleared, with a small number of youths looking after the farm through solesolevaki for the following three years. In 2010, the crops were harvested, and the planting materials were used to expand the farm. For every annual harvest, the youth farm makes an individual contribution of $15,000 to the vanua, church, and village development schemes, so tribe members are freed from contributing to the itavi and have more time and resources to look after their families. In 2020 during the pandemic, the youth farm used FJ$15 million from their account to build new houses for their youths and a village hall to be used as an evacuation centre during climate calamities. For Western innovation the focus would be on capital accumulation, and investments, but this form of Indigenous innovation looked within the community to support the resilience and well-being of the tribe as a whole, even if doing this meant engaging in the modern economy. Ultimately, Indigenous innovation is a means to sustain territorial resources and protect traditional ways of being from the forces of extractive development (see Figures 38.2 and 38.3).

Figures 38.2 and 38.3
Building a greenhouse at Nayarabale Youth Farm, Fiji

Source: Photo credit: Suliasi Vunibola

Conclusion

It is important to situate the idea and practice of Indigenous innovation within the notion of the 'pluriverse', framing and rooting such innovation in the narrative of solidarity. As this chapter argues, there is a need to expand our thinking around innovation beyond just the market definition towards more collaborative and place-based approaches. Such innovation is considerate to environmental, socio-cultural, and political justice while concentrating on the fundamental interdependency of all beings – indicating more than one way of understanding innovation within the pluriverse. These alternative visions stand firmly against both xenophobic nationalism and technocratic globalism, instead encouraging diverse theories and practices which showcase the geographic diversity of systems and approaches in our world. This means widening research, action agendas, and dialogues between a broader range of scholars and policymakers from pluralist worldviews and practices relating to a shared quest for a socially just world (Demaria and Kothari, 2017). Kothari et al. (2019) advocate the need to include approaches from marginal communities, including Indigenous peoples, peasants, and pastoral communities, as they can offer critical solutions. Indigenous innovation can significantly contribute to a global confluence of alternative cultural, economic, social, political, and **ecological** visions and practices.

Economic geographers have tended to focus their studies on the dominant form of innovation in the Global North. Their work has meant that geographers are well acquainted with conceptions of urban innovation districts, innovation and industrial parks, and regional innovation systems, and empirical research has shown how these are technocratic, market-oriented, and integrated into capitalism. This work has uncovered specific spaces and networks of innovation in the Global North and has shown how innovation lies at the heart of economic growth and productivity. Through diffusion, this notion of innovation has also gained traction in the Global South but the consequences, as we have seen, have led to a number of problems, including increased inequality and environmental destruction.

Indeed, innovation is now integrated into all aspects of daily life, from, buildings and iPhones, to computers and cars. The furniture we sit on, the utensils we cook with, the clothes we wear, and the spaces we walk through are all the result of particular practices of innovation, and through these, humans continue to devise a course of action to change existing conditions into preferred ones. Innovation is also becoming an international best practice maxim in a world where geopolitical and economic relations are critical in maintaining global order, and in most cases, Global South Countries have become subservient to their Northern counterparts (Ratuva, 2019).

More recently, however, there has been an interest in new forms of innovation which might drive different types of economic practices and form new types of businesses and economic geographies – ones that acknowledge and emerge from social and ecological considerations, based around Indigenous communities and Indigenous innovation.

The case study of Nayarabale Youth Farm shows how Indigenous communities look within to innovate and create a world for the tribe, rather than for the individual. Maintaining communal land or customary land is crucial to this notion of innovation, since land is not seen as property here, but as an extension of one's life, culture, and ethos, as people's way of life is inscribed on the land. Modernisation and market relationships also threaten customary land and Indigenous ways of life globally. To maintain control of their land and way of life, IAK has been used to understand the land, plants, seasons, and kinship using solesolevaki to use and manage land and crops sustainably. Ecological sustainability is interwoven into the Nayarabale ways of thinking due to the close connection to land and waterways, protecting the presence of totemic plants and fish. Solesolevaki is also an alternative to wage labour where people work communally without being paid, in order to support the tribe's future. A diverse form of economy is adopted (Gibson-Graham, 2008), which serves the community and not vice versa. In this way, alternative forms of innovation support alternative practices of economic, social, ecological, and cultural life and underpin new types of economic geographies in a globalised and changing world.

Discussion points

- How have economic geographers traditionally looked at innovation?
- Why is innovation an inherently geographical concept?
- How could innovation facilitate technologies which are friendly to human and planet heath, provide some examples?
- Discuss the ideologies of those innovations which are informed by the logic of the market, such as the extraction of rare metals by seabed mining in order to facilitate the production of electric cars to reduce carbon emissions.

References

Acemoglu, D., and Robinson, J. A. (2013). Economics versus politics: pitfalls of policy advice. *Journal of Economic Perspectives* 27(2): 173–192.

Alexiuk, E. (2013). *Exploring the Common Ground between Social Innovation and Indigenous Resurgence: Two Critical Indigenist Case Studies in Indigenous Innovation in Ontario, Canada*. Waterloo: University of Waterloo.

Bargh, M. (2012). Rethinking and re-shaping indigenous economies: Māori geothermal energy enterprises. *Journal of Enterprising Communities: People and Places in the Global Economy* 6(3): 271–283.

Bauer, J. M. (1997). Market power, innovation, and efficiency in telecommunications: Schumpeter reconsidered. *Journal of Economic Issues* 31(2): 557–565.

Brouwer, M. (2000). Entrepreneurship and uncertainty: innovation and competition among the many. *Small Business Economics* 15(2): 149–160.

Bryant-Tokalau, J. (2018). *Indigenous Pacific Approach to Climate Change: Pacific Island Countries*. Cham: Palgrave Macmillan.

Carbon Brief. (2021). *Analysis: Which Countries Are Historically Responsible for Climate Change?* https://www.carbonbrief.org/analysis-which-countries-are-historically-responsible-for-climate-change/

Corntassel, J. (2012). Re-envisioning resurgence: Indigenous pathways to decolonization and sustainable self-determination. *Decolonization: Indigeneity, Education & Society* 1(1): 86–101.

Dahms, H. F. (1995). From creative action to the social rationalization of the economy: Joseph A. Schumpeter's social theory. *American Sociological Association* 13(1): 1–13. https://www.jstor.org/stable/pdf/202001.pdf

Demaria, F., and Kothari, A. (2017). The post-development dictionary agenda: paths to the pluriverse. *Third World Quarterly* 38(12): 2588–2599.

Diamond, M. A. (1996). Innovation and diffusion of technology: a human process. *Consulting Psychology Journal: Practice and Research* 48(4): 221.

Diprose, G., Dombroski, K., Healy, S., and Waitoa, J. (2017). Community economies: responding to questions of scale, agency, and Indigenous connections in Aotearoa New Zealand. *Counterfutures* 4: 167–183.

Dombroski, K., Healy, S., and McKinnon, K. (2018). Care-Full Community Economies. In *Feminist Political Ecology and the Economics of Care: In Search of Economic Alternatives*, eds. W. Harcourt and C. Bauhardt. London: Routledge, 99–115.

Encaoua, D., Hall, B. H., Laisney, F., and Mairesse, J. (eds.) (2013). *The Economics and Econometrics of Innovation*. London: Kluwer Academic Publishers.

Escobar, A. (2018). *Designs for the Pluriverse: Radical Interdependence, Autonomy, and the Making of Worlds*. Duke University Press. https://doi.org/10.1215/9780822371816

Fagerberg, J., Mowery, D. C., and Nelson, R. R. (eds.) (2005). *The Oxford Handbook of Innovation*. Oxford: Oxford University Press.

Finau, G., and Scobie, M. (2022). Old ways and new means: Indigenous accountings during and beyond the pandemic. *Accounting, Auditing & Accountability Journal* 35(1): 74–84.

Fry, G. (2019). *Framing the Islands: Power and Diplomatic Agency in Pacific Regionalism*. Canberra: ANU Press.

Gertler, M. S. (2003). Tacit knowledge and the economic geography of context, or the undefinable tacitness of being (there). *Journal of Economic Geography* 3(1): 75–99.

Gertler, M. S. (2007). Tacit Knowledge in Production Systems: How Important Is Geography. In *The Economic Geography of Innovation*, ed. K. R Polenske. Cambridge: Cambridge University Press, 87–111.

Gibson-Graham, J. K. (2008). Diverse economies: performative practices for other worlds. *Progress in Human Geography* 32(5): 613–632.

Gudeman, S. (2001). Postmodern Gifts. In *Post-Modernism, Economics and Knowledge*, eds. J. Armariglio, S. Cullenberg, and D. Ruccio. London: Routledge, 475–490.

Harvey, D. (2001). *Spaces of Capital*. London: Routledge.

Harvey, D. (2010). *The Enigma of Capital and the Crises of Capitalism*. London: Profile Books.

Howaldt, J., and Kopp, R. (2012). Shaping Social Innovation by Social Research. In *Challenge Social Innovation*, eds. H.-W. Franz, and J. Howaldt Franz, Hochgerner, and Howaldt. Heidelberg; New York; Dordrecht; London: Springer, 43–55.

Howaldt, J., and Schwarz, M. (2017). Social innovation and human development—how the capabilities approach and social innovation theory mutually support each other. *Journal of Human Development and Capabilities* 18(2): 163–180.

Kadirov, D. (2018). Towards a theory of marketing systems as the public good. *Journal of Macromarketing* 38(3): 278–297.

Kothari, A., Salleh, A., Escobar, A., Demaria, F., and Acosta, A. (eds.) (2019). *Pluriverse: A Post-Development Dictionary*. Delhi: Tulika Books and Authorsupfront.

Peredo, A. M., McLean, M., and Tremblay, C. (2019). Indigenous Social Innovation: What Is Distinctive? And a Research Agenda. In *Handbook of Inclusive Innovation*, eds. G. George, T. Baker, P. Tracey, and H. Joshi. Cheltenham: Edward Elgar Publishing Limited, 107–128.

Ratuva, S. (2019). *Contested Terrain: Reconceptualising Security in the Pacific*. Canberra: ANU Press.

Ratuva, S. (2021). COVID 19, communal capital and the moral economy: Pacific Islands responses. *Cultural Dynamics* 33(3): 194–197.

Rosenberg, N., and Frischtak, C. R. (1984). Technological innovation and long waves. *Cambridge Journal of Economics* 8(1): 7–24.

Schumpeter, J. (1934). *The Theory of Economic Development. An Inquiry into Profits, Capital, Credit, Interest, and the Business Cycle* (Reprint 1983: Transaction Publishers – First Published in 1911 in German). Boston: Harvard University Press.

Schumpeter, J. (2003). *Capitalism, Socialism & Democracy*. London and New York: Taylor & Francis.

Science Museum. (2019). *The Age of Plastic: From Parkesine to Pollution*. https://www.sciencemuseum.org.uk/objects-and-stories/chemistry/age-plastic-parkesine-pollution#:~:text=Leo%20Baekeland.&text=The%2020th%20century%20saw%20a,fully%20synthetic%20plastic%20in%201907

Smith, T. S. J., and Wesley, L. (2017). Which 'being' in well-being? Ontology, wellness and the geographies of happiness. *Progress in Human Geography* 42(6): 807–829. https://doi.org/10.1177/0309132517717100

Tronto, J. (2017). There is an alternative: homines curans and the limits of neoliberalism. *International Journal of Care and Caring* 1(1): 27–43. https://doi.org/10.1332/239788217X14866281687583

Vunibola, S., and Scheyvens, R. (2019). Revitalising rural development in the pacific: an itaukei (indigenous Fijian) approach. *Development Bulletin* 81(1): 62–66.

Vunibola, S., and Scobie, M. (2022). Islands of Indigenous innovation: reclaiming and reconceptualising innovation within, against and beyond colonial-capitalism. *Journal of the Royal Society of New Zealand* 52(S1): 1–14; S4–S17.

Warf, B. (ed.) (2017). *Handbook on Geographies of Technology*. Cheltenham: Edward Elgar.

Waring, M. (2003). Counting for something! Recognising women's contribution to the global economy through alternative accounting systems. *Gender & Development* 11(1): 35–43. https://doi.org/10.1080/741954251

Online materials

- Indigenous Innovation Initiative, https://indigenousinnovate.org/

  'Innovation isn't always about creating new things. Innovation sometimes involves looking back to our old ways and bringing them forward to this new situation'. The Honourable Murray Sinclair, 2015 Indigenous Innovation Summit. This is an Indigenous innovation platform: The goal is to empower First Nation, Inuit and Metis innovators and communities to identify and solve their own challenges, transform lives, and drive inclusive growth and health through innovation.

- More than human worlds, https://www.morethanhumanworlds.com/

  In her own words, Sophie Chao stated: Addressing the anthropogenic crisis demands that we recognise and protect the more-than-human worlds that we inherit, inhabit, and pass on. More-than-human worlds encompass plants, animals, elements, climates, and humans who unequally bear the burden of ecological ruin and repair. These worlds invite us to rethink the diverse entanglements of humans with other-than-human life, matter, and meaning.

Further reading

Gibson-Graham, J. K., and Roelvink, G. (2014). Social Innovation for Community Economies. In *Social Innovation and Territorial Development*, eds. D. MacCallum, F. Moulaert, J. Hillier, and S.V. Haddock. Farnham: Ashgate Publishing Ltd, 41–54.
Social innovation within community economies is described as a way to include marginalised groups within social and political governance institutions and processes and pursue to utilise resources in the face of contemporary economic and social crises.

Maldonado-Villalpando, E., Paneque-Gálvez, J., Demaria, F., and Napoletano, B. M. (2022). Grassroots innovation for the pluriverse: evidence from Zapatismo and autonomous Zapatista education. *Sustainability Science* 17(4): 1301–1316.
Innovation that is driven by grassroots groups has been theorised in the academic literature as 'grassroots innovation'; the article assesses how grassroots innovation may contribute to building alternatives to development.

Peredo, A. M., McLean, M., and Tremblay, C. (2019). Indigenous social innovation: what is distinctive? And a research agenda. In *Handbook of Inclusive Innovation*, eds. G. George, H. Joshi, P. Tracey, and T. Baker. Cheltenham: Edward Elgar Publishing, 107–128.

This book chapter looks at similar attributes regarding Indigenous social innovation that could inform our effort to reduce social problems faced not only by Indigenous communities but also by other disadvantaged peoples and communities.

Vunibola, S., and Scobie, M. (2022). Islands of Indigenous innovation: reclaiming and reconceptualising innovation within, against and beyond colonial-capitalism. *Journal of the Royal Society of New Zealand* 52(S1): 1–14; S4–S17.

This study places the concept of innovation under a critical Indigenous lens to rethink and reclaim innovation as a crucial aspect of Indigeneity, within-and-against, and beyond the colonial-capital relation.

SECTION FOUR

ENVIRONMENTAL GEOGRAPHIES

Knowing environments

Kelly Dombroski and Junxi Qian

Introduction

Many students come to geography because of their interest in the environment. While students leaning more towards the human geography side of geography might also have a lot of interest in social, cultural, historical and other processes that shape place and **space**, at its core, human geography is about the relationship between humans and the environment. This interest in relationships pushes geography and geographers to approach places in holistic ways – which often leads to interdisciplinary work and approaches. The questions that have driven many geographers of our 'millennial' generation include the following:

- How do we create societies that live sustainably on the planet?
- How do we undo the damage humans have caused all over the world and make space for the other species and **ecologies** that inhabit it?
- How do we make sure each human gets what they need for a good life, without preventing anyone else from having a good life?

Geographers have approached these kinds of questions and at a variety of different scales – in specific places, within particular regions or nations, or across much wider global networks and planetary scales. As you will read in the chapters in this section on environmental geographies, geographical research and theories have informed the planning and organisation of human interactions with the environment, including the atmosphere, oceans, land masses, different ecological regions, as well as the built and social environment. Whatever and wherever the environment, environmental geography seeks insight on human-environment relationships.

The question has become imperative also because in an era of rampant global urbanisation, it is increasingly difficult to think of clear-cut boundaries between human landscapes and pristine nature. The idea of 'nature', instead, needs to be conceptualised as **socially constructed**, contingent on diverse social, economic and political forces. Indeed, ever since the heyday of modernist urban planning, nature has been squarely integrated into urban imaginations. Ebenezer Howard's early experiment on the garden city, for example, emerged from the belief that industrialisation and the artificiality of the built environment led to the moral decay of humans, to be redeemed by the re-introduction of nature into the cities. No wonder urban planners are always fascinated with the planning and conservation of green spaces in the city. In many ways, nature is thoroughly entangled in political economic processes, even in the production of economic

DOI: 10.4324/9780429265853-46

value – for example, closeness to the green and blue (water) spaces in cities might profoundly increase property values, which, nonetheless, heightens the unequal and unjust distribution of environmental amenities in the city (Heynen et al., 2006). More recently, the expanding literature on the socio-technical transition in the city has explored how new socio-technical **infrastructures** can be experimented with, to foster a transition towards more sustainable urban development models and lifestyles (Hodson and Marvin, 2010). In all of these analyses, the environment that geographers study includes both human and '**more-than-human**' elements (see Chapter 7).

In what follows, we explore some of the ways humans have tried to answer the questions of what is the place of 'nature' or 'the environment' in human-led social development or human-made settlements, and how we can live well together on this planet. But in order to do so, we also explore a question behind this: how do we come to know our environments? What are the diverse ways that different human groups have come to know their environments of origin, as well as those much further away? We begin by tracing some diverse ways of knowing environments that we are familiar with, with a focus on Chinese, Western and Indigenous traditions. We then trace the ways that geographers have approached human-environment relations in English-language literature. We touch on both 'natural' environments and environments that are more obviously produced by humans such as urban environments.

Summary

- Human geography explores the relationship between humans and the environment, aiming to create sustainable societies, undo human-caused damage and ensure equitable access to a good life.
- Geographers examine human-environment relationships at different scales and recognise the entanglement of nature with social, economic and political forces.

Diverse ways of knowing environments

Since the rise of industrialisation, many people around the world have become separated from the cycles of regeneration and seasons that characterise traditional agrarian cultures. Others have carried out colonial conquests, affecting environments far beyond their places of origin, indeed, changing the face of the planet profoundly (see Chapters 49 and 71). But we can also trace lines of tradition in our different cultural origins that seek to deeply know and be in tune with environments, seeing them as neither human nor natural, but entangled as specific places that are known and loved by their human and nonhuman inhabitants.

For Junxi, I grew up in a cultural tradition that sees humans' reverence to nature as a moral virtue and believes that there is a mutual enrichment between nature and human self. In ancient China, the literati-official class believed that the artificial landscapes in imperial capitals were not where the true self was anchored, and the quietude and richness of the self depended on their eventual return to the home villages. This idea is writ large in Taoist and Buddhist thought.

Buddhist ethics, for example, is famous for treating all living organisms as equal – including humans and nonhumans. This, however, does not mean that China has been immune to the human destruction of nature. Quite the contrary, as China gradually integrated into global **modernity** in the early twentieth century, it tended to see nature merely as the resource base of modern development and even campaigned to remove any obstacle to economic productivity. In the Maoist 1950s, for example, the state mobilised Chinese people to eliminate sparrows because the latter fed on crops, only leading to the unfettered spread of pests. Meanwhile, rampant environmental pollution has been a major side effect of China's spectacular urbanisation in the past four decades, and environmental protection and conservation have thus become a top priority for the Chinese state in remedying the negative externalities of economic growth. Although making a similar commitment to human-nature harmony, environmental protection as an imperative of state governance amidst extensive exploitation of natural resources is certainly very different from the organic cultural philosophies in the traditional Chinese society (see Figure 39.1).

In some cultures and places, people know the environment through understanding elements of the environment and its systems through kinship lines, creation myths and stories embedded in the landscapes. I (Kelly) grew up in 'Te Ika a Maui', otherwise known as the North Island of New Zealand. Te Ika a Maui refers to an Indigenous Māori origin story, where demigod and trickster Maui caught a huge fish and pulled it up to become what is known in English (rather unimaginatively) as the North Island. If you look at a map of Aotearoa New Zealand (Figure 39.2), you can see the North Island has the shape of a fish (perhaps a stingray). Different places around the island are named according to this and other stories. In many ways the story embodies a mental map of the island, allowing one to orient oneself in travel according to the parts of the fish – keeping in mind that for much of early history travel was by water. This is just one of many

Figure 39.1
An image of Mao Zedong overseeing the industrialisation and transformation of the Chinese landscape. Mao's vision of China was of rapid state-led industrialisation. This poster, typical in 1950s China, actually hangs in Kelly's office in New Zealand and was discovered in a back drawer in a geography classroom

Source: Photo credit: Kelly Dombroski

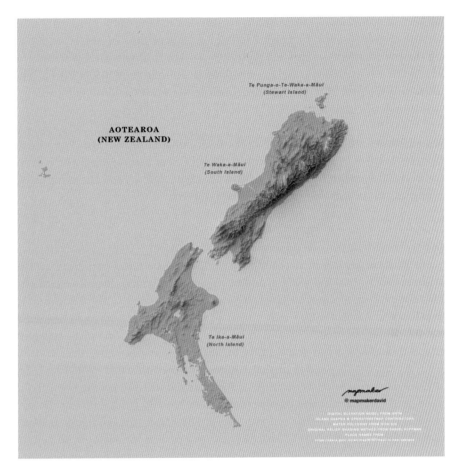

Te Punga-o-Te-Waka-a-Māui
(Stewart Island)

AOTEAROA
(NEW ZEALAND)

Te Waka-a-Māui
(South Island)

Te Ika-a-Māui
(North Island)

Figure 39.2
Aotearoa New Zealand map showing te reo Māori for the two main islands. Te Ika a Māui refers to the fish of Māui, while Te Waka a Māui refers to his canoe. This map is oriented with south at the top, rather than north. The South Island (Te Waka a Māui) is usually referred to as Te Wai Pounamu, as this is the name used by the tribal group of that area

Source: Figure credit: David Garcia

stories I heard as a young person about the landscapes around me, and every year I learn more – and this is as a person of European rather than Māori descent. Many of these stories embody important geographical, geological, horticultural, environmental and psychological knowledge all rolled into epic narratives that are told and retold.

In Aotearoa, many of these environmental stories are about ancestors, and in some the characters are rivers, mountains, islands and more, who are not objects to be studied as such, but kin from whom Māori tribal groups descend. This has a profound effect on the way such entities are studied even today: for Māori researchers such as Amanda Yates (2021), they are studied as more-than-human kin that we must care for and connect with. For John Patterson (1994, 1998), the narratives contain a set of environmental and community ethics that are part of a living tradition of relationship with the places and entities in these narratives. For both those authors and many other Māori, this entails a respect for the *mauri* or life force contained within all things, human and nonhuman. I write of Māori ways of knowing (rather than other Indigenous groups) because of growing up as a Pākehā settler descendent here in Aotearoa. But such ways of knowing the environment are not just present here – but in many parts of the world, such as the Indigenous environmental knowledge of peoples in Yunnan Province in China, where Junxi has been researching. Sherri Mitchell, an Indigenous *Penawahpskek* activist and writer from Turtle Island or North America, writes:

> Our songs, stories, and mythologies all speak of our interrelatedness. From birth, we are taught to be aware of the expanded kinship networks that surround us, which include other human beings along with the beings of the land, water, and air, and the plants, trees, and all remaining unseen beings that exist within our universe.
>
> *Mitchell, 2018: 9*

Her people have continuously been present in the same lands for 10,000 years and have developed ceremony and ritual to help others all around the world to connect and learn from the land. While **colonisation** and urbanisation for Māori and many other Indigenous peoples has often violently disconnected communities from their kinship connections to place, we also know that resistance, **decolonisation** and Indigenisation movements seek to reconnect with such ways of knowing, especially as the damage of modernity and industrialisation becomes ever more apparent.

In Western thought, we can trace shifts in knowing environments over time. Knowing environments as kin is also present in that history, but the influence of Roman colonisation, Christianity, and later enlightenment thinking has changed the way people come to know their environments and think about the environment more broadly (Hickel, 2020). Roman colonisation has often been credited with separating governance from the land and creating uniform and universalist forms of governance that do not require deep knowing of the environment. Throughout Europe and further afield, the Romans sought to alter the environment to suit their needs, whether through aqueducts, roads, massive earthworks and shifting people and animals all over the continent (Thommen, 2012). Later, this provided the infrastructure for the spread of Christianity, which began as a Jewish sect situated in the Middle East and ended up travelling throughout much of the world (Armstrong, 2022).

For some thinkers, Christian thought problematically sets up a division between humans and nonhumans, and humans and their environment, where humans are set up as God's chosen species and invited to dominate and subdue the rest of creation (Plumwood, 2002). Some different strands of Christian thought have rejected this **hyper-separation**, for example, the Franciscan tradition (see Healy, 2016, and see Chapter 73 for other strands). Yet others have endorsed such separation and built on it, which is considered the heritage of some of the problematic extractive relationships between Western peoples and their environments and the development of **capitalism** (Weber, 2001). Urbanisation and industrialisation also profoundly changed people's relationships with their environments and for many has broken the connection with the cycle of seasons and the cycle of food production from seed to harvest to compost and waste fertilising the next cycle – as Lefebvre (2004) pointed out, capitalism heralded the transformation of cyclical time into a linear time of development and progress. Karl Marx noted this as a key problem of capitalism in his book *Capital*, and scholars later named it 'the metabolic rift' (Foster, 1999) – but it is a point made by many Western scholars from many different areas of environmental thinking.

The Enlightenment was a period in Western history where many thinkers started to push away from Christianity and sought other universalist ideals of science and progress, which, combined with colonisation, lead to the development of the dominant forms of science today. In that form of knowing environment, scientists sought to separate themselves from the object being studied, understanding humans as separate from the environment and able to dominate and alter it (Haraway, 1988, Hickel, 2020). This led to incredible advances in technology in a short period of time, some of which have ended up being very destructive for the environment, even as ecological and geographical knowledge of the complex balance of systems also advanced. Scientific methods in the fields of ecology, biology, physical and biogeography, and more recently, the cross-disciplinary 'environmental science', have all contributed to the detailed documentation of knowledge of the environment that now informs 'resource management' in many parts of the world (Liboiron, 2021).

In Western thinking, we can therefore trace a distinctive shift from place-based and relational environmental knowing to more abstract and detached forms of knowing about the environment generally and scientifically. How did these historical and cultural shifts inform the way geographers came to know and study environments? Some of these will be present in the chapters that follow in this section on environmental geographies. But before we get to that, we must also review some historical shifts in environmental geographies over the last centuries to contextualise what has been included here. Geography, as the study of the Earth and the processes that shape it, has a long history of thinking about and studying the environment. In the English-language literature there have been a few major trends that we will discuss briefly next.

Summary

- Industrialisation and colonial conquests have led to a disconnection from traditional ways of knowing the environment in China and elsewhere, but cultural traditions still exist that emphasise deep knowledge and reverence for nature.
- Indigenous cultures can have kinship-based ways of knowing the environment, viewing nonhuman entities as more-than-human kin.
- Western thought has undergone shifts in knowing environments, influenced by Roman colonisation, Christianity, enlightenment thinking, urbanisation and industrialisation, leading to a separation between humans and nonhumans and a more abstract and scientific approach to understanding the environment.

Environmental determinism and regional geographies

Geography as a discipline was first associated with the descriptive projects of regional geographies (see Chapter 21). These studies were often carried out by geographical 'explorers', often European men travelling and documenting their observations for reporting back to Enlightenment-founded science societies back 'home' in Europe (see also Chapters 10 and 71). While on the one hand these descriptions carefully recorded and reflected on both human and physical geographies in a holistic way, they were also products of the **positionality** of the researchers: the thinking at the time was that different environments *determined* (rather than just influenced) the characteristics of the people who lived there and their social structures. This was reflected in their writing and often led to sweeping statements about **race**, **gender** and relations between people which are now usually understood to be racist stereotypes (see also Chapter 22).

One geographer who pulled together a massive volume of world geography, based on collating these kinds of writings, is Ellen Semple. Notwithstanding her achievements as one of the earliest women in geography, the racist assumptions of her time are evident in her works. She believed, for example, that 'man' originated and evolved in the tropical regions of the world but matured in the temperate regions and held that those cultures still in the tropics were less mature. Is it coincidence that her own race, white, predominated in those 'culturally mature' regions? In her book *Influences of Geographic Environment* (1911), she referred to one group as 'overbearing and marauding', another as 'cowardly' and others 'primitive' in some areas where agriculture is difficult to establish, while referring to other white groups in the same circumstances as 'resourceful' by economically dominating others. She stated that Japan's 'steep slopes... fertile only under spade tillage' would 'forever insure the persistence of numerous peasantry', unlike England where industrialisation had occurred in agriculture (Semple, 1911: 557). This stands in stark contrast to the current reality in Japan, where rural areas have been emptied of populations bound for the city, urban farming is widely practised, and the country is engaged in a globalised food supply chain (Manzenreiter et al., 2020).

Of course, it is easy to criticise someone writing more than 100 years ago for not predicting the future, but our aim here is to show how early geographers thought about the environment as the primary determining factor in cultural and social systems, with little analysis of power or inequality. This theory fell out of favour because it didn't adequately account for cultural variability within ecologically similar places and did not allow for genuinely curious scientific research into such variability because the answer was already determined by the theory. Environmental determinism is now seen as problematic because it naturalises inequality, poverty, and oppression and was used by white people as an excuse for dominating other races. It did highlight, however, that the study of the environment was initially dominated by an approach that thought about the relationships between people and their environments and, like any approach, was deeply influenced by the cultural context of the times.

Summary

- Regional geographies in the early days of geography focused on descriptive studies conducted by European explorers, reflecting both human and physical aspects of different environments.
- Environmental determinism, prevalent during that time, claimed that environments determined the characteristics of the people and their social structures, but it is now criticised for its racist assumptions and failure to account for cultural variability and power dynamics.

Cultural ecology and postmodern environmental geographies

In the middle of the twentieth century, environmental determinism was challenged by the approach known as 'cultural ecology'. It also tried to account for the influence of environment on human society but in a way that was 'possibilist' rather than 'determinist' (Haenn and Wilk, 2005). As an early cultural ecology researcher, Julian Steward, noted 'cultural ecology has been described as a methodological tool for ascertaining how the adaptation of a culture to its environment may entail certain changes', with a goal to research whether 'similar adjustments occur in similar environments' (Steward, 2005: 9). Carl Sauer, another influential cultural ecologist in the mid-twentieth century, was 'unimpressed by the arguments for similar environments creating similar cultures' (Carter, 1954: 262). He argued that cultural expansion and interaction across both near and far transformed both environments and cultures of agriculture, for example, north Pacific and Trans-Pacific navigators who spread different traditions and species to different regions of the world (such as sweet potato), and the expansion of grasslands under human influence.

Sauer's influence on environmental geography was significant: it moved thinkers in the Anglophone world from environmental determinism to an understanding of the human-environment relationship as interactive and geographically diverse. His concern with the influence of **extractive capitalist** practices of economy also prefigured the field of political ecology, discussed in Chapter 45. Cultural ecology has also been criticised for its tendencies to see culture as 'superorganic', that is, to use culture as an explanation for all human behaviour, rather than also recognising explanations in matters such as individual 'human behavior, attitudes and beliefs, social organisation and the characteristics and interrelationships of human groups' (Brookfield, 1964: 283). This is to say, cultural ecology may have traded environmental determinism for 'cultural determinism' (Duncan, 1980). Again, we can refer to Chapter 22 for the critique of cultural superorganism in cultural geography. In contemporary times, this interplay between structure and **agency**, continues, with some understandings of human-environment relationships focusing on the structures that shape human lives, such as cultures, environments, power relations and economies, while others focus on the individual agency that people have to make choices about how they relate to environments. But like any relationship, there is truth in both these positions – geographers have understood human relationships with the environment as influenced and partially determined by environment, culture and society, as well as the result of the collective of individual actions that people and smaller groups have taken.

In some ways, this concern with finding the 'one true theory' of how humans relate to their environment can be traced to the concerns of geography as a discipline in the mid-twentieth century. At that time, geographers were interested in 'elevating' their study to the level of a science such as physics or chemistry, where laws of nature were discovered and documented, tested and confirmed (Johnston and Sidaway, 2015). For those with an interest in physical geography and the study of hydrology, climate, geomorphology, biogeography, oceanography, coastal and mountain geographies and other Earth system geographies, the scientific method was, of course, central. But the concern with uncovering natural laws seen in a number of subdisciplinary areas of human geography eventually gave way to an explosion of quite different approaches in the 1990s, partly in response to the influence of postmodern thinking (Johnston and Sidaway, 2015). **Postmodern** thinking was and is suspicious of the kinds of 'grand narratives' and universalist thinking that inspired thinkers of the Enlightenment and other thinkers into the late twentieth century. Social theorists began to reject universalist and essentialist approaches to knowing environments (Gandy, 1996). Environmental geography began to engage with different ways of knowing environments as laid out by ecofeminists (Mies and Shiva, 1993, Plumwood, 2002), **postcolonial** thinkers from the **Majority World** (Chakrabarty, 2012, Escobar, 2018), Black geographies and ecologies (Moulton and Salo, 2022) and Indigenous scholars and activists (Coombes et al., 2013, Larsen and Johnson, 2017, Mitchell, 2018). As environmental degradation and ecological and climate crises deepened, the work of environmental geographers in both human and physical geography has become increasingly visible. Environmental geographers have had to work across different approaches to knowledge in order to contribute much-needed research for these rapidly changing times.

Summary

- Cultural ecology emerged as a possibilist approach challenging environmental determinism, studying how cultures adapt to their environments and examining the diverse interactions between humans and their surroundings.
- Postmodern environmental geographies rejected universalist thinking and embraced diverse ways of knowing environments, incorporating perspectives from ecofeminism, postcolonialism, Black geographies and Indigenous scholarship to address environmental degradation and climate crises.

Knowing environments in rapidly changing times

For those of you reading this book and training at a university in the field of geography and related environmental disciplines, you might be wondering 'what does all this have to do with today?' and 'what kind of knowing do we need in these times of ecological crisis?'. You may also be wondering why so much of the work in environmental geography at the moment mentions Indigenous ways of knowing the environment. In the chapters that follow in this section, the theme of Indigenous knowing comes up again and again – not least because some of the commissioned authors are Indigenous but also because for many environmental geographers, Indigenous environmental knowledge is seen to be leading the way in thinking about the relationship between humans and their environments. For some, this is dangerously romanticising Indigenous people's knowledges and lives, and putting pressure on minority people to 'save' the rest of the world from tragedy. But for others, it is an overdue recognition of the highly developed knowledges of human-environment relationships built on different **ontologies** of place.

The question for us is what does this framing exclude? For one, the environmental knowledges and relations of other non-white groups are obscured, such as those outlined by Alex Moulton and Inge Salo in their review of Black geographies and ecologies around the world (Moulton and Salo, 2022), and the many other traditional ecological knowledges of groups throughout Asia and elsewhere. For sure, some of these knowledges are in contemporary times being reframed as Indigenous knowledges due to shifts in terminology (see, for example, the discussion in Dahl and Tejsner, 2020 in the context of the Arctic). But others have and are being overlooked in the current academic interest in Indigenous environmental knowledges. As you read through the remainder of this section, continue to ask yourself about what is present, and what is missing in the accounts of environmental geography outlined.

In Chapter 40**, Global and local environmental problems and activism**, Amanda Thomas introduces us to some of the environmental problems of our times, and the kinds of activism being carried out to intervene in these problems. She notes that human relationships with the environment do not *have* to be problematic and gives examples of how activists are engaging with the nuances of environmental action – from eco-fascism to environmental justice movements, from local actions to global movements for change.

In Chapter 41, **Climate change**, Chie Sakakibara approaches the topic of climate change through her work in Point Hope, Alaska, and the example of Kiribati in the Pacific Ocean. While a lot of writing about climate change focuses on the work of the IPCC (Intergovernmental Panel on Climate Change) and global predictions of disaster, Sakakibara brings climate change down to the very real effects already happening in these two communities living in sensitive environments. She explores the role of emotions and **affect** in climate change, especially the grief and loss of solastalgia, a word referring to the physical and mental distress of people experiencing changing environments.

In Chapter 42, **Sustainability**, Kersty Hobson gives us an overview of the global efforts to embrace sustainability, a concept underlying the UN (United Nations) sustainable development goals. Sustainability as a concept and political goal has a relatively short history and has been critiqued for providing the grounds for 'greenwashing' activities and economies that are environmentally destructive. Yet it has also provided a language to start negotiating globally around transformations in economy and society, rather than just continuations of growth-oriented economies and consumerist societal norms.

In Chapter 43, **Nature culture**, a collective of Yolŋu Indigenous and ŋäpaki non-Indigenous authors in Australia reflect on the relationship between nature and culture from the perspective of Bawaka Country, the place where they live and write and research. They demonstrate the **ontological** start points of Yolŋu Indigenous understandings of nature and culture, which do not separate the two concepts. In this chapter you will be able to read direct messages to you, the student, from Yolŋu elders, asking you not to romanticise their relationship with the environment but to think about how everyone can relate well and respond to the environment or more-than-human entities.

In Chapter 44, **Political ecology**, Jessica Dempsey and Juanita Sundberg introduce political ecology, an approach to research human-environment relations that is very influential in human geography. For political ecologists, all social and political issues are also ecological – and all ecological issues are also social and political. The approach emphasises tracing power relationships in their multiple complexities but does not seek to just *describe* but to *change* such relationships to something better. They work through the example of energy transitions and mining to illustrate political ecology as an approach.

In Chapter 45**, Rethinking environmental governance**, Meg Parsons and Melissa Nursey-Bray discuss how environmental knowing is translated into environmental governance. They give some broader critiques of Western environmental governance modes, touching on the themes raised in this introductory chapter. But Parsons also gives some examples of how her Indigenous Māori understanding of *mauri* and kinship with more-than-human entities is being enacted into governance practice in Aotearoa New Zealand and discusses emerging forms of co-governance that might have wider global relevance such as 'living labs'.

The chapters in this section illustrate the current topics and approaches in environmental geography, which do differ from those previously reviewed in this chapter. While in some ways many of these chapters draw on place-based examples and approaches to environmental geography, overall, the chapters show the global shift in focus – rather than seeking to understand how the environment affects humans (as environmental determinism and cultural ecology began with), we now seek to understand and mitigate the effect of humans on the environment – or even, dismantle the problematic distinctions between humans (society, culture, economy, politics, governance) and environment at all scales. Increasing global recognition of the complex interconnections of ecologies and environments dissolves the distinctions between human-made environments and the 'natural' world, to the degree that environmental geography has made its way into many areas of human geography (as demonstrated in other sections of this book).

Discussion points

- How do you know about the environments around you? How do relate to the environments in your life?
- What historical and cultural traditions inform what you know about the environment in your place?
- What has made you curious in this chapter? What do you want to find out more about?
- What do you think of the statement 'the concept of nature is socially constructed'? Make some arguments for and against this idea.

References

Armstrong, K. (2022). *Sacred Nature: Restoring Our Ancient Bond with the Natural World*. Toronto: Knopf.

Brookfield, H. C. (1964). Questions on the human frontiers of geography. *Economic Geography* 40: 283–303.

Carter, G. F. (1954). Review of agricultural origins and dispersals, Carl O. Sauer. *American Journal of Archaeology* 58(3): 260–262.

Chakrabarty, D. (2012). Postcolonial studies and the challenge of climate change. *New Literary History* 43(1): 1–18, 179.

Coombes, B., Johnson, J. T., and Howitt, R. (2013). Indigenous geographies II: the aspirational spaces in postcolonial politics–reconciliation, belonging and social provision. *Progress in Human Geography* 37(5): 691–700.

Dahl, P. E., and Tejsner, P. (2020). Review and Mapping of Indigenous Knowledge Concepts in the Arctic. In *Routledge Handbook of Indigenous Peoples in the Arctic*. New York and London: Routledge, 233–248.

Duncan, J. S. (1980). The superorganic in American cultural geography. *Annals of the Association of American Geographers* 70(2): 181–198.

Escobar, A. (2018). *Designs for the Pluriverse: Radical Interdependence, Autonomy, and the Making of Worlds*. Durham: Duke University Press.

Foster, J. B. (1999). Marx's theory of metabolic rift: classical foundations for environmental sociology. *American Journal of Sociology* 105(2): 366–405.

Gandy, M. (1996). Crumbling land: the postmodernity debate and the analysis of environmental problems. *Progress in Human Geography* 20(1): 23–40.

Haenn, N., and Wilk, R. (2005). *Environment in Anthropology*. New York: New York University Press.

Haraway, D. (1988). Situated knowledges: the science question in feminism and the privilege of partial perspective. *Feminist Studies* 14(3): 575–599.

Healy, S. (2016). Saint Francis in climate-changing times: form of life, the highest poverty, and post-capitalist politics. *Rethinking Marxism* 28(3–4): 367–384.

Heynen, N., Kaika, M., and Swyngedouw, E. (2006). *In the Nature of Cities: Urban Political Ecology and the Metabolism of Urban Environments*. London: Routledge.

Hickel, J. (2020). *Less Is More: How Degrowth Will Save the World*. London: Random House.

Hodson, M., and Marvin, S. (2010). Can cities shape socio-technical transitions and how would we know if they were? *Research Policy* 39(4): 477–485.

Johnston, R., and Sidaway, J. D. (2015). A Changing Discipline? In *Geography and Geographers: Anglo-American Human Geography since 1945*. London: Routledge.

Larsen, S. C., and Johnson, J. T. (2017). *Being Together in Place: Indigenous Coexistence in a More than Human World*. Minneapolis: University of Minnesota Press.

Lefebvre, H. (2004). *Rhythmanalysis. Space, Time and Everyday Life*. London: Continuum.

Liboiron, M. (2021). *Pollution Is Colonialism*. Durham: Duke University Press.

Manzenreiter, W., Lützeler, R., and Polak-Rottmann, S. (2020). *Japan's New Ruralities: Coping with Decline in the Periphery*. London: Routledge.

Mies, M., and Shiva, V. (1993). *Ecofeminism*. London: Fernwood Publications/Zed Books.

Mitchell, S. (2018). *Sacred Instructions: Indigenous Wisdom for Living Spirit-Based Change*. Berkeley: North Atlantic Books.

Moulton, A. A., and Salo, I. (2022). Black geographies and Black ecologies as insurgent ecocriticism. *Environment and Society* 13(1): 156–174.

Patterson, J. (1994). Maori environmental virtues. *Environmental Ethics* 16(4): 397–409.

Patterson, J. (1998). Respecting nature: a Maori perspective. *Worldviews* 2(1): 69–78.

Plumwood, V. (2002). *Environmental Culture: The Ecological Crisis of Reason*. New York: Routledge.

Semple, E. C. (1911). *Influences of Geographic Environment, on the Basis of Ratzel's System of Anthropo-Geography*. New York: H. Holt.

Steward, J. (2005). The Concept and Method of Cultural Ecology. In *Environment in Anthropology*, eds. N. Haenn and R. Wilk. New York: New York University Press, 5–9.

Thommen, L. (2012). *An Environmental History of Ancient Greece and Rome*. Cambridge: Cambridge University Press.

Weber, M. (2001). *The Protestant Ethic and the Spirit of Capitalism* (trans. S. Kalberg). London: Routledge.

Yates, A. M. (2021). Transforming geographies: performing Indigenous-Māori ontologies and ethics of more-than-human care in an era of ecological emergency. *New Zealand Geographer* 77(2): 101–113.

Online materials

- Climate Action Tracker: https://climateactiontracker.org/. This website lets you see how different countries around the world are doing with climate action.
- Global Atlas of Environmental Justice: https://ejatlas.org/. This website documents environmental justice activism all over the world. You can register and upload your own.
- The Perils of Climate Activism: https://www.e-flux.com/architecture/survivance/410014/the-perils-of-climate-activism/. This short article reviews two activist music videos (among other things!) in India. It discusses the problems of solar panels taking up common spaces and highlights activism around air quality.
- Next City: https://nextcity.org/. This inspirational website contains thousands of examples of environmental justice from cities all over the world.

Further reading

Castree, N., Demeritt, D., Liverman, D., and Rhoads, B. (2016). *A Companion to Environmental Geography*. Chichester: John Wiley & Sons.
This book provides an introduction to environmental geographies, arguing that environmental geography is the middle ground between physical and human geography.

Gibson, K., Rose, D. B., and Fincher, R. (2015). *Manifesto for Living in the Anthropocene*. New York: Punctum Books.
This short readable open access book is made up of a series of chapters by geographers and others in the environmental humanities. It argues that social scientists and humanities scholars need to change the way we do research in response to the compounding environmental crises.

Moulton, A. A., and Salo, I. (2022). Black geographies and Black ecologies as insurgent ecocriticism. *Environment and Society* 13(1): 156–174.
This recent article discusses the contribution of Black geographies and Black ecologies to our thinking around environmental geographies.

Rocheleau, D., Thomas-Slayter, B., and Wangari, E. (2013). *Feminist Political Ecology: Global Issues and Local Experience*. London: Routledge.
This classic text introduces the idea of feminist political ecology, where the way we understand the environment is not only socially constructed but gendered. The authors give examples of where women's environmental knowledge is different from men's.

40 Global and local environmental problems and activism

Amanda Thomas

Introduction

On a low isthmus nestled between hills on two sides, and sea on the other two, Wellington Airport's single runway lies on a north-south axis. The isthmus was formed by accumulating sand dunes, and large earthquakes as recently as 1855, which lifted up the land. By the mid-twentieth century, the sand dunes were increasingly pushed aside, and hills bulldozed to make way for an airport. This was and is Māori land – but has been alienated from Māori through **colonisation**. It is now jointly owned by a private investment firm and the city council. The airport and Wellington city have grown together, and now the airport sits uneasily alongside residential neighbourhoods, including one of the most socio-economically deprived areas in the city.

In many ways, this airport represents the complexity of environmental problems at a moment in time where large societal shifts are needed. For an island nation, the airport connects people to the world. Almost 30% of people in Aotearoa New Zealand were born overseas, and as the climate changes, the need to welcome people across borders will become more urgent. And yet, the airport's activities produce significant pollution. In Wellington, flying is about 8% of the city's greenhouse gas emissions. Jet fuel fumes waft across local playgrounds, and the night-time glare from illuminated billboards and safety lighting confuse native birds. Noise pollution pervades neighbouring suburbs; people lie in bed, woken up by planes arriving from Australia at 1am and are kept awake by gnawing anxiety about the climate impacts of the airport's desire to double passenger numbers (Figure 40.1).

This example demonstrates the way environmental issues are complicated and also cross scales: from the globalised impacts of carbon emissions to the bodily experiences of eco-anxiety. Environmental geography is useful for exploring the complexity of issues but also for understanding how to produce change and environmental justice.

This chapter briefly explores what counts as an environmental problem, and how geographers have understood the underpinning causes of them. It also describes how people have intervened in these problems and tried to build more just and fair environments. Geographers have much to contribute to understanding why environmental problems are so hard to solve but also to understanding how communities work together to make change.

DOI: 10.4324/9780429265853-47

Figure 40.1
Aerial view of Wellington airport

Source: Photo credit: David Wall/Alamy

What are environmental problems?

In the broadest sense, environmental problems are issues that arise as people work out how to live well in the world. Human societies have always experienced these sorts of problems. However, we are living in an unprecedented time where problems like climate change and plastic pollution are reshaping environments everywhere. Many geographers working in critical and radical traditions argue that there are two overarching, or structural, causes of most environmental problems in the twenty-first century: **colonialism** and **capitalism**. These two exploitative systems of organising resources and relationships have had global reach and are often violently imposed.

Colonialism matters to environmental geography because the process of colonisation, and ongoing colonialism, remakes landscapes. In very basic terms, a lot of colonialism has been rooted in European empire building characterised by (i) the desire to extract value from people and places and (ii) ideas of cultural and racial superiority. Anna Tsing (2012a) writes about how the landscapes of the Americas, the Caribbean and the Pacific were remade through the spread of plantations, specifically sugar cane plantations. Plantations, she writes, '*were the engine of European expansion*. Plantations produced the wealth – and the modus operandi – that allowed Europeans to take over the world' (Tsing, 2012a: 148, emphasis in original). In places they colonised, the colonisers took land from Indigenous people (often extremely violently) and disrupted intimate entangled relationships, imported enslaved workforces and reproduced the same growing techniques for vast areas of uniform crops (Tsing, 2012b).

Notions of cultural and racial superiority have meant some ideas about what counts as nature, and 'good' environments have been forcibly rolled out in places, and excluded other understandings of the environment and how people are related to it. For example, geographers in Aotearoa New Zealand have described the way Eurocentric ideas about nature and how to manage it were imposed through British colonisation and have fundamentally altered the land and shaped national identity. Brad Coombes and Stephanie Hill (2005), drawing on **postcolonial** theory and working within Indigenous geographies, analyse national parks in Aotearoa New Zealand which make up a third of the total land area. These 'wild' and 'natural' spaces have underpinned the way this country is marketed through the 100% Pure international tourism campaign. They are firmly ingrained in a New Zealand national identity. But a closer look at how these parks were created, and what they continue to represent, shows the ongoing impacts on Māori.

Coombes and Hill write '[c]onventional management of protected areas has been based on an understanding of nature as separate from society, often leading to the expulsion of Indigenous people' and a severing of their access to resources and places with deep meaning (Coombes and Hill, 2005: 137). The idea of nature and society being separate has been important in the story of environmental management, and colonialism. First, understanding humans as separate from the environment enabled exploitation of nature, imagined as 'natural resources'. Then, when this began to be problematic, it was assumed that humans are inherently bad for the environment, and so human interactions with nature need to be carefully managed through further separation. For most national parks in Aotearoa New Zealand, no one is allowed to live there, gather native birds for food, or plants for medicine. Where many people would understand national parks and similarly protected areas as a solution to environmental problems – as a means to protect biodiversity, as important carbon sinks – Indigenous geographers reveal the injustice and exclusion inherent in the creation of national parks and game reserves. As Māori were excluded from parts of the country that became national parks, they were also excluded from things like food gathering and accompanying practices. These exclusions affected Māori economies but also the ability to engage in culture and care for place.

A lot of human interactions with places have led to more biodiversity, and healthier environments. The assumption common in Western societies that humans are inherently bad for the planet is not correct. For example, swidden, or slash and burn, agriculture in Southeast Asia is often portrayed as bad for the environment, out of place in modern states, and some development schemes have attempted to move forest-dwelling communities away from forested areas (McGregor and Thomas, 2017). However, Christensen (2002) found that just two swidden communities in Southeast Asia had identified and encouraged more than a thousand different forest products. In that example, the interactions of people and environments meant they both flourished. What counts as an environmental problem, and its solution, therefore may be different between populations and at different times. But more than this, geographers need to be aware of power relations – who is defining what is 'good' and 'bad', and why?

Colonialism has often been accompanied by capitalism, a way of organising the economy, society and nature. Capitalism is a system that organises societies into particular relationships of workers and business (or capital) owners. It is also premised on economic growth through ever increasing production and **consumption**; think here about the way consumption through Christmas shopping is reported as a positive indicator of economic health. **Marxist** geographers have highlighted the way capitalist systems have reorganised people and natures, in the interest of generating profit for a select few.

This approach to understanding environmental problems came to prominence in the 1970s and 1980s as a counter to natural hazards research, which took the view that environmental problems were technical rather than political. Marxist geographers argued that environmental problems are thoroughly social, economic, political and cultural in origin. In making this argument Michael Watts (1983) examined why there were increases in famine in northern Nigeria throughout the twentieth century, even though there weren't more droughts. Where some had described famine as the effect of drought and poor planning and management, Watts (1983) demonstrated the way colonisation and the imposition of capitalism had disrupted systems of subsistence. Taxes were imposed by the colonial government that forced people to grow crops they could sell rather than eat themselves. This then meant there was no excess food crop that could be gifted and stored in times of abundance, and shared back during times of drought. An environmental problem – drought – became a hazard – famine – through colonisation and the imposition of capitalism.

In the twenty-first century, it often feels like environmental problems are rapidly piling up – plastic pollution in the ocean from industrialised fishing vessels, waterway contamination from fast fashion factories, the impacts of agricultural intensification on soil and aquifers, habitat loss, and amplifying everything and pervading every aspect of life, climate change. As environmental geographers interested in the world around us, it's easy to feel overwhelmed and paralysed by the scale of these problems and the complexity of their origins. The legacy of critical and radical theory on environmental geographies has been attention to **power** and injustice. Many geographers have committed to exploring and participating in efforts to build a more just world.

Summary

- Environmental problems come from figuring out how to live in the world, but twenty-first-century environmental problems are having unprecedented impacts.
- Many critical and radical geographers have argued that colonialism and capitalism are the root causes of twenty-first-century environmental problems. These structures have changed how people understand and interact with nature and have extracted value from nature to concentrate in the hands of a few.
- These same geographers have argued for the importance of theorising and building more just and fair worlds.

Environmental activism and environmental justice

Environmental justice describes a concern for fairness in the processes that shape environments (like decision-making) as well as the outcomes. Fairness is about people – that is, no population bears unequal burdens – but also, all beings and things that people exist with. One way of building justice is through activism. Maybe the first things that come to mind in relation to activism are demonstrations and marches, or sit ins, lock ons and other forms of direct action. These are all important types of action that have a long and important history. But **feminist** geographers have argued that they are only *part* of the activity that makes up what counts as activism. Ian Maxey (1999: 201), drawing on feminist and poststructural theory, argues that activism is critically 'reflecting on the world and our place in it' which then enables people to contest oppressive power relations: 'activism means doing as much as I can from where I am at'. Feminist geographers have long drawn on the mantra that the personal is political. That is, every decision and action in day-to-day lives is loaded with politics and negotiations of power.

This kind of definition opens the way for all sorts of things to count as activism, from collectivising resources like gardens, or tools, to community predator trapping or neighbourhood meetings about building cycle lanes. For example, Dion Enari and Lisa Viliamu Jameson (2021) describe the way art (poetry, banner making, colouring books) and culture have been used to create conversations about climate change (see Figure 40.2). They write about art forms as public expressions of solidarity, awareness raising and a way to connect Pacific Islanders across the climate movement in Australia and beyond.

Not all environmental action works towards a fairer world, however.

There are many examples of action people might take in the interests of the environment that do not challenge uneven power and do not work towards justice. The civil rights and migrant justice movements have criticised, for example, the racism of some large environmental movements that blame immigrants, or 'overpopulation' in the Global South for environmental degradation (see Kosek, 2004). Evidence shows that it is the richest parts of the global population that are the most responsible for pollution because we consume much more, requiring more resources and creating more waste. For example, the richest 1% of the globe are responsible for 15% of all carbon emissions (Gore, 2021). In the United Kingdom, 70% of all flights are taken by just 15% of the population, and in India, 1% of households take 45% of flights (Hopkinson and Cairns, 2021). But more than consumption, many of the very rich became rich owning or investing in polluting activities, like fossil fuel production, plantations or running an airline (Huber, 2021).

Anti-immigrant and racist narratives are also clear in eco-fascism. Eco-fascism emphasises community, the importance of nature and pre-industrial ways of life. It is also authoritarian, violent, and imagines that white communities are always under threat and are the only people properly able to care for the environment. While eco-fascist groups may engage in organic gardening or beach clean ups, their actions do not produce a fairer world. Rather they seek to embed power inequalities and exclusion. Farhana Sultana (2022) makes a distinction between generic climate action and climate justice: the latter is distinct because it addresses colonialism and capitalism, the root causes of climate injustice.

In another example, as I write this chapter, Aotearoa New Zealand's climate response routinely emphasises a shift to privately owned electric, rather than fossil-fuelled, vehicles. Simultaneously, the founder of Tesla, Elon Musk, has announced plans to slash the Tesla workforce by 10% while taking home a $23 billion bonus. So while some people may buy Tesla vehicles in an effort to reduce their carbon emissions, this purchasing decision does not challenge oppressive power relations. Rather, it may contribute to widening economic inequality and the corrosion of workers' rights. Instead, a climate justice response recognises the need for just transitions. The idea of just transitions emerged from the union movement and asserts that a just climate future needs good, well-paid, respected jobs for everyone. No community should be left behind as economies and societies change; therefore, coal miners and oil rig workers need to be engaged and listened to, and people in green industries need protections and fair work places.

Environmental geography's concern with ideas of justice has often emerged out of the work of activist communities who have identified instances of injustice, brought visibility to them and contested them. For example, the concept of environmental justice, common within geography,

Figure 40.2

Banner making by activists

Source: Photo credit: Amanda Thomas

Figure 40.3
Marchers protested toxic waste dumping in Warren County, North Carolina, in 1982

Source: Photo credit: Jenny Labalme

emerged from grassroots mobilisations. In particular, the civil rights movement in the US was instrumental in challenging the way environmental burdens were heaped on Black communities. These concerns crystallised in 1982 during protests against a decision to dump contaminated soil in a largely Black part of North Carolina, in Warren County. There was no scientific reason behind the decision to site the landfill in a poor county with a majority Black population; the soil type and water table were not especially favourable. It was environmental racism – the fact that nonwhite people and communities are exposed to environmental hazards at much higher rates than white communities, whether that inequality was intentional or not, and exclusion from decision-making because of **race** and/or **class** (Pulido, 2016). Numerous geography studies have demonstrated that communities of colour and poor folks are much more likely to be exposed to environmental harm (see Schlosberg and Collins, 2014).

Led by Black women and church-based advocates, the civil rights community mobilised against environmental racism in Warren County and engaged in direct action to try and stop the trucks carrying the polluted soil to the dump (see Figure 40.3).

From that organising, as well as previous examples of toxic waste and chemical exposure, key principles of the environmental justice movement emerged.

Today, there are different ways of conceptualising what environmental justice looks like exactly, but it is common to include three particular elements:

- Who and what are seen as relevant actors or parties (recognition justice)?
- Who gets to have a say and how (procedural justice)?
- Is the distribution of goods and ills fair (distributive justice)?

At a more foundational level, Indigenous scholars like Kyle Powys Whyte (2020) have argued that the issue runs much deeper – who gets to define the environment and the issues at hand? For him, environmental injustice is characterised by the domination of one group over another, and by the disruption of relationships. Meg Parsons, Karen Fisher and Roa Crease (2021: 57) theorise an Indigenous environmental justice that includes responsibilities for 'animals, plants, weather, geology, spirits and supernatural beings', things that are often not accounted for in Western scientific studies. Indigenous environmental justice, they argue, is expansive – it means a fair world across humans and nonhumans and through multiple generations (see also Chapter 45).

Summary

- Activism involves thinking about power relations, and reflecting on everyday actions.
- Not all environmental activism works towards fairness or justice. Some embed unfair relationships along lines of race or class.
- Environmental justice has emerged from grassroots movements, particularly the civil rights movement in the US.
- Indigenous geographers have expanded on what justice is and who it is for by asking what the responsibilities are to nonhumans.

What kind of action has the most impact?

Geographers interested in environmental activism often debate what kinds of action are the most useful, and at what scale. The question of scale brings us back to feminist geographers and their argument that everything is political, and that people doing what they can, where they can counts as activism. Is this enough when it comes to addressing huge environmental problems like climate change with its roots in capitalism and colonialism, as Sultana (2022) and others argue (see also Routledge et al., 2018)? What is the role of the state? And globalised and local collective action? These debates highlight the influence of different traditions on the discipline of geography, as well as the way these influences overlap.

One example that generated a lot of debate in the 2000s and 2010s was the Transition Town movement. Transition Towns took shape in Ireland and the UK in the mid-2000s as a way of reducing energy consumption. The goal was to plan for both climate change and 'peak oil', the moment when oil production peaks and begins to decline. As well as reducing communities' reliance on fossil fuels, the Transition Town movement seeks to localise food production, waste cycles and revive skills through connected communities. In general terms, this is a localisation movement that tries to shrink networks of exchange so that there are only short distances to travel between where something is produced, and where it is consumed. It has led to countless community initiatives, from small local orchards and shared gardens, to networks of Transition Churches that are changing how they engage with climate change. For people involved in groups in Wellington, when they felt overwhelmed by the size of the change needed, they reminded themselves that they could 'only do so much' and they had to be 'ruthlessly realistic' about what they could achieve. Getting their hands in the soil, sharing abundance and knowledge, was their contribution to environmental change (Cretney et al., 2016).

However, there is a risk that localisation initiatives slip into injustice. In particular, using less energy or reducing consumption of disposable goods often means more work for women. For instance, in heterosexual relationships, laundry and cooking labour is often thought of as women's work, and so sourcing local, organic food or washing reusable nappies may be good for the environment but may add more household work for women (Parker and Morrow, 2017). Or some localisation initiatives that focus on active transport may reduce accessibility for people with disabilities who may not be able to walk or bike.

Another risk is that localisation is disengaged from wider structures. While supportive of Transition Towns' aims to shift ways of living and organising communities, the Trapese Collective (2008) argued that these initiatives need to be connected outwards with other communities and clearly be able to identify what has caused environmental injustice. Their argument is a warning against apolitical responses to environmental harm, those responses that avoid critique of broader economic and social systems, or that assume society simply needs technological fixes. In a similar vein, in her work on environmental racism, Laura Pulido (2017) argues activists and geographers need to be clear eyed about the structures causing injustice. She argues that the approach of many environmental justice movements in the US has failed because they have assumed justice can be secured through the legal system or appeals to the state. In that context, however, the state is not a neutral force – many states want capitalism to continue (think here, for instance, about the way countries are thought to be doing well if they have high GDP and economic growth, but the impacts on people and planetary well-being aren't factored into how they are calculated).

These are real and important risks. However, sometimes these debates reinforce hierarchical ideas of scale – that the global is always shaping community scale, but not vice versa (Coombes et al., 2012). Chapter 3 describes the way scale has been understood differently within geography. One of the important points that chapter makes is that there is a long tradition of thinking of scale as hierarchical, where the global is seen as more important, and separate from 'lower' scales.

But scale does not have to be seen in this hierarchical manner. In writing about Indigenous self-determination, Corntassel (2008) describes the importance of practices that maintain con-nection with the natural world, such as medicine gathering. Through this very local, community-centric practice, Indigenous communities demonstrate self-determination. This self-determination has implications that flow outward through multiple scales; through connections with other Indigenous communities to formulate strategies for progressing rights at a state-level, for instance. Furthermore, many local-community initiatives are connected through national or global political movements, for instance, the development of the United Nations Declaration on the Rights of Indigenous Peoples. Ideas and innovations can be shared, political demands coordinated, while also being adapted to be place specific.

Similarly, feminist geographers and postcolonial scholars have argued that scale is very messy and interconnected, with all sorts of connections that make places and politicise people. Anna Tsing has criticised the 'Matryoshka doll' approach to scale and instead used fungi as a way of exploring how scales are relational. That is, there are numerous connections that make up the world and geographers should be careful about thinking that power is fixed in particular scales. In her research, Tsing (2012a) has explored fungi, arguing that their relationships with multiple others (people and things) demonstrate the value of looking at relational scale. In one of her exam-ples, she writes about dry rot fungus, which used to be limited to the Himalayas. However, through colonisation in South Asia, the British Navy ships became home to this fungus. In doing so, they transported it around the world, but also these ships rapidly decayed leading to a crisis only solved through a radical reinvention of war ships (Tsing, 2012a). If fungi are seen as small, insignificant and low in a scalar hierarchy, we miss complexity and spaces where difference emerges. Returning to environmental activism, and the example earlier of the Pacific Island community in Australia shaping the climate movement, this politicisation also (re)connected and deepened connections across space (Enari and Viliamu Jameson, 2021). These connections across scales – Pacific Climate Warriors organising in Brisbane, to national and regional networks – also reflect the longstanding history of Pacific and island state leaders collaborating to push for global climate action.

Cases like this also demonstrate that there are already many, many examples of groups maintaining and building environmental justice. It's easy to miss these examples if we focus too much on big structures. If geographers only ever talk about capitalism, we start to imagine that it is the only way of organising an economy, and it becomes harder to see the many flourishing examples outside it (Gibson-Graham et al., 2013, see also Chapter 64 on postcapitalist geographies).

Activism at any scale has the potential to seed ideas, make new relationships, strengthen alliances and shape processes and outcomes at other scales. Feminist and Indigenous geographies show the dangers of taking a narrow, bounded approach to scale.

Summary

- Geographers have debated what scale environmental activism should be targeted at, given that the roots of environmental problems are big structures like capitalism and colonialism.
- Key geographers have argued that all activism needs to be clear about those big structures, but there is also a risk that focusing too much on them obscures all the examples of communities building justice and healthy environments.
- Feminist and Indigenous theorists have demonstrated the way scale is messy and non-hierarchical, so actions in one place can have influence in multiple other places across scales.

What counts as success?

If environmental justice activism can happen at any scale, then, how can success be measured? How does anyone know when activism has worked to address a problem? There are, of course, examples of activists issuing demands and a clear relationship of these being met. The Environmental Justice Atlas seeks to document, map and analyse the variety of initiatives to secure fairer processes and outcomes that relate to nature. There are 3,738 entries so far in the Atlas, which is just a tiny fraction of the environmental struggles happening globally. The Atlas authors and multiple others describe the positive effects that activism has in shaping the world. Arnim Scheidel and colleagues (2020) argue that 17% of mobilisations to prevent unwanted projects, such as nuclear plants or large dams, were successful in cancelling the development. This rose to 26% when mobilisation was also supported by legal action and deployed a diverse range of protest activities. Another approach is to draw out examples of communities going ahead and building the just societies they desire. Common Unity Project Aotearoa is a project based in Te Awa Kairangi Hutt Valley, just north of Wellington. It began as a project growing food and preparing it with a local school and has grown to include a range of enterprises, like a bike repair workshop, sewing collective using salvaged fabrics and micro farms with people currently or formerly incarcerated. Through a wide range of activities, Common Unity Project seeks to build collective resilience, while engaging people in climate change adaptation and mitigation (see Simon et al., 2020). Through initiatives like this, healthy environments and communities are built together.

There are wider, more diffuse ways of thinking about success as well. Writing about the possible long-term impacts of young peoples' mobilisation in climate activism, Sylvia Nissen and colleagues (2021) warn against success/failure binaries; they argue this is too simplistic. Typically outcomes are much more messy and complicated than that, and cause and effect is difficult to determine. Few politicians or corporations want to admit that they were forced to change a decision because of pressure from activists. Instead Nissen and colleagues describe 'legacies' that are hard to pin down. These legacies might be things like lasting empowerment for people, new subcultures that feed radical politics, the way movements sustain broader momentum for justice, or shape political narratives, like the recent mainstreaming of 'climate justice'. Many geographers have described the diffuse impacts of working collectively when tackling environmental problems, from friendships to sustaining activism. Success here means working with others, and connecting local and global struggles. In Warren County in the early 1980s, the fight against the toxic waste dump was ultimately lost. More than 500 people were arrested for civil disobedience. But the legacies of this activism were huge. It sparked research into environmental racism, conventions to spell out what environmental justice would look like, and countless other communities were politicised and began to organise in their own places (Cole and Foster, 2000).

Summary

- The success of environmental activism can be hard to measure.
- Taking a broader, more long-term view of what counts as success can reveal all sorts of impacts from people working together for environmental justice.

Conclusion

To return to Wellington Airport, the Airport has recently proposed expanding its footprint as part of plans to double passenger numbers. The airport managers argue that technology will mean flying will be less carbon intensive in time. Research has shown, however, that this technology is a long way off, especially at the scale needed to have any meaningful impact on the climate crisis (McLachlan and Callister, 2022). Youth-led environmental group, Generation Zero, initiated a community mobilisation to contribute to the planning process for expanding the airport. Community groups from neighbourhoods around the airport showed up to hearings and spoke about the existing effects of airport activity and dangers of expansion. When the Airport plans were largely approved, community groups presented to the city council, and lawyers and academics volunteered their time to contribute to mediation. With a few concessions, the airport has pushed forward with their plans. This may seem like a depressing note to finish on. Those of us who experience eco-anxiety feel the lack of progress in securing climate justice quite acutely. But this isn't the end. Through collective action, at messy and interconnected scales, communities continue to organise and push for debate and decisions about the airport's future, and therefore climate futures, that work towards justice for humans and the environment.

Just as the Wellington Airport examples demonstrate the messy, multi-scalar problems of environmental injustice, geographies of environmental activism demonstrate the need for multi-scalar action and connection. Geography shows the importance of scale but also of thinking about it in nuanced ways that see how social and environmental change can be seeded and won from all sorts of places. Geography is a useful way of approaching environmental problems and understanding some of the tools, like activism, that seek to bring about change. Through geography we can understand processes that occur across scales that both reflect and shape environments.

Discussion points

Discuss examples of environmental activism from around you:

- Do you think the action fits with ideas of environmental justice? Why?
- Thinking about the problem motivating the action, what scales are relevant to understanding the problem?

References

Christensen, H. (2002). *Ethnobotany of the Iban and the Kelabit.* Sarawak Forest Department, NEPCon Denmark: University of Aarhus.

Cole, L. W., and Foster, S. R. (2000). *From the Ground Up: Environmental Racism and the Rise of the Environmental Justice Movement.* New York: New York University Press.

Coombes, B. L., and Hill, S. (2005). 'Na whenua, na Tuhoe. Ko D.o.C. te partner'—prospects for comanagement of Te Urewera national park. *Society and Natural Resources* 18(2): 135–152.

Coombes, B., Johnson, J. T., and Howitt, R. (2012). Indigenous geographies I: mere resource conflicts? The complexities in Indigenous land and environmental claims. *Progress in Human Geography* 36(6): 810–821.

Corntassel, J. (2008). Toward sustainable self-determination: rethinking the contemporary Indigenous-rights discourse. *Alternatives: Global, Local, Political* 33(1): 105–132.

Cretney, R., Thomas, A. C., and Bond, S. (2016). Maintaining grassroots activism: transition Towns in Aotearoa New Zealand. *New Zealand Geographer* 72(2): 81–91.

Enari, D., and Viliamu Jameson, L. (2021). Climate justice: a Pacific Island perspective. *Australian Journal of Human Rights* 27(1): 149–160.

Gibson-Graham, J. K., Cameron, J., and Healy, S. (2013). *Take Back the Economy: An Ethical Guide for Transforming Our Communities.* Minneapolis: University of Minnesota Press.

Gore, T. (2021). *Confronting Carbon Inequality: Putting Climate Justice at the Heart of the COVID-19 Recovery.* Oxfam Media Briefing. https://oxfamilibrary.openrepository.com/bitstream/handle/10546/621052/mb-confronting-carbon-inequality-210920-en.pdf

Hopkinson, L., and Cairns, S. (2021). Elite status: global inequalities in flying. Possible. https://www.wearepossible.org/our-reports/elite-status-global-inequalities-in-flying. Last accessed February 2024.

Huber, M. (2021). Rich people are fueling climate catastrophe—but not mostly because of their consumption. *Jacobin*. https://jacobin.com/2021/05/rich-people-climate-change-consumption

Kosek, J. (2004). Purity and Pollution: Racial Degradation and Environmental Anxieties. In *Liberation Ecologies: Environment, Development, Social Movements*, eds. R. Peet and M. Watts (2nd edn.). New York: Routledge, 125–165.

Maxey, I. (1999). Beyond boundaries? Activism, academia, reflexivity and research. *Area* 31(3): 199–208.

McGregor, A., and Thomas, A. (2017). Forest-Led Development? A More-than-Human Approach to Forests in Southeast Asian Development. In *Routledge Handbook of Southeast Asian Development*, eds. A. McGregor, F. Miller, and L. Law. London: Routledge, 392–407.

McLachlan, R. I., and Callister, P. (2022). Managing New Zealand's Greenhouse Gases from Aviation. Working Paper 22/01. Institute for Governance and Policy Studies, Victoria University of Wellington.

Nissen, S., Wong, J. H. K., and Carlton, S. (2021). Children and young people's climate crisis activism – a perspective on long-term effects. *Children's Geographies* 3: 317–323.

Parker, B., and Morrow, O. (2017). Urban homesteading and intensive mothering: (re) gendering care and environmental responsibility in Boston and Chicago. *Gender, Place & Culture* 24(2): 247–259.

Parsons, M., Fisher, K., and Crease, R. P. (2021). *Decolonising Blue Spaces in the Anthropocene: Freshwater Management in Aotearoa New Zealand*. Cham: Palgrave Macmillan.

Pulido, L. (2016). Flint, environmental racism, and racial capitalism. *Capitalism Nature Socialism* 27(3): 1–6.

Pulido, L. (2017). Geographies and race and ethnicity II: environmental racism, racial capitalism and state sanctioned violence. *Progress in Human Geography* 41(4): 524–533.

Routledge, P., Cumbers, A., and Driscoll Derickson, K. (2018). States of just transition: realising climate justice through and against the state. *Geoforum* 88: 78–86.

Schlosberg, D., and Collins, L. B. (2014). From environmental to climate justice: climate change and the discourse of environmental justice. *WIREs Climate Change* 5: 359–374.

Scheidel, A., Del Bene, D., Liu, J., Navas, G., Mingorria, S., Demaria, F., Avila, S., Roy, B., Ertor, I., Temper, L., and Martinez-Alier, J. (2020). Environmental conflicts and defenders: a global overview. *Global Environmental Change* 63: 102104.

Simon, K., Diprose, G., and Thomas, A. (2020). Community led initiatives for climate adaptation and mitigation. *Kōtuitui* 15(1): 93–105.

Sultana, F. (2022). Critical climate justice. *The Geographical Journal* 188(1): 118–124.

Tsing, A. (2012a). Unruly edges: mushrooms as companion species. *Environmental Humanities* 1: 141–154.

Trapese Collective. (2008). The rocky road to a real transition. *The Commoner* 13: 141–167.

Tsing, A. L. (2012b). On nonscalability: the living world is not amenable to precision-nested scales. *Common Knowledge* 18(3): 505–524.

Watts, M. (1983). Hazards and crisis: a political economy of drought and famine in Northern Nigeria. *Antipode* 15(1): 24–34.

Whyte, K. P. (2020). Indigenous Environmental Justice: Anti-Colonial Action through Kinship. In *Environmental Justice: Key Issues*, ed. B Coolseat. London: Taylor and Francis, 266–278.

Online materials

- Rise: One Island to Another, a video of a collaborative poem by Kathy Jetñil-Kijiner and Aka Niviâna that demonstrates the scalar interconnections of climate injustice (who lives and dies, shared experiences across space of colonialism and the impacts of cultures of consumption) and is a call to action: https://350.org/rise-from-one-island-to-another/

- On environmental racism and the origins of the environmental justice movement: https://www. washingtonpost.com/climate-environment/interactive/2021/environmental-justice-race/
- The Environmental Justice Atlas documents struggles across the globe for environmental justice: https://ejatlas.org/
- This report by Oxfam demonstrates the unequal global share of carbon emissions, or carbon inequality: https://www.oxfam.org/en/research/carbon-inequality-2030

Further reading

Chatterton, P., and Pickerill, J. (2010). Everyday activism and transitions towards post-capitalist worlds. *Transactions of the Institute of British Geographers* 35(4): 475–490.
An important, and quite conceptual article that develops the idea of everyday activism.

Cretney, R., Thomas, A. C., and Bond, S. (2016). Maintaining grassroots activism: transition Towns in Aotearoa New Zealand. *New Zealand Geographer* 72: 81–91.
This article discusses scale and 'where' activism happens. We argue in it that we need to avoid simplistic ideas (e.g. local = good) and instead understand scales as entangled across space.

Martinez-Alier, J., Anguelovski, I., Bond, P., Del Bene, D., Demaria, F., Gerber, J.-F., Greyl, L., Haas, W., Healy, H., Marín-Burgos, V., Ojo, G., Porto, M., Rijnhout, L., Rodríguez-Labajos, B., Spangenberg, J., Temper, L., Warlenius, R., and Yánez, I. (2014). Between activism and science: grassroots concepts for sustainability coined by environmental justice organizations. *Journal of Political Ecology* 21: 19–60.
A really useful guide to the key concepts that have emerged from grassroots movements.

Nissen, S., Wong, J. H. K., and Carlton, S. (2021). Children and young people's climate crisis activism – a perspective on long-term effects, *Children's Geographies* 3: 317–323.
This article gives a really useful framing of activism beyond success/failure. Instead, the authors write about the many ripples activism generates.

Parsons, M., Fisher, K., and Crease, R. P. (2021). *Decolonising Blue Spaces in the Anthropocene: Freshwater Management in Aotearoa New Zealand*. Cham: Palgrave Macmillan.
The final chapter in this book theorises a decolonised, Indigenous environmental justice.

Pulido, L. (2016). Flint, environmental racism, and racial capitalism. *Capitalism Nature Socialism* 27(3): 1–6.
This is also reasonably conceptual, but is excellent at explaining environmental racism and the relationship to capitalism.

Thomas, A., Cretney, R., and Hayward, B. (2019). Geo-ed: the student strike 4 climate: justice, emergency and citizenship. *New Zealand Geographer* 75: 96–100.
Colleagues and I wrote this article to explore how the global Fridays for Futures/Student Strike 4 Climate movement played out in Aotearoa New Zealand.

41 Climate change

Chie Sakakibara

Introduction

As global attention shifts to the shrinking polar ice cap, rampaging wildfires in the Amazon, and extreme weather patterns and temperatures that immediately affect the future of our planet, concerns about global environmental change and cultural survival have become more prominent. This in turn has triggered attention to the knowledge and voices of historically marginalised groups of people at the forefront of global solutions to the climate crises. As one geographer writes, climate change 'is something students will have to contend with for the rest of their lives, regardless of their major or chosen career' (Wilson, 2016: 54). As such many students, perhaps yourself included, have chosen to study geography in order to make sense of these often overwhelming and concerning changes.

With interdisciplinary approaches that bring **space**, place, and time together, geographers are well-placed to explore climate change and its countless ripple effects. Geography is also a discipline of hope: it seeks to act on both the social dispiritedness and apathy with regard to climate change. Researchers investigate climate change as an intersection of environment and society through diverse perspectives and methodologies including climate science, simulating models of changing climates, developing qualitative methods and geospatial technologies such as **geographical information systems** (GIS) and remote sensing. We also need to take a critical and nuanced approach to climate change. As Farhana Sultana argues, 'although climate change is often framed as a global problem for all of humanity, the heterogeneity of its manifestations, impacts, and responses has to be carefully considered' (Sultana, 2014: 373). Hope must be cognizant that climate change affects some people and places more than others.

But what is climate change? More accurately, when we talk about climate change, we are referring to anthropogenic climate change. The *Framework Convention on Climate Change* defines climate change as follows:

> a change of climate which is attributed directly or indirectly to human activity that alters the composition of the global atmosphere and which is in addition to natural climate variability observed over comparable time periods.
>
> *UNFCCC, 1992: 3*

The human activities releasing carbon into the atmosphere result in a layer of gases (carbon dioxide, methane, nitrous oxide, HCFCS, HFCS, and ozone) surrounding the Earth, which act like a 'greenhouse', trapping warm air within. This has resulted in global warming, where increases in

DOI: 10.4324/9780429265853-48

average global temperatures are to be at least 2.6°C by 2100 unless we can aggressively mitigate greenhouse gas emissions. This means widespread climate changes for humans and the planet caused by the way that water and air currents move about the planet (IPCC, 2022). This affects the habitats of all kinds of plants, animals, bacteria, fungi and more, both on land and in the sea (IUCN, 2019). Ice caps and glaciers have begun melting, affecting the entire health of the planet. It also results in more frequent natural disasters (United Nations, 2021), which we are already seeing.

Climate change is, of course, not just about numbers and facts. The sea-level rises and glaciers melt as the wildfire dramatically spreads through the surface of the Earth. Many of the geographical regions that are most vulnerable to the effects of climate change are also the traditional homelands of Indigenous communities. Currently, a dominant strategy of climate change adaptation includes planning to remove entire Indigenous communities from their homelands. Many Indigenous groups and activists argue that adaptation strategies derived from such perspectives are genocidal (Wildcat, 2009, LaDuke, 2016) and instead seek recognition of an Indigenous right to environmental self-determination, which would allow the peoples to maintain their cultural and political status upon their traditional lands (Grossman, 2012, Watt-Cloutier, 2015). This chapter explores why adaptation by removal is so devastating for Indigenous communities, using ideas of home, place attachment, and place attachment disruption. It offers an argument for considering emotional geographies as an important aspect of climate change research and action, focusing primarily on Indigenous people's responses to climate change.

In 2024, there are approximately 476 million Indigenous peoples around the world spread over more than 90 nations. Indigenous peoples are often seen as vulnerable to climate change, and their vulnerability to climate change has been discussed extensively in the fields of public policy, sociology, anthropology, and geography. But few studies have engaged with Indigenous resilience built on the emotional aspects of human-environment relationships. Indigenous and rural communities often produce understandings of climate and climate change that are incompatible with statistical findings of climate science (Cochran et al., 2008). This difference highlights the significance of human diversity that grew in tandem with their relations with the environment: Indigenous ways of knowing, thinking about, and experiencing the world differ from the dominant episteme (Herman, 2015) and can and should contribute to policy formulations, especially those addressing climate change (Eisner et al., 2009).

Summary

- 'Climate change' is how we refer to the anthropogenic disruptions to the Earth's climate, caused by global warming. It is causing widespread environmental changes that affect all kinds of life on Earth.
- Climate change affects different groups of people differently. Some of the worst affected are Indigenous peoples in marginalised communities, who argue that removal from traditional lands is akin to genocide.
- Indigenous peoples deliberately invest in developing their relationship with their environment through emotional ties.

CASE STUDY
INDIGENOUS EXPERIENCES OF CHANGING CLIMATE IN POINT HOPE, ALASKA

Figure 41.1
Above: Point Hope new town; Below: Point Hope old town

Source: Photo credit: Chie Sakakibara

549

The Iñupiat are the first people at the top of the world, and they are the 'real' (piat or piaq) 'people' (iñu) or the authentic human beings (Sakakibara, 2020).[1] They are the residents of the northernmost rim of the United States, and their society and economy are heavily reliant upon the availability of wildlife species, including the bowhead whale, caribou, bearded seal, spotted seal, white fish, and avian species. Point Hope (population 716) is located approximately 125 miles north of the Arctic Circle. Point Hope's other name, Tikiġagq, means the index finger, and the peninsula points towards the migration path of the bowhead whale. The Tikiġaqmiut (the people of Point Hope) depend upon the bowhead for sustenance and cultural meaning. It is the northwesternmost settlement of North America and one of the longest continuously inhabited places in the Americas, with some of the richest archaeological resources that confirm the route that the ancestors of today's American Indians took millennia ago.

Residents of the largest of the villages outside of Utqiaġvik (pop. 4,676), Tikiġaqmiut maintain an active subsistence lifestyle and participate in Alaska Native **modernity** through institutions like the Tigkiġaq Corporation and the Native Village of Point Hope. In addition to the inland and coastal fish, animals, and birds that they harvest, Tikiġaqmiut have a strong history of environmental advocacy and are especially known for their grassroots activism. Young people go through family-based apprenticeships in their early years, and upon graduation from Tikiġaq High School, many youth specialise in daily subsistence activities in the village, while some attend universities elsewhere. Created in 1977, New Town of Point Hope is near the tip of the peninsula on a long spit of gravel jutting west into the Chukchi Sea. Approximately 90% of the original homeland is now underwater as global climate change accelerates its pace. In 2005 and 2006, I visited Point Hope to explore Indigenous adaptation to climate change and met Point Hope residents like Kunuyaq (a pseudonym), learning more about their experience as an Indigenous person in an area profoundly endangered by climate change.

Standing at the tundra's edge, Kunuyaq pointed out to sea and showed me the wound where Raven harpooned the giant whale that created Tikiġaq, or the land of Point Hope. To this day, Tikiġaqmiut relate that their land was once the sacred whale that became the foundation of their world. When I looked out upon the landscape symbolising the origin story of the people, it was under rising seas. The wound that once gave life to land and land to life is now a buried scar reminding Tikiġaqmiut that their home is drowning and with it, perhaps, their way of life. Climate change brings increasing uncertainties among Tikiġaqmiut by endangering special places. The sea ice and permafrost that once shielded the shore from storm surges are melting away. Indeed, what I felt most strongly during my time in Point Hope was a genuine fear about an unpredictable future.

Arctic climate change impacts Tikiġaqmiut lifeways on a cultural level by threatening their homeland, their sense of place, and their relationship with the whale and the environment. By expediting the destruction crucial ceremonial places for Tikiġaqmiut, the disappearance of the coastline challenges the survival of stories and traditional social institutions that keep people alive. When Tikiġaqmiut lost their ancestral homeland to the sea in the 1970s, the Village Council decided to move their settlement of Tiġara (today known as Old Town) to its present location, the New Town of Point Hope (see Figure 41.1). As the villagers resettled in a new town, the remaining land and houses in Old Town barely above sea level were abandoned. Old Town used to contain sod houses supported by whale jawbones. Though only two miles southeast of the original location, the impersonal rectangular grid of New Town only serves to remind them that their true home lies elsewhere.

Climate change affects the relationship between humans and whales. By influencing whale migration timings, routes, and population, climate change directly threatens the peoples' lifeways and well-being. Following storms, flooding, and erosion, the place that rooted Tikiġaqmiut to their land is now underwater. Born and raised in Old Town, Kunuyaq is the only villager who remains in his original family home: 'I don't have anywhere else to go … This [place] is all I am, and this is my home, nothing else'. As Old Town disappears deeper into the sea, the people's relatedness with the land, the whale, and their cultural identity are threatened. Since the mid-1970s relocation from their original settlement, the village has been experiencing a major transition. Ninety per cent of the original homeland has eroded into the ocean, and it is just a matter of a few decades before the remainder of Old Town vanishes into the Chukchi Sea. The shore-fast ice retreats too soon and exposes more open water to the action of the wind. Waves scour the land. Without enough of a sea ice buffer, the land has become vulnerable. The resulting coastal erosion is only increasing as sea level is estimated to rise by nearly 3 inches every century due to warmer sea water and melting glaciers. Worse still, the rate of sea-level rise has accelerated. The consensus among scientists is that the sea level will rise an average of one to four feet by 2100, submerging coastal cities like New Orleans and Miami (Walsh et al., 2014). But the future is already a reality in many coastal Alaskan communities.

A 2009 Government Accountability Office report found that of Alaska's 213 Native villages, 184 are battling floods and erosion. At least 30 communities must relocate their entire villages. Yet Alaska Native villages have difficulty qualifying for federal assistance for such moves because the economic costs of such projects exceed the economic benefits. The federal government does not recognise sea-level rise and erosion as qualifying environmental incidents that merit funding. Many other Native villages are also in imminent danger from flooding and in desperate need of finding a new homeland. Newtok, a Yup'ik village near the coast of the Bering Sea, has only been able to begin its relocation process after a wait of two decades. Erosion causes a host of problems. Because of inundation, saline intrusion of drinking water sources affects public health. Community **infrastructure** is deteriorating rapidly, severely exacerbated by the thawing tundra. In 2007 experts predicted Alaska would require $6.1 billion to repair the domino effects of climate change on public infrastructure like fallen bridges, burst sewer pipes, and disintegrating roads.

Relocation of climate refugees is quickly becoming a reality but as yet no federal or state agencies are designated to help implement their relocations. The impacted communities are in perilous positions and still need to relocate, even without federal financial support. It will cost $180 million to relocate a town of 600 people. Climate change plays a critical role in displacing marginalised communities, demanding an environmental justice approach. Many other coastal communities in the circumpolar Arctic experience disasters that impact the heart of cultural cohesion: maintenance of traditions, and physical and spiritual health rooted in place. These problems are intricately interwoven, augmenting the sense of crisis and urgency in the circumpolar coastal world.

Summary

- The Point Hope residents (Tikiġaqmiut) are already facing the loss of their land to the sea, as well as other losses, including their historic relationship with the migrating whales.
- Their homes have been destroyed by erosion after protective ice barriers have disappeared, but erosion is not recognised as an environmental emergency qualifying for federal assistance. Relocation is also not supported by federal finance.

Home, place attachment, and solastalgia in climate changing times

The narrative of the Point Hope relocation and ongoing coastal erosion flows through many key concepts in human geography. Here, I would like to highlight some examples and draw parallels with other Indigenous peoples elsewhere. I have organised these thoughts around the themes of home, place attachment, and solastalgia—the sadness and distress experienced when environments change.

Home: For Tikiġaqmiut, their home is the rapidly eroding tundra. Home is an important concept in human geography. It can be a material and tangible, and at the same time, it can be an intangible and **affective** space shaped by everyday experiences, practices, social and community relations, memories, and emotions that collectively serve as a foundation of one's well-being and identity. The memories of Old Town stay in the hearts of many Tikiġaqmiut. Maasak is in her 80s, one of the oldest villagers in Point Hope. To her, Old Town was where she was born, grew up, got married, gave birth to all her children, buried her ancestors, and where she believes her people belong. 'I fear the Tikiġaq Peninsula will be completely taken [by water] by the time of my great-grandchildren. I fear what will become of where our ancestors are buried'. Maasak puts her hand over her heart when she mentioned that it was also a matter of time before the people lose their current settlement, which is fortified with sandbags and stone break walls and gravel to alleviate erosion from wave action. These narratives of the villagers about their past and possible future home loss, however, could nevertheless resuscitate a sense of home through their memories and ongoing and evolving storytelling about home.

Place attachment: In the circumpolar region, people are attached to their place and environment, which in turn has nurtured them and gives meaning to the community. People remember, cope with, narrate, and respond to climatic and environmental changes through storytelling and social events. By telling stories and participating in community events, Iñupiat actively pursue place-making and place attachment—the process of cultivating a relationship with places where one resides, works, heals, and pursues other meaningful activities. This is also a process of nurturing a sense of place, which refers to some special meanings attached to certain places for particular people and community. Collectively, these experiences and stories tell a tale of community solidarity.

Despite ongoing disruptions to place attachment and home, Iñupiaq Elders are masters of converting despair into hope. This is where storytelling plays a vital role to elevate the community spirit. With the stories' emotional and sensational appeal to both villagers and outsiders, supernatural stories give a high visibility and a human sense of place. As ghosts haunt places, the increasing number of supernatural tales, perceptions, and experiences set in the original settlement makes the villagers' bond with Old Town more tangible. The new spirit-being stories tell us about the villagers' relation to and understanding of places, of climate change, and even of the changing behaviour of spiritual beings (see also Chapter 29). Through the telling of such stories, Elders pass on their emotional investments, traditional knowledge, and a sense of place to younger generations. Through receiving such gifts, younger villagers who were born after the relocation can claim their connectivity with the disappearing homeland. This shared sense of rootedness and understanding of a place augments communal unity and cultural solidarity to form resilience against environmental uncertainties.

Stories serve to maintain an attachment relationship and anchor Iñupiat to their submerging land for old and young alike. Overall, storytelling is an expressive form of adaptation that reflects environmental uncertainties and the long-term well-being of the community. 'Our homeland is going under water, but the place still lives with us through stories', said Anna, a mother in her mid-20s. Stories may change as the environment transforms itself, which reflects the flexible nature of the Iñupiaq worldview. This elasticity enables their adaptation through the power of culture. In this way, storytelling captures and contributes to the momentum for building resilience against the changes and distress incurred by climate change.

Solastalgia: In Point Hope and across the circumpolar Arctic, the current era of climate change coincides with the unprecedented rise in the rate of suicide, depression, substance abuse, and domestic violence among the youth in the Arctic. Some people have started to connect this kind of mental and physical distress with the idea of *solastalgia*. Solastalgia, a combination of the Latin word *solacium* (comfort) and the Greek root—*algia* (pain), is a term coined by an Australian philosopher Glenn Albrecht (2005). Unlike nostalgia, which is distress or sadness experienced when one is separated from a home, solastalgia is caused by environmental change affecting people while they are still directly connected to their home (environment). Solastalgia is thus the distress caused by environmental degradation—including the influences by climate change that continuously and increasingly impact people's well-being.

Solastalgia has two parts. First, it is the feeling that resembles nostalgia in a home that no longer resembles the original home. Second, it is the mental and physical health problems we face that correspond to the environmental crises that our planet is facing. While the concept was presented by a non-Indigenous scholar in rural Australia, Indigenous authors often indicate that this notion echoes the sentiments caused by the ongoing destruction of Indigenous lands and sense of place in a global context. Solastalgia is largely manifesting as emotional pain in the form of loss of control, identity, and isolation. Furthermore, primary solastalgia symptoms after climate change affected their homes manifested as a sense of sadness, fear, distress, and a lack of identity (Kingsley et al., 2013).

Solastalgia relates to home, place attachment, and disruption. And the issue is not confined to the Arctic, but it is becoming widespread. As the Arctic glaciers melt, the first climate domino falls as the sea-level rises. The emerging water from the ice directly and catastrophically affects the island nations of the Pacific. One example is the island nation of Kiribati (pronounced 'kiribas'), a seemingly idyllic atoll nation is destined to become the first victim of climate change in the lower latitude region. The intensity of climate-induced environmental change confronted by the 121,388 Indigenous people of Kiribati (who are known as I-Kiribati); whose island is going under water is nothing less than what their Arctic counterparts go through (Roman, 2018).

The nation of Kiribati nestles on a narrow strip of land that lies between the Pacific and a large lagoon. Human lives in Kiribati have been reliant upon the waters around them. The ocean has provided I-Kiribati with the means of survival, including food, and became a classroom for navigating the Pacific oceanic landscape. However, global climate change has permanently changed their relationship with the water as they became one of the first victims of climate change while they are only responsible for only 0.6% of world greenhouse gas emissions. As their crops fail due to the intrusion of the salt water into the island soil, the people lose their home to the sea. Many I-Kiribati have already left their homeland for New Zealand and other locations. Just like in Point Hope, however, others decide to stay in their homeland by building walls and moving communities inland as well as planting mangroves to protect the soil from erosion and

Figure 41.2
Aerial view of Kiritimati, Kiribati

Source: Photo credit: Travel Pix/Alamy

mitigate storm surges (Iberdrola, 2020). The Kiribati government has bought land in Fiji to grow crops and as potential evacuation site for the citizens. The youth of Kiribati, however, frequently reach out to their allies and Indigenous neighbours on the global scale to put them on the map. At the United Nations, conference of the partie's COP 27 meeting in Egypt, Kiribati expressed a strong demand to physically raise up their islands to escape the encroaching seas and sought support from the international community to raise the funds as a way to compensate for the level of environmental injustice their people have been going through in the times of global climate change. This plea draws a parallel with their Arctic counterpart whose land is eroding to the sea (Figure 41.2).

The reality is that this problem is not endemic to the Pacific or the Arctic. Kiribati and Point Hope are just the first two dominos to fall. As climate change progresses at its current pace, it is just a matter of time for cities like London and Los Angeles to disappear. Solastalgia will then no longer be a regional issue but rather become a global phenomenon. Indeed, we can trace solastalgia all over the globe already: in the southern hemisphere, Aboriginal and Torres Strait Islander peoples in Australia have also faced forced relocations and degradation of their homes. Mental health among Aboriginal peoples across Australia has been impacted by the recent droughts, environmental degradation and increasing dryland salinity and uranium mining (Kingsley et al., 2013). As the environment is central to human health and well-being, environmental justice is also an issue of health inequalities. When the communities confront the impacts of environmental **colonialism** and inequalities, the shared legacies and memories of pain, poverty, violence, and intergenerational trauma gather people and have them recreate songlines to reconfirm the connectivity with the land (see also Chapter 43).

As the examples of Point Hope and Kiribati reveal, climate change displaces many Pacific Islanders, and coastal villagers of the Pacific Northwest and high-latitude regions. For Indigenous Australian communities, rising sea levels pose a risk to coastal communities, and ongoing droughts jeopardise the environmental and cultural sustainability of the interior locations. Meanwhile, non-Indigenous regions often still have time and resources to implement adaptations. This uneven relationship is a form of environmental injustice (see Chapter 40).

Summary

- The loss of home for Indigenous peoples affected by climate change disrupts place attachment and prompts solastalgia, a set of feelings related to loss and grief as the environment changes.
- Disruption of place attachment is serious, as relationships with place are what sustains Indigenous communities culturally, and this loss of identity is profoundly affecting.

Emotional geographies of climate change

In such disruptive and distressing times, it is important to recognise that climate change is not just about facts, figures, and modelling outcomes. It is also entwined with emotion. In the Western tradition, overall, emotions are something we often hear about in a very anthropocentric way, as the dictionary defines emotions as 'physiological and behavioural changes in the body' in response to a certain event (see Chapter 24). On the other hand, many Indigenous philosophies do not characterise emotions as simple as a human response to an event or object; rather, emotions help humans to cultivate connections and reciprocal link with non-human persons including environments. The place attachment and solastalgia we have discussed previously fall into this category. There are other examples, too: many Arctic peoples understand that animals willingly give themselves to hunters in response to receiving respectful treatment as 'non-human persons' (Fienup-Riordan 1990, Brewster, 2004). Such relationships are key for Indigenous places and Indigenous identity, yet these relationships are affected by climate and climate change as animal communities face changes to habitat. The foundation of Indigenous identity is challenged by emotional obstacles that people face when their kinship with homeland is threatened.

It is thus important to recognise the importance of emotion in our climate change study and action. In this chapter, I have shown how it is not enough just to study the facts and figures of climate change, but to investigate what it *means* for people on an emotional level. This is different from studying what it means for the global economy, or our physical surroundings. The disappearance of the Arctic sea ice and glaciers as well as thawing of the tundra disrupt human-animal relations at the core of **more-than-human** reciprocity, affecting people's relationships, place attachments, emotions, and identity. When we recognise place attachment and kinship emotions, we can better comprehend and nurture the tight-knit relationship between human and environment in a number of different areas. In these times of heightened socio-environmental stress, many Indigenous communities rely on the power of cultural solidarity through traditions. This solidarity is a form of emotional and cultural resilience that can be found in hunting, religious worship, language retention efforts, and a variety of manifestations of expressive culture such as arts, music, dance, and heritage education. The emotional, the cultural, the ritual, and the environmental are all linked together and part of kinship relationships.

Music, in particular, has a power to resuscitate cultural and collective memories among Indigenous communities. These memories have an important role in the community members' responses to environmental uncertainties and their related emotional difficulties. For example, in northern Alaska, storytelling, dancing, singing, and drumming are powerful cornerstones for cultural survival. Dance reveals a strong sense of social integration and moral development. As ethnomusicologist and anthropologist Aaron Fox (2014: 544) writes, '[d]ancing saves lives'. Far away in southeast Montana, Supaman—a young Crow man with the given name Christian Parrish Takes the Gun—raps to the youths on the Crow Nation reservation to raise the shared emotional level of his community (Figure 41.3, see also online materials). Hip hop music was originally born in the **ghetto** in New York City but has been appropriated in solidarity to express the issues associated with difficult life, poverty, crime, drugs, alcohol, teen pregnancy, and other social problems shared within and beyond the Crow tribal community. By relating to the songs of the oppressed, youth merged urban music with more local concerns of their ancestral land, as it has often manifested in the Indigenous Peoples' and Communities' Pavilion at COP meetings.

FIGURE 41.3
Supaman, a Crow musician and artist

Source: Courtesy of Christian Takes The Gun

When we consider the holistic nature of Indigenous philosophies, human emotions matter. So do the practices, rituals, relationships, and contemporary strategies to attend to emotion.

Summary

- Emotions are important in climate change research.
- Emotional kinship relations with place and species are elements of Indigenous emotional geographies.
- Interventions and solidarity relationships that recognise the emotional elements of climate change include music, cultural traditions, and solidarity across different Indigenous groups.

Conclusion: Indigenous solidarity

We began this chapter with reference to the dispiritedness that many of us might feel around climate change, and a call for geographies of hope. But these geographies of hope are not just blind optimism. Such geographies of hope must connect with the real-life emotional experiences of those most affected by climate change, based on real stories of resilience from those whose ways of life are being most disrupted. This chapter has aimed to show how diverse groups are thinking about climate change when their cultures and ways of life are under threat. Resilience consists of the processes by which people overcome life challenges to achieve their sense of well-being and is often deeply rooted in their sense of place (Goldstein, 2012). The adaptability and elasticity of Indigenous peoples have been said to be the foundation of their resilience (Grossman, 2012). The most vital Indigenous responses to climate change are in the expanding capacity of community members to pass on cultures that respect the land. Such ability is not rooted in tribal government offices or negotiations over political rights with other governments.

The Indigenous communities we have discussed in this chapter have survived colonialism including wars, epidemics, poverty, and resource deprivations, but it was always the collective effort to keep the culture alive and strong that enabled their survival. While for some peoples, such as those in the Western world, climate change might be the first cultural environmental apocalypse on the horizon, other marginalised groups have been going through deep emotional and environmental disruption and experiencing solastalgia for generations. Cultivating an intimate relationship with the environment is a double-edged sword as the people with close ties to the land will feel the impacts of changes to the land such as melting ice, changing animal migration patterns, unpredictable weather for growing crops. On the other hand, this close connection to the land is an inseparable part of what makes Indigenous peoples resilient in the face of global climate change. The late Ojibwa environmentalist, activist, and leader Walter Bresette (1947–1999) proposed the Seventh Generation Principle, which crystalises an Indigenous way of relating to the environment: 'The right of the people to use and enjoy air, water, sunlight, and other natural resources determined to be common property, shall not be impaired, nor shall such use impair their availability for future generations' (LaDuke, 1999: 199). What would it look like for geographers to act in solidarity with Indigenous peoples, researching climate change not just in terms of modelling physical changes to the environment and the effects of sea-level rise on infrastructure and property, but researching climate change with full recognition of its disparate effects on marginalised cultures and places? We can hold on to the human geography concepts of home, place attachment, solastalgia, researching them with attentiveness to emotional geographies, solidarity with Indigenous peoples, and the relational experiences of marginalised peoples in climate-disrupted environments.[2]

Discussion points

- How do you define human geography? Why is it important to fully comprehend and discuss climate change?
- Why is it important to consider Indigenous voices and experiences when we discuss climate change policy for adaptation and mitigation?
- What are some examples of innovative responses emerging from the regions that are the most affected parts of the world by global climate change?
- How do different people experience different emotions around climate change?

Notes

1. The term Iñupiat is plural, but it also handles the possessive. The singular and the adjectival form of the word is Iñupiaq.
2. The author would like to thank colleagues, partners, and mentors in Arctic Alaska and beyond. Special thanks are due to Michael Roman. Thanks to University of Arizona Press for the permission to use a segment of my work *Whale Snow* (2020) in this publication.

References

Albrecht, G. (2005). 'Solastalgia': a new concept in health and identity. *Philosophy Activism Nature* 3: 41–44. https://doi.org/10.1080/10398560701701288

Brewster, K. (2004). *The Whales, They Give Themselves: Conversations with Harry Brower, Sr.* Fairbanks: University of Alaska Press.

Cochran, P., Marshall, C., Garcia-Dowing, C., Kendall, E., Cook, D., McCubbin, L., and Gover, R. M. S. (2008). Indigenous ways of knowing: implications for participatory research and community. *American Journal of Public Health* 98(1): 22–27. https://doi.org/10.2105/AJPH.2006.093641

Eisner, W., Cuomo, C. J., Hinkel, K., Jones, B., and Brower, R. Sr. (2009). Advancing landscape change research through the incorporation of Iñupiaq knowledge. *Arctic* 62(4): 429–442. https://www.jstor.org/stable/40513334

Fienup-Riordan, A. (1990). *Eskimo Essays: Yup'ik Lives and How We See Them*. New Brunswick: Rutgers University Press.

Fox, A. (2014). Repatriation as Reanimation through Reciprocity. In *The Cambridge History of World Music: Vol 1 (North America)*, ed. P. Bohlman. Cambridge: Cambridge University Press, 522–554. https://doi.org/10.1017/CHO9781139029476.029

Goldstein, B. E. (ed.) (2012). *Collaborative Resilience: Moving Through Crisis and Opportunity*. Cambridge, MA: MIT Press.

Grossman, Z. (2012). No Longer the 'Miner's Canary'. In *Asserting Native Resilience: Pacific Rim Indigenous Nations Face the Climate Crisis*, eds. Z. Grossman and A. Parker. Corvallis: Oregon State University Press, 175–188.

Herman, R. D. K. (2015). Traditional knowledge in a time of crisis: climate change, culture and communication. *Sustainability Science* 11(1): 163–176. https://doi.org/10.1007/s11625-015-0305-9

IPCC. (2022). *Climate Change 2022: Impacts, Adaptation, and Vulnerability.* Contribution of Working Group II to the Sixth Assessment Report of the Intergovernmental Panel on Climate Change. Cambridge University Press. doi:10.1017/9781009325844

IUCN. (2019). Species and Climate Change. https://www.iucn.org/resources/issues-brief/species-and-climate-change

Kingsley, J. Y., Townsend, M., and Henderson-Wilson, C. (2013). Exploring aboriginal people's connection to country to strengthen human-nature theoretical perspectives. *Ecological Health: Society, Ecology and Health Advances in Medical Sociology* 15: 45–64.

LaDuke, W. (2016). *Recovering the Sacred: The Power of Naming and Claiming.* Chicago: Haymarket Books.

Sakakibara, C. (2020). *Whale Snow: Iñupiat, Climate Change, and Multispecies Resilience.* Tucson: University of Arizona Press.

Sultana, F. (2014). Gendering climate change: geographical insights. *The Professional Geographer* 66(3): 372–381. DOI: 10.1080/00330124.2013.821730

United Nations. (2021 September 1). Climate and Weather Related Disasters Surge Five-Fold over 50 Years, but Early Warnings Save Lives—WMO Report. https://news.un.org/en/story/2021/09/1098662

Watt-Cloutier, S. (2015). *The Right to Be Cold: One Woman's Story of Protecting Her Culture, the Arctic and the Whole Planet.* Toronto: Penguin Canada.

Wildcat, D. R. (2009). *Red Alert! Saving the Planet with Indigenous Knowledge.* Golden: Fulcrum.

Online materials

- Allison Akootchook Warden (Aku-Matu) is an Iñupiaq intermedia artist and a tribal member of the Native Village of Kaktovik, Alaska. Warden explores contemporary Indigenous issues such as climate change, extractivism, and intergenerational trauma and seeks out for a hopeful future in her music, bringing her training in theatre to the stage. Allison Akootchook Warden (Aku-Matu) https://www.allisonwarden.com/aku-matu.html

- This film clip illustrates how climate change affects the environment and everyday life of Iñupiat in Point Hope, Alaska.
  CGTN America. 2015. Climate Change is Having a Drastic Impact on Point Hope, Alaska. https://www.youtube.com/watch?v=d9pZvStcTN0

- Climate change is a global problem. The following link encourages us to make a connection between the experiences of the North and the Pacific islands.
  Milman, Oliver. 'No Safe Place': Kiribati Seems Donors to Raise Islands from Encroaching Seas. https://www.theguardian.com/environment/2022/nov/18/cop27-kiribati-donors-raise-islands-sea-level-rise

- The Indigenous peoples in the circumpolar region are standing on the frontline of global climate change. The following link gives an overview of how climate change intersects with Indigenous social fabric.
  UN Chronicle. 'Climate Change in the Arctic: An Inuit Reality'. https://www.un.org/en/chronicle/article/climate-change-arctic-inuit-reality

- Listen to one of the songs by Crow artist Supaman, in this one raising awareness and affect around Indigenous water issues over the globe: https://youtu.be/C9-VTggwePA?si=Izcu7LR4lhyarWYO. See more of his work at https://www.supamanhiphop.net/videos

- The following interview elucidates the author's experience of working with the Iñupiat community of Arctic Alaska to confirm their cultural resilience and adaptation in the face of global climate change.
  University of Arizona Press. 2020. 'Whale Snow: Five Questions with Author Chie Sakakibara'. https://uapress.arizona.edu/2020/11/whale-snow-five-questions-with-author-chie-sakakibara

Further reading

Bondi, L., Davidson, J., and Smith, M. (eds.) (2005). *Emotional Geographies*. Farnham: Ashgate Publishing. This book explores the geographies of emotion.

Cochran, P., Marshall, C., Garcia-Dowing, C., Kendall, E., Cook, D., McCubbin, L., and Gover, R. M. S. (2008). Indigenous ways of knowing: implications for participatory research and community. *American Journal of Public Health* 98(1): 22–27.
This article explores the implications of Indigenous ways of knowing for participatory research and community engagement.

Sakakibara, C. (2020). *Whale Snow: Iñupiat, Climate Change, and Multispecies Resilience*. Tucson: University of Arizona Press.
My book examines the Iñupiat community's response to climate change and their practices of multi-species resilience.

Whyte, K. P. (2017). Indigeneity and US Colonialism. In *Oxford Handbook of Philosophy and Race*, ed. N. Zach. Oxford: Oxford University Press, 91–101.
This chapter discusses the relationship between Indigeneity and US colonialism, exploring these themes in the context of philosophy and race.

Wildcat, D. R. (2009). *Red Alert! Saving the Planet with Indigenous Knowledge*. Golden: Fulcrum.
This book emphasises the importance of Indigenous knowledge in addressing environmental challenges facing humanity and the planet.

Wilson, R. M. (2016). Will the End of the World Be on the Final Exam? Emotions, Climate Change, and Teaching an Introductory Environmental Studies Course. In *Teaching Climate Change in the Humanities*, eds. S. LeMenager, S. Siperstein, and S. Hall. New York: Routledge, 53–58.
This chapter discusses incorporating emotions and climate change in teaching an introductory environmental studies course.

42 Sustainability

Kersty Hobson

Introduction

> We are resolved to free the human race from the tyranny of poverty and want and to heal and secure our planet. We are determined to take the bold and transformative steps which are urgently needed to shift the world on to a sustainable and resilient path. As we embark on this collective journey, we pledge that no one will be left behind.
>
> *United Nations General Assembly, 2015: 1*

The above declaration is from the United Nations (UN) General Assembly resolution called 'Transforming our world: the 2030 Agenda for Sustainable Development'. This document sets out the UN's high-level vision of a future that is fairer and more sustainable than the world we live in now. This vision contains a comprehensive, global agenda of 17 headline areas—called the Sustainable Development Goals (SDGs)—that cover issues such as poverty, **gender**, education, climate change and economic growth. Below these headlines goals sit 169 targets, some of which set timelines for action e.g. 'by 2030, halve per capita global food waste at the retail and consumer levels' (United Nations, n.d.b). This level and scope of ambition continues on through the SDGs, linking issues of environmental and **ecological** sustainability to the social issues of equity and fairer societal processes and outcomes.

Perhaps this seems like an obvious link to make: that a fairer world is more environmentally sustainable. However, this chapter outlines how the above words can be seen as part of an important and relatively recent shift in the story of 'sustainability' over the past few decades. Prior to this, the debates and actions that aimed to foster sustainability were less clear on the importance of such social and environmental links: an approach labelled as 'weak' sustainability, because ensuing actions have failed to—and indeed, did not really try to—address the root causes of key issues. As a result, the world has continued to become less sustainable, despite decades of policies and interventions that aimed to do the opposite. In response, more and more commentators have argued that we urgently need 'strong' approaches to sustainability, which are 'bold and transformative' as the UN quote above suggests. This chapter explores these arguments, first introducing the ideas of sustainability and sustainable development, and then discussing the key issues of equality and decoupling, to show how 'strong' approaches (such as degrowth and sufficiency) are increasingly gaining ground.

DOI: 10.4324/9780429265853-49

Summary

- 'Weak' approaches to sustainability have prevailed in recent decades and have failed to address the root causes of key issues.
- The UN, amongst others, now aims to create 'strong' sustainability approaches and outcomes, to address the links between social and environmental problems.

What is sustainability?

As the verb 'sustain' suggests, sustainability fundamentally means the ability to maintain certain functions or actions at a particular rate over a defined time-period. This can refer to maintaining a delicate ecological balance; or a certain level of economic growth; or one's heartrate while out jogging. But in this chapter, we are looking at a particular journey the concept of sustainability has taken since the 1970s that relates to the relationship between society and the environment. Back then, increasing rates of (and improved techniques to detect) environmental problems and resource depletion raised serious questions about whether post-World War II levels of global economic growth could be sustained without causing irreversible ecological damage: damage that was already starting to drastically impact all flora and fauna on this planet, as well as atmospheric conditions, all those years ago.

Such mounting concern was captured by the controversial 1972 report 'Limits to Growth' (LtG). This research and subsequent publication brought to public attention the unsustainable consequences of human activity, stating that 'If the present growth trends…continue unchanged, the limits to growth on this planet will be reached sometime within the next one hundred years' (Meadows et al., 1972: 23). Given such dire predictions LtG was widely dismissed and critiqued, both when it was published and in the decades that followed. Some of these criticisms have held up over time. For example, LtG's focus on population growth as a key root of global unsustainability has been shown to overplay the importance of absolute population size, while underplaying the importance of who gets what and by how much—topics we will get to a bit later. But other criticisms have been roundly disproved. For one, we can now see that the LtG projections have been matched with decades of real-world data and impacts, with the LtG hypothetical models now lining up neatly with real-world experiences (e.g. Turner, 2008)—all of which underscore its messages of profound negative impacts and consequences into the twenty-first century.

Back in the 1970s, the core LtG message—that continued economic growth is fundamentally unsustainable for all life on Earth—brought concerns about ecological sustainability into public spheres of political and social debate, where they firmly remain today. Perhaps partially in response to the criticisms of the LtG, the 1980s saw a less threatening take on the idea of sustainability emerge. Here, 'sustainable development' became the key term and for decades remained a foundational concept in debates about global economic growth and its multiple negative impacts. Returning to the UN for a moment, their 1987 report 'Our Common Future' is pivotal here. Detailing the results of the 'Brundtland Commission'—named after Gro Harlem Brundtland, the former Norwegian Prime Minister who chaired the UN's World Commission on Environment and Development—this 383-page report gave us the often-quoted definition of

Figure 42.1
UNCED Earth Summit, Rio de Janeiro, Brazil, 1992

Source: Photo credit: Education Images/Universal Images Group via Getty Images

sustainable development: 'Development that meets the needs of the present without compromising the ability of future generations to meet their own needs' (Brundtland, 1987: 15). A lot has been said—both for and against—that particular take on sustainability, in terms of what it assumes, as well as what it includes and leaves out (see 'discussion points' below). For now, what is important is to follow the uptake of 'sustainable development' from the late 1980s onwards.

A key moment in this story of sustainability is the 1992 Earth Summit, where the above Brundtland definition was launched into the public sphere. Here government heads and many thousands more from around the world gathered in Rio de Janeiro, amidst much publicity and media fanfare, for two weeks 'of a massive effort to focus on the impact of human socio-economic activities on the environment' (United Nations, n.d.a). For those of us alive at the time, 'Rio' was indeed a big deal. It made global news headlines and evoked feelings of hope that we were now all coming together to address sustainability. Such optimism is captured in Figure 42.1. Here Brazilian Indigenous participants at Rio are standing in front of the 'Earth Pledge' wall that hundreds of delegates had already signed to signal collective promises of further action.

Amidst this excitement, the initial outcomes of Rio were hopeful. The conference gave rise to numerous Conventions, still active today (e.g. the UN Framework Convention on Climate Change); key programmes that aimed to act as a global 'blueprint for sustainability' (e.g. Agenda 21); and the Rio Declaration. In the aftermath of the conference, however, analyses unpacked the specifics of goals and outcomes, including the assumptions they contained. For example, the Rio Declaration placed 'Human beings at the centre of concerns for sustainable development' (Principle 1), asserting that 'development must be fulfilled so as to equitably meet

563

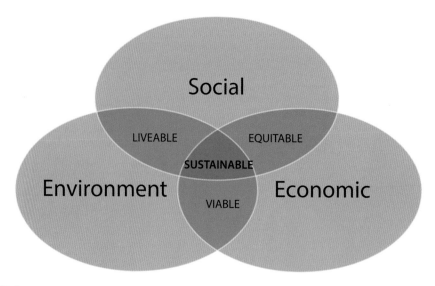

Figure 42.2
Diagram of the key spheres of sustainable development

Source: Adapted from Brusseau (2019)

developmental and environmental needs of present and future generations' (Principle 3). For some commentators, this anthropocentric version of sustainability—when married with a particular version of 'development'—suggested problems ahead, as ecological parameters were not being given equal weight to those of the economy. For others, that was not the case. For example, Figure 42.2 is a diagram often used to capture the post-Rio view of sustainable development, as the space where the social, environmental and economic can overlap, hitting a certain 'sweet spot' that balances these different demands.

In reality, the Rio Conference made it apparent that not all these three areas are deemed of equal importance to everyone, despite the ideals of Figure 42.1. During the conference, government and business leaders continually stressed how economic growth and the varieties of **neoliberal capitalism** taking hold around the world were not open to debate or amendment. Or as the then-US President George Bush (Senior) put it 'The American way of life is not up for negotiations. Period'. At the same time, Global South countries vocalised deep disquiet about any 'environmental' agenda that could impose restrictions upon their own national economic development: development needed to raise living standards and lift more people out of poverty. Therefore, from the offset, the 'economic' sphere in this form of sustainable development undoubtedly took precedence over the 'social' and 'environmental' spheres. This has led to many researchers, including geographers, to argue that 'sustainable development' is, in essence, an oxymoron. That is, a phrase that is internally contradictory, in that it suggests 'sustainability' and 'development' can go unproblematically hand-in-hand, when actually they cannot (Redclift, 2005). But why is this the case? Why was sustainable development—and the actions that ensured from Rio—increasingly held up to critical scrutiny, in the ensuing years after the positivity of Rio? In the next section we will explore what happened next, and how sustainable development in practice did little to stem the growth of the negative social and environmental impacts it was meant to address.

Summary

- Research since the 1970s, such as the LtG report, has been highlighting the causes and impacts of global ecological destruction.
- From the 1980s the concept of 'sustainable development' took centre stage, gaining significant international traction through the Brundtland Report and the 1992 Rio Earth Summit.
- Many have argued that this take on 'sustainable development' is an oxymoron due to its anthropocentrism and prioritisation of economic growth.

Weak sustainability and the failure of sustainable development

The phrase 'weak sustainability' emerged in academic analysis during the 1990s onwards, to capture the prevailing political and policy viewpoint that, for the most part, there is 'no need to transform either the predominant narrative on nature or the existing dominant **discourse** on what constitutes economic progress and development' (Williams and Millington, 2004: 100). That is, it assumes that we can and must continue along the path of focussing on global economic growth as the key measure of collective progress, with nature being a backdrop and 'resource' for humanity.

And this is certainly how sustainability was interpreted in mainstream policy and action from the early 1990s onwards. Here, there were many 'sustainability fixes' brought into established ways of thinking and acting. Rather than fundamentally altering the ways in which the three spheres of sustainable development were understood and put in practice, such 'fixes' were often a 'selective incorporation of ecological goals in the greening of urban governance' (While et al., 2004: 551), as well as the 'greening' of business and everyday life (see below). For example, some local governments around the world developed 'Local Agenda 21' action plans, which aimed to create more sustainable communities through consultation and attempts to 'join up' local initiatives, to deliver in the three areas of sustainability in Figure 42.1. While intentions here were sound, delivery often met many barriers, and differed from place to place. This gave rise to a 'hybridity of approaches and rationalities' (Raco, 2005: 325) with some places becoming seemingly more 'greener' than others (such as Portland, Oregon: see Goodling et al., 2015). As such, this sustainability agenda—when put into practice in real-world conditions and norms—was delivered in a piecemeal way with very mixed results.

Why this was the case is important, and we can make more sense of this by looking at who was setting this particular sustainability agenda. At Rio and beyond, Global South and Indigenous communities were definitely not the loudest and most powerful voices in the room, with their messages and input being repeatedly over-ridden by Global North leaders. Indeed, if you look at pictures of the 1992 Earth Summit (such as the ones listed in online materials at the end of this chapter), we can ask whether this is a sound representation of global **ethnicity** and gender, both at the time and now. Why such **representation** matters is discussed elsewhere in this book in more detail (see Chapter 9). Here, it matters because the mechanisms and pathways to creating more sustainable futures ended up mirroring the prevailing neoliberal approaches to governance of Global North countries, which favoured pro-business, non-regulatory methods of social change. As a result, a 'softly softly' or 'weak' approach was taken to fostering greater sustainability, which emphasised how we could indeed grow the economy and address sustainability issues through making goods and services more efficient, as well as 'greening' our values and attitudes. For example—despite clear evidence that Global North household consumption of resources far outstrips global ecological supply—addressing this issue has taken the form of voluntary and information-based approaches, which encourage us all to make 'greener' purchases while 'thinking global, acting local' (Burgess et al., 2003). This form of sustainability is no threat to the mass consumerism that has dominated economic growth patterns of the past few decades. Instead, we can all keep consuming but can do so more 'eco-consciously'.

Yet, research has repeatedly shown such forms of intervention are highly ineffective at changing our behaviour. This is because they assume many things that turn out to be untrue. For one, it assumes that new information has a notable impact on consumer behaviour, which it does not. Instead, habits, context, cost, norms and convenience—amongst many other factors—all play key roles in making it hard to 'green' household consumption. In fact, the very idea of 'green consumption' is highly questionable. For example, 'Greenwashing' has become a widespread practice, where the ecological credentials of products are presented to consumers in ways that falsely underestimates their environmental impacts (see the online materials section). This makes it hard for us all to know the actual environmental costs of what we are buying and using. In addition—and thinking more at a whole systems level—there is the important idea of 'decoupling'.

To understand a bit more about 'decoupling' and why it matters so much, you can watch the short video by the International Resource Panel listed in online materials for this chapter. But to explain briefly here, the idea of 'relative' decoupling suggests that it is possible to keep economic growth going but detach it from its environmental pressures: an argument that has been an underlying, fundamental ethos of 'weak' sustainability. Relative decoupling can be seen in Figure 42.3, above the 'Time' line, where the growth in resource use is not matched by the same magnitude of growth in environmental pressure. Making this happen entails, amongst other things, making goods and services more efficient by decreasing ecological intensity per unit. For example, over the past 20 years, washing machines have become a lot more energy efficient. Plus, we are collectively buying more of the efficient ones e.g. in the EU around 83% bought are in the top categories (A+, A++ and A+++: see Applia, 2023). As a result, resource use is still growing, but at a slower rate than previously, relative to economic growth.

This all sounds positive and is indeed an improvement. But the problem here is that as the overall demand for goods and services continue to grow, any environmental gains made by new energy efficiencies are outstripped by rising absolute numbers of goods being bought and used, e.g. more and more washing machines are being purchased and kept in use for shorter periods of time. And when looked at across all sectors, this is exactly what has been happening, as demand continues to outstrip any resource savings made through improved efficiencies. This has led many to argue that what we now need is 'absolute decoupling'—the line below 'Time' in Figure 42.3. This requires a decrease in overall, absolute resource use, untethered from a direct relationship with economic growth. Or, no matter how much the

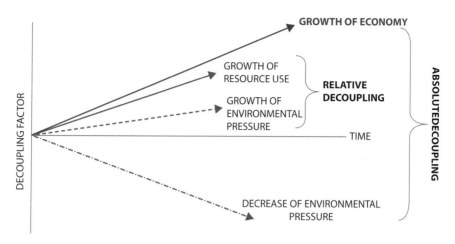

Figure 42.3
Relative and absolute decoupling

Source: Adapted from Ness (2009)

economy does or does not grow, the total amount of resources being used goes down and does so significantly.

The importance of this difference cannot be stressed enough. As one review of decoupling research put it, 'large rapid absolute reductions of resource use and GHG emissions cannot be achieved through observed decoupling rates, hence decoupling needs to be complemented by sufficiency-oriented strategies and strict enforcement of absolute reduction targets' (Haberl et al., 2020: 1). The last part of that quote is basically advocating for 'strong' sustainability, where 'rather than adapt the Earth to suit ourselves, we adapt ourselves to meet the finitude of nature' (Williams and Millington, 2004: 100). This moves us away from the pro-growth, anthropocentric view of sustainability that has prevailed towards more radical ideas and interventions. But how to do that? What sorts of sufficiency-oriented strategies and resource reduction interventions are being put forward; and how likely are they to be taken up and succeed? Before we explore those questions, we have to come back to a point that opened this chapter: the relationship between equality and sustainability.

Summary

- From the 1990s, sustainable development goals and interventions were dominated by Global North agendas and actors, favouring neoliberal approaches to economic growth.
- In this time, resource use has continued to grow, with approaches such as the 'greening' of consumerism failing to make any notable positive impacts.
- Rather than 'relative' decoupling, we now need sustainability interventions to work towards rapid 'absolute decoupling', to halt resource depletion and ecological deterioration.

'Are you doing your bit?': equality and sustainability

During the late 1990s, the UK Labour Government ran a campaign entitled 'Are you doing your bit?'. This national campaign aimed to promote widespread public environmental aware-ness, encouraging all individuals to take action to 'make the environment mainstream' (OECD, n.d.: 3). We have already looked at the ineffectual nature of such approaches to social change (see above). This campaign is mentioned here to make the point that, as it turns out, not all the 'bits' we can do are equal. This relates to questions of who has the most responsibility for both the causes and solutions to environmental issues—contentious arguments that have been a part of sustainability debates since LtG was published. What has become more apparent over the years is that such unevenness has dire consequences for the chances of achieving any level of sustainability.

For example, the international development charity Oxfam has repeatedly highlighted how global income and wealth inequality links directly with negative environmental consequences. They show how between 1990 and 2015 'the richest 10% of the world's population (c.630 mil-lion people) were responsible for 52% of the cumulative carbon emissions—depleting the global carbon budget by nearly a third (31%)'. At the same time, the 'poorest 50% (c.3.1 billion people) were responsible for just 7% of cumulative emissions and used just 4% of the available carbon budget' (Oxfam, 2020: 2). During this period, global greenhouse gas emissions continued to rise dramatically, which means that this growth—which now presents real threats to life on Earth—is being disproportionately caused by the richest amongst us. Thus, far from everyone 'doing their bit', a small percentage of people around the world need to drastically reduce their overall resource consumption, above and beyond the vast majority of the global population (see also Chapter 9).

And this is not just about holding those responsible to account. Research has shown there are clear links between inequality and poor environmental outcomes, which impact everyone, rich, poor or somewhere in between. As the geographer Danny Dorling (2017: no page) has put it: 'people in more equal rich countries consume less, produce less waste and emit less carbon, on average. Indeed, almost everything associated with the environment improves when economic equality is greater'. This may not be such a problem were it not for the extent of the stark inequality around the world. While it is often assumed that this is easily captured by binary geographical categories, e.g. Global North/'rich countries' and Global South/'poor countries', it is *within* country inequality that now accounts for most (i.e. 68%) of global figures (World Economic Forum, 2022). For example, in the United States, income inequality has continued to climb, with calculations suggesting it has increased by 20% from 1980 to 2016 (Pew Research Centre, 2020), putting its inequality at similar levels to some countries often considered part of the 'poorer' Global South, e.g. Papua New Guinea and Djibouti. This challenges how we may think about the causes and solutions to sustainability. While Figure 42.1 captures the importance of this overlap between the social, economic and environmental aspects of sustainability, the pervasiveness and importance of growing inequality around the world means that, when the UN talks of creating 'bold and transformative steps' that leave no-one behind (ibid.), we now need to go way beyond 'greening' consumption or local government attempts to foster more sustain-able communities. Instead, fundamental systems of governance and socio-economic provision need to be rethought and restructured, above and beyond the 'sustainability fixes' of old. In the final section of this chapter, we explore what this might look like and some of the significant challenges faced in making the 'sustainability' component of the SDGs a reality.

Summary

- The wealthier of the world have caused the majority of historical and current greenhouse gas emissions and therefore bear the greatest responsibility for taking action.
- Growing inequality, both between and within countries, creates poorer environmental outcomes for everyone, and thus tackling inequality must be central to any sustainability agenda.

From sustainable development to degrowth and sufficiency

Let us return one more time to the UN. As said above, there are 17 headline SDGs with a total of 169 targets. As we cannot consider the entire UN agenda here, let us look at one: SDG 12, 'responsible consumption and production'. Here, the rapid and continuing rise in global resource use—e.g. 40% rise in global material footprint per capita, from 8.8 metric tons in 2000 to 12.2 metric tons in 2017—is the main target for action. According to the UN, this growth will be addressed through countries participating in a '10 year framework of programmes', where countries are 'developing, adopting or implementing policy instruments aimed at supporting the shift to sustainable consumption and production' (United Nations, n.d.). This all sounds sensible and desirable. Yet, very little is said by the UN about what these policy instruments need to look like and do. Commentators on SDG 12 have suggested that how it is framed and acted on fails to address prevailing narratives of economic growth that continue to be steered by business interests. In addition, its broad goals and focus on production and design—rather than reducing absolute levels of consumption—do not, and cannot, tackle the roots of the issue (Gasper et al., 2019), if we think about to the difference between relative and absolute decoupling as shown in Figure 42.3.

What are these roots, though, and how do we address them? Coming back to the topic of inequality and sustainability, many argue that how and for what reasons global resources are shared and allocated must be fundamentally transformed, in ways that go beyond past understandings of sustainable development. One important concept here is that of 'degrowth'—a term translated from the original French notion of 'decroissance'. While much has been written and debated about this term and the ideas it contains, fundamentally: 'The goal is not a better (variously defined as more inclusive or greener) growth, but another kind of society altogether, in which growth and development are not central metrics or signifiers' (Demaria et al., 2019: 432). Here, diverse strategies across scales and spaces aim to transform the norms of current 'imaginaries' and practices through, for example, activism, sharing resources, voluntary simplicity and 'slow food', all of which aim to emphasise a shared, collective and fair quality of life for all—of 'doing more and better with less'—rather than the individual accrual of assets and wealth that has been the prevailing model of a 'good life' under capitalist growth norms.

Emerging from Global North countries such as France, it would be easy to view degrowth as fundamentally advocating for a 'greener lifestyle', probably for the socio-economically privileged. But many argue there is a 'bigger' politics at work here. That is, advocates emphasise the profound global injustices inherent in current systems, even those connected to the apparent 'greening' of society. For example, research has detailed how Global South countries have been increasingly subject to forms of 'eco-colonisation'. Here the resources extracted to create more efficient goods and services—often for Global North consumers—come at great cost to local communities, who often experience the loss of livelihoods, land and even violence, all to feed resources into global markets. As such 'reforming' capitalism into an eco-version of itself will not do. Instead, true sustainability can only be achieved if what is consumed, by whom, and for what ends, is reconfigured.

This puts a very different light on SDG 12 of 'responsible consumption and production'. Unavoidably, this means consuming less in absolute terms, and doing so on a scale that meets the challenges of bringing down overall resource use. This *can* involve individuals making different choices. For example, as 77% of the average UK 'carbon footprint' comes from food, travel and housing, there is a lot everyone can do, e.g. stop eating meat, travel less and cycle or walk more when we do. But—given that the average UK resident's carbon footprint is 12.7 tonnes CO_{2e} and we must reduce this to 2.3 tonnes CO_{2e} by 2030, according to Oxfam—individual action alone is going to be wholly inadequate. Those writing around the idea of 'sufficiency' (rather than efficiency) make this point. That is, multiple social, political and economic policies, interventions and **infrastructures** need to be in place to enable us all to be 'sufficient'. This is not something we as individuals can do by ourselves. For example, geographers writing on aspects of the 'Sharing Economy' show how borrowing, pooling and distributing surpluses face multiple challenges—challenges that can only be addressed if we look systems in their entirety (e.g. see Davies and Evans, 2019 on food).

Where does the leave us, in terms of the concept of sustainability? On the one hand, its fundamental premise—of sustaining viable existence on Earth—becomes more and more relevant as this century unfolds. On the other hand, this chapter has detailed how since the 1980s it became shorthand for one interpretation of viable global futures: a 'weak' interpretation that failed to deliver the widespread transformations required. As such, the UN's opening words to this chapter have never been more apt. Sustainability in any form cannot be achieved in an unequal world where the systems of growth and accumulation that got us here are our pathways to salvation. How politicians, business and individuals take up calls the growing degrowth and sufficiency movements remain to be seen. But there is no doubt that calls for 'strong' sustainability will only keep getting more frequent and louder as time goes on.

Summary

- Some of the SDGs have been argued as 'weak' and unable to deliver the 'bold and transformative steps' the UN now says are imperative.
- 'Degrowth' approaches call for a fundamental rethink of what is valued and why, with 'sufficiency' strategies replacing previous 'efficiency' approaches to sustainability.

Discussion points

- Look again at the definition of sustainable development put forward by the Brundtland Commission. What are some of the key ideas it contains? What do you think is missing from this definition, in terms of how you see sustainability?
- Why do you think there is such a clear correlation between more equal societies and more sustainable ones? What might be taking place in these countries that make them both fairer and greener, at the same time?
- Ideas of degrowth and sufficiency require us to all to rethink what makes a 'good life' and how we collectively go about it. What would a fairer and more sustainable society look like to you, and how might we all get there?

References

Adelman, S. (2018). The Sustainable Development Goals, Anthropocentrism and Neoliberalism. In *Sustainable Development Goals: Law, Theory and Implementation*, eds. D. French and L. J. Kotzé. Cheltenham: Edward Elgar Publishing, 15–40.

Applia. (2023). Statistical Report 2021–2022. https://statreport2022.applia-europe.eu. Accessed 20th February 2024.

Brundtland, G. (1987). *Report of the World Commission on Environment and Development: Our Common Future*. United Nations General Assembly document A/42/427.

Brusseau, M. L. (2019). Sustainable Development and Other Solutions to Pollution and Global Change. In *Environmental and Pollution Science*, eds. M. L. Brusseau, I. L. Pepper, and C. P. Gerba (3rd edn.). London: Academic Press, 585–603.

Burgess, J., Bedford, T., Hobson, K., Davies, G., and Harrison, C. M. (2003). (Un)sustainable Consumption. In *Negotiating Environmental Change: New Perspectives from Social Science*, eds. F. Berkhout, M. Leach, and I. Scoones. Cheltenham: Edward Elgar Publishing, 261–292.

Davies, A., and Evans, D. (2019). Urban food sharing: emerging geographies of production, consumption and exchange. *Geoforum* 99: 154–159.

Demaria, F., Kallis, G., and Bakker, K. (2019). Geographies of degrowth: Nowtopias, resurgences and the decolonization of imaginaries and places. *Environment and Planning E: Nature and Space* 2(3): 431–450.

Dorling, D. (2017). Is inequality bad for the environment? *The Guardian online*, Tuesday 4 July 2017. https://www.theguardian.com/inequality/2017/jul/04/is-inequality-bad-for-the-environment

Gasper, D., Shah, A., and Tankha, S. (2019). The framing of sustainable consumption and production in SDG 12. *Global Policy* 10: 83–95.

Goodling, E., Green, J., and McClintock, N. (2015). Uneven development of the sustainable city: shifting capital in Portland, Oregon. *Urban Geography* 36(4): 504–527.

Haberl, H., Wiedenhofer, D., Virág, D., Kalt, G., Plank, B., Brockway, P., Fishman, T., Hausknost, D., Krausmann, F., Leon-Gruchalski, B., Mayer, A., Melanie Pichler, M., Schaffartzik, A., Sousa, T., Streeck, J., and Creutzig, F. (2020). A systematic review of the evidence on decoupling of GDP, resource use and GHG emissions, part II: synthesizing the insights. *Environmental Research Letters* 15(6): 065003.

Meadows, D. H., Meadows, D. L., Randers, J., and Behrens III, W. W. (1972). *The Limits to Growth: A Report for the Club of Rome's Project on the Predicament of Mankind*. Earth Island, London.

Ness, P. (2009). *Eco-Efficient and Sustainable Urban Infrastructure Development in Asia and Latin America*. Expert Group Meeting 'Developing Eco-efficient and Sustainable Urban Infrastructure in Review of conceptual frameworks and available methodologies for the development of eco- efficient and sustainable urban infrastructure'. https://doi.org/10.13140/2.1.2285.6969

OECD. (n.d.). *Development of the UK's Campaign to Stimulate Public Action to Protect the Environment (March 1998–October 2000)*. https://www.oecd.org/environment/environment-development/37353858.pdf

Oxfam. (2020). *Confronting Carbon Inequality*. https://oxfamilibrary.openrepository.com/handle/10546/621052

Pew Research Center. (2020). *Trends in Income and Wealth Inequality*. https://www.pewresearch.org/social-trends/2020/01/09/trends-in-income-and-wealth-inequality/

Raco, M. (2005). Sustainable development, rolled-out neoliberalism and sustainable communities. *Antipode* 37(2): 324–347.

Redclift, M. (2005). Sustainable development (1987–2005): an oxymoron comes of age. *Sustainable Development* 13(4), 212–227.

Turner, G. M. (2008). A comparison of the limits to growth with 30 years of reality. *Global Environmental Change* 18(3): 397–411.

United Nations. (n.d.a). *Conference: Environment and Sustainable Development*. https://www.un.org/en/conferences/environment/rio1992. Accessed 21 March 2022

United Nations. (n.d.b). *Sustainable Development Goals*. https://sdgs.un.org/goals. Accessed 21 March 2022.

United Nations General Assembly. (2015). *Resolution Adopted by the General Assembly on 25 September 2015: A/RES/70/1*.

While, A., Jonas, A. E., and Gibbs, D. (2004). The environment and the entrepreneurial city: searching for the urban 'sustainability fix' in Manchester and Leeds. *International Journal of Urban and Regional Research* 28(3): 549–569.

Williams, C. C., and Millington, A. C. (2004). The diverse and contested meanings of sustainable development. *Geographical Journal* 170(2): 99–104.

World Economic Forum. (2022). *These Charts Show the Growing Income Inequality between the World's Richest and Poorest*. https://www.weforum.org/agenda/2021/12/global-income-inequality-gap-report-rich-poor

Online materials

- Osman, J. 2020. *Greenwashing: The Tipping Point*. https://www.clientearth.org/latest/latest-updates/stories/greenwashing-the-tipping-point/
- *Images of Earth Summit Showing the Lack of Ethnic and Gender Diveristy*. https://www.un.org/en/conferences/environment/rio1992
- To understand a bit more about 'decoupling' and why it matters so much, you can watch the short video by the International Resource Panel. https://www.youtube.com/watch?v=9zYEpPjYmJw
- Inequality: https://www.bloomberg.com/graphics/2022-wealth-carbon-emissions-inequality-powers-world-climate/
- The Sustainable Development Goals: https://sdgs.un.org/goals

Further reading

Meadows, D. H., Meadows, D. L., Randers, J., and Behrens III, W. W. (1972). *The Limits to Growth: A Report for the Club of Rome's Project on the Predicament of Mankind*. Earth Island, London.
This original report text is published as a book and provides some insight into how sustainability and limits to growth were first envisioned in the Anglophone world.

Redclift, M. (2005). Sustainable development (1987–2005): an oxymoron comes of age. *Sustainable development* 13(4): 212–227.
This classic article describes some of the tensions in the concept of sustainable development.

Haberl, H., et al. (2020). A systematic review of the evidence on decoupling of GDP, resource use and GHG emissions, part II: synthesizing the insights. *Environmental Research Letters* 15(6): 065003.
This paper summarises the evidence for decoupling GDP with emissions and resource use.

Hickel, J. (2020). *Less Is More: How Degrowth Will Save the World*. London: William Heinnemann.
This readable book introduces the reader to the limits of sustainability and the emerging degrowth movement.

43 Nature culture

Bawaka Country including Laklak Burarrwanga, Ritjilili Ganambarr, Merrkiyawuy Ganambarr-Stubbs, Banbapuy Ganambarr, Djawundil Maymuru, Sandie Suchet-Pearson, Sarah Wright, Lara Daley and Kate Lloyd

Editor's note: the formatting of this chapter is different from usual academic texts. The authors explain in a box later in the chapter.

Introductions and protocols

Country is the keeper of the knowledge we share with you. Country gives the knowledge … It guides us and teaches us. Country has awareness; it is not just a backdrop. It knows and is part of us (Burarrwanga et al., 2019: xxii).

We share in this chapter about nature and culture, about how nature and culture cannot be separated, are never separate. For us, sharing from a Yolŋu **ontology** from/as Bawaka in Northeast Arnhem Land from the continent now known as Australia, the idea that nature and culture could stand alone, separate each from the other, simply doesn't make sense. We share some of our ways of knowing and doing nature and culture in the hope this will help you reflect on your own ideas and think critically about mainstream accounts.

First let us introduce who we are. We write as Bawaka Country: we are Yolŋu and non-Yolŋu, a **more-than-human** Collective, guided and led by our places, particularly Bawaka homeland, Bawaka Country, Yolŋu Territory (see Box 43.1). The humans of this Collective are part of Bawaka Country, we are connected to it in our very beings, we are part of it, and the Yolŋu authors, Dr Laklak Burarrwanga, Ritjilili Ganambarr, Merrkiyawuy Ganambarr-Stubbs, Banbapuy Ganambarr, sisters and Datiwuy Elders and caretakers for Gumatj, and their daughter Djawundil, are Custodians and caretakers of this Country. The ŋäpaki, non-Yolŋu authors, Sandie Suchet-Pearson, Sarah Wright, Lara Daley and Kate Lloyd, are non-Indigenous geographers, settlers/migrants/colonisers, connected through relationships and responsibilities to this Country now, placed in cycles of gurruṯu, kinship, by and within Yolŋu family. These relationships are not a romantic move to innocence where non-Indigenous people become Yolŋu but are an assertion of Yolŋu Rom (Law).

DOI: 10.4324/9780429265853-50

BOX 43.1
WEAVING LIVES TOGETHER

When we write, we write together as a collective. We sit together, we listen, we learn and we have done this over a long period of time, since 2006 (see Figure 43.1). Our collective writes with Bawaka Country as lead author to honour the active agencies of Country and the ways in which they shape, enable and facilitate our work (Bawaka Country, 2016). Through our writing process, we try to privilege Yolŋu knowledges and ensure the four ŋäpaki authors

Figure 43.1
Dr L. Burarrwanga and Sarah working through draft material; Merrkiyawuy, Djawundil, Ritjilili and Dr L. Burarrwanga discussing our work with Kate, Sarah, Sandie and Lara via mobile phone (using the big pot to amplify the phone speaker!); Dr L. Burarrwanga and our first book *Weaving Lives Together*; Djawundil reading from our book at the *Songspirals* exhibition

Source: Photo credit: The Bawaka Collective

work to unlearn their whiteness and be accountable for their multiple privileges living on Dharug, Gumbaynggirr and Awabakal Countries in the south of Australia. The collective also tries to attend carefully to the voice used throughout the chapter. Please note that when we write 'we/our' in relation to Yolŋu people, it does not include the ŋäpaki authors.

Our *Songspirals* book (Burarrwanga et al., 2019) guides this chapter. Direct quotes from the book are not indented to make sure this knowledge is foregrounded. These quotes lead the chapter and are followed by our collective's indented commentary and explanations. We do this deliberately to privilege Yolŋu knowledge authorities and Yolŋu scholarship. We also explicitly link our commentary to Indigenous scholars both within the academy and beyond Australia.

In this chapter, we are led by Country and by **songspirals**, also known as songlines. We follow the teachings of Country, which is both nature and culture, the lands, dreams, waters, stories, currents, patterns, people, plants, and all beings that make up our homelands, and are guided particularly through quotes that come from our co-written book *Songspirals* (Burarrwanga et al., 2019). Being led by Country means this chapter is structured differently to many other mainstream academic works. Both the quotes, which are left justified, and the indented commentary, have been written by our collective (see box explaining our writing process). We invite you to journey with us in a different kind of learning.

Songspirals are deep and many layered songs, passed down through the generations and sung and cried by Yolŋu people to wake, make and remake Country, and the life-giving connections between people and place. They are an expression of **co-becoming**, of the beings of Country constantly emerging together as one (see Chapter 7 *More-Than-Human*).

We share just some layers of Yolŋu knowledge here in this chapter, an understanding of nature, culture, land and belonging that might be new to many people. We ask you to treat it with respect, reflect on what it means to you, what you can learn from it and how it can shape your own relations with your place, but do not to take it as your own.

This chapter is Indigenous-led and led by place. It follows protocols in which Indigenous ways of knowing and sharing are central; they are the stepping off point for this discussion of nature and culture. While many textbooks and much work within academia looks to different lineages, such as those from a Western **epistemic** tradition, we invite you to understand from a starting point of Yolŋu lineage, Yolŋu authority and the authorities of Yolŋu Country. Yolŋu ways of knowing and doing are situated and dynamic, are always in emergence from our Yolŋu place and Rom, Law.

Approaching the chapter in this way reveals how all ways of knowing, doing, and relating around nature and culture are situated; they always come from a specific set of place-based connections, politics and cultural understandings. And while these lineages are always specific, they are also always connected, so that the knowledges that you might learn in a class at a university in the United Kingdom, for example, are made possible because of complex and often violent histories and relationalities (see Chapter 49).

Many people have highlighted why it is important to privilege knowledges that sit outside the academy and/or outside the centres of a Western epistemic tradition. Māori writer Alice Te Punga Somerville, for example, points out that Indigenous scholarship is both important and diverse and is both within and beyond the academy. She insists we need to seriously engage with Indigenous theory on its own terms. Likewise, Māori researchers Hana Burgess, Donna Cormack and Papaarangi Reid say that academic knowledge and referencing should be approached 'as extensions of our relational world and as a way we can acknowledge and nurture the intergenerational relationships that constitute who we are, and how we come to know' (2021: 57). They emphasise the need to understand knowledges of community leaders and Elders as scholarship and respect it accordingly *as well* the need to attend to the power dynamics around how knowledge is shared and who is cited as an authority within academic work (see also Smith et al., 2021, Liboiron, 2022).

With these important protocols in mind, we now move on to share further about nature and culture.

Summary

- There are many rich ways of understanding nature-culture relationships. In this section, we introduced Yolŋu ontology from/as Bawaka in North East Arnhem Land, Australia. This chapter is Indigenous-led and led by place.
- It is important to respect Indigenous scholarship, which is sophisticated, diverse and occurs within and beyond the academy.
- Exploring nature-culture from a Yolŋu perspective gives readers an opportunity to critically reflect on other perspectives on nature and culture.
- Within a Yolŋu world, the idea that nature and culture could stand alone, separate each from the other, simply doesn't make sense.

Caring as Country

Country is our homeland. It is home and land, but it is more than that. It is the seas and the waters, the rocks and the soils, the animals and winds and people too. It is the connections between those beings, and their dreams and emotions, their languages and their Law. Country is the way humans and non-humans co-become, the way we emerge together, have always emerged together and will always emerge together. It is all the feelings, the songs and ceremonies, the things we cannot understand and cannot touch, the things that go beyond us, that anchor us in eternity, in the infinite cycles of kinship, sharing and responsibility. Country is the way we mix and merge, the way we are different and yet become together, are part of each other. It is the messages, languages and communication from all beings to all beings. And Country is the songspirals (xxii).

There is no separating nature from culture, not when we are Country and Country is us. Nature and culture co-become together. Many Indigenous ways of knowing/being/doing are underpinned by this fundamental connection. Mary Graham (2009: 74), an Aboriginal scholar, Kombu-Merri and Wakka Wakka woman, explains that place defines knowledge, it comes before and supersedes inquiry. She says place, 'informs us of where we are at any time, thereby at the same time informing us of who we are'. Place is not inert but a set of ongoing relationships. Place is kin, and as family, place has **agency** and shapes and enables everything humans and non-humans do (see also Watts, 2013, Smith et al., 2020).

As Ambelin Kwaymullina (2008: vi), who belongs to the Palyku people of the eastern Pilbara region of Western Australia, puts it, Country is both nature and culture and kinship and connection and more, Country 'is the whole of reality, a living story that forms and informs all existence'.

This understanding contrasts with how nature and culture are constructed as separate in many dominant ways of thinking, including popular and academic Western epistemic traditions. But humans are literally part of environments; humans shape them and are shaped by them. Indeed, 'nature' is inside humans, with human beings made of water and the very same elements that make up the rivers and the soils and ecosystems of this planet. Within geography, there is a renewed movement to understand this, to see the ways that humans and environments and places are co-constituted.

For Yolŋu people, the sense of our co-becoming as Country is strong and fundamental. It is emergent too, not something stuck in the past; please do not interpret our sharing into a stereotyped or **romanticised** vision. We live in this world too, with phones, racism and television shows that you and we have all possibly watched, music we might share. Our co-becoming takes place through our everyday as much as it does in ceremony, for all these things are deeply related. Songspirals encompass all this.

Songspirals bring Country into existence, songspirals bring people into existence. We can only understand people through Country, as Country. Songspirals are not just about hunting and looking at the water, they are about walking, feeling the sand, feeling the heat. Songspirals describe that person in a different way. That person is sitting down, looking, seeing dolphins jumping out of the water, seeing the tide coming in and out. We keen **milkarri** [Yolŋu women crying the songspirals] for the smell of the water, the salt spray on their body, we sing that too. And we dance it. When we dance the rain, we are the hands of the rain, we pat our hands down in a particular way, singing about how it is raining, how we are walking through the bush looking for a shelter. As we talk about and write this, the rain comes. We have to move our notebooks, we have to talk about mädirriny (the south wind) and the season. The songspirals, the rain, being wet, us, we become one (45–46).

Agency and care are fundamental to our more-than-human relations, to the inseparability of nature and culture. In Australian environmental management regimes, the term Caring for Country has become popular over the last few decades. This is important as it starts to recognise the active role of Aboriginal and Torres Strait Islanders play as Custodians caring for Country. However, it's equally important to recognise the active agencies of Country. Country also cares for us and for all the beings of place. This includes humans – humans, like plants, animals, rocks and even our dreams, are a part of Country. Therefore, instead of caring for Country we talk about Caring *as* Country (Bawaka Country, 2013), recognising, celebrating and nurturing the connections that are real and deep and healing.

In 2016, a very strong cyclone came through Bawaka, highlighting how connections of care flow in different, deeply emotional ways, to, from and as Country, as well as through the more-than-human generations.

All these trees, uprooted and damaged. When our kids first arrived after the cyclone, they just came and touched them. They said, 'Marrkapmi, my dear ones, it is alright'. That's why we take the children to the homelands, so they can see. Maybe they will have a tear or two.

We came back a month later. Our eldest sister, Laklak, had been sick. We all piled in the troopie to go out there. Sarah and her family were there too. It was a time when we were sharing this songspiral. We were working on it together, the Gathering of the Clouds, and we had gathered. We needed to be out there at Bawaka.

We saw the new leaves were coming, and knowing that everything was coming back again, that the sand was coming back, we felt happy. The first thing we did when we got out of the truck and we saw the sand coming back was feel happy. The land knows this; it communicates.

The young leaves were red and fresh. Country knows how to heal. Milkarri helps with that. It is a wondrous thing. If none of us came here, some of those trees would be dead. That beautiful tamarind tree that we sit under, the one that gives us shade, had a big piece of iron crashed into it and wounded it, but because it knows we are here, it is starting to grow back (92–93).

> Humans are part of Country and this is caring as Country. Yolŋu don't separate knowing from doing, being from acting, the sacred from the everyday. Sitting under the tamarind tree, whose ancestors (or even the seeds of the tree itself) would have travelled to the shores of Bawaka, assisted by Macassan traders from what is now known as Indonesia many, many years ago, is caring as Country. Drinking a cup of tea or weaving a basket, discussing the next lot of tourists to arrive or planning the next buŋgul (ceremonial dance) is caring as Country (Bawaka Country, 2013). It is care because Yolŋu are taught from the moment they are born about their more-than-human relationships as part of Country and about the responsibilities and obligations that come with this – in everything we do and say children learn about how they are related and what they need to do as a result of this, how they need to interact, how they need to share.

When we cry our milkarri, we are singing the map. We are singing about the dangers, the goodness on the land, what we will find, how we are going to find it, how we are going to survive. The manikay, the ceremonial singing, with the contributions of women and men; the buŋgul, the ceremonial dancing; the ochre body painting, its design; the yidaki; the bilma – they all have to be right. The women's tremulous voices keening the words, the men with their lower-pitched singing, the richness of sound and movement and emotion, the rising dust and sand, the vibrations through the air, the beings of Country coming together as one. This is the land that is never shown to the rest of Australia. We are sharing a layer of this with you through the milkarri. It is in the milkarri, in the bilma, in the movement of the dancing. It is all a map for Dhuwa and Yirritja (32).

> For Yolŋu 'nature' has agency and knowledge. Nature has vitality and life, knowledge beyond what humans could ever come to know. Yolŋu children come into being as part of Country, becoming together knowing their more-than-human kin and knowing what their responsibilities as humans are in this web of life. Through the songspirals, through milkarri and manikay, through vibrations in the air and ochre on their bodies, they know the boundaries of their Country, they come to know who they are and how to care as Country according to Rom, Yolŋu Law. Part of this is the relationship between mother and child, yothu-yindi. Yindi is the mother and yothu is the child. This relationship is not just between people but between people and the land. Yothu-yindi also exists beyond humans. It can be between two pieces of land like Bawaka and Yalaŋbara across the water. It exists between trees, animals, rocks, soil, winds, ancestors, clouds, stories and songs. This is one of the many ways that everything is connected for Yolŋu. It is a web that weaves and holds everyone and everything

together so that nature and culture are all a part of Country. One does not exist without the other. As Anishnaabe and Haudenosaunee woman Vanessa Watts (2013: 23), writes 'habitats and ecosystems are better understood as societies from an Indigenous point of view'.

The songs East Journey [a band from Arnhem Land] write and sing link to everything we're talking about … The songs are part of the songspirals, the music *is* the songspirals. They have the same meaning. They are singing from the heart, with emotion. They are giving the message to the world (156–157).

It is important not to romanticise Yolŋu ways of being and knowing. Caring as Country is real and although it is based on Yolŋu Rom, Law which never changes, it also embraces change and is always responding – responding to the violence of ongoing colonising processes and responding to everyday things including angst and conflict and running around after the kids and doing the shopping and cooking. Yolŋu culture is dances and song, rock music and artworks, tears and joy. Yolŋu culture is shopping, social media and watching television, Yolŋu culture connects everything to life. It is life. Everyone (every more-than-human thing) has culture, including ŋäpaki who may think they do not have culture because it has become so normalised as to be invisible. We have shown how culture is relational and always in emergence, how culture is politics and land, life and kinship and Country. How humans need to understand that to relate well, to recognise and respond to more-than-human obligations and responsibilities.

Summary

- Many Indigenous ways of knowing/being/doing are underpinned by an essential connection, or relationality, between nature and culture. Place is not solely either nature or culture but is kin, with agency, shaping and enabling everything humans and non-humans do.
- 'Nature' has agency and knowledge. Nature has vitality and life, knowledge beyond what humans could ever come to know.
- Within cultural geography, there is a movement to see and understand the ways that humans, environments and places are co-constituted.
- Caring *as* Country recognises humans as part of place, as part of the environment, as part of Country, and celebrates and nurtures intimate connections that are real, deep and healing.
- The message of caring as Country is not to see yourself as separate from nature and able to act on things or manage or control things as if they have no agency.

Learning and feeling Country with care and respect

In this section we look at how you come to know and feel connections and interrelationships with nature/culture. We share some ways that Yolŋu learn, feel and know. We acknowledge that there are many different knowledge systems and ways of knowing the world that are distinct to different places and contexts. These knowledge systems, for example from the Global South or other Indigenous nations, also know and relate to nature/culture differently to many dominant traditions and at times are also sidelined and ignored.

We [Yolŋu] need to keep our culture by getting other people to walk with us. We want you to touch, and hear, our world. Because when children are little, they learn from touching, feeling, doing. But when we talk, talk, talk, they don't learn. We invite you to sit on the ground with us. We can balance both cultures; we can share. We will treat you as family (xxvi).

> To keep our culture strong Yolŋu want you, the reader, to also learn. This is not only learning from talking, but is also learning through doing, through sitting and walking together, touching and hearing and sharing. Culture and being in the world is not solely in the head, not just found in academic textbooks, but it is part of us becoming together. And bodies and emotions, senses and heart, are central to this. Co-becoming, learning together, is not abstract. It is lived experience, learning from, with and as Country.

For us, this songspiral and this chapter are intensely personal, emotional and meaningful. Every mother, whether black, white or from a different background, cries with sorrow, love, happiness, joy and heartache … Tears represent a being or a belonging, a beginning or an end, a journey (7).

We can't be happy all the time. If something breaks, we must cry. If we are happy, we must laugh. It is the same with the land, with the wind and currents, the animals: they all have emotion. When milkarri comes, when us women cry, if something bad happens, we've got to cry, it's part of us. It's all about connecting us to the land (91).

> In some cultures, emotions and sensory experiences are often denigrated. Emotions and sensory experiences are seen as absent in nature, and are attributed to feminine aspects of culture, which are seen as inferior. But just as culture is not only in the head (or only in dances and paintings – though it is all those things too), nature is not 'wild', not empty or a wilderness (Rose, 1996, Suchet, 2002). Nature is woven together by relationships like yothu-yindi, or as more-than-human societies (Watts, 2013). When colonising processes disrupt these relationships and societies it is not just humans that grieve damaged relationships with more-than-human kin, but Country misses bodily and intimate connections with humans too (Yandaarra et al., 2022). Nature has emotions, it is agentic, sensory, rich and diverse (see Chapter 41). And nature is culture. Yolŋu not only embrace this but recognise the importance of emotions as part of the co-becoming and wellbeing of all life.

Most ŋäpaki who write about songspirals are professors, and they write about it in an academic way. It can be abstract and disconnected from life. Sometimes they don't do it well. The emotion isn't there. It's important to talk about this because we need to get the depth. Also, when some ŋäpaki come, they see our dances as decorative, like a disco or a performance only for tourists, but it is totally different. We don't just go in and dance. It must be done by the right people, in the right way, at the right time. We have strict laws about this. And it must be done with emotion (94).

When we dance the shark songspiral, it's very dangerous because it's about how the shark owns the territory. There is spiritual danger. It's very powerful. It can be calm, but it can also be angry, like us. There is a dangerous part of songspirals, a good part of songspirals, an emotional part of songspirals. All these together (91).

> The emotions and senses that guide us, while central, are not a matter of sentimentality or something over-romantic (Hatala et al., 2019). For Yolŋu, things must be done the right way, following the protocols of particular times and places, based on the Rom. This is how relationships are nourished and maintained between people, and between people and the land, so that Country and the Yolŋu world can continually be brought into existence. We must take care and do things properly; this is the Law.
>
> And there are limits and layers to this knowledge. In this chapter, we have only shared carefully selected aspects of the very top layers of Yolŋu knowledge. These aspects of Yolŋu knowledge have been authorised by the appropriate Yolŋu Custodians including the caretakers and owners of the different songspirals. This is important as not all humans can expect to know all knowledge (as is often assumed in Western academic practice).
>
> This means that dissolving false boundaries between nature and culture also requires knowing your (human) limits. Part of knowing the right way is knowing/attending/listening/hearing/learning/sensing/feeling how to respond to the knowledge that is shared. And the starting place is your place, bringing it to yourself, remembering the places and connections you have. Intimate culture/nature relations are central to everyone's more-than-human being – but these relations constantly emerge as every place is different as every time is different. Paying attention to this relational co-becoming as part of your own worlds will hopefully mean you respond more carefully to your obligations.

We share songspirals with you and we ask that you treat them with respect. Respecting the knowledge means not writing about things that you don't understand, not putting things into your own words. The words [in the book and this chapter] … are our knowledge, our property. You can talk about it, but don't think you can become the authority on it. You can use our words for reflection. You can talk about your own experiences and think about how to take lessons from our book [and chapter] into your life. You need to honour the context of our songspirals, acknowledge the layers of our knowledge. You can talk about the very top layer, but you need to be respectful and aware of the limits of what we are sharing and what you in turn can share (xxv).

> We hope you can reflect on what we have shared today. What we have shared is from our own ways of knowing, doing and being, it is from our Country, our own lands/seas/skies. Always this is situated. And we hope you have some insights into the ways that ideas of nature and culture are always situated, are not universal, most especially any construction that makes nature and culture seem separate.
>
> As we have shared with you and you have read, listened, absorbed, and hopefully will respond in ways appropriate to your place and your life, we have made a connection. Perhaps you have learned something through your heart. We have gathered, for this moment, as clouds do. We meet, make rain and pass on our way again. This is in the songspirals.

We all feel the emotion, as the clouds gather, as we do milkarri. The clouds point to our home-lands that have nurtured us, our source of life, the givers of knowledge and philosophy. They bring us together (92–94).

Summary

- There are multiple and diverse ways of knowing and relating to nature/culture, many of which are sidelined by dominant ways of knowing and being.
- Emotions and senses are often undervalued in dominant knowledge systems.
- Emotions and sensory experiences are a fundamental part of connections and relation-ships with all of life.
- It is important to recognise the limits of more-than-human knowing and treat knowledge that is shared with respect.
- As teachers and students, you are invited to learn from the sharing of knowledge in this chapter and to draw on our sharing for reflection on your own relationships with nature/culture.

Discussion points

- What are some of the taken-for-granted ideas and assumptions that inform how you think about nature and culture? Could you seek out community elders and knowledge holders where you live to help you understand culture-nature relationships in a new way?
- What, if any, assumptions and understandings do you have about nature and culture when reading this chapter?
- How can you see yourself caring as a part of nature/culture, not just a human caring for a separate nature?
- How can caring, responsible relationships with nonhumans and place/Country be embed-ded through your interactions?
- Can you think of a time when you have responded with care and emotion to your place/environment?
- What are some limits to your sharing, your right to share and to your knowledge? Are there times when you are aware of knowledge that you don't feel is appropriate to share with others?

References

Bawaka Country including Suchet-Pearson, S., Wright, S., Lloyd, K., and Burarrwanga, L. (2013). Caring as country: towards an ontology of co-becoming in natural resource management. *Asia Pacific Viewpoint* 54(2): 185–197.

Bawaka Country including Wright, S., Suchet-Pearson, S., Lloyd, K., Burarrwanga, L., Ganambarr, R., Ganambarr-Stubbs, M., Ganambarr, B., Maymuru, D., and Sweeney, J. (2016). Co-becoming Bawaka: towards a relational understanding of place/space. *Progress in Human Geography* 40(4): 455–475.

Burarrwanga, L., Ganambarr, R., Ganambarr-Stubbs, M., Ganambarr, B., Maymuru, D., Wright, S., Suchet-Pearson, S., and Lloyd, K. (2019). *Songspirals: Sharing women's Wisdom of Country through Songlines*. Sydney: Allen & Unwin.

Burgess, H., Cormack, D., and Reid, P. (2021). Calling forth our pasts, citing our futures. *MAI Journal* 10(1): 57–67.

Graham, M. (2009). Understanding human agency in terms of place: a proposed aboriginal research methodology. *PAN: Philosophy Activism Nature* 6: 71–78.

Hatala, A. R., Morton, D., Njeze, C., Bird-Naytowhow, K., and Pearl, T. (2019). Re-imagining miyo-wicehtowin: human-nature relations, land-making, and wellness among Indigenous youth in a Canadian urban context. *Social Science & Medicine* 230: 122–130.

Kwaymullina, A. (2008). Introduction: A Land of Many Countries. In *Heartsick for Country: Stories of Love, Spirit and Creation*, eds. S. Morgan, T. Mia, and B. Kwaymullina. Freemantle Press, 5–20.

Liboiron, M. (2022). 'Citational Politics in Tight Places'. CLEAR, 2 March 2022, https://civiclaboratory.nl/2022/03/02/citational-politics-in-tight-places/. Accessed 29 November, 2022.

Rose, D. B. (1996). *Nourishing Terrains: Australian Aboriginal Views of Landscape and Wilderness*. Canberra: Australian Heritage Commission.

Smith, A. S., Smith, N., Wright, S., Hodge, P., and Daley, L. (2020). Yandaarra is living protocol. *Social & Cultural Geography* 21(7): 940–961.

Smith, C. A., Williams, E. L., Wadud, I. A., Pirtle, W. N., and Cite Black Women Collective. (2021). Cite black women: a critical praxis (a statement). *Feminist Anthropology* 2(1): 10–17.

Suchet, S. (2002). 'Totally Wild'? Colonising discourses, indigenous knowledges and managing wildlife. *Australian Geographer* 33(2): 141–157.

Watts, V. (2013). Indigenous place-thought and agency amongst humans and non humans (First Woman and Sky Woman go on a European world tour!). *Decolonization: Indigeneity, Education & Society* 2(1): 20–34.

Yandaarra including Smith, S., Smith, N., Hodge, P., Daley, L., and Wright, S. (2022). Ngurrajili 'continued giving': Coming Together Around Yuraal, Food, as Decolonising Practice. In *Vegan Geographies: Spaces Beyond Violence, Ethics Beyond Speciesism*, eds. P. Hodge, A. McGregor, S. Springer, O.,Véron, and R. J. White. Brooklyn: Lantern Publishing & Media, 83–106.

Online materials

- https://www.allmyrelationspodcast.com/ a podcast hosted by Matika Wilbur (Swinomish and Tulalip) and Desi Small Rodriguez (Northern Cheyenne) to explore our relationship – relationships to land, to our creatural relatives, and to one another.
- https://bawakacollective.com/. The Bawaka Collective's website describes their work and includes links to videos and publications.
- https://bawakacollective.com/handbook/. The Bawaka Collective's Intercultural Communication Handbook, which inspired the discussion points for this chapter.
- https://emergencemagazine.org/ a website, podcast and magazine sharing stories aim to shift ways of thinking and being in our relationships with the living world.
- https://www.gumbaynggirrjagun.org/ is an Aboriginal organisation that has the aim of 'maintaining the integrity of the Gumbaynggirr Dreaming and its place in the world while strengthening cultural practice in a way that is relevant for today, and for the purpose of sharing wisdom of growing relationships with self, each other and the earth'.
- https://www.citeblackwomencollective.org is a website advocating for a critical rethinking of the politics of knowledge production.

Further reading

Bawaka Country including Suchet-Pearson, S., Wright, S., Lloyd, K., and Burarrwanga, L. (2013). Caring as country: towards an ontology of co-becoming in natural resource management. *Asia Pacific Viewpoint* 54(2): 185–197.
This paper introduces the concept of Caring as Country as a counter point to separating nature form culture.

Hughes, M., and Barlo, S. (2021). Yarning with country: an indigenist research methodology. *Qualitative Inquiry* 27(3–4): 353–363.
This paper invites the reader into a conversation about yarning with Country and discusses how to do research within a relational methodology with Country as a key participant.

Larsen, S. C., and Johnson, J. T. (2017). *Being Together in Place: Indigenous Coexistence in a More than Human World*. Minneapolis: University of Minnesota Press.
This book powerfully speaks to the vitalities of coexistence, drawing on examples where humans and more-than-humans are working to decolonise their relationships through Indigenous-led and place-based activisms.

Rose, D. B. (1996). *Nourishing Terrains: Australian Aboriginal Views of Landscape and Wilderness*. Canberra: Australian Heritage Commission.
This beautiful, evocative and seminal piece beautifully shares understandings of Country.

Watts, V. (2013). Indigenous place-thought and agency amongst humans and non humans (First Woman and Sky Woman go on a European world tour!). *Decolonization: Indigeneity, Education & Society* 2(1), 20–34.
This powerful paper speaks of agency in human and more-than-human worlds. Anishnaabe and Haudenosaunee scholar Vanessa Watts shares an Indigenous conception of Place-Thought and critiques the processes of colonisation that construct ideas of agency, so it is perceived as something only belonging to humans.

44 Political ecology

Jessica Dempsey and Juanita Sundberg

Introduction

Why are so many environmental problems so hard to solve? For political ecologists the primary barriers to solving climate change, deforestation, or pollution are not technical, scientific, or even philosophical – although these do matter. In most cases, we know what needs to be done: addressing climate change requires phasing out of fossil fuels and reducing biodiversity loss involves slowing land use change. In other words, barriers to change are political. Political ecologists are researchers who start from the premise that ecologies are entangled with power relations. As a stance and an approach, political ecology works across nature–culture binaries, scales, and silos (see Chapter 43) to disentangle how ecologies come to be produced, with the ultimate objective of changing these relations to be more equitable and liberatory.

This political ecology stance has a number of implications for research practice. First, the 'political' refers to the ways **power** is wielded and negotiated in relation to ecologies and ecological knowledge (Paulson and Gezon, 2004: 28). Wherever there are power struggles, there is politics. Ecology is the study of complex relationships between organisms and always changing biophysical homes. We live on a dynamic planet where a multiplicity of actors – humans, animals, plants, minerals, chemicals – have diverse relationships. For political ecologists the two parts of political ecology are intrinsically connected; as David Harvey (1996: 174) wrote, 'all socio-political projects are seen as ecological and vice versa'. From this perspective, no ecologies may be understood outside of politics and our politics are always material. Their effects are also unevenly distributed, raising questions about who or what is made 'killable', as Donna Haraway (2008) puts it, and who benefits from this living and dying.

For instance, political ecological research building on the Black Radical Tradition highlights the centrality of racial hierarchies in the development of racial **capitalism**, which depends on the devaluation of the lives and lifeworlds of racialised people (Pulido, 2017, Ranganathan, 2016, see also Chapter 71). White supremacy affords some actors (including other-than-humans) protection from risk, while others are made more vulnerable. Racialised people bear the disproportionate costs of **uneven development** and climate change and these inequalities drive species declines. When colonial actors dispossess Indigenous people from their **territories**, Indigenous knowledge of and relationships with the land are disrupted, as is the land itself (Daigle, 2018, Whyte, 2018, see also Chapter 10). In settler colonial societies, efforts to subjugate Indigenous peoples are accompanied by ecological domination and the transformation of land into property (see Chapters 49 and 72).

DOI: 10.4324/9780429265853-51

Second, political ecologists tend to take a normative stance, meaning they believe there are better, less coercive, and less damaging ways of living together. Normative research has long been central to the practice of political ecology (Peet and Watts, 2004). Political ecologists aim to contribute to more equitable relations between humans and other-than-humans by working in solidarity with communities directly involved in repairing relations with one another and the land, thus creating alternatives to existing oppressive institutions (Hardy et al., 2022, Mei-Singh, 2021). Rosemary-Claire Collard (2015) extends solidarity to other species and calls on political ecologists to reject speciesism and, instead, register how animals – as beings with their own lives and purposes – participate in world building.

Third, political ecologists are embedded in particular bodies of scholarship and physically located in an inequitable world; they also are marked by power relations along axes of **race**, **gender**, **class**, ability, and sexuality (see Chapters 12 and 13). Donna Haraway (1991) links **positionality** to **power** and knowledge, to show how one's **embodied** and geopolitical position informs one's analytical categories, research questions, as well as the collection and interpretation of data. Hence, political ecologists, like all researchers, offer a partial view.

Feminist political ecologists draw attention to how **masculinism** and whiteness – as dominant positionalities in the discipline of geography – limit analytical possibilities by restricting the categories used, the questions asked, and the conclusions reached (Pulido, 2002, Mollett and Faria, 2013, Bigger and Dempsey, 2018). In the 1990s, feminist political ecologists disrupted conventional framings of land managers as male to show how gender matters in understanding local resource use. Dianne Rocheleau (1995) and colleagues (Rocheleau et al., 1995) demonstrated that women in distinct societies use and manage resources differently from men and, therefore, develop particular environmental knowledges. Neglecting cultural differences in gendered roles and responsibilities may result in or reproduce inequities (Carney, 1996, Rocheleau et al., 1996, Schroeder, 1999).

The increasing presence of Indigenous, Black, Latinx, and other racialised scholars in the discipline of geography has brought new conceptual frameworks and areas of interest to political ecology. For instance, Alex Moulton and colleagues (2021) highlight a tendency to focus on the traumatic outcomes of structural violence, dispossession, and impoverishment. Building on calls to stop damage-centred research (Tuck, 2009), Moulton et al. (2021) suggest that centring destruction erases community articulations of desire, possibility, and liberation. In contrast, desire-centred approaches acknowledge violence while working *with* communities to affirm their visions and enactments of ethical futures. In this vein, Adam Bledsoe (2018), Willie Wright (2020) and Celeste Winston's (2021) research demonstrates how enslaved people escaped their oppressors to create communities in landscapes devalued by colonists, like thick forests (Shore, 2017, Moulton, 2022), swamps (Peixotto, 2017), and mangroves (Carney, 2017). There, African-descendant people cultivated political possibility and ecological diversity.

Finally, political ecology is a valuable stance for studying issues in a wide range of sites and spaces, even those that, at first glance, do not appear to be ecological. For example, the US military is an enormous contributor to climate change via greenhouse gas (GHG) emissions. Belcher and colleagues (2020) trace the energy-intensive global supply chains that fuel US **imperialism** across the globe and the weapons systems that will continue to drive hydrocarbon fuel consumptions for decades. Likewise, an academic/activist collective in Seattle and Tacoma on the US Pacific coast documents how a privately run immigration detention centre came to be located on a toxic waste site (Ybarra 2021). Their study exposes how the settler colonial state lays the groundwork for profiteering, by dispossessing Puyallup territory, allowing contamination, and making devalued land available to a private company to detain people devalued by the state.

Having presented political ecology as a stance concerned with power and positionalities, the rest of this chapter considers what this means in practice. First, we address how political ecology is done, how research topics may be approached, and what kinds of methods might be involved. Then we focus on a particular example, the energy transition and extractivist industries, and what questions political ecologists might ask.

Summary

- Political ecologists argue that environmental problems are challenging to solve because the primary barriers to addressing complex issues are not technical or scientific, but political, since power relations are entangled with ecological issues.
- Political ecologists take a normative stance, calling for less coercive and less damaging ways of living together by actively proposing alternatives to oppressive institutions.
- Political ecologists acknowledge their own positionalities and recognise how race, gender, class, ability, and sexuality influence research questions, analytical categories, and data interpretation. They also highlight the importance of diverse perspectives, for instance from feminist and racialised scholars, in expanding the conceptual frameworks and areas of interest within political ecology.

Doing political ecology

How do political ecologists do their research? As is true for all scholars, political ecologists develop methodologies to guide the research process. Methodological considerations include as follows:

- the research questions (e.g. what do I want to know? And why?)
- the assumptions underlying one's categories (e.g. am I assuming land managers are male?)
- the kinds of information needed to answer the questions (e.g. remote sensing data, oral histories, state documents)
- the best methods for producing this information (e.g. vegetation inventories, interviews, archives)
- where the research should be conducted and at what scale (e.g. in the lab, with land managers in the field)

All of these considerations are political; our choices are rooted in our experiences as embodied beings entangled with geopolitical processes and each decision will shape the knowledge produced.

A great strength of political ecology has been its attention to the politics of methodology. For instance, feminist political ecologists developed collaborative methodologies for understanding the categories used by local people themselves (Rocheleau, 1995, Nightingale, 2003, 2016). The purpose is to avoid assuming and imposing academic categories that may erase local knowledges and ways of being.

To demonstrate how questions about power factor into methodology, Paul Robbins (2012) compares political ecology to an *apolitical* ecology. An apolitical ecology typically focuses on the observable, proximate causes of environmental issues or conflicts, like local actors' forms of grazing or farming. As such, apolitical ecological explanations ignore the structures of power that manifest in policies (e.g. land tenure laws, free trade agreements), which inform the decisions of local actors.

For example, a prevalent apolitical explanation for GHG emissions is overpopulation. The Intergovernmental Panel on Climate Change (IPCC) 2014 Assessment Report identifies economic and population growth as primary drivers of climate change. Numerous scholars and political leaders recommend interventions (contraception, limits on family size, carbon taxes on babies) directed at women in low-income countries, where population growth rates tend to be higher (Ojeda et al., 2020). Pointing the finger at these women presumes that all humans are equally responsible for causing current environmental crises. However, affluent regions (and individuals) generate the highest levels of GHG emissions (Satterthwaite, 2009, Wiedmann et al., 2020). And, the systems – **colonialism**, racial capitalism, industrialisation – producing disproportionate emissions were driven by and benefit the Global North. Ojeda et al. (2021) conclude that apolitical narratives about climate change blame marginalised women in the Global South, making them vulnerable to invasive policies likely developed without their participation. In short, apolitical ecology ignores racial capitalism, policy frameworks, and consumerism, while political ecology addresses them.

To trace the connections between ecological change and sociopolitical dynamics, political ecologists tend to employ mixed methods (Rocheleau, 1995, Zimmerer, 2015). For example, in her study of a community forestry programme in Nepal, Andrea Nightingale (2003) combined aerial photo interpretation with ecological oral histories to analyse the effectiveness and sustainability of a community forest management project. These two methods are likely to produce different kinds of knowledge. With aerial photographs, researchers observe and interpret things that are visible to the eye: landforms and vegetation. The knowledge produced relies on an interpretation of observable phenomena and is therefore considered objective. In contrast, ecological oral histories ask local people to narrate landscape change over time. The knowledge produced sheds light on observable and unobservable phenomena as perceived by embodied actors; many of whom may not be considered legitimate knowledge producers due to their political marginalisation. Nightingale (2003) treated the results of both aerial photo interpretation and oral histories as partial and placed them into conversation to produce new insights about the pace and location of forest regeneration. Doing so showed how and why local people claimed the programme a success and framed them as legitimate producers of environmental knowledge.

Summary

- Political ecologists consider methodological factors such as research questions, assumptions, information needed, methods, and research location. These choices are politically influenced and shape the knowledge produced.
- Political ecology addresses power structures, unlike apolitical ecology that focuses solely on observable causes and disregards power dynamics.
- Political ecologists emphasise the politics of methodology and use mixed methods, combining objective observations with subjective perceptions. For instance, aerial photo interpretation provides objective data, while ecological oral histories capture local perspectives. Both sources are treated as partial and combined to gain a holistic understanding without erasing local knowledge.

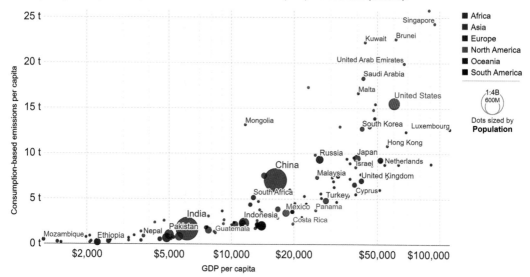

Consumption-based CO₂ emissions per capita vs. GDP per capita, 2020

– Consumption-based emissions[1] are national emissions that have been adjusted for trade. It's production-based emissions minus emissions embedded in exports, plus emissions embedded in imports.
– GDP per capita is adjusted for price differences between countries (PPP) and over time (inflation).

Source: Global Carbon Budget (2022); Gapminder (2022); UN (2022); HYDE (2017); Gapminder (Systema Globalis), Data compiled from multiple sources by World Bank
OurWorldInData.org/co2-and-greenhouse-gas-emissions • CC BY

1. **Consumption-based emissions**: Consumption-based emissions are national or regional emissions that have been adjusted for trade. They are calculated as domestic (or 'production-based' emissions) emissions minus the emissions generated in the production of goods and services that are exported to other countries or regions, plus emissions from the production of goods and services that are imported. Consumption-based emissions = Production-based – Exported + Imported emissions

Figure 44.1
Consumption-based CO₂ emissions per capita versus GDP per capita, 2020

Source: Figure credit: Our World in Data

Political ecologies of energy transitions and mining

This section elaborates the role of mining in renewable energy transitions to demonstrate what political ecologists do, the questions they ask, and the dilemmas they face in deciding how to approach and represent their research.

Global climate change is *the* issue of our time (see Chapter 41). It is also deeply political. The historical and contemporary unevenness/inequities of greenhouse gas production are stark, as Figure 44.1 demonstrates; the richest countries with the highest GDPs produce the most emissions per capita, versus the poorest, which are in a state of energy poverty. For decades scientists and environmentalists have been calling for massive decarbonisation of energy systems to protect people and ecosystems. At present, about 80% of energy worldwide is produced by burning fossil fuels (IEA, 2022a). With increasingly energy-reliant lives, especially in the Global North, the challenge of decarbonisation is enormous.

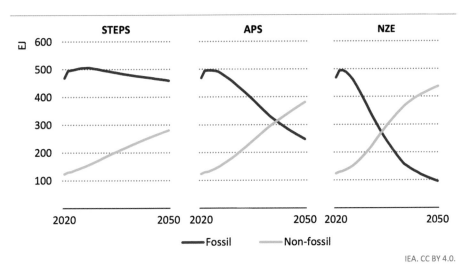

IEA. CC BY 4.0.

Figure 44.2
Fossil and non-fossil energy supply by scenario 2020–2050

Source: Figure credit: IEA

While efforts to phase out fossil fuels have been wildly insufficient, for the first time ever the World Energy Outlook (produced by the International Energy Association [IEA]) projects a peak use of fossil fuelss in 2025 due to government climate policies. Figure 44.2 presents three scenarios for 2050 and shows the associated decline of fossil fuels and growth of non-fossil energy (measured in exajoules [EJ] on the Y-axis) needed to achieve these scenarios. The Stated Policies Scenario (STEPS), which models climate policies governments are already enacting, will decrease fossil fuel use by 20% by 2050, leading to a 2.5°C global average temperature rise above pre-industrial levels. The Announced Pledges Scenario (APS) includes aspirational targets announced by governments; these models assume that all targets are met on time and in full, including their long-term net zero and energy access goals. The APS predicts 1.7°C increase. And finally, the Net Zero Emissions by 2050 (NZE) scenario maps out a way to prevent global temperatures from rising above 1.5°C. World governments have not yet agreed on the NZE. As climate ambition increases, so does the pace and scale of non- energy needed to replace fossil fuels.

Yes to an energy transition, and pronto! And yet, this transition is not entirely clean because minerals are crucial to many non-fossil fuel energy technologies. Minerals like lithium, nickel, cobalt, manganese, and graphite are used for batteries and rare earth elements are used for the magnets in wind turbines and electric vehicle (EV) motors. Electrification, in general, requires large quantities of copper and aluminium (International Energy Agency [IEA], 2022b). Figure 44.3 shows the predicted demand for minerals using the same three climate policy scenarios described above, with their demand quadrupling under the NZE scenario.

These minerals feature prominently in geopolitical struggles. Many states use the term 'critical minerals' to describe relatively scarce minerals (see Figure 44.3). With this designation, states indicate that securing access to these minerals is a national security priority.

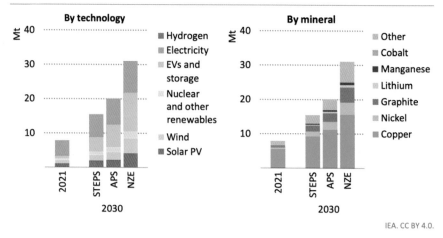

Mineral requirements for clean energy technologies quadruple to 2030 in the NZE Scenario, with particularly high growth for materials for electric vehicles

Notes: Mt = million tonnes; EVs = electric vehicles. Includes most of the minerals used in various clean energy technologies, but does not include steel and aluminium. See IEA (2021b) for a full list of minerals assessed.

Figure 44.3
Mineral requirements for clean energy technologies by scenario, 2021 and 2030

Source: Figure credit: IEA

Political ecology approaches to the energy transition

Does the energy transition require a mining boom? Who is slated to win and lose from this boom? What would it look like to more fairly share in these minerals and their benefits? To address these questions, political ecologists could pursue various lines of enquiry.

Historicising and accounting for costs and benefits: One option is to start by historicising the global mining boom. A political ecologist might trace the genesis of modern forms of extractivism, a political-economic system and mode of accumulation that emerged with European imperialism and **colonisation** in the Americas, Asia, and Africa. How do power relations organised during the era of European colonialism inform contemporary resource extraction and the energy transition?

During the colonial era in the Americas, European colonial regimes established systems of racial domination and land exploitation. As tonnes of silver were taken to Spain, mining dramatically modified landscapes far beyond mine sites, effectively dispossessing Indigenous communities and making them more vulnerable to colonisation (Studnicki-Gizbert and Schecter, 2010). Enslaved Indigenous and African peoples laboured in colonial mines, laying the groundwork for Anglo-Saxon Europe's industrialisation and further imperial conquest and exploitation. A 2019 UN human rights report suggests racial inequalities structure the costs and benefits of extractive industries at global and national scales, resulting in human rights violations and violence against racialised communities living at or near sites of extraction (Achiume, 2019). Building on these histories, political ecologists might ask how colonial extractivism informs possibilities for Indigenous and other racialised communities today.

Political ecologists also might ask if and how gender relations articulate with extractivism today (see also Chapter 12). Has gender-based violence increased in areas around mines? How do patriarchal power relations inform the critical mineral boom? These questions are crucial. A 2018 report by the Native Women's Association of Canada found that mining has disproportionately negative impacts on Indigenous women and girls. Likewise, a 2022 study of environmental assessments of mining projects in British Columbia found that the gendered impacts of mining were inadequately considered (Dempsey et al., 2022). In conversation with these historical patterns, political ecologists can work to better determine the direct positive and negative impacts from the critical mineral boom.

Despite narratives calling for 'green' technologies, the energy transition cannot simply be understood as 'clean'. While the mining sector brings benefits – jobs, resource rents – there also may be widespread negative effects: health problems for mine workers and nearby communities; Indigenous dispossession; boom and bust economies; water loss and contamination; and, declining habitat for wildlife. Minerals for energy transitions in the Global North, including those called for in progressive 'Green New Deals', deepen the burdens placed on the Global South and on rural/Indigenous communities. Political ecologists use the term 'green extractivism' to describe the lopsided costs and benefits of securing minerals essential to 'green' EVs like lithium and cobalt (Voskoboynik and Andreucci, 2022, Zografos, 2022), connecting long histories of exploitation to the present energy transition. Since communities are not uniformly impacted, political ecologists might study why and how. They can also better understand how domestic or international mining companies and even, say, EV manufacturers wield their wealth and power to secure development approvals.

Studying resistance and political power: Widespread negative impacts prompt many communities throughout the world to oppose mines and the terms of mine development. Resistance to mining across the globe has been met with violence, criminalisation, and stigmatisation (e.g. equating protest with terrorism). In 2022, Global Witness reported that 1733 land and environmental defenders were killed between 2012 and 2022. These murders are rarely resolved due to impunity for security forces, government actors, and corporations. Political ecologists studying these struggles might ask how communities negotiate with or resist mining companies and state authorities related to these developments. They also examine the stretched out geographies of solidarity and justice (Figure 44.4).

Not all communities oppose mining developments. Political ecologists can research the strategies communities use to increase the positive benefits and reduce negative impacts. For instance, a study of Indigenous communities in Chile's Salar de Atacama region found that communities negotiated with lithium mining companies to increase their share of benefits, yet still experienced negative impacts such as water scarcity and community tensions (Lorca et al., 2022). To understand and assess the uneven implications of 'green' energy transitions, political ecologists can ask how and why communities embrace or encourage mining developments, and how such decisions are informed by historical patterns of extractivism.

Regulation and re-regulation of mining: Likewise, political ecologists might study the regulatory apparatus that 'delivers nature to capital', as Parenti (2015) puts it. What are the laws that govern mining? How were they established? How do these legal frameworks enable or alter patterns of costs and benefits over the long term?

Political ecologists might ask how the past informs contemporary mining regulations. Dawn Hoogeveen (2015) found that mining laws established during the British colonial era contribute

Figure 44.4
Protestors during the Carnival of Dirt protest against mining companies, 2012. London, UK
Source: Photo credit: Cliff Hide News/Alamy

to Indigenous dispossession in Canada today. The British principle of 'free-entry' implies the right to stake a land claim and, therefore, rights to the subsurface minerals without consulting private landholders or Indigenous peoples. How do these types of regulatory regimes persist in Canada despite stated governmental commitments to reconciliation with Indigenous Peoples? To pursue this question, political ecologists might study relationships between the mining sector and political elites. This approach is crucial, for, as Hoogeveen's (2015) interviews reveal, Canada's mining industry defends free-entry through lobbying and maintaining close ties to decision makers.

At the end of the twentieth century, the shift to **neoliberalism** prompted a rise in extractivism, especially in formerly colonised regions where political economies facilitated the massive exportation of non-renewable natural resources. Between 1985 and 1995, over 90 states adopted new mining laws in an effort to produce the 'underground as a site for the circulation of international capital' (Bridge, 2007, 85). To expose the power relations generating regulatory shifts, political ecologists can study changes to domestic laws, including efforts to streamline mining approvals to fast track critical mineral extraction. What actors and interests motivate these shifts? How do tax and resource rent regimes distribute the benefits from mining? And, are they being used to reduce domestic inequalities?

Likewise, political ecologists might also study efforts by communities and Indigenous Nations to change regulations. For example, the Gitxaała Nation in British Columbia challenges the free-entry principle. In Chief Councillor Linda Innes' words, 'For too long, anyone with a computer and $34 has been able to acquire rights to minerals on the traditional territory of Gitxaała Nation. It is a complete disregard of our own laws and governance' (Follett Hosgood, 2021). Political ecologists can study these struggles and regulatory debates as well as participate in them.

One approach is to work collaboratively with Indigenous communities involved in pursuing such changes.

Is the mining boom inevitable? The headlines scream urgency, with a green facade: 'Canada vows to cut mining red tape as Canada risks falling behind in global critical minerals race'; 'The global race to secure critical minerals heats up'. Although the energy transition requires minerals and extraction, political ecologists might examine how policies could alleviate the demand for minerals, and advance ways of living together that are less damaging. Along with others, some political ecologists suggest a re-think of climate policy in light of extensive mineral demands. For instance, what if governments focused on incentivising public transit over personal EVs, which would also foster mobility justice (Henderson, 2020)? These types of questions can identify alternative strategies. Others point to a need for 'robust and complete end-of-life' approaches, pushing governments to focus on securing access to new sources of critical minerals but also on recovering and recycling them so we don't need to extract so much in the first place (Mulvaney et al., 2021). This could include advancing regulation with strong extended producer responsibility for end of life and recycling. By working on public-facing, collaborative, and action-oriented research, political ecologists can be involved in social and political change.

Summary

- Political ecologists studying the energy transition can explore the historical origins of extractivism and how power relations organised in the past inform contemporary resource extraction and the energy transition.
- They can investigate how gender relations intersect with extractivism and examine the gendered impacts of mining.
- Political ecologists can study community resistance to mining, strategies employed by communities to increase benefits and reduce negative impacts, and the regulatory frameworks governing mining and their historical roots.

Conclusion

Doing political ecology and applying it to research on a topic like transitioning to green energy poses challenges and choices. To illustrate, we draw out two such challenges in relation to mining. The first challenge relates to scale. As demonstrated, understanding the political ecologies of decarbonisation implies tracing factors related to capital investment (public and private), power, and knowledge. Indeed, addressing these factors distinguishes political ecology from 'apolitical ecology' (Robbins 2012). The power of capital and knowledge formations operate at scales that seem far removed from ordinary people affected by mining, from Indigenous communities in Bolivia to commuters in Vancouver. And yet, political ecologists are committed to working locally with people affected by issues like the energy transition, considering their knowledge and making visible their experiences.

One way to deal with this dual focus on both international economic processes and on-the-ground realities is to analyse how specific policies manifest in different places. Rather than broad analyses of capitalist accumulation, **globalisation**, or modernisation, political ecologists succeed at seeing the global in the local via multi-sited research.

Decisions about scale also relate to a second challenge: choosing which actors to privilege. In the energy transition story, the actors include multilateral organisations, multinational corporations, governments, and think tanks as well as NGOs, national bureaucrats, families, and ecosystems. Focusing attention on one set of actors over others will significantly shape each step of the analysis. For instance, a focus on the global arrangements that lead to dispossession in Bolivia may have the effect of portraying local people as helpless in the face of global forces. Conversely, attention to the efforts of displaced people to feed their families by, say, planting crops on land claimed by a mine without examining how and why they were displaced may end up portraying these people as illegal trespassers or 'the problem'. Many political ecologists therefore choose to study across a variety of scales and actors and employ mixed methods to produce a holistic portrayal. Ascertaining how particular arrangements come into being allows political ecologists to rob them of their 'naturalness' – one of their primary sources of power – and to reveal their potential for reconfiguration.

Discussion points

- Think about a contemporary environmental issue familiar to you. What would an 'apolitical ecology' analysis of this issue look like? What would a political ecology analysis look like?
- Thinking about your answer to the previous question, was your political ecology analysis more of a critique or do you identify alternatives? What are the respective dangers of critique versus alternatives in political ecology? Which one are you more inclined towards? How might you develop your skills in the other area?
- What do you think a political ecology approach adds to other ways of doing human geography? For example, population studies or urban studies?

References

Achiume, T. (2019). Global extractivism and racial equality. Report of the Special Rapporteur on contemporary forms of racism, racial discrimination, xenophobia and related intolerance. United Nations. Available at https://www.ohchr.org/en/documents/thematic-reports/ahrc4154-global-extractivism-and-racial-equality-report-special

Belcher, O., Bigger, P., Neimark, B., and Kennelly, C. (2020). Hidden carbon costs of the 'everywhere war': logistics, geopolitical ecology, and the carbon bootprint of the US military. *Transactions of the Institute of British Geographers* 45(1): 65–80.

Bigger, P., and Dempsey, J. (2018). The ins and outs of neoliberal natures. *Environment and Planning E: Nature and Space* 1(1-2), 25–43.

Bledsoe, A. (2018). Marronage as a past and present geography in the Americas. *Southeastern Geographer* 57(1): 30–50.

Bridge, G. (2007). Acts of Enclosure: Claim Staking and Land Conversion in Guyana's Gold Fields. In *Neoliberal Environments: False Promises and Unnatural Consequences*, eds. N. Heynen, J. McCarthy, S. Prudham, and P. Robbins. Abingdon: Routledge, 74–86.

Carney, J. (1996). Converting the Wetlands, Engendering the Environment. In *Liberation Ecologies. Environment, Development and Social Movements*, eds. M. Watts and R. Peet. New York: Routledge, 165–187.

Carney, J. (2017). 'The mangrove preserves life': habitat of African survival in the Atlantic world. *Geographical Review* 107(3): 433–451.

Collard, R.-C. (2015). Ethics in Research Beyond the Human. In *The Routledge Handbook of Political Ecology*, eds. T. Perreault, G. Bridge, and J. McCarthy. London: Taylor & Francis Group, 127–139.

Daigle, M. (2018). Resurging through Kishiichiwan: the spatial politics of Indigenous water relations. *Decolonization: Indigeneity, Education & Society* 7(1): 159–172.

Dempsey, J., Doebeli, A. G., Hoogeveen, D., Quinn, C., and Sosa-Aranda, I. (2022). Inconsistent, downplayed, and pathologized: how mining's gendered impacts are considered in BC environmental assessment. *The Canadian Geographer*, https://doi.org/10.1111/cag.12795

Follett Hosgood, A. (2021). The Gitxaala Nation Is Suing the Province Over Mining Claims. *The Tyee*. 26 October. Available at https://thetyee.ca/News/2021/10/26/Gitxaala-Nation-Suing-Province-Mining-Claims/

Haraway, D. (1991). Situated Knowledge: The Science Question in Feminism and the Privilege of Partial Perspective. In *Simians, Cyborgs and Women*. New York: Routledge, 183–201.

Haraway, D. (2008). *When Species Meet*. Minneapolis: University of Minnesota Press.

Hardy, D., Bailey, M., and Heynen, N. (2022). 'We're Still Here': An Abolition Ecology Blockade of Double Dispossession of Gullah/Geechee Land. *Annals of the American Association of Geographers* 112(3): 867–876.

Harvey, D. (1996). *Justice, Nature and the Geography of Difference*. Oxford: Blackwell-Wiley.

Henderson, J. (2020). EVs are not the answer: a mobility justice critique of electric vehicle transitions. *Annals of the American Association of Geographers* 110(6): 1993–2010.

Heynen, N. (2018). Toward an abolition ecology. *Abolition: A Journal of Insurgent Politics* (1): 240–247.

Heynen, N., and Ybarra, M. (2021). On abolition ecologies and making 'freedom as a place'. *Antipode* 53(1): 21–35.

Hoogeveen, D. (2015). Sub-surface property, free-entry mineral staking and settler colonialism in Canada. *Antipode* 47(1): 121–138.

International Energy Agency (IEA). (2022a). World Energy Outlook 2022. Available at https://www.iea.org/reports/world-energy-outlook-2022/key-findings

International Energy Agency (IEA). (2022b). The Role of Critical Minerals in Clean Energy Transitions. Available at https://www.iea.org/reports/the-role-of-critical-minerals-in-clean-energy-transitions/executive-summary

Lorca, M., et al. (2022). Mining indigenous territories: consensus, tensions and ambivalences in the Salar de Atacama. *The Extractive Industries and Society* 9: 101047.

Mei-Singh, L. (2021). Accompaniment through carceral geographies: abolitionist research partnerships with Indigenous communities. *Antipode* 53(1): 74–94.

Mollett, S., and Faria, C. (2013). Messing with gender in feminist political ecology. *Geoforum* 45: 116–125.

Moulton, A. A. (2022). Towards the arboreal side-effects of marronage: black geographies and ecologies of the Jamaican forest. *Environment and Planning E: Nature and Space*.

Moulton, A. A., Velednitsky, S., Harris, D. M., Cook, C. B., and Wheeler, B. L. (2021). On and beyond traumatic fallout: unsettling political ecology in practice and scholarship. *Journal of Political Ecology* 28: 678.

Mulvaney, D., Richards, R. M., Bazilian, M. D., Hensley, E., Clough, G., and Sridhar, S. (2021). Progress towards a circular economy in materials to decarbonize electricity and mobility. *Renewable and Sustainable Energy Reviews* 137: 110604.

Native Women's Association of Canada. (2018). Indigenous Gender-based Analysis for Informing the Canadian Minerals and Metals Plan. Policy Paper. Available at https://www.minescanada.ca/sites/minescanada/files/2022-06/indigenous-gender-based-analysis-cmmp_.pdf

Nightingale, A. (2003). A feminist in the forest: situated knowledges and mixing methods in natural resource management. *ACME: An International E-Journal for Critical Geographies* 2(1): 77–90.

Nightingale, A. J. (2016). Adaptive scholarship and situated knowledges? *Area* 48: 41–47.

Ojeda, D., Sasser, J. S., and Lunstrum, E. (2020). Malthus's specter and the Anthropocene. *Gender, Place & Culture* 27(3): 316–332.

Parenti, C. (2015). The environment making state: territory, nature, and value [AAG Lecture]. *Antipode* 47(4): 829–848.

Paulson, S., and Gezon, L. (2004). *Political Ecology Across Spaces, Scales, and Social Groups*. New Brunswick: Rutgers University Press.

Peet, R., and Watts, M. (eds.) (2004). *Liberation Ecologies. Environment, Development and Social Movements* (2nd edn.). London and New York: Routledge.

Peixotto, B. (2017). Wetlands in defiance: exploring African-American resistance in the great Dismal swamp. *Journal of Wetland Archaeology* 17(1): 18–35.

Pulido, L. (2002). Reflections on a white discipline. *The Professional Geographer* 54(1): 42–49.

Pulido, L. (2017). Geographies of race and ethnicity II: environmental racism, racial capitalism and state-sanctioned violence. *Progress in Human Geography* 41(4): 524–533.

Ranganathan, M. (2016). Thinking with flint: racial liberalism and the roots of an American water tragedy. *Capitalism Nature Socialism* 27(3): 17–33.

Robbins, P. (2012). *Political Ecology: a Critical Introduction* (2nd edn.). Oxford and Malden MA: Wiley-Blackwell.

Rocheleau, D. (1995). Maps, numbers, text, and context: mixing methods in feminist political ecology. *Professional Geographer* 47(4): 458–466.

Rocheleau, D., Thomas-Slayter, B., and Edmunds, D. (1995). Gendered resource mapping: focusing on women's spaces in the landscape. *Cultural Survival Quarterly* 18(4): 62–68.

Rocheleau, D., Thomas-Slayter, B., and Wangari, E. (1996). *Feminist Political Ecology: Global Issues and Local Experiences*. New York: Routledge.

Satterthwaite, D. (2009). The implications of population growth and urbanization for climate change. *Environment and Urbanization* 21(2): 545–567.

Schroeder, R. A. (1999). *Shady Practices: Agroforestry and Gender Politics in The Gambia*. Berkeley: University of California Press.

Shore, E. (2017). Geographies of resistance: quilombos, afro-descendants, and the struggle for land and environmental justice in Brazil's Atlantic forest. *Afro-Hispanic Review* 36(1): 58–78.

Studnicki-Gizbert, D., and Schecter, D. (January 2010). The environmental dynamics of a colonial fuel-rush: silver mining and deforestation in new Spain, 1522 to 1810. *Environmental History* 15: 94–119.

Tuck, E. (2009). Suspending damage: a letter to communities. *Harvard Educational Review* 79(3): 409–428.

Voskoboynik, D. M., and Andreucci, D. (2022). Greening extractivism: Environmental discourses and resource governance in the 'Lithium Triangle'. *Environment and Planning E: Nature and Space* 5(2): 787–809.

Whyte, K. (2018). Settler colonialism, ecology, and environmental injustice. *Environment and Society* 9(1): 125–144.

Whyte, K. P. (2018). Food Sovereignty, Justice and Indigenous Peoples: An Essay on Settler Colonialism and Collective Continuance. In *Oxford Handbook on Food Ethics*, eds. A. Barnhill, T. Doggett, and A. Egan. New York: Oxford University Press, 345–366.

Wiedmann, T., Lenzen, M., Keyßer, L. T. et al. (2020). Scientists' warning on affluence. *Nature Communications* 11: 3107.

Winston, C. (2021). 'Maroon geographies'. *Annals of the American Association of Geographers* 111(7): 2185–2199.

Wright, W. J. (2020). The morphology of marronage. *Annals of the American Association of Geographers* 110(4): 1134–1149.

Ybarra, M. (2021). Site fight! Toward the abolition of immigrant detention on Tacoma's tar pits (and everywhere else). *Antipode* 53(1): 36–55.

Zimmerer, K. S. (2015). Methods and environmental science in political ecology. In *The Routledge Handbook of Political Ecology*, eds. T. Perreault, G. Bridge, and J. McCarthy. Abingdon: Oxford University Press, 150–168.

Zografos, C. (2022). The contradictions of Green New Deals: green sacrifice and colonialism. *Soundings* 80: 37–50.

Online materials

- Pollen (Political Ecology Network) – https://politicalecologynetwork.org
- Political Ecology Working Group – https://www.politicalecology.org
- International Energy Association https://www.iea.org

Further reading

Robbins, P. (2012). *Political Ecology: A Critical Introduction* (2nd edn.). Oxford and Malden: Wiley-Blackwell.

This book provides an accessible introduction to the field of political ecology, offering a critical perspective on the complex interactions between nature, society, and power, making it a valuable starting point for understanding environmental politics.

Rocheleau, D., Thomas-Slayter, B., and Wangari, E. (1996). *Feminist Political Ecology: Global Issues and Local Experiences*. New York: Routledge.

Exploring the intersection of gender, environment, and power, this book offers a feminist perspective on political ecology, examining the experiences of women in relation to global environmental issues, making it an insightful resource for those interested in gender and environmental studies.

Moulton, A. A., Velednitsky, S., Harris, D. M., Cook, C. B., and Wheeler, B. L. (2021). On and beyond traumatic fallout: unsettling political ecology in practice and scholarship. *Journal of Political Ecology* 28: 678.

This article challenges conventional approaches in political ecology by exploring the concept of traumatic fallout and its implications for both research and real-world environmental issues, offering a thought-provoking perspective for scholars and practitioners engaged in political ecology.

Rethinking environmental governance

Meg Parsons and Melissa Nursey-Bray

Introduction

Human geographers are at the forefront of research into how humans seek to govern and manage different environments, including land and water, coasts and oceans, and natural resources, including plants, animals, minerals, and freshwater. A chorus of Indigenous voices, supported by non-Indigenous allies, are expressing concerns about the worsening state of their ancestral rivers, which they link to Western ways of governing water. Indigenous peoples around the globe governed their lands and waters for centuries or millennia prior to **colonisation**. Although Indigenous systems of governance changed over time and were disrupted by **colonialism** and colonial forms of governance, Indigenous people nevertheless continue to retain their knowledge about and governance approaches through their oral histories, stories, and on-the-ground practices of interacting with and caring for their ancestral **territories**. Indigenous peoples around the globe are actively seeking to preserve or re-assert their Indigenous governance systems over their ancestral lands and waters, which includes their rights to make decisions about how people interact with, utilise, and manage their rivers. In this chapter, we introduce some of the critical insights emerging into environmental governance and management focusing on Indigenous freshwater governance; these include Indigenous environmental guardianship, settler colonialism impacts on rivers, and new Indigenous-settler nations' arrangements to share the governance of rivers.

Different understandings of environments, natural resources, and waters

Environmental governance goes beyond governments and includes the interactions between government and society and how those relationships inform decision-making processes. Environmental governance, at its most simple, refers to a system that controls decision-making about how environments are used, protected, and managed. Specific laws and institutional arrangements help determine the rules under which decisions, planning, and actions are made

DOI: 10.4324/9780429265853-52

with regards to how people interact with land, rivers, and other environments. The ways in which each environment is governed and managed always reflect how a society or the dominant social group within that society knows their world as well as how they interact with the world. This chapter will illustrate these ideas more specifically using the case study focusing on water.

Conventional environment governance and management approaches are underpinned by Western ways of being and understanding the nature of reality (**ontology**), ways of knowing (**epistemologies**), and practices (methodologies). Western ontology, epistemologies, and methodologies are premised on the assumption that humans possess the inherent right to be in command of and control 'nature' (see Figure 45.1). In Western **cultures**, environments are conceived of as comprising natural resources, materials, or substances that humans can exploit for economic gain, such as freshwater, forests, fish species, and minerals. The focus of Western environmental governance is about institutional arrangements that determine who can make decisions about specific environments, which are seen as resource systems, and the management of resource users' access and usage of natural resources (see Figure 45.1).

There are key differences in how Western and Indigenous cultures conceptualise land, water, and other environments (see Figures 45.1 and 45.2), which in turn influence how these different cultures interact with environments; this includes how they govern and manage river systems. Before we proceed to discuss Indigenous freshwater governance, we first think it necessary to provide a brief overview of the distinct differences between Western and Indigenous environmental governance and management approaches. Although we recognise that there is incredible linguistic, political, and socio-cultural diversity both within and across Indigenous societies as there is with non-Indigenous societies, there are nevertheless some common features within the broad categories of 'Indigenous' and 'Western' that reflect how they know water and how they govern, manage, and use water.

Indigenous water worlds: a relational kin-centric ontology

One of the common features of Indigenous ontologies is the emphasis on relationality, wherein everything in the world exists in relationships with one another. Whereas Western ontologies and epistemologies emphasise division of things (culture and nature, plants and animals, rivers and oceans, land and water, animate and inanimate), Indigenous ontologies see everything as being interwoven together, connected rather than separated, and founded on their connections with their waters, be it a river, lake, stream or ocean, and lands, and with their ancestors, and future generations. Relationality does not negate the **agency** of individual actors; rather, all human and **more-than-human** entities are understood to be the embodiment of all things and exist in a relational orbit. These relations, moreover, are not always positive (Todd, 2014, Parsons and Fisher, 2020): as with human relatives, water relatives are not always kind or well behaved. A river, for instance, can be a giver of life but also damage or take life away (Parsons et al., 2021).

One example of Indigenous ways of thinking and how it relates to rivers comes from Meg's homeland of Aotearoa New Zealand (henceforth Aotearoa). For Māori, the world – known as Te Ao Māori (the Māori world) – is founded on interdependent kinship or family, relationships between humans and more-than-human entities (which include plants, animals, rocks, mountains, oceans, and rivers). Māori connect themselves to their environment through their genealogical connections (whakapapa) that tie to specific family (whānau), sub-tribal (hapū), and tribal (iwi)

WESTERN ENVIRONMENTAL GOVERNANCE & MANAGEMENT

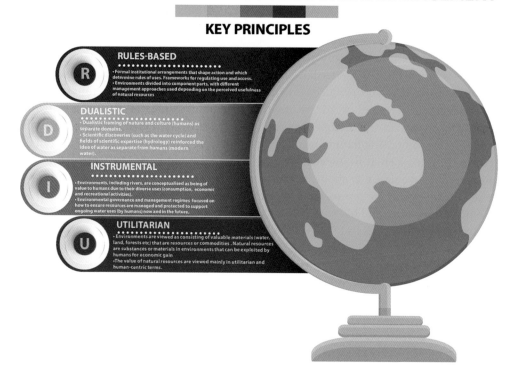

KEY PRINCIPLES

RULES-BASED

R
- Formal institutional arrangements that shape action and which determine rules of uses. Frameworks for regulating use and access.
- Environments divided into component parts, with different management approaches used depending on the perceived usefulness of natural resources

DUALISTIC

D
- Dualistic framing of nature and culture (humans) as separate domains.
- Scientific discoveries (such as the water cycle) and fields of scientific expertise (hydrology) reinforced the idea of water as separate from humans (modern water).

INSTRUMENTAL

I
- Environments, including rivers, are conceptualised as being of value to humans due to their diverse uses (consumption, economic and recreational activities).
- Environmental governance and management regimes focused on how to ensure resources are managed and protected to support ongoing water uses (by humans) now and in the future.

UTILITARIAN

U
- Environments are viewed as consisting of valuable materials (water, land, forests etc) that are resources or commodities. Natural resources are substances or materials in environments that can be exploited by humans for economic gain
- The value of natural resources are viewed mainly in utilitarian and human-centric terms.

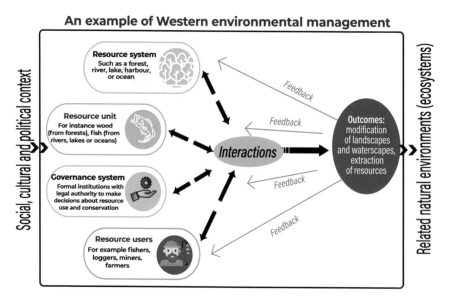

An example of Western environmental management

Social, cultural and political context

Resource system
Such as a forest, river, lake, harbour, or ocean

Resource unit
For instance wood (from forests), fish (from rivers, lakes or oceans)

Governance system
Formal institutions with legal authority to make decisions about resource use and conservation

Resource users
For example fishers, loggers, miners, farmers

Interactions

Feedback

Outcomes: modification of landscapes and waterscapes, extraction of resources

Related natural environments (ecosystems)

Figure 45.1

Western environmental governance and management – Key principles

Source: Image credit: Meg Parsons

Values-based

• Socially, culturally, and politically situated institutional arrangements that reflect local settings (both place-based and Indigenous Nation-based). Each Indigenous peoples (Nation, tribe, clan, language group) possess specific Indigenous Knowledge (IK) and legal systems that influence their systems of governance and management, as well as their practical management strategies.
• Behaviours and practices are influenced by shared (collective) social norms that reflect Indigenous peoples' worldviews, ethics, values, ways of life, which includes what behaviours are considered socially acceptable (ethical and just) in a diversity of contexts.

Holistic

• Land, freshwater, saltwater, and air systems are holistic, interconnected, and indivisible entities. Just as there is hard distinction existing between humans and non-humans or cultural and natural environments, there are no rigid divisions between different environments, be it land, freshwater (be it streams, rivers, wetlands, springs) and saltwater, as they are all connected.
• Geo-features such as rivers and mountains are afforded both vitality and agency within many Indigenous peoples.
• Governance and management approaches centre on the interconnectedness relationships across generations of humans and nonhumans.

Holism

Values and ethics

Scaredness

Relational relationships

Relationality

• Ecosystems are conceptualised as comprising both human and more-than-human entities that exist in partnership with one another.
• Human and more-than-human beings are linked through bonds of kinship.
• Humans and more-than-humans (including rivers) hold reciprocal duties and responsibilities based on ethics of intergenerational care for each other.

Scaredness

• Many geo-features, such as rivers, forests, and mountains, as well as specific plants and animals are of cultural and spiritual importance, which shapes how Indigenous peoples interact with those geo-features and plants and animals.
• Governance and management approaches are adopted that respect and honour the sacredness of land, water, forests, and plants and animals. These include specific connections and relationships with gods or other supernatural beings, or spiritual places or events.
• Water and specific plants and animals are used in the performance of sacred protocols and events.

INDIGENOUS ENVIRONMENTAL GOVERNANCE & MANAGEMENT: KEY PRINCIPLES

Figure 45.2
Indigenous environmental governance and management – Key principles

Source: Image credit: Meg Parsons

groupings as well as to their ancestral lands and waters (known as rohe), which include a specific river (awa) and a mountain (maunga), whom they consider to be their ancestor or tupuna and whom they must care for and show respect to. Within Te Ao Māori, rivers are alive with their own life force, filled with energy and spirit. Rivers are sacred treasures, home to supernatural beings, and the ancestors of specific tribal groups. One of the key principles of the Māori legal system known as tikanga Māori is that of environmental guardianship – termed kaitiakitanga – wherein each tribe, sub-tribe, and family is held responsible for acting as the kaitiaki, meaning guardian, of their ancestral lands and waters. Kaitiaki are expected to make decisions about governing their lands and waters and take practical management actions to protect their river. They are, in line with their kin-centric ontology, therefore responsible for actively caring for their river, just like they would a member of their human family (Parsons et al., 2021).

Other Indigenous peoples similarly stress the interconnections between humans and more-than-human beings and situate rivers as living beings. For instance, as Indigenous scholar Anne Poelina (Nyikina Warrwa First Peoples) (Poelina et al., 2019) notes, the Nyikina and Mangala First Peoples of the Western Kimberley region of Australia see their river the Mardoowarra and all its tributaries:

> as a living [sacred] ancestral being (the Rainbow Serpent), from the source to the seas, with its own 'life force' and spiritual essence. It is the 'River of Life' and has the right to Life.
>
> *RiverOfLife et al., 2021: 40*

Also in Western Australia, the Walalakoo Aboriginal Corporation (WAC) advocates for the protection of the entire 'Living Water' system (including its tributaries, wetlands, springs, and aquifers), and formal recognition of Indigenous Laws as the basis for new river co-governance arrangements, illustrating how the Walalakoo First Peoples, like Indigenous Māori, conceptualise rivers as interwoven spaces that are alive, sentient, and existing always in indivisible and enduring relationships with humans and more-than-humans. Water and caring for water are then integral parts of Indigenous peoples' identities, values, and ways of being. Access to, use of, and protection of water involve both rights and responsibilities.

Indigenous ways of seeing the world and rivers differ markedly from Western ways of seeing (see Figure 45.2). For Western cultures, including within White settler cultures in nations like Aotearoa, the USA, Canada, and Australia, rivers are seen as non-living resources or commodities, which humans can exploit, own, and sell, and can control, also referred to as a command-and-control mentality. Freshwater degradation is often described by Western scientists and government officials merely in terms of the specific activities or outcomes that are measurable and align with scientific standards. For Indigenous peoples though, the degradation of rivers and other waters extends beyond quantifiable and numeric accounts and is seen as a physical and spiritual attack on one's selfhood (Parsons et al., 2021) and is linked to settler-colonialism and its unsustainable and unethical ways of governing and managing rivers (Wilson et al., 2019). Common Māori sayings highlight this way of thinking about freshwater degradation: 'Harm the river and you harm my ancestors', … 'If the river is dying, so am I' (Hikuroa et al., 2021: 73).

Summary

- Indigenous ontologies about nature differ from Western understandings and are relational, seeing all thinks, human and non-human as connected.
- Māori and other Indigenous peoples conceive of rivers as living relatives with their own life force.
- These differences mean environmental decision-making is managed as a quantifiable, measurable, and outcome-driven process by Western science and policy makers.
- Environmental degradation of rivers is seen by Māori as a spiritual attack on selfhood.

Settler-colonial states and water colonialism

Settler-colonialism is a key factor that influences how water governance occurs. Settler colonialism is a specific type of ongoing colonisation. It involves a colonial power trying to displace and supplant the original inhabitants – Indigenous or First Nations – of a colonised territory with a new society comprised of 'settlers'. As such, it is a system that denigrates, marginalises, and excludes Indigenous peoples' knowledges of and ways of governing and managing their lands and waters (Berry and Jackson, 2018, Parsons et al., 2021): termed 'water colonisation' (Berry and Jackson, 2018). In this system, freshwater is distributed primarily to benefit 'white water citizens' (Berry and Jackson, 2018) at the expense of Indigenous peoples, who are less able to access freshwater supplies (for consumptive, economic and cultural purposes), including being unable to secure clean, safe drinking water in parts of Canada and Australia (Wilson et al., 2018). In Australia's largest river system – the Murray Darling Basin – Indigenous peoples are allocated by settler governments only a small number of water allocations as part of a water trading market, while in Northern Australia, settler-state sanctioned 'water grabs' are ongoing, which deny Indigenous water rights (Hartwig et al., 2022). In Aotearoa New Zealand, colonial governments continue to ignore Māori laws about how water health (both physical and spiritual) should be maintained. For instance, Aotearoa's local governments continue to discharge under-treated sewage directly into rivers, lakes, and harbours, even though such a practice breaches of Māori laws, which decrees that all water polluted with human effluent needs to be released onto the land to purify it (Parsons et al., 2021).

Settler-colonial legal systems thus fail to adequately allow for and enforce Indigenous water rights, entitlements, and obligations. Priority is given to Western scientific knowledge about water and settler-colonial laws, most notably about the ownership and allocation of water as a 'resource' rather than understanding it as a living being, and marginalising Indigenous knowledge and laws. This ongoing inability to exercise Indigenous laws, decision-making authority, and knowledge about their freshwater bodies is a source of ongoing hurt for Indigenous peoples and causes water insecurity, and poorer health for both rivers and peoples (Wilson et al., 2019). Indigenous peoples are forced to negotiate with multiple government agencies as well as private actors (such as energy companies, irrigators, and commercial fishers) to try to ensure Indigenous knowledge, laws, and priorities are taken into account in decision-making about their ancestral rivers. Colonial countries, however, continue to treat water as a resource that can and should be managed to maximise economic benefits to people (specifically settler resource users). Overall, settler-colonial societies generally remain unwilling to take seriously Indigenous ways of seeing water as living being whose life and health and wellbeing is interwoven with humans.

One of the ways settler-colonial societies and environmental governance agencies denigrate Indigenous peoples is by treating them as a stakeholder group. The term stakeholder refers to any person or group with a stake in the exploitation and use of a resource system (a river) or resource unit (water or fish). Most governments continue to treat Indigenous peoples as one of a number of stakeholders – such as fishers, irrigators, farmers, tourism operators, and energy companies – who governments consult with about freshwater policies, plans, and projects. Indigenous peoples argue they are not stakeholders, they are Indigenous nations; Indigenous peoples' decision-making rights and environmental guardianship responsibilities far exceed those of stakeholders and are recognised under various international legal agreements and national legislation (Wilson, 2020,

Parsons et al., 2021). A 'paradigm shift' is called for which ensures the **decolonisation** of freshwater governance and management to not only recognise Indigenous peoples' knowledge about and interests in water but also to empower Indigenous people to enact their ontologies and epistemologies, including their knowledge, governance, and management approaches, and laws. This includes the creation of new institutional arrangements wherein Indigenous people share or lead decision-making about their rivers. In doing so, the pathway to addressing historical and contemporary environmental injustices and social inequities experienced by Indigenous peoples would be established, while settlers could also learn much from Indigenous perspectives of water governance and management.

- Current systems of water management are impeded by the impacts of settler colonisation which causes water colonisation
- A paradigm shift in policy is needed that creates governance pathways for the recognition of water bodies as living beings
- Indigenous peoples need to be brought into policy as equal parties – nation-to-nation arrangements – not just as stakeholders
- Water governance needs to be decolonised in practice

Decolonising river governance and management

Decolonisation is an ongoing process (Smith, 1999). It often involves:

- acts of reframing the colonial present (challenging the dominance of Western knowledge, legal systems, and institutional arrangements);
- acts of envisioning the decolonial future; and
- efforts to transform decision-making processes to enable Indigenous cultures, knowledges, values, and political authority to be legally recognised and empowered (see Chapter 71).

The decolonisation of river governance is an ongoing process that supports and tangibly enables Indigenous people's self-determination rights, recognises Indigenous knowledge, alters inequitable power structures and mechanisms, and ensures that Indigenous peoples are able to exercise their decision-making authority about and material access to their waters. It is founded on the need to build new as well as maintain existing relationships between settler-colonial governments and Indigenous peoples. It also requires new relationships between Indigenous peoples, institutions or individuals within the water sector, such as infrastructure providers, commercial water users, and civil society. Rather than being a specific time or individual action, the decolonisation of freshwater is a dynamic iterative process, which leads not to the pre-colonial past but instead is directed at the potential for creating just decolonial futures.

Many Indigenous peoples are presenting new visions of freshwater governance based on their kin-centric worldviews, knowledge systems, and legal systems, and their aspirations for healthy rivers, lands, and peoples. In Western Australia, the First Peoples of Martuwarra (Fitzroy River), for instance, are engaged in ongoing efforts to reframe and challenge the legitimacy of the settler-colonial state's river governance system. This has involved the creation of a 'Living Waters, First Law Framework' based on their laws (Warloongarriy Law), and ongoing advocacy and negotiations, such as submitting petitions, meeting with governmental and non-governmental organisations, undertaking research, forming collaborative partnerships, all directed at the aim of establishing a co-governance arrangement over their ancestral river.

Summary

- Decolonisation of water governance systems requires new relationships among Indigenous peoples, knowledge systems, and institutions.
- Decolonisation is an active and ongoing process.
- Indigenous peoples across the world are active in their pursuit of decolonised environmental governance.

River governance and co-governance

There is a range of different types of freshwater governance arrangements that involve settler-colonial governments and Indigenous peoples in operation around the world and offer opportunities for decolonised policy in practice. Overwhelmingly, in settler-colonial societies, settler-colonial jurisdictions, where settler governance arrangements are prioritised take precedent over co-jurisdiction and Indigenous jurisdiction and contribute to the continuation of water colonialism.

Co-governance, however, is a model that occupies a middle ground between Indigenous and settler-colonial governance. It involves two or more governments – typically Indigenous and the settler-colonial governments – sharing jurisdiction over a specific geographical area, such as watershed or geo-feature, for example, a river or mountain. While co-governance arrangements differ greatly, they are more and more frequently being adopted in river governance within settler-colonial states as part of efforts to resolve Indigenous dispossession, exclusion, and freshwater degradation. Co-governance approaches acknowledge that Indigenous peoples are important political actors in the realm of river governance, and they are more than stakeholders because of their long occupation and use of their territories, sometimes for millennia prior to colonisation. Co-governance is meant to involve equitable power sharing between Indigenous and settler-colonial governments. In some cases, Indigenous peoples participate in river co-governance arrangements that are led by settler colonial governments. Often, these settler-led co-governance arrangements replicate long-standing colonial power structures and governance processes wherein Indigenous people are seen as one of a number of stakeholders (such as non-Indigenous commercial fishers, tourism operators, farmers, and energy companies) rather than as an Indigenous nation (more-than-a-stakeholder) and a co-governance partner. Examples include those in operation in Aotearoa's Rangitāiki River (Parsons et al., 2019) and Canada's Yukon, including the First Nations of Carcross/Tagish, Kluane, Tr'ondëk Hwëch'in, and White River (Wilson, 2020). In some parts of the world, such as Australia, river co-governance arrangements between Indigenous and colonial governments are still largely an aspirational goal rather than a reality. In other contexts, such as Aotearoa, co-governance is becoming more and more commonplace.

In Aotearoa, efforts to decolonise river governance through the creation of new laws and institutions have occurred since the 2010s. A number of formal agreements strengthen the role of

Māori in formal freshwater decision-making processes and constitute a fundamental shift in river governance and management. While each differs in terms of structure and functions, they all share the importance of Te Ao Māori, with an emphasis on the incorporation of Māori knowledge, values, and expertise in river governance and management. These new approaches, which include the Waikato River Authority, Rangitāiki River Forum, and Te Awa Tupua (Whānganui River), are all meant to allow Māori to participate actively in official decision-making procedures alongside government agents, particularly regional and district councils, with varied degrees of authority.

All these new co-governance arrangements in Aotearoa emerged as a consequence of legislation that recognised the significance of the Treaty of Waitangi as the nation's founding document and developed a process whereby Māori groups could file complaints known as Treaty claims about historic or contemporary instances where the New Zealand Government failed to honour its Treaty commitments (through a permanent commission of inquiry known as the Waitangi Tribunal) and also engaged in direct negotiations with the New Zealand Government to reach legal agreements.

Perhaps the most innovative co-governance approach is that of the Whanganui River (Awa Tupua). The Treaty settlement and its resulting legislation (TeAwa Tupua (Whanganui River Claims Settlement) Act, 2017) resulted in the river being named a legal person. The statute also created the position of two trustees (a representative of Whanganui Māori iwi and a representative of the Crown), whose job it is to act as the living face of river and advocate on behalf of the river. Known as Te Pou Tupuna, these trustees comprise 2 of the 17 members of a river governance body (known as Te Kōpuka), whose members also include representatives from local government bodies, community groups, and hapū (sub-tribes). Whanganui iwi and hapū argue that Te Kōpuka goes beyond co-governance and is an example of a local collaborative governance framework that is driven by Māori ways of knowing and doing, including the laws of Whanganui Māori iwi.

The concept of legal personhood being given to a river, a mountain, or 'Mother Earth' was first proposed by Western legal scholars as a way to protect 'rights of nature'. It does not reflect Māori legal traditions or Māori ways of understanding the world, but there are some similarities. While the river is the tupuna of Whanganui iwi, a tupuna is not the same as a person under Whanganui Māori laws. A tupuna is a powerful, more-than-human being that dwells in the ancestral realm. Likewise, a river is not an individual but rather a collective (of people, ancestors, water, plants, animals, and supernatural beings) who are all connected together through shared kinship. The Whanganui River (Awa Tupua) being named a legal person is an attempt to compromise between two different legal systems: settler-colonial state law and Māori law. For Whanganui iwi, they seek it as a new way forward that fills the knowledge gaps and bridges the differences between settler-colonial and Whanganui Māori governance and management approaches. For them, the legal personhood accommodates but does not necessarily fully represent their connections with and responsibilities towards their river. Some academics agree with Whanganui Māori iwi and see legal personhood as a decolonising action that recognises the cornerstones of Māori environmental governance and allows local Māori to be actively involved in decision-making about their river. However, other scholars warn that legal personhood is a **modernist** device that is or could potentially undermine Māori and other Indigenous peoples' self-determination and water rights (Hikuroa et al., 2021). Legal personhood does not, however, necessarily mean that colonial states are willing to fully recognise and provide for Indigenous self-determination rights or authority. Indeed, none of Aotearoa's river co-governance legislation explicitly mentions Māori tino rangatiratanga (self-determination rights), despite its guarantees under the Māori version of the Treaty as well as the United Nations Declaration on the Rights of Indigenous Peoples. The river, as a legal person, is ultimately set within the apparatus of the settler-colonial state and its legal regime and Western ontology and epistemological frames, thus potentially consolidating a form of water colonisation.

In other countries around the world, rivers are also being awarded legal personhood. In Colombia, Ecuador, and India, different governments and cultures are seeking a legal avenue to accommodate their diverse legal and socio-cultural traditions, colonial histories, knowledge systems, and communities' interests in specific river systems (Macpherson and Ospina, 2020). Legal personhood, some scholars argue, can mark the start of new collaborative relationships among different cultures, both Indigenous and non-Indigenous, wherein non-Western ways of knowing and interacting with water are situated at the heart – rather than the margins – of efforts to sustainably govern, manage, and restore river systems (Parsons et al., 2021).

Living Labs are another mode that may offer opportunities for productive and decolonised co-governance (Lupp et al., 2021). Living Labs, an idea coined in the early 1990s, originally sought to build innovative stakeholder-driven research and development, involving them in all the steps of creation (Bajgier et al., 1991). A Living Lab involves different people coming together and engaging in real-time experimentation. Transferred to policy and environmental governance, Living Labs could be developed as processes of co-governance that are then tested and refined to create decolonised policy regimes. In Canada, for example, Living Labs have been trialled to build collaborative and decolonised water regimes (Arsenault et al., 2018). Programmes have included:

- a Lab that institutes Indigenous community-based health practices using a two-eyed seeing philosophy in Saskatchewan;
- a lab that deploys collective knowledge sharing frameworks about water to build respectful and non-extractive engagement between Elders, traditional knowledge holders and policy makers in Ontario; and
- one based on decolonising water via the practice of reciprocal learning methodologies in British Columbia.

In this way, the idea of Living Labs used to establish new water governance frameworks that are informed and rooted in Indigenous epistemologies (Arsenault et al., 2018).

Summary

- Co-governance arrangements offer the possibility of providing a mechanism of management that meets both Western and Indigenous aspirations for and needs for water.
- However, these decolonised arrangements still need to embed means for Indigenous ontologies and understandings to be acknowledged, so that they don't perpetuate settler and water colonisation.
- The recognition of water bodies such as rivers as legal self-identities has both promise and pitfalls for future water governance.
- Living Labs are an emerging form of co-governance that may offer potential for decolonised collaborations.

Conclusion

Indigenous peoples are envisioning what decolonial river governance means. They are actively re-asserting their knowledge, laws, and ways of governing and managing their rivers. Many are agitating for colonial governments to share decision-making authority with them, in a real way that recognises Indigenous self-determination rights and is Indigenous-led. Co-governance arrangements need to build new forms of decolonised decision-making in practice, not perpetuate settler and water colonisation. Decolonial acts (reframing, envisioning, and enacting) provide Indigenous peoples with opportunities to assert their knowledge, values, and aspirations for healthy futures for all living things (Indigenous and non-Indigenous peoples as well as more-than-human beings).

Discussion points

- What do you think decolonisation means in the context of water governance and environmental decision-making?
- Within your own cultural being, what does water mean to you?
- What are the points of difference and similarity between Indigenous and non-Indigenous ways of conceiving water and its management?
- What examples can you find, and how do you think Indigenous-led co-governance works in your country?
- What are the advantages, disadvantages, and implications for water governance of the idea of legal personhood for water bodies?
- Using examples, discuss the idea of a Living Lab, and how could they work and be envisioned as modes of decolonised co-governance?

References

Arsenault, R., Diver, S., McGregor, D., Witham, A., and Bourassa, C. (2018). Shifting the framework of Canadian water governance through Indigenous research methods: acknowledging the past with an eye on the future. *Water* 10(1): 49.

Bajgier, S. M., Maragah, H. D., Saccucci, M. S., Verzilli, A., and Prybutok, V. R. (1991). Introducing students to community operations research by using a city neighborhood as a living laboratory. *Operations Research* 39(5): 701–709. https://doi.org/10.1287/opre.39.5.701

Berry, K. A., and Jackson, S. (2018). The making of white water citizens in Australia and the Western United States: racialization as a transnational project of irrigation governance. *Annals of the American Association of Geographers* 108(5): 1354–1369. https://doi.org/10.1080/24694452.2017.1420463

Hartwig, L. D., Jackson, S., Markham, F., and Osborne, N. (2022). Water colonialism and Indigenous water justice in south-eastern Australia. *International Journal of Water Resources Development* 38(1): 30–63.

Hikuroa, D., Brierley, G., Tadaki, M., Blue, B., and Salmond, A. (2021). Restoring Sociocultural Relationships with Rivers. In *River Restoration*, eds. B. Morandi, M. Cottet, and H. Piégay. John Wiley & Sons, Ltd., 66–88. https://doi.org/10.1002/9781119410010.ch3

Lupp, G., Zingraff-Hamed, A., Huang, J. J., Oen, A., and Pauleit, S. (2021). Living labs—a concept for co-designing nature-based solutions. *Sustainability* 13(1): 188. https://doi.org/10.3390/su13010188

Macpherson, E., and Ospina, F. C. (2020). The pluralism of river rights in Aotearoa New Zealand and Colombia. *SocArXiv*. https://doi.org/10.31235/osf.io/rdh4x

Martuwarra RiverOfLife, Taylor, K. S., and Poelina, A. (2021). Living Waters, Law First: Nyikina and Mangala water governance in the Kimberley, Western Australia. *Australasian Journal of Water Resources* 25(1): 40–56. https://doi.org/10.1080/13241583.2021.1880538

Parsons, M., and Fisher, K. (2020). Decolonising Settler Hazardscapes of the Waipā: Māori and Pākehā Remembering of Flooding in the Waikato 1900–1950. In *Disasters in Australia and New Zealand*, eds. S. McKinnon and M. Cook. Springer Singapore, 159–177. https://doi.org/10.1007/978-981-15-4382-1_9

Parsons, M., Fisher, K., and Crease, R. P. (2021). *Decolonising Blue Spaces in the Anthropocene: Freshwater Management in Aotearoa New Zealand*. Cham, Switzerland: Palgrave Macmillan. https://doi.org/10.1007/978-3-030-61071-5

Parsons, M., Nalau, J., Fisher, K., and Brown, C. (2019). Disrupting path dependency: making room for Indigenous knowledge in river management. *Global Environmental Change* 56: 95–113.

Poelina, A., Taylor, K. S., and Perdrisat, I. (2019). Martuwarra Fitzroy River Council: an Indigenous cultural approach to collaborative water governance. *Australasian Journal of Environmental Management* 26(3): 236–254. https://doi.org/10.1080/14486563.2019.1651226

Smith, L. T. (1999). *Decolonizing Methodologies: Research and Indigenous Peoples*. London: Zed Books.

Te Awa Tupua (Whanganui River Claims Settlement) Act 2017 Te Awa Tupua (Whanganui River Claims Settlement) Act 2017 No 7 (as at 30 November 2022), Public Act – New Zealand Legislation.

Todd, Z. (2014). Fish pluralities: human-animal relations and sites of engagement in Paulatuuq, Arctic Canada. *Études/Inuit/Studies* 38(1–2): 217–238. https://doi.org/10.7202/1028861ar

Wilson, N. J. (2020). Querying water co-governance: Yukon first nations and water governance in the context of modern land claim agreements. *Water Alternatives* 13(1): 93–118.

Wilson, N. J., Harris, L. M., Joseph-Rear, A., Beaumont, J., and Satterfield, T. (2019). Water is medicine: reimagining water security through Tr'ondëk Hwëch'in relationships to treated and traditional water sources in Yukon, Canada. *Water* 11(3): 624.

Wilson, N. J., Mutter, E., Inkster, J., and Satterfield, T. (2018). Community-based monitoring as the practice of Indigenous governance: a case study of Indigenous-led water quality monitoring in the Yukon River basin. *Journal of Environmental Management* 210: 290–298.

Online materials

- https://www.theguardian.com/world/2021/apr/30/canada-first-nations-justin-trudeau-drinking-water

  https://www.theguardian.com/australia-news/2022/mar/06/indigenous-fight-for-water-justice-intensifies-as-victoria-hands-back-murray-darling-entitlement

  https://www.theguardian.com/world/2019/nov/30/saving-the-whanganui-can-personhood-rescue-a-river

  The Guardian newspaper website is worth visiting for its coverage on environmental issues as well as topics relating to Indigenous peoples. It publishes a wide range of articles centred on Indigenous water issues (including First Nations' lack of safe access to drinking water, water colonialism in Australia, and the Whanganui River's legal personhood in Aotearoa) on as well as Indigenous peoples' efforts to re-assert their authority within environmental governance and management arrangements.

- https://www.awa.asn.au/resources/latest-news/community/engagement/overturning-aqua-nullius-the-change-needed-to-secure-indigenous-water-rights
  This blog post interviews the Australian Indigenous legal scholar Dr Victoria who argues that Australia's water laws need to radically change (overturning *aqua nullius*) to stop water colonialism and secure Indigenous water rights.

- https://www.keepersofthewater.ca/
  This website represents the Keepers of the Water movement, which began in Canada's Northwestern Territory in 2006 and involves First Nations, Métis, Inuit, environmental groups, concerned citizens, and local communities who are working together for the protection of water, land, air, and all living things within the Arctic Ocean Drainage Basin.

Further reading

Simms, R., Harris, L., Joe, N., and Bakker, K. (2016). Navigating the tensions in collaborative watershed governance: water governance and Indigenous communities in British Columbia, Canada. *Geoforum* 73: 6–16.
A classic example of the ways in which collaborative water governance operates and the struggles that Indigenous peoples (First Nations in Canda) encounter with water governance structures and processes that remain situated within colonial laws and Western (non-Indigenous) ways of thinking about human-water relationships.

Memon, P. A., and Kirk, N. (2012). Role of Indigenous Māori people in collaborative water governance in Aotearoa/New Zealand. *Journal of Environmental Planning and Management* 55(7): 941–959.
A good introductory essay on how Indigenous peoples (Māori in Aotearoa) engage in water governance and seek to ensure their values and knowledge are recognised and translated into changes to how land and water are managed.

Jackson, S. (2018). Water and Indigenous rights: mechanisms and pathways of recognition, representation, and redistribution. *Wiley Interdisciplinary Reviews: Water* 5(6): e1314.
A good review article that introduces readers to Indigenous peoples' water rights.

McGregor, D. (2013). Indigenous women, water justice and zaagidowin (love). *Canadian Woman Studies* 30(2): 71–78.
An introductory essay into Indigenous women's relationships with water introduces the concept of water justice.

O'Donnell, E., and Macpherson, E. (2019). Voice, power and legitimacy: the role of the legal person in river management in New Zealand, Chile and Australia. *Australasian Journal of Water Resources* 23(1): 35–44.
A more advanced essay, but still accessible, which explores legal personhood of nature in different national contexts.

SECTION FIVE

POLITICAL GEOGRAPHIES

46 Knowing political geographies

Andrew Williams and Mark Goodwin

Introduction: a journey through the political geography of Exeter

Political geography is one of those deceptive subjects, which at first glance can seem quite distant, even remote. Those new to the topic often associate it with the relatively inaccessible political machinery of political parties, elections and governments, or with the 'high' politics of states and nations, of the UN and G7 summits. In reality, while these elements are part of the concerns of political geography, the subject is much broader and encompasses a whole host of more informal political practices – those taking place locally as well as nationally and internationally, and in a variety of settings in the home, in the workplace, in the street and in the community. Let us illustrate this by taking you with Mark on his journey to work, a 30-minute walk across the city of Exeter, in the South West of England.

To the left as we leave the house, at the bottom of the hill, is a new barrier across the road, designed to prevent traffic from passing in order to reduce carbon emissions and promote cycling and walking. These 'Low Traffic Neighbourhoods' have been introduced in selected cities across England but have proved incredibly divisive amongst local communities. Some residents like the car free environment; others resent having to take longer routes to reach schools or shops. Others are concerned about more traffic being funnelled onto surrounding roads. Tensions have run high in some cities, and street furniture has been vandalised and petitions and marches organised. Things have been relatively quiet in Exeter, but we have our first glimpse of the potential for political dispute as soon as we leave the house. We turn right, and after crossing a main road at the top of the street, the first thing we see is a set of almshouses, built in the late nineteenth century 'to provide accommodation for people deemed to be unable to remain in their own homes by reason of reduced circumstances'. These nineteenth-century buildings replaced those knocked down elsewhere in the city which were first provided for the same purpose by a previous Mayor of Exeter around 1400 – a political decision taken over 700 years ago to provide welfare for the poor which has a continuing impact on the urban fabric of the city, and on the lives of those able to secure accommodation in these homes. A few minutes away are a further set of almshouses, these ones built in 1849 by Lady Rolle, widow of Baron Rolle of Stevenstone. A decade or so earlier, John Rolle had been awarded £4333 6s 9d compensation for the loss of 337 enslaved people after inheriting his father's plantation in The Bahamas, which itself was compensation for the

DOI: 10.4324/9780429265853-54

loss of his Florida estates in the American War of Independence. These second group of alms-houses serve as a physical reminder of the role of slavery and the plantation economy in building modern Britain, even in places not necessarily perceived to be central to Empire. (If you want to explore the legacies of slavery further, see the work of the *Centre for the Study of the Legacies of British Slavery* at University College London, available at https://www.ucl.ac.uk/lbs/.)

Next we pass a hospital, and then the former site of Exeter's main police station. Both of these are key public sector agencies, delivering vital services to the public, but both these sites have been the focus of recent debates over their usage, as the agencies concerned have looked to sell them in order to raise funding in the light of national public expenditure cuts (see Chapter 52). The entire police station site has now been sold for housing, and the police have moved to a new building on the edge of the city, and some of the hospital site is now occupied by a supermarket and a private student hall of residence – contemporary impacts of political decisions taken at both national and local scales which raise issues about the location of public services and their accessibility to the community. As we write, local residents are now opposing plans to build several hundred apartments on the former police station site, and planning permission has twice been refused because the density and volume of the proposed accommodation was too high.

A little further on we pass a local authority swimming pool that has been closed, and across the road from that we see a new public pool which has just been built. This is the first public pool and leisure centre in the UK to be built to Passivhaus standards and has been designed to be ultra-low energy and low carbon in its operation. Again we come back to the politics around the public provision of collective services, only this time combined with the contemporary politics of tackling climate change. Opposite the leisure centre stand the main buildings of Exeter City Council, which provides not only leisure services but also social housing, planning services and refuse collection for the residents of the city. Other public services, such as education, transport and social care are provided for the city by Devon County Council, which has a much larger **territorial** remit – an example of the territorial organisation of local government in England but one which is far from uniform. In fact, some areas in the country have unitary local authorities, which provide all the public services in their area, while others have elected Mayors who are responsible for some services. Exeter's two-tier provision is part of a patchwork quilt of administrative areas which have proved a fertile ground for political geographers to explore. In the window of a nearby community café we see a poster asking for donations for the local food bank, an indictment of the rapid normalisation of charitable responses to economic hardship brought about by funding cutbacks and welfare reform.

As we head downhill, we pass Exeter's mosque on the right, a reminder of the multicultural and multi-ethnic nature of contemporary cities but also sadly the site of occasional Islamophobic protests and counter-protests against far-right groups (see Chapter 53), highlighting that global geopolitics can have local repercussions. On the left we pass a small park – overgrown and derelict for many decades but now reclaimed for community use following a local campaign and neighbourhood planning initiative. According to Jane Wills (2016), who has written about this particular park as part of her research on localism, this example is part of an emerging uneven geography of English localism, facilitated by neighbourhood planning reforms at a national level, but taken up unevenly by different communities across the country. Between the park and the university, we pass the bronze statue of General Sir Redvers Buller, standing on a granite plinth in front of the local education college. Redvers Buller was a professional soldier and the commander of the British Forces during the Second Boer War in South Africa. The statue is engraved on the

Figure 46.1
Statue of General Sir Redvers Buller

Source: Photo credit: Mark Goodwin

front with all the countries Buller fought in – India, China, Canada, Ashanti, Egypt, Soudan and South Africa, along with the inscription 'He Saved Natal' (see Figure 46.1). This roll-call to **colonialism** is distasteful, and the inscription is, of course, contestable and would have been questioned by most of those living in Natal at the time, as well as by their descendants today. These monuments to colonialism and empire continue to be sites of contestation, and some have been pulled down by protestors, while others have been removed by the authorities. This statue has been kept but has been the subject of a 'remain and explain' policy, and on the opposite side of the road, we now find a new Information Board containing voices from the places where General Buller served that are listed on the plinth. The board concludes with the message that 'the voices on this board connect us to the places and times where Buller was posted. They remind us that there is no single story in any history'. They also remind us of the role of monuments in producing and memorialising particular aspects of national history and identity. As the Board goes on to say, 'statues are put up by people with the money and support to share a public message about what is important to them. Looking again at a statue can help us think about what is important today'. Leaving the statue behind, which often has a traffic cone on its head in an ironic subversion of the power it was originally meant to project, in a few minutes we turn right onto the university campus and eventually reach the Geography Department.

In our half-hour journey from home to work, we have encountered many of the key elements and concerns of political geography – local tensions over the use of space; conflicts over the location of public services; the nature of historical and contemporary welfare provision; the territorial scope of local government; legacies of both empire and more recent warfare; and community power and engagement, to name but a few, and running through all of these, the 'multiple intersections of "politics" and "geography"' (Jones et al., 2014: 3). The point is, this could be anywhere, and a comparable walk through any city will reveal similar intersections, albeit in a different form (see Sidaway, 2009, for a similar exercise). As Jones et al. (2014: 2) conclude, 'put simply, political geography is everywhere. From the "big P" Politics of elections and international relations, to the "small p" politics of social relations and community life, politics not only shapes and infiltrates our everyday lives, but is everywhere embedded in space, place and territory. It is this intersection of "politics" and "geography" that we understand as "political geography"'. They go on to explore and unpack these 'multiple intersections', as we set out in Box 46.1.

BOX 46.1
DEFINING POLITICAL GEOGRAPHY

'We define political geography as a cluster of work within the social sciences that seeks to engage with the multiple intersections of "politics" and "geography", where these two terms are imagined as triangular configurations (Figure 46.2). On one side is the triangle of power, politics and policy. Here power is the commodity that sustains the other two – as Bob Jessop puts it, "if money makes the economic world go round, power is the medium of politics" (Jessop, 1990: 322). Politics is the whole set of processes that are involved in achieving, exercising and resisting power – from the functions of the state to elections to warfare to

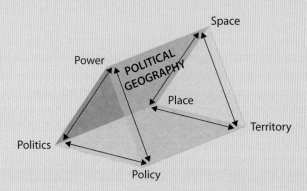

Figure 46.2
Political geography as the interaction of 'politics' and 'geography'

Source: Redrawn from Jones et al. (2014: 3)

office gossip. Policy is the intended outcome, the things that power allows one to achieve and that politics is about being in a position to do.

The interaction between these three entities is the concern of political science. Political geography is about the interaction between these entities and a second triangle of space, place and territory. In this triangle, space (or spatial patterns or spatial relations) is the core commodity of geography. Place is a particular point in space, whilst territory represents a more formal attempt to define and delimit a portion of space, inscribed with a particular identity and characteristics. Political geography recognises that these six entities – power, politics and policy, space, place and territory – are intrinsically linked, but a piece of political geographical research does not need to explicitly address them all. Spatial variations in policy implementation are a concern of political geography, as is the influence of territorial identity on voting behaviour, to pick two random examples. Political geography, therefore, embraces an innumerable multitude of interactions, some of which may have a cultural dimension that makes them also of interest to cultural geographers, some of which may have an economic dimension also of interest to economic geographers, some of which occurred in the past and are also studied by historical geographers' (Jones et al., 2014: 3).

Summary

- Political geography is not limited to formal government processes or political institutions.
- Everyday life is steeped in politics and is constituted by local, national and global processes.

A journey through the history of political geography

Let's go on another journey now, one that sets out to give you a sense of the academic development of political geography. Unsurprisingly, these multiple intersections between geography and politics have taken different forms across the history of the sub-discipline. As the chapters in this section testify, contemporary political geography is a very vibrant area of the discipline, exploring a lively and diverse range of subjects as academics seek to explore the intersections between **space**, place, territory, politics, **power** and policy. Yet at the end of the 1960s, Brian Berry, one of the most influential geographers of his generation, had described the sub-discipline as a 'moribund backwater' (Berry, 1969: 450). What is perhaps most damning about this description is that it came at a time when political turmoil was raging across the world – from anti-Vietnam war protests and race riots in the USA to student rebellions in Western Europe and Soviet tanks on the streets of Prague. And seemingly the 'moribund' field of political geography had little or nothing to say about the most momentous political events of the era. As well as introducing the seven chapters in this section, the rest of this introduction traces how we got from there to here – from being a moribund backwater to a position where political geography is not only thriving as a sub-discipline but is also influencing debates across the social sciences, as we will see in the chapters which cover Collaborations with Justice in the final part of the book. Space precludes consideration of the earlier history of political geography, but for very good analyses of the period up to the 1960s, see Agnew and Muscara (2012), Herb (2008) and Jones et al. (2014).

The statement that the 'personal is political' has achieved quite widespread currency since it was first used as part of the **feminist** movement in the 1960s. It neatly sums up the idea that politics is to be found in each and every aspect of our daily lives and is not restricted to the more formal machinery of parliament and government. The latter concern with formal politics dominated political geography for many years and led to an emphasis on a seemingly distant and specialised sphere of activity to do with political parties, elections, governments and public policy. Although there was the notion that everyday life was affected by such processes, there was little conception that politics was actually part of our day-to-day lives. It was something that was carried out by other people (politicians and civil servants) and that went on elsewhere (in government institutions).

More recently, however, this view has changed in three key ways. First, there has been a realisation that the formal politics of government and the state have much more impact on our daily lives than hitherto thought, and second, there has been a far broader examination of a whole host of informal politics – taking place in the home, in the workplace, in the street and in the community. Underlying both of these has been a huge increase in the theoretical and conceptual literatures that political geographers have turned to for inspiration. Third, the sub-discipline has responded to a number of cataclysmic events across the globe, which have generated new areas and avenues of enquiry. Let's take these issues one by one. First, while the role the state and government play in people's lives in a dictatorship, or an absolute monarchy, say North Korea or Saudi Arabia, has always been clear, in liberal democracies it was easier to promote the idea of a separate realm of government, distinct from people's everyday lives. However, in reality, the state touches every aspect of our lives (see Painter and Jeffrey, 2009: 19, for an example of how formal politics affects your night out – from where and when you can buy an alcoholic drink to what time the last bus goes). This has been particularly clear throughout the COVID-19 pandemic, when governments across the world brought in strict controls over people's travel and behaviour, but the advent of 'populist' governments in many western countries had already sought to control people's rights – their right to protest, their right to seek refuge, their right to migrate and in the USA their right to abortion (see Chapter 53). All these moves have come under investigation by political geographers, as government practices shifted those intersections between politics and geography that we described earlier.

Second, the scope of what was legitimate for political geography to study widened as the critical geography that we discussed in Chapter 1 gained a foothold across the discipline during the 1970s and 1980s. **Marxist political economy** was used to underpin analyses of urban development and community struggles; feminist geographers not only critiqued the masculine bias of much conventional political geography, but they also opened up avenues to study the **gendered** politics of the home, and the household, and identified the body as a site of political struggle; the 'cultural turn' of the 1980s and 1990s led to a focus on the politics of identity and **representation**, and on the **discourses** which carry particular political meanings and framings as they flow through the popular press, film, TV, news and photography; and **postcolonial** geography was used to critique conventional geopolitics and uncover the multiple political practices that have been used to maintain western dominance (see Chapter 49). Jones et al. (2014), Painter and Jeffrey (2009) and Squire and Jackman (2023) all provide excellent accounts of these shifting objects of study along with the changing ways of studying.

Third, like other areas of the discipline, political geography is constantly affected by what is happening across society and politics. The terrorist attacks on the USA in 2001 and the subsequent wars in Iraq and Afghanistan led to a renewed interest in international relations and geopolitics, as well as in war and security studies; the rise of Trump, Brexit and populist politics has resulted in a revitalisation of electoral geography, as well as major studies of the continuing effects of the **neoliberal** policies these governments have promoted; the continued effects of climate change on our environment and society and the moves towards net zero and carbon reduction have prompted a vital interest in environmental politics and in direct action; and of course, the global tragedy of COVID-19 has resulted in a new interest in bio-politics and bio-security, and in the links between geographies of health and political geographies, as well as in those between animals and humans.

Summary

- Political geography is a thriving and influential sub-discipline, exploring various intersections between space, place, territory, politics, power and policy.

A journey through this section

Political geography then continues to evolve, as new concepts and theories come into play and new subjects arise to study. Inevitably we can only present a slice of this in the chapters available to us, and there are many areas of political geography we have not been able to devote a chapter to, although some of these are touched on elsewhere in the book. As Jones et al point out in Box 46.1, the cultural dimensions of politics are of interest to cultural geographers, the social dimensions to social geographers, the environmental dimensions to environmental geographers, the urban dimensions to urban geographers and so on. So while we do not devote a chapter in this section to the politics of gender and sexuality, say, we do cover this topic in Chapters 12 and 72, and we cover the politics of **race** and **ethnicity** in Chapters 13 and 70, and the politics of the environment and climate change in Chapters 41, 44, 45 and 65. The seven chapters in this section provide a mixture, with some looking at key concepts in the sub-discipline – Territoriality, Borders, Neoliberalism – while others involve an analysis of particular substantive topics – Nationalism, Colonialism, Geopolitics and Protest. Between the concepts and the topics, we will showcase how power, politics and policy are related to space, place and territory and also explore how different theoretical currents continue to shape the development of political geography.

In Chapter 47, Sam Halvorsen and Rogério Haesbaert look at the foundational concept of territory, both as an academic term and as a practical category used by social groups. They begin by analysing the long association of territory with the ideas of state space, the **nation-state** and sovereignty, before covering the rescaling of territory beyond the nation-state – both 'upwards' to supra-national organisations, such as the UN and the EU, and 'downwards' to local agencies and social groups. They also introduce recent moves to recast territory as a relational concept, linked to social actors and communities beyond the state, and by using examples from Latin America, they describe the increasing richness of the term as it becomes increasingly used as a site for political identity and mobilisation.

Chapter 48, by Angharad Closs Stephens and Franz Bernhardt, explores a set of interlinked topics which have long been prominent within political geography, those of the nation, nation-state and nationalism. They use events from the 'exceptional' year of 2020 – especially the COVID-19 pandemic, and the Black Lives Matter protests – to expose different understandings of these three terms. In so doing they show how national identity is not fixed and stable but rather is performed and narrated through multiple sites and activities.

In Chapter 49, Amba Sepie looks at another long-standing topic in political geography, that of Colonialism and Colonisation, and she shows how these terms have been contested both within and outside academia. The chapter draws from Indigenous and postcolonial writings to examine European colonialism and its ongoing legacies in social and political life. Sepie argues Indigenous and traditional Earth minded land bases and cultures offer a worldview very different from those that Westernised peoples are accustomed to, and one from which people have much to learn.

In Chapter 50, Gabriel Popescu develops a theme introduced in Chapter 47 on Territory to explore another key concept within political geography, that of the Border. Gabriel shows how borders are typically understood as lines marking the limit of a territorial entity and explores how increasing **globalisation** has led to an increase in the number, types and complexity of borders and border geography. He uses the example of digital technology and 'smart' borders to uncover how nations are seeking to reconcile mobility across borders with security within them and shows how borders are not 'natural', as some would have us believe, but are, in fact, **social constructions**, grounded in cultural and political practice and power dynamics.

Chapter 51 brings us back to another long-established topic within political geography, that of Geopolitics. Indeed, as Sara Fregonese points out, some of the very first writings in political geography, at the turn of the twentieth century, were about geopolitics, by Sir Halford Mackinder, the first dedicated scholar of geography at a UK university, as well as a geopolitical theorist, MP and imperial statesman. The chapter then moves from coverage of this conventional geopolitics to a deeper examination of what is termed 'Critical Geopolitics', and Fregonese uses the examples of **embodied** and emotional geopolitics, and urban geopolitics, to chart how geopolitics has come to focus on the everyday 'little things' of life as well as the 'big things' of international politics and state power.

In Chapter 52, Julie MacLeavy examines a key concept which has recently become central, not just to political geography but also to the social sciences as a whole. This is the notion of **Neoliberalism**, and Julie analyses the understanding and use of the term within human geography. She shows how the idea of neoliberalism first gained prominence in the 1970s and 1980s when it emerged as a particular type of political project aimed at reducing the power of the state in favour of increasing market-led competition. The chapter charts how once state intervention had been 'rolled-back', neoliberalism then involved 'rolling out' a set of policies – but crucially, these were not rolled out evenly either within or between countries, and Julie examines how the work of geographers has been vital to exposing the uneven and varied nature of the neoliberal transition. The chapter ends by looking at the social, spatial and environmental impacts of neo-liberal policies.

The final chapter in this section, by Richard White, looks at the topic of Activism and Protest. Again, this topic has a long history within political geography, dating from the **anarchist** geography of Peter Kropotkin and Elisee Reclus in the late nineteenth century (Livingstone, 1992). Richard places the autonomous geographies of today in the context of anarchism and anarchist geographies, and also shows how place and space are often central to activism and protest. He shows how activism literally 'takes place' across a wide range of sites, from the household to the allotment and is not restricted to the popular notions of activism and protest which involve waving a banner and marching in a public space.

Taken together, these chapters provide excellent examples of the movement of political geography away from a concentration on formal politics to an exploration of the myriad spaces of informal politics. Yet they also show the continued importance of the formal political sphere, and of governments and nation-states. Indeed, if there is one thing that the COVID-19 pandemic and its aftermath have shown us, it is the continuing authority of the state to enact and pursue policies within their own borders and over their own territories – policies which are often very distinct and varied from those of other countries. The challenge for the future, perhaps, is to examine these two spheres together, by looking at how each affects the shaping of the other, rather than continuing to see them as separate. Each chapter gives a pointer to the very exciting areas of enquiry that emerge if this is done, as political geography continues to trace the multiple intersections between politics, power and policy, and place, space and territory.

Discussion points

* Try documenting your own journey to work or study. What everyday themes of political geography can you identify?
* How has the study of political geography evolved over time?
* What role have Marxist, feminist and postcolonial perspectives played in shaping the development of political geography?

References

Agnew, J., and Muscara, L. (2012). *Making Political Geography*. Lanham, Maryland: Rowman and Littlefield.

Berry, B. J. (1969). Book review. *The Geographical Review* 59(3): 450–451.

Herb, G. (2008). Chapter 1: The Politics of Political Geography. In *The Sage Handbook of Political Geography*, eds. K. Cox, M. Low, and J. Robinson. London: Sage, 21–40.

Jessop, R. (1990). *State Theory*. Cambridge: Polity.

Jones, M., Jones, R., Woods, M., Whitehead, M., Dixon, D., and Hannah, M. (2014). *An Introduction to Political Geography: Space, Place and Politics*. London: Routledge.

Livingstone, D. (1992). *The Geographical Tradition*. Oxford: Blackwell.

Painter, J., and Jeffrey, A. (2009). *Political Geography*. London: Sage.

Sidaway, J. (2009). Shadows on the path: negotiating geopolitics on an urban section of Britain's South West Coast Path. *Environment and Planning D: Society and Space* 27(2009): 1091–1116.

Squire, R., and Jackman, A. (2023). *Political Geography: Approaches, Concepts, Futures*. London: Sage.

Wills, J. (2016). Emerging geographies of English localism: the case of neighbourhood planning. *Political Geography* 53(2016): 43–53.

Further reading

Cox, K., Low, M., and Robinson, J. (eds.) (2008). *The Sage Handbook of Political Geography*. London: Sage.
An extensive, edited collection of chapters covering most aspects of political geography.

Flint, C., and Taylor, P. (2018). *Political Geography: World-Economy, Nation-State and Locality*. Harlow: Pearson.
The seventh edition of a now classic textbook, with a particular grounding in world-systems theory.

Jones, M., Jones, R., Woods, M., Whitehead, M., Dixon, D., and Hannah, M. (2014). *An Introduction to Political Geography: Space, Place and Politics*. London: Routledge.
A very readable textbook, with an excellent opening chapter which covers the history of political geography.

Painter, J., and Jeffrey, A. (2009). *Political Geography*. London: Sage.
The second edition of a thoughtful textbook, which deliberately interrogates politics and geography in order to explore the relationship between the two.

Smith, S. (2020). *Political Geography: A Critical Introduction*. Hoboken, New Jersey: Wiley-Blackwell.
A textbook which weaves postcolonial and feminist approaches into the concerns of political geography.

Squire, R., and Jackman, A. (2023). *Political Geography: Approaches, Concepts, Futures*. London: Sage.
A cutting-edge textbook for political geography students covering a wide range of topics, including feminist geopolitics, non-human worlds, decolonisation movements, popular culture, nationalism, peace, and resistance. It provides ideas for practical dissertation research and includes tasks to facilitate active follow-on learning.

Sultana, F. (2022). The unbearable heaviness of climate coloniality. *Political Geography* 99: 102638.
A critical introduction to how political geography is vital to understanding climate change.

For the most up-to-date writings on political geography, you should scan recent editions of the journals *Political Geography, Space and Polity* and *Environment and Planning C: Politics and Space*. These will all give you a sense of the current topics being pursued in the field.

47 Territory

*Rogério Haesbaert da Costa
and Sam Halvorsen*

Introduction

Territory is one of the most widespread and polysemic spatial concepts both within and outside the geographical discipline. It is often used to simply refer to the physical-material base of social processes. By tradition, in geography and political science, the term has a narrower association with the sovereign space of the **nation-state**. Nevertheless, today we are able to view territory in a much more open way through the different power relations exercised in processes of appropriating and/or dominating space, across multiple dimensions (e.g. state-military power, economic power, symbolic power). As such, to talk of territory necessarily implies appreciating the set of relations through which it is constructed, reconstructed and destroyed, what is sometimes referred to as a dynamic process of territorialisation, deterritorialisation and reterritorialisation.

The transdisciplinary character of territory is evident once we acknowledge that debate over its meaning and function was not only born within geography and political science but also in the natural sciences, in particular biology and the study of animal behaviour (ethology) in relation to the territoriality of different species. This has opened a recurring discussion on the relationship between territory and human and non- or more-than-human territorialities. We should also note the existence of a debate over territory/territoriality in disciplines such as sociology, economics (despite a preference for geographical concepts such as **space** and region), anthropology (especially over territoriality as an identity) and psychology (individual territory).

Beyond its intellectual treatment as an analytical category of the social sciences and in ethology, territory must also be recognised as a practical category, used in everyday life by many social groups. In some cases, such as Indigenous communities, it is used as a tool in their struggle for the defence of land and greater territorial autonomy. In this sense, we can also identify a normative characteristic of territory, often present in diverse policies of land and urban planning by the state or related institutions. We can thus distinguish between **hegemonic** or top-down territories and **subaltern** or bottom-up territories. In turn, we can locate territory as a core strategy of both **colonisation** and **decolonisation**.

Finally, territory is necessarily a relational category. By this we mean it is created (and destroyed) by social relations of power that are, in turn, part of a broader set of historically and geographically dependent contexts. Territory is necessarily related to the relations of power where people, things and environments are always intertwined (see Jessop et al., 2008). Territory cannot be understood without its relationship to multiple spaces and places, practices and meanings that are both relatively fixed in location and travel through networks and scales such as political institutions or the internet.

DOI: 10.4324/9780429265853-55

Territory as state space: foundational ideas

Territory has a long history going back at least to the juridical system of the Roman Empire (Elden, 2013). Its relationship with **power** and state sovereignty is the most pervasive element. From around the late nineteenth century, and through German geography and the work of Friedrich Ratzel (1897), the nation-state and its borders have been understood as part of a territorial strategy for controlling the flow and flux of economies, populations and information. The production/delimitation of territory has also served to strengthen the 'imagined community' of the nation (Anderson, 1983). From an economic perspective, territory as sovereign state space has had many tos and fros with the long history of **capitalism**, at times strengthening its capacity to control economic flows and consolidating them in a national market, at other times opening its frontiers and administering regional units such as the European Union or even facilitating the **globalisation** of the circulation of capital (Harvey, 2003).

Another classic geographer from this perspective is Jean Gottmann (1973) who deepened the debate on the institutionalisation of territory by states while also recognising the reproduction of their territorial logics across different scales, including the international. Gottmann understood there to be a double dimension of territory: material and symbolic ('iconographic', as he called it) and a difference between territory as a shelter/security and as a resource. Territory is thus caught between the search for securing and preserving existing communities while also seeking to open out to new opportunities. In practice, one of these dimensions may predominate. For example, a marginalised social group may look to territory as a shelter, as was the case with the formation of the gay area in San Francisco's Castro district in the 1970s and 1980s (Castells, 1983) (Figure 47.1).

Figure 47.1
The gay community of Castro, San Francisco

Source: Photo credit: Aurore Kervoerm/Getty

In contrast, capitalist corporations may seek, above all else, to exploit territory as a resource, as has been suggested regarding US corporations following the Iraq invasion (Harvey, 2003).

A large part of state territorial activity is orientated towards *planning* territory as an integrated and multi-scalar form. In its assumed role as a regulator of the distribution of services across the territory, the state appears to propose and develop a new order of space with the objective of reducing inequalities. Yet this logic finds itself in direct contradiction with capital's need to produce territory through **creative destruction** in which **uneven development** and territorial inequalities are in-built mechanisms (Smith, 1984).

The territorial trap and political technologies

By the late twentieth century, a particular understanding of territory, as a bounded 'container' of state-society relations, had become dominant in the social sciences. This definition was particularly strong in international relations, a discipline that tended to take for granted the co-existence of nation-states as territorially bound and mutually exclusive units. John Agnew (1994) noted three assumptions underlying such understandings: (i) the state's territory is a fixed, ahistorical unit of sovereign power (i.e. it is the only way to secure political organisation); (ii) territorial states are based on a clear distinction between domestic and foreign affairs; (iii) all of 'society' is contained within the state's territory. These assumptions reinforce each other and create a 'territorial trap' that fails to acknowledge how the territorial state is a historically and geographically specific form (i.e. it has not existed everywhere and at all times) and prevents us from appreciating diverse social activity (from trade to migration) that operate across multiple scales and networks.

State territory is a dominant way of organising and controlling space whose idea emerged in Western Europe with the Roman Empire and consolidated after its passage into **modernity**. In a landmark text, Stuart Elden (2013) meticulously traces how this modern idea of territory came into being. For Elden, territory is a *political technology*, by which he refers to two elements. On the one hand, the birth of territory was a response to modern technological advances in, for example, cartography, which made the strategy of mapping, demarcating and controlling political space a new historical possibility. On the other hand, territory is a modern technique of government that uses particular ideas and practices through legal, military, economic and other systems. As such Elden demonstrates that territory cannot be reduced to the related categories of land (economy) and terrain (political-strategic); it is a complex set of modern processes that allow space to be organised and controlled by the state and its sovereign power.

Summary

- Territory is a longstanding geographical idea and practice for organising and controlling space.
- State sovereignty is the dominant form of territory that consolidated in Europe after the medieval period and expanded around the world with the colonisation process.
- Nevertheless, the relations between the state and society are not contained by territory, they are dynamic processes.

Re-scaling territory in a globalising world

State territory is a dynamic process. The late twentieth century was a particularly intense period of social and spatial transformations in the world, usually summarised as globalisation, that reconfigured territory. The extension and intensification of global flows of people, goods, capital and communication since the 1970s, facilitated both by new technologies and political-economic arrangements, suggested that nation-states were either losing their capacity to manage sovereign, territorial power or else were having to adjust and reformulate their relationship to the society and the world.

During the 1990s, as 'free market' or **neoliberal** capitalism flourished in the wake of the collapse of the Soviet bloc, some commentators, often labelled as 'hyperglobalists', argued that territorial boundaries were increasingly insignificant, thus paving the way for the demise of the nation-state (Ohmae, 1990). Others argued that imperial state power, specifically the hegemony of the USA, was operating at a global level creating a new deterritorialised empire (Hardt and Negri, 2000). Few geographers supported these exaggerated arguments of the death of the territorial state and instead sought to examine the complex re-scaling of territorial power.

The territory of the state is produced as a particular scale of power that is historically tied to the creation of legal and political institutions through which social life is governed. Yet the scale of the nation-state (e.g. national government, supreme court) is not isolated from other scales, such as local governments and municipalities or supra-national bodies like the European Union. The transformation understood as globalisation can thus be seen as a complex process involving the shifting (or re-scaling) of political-economic institutions to scales beyond the nation-state (Brenner, 1999).

A combination of neoliberalism (and subsequent 'hollowing-out' of nation-state capacities) and a period of democratisation (deepening processes of democracy beyond national elections) led to a period of decentralisation of state power and the proliferation of local territorial institutions across much of the world (Peck and Tickell, 2002, Campbell, 2003). At the same time, new trade blocs (such as the North America Free Trade Agreement) and forms of international governance (e.g. World Trade Organisation) took on increased responsibility for managing political and especially economic organisations.

State territory evolves in response to shifting global and local processes. Rather than being rendered less important due to globalisation, we can instead appreciate its shifting scales of power in the context of glocalisation (Swyngedouw, 1997): that is, the simultaneous growth of both sub-national and intra-national territorial institutions. In so doing, however, the universality of state-centric understandings of territorial power starts to come under question once we appreciate the diversity of political actors and institutions involved in sustaining it.

Territory and networks

If one response to growing critiques of state-centred understandings of territorial power and the risks of the 'territorial trap' was to reassert the significance of territorial scales for governing society, another approach was to emphasise the importance of networks and extra-local relations for shaping how territories are constructed and experienced. The era of globalisation was heralded as 'the network society', according to sociologist Manuel Castells (1996), and few (if any) places on Earth were free from the cross-cutting flows of information, capital, people and things.

'Global cities' are a good example of territories (urban spaces organised under a global polit-ical-economic logic) that are impossible to understand without **transnational diasporas**, global financial hubs, cultural hybridisation and so on (Sassen, 2001, also see Chapter 16). Large corporations and finance capital began to assume some of the roles of the state, such as large-scale territorial planning. Territories may thus be governed by multiple scales of political and eco-nomic institutions but they are also produced by networks that intersect and flow through them.

Territories – as bounded spaces controlled by the political organisation of the state and cap-ital across multiple scales – are not opposed to extra-local flows and networks but may be seen as being constituted by them (as 'network-territories' [Haesbaert, 2004]). Joe Painter (2010) has argued that territory, like the state, is in fact an 'effect'. Rather than operating as a political subject in itself, territory is the product of a set of practices that exist through networks of peo-ple and things. Painter gives the example of English administrative regions and demonstrates how their territories are the result of the technical process of coding in which government agents use a range of computer software and hardware, as well a web of input from non-specialists, to determine how regions and their economic value should be calculated, in turn designating territories.

Territory, territoriality and power

In its expanded and relational sense, territory, aside from being an effect or outcome, must be seen as constitutive of relations or networks of power. Territorial power manifests multiple dimensions from the state and its alleged monopoly of legitimate violence through to economic power, symbolic power and **affective** power (for example today lots of power is exercised through territories of fear, such as some urban neighbourhoods). Territorial power can be under-stood as a strategy of territoriality.

Territoriality refers to what Robert Sack (1986: 5) defined as a 'powerful geographic strategy to control people and things by controlling area'. This is considered a universal feature of humans, rooted in their social relations, which have always been geographically embedded. This is con-trasted to animal (ethological) understandings that are rooted in biology. Examples are infinite, from a mother putting a child in a playpen through to the construction of modern electoral boundaries, or the activities of urban gangs. There is a universal attempt by humans to control the flows of people and things by delimiting and controlling space.

Borders and boundaries are core elements of territory, relying on multiple dimensions of power, from symbolic and affective through to direct violence. They are constructed at multiple scales, from offices divided into cubicles through to the shifting borders of the European Union. Boundary-making poses a tension to the dynamics of globalisation and has been oriented more towards people than capital in recent decades (see Chapter 50).

Through **discourses** of fear of the other, walls are built, **gated communities** are con-structed and territories are strictly demarcated into those who belong and those who do not. According to the Transnational Institute, in the last half-century over 60 border walls have been constructed (Figure 47.2). Immigration, terrorism and smuggling are the top three justifications for building walls, with the highest number in Asia.

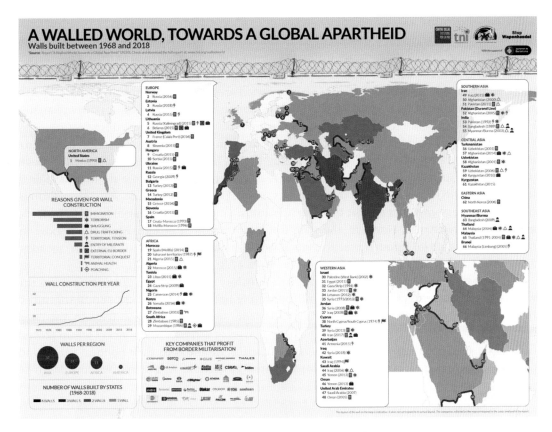

Figure 47.2
New border walls. For a more in-depth look at the figure, visit the link in the source

Source: TNI: https://www.tni.org/files/infographics_walledworld_centredelas_tni_stopwapenhandel_stopthewall_eng_def.jpg

Summary

- Territory is a dynamic process of controlling space that has been reconfigured by globalisation.
- The territorial power of the state has been re-scaled towards sub-national units and international institutions and is also a product of networks.
- Territorial power is often understood as a process of territoriality, understood as any attempt to control people and things in space, often with recourse to boundaries and borders that can reinforce identities.

Territories beyond the state

Once we acknowledge that the state is not the only actor seeking to control and organise space we open up the definition to a more expansive set of ideas and practices. In fact, such an open definition of territory, as the attempt by any actor to appropriate space in pursuit of its political objectives, is widely accepted outside of Anglophone literatures. The Swiss-French geographer Claude Raffestin (1980), who draws inspiration from the work of French intellectuals Michel Foucault and Henri Lefebvre, is a leading proponent of such a conceptualisation, which has also had a significant impact in other Latin geographies. For Raffestin, territory is produced when actors use their energy, through social relations of communication and multiple power relations, to represent and practice territory in line with their desires and material realities.

This definition could be applied to a wide array of examples. In the favelas of Rio de Janeiro, the territorial strategies of armed gangs and drug dealers have been well documented through popular media such as the hit film 'Cidade de Deus' (City of God). Here, we see that local drug lords interact with other grassroots organisations such as paramilitary groups who operate some-times alongside, sometimes against the state apparatus. This territorial control tends to be fickle and can quickly change. However, the state still attempts, often unsuccessfully, to impose its own territorial control through practices such as wall-building, in order to maintain 'security' and control the expansion of some favelas (see Figure 47.3).

Territories are also the focus of grassroots, emancipatory movements. In 2011 cities across the world witnessed uprisings, their inhabitants protesting both economic and political injustices. In the wake of a global financial crisis activists in Madrid the prominent public space: the Plaza del Sol (Figure 47.4), appropriating the square by masses of activists who quickly set up protest camps as a radically alternative way of organising space, in-line with their political values and objectives, including mutual aid and environmental protection. As in cities worldwide, these

Figure 47.3
Wall in a favela of Rio de Janeiro, labelled by the state as an 'ecolimit' to control the expansion of the community

Source: Photo credit: Rogério Haesbaert

Figure 47.4
Puerta del Sol, Madrid, Spain

Source: Photo credit: Julio Albarrán/Flickr

temporary occupations demonstrated that territory can very quickly transform but that some tend to be more lasting and others fickler.

In Madrid, as elsewhere, activists directly confronted the dominant production of territory by the state (controlled and enforced by the police who regularly used repression to disperse crowds) as well as capital (rejecting the highly consumerist or corporate use of urban centres), reclaiming a universal right to use the city as inhabitants see fit. Following eviction of the camp, activists successfully managed to reterritorialise their struggle in urban neighbourhoods. Later, they shifted their territorial focus to the state itself as some activists formed Podemos as a new political party (Fominaya, 2020).

There are countless examples of social movements worldwide where activists have made territory central to their strategy, such that their identities, values and institutional forms are all oriented towards the quest to occupy and control territory in pursuit of their objectives. In such cases, Halvorsen et al. (2019) suggest that we can refer to socioterritorial movements, such as the Brazilian Landless Workers Movement (MST), who used land occupation as a means of survival for its families as well as constructing a new logic of agriculture and development in the context of a neoliberal paradigm in the region.

Decolonising territory

There has been a growing recognition in Anglophone debates that territory, like other concepts, should not only be understood through hegemonic, universalising and Eurocentric readings (Radcliffe, 2022). Rather, attention needs to be given to other 'loci on annunciation' where

631

Figure 47.5
Central Square of autonomous municipality of Cherán, in the state of Michoacán, Mexico

Source: Photo credit: Rogério Haesbaert

territory is used and (re)interpreted. There is a move towards what some term the decolonisation of territory that seeks to criticise and undo the hegemonic, statist and patriarchal pretensions of territory that are constructed 'from above' and protected as if it were the only territorial model available across the entire planet. In contrast, 'bottom up' readings, often from the periphery or Global South, are multiple, diverse and essential for an understanding of territory that is (re)produced and used as a category in the practice of groups that suffer from exploitation, domination and oppression.

An excellent example of a decolonial territorial struggle is the one fought by the Purépecha Indigenous people of the municipality of Cherán, México (Figure 47.5). Fighting against 'narco entrepeneurs' who exploited their native forests, they managed to close their territory to the access of these groups and gain political autonomy being today governed by their uses and customs (*usos y costumbres*), in a self-government with the direct participation of their inhabitants. Similar initiatives are now expanding to other Mexican municipalities.

The Purépecha represents one of many Indigenous, peasant and Afro-descendent struggles against state- and capital-led 'terricide': the death of a territory that simultaneously marks the disappearances of their way of life. Inspired by different mixes of European political traditions (e.g. **Marxism** and **anarchism**) and Latin American ideas (e.g. 'indigenous marxism' from Mariátegui or 'pedagogy of the oppressed' from Paulo Freire), autonomy is central to the decolonial territorial struggle. This is clear, for example, in recent 'eco-territorial' movements against neo-extractivist modes of exploitation (Svampa, 2019).

Many of these territorial struggles start with the body itself as an instrument of resistance, or re-existence, in the sense of resisting in order to exist or to exist in a new and more autonomous way of life. The notion of body-territory (*cuerpo-territorio*) has been increasingly used by (eco)feminist Indigenous movements in Latin America (Zaragocin and Caretta, 2021). In Cherán, for example, women – and their bodies – played a key role during the insurrection movement in 2011.

This embodiment of territory also includes an **ecological** dimension such that the culture-nature binary is often dissolved in Indigenous or Afro-descendent territorialisations. A river, mountain and animal may be considered political agents alongside humans in the production of territory. A key element to decolonising territory is breaking the dichotomy between socially produced power and forces of nature. More broadly, we can say that territories are multiple in several senses: they contain a multiplicity of territorialities (e.g. human and more-than-human) and involve a 'multi' or 'transterritorial' movement across and between territories (Haesbaert, 2004). Indeed, we can see that Indigenous communities revindicate their condition as 'transterritorial people', such as the Guarani who search for recognition of their free movements across the borders of Brazil, Paraguay, Argentina and Bolivia.

Finally, decolonising territory implies the formation of new and transformative processes of reterritorialisation that include the search for cracks in the political-administrative territory of the state, making use of legal strategies. In the example of Cherán, autonomy has been secured through legal pluralism within the Mexican constitution and rereading international conventions (such as those of the United Nations). Decolonising territorial processes are also spreading across the poor peripheries of the large metropolises, where the identification of spaces of everyday reproduction is often consolidated not only through territory as a geographical category of analysis but as a category of practice and a tool of mobilisation and struggle by individuals, communities and peoples.

Summary

- Territories are also produced by non-state actors seeking to control and organise space in pursuit of their own political aims.
- The acknowledgement by scholars of diverse ideas, values and practices of territories has been facilitated by a dialogue with Latin American knowledges, often in line with decolonial tendencies and social movement strategies.
- Decolonising territory presents a political and **epistemological** challenge to dominant ideas and histories of territory, as can be seen in the struggle of Indigenous, Afro-descendent and urban peripheral communities in Latin America.

Conclusion

Territory is one of geography's core concepts yet has only recently been opened up to contestations over its multiple interpretations and practices. Although the idea is intimately bound up with the birth of the modern nation-state and the political technologies that made it possible, its use and understanding exceed and challenge such origins.

The chapter has drawn widely on examples from Latin America as this is a region in which territory has been actively and explicitly mobilised by a broad array of social actors in recent decades. It is also a region where there has been significant analytical diffusion of the concept by geographers such as Milton Santos (Santos, 2021). Yet, as a process of spatialised power relations, territory is a category that is relevant to all human (and indeed **more-than-human**) societies and worlds. A key challenge for us as geographers is to be alert to the Eurocentric universalising tendencies prevalent within territorial thought and practice and remain sensitive to its own set of geographies. We conclude by suggesting a few ways forward.

First, we can approach territory as a strategy of certain political organisations who are attempting to reconfigure who is able to control and organise space and to what ends. We can find this strategy almost everywhere we look as people attempt to use space in ways that serve their particular ends: whether it be their survival as an **ethnicity** or an attempt by a political party to win more votes.

Second, territory expresses and/or provides an identity to social groups who understand themselves based on their bonds with their environment, usually contained within demarcated boundaries. Some identities are more visible than others and we thus need to be alert to those territorial identities that are both hidden and actively destroyed. This involves taking seriously the claims of subaltern groups and people who do not always conform to state-capitalist-based traditions.

Third, examining territory involves moving through relations between people and things, society and environment, local and global processes. In short, to study territory is to study those relations and networks through which space is produced, organised and especially, governed and/or controlled. Here, a challenge is understanding which political processes are more significant than others, or which groups/social classes, scales, environments (and so on) are dominant in each geo-historical context. Territory is a dynamic entity that is never static yet has always been reproduced through contestations and insurgent claims.

Finally, given the large body of thought and experience in grappling with territory that has emerged, especially from Latin America, there is a political and linguistic challenge to take seriously those knowledges produced outside the Anglophone discipline (see Müller, 2021). This indicates challenges not only of language but of translation, dialogue and recognition of difference but also of concrete political practices from these knowledges as a starting point to learning and transformative processes.

Discussion points

- Why is territory so closely associated with the modern nation-state?
- What are the risks of falling into a 'territorial trap' when seeking to understand international relations or processes of globalisation?
- Can you think of different examples of territorial power? Who are the actors and what forms do they take on?
- What is at stake in decolonising territory? What implications does this have for how we 'do' geography? And what broader political and social transformations would be involved?
- Develop and discuss new examples of territorial decolonisation in the contemporary world.

References

Agnew, J. (1994). The territorial trap: the geographical assumptions of international relations theory. *Review of International Political Economy* 1(1): 53–80.
Anderson, B. (1983). *Imagined Community*. London: Verso.

Brenner, N. (1999). Beyond state-centrism? Space, territoriality, and geographical scale in globalization studies. *Theory and Society* 28: 39–78.

Campbell, T. (2003). *The Quiet Revolution: Decentralization and the Rise of Political Participation in Latin American Cities*. Pittsburgh: University of Pittsburgh Press.

Castells, M. (1983). *The City and the Grassroots: A Cross-Cultural Theory of Urban Social Movements*. London: Edward Arnold.

Castells, M. (1996). *The Rise of the Network Society. Vol. 1 of The Information Age: Economy, Society and Culture*. Oxford: Blackwell.

Elden, S. (2013). *The Birth of Territory*. London: University of Chicago Press.

Fominaya, C. F. (2020). *Democracy Reloaded: Inside Spain's Political Laboratory from 15-M to Podemos*. Oxford: Oxford University Press.

Gottmann, J. (1973). *The Significance of Territory*. Charlottesville: The University Press of Virginia.

Haesbaert, R. (2004). *O mito da desterritorialização: Do 'fim dos territórios' à multiterritorialidade*. Rio de Janeiro: Bertrand Brasil.

Halvorsen, S., Fernandes, B. M., and Torres, D. (2019). Mobilising territory: socioterritorial movements in comparative perspective. *Annals of the Association of American Geographers* 109(5): 1454–1470.

Hardt, M., and Negri, A. (2000). *Empire*. Cambridge, MA: Harvard University Press.

Harvey, D. (2003). *The New Imperialism*. Oxford: Oxford University Press.

Jessop, B., Brenner, N., and Jones, M. (2008). Theorizing sociospatial relations. *Environment and Planning D: Society and Space* 26: 389–401.

Müller, M. (2021). Worlding geography: from linguistic privilege to decolonial anywhere. *Progress in Human Geography* 45(6): 1440–1466.

Ohmae, K. (1990). *The Borderless World*. London: HarperCollins.

Painter, J. (2010). Rethinking territory. *Antipode* 42(5): 1090–1118.

Peck, J., and Tickell, A. (2002). Neoliberalizing space. *Antipode* 34: 380–404.

Radcliffe, S. (2022). *Decolonizing Geography: An Introduction*. Cambridge: Polity Press.

Raffestin, C. (1980). *Pour une geographie du pouvoir*. Paris: LITEC.

Ratzel, F. (1897). *Politische Geographie*. Munchen und Leipzig: R. Oldenbourg.

Sack, R. (1986). *Human Territoriality: Its Theory and History*. Cambridge: Cambridge University Press.

Sassen, S. (2001). *The Global City: New York, London, Tokyo*. Princeton: Princeton University Press.

Smith, N. (1984). *Uneven Development: Nature, Capital, and the Production of Space*. New York: Blackwell.

Svampa, M. (2019). *Neo-Extractivism in Latin America: Socio-Environmental Conflicts, the Territorial Turn, and New Political Narratives*. Cambridge: Cambridge University Press.

Swyngedouw, E. (1997). Neither Global Nor Local: 'Glocalisation' and the Politics of Scale. In *Spaces of Globalization: Reasserting the Power of the Local*, ed. K. Cox. New York and London: Guilford/Longman, 137–166.

Zaragocin, S., and Caretta, M. A. (2021). Cuerpo-territorio: a decolonial feminist geographical method for the study of embodiment. *Annals of the American Association of Geographers* 111(5): 1503–1518.

Online materials

- https://www.mstbrazil.org/

  Website of one of the largest socioterritorial movements in the world.

- https://www.tni.org/en/walledworld

  Overview of new border walls being constructed worldwide.

- https://www.occupy.com

  Website that documents some of the 'occupy' uprisings of 2011 and the movements that have flourished in their wake.

Further reading

Delaney, D. (2005). *Territory: A Short Introduction*. Oxford: Blackwell.
One of few textbooks on territory available to English speakers, a great introduction.

Elden, S. (2010). Land, terrain, territory. *Progress in Human Geography* 34(6): 799–817.
A summary of the key theoretical argument made by Stuart Elden, later presented as part of a large book.

Haesbaert, R. (2013). A Global Sense of Place and Multi-Territoriality: Notes for Dialogue from a 'Peripheral' Point of View. In *Spatial Politics: Essays for Doreen Massey*, eds. D. Featherstone and J. Painter. Oxford: Wiley-Blackwell, 146–157.
English-language overview of recent debates in Brazilian geography on the multiple dimensions of territoriality.

Halvorsen, S. (2019). Decolonizing territory: dialogues with Latin American knowledges and grassroots politics. *Progress in Human Geography* 43(5): 790–814.
Overview of recent Latin American literatures and attempt to build dialogue with approached to territory that are more dominant in Anglophone scholarship (such as that of Stuart Elden).

Raffestin, C. (2012). Space, territory, territoriality. *Environment and Planning D* 30: 121–141.
One of few English publications by the French geography who has been a key influence worldwide.

Santos, M. (2021). *The Nature of Space*. Durham: Duke University Press.
Recent translation of one of Brazil's most important geographers from the last century, includes key theoretical underpinnings of territory.

Storey, D. (2012). *Territories: The Claiming of Space*. London: Routledge.
Another useful introductory textbook for Anglophone audience.

Zaragocin, S., and Caretta, M. A. (2021). Cuerpo-territorio: a decolonial feminist geographical method for the study of embodiment. *Annals of the American Association of Geographers* 111(5): 1503–1518.
Summary of recent feminist work that starts from the body as a scale of territorial thought and action.

Zavala Guillen, A. L. (2022). Maroon socioterritorial movements. *Annals of the American Association of Geographers* 112(4): 1123–1138.
Historical overview that emphasises how territory has been central to Afro-descendent populations and their struggles for freedom.

48 Nationalism and nation-states

Angharad Closs Stephens
and Franz Bernhardt

Introduction

We are writing this chapter as the UK emerges from the COVID-19 global pandemic. This means that it is no longer obligatory to wear a face covering or keep a distance between ourselves and others in shops, on public transport and at schools and universities, although the harmful effects of this virus are not yet over. The COVID-19 global pandemic led to rapid and far-reaching changes in everyday habits, practices, and freedoms in advanced liberal democracies as well as in authoritarian states. It changed how people think of themselves and their relationship to the world around them. We begin this chapter by turning to the COVID-19 pandemic because of the ways it exposed many of the concepts we engage with in human geography: including the nation and state; borders, citizenship, and mobility; identity, memory, and solidarity. Young people who lived through the COVID-19 pandemic do not need to be taught many of these concepts: they have encountered them through their life experiences. In this chapter, we discuss moments from the pandemic as well as other events and protests that took place during the extraordinary year of 2020, to engage different understandings of 'nationalism' and '**nation-states**'.

Nations, states and 'imagined communities'

The COVID-19 pandemic offers a significant moment for reading the everyday ways in which ideas about the nation come into focus, materialise, and operate **affectively**, conjuring the image that we are part of a united community. Consider, for example, the experience of watching the Prime Minister make his ministerial broadcast to the nation, which ordered people to stay at home, commencing on 23 March 2020 the first UK-wide lockdown. According to *The Guardian* newspaper, this was one of the most watched TV broadcasts ever, as 27 million people watched it live (Waterson, 2020). Johnson wore a blue shirt and red tie to make his announcement, matching the Union Jack flag placed to the right of the screen. The experience of watching this broadcast made us feel part of what Benedict Anderson describes as an 'imagined community'. Anderson remains perhaps the most well-known theorist of nationalism, and this concept

DOI: 10.4324/9780429265853-56

has become central to many different disciplines, including geography. In describing the nation as imagined, he did not mean that it wasn't real. His point was that the nation comes alive through ideas, stories, symbols, objects, and media – such as in this ministerial broadcast, but it also materialises through bureaucratic forms, economic systems, and material **infrastructure**. As Anderson put it: the nation 'is imagined because the members of even the smallest nation will never know most of their fellow-members, meet them, or even hear of them, yet in the minds of each lives the image of their communion' (1991: 9). Whilst we will never meet all the other 27 million people who watched this broadcast with us, we experienced a sense of sharing something in common with them.

As human geographers, one of our tasks is to trace the affective and material processes through which the nation is felt, **embodied**, and activated – such as in this television broadcast. A key point here is that the nation will include processes of inclusion and exclusion: it can make us feel energised, recognised, comforted just as it can also be used to exclude and to harm. The sense that 'we' form a community is therefore achieved by also establishing what we are not, that is, how 'we' are different from 'them' (Mbembe, 2016). Ideas about 'us and them' travel across a range of genres, from novels and films to identity cards and school curriculums. They can operate in benign, friendly, and comical ways and in violent and destructive ways. This way of marking distinctions that establish who we are, and how we think we are different from others, matters, because it creates a powerful way of understanding our social worlds. Indeed, this was one of the major lessons of the twentieth century: people go to war based on the ways in which they see, imagine, and perceive others (Der Derian cited in Gregory, 2004: 18).

The histories of the twentieth century show us that the idea of the nation combined with the force, reach, economic, and military might of the state can be used to enable great achievements and positive societal changes – including national healthcare systems and job security schemes. However, the institutions of the nation-state can also be used against minority or unwanted populations. This is what the world witnessed during the Second World War, when Adolf Hitler, leader of the National Socialist German Worker's Party (Nazis), was in 1933 elected German Chancellor, and new citizenship laws, the 'Nuremberg Race Laws', passed in 1935, meant that the racist ideas favoured by the Nazis, which narrowed the idea of who counted as 'German', were put into law. These laws rendered not only Jewish people but also Roma and traveller communities, people with disabilities, and Black people outside of the 'imagined community' of Germany, making them stateless (Sharma, 2020: 27). After the war, the 50 countries representing the United Nations at that time met and agreed on 30 principles and values that belonged to all human beings equally, establishing on 10 December 1948, the Universal Declaration of Human Rights. This declaration was designed to confirm rights that people held as human beings, and which superseded people's rights as laid out in their respective nation-states. However, here lies one of the paradoxes of global politics: people's human rights, as declared in the Universal Declaration, still depend on a nation-state's willingness to recognise and act on them (Sharma, 2020: 125). Whichever nation-state we find ourselves living in determines to a large extent our everyday freedoms, capacities, life chances, and choices.

This world of nation-states, which is the dominant framework of international politics today, gradually emerged to replace a world of empires. It emerged in part through the dissolution of the Habsburg and Ottoman empires, after the end of the First World War, and more rapidly, through the **decolonisation** of Asia and Africa and the establishment of newly independent **postcolonial** nation-states that followed the Second World War. The Charter of the United Nations, agreed between 50 states at the end of the Second World War, codifies the principle that international relations should be organised among nation-states and that each state is sovereign and equal in the eyes of its members. This agreement declares how politics is organised in our contemporary world. One of the implications of this framework is that there remain hundreds of national liberation movements that each want a state of their own within which they can also be sovereign. Yet this dream of national sovereignty extends beyond such movements and is considered both the great aim and foundation of international politics. It represents what Maja Zehfuss calls the 'fantasy of control' (2021: 184): to maintain control over **territory** through borders and also, control over the future, that is, about what the nation might become.

This structural and historical context is important for understanding where our ideas about belonging to a nation have come from, and how this became the most legitimate model for being political in the **modern** world. However, geographers studying nations and nationalism have tended to focus on the more everyday ways in which ideas about the nation unfold, as we discuss in the next section. During the first period of the UK-wide COVID-19 lockdown, between March and June 2020, several different images and refrains, which may not strike us individually as anything to do with the 'nation' or 'nationalism', in their combination, ensured that ideas about national belonging were heightened and in the air. For example, during this period, children drew pictures of rainbows that were stuck in house windows, which resonated with signs placed on the side of roads and in closed shop windows thanking 'key workers' (those in jobs that were deemed essential under these emergency conditions) and the NHS (National Health Service). These rainbows were not designed to be a 'national' effort; they emerged by chance, and quite organically. However, as they travelled alongside more coordinated, top-down efforts to narrate the sense of a national community, including a special broadcast by Her Majesty the Queen, they were given a distinctive meaning that contributed to a 'national mood'.

In a special television broadcast, the Queen thanked those doing essential work 'outside the home' and said: 'I'm sure the nation will join me in assuring you that what you do is appreciated and every hour of your hard work brings us closer to a return to more normal times'. Showing images of people standing on doorsteps, in supermarkets, and outside hospitals, the Queen defined a sense of national identity by narrating how we the people share in a common past, present, and future. This is interesting because according to theorists of nationalism, it is precisely through the idea of feeling that we are sharing in a temporal journey that it becomes possible to imagine a nation (Anderson, 1991, Bhabha, 2004: 201). In repeating claims about a common journey, a sense of community and kinship is forged, creating the image of a 'homogenous' and 'horizontal society' (Bhabha, 2004: 202). We can see how this works by turning to the following passage from the Queen's address:

> 'we should take comfort that while we may have more still to endure, better days will return.
> We will be with our friends again,
> we will be with our families again,
> we will meet again'.

This final line was deliberately selected to echo the words of the song, 'We'll meet again', which was recorded and sang by Dame Vera Lynn in 1939, at the outbreak of the Second World War, to bring comfort to families, friends, and lovers in Britain who were separated by war. In this moment of crisis, the idea that we are sharing in a national community with others came sharply into focus, and other moments of Britain's history were recalled (Figure 48.1). However, as the next section goes on to discuss, which aspects of the past we choose to remember and which we forget makes a difference to how we understand the nation in the present.

Figure 48.1
The National Covid Memorial Wall, London. A public mural painted by volunteers to commemorate victims of the COVID-19 pandemic in the UK

Source: Photo credit: Angharad Closs Stephens

Summary

- The COVID-19 pandemic highlighted the ways in which ideas of national belonging are constructed through media, symbols, and shared experiences, creating an 'imagined community'.
- The idea of 'the nation' is deeply ambivalent: it can be used for positive societal change but also has a darker and exclusionary edge.

The nation and its others

Many geographers have paid attention to the mundane and ordinary ways in which ideas about the nation unfold. Perhaps this is no surprise, given that the idea of the nation does not unfold evenly over horizontal space. Rather, it comes into focus in particular sites, at certain times, and in ways that necessarily then involve a relationship to **space**. Whilst theorists of nations and nationalism have generally explained these phenomena through historical and structural accounts of the shift to an industrial age and to processes of modernisation (Gellner, 1983), through ideas about memory, culture, and invented traditions (Smith, 1995) and the waning of religious authority in Europe (Anderson, 1991), geographers, sociologists, and anthropologists including Tim Edensor, Paul Gilroy, Sara Ahmed, and Ghassan Hage (see further reading) have been drawn to the everyday elements and emotional moments through which ideas about a nation come into view. For example, Tim Edensor encourages us to look for how the nation is reproduced in moments from popular culture and in everyday life. He argues students of nations and nationalism to pay attention to the 'shared meanings, habits, rituals and ways of speaking' that 'facilitate communication and establish a sense of national belonging' (2002: 20). In examining everyday life, Edensor encourages us to start by making it unfamiliar: that is, look at everyday practices from the perspective of migrants or strangers, examine how familiar routines and spaces can become subject to social and economic change, or ask what happens when the 'habituated, embodied national subject' is placed in an unfamiliar context (2002).

During the summer of 2020, young people across the world marched as part of protests declaring 'Black Lives Matter'. They gathered to demonstrate their outrage at the murder of George Floyd, a 46-year-old Black man, by police officers on 25 May 2020 in Minneapolis. These powerful popular protests emerged alongside the pandemic, but they possibly also emerged because of this temporary break from the usual ways of doing things. Here lay an incomparable moment for challenging the racialised assumptions and presuppositions of everyday life. The intensified feelings of rage and anger combined with a determination to do something at this unique opportunity, when we were recalibrating the ways in which we live. Against the backdrop of quiet and empty streets, people took to them to demand large-scale change and justice for Black people as well as other racialised minorities.

These protests led to several immediate actions, and the gatherings folded into other spectacular acts, including when a large crowd of people in Bristol, England, carried a statue of Edward Colston, a seventeenth-century slave trader, and threw it into the river, cheering – a moment that was widely shared on social media. This high-profile event followed broader calls for Britain to acknowledge, research, and teach its colonial and imperial histories. The spectacular events in Bristol were accompanied by slow work, as several different British institutions, funding organisations, museums, and arts councils carried out reviews of the racial composition of their boards, managements, and awardees, as well as their own historical connections to slavery and **colonialism**. This included a high-profile investigation by the National Trust (a conservation charity that protects landmark buildings, gardens, castles, and land), which argued that although the 'country house' forms a quintessential image of Britishness (or Englishness), this is also a site of global histories, with many such houses' wealth based on connections to slave-ownership, or displaying an aesthetic taste for modernity and civilisation – a taste forged in opposition to ideas about blackness (see Huxtable et al., 2020: 9).

In this highly politicised context, during the summer of 2020, players in the England national football team – a multi-ethnic team – practised 'taking the knee' before football matches. This gesture of bending on one knee in advance of a match was designed to demonstrate their rejection of racism in football and to demand change. It echoes the actions of Colin Kaepernick, quarterback for the National Football League (US), who refused to stand for the American national anthem in 2016, in protest at the violence Black and minority ethnic people continue to endure in the US (Campbell, 2021). However, the gesture of taking the knee has a much longer history and has been used by many different athletes in sports to protest racial inequalities and injustices and used also by Martin Luther King as part of a campaign for voting rights in the US in 1965 (BBC, 2021). What was significant in the summer of 2020 was that the manager of the England football team, Gareth Southgate, supported the players' protests, which gave the whole team the authority to withstand the booing carried out by some members of the crowd. Indeed, the Home Secretary Priti Patel declined to support the players saying she did not agree with 'gesture politics' (ibid).

Sport is political, and there are political questions to be asked about sports. These range from questions about the numbers of Black and minority ethnic people in managerial and coaching positions in white majority countries to how many sports are divided between men's and women's matches and tournaments, and award different prizes and funding, as well as how transgender athletes face exclusion and/or limits on their participation. But let us turn to the role of the nation in sport and how ideas about the nation are closely connected to ideas about **race**, as each nation often relies on **ethnicity** to fuse an account of the unity of the people as 'the basis and origin of political power' (Balibar, 1991: 94). Paul Gilroy argues that sports is political because there is ultimately a connection between sports and war. To demonstrate, he discusses a chant that is heard at football grounds in the UK: 'two world wars and one world cup, doo dah, doo dah' (2004: 118). He argues that songs such as this one, sung in stadiums, recall and actively shape global politics. In this case, it recalls Great Britain's position as a victorious state against Germany in the Second World War, not unlike the way the Queen recalled the war during her pandemic address. What kind of images, narratives, and assumptions does such a song revive? In this case, we might say that this chant demonstrates how British nationalism has 'racialized contents' (Gilroy, 2004: 121). It intensifies ideas about 'us and them' and deflects attention from Britain's own histories of violence. According to Gilroy, the song also shows how so much of British culture maintains a sense of mourning for a 'once-imperial nation' and seems unable 'to accept its loss of prestige in a determinedly postcolonial world' (ibid: 117). Does it matter what songs we sing at football matches? Gilroy argues that it does.

In taking the knee, the players of the England national football team also suggested that our gestures and actions matter and that they contribute towards making worlds in which we and others can feel at home.

Summary

- Geographers have focused on how ideas of the nation are performed and reproduced in everyday life, in specific spaces and times.
- The politics of nationalism are often revealed when the 'habituated and embodied national subject' is transgressed or placed in an unfamiliar context.

National identities and devolution

We have so far engaged with two complexities of nationalism and national identity. The first one concerned the ideas of 'us and them' at the heart of nationalist thought and the political processes of inclusion and exclusion that follow. The second has addressed the mundane practices as well as more spectacular everyday ways through which ideas about the nation operate. We have not highlighted which of these range of different practices we consider to be 'nationalist'. Following Michael Billig (1995), we suggest that although nationalism is often understood to be a specific **ideology**, belonging to some people or some movement, it in fact encompasses a far wider range of institutional contexts and narratives (Gruffudd, 2014). When we treat nationalism as a specific ideology, we risk locating it on the peripheries of politics, overlooking its centrality to the system of nation-states. In contrast, we want to emphasise the prevalence and persistence of the nationalist assumption that cultural and territorial units must be joined together (Gellner, 1983). In this final section, we wish to illustrate some of the complexities of ideas about nations and nationalism, in so far as they do not represent a single political position.

If we return to our main example of the first year of the COVID-19 global pandemic, we can turn to another moment, involving public reactions and protests to refugees and asylum seekers in the UK. Specifically, in September 2020, amongst the ongoing Black Lives Matter protests, the UK Home Office announced that they would be repurposing former military barracks in the area of Penally, in Pembrokeshire, Wales, and using it to house 230 asylum seekers. This announcement led to protests in this part of Wales, as dozens of people campaigned over several weekends. Some gathered to demand that these people should be given better and proper housing, given that the Welsh Government had recently declared Wales a 'Nation of Sanctuary' (Figure 48.2). Others protested against giving refugees any housing at all, arguing that these people should be kept out of the nation.

The conditions inside and outside the former military camp are perhaps reflective of how the Home Office thinks it should treat populations who find themselves as refugees. From the outside, the barracks are reminiscent of a prison, surrounded by barbed wire and high fences. The Home Office claimed this was a temporary measure, brought on by a 'blockage' of the immigration system caused in part by the COVID-19 lockdown. But as a human rights group described

Figure 48.2
Sticker on a bus stop, Abertawe/Swansea, Wales. 'Welcome to refugees'

Source: Photo credit: Franz Bernhardt

it, the site is 'without the safeguards of a prison' (Townsend, 2020). Indeed, video footage and photographs of the site filmed by the *BBC* showed bunk beds in communal rooms with less than 2 m (6 ft) between them, bathrooms in which toilets were blocked, and the floors overflowing with water (Wells, 2021). At this point, there was still no vaccine against COVID-19, and maintaining good hygiene was critical. There was no privacy for sleeping or showering, and by March 2021, the Independent Chief Inspector of Borders and Immigration declared that the site was 'filthy' and should not be used for the purpose of providing accommodation to refugees and people seeking asylum.

The dominant perception of refugees and asylum seekers in the UK has long been negative and used to stoke fear and unease. Key expressions used by the popular press to describe refugees and asylum seekers include: 'illegal, criminal, a threat, a worry, to be feared' (Mavelli, 2017: 825). These hostile framings of refugees and asylum seekers form what many people would consider an extreme 'nationalist' politics, where the nation can only form a home for one identity group. However, the refugee policies of various governments, both Conservative and Labour, have at different points talked about 'asylum seekers threatening the identity, culture, wealth, and health of the British population' (ibid). What we find is that collective identities are often constructed through 'a simultaneous process of identification with and differentiation from selected **others**' (Barnett, 2005: 7), and that refugees often come to mark the limits of the nation, forming ideas about how 'we' are different from 'them'. Nevertheless, markers of national identity are not always framed in negative terms. Another effect of the decision to use the old barracks in Penally was that it led to conflict between the Welsh and British governments about how people who find themselves as refugees should be treated. This tells us something about the different forms of 'us and them' that can animate the nation. In its first written statement on the developments in Penally, the Welsh Government emphasised how the decision by the Home Office to use an old military camp as a centre to house asylum seekers was 'the direct opposite of the Nation of Sanctuary approach' and 'incompatible with the Welsh Government's approach to inclusive and cohesive communities' (Hutt, 2020). This statement demonstrated a contrasting national narrative and a different imaginary of welcome and hospitality in the context of a devolved Wales. Alongside the dominant association of refugees and asylum seekers as threatening 'others', the Welsh Government states its wish to be more welcoming. This case demonstrates how nationalism can be both a positive and a negative social force, one found in both the geographical core and in the periphery (Gruffudd, 2014).

There is a strong geographical and peripheral element to nationalism in the UK, which involves the context of **devolution**. Devolution refers to the transfer of power between different levels of government. Within the UK, certain powers are devolved to the Scottish Parliament, Senedd Cymru (Welsh Parliament), and the Northern Ireland Assembly. Importantly, these powers do not include immigration policy, which is reserved with the UK Government. However, the devolved Welsh Government has responsibility for running public services such as health and education, which makes a difference in the lives of those arriving as asylum seekers and refugees. This explains the political conflict over the treatment of refugees in Penally because in an official cabinet statement (released in February 2021), the Welsh Government emphasised that Wales has responsibility for the integration, community cohesion, local government, and health of these newly arrived populations – 'all areas which have been impacted negatively by the Penally site implementation' (Hutt, 2021). These are factors where the Welsh Government declared that *it* was sovereign.

Indeed, the devolved Welsh and Scottish Governments have repeatedly condemned British immigration policy. They have done so most recently by rejecting the UK Government's Nationality and Borders Bill in February 2022, introduced by Home Secretary Priti Patel. This Bill includes legislative changes to create a hostile environment for all 'illegally' arriving refugees and asylum seekers in the UK such as the removal of family reunion rights for many refugees or proposals for 'offshore processing'. One of their reasons for rejecting it is that some of the legislative changes to immigration rules would infringe upon the devolved governments' powers regarding the reception of refugees and asylum seekers. However, their objection to the Bill also points to a larger conflict between the devolved governments and the UK Government on how to approach immigration policy and the treatment of refugees and asylum seekers more generally. In the context of this conflict, the narrative of Wales as a welcoming 'Nation of Sanctuary' for refugees constitutes a form of national identity formation. It makes a claim about what

Figure 48.3
Sticker, Abertawe/Swansea, Wales

Source: Photo credit: Franz Bernhardt

'Wales' is, against what is considered a more hostile 'British' government and its exclusionary asylum regime (Figure 48.3). This shows how national identity, and competing national identities, almost always comes to be politicised through an inherent logic of 'us and them'. Yet how we imagine that national community makes a difference. As these examples show, the nation is open to be narrated in several different ways.

Summary

- Nationalism is more than a specific ideology and operates through a wide range of everyday practices and institutional contexts.
- Devolution adds an important element to nationalism in the UK, with conflicts arising between devolved governments and the UK Government over immigration policies and the treatment of refugees.

Conclusion

This chapter has taken the exceptional year of 2020, which saw COVID-19 become a global pandemic, leading to worldwide, unparalleled restrictions on people's movements, alongside high profile global and local protests – by 'Black Lives Matter' movements, athletes who 'took the knee' before football matches, and those who objected to housing refugees and asylum seekers in unsanitary and crowded conditions at army barracks. By way of these different examples, we have examined how the nation comes into view at different points, sites, and moments, both as part of ordinary life and as part of formal international relations. What is distinctive about the nation is the way it conjures a sense of sharing something in common. This can be powerful when it makes us feel that we belong to something bigger than ourselves, but it can also be oppressive and harmful when it works to suggest some people belong more fully than others, through racialised determinations. As all our examples show, the nation works by distinguishing between 'us and them': a logic that can be used against minority populations, as we know from the histories of the twentieth century but which can also, as we see in our final example, be used strategically to call for greater rights for vulnerable populations. Overall, the nation forms the most powerful understanding of the political community in our contemporary world, and it is this that makes it imperative for us as human geographers to understand how it works and what its effects are.

Discussion points

- If you were drafting a contemporary Universal Declaration of Human Rights, what essential elements would you include that were not addressed in the original 1948 declaration?
- What kind of rights should supersede the rights given to us by respective nation-states?
- Can you think of examples of events or traditions where we sing songs with others to establish a sense of togetherness? What is it about communal singing that contributes to a sense of unity and belonging within a community?
- Compare and contrast public reactions to people crossing international borders and becoming refugees in different countries such as the UK, US, Germany, and Brazil. What do these responses reveal about our perceptions of national identity?
- Can you think of examples of 'competing' national identities? What might this competition for a nation-state tell us about the nature of nationalism more broadly?

References

Anderson, B. (1991). *Imagined Communities*. London: Verso Books.

Balibar, É. (1991). The Nation Form: History and Ideology. In *Race, Nation, Class: Ambiguous Identities*, eds. É. Balibar and I. Wallerstein. London: Verso Books, 93–94.

Barnett, C. (2005). Ways of relating: hospitality and the acknowledgement of otherness. *Progress in Human Geography* 29(1): 5–21.

BBC. (2021). What's taking the knee and why is it important? *BBC*, 13 October. https://www.bbc.co.uk/news/explainers-53098516 (Last accessed 27 June 2022).

Bhabha, H. (2004). *The Location of Culture*. London: Routledge.

Billig, M. (1995). *Banal Nationalism*. London: Sage Publications Ltd.

Campbell, P. I. (2021). Taking the knee in football: why this act of protest has always been political. *The Conversation,* June 16.

Edensor, T. (2002). *National Identity, Popular Culture and Everyday Life.* London: Routledge.

Gellner, E. (1983). *Nations and Nationalism.* Oxford: Blackwell Publishing.

Gilroy, P. (2004). *After Empire: Melancholia or Convivial Culture?* London: Routledge.

Gregory, D. (2004). *The Colonial Present. Afghanistan, Palestine, Iraq.* Malden; Oxford; Victoria: Blackwell.

Gruffudd, P. (2014). Nationalism. In *Introducing Human Geographies,* eds. P. Cloke, P. Crang, and M. Goodwin. London: Routledge, 556–568.

Hutt, J. (2020). Written statement: use of Penally army training camp for asylum seekers. *Welsh Government* [Online], 15 October. Available at https://gov.wales/written-statement-use-penally-army-training-camp-asylum-seekers (Accessed 12 October 2021).

Hutt, J. (2021). Written statement: Penally asylum accommodation February update. *Welsh Government* [Online], 4 February. Available at https://gov.wales/written-statement-penally-asylum-accommodation-february-update (Accessed 12 October 2021).

Huxtable, S.-A., Fowler, C., Kefalas, C., and Slocombe, E. (2020). Interim report on the connections between colonialism and properties now in the care of the National Trust, Including links with historic slavery. *The National Trust,* September. Available at https://nt.global.ssl.fastly.net/binaries/content/assets/website/national/pdf/colonialism-and-historic-slavery-report.pdf (Last accessed 27 June 2022).

Mavelli, L. (2017). Governing populations through the humanitarian government of refugees: biopolitical care and racism in the European refugee crisis. *Review of International Studies* 43(5): 809–832.

Mbembe, A. (2016). The society of enmity. *Radical Philosophy* 200. https://www.radicalphilosophy.com/article/the-society-of-enmity (Accessed 27 June 2022).

Sharma, N. (2020). *Home Rule: National Sovereignty and the Separation of Natives and Migrants.* Durham and London: Duke University Press:

Smith, A. D. (1995). *Nations and Nationalism in a Global Era.* Cambridge: Polity Press.

Townsend, M. (2020). Revealed: the squalor inside ex-MoD camp being used to house refugees. *The Guardian,* 11 October. Available at https://www.theguardian.com/uk-news/2020/oct/11/revealed-the-squalor-inside-ex-mod-camps-being-used-to-house-refugees (Accessed 27 June 2022).

Waterson, J. (2020). Boris Johnson's COVID-19 address is one of most-watched TV programmes ever. *The Guardian,* 24 March 2020. https://www.theguardian.com/tv-and-radio/2020/mar/24/boris-johnsons-covid-19-address-is-one-of-most-watched-tv-programmes-ever (Last accessed 27 June 2022).

Wells, I. (2021). 'Run-down' Penally asylum camp to close on 21 March. *BBC News* [Online], 16 March. Available at https://www.bbc.com/news/uk-wales-politics-56418361 (Accessed 27 June 2022).

Zehfuss, M. (2021). 'We can do this': merkel, migration and the fantasy of control. *International Political Sociology* 15(2): 172–189.

Online materials

- https://www.nationaltrust.org.uk/features/addressing-the-histories-of-slavery-and-colonialism-at-the-national-trust

  This is the website of the *National Trust,* which is responsible for caring for places and collections on behalf of the nation. This report addressed the connections between 93 National Trust sites and British histories of colonialism and slavery.

- https://www.amnesty.org.uk/

  Amnesty International is a movement that campaigns for people's human rights across the world. It often highlights the ongoing violent effects of border controls across the UK, Europe, and the World and the plight of people who find themselves as refugees and asylum seekers.

- https://theconversation.com/why-wearing-a-poppy-and-taking-a-knee-in-football-should-not-be-dismissed-as-gesture-politics-171237

  The Conversation has many articles addressing the relationship between sport, national identity and politics – this one discusses why taking the knee and wearing a poppy represent more than 'gesture politics'

- https://www.theguardian.com/world/2021/jul/18/wall-of-love-the-incredible-story-behind-the-national-covid-memorial-led-by-donkeys

  The story of how the Covid Memorial Wall in London was built, described in *The Guardian* newspaper, to remember those who died from the pandemic.

Further reading

Ahmed, S. (2004). *The Cultural Politics of Emotion.* Edinburgh: Edinburgh University Press.
A superb introduction to why we might pay attention to emotions in the study of global politics.

Amin, A. (2012). *Land of Strangers.* Cambridge: Polity Press.
A significant effort to think about political belonging in non-nationalist terms.

Antonish, M., and Skey, M. (2017). *Everyday Nationhood: Theorising Culture, Identity and Belonging after Banal Nationalism.* London: Palgrave Macmillan
A publication that reviews Michael Billig's idea of 'banal nationalism' (1995) and brings debates on everyday nationalism up to date.

Ashutosh, I. (2019). On the grounds of the global Indian: tracing the disjunctive spaces between diaspora and the nation-state. *Environment and Planning C* 37(1): 41–58.
An article exploring ideas of distance and proximity to the nation among the Indian diaspora in Toronto.

Crang, M., and Tolia-Kelly, D. (2010). Nation, race and affect: senses and sensibilities at national heritage sites. *EPA: Economy and Space* 42(10): 2315–2331.
An example of how we might read the inclusions and exclusions inherent in ideas about national belonging at heritage sites.

Edensor, T., and Sumartojo, S. (2018). Geographies of everyday nationhood: experiencing multiculturalism in Melbourne. *Nations and Nationalism* 24(3): 553–578.
An example of the everydayness of multicultural ideas about belonging, as experienced in the city of Melbourne, Australia.

Hage, G. (2017). *Is Racism an Environmental Threat?* Cambridge: Polity Press.
Following on Hage's landmark text, *White Nation: Fantasies of White Supremacy in a Multicultural Society,* this text connects nationalism to many other practices of inclusion and exclusion – from racism to how we engage with the environment.

Sharma, N. (2020). *Home Rule: National Sovereignty and the Separation of Natives and Migrants.* Durham and London: Duke University Press.
A wide-ranging tour de force that develops an argument about the prevalence of the 'us and them' logic in the modern world.

Smith, S. (2020). *Intimate Geopolitics. Love, Territory and the Future of India's Northern Threshold.* New Brunswick, NJ: Rutgers University Press.
A book that prioritises the everyday impacts of the geopolitics of borders and national identity by focusing on stories of love and belonging.

Wilson, H. F., and Anderson, B. (2020). Detachment, disaffection and other ambivalent affects. *Environment and Planning C: Politics and Space* 38(4): 591–598.
A unique insight into how national affects are not necessarily always spectacular or highly emotional but sometimes very ordinary and deeply ambivalent.

49 Colonisation and colonialism

Amba J. Sepie

Introduction: Colonisation affects us all

Colonisation is an extended process of denying relationships. Everybody has been colonised. It doesn't matter what colour your skin is, or where you're from.

Papaschase Cree scholar, Dwayne Donald, 2010

Much of the world's population (albeit not the majority) enjoy the relative comfort and convenience proffered by **modernity** without necessarily knowing much about how urbanised, technologically proficient societies came to be considered 'normal'. If you live in an affluent place, it can be easy to take this for granted. Does history really matter? This is geography, right? Well, geography needs some input from history, and maybe anthropology too, if we are to make sense of humans and places in ways that lead us to better conclusions on where we are heading as a species.

Although it may not seem as if the relative comforts of modern life, the plight of the orang-utan in Indonesia's diminishing rainforests, the civil war in the Central African Republic, or the global homelessness epidemic have all that much in common, they nonetheless share a shady ancestor in the form of colonisation. In short, colonisation refers to a historical process of consuming people and places by asserting power, usually through violent means, to the extent that the host population and place are overwhelmed. The process of colonisation is not new. Among some early examples of colonisation was the expansion of ancient Mesopotamian city-states, such as Ur, Uruk, and Lagash, around the 3rd millennium BCE; the colonies of Ancient Greece and Phoenicia, 550 BCE; the assaults on the peoples of pastoral Europe and the British Isles prior to the onset of Christianity; the Bantu colonisation of African nations; multiple migrations throughout the South Pacific, and the ingress into Central and South America by Aztecs and Nasca forces (Shifferd, 1987). In contemporary times, many people will be familiar with maritime British **colonialism** as perhaps the most well-known recent example.

But it is important to distinguish ancient process of colonisation from what is conventionally referred to as colonialism. Colonialism broadly refers to the practice of acquiring, controlling, and exploiting **territories** and peoples outside of one's own borders for economic, political, and social gain. The meaning and preferred terminology – colonisation or colonialism – varies geographically and often reflects the ways in which people are located socially and historically in relations of

DOI: 10.4324/9780429265853-57

BOX 49.1
MOANA JACKSON ON COLONISATION

'Colonisation' has a history as old as humankind. For as long as people have imagined that the grass was greener on the other side of the fence, they have embarked on the bloody and costly business of dispossessing each other... In 1492, the dispossession took a new and especially destructive turn...[this] marked the beginnings of a haphazard but deliberately learned process of political domination and commercial exploitation that was quite specific in its intent and unlimited in its reach.

Ngāti Kahungunu, Rongomaiwahine, and Ngāti Porou (Māori) scholar,
Moana Jackson, 2007: 167

domination. As Moana Jackson (Box 49.1) stresses, **colonisation** took on a 'new and especially destructive turn' following the European search of new trade routes, resources, and wealth in 1492. This form of colonialism was characterised by its global reach and by its openly violent means of accumulating capital to fuel development and expansion of **capitalism** in the metropole. Relations of slavery, land-grabs, genocide, and systems of indentured labour underpinned the mercantile capitalism, the industrial revolution, and the expansion of the financial capitalism (Melamed, 2015). In all of this, colonial relations of domination and/or dispossession were established and maintained through political, economic, and cultural power. From the fifteenth century onwards, Britain, The Netherlands, France, Spain, and Portugal, among others, embarked on voyages of exploration and conquest and sought to establish colonies, trade ports, and plantation economies in various parts of the world, including the Americas, Africa, Asia, and Oceania.

From the first instances of colonisation in ancient times to contemporary instances of **neo-colonialism**, we have all been affected by it in some way. Elements of colonisation live on in latter-day processes of **globalisation**, Euro-Americanisation, modernisation, and development, slowly consuming people and places by introducing new ways of thinking and being which can eventually eradicate what existed before. Despite its ubiquity, colonisation continues to have a highly uneven impact on people and places worldwide. Some people remain embroiled in battles for their cultural survival and land because of colonialism, and for others, the recovery of knowledges and relationships to land have been lost so long ago that the retrieval of a sense of place and belonging is very difficult.

In this line of thinking, we can understand European colonisation as a process that consumes its host – as a territory, culture, society, political structure, and economy. Over time, it has erased or transformed many of those cultures and traditions which gave people a sense of connection to places, to other species and our wider environment, and to one another, as linked to place-based kinship-oriented value systems (Wahinkpe Topa and Narvaez, 2022). It destroyed bonds, or relationships between people and places, as suggested by Dwayne Donald in the quotation at the beginning of this introduction (see also Chapters 5 and 71).

Take the orangutans, whose habitat is being destroyed by modern plantations, and around whom many international rescue programmes have arisen (Chua et al., 2021). Reframed by many groups as a 'resource', they have become part of a value system that is no longer connected to people and place. Respect for the personhood of other species, which is a well-known precept held by place-based peoples, is just not compatible with societies that are based on intensive and extractive resource consumption. Other chapters in this textbook, such as those which cover the **more-than-human** (Chapters 7, 43), environmental (Chapters 39, 44), and Indigenous geographies (Chapters 10, 45), deal with related aspects of this problem. You might have noticed that although there is a lot of attention given to environmental issues, endangered species, and wars, we are not always entirely sure how they happened, or what we should do about them. Understanding colonisation and the ways in which it continues to affect us is critical to the process of finding answers to these quandaries (Kiddle, 2020).

Summary

- Colonisation can be defined as a process of spatial and territorial consumption of places, peoples, and culture, whilst colonialism tends to refer to the historical period in which a very specific kind of socio-political system, wielding significant power and influence, was extended in a manner that captured people and places and bound them to the new system.
- Colonisation continues in its altered form as globalisation, Euro-Americanisation, modernisation, and development, introducing new ways of thinking and being which eventually eradicate the values and practices of the host population.

Colonialism, empire, and imperialism

The scale and global reach of European colonialism were unprecedented, as was the catastrophic loss of human life and environment – justified through racial and cultural hierarchies and the precedence of profit. European colonialism had profound and far-reaching impacts: from forming the world economic system and entrenched relations of extraction and underdevelopment (Chapter 37); to concentrating wealth and power in the metropole, birthing financial, political, and cultural institutions – and persistent inequalities – that continue to exist in the present day (Hickel, 2017); to reshaping the geography of the world's population. Paul Gilroy's notion of the *Black Atlantic*, for example, examines the **transnational** African **diaspora** and Black cultural politics following the forced migration of 12 to 15 million enslaved people from West Africa to the Americas.

The motivations behind colonialism were diverse and included economic gain, the search for new trade routes, religious missions, geopolitical rivalry, and the desire for national prestige. Competition over colonies was rife as global powers sought to acquire and control new territories. Colonialism was closely tied to **imperialism**, understood as the extension of a state's power and influence over other territories, often by establishing colonies, but which can also involve indirect means of dominance/subjugation through economic control, political influence, and cultural **hegemony**. Although colonialism is often associated with a specific historic period, the concept of imperialism can be applied to different timeframes, including contemporary geopolitics (Chapter 51). Economically, colonies were often seen as sources of valuable resources, such as minerals, spices, agricultural products, and labour, which could be exploited for the benefit of the incoming powers. Additionally, colonies provided markets for manufactured goods, ensuring a steady flow of trade and profits, and colonial establishment of military outposts or naval bases in the new territory provided strategic advantages and facilitated further expansion. Authorities also imposed trade restrictions, monopolies, and taxes that favoured the interests of the colonisers at the expense of the local Indigenous and Traditional populations.

In practice, colonialism typically involved initial exploration, followed by the arrival of colonisers, who would immediately assert their control over the land (see Chapter 10 for more about how geographers were part of this process). When settlers accompanied this arrival, their intent to create permanent homes in the new lands (as sanctioned by the governing powers 'back home') often led to conflicts with the local peoples, ranging from civil, somewhat peaceful, negotiations and trade, to violent clashes and wars. Settlers occupied and transformed the land, often displacing resident populations to create a society that reflected the values and interests of the settlers (see Chapter 71). We refer to this phenomenon as settler colonialism, and it is technically a subset of colonisation and its younger sibling, colonialism. Notable examples of settler colonialism include the British, French, Dutch, and Spanish occupations of North America in the 16th and 17th centuries, and the British colonisation of Australia in the late eighteenth century (Box 49.2). Settler colonial states did not appear ex nihilo but were imposed on pre-existing societies – often these were already complex and large-scale. Archaeological evidence suggests that most pre-colonial societies operated without a centralised European-style state with clearly demarcated borders (Ince and Barrera de la Torre, 2017). Territorial state demarcation is quite specific to European models of statehood. In southeast Asia, for example, there were many other forms of governance with quite different territorialities, which have since been erased by colonisation and the rise of the **nation-state** as a globalised model of governance (Anderson, 2006). According to Wolfe (2006), settler colonialism utilises a 'logic of elimination' (otherwise known as a replacement ethos) as a necessary precursor to colonisation and ultimate control over territory. In this mode of colonialism, access to territory was predicated on eliminating original inhabitants in whatever way was acceptable – in some cases, direct war, and in other cases, insidious forms of violence, such as residential schools, discriminatory laws, and many more (see, for example, Zaragocin's [2019] work with Epera Indigenous women in the Ecuador–Colombia borderland).

Alongside military occupation, purchase of land from Indigenous groups was a key technique in many areas: transferring from common or ancestral land that could not be owned by anyone, to private property; introduction of European-style laws and contracts; conceptions of land as real estate to be bought and sold; principles of 'freedom', 'property', and 'free enterprise' enshrined in founding documents such as the US constitution. In North America, as it was in Australia and many other places, the **ideology** of white supremacy was central to legitimising settler colonial practices. Take John Gast's (1872) painting, 'American Progress' (Figure 49.1), a classic example of the settler colonial imaginary. Whiteness is depicted in various ways: as purity and progress, personified by a woman representing the United States carrying a book of learning and knowledge, calling settlers to follow her westward to bring sunlight; as technological superiority with the presence of trains, stagecoaches and telegraphs; and as the taming and domination of 'nature' portrayed through scenes of farming, the displacement of Indigenous people, and fleeing herds of buffalo and wild animals. The painting powerfully represents 'Manifest Destiny', a 19th-century belief that American settlers were destined by God to expand westward across North America.

By imposing their own legal, political, and social systems, colonial authorities effectively supplanted or assimilated local cultures into the coloniser's language, education and health systems,

Figure 49.1
A 1873 chromolithograph of John Gast's (1872) painting 'American Progress': An allegorical representation of manifest destiny

Source: Granger NYC, Alamy Stock Photo

BOX 49.2
CASE STUDY: BRITISH COLONIALISM IN AUSTRALIA

The Indigenous peoples we refer to as Aboriginal or First Nations Australians have occupied **Country** for tens of thousands of years. Their communities are place-based, with complex systems of governance, and they maintain reciprocal relationships with the environment and other species alongside a rich spiritual and artistic tradition.

Colonialism began when Captain James Cook claimed the continent in the name of the British Crown in 1770, and emissaries of the Crown determined upon settling the region with convicts. They declared the continent of Australia *terra nullis*, which means unoccupied land, despite the presence of Aboriginal peoples. The First Fleet arrived in 1788, and by 1830, there were around 60,000 convicts and free settlers in residence.

This settlement initiated a genocide against the Aboriginal peoples and Torres Strait Islanders, with over 10,951 massacred by colonists between 1788 and 1930 (Ryan et al., 2022). Starvation, enslavement, brutal working conditions, and direct settler violence were routinely ignored by the authorities. Aboriginal women and girls were treated as slaves and routinely used for sex on pastoral stations, and Aboriginal children were forcibly removed to Missions (known as the Stolen Generations). Racial segregation, which included limited movement, refusal of basic rights, education, medical care, etc., continued into the 1960s. In theory, Aboriginal peoples were recognised as Australian citizens with full voting rights in 1967; however, they do not presently receive the full benefit of these rights. Despite efforts towards reconciliation and minor recognition of Aboriginal rights in recent decades, Aboriginal Australian cultural identity and peoples remain in a threatened state within the present socio-political environment of Australia (Figure 49.2).

Figure 49.2
Graffiti proclaiming Noongah ownership of land, Perth, Western Australia

Source: Photo credit: DustyDingo/Alamy Stock Photo.

gender codes, religious beliefs, administrative structures, and legal frameworks (for a contemporary example, see Smiles' (2018) paper on Indigenous resistance to the practice of autopsy in Minnesota). The nature of colonial rulership was hierarchical (a social and governance model we still have), highly mobile and acquisitional, and informed by a value system inherited from monotheistic religion, in which strict binaries (us and them, human and animal, good and evil, etc.) were enforced and used to structure the new societies. The violence, both subtle and overt, that colonial powers utilised to establish and maintain control over their colonies was directed by military force, socio-political manipulation, the imposition of religious, legal, and administrative systems, and the physical dismantling of the communities themselves.

Throughout history, colonial powers faced significant resistance from the colonised populations. A classic account is C.L.R. James' (1938) study of the Haitian revolution (1791–1804), in which

African slaves, led by Toussaint L'Ouverture, mounted a lasting insurrection against their French overlords, extending to themselves the very same principles of freedom and humanity being fought over in revolutionary France. More recent work by Priyamvada Gopal (2019) explores the significance of anti-colonial struggles throughout the British Empire. From the 1950s to the 1970s, many former colonies gained independence, either peacefully or through revolution, marking the end of the formal colonial era. However, many former colonies, especially those whose economies had been purposively designed for resource extraction and export of cash crops, remained locked into economic and social relationships that heavily benefited former colonial powers (Nandy, 1992). In contemporary times, the concept of neo-colonialism refers to economic and political relationships of domination and dispossession between the metropole and former colonies that continue after formal independence. This includes strategic interventions of nation-states, the terms of trade established by transnational institutions such as the World Trade Organisation, and the substantial power of multinational corporations over local and regional economies.

Summary

- The deployment of colonising practices can be identified in the histories of many diverse cultures, although European colonialism provides the spatiotemporal reference many of us are now most familiar with.
- Colonialism usually refers to an era which began with the Age of Exploration and spanned roughly from the 15th to 20th centuries, but it is important to recognise new forms of colonial extraction in different parts of the world.
- Settler colonialism is a subset of colonialism. It was immensely profitable for the colonising peoples and nations and caused immense damage to local traditional and Indigenous economies and environments.

Systemic legacies of colonisation

Growing attention has been given to the ongoing legacies of colonialism. As global movements for reparations for slavery and colonialism, such as the CARICOM Reparations Commission, receive greater publicity, there is still in some quarters a persistent denial and disavowal when talking about the violence of colonialism. In the UK, for example, research into British imperialism has become deeply politicised in so-called culture wars with politicians and right-wing media denouncing as 'woke' academics and cultural institutions that transgress nostalgic versions of Britain's colonial past (for an overview, see Lester, 2023). Ideas of indigeneity and 'replacement theory' have again become weaponised and politicised by fascist and Islamophobic groups advocating white nationalism in Europe and settler colonial societies.

Colonialism continues to shape geopolitical realities, influence **ecological** decision-making, perpetuate economic dependencies, and impact cultural and societal dynamics around the world (Nandy, 1992, Liu et al., 2020). Colonialism and the colonised mindset, which stem from systematic cultural assimilation reaching far back into our histories, have profoundly transformed the modern world (Rose, 2004). Everyday experiences of racialisation have their roots in colonial classifications. The concept of 'double consciousness', for example, was developed by W.E.B. Du Bois (1903) to address the inner conflict faced by marginalised or colonised groups within an oppressive society. He argued that African Americans grappled with a divided sense of self between their own authentic identity and the externally imposed identity structured by racially biased white society. Albert Memmi (1965) linked this to assimilation, or the defeatist acceptance of oppression, only one of two options he saw as a solution to a state of colonisation (the other being revolt). Similarly, the work of Frantz Fanon (1961), a key thinker of African **decolonisation**, argued anti-colonial struggle required the formation of a national consciousness different to that of the elite 'national bourgeoisie' of colonised countries. In *Black Skin, White Mask*, Fanon also highlighted how colonialism resulted in the psychological internalisation of colonial and racial hierarchies that need to be challenged if lingering processes of racialisation and racial **alienation** are to be overcome. More recently, Sylvia Tamale in *Decolonization and Afro-Feminism* (2020) underscores of role Afro-feminism can play in 'shaking off' colonial ways of thinking about law, education, religion, family, and sexuality. As the movement grows towards recognising colonisation as a phenomenon that has affected *all* humans, in racialised and non-racialised ways, the profound insights of these scholars can be reflected upon as relevant to both colonialism and older instances of colonisation. In both cases, connections among humans, culture, kinship, and place have been profoundly diminished.

Colonisation is a total system, distributing various physical, social, and psychic goods of the incoming powers in a manner that overwhelms the host population and their lands. The dissolution of kinship bonds, dispossession of land, and substitution of belief systems with new gods were key elements of successful conquest. Whilst Traditional and Indigenous peoples possess a living ancestral memory of the collective losses wrought by colonialism and can make concrete connections between colonial violence and cultural and physical losses, those who were colonised by processes prior to living ancestral memory do not. All over the world, we find half-remembered traditions, such as in Britain, Ireland, and Wales, of a way of life prior to colonisation, sometimes referred to as folkways or superstitions. These cultural repositories, which suggest a history that is very similar to Traditional and Indigenous ecologically oriented communities, carry echoes of a time prior to colonisation. We can therefore locate colonialism in a continuum with colonisation, as a process and method of destroying relationships between people and places that has ancient roots.

A brief account of strategies undertaken during the colonial era serves as good illustrations of how these bonds are targeted. Families and communities are often physically displaced from their homes (to allotments, reservations, **ghettos**, or urban sectors), severing their land kinship and food sovereignty. A sector of the community can be bound to labour requirements, which mean they work away from home, with the governing powers compelling labour from husbands, fathers, and sons for mining, logging, and other industrial forces. Child removal policies and residential school systems separate the children, directly impacting the ability of communities to pass on cultural traditions through child rearing and education, with profound intergenerational effects (Figure 49.3). Education, oppressive laws, and assimilative practices undermine and eliminate language use, customary ceremonial practice, body sovereignty, and cultural identity. Forced sterilisation disproportionally targeted racialised and indigenous women in America (Davis, 2003) and Canada (Clarke, 2021). Destructive and culturally interruptive strategies such as these have been shown to destroy the cultural foundations of a people within just two generations.

Figure 49.3
Cree students and teacher in class at All Saints Indian Residential School (Anglican Mission School),
Lac La Ronge, Saskatchewan, March 1945

Source: Photo credit: Bud Glunz. Library and Archives Canada, PA-134110

This is by no means an exhaustive list and does not include assimilation by choice or assimilation as a result of forced economic adaptation or acquiescence to political regimes. But it is important to remember that colonisation takes over the hearts, minds, actions, and beliefs of the colonised population to such a degree that it is easy to think that this is indeed 'who they are' at core, and that they have always been this way.

Summary

- Colonisation can be thought of as a systematic method for the displacement of beliefs, relationships, and people.
- Colonisation is a total package, distributing the various physical, social, and psychic goods of the incoming powers in a manner that overwhelms the host population and the lands they occupied.
- Traditional and Indigenous populations faced family separations, land dispossession, forced labour, cultural suppression, and the loss of language, autonomy, and self-governance.

Colonisation and human nature

Assimilation into the colonised mode of being, when successful, creates a coloniser from the colonised: a mobile and acquisitional, hierarchically organised, violent, and accumulative group, from which we derive the notion that the human being is aggressive and selfish by nature, with an interest in organised warfare. Colonial forces, who were singularly motivated to pursue new horizons and new resources, were carrying the colonised mindset and associated value system well prior to their incursion into other lands.

To understand colonisation more completely, however, it is necessary to review some misconceptions about human nature; specifically, the idea that humans are curious and competitive explorers. The greater majority of evidence suggests that humans are essentially *cooperative*, only behaving competitively or engaging in war when they are directly under threat and believe they have no other choice – or are socialised into it because of a dysfunctional culture (see de Waal, 2008, Singh, 2017, Tronto, 2017 for different perspectives). The depth of human history reveals people living sustainably in places they have strong bonds with, rarely venturing far from home territories, and cooperating with their neighbours (Mohawk, 1978). This way of life was necessary for our survival.

A century of anthropological studies investigating the habits and mindset of Traditional and Indigenous peoples shows very clearly that Earth-oriented, place-based peoples do not readily give up their homes and land. Indigenous protests over land dispossession have been global and continuous. In Aotearoa, in 1844, Hōne Heke cut down the flagstaff flying the Union Jack

Figure 49.4
The Aboriginal Tent Embassy was established in 1972 in Ngunnawal Country, outside what is now referred to as Old Parliament House, in Canberra. The protest over Aboriginal land rights and self-determination is still ongoing

Source: Photo credit: Travelscape Images/Alamy Stock Photo

Figure 49.5
On June 30, 2021, Indigenous people from various ethnicities gathered in Sao Paulo, Brazil, to oppose a controversial land reform bill that was being reviewed by the Supreme Court. The bill curtails the rights of Indigenous peoples to their ancestral lands by imposing an arbitrary cut-off date for establishing Indigenous territories and opens previously protected Indigenous land to mining and infrastructure projects

Source: Photo credit: Cris Faga/NurPhoto Stock Photo – Alamy

(at Kororāreka, Bay of Islands) four times as a protest against the Crown, and other Māori leaders have opposed land confiscations up to the present day (see Chapter 5). In America, modern protests began with the landmark occupation of Alcatraz Island in San Francisco in 1969. Other notable examples are the Aboriginal Day of Mourning (1938), the Aboriginal Tent Embassy in Australia (Figure 49.4), and more recently, the protests at Standing Rock against the Dakota Access Pipeline (Grote and Johnson, 2021). Indigenous resistance against land occupation in South American countries is constantly hitting the news (Figure 49.5; see also Chapter 10). Earth-oriented, place-based peoples *do not* readily give up their homes and land (Whyte, 2018).

It is correct that once survival as a group no longer depends directly on the environment, human groups will keep moving, conquering, and acquiring resources in the form of people and land in order to sustain a life in which bonds to the natural world have been eliminated. With the gradual and systematic annihilation of Traditional and Indigenous peoples, especially in the last 500 years, this moving and conquering business now seems so normal that many have made the error of calling it human nature. But thankfully, the recent attempts at colonisation did not entirely eradicate the Indigenous and Traditional communities upon whom this process was most recently inflicted. There are still many humans who can recall what it was to cultivate kinship bonds with place and be directed by a sustainable value system (Whyte, 2018, Yates, 2021, Yates et al., 2022). We can, and should, learn from this as we consider what to do about the orangutans and the wars (Wahinkpe Topa and Narvaez, 2022).

Summary

- Humans are cooperative, although they can and do behave competitively.
- Traditional and Indigenous place-based peoples do not readily give up their homes and land.
- Indigenous protests over land dispossession have been global and continuous.

Conclusion

The study of colonisation remains an important field in understanding historical, social, and political dynamics across the globe. The extent to which this phenomenon has affected us all, the degree to which both Majority and Minority World values and practices are afflicted in a manner that does not prioritise people's cooperative natures, and the relationship of these issues to the social and ecological obligations which entangle us all are slowly becoming clearer (Rose, 2004). It would be constructive to engage more directly with decolonisation, which is the project of undoing some of the more harmful effects of colonisation, colonialism, and settler colonialism by targeting the physical, social, mental, and spiritual legacies of our collective human history (see Chapter 71). Decolonisation requires the interrogation of history, biases, and relationships with oppression or with unequal power relations, in a manner that can effectively reconfigure perceptions of humanity. This amounts to improved human-to-human relationships, whilst encompassing proper stewardship of the wider more-than-human environment in which we are all embedded, as co-inhabitants of a planet. Whenever projects are oriented towards 'queering westernisation', or interrogating a dysfunctional norm that originates with colonising practices, processes, and ideologies, such projects are employing the philosophical perspectives of decolonisation. As such, geographers have a role in strategic and well-informed assessments of the contemporary social, political, and ecological dysfunctions of modern societies and action towards making visible the best practices for our collective future.

Discussion points

- The geopolitics of the globe has been deeply affected by processes of colonisation and colonialism. In what ways has colonisation and colonialism affected you, the places you live, and the people you descended from?
- Can you think of any links between our present-day socio-ecological problems and colonialism? A good starting point is to consider how our values are connected to how we treat our environment and other species.
- What are some of the lasting effects of colonialism on contemporary Traditional and Indigenous communities? Discuss some of the ways we might collectively assist with mitigating these effects.
- In the Western tradition, Joan Tronto (2017) and Val Plumwood (2007) have both suggested that many of us need different kinds of political and economic '**subjectivities**' (or

understandings of ourselves) in order to transform societies built on settler colonialism and its values. To what degree do you draw on competitive understandings of yourself? To what degree do you draw on cooperative ones? How does this affect your political decisions?

References

Anderson, B. (2006). *Imagined Communities: Reflections on the Origin and Spread of Nationalism*. London: Verso Books.

Chua, L., Fair, H., Schreer, V., Stępień, A., and Thung, P. H. (2021). Only the orangutans get a life jacket. *American Ethnologist* 48: 370–385.

Clarke, E. (2021). Indigenous women and the risk of reproductive healthcare: forced sterilization, genocide, and contemporary population control. *Journal of Human Rights and Social Work* 6: 144–147.

Davis, A. (2003). Racism, Birth Control and Reproductive Rights. In *Feminist Postcolonial Theory: A Reader*, eds. R. Lewis and S. Mills. New York: Routledge, 353–367.

de Waal, F. (2008). Putting the altruism back in altruism: the evolution of empathy. *Annual Review of Psychology* 59: 279–300.

Donald, D. (2010). 'On What Terms Can We Speak? Aboriginal-Canadian Relations as a Curricular and Pedagogical Imperative'. Paper Presented at the Big Thinking Lecture Series for the Congress of the Humanities and Social Sciences, University of Lethbridge, Alberta, Canada. Available online: https://vimeo.com/21534649

Gast, J. (1872). American Progress. Oil, 45.1 x 54.6 cm (17 3/ x 21 /2 in.). Autry Museum of Western Heritage, Los Angeles.

Gopal, P. (2019). *Insurgent Empire: Anticolonial Resistance and British Dissent*. London: Verso Books.

Grote, K. M., and Johnson, J. T. (2021). Pipelines, protectors, and settler colonialism: media representations of the Dakota Access Pipeline protest. *Settler Colonial Studies* 11(4): 487–511.

Hickel, J. (2017). *The Divide: A Brief Guide to Global Inequality and Its Solutions*. London: Routledge.

Ince, A., and Barrera de la Torre, G. (2017). Future (pre)Histories of the State: On Anarchy, Archaeology, and the Decolonial. In *Historical Geographies of Anarchism: Early Critical Geographers and Present-Day Scientific Challenges*, eds. F. Ferretti, G. Barrera de la Torre, A. Ince, and F. Toro, Routledge Research in Historical Geography. London: Routledge, 51–78.

Jackson, M. (2007). Globalisation and the Colonising State of Mind. In *Resistance: An Indigenous Response to Neoliberalism*, ed. M. Bargh. Wellington: Huia, 167–182.

James, C. L. R. (1938). *The Black Jacobins: Toussaint l'ouverture and the San Domingo Revolution*. London: Secker & Warburg.

Kiddle, R. (2020). Colonisation Sucks for Everyone. In *Imagining Decolonisation*, eds. R. Kiddle, B. Elkington, M. Jackson, O. R. Mercier, M. Ross, J. Smeaton, and A. C. Thomas. Wellington: Bridget Williams Books, 83–106.

Lester, A. (2023). The British Empire in the culture war: Nigel Biggar's colonialism: a moral reckoning. *The Journal of Imperial and Commonwealth History* 51(4): 763–795.

Liu, A., Waliuzzaman, S., Do, H. T., Haryani, R., and Pem, S. (2020). Journeys of Postdevelopment Subjectivity Transformation: A Shared Narrative of Scholars from the Majority World. In *The Handbook of Diverse Economies*. Edward Elgar Publishing, 444–451.

Melamed, J. (2015). Racial capitalism. *Critical Ethnic Studies* 1(1): 76–85.

Nandy, A. (1992). Development. In *The Development Dictionary*, ed. W. Sachs. London: Zed Press, 264–274.

Plumwood, V. (2007). A review of Deborah Bird Rose's reports from a wild country: ethics for decolonisation. *Australian Humanities Review* 42(August): 1–4.

Rose, D. B. (2004). *Reports from a Wild Country: Ethics for Decolonisation*. Sydney: UNSW Press.

Ryan, L., Debenham, J., Pascoe, B., Smith, R., Owen, C., Richards, J., Gilbert, S., Anders, R. J., Usher, K., Price, D., Newley, J., Brown, M., Le, L. H., and Fairbairn, H. (2022). *Colonial Frontier Massacres in Australia 1788–1930*. Newcastle: University of Newcastle, 2017–2022. https://c21ch.newcastle.edu.au/colonialmassacres/map.php

Shifferd, P. A. (1987). Aztecs and Africans: Political Processes in Twenty-Two Early States. In *Early State Dynamics* (vol. 2), eds. H. J. Claessen and P. Van De Velde. Leiden, The Netherlands: Brill, 39–53. https://doi.org/10.1163/9789004617995_005

Tamale, S. (2020). *Decolonization and Afro-Feminism*. Ottawa, Canada: Daraja Press.

Singh, N. (2017). Becoming a commoner: the commons as sites for affective socio-nature encounters and co-becomings. *Ephemera: Theory & Politics in Organization* 17: 751–776.

Smiles, N. D. (2018). '… to the Grave …': autopsy, settler structures and indigenous counter-conduct. *Geoforum* 91: 141–150.

Tamale, S. (2020). *Decolonization and Afro-Feminism*. Ottawa, Canada: Daraja Press.

Tronto, J. (2017). There is an alternative: homines curans and the limits of neoliberalism. *International Journal of Care and Caring* 1: 27–43.

Watts, M. (2000). Colonialism. In *The Dictionary of Human Geography*, eds. R. J. Johnston, D. Gregory, G. Pratt, and M. Watts (4th edn.). Chichester: Wiley-Blackwell, 93–95.

Whyte, K. (2018). Settler colonialism, ecology, and environmental injustice. *Environment and Society* 9: 125–144.

Wolfe, P. (2006). Settler colonialism and the elimination of the native. *Journal of Genocide Research* 8(4): 387–409.

Yates, A. M. (2021). Transforming geographies: performing Indigenous-Māori ontologies and ethics of more-than-human care in an era of ecological emergency. *New Zealand Geographer* 77: 101–113.

Yates, A., Dombroski, K., and Dionisio, R. (2022). Dialogues for wellbeing in an ecological emergency: wellbeing-led governance frameworks and transformative indigenous tools. *Dialogues in Human Geography* 13(2): 268–287.

Zaragocin, S. (2019). Gendered geographies of elimination: decolonial feminist geographies in Latin American settler contexts. *Antipode* 51(1): 373–392.

Online materials

- Mapping Indigenous L.A. https://mila.ss.ucla.edu/
  Story map project that uses digital storytelling and oral history to explore the history of colonialism and Indigenous dispossession in the Los Angeles region.

- Cultural Survival https://www.culturalsurvival.org/
  Cultural Survival is a fantastic resource for collated information, news, and articles on issues affecting present-day Traditional and Indigenous communities in the wake of colonisation.

- Proven Sustainable https://provensustainable.org/
  Proven Sustainable is a website that produces and collates audiovisual material from global Earth Elders and Traditional and Indigenous voices on the sustainable practices that they assert will maintain our collective future as a species.

- Colonial Voyage https://www.colonialvoyage.com/
  A website dedicated to the Age of Exploration and colonial history.

- Colonial Frontier Massacres in Australia, 1788–1930 https://www.theguardian.com/australia-news/ng-interactive/2019/mar/04/massacre-map-australia-the-killing-times-frontier-wars
  An interactive map produced by *The Guardian* using data from University of Newcastle's Colonial Frontier Massacres Project team.

Further Reading

Du Bois, W. E. B. (1903). *The Souls of Black Folk*. New York: Barnes and Noble. Available to read online at the Internet Archive: https://archive.org/details/soulsofblackfol300dubo
This text is a record of the African American experience of double consciousness, or the dual self-perception experience by colonised groups within an oppressive society. This text sets a framework for understanding what it is to live in the partially colonised state.

Fanon, F. (1961). *The Wretched of the Earth*. New York: Grove Press. A 2004 translation is available to read online at the Internet Archive: https://archive.org/details/wretchedofearthf0000fano
Fanon's book is an analysis of the lived experience and psychology of being colonised and potential pathways to liberation.

Memmi, A. (1965). *The Colonizer and the Colonized*. New York: Orion Press. Available to read online at the Internet Archive: https://archive.org/details/colonizercoloniz0000memm_w8w9
A historical classic written by an author with an Algerian Jewish background, on the relationship between local people and those who colonise them, notable for the identification of Memmi with the European coloniser.

Mohawk, J. (ed.) (1978). *Basic Call to Consciousness*. New York: Akwesasne Notes/Book Publishing Company. Available to read online at the Internet Archive: https://archive.org/details/basiccalltoconsc00summ/page/n131/mode/2up
Mohawk's book contains the story of the Iroquois Confederacy, more properly known as the Haudenosaunee, detailing their first experience of colonisation before the time of the Peacemaker, who restored the soul of their people to 'proper relationship', and then additionally, with the advent of European colonialism. It also contains the address made to the United Nations in 1977 regarding the future of Earth from the Haudenosaunee perspective.

Topa, W., and Narvaez, D. (2022). *Restoring the Kinship Worldview: Indigenous Voices Introduce 28 Precepts for Rebalancing Life on Planet Earth*. Berkeley: North Atlantic Books.
This text is a collection of essays from Indigenous and other scholars on the topics covered in this chapter, with discussion regarding collaborative ways to approach a return to social and ecologically sound values as we navigate towards the possibility of a decolonised future.

50 Borders

Gabriel Popescu

Introduction

When you browse through a world atlas, check places on search engines, watch news programmes, or walk inside classrooms, businesses, and government offices, you notice that the most common map is the one where the Earth's surface is divided by irregular lines called borders. This map represents our taken-for-granted view of the Earth's surface. However, taking a look at the Earth's map as seen from outer space borders are nowhere to be found, showing that the natural condition of the Earth is borderless (see Cosgrove, 1994). The two maps hardly resemble each other, although they represent the same space. The first is a political **representation** of the Earth, the second a physical representation, and it's the former, with all the borders firmly marked out, that has become the conventional map of the world, the one most people are most familiar with.

In recent years, borders have featured prominently in political and popular culture, from Europe, to the USA, to Australia, to India. Borders are presented as both causes and solutions to an assortment of issues confronting today's societies, creating a perception that if only people can get the borders right then all problems would go away. What it is about borders that makes them such significant features in contemporary societies?

Our lives have long been geographically ordered by a nested hierarchy of **territorial** and administrative borders, such as neighbourhood, city, county, region, state, and supra-state borders. Amongst these, **nation-state** borders are arguably the most recognisable. At the same time, we also live in a world defined by mobility that necessitates constant border crossing. Paradoxically, we have been busy surrounding ourselves with borders only to realise that we have to cross them all the time. Contemporary patterns of spatial interaction are creating a complex web of relationships that crisscross the fixed geography of territorial borders. Today, our lives are geographically ordered by a maze of borders that often have no clear territorial hierarchy.

Despite unprecedented opening up to various **globalisation** exchanges, borders are far from fading away. Instead, they are undertaking both a qualitative and a quantitative transformation by changing their nature and multiplying in number. They are losing some of their territorially linear aspects while acquiring more network-like characteristics. Simultaneously, bordering practices are increasingly reliant on digital technologies and are becoming embedded into our own bodies through the use of biometric measurements (Amoore, 2006). Border control has been unsettled as well, as more and more authority is transferred from public to private and

DOI: 10.4324/9780429265853-58

quasi-public institutions. The outcome is that we have to negotiate more borders, in more places, and of more kinds than ever before. Borders have become intrinsic to everyday life, affecting people and places in a highly unequal manner, and influencing how we think about the world.

The goal of this chapter is to offer an understanding of border-making by describing its underlying causes, discussing the functions it performs, showing the shapes it takes, examining the contemporary processes that drive it, and discussing its impact on society.

Making sense of borders

Borders are typically understood as lines separating two territorial entities or marking the limit of a territorial entity. Borders are **social constructions**, made by people to help them organise their lives. They are not naturally occurring divisions between people and places, even when they are placed on top of mountain ranges, shorelines, or rivers. All borders are made by someone, since humans decide their location. People have used the process of border-making for a long time as a **power** strategy to assert control over territory by marking difference in territory. However, the difference that borders mark does not have a fixed, preexisting meaning. It is humans who determine what difference means, at what times, and in what places. Throughout history, border change has been the norm rather than the exception. Borders have not existed in the same location since primordial times, they were not always imagined as lines, and they have not always performed the same functions (Popescu, 2011).

Border-making has significant structuring effects on societies as it determines who belongs where, and who is an insider and who is an outsider. As a consequence, borders have traditionally served the role of ordering society. Making borders is a means for organising human behaviour in space by regulating movement across space.

Today, borders are commonly understood as the geographical limits of the nation-state. For the most part, their rationale is taken for granted in daily life, even though the majority of today's state borders have only come into existence during the past 60 years. Early states such as Rome and China had porous frontiers, which were sparsely populated and loosely controlled areas that provided a gradual territorial transition to their neighbours. By the early twentieth century, these somewhat porous frontiers had come to be replaced by sharp border lines that provided abrupt territorial transitions from one state to another and increased control over movement. At the same time, the **ideology** of nationalism and its attempt to create national states by assuming a close overlap between the territorial sovereignty of a state and the identity of the people living inside its borders helped to consolidate the grid of border lines as the ubiquitous framework for thinking about the world (see also Chapter 48). **Colonialism** helped to globalise this particular border geography by exporting it from Europe to the rest of the world. There are currently over 300 land borders and over 400 maritime international borders, and their number continues to grow with the emergence of new states. Borders exist in a state of flux, they are always being imagined and reimagined as they constantly appear and disappear.

As divisions between nation-states, borders accumulate multiple functions and characteristics that aim to organise social life inside the territory of a state while simultaneously regulating interaction between states. Politically, borders imply the end of the authority of a state and the beginning of another. Economically, they are assumed to define the extent of the national economy. Socially, they suggest a shared national identity and cultural cohesiveness. Militarily, they are seen as defence lines to protect the state against external threats. In reality things are slightly messier than this, as borders routinely separate ethnic groups, governments claim territories inside neighbouring states, and the need for cross-border trade and migration constantly raises challenges to the capacity of borders to fully contain social relations inside state territories. As a result, borders have always functioned with various degrees of permeability as a regulatory mechanism for flows of people, goods, and money. The managing of border permeability across the world is codified in a variety of border regimes that range from virtually closed, as in the case of North Korea, to quite open, as in the case of the internal borders of the European Union. According to the context in which they operate, borders can work as barriers or bridges in relation to neighbouring countries (Sidaway, 2002).

An essential characteristic of state borders consists in their double meaning as lines of separation and contact in space. Whenever a border is erected, it acquires two meanings simultaneously. On the one hand it separates two groups of people, while on the other it links them by bringing them into contact. This makes border-making a tricky business, as it is impossible to address only one aspect of borders without considering the other. Whenever governments choose to restrict cross-movement, for example, the forces responsible for this phenomenon react by pushing back for more cross-movement.

Borders also have a symbolic dimension. They are continually produced and reproduced through a series of **discourses** aimed at maintaining their relevance in people's lives. Geography and history textbooks, media images of checkpoints and fences, patriotic songs, national maps, and passports, all constitute powerful symbols that serve to perpetuate and reinforce state borders in people's minds.

Summary

- Borders are not naturally occurring divisions between people. They are social constructions made by people.
- Borders are the outcome of power relations and they serve the purpose of marking perceived differences in space.
- They perform multiple functions aimed at organising social life inside a territory and regulating interaction between countries.

Borders in the era of globalisation

In the late twentieth century, state border lines came under steady pressure from various globalisation processes whose logic of movement required increased permeability. Different aspects of social and economic life such as economic trade and global consumption; the management of the environment and climate change; the tackling of pandemics; combatting organised crime, and the rise of social media have all helped to develop patterns of geographical organisation that are **transnational** and which cut through state borders. These developments led to a growing disconnection between the geography of globalisation and the ability of border lines to regulate it. For example, it is useful to think how electronic money flows circle the globe with the speed of light every day between financial centres such as London, New York, and Tokyo with little regard to national borders (see Chapter 31), and how borders have done little to contain viral outbreaks such as COVID-19 that has spread from continent to continent through global travel.

To maintain the relevance of national borders, the production of borders today is driven by the tension between simultaneous demands for unimpeded cross-border mobility on the one hand and for reliable territorial security on the other. The main objective is to achieve a border regime of highly selective permeability that can allow the free flow of exchanges that powerful stakeholders consider desirable, while also blocking the exchanges that these stakeholders consider less desirable. For example, borders may be porous for most forms of capital but not for most categories of labour. In other words, borders are expected to function much like 'firewalls', designed to allow the smooth functioning of legitimate traffic while blocking unwanted intruders. The key questions that emerge now are who decides what constitutes legitimate traffic, and how can we be confident that our own mobility, taken for granted today, will not be deemed illegitimate tomorrow?

To implement this new regime, borders have taken on additional functions and territorial configurations in order to become articulate and mobile. One way to make sense of how and what kind of new borders are being produced is to think in terms of de- and re-bordering dynamics. While some borders in some places have their barrier functions significantly diminished, other borders in other places are erected. These new borders often do not maintain a linear appearance and are not located at the edges of a state's territory.

Three main types of border spaces can be associated with globalisation's current political, economic, and cultural geographies – borderlands, networked borders, and border lines. In the first case, the territorial depth of borders is acknowledged and is managed as transitional regions that connect state territories. Borderlands can range anywhere from narrow strips of land adjacent to the border line, to large regions like the U.S.-Mexico borderland or Pakistan's Northwest Territories. In the second case, borders acquire territorial mobility by being embedded into flows so that border functions can be performed in any location in the world. We can think of borders as 'portable', or projected at distance from the margins of states. Consider the examples of an immigration raid in a poor neighbourhood, an immigration status check in a hospital, an offshore refugee camp, or the online software that verifies our personal identity data when purchasing airplane tickets from the comfort of our homes.

In the last case, borders preserve the appeal of sharp lines and become reinforced by fences and walls. Despite the highly problematic utility of such structures and their exorbitant price tags, fencing people in and out of territories has become a major business as well as a political panacea. The political popularity of reinforced border lines resides primarily with their symbolic value as simplified blueprints for organising identity along 'us versus them' binary oppositions. Tens of thousands of kilometres of border fences have been built worldwide, from the U.S. fence at its border with Mexico, to the EU borders in Europe and North Africa, and from Saudi Arabia and Israel to the India-Bangladesh border.

The result of these restructuring dynamics is the multiplication and diversification of borders and their diffusion inside state territories and increasingly into everyday lives. Globalisation, despite being commonly associated with a 'borderless world', has in fact produced more rather than fewer borders and has increased rather than decreased their complexity.

Summary

- With globalisation, borders came under pressure to allow for increased permeability of exchanges.
- In response, borders changed their functions and multiplied their shapes to include borderlands, networks, and lines.
- Globalisation has led to a more complex border geography and an increase in the number and type of borders.

Border security discourses and the management of mobile threats

In recent years, security discourses have reframed national security threats in terms of transnational phenomena to be managed with the help of borders. In particular, it is the mobility aspect of these phenomena that has become the core security concern. The fact that migration, terrorism, economic flows, electronic crime, and environmental pollution can originate both inside and outside a state's territory has significantly blurred the distinction between internal and external security to the point of fusing the two realms. Various aspects of transnational flows with significantly different causes and behaviours are frequently lumped together in public discourse and are presented as potential threats to the personal livelihoods of citizens. A key outcome is that security issues are increasingly perceived as being more directly connected to everyday life. Certain fears people have in their private lives, such as job insecurity or being victims of crime, become more easily projected into the realm of national security. The result has been the penetration of security policies and practices deep into the fabric of society to the level of the individual. It is seemingly everyday life, rather than state territory, that now must be secured first in order for the people to feel secure.

This worldview casts mobility and security in antagonistic terms and sees borders as tools for securing global flows. The belief is that enhanced border surveillance covering various aspects of daily life would allow risks to be identified and prevented. Then, risk management strategies can be employed with the help of highly mobile borders to predict risks by meaningfully differentiating between 'good' and 'bad' mobility. Risks, however, are about probabilities. Deciding which of the numerous risks people face in their daily lives constitutes an existential threat to society is a complex task. Accordingly, seeing borders as tools for risk management opens up space for the politicisation of risk and makes borders more contested. For example, the recent security discourses emphasise risks from migration and organised crime, while playing down the social risks associated with free trade and environmental pollution.

In recent decades, the issue of migration has been constructed as a major border security risk throughout the developed world. Transnational migration today is largely a result of widening

Figure 50.1
Migrants and refugees in Italy together with the USB union demonstrate against the Meloni government and the Cutro Decree which will cancel the special protection for refugees. Under the new law, migrants will no longer be able to convert the special protection into a work permit: a change likely to increase the number of undocumented workers in Italy

Source: Photo credit: Alamy, taken on 28 April 2023 in Rome

unevenness in global development and conflict-generated violence. It encompasses various aspects, ranging from short-term to permanent situations, and covering work-related to refugee-specific mobilities. Political discourses and media reports often overlook these differences and associate migration with criminality, helping to create an image of migrants as threatening **Others**. In countries as diverse as the USA, the UK, Australia, and in the European Union, several rounds of legislation have been passed over the years to criminalise migration and establish border security as central to the regulation of migration (Figure 50.1). Shilliam (2018) and El-Enany (2020) both provide an excellent historical account of these policies in the UK context. Every new round of legislation has enhanced border policing capacity, expanded the list of infractions that made migrants eligible for deportation, and increased investment in border **infrastructure**. As a result, migration legislation tends to ignore differences between various types of migration, focusing instead on tightening the requirements for legal admission across the board. As more avenues to migrate legally are closed, large migrant categories such as refugees and temporary migrants increasingly turn to illegal migration. Illegal migration continues to grow, and migration fears in host societies become self-fulfilling security risks. The issue is that border security makes a poor solution to migration management because it cannot address its root causes.

CASE STUDY
'EVERYDAY BORDERING'

Over the last few decades, countries such as the USA, Australia, and the UK have enacted migration management policies that have expanded national borders inside their territories and into people's everyday lives. In 2012, the UK government formally announced a set of policies aimed to create a 'hostile environment' for undocumented migrants that would make their lives unbearable to the point where they would choose to leave (Figure 50.2). The intention was to prevent undocumented migrants from accessing a wide range of public services. It is important to note that the hostile environment for immigrants is not new; the logics of deportation (or 'repatriation') and racialised exclusions in welfare, housing, and employment are centuries old (see Jacobs, 1985, El-Enany, 2020, also see Chapter 55).

New laws were passed requiring people's immigration status be checked by staff in hospitals, universities, workplaces, housing agencies, and banks. Employers, landlords, doctors, social workers, educators, and bank clerks had to determine their workers', tenants', patients', students', and clients' rights to receive services. Essentially, private citizens are called upon to assume border policing roles in their everyday life, and report on other private citizens suspected of being 'illegally' in the country. Such policies create suspicion

Figure 50.2
In 2013 UK Home Office used vans with adverts urging 'illegal immigrants' to 'go Home or face arrest'

Source: Photo credit: UK border Agency/Home Office/PA

Figure 50.3
An Immigration Enforcement van in Kenmure Street, Glasgow was surrounded by hundreds of protesters on the 13 May 2021. Inside the van, two men had been detained for 'suspected immigration offences' and were later released

Source: Photo credit: Andrew Milligan/Alamy

and fear in people's daily lives and within communities. They disproportionately affect minority groups and work to undermine trust in authorities. However, such measures have generated citizen-led movements of solidarity and resistance, as shown in Figure 50.3 (also see Brambilla and Jones, 2020).

Summary

- Borders are employed as tools to secure highly mobile transnational exchanges by expanding surveillance inside society and utilising risk management strategies.
- These practices have increased the politicisation of borders and made them more contested.
- Migration has been constructed as a major security risk, pushing borders inside the daily lives of citizens.

Embodied borders and the digital connection

Imagining borders as tools to control mobile risks works to embed borders in the human body. The body has become the ultimate mobile border that can allow constant and accurate monitoring of movement at the smallest spatial scale. Mobile risks can be estimated from mobile bodies and efficiently eliminated at the border so that traffic flows are not disrupted. A vast array of digital technologies work as interfaces for integrating **embodied** borders and risk assessment systems in order to automate border crossing. Biometric technology, used to digitise bodily data such as fingerprints and iris patterns in order to store them on passport chips and border security databases, is one such example. Radio frequency identification (RFID) technology, used to wirelessly broadcast these bodily data stored on chips so that their owners' movement can be tracked without being stopped at the border, is another example.

Today, biometrics and RFID are mainstays of border securitisation regimes from Thailand and Australia to Nigeria and the USA. They are being used in large-scale applications affecting hundreds of millions of people, most notably through government-issued e-passports and through the setup of numerous border-related databases. The appeal of border digital technologies lies in the possibility of automated remote-control identification while on the move, which reduces transaction costs and speeds up flows by minimising human intervention. Consequently, these technologies are entrusted with key decision-making powers about people's lives.

This technology-driven border regime, often called 'Smart Borders', works under the assumption that identifying a person's body is similar to knowing a person's identity, and that the identity of an individual makes a reliable risk predictor (Pötzsch, 2015). Accordingly, biometric identification at the border is used in two major ways. The first purpose is to verify someone's identity and is most commonly associated with current e-travel documents. In this instance, the biometrics stored in our passports serve to verify our identity to confirm that we are who we say we are (Figure 50.4).

Figure 50.4
Biometric passport in Essen, Germany

Source: Photo credit: Oberhaeuser/Alamy

Our bodies work much like passwords, providing personal identification on the move. Nonetheless, simply verifying our identities does little to increase security, as verification cannot meaningfully determine who is a security risk. For this to happen, the second use of biometrics is to establish someone's identity to address the question, 'Who is this person?'. This task necessitates the establishment and maintenance of vast databases to include information about our everyday lives that can be electronically mined to reveal patterns of behaviour and association. Once our biometrics are recorded into a database, personal information can be collected every time there is a hit on them. Every time our identity is checked biometrically, this leaves a trace in a database that is stored under our profile according to predetermined criteria such as name, address, country of origin, how many times we cross a border, which borders we crossed and in what places, means of transportation used, form of payment for the trip, duration of stay, driving history, type of meal consumed in flight, seating preference, and more. This is how our digital identity takes shape in a database without us even being aware of it. When this entire digital infrastructure is in place at the border-crossing points, computerised software reads the passport chip and the body part, identifies personal data in the database, and then analyses them according to an obscured algorithm that produces our identity profile with a calculated risk score assigned to it. The end product is a computer-generated identity that few understand but that everybody must trust.

CASE STUDY
'THE MAKING OF THE REFUGEE CRISIS'

During the fall of 2015, more than one million refugees from war-torn countries like Syria, Iraq, and Afghanistan rushed to reach the European Union in search of asylum. Their sudden movement was triggered by a generous pledge from the German government to take in a substantial number of refugees in need of protection. The German offer, however, included no provision for the transport of refugees from the Middle East to Germany. In the absence of designated transportation corridors, refugees' only option was to make it to Germany on their own.

The EU's asylum laws require refugees to apply for asylum in the EU country of first arrival and wait there for the necessary documents to relocate to the destination country. The procedure demands refugees provide their fingerprints to be entered into an EU-wide biometric database in order to digitally tie their place of residence to the country of first entry. In this way, territorial borders are coded into refugees' bodies. This is precisely what many refugees crossing the Mediterranean from Turkey wanted to avoid when they refused registration upon arrival to Greece. Instead, they proceeded to move on overland to reach Germany through countries like Macedonia, Serbia, Croatia, Hungary, and Austria, creating the appearance of a chaotic movement overwhelming the capabilities of transit countries to provide humanitarian services for them.

The sense of crisis further escalated when the government of Hungary scrambled to erect barbed wire fences along their southern borders with Serbia in a desperate attempt to stop refugees from entering EU territory. The outcome was that refugees become stranded in makeshift camps and changed their border crossing attempts to neighbouring countries, which led to them being perceived by some in Europe as a threat to public order. In effect, the lack of coordination between the EU governments, together with inadequate EU asylum legislation, has been central to transforming the movement of refugees into a crisis. To put this event into perspective, the 2022 arrival of Ukrainian refugees into the EU has been much more effectively managed but also reflects the racialisation of refugees.

A closer examination of the 'Smart Borders' regime raises significant concerns over its capability of reconciling mobility and security via risk-based identity management. Overreliance on technology promotes a view of security as a problem that requires a technical fix and assumes that the world's structural problems can be addressed by bordering them away with the help of technology. Risk scores, biometric data, and other information on hundreds of millions of bodies have done little to improve societal or personal security. People who go on to commit terrorist acts continue to get through the 'Smart borders'; migration and smuggling show few signs of letting up; and the adverse effects of unregulated cross-border economic flows continue to widen the gap between the rich and the poor.

The issue is that the data in a database can be made to tell multiple stories about a person according to what type of information the algorithmic software is programmed to look for. The algorithms define good and bad citizens according to how they are written. As the criteria by which the algorithms work are kept secret and can change with the powers that govern us, the politics of biometrics becomes crucially important going forward (Amoore, 2006). The concern is that without a thorough understanding of what these new technologies of power can and cannot do, bordering practices can incorporate racial, **class**, ethnic, or **gender** stereotypes and prejudices that perpetuate existing inequalities. At the same time, relying on impersonal technologies to incorporate mass surveillance activities into the fabric of societies in the name of border security risks shedding accountability for control and reduces opportunities for democratic participation in the making of the new border regimes.

Summary

- Digital technologies such as biometrics have allowed borders to become embedded into human bodies. In this way, borders have become highly personal and mobile.
- The goal is to achieve highly individualised control of mobility in order to allow flows to travel unimpeded through space.
- This technology-driven border regime rises concerns regarding personal liberties and democratic participation.

Conclusion

Borders continue to play central roles in organising how people and societies interact across space. We are living through a period of border change with long-lasting implications for the prospects of democratic life and personal freedoms. When borders change functions, shapes, and meanings, people's lives change as well. This chapter has sought to help readers uncover the inherent complexities borders involve, their unfinished character, and their fundamentally contested nature.

Often taken for granted as natural divisions between countries, borders are better understood as social constructions grounded in cultural practices and power dynamics. Far from being the remote limits of states, borders take on a plurality of shapes, types, and functions that reach deep into societies to the level of our bodies. Today, national borders throughout the world have been entrusted with a new long-term rationale of being the guarantors of our security in a globalising world. Understanding borders helps us recognising the power relations they involve and enables us to act in a way that maximises our rights and improves social justice.

Discussion points

* Why and how have borders emerged?
* What is the purpose of borders?
* What new types of borders have emerged with globalisation?
* How do borders impact everyday life far away from the margins of countries?
* Beyond the nation-state, can you think of other examples of borders and bordering?

References

Brambilla, C., and Jones, R. (2020). Rethinking borders, violence, and conflict: from sovereign power to borderscapes as sites of struggles. *Environment and Planning D: Society and Space* 38(2): 287–305.

Cosgrove, D. (1994). Contested global visions: one-world, whole-earth and the Apollo space photographs. *Annals of the Association of American Geographers* 84: 270–294.

El-Enany, N. (2020). *Bordering Britain: Law, Race and Empire*. Manchester: Manchester University Press.

Jacobs, S. (1985). Race, empire and the welfare state: council housing and racism. *Critical Social Policy* 5(13): 6–28.

Pötzsch, H. (2015). The emergence of iBorder: bordering bodies, networks, and machines. *Environment and Planning D* 33: 101–118.

Shilliam, R. (2018). *Race and the Undeserving Poor: From Abolition to Brexit*. Newcastle-upon-Tyne: Agenda Publishing.

Sidaway, J. (2002). Signifying boundaries: detours around the Portuguese-Spanish (Algarve/Alentejo-Andalucía) borderlands. *Geopolitics* 9(1): 139–164.

Online materials

* Right to Remain – YouTube – A series of accessible videos produced by Right to Remain who work with groups across the UK supporting migrants to establish their right to remain with dignity, safety, and humanity, and to challenge injustice in the UK's asylum and immigration system [https://www.youtube.com/c/RighttoremainOrgUk].

- The Virtual wall of Europe – VPRO documentary – 2014 – YouTube – A Dutch documentary that considers the array of digital surveillance technologies – from drones to the storage of biometric data – used to control Europe's borders [https://youtu.be/a8IKhmpYRws].

Further reading

Amoore, L. (2006). Biometric borders: governing mobilities in the war on terror. *Political Geography* 25: 336–351.
This paper addresses the emergence of risk profiling and surveillance of mobility within the War on Terror. It develops the concept of the 'biometric border' to analyse the place of digital technology and private security firms in border management, and the ways power is encoded in and through the body of migrants and travellers.

Darling, J. (2022). *Systems of Suffering: Dispersal and the Denial of Asylum*. London: Pluto Press.
This book critiques the structural violence embedded in UK's asylum system and foregrounds the voices and experiences of refugees and asylum seekers.

Dean, K., Sarma, J., and Rippa, A. (2022). Infrastructures and b/ordering: how Chinese projects are ordering China–Myanmar border spaces. *Territory, Politics, Governance*. DOI: 10.1080/21622671. 2022.2108892
A useful case study of how infrastructural projects, such as China's Belt and Road Initiative, can be used as a technology of b/ordering.

Fauser, M., Friedrichs, A., and Harders, L. (2019). Migrations and borders: practices and politics of inclusion and exclusion in Europe from the nineteenth to the twenty-first century. *Journal of Borderlands Studies* 34(4): 483–488.
A special issue that takes a historical perspective to the relationship between borders and migratory movements in Europe, and the shifting borders of modern (nation-)states.

Jones, R. (2016). *Violent Borders: Refugees and the Right to Move*. London: Verso.
This accessible book highlights the devastating impact borders have on human and non-human life. It draws on case studies from the European Union, the US-Mexico border, the West Bank, Australia, the India-Bangladesh border, and the Bangladesh-Myanmar (Burma) border.

Popescu, G. (2011). *Bordering and Ordering the Twenty-First Century: Understanding Borders*. New York: Rowman & Littlefield Publishers.
This book examines why and how interstate borders have emerged, whose interest they serve, who is involved in border-making, and how border-making practices affect societies. Case studies focus on how migration, terrorism, global warming, pandemics, the international human rights regime, outsourcing, the economic crisis, supranational integration, **regionalisation**, and digital technology relate to borders and influence our lives.

Wastl-Walter, D. (ed.) (2011). *The Ashgate Research Companion to Border Studies*. Farnham: Ashgate.
An accessible and comprehensive introduction to interdisciplinary work on border studies, and the different methods geographers might use to study borders.

51 Critical geopolitics

Sara Fregonese

Introduction

This chapter introduces some of the strands through which a sustained critique of geopolitical power mechanisms has unfolded in political geography over the course of the last 30 years. These critical strands in what has become known as critical geopolitics have not developed in neat succession, and there are overlaps, parallels and gaps in and between approaches. For the sake of structure, however, here I review critical geopolitics scholarship along two different but related approaches. The first approach focuses on how geopolitical *meaning* is constructed and legitimated; it employs ***representations*** (such as texts and images) as its main tools for deconstructing spatial narratives of global politics. The second focuses on geopolitics as *experience* that emerges, unfolds and is encountered in ordinary life beyond and besides representations; this approach considers *practices* (including **embodiment**, materiality, experience and **performativity**) as starting points for its critique. Either via analyses of representation or engagements with experience, critical geopolitics considers spatial representations of world politics as contextual and situated rather than objective and scientific, and as present to everyday life rather than detached from it. Both approaches – the **discursive** and the experiential – advocate imagining alternative, more just and sustainable geopolitical arrangements and futures.

Conventional geopolitics

Geopolitics can be succinctly defined as the body of knowledge through which, in the last two centuries, world politics have been understood and represented geographically, and as the actions in international policy taken on the basis of those understandings and representations.

In everyday contemporary contexts, such as news reporting, geopolitics often coincides with international conflict, mostly related to **territorial** contestation and control. In academic Human Geography, however, geopolitics has a complex scholarly history. Ó Tuathail (2013) has identified four main areas where conventional geopolitics focuses its concern: first, how the physical geographic features of the Earth influence the exercise of international power; second, the exercise of state power through territoriality and governing populations; third, the competition for space and resources between states or polities like empires; and fourth, the practices and ideas of resistance to predominant territorial schemes.

DOI: 10.4324/9780429265853-59

One overarching mechanism within traditional geopolitics is that of broad spatial general-isations of political phenomena. This kind of analysis reduces complex realities to simplified, worldwide formulas of explanation. The representational power of geopolitics relies on provid-ing at-a-glance visions of the world political map, relating local and regional dynamics to a 'global system' of human actors and organisations – states, polities, armies, peoples and cul-tures – arranged across (and often seen as influenced by) a world of uneven continents, oceans, resources and people. This 'big picture vision' offers a coherent system of representation and analysis of any geographical scale.

This type of traditional geopolitical analysis has existed for a long time. Sir Halford Mackinder, one of the very first Professors of Geography at a British university, who created the School of Geography at Oxford University in 1899 and helped to found the London School of Economics in 1895, was a geopolitical theorist. At the turn of the twentieth century, he offered the *Heartland* theory, in which world political relations centred on one strategic continental 'pivot area' – the heartland Russia and central Asia; the control of Heartland, he theorised, was the key to world domination. A century later, after the end of the Cold War, Samuel Huntington's *Clash of Civilizations* thesis imagined a world of separate rival cultural regions. Huntington imagined these 'civilisations' as being like tectonic plates, along whose fault lines inevitable clashes and conflicts would occur. America and the West, he predicted, would clash with the civilisations of China and Islam. Huntington's work was widely read and cited in the media as the 'War on Terror' started late in 2001. These classic geopolitical visions remain powerful, alluring and persuasive; perhaps because they reduce complex realities to simplified explanations and thus offer clear practical recommendations for government policy: for instance, around strategic pri-orities in international policy; identifying threats to national interest; devising responses to such threats.

This conventional geopolitics and the foreign policy visions and actions that they shape have been subjected to sustained analysis and critique in political geography over the past 30 years. The critique is mainly aimed at teasing apart the gaps, silences and the (neo)colonial and/or exclusionary actions and policies that these essentialised views promote. The next section out-lines the first of two critical approaches to conventional geopolitics – one that focuses on the production and use of representations (such as texts and images) to trace how geopolitical nar-ratives are made meaningful, legitimate, predominant over others, and how they shape interna-tional understanding and action in international foreign policy.

Deconstructing geopolitical meaning

In the past 30 years, political geographers have advanced a sustained critique of the representa-tions and **discourses** through which conventional geopolitics legitimises and normalises spe-cific political views of the global power and annexed international policy decision. This critical current has engaged geopolitics 'as a social, cultural and political practice, rather than as a man-ifest and legible reality of world politics' (Dalby and Ó Tuathail, 1998: 2) and has used represen-tation and discourse deconstruction as its main lenses and methods of enquiry.

This type of critical geopolitics, especially in its early days, has had at its core 'deconstruct[ing] policy texts to examine the use of geographical reasoning in statecraft' (Dodds and Sidaway, 1994: 515) that is to say, understanding how specific spatial representations of world power are made meaningful, but also importantly, how they come to underpin and legitimate specific agendas for action in international politics.

The philosophical underpinnings of this discursive type of critical geopolitics lie in post-structuralism and scholars in this area have drawn from theorists like Michel Foucault, Edward Said and Gayatri Chakravorty Spivak. At the core of discursive critical geopolitics has been an attempt to redress conventional geopolitics' claims of scientific objectivity around the interpre-tation of global politics and power and to expose it instead as a type of knowledge about world politics that is always partial and contingent to context where it is produced.

The discursive critique mainly tackles three representational mechanisms underpinning tradi-tional geopolitics. The first mechanism has to do with vision. Conventional geopolitics' compre-hensive narratives of the world are what Agnew (2003) calls *God's trick*. They offer a supposedly detached and objective 'view from nowhere' onto a world conceived as an orderly and coherent whole. Critical geopolitics shows us instead how these representations are not god tricks, but situated knowledges produced by real people (predominantly men) thinking and acting within specific contexts of power, culture, and place. And those geopolitical visions often say as much about the people who come up with them – their cultural contexts, their **ideological** alle-giances, their political priorities – as they say about the world 'out there' that those experts claim to describe.

The second mechanism has to do with scale. Traditional geopolitics predominantly offers a state-centred view. The main actors on the world map are states: enemy or friendly states, groups, pan-regions, axes, rims, blocs of states. The narrator of these maps, and its main unit of measure and meaning, is almost solely the state (Ó Tuathail, 1996). Agnew (2003) calls this process of conceiving the state and its territorial borders as the exclusive spatial units to understand world politics a *territorial trap*.

The third mechanism has to do with value and is connected with the imperial enterprises that much of classical geopolitics underpinned in the 19th and early 20th centuries. It is what Agnew (2003: 25) called *global cultural hierarchy*. This mechanism projected homogenised and exoticised **imaginative geographies** (Gregory, 1998, Said, 1995) onto other places and people other than those in Europe, and especially those in colonised lands, that pictured them onto different '"levels" of civilisation with Europe at the top' (Agnew, 2003: 25). By designating places on the map as 'inner' and 'marginal' (MacKinder), or as 'first-', 'second-' or 'third world' (like during the Cold War) or as 'axis of evil' (as during the War on Terror), conventional geopolitical repre-sentations have been deconstructed by discursive critical geopolitics in their creation of moral and identity hierarchies between places on the world map, thus facilitating assumptions about cultural superiority, rights of expansion, perceptions of threat and us versus them outlooks.

Over three decades, unsurprisingly, discourse-based critical geopolitics has developed into a very diverse array of conceptual approaches and topics spanning sovereignty (McConnell, 2009), popular culture and art (Dodds, 2007, Dittmer and Gray, 2010, Ingram, 2019, Benwell and Pinkerton, 2020) (Figure 51.1), and violence and peace (Megoran and Dalby, 2018) among others. However, political geographers have also, and in parallel, argued that, with its focus on discourse and textual deconstruction of the official and large-scale representations of global politics, critical geopolitics does little to provide workable alternative views of world and, most importantly, has made invisible the ways geopolitics affects our ordinary experience and 'the everyday ways in which people *live* geopolitics' (Dittmer and Gray, 2010: 1671; see also Ó Tuathail, 2021).

Figure 51.1
A screenshot of *Call of Duty: Modern Warfare*. Geographers have long considered the interconnections between popular culture and geopolitics. Geopolitical imaginations do not emerge ex nihilo but are constructed, circulated and contested through popular practices of film, television, newspapers, podcasting, and computer games (see, for example, Dodds, 2019, Bos, 2021)

Source: Photo credit: Inge Flinte

Maggie O'Kane and the anti-geopolitical eye

Perhaps one of the best examples of critical geopolitics' deconstruction of conventional geopolitical discourse is that of Maggie O'Kane. In his *Critical Geopolitics*, Ó Tuathail (1996) put forward the notion of the *anti-geopolitical eye* as an embodied, close-up and non-official view that provides a counter-narrative to dominant framings and representations of geopolitical issues and, by extension, violent conflict. To exemplify this, Ó Tuathail discusses the work of journalist Maggie O'Kane, who reported on the conflict in Bosnia in the early 1990s during the breakup of former Yugoslavia (Figure 51.2). O'Kane's very personal and close-up reports from the streets and cities of the Bosnia war rather than from a newsroom showed the impacts of violence on people's everyday lives and used these to call for the international community to intervene to stop the conflict. Jennifer Hyndman described O'Kane's journalism as 'as kind of **feminist** geopolitics at work' (Hyndman, 2004: 311). Through this reporting approach, O'Kane displaced the conventional representations and expertise that had made sense of the conflict until then. O'Kane didn't offer the detached and impartial view usually adopted by geopolitics experts and pundits; her reports were a situated perspective – not the disembodied vision from nowhere of classical geopolitical reasoning, but a view *from somewhere*. By using 'the experience of ordinary people as the central register for recording highly personal stories of war', O'Kane's reporting points to 'embodied ways of seeing war, witnessing and protesting violence' (Hyndman, 2004: 319) as alternative visions, oppositional analyses, which counter the grand narratives of conventional

Figure 51.2
Geopolitical processes manifest in ordinary lives. During the Bosnian War, Sarajevo was besieged by
the Army of Republika Srpska from 5 April 1992 to 29 February 1996 (1,425 days). Amid the blockage
and facing severe food and water shortages, residents risked their lives to source essentials and were
frequently exposed to snipers and artillery shells

Source: Photo credit: Johnny Saunderson/Alamy Stock Photo

geopolitics. O'Kane's example of embodied and oppositional geopolitical gaze is ideal to move
on to the next section. Here, I review a wide scholarship in critical geopolitics, comprising feminist, non-representational and urban scholarship, which has extended the object and method of
enquiry beyond the critique of discourse and representation, and into the everyday experience
of geopolitics.

Summary

- Geopolitics signifies the geographical understanding and representation of world politics, and the actions taken based on those understandings and representations.
- Conventionally, geopolitics offers simplified explanations and practical recommendations for governments on international strategic priorities; national security threats and responses. However, such visions also tend to reduce complex realities to simplified representations.
- Political geographers – using deconstruction as their methods of enquiry – have critiqued established geopolitical representations and how they normalise specific views of global power.

Little things, big impacts. Critical geopolitics besides discourse

At the end of *Geopolitical Traditions* (Dodds and Atkinson, 2000), cultural geographer Nigel Thrift authored a short but incisive chapter titled *It's the little things*. Like arguments made by feminist geographers at the time of his writing, Thrift observed how the focus of critical geopolitics until then had tended to be on deconstructing representations and discourses of state power. Drawing on philosophies such as **non-representational theory** (NRT), and feminist and **postcolonial** approaches, Thrift noted that critical geopolitics had a limited **epistemological** approach to the critique of geopolitics, and also a narrow view of discourse as purely text or image. What discourse-based critical geopolitics left out, Thrift argued, were 'the little things': objects, humans and emotions where the geopolitical becomes present to our ordinary lives. To reclaim these ordinary workings of geopolitics within critical scholarship, Thrift (2000) called for 'a parallel agenda' going beyond the deconstruction of geopolitical representations and discourses, and focusing instead on the practices where geopolitical events, agendas and representations become intermingled with everyday experience.

Think for example of the UK's exit from the European Union on 31 January 2020 and the gradual but tangible impacts that this change in international relations has brought to UK road and traffic **infrastructure**. Since 1 January 2021, a series of inland border facilities have been gradually put in place. These are sites, far from ports, where customs and checks for transiting goods are implemented on Heavy Goods Vehicles (HGVs). These infrastructures, necessary under Brexit and the new set of relationships between the UK and the EU, require construction and development that has several everyday implications and contentions. While the inland border facilities are often seen as opportunities for local investment by the government in the context of the UK Government's Levelling Up agenda, communities in the vicinity of the sites – such as the White Cliffs Inland Border Facility near Dover – have been vocal about the negative impact of these sites, from increased HGV traffic, to noise and light pollution due to night-time construction floodlights (O'Carroll, 2021). From this viewpoint, it becomes clearer how the geopolitical and the everyday are not separate but connected realms bound together intimately by embodied, material and emotional connections that are made of 'events, **encounters**, movements, dialogues, actions, **affects** and things' (Pain and Smith, 2008: 7).

Embodied and emotional geopolitics

The body has gained 'a steady and significant increase in interest and analytical centrality' (Mountz, 2018: 760) in political geography literature for the past 20 years, reflecting a related increase in feminist approaches in the sub-discipline. Cynthia Enloe's book *Bananas, Beaches and Bases* (Enloe, 2000) was a precursor of these feminist debates around bodies (and especially female bodies) in political geography. Enloe brought to the fore the everyday spaces and mechanisms of **gender**, **class** and **ethnicity** – from military women to female labourers, from diplomatic wives to stewardesses – that are an inseparable yet silenced part of a type of representation of international politics that is focused on masculinity and officiality. Feminist approaches to geopolitics focus on the body by 'reposition[ing] the body not as passive matter of empirical exclusion but as an active site of political engagement and resistance' (Mountz, 2018: 761). Dynamics of geopolitical power become reflected on and shaped by specific bodies – as well as those excluded from specific geopolitical narratives. Of note here is Sara Smith's (2012) work on religious-led pro-childbearing campaigns and the ban of religious intermarriage in India's northern contested region of Jammu and Kashmir as part of a geopolitical project to defend territorial presence, identity and sovereignty of populations against the real or perceived risk of 'dying out'. 'In this narrative' Smith argues, 'the birth of a baby is more than a family event; it is part of a struggle to populate space with the right kinds of bodies' (2012: 1519), thus showing the body as a terrain where geopolitics becomes lived, grounded and embedded in everyday (contested) practices.

Emotions are a further realm where the connectedness between official and everyday geopolitics comes into view. Rachel Pain (2009) argued that many discussions around the emotional facets of the geopolitical agendas and public reactions in the wake of the 9-11 attacks against the Twin Towers in New York and the US Pentagon (Ó Tuathail, 2003) relied on a universalised and disembodied notion of fear, as if felt by everyone in the same way. This approach, Pain argues, divorces fear from the ways it plays out in everyday social and spatial contexts and overlooks how fear (and, by extension, security) is actually experienced and prioritised, where and by whom (see also Pain, 1991, Sidaway, 2008). Arguing for 'rupturing the very idea of these spaces and scales, because they tend to fix commanding notions about emotions, power, **human agency** and being' (Pain, 2009: 472–473), Pain proposes an emotional geopolitics of fear that, firstly, enquiries how emotions are deployed – individually and collectively – for political purposes and, secondly, how emotional dispositions politicise subjects and mobilise collective action at the conscious level.

More recently, addressing an existing scholarly gap between cultural geographies of affect and political geography, critical geopolitics is employing experience and affective **atmospheres** as lenses to provide analyses of armed conflict (Fregonese, 2017), post-conflict cities (Laketa, 2016), (counter)terrorism (Fregonese and Laketa, 2022) and diplomacy (Jones, 2020, Legg, 2020) that account for the role of the non-human, e.g. objects, and affective atmospheres in an effort to step beyond purely discursive critiques and tap into the everyday experience and agency of ordinary people and non-humans in war, peace, violence and diplomacy.

In the next and final section, I take note of Thrift's parallel agenda for critical geopolitics and consider the role of objects and materiality to convey, mediate and ground geopolitics in everyday experience. Here, I take this material focus broadly, to point to how the built environment of cities and towns connects large-scale geopolitics with localised everyday dynamics of more or less overt violence.

Summary

- Based on feminist and non-representational philosophies, a more recent strand of critical geopolitics focuses on geopolitics as experienced and practised in ordinary and everyday life.
- This approach considers embodiment, materiality, experience and performativity as lenses for its critique of conventional geopolitics.

Urban geopolitics: theorising world politics from the city

From the war in Ukraine to the uprisings in Chile and Lebanon; from the destruction and reconstruction of Syrian cities, to terrorist attacks against public spaces in Europe and beyond, urban spaces are central to today's international politics headlines.

This is unsurprising, as cities are some of the central and constitutive terrains of geopolitical dynamics today. According to the United Nations Conference on Trade and Development (2022), today 58% of the world's population lives in urban areas, with the highest rates of urban growth taking place in developing economies. Cities are hubs in networks of global productivity, 'complex actors with multiple capabilities who find themselves at the forefront of many of our major challenges – from the environment to terrorism' (Sassen, 2012), which makes them strategic places, including for global politics. Cities also are places where identity and difference are produced, encountered and can become contested.

Geopolitics and accounts of conflict and contestation have been long dominated by state-centred views: how states wage war against each other, how they weave diplomatic relations and how they see themselves strategically in the world. Lesser attention has been paid to how global politics are reflected in, and shaped by, cities. There has been, as Stephen Graham put it, an 'almost complete dominance of national, rather than subnational spaces and politics within international relations and political sciences' (Graham, 2004: 24).

For the last 20 years, an interdisciplinary corpus of geography, planning and urban studies literature under the banner of urban geopolitics has studied how geopolitics translates onto the urban ground, and how global and localised power and politics become connected in cities. Urban geopolitics scholarship initially engaged with a limited range of empirical case studies, notably militarised spaces in conflict zones like Israel/Palestine. In the past decade, the conceptual focus has been on military technology and weaponry, the impact of armed aggression on civilian infrastructures, and the visual politics of representation of urban spaces for military means. Of late, however, urban geopolitics has diversified its conceptual frameworks, drawing on theories of lived experience, new materialism (Slesinger, 2022), verticality and ordinariness

Figure 51.3
Everyday spaces of securitisation in cities: temporary Hostile Vehicle Mitigation (HVM) structures
installed around the annual Christmas market in Birmingham (UK)

Source: Photo credit: Carrie Ann Benjamin, ©Atmoct 2021 – www.atmoct.org

(Harker, 2014, Harris, 2015, Shtern, 2022), embodiment (Jackman and Brickell, 2022) as well
as treating a wider range of case studies through new comparative perspectives (Rokem, 2016,
Fregonese, 2021, Bădescu, 2022). These transcend the narrow terrain of war zones and armed
conflict and shift the attention instead towards the everyday and even informal spaces of securitisation (Figure 51.3), militarisation (Paasche and Sidaway, 2021; also see Sidaway, 2009) and
contestation around housing (Shtern and Yacobi, 2019), planning (Bou Akar, 2018) migration
(Kutz and Wolff, 2022), counter-radicalisation (Saberi, 2019), and counter-terrorism (Fregonese
and Laketa, 2022) among others.

Geopolitics and urban planning: *planning on the dark side and For The War Yet To Come*

Urban geopolitics is an interdisciplinary corpus of work and some of its scholarly debates are
around planning as deeply implicated in urban politics of contestation and even conflict. The
accepted axiom in western urban theory assumes that urban planning improves the spatial
organisation of cities for progress, stability and peace. As a necessity to regulate space, society
and hygiene in industrial inner cities in the 19th and 20th centuries, the spatial principles of
European urban planning have been exported to colonial cities (Çelik, 1997). Looking at western urban theory and planning from a very contested and conflictual viewpoint in the Middle
East – that of Israel/Palestine – Israeli planner Oren Yiftachel (1998) argued instead that this is a

narrow, and Eurocentric, view of planning. He shifts our attention to what he describes as spatial policies and reorganisations of space that create the conditions for social oppression, economic inefficiency, environmental damage, social isolation, group domination and ethnic marginalisation. The contexts where the 'dark side' of planning, as Yiftachel calls it, becomes blatant are cities with high degrees of ethnic, sectarian and political conflict.

An illustration of divisive planning practices at work has been provided more recently by US-based Lebanese planner Hiba Bou Akar. In *For The War Yet To Come* (Bou Akar, 2018) the spatial planning, property and land transactions, and building practices for the reconstruction of a post-conflict city like Beirut (Lebanon) are analysed in their implications with the interests of political-religious groups, with resulting disadvantages (social, economic and environmental) for great portions of the local population and everyday life. Bou Akar studied three neighbourhoods in Beirut, showing how what look like apolitical planning considerations and financial transactions around property and land around post-conflict reconstruction actually contain the dynamics of a war through other means. This war is not waged with weapons, but through planning decrees, zoning regulations and building practices, aimed at reorganising urban space in a way that – should there be another, future war – is favourable to the political and sectarian groups rivalling each other. For example, Bou Akar describes how in the city's suburbs religious and political organisations 'hold ground' against each other in the eventuality of future conflict by purchasing land (including where derelict buildings stand and are left as such), to signal the presence of specific religious communities in neighbourhoods facing major socio-demographic changes.

Summary

- Geopolitics has been long dominated by accounts centred around the **nation-state**. Less attention has been paid to how global politics are reflected in, and shaped by, cities and urban spaces.
- In the past 20 years, an interdisciplinary corpus study including geography, planning and urban studies under the name of urban geopolitics has developed to study how geopolitics becomes grounded in cities, and how global politics becomes localised in urban space.
- A strand of urban geopolitics has focused on how urban planning is deeply implicated in politics of contestation, inequality and conflict.

Conclusion

Almost exactly 30 years ago, Dodds and Sidaway (1994) called for broadening 'the empirical base [of critical geopolitics] so that research is less tied to empirical studies of the Anglo-American world' (p. 521), for developing feminist approaches to geopolitical discourse and for the engagement with 'credible alternatives to the contemporary world (dis)order' (p. 522). Since then, critical geopolitics has encompassed diverse approaches, methodologies and empirical foci but continues to share a common 'effort to think critically [...] and to challenge inherited legacies of imperial practices in the name of greater emancipation' (Dodds et al., 2013: xxi). Most importantly, as shown in this chapter, geopolitics doesn't simply happen far away outside our spheres of experience. Geopolitics happens in everyday lives – the everyday lives of the past Bosnian war that Maggie O'Kane showed the world; the everyday encounters in cities, at borders, or in the deliberations of urban planners; the everyday lives of refugees who become homeless through conflict and fall between the cracks of the nation-state system. The idea that geopolitics and everyday life are not separate is one imbued with political agency and possibilities for hope and resistance. Geopolitics is ultimately about power; it happens both in official diplomatic circles but connects to our everyday lives by playing out in myriad ways in the ordinary detail. Precisely because of their ordinariness, these everyday spaces can be impacted upon, resisted or changed. Acknowledging and tracing these everyday geopolitical connections therefore become politically enabling in the opportunities they present 'to resist, have dialogue, influence and act' (Pain and Smith, 2008: 7) politically.

Discussion points

- How can we define geopolitics?
- What kinds of representations do conventional geopolitics rely on?
- Why do we need a critical geopolitics?
- Why is important to understand geopolitics in the everyday?
- How are cities and geopolitics interconnected?

References

Agnew, J. A. (2003). *Geopolitics: Re-Visioning World Politics* (2nd edn.). London; New York: Routledge.

Bădescu, G. (2022). Urban geopolitics in 'ordinary' and 'contested' cities: perspectives from the European South-east. *Geopolitics*: 1–26. https://doi.org/10.1080/14650045.2022.2129010

Benwell, M. C., and Pinkerton, A. (2020). Everyday invasions: *Fuckland*, geopolitics, and the (re)production of insecurity in the Falkland islands. *Environment and Planning C: Politics and Space* 38: 998–1016. https://doi.org/10.1177/2399654420912434

Bos, D. (2021). Popular geopolitics 'beyond the screen': bringing modern warfare to the city. *Environment and Planning C: Politics and Space* 39(1): 94–113.

Bou Akar, H. (2018). *For the War Yet to Come: Planning Beirut's Frontiers*. Stanford: Stanford University Press.

Çelik, Z. (1997). *Urban Forms and Colonial Confrontations: Algiers under French Rule*. Berkeley and Los Angeles: University of California Press.

Dalby, S., and Tuathail, G. Ó. (eds.) (1998). *Rethinking Geopolitics*. New York: Routledge.

Dittmer, J., and Gray, N. (2010). Popular Geopolitics 2.0: towards new methodologies of the everyday. *Geography Compass* 4: 1664–1677. https://doi.org/10.1111/j.1749-8198.2010.00399.x

Dodds, K. (2007). Steve Bell's eye: cartoons, geopolitics and the visualization of the 'war on terror'. *Security Dialogue* 38: 157–177. https://doi.org/10.1177/0967010607078536

Dodds, K. (2019). *Geopolitics: A Very Short Introduction* (3rd edn.). Oxford: Oxford Academic. https://doi.org/10.1093/actrade/9780198830764.001.0001

Dodds, K., and Atkinson, D. (eds.) (2000). *Geopolitical Traditions: A Century of Geopolitical Thought, Critical Geographies*. London; New York: Routledge.

Dodds, K., Kuus, M., and Sharp, J. P. (eds.) (2013). *The Ashgate Research Companion to Critical Geopolitics*. Farnham; Burlington, VT: Ashgate.

Dodds, K.-J., and Sidaway, J. D. (1994). Locating critical geopolitics. *Environment and Planning D: Society and Space* 12: 515–524. https://doi.org/10.1068/d120515

Enloe, C. H. (2000). *Bananas, Beaches and Bases: Making Feminist Sense of International Politics.* Berkeley: University of California Press.

Fregonese, S. (2017). Affective atmospheres, urban geopolitics and conflict (de)escalation in Beirut. *Political Geography* 61: 1–10. https://doi.org/10.1016/j.polgeo.2017.04.009

Fregonese, S. (2021). Shockwaves: atmospheres beyond the conflict city/ordinary city divide. *Conflict and Society* 7: 26–41. https://doi.org/10.3167/arcs.2021.070103

Fregonese, S., and Laketa, S. (2022). Urban atmospheres of terror. *Political Geography* 96: 102569. https://doi.org/10.1016/j.polgeo.2021.102569

Graham, S. (2004). *Cities, War, and Terrorism: Towards an Urban Geopolitics.* Malden: Blackwell.

Gregory, D. (1998). *Geographical Imaginations* (Reprinted. edn.). Cambridge: Blackwell.

Harker, C. (2014). The only way is up? Ordinary topologies of Ramallah: ordinary topologies of Ramallah. *International Journal of Urban and Regional Research* 38: 318–335. https://doi.org/10.1111/1468-2427.12094

Harris, A. (2015). Vertical urbanisms: opening up geographies of the three-dimensional city. *Progress in Human Geography* 39: 601–620. https://doi.org/10.1177/0309132514554323

Hyndman, J. (2004). Mind the gap: bridging feminist and political geography through geopolitics. *Political Geography* 23: 307–322.

Ingram, A. (2019). *Geopolitics and the Event: Rethinking Britain's Iraq War Through Art, RGS-IBG Book Series.* Hoboken: Wiley.

Jackman, A., and Brickell, K. (2022). 'Everyday droning': towards a feminist geopolitics of the drone-home. *Progress in Human Geography* 46: 156–178. https://doi.org/10.1177/03091325211018745

Jones, A. (2020). Manipulating diplomatic atmospheres: the United Nations Security Council and Syria. *Annals of the American Association of Geographers* 110: 1369–1385. https://doi.org/10.1080/24694452.2019.1696665

Kutz, W., and Wolff, S. (2022). Urban geopolitics and the decentring of migration diplomacy in EU-Moroccan Affairs. *Geopolitics* 27: 703–728. https://doi.org/10.1080/14650045.2020.1843438

Laketa, S. (2016). Geopolitics of affect and emotions in a post-conflict city. *Geopolitics* 21: 661–685. https://doi.org/10.1080/14650045.2016.1141765

Legg, S. (2020). 'Political atmospherics': the India round table conference's atmospheric environments, bodies and representations, London 1930–1932. *Annals of the American Association of Geographers* 110: 774–792. https://doi.org/10.1080/24694452.2019.1630247

McConnell, F. (2009). De facto, displaced, tacit: the sovereign articulations of the Tibetan Government-in-exile. *Political Geography* 28: 343–352. https://doi.org/10.1016/j.polgeo.2009.04.001

Megoran, N., and Dalby, S. (2018). Geopolitics and peace: a century of change in the discipline of geography. *Geopolitics* 23: 251–276. https://doi.org/10.1080/14650045.2018.1459098

Mountz, A. (2018). Political geography III: bodies. *Progress in Human Geography* 42: 759–769. https://doi.org/10.1177/0309132517718642

O'Carroll, L. (2021). 'Betrayed': Dover residents furious over building of Brexit lorry park. *The Guardian*, 1st Jan 2021. https://www.theguardian.com/politics/2021/jan/01/residents-furious-brexit-lorry-park-kent-village

Paasche, T. F., and Sidaway, J. D. (2021). *Transecting securityscapes: dispatches from Cambodia, Iraq and Mozambique.* Athens, GA, USA: University of Georgia Press.

Pain, R. (1991). Space, sexual violence and social control: integrating geographical and feminist analyses of women's fear of crime. *Progress in Human Geography* 15: 415–431. https://doi.org/10.1177/030913259101500403

Pain, R. (2009). Globalized fear? Towards an emotional geopolitics. *Progress in Human Geography* 33: 466–486. https://doi.org/10.1177/0309132508104994

Pain, R., and Smith, S. (2008). *Fear: Critical Geopolitics and Everyday Life, Re-Materialising Cultural Geography*. Aldershot; Burlington, VT: Ashgate.

Rokem, J. (2016). Learning from Jerusalem: rethinking urban conflicts in the 21st century introduction. *City* 20: 407–411. https://doi.org/10.1080/13604813.2016.1166699

Saberi, P. (2019). Preventing radicalization in European cities: an urban geopolitical question. *Political Geography* 74: 102039. https://doi.org/10.1016/j.polgeo.2019.102039

Said, E. W. (1995). *Orientalism*. Harmondsworth: Penguin.

Sassen, S. (2012). *OP-ED August 2012. An emergent urban geopolitics*, 3.

Shtern, M. (2022). Passing as a tourist: exploring the everyday urban geopolitics of tourism. *Political Geography* 93: 102526. https://doi.org/10.1016/j.polgeo.2021.102526

Shtern, M., and Yacobi, H. (2019). The urban geopolitics of neighboring: conflict, encounter and class in Jerusalem's settlement/neighborhood. *Urban Geography* 40: 467–487. https://doi.org/10.1080/02723638.2018.1500251

Sidaway, J. D. (2008). The dissemination of banal geopolitics: webs of extremism and insecurity. *Antipode* 40: 2–8. https://doi.org/10.1111/j.1467-8330.2008.00568.x

Sidaway, J. D. (2009). Shadows on the path: negotiating geopolitics on an urban section of Britain's South West Coast Path. *Environment and Planning D: Society and Space* 27: 1091–1116. https://doi.org/10.1068/d5508

Slesinger, I. (2022). A strange sky: security atmospheres and the technological management of geopolitical conflict in the case of Israel's Iron Dome. *The Geographical Journal* 188: 429–443. https://doi.org/10.1111/geoj.12444

Smith, S. (2012). Intimate geopolitics: religion, marriage, and reproductive bodies in Leh, Ladakh. *Annals of the Association of American Geographers* 102: 1511–1528. https://doi.org/10.1080/00045608.2012.660391

Thrift, N. (2000). It's the Little Things. In *Geopolitical Traditions: A Century of Geopolitical Thought*, eds. Dodds, K., and Atkinson, D. London and New York: Routledge, 380–387.

Tuathail, G. Ó. (1996). *Critical Geopolitics: The Politics of Writing Global Space* (1st publ. edn.). London: Routledge.

Tuathail, G. Ó. (2003). 'Just out looking for a fight': American affect and the invasion of Iraq. *Antipode* 35: 856–870. https://doi.org/10.1111/j.1467-8330.2003.00361.x

Tuathail, G. Ó. (2013). Foreword: Arguing about Geopolitics. In *The Ashgate Research Companion to Critical Geopolitics*, eds. K. Dodds, M. Kuus, and J. P. Sharp. Farnham; Burlington, VT: Ashgate, xix–xxi.

Tuathail, G. Ó. (2021). Reflection on Criticisms of Critical Geopolitics. *Geopolítica(s). Revista de estudios sobre espacio y poder* 12(2): 191–206. https://doi.org/10.5209/geop.78616

United Nations Conference on Trade and Development. (2022). *UNCTAD Handbook of Statistics 2022 'Total and Urban Population'*. Available from https://hbs.unctad.org/total-and-urban-population/

Yiftachel, O. (1998). Planning and social control: exploring the dark side. *Journal of Planning Literature* 12: 395–406. https://doi.org/10.1177/088541229801200401

Online materials

- Ó Tuathail's Critical Geopolitics lectures: https://www.youtube.com/@criticalgeopolitics8523
- International Committee of the Red Cross (ICRC) video report on the impact of war in cities: https://www.youtube.com/watch?v=8GyzesoiT6I
- A conversation with Cynthia Enloe: https://www.youtube.com/playlist?list=PLfcRzkscDMdu K7Bfk3aYhZPESd7pQ1uZ_

- 2022 AAG IJURR Plenary Session – Planning for the War Yet to Come by Hiba Bou Akar –YouTube. In this lecture Hiba Bou Akar highlights the ways geopolitical tensions play out in urban planning decisions within conflict and post-conflict cities. https://www.youtube.com/watch?v=Dgr4J9xckvY
- Reporting Bosnia's war: Maggie O'Kane remembers – video | World news | The Guardian Maggie O'Kane recalls working in Sarajevo while it was under siege between 1992 and 1996. https://www. theguardian.com/world/video/2012/apr/05/bosnia-and-herzegovina

Further reading

Carter, S. R., and McCormack, D. P. (2006). Film, geopolitics and the affective logics of intervention. *Political Geography* 25(2): 228–245.
This book analyses the 2002 film *Black Hawk Down* that depicts the US involvement in Somalia in 1993. The case-study foregrounds the role played by the logics of affect in contemporary geopolitical cultures.

Dittmer, J., and Bos, D. (2019). *Popular Culture, Geopolitics, and Identity*. London: Rowman & Littlefield. This book highlights the importance of examining the role film, television, videogames and social media play in shaping geopolitical ideas within everyday life. An excellent resource that engages political geography concepts through accessible case-studies.

Dittmer, J., and Sharp, J. (eds.) (2014). *Geopolitics: An Introductory Reader*. London and New York: Routledge. A introductory resource for students thinking through Imperial Geopolitics, Cold War Geopolitics, Geopolitics after the Cold War and more recent thinking on geopolitics in human geography and beyond.

Massaro, V. A., and Williams, J. (2013). Feminist geopolitics. *Geography Compass* 7(8): 567–577.
This paper reviews the development of feminist geopolitics – an analytic that focuses on the relationship between geopolitics and everyday life, especially the ways individuals and communities push back, challenge and rewrite geopolitical relations.

Smith, S. (2020). *Political Geography: A Critical Introduction*. Chichester: John Wiley & Sons.
A clear and accessible introduction to how power is related to space, place and territory, with numerous case-studies illustrating how everyday life and the world of global conflict and nation-states are inextricably intertwined.

Neoliberalism

Julie MacLeavy

Introduction

Neoliberalism is a term that has gained significant attention in human geography over the past two decades, but its meaning and significance are still debated. It is generally used to refer to economic, political, and social arrangements that prioritise market relations and a reduced state role, while emphasising the responsibility of individuals to secure their own wellbeing. Neoliberalism promotes the idea that, rather than relying on the state or other collective entities, individuals should take ownership of their own economic and social success. This includes taking on personal responsibility for securing employment, investing in their own human capital, and managing their own financial and economic risks. The state is expected to create an environment that supports the operation of markets but to play a minimal role in providing for the social welfare of citizens. This means that policies which seek to reduce the size and role of the state are favoured, including the privatisation of state-owned enterprises and public services, and the reduction of regulations and taxes. The emphasis on individual responsibility is also reflected in the way that government welfare programmes are designed, with a focus on personal responsibility and work requirements for those in receipt of financial support. This approach is usually justified by the idea that individuals are, at heart, rational self-interested actors. If encouraged to take personal responsibility for their own economic and social success, they will be empowered to make better choices and act in ways that are socially beneficial. In short, by treating individuals as 'entrepreneurs of their own lives' (see Foucault, 2004: 215), the assumption is that they will be able to better themselves, by taking opportunities, starting new businesses, and innovating, all of which will ultimately benefit society.

Geographers acknowledge that the form neoliberalism takes varies depending on location and history. There is no single or unchanging version of neoliberalism, and so the focus is on understanding how its core principles are applied in a dynamic and evolving way. For this reason, many geographers use the term 'neoliberalisation' to better capture the different variations of neoliberalism that exist around the world and how they change over time. Yet this attention to variegation has been criticised by some, who argue that there are not enough common features to justify a provisional concept. This has given rise to a tension between efforts to understand (and resist) neoliberalism and efforts to reject the concept because of its ambiguous and contradictory application. While some scholars work to unravel the complex geographies of neoliberalism, others view it as an empty or structuralist term that obscures the multiple and contested processes by which arguments for free markets, deregulation, privatisation, and minimal state intervention in the economy have gained traction.

DOI: 10.4324/9780429265853-60

This chapter examines the understanding and use of neoliberalism within human geography. Beginning with its emergence as a descriptive term for policies that transformed post-war forms of economic practice and governance during the 1970s and 1980s, it discusses how the understanding of neoliberalism has evolved as its production and implementation have shifted in response to market failures and resistance. It proceeds to highlight the 'comparative topographies' (Martin, 2005: 203) of neoliberalism, and how the ambition to establish and defend free markets in all spheres of life has been materialised differently in different places. The chapter then turns to the social and distributional consequences of neoliberalism, including its impact on poverty, inequality, and migration. The chapter summarises the uneven impacts of neoliberalism with respect to the economic insecurity, social dislocation, and environmental degradation that result from unregulated development and, in closing, notes the role of geography in confronting these impacts, resisting them, and cultivating alternative economic forms.

Neoliberalism: from its origins to the present day

The history of neoliberalism can be traced back to the early twentieth century, with the emergence of classical liberal thought, which emphasised the importance of free markets and limited government intervention in the economy (Harvey, 2005). However, the term 'neoliberalism' was not coined until the 1930s, when a group of economists and intellectuals who were critical of the interventionist policies that had become popular during the Great Depression (1929–1939) advocated for a market-based approach to political and economic affairs. One of the most influential figures in the development of neoliberal thought was the economist Friedrich Hayek, who argued that centralised economic planning leads to inefficiency, and that market forces should be allowed to operate freely. Hayek's ideas were developed further by other economists such as Milton Friedman and George Stigler, who emphasised the importance of deregulation and the reduction of government spending to foster individual entrepreneurial freedoms and skills. At the time, these were fringe 'utopian' (Bourdieu, 1998) ideas that ran counter to Keynesian demand management, which saw post-war governments around the world implementing policies aimed at promoting full employment and economic growth through spending and regulation. However, by the 1970s, a period of economic 'stagflation' with concurrent high unemployment and high inflation led to a crisis of confidence in Keynesian management, and growing interest among political elites in the economic benefits of deregulation, privatisation, and trade liberalisation.

Countries such as Chile under the dictatorship of Augusto Pinochet and Uruguay under the direction of the US-backed military junta were among the first to implement policies that would ensure market-like order 'based on the conviction that where effective competition can be created, it is a better way of guiding individual efforts than any other' (Hayek, 2005 [1945]: 45). Changes were pushed through quickly, without democratic debate, and with violence used to suppress any resistant forces (Figure 52.1). Although neoliberalism is associated with ideas about limited state powers, its implementation relied upon on strong government intervention. The first experiments with neoliberalism in Latin America required the political sphere 'to be *regulated* – and heavily so – in order to *deregulate* the economy to the extent that neoliberal **ideology** demanded' (Hickel, 2016: 144). Elsewhere, the battle for this form of 'laissez-faire' was fought through the manipulation of accepted wisdoms about economic and social freedoms (Peck, 2008). Against the backdrop of the Cold War, voters in Great Britain and the United States were

Figure 52.1
Chilean Army troops positioned on a rooftop fire on the La Moneda Palace 11 September 1973
in Santiago, during the military coup led by General Augusto Pinochet, which overthrew Chilean
constitutional president Salvador Allende, who died in the attack on the palace

Source: Photo credit: Agence France-Presse (AFP) – Getty Images

warned that if the government continued to intervene in the economy, it would result in a total-
itarian state. The argument was also put forward that government efforts to improve the welfare
of the general population would ultimately lead to the loss of political freedoms that were currently enjoyed. Lobbying groups suggested that implementing policies that were instead based
on free-market principles would lead to economic growth, and the benefits of this growth would
eventually reach the general population through a process known as the 'trickle-down' effect.
Part of this involved the reduction of taxes to ensure individuals were incentivised to earn more
money, the spending of which – it was assumed – would result in more economic activity, which
would be good for everyone (see Figure 52.2).

Through the 1980s, political leaders such as Margaret Thatcher in Great Britain and Ronald
Reagan in the United States adopted policies influenced by the 'proto'-neoliberalism that had
been implemented in Latin America. The effect was a reversal of equality gains that had been
made when higher taxes on the rich had enabled state spending to ensure full employment and
the establishment of a social safety net, which helped to redistribute wealth and power between
classes and reduce the inequality gap that had existed since the late nineteenth century. As the
gap between the rich and poor widened, the core tenets of neoliberalism were reworked to address
issues of inequality and exclusion caused by these first neoliberal reforms. These outcomes were
framed as a motivation for individuals to work hard(er) and pursue (more) entrepreneurial opportunities, rather than taken as evidence of policy failure or justification for a return to policies that
would seek to ensure the benefits of economic prosperity were distributed fairly and so protect
the welfare and wellbeing of citizens, particularly those who were disadvantaged or marginalised.

THE TRICKLE-DOWN EFFECT

Figure 52.2
The theory of trickle-down economics, which has not been borne out by reality

Source: https://www.independent.co.uk/news/business/analysis-and-features/the-wealth-that-failed-to-trickle-down-report-suggests-rich-do-get-richer-while-poor-stay-poor-9989183.html)

Following the 'roll back' of Keynesian forms of intervention, this second stage involved the 'rolling out' of core neoliberal sensibilities (Peck and Tickell, 2002). Most often exemplified by the Third Way approaches of Bill Clinton in the United States and Tony Blair in Britain, who adapted the neoliberal projects of Reagan and Thatcher in certain ways, this phase saw a commitment to free market **capitalism** combined with policies that sought to reduce poverty and increase access to education, employment, healthcare, and conditional forms of welfare. Recognising that the first wave of neoliberalism had led to stagnating wages, cuts in welfare services and support, as well as increasing personal debt, as people invested in housing and other assets, or simply tried to maintain standards of living amid a growing share of income and wealth being channelled towards an emerging corporate elite (Piketty, 2014), they cut a more interventionist path. Minimum wage legislation was accompanied by the reformulation of welfare programmes with an emphasis on paid employment – the intention being to address increasing levels of inequality by helping individuals to become self-sufficient and move out of poverty through work. Arguments about the fiscal and social costs of welfare were expounded to usher in the use of work requirements to keep payments down and ensure that systems of income support did not restrict the development of a flexible labour market. In this way, the commitment to market rule was progressed but through policy mechanisms that changed the way that individuals understood themselves and their relationship to society and the state.

Through the 1990s and 2000s, then, political **subjectivity** was transformed from a collective, welfare-based understanding to a more individualised, responsibility-based understanding. Through policies that encouraged individuals to see themselves as autonomous, self-reliant actors, rather than as members of a collective society, economic risk was downloaded to the level of individual, and there was a corresponding decline in social cohesion and increase in social inequality, as individuals who were unable to achieve self-sufficiency were (increasingly) left to fend for themselves. Inequality is not only morally problematic and unjust, but it also harms overall economic growth. When a large portion of the population lacks the capacity to consume, aggregate demand decreases. This meant investment in assets, such as housing and financial products, became more profitable than investing in production for mass consumption, causing, in turn, the further concentration of wealth. Because asset ownership does not create job opportunities, only asset-holders and finance capital benefit from this investment (Adkins et al., 2020). Others face increasing job and housing insecurity and insurmountable debt.

The Global Financial Crisis of 2007–2008, which for a time affected faith in the market in addition to its actual performance, was caused by the inequality resultant from the further and more intense application of neoliberal policies and programmes (Stockhammer, 2015). Workers, especially in countries with high homeownership, took on high levels of debt to compensate for stagnant wages. This allowed for the creation and sale of securities backed by mortgages. It also increased risky financial investments in this high-risk debt, which ultimately led to the crisis as their value decreased. The response from governments around the world was to bail out the banks to prevent them from failing and causing further damage to the economy. This was done by providing large sums of money to financial institutions, either in the form of direct capital injections or through guarantees on bad loans. Organisations like the International Monetary Fund (IMF), European Commission and European Central Bank also provided credit to stabilise the financial system and prevent a complete collapse of the economy. These bailouts were controversial as they were seen by some as rewarding banks for their risky behaviour, and many governments faced criticism for the large sums of public money used to rescue privately owned concerns.

Contrary to initial expectations, the implementation of neoliberal policies increased during and after this period. Instead of addressing the conditions that caused the crisis, many countries in Europe, as well as the United States, Canada, and Australia, continued to pursue a neoliberal agenda, taking advantage of the economic turmoil to push through further cuts to spending, as well as increases in taxes and fees. Additionally, many governments reduced public sector employment and privatised state-owned assets. These measures were intended to reduce national debt and restore confidence in the economy. However, they also had the effect of passing on the losses from the bank bailouts to the general population. Many people have felt the impact of austerity measures through reduced access to public services and increased costs of living, but disadvantaged groups have been disproportionately affected as they are more likely to be employed in the public sector, have less disposable income to absorb rising costs, and fewer resources to access private services to compensate for service cuts (see Figure 52.3).

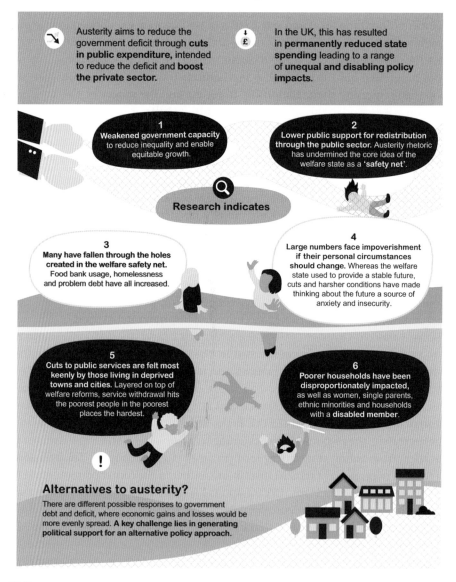

Figure 52.3
The effects of neoliberal austerity in the UK

Source: This visual summary was produced by Julie MacLeavy in collaboration with the Research Retold team at www.researchretold.com based on British Academy funded research EN\170147

The idea that cutting public services and reducing government spending is necessary to recuperate the private sector was used, once again, to discourage government investment as a means of boosting growth. Proponents of austerity argue that governments and households need to be financially responsible to create the conditions for private sector recovery and improve growth prospects. They also suggest that austerity is necessary to fix the poor financial management and excessive welfare spending of previous governments, which they assert led to the Global Financial Crisis. However, critics contend that by continuing and deepening neoliberalism, austerity prolongs the effects of the crisis, the real causes of which can be traced to:

- growing inequality, which reduces aggregate demand as the wealth of a growing number of workers is insufficient to support consumption;
- high levels of household debt, which led to much of the consumption that did take place being financed through increasingly expensive credit; and
- risky financial speculation, which led to the formation of investment bubbles as concentrated wealth flowed into new financial products.

It is important to understand that neoliberalism is a *political* project that adapts and evolves to address and absorb criticism, rather than a fixed set of economic principles. By re-framing social issues such as inequality and **uneven development** as technical problems that can be solved through a more intense market approach, it dismisses challenges to its organisational and institutional ideals. This ability to adapt is evident in the response to the Global Financial Crisis, where measures to restore faith in the market, such as liquidity support and bank recapitalisation, were implemented despite state intervention being previously seen as opposed to the neoliberal project. It also meant that the outcome of the crisis response was that corporate and financial elites reaped the benefits of state intervention, rather than those segments of society that had been negatively impacted by earlier stages of state 'retreat' (Lobao et al., 2018). The crash and recession ultimately led to austerity policies that emphasise economic growth over re-evaluating and reorganising economic practices as necessary to repair the damaged social structure and dismantled social protections and rehabilitate the individuals, communities, and neighbourhoods that have been negatively impacted by the long-term priority afforded to the market.

Summary

- Neoliberalism is an economic and political ideology that rose to prominence in the 1970s when many countries, including Great Britain and the United States, experienced 'stagflation'.
- Some of the key principles of neoliberalism include the following:
  - The belief that free markets are the most efficient way to allocate resources and that government intervention in the economy should be minimised.
  - The promotion of free trade and the reduction of tariffs and other trade barriers.
  - The privatisation of state-owned enterprises and the deregulation of industries.

> ○   The reduction or restructuring of the role of the government in welfare provision.
>
> ○   The use of monetary policy, particularly interest rate adjustments, to control inflation.
>
> •   Critics of neoliberalism maintain that it has led to increased inequality, as the benefits of economic growth have not been evenly distributed. Some also argue that it has led to a global race to the bottom, in which countries are forced to lower taxes, weaken labour laws, and reduce regulations to attract private investment.

The uneven and varied nature of neoliberal transformations

Neoliberalism is not a uniform and unchanging approach. As the above discussion makes clear, there are a range of policies and agendas that can emerge from the belief that 'open, competitive, and unregulated markets, liberated from all forms of state interference, represent the optimal mechanism for economic development' (Brenner and Theodore, 2002: 350). The experiences of individual countries can therefore be quite different from those portrayed within the '**hegemonic** story' (Larner, 2003: 509) of neoliberalism, which affords priority to the trajectories of nations in the global North and neglects the uneven take up of neoliberal ideas and practices in peripheral and semi-peripheral locations (Weller and O'Neill, 2014). In recent years, geographers have sought to recognise this and enact a shift from viewing neoliberalism as a cohesive project formulated and imposed in a top-down manner to observing its variegated production.

This has led to a wider recognition that the objectives and practices of neoliberalism vary globally. Beyond the North American and European context, policymakers have not pursued neoliberalism with a view to cutting back a 'bloated' post-war welfare state. Instead, states with minimal welfare provisions have seen neoliberal principles applied with the primary aim of facilitating development through the establishment export-oriented industries relying on comparative advantage in global markets. Aided by international institutions such as the IMF and World Bank, and the Washington Consensus on global economic policy, policymakers in Southern nations have instigated economic reforms with the goal of stimulating growth by opening up the economy to foreign investment. From this perspective, neoliberalism does not involve 'a projection of Northern ideology or policy, but a re-weaving of worldwide economic and social relationships', where the form of world trade, developmental state strategies, and the outcome of agriculture are all significant topics of concern (Connell and Dados, 2014: 124).

Southern discussions of neoliberalism also highlight the pivotal role of military power in extending neoliberalism across the globe. While the prevalence of democratic politics and well-established human and civil rights have militated against the 'crude' implementation of neoliberalism in the global North, it has been enacted with more 'purity' in Latin America, Africa and more recently parts of the Pacific, where human, civil, and democratic rights are less well protected and the possibility of resistance is reduced (Murray and Overton, 2016). In the case of Chile, discussed previously, neoliberalism was pursued in large part because it helped to increase the power of the Pinochet regime (Connell and Dados, 2014). The previous industrialisation strategy was replaced, which weakened the power of the industrial working class and its unions, and an export-orientated approach followed, which boosted economic growth through the expansion of mining and commercial agricultural industries, supporting the shift towards international trade. This change was well received by the Chilean property-owning class and further secured the diplomatic support of the United States, where political and economic elites were keen to create new openings for global investment and trade.

Export-led industrialisation has equally been a feature of the Chinese Communist Party (CCP)'s development strategy since the late 1970s. But what is distinctive in this instance is the CCP's effort to stop the formation of a unified capitalist group within the country to preserve their hold on power. The Chinese state retains a significant ownership stake in large companies in crucial industries, and state-owned banks continue to exert a significant level of control over the financial operations of these enterprises (Duckett, 2020). In other ways, China's economic and social policies resemble those of right-wing parties in parts of the global North, who tend to favour 'conservative' welfare regimes characterised by limited government intervention and a focus on self-sufficiency (Harvey, 2005). But as the CCP need not concern itself with gaining mass support through appealing to voters, measures to transform the economy are not presented with a view to promoting neoliberal reforms as the only way to maintain individual freedoms. Instead, market efficiency is presented as being consistent with socialism's core values of equality and economic security.

The varied political leanings and objectives of actors involved in advancing and executing neoliberal reforms show that while there is a 'common mantra' that government intervention crowds out economic activity and slows down economic growth, there is no blueprint for policy, which is enacted differently in different places, owing to variations in state forms and democratic freedoms. By this reading, neoliberalism emerges from the complex interaction of global economic and local social factors. The world is not a borderless terrain but rather 'a doubled world' where the global economy exists, albeit in ongoing tension with a constellation of communities within **nation-states** (Slobodian, 2018). This means that the forms of individualism and competition that are required to sustain a global market economy must be balanced with and against demands for the equal distribution of resources and fairness within nations. Demands may fluctuate in response to shifting circumstances and perspectives, resulting in outcomes that can conflict with intended policy goals.

Exemplifying this, Quinn Slobodian's (2018) study of South African apartheid details the considerable tensions amongst proponents of neoliberalism about how to implement a neoliberal approach to market development within a racially segregated society. He highlights that while generally opposed to apartheid for economic reasons – namely that preventing Black South Africans from participating in the market stopped them from using their talents and labour efficiently – key advocates such as Hayek were also against the granting of suffrage rights to Black South Africans owing to fears that it would lead to a redistribution of property, since the Black majority would want a return of land that had been previously taken by White settlers. Additionally, calls for sanctions on South Africa were disregarded because of fears that market restrictions would disrupt the global order. His work illustrates how, in the historical case of South Africa, an emphasis on protecting markets reinforced a system of racial exclusion, contradicting espoused claims that market-led governance would be impartial in the sense that it would treat all participants equally, without showing favouritism or prejudice.

More recently, contradictory reforms have arisen through a 'muddling through' of the problems emergent from applied neoliberalism, leading to a growing recognition of the propensity of market-led reforms to exploit group-based distinctions. In Great Britain, for instance, the failure of neoliberal policies to deliver trickle down benefits has led to a growing distrust in elites and their claims that suppressing wages will maintain competitiveness, or that reducing government services through austerity will eventually lead to private investments and improved standards of living. Political leaders have responded to declining support with a promise of economic and social revival through a developmentalist approach comprising (re)industrialisation, **infrastructure** construction, and – with Brexit – the insulation of local communities from global economic forces (MacLeavy, 2019). These objectives appear to contradict the central edicts of neoliberalism, namely the belief in self-regulating markets and the free movement of goods if not people. Yet they also remain consistent with its *modus operandi* in the sense that they continue to afford primacy to economic growth over all other values. There is, arguably, a continuation of the neoliberal order within contemporary developmentalism despite the fact that it uses nationalism, patriotism, and a strengthening of borders to (re)establish a policy agenda of tax cuts, deregulation, and continued state austerity (Arsel et al., 2021). What is notable is the propensity for this to deepen existing divisions between and within cities, states, and regions, as the areas that have already suffered the most severe effects of earlier rounds of economic restructuring are also the ones to experience the greatest loss of European Union funding, as well as the redundances resultant from multinational companies moving their operations to maintain access to the European single market.

Summary

- The implementation of neoliberal policies is complex and varies according to local conditions.
- Attempts to adapt to changing local conditions and perspectives can result in unintended consequences and the use of policy instruments that conflict with neoliberal goals.
- Acknowledging the uneven and contested development of neoliberalism in practice is crucial for understanding its multifaceted and conflicting impacts on societies and individuals.

The social, spatial, and environmental impacts of neoliberalism

The effects of neoliberalism can be complex and varied as what happens when policy mechanisms are articulated in specific domains depends on contextual factors and may also change over time as reform modalities elicit resistance. Nevertheless, common outcomes and trends can be observed. At a global level, the movement from a regulated economy organised in nation-states to one that is built around the primacy of capital, with an emphasis on global markets, the deregulation of industry, insecure labour, and the entrepreneurial self has had the effect of transferring wealth from the poor to the rich, increasing levels of inequality, and exacerbating existing spatial divides. This is because affluent individuals and nations are better positioned to take advantage of the opportunities created by neoliberal reforms, while those with fewer resources suffer as the commodification and marketisation of goods and services generate new sources of income for appropriation by political and economic elites. As elites can additionally use their wealth and connections to shape government policies to favour their interests and provide them with further advantages in the market, income and wealth disparities increase and are reflected in spatial configurations. The geographical consequences of neoliberal policies can be seen not only in processes of capital flight and outsourcing, which involve the movement of money and jobs from one area to another to secure economically and politically favourable conditions, but also in the widening gap between areas of decline and areas of growth, which affects the lived experiences of different populations.

The uneven outcome of neoliberal policies, where some individuals and communities bear the negative impacts, while others benefit, is a significant concern. These impacts often reflect pre-existing social cleavages, along the lines of class, **gender**, and **race**, as well as neo-colonial dynamics, and can modify the way in which modalities of difference are understood and experienced within society. Geographers have detailed how the implementation of neoliberal reforms uses already-existing social hierarchies to enable the enclosure of common goods and resources, reinforcing and deepening inequality. In some instances, the implementation of neoliberal reforms entails the clear use of violence against 'superfluous' populations that are characterised as being 'out of place' making them redundant and disposable (Bledscoe and Wright, 2019: 11). In Cambodia, for example, violent acts of 'accumulation by dispossession' have seen peasants evicted from land to facilitate the transformation of collective rights to land and resources into private ownership (Springer, 2015). Peasants are viewed as obstructing the creation of new areas of accumulation, and therefore as not deserving of their current location. This notion of 'undeservingness' provides justification for the use of harsh or corrupt methods to forcibly remove them. Other forms of neoliberal violence can be less direct, including processes of urban **gentrification** and the displacement of communities that happens alongside these processes – although in the United States there are many instances where the intense policing of Black people ousted from areas considered to be '**ghettos**' to enable their redevelopment has entailed overt 'extra-legal, terroristic violence' (Jefferson, 2016, n.p.).

A closer look at the links between neoliberal policies and their social and spatial outcomes reveals the subtle aspects of **power** that accompany state-sanctioned violence. It highlights that neoliberalism works not only through force and enforcement but also by infiltrating people's everyday lives and changing their thoughts, value systems, and beliefs. This reveals a deeper level of control and influence in which the people are encouraged to think of themselves and others in relation to the (labour) market and the norm of competition. In parts of Europe and North America, this is evident in the strong tendency to describe immigrants in terms of their economic utility, as workers in areas of labour shortage, or alternatively as a drain on resources, potentially unable or unwilling to 'give back' as much as they could potentially 'take' from society. It may also explain the rise and expansion of right-wing populism, which frequently involves the creation of an opposing '**other**' that is perceived as either receiving unfair help and advantage and therefore as a threat to modern, neoliberal ways of life or alternatively as an unwelcome competitor for jobs and opportunities that are growing increasingly scarce. Interestingly, within the context of right-wing populism, it is the (predominantly) White residents of immigration host countries who are portrayed as redundant or 'left behind' but deserving of rescue and recuperation.

In multiple ways, neoliberalism produces disposable people who have been dispossessed of their ability to live well among kin and community. Faced with limited options for making a living, people can migrate to secure their basic needs. Migration is a reaction to the economic forces and processes that produce 'human waste' (Bauman, 2004: 7) in conjunction with a decline in jobs and wages. It can also exacerbate social disparities by reinforcing culturally subjective divisions between communities or ethnic groups. In essence, the casting of migrants as disposable individuals no longer needed in their home economies opens the door to their exploitation as an inexpensive and dispensable source of labour and profit elsewhere. Furthermore, their collective portrayal as a 'threat' disempowers and individualises them, paving the way for their more forceful restraining and confinement through new, neoliberal forms of policing, incarceration, bordering, and surveillance (Axster et al., 2021). Scholars have frequently centred their attention on the United States as a key exemplar of how border controls, police practices, and incarceration shape the everyday realities of marginalised and racialised groups in the neoliberal era. While economic forces generate pressures for liberalised cross-border business movement in the context of the North American Free Trade Agreement, political and cultural forces lead to heightened border surveillance and more militarised border enforcement, especially along the US-Mexico border (Figure 52.4). These dynamics have been conceptualised in relation to the histories of carceral technologies and penal practices, breaking down any separation among the labour, migration, and security spheres. What is termed the 'prison-industrial complex' (Gilmore, 2017) provides an expansive means to think about the disciplinary practices along and beyond the

Figure 52.4
The US/Mexico border barrier in Texas

Source: Photo credit: Phil Gingrey/US Congress/Wikipedia Commons https://commons.wikimedia.org/wiki/File:US-Mexico_border_fence.jpg

border, which provide for the greater extraction of profit from labour by sustaining uneven geographies – as well as the importance of race and environment as interconnected systems of domination and resistance.

Neoliberal social relations are always interlinked with spatial environmental relations in the sense that they are embedded in and through **territory** and place. Recognising this, geographers have detailed how ecological and racial violence are co-constituted within neoliberal formations, thereby enabling an understanding of why people of colour are particularly vulnerable to environmental degradation (Pulido, 2017). Economic expansion and deregulation, which permits corporations to disregard green upgrades that could raise the costs of production, can have significant impacts on poor and minority communities as the economic costs of cleaner and more efficient technology and production methods are shifted onto those living adjacent to industrial plants and transport corridors. The residents of these neighbourhoods, who are predominantly non-White, face greater exposure to pollution and waste from unrestrained industrial production, which puts them at a higher risk of poor health and premature death. The violence of neoliberalism does not always manifest in the form of high-profile cases of police brutality and vehement border control. It is more often a slow, insidious form of harm and death, particularly in outlying and impoverished areas where the state uses its power and resources to implement reforms that alter the built environment by promoting private ownership and accumulation. This results in the suppression and containment of marginalised groups, particularly non-White individuals, as they are integrated into a political system that caters primarily to the needs and desires of those holding sway over capital.

Summary

- Neoliberalism relies on the unequal categorisation of people, communities, and regions.
- It reinforces and deepens inequality by exploiting existing social hierarchies to appropriate common resources, extract profits for private gain, and pass on the costs to others.
- Neoliberalism can be viewed as a form of state-sponsored violence that primarily impacts racialised communities, resulting in severe consequences, such as death, deterioration of health, and ecological degradation.

Conclusion

To confront the inequality, injustice, environmental destruction, and human suffering caused by neoliberalism, geographers have sought to equip movements of resistance with adequate conceptual tools. This means not only building up concepts to describe it but also deciphering its various effects, including how neoliberalism has led to extreme inequality, racist violence, and ecological disaster. In some cases, geographers have also collaborated with activists and advocates of organisations dedicated to creating a more just and equitable world in efforts to change the conditions emergent from market-led rule. Simply naming and exposing its consequences is not enough to challenge its power or empower marginalised communities. That requires 'a different form of critical conduct' (Cruikshank, 2018: 240), which acknowledges the alternative subjectivities that exist and supports them as a form of radical practice. Contrary to literature that suggests that neoliberalism is so deeply entrenched and ubiquitous that no viable alternative exists, this work is significant in promoting the notion that neoliberalism is not an inevitable formation but rather a contingent one. It also opens up the possibility of capturing resistances to neoliberalism, which do not simply refuse or reject its power and ideas but resist by enacting alternative economic practices that might change social, political, and environmental relations (Gibson-Graham et al., 2013). Such a perspective upholds a view of resistance as open-ended and emergent, while also enabling the enfolding of movements that are not (explicitly) directed towards neoliberalism into accounts of political struggles against it. Connecting struggles for Black liberation, migrant justice, **decolonisation**, housing justice, worker rights, gender equality, and environmental justice, into the fight against neoliberalism yields a view of how individuals and communities *can* act to gain political power and the role of geographical theory and practice in helping to create a vision for change.

Discussion points

- What are the key principles and polices of neoliberalism?
- How have politics, economy, and society been organised around the notion of 'the market'?
- How do we account for commonalities and differences in 'actually existing neoliberalism'?
- What are the critiques of neoliberalism, and how do they differ from the arguments of its proponents?
- What is the future of neoliberalism and what potential alternatives to this economic and political ideology are there?

References

Adkins, L., Cooper, M., and Konings, M. (2020). *The Asset Economy*. Cambridge: Polity Press.

Arsel, M., Adaman, F., and Saad-Filho, A. (2021). Authoritarian developmentalism: the latest stage of neoliberalism? *Geoforum* 124: 261–266.

Axster, S., Danewid, I., Goldstein, A., Mahmoudi, M., Tansel, C. B., and Wilcox, L. (2021). Colonial lives of the carceral archipelago: rethinking the neoliberal security state. *International Political Sociology* 15(3): 415–439.

Bauman, Z. (2004). *Wasted Lives: Modernity and Its Outcasts*. Malden: Blackwell.

Bledscoe, A., and Wright, W. J. (2019). The anti-Blackness of global capital. *Environment and Planning D: Society and Space* 37(1): 8–26.

Bourdieu, P. (1998). The essence of neoliberalism: utopia of endless exploitation. *Le Monde Diplomatique*, December. https://mondediplo.com/1998/12/08bourdieu

Brenner, N., and Theodore, N. (2002). Cities and the geographies of 'actually existing neoliberalism'. *Antipode* 34(3): 349–379.

Connell, R., and Dados, N. (2014). Where in world does neoliberalism come from? *Theory and Society* 43(2): 117–138.

Cruikshank, B. (2018). Neoliberalism: Towards a Critical Counter-Conduct. In *Rethinking Neoliberalism: Resisting the Disciplinary Regime*, eds. S. F. Schram and M. Pavlovskaya. Abingdon: Routledge, 238–257.

Duckett, J. (2020). Neoliberalism, authoritarian politics and social policy in China. *Development and Change* 51(2): 523–539.

Foucault, M. (2004). *The Birth of Biopolitics: Lectures at the College de France 1978–1979* (trans G. Burchell). Hampshire: Palgrave Macmillan.

Gibson-Graham, J.-K., Cameron, J., and Healy, S. (2013). *Take Back the Economy: An Ethical Guide for Transforming Our Communities*. Minneapolis: University of Minnesota Press.

Gilmore, R. W. (2017). Abolition Geography and the Problem of Innocence. In *Futures of Black Radicalism*, eds. G. T. Johnson and A. Lubin. London: Verso, 225–240.

Harvey, D. (2005). *A Brief History of Neoliberalism*. Oxford: Oxford University Press.

Hayek, F. A. (2005 [1945]). The Road to Serfdom. In Institute of Economic Affairs, *The Road to Serfdom with the Intellectuals and Socialism*. London: Institute of Economic Affairs, 39–70.

Hickel, J. (2016). Neoliberalism and the End of Democracy. In *Handbook of Neoliberalism*, eds. S. Springer, K. Birch, and J. MacLeavy. London: Routledge, 142–152.

Jefferson, B. J. (2016). Policing, whiteness, and the death-wage. Society and Space. https://www.societyandspace.org/articles/policing-whiteness-and-the-death-wage

Larner, W. (2003). Neoliberalism? *Environment and Planning D* 21(5): 509–512.

Lobao, L., Gray, M., Cox, K., and Kitson, M. (2018). The shrinking state? Understanding the assault on the public sector. *Cambridge Journal of Regions, Economy and Society* 11(3): 389–408.

MacLeavy, J. (2019). Neoliberalism and the new political crisis in the West. *Ephemera* 19(3): 627–640.

Martin, P. M. (2005). Comparative topographies of neoliberalism in Mexico. *Environment and Planning A: Economy and Space* 37(2): 203–220.

Murray, W. E., and Overton, J. (2016). Peripheries of Neoliberalism: Impacts, Resistance and Retroliberalism as Reincarnation. In *Handbook of Neoliberalism*, eds. S. Springer, K. Birch, and J. MacLeavy. London: Routledge, 422–432.

Peck, J. (2008). Remaking laissez-faire. *Progress in Human Geography* 32(1): 3–43.

Peck, J., and Tickell, A. (2002). Neoliberalizing space. *Antipode* 34(3): 380–404.

Piketty, T. (2014). *Capital in the Twenty-First Century*. London: Harvard University Press.

Pulido, L. (2017). Geographies of race and ethnicity II: environmental racism, racial capitalism and state-sanctioned violence. *Progress in Human Geography* 41(4): 524–533.

Slobodian, Q. (2018). *Globalists: The End of Empire and the Birth of Neoliberalism*. Cambridge, MA: Harvard University Press.

Springer, S. (2015). *Violent Neoliberalism: Development, Discourse, and Dispossession in Cambodia*. New York: Palgrave Macmillan.

Stockhammer, E. (2015). Rising inequality as a cause of the present crisis. *Cambridge Journal of Economics* 39(3): 935–958.

Weller, S., and O'Neill, P. (2014). An argument with neoliberalism: Australia's place in a global imaginary. *Dialogues in Human Geography* 4(2): 105–130.

Online materials

- Podcast: Neoliberalism and its discontents
  https://podtail.com/en/podcast/the-ezra-klein-show/neoliberalism-and-its-discontents/
  This podcast comprises a discussion with Wendy Brown, a renowned political theorist and professor at UC Berkeley, who is a leading critic of neoliberalism and Noah Smith, a prominent economist and Bloomberg columnist, who is famous for his strong support of some neoliberal policies.

Further reading

Chomsky, N. (1999). *Profit Over People: Neoliberalism and Global Order*. London: Seven Stories Press.
A book that stands out as one of the most influential texts on neoliberalism which offers a powerful indictment of the practices and policies of international financial institutions.

Harvey, D. (2005). *A Brief History of Neoliberalism*. Oxford: Oxford University Press.
A watershed text, Harvey's book has been tremendously influential in the ongoing debates that frame neoliberalism.

Ward, K., and England, K. (eds.) (2007). *Neoliberalization: States, Networks, Peoples*. Oxford: Wiley-Blackwell.
This book features contributors from a wide range of disciplinary backgrounds, writing from different locations, using varying methodologies, and working on diverse issues.

Smith, A., Stenning, A., and Willis, K. (eds.) (2008). *Social Justice and Neoliberalism: Global Perspectives*. London: Zed Books.
An important intervention that explores the entanglement of neoliberalism with identity formation and subjectivation to tease out how neoliberalism shapes the way individuals see themselves and the world around them.

Peck, J. (2010). *Constructions of Neoliberal Reason*. Oxford: Oxford University Press.
This is a key text, written by one of human geography's most innovative and prolific scholars.

53 Activism and protest

Richard J. White

We want to create freedom in our lives, to bring the poetic joy of being in the world to each moment of breath, and to fill the spaces of our existence with a deep and unshakable love for the mystery known as 'life'. To do this requires us to revolt. To bring light we must pursue a trajectory that refuses the darkness.

White et al., 2016: 1

Introduction: geographies of activism and protest

Activists and protest movements have been the subject of interest for geographers for a long time (see Panelli and Larner, 2010). One of the hopes of this chapter is that it will impress upon you that the more consciously we think about the *geographies* of activism and protests, the deeper and more enriched our understanding becomes. That geography matters can be seen in many ways. For example, geography is present when we ask questions such as: 'How do protesters think about the world?', or 'How do they position themselves, or organise with others, in ways that will help them bring about the desired changes they wish to see?'. We can complement these questions by exploring their symbolic, virtual, or material geographies: what impacts do protests have across **space** and place (see Salmenkari, 2009)? As Routledge (n.d.) observed:

> All protesters draw from and deploy a strategic geographical imagination that enables us to make sense of the world of protest and build effective campaigns. From Palestinian struggles against occupation to Nepalese citizens waging revolution, protests are generated and influenced by the material conditions and cultural practices of their places of work, livelihood and home. From the recent anti-fracking protests of Reclaim the Power in Lancashire, U.K. to landless farmers occupying land in Bangladesh, activists use and transform everyday landscapes, creating not only sites of resistance, but also spaces where alternative imaginaries and symbolic challenges can be made 'real'.

In short, geography can be immensely helpful in helping frame and address a range of 'who', 'how', 'why', and 'when' questions that are relevant to activism and protest movements across the world. This argument holds true whether we are looking towards the past, the present, or potential futures. It's remarkable to consider just how rapidly things have changed in terms of the rise of digital expressions of activism within the last 25 years (see Kahn and Kellner, 2004,

DOI: 10.4324/9780429265853-61

McLean et al., 2019). In 1999 when I was an undergraduate geography student, the internet was in its infancy, mobile phones were rarely seen, and if they were, they tended to be the size of small dogs! Digital activism, of course, has only been made possible through technological developments, with the internet being at the heart of this, and has made an incredible impact on the geographies of activism over the last 25 years. There is every reason to believe, as technology continues to evolve, and the battle for social and spatial justice continues to escalate, that the contested geographies upon which activism stands will keep unfurling in equally radical, unpredictable, and unprecedented directions over the next generation of time. As I begin this paragraph (on Friday 14 October 2022) Just Stop Oil activists are making headline news. Reporters have been busy covering the controversial sequence of events that took place at the National Gallery in London, where two young activists threw tomato soup over Vincent van Gogh's much-loved artwork *'Sunflowers'* and then glued their hands to the wall underneath the painting. To justify this specific form of protest, the activists posed several rhetorical questions, namely

> 'What is worth more, art or life?' said one of the activists, Phoebe Plummer, 21, from London. She was accompanied by 20-year-old Anna Holland, from Newcastle. 'Is it worth more than food? More than justice? Are you more concerned about the protection of a painting or the protection of our planet and people?' 'The cost of living crisis is part of the cost of oil crisis, fuel is unaffordable to millions of cold, hungry families. They can't even afford to heat a tin of soup'.
>
> *Gayle, 2022: n.p.*

Debating the relative merits of this specific type of activism and protest is largely beyond the scope of the chapter. However – setting aside the question as to whether (you think) these protestors were justified in taking the action they did – most of us would agree that this spectacle constituted an act of protest. 'Why might we believe this?' is an interesting question to consider: why should we interpret this as an act of protest, and not say as a reckless act of vandalism (as indeed some media outlets have suggested)? To find an answer to this means interrogating our geographical imaginaries: what beliefs and feelings do we have about protest and activism?

When we stop and think about it, protests seem to be taking place everywhere, all the time. Indeed, if you type 'protest' into a Google search engine, over 862,000,000 results will be available to you in under a second! At any given moment we can point to examples where individuals or groups have taken – or are taking – an active stance for (or against) all sorts of things. When reading the papers, listening to the radio, or watching the television, it won't be long before you come across news of protests focused on issues ranging from the rising cost of living, high fuel prices, university pensions, and working conditions, to abortion rights, COVID-19 restrictions, police racism, the destruction of the rainforest in Brazil, government repression in China, and the war in Ukraine. While unique in being contemporary examples, these acts do not suggest we live in an exceptional time: rather, we can trace the rich and knotted threads of protest throughout human history.

Before continuing any further, it is important to think through what you understand by the reference to activism and protest movements. For many people their impression of these is strongly aligned with the definitions we might find in a standard dictionary. Here protest is understood as either a noun, 'a strong complaint expressing disagreement, disapproval, or opposition' (Cambridge Dictionary, 2023a: n.p.) or as a verb, 'an occasion when people show that they disagree with something by standing somewhere, shouting, carrying signs, etc' (ibid). Activism, meanwhile, suggests 'the use of direct and noticeable action to achieve a result, usually a political or social one' (Cambridge Dictionary, 2023b: n.p.)). In this interpretation then, an activist would be considered someone who 'uses direct and public methods to try to bring about esp. social and political changes that [they] and others want' (ibid). Do these definitions sit well alongside your own at this moment in time?

The illustration of the Just Stop Oil protest in the National Gallery seems to be in keeping with the definitions highlighted: there is the use of direct and noticeable action, and they are expressing a desire for change that they want, and on behalf of the action group they stand for. As a relevant aside though without the two young people's voices being heard, we might have come to very different conclusions. Without knowing 'why' they threw tomato soup over van Gogh's art, maybe we could conclude that they were just mindless thugs seeking attention and notoriety. Maybe they just both really *really* hated *Sunflowers* and were intent on destroying it: nothing more and nothing less.

When responding to the questions posed: 'What is protest? What is activism?', we could also look to respond to these by drawing on our own personal experiences. Based on the above dictionary definitions, have there been occasions where we might consider ourselves an activist, as being involved in a protest movement? The instinctive response may be to reflect on instances where 'being' an activist has meant giving our time and energy to act out our displeasure and disagreement with a group of other like-minded individuals something. These examples involve exceptional situations and geographies that lie beyond our 'normal' everyday day-to-day actions and spaces. At school, for example, you might have had the opportunity to act on your concern about environmental issues, perhaps make protest poster and banners and then – with others in your class – go out onto the streets to express solidarity with other activists on climate change. One personal example that I might offer would be the activist poster-creating-session and subsequent march I joined in through the streets of Boston (US) in 2018 by the 'Geographers Against Trump'! See ACME Resistance (2018) for the motivations and reflections of those who participated.

So far the discussion on activism and protest has been largely in keeping with the popular narratives, succinctly captured by the Cambridge Dictionary, and this does give us a window with which to view the range of common geographies that identify and connect diverse protest moments that we see in the world: for example, where the decision to act is pre-determined, organised to take place in a very public way, and where participants raise awareness around the specific issues. Such a view risks obscuring and distracting us away from paying attention to other windows; windows which open out onto powerful geographies of activism and protest which are equally influential in shaping the world we live in and may well play an even greater role in shaping the world moving forward. This is particularly true when we think about the necessary steps needed to address the greatest challenges we face, including climate catastrophe, species extinction, social and economic inequality, and human-on-human war. The next section considers how a deeper more extensive reading of geographies of activism and protest allows us to see, re-think and re-value and re-animate our activist imaginaries.

Summary

- Geography plays a significant role in activism, influencing how protesters perceive the world, organise themselves, and create symbolic and material impacts across different spaces.
- The rise of digital activism in the past 25 years has reshaped the geographies of activism and politics.
- It is important to reflect on what we and others understand as 'activism' and 'protest' and critically assess the accuracy of how activist and protest movements are represented in the media.

Re-imagining geographies of activism and protest

When we think about 'who do activist and protest movements appeal to?', there is a credible argument to be made that many movements focus their attention on directly appealing to their elected government, or a particular private company to 'Do the right thing!'. This can be frequently seen in activists who demonstrate in public spaces waving colourful flags and banners (appealing to the government to take greater action on tackling climate change) or organise boycotts of certain goods and products and draw attention to injustices through occupying strategic places (the Animal Save Movement, for example, stand in public places, outside slaughterhouses, and abattoirs to raise consciousness and awareness about what takes place there) (see also Figure 53.1). Others might seek to cause maximum inconvenience (by preventing access to a particular place or disrupt traffic by blocking roads as Extinction Rebellion has done) or embarrassment (protestors targeting Shell's Annual General Meeting to highlight the firm's culpability in climate catastrophe, see Lawson and Gayle, 2022). Seen in this way, should the company in question go on to conduct its business differently, or if the government brings forward new and tighter regulations (to stop pollution or reduce carbon footprints), then the goal of the protest movement will be deemed to have enjoyed (a degree of) success, even if the wider battle is still ongoing.

However, the nature of the current crises that we see, crises that we are told threaten to end the world as we know it, have increasingly brought into popular focus serious reservations about whether either the market (**capitalism**) or the state are capable of being a key part of the solution. After all, capitalist businesses and the state are fundamentally a part of the crisis. For some activists, therefore, even if it were desirable, it would be impossible to take any meaningful action (see Cudworth et al., 2021). Consequently, what possible hope of success is there in making demands for these economic and policy processes to change and remake the world? That would be demanding the impossible, to capture a popular slogan!

However, what I want to impress upon you is that 'above-the-ground, visible and demonstrable' expressions of activism and protest do not define where activism and protest begin and end. It might be helpful to use an iceberg analogy here. So far, the discussion has focused on what lies 'above the water' on the activist iceberg. The deeper and more extensive iceberg mass that lies beneath the surface is where the focus of the chapter turns. These are the worlds composed

Figure 53.1
Occupy Wall Street protest. 2011 witnessed a global rise of protests against economic inequality and corporate greed, with protest camps often built nearby prominent financial institutions

Source: Photo credit: Richard White

of more informal, autonomous, and perhaps anarchistic geographies of activism and protest: worlds that are well known to us all!

Surveying the underbelly of the activist iceberg

If we imagine jumping off the top of the activist iceberg and plunging into the dark waters beneath, what might the underbelly of this splendid iceberg reveal? It might be a surprise that many of these hidden geographies of activism and resistance are familiar and well known to us; we just haven't been encouraged to see them as such. Here I am thinking about the work of James. C. Scott and his concept of 'infrapolitics'. For Scott, infrapolitics designates 'a wide variety of low-profile forms of resistance that dare not speak in their own name' (1990: 19). Some illustrations of infrapolitics include 'rumors, gossip, folktales, songs, gestures, jokes ... poaching, foot-dragging, pilfering, dissimulation, flight' (xiii). 'Together', Scott argues, 'these forms of insubordination might suitably be called the infrapolitics of the powerless' (ibid). In an instant we are swimming in waters that stretch well beyond the comparative shallows of activism and protest suggested and defined by dictionary and popular definitions. What possibilities, therefore, emerge from such recognition? How might we re-value and think more constructively about harnessing the potential and power of these forms of activism and resistance that Scott speaks to?

We should always be mindful of the productive and constructive capacity that activism and protest movements bring to the world: visions of hope and possibility that can be imagined, envisaged, and enacted. Here, the academic-activist scholarship of Professors Jenny Pickerill and Paul Chatterton has been particularly influential in the way in which geographers have come to think about and articulate autonomous geographies. Autonomous geographies concern:

> those spaces where people desire to constitute noncapitalist, egalitarian and solidaristic forms of political, social, and economic organization through a combination of resistance and creation.
>
> *Pickerill and Chatterton, 2006: 730*

The *praxis* (theory and action) of autonomous geographies has a rich and colourful history. Individuals who are inspired to engage with and create autonomous geographies do so for a whole number of reasons. It is interesting to note how influential **anarchism** and anarchist geographies have been and continue to be in informing the type of geographies that we see in contemporary expressions of activism. You might have read that last sentence twice: anarchism – aren't anarchists violent thugs, who use violence to bring forward chaos, disorder, and disaster into the world! You wouldn't be alone in thinking this: the negative stereotypes that are commonly used in Hollywood movies, or in the mainstream media, reinforce this popular impression. However, nothing could be further from the truth: anarchism is committed to rejecting all forms of dominion, oppression, and violence in the world (see Springer, 2016). The way in which it looks to achieve this is by focusing on mutual aid, volunteerism, horizontal forms of organising, and prefigurative praxis. What might surprise you is to know that many of the ways you and I (and our friends and family and neighbours) think and act in our everyday lives is consistent with an anarchist praxis (see White and Williams, 2014). Attending to these hidden – sub-surface – types of activism helps us focus on a series of everyday or familiar spaces that we have never recognised, let alone appreciated or valued, as being potential spaces of activism! I want to illustrate this by focusing on two sites: the household and the garden.

The household

That the household might be consideredas being a radical space of activism doesn't seem plausible at first glance. However, many (not all I realise) households are organised in ways that embody an ethics of care, mutual support, and love that many of us would like to see nurtured in the society at large (see White and Williams, 2014). When household members – a family, for example – are faced with a problem, how is this raised, and how do they generally work to solve it? Do they appeal to the government to make things right? Or do they engage in means that address the problem directly through working together in a way that is fair and equitable for all members of the household? Yet this way of organising and acting surely can be understood as an important and ongoing form of activism that we have all participated in and know well. Moreover, the lessons we learn here provide transformative potential for other spaces and sites across society at large. What possibilities open up for better futures, when we give ourselves permission to recognise, re-think, and re-value these spaces as part of a broad tapestry of activism and protest? For Bryne et al (cited in White and Williams, 2012: 125), this is a matter of perspective:

> We can view the household as hopelessly local, atomized, a set of disarticulated and isolated units, entwined and ensnared in capitalism's global order, incapable of serving as a site of class politics and radical social transformation. Or we can avoid conflating the micro logical with the merely local and recognize that the household is everywhere; and while it is related in various ways to capitalist exploitation, it is not simply consumed or negated by it.

When we read the household as an activist space, we can also illustrate this by reference to specific sites and locations within the household. Take the kitchen, for example. Is the labour used to complete key tasks there (e.g. washing dishes, putting out the bins, cooking, cleaning, ironing) fairly and evenly distributed across all household members? How does the food brought in and consumed by the household reflect broader common ethics to 'do least harm'? A vegan household, for example, would clearly position their resistance to the suffering of fellow sentient animals in factory farms and slaughterhouses, by choosing plant-based foods and drinks. A powerful activist stance – and a protest about the suffering of others – can be made through the ordinary everyday choices we make (what we eat and drink) and the spaces we inhabit (how we travel). The lesson to take may be that if we wish to change the world 'out there', then we should begin by recognising that activism often begins in our everyday environments and radiates from there (Figure 53.2).

Figure 53.2
This street art is part of Berlin's East Side Gallery painted on former Berlin Wall

Source: Mark König on Unsplash

(Radical) Gardening

A second, perhaps more unexpected, illustration of activism is gardening (Figure 53.3). In recent years I have rented a small allotment plot, and I'm aware that many people view allotments (as I did not so long ago) as 'simply' a place where people grow vegetables and fruit (with varying degrees of success!). Such a view does not acknowledge how these spaces – and the people in them – can be also construed as another important space of activism and protest. As McKay (2011: 6) notes:

> Radical Gardening is about the idea of the 'plot', and its alternate but interwoven meanings …
> Many of the plots… are inspiring, and allow us to see how notions of utopia, of community,
> of activism for progressive social change, of peace, of environmentalism, of identity politics,
> are practically worked through in the garden, in floriculture, and through what Paul Gough
> has called 'planting as a form of protest '.

Planting as a form of protest may be symbolic: growing coriander on the kitchen windowsill as an act of defiance against the big supermarkets! Equally, seeds can be sown in ways that encourages greater forms of self-sufficiency and reciprocity especially when surplus crops are exchanged with other growers (see Pottinger, 2017). They may be sown in places where local communities lack access to good quality fruit and vegetables, and thus – in addition to sharing knowledge, and developing skills and confidence – a ready supply of high-quality plant-based foods becomes available. The Food Empowerment Project referenced in the online materials section at the end of the chapter is an excellent case study about what is possible to achieve here.

Figure 53.3
Radical Gardening

Source: Photo credit: Richard White

Summary

- Activism extends beyond visible demonstrations and includes informal and autonomous forms of resistance.
- These everyday actions often 'go under the radar' and take place in familiar spaces.

Concluding thoughts: future geographies of activism and protest

In this final reflection, I want to encourage you to recognise how contemporary expressions of protest and activism recognise and reflect an awareness of how seemingly discrete geographies of oppression, violence, and domination overlap and interlock in significant ways. Kimberle Crenshaw (1989) coined the term **intersectionality** to help draw attention to the complex realities faced by individuals discriminated against based on their **race** and sex (e.g. African American women). We can see many examples where social justice movements embrace an intersectional approach within their activism (see Liinason, 2020). Key examples include Black Lives Matter (BLM), LGBTQIA+ movements (Figure 53.4), and Antifa. Antifa – a left-wing movement

Figure 53.4
George Floyd protests in Uptown Charlotte, North Carolina

Source: Photo credit: Clay Banks on Unsplash

of activists – gained much momentum and visibility in the US during the Presidency of Donald Trump and the rise of the 'alt-right' movement. Antifa's anti-fascist and anti-racist stance has consistently highlighted the danger that 'alt-right' views have for vulnerable groups, and they emphasise the importance of standing in solidarity with these groups. As Bogel-Burroughs and Garcia (2020: n.p.) highlight:

> Supporters generally seek to stop what they see as fascist, racist and far-right groups from having a platform to promote their views, arguing that public demonstration of those ideas leads to the targeting of marginalized people, including racial minorities, women and members of the L.G.B.T.Q. community.

Given existential threats to the global environment, biodiversity, and climate, activist movements are also taking seriously how the futures of humans are intimately bound with the futures of non-human animals and **more-than-human** communities (see Hodge et al., 2022). These intersections invite a radical departure from traditional forms of activism perhaps, in so far as they encourage an even greater radical politics to come to the fore: namely a politics of Total Liberation. One of the key thinkers here has been Steven Best, particularly through his book *The Politics of Total Liberation: Revolution for the 21st Century*. For Best:

> It is imperative that we no longer speak of human liberation, animal liberation, or earth liberation as if they were independent struggles, but rather that we talk instead of total liberation.
>
> *Best, 2014: 81*

The call for a holistic politics of Total Liberation has been embraced most fully by animal liberational activists that have sought inter-species justice for humans, non-humans, and ecosystems. Two prominent examples here include Earth Liberation Front (ELF) and the Animal Liberation Front (ALF). As Pellow and Brehm (2015: 193) argue, '[t]he idea that we can no longer understand, analyze, or resist a single form of oppression in isolation from other forms materialized in **feminist** and antiracist activist and intellectual circles across the nation, and we saw these ideas appear in the writings, speeches, and actions of radical animal rights and environmental activists'.

Finally, it is important to acknowledge how vital – and powerful – are the messages and alternative futures that activists desire to bring into the world. I hope this chapter has helped show how activism literally takes place across an impressively broad spectrum of sites, which conventional narratives – that is, those that only identify activists as those who wave banners in public spaces – rarely consider. Yet it is so vital that these **'othered'** and hidden forms of activism – the infrapolitics and autonomous geographies – are recognised and valued more fully moving forward.

Activists pose a terrific threat to authority and the vested interests of the powerful – from 'the global' to 'the local', and all the spaces in-between. The threat can be clearly seen in the draconian set of responses that 'the powerful' seek to use to hinder or prevent activism from taking place. To be an activist in the twenty-first century, to bring hope to a world that is in deep and perhaps terminal crisis brings with it greater threat of harassment, intimation, incarceration, or even death. In Latin America, for example, Global Witness (2021) reported that '227 land and environmental activists [had been] murdered in a single year, the worst figure on record' (see also Blackmore, 2020).

Offering an antidote to any sense of being overwhelmed about the state of the world today, we must recognise that:

> There is no ideal scale, no ideal mode or working, nor ideal activist. We see a diversity of forms and degrees of organization, and sometimes basically none, just spontaneous outrage.
>
> *White and Wood, 2016: 571*

There is no blueprint for 'being an activist' or how to do activism: be very sceptical of anybody who tries to tell you differently! This chapter may well have encouraged you to think about how you already act in ways that could be considered 'activist', but you have never thought of it in this way. It may have also encouraged you to be more conscious of the ubiquity of activism and think through ways in which we can all offer our unique skills, experiences, and time to directly address the problems that we see around us. Activism and protest is as much 'in here', as 'out there' (see Chapter 73). There is always the hope and possibility that the activist geographies that everyday people across the world commit to creating, nurturing, and willing-into-being in the world may yet prove to be the difference that makes all the difference. The fundamental question to consider maybe is one of reflection: what part will I play in the activist geographies of the morrow?

Discussion points

- Think of three examples of social injustice that concern (a) humans, (b) non-human animals, and (c) the environment. Make a list of the different forms of oppression that maintain this injustice and consider how injustice in one of these three areas may well extend into the others.
- Why is it important to question the accuracy of how activist and protest movements are represented, particularly if we haven't witnessed them first hand, or spoken to participants directly?
- What are some ordinary spaces and practices of activism and how might these connect to more visible and spectacular activist geographies?
- What challenges does intersectionality pose for activist and protest movements? What does – or what should – intersectional activism look like in practice?

References

ACME Resistance. (2018). Geographers against Trump: reflections on the first annual ACME protest. *ACME: An International Journal for Critical Geographies* 17(1): 1–16. Retrieved from https://acme-journal.org/index.php/acme/article/view/1703

Best, S. (2014). *The Politics of Total Liberation: Revolution for the 21st Century*. New York: Palgrave Macmillan.

Blackmore, E. (2020). How a peaceful protest at Tiananmen Square turned into a massacre. *National Geographic*. (Available at https://www.nationalgeographic.com/history/article/how-protest-tiananmen-square-turned-into-massacre [last accessed 26.10.2022].)

Bogel-Burroughs, N., and Garcia, S. E. (2020). What Is Antifa, the Movement Trump Wants to Declare a Terror Group? *The New York Times*. (Available at https://www.nytimes.com/article/what-antifa-trump.html [last accessed 06.11.2022].)

Cambridge Dictionary. (2023a). *Protest*. (Available at https://dictionary.cambridge.org/dictionary/english/protest [last accessed 29.06.2023].)

Cambridge Dictionary. (2023b). *Activism*. (Available at https://dictionary.cambridge.org/dictionary/english/activism [last accessed 16.03.2023].)

Crenshaw, K. (1989). Demarginalizing the Intersection of Race and Sex: A Black Feminist Critique of Antidiscrimination Doctrine, Feminist Theory and Antiracist Politics. *University of Chicago Legal Forum*, 139–67.

Cudworth, E., Boisseau, W., and White, R. J. (2021). Guest editorial: introduction for a critically posthumanist sociology in precarious times. *International Journal of Sociology and Social Policy* 41(3–4): 265–281.

Gayle, D. (2022). Just Stop Oil activists throw soup at Van Gogh's Sunflowers. *The Guardian*. (Available at https://www.theguardian.com/environment/2022/oct/14/just-stop-oil-activists-throw-soup-at-van-goghs-sunflowers [last accessed 26.10.2022].)

Global Witness. (2021). Global Witness reports 227 land and environmental activists murdered in a single year, the worst figure on record. *Global Witness*. (Available at https://www.globalwitness.org/en/press-releases/global-witness-reports-227-land-and-environmental-activists-murdered-single-year-worst-figure-record/ [last accessed 08.11.2022].)

Hodge, P., McGregor, A., Springer, S., Véron, O., and White, R. J. (eds.) (March 2022). *Vegan Geographies: Spaces beyond Violence, Ethics beyond Speciesism*. Brooklyn: Lantern Books.

Kahn, R., and Kellner, D. (2004). New media and internet activism: from the 'Battle of Seattle' to blogging. *New Media & Society* 6(1): 87–95.

Lawson and Gayle. (2022). Three arrested at Shell AGM as protesters chant 'We will stop you'. *The Guardian*. (Available at https://www.theguardian.com/business/2022/may/24/shell-pause-london-agm-protesters-oil-gas-green [Last accessed 07.110.2022].)

Liinason, M. (2020). Multiplicities of Power – Multiplicities of Struggle. Intersectional Movements and Feminist and Queer Grassroots Activism. In *Handbuch Intersektionalitätsforschung*, eds. A. Biele Mefebue, A. Bührmann, and S. Grenz. Wiesbaden: Springer VS. https://doi.org/10.1007/978-3-658-26613-4_25-1

McKay, G. (2011). *Radical Gardening: Politics, Idealism and Rebellion in the Garden*. London: Frances Lincoln.

McLean, J., Maalsen, S., and Prebble, S. (2019). A feminist perspective on digital geographies: activism, affect and emotion, and gendered human-technology relations in Australia. *Gender, Place & Culture* 26(5): 740–761. DOI: 10.1080/0966369X.2018.1555146

Panelli, R., and Larner, W. (2010). Timely partnerships? Contrasting geographies of activism in New Zealand and Australia. *Urban Studies* 47(6): 1343–1366. https://doi.org/10.1177/0042098009360226

Pellow, D. N., and Brehm, H. N. (2015). From the New ecological paradigm to total liberation: the emergence of a social movement frame. *The Sociological Quarterly* 56(1): 185–212. DOI: 10.1111/tsq.12084

Pickerill, J., and Chatterton, P. (2006). Notes towards autonomous geographies: creation, resistance and self-management as survival tactics. *Progress in Human Geography* 30(6): 730–746. https://doi.org/10.1177/0309132506071516

Pottinger, L. (2017). Planting the seeds of a quiet activism. *Area* 49(2): 215–222.

Routledge, P. (n.d.). *We Are All Space Invaders Now*. Blog, Pluto Press. (Available at https://www.plutobooks.com/9780745336244/space-invaders/ [last accessed 10.08.2022].)

Salmenkari, T. (2009). Geography of protest: places of demonstration in Buenos Aires and Seoul, *Urban Geography* 30(3): 239–260. DOI: 10.2747/0272-3638.30.3.239

Scott, J. C. (1990). *Domination and the Arts of Resistance: Hidden Transcripts of Acgi*. New Haven and London: Yale University Press.

White, R. J., Springer, S., and de Souza, M. L. (eds.) (2016). *The Practice of Freedom: Anarchism, Geography and the Spirit of Revolt*. Lanham: Rowman & Littlefield.

White, R. J., and Williams, C. C. (2012). Beyond Capitalist Hegemony: Exploring the Persistence and Growth of 'alternative' Economic Practices. In *The Accumulation of Freedom: Writings on Anarchist Economics*, eds. A. Nocella, J. Asimakopoulos, and D. Shannon. Edinburgh: AK Press, 117–139.

White, R. J., and Williams, C. C. (2014). Anarchist economic practices in a 'capitalist' society: some implications for organisation and the future of work. *Ephemera: Theory and Politics in Organization* 14(4): 971–975.

White, R. J., and Wood, P. B. (2016). Guest editorial. *International Journal of Sociology and Social Policy* 36(9/10): 570–577. https://doi.org/10.1108/IJSSP-07-2016-0092

Online materials

- Achuar
  Achuar, a group of Indigenous peoples from the Amazon rainforest in Ecuador, illustrate activism and protest in contemporary times. Many Achuar reside in the rainforest and partner with Pachamama Alliance to preserve their ancestral lands and culture. https://pachamama.org/achuar

- Anarcha Feminist Group Amsterdam
  'We are anarchists, and we believe in intersectionality. We are against all forms of exploitation and oppression including but not limited to those based on class, race, sex, sexuality, gender, or ability. Our feminism is trans and sex-worker inclusive. We believe that we can not effectively challenge the patriarchy if we do not also fight to abolish capitalism and the state. At the same time, we are tired of waiting for our own liberation, too often other forms of oppression are seen as an afterthought or as coming secondary to the class struggle. Our spaces, although they are anarchist, are not exempted from structural forms of violence and oppression. As long as we do not have effective structures in places to challenge these forms of violence, they will not go away by themselves'. https://radar.squat.net/en/amsterdam/anarcha-feminist-group-amsterdam

- El Cambalache: we exchange Economy without money, disarming capitalism
  El Cambalache was founded in 2015 and is a moneyless economy project located in San Cristóbal de las Casas, Chiapas, made by and for women and everyone in their everyday networks, as featured in the documentary, Inter-Change Value (2016). https://cambalache.noblogs.org/post/2021/05/18/taller-en-linea-junio-2021-online-workshop-june-2021/ and https://www.youtube.com/channel/UCslgLGj8V0LFxSaDnL8iYQg

- **Food Empowerment Project** is a vegan organisation founded by a woman of colour. Their values include 'a stance against racism, casteism, sexism, homophobia, transphobia, ableism, ageism, and body shaming. That is not to say we have never made mistakes or we never will, but we do our best to learn and listen to those impacted to make any necessary changes'. https://foodispower.org/mission-and-values/

- **VINE Sanctuary**: VINE is an LGBTQ-led farmed animal sanctuary that works for social and environmental justice as well as for animal liberation. Hundreds of animals co-create a multi-species community. https://vinesanctuary.org/incontext

Further Reading

Bond, S., Thomas, A., and Diprose, G. (2023). *Stopping Oil: Climate Justice and Hope*. London: Pluto Press.
By focusing on the experiences of a powerful climate justice campaign that emerged to resist deep-sea oil exploration in Aotearoa (New Zealand), the authors draw attention to, and inspire us to think creatively about, a range of geographies of hope and possibility.

Firth, R. (2022). *Mutual Aid and Radical Action*. London: Pluto Press.
This book provides another wonderful testimony to the importance and power of mutual aid (anarchy in action) in society, not least in the aftermath of crisis. It makes a powerful call to recognise and harness mutual aid as a means of better organising society beyond capitalism and the state.

Hsiao, A., and Lim, A. (eds.) (2020). *The Verso Book of Dissent: Revolutionary Words from Three Millennia of Rebellion and Resistance*. London: Verso.
Inspiring illustration of the many ways in which people have expressed dissent and protest. Wonderful historical and contemporary examples, and truly global in context.

Routledge, P. (2017). *We Are All Space Invaders Now*. London: Pluto Press.
A compelling case for radical geographic perspectives that helps us understand, value, and take inspiration from a wide range of global protests and social movements (past and present).

Springer, S. (2016). *The Anarchist Roots of Geography: Toward Spatial Emancipation*. Minneapolis: University of Minnesota Press.
Quite simply an outstanding book on anarchist geographies. Reading this will help you dispel any popular negative stereotypes about what anarchism is or is not; it will also encourage you to think of the radical and beautiful potential that anarchism has in inspiring and informing better futures.

Truscello, M. (2021). *Infrastructural Brutalism. Art and the Necropolitics of Infrastructure*. Cambridge, MA: MIT Press.
This book makes a series of powerful connections between infrastructure, power, injustice, exploitation, and death. It focuses on what radical activism should mean at a time of acute crisis, and what needs to be done to defeat this infrastructural power. You will never look at transport in the same way again!

SECTION SIX

SOCIAL GEOGRAPHIES

54 Knowing social geographies

Andrew Williams and Kelly Dombroski

Introduction

Social geography is a diverse and vibrant subdiscipline that considers how 'social relations, social identities, and social inequalities are produced, their spatial variation, and the role of **space** in constructing them' (Pain et al., 2001: 1). Social geographers tend to focus on how spatial processes construct social aspects of everyday life, social difference, and power relations (Smith et al., 2010). The subdiscipline is concerned with 'the interrelationships between society, space and place, asking how the nature and activity of societies are geographically constituted (created or changed by spatial patterns and processes) and geographically expressed (manifested in spatial patterns and processes)' (The Newcastle Social Geographies Collective, 2021: 9). Perhaps one of the most longstanding intellectual currents underpinning social geography is a concern with social and spatial justice (Chapter 55), especially geographies of inequality, identities, and disadvantage. Much of the scholarship is animated by political activism, community engagement, and participatory (or 'action-oriented') praxis.

Social geography: past and present

Writing disciplinary histories is always political. Who or what to include (and exclude)? To whom and where is credit allocated? As Sara Ahmed reminds us, citation is a **feminist** practice; it is 'how we acknowledge our debt to those who came before; those who helped us find our way when the way was obscured because we deviated from the paths we were told to follow' (2017: 15–16). Choosing not to cite any 'white men' was a deliberate decision by Ahmed to begin dismantling institutional structures of patriarchal whiteness. Any account of a (sub)discipline that simply rehearses a family tree of the 'big boys' not only reproduces racialised and **gendered** hierarchies of knowledge, but does so at the expense of feminist, Black and Indigenous scholars and knowledges (Mott and Cockayne, 2017, Hall, 2019). After all, citation is academic currency: a source of scholarly reputation that not only constitutes what counts as credible knowledge but also delimits people's livelihoods in an increasingly precarious higher education sector (Baker, 2019).

Disciplinary histories will always be a situated and partial story: no one has a 'godlike' view that sees and knows everything (Haraway, 1988). For instance, the origins of Western social

DOI: 10.4324/9780429265853-63

geography are usually traced back to the nineteenth-century 'French School' of human geography, known as *la géographie humaine*. This school played a pivotal role in challenging the prevailing environmental determinism of its day and emphasised instead the **agency** of people (a precursor to **humanist geography**, see Ley, 1983). Concurrently, within the **anarchist** tradition, geographers such as Peter Kropotkin (1842–1921) and Elisee Reclus (1830–1905) challenged the ways the geographical tradition of mapping and cataloguing of 'the **Other**' was fist-in-glove with the racist, sexist, and classist project of **Imperialism** (see Nayak and Jeffrey, 2011).

While debates persist regarding the definition of geography's 'canon' (Powell, 2015), ongoing discussions also centre around the overlooked traditions of radical social geography shaped by feminist, **decolonial**, and **subaltern** perspectives beyond the dominant Anglo-centric context (Barnes and Sheppard, 2019, Ferretti, 2020). Scholars like Ibarra García and Talledos Sánchez (2020) and Ferretti (2021, 2022), for example, highlight the contributions of Brazilian geographer Josué de Castro (1908–1973) and Cuban revolutionary geographer Antonio Núñez Jiménez (1923–1998) that deserve greater recognition than they currently receive in shaping critical geography and development studies. Such contributions complicate neat accounts of the evolution of social geography and underline the importance of comparative work that traces the development of the subdiscipline in different geographical contexts (see, for example, Craggs and Neate's [2020] account of the intellectual contribution of Nigerian geographers since the 1940s, alongside a series of Country Reports published in the journal *Social & Cultural Geography*).

The dominant account, at least in an Anglo-American context, usually draws attention to the influence of the 'quantitative revolution' in Human Geography in the late-1940s and 1950s – which, by the early 1960s, had inspired many social geographers to map and statistically analyse social phenomena such as social inequality and patterns of segregation. However, the influence of humanist geography challenged the dominance of positivist approaches in social geography that had sought to establish – through the application of scientific methods – universal laws that explained spatial patterns and processes (for a review, see Kitchin, 2015). Instead, attention shifted to the subjective meanings and experiences derived by humans from their surrounding environments (Buttimer, 1976, Tuan, 1976, Ley, 1983). Social geography also became more intertwined with radical geography, aligning with the emergence of various social movements, including civil rights, feminism, gay and lesbian rights, disability rights, anti-racism, **postcolonial** struggles, and environmentalism.

This 'radical turn' unfolded in the 1980s, influenced by **Marxist**, postcolonial, and feminist geography. It propelled research on poverty, health, housing, sexism, racism and labour exploitation (Massey, 1994) and, within this, offered critical insights on the spatial relationships produced by capitalism, imperialism, and **colonialism**. Furthermore, it prompted investigations into the intricate ways in which everyday life is experienced and negotiated across various dimensions of social difference, encompassing **gender**, age, **class**, **ethnicity**, **race**, sexuality, and dis/ability.

In the late 1980s and 1990s, the 'cultural turn', closely associated with poststructuralist thinking, broadened the scope of geographic analysis and sharpened focus on the role of identity, **representation** and meaning in constituting social relations, exclusion and everyday life. Underpinning all of this was a practice of anti-essentialism, a word which describes the desire to de-naturalise categories of difference and recognise how 'race', gender, sexuality, age, and dis/ability are **socially constructed** and reproduced through socio-spatial practices rather than being 'essential' to human nature (see Chapters 12, 13, and 58–60).

Identities play a fundamental role in shaping who we are as individuals, both in our own perception and that of others. In many ways, identity is geographically constituted. Firstly, identity is dynamic and changes over time and space (so what it means to be a woman, say, is not fixed but varies in different places, times, and contexts). Secondly, identities are multifaceted and intersect with markers of social difference such as class, gender, ethnicity, age, sexuality, religion, and dis/ability. These intersecting identities collectively structure our lives, influencing how we are treated, the life chances we have, and the expectations placed upon us. Thirdly, identities are relational – to where they belong, where they are 'in and out of place'. They are formed in relation to others rather than being solely derived from innate characteristics. In this sense, identities encompass both self-assertion ('this is me') and social judgement ('that is you'). What is more, how we 'form' our identities is shaped by wider historical currents and processes. Many writers argue that today our identities are less something we inherit through our social and geographical locations and more something that we partly fashion for ourselves within wider social fields in which we are judged and socially positioned.

Summary

- Social geography examines the interrelationships between society, space, and place, analysing how societies are constituted and expressed through spatial patterns and processes.
- Social and spatial justice, including geographies of inequality, identities, and disadvantage, are significant concerns in this field, often driving political activism, community engagement, and participatory approaches.
- Social geographers also examine the ways in which social identities, such as gender, age, race, ethnicity, religion, class, ability, and sexuality, are constructed, experienced, and contested in different geographic contexts.

Knowing social geography in changing times

While subdisciplines such as social geography provide ways of organising scholarly debates and areas of shared interest, it is important to acknowledge that the boundaries between these subdisciplines are – and always have been – porous, mutually constructed, and continually evolving. It is increasingly difficult to separate 'social' from 'cultural' geography, or from 'political', 'economic', 'historical', or 'environmental' geography for that matter. The longstanding debate on what constitutes 'social' and 'cultural' geography has led scholars such as Nayak (2011) and others (Cresswell, 2010, Smith et al., 2011) to recognise their inseparability, and ultimately, this has been fruitful in generating new avenues of thought and fostering new 'communities of practice'. Far from being static, the interests, approaches, and commitments of social geographers are constantly in motion. They are shaped by theoretical and methodological shifts; urgent social, political-economic, and environmental crises; and the personal experiences of academics themselves. Just as the nature of research has become more interdisciplinary, it is increasingly the case that social geography research is reoriented around topics (e.g. food, animals, **infrastructures**) that draw upon the whole breadth of the discipline, including but not restricted to social, cultural, physical, historical, and economic geography. Contemporary social geography continues to develop new topics that have become areas of research in their own right: mobilities (Chapter 11), emotion (Chapter 24), sexuality (Chapters 12 and 72), and health (Chapter 60). Food geographies, for example, have become a fulcrum for social, cultural, political, and economic geographers to examine the centrality of food in everyday life, address-ing wide-ranging concerns from food insecurity, alternative proteins, consumer cultures, to environmental and labour exploitation on plantations (see Kneafsey et al., 2021).

The connections between social and historical geography also have grown in recent years. Historical geography as a distinct subdiscipline continues to offer important insights into past geographies: from historical accounts of **capitalism**, **globalisation**, the state, and **territory**; the production of knowledge; heritage and the politics of memory; landscape and environment change; and identities, social hierarchies, and resistance stories that are all-too-often marginalised (see Ogborn, 1998, Morrissey et al., 2014, Naylor, 2017). Much of this work animates contem-porary struggles, such as histories of South Indian anticolonialism (Davies, 2019) and **transna-tional** networks of Black internationalism and anti-fascism (Featherstone, 2013). For example, Caroline Bressey has traced the presence of Black women in urban and rural Victorian England who are frequently written out of **hegemonic** accounts of Britain's past. Bressey highlights their experiences of welfare institutions, education, employment, and mobilising an anti-racist poli-tics (Bressey, 2013, 2015). The past is often shrouded in denial and discomfort – a phenomenon that has very real political effects in the present. For a long time Britain's relationship to Empire and slavery was not simply a matter of forgetting, but one of deliberate displacement and dis-connection (Stoler, 2016).

Wales – where Andy lives and works – has faced a peculiar kind of 'disavowal' different to that of England (Lester, 2022). In many ways, its complicity is concealed in cultural narratives of Welsh victimhood and English imperialism that feed calls for Welsh Independence.[1] Or Wales narrates itself as 'not as bad' in the role it played in slavery as the major ports of Bristol, Liverpool, and London. If its complicity is acknowledged at all, it is confined to a particular group of people whose direct involvement in transatlantic slavery can be traced, namely, the landed gentry (e.g. the Tredegar Morgans, who had shares in the Royal African Company) or the industrialist class (e.g. the Pennant family's slate mines financed by slavery). Yet the export economy of Wales – woollens, copper, coal – was integral to slavery and the British Empire (Evans, 2010). Buried underneath Swansea's Parc Tawe retail park – where Andy went to the cinema as a teenager – are the remains of the old North Dock and the 'Cobre Wharf', where copper masters attended weekly auctions to buy and sell copper ore imported from El Cobre mine in Cuba. After the abo-lition of slavery in British territories (1833–1838), industrialists in South Wales established the Cobre Mining Company that used enslaved African and indentured Chinese labour in the mine between 1835 and 1869. In contemporary times, Welsh nationalism is animated by the maxim 'Cofiwch Dryweryn' ('Remember Tryweryn') – to signify the decision by Liverpool City Council to ride roughshod over Welsh authorities and flood the community of Capel Celyn to create the Llyn reservoir for the water supply of Liverpool and the Wirral. However, as exemplified above, for Welshness to cultivate a radical and inclusive politics of reparation, it must also say in the same breath 'Cofiwch El Cobre'.

We have witnessed growing crossovers between social and historical research, particularly in the methods used by geographers to foster more collaborative, community-engaged scholarship, ranging from exhibition-making and museum curation, film, and digital media (see Figure 54.1), to citizen archaeology and public history (for an overview, see Driver, 2014).

Figure 54.1
Screenshot from Kyle Legall's digital graphic novel Cardiff 1919: Riots Redrawn (https://www.cardiff1919.wales/). The interactive novel combines spoken text and illustration to conjure up the atmosphere, people, and places involved in four day-long race riots in which homes were looted, hundreds injured, and three killed

Source: Reproduced with permission from Kyle Legall, available from https://www.cardiff1919.wales/

Summary

- The changing research agendas of social geographers largely speak to pressing social, political-economic, and environmental crises and how these connect to the commitments and experiences of academics themselves.
- Theoretical and methodological frameworks continue to change, but the radical commitment to tackling oppression and inequality, in all its guises, remains.

Expanding 'the social'

In the past three decades, social geography has undergone a significant expansion in its conceptualisation of 'the social' (Smith et al., 2010). Posthumanist social geography, or **more-than-human** social geography, emerges as part of a shift away from a human-centric perspective towards recognising the significance of materiality, technology, and non-human actors in shaping social life (see Whatmore, 2002 on hybrid forms of social/nature). An area of increasing scholarly attention within this field pertains to the intricate relationships between humans and non-human animals. Animal geographies transcend the mere cataloguing of animal species, aiming instead to explore the intricate social, ethical, and political dynamics entwined with pets, captive animals, research animals, animal welfare, including wild and farmed animals, and veterinary governance (Urbanik, 2013). Henry Buller (2014, 2015) provides a comprehensive overview of animal geographies, elucidating the diverse methodologies employed by geographers to gain a deeper understanding of animal **subjectivity**. Similarly, recent research in health geographies and medical humanities has drawn upon **non-representational** and posthumanist approaches to better understand how pathologised and medicalised phenomena, such as compulsion (Tourette syndrome) and other neurodiversities (Beljaars, 2020), 'obesity' (Berlant, 2007), or drug use and 'addiction' (Duff, 2012) are all co-constituted by the socio-material environment (Andrews and Duff, 2019; see Chapter 60). A growing body of work has emerged from this turn towards materiality, examining infrastructural geographies, from the role of libraries, playgrounds, and sidewalks in facilitating **sociality** and encounter (Latham and Layton, 2019), to the politics of water sanitation and its importance not only for hygiene but for democratic rights to public life and health (McFarlane, 2023).

Finally, while 'social' geography substantively refers to the study of social relations across space and place, it also refers to more collaborative and collective ways of working in the geographical production of knowledge (The Newcastle Social Geographies Collective, 2021). This has tended to denote **participatory geographies** – 'research by, with, and for people affected by a particular problem, which takes place in collaboration with academic researchers' (Kindon et al., 2009: 90) – but is gradually seeping into decisions over academic authorship and the pace and purpose of academic scholarship.

Theoretical and methodological frameworks within the field continue to evolve while maintaining a steadfast commitment to addressing various forms of **power**, oppression, and inequality (see Box 54.1). The discipline's pluralistic approach recognises the necessity of employing diverse methods and methodologies to serve different research purposes. Mapping and statistical analysis of inequalities remain crucial, alongside in-depth **ethnographic** case studies and other qualitative methods, including participatory action research. Contemporary social geography continues to explore a diverse range of topics through different analytical starting points: from the very intimate scale of the body; moments of conviviality and encountering difference; schools, hospitals, prisons, and other institutions; to city, rural, and regional inequalities; to global mobilities and transnational solidarities. Recent work includes investigating the racial-spatial politics of immigration (Ehrkamp, 2019); the geographies of friendship and loneliness (Bunnell et al., 2012); rethinking public space (Qian, 2020); student practices of homemaking (Holton and Riley, 2016); exploring care and activism in times of austerity (Hall, 2020, Jupp, 2022); dilemmas over children and young people's 'screen time' (Wilson, 2016) and play spaces (Holloway and Pimlott-Wilson, 2014); understanding domestic abuse and safety (Pain, 2014, Little, 2023), contesting gender-based violence (Brickell, 2020), to examining the phenomenon of veganism (Oliver, 2021), and navigating the complexities of sexual harassment and white heteropatriarchy within university spaces (Smyth et al., 2020, Boycr, 2022).

BOX 54.1
ANTI-BEGGING CAMPAIGN IN THE UK 2014

Geographers often use visual methodologies to deconstruct representations and the power they have in shaping everyday understandings of phenomena. Figure 54.2 shows a 2016 anti-begging poster from the Ipswich Locality Homelessness Partnership, UK, a derivative from a 2003 campaign launched by Thames Reach charity in London called 'Your kindness can kill'. Its aim was to discourage the public from giving money to homeless people.

Figure 54.2
An 'anti-begging' campaign in Ipswich, UK (https://web.archive.org/web/20170422140523/ http:/www.ilhp.org.uk/yourkindnesscouldkill.php)

Source: Ipswich Locality Homelessness Partnership, available from https://web.archive.org/web/20170422140523/ http:/www.ilhp.org.uk/yourkindnesscouldkill.php

Using questions inspired by Gillian Rose's (2022) framework for understanding visual culture, consider what power this representation has in shaping ethical action, its effectiveness, and the reasons why you think this leaflet was produced. Think about the image itself: its composition and visual meanings. How is homelessness represented? Think about the production of the image: how was it made? By whom? For whom? Why? Finally, think about the audience: How is it interpreted? By whom? Why?

Summary

- Social geography has expanded its understanding of 'the social' by embracing posthumanist perspectives that recognise the influence of materiality, technology, and non-human actors in shaping social life.
- Social geographers draw on a wide range of theoretical and methodological frameworks and increasingly emphasise collaborative knowledge production through participatory action research.

Chapter summaries

In Chapter 55, Andrew Williams begins by discussing patterns of social and spatial inequality, including the uneven distribution of resources, opportunities, and power, and their impacts on individuals and communities. After reviewing some of the ways geographers have theorised social and spatial justice, the discussion turns to the production of poverty and the racialisation of class and segregation in the USA. The chapter uses the concept of welfare racism to examine socio-spatial inequalities in the UK. He then contrasts the growing power of the superrich and elites in changing urban and rural places, with the work in feminist **political economy** that highlights how economic crises impact people's everyday lives, gendered relationships, and future aspirations.

In Chapter 56, Jon May explores the processes and politics of stigma and exclusion. Exclusion here is understood as a simultaneously social and spatial process in which some members of society are placed outside 'the norm' or the mainstream. A key writer in this area is the social geographer David Sibley, through his work on those cast as 'outsiders' and on the psychic underpinnings of our desires to distinguish between an included 'us' and an excluded 'them'. The chapter draws on the work of Erving Goffman, Imogen Tyler, Tom Slater, and others to show how geographers have theorised stigma. Illustrating these ideas with reference to the stigmatisation and exclusion of street homeless people in British and North American cities, it then considers the political economy of territorial stigma: examining its role in the destruction of social housing and processes of 'domicide'.

In Chapter 57, Joris Schapendonk and Maggie Leung address complex belongings, associated with combined processes of migration and globalisation, increasingly prevalent within modern formations of identity. Social geographies of identity are no longer nationally contained. Other, 'transnational' and '**diaspora** spaces', have emerged within which nationalised territories are disturbed and diasporic identities developed. But rather than starting with the dominant position of the migrant-receiving society, Schapendonk and Leung offer a perspective based on the ubiquity of mobility. They challenge the notion that being in one place (e.g. a country) is normal, while cross-border mobility is abnormal; and explore how diasporic identities and senses of belonging are formed and contested.

In Chapter 58, Carl Bonner-Thompson reviews recent trends in how geographical research on identity and difference is increasingly embracing **embodied** and relational approaches, influenced by feminist, queer, trans, fat, and dis/able geographies. These perspectives highlight the significance of considering the material, physical, and visceral aspects of the body. By acknowledging these realities, geographers gain insights into how identity and difference emerge in relation to various factors, such as places, people, meanings, **discourses**, and emotions. In all of this, thinking intersectionally is vital. **Intersectionality** – as Hopkins (2019) reminds us – 'is not only about multiple identities … [but the] "mutually constitutive forms of social oppression"' (p. 937), and using such a perspective allows us to examine the multiple ways in which race, gender, class, sexuality, age, religion, and dis/ability intersect with one another, and with social context, to shape relations of privilege and disadvantage.

In Chapter 59, Peter Kraftl and Sophie Hadfield-Hill look at a key element of any identity: age. This chapter provides a rich introduction to geographical research on age and the lifecourse. They examine why and how geographers have studied children and youth – how young people's experiences of the world vary with social and geographical contexts, and how understanding their voices and perspectives is crucial to making more inclusive places. The chapter then turns to 'relational' approaches to age, looking, for instance, at how people from different generations relate to one another in different private, institutional, and public settings, and at how 'family' is a contested and complex term. It ends with a consideration of the politics of (young) age, charting how geographers have critically evaluated the ways in which some young people become privileged – and others marginalised – within global political-economic processes.

In Chapter 60, David Conradson turns his attention to health and wellbeing, a subject matter that has received considerable attention in recent years. Geographical work in this area has gone beyond the study of spatial patterning of disease and illness and has focused on the mutually constitutive relationship between health and place. The chapter provides an overview of contemporary debates related to happiness and wellbeing, healthy cities, stigmatised 'unhealthy' bodies, health inequalities, and therapeutic landscapes as well as identifies new research in disability geography and medical humanities.

In Chapter 61, Emma Power and Miriam Williams provide a review of critical geographical scholarship on care and its relationship to feminist economic, political, and urban geography. It provides insight into how geographers approach the concepts of care and responsibility. In the first part of the chapter, they explore what care is and why it is an important concept in social geography. Secondly, they consider the different political approaches to who is responsible for care, bringing insights from feminist care ethics, which argue that we have collective rather than individual care responsibility. Thirdly, they examine how responsibility for care might extend across place and time. They end by reflecting on the transformative potential of care as a framework that challenges geographers to work towards more equal and caring worlds.

Finally, we would advise that you also consult the preceding section in this book on 'political geographies', which, with its foci on '**neoliberalism**', 'territory', 'colonialism', and 'protest and activism', has particularly strong resonances with the field of social geography.

Discussion points

- Make a list of the different aspects of your identity. Has your identity changed over time? If so, how and why?
- How do power relations play out spatially, and how are they influenced by factors such as social class, gender, race, and ethnicity? Discuss examples of power struggles and contestations over space.
- Discuss potential strategies and approaches that researchers, policymakers, and communities might employ to address social inequalities and promote spatial justice.
- Why is it important for social geographers to expand definitions of 'the social'?

Note

1   The language of colonialism for a long time flavoured calls for Welsh Independence, see Price, A. (2018). *Wales, the First and Final Colony: Speeches and Writings 2001–2018*.

References

Ahmed, S. (2017). *Living a Feminist Life*. Durham: Duke University Press.

Andrews, G. J., and Duff, C. (2019). Matter beginning to matter: on posthumanist understandings of the vital emergence of health. *Social Science & Medicine* 226: 123–134.

Baker, K. J. (2019). *Citation Matters, Women in Higher Education [Online]*. https://www.wihe.com/article-details/124/citation-matters/

Barnes, T. J., and Sheppard, E. (eds.) (2019). *Spatial Histories of Radical Geography: North America and Beyond*. Hoboken, NJ: John Wiley & Sons.

Beljaars, D. (2020). Towards compulsive geographies. *Transactions of the Institute of British Geographers* 45(2): 284–298.

Berlant, L. (2007). Slow death (sovereignty, obesity, lateral agency). *Critical Inquiry* 33(4): 754–780.

Boyer, K. (2022). Sexual harassment and the right to everyday life. *Progress in Human Geography* 46(2): 398–415.

Bressey, C. (2013). *Empire, Race and the Politics of Anti-Caste*. London: Bloomsbury.

Bressey, C. (2015). Race, antiracism, and the place of blackness in the making and remaking of the English working class. *Historical Reflections* 41(1): 70–82.

Brickell, K. (2020). *Home SOS: Gender, Violence and Survival in Crisis Ordinary Cambodia*. Oxford: Wiley-Blackwell.

Buller, H. (2014). Animal geographies I. *Progress in Human Geography* 38(2): 308–318.

Buller, H. (2015). Animal geographies II: methods. *Progress in Human Geography* 39(3): 374–384.

Bunnell, T., Yea, S., Peake, L., Skelton, T., and Smith, M. (2012). Geographies of friendships. *Progress in Human Geography* 36(4): 490–507.

Buttimer, A. (1976). Grasping the dynamism of lifeworld. *Annals of the Association of American Geographers* 66: 277–292

Craggs, R., and Neate, H. (2020). What Happens If We Start from Nigeria? Diversifying Histories of Geography. *Annals of the American Association of Geographers* 110(3): 899–916, DOI: 10.1080/24694452.2019.1631748

Cresswell, T. (2010). New cultural geography—an unfinished project? *Cultural Geographies* 17: 169–174.

Davies, A. (2019). *Geographies of Anticolonialism Political Networks Across and Beyond South India, c. 1900–1930*. Wiley: London.

Driver, F. (2014). Historical geography at large: towards public historical geographies. *Journal of Historical Geography* 46: 92.

Duff, C. (2012). Accounting for context: exploring the role of objects and spaces in the consumption of alcohol and other drugs. *Social & Cultural Geography* 13(2): 145–159.

Ehrkamp, P. (2019). Geographies of migration II: the racial-spatial politics of immigration. *Progress in Human Geography* 43(2): 363–375.

Evans, C. (2010). *Slave Wales: The Welsh and Atlantic Slavery, 1660–1850*. Cardiff: University of Wales Press.

Featherstone, D. (2013). Black internationalism, subaltern cosmopolitanism, and the spatial politics of antifascism. *Annals of the Association of American Geographers* 103(6): 1406–1420.

Ferretti, F. (2020). History and philosophy of geography I: Decolonising the discipline, diversifying archives and historicising radicalism. *Progress in Human Geography* 44(6): 1161–1171.

Ferretti, F. (2021). A coffin for Malthusianism: Josué de Castro's subaltern geopolitics. *Geopolitics* 26(2): 589–614.

Ferretti, F. (2022). Geographies of revolution: prefiguration and spaces of alterity in Latin American radicalism. *Environment and Planning C: Politics and Space* 40(5): 1147–1164.

Hall, S. M. (2019). Everyday austerity: towards relational geographies of family, friendship and intimacy. *Progress in Human Geography* 43(5): 769–789.

Hall, S. M. (2020). The personal is political: Feminist geographies of/in austerity. *Geoforum* 110: 242–251.

Haraway, D. (1988). Situated knowledges: the science question in feminism and the privilege of partial perspective. *Feminism Studies* 14(3): 575–599.

Holloway, S. L., and Pimlott-Wilson, H. (2014). Enriching children, institutionalizing childhood? Geographies of play, extracurricular activities, and parenting in England. *Annals of the Association of American Geographers* 104(3): 613–627.

Holton, M., and Riley, M. (2016). Student geographies and homemaking: personal belonging(s) and identities. *Social & Cultural Geography* 17(5): 623–645.

Hopkins, P. (2019). Social geography I: intersectionality. *Progress in Human Geography* 43(5): 937–947.

Hopkins, P. (2020). Social geography II: Islamophobia, transphobia, and sizism. *Progress in Human Geography* 44(3): 583–594.

Hopkins, P. (2021). Social geography III: committing to social justice. *Progress in Human Geography* 45(2): 382–393.

Ibarra García, M. V., and Talledos Sánchez, E. (2020). Pioneers of Latin American Critical Geography: Josué de Castro and Antonio Núñez Jiménez. In *Decolonising and Internationalising Geography. Historical Geography and Geosciences*, eds. B. Schelhaas, F. Ferretti, A. Reyes Novaes, and M. Schmidt di Friedberg. Cham: Springer, 17–26.

Jupp, E. (2022). *Care, Crisis and Activism: The Politics of Everyday Life*. Bristol: Policy Press.

Kindon, S., Pain, R., and Kesby, M. (2009). Participatory Action Research. In *International Encyclopedia of Human Geography*, eds. R. Kitchin and N. Thrift. London: Elsevier, 90–95.

Kitchin, R. (2015). Positivistic geography. In *Approaches in Human Geography*, eds. S. C. Aitken and G. Valentine. London: Sage, 23–34.

Kneafsey, M., Maye, D., Holloway, L., and Goodman, M. K. (2021). *Geographies of Food: An Introduction*. London: Bloomsbury Publishing.

Latham, A., and Layton, J. (2019). Social infrastructure and the public life of cities: studying urban sociality and public spaces. *Geography Compass* 13: e12444.

Lester, A. (2022). *Deny and Disavow: The British Empire in the Culture War*. London: Sunrise Publishing.

Ley, D. (1983). *A Social Geography of the City*. London: Harper & Row.

Little, J. (2023). Caring for survivors of domestic abuse: love, violence and safe space. *Social & Cultural Geography* 24(1): 67–85.

Massey, D. (1994). *Space, Place, and Gender*. Minneapolis: University of Minnesota Press.

McFarlane, C. (2023). *Waste and the City: The Crisis of Sanitation and the Right to Citylife*. London: Verso.

Morrissey, J., Nally, D., Strohmayer, U., and Whelan, Y. (2014). *Key Concepts in Historical Geography*. London: Sage.

Mott, C., and Cockayne, D. (2017). Citation matters: mobilizing the politics of citation toward a practice of 'conscientious engagement'. *Gender, Place & Culture* 24(7): 954–973.

Nayak, A. (2011). Geography, race and emotions: social and cultural intersections. *Social & Cultural Geography* 12: 548–562.

Nayak, A., and Jeffrey, A. (2011). *Geographical Thought: An Introduction to Ideas in Human Geography*. London: Routledge.

Naylor, S. (2017). Historical geography in transactions. *Transactions of the Institute of British Geographers* 42(4): 485–488.

The Newcastle Social Geographies Collective. (2021). *Social Geographies: An Introduction*. Lanham: Rowan & Littlefield.

Ogborn, M. (1998). *Spaces of Modernity: London's Geographies 1680–1780*. London: Guildford Press.

Oliver, C. (2021). *Veganism, Archives, and Animals: Geographies of a Multispecies World*. London: Routledge.

Pain, R. (2014). Everyday terrorism: connecting domestic violence and global terrorism. *Progress in Human Geography* 38(4): 531–550.

Pain, R., Barke, M., Gough, J., Fuller, D., MacFarlane, R., and Mowl, G. (2001). *Introducing Social Geographies*. London: Arnold.

Powell, R. C. (2015). History and philosophy of geography III: charting the Anabasis? *Progress in Human Geography* 39(6): 827–843.

Qian, J. (2020). Geographies of public space: variegated publicness, variegated epistemologies. *Progress in Human Geography* 44(1): 77–98.

Rose, G. (2022). *Visual Methodologies: An Introduction to Researching with Visual Materials*. London: Sage.

Smith, D., Browne, K., and Bissell, D. (2011). Reinvigorating social geographies? A 'social re/turn' for a changing social world: (re)opening a debate. *Social & Cultural Geography* 12(6): 517–528.

Smith, S. J., Pain, R., Marston, S. A., and Jones, J. P. (2009). *The SAGE Handbook of Social Geographies*. Los Angeles: Sage.

Smyth, A., Linz, J., and Hudson, L. (2020). A feminist coven in the university. *Gender, Place & Culture* 27(6): 854–880.

Stoler, A. L. (2016). *Duress: Imperial Durabilities in Our Times*. Durham, NC: Duke University Press.

Tuan, Y.-F. (1976). Humanistic Geography. *Annals of the Association of American Geographers* 66(2): 266–276.

Urbanik, J. (2013). Animal Geographies. *Oxford Online Bibliographies*. doi: 10.1093/obo/9780199874002-0049. www.oxfordbibliographies.com

Whatmore, S. (2002). *Hybrid Geographies*. London: Sage.

Wilson, S. (2016). Digital technologies, children and young people's relationships and self-care. *Children's Geographies* 14(3): 282–294.

Online materials

- What is intersectionality? – YouTube – A short animation that explains the concept of intersectionality (Produced by Peter Hopkins) https://www.youtube.com/watch?v=O1islM0ytkE
- Kyle Legall's digital graphic novel Cardiff 1919: Riots re-drawn https://www.cardiff1919.wales/

Further reading

Del Casino, V. J. (2009). *Social Geography. A Critical Introduction*. Oxford: Wiley-Blackwell.
A slightly more advanced summary of the field. In some parts it mirrors the structure of the discussion in the chapters here; for example there is an extended discussion of the Social Geographies of the life-course, ranging across childhood, mid-age and older-age. In other parts, it discusses issues with a slightly different emphasis; for example, in chapters on geographies of health, communities and organisations, and social activism and social justice.

Peter Hopkins' *'Progress Reports'* on Social Geography (Hopkins, 2019, 2020, 2021 in the reference list). Progress reports review current trends in the discipline and provide new theoretical developments.

Smith, S. J., Marston, S. A., Pain, R., and Jones, J. P. (2009). *The SAGE Handbook of Social Geographies*. Los Angeles: Sage, 1–632.
A comprehensive edited volume that will let you read further on how Social Geographers have studied various dimensions of social difference and diversity (gender, race, sexuality, disability, nation, age, and indigeneity), economy and society (markets, consumption, and everyday life), geographies of wellbeing (risk, fear, disability, and health inequalities), and geographies of social justice and ethics.

Social & Cultural Geography. https://www.tandfonline.com/journals/rscg20
As the title suggests, this journal is not limited to social geography alone, representing wider confluences of social and cultural geography. A survey of recent volumes will give you a feel for the breadth of social geography; more generally, the journal is a principal resource for reading the best contemporary research in the field.

The Newcastle Social Geographies Collective. (2021). *Social Geographies: An Introduction*. Lanham: Rowan & Littlefield.
An accessible introduction to the breadth and political relevance of current social geography written by a group of forty professors, lecturers, postdoctoral and postgraduate researchers based in Newcastle University, UK.

55 Social inequality

Andrew Williams

Introduction

Social inequality is one of the twenty-first century's most pressing social and geographical issues and has profound implications for individuals and societies. Perhaps it is one of the reasons you choose to study the discipline of human geography. After all, it is all about how people and places are different and recognising that disparities in wealth, income, education, employment, health-care, environment and opportunities are far from 'natural' but the outcome and medium of specific political, economic and social processes. You may have seen iconic images that show **gated communities** or high-rise financial buildings adjacent to extreme poverty and informal settlements across the globe (see, for example, the work of American Photographer Johnny Miller's *Unequal Scenes*, or Figure 55.1). But beyond this, social inequality refers more broadly to the unequal distribution of resources, opportunities and **power** across the world, between and within countries, regions, cities, neighbourhoods and among different social groups (see Chapter 9).

Inequality triggers moral and philosophical questions of what is considered fair, right and just, and, for that reason, it is closely associated with different philosophical approaches to 'social justice'. For instance, a liberal approach to justice, such as that of John Rawls, advocates the equal distribution of social and economic goods (liberty, opportunity, income and wealth) but accepts unequal distribution only if it benefits the least advantaged. The fair distribution of benefits and burdens, according to Rawls, should be allocated behind a 'veil of ignorance' – with the acknowledgement that circumstances of advantage/disadvantage we are born into (wealth, familial, **gender**, **race**, ability, geography) are entirely arbitrary. In this line of thinking, principles of justice mean ensuring equal access to opportunity and might include systems of guaranteed minimum (income and wealth) to protect equal basic liberties (see Waterstone, 2010, Barnett, 2018).

Marxist geographers such as David Harvey (1973) question whether we can achieve a socially just society unless we fundamentally alter the existing production system. Radical approaches to justice insist we must go beyond the mere redistribution of resources within the confines of **capitalism** and argue that any attempt to rectify these injustices through incremental reforms or social policies within the capitalist framework will only provide temporary relief and fail to address the root causes of inequality. Instead, radical approaches to justice require a reimagining and restructuring of the production system according to principles of collective ownership, democratic control over resources, and the equitable distribution of wealth and power.

Meanwhile, geographers inspired by **feminist** and poststructural thinking foreground other sources of oppression and exploitation that intersect with but are not determined by the capitalist production system: adding dimensions of identity and difference (especially race and gender)

DOI: 10.4324/9780429265853-64

Figure 55.1
Informal settlement with skyscrapers in Mumbai, India

Source: Photo credit: Sven Kurrle/Alamy Stock Photo

alongside distributional justice (Young, 1990, Fraser, 1995). Thus, for Young, justice goes beyond the fair allocation of benefits and burdens and 'includes the potential for people to participate fully in the conditions, situations and decision processes that give rise to particular distributions in the first place' (Waterstone, 2010: 423). Young also discusses *cultural imperialism* – the ways social hierarchies are constructed by dominant groups rendering their own experience and culture as natural and universal, and devaluing others as subordinate – and *violence* – the ways systematic violence is construed 'as possible and acceptable' as the combined result of different faces of oppression (Young, 1990: 61–62).

From these different theorisations of justice, we can begin to grasp different dimensions of social inequality: 'whether forged through the *spatial relations of production* (income and class), embedded in *patterns of distribution* (the provision and consumption of education, health care, housing and financial services, as well as the acquisition of commodities and experiences), or ingrained in the *structures of participation* (the entitlements and obligations of citizenship)' (Smith et al., 2010: 7 emphasis added).

Geographers have used a wide range of methodological approaches to study social inequality. Qualitative research, including **ethnographic** description, has a long history in showing how inequality is materialised, experienced and contested in particular sites and practices. See, for example, the pioneering work of W.E.B. Du Bois (1868–1963) and Jane Addams (1860–1935) whose qualitative research and activism located structural racism as the driver of racial inequality and challenged the explanatory logic crafted in ideologies of white supremacy. Quantitative research also remains a powerful tool with which to analyse and map attributes, such as income or education, aggregated into different spatial and scalar units. Geographers have revealed stark inequalities in health and life expectancy between neighbourhoods, cities, regions and countries (see Chapter 60), while others have used the Gini coefficient to quantify the degree of income or wealth inequality within a population (Dorling, 2015).

Summary

- Social inequality refers to the uneven distribution of resources, opportunities and power within and between countries, regions, cities, neighbourhoods and people.
- Different philosophical approaches to social justice, such as liberalism, Marxism, and feminism, offer distinct views on addressing inequality, with considerations of redistribution, decision-making processes, production system transformation, and intersectionality.
- Geographers employ quantitative methods such as statistical analysis and mapping to analyse income and education disparities, as well as qualitative research methods like interviews and ethnographic description to understand how social inequality is experienced and contested in specific contexts.

How and why have geographers studied spatial inequality?

Geographical work on social inequality draws on a rich theoretical tradition, especially from Marxist urban **political economy**, poststructuralist, feminist and **postcolonial** thinkers, amongst others. But geographers also offer a distinct focus on the different ways inequalities are spatialised. Spatial inequality is a distinct concept and field of enquiry that involves the ways in which **space**, place and scale are implicated in the creation and sustaining of inequality. Spatial inequality is not simply the geographical expression of social inequality. As Soja argues, 'justice, however it might be defined, has a consequential geography, a spatial expression that is more than just a background reflection or set of physical attributes to be descriptively mapped' (2010: 1). We need to understand that space is not simply a passive backdrop or container for inequalities but is an active constituent in injustice. Studying inequality geographically is not simply an exercise in mapping spatial variations across different scalar units (neighbourhood, region, country, etc.). Rather, by examining the interrelations between society, space and place, geographers trace the multiple ways in which spatial patterns and processes are shaped by, but also shape, the nature of inequality (Smith et al., 2010).

One important thinker is Edward Soja. He advocated for understanding social inequality through a socio-spatial **dialectic**. What he meant by this is that people create and modify spaces even as they are shaped and modified by those spaces (Knox and Pinch, 2010). Another way to frame this is that social relations construct certain spaces, and at the same time, those spaces act upon social relations. The same is true with injustice: injustice is embedded in space, while **spatiality** reproduces injustice (see Soja, 2010 for more context). For example, residential segregation (income, race, **ethnicity** or social **class**) reinforces and perpetuates social inequalities by concentrating advantages and disadvantages (for example, in housing, education, employment opportunities, transportation, green space and environmental hazards) in specific areas.

Another important thinker is Doreen Massey (1994). She also offers a processual and relational framework to analyse spatial inequalities. Space, she argues, is not fixed but constantly being made and remade by heterogeneous relationships between and across different scales of the local and global. Analysis of spatial inequality therefore focuses on the flows, relations and networks that constitute space and place; a perspective that draws attention to the interconnections and power relations involved in the production and practice of space. Spatial inequalities are constituted by the 'interlocking of "stretched-out" social relations' (Massey, 1994: 22).

Much of the geographic work on social inequality has focused on the persistence of poverty and global inequality at different scales brought about by various processes of political-economic restructuring – **neoliberalism** (Chapter 52), global cities (Chapter 16) and **financialisation** (Chapter 31). For thinkers like Saskia Sassen (2001), postindustrial global cities are at the extremes of polarisation, as they feature the sharpest concentration of both high- and low-income groups, the latter of which is increasingly dominated by immigrants from disadvantaged parts of the world (Figure 55.2). Globally, numerous governments have successively (re)organised economies according to neoliberal principles of free markets, deregulation and individual responsibility, deepening local, regional and global inequalities (Chapter 52). The growth of state-led **gentrification** in cities across the Global South, especially in China, India and South America (Lees, 2015, Slater, 2021), is also widening inter- and intra-neighbourhood inequalities, often displacing lower income populations (see Chapter 56).

Gentrification is an important idea for geographers thinking about social inequality. The concept was coined by Ruth Glass in the 1960s and refers to the 'class-based colonisation of cheaper residential accommodation and a reinvestment of the physical housing stock' (Atkinson, 2019: 2343–2344). While definitions vary, gentrification typically involves physical, economic and cultural changes within a neighbourhood, leading to shifts in demographics (displacement), land use and property values. Neil Smith's (1996) classic rent-gap hypothesis has been influential in analysing how differences between potential ground rent and actual ground rent lead to capital's renewed interest in disinvested areas. This line of thinking helps us focus on the wider political-economic structures and alliances between the state and the market in creating conditions for profit in the real estate and housing market. Recent work has also traced the place of the creative industries, housing financialisation and the tourist economy (AirBnB) in driving gentrification and exacerbating inequalities across the world (see Lees, 2015 for an overview). Research on gentrification in North American and European cities also has revealed racist and class-based processes that play a central role in cycles of divestment and reinvestment (Fields and Raymond, 2021). Race here is understood as a social construct, that is, natural human diversity is

Figure 55.2
Los Angeles is one of the most unequal cities in the USA

Source: Photo credit: trekandshoot/Alamy Stock Photo

made more rigid through racial categorisations which are reinforced through material and social processes (see Chapter 13). Similarly, class is a process involving the appropriation of surplus labour, with class identities and judgements intersecting with other aspects of identity, and in relation to different social contexts (Gibson-Graham et al., 2001).

In recent years geographers have increasingly used the analytic of racial capitalism to study the interrelationships between capital accumulation and processes of racialisation across different times and spaces (see McKittrick, 2006, Gilmore, 2007, Pulido, 2017, Bhattacharyya, 2018, Bledsoe and Wright, 2019, Hawthorne, 2019, Saha, 2022). Drawn from the Black Radical Tradition, particularly the writings of Cedric Robinson (1983), the concept emphasises how relations of racial differentiation and racialised violence, dispossession and extraction have underpinned the development of capitalist **modernity** (see Gilmore, 2007 and Chapter 70). We can illustrate this through two examples: one from the USA and the other from the UK.

Summary

- Spatial inequality is a distinct concept that focuses on how space, place and scale contribute to the creation and perpetuation of inequality.
- Geographers explore a range of spatial inequalities (health, education, income, poverty, housing) across different scales (neighbourhoods, cities, regions, countries).
- Racial capitalism provides an important analytical framework through which to understand the varied and interlocking processes of racialisation, inequality and capital accumulation.

CASE STUDY 1
RACIST MORTGAGE POLICIES AND INEQUALITY IN THE USA

Race and class are interconnected and mutually reinforcing systems of inequality. Neither is a natural or inherent category but has been **socially constructed** and maintained through systems of power and privilege. Geographers have traced the ways race and class have been produced through specific alliances, institutions and practices that contribute to and perpetuate racial and socioeconomic hierarchies. Tracing these developments in the USA, for example, entails an analysis of the evolving geographies of racial capitalism: from systems of slavery, lynching and settler colonialism (see Chapter 49); to exploitative sharecropping, indebtedness and prison labour camps (Gilmore, 2007); and the 'Jim Crow' laws introduced after the Civil War to restrict the freedom of African Americans and legalised racial segregation in housing, education, employment and public space. White racial violence was ubiquitous and included widespread massacres such as that in Tulsa 1921 where a prosperous Black neighbourhood known as Black Wall Street was attacked and burned by a white supremacist mob who in 18 hours killed an

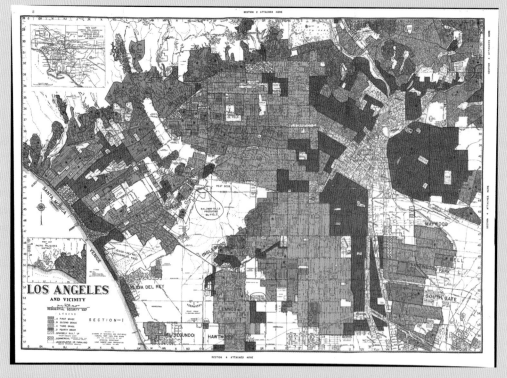

Figure 55.3
'Redlining' map of Los Angeles 1939

Source: Photo credit: Nelson et al. (2023) Mapping Inequality: Redlining in New Deal America (available from https://dsl.richmond.edu/panorama/redlining/)

estimated 300 African Americans and made more than 8,000 people homeless. Tulsa was one of over 100 massacres between 1865 and the 1940s that had an intergenerational impact on Black wealth and economic opportunities (Darity Jr and Mullen, 2022).

Structural violence was more insidious and worked through structures of federal government, policing, housing and city planning (for a broad overview, see Brown and Barganier, 2018). Racial segregation was enforced through racially restrictive housing covenants written into property deeds. In 1934 the Federal Home Loan Bank Board and the Home Owners' Loan Corporation established the discriminatory practice of drawing red lines on maps to mark neighbourhoods where banks and other financial institutions would refuse to provide loans, insurance policies or other services (Figure 55.3). Under redlining, predominantly Black and Latinx neighbourhoods were deemed 'high risk' or 'undesirable' by lenders and insurance companies who frequently used racist stereotypes to justify their decisions. With limited access to capital, racialised neighbourhoods were subject to a cycle of disinvestment, declining property values and limited economic opportunities, thereby reinforcing the classification of redlining and perpetuating racial and economic disparities and intergenerational wealth gaps. Rashad Shabazz (2015) excavates these themes in his account of how Black neighbourhoods in Chicago were consecutively stripped of capital and criminalised by the police over the last 125 years. This is one of many examples of state-sanction violence that has given rise to landscapes of environmental racism – a concept that helps us grasp the historical development of racial disparities in **infrastructures** (e.g. water, air quality, heat, shelter, sunlight, green space) and the tendency for poor and racialised populations to suffer disproportionately from pollution, including the process of siting environmentally hazardous facilities such as landfill, incinerators, heavy industry and waste disposal (Pulido, 2017).

The legacies of redlining and segregation are still visible in contemporary racial and spatial inequalities in housing, education, income, health, food deserts. These inequalities underpin the evolving frontier of gentrification (Gibbons, 2023) and the accumulation of capital through racialised dispossession (Dantzler, 2021), for example, through predatory lending, subprime mortgage foreclosure and exploitative rental sector (Taylor, 2020). But various forms of 'redlining', racial segregation and displacement continue in different guises, through **ghettoisation** and through allegedly 'colourblind' financial processes such as automated home valuation systems, appraisal systems and market tiering, alongside overt racial discrimination by lenders (Fields and Raymond, 2021).

Summary

- White racial violence combined with structural violence (redlining, displacement, segregation, discrimination) led to systematic racial dispossession in areas of housing and intergenerational wealth.
- The social construction of race and class is contingent on specific alliances, **discourses** and practices over a long period of time and will manifest differently around the world.

CASE STUDY 2
WEALTH AND POVERTY IN AUSTERITY BRITAIN

The financial crisis of 2007/2008 originated in the USA with the collapse of the subprime mortgage market and quickly spread across the globe leading to a severe recession and government bailout of the banks. Many governments worldwide embarked on fiscal cuts to public spending aimed at reducing government deficits and debt levels and restoring confidence in financial markets. In the UK and elsewhere, geographers have shown the impact of austerity cuts and welfare reform to be socially and spatially uneven, hitting the poorest places the hardest (Beatty and Fothergill, 2014, Gray and Barford, 2018) and disproportionately impacting Black, Asian and minority ethnic populations already marginalised by wider effects of societal racism (Emejulu and Bassel, 2015, Sandhu and Stephenson, 2015) (Box 55.1). Since 2010 Black and Asian households in the lowest fifth of incomes have experienced the biggest drop in living standards (19.2% and 20.1%, respectively) an average annual loss of £8,407 and £11,678 each year (Hall et al., 2017). Black and minority ethnic groups in the UK face a disproportionate risk of persistent poverty (JRF, 2023), food insecurity (Loopstra et al., 2018) and homelessness (Bramley et al., 2022), with the homelessness applications rates for Black-headed households 5.1 times higher in London, 3.5 times higher in the South West and 2.5 times higher in the North East, than that of white British households, respectively (ibid: 21). Such examples illustrate the ongoing need to challenge and expose the racial inequalities and their geographies (Box 55.1).

BOX 55.1
WELFARE RACISM

Welfare racism is a critical lens through which to examine the intersection of race, social policy and inequality. The concept sharpens the analysis of discriminatory practices and policies within the welfare system that disproportionately target and disadvantage racially minoritised groups. Welfare racism is not an 'aberration' in an otherwise balanced system; rather, it denotes a structural phenomenon rooted in **colonial**, racial and anti-immigrant thinking that has long characterised systems of welfare provision in different contexts.

The history of welfare racism in the UK, for example, can be traced at least as far back as Elizabethan Poor Laws which mandated parish authorities provide assistance to individuals who were either long-term residents or born within the parish. Even in the 1910s, parishes retained the right to send the poor to their parish of origin, meaning people categorised as 'aliens' were 'deterred from applying for support and this exposed them to labour exploitation' (El-Enany, 2020: 48). Exclusion from public welfare and financial support on grounds of citizenship and immigration status also has a long history. The Aliens Act 1905, for example, prevented impoverished Jews from entering the UK and allowed the expulsion of 'convicted foreigners' and those who had received poor relief for 12 months. From 1922 the Ministry of Labour decreed that 'aliens' could not claim benefits for longer than 16 weeks, building on earlier decrees that enabled expulsion orders of 'people found to be in receipt of Poor Law payments within twelve months of having arrived in Britain' (ibid: 56). Research has documented the overt and covert forms of racial discrimination in education, employment and housing in the post-war Welfare State (Williams, 1987), including Britain's own practice of redlining ('bluezones') which excluded areas of Black settlement from the mortgage loan market (Jacobs, 1985).

Given the role of transatlantic slavery in financing charitable institutions in the eighteenth and nineteenth centuries, and of colonial extraction and taxation in bankrolling the British Welfare State, surely 'colonial subjects' who were made to pay for the welfare of British citizens in the metropole should have a right to welfare citizenship (Bhambra, 2021).

Instead, the logics of deportability and disposability still shape the geographies of race, poverty and welfare. This was clearly illustrated in the Windrush scandal in 2017. The 'Windrush generation' were those who had immigrated to the UK from Caribbean countries between 1948 and 1971, having been invited by the UK government to help fill post-war labour shortages. Despite having the right to live and work in the UK, in the years following the 2012 Immigration Act, many were wrongfully categorised as 'illegal immigrants' due to a lack of documentation. This was primarily due to the loss of records by the Home Office. As a result, people, who had lived and worked in the UK for decades, suddenly found themselves facing challenges in proving their legal status, obtaining employment, accessing healthcare, and even facing detention or deportation.

Feminist geographers have highlighted how these social and economic processes are fundamentally gendered, both in terms of their uneven distributional impact, and in the way austerity has impacted everyday life. Using the concept of social reproduction (see also Chapter 33), Sarah Marie Hall documents how austerity reconfigures family, friendship and intimate relationships, care-responsibilities, and everyday consumption practices and decision-making. While revealing austerity's stark emotional and material effects, Hall (2019) also shows how people seek to support each other through difficult times through informal monetary arrangements and material exchange (e.g. sharing childcare, shopping, food, crafting, second-hand clothes).

For others, austerity has been profitable. The financialisation of the UK and global economy has led to a significant concentration of wealth among the super-rich, who have benefited the most from financial deregulation and speculation, inflated asset prices in housing and real estate, and the changing balance of power in corporations to favour shareholder profits over wages (The Equality Trust, 2022). The wealth of the UK's billionaires rose by £600bn (over 1000%) between 1990 ($n=15$) and 2022 ($n=177$), almost £150bn of that wealth came between 2020 and 2022 alone. Growing attention is now given to the geographies of the super-rich, their wider environmental impact, lobbying power, philanthropic control and their impact on **super-gentrification**.

Figure 55.4
Cornish resistance to second-home ownership in St Agnes where the lack of affordable housing and an overheated rental market compound the issue of rural poverty and homelessness. As of the start of April 2023, there were 12,679 second homes and more than 11,000 holidays lets in Cornwall, while 22,975 people were on its housing register (Cornwall Council 2023)

Source: Photo credit: Alamy

Over 7000 luxury basements have been built in London since 2008 to feed the aspirations of the global super-rich and the speculative real estate market, with a growing proportion remaining empty (Burrows et al., 2022) and near some of the most deprived parts of London (Box 55.2). But it is not only London, Sheppard and Pemberton (2023) document the growing trend of super-rich gentrification in rural England (Figure 55.4).

BOX 55.2
GRENFELL TOWER FIRE

On 14 June 2017, a fire broke out in the Grenfell Tower, a 24-storey residential tower block in West Lancaster Estate in Kensington and Chelsea – a London Borough 'where the average annual salary – at £123,000 – is the highest in the UK, but also where over one-third of workers earn below £20,000 and 4,500 children live in poverty (Bell 2017)' (cited in MacLeod, 2018: 464). The fire caused 72 deaths (see Figure 55.5) and over 70 injuries, and it is considered one of the worst fire disasters in the UK for decades.

The Grenfell Tower fire has become synonymous with inequality and injustice – in terms of the juxtaposition of extreme wealth and poverty but also the institutional

Figure 55.5
A list of names of the 72 people who lost their lives in the Grenfell Tower block fire on a sign, outside Grenfell Tower, London, during a silent walk to mark the two-year anniversary

Source: Photo credit: Alamy

violence (Cooper and Whyte, 2022) and disavowal of democratic process (MacLeod, 2018). Prioritising 'value for money' over safety concerns led to the use of cladding made from highly flammable polyethylene plastic sandwiched between two very thin sheets of aluminium – a cladding that had consistently failed fire tests for 12 years before Grenfell. Residents raised regular concerns about the safety of Grenfell Tower both before and after its 2015–2016 renovation, only to be disregarded by the municipal authority and the Kensington and Chelsea Tenant Management Organisation (TMO) (MacLeod, 2018). Downgrading fireproof zinc panels to aluminium cladding saved £293,368 from the £8.6 million renovation project (Forster, 2017).

Due to a lack of affordable housing and social housing, it took several years for households to be rehoused with many still living in temporary and emergency accommodation in 2020. For Shildrick (2018), the Grenfell Fire and institutional responses illustrate the effects of poverty propaganda that was used to deflect attention away from the real causes of inequality and maintain the status quo of neoliberal capitalism. Other scholars have contextualised Grenfell and the racialised urban landscape of poverty to a longer durée of racial capitalism (Danewid, 2020).

Summary

- Austerity and welfare reform compounded existing regional, gendered and racial inequalities in the UK.
- The financialisation of the UK and global economy has led to a significant increase in wealth for the super-rich, with the wealth of the UK's billionaires rising by over 1000% between 1990 and 2022.
- The Grenfell Tower fire highlighted the institutional violence and political economy that underpins the rise of global cities, which often involve racialised displacement, dispossession and structural violence.
- Welfare racism refers to the overt and covert ways in which welfare systems operate to disproportionately target and disadvantage racially minoritised groups.

Conclusion

Social inequality remains a key focus for human geographers, and one that recognises the need for a range of understandings and definitions of in/justice, and different methods for investigating it. From this brief account – spanning 'redlining', welfare racism and institutional violence – we can begin to grasp the importance of taking a structural view of racism understood as 'the state-sanctioned and/or extra-legal production and exploitation of group-differentiated vulnerabilities to premature death, in distinct yet densely interconnected political geographies' (Gilmore, 2002: 261). This line of thinking seeks to abolish structures that perpetuate racial hierarchies and violence and envision alternative, just and equitable ways of organising society and space. Though illustrating these points with recourse to USA and UK examples, geographers across the world have examined how systems of **colonialism**, racism and capitalism – past and present – shape contemporary power relations and geographies of social inequality.

Discussion points

- Why are different theories of justice important for understanding social inequality?
- How and why should geographers take a historical perspective when addressing contemporary social inequalities?

References

Atkinson, R. (2019). Necrotecture: lifeless dwellings and London's super-rich. *International Journal of Urban and Regional Research* 43(1): 2–13.

Barnett, C. (2018). Geography and the priority of injustice. *Annals of the American Association of Geographers* 108(2): 317–326.

Beatty, C., and Fothergill, S. (2014). The local and regional impact of the UK's welfare reforms. *Cambridge Journal of Regions, Economy and Society* 7(1): 63–79.

Bhambra, G. K. (2021). Relations of extraction, relations of redistribution. *British Journal of Sociology* 73(4): 4–15.

Bhattacharyya, G. (2018). *Rethinking Racial Capitalism*. London: Rowman & Littlefield.

Bledsoe, A., and Wright, W. J. (2019). The anti-Blackness of global capital. *Environment and Planning D: Society and Space* 37(1): 8–26.

Bramley, G., Fitzpatrick, S., McIntyre, J., and Johnsen, S. (2022). *Homelessness amongst Black and Minoritised Ethnic Communities in the UK: A Statistical Report on the State of the Nation*. Edinburgh: Heriot-Watt University.

Brown, E., and Barganier, G. (2018). *Race and Crime: Geographies of Injustice*. Oakland, California: University of California Press.

Burrows, R., Graham, S., and Wilson, A. (2022). Bunkering down? The geography of elite residential basement development in London. *Urban Geography* 43(9): 1372–1393. DOI: 10.1080/02723638.2021.1934628

Cooper, V., and Whyte, D. (2022). Grenfell, austerity, and institutional violence. *Sociological Research Online* 27(1): 207–216.

Cornwall Council. (2023). *Housing intelligence*. https://www.cornwall.gov.uk/housing/housing-intelligence/ (accessed 12/06/2023)

Danewid, I. (2020). The fire this time: Grenfell, racial capitalism and the urbanisation of empire. *European Journal of International Relations* 26(1): 289–313.

Dantzler, P. A. (2021). The urban process under racial capitalism: race, anti-blackness, and capital accumulation. *Journal of Race, Ethnicity and the City* 2(2): 113–134.

Darity Jr, W. A., and Mullen, A. K. (2022). *From Here to Equality: Reparations for Black Americans in the Twenty-First Century* (2nd edn.). Chapel Hill: UNC Press Books.

Dorling, D. (2015). *Injustice: Why Social Inequality Still Persists*. Bristol: Policy Press.

El-Enany, N. (2020). *(B)ordering Britain*. Manchester: Manchester University Press.

Emejulu, A., and Bassel, L. (2015). Minority women, austerity and activism. *Race & Class 57*(2): 86–95.

Fields, D., and Raymond, E. L. (2021). Racialized geographies of housing financialization. *Progress in Human Geography* 45(6): 1625–1645.

Forster, K. (2017). Grenfell Tower's fireproof cladding was 'downgraded to save £293,000', show leaked documents. *The Independent*. 30th June 2017. https://www.independent.co.uk/news/uk/home-news/grenfell-tower-cladding-fireproof-downgrade-save-money-cut-cost-ps293000-leak-documents-north-kensington-rydon-a7815971.html

Fraser, N. (1995). From redistribution to recognition? Dilemmas of justice in a 'postsocialist' age. *New Left Review* 212: 68–93.

Gibbons, J. (2023). Examining the long-term influence of New Deal era redlining on contemporary gentrification. *Urban Studies* 60(14): 2816–2834.

Gibson-Graham, J. K., Resnick, S., and Wolff, R. (eds.) (2001). *Re/presenting Class: Essays in Postmodern Marxism*. London: Duke University Press.

Gilmore, R. W. (2002). Race and globalization. In *Geographies of Global Change: Remapping the World*, eds. R. J. Johnston, P. J. Taylor, and M. J. Watts. New York: Wiley-Blackwell, 261–274.

Gilmore, R. W. (2007). *Golden Gulag: Prisons, Surplus, Crisis, and Opposition in Globalizing California*. Berkeley: University of California Press.

Gray, M., and Barford, A. (2018). The depths of the cuts: the uneven geography of local government austerity. *Cambridge Journal of Regions, Economy and Society* 11(3): 541–563.

Hall, S. M. (2019). *Everyday Life in Austerity: Family, Friends and Intimate Relations*. London: Palgrave Macmillan.

Hall, S. M., McIntosh, K., Neitzert, E., Pottinger, L., Sandhu, K., Stephenson, M. A., Reed, H., and Taylor, L. (2017). *Intersecting Inequalities: The Impact of Austerity on Black and Minority Ethnic Women in the UK*. Runnymede Trust and Women's Budget Group. https://www.runnymedetrust.org/publications/intersecting-inequalities-the-impact-of-austerity-on-bme-women-in-the-uk

Harvey, D. (1973). *Social Justice and the City*. London: Edward Arnold.

Hawthorne, C. (2019). Black matters are spatial matters: Black geographies for the twenty-first century. *Geography Compass* 13(11): e12468. https://doi.org/10.1111/gec3.12468

Jacobs, S. (1985). Race, empire and the welfare state. *Critical Social Policy* 5(3): 6–28.

JRF. (2023). UK Poverty 2023, York: Joseph Rowntree Foundation. https://www.jrf.org.uk/report/uk-poverty-2023

Knox, P., and Pinch, S. (2010). *Urban Social Geography: An Introduction* (6th edn.). London and New York: Routledge.

Loopstra, R., Fledderjohann, J., Reeves, A., and Stuckler, D. (2018). Impact of welfare benefit sanctioning on food insecurity: a dynamic cross-area study of food bank usage in the UK. *Journal of Social Policy* 47(3): 437–457.

MacLeod, G. (2018). The Grenfell Tower atrocity: exposing urban worlds of inequality, injustice, and an impaired democracy. *City* 22(4): 460–489.

Massey, D. (1994). *Space, Place, and Gender*. Minneapolis: University of Minnesota Press.

McKittrick, K. (2006). *Demonic Grounds: Black Women and the Cartographies of Struggle*. Minneapolis: University of Minnesota Press.

Pulido, L. (2017). Geographies of race and ethnicity II: environmental racism, racial capitalism and state-sanctioned violence. *Progress in Human Geography* 41(4): 524–533.

Saha, J. (2022). Racial capitalism and peasant insurgency in colonial Myanmar. *History Workshop Journal* 94: 42–60.

Sandhu, K., and Stephenson, M. A. (2015). Layers on inequality. *Feminist Review* 109: 169–179.

Sassen, S. (2001). *The Global City*. Princeton: Princeton University Press.

Shabazz, R. (2015). *Spatializing Blackness: Architectures of Confinement and Black Masculinity in Chicago*. Chicago: University of Illinois Press.

Sheppard, D., and Pemberton, S. (2023). The actions of key agents in facilitating rural super-gentrification: evidence from the English countryside. *Journal of Rural Studies* 97: 485–494.

Shildrick, T. (2018). Lessons from Grenfell: poverty propaganda, stigma and class power. *The Sociological Review* 66(4): 783–798.

Slater, T. (2021). *Shaking Up the City: Ignorance, Inequality, and the Urban Question*. Oakland: University of California Press.

Smith, N. (1996). *The New Urban Frontier: Gentrification and the Revanchist City*. London and New York: Routledge.

Smith, S., Pain, R., Marston, S., and Jones III, J. P. (2010). Introduction: Situating Social Geographies. In *Handbook of Social Geographies*, eds. S. Smith, R. Pain, S. Marston, and J. P. Jones III. London: Sage, 1–40.

Soja, E. (2010). *Seeking Spatial Justice*. Minneapolis: University of Minnesota Press.

Taylor, H. L., Jr. (2020). Disrupting market-based predatory development: race, class, and the underdevelopment of Black neighborhoods in the US. *Journal of Race, Ethnicity and the City* 1(1): 1–6.

The Equality Trust. (2022). *Billionaire Britain. Inequality from the top down*. https://equalitytrust.org.uk/news/equality-trust-finds-1000-increase-billionaire-wealth

Waterstone, M. (2010). Geography and Social Justice. In *The SAGE Handbook of Social Geographies*, eds. Smith, S. J., Pain, R., Marston, S. A., and Jones, J. P. London: Sage, 419–434.

Williams, F. (1987). Racism and the discipline of social policy: a critique of welfare theory. *Critical Social Policy* 7(20): 4–29.

Young, I. M. (1990). *Justice and the Politics of Difference*. Princeton: Princeton University Press.

Online materials

- Home – WID – World Inequality Database user friendly graphs and downloadable country data. https://wid.world/
- Census Maps – Census 2021 data interactive, ONS an interactive resource produced by UK Office of National Statistics that allows you to explore and download 2021 Census data. https://www.ons.gov.uk/census/maps/

- Geographies of Racial Capitalism with Ruth Wilson Gilmore – An Antipode Foundation film – a short introduction to racial capitalism and abolition geography. https://antipodeonline.org/geographies-of-racial-capitalism/
- Mapping Inequality (richmond.edu) – It explores historical redlining maps from 1930s America. Produced by Nelson, R. K., Winling, L., Marciano, R., Connolly, N., et al. (2023). 'Mapping Inequality', American Panorama, (ed.) Robert K. Nelson and Edward L. Ayers. https://dsl.richmond.edu/panorama/redlining/
- What the 1921 Tulsa Race Massacre Destroyed – The New York Times (nytimes.com) – interactive resource about Tulsa Massacre 1921. https://www.nytimes.com/interactive/2021/05/24/us/tulsa-race-massacre.html
- Oxfam International recent research on global wealth disparities. https://www.oxfam.org/en/tags/extreme-inequality
- The Fight over L.A.'s Skid Row – YouTube A short film showing how Los Angeles Community Action Network tries to align community and business interests to promote more equitable downtown development and prevent the criminalisation of poverty in the battle over valuable downtown real estate. https://www.youtube.com/watch?v=ikN2E2j57xE
- Stream City Rising Seasons & Full Episodes | KCET 'City Rising' illuminates the history of discriminatory laws and practices at the root of the gentrification and affordable housing crisis in the USA. https://www.pbssocal.org/shows/city-rising#episodes
- How Austerity Alters Lives and Futures – YouTube – a short video by Sarah Marie Hall on how austerity policies have changed people's decisions to have children. https://www.youtube.com/watch?v=skIy0oskzNE

Further reading

Bhattacharyya, G., Elliott-Cooper, A., Balani, S., Nişancıoğlu, K., Koram, K., Gebrial, D., El-Enany, N., and de Noronha, L. (2021). *Empire's Endgame*. London: Pluto Press.
An accessible introduction to issues of race, class and the colonial **nation-state**.

Coates, T. N. (2014). The case for reparations. *The Atlantic* (June). Available here https://www.theatlantic.com/magazine/archive/2014/06/the-case-for-reparations/361631/
A classic text on the need to acknowledge and address the historical and ongoing injustices – of slavery, theft, and legalised discrimination - that have shaped the economic and social conditions of African Americans in the USA.

Shabazz, R. (2015). *Spatializing Blackness: Architectures of Confinement and Black Masculinity in Chicago*. Chicago: University of Illinois Press.
A rich account of the underdevelopment of Black neighbourhoods over the last 125 years that highlights how the politics of incarceration is imbricated throughout the everyday lives of Black Chicagoans.

Shilliam, R. (2018). *Race and the undeserving poor: From abolition to Brexit*. Agenda Publishing.
A historical account that traces the distinctions between the 'deserving' and 'undeserving' poor in British society and how changing constructions of race continue to serve powerful interests.

Wei, Y. D. (2017). Geography of inequality in Asia. *Geographical Review* 107(2): 263–275.
A review of literature on spatial inequality and uneven development in Asia.

56 Stigma and exclusion

Jon May

Introduction

At its simplest, *stigma* can be defined as the process of labelling an individual or group with undesirable or shameful characteristics. A focus for scholars in sociology and psychology for several decades, the concept has until recently been of less interest to geographers (though see Takahashi, 1996, Davidson and Henderson, 2010, Laurie and Richardson, 2019). But in the last few years, a new and exciting body of work has emerged, setting out a distinctively geographical contribution to the study of stigma (Butler et al., 2018, Sisson, 2022, Slater, 2017, 2018, Tyler and Slater, 2018). Drawing on the concept of 'territorial stigmatization' developed by the French sociologist Loic Wacquant (2007), geographers have begun to explore the different ways in which places become stigmatised, and people become '"contaminated" by their area of residence' (Pearce, 2012: 1922, cited in Slater, 2017: 116). For Slater, 'territorial stigma' refers to a form of 'spatial disgrace ... so powerful that it is partially autonomized from other forms of stigmatization, exerting its own very real and deleterious effects' (2017: 111): whether making it almost impossible for people to get a job because of the address on their application, or legitimating the forced eviction of tenants from a stigmatised 'sink estate' slated for demolition.

For Wacquant, stigma is a political-economic process and a key means through which unequal social relations are managed, resources re-distributed and profit extracted under **capitalism** (Strobl, 2022). It is also a *violent* process. This violence is captured in the etymology of the word itself, which has its origins in the Ancient Greek word for a mark made on the skin by pricking or branding. Though no longer usually associated with acts of physical wounding, as the examples above suggest, territorial stigma 'does violence to' both people and places.

This focus on violence and expulsion suggests parallels with earlier studies of the geographies of *exclusion* – defined by Philo (2000: 751) as the 'simultaneously social and spatial process' – by which stigmatised groups are 'banished' to (and sometimes subsequently contained within) similarly stigmatised spaces – pioneered by the social geographer David Sibley (1981, 1995; see also Mohen, 2000, Herbert, 2011 Nagel and Grove, 2021). This chapter charts the different ways ideas about stigma, territorial stigma and exclusion have been developed by geographers. It begins by examining the classic accounts of stigma outlined by the Canadian sociologist Erving Goffman, and of the geographies of exclusion by David Sibley. Illustrating these ideas with reference to the stigmatisation and exclusion of street homeless people in British and North American cities, it then moves on to consider the **political economy** of territorial stigma: examining its role in the destruction of social housing and processes of 'domicide'.

DOI: 10.4324/9780429265853-65

Stigma

Much contemporary thinking about stigma traces its lineage to the work of the Canadian sociologist Erving Goffman and his ground-breaking book *Stigma: Notes on the Management of Spoiled Identity*, first published in 1963. For Goffman, stigma described attributes or behaviours that lead an individual or group to be classified by others as undesirable because 'spoiled' in some way. Once so identified, the stigmatised are discriminated against, devalued or shunned. Those who internalise their 'spoiled identity' are liable to suffer feelings of shame and psychological distress.

Goffman identified three types of stigma: relating to, in his words, 'flaws of character' (for example, 'mental disorder, imprisonment, addiction, alcoholism, homosexuality, unemployment, suicidal attempts, and radical political behavior'); 'abominations of the body'; and group stigma associated with particular 'races', nations and religions (ibid: 4). Importantly, Goffman understood stigma to be a relational and contextual process, arguing that it existed in the relationships between the 'attribute' and the 'audience' rather than in a particular attribute itself, such as skin colour.

Goffman was a leading proponent of 'symbolic interactionism' and his interest in stigma stemmed from his broader interest in what he called the 'interaction order'. For Goffman, social life unfolds through **encounters** in which we communicate with each other through our speech, body language and behaviour. Such interactions move around a series of unwritten rules and 'scripts' which are learnt at an early age and ensure 'normal' life unfolds in relatively calm and predictable ways. To maintain 'normal life' (defined by Goffman as, for example, 'having "a spouse and children" and "spending Christmas and Thanksgiving with the family"' (1963: 7 in Misztal, 2001: 317) stigmatised groups were expected to try and 'fit in', whether by denying their own differences or agreeing to be 'helped' to overcome them, with those that would not or could not conform being shunned.

A common critique of Goffman's work is that he paid too little attention to the ways in which social interactions and stigma are structured by wider inequalities of power. For example, even though working – at Berkeley, California – at the height of a civil rights movement aiming to abolish legalised racial segregation in America, he never acknowledged the systemic power of whiteness: noting instead, in his discussion of stigma as a relational construct, that just as a person with dark skin might be stigmatised by people with light skin, so too is a person with light skin is liable to be stigmatised by people with dark skin (Tyler, 2020). Nor did he investigate the classed, **gendered** and heteronormative assumptions structuring the constructions of 'normal' life in 1960s North American society.

Summary

- Much of the work on stigma draws on the ideas of Erving Goffman.
- For Goffman (1963), stigma described attributes or behaviours that lead an individual or group to be classified by others as undesirable because 'spoiled' in some way. Once so identified, the stigmatised are discriminated against, devalued, or shunned.
- A common critique of Goffman is that he paid too little attention to the ways in which social interactions and stigma are structured by wider inequalities of power.

Exclusion ... in theory

Though interested in processes of exclusion rather than stigma per se, the first geographer to explicitly explore processes of stigma and exclusion in detail was David Sibley. In his 1981 book *Outsiders in Urban Society*, Sibley noted how stigmatised groups often occupy the geographical margins of society. Through an investigation of the life-worlds of Gypsies, Travellers and North American Inuit, he examined the role that spatial boundaries play in maintaining social boundaries. Sibley recognised that as those considered socially 'marginal' are either pushed towards or, to avoid confrontation and abuse, seek out geographically marginal spaces, space emerges as both an expression of and a means by which exclusionary practices gain purchase and meaning.

In his 1995 book *Geographies of Exclusion*, Sibley turned to Julia Kristeva's psychoanalytical theory of *abjection* to argue that human identity is structured by an innate need to differentiate between those considered to be broadly the same, and those identified as fundamentally different or '**Other**'. For Kristeva, abjection – feelings of disgust or revulsion – initially emerge in response to, and as a necessary driver of, the moment at which an infant first experiences a sense of itself as separate to its mother: an awareness that produces feelings of nausea and a rush of adrenaline and fear (Pentony, 1996). For Kristeva, 'this memory of maternal dependency is deeply etched within the bodily and psychic lives of each of us' (Tyler, 2009: 80). As such, these feelings of abjection continue to be 'acted out' throughout our lives in 'both individual and group rituals of exclusion' (p. 78) with these 'subsequent "abjections" ... repetitions that contain within an echo of this earlier cathartic event' (p. 80). There are three broad categories of abjection in Kristeva's work, relating to certain foods, bodily waste and sexual difference (Ayra, 2017). Because a revulsion to bodily waste – and, in particular, any possibility that it may (re) enter the body – is especially powerful and so widespread, those perceived to be 'dirty' in some way are especially vulnerable to exclusion.

Drawing on these ideas, Sibley (1995) thus argues that people are engaged in a lifelong struggle to maintain a distinction – and safe distance – between themselves and 'abject Others' with this distancing both reflecting and re-enforcing inequalities of power between different social groups. Geographers have drawn on Sibley's work in two main ways: examining the experiences of a range of 'abject Others' rejected because of their age, physical or cognitive differences, gender, sexuality, ethnic or religious identity (Philo, 1997); and the role that spatial boundaries play in maintaining the distinctions between these outsider groups and others.

Summary

- Concepts of stigma are closely related to the concept of exclusion.
- The first geographer to explore processes of stigma and exclusion in detail was David Sibley who noted how stigmatised groups often occupy the geographical margins of society.
- Sibley drew on Julia Kristeva's psychoanalytical theory of abjection to argue that people are engaged in a lifelong struggle to maintain a distinction – and safe distance – between themselves and 'abject Others'.

... and practice

It is possible to think of numerous examples of such 'boundary marking'. Two of the most obvious – because literally set in stone – would be the ways in which prisons (Moran et al., 2018) and asylums (Philo, 1989) are designed to keep prisoner and patients at a safe distance from 'decent society' (see Figure 56.1), with those who break the rules further isolated in solitary confinement lest their bad behaviour 'infects' others (Ogborn, 1995). A more commonplace example would be stigmatisation and exclusion of street homeless people (see Box 56.1).

There are several reasons why people who become street homeless become stigmatised (Takahashi, 1996). In-so-far as they are usually under or unemployed, homeless people tend to be viewed as unproductive. In a society that accords a privileged status to economic productivity, homeless people are therefore afforded at best a marginal position and, at worst, come to be viewed as a drain on collective resources. Having apparently lost contact with friends and family, homeless people may also be perceived as 'disaffiliated' – as existing outside the comforts (and constraints) of mainstream life (and values). And, whether because of their own habits or because of stereotyping, people who become homeless often come to be associated with other stigmatised groups: drug addicts, alcoholics and the mentally ill, for example.

But using the concepts explored above, we can elaborate on the roots of this stigma in interesting and useful ways. For example, as it becomes more and more difficult to find free and easily accessible places to wash or relieve oneself, people who have been on the streets for some time may start to challenge normative understandings of personal hygiene. As Samira Kawash (1998) has argued, once marked as dirty or diseased, homeless people may subsequently be identified as

Figure 56.1
HM Dartmoor Prison is located in an isolated moorland area (Dartmoor) in South-West England. Because it is so isolated, it has been used to house some of Britain's most violent offenders

Source: Photo credit: Rich Walker

BOX 56.1
HOMELESSNESS

Though the most visible, street homelessness is only the most extreme form of homelessness, which is often conceptualised as a continuum of housing needs reaching from people in poor quality, insecure and/or overcrowded housing at one end to absolute rooflessness at the other. Distinctions are also often drawn between various forms of 'visible' homelessness (people 'sleeping rough' or living in encampments or temporary accommodation designated for homeless people) and 'hidden' homelessness: people who may be considered homeless but whose housing situation is not visible on the streets or in official statistics (because, for example, squatting or moving between friends and relatives). Homelessness may also usefully be thought of as an emotional or psychological state, being the absence of feelings of privacy, safety and security associated – in theory at least, if for many people not in practice, with feelings of 'home'. Different countries also define homelessness – and any support and/or accommodation homeless people may be entitled to – differently. In 2022, the UK government reported 3069 people 'sleeping rough' on any one night across England, though this is almost certainly an underestimate. By contrast, English local authorities offered help to prevent or relieve homelessness to 278,000 households between April 2021 and March 2022 (Geraghty, 2023). Whilst there are no official statistics on the size of the UK's hidden homeless population, in 2017, the London Assembly's Housing Committee estimated there to be approximately 13 times as many hidden homeless people in London as people sleeping rough (LAHC, 2017). If the hidden homeless include people living in temporary, insecure or 'informal' housing even these figures are dwarfed by the millions of people living in such conditions in the Global South (Busch-Geertsema et al., 2016)

a source of potential abjection: not only 'filthy', but the 'filth' of society. For Goffman, it is not only that street homeless people may be 'awkward or unkept' but that they disrupt the norms of social interaction. They may walk and talk 'wrongly': moving around the city seemingly without purpose, and making unsolicited and uncomfortable requests (for food, or money) of passers-by.

Street homeless people disrupt the 'interaction order', and its underlying geographies, in other ways too. By lying rather than sitting on public benches, and 'setting up home' in rather than moving through the streets, they disrupt normative understandings of the various **infrastructures** that facilitate public life and – because by necessity, eating, sleeping and bathing in public rather than behind closed doors – shatter deeply rooted notions of public and private space and the behaviours associated with each. In doing so, a homeless person may come to be seen not only as 'Other' but as a threat – 'a dangerous giant, a destroyer of worlds' in Goffman's words (1961: 72, cited in Gerrard and Farugia, 2015: 2223).

So stigmatised, it is perhaps unsurprising that street homeless people are also often excluded not only from private spaces such as shops and restaurants (where they might otherwise find something to eat or a restroom to use) but from more highly valued – or 'prime' – city spaces, and in North American cities authorities now deploy a range of strategies to 'protect' higher value areas from the 'polluting' presence of street homeless people (see Box 56.2).

BOX 56.2
SKID ROW AND HOMELESS CONTAINMENT

In Los Angeles, many downtown businesses defend their premises from the incursions of homeless people with private security guards, electronic surveillance and both highly visible and more subtle forms of 'defensive architecture': padlocks, gates, and spikes, sprinkler systems and 'bum-proof' seats (Figure 56.2). To further protect the downtown core, city authorities have introduced site-specific 'quality of life' ordinances designed to 'protect' the (housed) public from the 'nuisance' caused by homeless people setting up camp, eating, sleeping or bathing in prime public space. The Los Angeles Police Department (LAPD) also conduct regular sweeps to drive street homeless people out of downtown and into nearby 'Skid Row' where such ordinances are less rigorously (or perhaps, less regularly) enforced. Combining clearance with containment, by restricting the siting of homeless shelters, soup

Figure 56.2
The term 'defensive architecture' was first coined in the early 1990s by the American geographer Mike Davis. He used it to refer to the use of new styles of street furniture by businesses and city authorities in Los Angeles to 'defend' downtown from infringement by street homeless people but such furniture is now common in the UK too (see below). Such architecture takes different forms. Whilst some may be obvious, such as spikes set into doorways and alcoves to make it impossible for someone to shelter there, others are more subtle. The most insidious are perhaps designs that many may embrace as an attractive piece of street furniture, with their 'defensive' qualities evident only to those who need to use them for other purposes (as with the 'dividers' which make it difficult to sleep on this bench outside the High Courts of Justice in central London)

Source: Photo credit: Jon May

kitchens, detox programmes and drop-in centres into an area of approximately 50 city blocks on the edge of downtown, Skid Row has effectively become an unofficial 'containment zone' for the city's homeless, with reports of hospitals and the police 'dumping' homeless and mentally ill prisoners and patients in the neighbourhood on discharge. Even so, Skid Row too is also subject to the periodic clearance of encampments as social services and police seek to compel people to enter rehabilitation and related services (Stuart, 2014). Whilst it still regularly tops the charts, such developments are far from limited to Los Angeles with the National Coalition for the Homeless (n.d.) now publishing an annual list of America's 'meanest cities' (https://nationalhomeless.org/dirty-dozen-meanest-cities/).

Some of these strategies have crossed the Atlantic. Defensive – or more accurately, perhaps, offensive – architecture is now commonplace on the streets of many UK cities. The UK also has its own version of 'quality of life' ordinances. For example, *Public Spaces Protection Orders* (introduced as part of the *Anti-Social Behaviour, Crime and Policing Act 2014*) are designed to exclude 'troublesome' activities (such as street drinking) and hence 'troublesome people' from designated places. Research shows the policing and enforcement of such orders have been disproportionately directed towards homeless people, with reports of the continual dispersal and displacement of street homeless people from these areas and even of their verbal and physical abuse by officers (Heap et al., 2022).

Importantly, research also shows that not all homeless people are treated the same, with these differences playing out in variegated geographies of stigma and exclusion. For example, as Takahashi (1996) has shown, the degree of stigma suffered by homeless people differs according (in part) to the extent to which a person might be understood as responsible for the circumstances in which they find themselves, as well as according to their age, gender and **ethnicity**. Hence, young homeless people may be afforded more sympathy (by members of the housed public and police alike) than older homeless people, and research from Los Angeles shows clear differences in the policing of homeless people according to **race** and ethnicity, with a higher proportion of white people amongst the homeless in the city's wealthier beach-side communities and over-representation of Black homeless men and women in Skid Row.

Intersecting with its racialisation is what, drawing on Wacquant, Imogen Tyler calls the 'political economy of stigma' (2020: 26): that is, the role that these processes play in helping to secure capital accumulation and contain **class** struggle. In the current example, the stigmatisation and exclusion of street homeless people from the prime spaces of North American and European cities is vital to the efforts of those cities to secure investment in a period of intense 'inter-urban competition'. With city managers acutely aware of the need to project an image of 'success' if they are to attract increasingly footloose capital, they are also aware that nothing threatens the image of a prosperous and successful city so much as the presence of homeless people on its streets. As capitalism places ever-greater emphasis on the ability to consume as an indicator of success, street homeless people simultaneously offer a powerful 'Other' against whom members of the wider public might differentiate themselves: reassuring that public they belong amongst society's 'winners' and reducing the likelihood of people objecting to the control and exclusion of these 'losers', even if (or perhaps because) they secretly harbour doubts as to their own financial security in such an uncertain world.

Significantly, and in contrast to the stigmatisation of particular spaces and places, the stigma associated with street homeless people attaches to the person: moving with them as they move through the city and – even if eventually finding a home – often lingering with them in the physical and mental traumas that can scar someone who has lived on the streets (Homeless Link, n.d.). However, it is also important to recognise that just as different homeless people do not all face the same stigma, nor should it be assumed that the stigmatisation of homeless people will necessarily lead to their exclusion. As Gerrard and Farrugia note, an encounter with a homeless person can provoke a judgement of that person as 'filthy' and/or as the 'filth' of society. But it may also provoke judgements of homelessness as the '"filthy" outcome of capitalist society' and decisions whether to 'ignore, avert eyes, give money … smile, speak or don't speak, are enmeshed with individual understandings and experiences of social inequality, and moral and political judgements surrounding its causes and effects' (2015: 2224). The stigmatisation and exclusion of street homeless people also continues to produce a variety of more progressive, collective responses: ranging from the dismantling by activists of various forms of defensive architecture (Figure 56.3), to the provision of food, shelter and care of different kinds by a wide variety of individuals and organisations. These responses too have been a focus of work by geographers (see, for example, Cloke et al., 2010).

Figure 56.3
Better than Spikes is a group of activists working to turn the 'travesties of urban design into hospitable spaces', such as here by covering the spikes set to deter street homeless people in Shoreditch, London. See more at: https://betterthanspikes.tumblr.com/

Source: The Space, Not Spikes intervention. Photo credit: Courtesy Space, Not Spikes. https://news.artnet.com/art-world/space-not-spikes-homeless-intervention-320146

Summary

- Street homeless people are often highly stigmatised as 'abject Others' because of their association with 'dirt' and 'filth', and because they disrupt the norms of social interaction and the boundaries of public and private space and the behaviours 'appropriate' to each.
- In many North American and European cities, this exclusion takes the form of their dispersal from prime urban space and (in the US) containment in skid row districts on the edge of downtown areas.
- This dispersal is achieved through more intense policing and the use of new forms of 'defensive architecture' and legislation which make it harder for homeless people to engage in the activities they need to if they are to survive on the streets.
- It is also possible to relate this exclusion to a 'political economy of stigma'; with city managers seeking to exclude groups that disrupt the image of a prosperous and successful city necessary to attract capital investment.
- These processes of stigma and exclusion are both gendered and racialised, with different homeless people facing different forms and degrees of stigma.
- Encounters with homelessness may also provoke more progressive attempts to care for homeless people.

The political economy of stigma and territorial stigmatisation

Rather than in relation to psychoanalytical processes, or symbolic and interactional orders, most recent work by geographers on stigma starts from an understanding of stigma as something that is produced and 'put to work' by more powerful groups to further their interests within particular **political economic** contexts. Imogen Tyler, for example, has sought to retheorise stigma as a 'form of power ... [that] functions to devalue entire groups of people with the purpose of ... fortifying existing social hierarchies and creating new opportunities for the redistribution of wealth upwards' (2020: 26–27). One of the clearest examples of these 'political economies' of stigma is the stigmatisation of welfare recipients in austerity Britain.

Austerity is often defined simply as a budgetary policy of fiscal retrenchment designed to restore growth. But it is also possible to read austerity as an **ideological** smokescreen designed to obscure continuing efforts to 'shrink the state' under **neoliberalism** (Chapter 52), and as a form of 'regressive redistribution' (Hastings et al., 2017). Most obviously, in the period since 2010, 45 separate welfare benefits have been capped, scrapped, frozen or reduced and more than 3.5 million claimants (900,000 of whom are disabled) sanctioned following an alleged infringement of the rules; for example, missing an appointment or failing to apply for enough jobs. Once sanctioned a person may have their benefits stopped for a period of between four weeks and three years (May et al., 2020).

Cuts to welfare have become one of the most enduring symbols of austerity, as too have some of the effects of these cuts, most notably perhaps a staggering rise in the number of food banks operating in Britain: now numbering more than 2500, almost twice the number of McDonald's restaurants (Dawson, 2022). Yet even whilst millions of people have seen their household income slashed, others have made millions from these same changes. For example, from April 2010 to April 2019, the Department of Work and Pensions (DWP) paid the outsourcing giants *Atos*, *Capita* and *Maximus* nearly £2.3 billion to deliver Personal Independence Payment (PIP) and 'Work Capability' assessments on its behalf (Pring, 2021).

Rather than leading to widespread public disquiet, these changes – and the gaping inequalities they have exacerbated – have secured support from large swathes of the British electorate. That they have done so is in part at least a result of the successful stigmatisation of welfare recipients by successive Coalition and Conservative governments. Drawing on the same language to be found in the right-wing press (see Figure 56.4) and television programmes like *Shameless* and

Figure 56.4

Since the onset of austerity in 2010, headlines like these have become more common as the right-wing media and politicians have sought to secure electoral support for cuts to welfare spending by demonising welfare recipients. Imogen Tyler (2020) has referred to this process as the 'weaponisation of stigma'

Source: Image credit: Mirrorpix

Benefits Streets, Conservative politicians have routinely represented benefit recipients as dishonest, profligate and workshy, trapped in a cycle of 'dependency' and – driving a wedge between benefit claimants and others – fundamentally 'undeserving' of the support of society's 'strivers'. In a powerful example of such rhetoric, in 2014, then Conservative MP Edwina Currie tweeted that she was 'very, very troubled at the number of people … using food banks … [who] … never learn to cook … never learn to manage and the moment they've got a bit of spare cash [are] off getting another tattoo' (May et al., 2020; for other examples of this stigmatising rhetoric and its effects, see Bolton et al., 2022).

Exploring processes of territorial stigma, Tom Slater and others have traced a similar stigmatisation of working-class spaces and places in recent years. Slater is especially interested in the production and deployment of a stigmatising discourse on so-called sink estates: a '"derogatory designator", signifying social housing estates that supposedly *create* poverty, family breakdown, worklessness, welfare dependency, antisocial behaviour and personal irresponsibility' (2018: 1, emphasis added, see Box 56.3).

Just as the cuts made under austerity have been made possible by the stigmatisation of welfare recipients, Slater shows how social housing tenants have come to be similarly stigmatised because they are somehow 'infected' by the places they live. Having established this image, the demolition of these estates (calculated to have led to the displacement of up to 135,658 council

BOX 56.3
THE PRODUCTION OF 'SINK ESTATES'

The term 'sink estate' first entered common parlance when used by Tony Blair in his first speech as Prime Minister, made when visiting the *Aylesbury Estate* in South-East London in May 1997. From there, Slater (2018) traces its subsequent adoption by and circulation among a growing number of right-wing commentators, think tanks and politicians over the next two decades. For example, in 2013, it reappeared in a report called *Create Streets* published by the Conservative think tank *Policy Exchange*. In a chapter entitled 'Multi-storey Housing Creates a Spiral of Decline' the report again singled out the *Aylesbury Estate* as a classic example of a 'sink estate' and castigated it and high-rise estates more generally for making their inhabitants 'sadder, badder and lonelier' (cited in Slater, 2018: 13).

Another report for *Policy Exchange* published in 2015 went further, concluding that 'Although Estate Recovery Plans … offer the opportunity to turn around social housing estates … where … an estate is beyond recovery, the government must commit to demolishing and replacing it' because of what – in a reference to *Create Streets* – the author referred to as 'the strong evidence that tower blocks and multi-storey living leads to higher crime rates, weaker communities, and poorer health and education outcomes for residents' (*The Estate We're In*, cited in Slater, 2018: 14). Though clearance of parts of the Ayslebury Estate had already begun, in the same month the report was published (January 2016) then Prime Minister David Cameron announced the forthcoming demolition of a further 100 of Britain's 'worst sink estates' (Slater, 2018).

BOX 56.4
DEMOLITION OF THE HEYGATE ESTATE

In 2013, the *Heygate Estate* (a neighbour of the *Ayslebury Estate*) was sold by Southwark Council to the Australian developer Lend Lease for £50 million. Before the redevelopment began, the council spent £44 million of that money moving residents off the estate so as to provide Lend Lease with a clear site. After redevelopment, the site had a higher housing density (with 1300 rather than 1212 units) and was valued at £3.4 billion. But whilst 1020 of the original 1212 units had been rented out as council flats, post-redevelopment only 5% of units were set aside for 'affordable' housing with the rest marketed as prestige rental and owner-occupied homes (BBC News, 2013, Flynn 2016: 279–280). Significantly, as Mara Ferreri has argued, 'The dispossession of the Heygate began, as with much other low-income housing ... in its discursive association with social failure and urban decay' ... [accounts of the estate before the sale depicted it] 'as "infamous" (The Independent, 29 March 2010), "a notorious sink estate" (Evening Standard, 8 July 2010) and "a sort of human dustbin" (The Telegraph, 18 September 2010). By the time the council signed the regeneration agreement   with Lend Lease ... the estate was presented as vacant and derelict, which conveniently supported the argument for its disposability' (2020: 1011–1012).

tenants in London alone between 1997 and 2014) (Lees, 2014) can in turn then be presented as not only justified but just: the only way to both 'save' these tenants and to protect neighbouring communities from infection.

Tracing the anxiety created by years of living under the threat of demolition, and the distress that follows the breaking up and displacement of these communities, Mel Nowicki has argued that the demolition of such estates constitutes a form of *'domicide'*: the intentional destruction of someone's home leading to intense feelings of loss, anger and despair (Nowicki, 2017; see also Elliot-Cooper et al., 2020). In-line with an understanding that territorial stigma always works within and supports particular political economies, their demolition can also be read as a form of 'accumulation by dispossession' (Harvey, 2004, see Box 56.4).

Summary

- The most recent work by geographers understands stigma as a form of power put to work to the benefit of powerful groups to reenforce social hierarchies and enable capital accumulation and the redistribution of wealth upwards.
- An obvious example of this is the way in which right-wing politicians stigmatised welfare recipients to legitimate cuts to welfare spending during a period of austerity whilst private companies profited from new contracts for the delivery of benefit assessments.

- A discourse of 'sink estates' has led social housing tenants to become similarly stigmatised as they are constructed as having been 'infected' by the places they live.
- The stigmatisation of these estates has legitimated their demolition, and the displacement of tenants, and their replacement by private housing – leading to significant profits for private development companies.

Conclusion

This chapter has traced several different ways in which geographers have worked with the concepts of stigma and exclusion. These include Erving Goffman's concept of stigma as the 'spoiled' identity of those who disrupt the interaction order, and Julia Kristeva's account of abjection and its role in the exclusion of 'abject Others'. Especially when tracing the connections between the two – that is, how the stigmatisation of individuals or groups leads to their physical exclusion from more highly valued (or, in the case of 'sink estates', potentially valuable) spaces and places – it may be most useful to understand stigma as a form of 'classificatory violence 'from above' which devalues people, places and communities' (Tyler, 2020: 27). Such an understanding helps draw attention to the 'work' that stigma and exclusion do in helping secure social hierarchies, redistribute resources and secure the continuing extraction of profit under capitalism.

Discussion points

- Identify a group you feel is stigmatised. Which (if any) of Goffman's three types of stigma best explains their stigmatisation? In what ways might their stigmatisation relate to processes of 'abjection'?
- How might their stigma (also) be related to inequalities of class, race, gender, age or sexuality?
- Does this group suffer any kind of spatial exclusion?
- How (if at all) does their stigmatisation and/or exclusion work to further enforce social inequalities and an uneven distribution of resources?
- What kinds of methods are best suited to geographers' study of stigma and exclusion?

References

Arya, R. (2017). Abjection interrogated: uncovering the relation between abjection and disgust. *Journal of Extreme Anthropology* 1(1): 48–61.

Atkinson, R. (2003). Introduction: Misunderstood Saviour or Vengeful Wrecker? The Many Meanings and Problems of Gentrification. *Urban Studies* 40(12): 2343–2350.

BBC News. (2013). *Heygate Estate sold for £50m by Southwark Council*, 5 February 2013: https://www.bbc.co.uk/news/uk-england-london-21338296

Bolton, R., Whelan, J., and Dukelow, F. (2022). What can welfare stigma do? *Social Policy and Society* 21(4): 632–645.

Busch-Geertsema, V., Culhane, D., and Fitzpatrick, S. (2016). Developing a global framework for conceptualising and measuring homelessness. *Habitat International* 55: 124–132.

Butler, A., Schafran, A., and Carpenter, G. (2018). What does it mean when people call a place a shithole? Understanding a discourse of denigration in the United Kingdom and the Republic of Ireland. *Transactions of the Institute of British Geographers* 43(3): 496–510.

Cloke, P., May, J., and Johnsen, S. (2010). *Swept up Lives? Re-envisioning the Homeless City*. London: Wiley-Blackwell.

Davidson, R., and Henderson, V. (2010). 'Coming out' on the spectrum: autism, identity and disclosure. *Social & Cultural Geography* 11(2): 155–170.

Dawson, B. (2022). Many in the UK face a grim choice this winter between eating and heating as a cost-of-living crisis grips the nation. *Business Insider*, 9 October 2022: https://www.businessinsider.com/cost-of-living-there-are-more-food-banks-mcdonalds-uk-2022-9?r=US&IR=T

Elliot-Cooper, A., Hubbard, P., and Lees, L. (2020). Moving beyond Marcuse: gentrification, displacement and the violence of un-homing. *Progress in Human Geography* 44(3): 492–509.

Ferreri, M. (2020). Painted bullet holes and broken promises: understanding and challenging municipal dispossession in London's public housing 'Decanting'. *International Journal of Urban and Regional Research* 44(6): 1007–1022.

Flynn, J. (2016). Complete control: developers, financial viability and regeneration at the Elephant and Castle. *City* 20(2): 278–286.

Goffman, E. (1961). *Encounters: Two Studies in the Sociology of Interaction*. Middlesex: Penguin University Books.

Geraghty, L. (2023). Homelessness facts and statistics. *Big Issue*, 2 November: https://www.bigissue.com/news/housing/britains-homelessness-shame-cold-hard-facts/

Gerrard, J., and Farrugia, D. (2015). The 'lamentable sight' of homelessness and the society of the spectacle. *Urban Studies* 52(12): 2219–2233.

Goffman, E. (1963). *Stigma: Notes on the Management of Spoiled Identity*. New York, London and Toronto: Simon and Schuster Inc.

Harvey, D. (2004). The 'new' imperialism: accumulation by dispossession. *Socialist Register* 40: 63–87.

Hastings, A., Bailey, N., Bramley, G., and Gannon, M. (2017). Austerity urbanism in England. *Environment and Planning A* 49: 2007–2024.

Heap, V., Black, A., and Devany, C. (2022). *Living within a Public Spaces Protection Order: The Impacts of Policing Anti-Social Behaviour on People Experiencing Street Homelessness*. Sheffield Hallam University: https://shura.shu.ac.uk/30783/1/LivingwithinaPSPO_FullReport_Sept2022.pdf

Herbert, S. (2011). Contemporary geographies of exclusion III: to assist or punish? *Progress in Human Geography* 35(2): 256–263.

Homeless Link. (n.d.). *Tackling Trauma to Help end Homelessness*. https://homeless.org.uk/news/tackling-trauma-to-help-end-homelessness/

Kawash, S. (1998). The homeless body. *Replika* 71: 67–84.

LAHC. (2017). *Hidden Homelessness in London*. London Assembly Housing Committee. https://www.london.gov.uk/sites/default/files/london_assembly_-_hidden_homelessness_report.pdf

Laurie, N., and Richardson, D. (2019). Geographies of stigma: post-trafficking experiences. *Transactions of the Institute of British Geographers* 46: 120–134.

Lees, L. (2014). The urban injustices of new labour's 'New Urban Renewal': the case of the ayelsbury estate in London. *Antipode* 46(4): 921–947.

Lees, L., Shin, H. B., and Morales, E. L. (Eds.) (2015). *Global Gentrifications: Uneven Development and Displacement*. Bristol: Policy Press.

May, J., Williams, A., Cloke, P., and Cherry, L. (2020). Food banks and the production of scarcity. *Transactions of the Institute of British Geographers* 45(1): 208–222.

Misztal, B. (2001). Normality and trust in Goffman's theory of interaction order. *Sociological Theory Volume* 19(3): 237–402.

Mohen, J. (2000). Geographies of welfare and social exclusion. *Progress in Human Geography* 24(2): 291–300.

Moran, D., Turner, J., and Schliehe, A. K. (2018). Conceptualizing the carceral in carceral geography. *Progress in Human Geography* 42(5): 666–686.

Nagel, C., and Grove, K. (2021). Virtual forum introduction: populist nationalisms and new geographies of exclusion. *Political Geography* 89. 102429 e1–e3.

National Coalition for the Homeless. (n.d.). *Dirty Dozen Meanest Cities in the US*. https://nationalhomeless.org/dirty-dozen-meanest-cities/

Nowicki, M. (2017). Domicide and the Coalition: Austerity, Citizenship and Moralities of Forced Eviction in Inner London. In *Geographies of Forced Eviction*, eds. K. Brickell, M. Fernández Arrigoitia, and A. Vasudevan. London: Palgrave Macmillan, 121–143.

Ogborn, M. (1995). Discipline, government and law: separate confinement in the prisons of England and Wales, 1830–1877. *Transactions of the Institute of British Geographers* 20(3): 295–311.

Pearce, J. (2012). The 'blemish of place': Stigma, geography and health inequalities. A commentary on Tabuchi, Fukuhara & Iso. *Social Science & Medicine* 75(11): 1921–1924.

Pentony, S. (1996). How Kristeva's theory of abjection works in relation to the fairy tale and post colonial novel. *Deep South* 2(3): np. https://www.otago.ac.nz/deepsouth/vol2no3/pentony.html

Philo, C. (1989). 'Enough to drive one mad': The Organization of Space in 19th-Century Lunatic Asylums. In *The Power of Geography*, eds. J. Wolch and M. Dear. London: Unwin Hyman, 258–290.

Philo, C. (1997). Of Other Rurals? In *Contested Countryside Cultures: Otherness, Marginalisation and Rurality*, eds. P. Cloke and J. Little. London: Routledge, 19–50.

Philo, C. (2000). Social Exclusion. In *The Dictionary of Human Geography*, eds. R. J. Johnston, D. Gregory, G. Pratt, and M. Watts. Oxford: Blackwell, 751–752.

Pring, J. (2021). DWP assessment contracts will see another £2 billion handed to outsourcing giants. *Disability News Service*, 18th November. https://www.disabilitynewsservice.com/dwp-assessment-contracts-will-see-another-2-billion-handed-to-outsourcing-giants/

Sibley, D. (1981). *Outsiders in Urban Society* London: Palgrave Macmillan.

Sibley, D. (1995). *Geographies of Exclusion: Society and Difference in the West*. London: Routledge.

Sisson, A. (2022). Public housing and territorial stigma: towards a symbolic and political economy. *Housing Studies*. https://doi.org/10.1080/02673037.2022.2108383

Slater, T. (2017). Territorial Stigmatization: Symbolic Defamation and the Contemporary Metropolis. In *The SAGE Handbook of New Urban Studies*, eds. J. Hannigan and G. Richards. London: Sage, 111–125.

Slater, T. (2018). The invention of the 'sink estate': consequential categorisation and the UK housing crisis. *The Sociological Review* 66(4): 877–897.

Strobl, S. (2022). Social Theory: Loic Wacquant. *SEPAD*. https://www.sepad.org.uk/announcement/social-theory

Stuart, F. (2014). From 'Rabble Management' to 'Recovery Management': policing homelessness in marginal urban space. *Urban Studies* 51(9): 1909–1925.

Takahashi, L. (1996). A decade of understanding homelessness in the USA: from characterization to representation. *Progress in Human Geography* 20(3): 291–310.

Tyler, I. (2009). Against abjection. *Feminist Theory* 10(1): 77–98.

Tyler, I. (2020). *Stigma: The Machinery of Inequality*. London: Zed Books.

Tyler, I., and Slater, T. (2018). Rethinking the sociology of stigma. *The Sociological Review* 66(4): 721–743.

Wacquant, L. (2007). *Urban Outcasts: A Comparative Sociology of Advanced Marginality*. Cambridge: Polity.

Online materials

- The *Hostile Design* website aims to raise awareness about anti-homeless and 'hostile' design more generally. It includes links to numerous examples of such design across the UK: https://hostile design.org/
- *Southwark Notes – whose regeneration?* website is a huge archive documenting the history of the *Heygate Estate* and attempts to resist its demolition. It highlights several valuable collaborations between local residents and academic activists: https://southwarknotes.wordpress.com/heygate-estate/
- In this video Imogen Tyler talks to the title of *How does stigma contribute to social inequalities?* in a webinar at the University of Lancaster recorded in 2020: https://www.youtube.com/watch?v=27HVFIpJuew

Further reading

Cloke, P., May, J., and Johnsen, S. (2010). *Swept Up Lives? Re-envisioning the Homeless City*. London: Wiley-Blackwell.
Reviews work on the exclusion of street homeless people in North America and Britain and explores sites of support and care (soup runs, drop-in centres and night shelters) for homeless people in the UK.

Elliot-Cooper, A., Hubbard, P., and Lees, L. (2020). Moving beyond Marcuse: gentrification, displacement and the violence of un-homing. *Progress in Human Geography* 44(3): 492–509.
An excellent overview of work on displacement and related concepts including domicide.

Sibley, D. (1995). *Geographies of Exclusion: Society and Difference in the West*. London: Routledge.
A pioneering work on the geographies of exclusion. Includes a discussion of the exclusion of racialised and gendered knowledge in Geography not discussed here.

Slater, T. (2017). Territorial Stigmatization: Symbolic Defamation and the Contemporary Metropolis. In *The SAGE Handbook of New Urban Studies*, eds. J. Hannigan and G. Richards. London: Sage, 111–125.
A definitive outline of ideas on territorial stigma.

Smith, G. (2006). *Erving Goffman*. London: Routledge.
Part of Routledge's Key Sociologists series covering the wide range of Goffman's work.

Tyler, I. (2020). *Stigma: The Machinery of Inequality*. London: Zed Books.
A powerful retheorisation of stigma as a political-economic weapon, including chapters on racial stigma, the stigmatisation of migrants and of the anti-poor rhetoric of austerity Britain. Extremely readable.

Migration and diaspora

Joris Schapendonk and Maggi Leung

Introduction

Geography plays a key role in discussions around migration. We highlight three reasons for this opening statement. First, from erratic processes of forced displacement to the more privileged status of so-called lifestyle migration, geographical differences in terms of, among others, protection, economic opportunities, environmental conditions and amenities are vital to our understanding of why people move across borders in the first place (King, 2012). Second, besides explaining migratory moves, a geographical lens is very helpful in unpacking the politics of migration. In other words, thinking about spatial relations, scales and power inequalities helps us to analyse how states and supra-states react to migration, including their fortified borders as expressions of **territoriality** and the multiple scales of migration governance (Mainwaring, 2019, Collyer, 2023). With the signing of the Global Compact for Migration in 2018, for instance, migration has now fully entered the global governance arena. Finally, geography is important to think about the socio-spatial consequences of migration. What does migration mean for communities they depart from? How do they stay connected with the people they feel related to? How do migrants socially embed themselves in their new living places, and to what extent do societies allow for this embeddedness? When does somebody belong to a community? Where is home? This chapter on migration and **diaspora** particularly focuses on the latter dimension of geographies of migration.

Probably we have all raised the question *where do you come from?* in one way or the other. All too frequently, this question is posed on migrant bodies in diversified societies to indicate that they are not from here and hence belong somewhere else. As was so clearly shown by the prominent case of Ngozi Fulani in the context of a Buckingham Palace royal reception in 2022, the 'Where do you come from?' question is far from innocent and can actually become abusive when the interrogation highlights colonial and racial fault lines (see also the TED talk by Taye Selasi, referenced in the online materials at the end of the chapter). Whereas Fulani stressed how she was born and raised in Britain, her nationality and belonging was continuously questioned by the former Queen's Lady-In-Waiting and pinned down to a certain place of origin in the Caribbean. This continuous tendency to *root* certain populations to particular places of origin, located outside the spaces they actually live in, is part of the everyday *national geographics* of many 'multicultural societies' (Malkki, 1992). Some 30 years ago Malkki already pointed to the

DOI: 10.4324/9780429265853-66

ways territorialised interpretations of community and identity had negative consequences for people who are considered 'uprooted' or 'displaced'. This rooting is thus an inherent part of how difference is continuously made and perpetuated through our **imaginative geographies** of societies (Gregory, 1995, Samaddar 2020) and, as have seen in the case of Fulani, our specific imaginative geographies of particular people within societies (Bhambra, 2017).

This chapter delves into geographies of migration and community, but it deliberately does not start from the dominant position of the migrant-receiving society. This implies two shifts in our thinking. First, we move away from conventional 'sedentarist' thinking that considers being in a place (e.g. a country) as normal and treats cross-border mobility as abnormal and exceptional. Furthermore, sedentarist thinking reduces migration to a simplistic bipolar process: as if it is always a process of departure/arrival, push/pull or emigration/immigration. Indeed, this sedentarist way of thinking starts from a sense of spatial fixity, leaving boundaries of communities unquestioned and inflexible. As an alternative, we advocate mobility thinking that considers mobility not an enemy to community, but actually its social glue (Cresswell, 2010, Sheller, 2021).

The second shift is that we move away from policy-oriented discussions on community-building that expect migrants to fit in the countries they now live in. As it is recently argued, omnipresent debates on integration and assimilation (especially in North America and Western Europe) usually follow the kind of national and rooted geographies that we introduced above. Put plainly, the concept of integration automatically locates migrants outside the social spaces they live in (Schinkel, 2018), assuming they do not belong. Critical migration scholars have explained and criticised such expectations of integration and highlight the 'colonial logics' that underpin policy legislation (El-Enany, 2020; also see Chapter 13). Adrian Favell, for instance, notes how integration is a 'default concept' for **nation-states** to re-imagine their 'ongoing civilizational mission in the face of global diversity' (Favell, 2022: 2). Integration is, therefore, a matter of bordering and ordering (Van Houtum and Van Naerssen, 2002).

As an alternative, we start from a different community space: diaspora. This age-old term denotes a **transnational** space of community-building where parts of migrant identities and senses of belonging are formed, contested and reconfigured. However, as will be discussed, diasporic spaces are not romantic, apolitical, borderless and homogenous spaces per se. After exploring different dimensions of diasporas, we address the question of diasporic belonging and engagement from a critical geographical lens, asking ourselves: to what extent do diasporic spaces transcend the rooted order of things that we started with?

The chapter is structured as follows: first, we provide a concise introduction to the concepts of migration and mobility; second, we define diasporas and challenge the boundaries of diasporic communities.

Approaching migration and mobility

Migration has been approached from diverse theoretical angles, and it is an impossible task to provide an all-inclusive overview here. However, it is safe to state that the theorisation of migration has followed wider trends in social sciences. We could easily distinguish neoclassical economic theories that focus on migrant decision-making, such as the well-known push-pull model, from structuralist models of migration starting from centre-periphery thinking or the segmentation of labour markets. Whereas the former approach tends to position migrants as rational

BOX 57.1
THE TRANSNATIONAL TURN

Emerging in the early 1990s, the field of transnational migration moved away from the idea that migration is a permanent rupture from a country of origin (e.g. Schiller et al., 1992). Transnational migration scholars, including Nina Glick Schiller, Alejandro Portes and Thomas Faist, were sensitive to the ways migrants built networks and created communities as well as patterns of life that cut across national boundaries. This approach stimulated new debates on migration and community, as we will discuss below.

economic actors and profit maximisers that voluntarily act on the basis of wage differences, the latter foregrounds the idea that migration predominantly reflects a world order in which wealthy economies dominate over other parts of the world. Critiques of both approaches have argued that they ignore the way migration is a socially embedded phenomenon. As an alternative, many scholars started to work on households, migration networks and later, transnationalism or transnational migration (Box 57.1; see also Samers and Collyer, 2017 for an overview).

After the transnational turn, we have seen many more turns in the field of migration theories, including the 'reflexive turn' (Amelina, 2021), 'material turn' (Wang, 2016) and 'spatial turn' (Smith, 2011). Arguably, the 'mobility turn' has been one of the most influential in the past 15 years (Faist, 2013). In the context of migration, the mobilities turn challenges the idea that mobility is just a residual in-between phase for migrants between their old and their new home: as if people live place-bound and settled lives in the places of origin and in their destinations. Instead, it positions migration in the broader category of mobilit*ies* (indeed, in plural) (see Chapter 11; Figure 57.1). In so doing, migration is considered to be an inherent part of wider **globalisation** processes that include the mobilit*ies* of people (tourism, business travels, visiting of friends and family) but also non-human mobilities, most notably money, goods and information. This approach has great influence on how we understand society and community (Box 57.2). Society or community are not so much stable, static and bounded social entities; rather, they are actively constituted by the constant intermingling of different mobilities (Sheller, 2021). This mobility mindset also implies that pre- and post-migration phases in people's lives are filled with different mobilities too. As such, it is a rather different way of approaching questions of migration compared to the conventional departure-movement-arrival model (Schapendonk, 2020).

Evidently, people move in very different ways, and under very different conditions. For some, mobility resembles utopian freedom; for others it is a stressful undertaking, especially when the right documents are lacking (Van Liempt et al., 2023), or constitutes a life-threatening quest for safety, as we know from the humanitarian crises in the Mediterranean (Mainwaring, 2019). In this context of unequal mobility, it is important to note that any form of categorisation – whether it is an asylum seeker, refugee, expat – is a mediated outcome of policy-related and **discursive** practices, shaped by many intermediaries (Shubin and Findlay, 2014). In other words, some people who cross borders are *turned into* migrants of some kind (Amelina, 2021), while others (like in the cases of '**expatriate**', 'global nomads' or sports professionals) are freed or excused

BOX 57.2
EDUCATION THROUGH A MOBILITIES LENS

We invite you to think about your education experience from a mobilities perspective. How would the community of students be like without mobilities? How would it look like without migratory mobilities, that is, movements across international borders? What would your university be like without the daily incoming and outgoing mobility of students, lecturers, administrative staff, canteen staff and their cleaners? How would your programme look like without the mobility of information and materials? And finally, what does your study do to *your (future) mobility*? How does your study of geography affect your geographical and mental horizons, your imaginaries of, and relation to, the other parts of the world?

By raising these questions, you might get a sense of how multiple mobilities constitute societies and personal experiences. While thinking about these questions, it is important at the same time to be sensitive to the ways mobilities become a factor of differentiation. The latter notion implies that some mobilities are facilitated and promoted, while others are hampered and blocked. This is called 'the politics of mobility' (Cresswell, 2010).

Figure 57.1
Migration as a global phenomenon

Source: Vector credit: © Shutterstock/Doom.ko

from such labels (Kunz, 2020). For example, the work of Sophie Cranston (2016, 2017) shows how numerous commercial actors do not only facilitate the mobility of privileged migrants but also construct *the expat* as an identity marker through the services they offer. Through this discursive selectivity, the notion of migration is more and more associated with the idea of an act of underprivilege. This is clearly the case in discussions around migration and mobility in Europe. Here, *mobility* is often used as a more positive term that relates to the post-national lives of free European citizens, as in the case of Favell's book *Eurostars and Eurocities* (2008). While terms like *onward migration* or *secondary movements* are used to describe the mobility of **Others**, including non-European national workers and asylum seekers. However, critical migration studies and mobility approaches refuse to take common-sense and policy-induced terminologies for granted but instead further unpack the politics of the same (e.g. Crawley and Skleparis, 2018, Aparna, 2020, Schapendonk, 2021). The latter implies that, instead of seeing labels and categories as neutral terms, we might raise the question who makes these labels, when are labels seen as natural orders, and what do these labels enact?

The latter issue of labelling might appear to you merely as an academic reflection, but the real effects are all around us. Take the issue of skilled migration, for instance. As argued by Hof (2021) in her work on European migration to knowledge economies of Singapore and Japan, the skilled migrant is a **social construct** that intersects with **class** and whiteness leading to certain forms of white privilege and desirability. Lan (2022) has recently offered nuanced interpretations on this matter. Her research on whiteness in China underlines the fluid and contested nature of whiteness. While being privileged, 'white' low-income knowledge workers in China are also confronted with precariousness, especially during the COVID-19 pandemic period (Lan et al., 2022). Similar intersections of **gender**, **race** and class are foregrounded in studies on educational or skilled mobility to the United States or Europe and they help to explain how migration is a matter of social stratification (Raghuram, 2004, Koskela, 2019).

Regarding the latter issue, a series of studies have underlined the complex links between geographic and social mobilities. Straddling transnational spaces, migrants often experience 'contradictory social mobility' (Parreñas, 2001) across the societies in which they are embedded. As such, migrants are positioned simultaneously in the social stratification orders of multiple political-economic and socio-cultural contexts. In her study on Filipino domestic workers overseas, Parreñas (2001) underlines the commonly experienced contradictions between the capacity to earn a higher income (hence, upward social mobility) and having to take up work that is categorised as lower skilled such as domestic care work (hence, downward social mobility). Rutten and Verstappen (2014) make a similar observation among Indian migrant youth in London. Leung (2017) weaves in a temporal perspective to this discussion, echoing and substantiating the 'temporal turn' in migration studies (see, e.g. Baas and Yeoh, 2019, Griffiths et al., 2013, Mavroudi et al., 2017). In her academic mobility research, she illustrates how upper and middle-class students or researchers from Asia pursuing their advanced degrees at prestigious institutions in Europe often worked long hours in 'low skilled' jobs to finance their (and their family's) cost of living. Very often they were confronted with living conditions in poorer neighbourhoods that contrasted heavily with their more luxurious living standards in their places of origin. In time, however, many of her research participants ended up achieving their professional ambition. This pain-and-then-gain process exemplifies a common Cantonese Chinese saying about overseas education. People who have had international education are described as having 'soaked in sea water' (*jum guo ham sui* 浸過鹹水) – as in having crossed the ocean. Indeed, the expression captures the **temporality** described above. As such, 'before student and academic migrants can capitalise on what they have set out for, they will most likely first have to get wet and salty, and sometimes the sea salt hurts and brings tears' (Leung 2017: 2714).

Summary

- Theorising migration has evolved from neoclassical economic theories (individual decision-making and wage differences) and structuralist models (dominance of wealthier economies). Both approaches have been criticised for neglecting the social embeddedness of migration.
- In the 1990s, theory shifted its focus from perceiving migration as a permanent rupture from the country of origin to recognising the building of networks and communities across national boundaries.
- The 'mobility turn' marked a change in theory understanding migration as part of broader global processes of mobilities, including the movement of people, goods and information. This perspective challenges the notion of stable and bounded societies, emphasising the intermingling of different mobilities, departing from the conventional departure-movement-arrival model.

Defining diasporas

The age-old term diaspora is generally defined as a scattered population with a shared and imagined homeland (Safran 1991, Van Hear 2014). There is a narrow interpretation of this concept that limits diaspora to the notion of exile and displacement. In more contemporary discussions, however, diaspora has a broader connotation that is not only related to conditions of forced displacement (Ponzanesi, 2020). The term usually refers to a transnational migrant community that is spread across different places in the world and shares some socio-economic, cultural and/or political engagements in relation to places they feel connected to. These places are often described as 'homelands' or 'countries of origin'. In his seminal work *The Black Atlantic,* Gilroy (1993) 'mobilises' the concept of diaspora as both about 'routes' and 'roots' in order to offer a rich account of the cultural and historical connections between people of African descent living in America, the Caribbean, and Europe. Building on such emphasis on the journeys, Leung (2004: 21) defines diaspora as

> a dynamic patchwork, a fluid collage made up of multiple, diverse, sometimes diverging while other times overlapping, journeys embarked upon by individuals of a dispersed community, sharing a homeland, sometimes mythical or imagined, and a collective sense of belonging. 'Journeys', in this sense, do not only mean migrants' movements across geographical space. They also entail long-term or life-long processes which migrants undergo, interacting with their social environment in different geographical scales as part of their identity (re)construction and (re)interpreting their positions within the host society. Central to this is their ongoing negotiation in defining home(s) and how the perceptions they glean evolve into daily life practices.

The processes of homemaking and enacting diaspora membership are, however, not always self-determined. In the everyday, diasporic identities might also be imposed on individuals in multicultural **encounters** as an act of Othering (as in the case of Ngozi Fulani above) (see also Peterson, 2020 for a Scottish case). Recent waves of racialised discrimination and aggression reported during the COVID-19 pandemic also help illustrate such daily structural violence. People with Chinese and Asian (and other) appearances, for instance, were seen as threats merely because of their physical appearance and hence put in the 'yellow peril' box (Pew Research Center 2020, Wang et al., 2021).

Diasporic communities are often regarded as an inherent element of cultural globalisation (Dwyer, 2013). They find common ground in cultural expressions like music, film and fashion. In so doing, the concept of diaspora often has a positive or emancipatory connotation as it indicates that senses of belonging may indeed transcend the territorial boundedness, homogenous identity and assimilating geographies of the nation-states (e.g. Ponzanesi, 2020). In other words, there are other forms of communities that are formed across borders (Box 57.3), and they might have their own bottom-up narratives and geopolitics of belonging (Hyndman et al., 2022). However, we should also note the paradox that diasporic spaces are often actually defined by national or ethnic boundaries. In line with this, Ien Ang argues that it is important to articulate the double-edged character of diaspora, as she writes: 'it can be a site of both support and oppression, emancipation and confinement, solidarity and division' (Ang, 2003: 142).

Avtar Brah's (1996) concept of diaspora space is useful in helping us make sense of such processes of in/exclusion. She emphasises the 'entanglement of genealogies of dispersion with those of staying put' (p. 181), who can be either on the origin and destination side. She goes on to assert, '[t]he question of home, therefore, is intrinsically linked with the way in which processes of inclusion and exclusion operate and are subjectively experienced under given circumstances' (p. 192). Diaspora space is thus inhabited by those constructed as 'locals' and 'migrants'. Brah's call shifts the discourse of migration from the 'exotic', 'displaced migrants', 'the others' to the links between those who move and those who do not. This relational thinking has multiple implications. For one, it underlines the politics of social citizenship. It alerts us the power of the 'Where are you from?' question. It cautions us not to fall in the pitfall of *rooting* people with

BOX 57.3
DIGITAL DIASPORAS

Much of the transnational connectivity, and hence identify formation, that is so central to the notion of diaspora happens online. Consequently, the term *digital diaspora* has become a common term. Apps on mobile phones help to remit money, social media facilitates social bonding as videos are shared, politics is discussed, emotions travel, festivals are celebrated, and solidarity and activism is advertised and practised (Kok and Rogers, 2017). Digital presence and practice is not unique to diasporic social spaces, but the online world does stretch the meaning of diasporic spaces. As Ponzanesi (2020: 990) writes: 'the ubiquity, speed and instantaneousness of connectivity allowed by new digital technologies have changed the way in which migration is experienced and distance is mediated'.

Figure 57.2
Diasporic spaces are not necessarily homogenous. The Tigray Diaspora in the US, for example, has
been actively engaged in protesting against the war in Tigray, a conflict between the Ethiopian federal
government and Eritrea on one side, and the Tigray People's Liberation Front (TPLF) on the other

Source: Image credit: © Alamy/AP Photo/Alex Brandon

such an 'innocent' or 'friendly' question, especially to offspring of migrants who might or might
not view themselves as part of a diaspora. Taking one further step, we can and should incorporate those who have not moved, the 'locals', into the adaptation (or 'integration' processes)
hitherto expected only from the migrants.

To move beyond romantic and homogeneous interpretations of diasporas, two aspects are
worth unpacking further: (i) multiplicity and representation and (ii) the role of the state. Diaspora
communities across the globe bring their own institutions, including home associations, cultural centres and NGOs. These institutions are frequently embraced in policy arenas, such as the
migration-development nexus. However, it is important to note that even in situations diasporic
groups share a notion of home, they should not be seen as homogenous spaces, raising questions
around representation and visibility (Figure 57.2). For example, in the period that NATO intervened in Libya to overthrow the Gaddafi regime, we have seen pro- and anti-Gaddafi demonstrations organised by Libyan communities in European countries. Similarly, it is misleading
to talk about the Surinamese diaspora in the Netherlands, as it does not only consist of black
Surinamese groups (with histories related to Dutch slave trade from Africa) but also groups that
identify as Hindu (who were moved as contract labourers from Kolkata/India to Suriname just
after slavery formally ended) as well as a considerable number of Chinese Surinamese people
who moved to the Netherlands after Suriname's independence. Thus, diasporic spaces can be as
complex and multicultural as many other forms of community.

To focus on the role of the state, we start with a remarkable advertisement: Lebanon Calling.
When you have watched this short clip, https://www.youtube.com/watch?v=BfHig3Yh6iA,
you may ask *why* is Lebanon calling in the first place? And *why* does Lebanon reach out to

this particular person? What does Lebanon want from him? What this advertisement indicates is that states may have a keen interest in engaging in *diasporic politics*. Hence, there is a difference between *transnationalism from below*, i.e. the bottom-up initiatives from migrant communities to connect across borders and create social spaces, and *transnationalism from above* when states are actually forging relations with what they regard as *their population* (e.g. Levitt and Jaworsky, 2007). The advertisement mainly hints at the possibility to invest in, or even return to, the imagined homeland. This is evidently linked to questions of development (see Box 57.4) and nation-building agendas.

BOX 57.4
MIGRATION, DIASPORA AND DEVELOPMENT

The question of the relation between migration and development has been discussed for many decades. Whereas pessimistic views see migration as a sign of 'underdevelopment' (and conditions get worse when more people move out), more optimistic interpretations regard migration not as an undesirable phenomenon for development per se but rather as a developmental potential for the flow of capital and possible innovations as a result of emigration (e.g. de Haas et al., 2019). Based on the more optimistic viewpoints, migrants are considered to be important actors in the field of development cooperation. In both high- and low-income countries, governmental agencies and development organisations are increasingly active to materialise the 'development potential' of migration. Initially, discussions were mainly concentrated on remittances (the economic capital that people send to their communities 'back home') or concerns over brain drain (when people with higher education and more capital move out). At a later stage, discussions on the migration-development nexus broadened to the issue of how migrant communities – or indeed diaspora organisations – may be involved in development cooperation. The basic idea is that diaspora organisations form the perfect bridge as they know both the socio-economic realities and development needs 'on the ground' at the receiving end of development, as well as the rules of the game and institutional complexities in the countries where development policies are designed through international cooperation. While this trend in policy making and development aid is moving away from a mere negative interpretation of migration, there are certainly important questions to be raised. First of all, development (as a policy field) becomes more and more a tool for migration and border management (Samaddar, 2020). This does not only translate in development projects that seek to discourage outmigration (Bakewell, 2008) but also to political conditionality ('you only receive development money, if you cooperate with our migration agenda') (Adepoju et al., 2010). Second, the development issue raises questions about migrant positionalities. Critical voices see the incorporation of migrants in migration-development initiatives as an attempt by powerful states 'to regulate those who live in faraway places through proximate subjects' (Raghuram, 2009: 113). It also heightens the burden for migrants, as societies ask them to both adapt to their new environments and to invest along the lines of moral duties to their countries of origin. In a way, the message is, while you take root *here*, you should not forget about where you have been *rooted* before.

Leung (2015) elaborates these connections in her analysis of the role of the state in cultivating and claiming the Chinese knowledge diaspora – a term that refers to the global spread of individuals of Chinese descent who have expertise, knowledge, or skills in various fields such as academia, technology, and science. Rather than fixing the state on a national level, she underlines the at times collaborative, at other times competitive relationship among different levels (national to communal) and locations (different cities and provinces) of the Chinese state. She also underlines the role of 'other' states in the global knowledge economy in shaping and utilising the Chinese knowledge diaspora. Her recent work on role of the Chinese state during the COVID-19 pandemic further illustrates its care and control exercised on its diaspora subjects (Leung, 2022). While appreciating the homeland state's care during times of trouble, some of her research participants expressed concern about its attempt to surveil and exert control from a distance. Similar sentiments are also present in the case of the Eritrean diaspora. People fleeing the Eritrean authoritarian regime in the last decades have been confronted with state taxes and monitoring practices by agents related to the same regime they tried to escape from (Belloni, 2019).

Summary

- Diaspora is a scattered population with a shared homeland and includes transnational migrant communities.
- Diasporic identities can be imposed as an act of Othering and may face discrimination and aggression.
- Diasporas are part of cultural globalisation and often find common ground in cultural expressions.
- Diasporic spaces can be complex and multicultural, and it is important to consider the politics of representation and visibility within these spaces.

Conclusion

The discussion on migration and community often takes the position of the receiving society. This chapter indicates that it is worthwhile to explore other positionalities and other spaces to better understand the social and spatial consequences of human movements across the globe. We highlighted that particular categorisations based on homeland imaginations can be problematic, as it articulates *non*-belonging and essentialises identities according to bounded and homogeneous geographies. This problem of boundary-making (of who belongs where) does not only occur in discussions of immigration and integration. It also resonates in ways we approach diasporic communities, as transnational spaces that are still very much bounded by ethnic and national identity markers. Like nations, diasporas are *imagined communities* (Anderson, 1991). It is therefore important to underline that linkages with so-called homelands vary considerably between individuals. Heterogeneity within each diaspora along lines of gender, class, generation, geographies (where one is from, gone to and in other ways linked to) and other internal differences of power and positions all affect individual's engagements and sentiments. Moreover, specific relations and emotions may become highly visible during particular events (whether it is sports or more dramatic events such as humanitarian crises or conflict) and remain dormant for other periods of time. In line with this, a mobility perspective encourages us think about people moving in and out of diasporic spaces. The latter was illustrated so clearly by a Ghanaian pastor living in Amsterdam. When the question was raised how the Ghanaian community looked like from his perspective, he said that the number of people in his church remained more or less the same, but the faces of the people change all the time.

Discussion points

- In what ways does a geographical lens help us understand the politics of migration? Explore the relationship between spatial relations, power inequalities and migration governance, including the fortification of borders and the global governance of migration.
- How and why does the concept of diaspora challenge rooted geographies and conventional notions of community?
- Think about your own neighbourhood, town or city and explore the ways in which diasporas shape identities, senses of belonging and community-building beyond traditional boundaries.

References

Adepoju, A., Van Noorloos, F., and Zoomers, A. (2010). Europe's migration agreements with migrant-sending countries in the global south: a critical review. *International Migration* 48(3): 42–75.

Amelina, A. (2021). After the reflexive turn in migration studies: towards the doing migration approach. *Population, Space and Place* 27(1): e2368, 1–11.

Anderson, B. (1991). *Imagined Communities: Reflections on the Origin and Spread of Nationalism.* London: Verso.

Ang, I. (2003). Together-in-difference: beyond diaspora, into hybridity. *Asian Studies Review* 27(2): 141–154.

Aparna, K. (2020). *Enacting Asylum University: Politics of Research Encounters and (Re)producing Borders in Asylum Relations* (PhD). Nijmegen, The Netherlands: Radboud University.

Baas, M., and Yeoh, B. S. A. (2019). Introduction: migration studies and critical temporalities. *Current Sociology* 67(2): 161–168. doi:10.1177/0011392118792924.

Bakewell, O. (2008). 'Keeping Them in Their place': the ambivalent relationship between development and migration in Africa. *Third World Quarterly* 29(7): 1341–1358.

Belloni, M. (2019). Refugees and citizens: understanding Eritrean refugees' ambivalence towards homeland politics. *International Journal of Comparative Sociology* 60(1–2): 55–73.

Bhambra, G. K. (2017). Postcolonial Europe: Afterword. In *Postcolonial Europe: Comparative Reflections after the Empires*, eds. L. Jensen, J. Suárez-Krabbe, C. Groes, and Z. L. Pecic. London: Rowman & Littlefield, 215–220.

Brah, A. (1996). *Cartographies of Diaspora: Contesting Identities.* London: Routledge.

Collyer, M. (2023). Helping People Feel That Their Future Lies at Home: The Geopolitics of Externalizing Irregular Migration Control in the European Union. In *Research Handbook on Irregular Migration*, eds. I. van Liempt, J. Schapendonk, A. Campos-Delgado. Cheltenham, UK and Northampton, USA: Edward Elgar Publishing, 270–280.

Cranston, S. (2016). Producing migrant encounter: learning to be a British expatriate in Singapore through the global mobility industry. *Environment and Planning D: Society and Space* 34(4): 655–671.

Cranston, S. (2017). Expatriate as a 'good' migrant: thinking through skilled international migrant categories. *Population, Space and Place* 23(6): e2058, 1–12.

Crawley, H., and Skleparis, D. (2018). Refugees, migrants, neither, both: categorical fetishism and the politics of bounding in Europe's 'migration crisis'. *Journal of Ethnic and Migration Studies* 44(1): 48–64.

Cresswell, T. (2010). Towards a politics of mobility. *Environment and Planning D: Society and Space* 28(1): 17–31.

de Haas, H., Castles, S., and Miller, M. J. (2019). The Age of Migration: International Population Movements in the Modern World (6th edn.). London, New York and Dublin: Bloomsbury Academic.

Dwyer, C. L. (2013). Diasporas. In *Introducing Human Geographies*, eds. P. Cloke, P. Crang, M. Goodwin (3rd edn.). London: Routledge, 669–685.

El-Enany, N. (2020). *(B)ordering Britain: Law, Race and Empire*. Manchester: Manchester University Press.

Faist, T. (2013). The mobility turn: a new paradigm for the social sciences? *Ethnic and Racial Studies* 36(11): 1637–1646.

Favell, A. (2008). *Eurostars and Eurocities: Free Movement and Mobility in an Integrating Europe*. Oxford: Blackwell.

Favell, A. (2022). *The Integration Nation: Immigration and Colonial Power in Liberal Democracies*. Cambridge: Polity Press.

Gilroy, P. (1993). *The Black Atlantic. Modernity and Double Consciousness*. London: Verso.

Gregory, D. (1995). Imaginative geographies. *Progress in Human Geography* 19(4): 447–485.

Griffiths, M., Rogers, A., and Anderson, B. (2013). *Migration, Time and Temporalities: Review and Prospect*. COMPAS Research Resources Paper. Oxford: Centre on Migration, Policy and Society.

Hof, H. (2021). Intersections of race and skills in European migration to Asia: between white cultural capital and 'passive whiteness'. *Ethnic and Racial Studies* 44(11): 2113–2134.

Hyndman, J., Amarasingam, A., and Naganathan, G. (2022). Diaspora geopolitics in Toronto. Tamil nationalism and the aftermath of war in Sri Lanka. *Geopolitics* 27(2): 424–443.

King, R. (2012). Geography and migration studies: retrospect and Prospect. *Population, Space and Place* 18(2): 134–153.

Kok, S., and Rogers, R. (2017). Rethinking migration in the digital age: transglocalization and the Somali diaspora. *Global Networks* 17(1): 23–46.

Koskela, K. (2019). Intersecting experiences: class, gender, ethnicity and race in the lives of highly skilled migrants in Finland. *Nordic Journal of Migration Research* 9(3): 311–328.

Kunz, S. (2020). Expatriate, migrant? The social life of migration categories and the polyvalent mobility of race. *Journal of Ethnic and Migration Studies* 46(11): 2145–2162.

Lan, S. (2022). Between privileges and precariousness: remaking whiteness in China's teaching English as a second language industry. *American Anthropology* 124(1): 118–129.

Lan, S., Sier, W., and Camenisch, A. (2022). Precarious whiteness in pandemic times in China. *Asian Anthropology* 21(3): 161–170. DOI: 10.1080/1683478X.2022.2099081

Leung, M. W. H. (2004). *Chinese Migration in Germany: Making Home in Transnational Space*. Frankfurt am Main and London: IKO-Verlag für Interkulturelle Kommunikation.

Leung, M. W. H. (2015). Engaging a temporal–spatial stretch: an inquiry into the role of the state in cultivating and claiming the Chinese knowledge diaspora. *Geoforum* 59: 187–196.

Leung, M. W. H. (2017). Social mobility via academic mobility: reconfigurations in class and gender identities among Asian scholars in the global north. *Journal of Ethnic and Migration Studies* 43(16): 2704–2719.

Leung, M. W. H. (2022). COVID-19 care circuits: the Chinese transnational state, its diaspora, and beyond. *China Perspectives* 2022/04: 29–37. https://doi.org/10.4000/chinaperspectives.14358

Levitt, P., and Jaworsky, B. N. (2007). Transnational migration studies: past developments and future trends. *Annual Review of Sociology* 33: 129–156.

Mainwaring, C. (2019). *At Europe's Edge. Migration and Crisis in the Mediterranean*. Oxford: Oxford University Press.

Malkki, L. (1992). National geographic: the rooting of peoples and the territorialization of national identity among scholars and refugees. *Cultural Anthropology* 7(1): 24–44.

Mavroudi, E., Page, B., and Christou, A. (eds.) (2017). *Timespace and International Migration*. Cheltenham: Edward Edgar.

Parreñas, R. (2001). *Servants of Globalization: Women, Migration and Domestic Work*. Stanford: Stanford University Press.

Peterson, M. (2020). Micro aggressions and connections in the context of national multiculturalism: everyday geographies of racialization and resistance in contemporary Scotland. *Antipode* 52(5): 1393–1412.

Pew Research Center. (2020). Many Black and Asian Americans Say They Have Experienced Discrimination Amid the COVID-19 Outbreak. https://www.pewsocialtrends.org/wp-content/uploads/sites/3/2020/07/PSDT_07.01.20_racism.covid_Full.Report.pdf

Ponzanesi, S. (2020). Digital diasporas: postcoloniality, media and affect. *Interventions* 22(8): 977–993.

Raghuram, P. (2004). The difference that skills make: gender, family migration strategies and regulated labour markets. *Journal of Ethnic and Migration Studies* 30(2): 303–321.

Raghuram, P. (2009). Which migration, what development? Unsettling the edifice of migration and development. *Population, Space and Place* 15(2): 103–117.

Rutten, M., and Verstappen, S. (2014). Middling migration: contradictory mobility experiences of Indian youth in London. *Journal of Ethnic and Migration Studies* 40(8): 1217–1235. DOI: 10.1080/1369183X.2013.830884

Safran, W. (1991). Diasporas in modern societies: myths of homeland and return. *Diaspora: A Journal of Transnational Studies* 1(1): 83–99.

Samaddar, R. (2020). *The Postcolonial Age of Migration*. London: Taylor & Francis.

Samers, M., and Collyer, M. (2017). *Migration*. New York: Routledge.

Schapendonk, J. (2020). *Finding Ways Through Eurospace. West African Movers Re-Viewing Europe from the Inside*. Oxford: Berghahn Books.

Schapendonk, J. (2021). Counter moves. Destabilizing the grand narrative of onward migration and secondary movements in Europe. *International Migration* 59(6): 45–58.

Schiller, N. G., Basch, L., and Blanc-Szanton, C. (1992). Transnationalism: a new analytic framework for understanding migration. *Annals of the New York Academy of Sciences* 645(1): 1–24.

Schinkel, W. (2018). Against 'immigrant integration': for an end to neocolonial knowledge production. *Comparative Migration Studies* 6(1): 1–17.

Sheller, M. (2021). *Advanced Introduction to Mobilities*. Cheltenham, UK and Northampton, MA, USA: Edward Elgar Publishing.

Shubin, S., and Findlay, A. (2014). Imaginaries of the ideal migrant worker: a Lacanian interpretation. *Environment and Planning D: Society and Space* 32(3): 466–483. https://doi.org/10.1068/d22212

Smith, D. P. (2011). Geographies of long-distance family migration: moving to a 'spatial turn'. *Progress in Human Geography* 35(5): 652–668. https://doi.org/10.1177/0309132510394011

Van Hear, N. (2014). Refugees, Diasporas and Transnationalism. *The Oxford Handbook of Refugee and Forced Migration Studies*, 176–187.

Van Houtum, H., and Van Naerssen, T. (2002). Bordering, ordering and othering. *Tijdschrift voor economische en sociale geografie* 93(2): 125–136.

van Liempt, I., Schapendonk, J., and Campos-Delgado, A. (eds.) (2023). *Research Handbook on Irregular Migration*. Cheltenham, UK and Northampton, MA, USA: Edward Elgar Publishing, 1–12.

Wang, C. (2016). Introduction: the 'material turn' in migration studies. *Modern Languages Open*. DOI: http://doi.org/10.3828/mlo.v0i0.88

Wang, S., Chen, X., Li, Y., Luu, C., Yan, R., and Madrisotti, F. (2021). 'I'm more afraid of racism than of the virus!': racism awareness and resistance among Chinese migrants and their descendants in France during the COVID-19 pandemic. *European Societies* 23(sup1): S721–S742.

Online materials

- Taiye Selasi: Don't ask where I'm from, ask where I'm a local | TED – YouTube. Taiye Selasi speaks on behalf of 'multi-local' people, who feel at home in the town where they grew up, the city they live now and maybe another place or two. 'How can I come from a country?' she asks. 'How can a human being come from a concept?' https://www.youtube.com/watch?v=LYCKzpXEW6E
- The Best Of Migration Matters: six short videos, big questions. This is an excellent resource made by *Migration Matters* – over 150-bite-sized videos on topics ranging from the relationship between migration and climate change to integration and diversity and migrant lives during the pandemic that feature academic experts, practitioners, the public and those with lived experience. https://migrationmatters.me/best-of/
- Six Impossible Ideas (After Brexit) – Migration Matters: A collaboration between Migration Matters and London School of Economics produced 6-byte-sized videos (3–5 mins) on big questions shaping the public debate in the UK: Are migrants city-makers or city-takers? Do migrants take away jobs? Do borders affect your freedom? Should borders separate or connect? Can the media make us more welcoming? Integration: What works and what doesn't? Each video has resources for further thought and exploration. https://migrationmatters.me/course/six-ideas/
- Calcutta, A Migrant City – YouTube: 'Calcutta, A Migrant City' is a short film by Mahanirban Calcutta Research Group in collaboration with Rosa Luxemburg Stiftung and directed by Saibal Mitra. It shows despite the contribution of migrant labourers in building Kolkata since the 14th century, they have been under-represented in the mainstream discourses. https://www.youtube.com/watch?v=fpREEq7Ar-Y
- COVID doesn't discriminate (English) – YouTube: In this short video, Wendy Wang looks at some shocking examples of discrimination against people of Asian descent during the COVID-19 pandemic; from the former US president to a Dutch radio station's mocking and discriminatory song. She reflects on these examples and tells personal experiences from her own life. A vivid example of the implications discrimination can have upon its victims. Video made by Issa Shaker and Ena Omerovic (Common Frames) and funded by Migration and Societal Change Focus Area of Utrecht University. https://www.youtube.com/watch?v=RceZVuzPpIM
- Lebanon calling: An advert aired during 2016 US elections. The producer Demco Properties wanted to send a message to all Lebanese expats to put their trust again in their country and come back to invest and help it walk towards a better future. https://www.youtube.com/watch?v=BfHig3Yh6iA

Further reading

Boyle, P., Halfacree, K., and Robinson, V. (2014). *Exploring Contemporary Migration*. New York: Routledge.
An accessible and comprehensive introduction to migration and population research.

Collins, F. L. (2021). Geographies of migration I: platform migration. *Progress in Human Geography* 45(4): 866–877.
This paper reviews work on the migration industry and the infrastructures underpinning migration.

Collins, F. L. (2022). Geographies of migration II: decolonising migration studies. *Progress in Human Geography* 46(5): 1241–1251.
This paper reflects on the **coloniality** of migration governance and provides a good entry into **post-colonial** and decolonising debates in the field of migration.

58 Identity and difference

Carl Bonner-Thompson

Introduction

Identity is a tricky idea to think about. If someone asked you to talk about your identity, where would you start? You might start with your age, **gender,** or if you work or study. There might be easier parts of your identity to talk about in certain contexts. For example, at work, I would feel comfortable saying I'm a man, but I might feel less comfortable talking about my sexual identity. Of course, this will vary in different situations and in different parts of our lives (or across **space** and time), and there will be certain moments when you feel very uncomfortable talking about parts of your identity. Then we have ideas of difference. How comfortable are we at talking about how different we feel from one another? When do we feel different from others? Again, this might be something that *some* people find easier to do in some **encounters** than others. These moments of comfort and discomfort might alert us – as people interested in social and cultural geography – to the times and places where some identities are included/ excluded, the reasons behind the boundaries of inclusion, and their origins. For example, in the UK young white working-class men have some of the lowest rates of entering higher education and black young people experience racism across university spaces (Dumangane, 2016, Gamsu et al., 2019), and therefore both groups might not feel fully comfortable speaking in lecture theatres and seminars. This observation might enable us to question what forms of **class** and gender **performances** are welcomed/accepted/normalised in universities. It is issues like that are explored in this chapter. I will explore how geographers understand issues of identity difference, particularly focusing on relational geographies, **intersectionality** and **embodiment**. I then move to explore some marginalised identities that geographers are grappling with, particularly transgender and gender variant lives, body size and fatness, class and disabilities.

Identities: relationality, self/other and intersectionality

Identities are the ways that we understand ourselves and the world understands us. We often think about identities along the lines of gender, **race**, class, age, sexuality (dis)ability and age, all of which shape our identity. Our identities are how we experience different spaces (for example, homes, streets workplaces, schools and hospitals), whether it be through inclusion, exclusion, fear, safety or violence. At the same time, as you will find out in this chapter, these spaces also shape how our identities are *made*.

DOI: 10.4324/9780429265853-67

Identity might not be what you expected – it is not just how you think about yourself (although it can be part of it). One thing to remember is that identities are sets of different processes, meanings and ideas. Geographers, among other social scientists, have argued that identities are **socially constructed**. This means that we think about identities as not something natural or 'pre-existing', but that they have been 'created' by societies, through institutions, politics, culture, language and conversations. For example, the difference between man/woman has been created in scientific and medical knowledge, but they get reaffirmed at work, at home, by politicians and by what we see on TV. Something important to remember as we go forward – identities are not something that 'just' exist, but they are *made*. This implies that identities are always in a process of being created in and across society and space – a social and spatial construction.

How do identities get made? Well, geographers would argue that this happens *relationally*. A relational approach to identity argues that we make sense of ourselves *in relation* to other people and places. This means that we understand ourselves through a shared or collective identity with others (for example, it could be people we share a gender or sexual identity or those whom we share similar interests with or are in the same profession), and by marking ourselves out from those we consider different. This, of course, means that these can change over time and space, as our tastes, employment status and age, for example, do. Therefore, identities are always being constructed relationally as we move through space and time. It is not a process that only happens once but continuously occurs as we encounter people and places across our lives. This relational way of making sense of ourselves creates a way of understanding identities through the relationship of self/other.

Understanding identity through notions of self/other is rooted in psychoanalytical thinking. In such ideas, the self comes to distance itself or creates boundaries between abject things or the **other**. By othering something, or someone, we mark them out as different, often associating them with ideas or feelings that would make us want to repel them, for example, we might associate certain people with disgust or abnormality (see Chapter 56). This process of othering is therefore very powerful and can legitimise the exclusion or persecution of people. We can see self/other operating in so many of the binaries that shape our social and spatial lives. For example, in the straight/gay binary, it is gay that becomes the 'other'. Non-heterosexuality is often marked as different (in different ways across different places and to different intensities) and can become associated with abnormality, disgust and shame, where sexual and romantic relationships between people of the same gender are marked out as 'wrong'. Therefore, heterosexuality *becomes* the self – normal and included – whereas non-heterosexuality becomes the other (see Chapter 12 on gender/sexuality for more details) – and this happens in and across spaces. Think about 'gay bars', for example. These spaces, whilst important for some LGBTQ+ people, mark out 'gay' spaces as different to 'non-gay' spaces, which operate as the 'norm'. It is important to note that these are social and cultural processes that often can be traced back to shifts in medical, scientific and religious thinking. Processes of othering do not only construct places and people as 'disgusting' but as exotic or remote. You might think about how places like Thailand or India are represented in Western advertising – often as 'exotic' places that are there to be 'consumed' by white Western tourists. Geographers make unique contributions to these ideas on self/other, thinking about spatial dynamics. People may become othered across different places in different ways. For example, people might become othered in different countries due to their race or nationality or some people might become othered at work or school compared to their home life. So, othering can take on multiple forms, but it is important to note that they do form how places and people are understood by society, and if we look closely, we may see underlying relations of power that have shaped the 'other'.

As well as exploring how people come to be marked out as different, geographers have also been exploring how people come to be and live with difference. Thinking with the idea of multiculturalism, geographers have explored how urban places enable people to encounter difference in parks, on buses, in shops and on the streets (Vertovec, 2007, Wilson, 2011, Oke et al., 2018). Some geographers argue that the ways people are brought together in these fleeting encounters enable a way of becoming comfortable with different racial, gendered, sexual, aged and national identities. Neal et al. (2015), for example, argue that parks are important sites for bringing diverse people and strangers together in ways that allow difference to become part of everyday experiences and for people to develop multiple place attachments. However, geographers like Nayak (2017) argue that we should not accept cities as multicultural 'utopias'. For Nayak (2017) we need to be critical of any romanticising of multiculturalism and continue to pay attention to the ways racism continues to shape urban encounters, especially in contexts where nations are constructed through whiteness (see Chapters 13 and 72), like the UK.

These approaches to understanding identity have offered human geographers useful ways of understanding how certain groups live together but have also been marginalised in and across social, cultural, economic and political spaces and places. To help reveal how these differences operate, some geographers have found the tools offered by intersectionality useful (Rodó-de-Zárate, 2016, Hopkins, 2019). Intersectionality is a concept developed by Kimberlé Crenshaw (1991) to address the lack of understanding of how identities work together to shape experiences of the world. Dissatisfied with the ways (first and second wave) **feminist** politics of the time assumed all women had the same gendered experiences, Black feminist scholars (like bell hooks) argued that black women do not experience the world in the same way that white women do, as black women encounter misogyny and racism simultaneously. Such insights led to the development of intersectionality and sharpened understanding of identity as something that is made up of gender, race, class, sexuality, (dis)ability and age all at the same time, and that ultimately our experiences of the world (of identity and difference) are shaped by these aspects working together. For example, the work of Irazábal and Huerta (2016) in New York explores the lives of LGBTQ+ young people of colour and shows how their rights to the city are always being shaped by their racial, sexual and aged identities. LGBTQ young people of colour were made to feel uncomfortable in LGBTQ+ spaces that were dominated by white (and middle-class) LGBTQ+ people, which meant there were very few spaces these young people could be openly queer without fear for their own safety and well-being. Many geographers have critically interrogated queer spaces as 'inclusive' for all queer people, often arguing that many queer bodies are excluded based on gender, age, race, **ethnicity** and class (Browne, 2006, Oswin, 2008), as only certain queer bodies are deemed to 'fit in'. How different people are enabled to belong in different places is always being shaped by the multiple aspects of their identities. By thinking intersectionally, geographical scholarship has sharpened analysis of the various relationships between identities and place, and the experiences and bodies that have otherwise erased (McKittrick, 2011).

Summary

- Identities are understood as relational. That means that identities are always formed in relation to something – people, places or objects.
- Identities do not exist on their own but are always being made by different processes.
- Self/other has been an important approach to understanding identity and difference, especially when thinking about how some people are excluded from places and are subject to violence.
- Intersectionality, a key idea from black feminist scholarship has helped geographers understand how identity and difference are always produced and experienced through all aspects of our identities – race, gender, sexuality, age, ability and class.

Bodies

Not only do geographers understand identity as intersectional, but interventions have championed the importance of the body. Early work on identity in geography often didn't consider the importance of bodies, which sounds strange when you consider that we experience the world through our bodies and we change and manage our bodies to conform or resist certain parts of our identities. Feminist geographies (and later trans geographies – as I discuss later) were central to the inclusion of bodies in the conceptualisation of identity and difference. They argued that the exclusion of anything 'bodily' from the discipline is a symptom of the **masculinist**, heteronormative and colonial ideas of legitimate knowledge (Longhurst, 1995). So often, knowledge, theory and thinking are kept separate from flesh, corporeality and emotions, where rational academic research was somehow an objective 'thing' that was in no way related to our bodies – this is often called the mind/body dualism.

Geographical writing on bodies often agrees that they are critical sites for the ways identities are formed and negotiated, power relations are enacted and resisted, and knowledge is produced. Geographers would argue that bodies are themselves sites where power is negotiated. In this work, gender, sexuality, race, ethnicity, age, (dis)ability, size and class are **embodied**, which means that they do not exist independently of our bodies. This does not just mean that our bodies are the site where identities are mapped onto; rather, bodies are active in creating identity. For example, the ways that women might wear makeup may be a result of the expectations of what it means to be a woman; at the same time makeup becomes part of how women experience gender across different places. Thinking about the body has also enabled a range of research on emotions, recognising that economic, political, social and cultural processes are felt (Bondi et al., 2005).

Influential feminist geographers such as Longhurst and Johnston (2014) have long been concerned that the concept of embodiment has become accepted in mainstream geographic ideas but in very 'incorporeal' ways. They suggest that bodies have become a way to talk about differences, but the research rarely addressed the messy, fleshy, wet and hairy bits of bodies – the smell and touch of sweat, the sound and smell of shit and the folds of fat – or the emotional parts of our bodies and how we feel. For Longhurst and Johnston (2014) these messy parts of our bodies are themselves still too much of a taboo – or 'other' – for inclusion in geographical research.

There are, of course, researchers who are taking up this task. Work that explores fluids, flesh and hair is often referred to as taking 'materialist' or 'corporeal' approaches to their study. This means that geographers have started to think about the fleshy body in the way identity and difference are formed and experienced. When we say 'fleshy' or 'material', we are talking about the parts of our bodies that we can touch, feel, smell, hear and even taste. Krishnan (2021) explores the ways that young women living in hostels in Chennai, India, negotiate the regulation of their bodies to live out sexual practices across urban places. Waitt and Stanes' (2015) research in Australia explores how the sight, smell and touch of sweat mean different things across different places for men. For example, at the gym sweat comes to symbolise hard work and strength, whereas at work sweat might get in the way of embodying professional masculinity and therefore requires bodily regulation (e.g. shaving armpit hair and using deodorant). In my research with gay, bisexual and queer men in Newcastle, UK, I have explored how the sight, touch, smell, sounds and tastes of bodies and places shape how people understand sexual encounters (Bonner-Thompson, 2021). Drawing on **postcolonial** and **decolonial** geographies, Noxolo (2018) also encourages geographers to engage more deeply with embodiment through dance. She reflects on the closure of a black-run community arts centre in Birmingham, UK, during austerity, and the ways that diverse dance (and creative arts) practices and movement are important for the ways urban environments are made and mobilised (see Chapter 25 on **performativity**). Geographical contributions on bodies remind us how spaces and bodies are co-constituted – meaning that are created together. The specific social and cultural norms of places cause us to manage our bodies in certain ways (for example, not wanting to be sweaty/smelly in certain working environments, or where/how we have sex), whilst our embodied practices also shape how places and spaces are made (for example, how dance reimagines urban environments). Research on the body is therefore developing, and research on trans geographies also reminds academics of the importance of paying attention to embodied experience.

Summary

- Feminist geographers critiqued geographical research as being disembodied.
- Refocusing geographical research on bodies and embodiment meant rethinking how identity and difference might be conceptualised.
- Feminist, queer and postcolonial geographers are continuing to challenge disembodied ways of doing research, understanding the importance of flesh, materiality and movement to the experience of power and place. Such challenges are important in disrupting 'masculinist' ways of thinking about the world.

Transgender geographies

Transgender lives are receiving increasing attention at a global scale, with high-profile politicians and celebrities challenging trans rights and existence. This makes it a pivotal time for researchers to critically engage in the ways gender is produced and negotiated across different spaces and scales. Geographers who have focused on trans lives and trans geographies have tended to challenge the ways that identity and difference have been researched and represented *within* human geography. This area of work has been heavily influenced by trans studies – an interdisciplinary area of work that has challenged how feminist, queer and gender studies think about bodies and identities. One of the key critiques that trans studies have contributed is the ways that trans people are often 'used' as a way to exemplify the instability of gender binaries which can deny trans people the lived and embodied experience of gender (Nash, 2010). Trans geographies have therefore foregrounded the lived, subjective and embodied experience of trans people (Doan, 2010, Hines, 2010, Johnston, 2019). As mentioned in the previous section, this means trans research is often concerned with the material and 'fleshy' experiences of identity and difference rather than simply focusing on **social construction** (Johnston, 2019). Trans geographies, therefore, call us to challenge not only the understanding of gender but the very ways that geographers understand place, space and time (March, 2021).

Geographers have exposed how everyday spaces and places are gendered in ways that can make trans people feel out of place and excluded and how this can lead to forms of violence (Doan, 2010, Johnston, 2019, Bonner-Thompson et al., 2021). Geographers have documented such experiences with bathrooms (Bender-Baird, 2016), higher education (Bonner-Thompson et al., 2021), work (Hines, 2010) and urban spaces (Doan, 2010, Johnston, 2019). In a landmark study, Doan (2010) reflects on her own lived experiences as a trans person (what we call autoethnographic methods) to highlight the ways they experience the violence of gender binaries across public and private spaces, including car parks, public restrooms, shopping malls, the workplace and the home. This research is critical of previous understandings of gender and space that have only focused on women's access/experience as it fails to account for trans and genderqueer people. In focusing on the lived experiences of the material body, Misgav and Johnston (2014) highlight how sweat becomes a source of collective eroticism for gay men on a nightclub dance floor in Tel Aviv, yet is something to be regulated by trans women. They make an important claim that whilst, as academics, we claim gender identities are fluid, body fluids themselves might alert us to the moments when we attempt to stabilise gendered bodies. Meanwhile, Rosenberg and Oswin (2015) explore the experiences of 23 trans feminine people in prisons in the USA, who expose the intense sexual, gendered and physical violence incarcerated trans people experience. They also explore how many trans feminine people are often denied control of their bodies, often denied hormones and certain types of clothing which prevented feminine gender presentation. Bathrooms have become very politicised spaces for trans people, where debate has intensified over who should be allowed in which bathrooms, turning them into sites of fear, anxiety and surveillance (Bender-Baird, 2016). As a form of inclusion, you may have noticed that some bathrooms have become 'for all genders' (Figure 58.1).

Figure 58.1
A sign outside a toilet for everyone, a unisex or gender-neutral toilet, with handicapped access and Braille lettering saying 'gender neutral accessible'
Source: Photo credit: O'Dea/Wikimedia Commons

Summary

- Trans geographies have criticised how trans people's identities have been used to exemplify the instability of gender as it overlooks the lived and embodied experiences of trans people themselves.
- Trans scholarship has been important in reminding geographers of the importance of material bodies.
- Research in trans geographies has highlighted the ways that everyday spaces are shaped by man/woman binaries which produce experiences of violence and exclusion for trans and genderqueer people.

Body size

In a context where fatness is often conflated with bad health and slimness as healthy, fat activists have challenged essentialist ideas of body size. As geographers become increasingly interested in bodies, body size and shape have become important markers of difference. Focusing on the materiality of bodies, research on body size explores the ways bodies *actually* take up space as well as how they're represented and talked about. According to popular public opinion – or **discourse** – we live in an obesity pandemic (Monaghan et al., 2013) and we are constantly reminded through advertising, diet companies and public health campaigns that we must not be fat (see Figure 58.2). Many people who work on body size and fatness argue that being fat is not unhealthy and suggest that measures of health that are based on body size are limiting and problematic (Monaghan et al., 2013, Colls and Evans, 2014). Geographers interested in body size

Figure 58.2
Anti-obesity campaign in the UK

Source: Photo credit: Inge Flinte

and fatness have explored everyday experiences of being fat (Hopkins, 2012), for example when shopping for clothes (Colls, 2006). Colls and Evans (2014) critique the idea of obesogenic environments – a term that suggests that fatness and obesity are symptoms of a set of social, cultural, political and economic circumstances (for example, access to public spaces or affordable food) that subsequently cause bodies to be unhealthy. They suggest that it is not necessarily environments that make people fat, but that the spaces and places that people encounter construct fat bodies as 'unhealthy' or 'problematic'. For Colls and Evans (2014: 744), this would mean understanding that size does not always shape the health of bodies, but that 'what matters in terms of inequalities is how physical, social and legal barriers may prevent (fat) bodies from being well/healthy'. They are very clear that this doesn't mean if fat people can freely access different foods and public spaces they will soon become less fat, but that fat people have the right to access public spaces, just as any other bodies.

More recent work on body size and fatness has explored the relations between size and sexuality in supposed fat-inclusive/accepting spaces. McGlynn's (2022) research, for example, explores how fat gay/bisexual/queer (GBQ) men navigate 'bear spaces' – bars, pubs, clubs and social meetups used and created by large-bodied and hairy GBQ men. He highlights how spaces that are shared with other fat GBQ men are important in feeling a sense of comfort and belonging in relation to gay and queer spaces that celebrate thin and muscular bodies. However, McGlynn also discusses how fat stigma still permeates fat-inclusive spaces, as people often feel comfortable as they are not 'the fattest one in the room'. Therefore, he argues that comfort does not necessarily mean that stigma is removed from inclusive spaces but instead shapes how comfort is experienced and embodied.

Summary

- Research on body size makes important contributions to the inclusion of the fleshy body as a legitimate form of knowledge.
- Geographers are critical of dominant discourses that suggest fat bodies are unhealthy, suggesting that 'particular social, cultural, political and economic environments make *living* as a fat body problematic' (Colls and Evans, 2014: 735).

Class

The geographies of social class have changed over the years. Traditionally taking **Marxist** approaches to class, geographers were interested in the ways **capitalism** and labour markets created class structures that resulted in social inequality among working- and middle-class people (see Chapter 55). The famous geographer, David Harvey, has used Marxist perspectives to explore how global systems create and reinforce patterns of inequality. However, since the cultural turn, geographers have been exploring how class is lived, experienced and embodied, whilst understanding how the class system is a system of exploitation that relies on spatially uneven relations of power that are a product of global relations between nations and connections with local lives. **Gentrification**, for example, is a product of urban transformation that occurs when middle classes move into 'trendy' areas bringing investment, changing the cultural identity of the places and raising house prices. Such processes can create conflict between social classes but also lead to the displacement of working-class residents (Elliott-Cooper et al., 2019).

Social class can often mean different things. It might be used to refer to someone's occupation or financial wealth and it can also refer to the cultural tastes that one might have. What is important to note is that social class is also a set of social relations that shift and change on local, regional, national and global scales. Exploring how class identities are lived and experienced, McDowell's (2003) early work with young white working-class men engages in intersectional principles by exploring how unemployment shapes young working-class masculinities as they attempt to transition to adulthood. McDowell highlights the importance of education, the home and the street as places where young men try to practice masculinity in different ways when employment is difficult to access. McDowell et al. (2020) revisit these ideas almost 20 years later in deprived seaside towns, arguing that traditional ideas of masculinity (particularly men as breadwinners) intensify a feeling of failure when work is scarce, blaming themselves rather than the structural violence of economic relations and policies (the 2007/2008 financial crash and austerity policies) that have led to the lack of jobs and support (and subsequent poverty) in deprived places.

Other research has explored the ways class is embodied across time and space. Nayak and Kehily (2014) explore how marginalised young men and women, referred to as 'chavs' in the UK, embody and negotiate working-class stigma. In the UK, chav is a derogatory term used to categorise a certain type of working-class identity, one that wears tracksuits, wears chunk gold jewellery, might smoke, speak in 'rough' accents, and they might rely on the welfare state. People who fall into this category are often 'othered', constructed as lesser in society, as lazy and often blamed for the economic downfall. Nayak and Kehily (2014) highlight how such ideas are part of a politics of disgust – attempting to label certain embodied practices as disgusting. The young men and women who are labelled as such are aware of the identities society labels them with but attempt to negotiate, appropriate and/or contest them. Geographical scholarship on class continues to focus on the multifaceted ways in which class is lived, represented and negotiated in different spaces and places, and how identity constructions perpetuate inequalities and stigma (see Chapters 55 and 56).

Disabilities

Work on disability and illness in geography has undergone shifts in how disability has been understood and conceptualised. Disability was once conceptualised using the *medical model*, where disability was understood as a form of tragedy and individual bodies are unable to perform everyday practices or activities. In this sense, disabled people were to be deserving of sympathy. However, as an important political intervention in the understanding of disability, scholars turned to the social model of disability to help understand the relationship between ability and places. The *social model* of disability was a useful critique, arguing that bodies become disabled as environments, **infrastructures** and places are not built/created for different types of bodies. Therefore, it is spaces and environments that disable bodies. For example, it could be that urban environments are constructed in a way that fails to accommodate people with different mobility needs (Hall and Bates, 2019). Further research has extended this approach to explore how social relations can disabled people, for example, how work culture and policy might disable participation, which is more than the built environment. In this view, disability is perceived as a social construction, where the ways societies are organised and produced become the root causes of issues related to a person's medical condition.

Whilst this approach did – and still does – enable a reimagination of disability, some writers argue that the social model may fail to account for the felt experience of pain that illness and disability may bring (Parr and Butler, 1999, Hall, 2000, Moss and Dyck, 2002). Whilst environments may generate disabling experiences, some ill and disabled bodies continue to feel pain which is a key part of everyday experiences. It is here where appreciating bodies and embodiment is important to more fully understand how identity and difference are constructed and experienced. In such approaches, spaces and places are not thought of as already oppressive and exclusionary 'rather as contexts in which people engage and perform their embodiment and in so doing re/produce and transform both themselves and their surroundings' (Hall and Wilton, 2017: 728). Such ideas have enabled the start of a *relational approach* to disability, where disability and place are understood as co-constituted and neither pre-determined by the other. In her work with visually impaired young people in the UK, Worth (2013) highlights how what it means to be visually impaired is always changing in relation to other students, teachers, and the different spaces in schools. Her argument is not simply about the degree to which schools disable visually impaired young people; instead, she shows how young people actively make sense of their bodies and selves as they negotiate disablism, friendships and other social networks. This is not to say that disabled people do not face discrimination, but that embodied experiences are neither simply bad/good, and that they *emerge* in different ways across different socio-spatial contexts (Hall and Bates, 2019). It is also through such relational approaches that geographers are beginning to attend to able bodies, with calls to critically engage with the idea of the able body to decentre it from the self/other binary of able/disable (Hall and Wilton, 2017).

Summary

- Disability is not just something that belongs to or is part of individuals; it is part of complicated socio-spatial contexts.
- The social model of disability was important in critiquing essentialist ideas of disability and illness but has since been critiqued for disembodied understandings.
- Using relational approaches to disability geographers are now interested in researching the embodied experience of disability to understand how it is made meaningful across time and space.

Conclusion

Geographies of identity and difference are a lively area of research, which has seen significant shifts over the last few decades. Embodied and relational approaches are becoming the norm in geographical research thanks to interventions from feminist, queer, trans, fat and dis/able geographies. Such areas of work have prompted geographers to take seriously the material, corporeal and fleshy realities of the body, and have enabled an understanding of the ways identity and difference *emerge* in relation to places, people, meanings, discourses and emotions.

What is important is that in understanding identity and difference, we should think intersectionally. People's experiences are always shaped by gender, race, sexuality, class, age and dis/ability at the same time. To universalise experience by only focusing on one would fail to consider the complexity of socio-spatial experiences. You can see this in some of this work, whether it is about exploring the experiences of fat gay men, disabled young people or young white working-class men, each of these creates unique relations with the world. The challenge for geographers now is to continue disrupting the way we have come to know the world by exploring how different identities and differences are configured across the Majority (Global South) and Minority World (Global North), using the critical tools provided by feminist, queer, Marxist and postcolonial theory.

Discussion points

* Make a list of the different ways in which geographers have understood identity.
* What does it mean to call identity relational?
* Why have geographers turned to 'bodies' to understand identity?
* What are the unique contributions of embodied geographies to understanding identity and difference?
* What is the importance of researching the embodied experiences of the world?
* How might identity and difference be experienced in relation to space and place?
* How can intersectionality help us to understand identity and difference?
* How do you experience places and spaces through your body?
* How do the multiple parts of your identity shape how you experience different places?

References

Bender-Baird, K. (2016). Peeing under surveillance: bathrooms, gender policing, and hate violence. *Gender, Place & Culture* 23(7): 983–988. https://doi.org/10.1080/0966369X.2015.1073699

Bondi, L., Davidson, J., and Smith, M. (2005). *Emotional Geographies*. London and New York: Routledge.

Bonner-Thompson, C. (2021). Anticipating touch: haptic geographies of Grindr encounters in Newcastle-upon-Tyne, UK. *Transactions of the Institute of British Geographers* 46: 449–463. https://doi.org/10.1111/tran.12417

Bonner-Thompson, C., Mearns, G. W., and Hopkins, P. (2021). Transgender negotiations of precarity: contested spaces of higher education. *The Geographical Journal* 187: 227–239. https://doi.org/10.1111/geoj.12384

Browne, K. (2006). Challenging queer geographies. *Antipode* 38(5): 885–893. https://doi.org/10.1111/j.1467-8330.2006.00483.x

Colls, R. (2006). Outsize/Outside: bodily bignesses and the emotional experiences of British women shopping for clothes. *Gender, Place & Culture* 13(5): 529–545. https://doi.org/10.1080/09663690600858945

Colls, R., and Evans, B. (2014). Making space for fat bodies?: A critical account of 'the obesogenic environment'. *Progress in Human Geography* 38(6): 733–753. https://doi.org/10.1177/0309132513500373

Crenshaw, K. (1991). Mapping the margins: intersectionality, identity politics, and violence against women of color. *Stanford Law Review* 43(6): 1241–1299. JSTOR. https://doi.org/10.2307/1229039

Doan, P. L. (2010). The tyranny of gendered spaces – reflections from beyond the gender dichotomy. *Gender, Place & Culture* 17(5): 635–654. https://doi.org/10.1080/0966369X.2010.503121

Dumangane, C. (2016). Exploring the narratives of the few: British African Caribbean male graduates of elite universities in England and Wales. Doctoral dissertation, Cardiff University.

Elliott-Cooper, A., Hubbard, P., and Lees, L. (2019). Moving beyond Marcuse: Gentrification, displacement and the violence of un-homing. *Progress in Human Geography* 0309132519830511. https://doi.org/10.1177/0309132519830511

Gamsu, S., Donnelly, M., and Harris, R. (2019). The spatial dynamics of race in the transition to university: Diverse cities and White campuses in U.K. higher education. *Population, Space and Place* 25:e2222. https://doi.org/10.1002/psp.2222

Hall, E. (2000). 'Blood, brain and bones': taking the body seriously in the geography of health and impairment. *Area* 32(1): 21–29. https://doi.org/10.1111/j.1475-4762.2000.tb00111.x

Hall, E., and Bates, E. (2019). Hatescape? A relational geography of disability hate crime, exclusion and belonging in the city. *Geoforum* 101: 100–110. https://doi.org/10.1016/j.geoforum.2019.02.024

Hall, E., and Wilton, R. (2017). Towards a relational geography of disability. *Progress in Human Geography* 41(6): 727–744. https://doi.org/10.1177/0309132516659705

Hines, S. (2010). Queerly situated? Exploring negotiations of trans queer subjectivities at work and within community spaces in the UK. *Gender, Place & Culture* 17(5): 597–613. https://doi.org/10.1080/0966369X.2010.503116

Hopkins, P. (2012). Everyday politics of fat. *Antipode* 44(4): 1227–1246. https://doi.org/10.1111/j.1467-8330.2011.00962.x

Hopkins, P. (2019). Social geography I: intersectionality. *Progress in Human Geography* 43(5): 937–947. https://doi.org/10.1177/0309132517743677

Irazábal, C., and Huerta, C. (2016). Intersectionality and planning at the margins: LGBTQ youth of color in New York. *Gender, Place & Culture* 23(5): 714–732. https://doi.org/10.1080/0966369X.2015.1058755

Johnston, L. (2019). *Transforming Gender, Sex and Place: Gender Variant Geographies*. Abingdon and New York: Routledge.

Krishnan, S. (2021). Where do good girls have sex? Space, risk and respectability in Chennai. *Gender, Place & Culture* 28(7): 999–1018. https://doi.org/10.1080/0966369X.2020.1770204

Longhurst, R. (1995). VIEWPOINT The body and geography. *Gender, Place & Culture* 2(1): 97–106. https://doi.org/10.1080/09663699550022134

Longhurst, R., and Johnston, L. (2014). Bodies, gender, place and culture: 21 years on. *Gender, Place & Culture* 21(3): 267–278. https://doi.org/10.1080/0966369X.2014.897220

March, L. (2021). Queer and trans* geographies of liminality: a literature review. *Progress in Human Geography* 45(3): 455–471. https://doi.org/10.1177/0309132520913111

McDowell, L. (2003). *Redundant Masculinities?: Employment Change and White Working Class Youth*. Maiden, MA, USA; Oxford, UK; Victoria, Australia: Blackwell Publishing.

McDowell, L., Bonner-Thompson, C., and Harris, A. (2020). On the margins: young men's mundane experiences of austerity in English coastal towns. *Social & Cultural Geography* 1–18. https://doi.org/10.1080/14649365.2020.1795233

McGlynn, N. (2022). 'Fat boys make you feel thinner!': fat GBQ men's comfort and stigma in UK bear spaces. *Gender, Place & Culture* 1–20. https://doi.org/10.1080/0966369X.2022.2126827

McKittrick, K. (2011). On plantations, prisons, and a black sense of place. *Social & Cultural Geography* 12(8): 947–963. https://doi.org/10.1080/14649365.2011.624280

Misgav, C., and Johnston, L. (2014). Dirty dancing: the (non)fluid embodied geographies of a queer nightclub in Tel Aviv. *Social & Cultural Geography* 15(7): 730–746. https://doi.org/10.1080/14649365.2014.916744

Monaghan, L. F., Colls, R., and Evans, B. (2013). Obesity discourse and fat politics: research, critique and interventions. *Critical Public Health* 23(3): 249–262. https://doi.org/10.1080/09581596.2013.814312

Moss, P., and Dyck, I. (2002). *Women, Body, Illness: Space and Identity in the Everyday Lives of Women with Chronic Illness*. Lanham, Boulder, New York, and Oxford: Rowman & Littlefield.

Nash, C. J. (2010). Trans geographies, embodiment and experience. *Gender, Place & Culture* 17(5): 579–595. https://doi.org/10.1080/0966369X.2010.503112

Nayak, A. (2017). Purging the nation: race, conviviality and embodied encounters in the lives of British Bangladeshi Muslim young women. *Transactions of the Institute of British Geographers* 42(2): 289–302. https://doi.org/10.1111/tran.12168

Nayak, A., and Kehily, M. J. (2014). 'Chavs, chavettes and pramface girls': teenage mothers, marginalised young men and the management of stigma. *Journal of Youth Studies* 17(10): 1330–1345. https://doi.org/10.1080/13676261.2014.920489

Neal, S., Bennett, K., Jones, H., Cochrane, A., and Mohan, G. (2015). Multiculture and public parks: researching super-diversity and attachment in public green space. *Population, Space and Place* 21(5): 463–475. https://doi.org/10.1002/psp.1910

Noxolo, P. (2018). Flat out! Dancing the city at a time of austerity. *Environment and Planning D: Society and Space* 36(5): 797–811. https://doi.org/10.1177/0263775818782559

Oke, N., Sonn, C. C., and McConville, C. (2018). Making a place in Footscray: everyday multiculturalism, ethnic hubs and segmented geography. *Identities* 25(3): 320–338. https://doi.org/10.1080/1070289X.2016.1233880

Oswin, N. (2008). Critical geographies and the uses of sexuality: deconstructing queer space. *Progress in Human Geography* 32(1): 89–103. https://doi.org/10.1177/0309132507085213

Parr, H., and Butler, R. (eds.) (1999). *Mind and Body Space: New Geographies of Illness, Impairment and Disability*. London: Routledge.

Rodó-de-Zárate, M. (2016). Feminist and Queer Epistemologies Beyond the Academia and the Anglophone World: Political Intersectionality and Transfeminism in the Catalan Context. In *The Routledge Research Companion to Geographies of Sex and Sexualities*, eds. G. Brown and K. Browne. London and New York: Routledge, Taylor & Francis Group, 155–164.

Rosenberg, R., and Oswin, N. (2015). Trans embodiment in carceral space: hypermasculinity and the US prison industrial complex. *Gender, Place & Culture* 22(9): 1269–1286. https://doi.org/10.1080/0966369X.2014.969685

Vertovec, S. (2007). Super-diversity and its implications. *Ethnic and Racial Studies* 30(6): 1024–1054. https://doi.org/10.1080/01419870701599465

Waitt, G., and Stanes, E. (2015). Sweating bodies: men, masculinities, affect, emotion. *Geoforum* 59(0): 30–38. http://dx.doi.org/10.1016/j.geoforum.2014.12.001

Wilson, H. F. (2011). Passing propinquities in the multicultural city: the everyday encounters of bus passengering. *Environment and Planning A: Economy and Space* 43(3): 634–649. https://doi.org/10.1068/a43354

Worth, N. (2013). Making friends and fitting in: a social-relational understanding of disability at school. *Social & Cultural Geography* 14(1): 103–123. https://doi.org/10.1080/14649365.2012.735693

Online materials

- What Is Intersectionality? https://www.youtube.com/watch?v=O1islM0ytkE&t=14s A video commissioned by Peter Hopkins that explains intersectionality.
- Queer Lit podcast – https://www.spreaker.com/show/queer-lit: A podcast that hosts conversations with people in queer academia/art/media that explores ways of understanding the world and the politics of identity.

Further reading

Doan, P. L. (2010). The tyranny of gendered spaces – reflections from beyond the gender dichotomy. *Gender, Place & Culture* 17(5): 635–654. https://doi.org/10.1080/0966369X.2010.503121
A key text in trans geographies.

Hall, E., and Wilton, R. (2017). Towards a relational geography of disability. *Progress in Human Geography* 41(6): 727–744. https://doi.org/10.1177/0309132516659705
An introduction to the relational approach to disability.

Hopkins, P. (2019). Social geography I: intersectionality. *Progress in Human Geography* 43(5): 937–947. https://doi.org/10.1177/0309132517743677
A useful overview of the ways intersectionality has been engaged with in Human Geography, recognising the important work of Black feminist scholarship.

Longhurst, R., and Johnston, L. (2014). Bodies, gender, place and culture: 21 years on. *Gender, Place & Culture* 21(3): 267–278. https://doi.org/10.1080/0966369X.2014.897220
The review of the field of geography provides an understanding of how bodies are being incorporated into academic research.

Noxolo, P. (2018). Flat out! Dancing the city at a time of austerity. *Environment and Planning D: Society and Space* 36(5): 797–811. https://doi.org/10.1177/0263775818782559
A key text on the corporeality of black bodies.

The Newcastle Social Geography Collective (2021). *Social Geographies: An Introduction*. London: Rowman and Littlefield.
This edited volume draws together research in social geography exploring a wide range of issues around identity and difference. A range of identities and issues are explored.

59 Age and the geographies of childhood and youth

Peter Kraftl and Sophie Hadfield-Hill

Introduction

Ageing is something that happens to all of us in some form. Simply put, ageing describes an inescapable biological process that sees bodies grow and shrink, their capacities coming and going. In most cultures of the Minority Global North, ageing is viewed as a linear process: from birth, through childhood, into adulthood, to older age. In other contexts, there may not be such clear-cut boundaries – for instance, definitions of childhood and adulthood may be blurred or non-existent. But even if ways of perceiving and classifying age might vary, our ways of interacting with the world around us change as we age. It is therefore worth stopping and thinking about age and the ageing process. It is important to understand the implications of 'being of a certain age' (whatever that age is), to question how ageing is experienced in different geographical contexts and to analyse how social, economic and political forces shape what it means to be a 'teenager' or 'older person'. Consider the following five (of many) ways of thinking about age and ageing:

1. Age is commonly denoted by a number. That number defines a person's legal status ('child' or 'adult'). That number is used as an instrument to control where citizens of a given country may or may not go (school, work) and what they may or may not do (smoke, drink, vote, have sex). The control of children by adults has led to global calls for greater rights for people deemed 'not-yet adult' – principally through the *United Nations Convention on the Rights of the Child* (1989).
2. Age is one of several indicators of a person's identity. Youth cultures and subcultures – around music, fashion, sport or technology – are examples of this. But, do you have to be of a young age to be part of a youth subculture? (Figure 59.1)
3. Ageing is accompanied by a series of changes in the material stuff that surrounds us. From school uniforms to wedding rings, our material belongings, however meagre, represent transitions we make throughout the lifecourse.
4. In different geographical contexts, age categories bring with them assumptions about how people should act. In several contexts, children are viewed as both angels (naturally innocent) and devils (naturally evil) (Valentine, 1996). Older people tend to be viewed quite

DOI: 10.4324/9780429265853-68

Figure 59.1
Skateboarding – a youth subculture? While skateboarding is typically viewed as a 'youth' sport, many riders are adults in their 20s, 30s and 40s. Women-and-girl-only sessions now run in some managed skateparks to address the exclusive forms of masculinity that dominate skate spaces (Paechter et al., 2023)

Source: Photo credit: Hero Images Inc./Alamy Stock Photo

negatively in the UK, while in Japan they are viewed as 'cute'. These are, of course, generalisations, but they demonstrate that age is the product of **socially constructed** values as much as natural processes.

5.   In contexts where there are clearer definitions of 'child' and 'adult', groups of people of the same age are often thought about as being part of generations (Punch, 2020). During the early 2020s, there were deeply held concerns about the generational inequalities and challenges faced by young people, who were growing up with the combined impacts of climate change, COVID-19 and fears over resource insecurity and increased living costs.

Just like other aspects of identity, ageing is a fundamentally complex and contested process. Age is also a key marker of social difference and inequality, which are felt very differently in different places. This chapter explores why age has become such an important topic of debate among geographers. It begins by exploring geographers' work on childhood and youth, showing how **space** and place matter profoundly to the lives of younger people. It then outlines some of the ways geographers have studied age in different contexts.

Geographies of children and young people

We have already considered how age and ageing are the result of both biological and social processes. The experiences of children and young people during COVID-19 lockdowns around the world between 2020 and 2022 are a case in point (Kusumaningrum et al., 2022). And geography *really* mattered to their experiences. On the one hand – in general – children were least vulnerable to the COVID-19 virus itself – both in terms of being infected and of displaying symptoms. On the other hand, research from around the world has shown that the associated lockdowns – the major social and political response to the virus – disproportionately affected children and young people. We know that some children lost out on learning opportunities, that many developed mental health issues, and that unequal access to digital technologies meant that being confined at home led to very different experiences for different young people. While each of these issues speaks of social and geographical inequalities, perhaps the most obviously 'geographical' feature of the lockdowns were the limitations placed on time and activities in public spaces – with children simply unable to play outside in many places around the world (Cortés-Morales et al., 2022).

Take a look at Figure 59.2. This infographic from research in Canada shows some of the many impacts of COVID-19 and associated lockdowns on children and young people. The image indicates some of the many challenges that children and young people faced during lockdown. But, as you look at the infographic, consider two questions:

1. How many of the issues faced by children and young people were somehow spatial in nature? From feelings of isolation to schools no longer providing 'safe spaces' for children at risk of domestic violence, how were spatial boundaries, rules and experiences at the heart of these issues?
2. How was (young) age cross-cut by other social and spatial differences? In particular, it was noteworthy how COVID-19 and responses to it amplified already existing inequalities and vulnerabilities – for instance, in terms of income. These cross-cutting influences are an example of **intersectionality** – a key concept in the geographical study of age and social difference, which we look at in more detail in the next section.

The kinds of questions raised by children and young people's experiences of COVID-19 are exemplary of the broader issues that are considered by geographers of childhood and youth. Within the now-established sub-discipline of *children's geographies*, researchers have sought to ask how and why space and place matter to the lives of children and young people (Holloway and Valentine, 2004, Aitken, 2018). There are at least three important features of this work.

First, children's geographers have increasingly emphasised *diversity* in the lives of children and young people. Although, as the example of COVID-19 demonstrates, children globally are to some extent treated similarly by adults through their comparative lack of **agency** and rights, their experiences vary enormously depending on their geographical and social position. As Wells (2021) shows, different types of institutions in different settings (schools, childcare, councils) treat children differently, thereby setting the parameters for their future life chances. Moreover, the very conditions in which they live can also affect their current and future lives: we know that children – particularly from monetary-poor backgrounds – are some of the most vulnerable groups in places affected more intensely by climate change (Helldén et al., 2021). Meanwhile, scholars have become increasingly critical of the Eurocentric lineage of the term 'childhood' – both as it is applied in policy-making around the world and in geographers' own analyses of non-European childhoods. Thus, along with geographers more widely, they call for the **decolonisation** of the sub-discipline (see Chapters 1 and 71) in a way that recognises

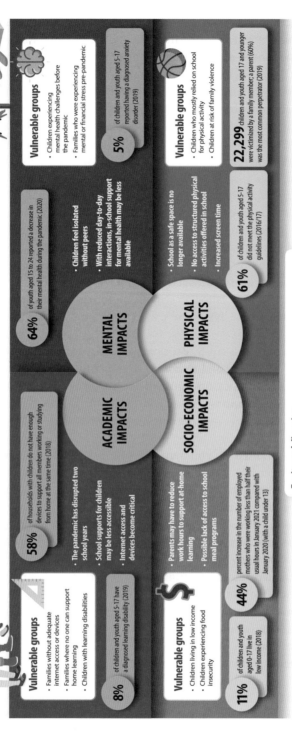

Figure 59.2
School closures and COVID-19: impacts on children

Source: Image credit: Statistics Canada

diverse understandings of generations and lifecourse (Khan, 2021) and hence of 'multiple childhoods' (Balagopalan, 2018).

Second, children's geographers have called for greater attention to the experiences of children and young people themselves – to how they have 'agency' (or a role to play) in the world. They emphasise a need to listen to their voices – both in hearing what they have to say about their lives in research and in enabling children to participate in (for instance) local decision-making processes that affect their lives (Holloway and Valentine, 2000). In other words, children should have rights; in different contexts, there may be debate about the extent to which these should be the same adults, but children have the right to be heard and taken seriously. Indeed, the many problems associated with COVID-19 (see Figure 59.2) might at least have been reduced, if not mitigated, had decision-makers taken greater time to listen to children's experiences.

At the same time, geographers have questioned what exactly is meant by 'children' and their 'agency'. Often, this means seeing children as highly individual subjects. One risk of doing this is that we downplay their relationships with others of the same generation and others more generally (see discussion of *Intergenerationality*, below). Another risk is that we ignore the ways in which children's lives are made up of all kinds of non-human stuff: of the foods and bacteria that pass through their bodies; of the toys, tools and technologies they use or wear; of the very environmental processes in which they – like the rest of us – are inescapably entangled (Kraftl, 2020). For instance, fascinating work by Taylor and Pacini-Ketchabaw (2018) shows how children interact with a range of what they call 'companion species' – from domesticated animals to 'wild' creatures, such as kangaroos. They show that these encounters may not always be cute and cuddly but may be uncomfortable and call into question (particularly) Minority North ways of viewing 'natures' – for instance, as children display a fascination with the carcasses of dead mammals.

Third, children's geographers have shown that children and young people are exposed – in both an individual and generational sense – to some of the most pressing concerns of the twenty-first century. At the same time, children may also be at the forefront of attempts to question, adapt, innovate and address those challenges. For instance, even though they may be some of the most vulnerable to climate change, children and young people have – at least in some contexts – been increasingly prominent in both activism and protest, and in everyday efforts to mitigate the effects of climate change (Skovdal and Benwell, 2021). Similarly, geographers have sought to examine the everyday practices, hopes and fears of young people growing up in financial hardship. In the UK context, for instance, several authors have explored how the UK Government's austerity policies – which reduced or removed State support for a range of welfare services – have dramatically affected the current lives and future aspirations of young people (Horton et al., 2021, and see Chapter 52 on **Neoliberalism**). Finally, among much work on children's experiences of an increasingly urbanised world, some authors have focused on the ways in which more inclusive, sustainable cities could be built in a way that meets the needs of children and where children can be active participants in planning those cities (Christensen et al., 2017). UNICEF's *Child-Friendly Cities* initiative (https://childfriendlycities.org/) provides an excellent example of how an international organisation, national governments and city authorities have worked together to try to create cities that meet the needs of children – from education to health, and from the physical environment to transport.

Summary

- Age and ageing are the result of biological and social processes, and it is important to understand age in relation to specific social constructions, identities and material cultures.
- Childhood and youth are key topics studied by geographers. Children and young people's experiences of the world and their environments may be dramatically affected by their social and geographical positioning.
- Children and young people may be vulnerable to a range of intersecting challenges – from climate change to resource insecurity. However, they may also be important voices and actors in addressing those issues.

Relational geographies of age

So far, we have concentrated primarily upon research that looks at one particular age group: children and young people. Other scholarship in human geography has looked at older age (e.g. King et al., 1998, Andrews et al., 2007, Tarrant, 2010, Stockdale, 2011). The problem, however, as Hopkins and Pain (2007) point out, is that these two age groups tend to be studied in isolation. The effect is that interactions among different age groups tend to be downplayed (Vanderbeck, 2007).

Hopkins and Pain (2007) make a powerful case for what they call more 'relational geographies of age'. They suggest that geographers could focus on three features of age and ageing that emphasise the relations between age groups:

1. Intergenerationality: how people of different age groups mix, care for, conflict or collaborate in their everyday lives.
2. Intersectionality: how other kinds of identity categories – like **ethnicity**, dis/ability, religion or socio-economic **class** – cut across age and may offer important commonalities among people of different age groups.
3. The lifecourse: how an individual does not experience 'phases' of life in isolation – one's life is a flow through childhood and adulthood, marked by complex transitional periods.

On this list, a fourth feature is important: families. This focuses explicitly on family units, how families are done and undone, and the everyday impacts of family geographies on people and place. In this section, we will look at each of these ideas in turn to outline how human geographers have developed studies of age. We finish the section by looking at a couple of broad criticisms of these approaches.

Intergenerationality

Much of the work on intergenerationality by geographers has (as we return to later) focused on family contexts; the diverse ways in which families care for each other across generations (see, for example, Holloway 1998, Hallman, 2010). Anna Tarrant, for example, focused on the roles and responsibilities of grandparents, arguing that 'the family is perhaps one of the most influential networks a child is born into, where generational identities, intersected by various axes of social difference including age and generation, influence one another' (Tarrant, 2010: 190). Tarrant argues that grandparenthood brings with it lifestyle changes – like making time and space for new relationships with their grandchildren. She focuses on the body as a space where intimate intergenerational relationships take place. Sometimes these can be as welcome as they can be awkward to come to terms with. Of course, we know that children can also be carers for other family members (see, for example, Becker's 2007 study of young carers in the UK, Australia, and USA; Day's 2017 study of young caregivers in Zambia). While the type of carework and level of responsibility varies substantially according to household structure and geographical context, Evans (2010: 1478) suggests that 'well over 4% of children in many African countries may be regularly involved in caring for parents, siblings and relatives'. Drawing on qualitative research in Tanzania, Uganda and Senegal, Evans documents young people's experiences of caregiving, bereavement and chronic illness, calling for comparative research that sharpens understanding of the 'commonalities and diversities of children's caring lives globally' (see also Evans and Becker, 2019: 231, Evans, 2012, 2014, Evans et al., 2022).

Notwithstanding the importance of the 'family' – however understood – as a core unit where intergenerational care is done, what about other kinds of intergenerational relations, in other contexts? Take, for instance, the planning and design of urban spaces. There is the *Child-friendly Cities* movement as mentioned above, where priorities are given to the ways in which city spaces, neighbourhoods, towns, communities and streets are *child-friendly* – where thought has gone into their design for smaller bodies and where children and young people have been active in the process of design and use (see, for example, Khan et al., 2023).

At the other end of the lifecourse, there is the commitment to age-friendly cities, where the priority is on designing and planning for older generations. In 2007, the World Health Organisation published an Age-friendly Cities guide which provides a framework for creating and sustaining communities that include the participation and needs of older generations, ranging from their housing needs, healthcare support, civic participation and transportation (WHO, 2007). In the UK context, this has been implemented in a network of age-friendly communities which 'make it possible for people to continue to stay living in their homes, participate in the activities that they value and contribute to their communities, for as long as possible' (Centre for Ageing Better, 2023). The network is supported by *Age UK*, a national charity that recognises that 'too many of our communities are significantly underprepared to manage the challenges and unlock the potential of our ageing population' (Age UK, 2023: n.p.). However, despite these two priorities in the planning for our cities and communities, there seem to be missed opportunities for intergenerational design and planning (Figure 59.3). For instance, how might we work towards a framework where we can create cities that support both young and old residents more equitably?

Intersectionality

The second key conceptual frame is intersectionality. It is particularly powerful because it reminds us that, for instance, it is impossible to place all children in the same category (Matthews and Limb, 1999). What it means to be a young person may vary substantially depending upon that child's **gender**, religion, ethnicity or sexuality (Konstantoni and Emejulu, 2017). Linda McDowell's (2003) work on young working-class men was a relatively early example of this work in geography. She showed how a combination of factors influenced their aspirations for future

Figure 59.3
'You're never too old to play': the UK's first 'Older People's Play Area' was opened in Blackley in 2008

Source: Photo credit: © Alamy/PA Images/Martin Rickett

employment: from the expectations of working-class families upon young males, to their senses of masculine identity that were reinforced through the places they frequented in their daily lives (including the workplace).

Peter Hopkins' work on young religious identities (Hopkins et al., 2010) and Anoop Nayak's (2017) work on young Muslim women's experiences of growing up in North East England are good starting points for seeing how geographers are using an intersectional lens to further understand youth experiences. Most recently, Kapinga et al. (2022) have written about young Muslims' religious identities in relation to places beyond the UK. Here, they argue that 'young people's identity negotiations in relation to places beyond where they are growing up can play an important role in their transition to adulthood' (2022: 2). Using map-making techniques, they explored spatially embedded religious identities and how young Muslims, as they are growing up, make sense of their Muslim identity. They also highlight an important intergenerational dimension here too, in terms of family negotiations around identity and the wider Muslim community – particularly in terms of exploring their own Muslim identity independently (i.e. freedom to make their own decisions and explore religion in their own way).

Lifecourse

A third way of studying age is to look at the lifecourse. Bailey (2009) argues that:

> … interested in patterns of order and orders of patterns in the often banal practices of everyday life, lifecourse scholarship seeks to describe the structures and sequences of events and transitions through an individual's life.

> *Bailey, 2009: 407*

Thus, it is possible to discern three features of lifecourse scholarship (after Hopkins and Pain, 2007, Bailey, 2009):

1. A focus on individual biographies: on the transitions that, for instance, mark an increase (or decrease) in a person's mobility.
2. An interest in how individuals synchronise their lives in relation to others – how, for instance, adult children and elderly parents may decide where to live upon the event that the latter reach a certain age (also Pettersson and Malmberg, 2009).
3. A critical examination of the inequalities that present themselves over the lifecourse – for instance, how health inequalities between different socio-economic status groups may start in childhood but become accentuated with age.

Geographers have also attended to lifecourses that do not conform with predominant expectations in countries of the Majority Global North (Jeffrey and McDowell, 2004). Research by Butcher and Wilton (2008) shows how young people with intellectual disabilities remain, in essence, 'stuck in transition'. While those young people may take part in educational courses designed to enable them to secure paid work, a shortage of relevant jobs often means that 'youths spend considerable time in "transitional spaces", such as the vocational training centre, sheltered workshop, and supported placements' (Butcher and Wilton, 2008: 1079). In a different context, van Blerk's (2008) research in Ethiopia looked at unconventional routes to adulthood taken by 60 children living in poverty. Those children had moved from agricultural regions of Ethiopia to the cities of Addis Ababa and Nazareth to find work. van Blerk showed how sex work provided a risky, although frequently successful, way for children to achieve the independence that is often symbolic of adulthood. Both studies show that geographers are steadily acquiring a more nuanced picture of the diversity of ways in which the lifecourse can be experienced in different geographical contexts. They also demonstrate some of the places (vocational training centres) and spatial processes (rural–urban migration) that form an inescapable part of lifecourse transitions.

In line with a recent interest in material things in human geography, research by Owen and Boyer (2022) asks us to consider the materialities of the lifecourse and the impact of childhood material objects on family life. They look at the 'material things' owned by parents and children in the UK, including teddies, instruments, clothes, books, school projects and technologies, to show how these objects define relationships over the transition of youth to adulthood and how materialities and memories are embedded in the lifecourse of parent and child.

Family geographies

The fourth lens through which we can consider the relational geographies of age is the family. To some extent, the family has already been figured out in previous sections, whether it be (i) the care narratives which circulate in understandings of intergenerational relations; (ii) the family dynamics when working through youth identities and religion; or (iii) the material objects and materialities which shape the lifecourse and family life. However, family geographies have more to offer in terms of our broader understanding of the geographies of age. Here we consider three axes of geographical work on the family: care, austerity and technology.

First, Kate Boyer's work on care, motherhood and families has been particularly influential. She and others reflect on the re-gendering of care following financial recession in the UK (Boyer et al., 2017). They highlight the shifting roles of men – including fathers and grandfathers – in the everyday responsibilities of social reproduction (also acknowledging the shifting patterns of male caring with the increased acceptance and legal protection for non-heterosexual families). They argue that these trends of male engagement in family responsibilities are 'critical for the future of work, family and new household dynamics' (2017: 67).

Second, Sarah Marie Hall's work on everyday austerity and the family holds an important place in recent work on relational geographies of age. Hall uses the family as a central lens to understand the impact and experience of austerity on everyday life and argues that 'the notion of family is deep rooted in how most governments convey messages of responsibility and distribute social benefits to citizens, and of key importance in the context of cuts to public expenditure' (Hall, 2018: 773). Wary of romanticising family relationships, Evans et al. (2019: 503) along with Hall encourage geographers to examine the awkward, turbulent, conflict-ridden relationships that may make up family life.

The third axis explores how families work and are 'done' at a distance, alongside the importance of digital technologies in supporting distant family relationships. In the context of Sweden, where it is estimated that a quarter of all children live with only one parent, with separation being the dominant factor, Stjernstrom and Stromgren (2012) highlight that parental separation gives rise to new forms of social planning, shared parenting and communication. This is just one context where families are 'doing family' in a certain way, shaped by diverse cultures of communication and mobility. In a slightly different vein, Longhurst's (2016) research with 35 mothers in Aotearoa New Zealand, explores how women use digital media to connect with their children on an everyday basis and the emotional geographies of these interactions – unlike the scholarship on doing family at a distance, the focus of this research is how families who live *together* communicate digitally. Indeed, Valentine (2006) has argued that the digital world was 'globalising intimacy' – as digital technologies shape our everyday interactions with family, both near and far, and are an important tool for intergenerational relations, identity formation and more.

These four interrelated lenses offer powerful ways to explain how identities and social spaces shape and are shaped by age. However, some geographers have offered words of caution or, rather, sought to supplement these approaches (Horton and Kraftl, 2008). A key criticism of work on intergenerationality and intersectionality is that it remains too focused upon identifiable, classifiable traits of identity – like generation, class or gender. It has been suggested that there are additional ways to understand age that cannot be captured by such neat terms. Geographers, for instance, have challenged understandings of the lifecourse as a relatively linear progression from young to old age. Instead, they have emphasised understand how life simply 'goes on' in ways that involve more complex temporalities (Philo 2003, Horton and Kraftl, 2008). If you have left home, for example, do you slip into the same old habits you had as a child when you 'go home'? On a different tack, there remain good reasons for focusing upon age categories, not least because certain age-based traits (like youthfulness) become political issues in themselves, as we see in the next section.

Summary

- Studies of intergenerational relations have helped geographers overcome the compartmentalisation of different age groups.
- The notion of intersectionality is significant because it breaks down catch-all categories like 'child' and 'elderly'.

- Research about the lifecourse helps tie together different geographical scales – from the transitions that individuals make to the expectations made upon them by family, peers or wider society.
- Research on family geographies has much to offer our understanding of intergenerational relations, care and the ways that people deal with crises (such as recession).
- Some geographers have criticised ideas of intergenerationality, intersectionality and the lifecourse, seeking to supplement these with non-linear approaches that emphasise more complex temporalities.

The politics of ageing

The previous section examined ways in which geographers can produce more balanced studies of ageing. In this section, we explore how age and ageing have become politicised. By this, we do not simply mean that ageing is now 'on the agenda' because of the kinds of issues faced by (for instance) children, as exemplified in Figure 59.2. Rather, we mean that age has become involved in politicised debates about, for instance, education, economic development and health. Many geographers have taken a critical stance on these issues, attempting to pick apart the dominant assumptions that policy makers and the media are making about age. In this section, we highlight three features of that work, focusing again on young age.

The first point relates to the use of age categories as a justification for a particular political or economic system (take **capitalism**, for instance). Several commentators have noted that childhood is far from a simple by-product of capitalism. Instead, as Sue Ruddick (2003: 327) argues, 'youth and childhood can be located at [the] literal and figurative core' of industrial capitalism. So, doing something 'for the good of children' has been used as a justification for all kinds of projects associated with capitalism. This argument can be made about policies initially aimed at children – like education for citizenship or IT skills training – but which have been central to ways in which societies define their future priorities (Hanson Thiem, 2009). Those priorities can be as diverse as social inclusion and economic competitiveness and may, actually, have very little to do with what is genuinely 'good' for today's children.

A second feature of work on the politics of ageing is its analysis of age as an 'investment'. Focusing on childhood, Cindi Katz (2008) argues that better-off families in the Majority Global North harbour deep-set fears about the future – about the economy, security or the environment. In the face of such insecurity, those families have increasingly used children as a 'safety net'. Katz (2008: 10) argues that a major strategy for doing this has been to commodify children – to view them as a spectacular 'accumulation strategy'. This could happen in a number of ways (after Katz, 2008: 10–12):

- through the 'over-elaboration' of child-rearing in self-help guides, support groups, educational toys and all manner of other paraphernalia
- in the appearance of such over-elaboration at ever-earlier stages in the lifecourse – for instance, in competition for 'prestigious' pre-school places

- through the practice of moving house to ensure that a child falls into the catchment area for a 'good' school
- in the phenomenon of the 'overscheduled' child – rushed from school, to play dates, to sport clubs, to dance classes.

Katz (2018) also argues that the flip-side of the notion of the child as accumulation strategy is the way in which some children are viewed as 'waste'. This provocative and challenging argument exposes the ways in which some children, in some places around the world, are positioned by global capitalism. These children, who are, in fact, in the majority globally, grow up in socially, economically and environmentally precarious circumstances. They suffer from a lack of social investment (for instance, in welfare support) and may in effect be invisible to most of the world, particularly in the Minority Global North. They may not be in school or paid work, or they may be called upon to work in dangerous settings: for example, on rubbish dumps or recycling sites, in textile factories, or in cobalt mines, all of which constitute the unseen labour in the clothes and digital technologies used by the wealthy. Since they are viewed as dispensable, Katz critically draws attention to their treatment by arguing that they are positioned as 'waste'.

Summary

- Age has become involved in politicised debates about education, economic development and health.
- Childhood has become a key site of accumulation and commodification in different geographical contexts.
- Some children – particularly in the Majority World – are positioned as 'waste' within global capitalism.

Conclusion

This chapter has highlighted some of the diverse approaches that geographers have taken to studying age. Age cuts across various areas of the discipline – taking in population geography, development geography, cultural geography and social geography. We have also indicated that there are healthy debates about how geographers conceptualise age. However, it should be apparent from reading this chapter that these approaches complement one another and that geographers are making important contributions to the study of age. A central contribution has been to show that age denotes far more than a person's numerical age or their stage in the lifecourse. Ageing is not simply something that happens to people. Instead, age is as much a product of government policy-making, family circumstances, economic conditions and individual feelings as it is a biological process. Thus, age is entwined with geographical processes in all kinds of ways. Children and young people experience, feel and respond to social and environmental challenges in diverse ways – from climate change to the building of cities. Moreover, we have seen that the idea of 'childhood' may be a foundational concept on which entire political-economic systems are built, including the global economy. Ultimately, geographers play an important role in questioning how societal assumptions about age are central to the organisation of social spaces.

Discussion points

- Can you think of other ways in which age 'matters' than those presented here? How are these expressed in spatial processes or particular places?
- What are the advantages and disadvantages of living in a society that emphasises 'youthfulness' but where children and young people are still very often marginalised?
- How could societies better plan for cities and communities which are age-friendly, across generations?
- Think about your current age and your own relations with different generations, how do you feel that your own body and experiences are positioned within society? What more could be done to make you feel more supported?
- In the context in which you are reading this book, can you describe how generations are viewed? What are relationships like between different generations? Are these largely positive or negative?
- Imagine that you are picking up this piece in 50 years' time: what might be some of the future challenges related to age?

References

Age UK. (2023). *Age-Friendly Communities*. Accessed from: https://www.ageuk.org.uk/our-impact/politics-and-government/age-friendly-communities/#skipToContent. Accessed 28 March 2023.

Aitken, S. C. (2018). Children's geographies: Tracing the evolution and involution of a concept. *Geographical Review* 108(1): 3–23. https://doi.org/10.1111/gere.12289

Andrews, G., Cutchin, M., Mccracken, K., Phillips, D., and Wiles, J. (2007). Geographical gerontology: the constitution of a discipline. *Social Science and Medicine* 65: 151–168.

Bailey, A. (2009). Population geography: lifecourse matters. *Progress in Human Geography* 33: 407–418.

Balagopalan, S. (2018). Childhood, Culture, History: Redeploying 'multiple childhoods'. *Reimagining Childhood Studies*, 23–39.

Becker, S. (2007). Global perspectives on children's unpaid caregiving in the family: research and policy on 'young carers' in the UK, Australia, the USA and Sub-Saharan Africa. *Global Social Policy* 7(1): 23–50.

Boyer, K., Dermott, E., James, A., and Macleavy, J. (2017). Regendering care in the aftermath of recession? *Dialogues in Human Geography* 7(1): 56–73.

Butcher, S., and Wilton, R. (2008). Stuck in transition? Exploring the spaces of employment training for youth with intellectual disability. *Geoforum* 39: 1079–1092.

Centre for Ageing Better. (2023). UK Network of Age-friendly communities. Accessed from: https://ageing-better.org.uk/uk-network-age-friendly-communities. Accessed 28 March 2023.

Christensen, P., Hadfield-Hill, S., Horton, J., and Kraftl, P. (2017). *Children Living in Sustainable Built Environments: New Urbanisms, New Citizens*. London and New York: Routledge.

Cortés-Morales, S., Holt, L., Acevedo-Rincón, J., Aitken, S., Ekman Ladru, D., Joelsson, T., Kraftl, P., Murray, L., and Tebet, G. (2022). Children living in pandemic times: a geographical, transnational and situated view. *Children's Geographies* 20(4): 381–391.

Day, C. (2017). Children and Young People as Providers of Care: Perceptions of Caregivers and Young Caregiving in Zambia. In *Children, Young People and Care*, eds. J. Horton, and M. Pyer. London: Routledge, 144–155.

Evans, R. (2010). Children's caring roles and responsibilities within the family in Africa. *Geography Compass* 4: 1477–1496.

Evans, R. (2012). Sibling caringscapes: Time–space practices of caring within youth-headed households in Tanzania and Uganda. *Geoforum* 43(4): 824–835.

Evans, R. (2014). Parental death as a vital conjuncture? Intergenerational care and responsibility following bereavement in Senegal. *Social & Cultural Geography* 15(5): 547–570. https://doi.org/10.1080/14649365.2014.908234

Evans, R., Bowlby, S., Gottzen, L., and Mccarthy, J. R. (2019). Unpacking 'family troubles', care and relationality across time and space. *Children's Geographies* 17(5): 501–513.

Evans, R., and Becker, S. (2019). Comparing Children's Care Work Across Majority and Minority Worlds. In *Global Childhoods beyond the North-South Divide*, eds. A. Twum-Danso Imoh, M. Bourdillon, and S. Meichsner. Cham: Palgrave Macmillan, 231–253. https://doi.org/10.1007/978-3-319-95543-8_12

Evans, R., Aduyai Diop, R., and Kébé, F. (2022). Familial Roles, Responsibilities and Solidarity in Diverse African Societies. In *Oxford Handbook of the Sociology of Africa*, eds. R. Sooryamoorthy, and N. E. Khalema. Oxford: Oxford University Press, 485–502. https://doi.org/10.1093/oxfordhb/9780197608494.013.30

Hall, S. M. (2018). Everyday austerity: towards relational geographies of family, friendship and intimacy. *Progress in Human Geography* 43(5): 769–789.

Hallman, B. (2010). *Family Geographies: The Spatiality of Families and Family Life*. Oxford: OUP.

Hanson Thiem, C. (2009). Thinking through education: the geographies of contemporary educational restructuring. *Progress in Human Geography* 33: 154–173.

Helldén, D., Andersson, C., Nilsson, M., Ebi, K. L., Friberg, P., and Alfvén, T. (2021). Climate change and child health: a scoping review and an expanded conceptual framework. *The Lancet Planetary Health* 5(3): e164–e175.

Holloway, S. L. (1998). Geographies of justice: preschool-childcare provision and the conceptualisation of social justice. *Environment and Planning C: Government and Policy* 15: 85–104.

Holloway, S. L., and Valentine, G. (eds.) (2004). *Children's Geographies: Playing, Living, Learning*. London and New York: Routledge.

Hopkins, P., and Pain, R. (2007). Geographies of age: thinking relationally. *Area* 39: 287–294.

Hopkins, P., Olson, E., Pain, R., and Vincett, G. (2010). Mapping intergenerationalities: the formation of youthful religiosities. *Transactions of the Institute of British Geographers* 36: 314–327.

Horton, J., and Kraftl, P. (2008). Reflections on geographies of age: a response to Hopkins and Pain. *Area* 40: 284–288.

Horton, J., Pimlott-Wilson, H., and Hall, S. (eds.). (2021). *Growing up and Getting by: International Perspectives on Childhood and Youth in Hard Times*. Bristol: Policy Press.

Jeffrey, C., and Mcdowell, L. (2004). Youth in a comparative perspective: global change, local lives. *Youth and Society* 36: 131–142.

Kapinga, L., van Hoven, B., Bock, B. B., and Hopkins, P. (2022). Young Muslims' religious identities in relation to places beyond the UK: a qualitative map-making technique in Newcastle upon Tyne *Children's Geographies*. https://doi.org/10.1080/14733285.2022.2100691

Katz, C. (2008). Cultural geographies lecture: childhood as spectacle: relays of anxiety and the reconfiguration of the child. *Cultural Geographies* 15: 5–17.

Katz, C. (2018). The angel of geography: Superman, Tiger Mother, aspiration management, and the child as waste. *Progress in Human Geography* 42(5): 723–740.

Khan, A. A. (2021). Advancing children's geographies through 'grey areas' of age and childhood. *Geography Compass* 15(8): unpaginated.

Khan, M., Nekeb, S., Smith, T., Harris, N., and McVicar, M. (2023). A Grangetown to grow up in: A children and young people's plan for Grangetown, Cardiff. https://orca.cardiff.ac.uk/id/eprint/156361/1/M%20Khan%20T%20Smith%20N%20Harris%202023%20a%20grangetown%20to%20grow%20up%20in%20report%20pub%20ver.pdf

King, R., Warnes, A., and Williams, A. (1998). International retirement migration in Europe. *International Journal of Population Geography* 4: 91–111.

Konstantoni, K., and Emejulu, A. (2017). When intersectionality met childhood studies: the dilemmas of a travelling concept. *Children's Geographies* 15(1): 6–22.

Kraftl, P. (2008). Young people, hope and childhood-hope. *Space and Culture* 11: 81–92.

Kraftl, P. (2020). *After Childhood: Re-Thinking Environment, Materiality and Media in Children's Lives.* London and New York: Routledge.

Kusumaningrum, S., Siagian, C., and Beazley, H. (2022). Children during the COVID-19 pandemic: children and young people's vulnerability and wellbeing in Indonesia. *Children's Geographies* 20(4): 437–447.

Longhurst, R. (2016). Mothering, digital media and emotional geographies in Hamilton, Aotearoa New Zealand. *Social & Cultural Geography* 17(1): 120–139.

Matthews, H., and Limb, M. (1999). Defining *an* agenda for the geography of children. *Progress in Human Geography* 23: 61–90.

Mcdowell, L. (2003). *Redundant Masculinities: Employment Change and White Working Class Youth.* Oxford: Blackwell.

Nayak, A. (2017). Purging the nation: race, conviviality and embodied encounters in the lives of British Bangladeshi Muslim young women. *Transactions of the Institute of British Geographers* 42(2): 289–302.

Owen, J., and Boyer, K. (2022). Holding on to childhood things: storage, emotion and curation of children's material biographies. *Social & Cultural Geography* 23(2): 192–209.

Paechter, C., Stoodley, L., Keenan, M., and Lawton, C. (2023). What's it like to be a girl skateboarder? *Women's Studies International Forum* 96: 102675.

Pettersson, A., and Malmberg, G. (2009). Adult children and elderly parents as mobility attractions in Sweden. *Population, Space and Place* 15: 343–357.

Philo, C. (2003). To go back up the side hill: memories, imaginations and reveries of childhood. *Children's Geographies* 1: 3–24.

Punch, S. (2020). Why have generational orderings been marginalised in the social sciences including childhood studies? *Children's Geographies* 18(2): 128–140.

Reher, D. (2004). The demographic transition revisited as a global process. *Population, Space and Place* 10: 19–41.

Ruddick, S. (2003). The politics of aging: globalization and the restructuring of youth and childhood. *Antipode* 35: 334–362.

Skovdal, M., and Benwell, M. C. (2021). Young people's everyday climate crisis activism: new terrains for research, analysis and action. *Children's Geographies* 19(3): 259–266.

Stjernstrom, O., and Stromgren, M. (2012). Geographical distance between children and absent parents in separated families. *Geografiska Annaler: Series B, Human Geography* 24(3): 239–253.

Stockdale, A. (2011). A review of demographic ageing in the UK: opportunities for rural research. *Population, Space and Place* 17: 204–221.

Tarrant, A. (2010). Constructing a social geography of grandparenthood: a new focus for intergenerationality. *Area* 42: 190–197.

Taylor, A., and Pacini-Ketchabaw, V. (2018). *The Common Worlds of Children and Animals: Relational Ethics for Entangled Lives*. Abingdon and New York: Routledge.

Valentine, G. (1996). Angels and devils: moral landscapes of childhood. *Environment and Planning D: Society and Space* 14: 581–599.

Valentine, G. (2006). Globalising intimacy: the role of information and communication technologies in maintaining and creating relationships. *Women's Studies Quarterly* 34: 365–393.

van Blerk, L. (2008). Poverty, migration and sex work: youth transitions in Ethiopia. *Area* 40: 245–253.

Vanderbeck, R. (2007). Intergenerational geographies: age relations, segregation and re-engagements. *Geography Compass* 1: 200–221.

Wells, K. (2021). *Childhood in a Global Perspective*. 3rd edition. Cambridge, UK; Medford, MA: Polity Press.

WHO. (2007). Global Age-Friendly Cities: A Guide. Accessed from: https://apps.who.int/iris/bitstream/handle/10665/43755/9789241547307_eng.pdf?sequence=1&isAllowed=y. Accessed 28 March 2023.

Online materials

- VCS Adventure Playground, 1972 – YouTube – A short clip about life as a child in 1970s Cardiff, including the building of an adventure playground. https://www.youtube.com/watch?v=teCaieAQOk4
- World Day Against Child Labour: Five must-watch documentaries | Child Rights | Al Jazeera – A series of short documentaries about child labour in USA, Bangladesh, Bolivia, Myanmar, and Haiti. https://www.aljazeera.com/program/featured-documentaries/2019/6/12/world-day-against-child-labour-five-must-watch-documentaries
- Researching Age-Friendly Cities (2015) – Full Film – YouTube – A short introduction to designing cities for older populations. https://www.youtube.com/watch?v=WXELgwHQ34o

Further reading

Children's Geographies
This journal is an excellent starting point to get a sense of the sheer diversity of children's spatial experiences – take a look through previous issues to find examples of research in this area, or use the journal homepage's search function to look for particular topics: https://www.tandfonline.com/toc/cchg20/current

Del Casino, Jr., V. (2009). *Social Geography: A Critical Introduction*. London: Wiley.
An accessible, thought-provoking introduction to social geography. Chapters 4–6 deal specifically with age categories throughout the lifecourse. The book also sets age into the wider context of other identity categories.

Hall, S. M. (2018). Everyday austerity: towards relational geographies of family, friendship and intimacy. *Progress in Human Geography* 43(5): 769–789.
A key intervention in scholarship on the family, which exemplifies the relational approach to age that many human geographers adopt.

Hopkins, P., and Pain, R. (2007). Geographies of age: thinking relationally. *Area* 39: 287–294.
The authors make a clear case for a focus on intergenerational relations, intersectionality and the lifecourse, as well as the use of participatory methods in research on age. This paper spawned a debate with Horton and Kraftl (2008), available in *Area* 40: 284–292.

Khan, A. A. (2021). Advancing children's geographies through 'grey areas' of age and childhood. *Geography Compass* 15(8): unpaginated.
A newer review piece that explores children's geographies and age by arguing that we need to look beyond neat definitions at the 'grey areas' and ambiguities associated with age in different contexts. It is also a call to decolonise previously Eurocentric research on age and childhood in geography.

Reher, D. (2004). The demographic transition revisited as a global process. *Population, Space and Place* 10: 19–41.
The demographic transition model is a classic one for population geographers. Using large-scale quantitative analyses, Reher explores how contemporary global trends in ageing intersect with other trends, such as in healthcare and economic development.

Ruddick, S. (2003). The politics of aging: globalization and the restructuring of youth and childhood. *Antipode* 35: 334–362.
An important example of a critical stance on the political uses (and abuses) of age. Ruddick explores how young age has been central to the development of capitalism and looks at cultures of youthfulness among older generations.

60 Health and wellbeing

David Conradson

Introduction

Across the world today, there are stark variations in the health of human populations. If we were to compare Sudan and Switzerland at a country level, for instance, large differences in population health indicators such as infant mortality, life expectancy, heart disease, cancer incidence and survival rates are evident. Within these countries, there are then variations in health outcomes among regions, cities and neighbourhoods. Alongside this variability in health outcomes, there are also geographical differences in the provision of healthcare. In some towns and villages in the Majority World, there are few, if any, collectively organised health services. By contrast, there are many places in the Minority World where the sick can readily access a range of medical and surgical treatments, including gene therapies and other advanced health interventions.

Geographical enquiry can assist us to understand these uneven landscapes of health outcomes and healthcare provision. For a start, geographers recognise that the places in which people live afford them certain qualities of air, food, water and housing, as well as particular opportunities for employment, social community and interaction, rest and recreation. All of these contextual factors affect people's health, and the factors in turn reflect broader political and economic systems and the philosophies that inform them (Bambra, 2018).

As an introduction to geographical perspectives on health and wellbeing, this chapter reviews three related bodies of work. The first is disease ecology, which is explored with reference to waterborne disease in Bangladesh. The second concerns health and place, and here consideration is given to greenspace, bluespace and obesogenic (obesity-generating) environments. The third body of work, critical geographies of wellbeing, includes analysis of government wellbeing initiatives as well as the examination of various settings and practices intended to foster wellbeing, therapeutic landscapes and Indigenous knowledges and frameworks.

Geographical work on health and wellbeing

In broad terms, it is possible to identify three bodies of geographical scholarship on health and wellbeing. The first of these, medical geography, came to prominence in the 1960s and had a twin focus on 'disease ecology' and the distribution of health services (Mayer, 1982, Meade and Emch, 2011, Moon, 2020). Disease ecology was concerned with identifying the biological and environmental determinants of disease incidence and its progression (May, 1958, Learmonth, 1988). Work in this field has analysed the incidence and spatial diffusion of communicable

DOI: 10.4324/9780429265853-69

diseases such as malaria, cholera, influenza, smallpox, HIV and COVID-19, and some medical geographers have used their research to inform health policy and practice. Work on health services then examines the spatial distribution of healthcare facilities such as doctor surgeries and hospitals and considers how variations in healthcare provision may influence local health outcomes (e.g. limited screening for certain forms of cancer might lead to late or no diagnosis, thus compromising a person's chance of survival) (Joseph and Phillips, 1984, Ricketts, 2010, Cloutier and Brendle-Moczuk, 2019).

A second body of work, which has become known as health geography, emerged during the 1990s as part of a critical response to medical geography (Kearns, 1993, 1995, Kearns and Moon, 2002, Moon, 2020). It was argued that geographers should give greater attention to the properties of places that support health rather than focusing primarily or exclusively on disease and illness (Kearns, 1993, 1995). There was a call to employ qualitative as well as quantitative methods and to engage more directly with social theory (Gesler and Kearns, 2002, Moon, 2020). Although this critique was not universally welcomed, the provocation to focus more directly on health and place prompted a number of new areas of enquiry, including work on neighbourhood and city-level health, as well as investigations of therapeutic landscapes, greenspace and bluespace.

In recent years, a further strand of geographical work has emerged that critically examines wellbeing, both as a phenomenon in itself and as a focus of contemporary societal, political and economic attention (Kearns and Andrews, 2010, Atkinson et al., 2012, Smith and Reid, 2018). Researchers have examined government wellbeing initiatives (e.g. Atkinson, 2021), investigated settings and practices intended to foster wellbeing (e.g. Lea, 2008, Philo et al., 2015, Smith, 2021) and developed novel frameworks for conceptualising wellbeing (e.g. Fleuret and Atkinson, 2007, Andrews and Rishworth, 2023). This scholarship has been shaped by its engagement with **feminist** thought, which has prompted attention to the body and emotions; by an interest in processual perspectives, **non-representational theory** and **vital materialism** (e.g. Andrews, 2018, 2019, 2020); and by attention to Indigenous health knowledges and practices (e.g. Wilson and Young, 2008).

There is significant ongoing research in each of these three areas of geographic work on health and wellbeing, as well as interaction and cross-fertilisation between them. To illustrate something of their nature, the following sections consider examples of geographic work on disease ecology, health and place, and wellbeing.

Contemporary disease ecology: water quality in Bangladesh

Access to clean water for drinking, washing and cooking is critical for human health. While many people in the Minority World are able to access relatively clean and drinkable water from a tap in their homes, millions in the Majority World have no such facility. Instead, they must gather water from wells or from streams and rivers, lakes and ponds. In densely populated regions or areas with limited sanitation **infrastructure**, these sources of surface water may become contaminated by human and animal waste. Those drinking from them then risk contracting diseases such as cholera, dysentery and typhoid. These diarrheal diseases are a major global health problem, with an estimated 2 billion cases annually that then lead to the death of around 1.5 million

Figure 60.1
Gathering water from a shallow tubewell in Bangladesh

Source: Photo credit: © Alamy/Piyas Biswas/SOPA Images/ZUMA Wire

children each year. Diarrheal diseases are, in fact, the leading cause of child mortality and morbidity worldwide, a situation which is all the more remarkable given that these diseases are both treatable and preventable.

One country in which diarrheal diseases have been a particular challenge is Bangladesh, as sanitation systems remain unevenly developed and surface water sources are prone to contamination by human waste. As part of ongoing efforts to mitigate this problem, around ten million shallow domestic wells – typically less than 45m in depth – have been installed across the country since the 1970s, enabling water to be drawn from underground aquifers (Figure 60.1). Over 90 per cent of Bangladeshi households now obtain their water from these shallow wells, and the use of these wells has been a significant factor in the reduction of diarrheal disease in recent decades (Escamilla et al., 2011).

In the 1990s, however, a number of these shallow wells were found to contain dangerous levels of naturally occurring arsenic (van Geen et al., 2011). The World Health Organisation (WHO) guideline limit for arsenic exposure is 10μg/l, but around a third of the Bangladeshi population were found to be drinking water that exceeded even their own national limit of 50μg/l. Exposure to arsenic at these levels is known to cause cardiovascular disease, as well as cancers of the lung, liver and bladder (Escamilla et al., 2011). So there was widespread concern that the shallow well solution to diarrheal disease had inadvertently created another major health problem, albeit one likely to emerge over longer time scales.

The community response has been to install deep wells, typically of over 150m depth, to tap into parts of the sub-surface aquifers that avoid both arsenic and faecal contamination. Around 165,000 of these wells have been installed across Bangladesh since the mid-1990s. However because deep wells are more expensive and time-consuming to install than shallow wells, relatively few individual households can afford them. Instead, these wells have typically been located in the central areas of villages, so as to maximise community access to them.

To investigate the health impact of these deep wells in Bangladesh, geographers have examined how exposure to microbial pathogens (e.g. *Escherichia coli*, rotavirus, *Shigella*) and arsenic varies with well type and depth (Emch, 1999, Escamilla et al., 2011, van Geen et al., 2011, Wu et al., 2011a, 2011b, Goel et al., 2019). One place in which this work has been conducted is Matlab, a rural area about 50 km southeast of the capital Dhaka, with over 100 villages and a total population of around 220,000. Here, researchers have investigated how water quality is affected by well type and depth and by environmental and biological processes (e.g. water percolation and flushing within the aquifer; the capacity of bacteria such as *E. coli.* to survive in sub-surface sediments; the periodic contamination of some wells by the ingress of surface water during floods). The cultural factors which influence the use of well technologies and education around sanitation practices have also been of interest.

One key study found that among households drawing their water from deep wells, levels of childhood diarrhoea were almost half those using shallow wells (Escamilla et al., 2011). This suggested that deep wells not only reduced exposure to arsenic but also to the microbial pathogens that cause diarrheal disease. As noted, deep wells are expensive, however, especially in comparison to the shallow wells that individual households had previously been able to self-fund. The ability of households and communities to resource further deep wells has thus been closely dependent upon collaboration between Bangladeshi government agencies and their international development partners.

A further challenge for Bangladeshi households over the past two decades has been the increased frequency of high-intensity rainfall events, which have emerged as part of global climate change (Wu et al., 2014). In urban areas, in particular, these high-intensity rainfall events have generated increased surface flooding, which in turn has increased the risk of surface water contamination. In some cases, the contaminated floodwaters have infiltrated unprotected shallow tubewells, increasing the exposure of households to cholera and other waterborne diseases. Studies of these phenomena represent a new wave of disease ecology research that actively considers the regional effects of global climate change. In Bangladesh, where one of these effects is increased high-intensity rainfall events, researchers have been examining the consequences of this rainfall for surface flooding and the introduction of waterborne pathogens into underground aquifers.

This research in Bangladesh exemplifies several features of contemporary disease ecology. The overall aim is to understand how environmental and social factors contribute to disease in a particular place or region. As is the case here, disease ecology studies are typically undertaken by multidisciplinary teams, drawing on field observations and measurements as well as previously collated health and environmental data. In contemporary disease ecology research, **geographic information science** (GIS) and spatial analytical techniques are also commonly employed (e.g. Faruque, 2022, Laituri et al., 2022). When developing recommendations for future action and policy, disease ecology researchers generally seek to take account of local cultural, social and political dynamics. In Matlab, for instance, there was recognition of the difficulties of digging additional deep wells in such a resource-constrained setting, even though these wells were the best available mitigation strategy at the time.

Summary

- Contemporary disease ecology considers how environmental and social factors contribute to the emergence and diffusion of disease in particular places. This research makes an important contribution to the global effort to combat and eradicate infectious diseases.
- Disease ecology research is typically undertaken in multidisciplinary teams which, among others, may include medical and health geographers, epidemiologists, public health specialists, engineers and ecologists. The data and methods employed are typically quantitative in nature, and geospatial analysis techniques may be used to explore the relationships between disease and environmental factors.

Health and place: greenspace, bluespace and obesogenic environments

In many countries, there are significant differences in health outcomes among people living in different towns, cities and neighbourhoods (Kawachi and Berkman, 2003). A proportion of these geographical variations in health outcomes reflect differences in the *composition* of local populations, including their socio-economic status, age and **ethnicity**. Place-based or *contextual* effects have also been observed, however, such that people in disadvantaged areas typically experience worse physical and mental health than those in more affluent areas, even after the influence of demographic composition has been taken into account (Diez Roux, 2001, Macintyre et al., 2002, Kawachi and Berkman, 2003, Bambra, 2018).

These contextual or place effects derive from the influence of social, built and natural environments on health. Social environments may influence health-related behaviours in a number of ways, as people may adjust their diet, levels of physical activity, smoking and drinking in relation to the behavioural norms and culture of those around them. The nature of a built environment can influence health by virtue of its impact on levels of physical activity, exposure to environmental pollutants and stress-generating or stress-attenuating effects. When these factors are considered together, it is not surprising that where one lives is correlated with the likelihood of experiencing a range of illnesses, including coronary heart disease (Ellaway and Macintyre, 2010).

Researchers are often interested to disentangle place effects on health from the influence of population or compositional characteristics. Studies have also attempted to identify the causal pathways by which a particular aspect of the social, built or natural environment is able to influence health. If a clear link can be drawn between a particular environmental factor (e.g. the presence of fast food 'restaurants'), a particular health-related behaviour (e.g. purchasing and eating high calorie, low nutrition food) and a health outcome (e.g. obesity), then this provides a stronger basis for specific health promotion interventions (e.g. changing the local planning laws, to make it more difficult for fast food restaurants to operate near residential or school areas) (Lake et al., 2010).

Figure 60.2
Urban greenspace in Barcelona

Source: Photo credit: Eric Fisher/Wikimedia Creative Commons

One feature of cities and neighbourhoods that has attracted attention from health researchers in recent years is the presence of 'greenspace', in the sense of publicly accessible parks and other vegetated areas (Bell et al., 2014, Foley, 2018) (Figure 60.2). Groenwegen et al. (2006) evocatively refer to greenspaces as 'vitamin G', noting studies which link access and proximity to greenspace with better cardiovascular and mental health, and with opportunities for social contact (Maas et al., 2008, Maas et al., 2009). Early research in this area suggested that simply being able to view greenspace, irrespective of whether or not one was physically present within it, could foster mental relaxation and relieve stress (Ulrich, 1984). An independent and positive health effect of access to greenspace has been observed in several places (Sugiyama et al., 2008), although the strength of this effect varies socially and geographically (Maas et al., 2006).

In a densely populated country such as the Netherlands, the positive relationship between greenspace and health is strongest for youth, the elderly and those of lower socio-economic status (Maas et al., 2006). These groups may be more inclined to use greenspace, or perhaps they have the greatest potential to benefit from using it. In any case, such a finding accords with Macintyre et al.'s (2002) observation that place effects on health are often strongest for particular social groups rather than being similar for all members of a population. In New Zealand, where residential densities are typically much lower than in the Netherlands, the positive health effect of urban greenspace is less clear (Richardson et al., 2010). This may be because urban greenspace presents less of a contrast to the typical residential environment in New Zealand, as many homes come with surrounding land and gardens, and the cities are relatively 'green' in international terms.

Building upon this work on greenspace, a number of health geographers in recent years have turned their attention to bluespace (Foley and Kistemann, 2015). Foley (2018: 251) writes that bluespace 'broadly refers to a range of natural and artificial spaces associated with water, including lakes, rivers, seas, reservoirs and other pooled waters'. Some people experience these aquatic environments as relaxing, perhaps as a result of immersion in them through activities such as swimming and boating, and as enabling both physical health and mental wellbeing. The research on greenspace and bluespace has implications for urban planning, as it suggests that cities might usefully be designed or (re)developed so as to enable increased human interaction with both green and blue environments, thereby promoting health and wellbeing (Foley, 2018, Kent and Thompson, 2019).

As a less positive form of place effect, health geographers have also identified certain features of cities and neighbourhoods that can contribute to obesity (Pearce and Witten, 2010). Although genetic factors and diet play a role in obesity, the characteristics of some environments render them potentially obesogenic or obesity-generating (Lake et al., 2010). The low density of many North American, Australian and New Zealand cities has been identified as problematic in this regard, for instance, as it encourages the use of private cars rather than more active forms of transport such as walking and cycling. To address this problem, urban planners in many cities are attempting to encourage increased active transport, in part by introducing infrastructure such as dedicated bike lanes (Figure 60.3). These interventions in the built environment may sometimes

Figure 60.3
A bike lane in Boston, United States

Source: Photo credit: Adam Coppola

be accompanied by public health measures that seek to reduce the consumption of high energy, highly processed foods.

Summary

- Across the world, there are significant variations in population health and life expectancy between places. Some of these variations reflect the demographic composition of the local populations, but the physical, social and built characteristics of places are also important influences on health.
- Greenspace and bluespace have been shown to promote health, though their significance appears to vary between places and for different social groups. Greenspace is thought to promote health because it has the potential to facilitate physical activity, enable social interaction and connectedness, reduce stress and increase mental relaxation.
- Work on obesogenic environments has highlighted the potentially negative health impacts of low-density cities and sedentary forms of work, both of which tend to reduce physical activity levels. In response, there are efforts in many cities to encourage more active forms of urban mobility, such as walking and cycling, by developing new transport infrastructures.

Wellbeing: government initiatives, settings and practices, Indigenous knowledges

A third and more recent body of geographical scholarship engages with the academic and political rise of wellbeing. Following the WHO's (1948) definition, wellbeing is broadly understood in this work as not simply the absence of disease but rather as the presence of physical, mental and social health. Although Anglophone geographical engagement with wellbeing extends back to work in the 1970s on **territorial** social indicators (Conradson, 2016), this more recent engagement has some specific features. Firstly, it has critically examined the attention that the governments of several Western countries – including the UK, France, Canada and New Zealand – have given to wellbeing as a public policy focus. In emphasising the importance of individual responsibility and self-initiative, some government framings of wellbeing have been similar to **neoliberal** formulations of the self-actualising subject, in ways that underplay the importance of social support and collective resources in facilitating wellbeing (Atkinson, 2017, 2021). Secondly, geographers have examined a number of settings and practices that seek to foster wellbeing, with research projects that span contemporary activities such as yoga (e.g. Hoyez, 2007, Philo et al., 2015, Eagar and Kearns, 2022), mindfulness (e.g. Whitehead et al., 2016) and walking (e.g. Doughty, 2013). Many of these studies pay attention to **embodiment**, are informed by **feminist** thought and vital materialism, and investigate the subjective lived experience of particular wellbeing practices. There has also been some engagement with the field of medical humanities (Alan, 2019), drawing upon its interest in the lived experience of health and illness (e.g. de Leeuw et al., 2018). Finally, geographers have given attention to the spatial variability of wellbeing within and between places. This work has brought a distinctive spatial lens to the multidisciplinary field of wellbeing research (Searle et al., 2021).

When Gesler (1992) first developed the notion of therapeutic landscape, he was investigating places with longstanding reputations for healing and health enhancement. These sites included the city of Bath in England, with its natural hot springs, and Epidaurus in Greece, the site of a revered healing temple in the classical world. Gesler examined how the environmental, social and symbolic dimensions of such places converged to facilitate subjective wellbeing for a proportion of the people who visited them. Since Gesler's initial work, a number of geographers have employed and developed the notion of therapeutic landscapes. Their research has examined mountain and forest environments, coastal and lake areas and sites of spiritual pilgrimage and retreat (Williams, 2007).

Although early scholarship on therapeutic landscapes tended to focus primarily on exceptional places, contemporary work now encompasses everyday settings that foster wellbeing (Finlay, 2018). This has included domestic gardens, urban parks, campsites, the beach and people's homes. The material, virtual and imagined dimensions of these environments have been considered. In contrast to the quantitative methods and statistical analysis employed in medical and some health geography, therapeutic landscape researchers have typically used qualitative methods to explore how these settings are able to foster subjective wellbeing (Williams, 2009, Bell et al., 2018). With the increasing prevalence of GPS-enabled devices such as smartphones and sports watches, however, there are now new possibilities for tracking the physiological effects of spending time in these environments and landscapes (Bell et al., 2015).

When examining how particular settings and practices seek to facilitate wellbeing, researchers have sometimes encountered worldviews that lie outside the norms of Western biomedicine. In the west, complementary and alternative medicine is significant in this regard (Andrews et al., 2004). As exemplified by yoga and acupuncture, such health practices typically work with an integrated conception of *bodymind*. In contrast to mainstream Western medicine, they may also posit the existence of forms of energy, seen and unseen, that affect human health but which are not apprehensible through contemporary Western scientific tests and measurement devices. The origins of illness may then be understood in terms that differ from the standard biomedical accounts of toxins, viruses, bacteria and inflammatory processes. Instead, phenomena as diverse as family disagreements, energy meridians, notions of 'curses' and the activity of unseen beings may be brought into consideration.

A number of geographers are now engaging with Indigenous health knowledge and practices, whether in settler colonial states such as Australia, Canada, the United States and New Zealand (e.g. Panelli and Tipa, 2007, Wilson and Young, 2008, Gall et al., 2021), or in countries in the Majority World, such as Ghana (e.g. Hausermann, 2021). In Aotearoa New Zealand, Te Whare Tapa Whā is one well-known Indigenous model of wellbeing (Durie, 1994). Developed by the prominent Māori psychiatrist and research academic Sir Mason Durie, the model emphasises the multidimensional nature of wellbeing. Represented visually as a four-walled house, the model stresses the importance of the physical, mental, social and spiritual dimensions of life, all of which are considered necessary components for the emergence of individual and collective wellbeing (Figure 60.4).

In Te Whare Tapa Whā, the importance of a person's connection to place is marked by reference to *whenua* (land), the label for which is placed in a foundational position beneath the

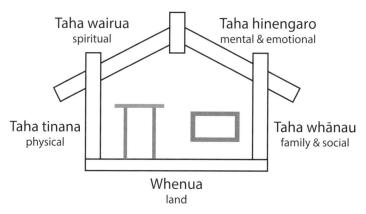

Figure 60.4
Te Whare Tapa Whā

Source: Image credit: Nick Brennan adapted from Sir Mason Durie

house. For Māori and many other Indigenous peoples, connection to land has been severely disrupted by **colonisation**. In Māori models of wellbeing, strengthening the connection that a local tribe has to land and place is thus typically a key consideration and aspiration (Panelli and Tipa, 2007). Land can be a critical source of food, water and other material resources, for both current and future generations. It is also an important site for belonging and spiritual wellbeing (Yates, 2021, Yates et al., 2023).

Summary

- Contemporary geographical work on wellbeing includes critical analyses of government wellbeing initiatives; investigations of settings and practices intended to foster wellbeing; the development of the therapeutic landscape framework; and examinations of the spatial variability of wellbeing within and between places.
- The notion of therapeutic landscapes, which emerged during the early 1990s, has become an important research focus in geographical work on health and wellbeing. A number of studies have employed Gesler's conceptual framework to examine the physical, social and symbolic dimensions of places which some people experience as health enhancing. Recent work on therapeutic landscapes has extended beyond exceptional places to consider everyday settings that foster wellbeing.
- In contrast to biomedical approaches, complementary and alternative medicine practices typically emphasise the integrated nature of the *bodymind*. They may also work from a worldview that acknowledges and perhaps seeks to influence the activities of unseen beings and energies as they relate to human health.
- Indigenous models of wellbeing, such as Te Whare Tapa Whā in Aotearoa New Zealand, typically have a multidimensional conception of the factors that determine health and wellbeing (e.g. physical, mental/psychological, social and spiritual).

Conclusion

For several decades now, geographers have investigated different aspects of health and wellbeing. The earliest expression of this work, medical geography, had a twin focus on disease ecology and health services. In the 1990s, a critical assessment of medical geography's attention to illness led to the development of health geography, which was distinguished by a concern for health and place, openness to qualitative methods and a stronger engagement with social theory. A third and more recent area of geographic enquiry is the critical examination of wellbeing. This research includes the analysis of government wellbeing initiatives, settings and practices intended to foster wellbeing, therapeutic landscapes and Indigenous models of health and wellbeing.

Each of these three bodies of research is subject to ongoing development and evolution. The work within them spans a variety of places in the Majority and Minority Worlds, employs a range of quantitative and qualitative methods, and draws upon analytical tools and techniques from geospatial science as relevant. Understanding how health and place are intertwined remains a crucial task for geographers, and there is a range of important research yet to be undertaken. Which topics catch your attention? Which seem most ethically pressing to you? What would you like to investigate?

Discussion points

- Consider some of the different settings in your everyday life: your home, neighbourhood, places of study and (perhaps) work and where you relax. How might these settings affect your health? Over what kinds of time scales might their influence on your health become apparent?
- Research on greenspace, bluespace and obesogenic environments suggests that planners and policy makers should intervene in particular ways to foster healthier cities. What kinds of interventions might help in this regard? Who should pay for them? What factors might inhibit the development of healthier cities where you live?
- What places, if any, do you experience as enhancing your wellbeing? Can you identify what, in particular, about them has this effect on you?
- What might healthcare systems in Western countries learn from Indigenous models of health and wellbeing? How might some of these Indigenous models be better integrated into dominant healthcare systems?
- What are some of the strengths and limitations of quantitative and qualitative methods when examining the dynamic relationship among health, places and the environment? How might these methods be combined in a productive fashion?

References

Alan, B. (ed.) (2019). *Routledge Handbook of the Medical Humanities*. Abingdon and New York: Routledge.

Andrews, G. J. (2018). *Non-Representational Theory & Health: The Health in Life in Space-Time Revealing*. London: Routledge. https://doi.org/10.4324/9781315598468

Andrews, G. J. (2019). Health geographies II: the posthuman turn. *Progress in Human Geography* 43(6): 1109–1119. https://doi.org/10.1177/0309132518805812

Andrews, G. J. (2020). Health geographies III: more-than-representational pushes and expressions. *Progress in Human Geography* 44(5): 991–1003. https://doi.org/10.1177/0309132519888690

Andrews, G. J., and Rishworth, A. (2023). New theoretical terrains in geographies of wellbeing: key questions of the posthumanist turn. *Wellbeing, Space and Society* 4: 100130.

Andrews, G. J., Wiles, J., and Miller, K. L. (2004). The geography of complementary medicine: perspectives and prospects. *Complementary Therapies in Nursing and Midwifery* 10(3): 175–185.

Andrews, G. J., Crooks, V. A., Pearce, J. R., and Messina, J. P. (eds.) (2021). *COVID-19 and Similar Futures: Pandemic Geographies*. Cham, Switzerland: Springer.

Atkinson, S. (2017). Health and Wellbeing. In *International Encyclopedia of Geography: People, the Earth, Environment and Technology*, eds. D. Richardson, N. Castree, M. F. Goodchild, A. Kobayashi, W. Liu, and R. A. Marston. https://doi.org/10.1002/9781118786352.wbieg0770

Atkinson, S. (2021). The toxic effects of subjective wellbeing and potential tonics. *Social Science & Medicine* 288: 113098. https://doi.org/10.1016/j.socscimed.2020.113098

Atkinson, S., Fuller, S., and Painter, J. (eds.) (2012). *Well-Being and Place*. Aldershot: Ashgate.

Bambra, C. (2018). Placing Health Inequalities: Where You Live Can Kill You. In *Routledge Handbook of Health Geography*, eds. V. A. Crooks, G. J. Andrews, and J. Pearce. London: Routledge, 28–36.

Barnett, R., and Barnett, P. (2009). Health Systems and Health Services. In *International Encyclopedia of Human Geography*, eds. R. Kitchin and N. Thrift. Oxford: Elsevier, 58–70.

Bell, S. L., Foley, R., Houghton, F., Maddrell, A., and Williams, A. M. (2018). From therapeutic landscapes to healthy spaces, places and practices: a scoping review. *Social Science & Medicine* 196: 123–130.

Bell, S., Phoenix, C., Lovell, R., and Wheeler, B. (2014). Green space, health and wellbeing: making space for individual agency. *Health & Place* 30: 287–292.

Bell, S., Phoenix, C., Lovell, R., and Wheeler, B. (2015). Using GPS and geo-narratives: a methodological approach for understanding and situating everyday green space encounters. *Area* 47(1): 88–96.

Cloutier, D., and Brendle-Moczuk, D. (2019). Health Services and Service Restructuring. In *International Encyclopedia of Human Geography*, ed. A. Kobayashi (2nd edn.). Oxford: Elsevier, 335–345. https://doi.org/10.1016/B978-0-08-102295-5.10390-7

Conradson, D. (2016). Wellbeing: Reflections on Geographical Engagements. In *Wellbeing and place*, ed. S. Atkinson. London: Routledge, 15–34.

de Leeuw, S., Donovan, C., Schafenacker, N., Kearns, R., Neuwelt, P., Squier, S. M., and Anderson, J. (2018). Geographies of medical and health humanities: a cross-disciplinary conversation. *GeoHumanities* 4(2): 285–334.

Diez Roux, A. V. (2001). Investigating neighbourhood and area effects on health. *American Journal of Public Health* 91(11): 1783–1789.

Doughty, K. (2013). Walking together: the embodied and mobile production of a therapeutic landscape. *Health & Place* 24: 140–146.

Durie, M. (1994). *Whaiora—Māori Health Development*. Auckland: Oxford University Press.

Eagar, E., and Kearns, R. (2022). Contemplative practices: the body as therapeutic site linking health and place. *Health & Place* 76: 102826.

Ellaway, A., and Macintyre, S. (2010). Neighbourhoods and Health. In *A Companion to Health and Medical Geography*, eds. T. Brown, S. Mclafferty, and G. Moon. Oxford: Wiley-Blackwell, 399–417.

Emch, M. (1999). Diarrheal disease risk in Matlab, Bangladesh. *Social Science & Medicine* 49(4): 519–530. https://doi.org/10.1016/S0277-9536(99)00146-X

Escamilla, V., Wagner, B., Yunus, M., Streatfield, P. K., van Geen, A., and Emch, M. (2011). Effect of deep tube well use on childhood diarrhoea in Bangladesh. *Bulletin of the World Health Organization* 89(7): 521–527.

Faruque, F. S. (2022). *Geospatial Technology for Human Well-Being and Health.* Springer. https://doi.org/10.1007/978-3-030-71377-5

Finlay, J. (2018). Therapeutic Landscapes: From Exceptional Sites of Healing to Everyday Assemblages of Well-Being. In *Routledge Handbook of Health Geography*, eds. V. A. Crooks, G. J. Andrews, and J. Pearce. London: Routledge, 116–123.

Fleuret, S., and Atkinson, S. (2007). Wellbeing, health and geography: a critical review and research agenda. *New Zealand Geographer* 63(2): 106–118.

Foley, R. (2018). Palettes of Place: Green/Blue Spaces and Health. In *Routledge Handbook of Health Geography.* eds. V. A. Crooks, G. J. Andrews, and J. Pearce. London: Routledge, 251–258.

Foley, R., and Kistemann, T. (2015). Blue space geographies: enabling health in place. *Health & Place* 35: 157–165.

Gall, A., Anderson, K., Howard, K., Diaz, A., King, A., Willing, E., and Garvey, G. (2021). Wellbeing of Indigenous peoples in Canada, Aotearoa (New Zealand) and the United States: a systematic review. *International Journal of Environmental Research and Public Health* 18(11): 5832.

Gesler, W. M. (1992). Therapeutic landscapes: medical issues in light of the new cultural geography. *Social Science & Medicine* 34: 735–746.

Gesler, W. M., and Kearns, R. A. (2002). *Culture/Place/Health.* London: Routledge.

Goel, V., Islam, M. S., Yunus, M., Ali, M. T., Khan, A. F., Alam, N., Faruque, A. S. G., Bell, G., Sobsey, M., and Emch, M. (2019). Deep tubewell microbial water quality and access in arsenic mitigation programs in rural Bangladesh. *The Science of the Total Environment* 659: 1577–1584. https://doi.org/10.1016/j.scitotenv.2018.12.341

Groenewegen, P., van den Berg, A., de Vries, S., and Veheij, R. (2006). Vitamin G: effects of green space on health, well-being, and social safety. *BMC Public Health* 6(149): 1–9.

Hausermann, H. (2021). Spirit hospitals and 'concern with herbs': a political ecology of healing and being-in-common in Ghana. *Environment and Planning E: Nature and Space* 4(4): 1313–1329. https://doi.org/10.1177/2514848619893915

Hoyez, A. C. (2007). The 'world of yoga': the production and reproduction of therapeutic landscapes. *Social Science & Medicine* 65(1): 112–124.

Joseph, A. E., and Phillips, D. R. (1984). *Accessibility and Utilization: Geographical Perspectives on Health Care Delivery.* New York: Harper & Row.

Kawachi, I., and Berkman, L. (2003). *Neighbourhoods and Health.* Oxford: Oxford University Press.

Kearns, R. A. (1993). Place and health: towards a reformed medical geography. *The Professional Geographer* 45(2): 139–147.

Kearns, R. A. (1995). Medical geography: making space for difference. *Progress in Human Geography* 19(2): 251–259.

Kearns, R., and Andrews, G. (2010). Geographies of Well-Being. In *The Sage Handbook of Social Geographies*, eds. S. J. Smith, R. Pain, S. A. Marston, and J. P. Jones. London: Sage, 309–328.

Kearns, R. A., and Moon, G. (2002). From medical to health geography: novelty, place and theory after a decade of change. *Progress in Human Geography* 26(5): 605–625.

Kent, J., and Thompson, S. (2019). *Planning Australia's Healthy Built Environments.* New York: Routledge.

Lauturi, M., Richardson, R. B., and Kim, J. (eds.) (2022). *The Geographies of COVID-19: Geospatial Stories of a Global Pandemic.* Springer. https://doi.org/10.1007/978-3-031-11775-6

Lake, A., Townshend, T. G., and Alvanides, S. (eds.) (2010). *Obesogenic Environments: Complexities, Perceptions and Objective Measures.* Oxford: Wiley-Blackwell.

Lea, J. (2008). Retreating to nature: rethinking 'therapeutic landscapes'. *Area* 40(1): 90–98.

Learmonth, A. (1988). *Disease Ecology: An Introduction.* Oxford: Wiley-Blackwell.

Maas, J., van Dillern, S., Verheij, R., and Groenewegen, P. (2009). Social contacts as a possible mechanism behind the relationship between green space and health. *Health and Place* 15(2): 586–595.

Maas, J., Verheij, R., Groenewegen, P., de Vries, S., and Spreeuwenberg, P. (2006). Green space, urbanity and health: how strong is the relation? *Journal of Epidemiology and Community Health* 60(7): 587–592.

Maas, J., Verheij, R., Spreeuwenberg, P., and Groenewegen, P. (2008). Physical activity as a possible mechanism behind the relationship between green space and health: a multi-level analysis. *BMC Public Health* 8(1): 206.

Macintyre, S., Ellaway, A., and Cummins, S. (2002). Place effects on health: how can we conceptualise, operationalise and measure them? *Social Science and Medicine* 55(1): 125–139.

May, J. M. (1958). *The Ecology of Human Disease*. New York: MD Publications.

Mayer, J. D. (1982). Relations between two traditions of medical geography: health systems planning and geographical epidemiology. *Progress in Human Geography* 6: 216–230.

Moon, G. (2020). Health Geography. In *International Encyclopedia of Human Geography*, ed. A. Kobayashi (2nd edn.). Oxford: Elsevier, 315–321. https://doi.org/10.1016/B978-0-08-102295-5.10388-9

Panelli, R., and Tipa, G. (2007). Placing well-being: a Māori case study of cultural and environmental specificity. *EcoHealth* 4: 445–460.

Pearce, J., and Witten, K. (eds.) (2010). *Geographies of Obesity: Environmental Understandings of the Obesity Epidemic*. Aldershot: Ashgate.

Philo, C., Cadman, L., and Lea, J. (2015). New energy geographies: a case study of yoga, meditation and healthfulness. *Journal of Medical Humanities* 36: 35–46.

Richardson, E., Pearce, J., Mitchell, R., Day, P., and Kingham, S. (2010). The association between green space and cause-specific mortality in urban New Zealand: an ecological analysis of green space utility. *BioMed Central Public Health* 10(1): 240, 1–14.

Ricketts, T. C. (2010). Accessing Health Care. In *A Companion to Health and Medical Geography*, eds. T. Brown, S. Mclafferty, and G. Moon. Oxford: Wiley-Blackwell, 521–539.

Searle, B. A., Pykett, J., and Alfaro-Simmonds, M. J. (eds.) (2021). *A Modern Guide to Wellbeing Research*. Cheltenham, UK; Northampton, MA: Edward Elgar Publishing.

Smith, T. S. (2021). Therapeutic taskscapes and craft geography: cultivating well-being and atmospheres of recovery in the workshop. *Social & Cultural Geography* 22(2): 151–169.

Smith, T. S., and Reid, L. (2018). Which 'being' in wellbeing? Ontology, wellness and the geographies of happiness. *Progress in Human Geography* 42(6): 807–829.

Sugiyama, T., Leslie, E., Giles-Corti, B., and Owen, N. (2008). Associations of neighbourhood greenness with physical and mental health: do walking, social coherence and local social interaction explain the relationships? *Journal of Epidemiology and Community Health* 62(5): e9.

Ulrich, R. S. (1984). View through a window may influence recovery from surgery. *Science* 224(4647): 420–421.

van Geen, A., Ahmed, K., Akita, Y., Alam, M., Culligan, P., Emch, M., Escamilla, V., Feighery, J., Ferguson, A., Knappett, P., Layton, A., Mailloux, B., Mckay, L., Mey, J., Serre, M., Streatfield, P., Wu, J., and Yunus, M. (2011). Fecal contamination of shallow tubewells in Bangladesh inversely related to arsenic. *Environment, Science and Technology* 45: 1199–1205.

Whitehead, M., Lilley, R., Howell, R., Jones, R., and Pykett, J. (2016). (Re)inhabiting awareness: geography and mindfulness. *Social & Cultural Geography* 17(4): 553–573.

WHO. (1946[2006]). Constitution of the World Health Organization. In: *World Health Organization: Basic documents*. *45th ed*. Geneva: World Health Organization. https://www.who.int/publications/m/item/constitution-of-the-world-health-organization

Williams, A. (ed.) (2007). *Therapeutic Landscapes*. Aldershot: Ashgate.

Williams, A. (2009). Therapeutic Landscapes as Health Promoting Places. In *A Companion to Health and Medical Geography*, eds. T. Brown, S. McLafferty, and G. Moon. Wiley Chichester and Oxford, UK; Malden, MA: University Press of America, 207–223.

Wilson, K., and Young, T. (2008). An overview of Aboriginal health research in the social sciences: current trends and future directions. *International Journal of Circumpolar Health* 67(2–3): 179–189.

Wu, J., van Geen, A., Ahmed, K. M., Akita, Y., Alam, J., Culligan, P. J., Escamilla, V., Feighery, J., Ferguson, A. S., Knappett, P., Mailloux, B. J., Mckay, L., Serre, M., Streatfield, P. K., Yunus, M., and Emch, M. (2011a). Increase in diarrheal disease associated with arsenic mitigation in Bangladesh. *PLoS One* 6(12): e29593.

Wu, J., Yunus, M., Streatfield, P. K., van Geen, A., Escamilla, V., Akita, J., Serre, M., and Emch, M. (2011b). Impact of tubewell access and depth on childhood diarrhea in Matlab, Bangladesh. *Environmental Health* 10: 109.

Wu, J., Yunus, M., Streatfield, P. K., and Emch, M. (2014). Association of climate variability and childhood diarrhoeal disease in rural Bangladesh, 2000–2006. *Epidemiology and Infection* 142(9): 1859–1868. https://doi.org/10.1017/S095026881300277X

Yates, A. M. (2021). Transforming geographies: performing Indigenous-Māori ontologies and ethics of more-than-human care in an era of ecological emergency. *New Zealand Geographer* 77(2): 101–113.

Yates, A., Dombroski, K., and Dionisio, R. (2023). Dialogues for wellbeing in an ecological emergency: wellbeing-led governance frameworks and transformative indigenous tools. *Dialogues in Human Geography* 13(2): 268–287. https://doi.org/10.1177/20438206221102957

Online materials

- The Changing Geography of Ill Health – YouTube. A lecture by Prof Chris Whitty that examines the shifting geography of ill health in the UK and globally, and its implications. https://www.youtube.com/watch?v=XmVjXzJcTE4
- WHO: Making cities healthier – improving health for all. An international focus on many of the challenges urban residents face with regard to air quality, active transport, greenspaces, healthy foods and access to healthcare services. https://www.youtube.com/watch?v=cmSLlKLHjVo
- Building Healthy Cities: Healthy Urban Planning in Asia. A short video on how three Asian Smart Cities are working to create healthy urban environments. https://www.youtube.com/watch?v=8Y-jR038Zig
- Indigenous Knowledge to Close Gaps in Indigenous Health | Marcia Anderson-DeCoteau | TEDxUManitoba – YouTube. Dr. Anderson DeCoteau is a Cree-Saulteaux physician who challenges the coloniality of healthcare systems. This short video provides an accessible introduction to Indigenous understandings of health and gives particular attention to equity, access and institutional racism in healthcare. https://www.youtube.com/watch?v=IpKjtujtEYI

Further reading

Bell, S. L., Foley, R., Houghton, F., Maddrell, A., and Williams, A. M. (2018). From therapeutic landscapes to healthy spaces, places and practices: a scoping review. *Social Science & Medicine* 196: 123–130.

An overview of the progression from geographic work on therapeutic landscapes to a broader interest in healthy spaces, places and practices.

Brown, T., McLafferty, S., and Moon, G. (eds.) (2010). *A Companion to Health and Medical Geography*. Malden, MA, Oxford and Chichester, UK: Wiley-Blackwell. https://doi.org/10.1002/9781444314762

A comprehensive overview of contemporary health and medical geography, with chapters on a range of topics written by leading researchers in the field.

Cliff, A. D., Haggett, P., and Smallman-Raynor, M. (2004). *World Atlas of Epidemic Diseases*. London: Arnold.
A wide-ranging cartographic exploration of the major epidemic diseases which have impacted human life in the past and present. The volume predates the COVID-19 pandemic, but can be read alongside work on that (e.g. Andrews et al., 2021).

Crooks, V. A., Andrews, G. J., and Pearce, J. (2018). *Routledge Handbook of Health Geography*. London: Routledge. https://doi.org/10.4324/9781315104584
An overview of key strands within the wide ranging scholarship of health geography, with accessible contributions from both emerging and established scholars.

Foley, R., Kearns, R., Kistemann, T., and Wheeler, B. (2019). *Blue Space, Health and Wellbeing. Hydrophilia Unbounded*. London: Routledge. https://doi.org/10.4324/9780815359159.
A valuable introduction to geographical thought and work on bluespace.

Gatrell, A. C., and Elliott, S. J. (2015). *Geographies of Health: An Introduction* (3rd edn.). Chichester, UK; Malden, MA: Wiley Blackwell.
An upper level undergraduate textbook on the geographies of health, with an emphasis on health inequalities, health services and environmental determinants of health. Attention is given to key concepts and methods in health geography.

Meade, M. S., and Emch, M. (2011). *Medical Geography* (3rd edn.). New York: Guilford Press.
An upper level undergraduate textbook that exemplifies the North American tradition of medical geography, emphasising disease ecology, health-environment interactions and quantitative methods, including the use of GIS.

61 Care and responsibility

Miriam J. Williams and Emma R. Power

Introduction

When you buy a cup of coffee at a café, that coffee connects you with people who are involved in growing, processing, selling and making coffee (Figure 61.1). But do you know if the coffee producers received a living wage for growing the coffee you are drinking? Was there slavery or child labour in the supply chain, or was the environment damaged by the production process? Does the Barista who made your coffee have reasonable pay and working conditions?

There are many actors involved in coffee production: from the corporations that own the coffee plantations and land, to the manufacturing, logistics, importers, roasters and others that are involved in moving coffee from farm to cup. When you buy and drink coffee, you are connected to other people and places through the supply chain, but is it your responsibility to care about these aspects of how your coffee was made? Would knowing the answers to the questions above make a difference to your coffee buying decisions?

Many coffee drinkers in the Global North have either intentionally or unintentionally thought about their responsibility to coffee growers because of Fair Trade certification schemes, which prompt consumers to consider the working conditions of coffee producers (see Figure 61.2). Although we commonly think about responsibility to those who live around or nearby to us, Fair Trade schemes and research about ethical consumption prompt us to see how responsibility for other people and places might stretch across the globe in line with the extension of global economic supply chains (Barnett et al., 2011). It also shows us some ways that people seek to care for others through their consumption choices (Kneafsey et al., 2008).

Thinking with coffee helps to show how the everyday practices that we take part in connect us to people all over the world, because they too have been involved somewhere, somehow, in activities that make that practice possible. Thinking about these connections raises ethical questions about care and responsibility, including (in the case of coffee) if we have a responsibility to care about others who are part of the global supply chain and, if we do, what the nature of that responsibility is. While it is possible to ignore these connections, coffee provides an interesting example of how different people do take responsibility to care for each other through their daily practices, including the products that they consume. It also shows the work of various organisations that are involved in provoking and supporting people to care about others. At the same time, such case studies raise important ethical questions, including whether and to what extent

DOI: 10.4324/9780429265853-70

Figure 61.1
Morning coffee

Source: Photo credit: Authors

Figure 61.2
Provoking care? Fair Trade coffee packaging

Source: Photo credit: Authors

individual consumers are responsible for the harmful effects of supply chains that they take part in. Such examples challenge us to contemplate the varied ways that care and responsibility do and do not extend across place and time through relations that we are part of and the practices we perform. Care is a concept that can assist us to think through the geography of such relationships and many others: about how we are connected to others, including those who live close by, or far away, as well as those '**others**' whose lives are vastly different to our own (Raghuram, 2016: 511).

This chapter has four sections that address some of these questions as it provides insight into how geographers approach the concepts of care and responsibility. In the first part of the chapter, we explore what care is and why it is an important concept in social geography (Lawson 2007, Raghuram et al., 2009). Secondly, we consider who is responsible for care and explore different political approaches to this question, bringing insights from **feminist** care ethics which argues that we have both collective and individual care responsibility. Thirdly, we examine how responsibility for care might extend across place and time. We end by reflecting on the transformative potential of care as a framework that challenges geographers to work towards more equal and caring worlds.

Care: a practice and ethics

Care is a concept that describes both an ethic and orientation to the world and others (for example, to care for an issue, another person or place) and a practice (something that is done; to take care of something or someone) (Conradson, 2011: 454). Care is a practice that sees us look beyond our selves to consider others. It is vital to our lives and societies (Lawson, 2007: 3) and is a universal need that everybody requires so that they can survive and live a flourishing life (Power and Williams, 2020).

For a long time, care was seen as a practice that took place within families in the private domain of the home. It was understood as a domestic and **gendered** practice performed primarily by women (Milligan and Wiles 2010, Green and Lawson, 2011). This assumption meant that care was often invisible within public and political debates (Lawson, 2007). The integral nature of care to our everyday lives has also led it to be frequently taken for granted (Williams, 2020). Feminists and geographers have established that the confinement of care to the domestic sphere is a very limited and problematic understanding of care. They have shown that care is an essential practice that is performed by diverse actors and that takes place in multiple places, which extend well beyond the home (Smith, 2005, Green and Lawson, 2011, Power and Williams, 2020). Fisher and Tronto (1990) have argued that we can begin to see this broader significance of care when we recognise that it is:

> a species activity that includes *everything* that we do to maintain, continue, and repair our 'world' so that we can live in it as well as possible. That world includes our bodies, our selves, and our environment, all of which we seek to interweave in a complex, life-sustaining web.
>
> *Fisher and Tronto, 1990: 40, emphasis added*

Care practices include everyday activities like making someone a cup of tea, cooking, gifting, cleaning and taking care of children; they also include the work of maintaining and repairing the places that we live in, from our homes, to schools, workplaces and **more-than-human** environments that make up our worlds. Care can be hard work, difficult, messy and burdensome (Puig de la Bellacasa, 2017, Williams, 2020). Care can also inform our political beliefs, the causes that we support or are part of, as well as consumption decisions we make.

Care takes place across a series of phases or stages, from caring about, to taking care of, care giving and care receiving which are outlined by Tronto (1993). Each of these phases involves a practice (an action) as well as an accompanying disposition. *Caring about* is the first phase of care. When people 'care about', they are recognising that someone or something has a need for care. Caring about involves attentiveness as people pay attention to their own needs and those of others. The second phase, *taking care of*, is connected to responsibility. It involves the step of taking responsibility for the care need that was identified in stage one. Taking care of does not necessarily involve personally meeting that need; instead, it can entail organising someone else to meet that need. The third phase, *care giving*, is the phase where the need for care is met in practice. It describes the practical work of care, of directly meeting the need for care that was identified in phase one and is connected to competence. The fourth phase, *care receiving*, involves listening and paying attention to the object or person who received care to evaluate if their needs have been met and is connected to the disposition of responsiveness. Tronto (1993: 136) explains that this phase involves that 'we consider the other's position as that other expresses it'.

While a complete act of care would involve each of the four phases of care, actions can also involve just one or a few of the phases. For example, you may care about the working conditions and life of food producers but not take any action to respond to those needs. Alternatively, you may decide to contribute to *taking care of* through researching the working conditions and environmental commitments of companies that grow and produce the food you consume. These two phases can also be complicated by other factors. For example, Fair Trade products often cost more than standard products and so you may care about these issues but not have the budget to afford the higher cost of food. Care practices can also be distributed, with a different person or set of people actioning each phase.

Care is also an ethics and way of relating to others that 'begins from [recognising] the centrality of care work and care relations to our lives and societies' (Lawson, 2007: 3). To care is to recognise and engage with other's needs, including simply recognising that we all require care to survive and live flourishing lives. Scholars have developed a specifically feminist ethics of care (also referred to as a relational ethics of care) that is founded on recognition that all beings give and receive care and are always interdependent with others (Lawson, 2007: 3). This understanding of people and care challenges the currently dominant idea that only some people need care, or that care is only a private practice that takes place within families. Instead, it prompts us to see care as a central social and political practice that might be part of any relationship that we have with other people, or activity that we take part in. Feminist care ethics challenge us to think with care in our everyday lives, recognising the needs of others and sharing the burden of care work collectively (Puig de la Bellacasa, 2017).

This discussion shows care as an ethics can be part of all sorts of relationships, from those that are intimate and personal (such as within families or between friends), to those that take place inside professional settings (such as in health care or childcare), and those that take place across distance (such as through internet technology or food systems). Although we commonly think of care as a practice and ethic that takes place between individual people, ethics of care can also be practised within organisational cultures, for example, employers might engage with staff via an ethics of care or care might be part of the ethos of a charitable food bank (Cloke et al., 2017) or housing provider (Mee, 2009, Power and Bergan, 2019). However, care also raises questions about responsibility, including who is responsible to care in different contexts, places and times, and whether responsibility for care stretches across different places and times, or is something that takes place more locally. We take these questions up in the next section.

Summary

- Care is both a practice and an ethics.
- Care takes place across a series of phases or stages, from caring about, to taking care of, care giving and care receiving.
- Feminist care ethics challenge dominant understandings of care as a private practice and highlight the ways care is a central social and political practice.

Who is responsible for care?

Because care is an essential practice that includes the work of maintaining, continuing and repairing our worlds, it is important to understand who is responsible for care, who takes responsibility for care and the different scales at which responsibility might operate. These are ethical considerations that go to the heart of how needs for care are met, and how care is organised in society.

Different social and political traditions have distinct beliefs about who is responsible for care giving or ensuring that needs are met. In places like the United Kingdom, the United States and Australia, the western liberal tradition is dominant. This tradition understands care as a private practice that takes place within the home and that is the responsibility of individuals and their families (Green and Lawson, 2011, Power, 2019). **Neoliberal** philosophies in the past three decades have seen these ideas shift slightly. Care is still seen as a private responsibility, but it is increasingly seen as a need that people meet privately through the market: through buying goods and services that meet their needs (Green and Lawson, 2011, Tronto 2013. See also Chapter 36). This understanding of care assumes that everyone has equal access to well-paying work and to buying the goods that best meet their needs. It ignores the structural constraints that shape access to job and consumer markets, including racism, sexism, ageism and geography (including where a person lives). In other countries care responsibility is understood differently. Raghuram (2016: 517), for instance, explains that

> in Scandinavia, care is seen as an inherent duty of the state. Here, the state is seen as responsible for care, not just the safety net which is offered when familial and community care fails.

States that take responsibility for care in this way are more likely to have social policy that supports care needs, from housing and welfare through to labour policy and paid parental leave. The goal of these policies is to ensure that most, or all, people who live within the country can meet their needs; particularly everyday needs such as food and housing.

While in Scandinavia there is a sense that care is to some extent a collective and public responsibility, a consequence of the western liberal view that care is a private practice is that care has become less visible within the public sphere. It is also undervalued and increasingly unevenly socially distributed, with some people overburdened with responsibility for care giving. Women and other marginalised groups are more likely to be responsible for giving care and to be under-recognised and under-rewarded for that work, including through lower pay and poorer working conditions, as explored further in Chapters 36 and 55 (also see Lawson, 2007, England, 2010, Green and Lawson, 2011, Puig de la Bellacasa, 2017). Feminist care theorists challenge this way of understanding and organising care by pointing to the universal need for care and that all beings require care across the lifecourse (Puig de la Bellacasa 2017, Power and Williams, 2020). From this standpoint they argue for a redistribution of care responsibility, challenging the individualisation of care responsibility (of making care the sole responsibility of any one person), instead 'arguing that care has relational, spatially extensive, and public dimensions' (Lawson, 2007: 6).

To think about care as a practice that has relational, spatially extensive and public dimensions is to begin to dramatically expand who is understood as being responsible for care. If individuals are responsible for meeting their care needs independently, then their working and pay conditions are their own private concern. If they do not receive sufficient pay, or their conditions are inadequate, then an individually focused philosophy of care would suggest that they should leave that work and find a different job. However, this is not always straightforward, or possible. Many groups face barriers to employment due to discrimination, based on **race**, age or gender. Some industries (particularly caring industries) are also typically lower paid, despite their social importance. There are also global inequalities, with work in some countries have little or no regulation and workers exposed to poor and dangerous working conditions, underpay, and even conditions of slavery. Relational ethics of care recognise these structural barriers to care and take a different perspective, considering how care responsibility might accrue relationally, with anyone who benefits from the activity that another person performs having some form of responsibility to that person. For scholars such as Iris Marion Young (2011) and Barnett et al. (2011), responsibility is not only prompted by being near to the person or thing that requires care (such as within the family in the western liberal tradition) but is also connected with questions of inequality, power and privilege in the past, present and future. Geographers give us tools for thinking about how responsibility can extend across time and place, and we consider these in the next section.

Summary

- Western neoliberal views of care as an individual responsibility have become dominant.
- Feminist care ethics emphasise the universal need for care and ways in which care is a collective and public responsibility.
- Relational, spatially extensive, and collective understandings of care begin to expand who is understood as being responsible for care.

Care responsibility across time and place

Geographers have played a significant role in generating new understandings of how care might be practised across time and **space** and how responsibility for care might be a shared, even if unequal, responsibility (Kneafsey et al., 2008, Milligan and Wiles, 2010, Barnett et al., 2011). As we have seen, care has often been understood as a practice enacted through close relations between people who know one another (Silk, 1998). This way of thinking suggests that you are responsible to care for your family, but not the people who you do not know. However, over time this restrictive framing of care has been challenged. Smith (1998) identifies multiple ways that care might be practised outside of close family relationships, including to those unknown or known – at a distance – by delineating between the practices of *caring about* and *caring for* others. Similarly, scholars have begun to conceptualise how care might be practised through supply chains, policies or regulations. For example, people might practise *caring about* by providing money or donations to people in need, while charities or aid organisations give care on the ground (Silk, 1998, 2004). Care provides a lens through which to understand the relationships between spaces and places and how these relationships shape obligations of responsibility (Raghuram, 2016: 515).

The work of Doreen Massey has been important in providing a relational understanding of responsibility that starts from recognising connectedness (Massey, 2004, 2006). 'Connectedness' can help us to understand how responsibility extends across space (e.g. when practices connect people in one place with those in another, as well as across time such as by acknowledging and addressing the wrongs of the past, or taking responsibility to ensure a habitable planet for future generations) (Massey, 2004, 2006). Fair Trade, for example, has been studied as a form of shared responsibility for care that is practised through supply chains, certification systems and the workings of non-government organisations '…to extend the consumers' sense of caring beyond the "here" and "now" to include the "there" and "then" of producers' place-based livelihoods' (Goodman, 2004: 903). Knowledge of the plight of growers, or the injustices of supply chains, is seen as a means for enhancing a sense of responsibility for others (Kneafsey et al., 2008: 45). Responsibility enacted through consumption is both a problem and possibility as it connects to broader discussions about the role of different actors such as the state and corporations in taking responsibility for care, as we saw in the previous section.

In addition to thinking about how responsibility might extend across time and place, feminist care theorists challenge us to think about how care might be a public, as well as private or individual, responsibility. In recent writing Tronto (2013) identified a fifth phase of care that follows the four outlined above. This fifth phase, 'caring with', describes an ideal phase of care, when care is recognised as being a public responsibility and where people and societies take responsibility to 'care with' one another (Power, 2019). Caring with recognises that care practices take place in the context of social relations, including social policy, that impact upon the social distribution of care responsibility and make it more or less possible for some to meet their needs for care (Power, 2019). States can introduce policies that care for citizens and non-citizens, or that support care work, for example, supporting the right to fair pay, safe working conditions and carers leave, including parenting leave. They can also introduce welfare policies that ensure equitable access to resources to meet basic needs. This is one way that states can 'care with' citizens, ensuring that everyone is able to meet their essential needs, and has the time, and financial capacity for caring. Fair Trade is an example of individuals and organisations attempting to 'care with' others who exist in other parts of the world and the global supply chain. Scholars such as Herman (2021) have drawn upon an ethics of care to think through how Fair Trade might be become more caring by suggesting that a place-based ethics of care might enhance the universal application of justice principles through Fair Trade, paying attention to the particular needs that exist for different communities in different places.

Summary

- Scholars have focussed on how care might be practised across time and place.
- Massey's work has been particularly important in shaping geographers' relational understanding of responsibility and the connectedness of places.
- The fifth phase of care, caring with, recognises the ways in which care is enacted in the context of social relations, where these relations actively delineate the distribution of responsibility and possibilities for care.

Transforming for care

Care can also be a tool for change. Many scholars in geography and beyond draw upon an ethics of care to shape their vision for more just and caring worlds (see for example Williams, 2017, Power and Williams, 2020, Hobart and Kneese, 2020, The Care Collective, 2020, Williams, 2020, Wood et al., 2020). Feminist ethics of care has informed understandings of what it is to 'be' an academic with scholars advocating for the practice of slow scholarship (Mountz et al., 2015), gentle methodological approaches (Pottinger, 2020) and modest activisms (Horton, 2020). An ethics of care is a way to repair and transform our worlds, putting care for others and the material conditions of other lives at the centre of research and politics (Lawson, 2007, Wood et al., 2020). For instance, Lawson (2007: 8) explains how care ethics can help us construct 'new forms of relationships, institutions and action that enhance mutuality and well-being'.

The transformative power of an ethics of care has shaped visions for more just and caring worlds. For example, Williams (2017: 826) advocates for *care-full justice*, a concept that recognises the possibility of more caring and just cities, and provides a framework for recognising how people are responding to injustice through their everyday practices. The concept of care-full justice recognises the interdependence of everyday practices of care and justice and the importance of caring justice and just care (Williams, 2017). Rather than an abstract conception of justice which applies universal norms such as fairness, freedom and equity and evaluates practices based upon the presence or absence of such norms, a care-full justice approach provides a means through which to uncover contextually dependent expressions of care and justice in everyday practices (Williams, 2017). Applying the concept of care-full justice in her work on Fair Trade wine, Herman (2021) emphasises that there is a disconnect between the universal standards of Fair Trade and the capacities of small-scale wineries on the ground. Herman (2021) highlights how an ethics of care might assist certifying organisations tailor place-based responses to ensure greater equity and care for producers.

Additionally, scholars have developed the concept of radical care as both a survival strategy for living in unequal worlds and a way to envision more caring worlds (Hobart and Kneese, 2020). Hobart and Kneese (2020) argue that care is an ethics that makes collective work to imagine lives and worlds outside of contemporary structures of advantage and disadvantage possible. They explain how 'radical care' draws attention to and strives to challenge oppressive social, political and economic structures and violence. Drawing attention to oppressive structures and the everyday violence that they cause is one way of taking care of oneself and others through recognising that challenging or oppressive circumstances (such as poor health, or housing unaffordability, or difficulties affording food) are a product of the wider system, rather than representing a personal failing. This offers a direct challenge to western liberal traditions that typically suggest that this type of inequality represents a failure to take responsibility for oneself. Radical care can also entail collective work to build *alternatives* to oppressive systems like **colonialism** and **capitalism**, as well as smaller and more modest acts of care for others and oneself in order to survive within these structures (Hobart and Kneese, 2020).

For example, Okoye (2021) highlights how Black scholars are 'made absent' in academia through under-representation and 'everyday practices: silences, micro-aggressions exclusions of our knowledges and knowledge traditions from the classroom, centring of white scholars(hip) in knowledge production, and funding opportunity' (Okoye, 2021: 806). Okoye's (2021) contribution is **performatively** written as a tweet thread and reflects upon the radical caring connections built between Black PhD students, scholars and activists on twitter. These reflections on the care-full methods, spaces of co-learning, mutuality, relationality and care highlight how such caring relations enacted in myriad of ways might assist Black scholars 'shape a space-time where and when we learn, we heal; we find opportunities to re-make ourselves – whether as activists, as scholars, or even just as Black peoples' (Okoye, 2021: 808). Such examples provide insight into the ways in which radical care is enacted in the here and now to challenge colonialism and the importance of everyday practices of care in creating such spaces.

Summary

- Scholars in geography and beyond focus on the transformative potential of an ethics of care which shapes their vision for more just and caring worlds.
- Care-full justice (Williams, 2017) recognises the inter-dependence of everyday practices of care and justice and the importance of caring justice and just care.
- Radical care (Hobart and Kneese, 2020) scholars challenge oppressive social, political and economic structures and violence through building alternatives to oppressive systems.

Conclusion

Questions of care and responsibility are central to scholarship in social geography. A focus on care assists us think about how care is practised by different actors to maintain, continue, repair and transform our worlds. Although care is often believed to be a private practice that takes place inside the home, research identifies care as a practice and ethics that can be part of all sorts of relationships, including personal and professional relationships, those that are mediated, and those that take place in diverse settings, including outside the home.

Much care research in geography is informed by a relational or feminist ethics of care. These approaches help re-centre care as a practice that all people are dependent upon, and in doing so bring into focus what it is that makes care possible, including policy settings that make it more or less possible for people to meet their needs.

Relational approaches to care responsibility also offer geographers a tool for thinking critically across space and place and the spatial extensiveness of care. Such approaches help us to see how we are connected to others across the world, and from that starting point to raise questions about who is responsible for care in our world, and how inequalities might be addressed.

Feminist care scholars, in particular, propose solutions for how care responsibilities might be shared more equally to transform our worlds. Thinking back to the example of coffee with which we started this chapter, a focus on care helps us understand how care and responsibility extends across place and time as well as how care might become a shared responsibility.

A body of work on the transformative potential of care has emerged which centres the importance of care for survival and responding to injustice. Such work challenges social geographers to continue to grapple with how care is practised in the everyday and how focusing on care inequalities and injustices might facilitate understandings of how worlds might become more caring.

Discussion points

- Why is it important for geographers to understand how care is practised and who is taking responsibility for care?
- Who do you care for and who cares for you in your everyday life? Create a map that shows the people whom you are connected to in your everyday life (including your family, friends, local community, work colleagues, people who are part of the supply chain for products you buy). How is care part of (or not part of) these relationships?
- Thinking about the example of coffee, how might the five phases of care (caring about, taking care of, care giving, care receiving and caring with) be practised through a Fair Trade coffee supply chain? What are some of the complexities and inequalities that might emerge when we think about these relationships and geographies of care?
- Identify who takes responsibility for care in your society and how this responsibility is expressed. To what extent are governments, businesses, community and individuals tasked with responsibility to care for particular groups (e.g. children, homeless people, coffee farmers)? How might responsibility for care be more equitably shared?

References

Barnett, C., Cloke, P., Clarke, N., and Malpass, A. (2011). *Globalizing Responsibility: The Political Rationalities of Ethical Consumption*. Chichester: Wiley-Blackwell.

Cloke, P., May, J., and Williams, A. (2017). The geographies of food banks in the meantime. *Progress in Human Geography* 41(6): 703–726. https://doi.org/10.1177/0309132516655881

Conradson, D. (2011). Care and Caring. In *A Companion to Social Geography*, eds. V. J. Del Casino Jr, M. E. Thomas, P. Cloke, and R. Panelli. Oxford: Blackwell Publishing, 454–471.

England, K. (2010). Home, work and the shifting geographies of care. *Ethics, Place & Environment* 13(2): 131–150.

Fisher, B., and Tronto, J. C. (1990). Towards a Feminist Theory of Caring. In *Circles of Care: Work and Identity in Women's Lives*, eds. E. K. Abel and M. Nelson. Albany: State University Press of New York, 35–62.

Goodman, M. K. (2004). Reading fair trade: political ecological imaginary and the moral economy of fair trade foods. *Political Geography* 23(7): 891–915. https://doi.org/10.1016/j.polgeo.2004.05.013

Green, M., and Lawson, V. (2011). Recentring care: interrogating the commodification of care. *Social & Cultural Geography* 12(6): 639–654.

Herman, A. (2021). Governing fairtrade: ethics of care and justice in the Argentinean wine industry. *Social & Cultural Geography* 22(3): 425–446. https://doi.org/DOI:10.1080/14649365.2019.1593493

Hobart, Hi'ilei Julia Kawehipuaakahaopulani, and Kneese, T. (2020). Radical care, survival strategies for uncertain times. *Social Text* 38(1 (142)): 1–16. https://doi.org/10.1215/01642472-7971067

Horton, J. (2020). For diffident geographies and modest activisms: Questioning the ANYTHING-BUT-GENTLE academy. *Area*, early view. https://doi.org/10.1111/area.12610

Kneafsey, M., Holloway, L., Venn, L., Cox, R., Dowler, E., and Tuomainen, H. (2008). *Reconnecting Producers, Consumers and Food: Exploring Alternatives*. London: Berg.

Lawson, V. (2007). Geographies of care and responsibility. *Annals of the Association of American Geographers* 97(1): 1–11.

Massey, D. (2004). Geographies of responsibility. *Geografiska Annaler Series B: Human Geography* 86(1): 5–18.

Massey, D. (2006). Space, time and political responsibility in the midst of global inequality. *Erdkunde* 60(2): 89–95. https://doi.org/DOI:10.3112/erdkunde.2006.02.01

Mee, K. J. (2009). A space to care, a space of care: public housing, belonging, and care in inner Newcastle, Australia. *Environment and Planning A* 41: 842–858.

Milligan, C., and Wiles, J. L. (2010). Landscapes of care. *Progress in Human Geography* 34(6): 736–754.

Mountz, A., Bonds, A., Mansfield, B., Loyd, J., Hyndman, J., Walton-Roberts, M., Basu, R., Whitson, R., Hawkins, R., Hamilton, T., and Curran, W. (2015). For slow scholarship: a feminist politics of resistance through collective action in the neoliberal university. *ACME: An International Journal for Critical Geographies* 14(4): 1235–1259.

Okoye, V. O. (2021). Black digital outer spaces: constellations of relation and care on Twitter. *Transactions of the Institute of British Geographers* 46(4): 806–809. https://doi.org/10.1111/tran.12495

Pottinger, L. (2020). Treading carefully through tomatoes: Embodying a gentle methodological approach. *Area*, early view, 1–7. https://doi.org/10.1111/area.12650

Power, E. (2019). Assembling the capacity to care: caring-with precarious housing. *Transactions of the Institute of British Geographers* 44: 763–777. https://doi.org/DOI:10.1111/tran.12306

Power, E., and Bergan, T. L. (2019). Care and resistance to neoliberal reform in social housing. *Housing, Theory and Society* 36(4): 426–447. https://doi.org/10.1080/14036096.2018.1515112

Power, E., and Williams, M. J. (2020). Cities of care: a platform for urban geographical care research. *Geography Compass* 14(1): 1–11. https://doi.org/10.1111/gec3.12474

Puig de la Bellacasa, M. (2017). *Matters of Care: Speculative Ethics in More than Human Worlds*. Minneapolis: University of Minnesota Press.

Raghuram, P. (2016). Locating care ethics beyond the global North. *ACME: An International Journal for Critical Geographers* 15(3): 511–533.

Raghuram, P., Madge, C., and Noxolo, P. (2009). Rethinking responsibility and care for a postcolonial world. *Geoforum* 40: 5–13.

Silk, J. (1998). Caring at a distance. *Ethics, Place & Environment* 1(2): 165–182.

Silk, J. (2004). Caring at a distance: gift theory, aid chains and social movements. *Social & Cultural Geography* 5(2): 229–250.

Smith, D. M. (1998). How far should we care? On the spatial scope of beneficence. *Progress in Human Geography* 22(1): 15–38.

Smith, S. (2005). States, markets and an ethic of care. *Political Geography* 24: 1–20.

The Care Collective [Chatzidakis, A., Hakim, J., Litter, J., and Rottenberg, C.] (2020). *The Care Manifesto: The Politics of Interdependence*. London and New York: Verso [Verso Pamphlet Series].

Tronto, J. (1993). *Moral Boundaries, A Political Argument for an Ethic of Care*. New York and London: Routledge.

Tronto, J. (2013). *Caring Democracy: Markets, Equality, and Justice*. New York: NYU Press.

Williams, M. J. (2017). Care-full justice in the city. *Antipode* 49(3): 821–839. https://doi.org/10.1111/anti.12279

Williams, M. J. (2020). The possibility of care-full cities. *Cities* 98: 1–7. https://doi.org/10.1016/j.cities.2019.102591

Wood, L., Swanson, K., and Colley, D. (2020). Tenets for a radical care ethics in geography. *ACME: An International Journal for Critical Geographers* 19(2): 424–447.

Young, I. M. (2011). *Responsibility for Justice*. New York: Oxford University Press.

Online materials

- http://www.followthethings.com/ – a 'shopping' website and database organised by Prof Ian Cook et al. (Exeter) and of Keith Brown (Arizona) that traces the hidden relations between producers and consumers of everyday things. A great resource for trade justice teaching and research.

Further reading

Lawson, V. (2007). Geographies of care and responsibility. *Annals of the Association of American Geographers* 97(1): 1–11.
A highly influential paper focusing on the centrality of care and questions of responsibility for Human Geography scholarship and research practice.

Power, E., and Williams, M. (2020). Cities of care: a platform for urban geographical care research. *Geography Compass* 14(1): 1–11.
A helpful overview of urban care scholarship to date and potential opportunities for future research.

Raghuram, P., Madge, C., and Noxolo, P. (2009). Rethinking responsibility and care for a postcolonial world. *Geoforum* 40: 5–13.
The introductory paper to a special issue on Care and Responsibility in a post-colonial world.

PART FOUR

COLLABORATIONS

SECTION ONE

COLLABORATIONS FOR THE ANTHROPOCENE

62 Anthropocene collaborations

Noel Castree

The Anthropocene is different. It is one of those moments where a scientific realisation, like Copernicus grasping that the Earth goes round the sun, could fundamentally change people's view of things far beyond science. It means more than rewriting some textbooks. It means thinking afresh about the relationship between people and their world and acting accordingly.

The Economist, 2011

Introduction

The Holocene is the inter-glacial period during which *Homo sapiens* have flourished, despite various setbacks. Since the turn of the new millennium, a number of geoscientists have claimed that this approximately 11,500-year period has ended. However, unlike all previous geological epochs, the end of the Holocene has *human* rather than natural causes. Geoscientists, starting with the late Paul Crutzen (a distinguished atmospheric chemist) and Eugene Stoermer (a freshwater biologist), have adduced evidence that the magnitude, scope and scale of peoples' impacts on the Earth are unprecedented. We now live, it seems, on a 'human planet'. Geoscientists have coined the term 'the **Anthropocene**' in order to formalise this startling insight. Humans' combined activities since around 1800, if not sooner, have significantly affected not only the world's climate but also the pedosphere, hydrosphere, lithosphere, biosphere and cryosphere. The implications are game-changing for everyone, whether they recognise it or not. The entire world's physical geography is now altering rapidly, through a combination of intentional human activities and unintended impacts. In turn, this means that the world's human geography will be reshaped as people adapt to or are taken surprise by momentous changes to what geoscientists call 'the Earth System'.

Unsurprisingly, geographers – both physical and human – have been key players in the analysis of the Holocene-Anthropocene transition. But many other disciplines and interdisciplines have been involved too, spanning the full spectrum from 'hard' geoscientific research through the social sciences to the humanities and the arts. This is because the Anthropocene is not just a scientific question about the nature, rate and size of environmental change. It's also a question of people's attitudes to 'nature', of economic activities, of politics and policy, of moral values, of what constitutes 'progress' and so on. So, geographers have no monopoly on Anthropocene analysis within the academic world, let alone beyond it. Instead, they find themselves contributing to a wide and very diverse discussion about how different forms of knowledge – factual, scientific, conceptual, ethical,

DOI: 10.4324/9780429265853-73

applied and so on – can help us understand the Anthropocene. In this chapter, I will explain how the Anthropocene proposition is inciting several new interactions between human and physical geographers, as well as across the full spectrum of academic disciplines. These interactions stand to shape wider societal understandings of the emerging Anthropocene and how, in practical terms, humans should respond to the end of the Holocene. But I begin by tracing the origins and evolution of geoscientific claim that the Earth System has been knocked out of its inter-glacial state.

A new geological epoch?

The Earth has undergone extraordinary changes during its 4.5-billion-year history. These changes have been driven by a mixture of endogenous interactions between gas and matter, and external drivers (such as the huge comet that wiped out the dinosaurs 60 million years ago). In the last 250,000 years, the Earth has cycled through glacial and inter-glacial phases. During the most recent phase, when ice has been concentrated at the poles and sea levels are lower than they would otherwise be, human beings have made extraordinary leaps forward. This phase is called the Holocene (see Figure 62.1). Starting with the birth of crop cultivation and animal

Figure 62.1
The geological spiral of time

Source: https://pubs.usgs.gov/gip/2008/58/, designed in 2008 by J. Graham, W. Newman & J. Stacy courtesy of the U.S. Geological Survey. Is 'the human age' already underway?

domestication at least 2500 years ago, people have progressively (if unevenly) modified their local environments rather than simply adapted to them. By the late 1960s, it was becoming clear to some observers that the negative impacts of this modification were not only increasingly severe but also quite widespread. The first Earth Day, in 1970, captured the new awareness that a particular model of 'development' in North America and Western Europe, in particular, was adversely affecting water, air, soils, wildlife and more besides. The United Nations, an organisation formed after the Second World War (1939–1945), created an environment programme two years later to coordinate the identification and remediation of emerging problems, such as desertification and ozone layer thinning (the latter being discovered by Paul Crutzen and others in the mid-1970s). Relatedly, in the following 20 years, geoscientists of various kinds (based mostly in universities) established several long-term research programmes to study aspects of global environmental change.

One was the World Climate Research Program (established in 1980), and another was the International Geosphere-Biosphere Program (IGBP, 1987–2015). The first has been pivotal to the detection and tracking of anthropogenic climate change, reported to governments via the Intergovernmental Panel on Climate Change. But the second had a far grander focus on the changing dynamics of the contemporary Earth System – that is, the interactions between the atmosphere, hydrosphere, cryosphere, pedosphere and biosphere under human forcing. Paul Crutzen was one of the senior geoscientists in the IGBP. The accumulating evidence gathered by Program scientists led him to coin a term already formulated, independently, by Eugene Stoermer: 'the Anthropocene'. In a subsequent joint article, Crutzen and Stoermer (2000) suggested that the intentional activities of people, such as commercial farming, travelling by car and the burning of fossil fuels, had unintentionally altered the 'boundary conditions' defining the Holocene. Thereafter, the Anthropocene neologism slowly attracted attention, initially in the wider family of geoscience specialisms such as climatology, palaeoarchaeology and hydrology.

Geoscientists have explored three key questions about the Anthropocene since 2000: What bodies of evidence are needed to detect Earth System change today? How much change is required to declare the Holocene is at an end? And when, precisely, did humans' combined activities instigate such change? The answers are open to considerable debate. Broadly, researchers have fallen into two camps when approaching them. There have been IGBP-related investigators like Crutzen (who died in 2021) and the Australian-American geoscientist Will Steffen (1947–2023). They have synthesised disparate bodies of evidence about changes to climate, land cover and so on to suggest that the Anthropocene has arrived and began around 1950 – the start of what they call 'The Great Acceleration' in human affairs (see, e.g. Steffen et al., 2004). Somewhat distinct from this group, there have been stratigraphers who inhabit the discipline of geology (the study of rocks). Chief among them is British stratigrapher Jan Zalasiewicz (1954–). He led the Anthropocene Working Group (AWG, established in 2009) for several years. The AWG worked assiduously to see if the global anthropogenic signal might be visible in future stratigraphic layers – thus being equivalent to prior naturally-caused Earth System changes visible in boundaries between rock types. With its work ongoing, the AWG has recommended to the International Commission on Stratigraphy that the Anthropocene be recognised formally in the geological time scale. It dates from the beginning to the 1950s, confirming the IGBP view.

Despite these efforts, the three scientific questions posed above still remain open. For instance, the American Bill Ruddiman (2016) has adduced evidence of an 'early Anthropocene' triggered by land clearing for agriculture many thousands of years ago. Meanwhile, physical geographers

Simon Lewis and Mark Maslin (2018) propose that a global climate impact occurred in the seventeenth century as Spanish and Portuguese imperialists greatly influenced land cover (and thus atmospheric carbon dioxide levels) in Latin America. While stratigraphers use very exacting evidence to establish new entries into the geological time scale, researchers in or adjacent to the IGBP are more ready to accept that the Holocene is ending. Regardless of these ongoing disagreements, geoscientists of various stripes increasingly use the term 'the Anthropocene' routinely to describe the present and future state of the Earth System. It has, through a mixture of formal and informal use, become part of the *lingua franca* in physical geography, stratigraphy, environmental science and other established geoscientific research fields.

Relatedly, so too have a couple of other key ideas about Earth System change. One is the notion of so-called planetary boundaries which, according to Swedish researcher Johan Rockström and colleagues (2009), define a 'safe operating space for humanity' (see Figure 62.2). The other is the notion of 'tipping points' whereby small additional changes to an already perturbed Earth System can take it across irreversible thresholds (e.g. shrinking polar ice cover may reach a point where albedo loss facilitates still more atmospheric warming, which leads to further loss of ice in a positive feedback spiral – see Chapter 41, Climate Change). The tipping point idea implies the need to detect early signs of systemic transitions well before they occur (see Brovkin et al., 2021). The implication of these ideas is that the Anthropocene has only just begun: the rate, magnitude and scope of global environmental change will intensify unless humans take immediate and significant action to arrest it. This gives these otherwise scientific propositions a sharp political edge (see Chapter 44, Political Ecology). Indeed, leading geoscientists like Steffen and Rockstrom have frequently warned that humanity risks pitching itself into an unmanageable

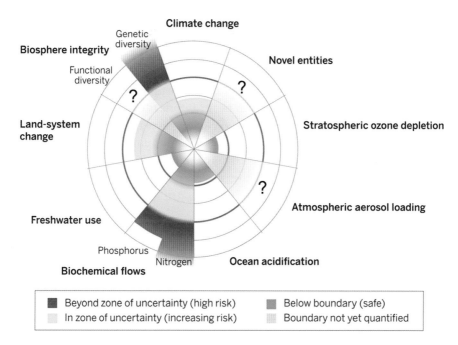

Figure 62.2
Exceeding 'planetary boundaries'? An unsafe operating space for humanity

Source: Steffen et al. (2015)

global environmental crisis. This is because, while humans have the *power to alter* the entire Earth System, they lack the *power to control* the major impacts of that alteration. The German sociologist Ulrich Beck recognised this disjuncture 30 years ago when he proposed we now live in 'risk societies'. The Anthropocene is, in effect, a massive, uncontrolled experiment. The crisis it foments, if it comes to pass, will be a legacy we impose on hundreds of generations of human beings to come, as well as countless non-human species. For instance, it may in future be extremely difficult to protect major coastal cities like Shanghai, Sydney and San Francisco from rising sea levels or temperatures. 'Planned retreat' on an epic scale may need to occur over a 100–400-year time period. The financial costs, logistics and material requirements to achieve this will be quite formidable.

Summary

- The Anthropocene concept originates in geoscience, with Earth System scientists and stratigraphers the two main groups to test its validity using evidence since around 2000.
- The concept is closely linked to the concepts of 'planetary boundaries' and global 'tipping points'.

Implications for research, policy and practice

If one takes the claims of geoscientists to be robust, then the Anthropocene proposition has very clear and significant implications for any researchers (and educators) interested in people-environment relationships. As noted above, it describes what, for humans, will be an unprecedented degree of change that will 'scramble' the world's existing geography (see Figure 62.3). To be more specific, there's a set of key implications for future enquiry we need to acknowledge. Each implies the need for some sort of cooperation among experts possessed of different expertise about societies and their physical environments near and far. Indeed, more than cooperation, each implies a new form (or forms) of 'combinatorial expertise' that needs to be fostered among new generation of researchers so that they are less specialised than their predecessors. The implications are as follows:

1. *All environmental analysis needs also to be social analysis* – The Anthropocene marks the 'end of nature' on a global scale. Global environmental change, in other words, has societal *causes* and societal *impacts* and will require well considered societal *responses*. 'Pure' natural science and 'pure' social science and humanities disciplines will thus need, in future, to join forces more often and more effectively. In the case of geography, this means that human and physical geographers need to find common cause, where they don't already.
2. *Local-scale analysis (place) requires global-scale analysis (space), and vice versa* – Clearly, the Anthropocene has been triggered by a myriad of local level activities whose cumulative effect has been to instigate systemic change at the level of Earth as a whole. This means that, moving forward, close attention to causes and effects across different geographical scales of

Figure 62.3
Unnatural life on a human planet. This striking image of polar bears – normally quite solitary animals –
scavenging for food on a waste dump in Belushya Guba in Siberia was taken in 2018. The bears
became something of a menace to local people. The image raises important questions about what
caused such atypical behaviour and whether the disruption to the bears' icy habitat can be reversed.
The photograph is a quintessential Anthropocene image whereby human activities and nature become
fused together quite profoundly

Source: Photo credit: Alexander Grir/AFP via Getty images

socio-environmental analysis is an essential requirement. For instance, as climatic belts shift
location, particular places may need to embrace 'alien species' (of trees and grasses) in order
to 'store' carbon dioxide, rather than seek to turn back the clock to the natural ecosystems
of the Holocene. In other cases, transborder environmental changes will shape patterns of
international conflict and cooperation (see Dalby, 2020).

3. *Present-day analysis requires long-term analysis too* – If cross-scalar analysis is required geographically, it is also required temporally. A key point about the Anthropocene is that events
and processes occurring today will impact the physical environment and humanly created
environments long into the future. For instance, just how rigorous governments are in
reducing GHG emissions between now and 2050 will make a major difference to the Earth's
geography by 2150, 2250 and so on. If analysts only focus on the short- and medium-term,
they will therefore fail to spot temporally distant but very significant processes, events and
outcomes. In short, the Anthropocene's onset requires that description and explanation of
the present must be accompanied by robust predictions about the future, as well as scenario-
building about the futures we humans want (and want to avoid). Consideration of the rights
of the unborn would need to be part of this.

4. *Analysis has to both live with, and attempt to tame, uncertainty and unknowability* – As the three
points above indicate, the Anthropocene calls for a form of 'total analysis' that can illuminate the dynamics of an extremely large, layered and complex Earth System that's no longer

wholly natural. This makes huge demands on researchers in terms of data/information gathering, analytical methods/techniques and concepts that can characterise cause-effect relationships that mix linearity and non-linearity across different scales and involve communities with very different perspectives on development and how to solve problems. An upshot is that precision may prove elusive, especially when it comes to predictive knowledge and especially at larger and longer term scales. There will be limits to knowledge, with some things always eluding researchers' capacity to comprehend. Yet key decisions about how to act in the face of global environmental change will still be required. Taming uncertainty will allow better – but never perfect – decision-making in what will often be high-stakes situations.

5. *Cognitive analysis must be balanced with normative analysis* – Geoscience is a largely cognitive endeavour, focussed on producing accurate descriptions, explanations and predictions of Earth surface phenomena. However, the onset of the Anthropocene inevitably raises extra-scientific questions of a *normative* kind. These questions pertain to what humans could and should do to mitigate, and adapt to, global environmental change. At base, the questions require a mixture of moral-ethical reasoning (involving values, like care, rights, the avoidance of suffering and so on) and practical reasoning (involving considerations about what is financially and technologically possible). These questions, and forms of reasoning, loom large in the social sciences and humanities, including human geography. The questions do not yield single 'true' answers, however. The reason is that values – the different things that different people believe matter – vary considerably and are, at base, a question of both conviction and convention. For instance, the values of a mining company like BHP or not those of the radical 'green' organisation Earth First! They wear different 'spectacles' and so do not see the same world, normatively speaking. They therefore identify different implications for action arising from the 'facts' of global environmental change provided by the geoscientists. Accordingly, normative questions require more than evidence to be answered: arguments and justifications are also needed, which are the stuff of politics. And all politics involves winners and losers as rival viewpoints clash and collide.

As these five points make clear, the Anthropocene requires great acts of knowledge synthesis that span geoscience and the various 'people disciplines' like economics and anthropology. After all, the Anthropocene is a multidimensional phenomenon that, in practical terms, confronts humanity with a set of 'grand challenges'. We need to join the proverbial dots or, to use systems language, properly identify the various couplings, positive feedbacks, negative feedbacks, cascading effects, recovery periods and tipping points (see Figure 62.4). In general terms, the big research agenda demanded by the Anthropocene needs to focus on five main questions:

- *What, fundamentally, is causing the Holocene to end?* (This is a social science and humanities question, fundamentally.)
- *What changes to the global environment are occurring and will occur?* (This is a geoscience question, largely.)
- *What material impacts will the changes have in different parts of the world in the short-, medium- and long term?* (This is a geoscience and social science question, mainly.)

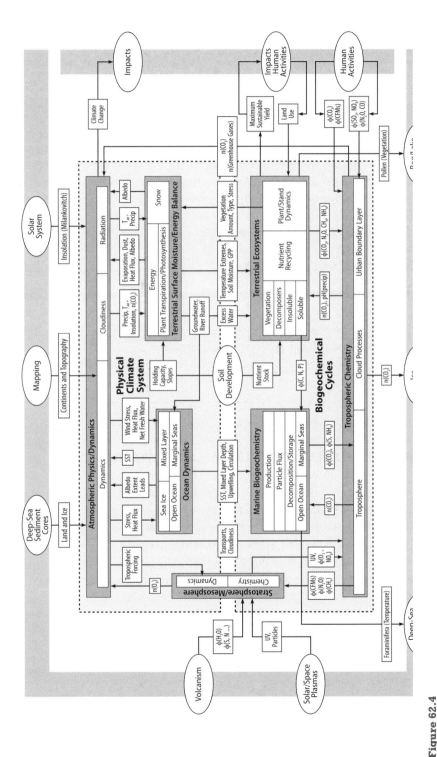

Figure 62.4

The Earth System under human forcing. The right side of the diagram depicts processes that are growing in relative importance, suggesting the need for massive acts of cross-disciplinary research

Source: Figure credit: Noel Castree

- *What should people collectively do to avoid a 'bad Anthropocene' from occurring, for us and future generations?* (This is largely a social science and humanities question, aided by geoscience insights into what is technically possible.)
- *What sort of future do we* want, *for our children and the non-human world, if we are able to create it?* (This is largely a social science, humanities and arts question, aided by geoscience insights into what is technically possible rather than merely normatively desirable.)

In the eyes of many, tackling this five-part agenda is *extremely* urgent: we simply cannot delay. Yet, historically, the world of research (especially in universities) has been characterised by divisions of labour that often favour specialisation – numerous researchers have based whole careers on 'splitting' rather than 'lumping'. In the case of geography, the Holocene's end may therefore seem like a special opportunity to flourish. After all, its late nineteenth-century founders in European universities presented it as a 'bridging' discipline that could offer a holistic perspective on people and planet. So how are human and physical geographers responding to the Anthropocene challenge? And are they responding differently to researchers in other disciplines?

Summary

- The Anthropocene concept, if scientifically valid, has major implications for research across multiple disciplines, but especially for geography.
- Five overarching research questions stand to preoccupy many researchers for decades to come. The questions cover cognitive and normative issues.

Geography, geographers and the Anthropocene

As we have seen, the Anthropocene is a profoundly geographical phenomenon. But geographers, clearly, are not the only ones studying it. As we'll now see, different geographers have – variously – worked alone or with others, sometimes within geography, other times with researchers in other disciplines. For reasons to be explained, these efforts don't amount to a new commitment to a grand synthesis of knowledge that would make geography the quintessential Anthropocene discipline. However, this is not necessarily a sign of failure, as we will discover.

- *Proposing, testing and elaborating the Anthropocene hypothesis*: A number of physical geographers have been part of the various multi-disciplinary geoscience teams researching whether the Holocene is, in fact, ending. Among them are Frank Oldfield (Liverpool University) and Billie Lee Turner (Arizona State University) – both involved in the IBGP – and American biogeographer Erle Ellis (who has been part of the AWG). Then there's Exeter University's Tim Lenton (who has studied tipping points closely) and British-American Diana Liverman, who (with Lenton and many others) has authored key articles about planetary boundaries. Independent of these individuals and their teams, other physical geographers have adduced evidence that has shaped scientific understanding of the Anthropocene. Among them are British physical geographers Simon Lewis and Mark Maslin, as noted above.

- *Explaining what has caused the Earth System to leave its Holocene state*: There are many possible ways to explain how humans have perturbed the atmosphere, hydrosphere, cryosphere, biosphere and pedosphere. Has the Anthropocene been caused by too many people being born?; by the discovery and use of fossil fuels, a one-off energy bonanza?; by an instrumental attitude towards the non-human world that developed in Western Europe during the so-called Enlightenment period? and so on. To illustrate: American Jason Moore is among those who has proposed one of several explanations. In his book *Capitalism in the Web of Life* (2015), he argues that the **globalisation** of a profit-seeking economic system – originally based in Europe in the seventeenth century – has wreaked **ecological** havoc (especially by using stored energy in fossil fuels to power the Great Acceleration since around 1950). This led him to propose the term Capitalocene as a more accurate neologism than the Anthropocene. For Moore, eliminating fossil fuel use in **capitalism** is essential, better still replacing it with an economic system whose goals are to steward the Earth and share its resources more equitably among people.

- *Tracking the impacts of Anthropocene change through time and across space*: Many human and physical geographers are involved in a mix of place-specific and more general projects about likely impacts unfolding over time. These projects focus on things like urban heat extremes, floods, droughts, land cover loss and ice melting, along with associated risk assessments about potential harm to people. In other cases, what's tracked is the meaning of impacts for different communities, such as Aboriginal people in Australia (where this author resides at the time of writing). In still other cases, geographers are part of large, multi-disciplinary teams building and running so-called integrated assessment models about large-scale future changes to society and environment.

- *Considering Anthropocene futures*: A range of work about local, regional and global futures is ongoing in geography. For instance, some geographers are part of teams that design formal scenarios about futures we want, and those most people would *not* want to see eventuate. By contrast, there are studies of how different people within and beyond universities are envisaging 'good' and 'bad' Anthropocene futures in a range of writings, be they academic or not. These allow us to understand current framings of where people think we are heading, allowing us to see the parameters of current debate (e.g. Dalby, 2016). Then, finally, there are pieces of reasoned advocacy for certain futures seen to be desirable – futures predicated on contestable values and which imply specific bundles of reformist or revolutionary action. An example is Nigel Clark's book *Inhuman Nature* (2011). He argued for a new humility in the face of a planet likely to be more hostile to humanity in the future. Rather than hubristically try to 'green' current economic and consumption practices, Clark called for a mind-shift towards respect for the non-human world and full acknowledgement of our vulnerability to the Earth's power. Relatedly, Australian geographer Lesley Head (2016) has reflected on how different communities can remain hopeful in the face of potentially bleak, grief-inducing news about the future. Meanwhile, Mike Hulme (2014) has strongly argued against any future plans to seed the upper atmosphere with 'sun reflecting' particles in order to cool and over-heating Earth. This sort of 'techno-fix' for global environmental problems is, in his view, risky and ill-advised.

- *Analysing the 'social career' of the Anthropocene concept*: It's easy for people to defer to the Anthropocene concept because it comes from the world of science and must therefore, presumably, be legitimate. But many human geographers, so too other social scientists and humanists, take a different view. They have enquired into the 'work' that the Anthropocene concept can perform in domains beyond geoscience, both for good and ill. For instance, Swedish geographers Anders Malm and Alf Hornborg(2014) have pointed out that the Anthropocene risks presuming that *all* of humanity is culpable for the Holocene's end. In this way, a seemingly 'neutral' scientific concept can negatively shape public understanding, occluding how a small number of wealthy countries have, in fact, imposed planetary change on the rest of humanity and all of nature. This means that there's a surreptitious politics embedded in the Anthropocene concept *itself*, not only in the extra-scientific implications of the concept. Without denying the seriousness of the Earth System changes afoot, there's a need to be alert to how the Anthropocene idea gets used for good and ill in an era of misinformation, spin, fake news and so on.

Summary

- Geographers have, for good reasons, made a wide range of contributions to understanding the Anthropocene.
- Their contributions have not converged, however, and remain varied.

Collaborative research about the Anthropocene

What explains the diversity of ways that geographers have approached the research agenda inspired by the Anthropocene proposition? And is this diversity a sign of failure to properly explore that agenda? Let's take each question in turn.

The research agenda outlined earlier is very large. It's therefore no surprise that different geographers have tackled different parts of it, in relative isolation in many cases. But beyond this, there are different ways to investigate any one part of that agenda. As noted above, investigations of cognitive issues are different in kind from those of normative issues, even though both sorts of investigations need to be combined in the end. Then there's sheer fact that many Anglophone geographers have been trained to be specialists (e.g. biogeographers versus economic geographers): this can make dialogue between specialists time-consuming and hard work as they seek common ground. It's perhaps no surprise that the geographers seemingly most adept at collaborating with others regarding the Anthropocene are physical geographers, perhaps because they share a broadly 'scientific' ethos in the research they do. By contrast, wider forms of intra-disciplinary collaboration seem quite rare at present.

So are geographers missing a vital opportunity? Should there be a huge push to 'cross-train' younger geographers so that they can converge on tacking the large and important Anthropocene research agenda in the years ahead? The answer, for some, would be a resounding 'yes'. For instance, a number of geographers are part of a transdisciplinary field called 'sustainability science' that aspires to such unity of focus. Their viewpoint is predicated on the idea – alluded to earlier in this chapter – that the Anthropocene is creating one, super-complex new reality organised at many scales. This reality, they contend, demands to be understood cognitively so that we know what to do to avoid a 'bad Anthropocene' through operationalising the right solutions. However, not all geographers accept this 'one world **ontology**'. Instead, they suggest that different societies have different views about what the 'fact' of planetary change *means* and what, therefore, needs to be *done* about it – where, when, and how. We need to elucidate these differences, they argue, to ensure there is fairness and mutual learning underpinning the serious decisions humans need to take about what sort of future Earth we want to inhabit (Grove and Rickards, 2022). Though there's an obvious sense in which humans inhabit one Earth, in another sense we live in a world of worlds morally, **affectively** and otherwise.

The upshot is that we have two rival views about the goals of collaborative research on the Anthropocene in Geography and other disciplines. *Multi*-disciplinary work (where different expertise is combined), *cross*-disciplinary work (where each expert is adept in more than one specialism) and *trans*-disciplinary research (where experts work closely in teams with non-academic actors to forge real-world solutions to problems like global warming): there is no agree-ment on the 'right' way to pursue any of these forms of collaboration so far as present-day geographers are concerned. This is arguably a sign of intellectual good health, even though some will lament the lack of unity in the face of huge Anthropocene challenges.

Summary

- The Anthropocene research agenda seems to call for deep and wide collaboration across all of Geography's branches, as well as almost all the branches of academia.
- However, there's more than one form of collaboration that the Anthropocene calls for, and there is arguably value in maintaining different perspectives on how to study, and respond practically, to the end of the Holocene.

Conclusion: sustaining a vibrant 'Anthropo*scene*'

The Anthropocene is among the grandest concepts of our age. It implies serious threats to, as well as significant opportunities for, *Homo sapiens*. Research into the Holocene's end reaches beyond geography, but geographers have played their role in enriching current understandings of Earth System change. While the Anthropocene calls on researchers to dissolve old divides between natural science, social science, the humanities and the arts, there are good reasons why a convergence on understanding the Anthropocene in one 'super synthesis' mode is both impractical and arguably undesirable. The challenge is to understand Earth System change at a range of scales, without presuming there's one or other 'right way' for humans to respond to such change. Researchers in geography and elsewhere can help to inform what ought to be rich political debates about what an achievable and desirable Anthropocene future will look like. This means striking a balance being working together while also retaining the distinctive insights provided by human and physical geography perspectives.

Discussion points

- Why don't geographers have a monopoly on the analysis of the Anthropocene?
- What kind of questions and answers can human geographers provide as compared to physical geographers studying the Anthropocene?
- Are geographers missing a vital opportunity by not reorganising their discipline in order to coherently explore the Anthropocene research agenda?

References

Brovkin, V. et al. (2021). Past abrupt changes, tipping points and cascading impacts in the Earth System. *Nature Geoscience* 14(5): 550–558.

Clark, N. (2011). *Inhuman Nature*. London: Sage.

Crutzen, P. J., and Stoermer, E. (2000). The Anthropocene. *Global Change Newsletter* 41: 17–18.

Dalby, S. (2016). Framing the Anthropocene. *The Anthropocene Review* 3(1): 33–51.

Dalby, S. (2020). *Anthropocene Geopolitics*. Ottawa: University of Ottawa Press.

Grove, K., and Rickards, L. (2022). Contextualizing narratives of geography's past, present, and future: synthesis, difference, and cybernetic control. *Environment and Planning F* 1(1): 26–40.

Head, L. (2016). *Hope and Grief in the Anthropocene*. London: Routledge.

Hulme, M. (2014). *Can Science Fix Climate Change?* Cambridge: Polity.

Lewis, S., and Maslin, M. (2018). *The Human Planet*. Harmondsworth: Penguin.

Malm, A., and Hornborg, A. (2014). The geology of mankind? *The Anthropocene Review* 1(1): 62–69.

Moore, J. (2015). *Capitalism in the Web of Life*. London: Verso.

Rockström, S. J. et al. (2009). A safe operating space for humanity. *Nature* 461: 472–475.

Ruddiman, W. (2016). *Plows, Plagues and Petroleum* (2nd edn.). Princeton: Princeton University Press.

Steffen, W. et al. (2004). *Global Change and the Earth System*. Berlin: Springer.

Steffen, W. et al. (2015). Planetary boundaries: guiding human development on a changing planet. *Science* 347(6223): 1259855.

Online materials

- https://theanthropocene.org/film/ A documentary film by Jennifer Baichwal, Nicholas de Pencier and Edward Burtynsky that reflects on humans' out-size global impact.
- https://futureearth.org A very resource-rich website of the global scientific research platform for research into Anthropocene change. It includes *Anthropocene Magazine*, a good source of regular online insight into global environmental change issues.
- http://www.youtube.com/watch?v=1RlVnaxTUv4 A short overview of the Anthropocene by American biographer Erle Ellis, author of the short book *Anthropocene* (see Ellis, E. C. (2018). *Anthropocene: a very short introduction*. Oxford: Oxford University Press).
- https://www.youtube.com/watch?v=Y89DTM8WcAo Another overview, but this time from the distinguished American anthropologist Anna Tsing.

Further reading

Castree, N. (2018). The Anthropocene and Planetary Boundaries. In *The International Encyclopedia of Geography*, eds. D. Richardson et al. Oxford: Wiley-Blackwell.
This encyclopaedia article details the origins, meaning and evolution of the geoscience ideas of the Anthropocene and planetary boundaries, with a focus on their relevance to geographers.

Steffen, W. et al. (2018). Trajectories of the Earth System in the Anthropocene. *Proceedings of the National Academy of Sciences* 115(33): 8252–8259.
This article presents research on the trajectories of the Earth System in the Anthropocene, examining the complex interactions between human activities and Earth's processes, highlighting the need for sustainable practices to avoid irreversible and significant environmental changes.

Environmental humanities

Donna Houston and Emily O'Gorman

Introduction: a (reprised) invitation

In 2004, environmental humanities scholars Deborah Bird Rose and Libby Robin wrote an invitation to the 'ecological humanities in action' in *Australian Humanities Review*. The invitation was a call to action: for humanities scholars to respond to rapid social and environmental change taking place in Australia and around the world. Rose and Robin called on humanities and social science scholars to work in modes of 'connectivity' and 'commitment' to confront cascading and compounding environmental crises fuelled by globalised **capitalism** and ongoing settler-colonial practices of erasure, violence and destruction of land, life and futurity. They called for settler and non-Indigenous scholars to become responsive to First Nations peoples' sovereign knowledges, places, land-management practices and aspirations for justice.

Rose and Robin entreated humanities scholars to undertake applied, public, environmental scholarship and communication; to work across disciplinary boundaries in cross-cultural, multispecies and multi-being contexts. The themes of 'connectivity' and 'commitment' emphasised a renewed role for environmentally focused humanities and social sciences. *Connectivity* highlighted the key challenge for Western-dominated humanities disciplines to think beyond the idea of humanity as being exceptional and therefore above or outside of interdependent webs and relations that support planetary life (Plumwood, 2008). *Commitment* highlighted the ongoing and difficult task of confronting environmental catastrophes and dismantling the racist and extractive pasts and presents which continue to perpetuate injustice and environmental damage (Nixon, 2011, Todd, 2017).

It is 20 years since Rose and Robin published 'ecological humanities in action'. In manifest ways, the environmental humanities continue to be 'an effort to inhabit a difficult space of simultaneous critique and action' (Rose et al., 2012: 3). This chapter aims to draw out some of this tension. We begin with a discussion of burgeoning scholarship in the environmental humanities, including contributions to the field by human geographers. We identify key threads and themes running through environmental humanities scholarship and outline some critiques and reflections. We conclude by reprising Rose and Robin's invitation, underscoring how the interconnections and interdisciplinary collaborations of the environmental humanities continue to story new possibilities for just human-environment relations in a time of great unravelling of Earth's life.

DOI: 10.4324/9780429265853-74

We present this chapter with the following caveats. The environmental humanities are incredibly diverse and they have developed with different inflections in different places (O'Gorman et al., 2019). We are not able to cover the full scope of environmental humanities work or the overlapping genealogies of political ecology, science and technology studies (STS), posthuman and ecological feminist thought here (see for example Ojeda et al., 2022). We are writing as settler scholars living and working on unceded sovereign lands of the Gadigal, Birrabirragal, Dharug, Dharawal and Gundungurra peoples in Australia. Our understanding of environmental humanities is enlivened and limited by our situated perspectives.

Summary

- 'Connectivity' and 'commitment' were important early themes in environmental humanities scholarship.
- The environmental humanities have continued to be driven by the need for both critique and action, with burgeoning new directions.

What are the environmental humanities?

The field of environmental humanities has consolidated and flourished over the last two decades in response to the multiple and mounting environmental crises, from climate change to plastic pollution and deforestation. Researchers in this field have aimed to further develop and consolidate the role of the humanities and social sciences in better understanding and addressing these and other issues. At the same time, they have sought to show the importance of approaching 'environmental' issues as also deeply social and cultural. They have resisted the notion that there are merely 'human dimensions' to 'environmental problems' and instead revealed the interconnections of human and non-human worlds. Environmental humanities researchers have proposed new framings and approaches to these issues as 'nature-culture' (Haraway, 2008).

The field has served as an umbrella for environmental sub-disciplines across the humanities and social sciences, such as human geography, environmental history, environmental philosophy, eco-criticism, anthropology and many others, as well as artistic practice. It has also aimed to foster closer dialogue and collaborations between them, advocating for the value of multi- and interdisciplinary approaches in addressing socio-ecological dilemmas. Indeed, it has increasingly become an interdisciplinary field with distinctive concepts and approaches (Emmett and Nye, 2017).

Echoing the assertion that the environmental humanities are simultaneously a critique and a call to action, we understand environmental humanities scholarship, artistic practice and storytelling to include various configurations of the following themes:

1. The critique (and dismantling) of dominant Western knowledge systems, settler-colonial and extractive histories and economic practices that separate humans from the living world and which perpetuate the ongoing destruction of lands, waters, atmospheres, undergrounds, human and non-human life.

2. The communication of the urgency and uneven impacts of unstable and changing climates; proliferating environmental and toxic pollution; and irreversible losses of the Earth's biodiversity.
3. The centring of, and responsiveness to, the resurgence of First Nations, Black, Asian and non-Western onto-epistemologies of being and relationality.
4. Interdisciplinary and multidisciplinary research focused on the multispecies, multi-being entanglements of humans and the interdependent worlds on which all life depends.
5. The development of enlarged modes of thinking and doing to enact just, plural, anti-colonial, **more-than-human** living praxes.
6. A focus on creative methodologies such as storytelling, **ethnography**, counter-mapping and artistic production which frequently take the form of multidisciplinary collaborations.

In the next section, we discuss the above themes in more detail and in relation to key ideas that shape the environmental humanities. This is illustrated with specific works from environmental humanities scholars and artists.

Summary

- Over the last two decades, environmental humanities scholarship has sought to consolidate the role of the humanities and social sciences in addressing socio-environmental dilemmas and reveal the interconnections of human and non-human worlds.
- Environmental humanities continue to serve as an umbrella for multiple sub-disciplines but is increasingly an interdisciplinary field.
- There are a number of distinctive themes that characterise scholarship in the field, from decentring Western knowledge systems to creative multidisciplinary methodologies.

Key ideas shaping environmental humanities

Beyond human exceptionalism

A common thread across the diversity of scholarly and artistic concerns in the environmental humanities is the staunch critique of Western philosophical, cultural and scientific knowledges and practices that have separated questions of what it means to be human from the existence of other-than-human beings and entities. The separation of 'humans' from 'nature' is a specifically Western Enlightenment conceptualisation, which masquerades as a universal human condition and way of being in the world. Ecofeminist philosopher Val Plumwood (1993) in her book *Feminism and the Mastery of Nature* further argued that in separating 'humans' from 'nature' this worldview also then positioned 'humans' as dominant to 'nature'. Environmental humanities researchers have argued that this 'dualism' and **'hyper-separation'** (Plumwood, 1993, 2008) of 'humans' and 'nature' have underpinned many of the crises we are now facing. They instead seek to decentre humans and reposition them with lively more-than-human relationships in which there are a diverse array of actors – both human and not. This repositioning of humans as diverse participants within dynamic social-historical ecologies is more closely attuned to relational cosmo-ecologies of many Indigenous and non-Western systems of science and knowledge (Rose, 2014, see also Chapter 43). Environmental humanities scholars have emphasised how the destructive 'hyper-separations' of people and nature contributing to the current climate and biodiversity crises are predicated on the (ongoing) violent structures of Western **imperialism**, hetero-patriarchy, racialised capitalism and settler-colonialism (Nixon, 2011).

Entangled life on a damaged planet

At the heart of environmental humanities work (including research, storytelling and praxis) are efforts to re-imagine and explore new and alternative vocabularies, narratives and practices, particularly ones which are calibrated to the pressing environmental realities of our times (Rose et al., 2012, Neimanis et al., 2015). Environmental humanities scholars approach this task of re-imagining human-nature relationships in different ways. For example, environmental humanities scholars focus on research topics that have traditionally fallen to the Earth, environmental and life sciences, including but not limited to, plastic pollution (Liboiron, 2021) and genetics (Tallbear, 2013). Some of this work is discussed in the next section on 'more-than-human and multispecies approaches'.

Environmental humanities scholars have devoted considerable attention to the **Anthropocene** (see Chapter 62) – a term first used by Earth and atmospheric scientists in the early 2000s to describe the planetary scale environmental changes that are being caused by humans (Steffen et al., 2011). As discussed in Chapter 62, the Anthropocene ('the age of humans') is evoked to communicate the vast scale of anthropogenic environmental change to Earth systems and processes. But for many scholars in the humanities and social sciences, the Anthropocene is a contesting and contested idea. As Elaine Gan, et al. (2017: G1) write: 'The word tells a big story: living arrangements that took millions of years to put into place are being undone in the blink of an eye. The hubris of conquerors and corporations makes it uncertain what we can bequeath to our next generations human and nonhuman'.

The 'big story' of the Anthropocene is also deeply contested. The prospect of world-unravelling environmental change encourages *enlarged thinking* – capacities to think-*with* timescales, responsibilities, interrelations and consequences beyond that of which are typical of Western humanities research (Rose and Robin, 2004, Gan et al., 2017). Yet, 'big stories' can affirm universal and monocultural thinking in ways which erase historical, **ontological**, cultural and social differences (Neimanis et al., 2015, Gergan et al., 2020).

Potawatomi scholar and activist Kyle Powys Whyte discusses the 'white fantasies' of the climate crisis and the Anthropocene (2018). He shows how stories of the Anthropocene in Western mainstream science and environmental culture are largely shaped in and through white male protagonists who present environmental crises as something that 'we (humans)' have arrived at and require saving from. For Whyte, and other First Nations, Black, Asian, Latin and allied scholars such as Heather Davis and Zoe Todd (2017), Davis et al. (2019), and Gergan et al. (2020), the Anthropocene unfolds in a time when **colonialism**, racism, hetero-patriarchy and anti-Blackness continue to reproduce ontological, spatial and place-based injustices. Bound up in white, Western, settler framings: the Anthropocene evokes a singular story of undifferentiated humans who have created and now face a dystopic future (Gergan et al., 2020). But as Whyte (2018) argues, what is it that is 'unprecedented' for First Nations peoples already living with conditions their ancestors would likely characterise as dystopic? Whyte draws attention to the dissonances of Anthropocene thinking for many Indigenous and non-Western peoples and highlights the ways in which such thinking forecloses on the living futurities entailed in the resurgence of First Nations, Asian and Afro-descendent sciences, onto-epistemologies, land management and legal orders (Davis and Todd, 2017, Winter, 2021, McKittrick, 2020, see also Chapter 45).

Critiques of the Anthropocene thus emphasise that the task of confronting 'big stories' of planetary environmental crises which entangle all of Earth life and processes also involves confronting and eliminating unequal relations among humans. Janae Davis et al. (2019: 5) contend: 'Such **epistemological** blinders in Anthropocene scholarship to the role of racism and resistance are not simply academic oversights: They have implications for how we might envision (or fail to envision) just responses to global ecological change' (see also Chapter 10 on Indigeneity).

Multispecies and more-than-human approaches

Interdisciplinary multispecies and more-than-human approaches are closely related bodies of scholarship that have thrived within the environmental humanities over the last decade (see Chapter 7). This scholarship is characterised by relational approaches in which people, plants, animals, bacteria, fungi, elements exist not in and of themselves but are always **co-becoming** in dynamic interconnection. This approach is in keeping with environmental humanities' interest in decentring the human. It instead centres the more-than-human world as a set of nested relationships. These approaches emphasise that our worlds are deeply material and are also full of more-than-human stories and meanings that are co-created between multiple entities (Giraud et al., 2018). They further seek to examine how these relationships are formed by asymmetrical power relationships and are animated by concerns for justice. As noted by van Dooren et al. they are 'precisely about multiplying differences and modes of attention, about the specificity of lived natural-cultural entanglements in thick contact zones, with their own very particular histories and possibilities' (2016: 13). In keeping with this goal, these approaches emphasise not only diversity of organisms and beings but also diversity in experiences, including diversity in people's situated experiences shaped by **race**, **class**, sexuality and **gender** (Ojeda et al., 2022).

These approaches have drawn together threads from multiple bodies of scholarship. This includes scholarship in more-than-human geography, the formation of which was influenced by the work of Sarah Whatmore (2006) and later Jamie Lorimer (2015). These approaches have also been heavily influenced by multispecies ethnography, a field formed through the work of anthropologists (e.g. Paxson, 2008, Kirksey and Helmreich, 2010, Tsing, 2015). In turn these fields built upon the work of **feminist** STS scholars such as Donna Haraway, who advocated for a radical decentring of the human, for the importance of recognising human co-becoming with many other organisms and forces, and the need to rethink the relationship between science and society including 'situating' these and other knowledges (1988). They were also influenced by the arguments of STS scholars such as Bruno Latour who developed **Actor-Network-Theory** (ANT) as a way of examining multiple relationalities (e.g. 1993). More recently, environmental history has begun to consolidate work in 'more-than-human histories' (O'Gorman and Gaynor, 2020). 'More-than-human histories' aim to foster dialogue between environmental history and multispecies studies and centre more-than-human relationships in their historical analyses.

Interdisciplinary and participatory collaborations

Interdisciplinarity and multidisciplinary collaborations have been a defining feature of the environmental humanities. Individuals or groups of researchers have together sought approaches around a central matter of environmental/ecological concern. The precise combinations of disciplines being drawn on in either individual interdisciplinary work or multidisciplinary collaborations vary according to available expertise, collaborative relationships and the issues being addressed, as do the modes of communicating this work. The 'Shadow Places Network' specifically aims to form collaborations between artists, activists and scholars in order to address questions of justice in an era of climate change (https://www.shadowplaces.net/, Potter et al., 2022, Figure 63.1). The 'Feral Atlas' is an interactive web-based environmental humanities collaboration between artists and humanities and social science researchers. It seeks to present a public audience with a means of exploring the Anthropocene through sets of visualised and written stories, often centred on a specific non-human (see online materials).

Environmental humanities collaborations have also sought to build sustained dialogue and research relationships beyond the academy, artists and activists. For example, the Bawaka Collective comprises Indigenous custodians and non-Indigenous academics who foreground Yolŋu ontologies (see online materials), including through acknowledging the role of **Country** in shaping their research by naming Bawaka Country as first author in publications (e.g. Bawaka Country et al., 2016, and Chapter 43). Country is an Australian Aboriginal English term used to refer to sets of nourishing relationships between different plants, animals, ancestors and entities in a particular place. These publications have included scholarly research articles that seek to decolonise the academy and public-facing books (e.g. Burarrwanga et al., 2013) and art exhibitions that aim to communicate Yolŋu stories in culturally appropriate ways.

Environmental humanities researchers have also initiated collaborative projects that are oriented towards public participation. For example, 'Toxic Bios' is a public environmental humanities

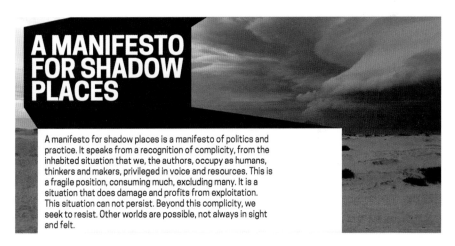

A manifesto for shadow places is a manifesto of politics and practice. It speaks from a recognition of complicity, from the inhabited situation that we, the authors, occupy as humans, thinkers and makers, privileged in voice and resources. This is a fragile position, consuming much, excluding many. It is a situation that does damage and profits from exploitation. This situation can not persist. Beyond this complicity, we seek to resist. Other worlds are possible, not always in sight and felt.

Figure 63.1

Extract from Shadow Places Network Manifesto. Shadow Places Network website (https://www.shadowplaces.net/)

Source: Screenshot reproduced here with the authors' permission. The SPN was originally funded by a Swedish government Seed Box grant

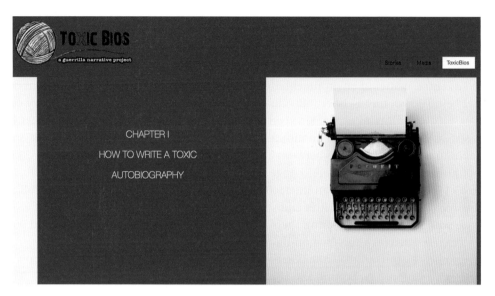

Figure 63.2
How to write a toxic biography. Extract from the Toxic Bios website (Armiero et al., 2019)

Source: Image by Florian Klauer in Upsplash. Screenshot reproduced here with the author's permission

project led by Marco Armiero initially funded by a Swedish government Seed Box grant. Developed as a digital participatory project, 'Toxic Bios' allows people to tell autobiographies of their own experiences of environmental injustices. Its purpose is to give voice to marginalised narratives that are overrun by dominant stories of progress (Armiero et al., 2019, Figure 63.2). As another example, multidisciplinary environmental humanities collaborations have also experimented with ways of incorporating non-humans into research as active participants, highlighting methodological innovations that thinking-with, and becoming attuned to, more-than-human worlds entail (Bastian et al., 2016).

Summary

- Some key ideas that are shaping environmental humanities research are as follows:

  ○ Debunking the Western idea of humans as separate from and superior to the rest of 'nature'.

  ○ Examining and addressing the asymmetrical power relationships and injustices that have emerged in, with and through our era of environmental crises and the Anthropocene.

  ○ Developing interdisciplinary multispecies and more-than-human approaches that decentre humans while still examining questions of power.

  ○ Actively forming interdisciplinary and participatory collaborations as a means to both critique and address socio-environmental problems.

'Staying with the trouble': reflections and future directions

This chapter has discussed some of the ways in which the environmental humanities offer a sustained critique of ecocidal and extractive ways of thinking and doing, while at the same time, exploring new and alternative narratives and practices for living justly and ethically in multi-species and more-than-human worlds. The environmental humanities are thus unsettling of the intellectual traditions from which they arise; but they are, and will continue to be, profoundly unsettled. Reflecting on the contested terrains of the Anthropocene, Donna Haraway writes: 'It matters what thoughts think thoughts. It matters what knowledges know knowledges. It matters what worlds world worlds. It matters what stories tell stories' (2016: 35). Haraway asks us to 'stay with the trouble' – the *trouble* being how to attend and be attentive to the diverse and unequal human and other-than-human agencies, stories and histories that entangle life on our damaged planet. With Haraway's words in mind, we conclude this chapter by reflecting on future directions for the environmental humanities.

The collaborative spirit of the environmental humanities makes it a lively field for translating environmental research into civic action. As we have shown, environmental humanities and social science scholars continue to develop and experiment with new ways of conducting public facing, feminist and anti-colonial research across many different human-environment domains. However, the uptake of environmental humanities methods and approaches by science-based disciplines is far less evident (Emmett and Nye, 2017). The CLEAR Lab (Civic Laboratory for Environmental Action Research) founded by Max Liboiron is an exemplary example of science-environmental humanities-inspired collaboration which draws together many of the themes discussed in this chapter (see also, Liboiron, 2021). The CLEAR Lab uses feminist and anti-colonial approaches to conduct ethical scientific research on plastic pollution in oceans and rivers in Inuit Nanangat and the Arctic. The lab conducts openly ethical, transparent, community-driven and accountable research, which means challenging the idea that science is neutral and especially the idea that science is neutral on sovereign First Nations lands and waters:

> Thus, in every step of our scientific process, we aim to be in good relations with land and the wider environment, work with humility and recognize the limits to our own knowledge and methods, and to be accountable to the communities who our research effects the most.
> *https://civiclaboratory.nl*

As environmental humanities develop interdisciplinary concepts and collaborations, its multidisciplinary fields are also generating new capacities for sharing and interaction with other fields (for example, civically engaged science/social science, more-than-human histories). Other recent examples of fruitful interchange include a burgeoning interest in inhabiting, planning and designing more-than-human, multispecies cities (Houston et al., 2018) and recent developments of the digital environmental humanities (Travis et al., 2022).

An important future direction of the environmental humanities is led and inspired by Indigenous relational realities, plural legal orders and multi-being personhood (Todd, 2017, Winter, 2021), where scholars bring together more-than-human, feminist, anti-colonial perspectives to consider alternate models of law and governance grounded in **multispecies justice**

Figure 63.3
The Whanganui River Te Awa Tupua in the North Island of Aotearoa New Zealand
Source: Photo credit: Duane Wilkins/Wikimedia Commons under CC by 3.0 https://creativecommons.org/licenses/by/3.0/deed.en

(Chao et al, 2022, Tschakert, 2022) and pluriversal politics (Escobar, 2020). Here, alternate politics and practices for how to live well together in plural worlds comprising many different human cultures, beings and entities emphasise what just societies look like beyond the logics of colonialism and extraction. The **pluriverse** describes the ways in which **decolonial** and multi-being relations can be ethically negotiated and practised. It includes but is not limited to cosmo-ecological movements such as the 2011 Universal Declaration on the Rights of Mother Earth and Ecuador's revised constitution that 'grants "Pachamama" the right [of nature] to maintain and regenerate its life cycles, structures, functions, and evolutionary processes' (cited in Adamson, 2013: 176); and establishing the legal personhood of rivers and other non-human entities, for example, Te Awa Tupua, Te Urewera and Taranaki Maunga regions in Aotearoa New Zealand (Winter, 2021, see also Chapter 45) (Figure 63.3).

Honouring Earth's relational diversities are not new to Indigenous, Asian and Afro-descendant peoples. And while such visions and alter-politics have the potential to transform legal and political systems based in Western hyper-separations and extractive values, it is important to recognise that specific relational, kinship and place-based responsibilities are not so easily translated into writing or research. As Trawlwulwuy scholar Lauren Tynan (2021: 604) reflects:

> As an ethic of responsibility, relationality is something that is practiced. Often, the processes of engaging with Indigenous Peoples and knowledges does not mimic the relational ethos through which knowledge and relationships are offered. Relationality is often discarded in the quest for fragments of Indigenous knowledge to be extracted, assimilated and consumed by the settler colony.

Robin and Rose's invitation to action asked researchers to work in ways that are informed by connectivity and commitment. They called on researchers to be reflective of the way they *do* research as this matters; it helps to shape and story worlds. This is an imperative that still deeply informs the environmental humanities. These sorts of approaches – which both stay with the trouble and are experimental, collaborative, reparative and responsible – remain urgently needed to dwell ethically, justly, in difference and in common, in a time of environmental crises.

Summary

- Environmental humanities continues to develop as it 'stays with the trouble' (Haraway, 2016).
- Recent and future directions include continuing to forge multidisciplinary collaborations, including with the sciences; and, to be attentive to Indigenous relational realities, including through concepts such as multispecies justice.

Discussion points

- What is human exceptionalism and what are some of the ways in which it can be decentred?
- What kinds of social and environmental issues are associated with the Anthropocene and what are some of the criticisms of the term?
- What are key differences between 'universal' and 'pluriversal' understandings of world?
- How does 'relational' and 'more-than-human' thinking help to redefine understandings of justice?

References

Adamson, J. (2013). Cosmovisions: Environmental Justice, Transnational American Studies, and Indigenous Literature. In *The Oxford Handbook of Ecocriticism*, ed. G. Gerrard. London: Oxford University Press, 172–187.

Armiero, M., Andritsos, T., Barca, S., Brás, R., Ruiz Cauyela, S., Dedeoğlu, Ç., Di Pierri, M., Fernandes, L. D. O., Gravagno, F., Greco, L., and Greyl, L. (2019). Toxic bios: toxic autobiographies—a public environmental humanities project. *Environmental Justice* 12(1): 7–11.

Bastian, M., Jones, O., Moore, N., and Roe, E. (2017). *Participatory Research in More-than-Human Worlds*. London and New York: Routledge – An interdisciplinary collection on participatory methods and approaches in more-than-human research.

Burarrwanga, L., Ganambarr, R., Ganambarr-Stubbs, M., Ganambarr, B., Maymuru, D., Wright, S., Suchet-Pearson, S., and Lloyd, K. (2013). *Welcome to My Country*. Sydney: Allen & Unwin.

Bawaka Country, Wright, S., Suchet-Pearson, S., Lloyd, K., Burarrwanga, L., Ganambarr, R., Ganambarr-Stubbs, M., Ganambarr, B., Maymuru, D., and Sweeney, J. (2016). Co-becoming Bawaka: towards a relational understanding of place/space. *Progress in Human Geography* 40(4): 455–475.

Davis, J., Moulton, A. A., Van Sant, L., and Williams, B. (2019). Anthropocene, capitalocene, … plantationocene?: a manifesto for ecological justice in an age of global crises. *Geography Compass* 13(5): 1–15.

Davis, H., and Todd, Z. (2017). On the importance of a date, or, decolonizing the Anthropocene. *ACME: An International Journal for Critical Geographies* 16(4): 761–780.

Emmett, R. S., and Nye, D. E. (2017). *The Environmental Humanities: A Critical Introduction.* Boston: MIT Press.

Escobar, A. (2020). *Pluriversal Politics: The Real and the Possible.* Durham and London: Duke University Press.

Gan, E., Tsing, A., Swanson, H., and Bubandt, N. (2017). Haunted Landscapes of the Anthropocene. In *Arts of Living on a Damaged Planet*, eds. A. Tsing, H. Swanson, E. Gan, and N. Bubandt. Minneapolis and London: University of Minnesota Press, G1–G14.

Gergan, M., Smith, S., and Vasudevan, P. (2020). Earth beyond repair: race and apocalypse in collective imagination. *Environment and Planning D: Society and Space* 38(1): 91–110.

Giraud, E., Hollin, G., Potts, T., and Forsyth, I. (2018). A feminist menagerie. *Feminist Review* 118(1): 61–79.

Haraway, D. J. (2008). *When Species Meet.* Minneapolis and London: University of Minnesota Press.

Haraway, D. J. (2016). *Staying with the Trouble: Making Kin in the Chthulucene.* Durham and London: Duke University Press.

Houston, D., Hillier, J., MacCallum, D., Steele, W., and Byrne, J. (2018). Make kin, not cities! Multispecies entanglements and 'becoming-world' in planning theory. *Planning Theory* 17(2): 190–212.

Kirksey, E., and Helmreich, S. (2010). The emergence of multispecies ethnography. *Cultural Anthropology* 25(4): 545–576.

Latour, B. (1993). *We Have Never Been Modern.* Cambridge and London: Harvard University Press.

Liboiron, M. (2021). *Pollution Is Colonialism.* Durham and London: Duke University Press.

Lorimer, J. (2015). *Wildlife in the Anthropocene: Conservation after Nature.* Minneapolis and London: University of Minnesota Press.

McKittrick, K. (2020). *Dear Science and Other Stories.* Durham: Duke University Press.

Neimanis, A., Åsberg, C., and Hedrén, J. (2015). Four problems, four directions for environmental humanities: toward critical posthumanities for the Anthropocene. *Ethics and the Environment* 20(1): 67–97.

Nixon, R. (2011). *Slow Violence and the Environmentalism of the Poor.* Cambridge, MA; London: Harvard University Press. https://doi.org/10.4159/harvard.9780674061194

O'Gorman, E., and Gaynor, A. (2020). More-than-human histories. *Environmental History* 25(4): 711–735.

O'Gorman, E., van Dooren, T., Münster, U. et al. (2019). Teaching the environmental humanities: international perspectives and practices. *Environmental Humanities* 11(2): 427–460.

Ojeda, D., Nirmal, P., Rocheleau, D., and Emel, J. (2022). Feminist ecologies. *Annual Review of Environment and Resources* 47(1): 149–171.

Paxson, H. (2008). Post-pasteurian cultures: the microbiopolitics of raw-milk cheese in the United States. *Cultural Anthropology* 23(1): 15–47.

Plumwood, V. (1993). *Feminism and the Mastery of Nature.* New York and London: Routledge.

Plumwood, V. (2008). Nature in the active voice. *Australian Humanities Review* 44. online: http://australianhumanitiesreview.org/2009/05/01/nature-in-the-active-voice/ (accessed 15 November 2022).

Potter, E., Miller, F., Lövbrand, E., Houston, D., McLean, J., O'Gorman, E., Evers, C., and Ziervogel, G. (2022). A manifesto for shadow places: re-imagining and co-producing connections for justice in an era of climate change. *Environment and Planning E: Nature and Space* 5(1): 272–292.

Rose, D. B., and Robin, L. (2004). The ecological humanities in action: an invitation. *Australian Humanities Review*. online: http://australianhumanitiesreview.org/2004/04/01/the-ecological-humanities-in-action-an-invitation/

Rose, D. B., van Dooren, T., Chrulew, M., Cooke, S., Kearnes, M., and O'Gorman, E. (2012). Thinking through the environment, unsettling the humanities. *Environmental Humanities* 1(1): 1–5.

Steffen, W., Grinevald, J., Crutzen, P., and McNeill, J. (2011). The Anthropocene: conceptual and historical perspectives. *Philosophical Transactions of the Royal Society A* 369: 842–867.

Tallbear, K. (2013). *Native American DNA: Tribal Belonging and the False Promise of Genetic Science*. Minneapolis and London: University of Minnesota Press.

Todd, Z. (2017). Refracting Colonialism in Canada: Fish Tales, Text and Insistent Public Grief. In *Coloniality, Ontology and the Question of the Posthuman*, ed. M. Jackson. London: Routledge, 131–146.

Travis, C., Dixon, D. P., Bergmann, L., Legg, R., and Crampsie, A. (2022). *Routledge Handbook of the Digital Environmental Humanities*. London and New York: Routledge.

Tschakert, P. (2022). More-than-human solidarity and multispecies justice in the climate crisis. *Environmental Politics* 31(2): 277–296.

Tsing, A. (2015). *The Mushroom at the End of the World: On the Possibility of Life in Capitalist Ruins*. Princeton: Princeton University Press.

Tynan, L. (2021). What is relationality? Indigenous knowledges, practices and responsibilities with kin. *Cultural Geographies* 28(4): 597–610.

van Dooren, T., Kirksey, E., and Münster, U. (2016). Multispecies studies: cultivating arts of attentiveness. *Environmental Humanities* 8(1): 1–23.

Whatmore, S. (2006). Materialist returns: practising cultural geography in and for a more-than-human world. *Cultural Geographies* 13(4): 600–609.

Whyte, K. P. (2018). Indigenous science (fiction) for the Anthropocene: ancestral dystopias and fantasies of climate change crises. *Environment and Planning E: Nature and Space* 1(1–2): 224–242.

Winter, C. (2021). A seat at the table: Te Awa Tupua, Te Urewera, Taranaki Maunga and political representation. *borderlands* 20(1): 116–139.

Online materials

- Bawaka Country Collective: https://bawakacollective.com/ The Bawaka Collective comprises Indigenous custodians and non-Indigenous academics who have sought to foreground Yolŋu ontologies.
- Shadow Places Network: https://www.shadowplaces.net/ The 'Shadow Places Network' specifically aims to form collaborations between artists, activists and scholars in order to address questions of justice in an era of climate change.
- Feral Atlas: https://feralatlas.org/index.html The 'Feral Atlas' is an interactive web-based environmental humanities that is a collaboration between artists and humanities and social science researchers.
- CLEAR Lab: https://civiclaboratory.nl: The CLEAR Lab uses feminist and anti-colonial approaches to conduct ethical scientific research on plastic pollution in oceans and rivers in Inuit Nanangat and the Arctic.

Further reading

Chao, S., Bolender, K., and Kirksey, E. (2022). *The Promise of Multispecies Justice*. Durham and London: Duke University Press.
Develops the concept of multispecies justice through interdisciplinary case studies.

Tsing, A., Swanson, H., Gan, E., and Bubandt, N. (2017). *Arts of Living on a Damaged Planet*. Minneapolis and London: University of Minnesota Press.
Interdisciplinary collection exploring relationality and damage in the Anthropocene.

Tynan, L. (2021). What is relationality? Indigenous knowledges, practices and responsibilities with kin. *Cultural Geographies* 28(4): 597–610.
Excellent article on relationality that highlights some tensions in scholarly relational thinking for Indigenous people who inhabit and have specific responsibilities to human and non-human kin.

van Dooren, T., and Rose, D. (2016). Lively ethnography: storying animist worlds. *Environmental Humanities* 8(1): 77–94.
Classic essay highlighting key themes and approaches to storytelling in lively/living worlds.

Yusoff, K. (2019). *A Billion Black Anthropocenes or None*. Minneapolis: University of Minnesota Press.
Explores the relationship between race and geology and offers a significant counterpoint to white and Western framings of the Anthropocene.

Postcapitalist geographies

Thomas S.J. Smith and Benedikt Schmid

Introduction

Given today's rapid global communication and interconnection, there is probably more familiarity than ever with global harms – whether social or **ecological** – faced by societies around the world. We can easily list the abundance of challenges: the increasing concentration of wealth and power, mental and physical health crises, climate crisis, habitat destruction and species extinction, and pervasive pollution, to name just a few. The underlying cause of many of these challenges is often attributed to a system called '**capitalism**'. While the precise definition of capitalism is contested, the term is generally used to describe economic relations oriented towards private capital accumulation and economic growth, grounded in wage labour, **commodity** markets and for-profit enterprises. Mainstream politics – when not actively part of the problem – seems inept at confronting the destructive effects of these relations. Instead, the crises intensify while the global majority are left to suffer the consequences of living in what has been called (with much debate) the '**Anthropocene**' (see Chapters 62 and 63).

Amidst discontent at the current state of things, it can be hard to imagine the world as anything other than entirely dominated by economic exploitation and environmental injustice, driven by an out-of-kilter economic system built around profits and growth. Particularly since the great geopolitical rivalry between capitalist and communist powers came to an end with the collapse of the Soviet Union in the late 1980s, it has been asserted that capitalism – even with all its flaws – is the best possible economic model. We had reached the 'end of history', as Francis Fukuyama famously proposed. For this reason, the early twenty-first century was described as a time of 'capitalist realism' – the assumption that capitalism is the only imaginable way to organise **modern** societies (Fisher, 2009).

Yet, the story does not end there. Postcapitalist geography has emerged to challenge such assumptions. While this capitalist economic order is often referred to as if it were an unavoidable and seamless container in which almost everyone around the world conducts their affairs, it is not as dominant or supreme as it is often made to seem. Journeys within and beyond capitalism regularly take place across all societies, every day.

Box 64.1 invites us to consider an imagined scenario, portraying a day in just one person's life.

This small scenario illustrates that, on a daily basis, many of us are likely to move in and out of spaces which take a wide range of economic forms. There are more than just 'capitalist' forms

DOI: 10.4324/9780429265853-75

BOX 64.1
ALEX'S EVERYDAY ENGAGEMENTS BEYOND CAPITALISM

The morning arrives. Alex wakes up in her apartment in Berlin, which is owned through a cooperative housing association and provided below market rents. She gets out of bed and gets dressed in a shirt made from ethically traded cotton, imported from an organic farmer's organisation in India.

In the kitchen, she begins to prepare her breakfast. The majority of ingredients come from a local community-supported agriculture (CSA) scheme, topped up with some fruit gleaned from the autumn surplus in a neighbour's back garden. The honey on top was given to her by a relative: a gift after she volunteered to give some help around their garden last month.

After breakfast, she travels to her office in municipal public transport, gazing out the window at an array of high-street enterprises – big and small, incorporated and family-owned and everything in between. On her lunch break, she goes to the credit union to pay some bills and, when the evening comes, meets up with some friends to play chess in a public park. Before nightfall, she returns home to take over care for her elderly parent.

of labour, transaction and organisation, and this has deep implications for how we view social geographies and our relations with one another. Just as the places discussed in the vignette above vary widely – from the home to the credit union, and from the corner shop to the community garden – so does the form of **subjectivity** and relationships which they imply. As we go about our lives, we may at once be citizen, worker, consumer, rebel, neighbour, carer, taxpayer, friend, relative and producer.

With societies stumbling from one deep socio-economic crisis to another (think of the global financial crisis of 2008, or the fallout from the COVID-19 pandemic), criticisms of capitalism have gained momentum. Activists involved in street protests have argued that capitalism must first be smashed and overcome, if there is to be any equitable and ecological path forward. For example, the occupation of central city spaces by the post-financial crisis Occupy movement often featured these kinds of arguments (Routledge, 2017). This is also the approach proposed by many eco-socialists and other critics. But as far back as the 1990s, the **feminist** economic geographer JK Gibson-Graham argued that even those opposed to capitalism seemed to orient all their thinking and analysis around it, rather than really going beyond it (see Chapter 30). They called this 'capitalocentric' thinking: the habit exhibited by both supporters and critics of capitalism alike, to place this one economic form at the centre of geographical analysis of the economy, above all others (Gibson-Graham, 1996). Gibson-Graham argued that this tended to hide the diversity of postcapitalist activities that people are already engaged in (see, for instance, Alex's daily routine above) and limit understandings of what economies are and the imagination of what they could be. Postcapitalist geographers are therefore interested in diverse economies: the multiplicity of ways – both within and beyond capitalism – in which individuals and communities produce, exchange, care and organise their lives across space and time.

Indeed, feminist scholars have long argued that unpaid labour – hidden from most formal, national accounting tools and economic models – actually makes up the majority of work undertaken in most societies (see Chapter 33). Much of this comprises care work that is dispro-portionately undertaken by women. Overall, diverse forms of labour predominate, with for-mal paid work as the exception rather than the rule: according to the International Labour Organisation (ILO), more than 60% of the world's employed population (roughly 2 billion) work in the informal economy, with 93% of that figure working in so-called emerging and developing countries (see Chapter 34).

Moving from antagonism (being *against* capitalism) to a project of imagination and **agency** (fostering economic plurality and diversity), postcapitalist geographers seek to understand and enact spatial strategies where human and non-human come together to coexist, without the domination of capital and its tendency towards incessant growth. This, broadly understood, is the field of *postcapitalist geography*, and it turns the conversation towards real, transformative eco-social forms of economy.

There is no sharp line separating postcapitalist practices from more antagonistic forms of resistance and protest – in practice they often coexist and complement each other. The tradition of reclaiming gentrified or disused space through squatted housing and radical social centres, for instance, serves also as a practical opening into decentralised, non-market and non-hierarchical ways of organising. The same can be said of many protest camps which have emerged in recent years, such as ZADs (*zone à défendre*) which occupy land to prevent unjust and profit-oriented development projects (most famously, airports). These are often run as sites of economic and social experimentation by affinity groups and activists along the lines of the classic socialist dic-tum, 'from each according to his ability, to each according to his needs'.

Geography has long recognised that 'another world is possible', with postcapitalist agitation far from being a new trend in the geographical tradition. Peter Kropotkin and Élisée Reclus were both **anarchists** and well-known geographers from the nineteenth century, who advocated kinship and equality across species and nations. Both were banished from their home countries for their political commitments and activism. Today, rather than being confined to one sub-discipline, post-capitalist geography is a growing presence across economic, political and cultural geography, par-ticularly aligning with sub-fields categorised under 'critical' and 'radical' geography. Inspired and led by feminist geographers, it has become part of a more plural academy embracing Indigenous, feminist and other knowledges, beyond what had been a more homogeneous and masculinised discipline, historically complicit in **coloniality** and domination. This newer sub-field includes contemporary interests in autonomous geographies, anarchist geography (Springer et al., 2012), **Marxist** geography, feminist economic geography, geographies of degrowth and collaboration with other relevant disciplines such as political ecology, ecological economics, political theory, radical organisational studies and socio-technical transitions (Chatterton, 2016), among others.

Summary

- Capitalist forms of production, exchange, consumption and governance are only one among many forms of economic practices.
- They exist alongside and are interwoven with community-led economies, solidarity-based relations, alternative markets, state led economies, slave and feudal economic relations and many others.

- Scholars have moved beyond thinking of capitalism as the only imaginable way to organise modern societies, which opens perspectives on other forms of economic organisation.
- Geography has had a critical engagement with capitalism and social domination going back to some of its founding figures.

Towards postcapitalist politics

Postcapitalist geographers are most interested in exploring the spaces and places in which capitalist market relations are marginalised or under ethical control, where private property is subordinate to communal well-being, and where enterprises operate for some common good, not just private profit and accumulation. This is a provocative and contested field, however (Chatterton, 2016). The 'post-' can refer to **imaginative geographies** of a utopian future in which capitalism has been replaced root-and-branch by a new system, in which social life is not dictated by capital. While the future features as a horizon or vision, postcapitalist geographers are primarily curious about concrete social geographies of the here and now. The resulting research explores practices and approaches in the present, which move us away from capitalism as the centre or locus of analysis and practice (see Table 64.1 for one way of analysing and categorising these practices). These can shed light on the possibility of ethical, more-than-capitalist livelihoods (Cameron, 2022). We can therefore think of the term 'postcapitalist' in similar terms as other social scientific 'posts' which indicate the emergence of new forms and understandings, rather than clean breaks with the past – such as **postmodern**, **postcolonial** and **postdevelopment**.

Given that exploitation is a real threat even in the diverse economy which exists outside of capitalism (think, for instance, of slavery, feudalism, or the social and ecological horrors inflicted in the twentieth century in the name of top-down socialism), postcapitalist geographers are normatively drawn to the study of livelihoods which are conducive to human and **more-than-human** well-being and sustainability. These livelihoods and practices which allow us to sustainably survive and thrive together are referred to in this literature as 'community economies' (Gibson-Graham and Dombroski, 2020). Geographers working in this area therefore confront the messy realities of organising social production and reproduction according to practices and principles of care and commoning. This implies scalar complexity too: postcapitalist geography investigates the spaces and places of everyday liberation across a diverse range of intertwined scales – from the neighbourhood and household to the municipality, the city, the region and the global, albeit not necessarily in any linear order.

Some critics argue that the postcapitalist practices studied thus far are too distributed and small-scale to ever challenge a supposedly global capitalist system. Initiatives like alternative currencies, workers cooperatives, ethical procurement, eco-social enterprises, bike kitchens (Figure 64.1), community gardens (Figure 64.2) and CSAs might be nice adornments or niches, critics say, but how could they ever get to the root of the problems of global capital? Feminist economic geographers, however, have proposed that to start with the idea that there is one

Table 64.1 A diverse economy table

Enterprise	Labour	Transactions	Property	Finance
Non-capitalist	**Unpaid**	**Non-market**	**Open access**	**Non-market**
Communal or worker-owned cooperative	Earth Others	Household flows	Atmosphere	Sweat equity
Independent or Sole proprietorship	Housework	Gift giving	Oceans beyond national zones	Crowd sourced funding
Feudal estate	Family care	Indigenous ritual exchange	Open source intellectual property	Family lending
Slave enterprise	Emotional labour	Gleaning		Migrant remittances
	Neighbourhood work	Hunting, fishing, foraging		Rotating credit and savings associations
	Volunteering	Theft		Donations
	Slave labour	Poaching		Interest–free loans
		Earth Other exchanges		Treaty finance
		State allocations		Debt bondage
		State appropriations		Bribery
				Patronage
Capitalist	**Waged**	**Market exchange**	**Privately owned**	**Market**
Family firm	Salaried	'Free'	Private individual	Retail banks
Private unincorporated firm	Unionised	Naturally protected	Private corporate	Commercial banks
Public company	Non-unionised	Artificially protected	Feudal	Investment banks
Multinational	Part time	Monopolised	Stolen	Insurance companies
	Temporary	Regulated		Other financial institutions
	Seasonal	Niche		
	Familial			
More than capitalist	**Otherly remunerated**	**Other market**	**Collectively 'owned'**	**Other market**
State capitalist enterprise	Self-employed labour	Sale of public goods	Indigenous land, rivers, sea	State banks
Green capitalist firm	Self-provisioning labour	Ethical 'fair trade' markets	Collective property	Islamic banks and financial instruments
Socially responsible capitalist firm	Cooperative labour	Local trading systems	State managed assets	Credit unions
Non-profit enterprise	Indentured labour	Alternative currencies	Common property	Cooperative banks
Social enterprise	Feudal labour	Underground market		Community currencies
Producer and consumer cooperatives	Reciprocal labour	Co-op exchange		Pay day lending
Tribal enterprise	Bartered labour	Barter		
	Work for welfare	Informal market		
	Intern labour			

Source: Adapted from Gibson-Graham and Dombroski (2020)

Note: Divided into the categories of enterprise, labour, transactions, property and finance. A diverse economy table is one possible framework for exploring economies beyond capitalism.

Figure 64.1
Community-driven repair takes place in a Bike Kitchen

Source: Patrick Kolesa, Bikekitchen München

Figure 64.2
Community gardening in Newcastle, Australia

Source: Photo credit: Jenny Cameron

over-arching, all-powerful global system is misleading and counterproductive. After all, if capitalism is seen as an all-pervasive system that inevitably incorporates, co-opts or crushes any community-led alternative, any mobilisation to create non-capitalist circuits of value is prematurely nipped in the bud. Taking postcapitalist practices seriously, on the other hand, acknowledges that there are already worlds within worlds even within 'capitalist' societies, the power and potential of which we may not yet know.

The postcapitalist politics which result go beyond any simple global versus local, powerful versus subordinate binaries. Conventional spatial imaginaries of global to local, or top-down and bottom-up can be destabilised or subverted when we realise that change also happens in surprising and unpredictable ways, along translocal networks, through solidarity-at-a-distance, through scaling 'out' rather than scaling 'up' or through diffusion akin to the power of rhizomes spreading under the soil. This distributed approach has been described as a 'politics of ubiquity' by Gibson-Graham and Dombroski (2020). No one form dominates and, from this, a variegated 'tapestry of alternatives' emerges, or a 'movement of movements' (Pickerill and Chatterton, 2006: 740). This rich geographical tapestry is woven from historic and contemporary movements like Italian autonomism, the Zapatistas of Chiapas, the MST (*Movimento dos Trabalhadores Sem Terra*) of Brazil, various waves of feminism, Indigenous activism for *Buen Vivir* in South America and so on. Postcapitalist geography is, above all, sensitive to the place-based, local forms of struggle against and beyond capitalism.

The strategies engaged in by these eco-social movements will differ. Some spaces may attempt to retreat from exploitative economic practices in order to cultivate alternatives – for instance, in the case of rural eco-communities and eco-villages – while others are much more interventionist in broader social patterns – such as 'infrastructural' organisations that provide a basis for further non-market practices. An example of the latter is the German 'Mietshäusersyndikat', a fast-growing organisation that supports housing projects to take properties permanently off the real estate market. These differing approaches play their own role and, indeed, can be mutually beneficial. The space for learning, practice and experimentation provided by the eco-community, for instance, can often filter through to movement practices elsewhere, and vice versa. Such debates are evident in the literature on 'autonomous geographies', for instance, which focuses on 'those spaces where people desire to constitute non-capitalist, egalitarian and solidaristic forms of political, social, and economic organization through a combination of resistance and creation' (Pickerill and Chatterton, 2006: 730). Autonomy here is not the selfish autonomy idealised in the free-market **ideology** of the individual, but rather autonomy sought through collectivity, reciprocity and mutualism.

Another important and growing locus of discussion is the '**commons**' – a spatial entity or process governed collectively by those with an interest in its sustainable maintenance. (see Chapter 65). Classic examples of commons are community woodlands or fisheries, and a variety of work by geographers has examined how such commoning processes come into being or are managed. While much hope has been pinned on the commons as a fulcrum for ethical futures, an important consideration 'is that commons are always partial, coexisting with a myriad of other public and private forms of ownership and governance' (Chatterton, 2016: 408). Historically, for instance, a commons was used as an extension of the private or familial domain, for grazing cattle or gathering firewood, and thus supplementary to other domestic or public logics. In other words, postcapitalist geographies are diverse, rather than all-or-nothing.

Summary

- 'Postcapitalist' is a term commonly used to describe diverse economic practices and approaches *in the present*, which move us away from capitalism as the centre or locus of analysis *and* practice.
- It engages with the complex realities of social production and reproduction, acknowledging both the everyday and broader patterns of socio-ecological transformation.
- Postcapitalist thinkers seek to cultivate an openness towards other possibilities without neglecting the power relations within which social struggles play out.
- There is a distinction between 'diverse economies', which include a number of unjust and unwanted economic practices, and 'community economies', which are ethically negotiated for collective well-being.
- Postcapitalist scholars are interested in different organisational forms and strategies that range from integrative to autonomous to interventionist ones.

Researching postcapitalist practices – geographical collaborations for knowledge and action

What forms of geographical research are appropriate for a world facing extreme inequalities and the rapid degradation of ecosystems and livelihoods? Many postcapitalist scholars are academic-activists who are explicit about their appreciation for the movements which they study. Aware of the litany of collective crises facing humans and planet, they often choose to move beyond passive observation or critique. Instead, they engage in practical, creative and **embodied** ways with the very communities they are interested in researching. While governments and multi-lateral organisations tend to promote and fund market-based approaches, green growth and capitalist techno-fixes, postcapitalist scholars look to escape the well-worn maps of modernism and top-down control in their research. As Cameron (2022: 48) writes, 'there is no predetermined blueprint or recipe for how to proceed with strengthening postcapitalist worlds'. The work which emerges from this is often context-sensitive, focusing on the specific assets, strengths and interests evident in a particular locale, without turning a blind eye to the broader patterns and power relations amongst which place-based experiments are embedded.

Many postcapitalist geographers go beyond academic description and analysis and recognise that their research has real formative impacts on the world. In other words, a particular research focus or theoretical approach can make certain initiatives or endeavours more real, and the application of a particular research methodology can aid or constrain the creation of postcapitalist economies. Research is therefore not innocent or neutral. Postcapitalist scholars, in this sense, acknowledge and cultivate the ethical and political dimensions of research.

A key waymarker for postcapitalist research is J.K. Gibson-Graham's diverse and community economies approach (1996, 2006) which has led to a flourishing of experimental work attuned to the many culturally embedded economic relations which exist across space and time. Action research or participatory action research (PAR) has been one social science research approach employed in this tradition which emphasises collaboration and solidarity with (often marginalised) groups to produce positive and consequential change. Subverting hierarchical or extractivist relations between researchers and participants, the latter ideally become co-investigators in action research, setting the research agenda and responding to internal concerns.

Cameron et al. (2011) provide an accessible example of community economies research, through their work on the Newcastle Community Garden Project. Their research intervention involved gathering community gardeners who would otherwise not have met, and facilitating discussions, exchanges and field trips over a number of weeks, in collaboration with local organisations. The result was not just strengthening place-based networks and learning about different management and organisational approaches but also a sensitivity to the **more-than-human** specificity of each garden; participants engaged with each space through all their senses – including taste, touch and smell. This then led to several new garden and social projects being implemented in the community gardens (Figure 64.3).

Diverse and community economies scholars also often begin their place-based research by identifying or inventorying the diverse ways in which communities meet their needs. Dombroski

Figure 64.3
These images show new inter-generational garden projects emerging at the Newcastle Community Garden Project, New South Wales, Australia

Source: Photo credit: Jenny Cameron

and Roelvink (2022: 284) write that 'bringing other processes to light is a way of making them seem more 'possible' as building blocks for different kinds of economies'. For this, certain imaginative and representational tools are used, such as the well-known 'iceberg diagram', which demonstrates capitalism as just the tip of the iceberg of economic life (see Chapter 30, Figure 30.3). Rather than uniformity and domination, a language of economic difference is allowed to emerge: local, traditional and Indigenous practices, for example, are unveiled or re-evaluated, and non-exploitative ways of relating to each other are brought to light. Gibson et al. (2018: 11), for example, convened workshops to identify community economies practices in Asia using many different languages, intertwining ecological knowledge with 'relations marked by cycles of life and death (*yuu kam, pha kwan, hamutu moris hamutu mate, dāna*), and practices that seek to mitigate misfortune through careful opportunities to redistribute risk (*arisan*) and wealth (*jimpitan*) as well as encourage reciprocity (*bayanihan, kamañidungan, provas, dāna*) and mutual obligation (*punggawa–sawi*)'.

However, while ethically committed geographical research has been growing in recent decades, it strains against the assumptions, limits and normalising demands of scientific 'objectivity' in today's higher education (Autonomous Geographies Collective, 2010). Research projects such as those outlined above admit their **positionality**, acknowledging who is doing the research and what assumptions lay behind it. Postcapitalist geographers highly value this reflection on the role of normativity and the research process itself. In doing so, the so-called objective researcher whose normative orientation remains hidden behind normalised concepts (such as economic growth or modernisation) is replaced by a situated activist-scholar who is explicit about the (postcapitalist) politics of their research.

Summary

- Postcapitalist geographers foreground **performativity**, positionality and politics in the research process.
- Building on an explicitly normative orientation, postcapitalist scholarship is often about capacity building, empowerment and strategy.
- (Participatory) action research collects a variety of approaches that move from doing research *on* individuals and communities to including them as co-researchers.

Discussion points

- What economic practices are you involved in that could be described as non-capitalist? Take inspiration from the example of Alex (Box 64.1) if you want to.
- Reflecting on places you are familiar with, can you identify any specific traditional and/or Indigenous economic practices which have underpinned local livelihoods? See the iceberg diagram (in Chapter 30) for an example.
- In what ways does care for the commons challenge mainstream economic assumptions around property and society?

- Are postcapitalist practices and relations always 'local'? Can you think of any economic initiatives or networks you are familiar with which might operate at different scales?
- What ethical dilemmas could arise in the research process, when undertaking participatory action research?

References

Autonomous Geographies Collective. (2010). Beyond scholar activism: making strategic interventions inside and outside the neoliberal university. *ACME: An International Journal for Critical Geographies* 9(2): 245–275.

Cameron, J. (2022). Post-Capitalism Now: A Community Economies Approach. In *Post-Capitalist Futures: Paradigms, Politics, and Prospects*, eds. S. Alexander, S. Chandrashekeran, and B. Gleeson. Singapore: Palgrave MacMillan, 41–52.

Cameron, J., Manhood, C., and Pomfrett, J. (2011). Bodily learning for a (climate) changing world: registering differences through performative and collective research. *Local Environment* 16(6): 493–508.

Chatterton, P. (2016). Building transitions to post-capitalist urban commons. *Transactions of the Institute of British Geographers* 41(4): 403–415. DOI: 10.1111/tran.12139

Dombroski, K., and Roelvink, G. (2022). Economic Geographies: Navigating Research and Activism. In *Handbook of Methodologies in Human Geography*, eds. M. Rosenberg, S. Lovell, and S. Coen. Routledge, 279–294.

Fisher, M. (2009). *Capitalist Realism: Is There No Alternative?* Winchester: Zero Books.

Gibson, K., Astuti, R., and Carnegie, M. et al. (2018). Community economies in monsoon Asia: keywords and key reflections. *Asia Pacific Viewpoint* 59(1): 3–16.

Gibson-Graham, J. K. (1996). *The End of Capitalism (as We Knew It): A Feminist Critique of Political Economy*. Oxford: Blackwell.

Gibson-Graham, J. K., and Dombroski, K. (eds.) (2020). *The Handbook of Diverse Economies*. Cheltenham: Edward Elgar Publishing.

Pickerill, J., and Chatterton, P. (2006). Notes towards autonomous geographies: creation, resistance and self-management as survival tactics. *Progress in Human Geography* 30(6): 730–746. DOI: 10.1177/0309132506071516

Routledge, P. (2017). *Space Invaders: Radical Geographies of Protest*. London: Pluto Press.

Springer, S., Ince, A., and Pickerill, J. et al. (2012). Reanimating anarchist geographies: a new burst of colour. *Antipode* 44(5): 1591–1604. DOI: 10.1111/j.1467-8330.2012.01038.x

Online materials

- https://www.communityeconomies.org/ – Home to a wide range of publications and resources from the Community Economies Institute and members of the Community Economies Research Network.
- https://www.exploring-economics.org – An extensive bottom-up e-learning platform exploring economic pluralism. Includes texts, videos, podcasts and much more.
- https://www.globaltapestryofalternatives.org – A network website for the Global Tapestry of Alternatives, providing a rich repository of publications, event recordings, webinars and other resources.
- https://www.centerforneweconomics.org – The Schumacher Center for a New Economics organises lectures, events and activities related to just and regenerative economies.

Further reading

Bollier, D., and Helfrich, S. (2019). *Free, Fair, and Alive: The Insurgent Power of the Commons*. Gabriola Island: New Society Publishers.
Two leading scholars and practitioners of the commons undertake a deep-dive into the emancipatory patterns of commoning and self-organised economies.

Gibson-Graham, J. K., Cameron, J., and Healy, S. (2013). *Take Back the Economy: An Ethical Guide for Transforming Our Communities*. Minneapolis: University of Minnesota Press.
An accessible and practical guide to how individuals and communities can create ethical and postcapitalist economies.

Gibson-Graham, J. K., and Dombroski, K. (eds.) (2020). *The Handbook of Diverse Economies*. Cheltenham: Edward Elgar Publishing.
A comprehensive handbook which presents insights into a vast range of postcapitalist research, from exploration of different enterprise forms to diverse research methodologies.

Kothari, A., Salleh, A., and Escobar, A. et al. (2019). *Pluriverse – A Post-Development Dictionary*. New Delhi: Tulika Book.
A landmark publication of over 100 essays exploring economic plurality from some key voices of the Global North and South.

65 Commons

Jenny Cameron

Introduction

In recent years and across multiple disciplines, there has been increasing interest in the concept of the commons. For many researchers, and activists, the concept speaks to an interest in understanding how we are to live 'in common'—with other people and with the world around. What are the things we share? How can we manage these commons so that current generations benefit while the commons are still protected and sustained for future generations?

As these questions suggest, this area of research is exciting and dynamic. Researchers continue to study the topic area that is foundational to understanding the commons—the ways that humans interact with and manage so-called natural resources. But the concept is being extended into novel areas of research, such as digital commons, knowledge commons, urban commons, educational commons and health commons.

This diversity of research, of course, begs the question, what are commons? David Bollier, a long-time writer about the commons, presents us with a compelling definition: '*The commons is not a resource*. It is a resource *plus* a defined community *and* the protocols, values and norms devised by the community to manage its resources' (2011: np, original emphasis). This three-pronged definition draws our attention to the resource that comprises a commons, for example: a river; a children's playground; an open-source software program. But we also have to consider the people who gather around that commons, for example: a diverse group of recreational kayakers, tourist operators and Indigenous custodians; a group of parents and children who meet regularly at the playground; a collaboration of developers, coders and programmers from around the world. And we have to include the agreed-to 'rules' by which the group governs their shared resource, for example: take all waste home with you; take turns on the equipment; acknowledge the contribution of others.

This definition highlights three qualifications that come with commons thinking. Notice how there is no mention of legal forms of property. Commons can be created on any form of property, whether private property, public property or open access 'property'. Notice too how there is no mention of government bodies. State agencies may be part of the group that gather around the commons but their involvement is not always necessary (and sometimes state involvement undermines a commons). Finally, there is a temporal element to the commons. Some commons such as a river that has been cared for by generations of Indigenous custodians may be thousands of years old; some such as a children's playground may only function for short periods during the day (indeed, other users at other times of the day, or night, may create their own commons around that same resource with a different set of shared 'rules').

DOI: 10.4324/9780429265853-76

Two researchers whose work has been pivotal to the study of commons are Garrett Hardin, an ecologist, and Elinor Ostrom, a political scientist. Their work has shaped how others, including geographers, study the commons especially those based on natural resources. This chapter starts with the contribution of Hardin and Ostrom and then highlights how geographers have built on their insights, with examples of commons based on land, air and sea. The chapter concludes by outlining some of the ways that geographers are extending commons research into novel areas.

Summary

- The concept of the commons explores how humans interact with and manage shared resources, extending beyond natural resources to include digital, knowledge, urban, educational and health commons.
- Commons are not just resources but also resources *combined with* a defined community and the protocols, values and norms devised by the community to manage the resources.

The contribution of an ecologist and a political scientist

In December 1968, the journal *Science* published an article by the ecologist Garrett Hardin, entitled 'The Tragedy of the Commons'. The article was significant in two respects. It was one of the first academic publications to focus on the commons (and worth noting that the article was published in *Science*, one of the most prestigious scientific journals). As Elinor Ostrom later noted, until this article was published there were virtually no academic publications on the commons (van Laerhoven and Ostrom, 2007: 5). However, Hardin's article introduced a catchy phrase, the tragedy of the commons, that has entered popular parlance and is frequently used in a misleading way to claim that self-interest inevitably overrides people's capacity to work together for shared benefit. Given the significance of Hardin's article—and his later recanting of parts of his article—it is worth spending a moment on this work.

Hardin explained the tragedy of the commons through an imagined example, a pasture that is shared by cattle herders. For a while, the number of cattle using the commons pasture is in balance with the carrying capacity of the pasture. However, over time, each herder adds more and more cattle to their individual herd. This leads to overgrazing and collapse of the pasture. From this example, Hardin concludes, 'Ruin is the destination toward which all men rush, each pursuing his own best interest in a society that believes in the freedom of the commons. Freedom in a commons brings ruin to all' (1968: 1244). Hardin also proposed that the commons can be ruined in other ways, for example, when pollutants are dumped into waterways because the cost of discharging waste into this commons is less than the cost of treating waste on-site.

As an antidote to the inevitability of ruin, Hardin advocated for closing the commons through institutions such as private property (to make each herder responsible for their own pasture) and taxation (to make waste generators pay for the cost of polluted waterways). Hardin saw this course of action, which he called 'mutual coercion' (p. 1247), as a continuation of the historical enclosure of shared agricultural land in Western Europe, which in Britain culminated in the

Enclosure Act of 1773. In essence, Hardin was arguing for private property and centralised government as the means for governing shared resources (Dietz et al., 2003).

Provoked by Hardin's article and his reliance on an imagined example, researchers undertook empirical studies of commons, especially of agricultural commons such as pastures, forests and fisheries, to better understand how commons worked in practice. Contrary to Hardin's imagined tragedy of the commons, these researchers found that commons were flourishing in diverse contexts around the world.

One researcher whose work has been pivotal to these studies is Elinor Ostrom. Her contribution was recognised by the awarding of the Nobel Prize in Economic Sciences in 2009 (the first woman to be awarded the prize) for her 'analysis of economic governance, especially the commons' (The Nobel Prize, 2009: np). Ostrom's research has shown how shared resources can be effectively self-governed when two elements come into play. First, there have to be 'evolved norms' (Ostrom et al., 1999: 279) which develop over time as users build a shared understanding of the resource and how it is wisely used. Second, out of these norms, users need to establish rules of use that confirm things such as how much can be used, when use can occur, monitoring arrangements and sanctions for when the rules are not followed.

Initially, Ostrom studied agricultural commons at a local scale. One of her examples was the *zanjera* irrigation commons in the northwest region of Luzon in the Philippines (Ostrom, 1990). There are between 1,000 and 1,200 *zanjera*, and they range in size from 2 to 4,000 acres. The centuries-old *zanjera* commons is based on an ingenious method of apportioning land so that farmers have access to equal amounts of water, even during dry times. This helps to minimise conflict during drought. There are rules too that govern how the irrigation channels are maintained and managed. Some of the farmland on which *zanjera* are built is privately owned. But the evolved norms mean that access agreements with the landowners are respected, and that as a rule farmers pay landowners 25 per cent of their crop (or the cash equivalent) for use of the land.

Other self-organising agricultural commons that Ostrom and her colleagues have written about include mountain commons in Switzerland (see Figure 65.1) and Japan, forest commons in Nepal and pastural commons in Eastern and Southern Africa. From this basis, research has examined commons in which institutions play an important role (such as the groundwater basins located beneath the Los Angeles metropolitan area), commons that are in a fragile state (such as some inshore fisheries in parts of Nova Scotia, Canada) and commons that have failed (such as some inshore fisheries in parts of Sri Lanka and Turkey). In research before her death in 2012, Ostrom was extending her work to look at knowledge commons (and pressures to privatise or enclose knowledge) and the digital commons.

As a result of the extensive empirical work of Ostrom and other researchers, Hardin reconsidered his initial proposition, and in 1998 he wrote a statement acknowledging that he made a 'mistake' through 'omission of the modifying adjective "unmanaged"' (p. 683). In other words, the tragedy is that of the *unmanaged* commons that are not governed by the types of norms and rules identified by Ostrom and others. We only need to think of the current context to recognise what can result when commons are unmanaged. Globally, we are experiencing a climate breakdown that is occurring because decades of greenhouse gases have been pumped into the unmanaged atmosphere that encases our planetary home. As researchers such as Ostrom have pointed out, it is crucial for the commons to be well-governed so that resources, including the resources on which life on this planet depends, will be sustained now and into the future. Geographers have contributed to this understanding of how these types of commons might be governed

Figure 65.1
Self-organising agricultural commons such as those found in the mountains of Switzerland have been a long-standing focus of research

Source: Photo credit: Daniel Seßler on Unsplash

effectively. In what follows we look at the work of geographers who are researching commons based on land, air and sea.

Summary

- Garrett Hardin's article 'The Tragedy of the Commons' highlighted the potential downfall of unmanaged shared resources and advocated for closing the commons through private property and taxation.
- Elinor Ostrom's research showed that effective self-governance of shared resources is possible through evolved norms and established rules, challenging Hardin's initial proposition. Her work focused on various examples of successful commons worldwide.

Dimensions of the commons

One of the contributions for geographers has been to expand on the idea of evolved norms and rules that are used to govern commons. Gibson-Graham et al. (2013) have done this through their Commons Identi-Kit which identifies six dimensions of the commons and emphasises

Table 65.1 The Commons Identi-Kit					
Access	Use	Benefit	Care	Responsibility	Property
Shared and wide	Negotiated by a community	Widely distributed to community members and beyond	Performed by community members	Assumed by community	Any form of ownership (private, state or open access)

Source: Adapted from Gibson-Graham et al. (2013) under creative commons licence, https://www.communityeconomies. org/take-back-economy/tools-taking-back/5-property

the relationships within a community that are drawn on to navigate these dimensions (see Table 65.1).

One of the examples Gibson-Graham et al. use to explore these dimensions of commoning is the West Arnhem Land Fire Abatement (WALFA) project in the Northern Territory of Australia. This initiative is based on the traditional practice of fine-scale mosaic burning in which regular controlled fires are used to prevent large-scale and highly destructive savanna wildfires. WALFA and four adjacent fire abatement areas cover over 80,000 square kilometres of land (an area slightly larger than Scotland). *Access* to the WALFA land is shared between five Indigenous ranger groups, and they negotiate *use* of the land through an annual meeting to plan and map the areas for burning. Each Indigenous group takes *responsibility* for the one of the five fire areas (including responsibility for following rules for monitoring, record-keeping and reporting), and they exercise *care* for the country by conducting mini-burns early in the dry season.

What is striking about this example is how widespread the *benefits* are. The impetus for the project came from Indigenous custodians who were concerned that without customary fire management the country had become physically and spiritually sick. With traditional practices reintroduced the ecosystem is being rejuvenated and the destructive impact of uncontrolled wildfires is minimised. This includes a reduction in the damaging greenhouse gases (especially methane and nitrous oxide) that are concentrated in the high-intensity wildfires that typically occur late in the dry season. Using technological know-how, WALFA is able to quantify the contribution the smaller early season burns make to reducing GGE. As a result, WALFA is registered with the Australia's Clean Energy Regulator, and they are issued Australian carbon credit units which they sell on carbon markets. The funds raised are used for initiatives such as Indigenous-led educational, employment and training activities, long-term management programmes for threatened flora and fauna, and protection of customary ecological knowledges.

The WALFA commons is held on land with Aboriginal tenure, which means it is a form of *private property* 'owned' by traditional custodians. Gibson-Graham et al. use this example to highlight how commons can be created on any type of property. As they argue, 'ownership of property is largely a legal matter and does not deter land or other resources from being managed as a commons' (2013: 132).

Implicit in the Commons Identi-Kit is a focus on the community that gathers around the commons and the ways the community draws on evolved norms to navigate the various dimensions of the commons. In the case of the WALFA commons, these evolved norms are based on tens of thousands of years of living 'on country' and a deep and **embodied** understanding of the ways that humans are inseparable from the world around. The community that gathers around a commons need not be homogenous. Gibson-Graham illustrates this through the example of the Avocet Nature Reserve, a 2,700-acre reserve on privately owned land that has been protected from development (in perpetuity) through a voluntary conservation agreement with the state government. The Spooner family established the reserve on their cattle property to protect the endangered bridled nailtail wallaby, a small kangaroo species also known as 'flashjack' wallabies. Around this flashjack commons a community comprising diverse members has formed. This includes cattle pastoralists, researchers, conservation volunteers, state government programme officers and sporting shooters (who shot the wild pig population that would otherwise damage the grasses on which the wallaby depends for both food and shelter). This diverse group works together to navigate use and access and take care and responsibility for the wellbeing of the flashjack commons.

Summary

- Geographers have expanded on the concept of evolved norms and rules to govern commons, identifying six dimensions of the commons that emphasise community relationships.
- The six dimensions of the commons they consider are access, use, benefits, responsibility, care and ownership.

Commoning as doing

A second contribution from geographers has been to deepen the understanding of commoning as a process. The historian Peter Linebaugh has argued emphatically for the importance of this approach:

> To speak of the commons as if it were a natural resource is misleading at best and dangerous at worst—the commons is an activity and, if anything, it expresses relationships in society that are inseparable from relations to nature. It might be better to keep the word as a verb, an activity, rather than as a noun, a substantive.
>
> *Linebaugh 2008: 279*

Building on this insight, geographers Gibson-Graham et al. (2013) have expanded their Commons Identi-Kit to incorporate processes of commoning (see Figure 65.2). The Ways of Commoning diagram shows how commoning can involve reconfiguring enclosed property, on the one hand, or unmanaged open-access resources, on the other. The example of the flashjack commons above illustrates how what was once private individual property has been commoned. The WALFA commons is an example of commoning an unmanaged resource that was to some extent open access because **colonisation** removed people from their traditional homelands. Thinking of commons in this way draws our attention to the work that goes into creating new commons as

	Access	Use	Benefit	Care	Responsibility	Ownership
Commoning enclosed property	Narrow	Restricted by owner	Private	Performed by owner or employee	Assumed by owner	Private individual Private collective State
Creating new commons	Shared and wide	Negotiated by a community	Widely distributed to community and beyond	Performed by community members	Assumed by community	Private individual Private collective State Open access
Commoning unmanaged open-access resources	Unrestricted	Open and unregulated	Finders keepers	None	None	Open access State

Figure 65.2
Ways of commoning

Source: Adapted from Gibson-Graham et al. (2013) under creative commons licence. https://www.communityeconomies.org/take-back-economy/tools-taking-back/5-property

well as the ongoing work of maintaining commons, whether those that have only recently been created (such as the flashjack commons), those that are centuries old (such as the zanjera commons) or those that have been reclaimed (such as the WALFA commons).

The commons discussed so far involve relatively localised endeavours. What of enclosed property and unmanaged resources that are more large-scale? Can processes of commoning apply at these scales? As alerted to earlier, we can think of the atmosphere as an unmanaged open-access resource into which humans have pumped decades of greenhouse gases—with devastating impacts for life on this planet. With each passing United Nations Climate Change Conference, it seems that time is ticking away, and the likelihood of building a robust global atmospheric commons is being lost. Yet, there is an example of an atmospheric agreement, discussed by Gibson-Graham et al. (2016), that shows how commoning is possible at a global level.

From the 1930s to the 1970s chlorofluorocarbons (CFCs) and other ozone-depleting chemicals (ODCs) were widely manufactured and used in products such as aerosol sprays, foams and other packing materials, and refrigerators. In 1974, two researchers hypothesised that ODCs were depleting the Earth's ozone layer, that part of the stratosphere that absorbs most of the sun's damaging ultraviolet radiation. This could not be confirmed until 1985 when two research teams using different types of technology found that the layer was indeed being depleted. One team even produced images of a hole in the ozone layer. The impact was like a scene from a disaster film. One of the scientists recounted that when the images were first shown 'All hell broke loose, particularly in the media. People were scared and thought this could be a real disaster that could kill us, give us cancer' (Hansen, 2012). The global response was rapid. Within two years the Montreal Protocol on Substances that Deplete the Ozone Layer was agreed to, and it came into force two years later in 1987. By 2005 all 191 countries that ratified the Protocol had cut their production and consumption of ODCs by 95 per cent. Gradually the ozone layer is being replenished, and the hole is repairing itself.

In their analysis of what enabled this global commoning of a previously unmanaged open-access resource, Gibson-Graham et al. (2016) highlight how a diverse community gathered to take responsibility for this component of our atmospheric commons. As expected, it included scientists, politicians and national and international policymakers, but other groups were involved as well. Media reporting on the status of the hole had a large public impact; this helped raise awareness and led to citizens pressuring for action. Unionists refused to work with ODCs and multi-national corporations that produced ODCs pro-actively developed alternatives. There was a concerted effort on multiple fronts to care for the ozone layer, and to agree to standards for use and access. All this has resulted in significant benefits for life on the planet with humans, plants, animals and ecosystems being protected from excessive ultraviolet radiation.

In reflecting on the process of commoning, the political economist Massimo de Angelis argues that 'there are no commons without *incessant* activities of commoning' (2006: 1, added emphasis). This statement is a reminder of two important aspects of commoning. First, it is a reminder that commoning is not a one-off activity. Once created, commons need to be continually maintained and nourished. For example, even the highly successful Montreal Protocol has had to be revisited and revised. In 2016, the Kigali Amendment was introduced to address the new risk that comes from the use of hydrofluorocarbons as a replacement for ODCs. In the same way, groups that gather around a commons such as WALFA commons meet regularly to review and plan their activities and to respond to changes that inevitably occur. To reiterate, commoning is a doing.

De Angelis's statement is also a reminder of how we need to be vigilant about those commons that we take for granted and be alert to attempts to enclose these commons. Currently there is a commons battle raging over outer space. The 1967 UN Outer Space Treaty establishes that outer space is *terra communis* or common 'land'. The first principle of this treaty is a pretty good statement of the widespread benefit that should come from the commons: 'the exploration and use of outer space shall be carried out for the benefit and in the interests of all countries and shall be the province of all mankind' (United Nations Office for Outer Space Affairs [UNOOSA], no date). However, this commons is at risk. There are pressures to change the legal status of outer space to *terra nullius*, literally 'land' belonging to no one (see Figure 65.3). This would open up outer space as a new frontier for nations to colonise and corporations to privatise. This form of enclosure would bring individual nations and corporations new-found wealth and power through activities such as asteroid mining for so-called rare earth minerals. Closer to home, there are similar pressures on our polar regions and the deep ocean seabed. The same sort of effort that was needed to build a commoning community around the ozone will be needed for these and other commons that are under threat.

Summary

- Recently, commons scholars have emphasised that commoning is a process rather than viewing the commons as a static resource.
- Commoning involves reconfiguring enclosed property or unmanaged open-access resources into shared use, benefit, care, responsibility and so on.
- The example of the Montreal Protocol highlights the global commoning of the ozone layer, involving diverse communities and resulting in significant benefits.

Figure 65.3
With interest in the potential of outer space for activities such as asteroid mining, debates about the commons are being applied in new settings

Source: Photo credit: © Getty Images/Marc Guitard

Mapping the commons

A final contribution that geographers have made to the study of commons is through mapping activities that highlight not just the extent of commons but also the communities that help to constitute the commons through their commoning activities.

In much the same way that Hardin talked about the tragedy of the commons in his initial *Science* publication, there is a widespread view that the oceans currently represent a tragedy of the commons with fish and other marine life being depleted and degraded through overfishing, pollution and ocean warming. There is no doubt that the oceans are under great pressure; however, just as Ostrom and her colleagues told a more nuanced story of commons on land, so too there is a more nuanced story to tell about our ocean commons. Kevin St Martin is one geographer who is doing so through using **GIS** technologies in a novel way with fishers to map communities and commons at sea (see also Chapter 67)

In the northeast of the US, where St Martin is based, fisheries scientists and managers tend to think of commercial fishing as an activity carried out by utility-maximising fishers who are tragically overfishing the marine commons and therefore need to be policed. In discussions about the future of these fisheries, the voice of the commercial fishers has been largely silenced. However, St Martin worked with the fishers along the coast to map their use of the ocean, thereby making visible the ways that fishers from different ports and using different fishing gear interacted in different ways with the marine environment (St Martin and Hall-Arber, 2007, St Martin, 2009). These maps become a talking point for fishers helping them to articulate the contribution they were already making to the management of the marine commons (for example, by using their local knowledge to fish only in certain areas so that other areas had time to replenish, and by fishing in collaboration rather that competition with each other).

Through these discussions, the commercial fishers became interested in devising their own area-based fisheries management plans. One plan had the commercial fishers catching fewer fish to achieve a balance between conserving fish stock while providing them with viable livelihoods that would support their land-based families and the local communities in which they lived (Snyder and St Martin, 2015). To help make this plan feasible, the fishers formed a community-supported fishery which is based on community members purchasing a share of the catch in advance, with the fish delivered each week. This gives the fishers certainty about their income and means that they only catch what they have already pre-sold. The model has been taken up by over 40 fishing-based communities across the US and Canada as a means of contributing to the sustainability of the marine commons while securing ongoing livelihoods for fishers. This

Figure 65.4
Concerns about the entwinement of environmental and human wellbeing are prompting users of open access spaces, such as the oceans, to act as responsible commoners

Source: Photo credit: Marc Guitard/Getty images

work of negotiating how the marine commons is used and accessed by the commercial fishers and how they enact their responsibility and care for the commons is ongoing (see Figure 65.4) with the fishers now involved with the fisheries scientists and managers to deliberate on what fishing futures might look like in oceans that are under pressure from climate change and other threats (see also Bresnihan, 2016).

Summary

- Geographers have contributed to mapping activities that highlight the extent of commons and the communities involved in commoning.
- Kevin St Martin's participatory mapping work with commercial fishers in the northeast US helped them articulate their contribution to the management of the marine commons, leading to the development of area-based fisheries management plans and community supported fisheries.

Conclusion

This chapter has focused on the ways that humans interact with and manage so-called natural resources and in so doing help to create commons that provide benefits for humans and the diversity of other forms of life on this planet. Through this focus we have seen how research conducted by human geographers is in conversation and collaboration with the work of others, including ecologists, political scientists, historians and political economists. But this is only one area of study through which geographers are making a contribution to our understanding of commons and processes of commoning. This contribution is perhaps most notable in the study of urban commons, with geographers exploring the role of initiatives such as community gardens and community centres, housing cooperatives, food-rescue networks, refugee and asylum-seeker camps in building urban commons (e.g. Huron, 2018). Others are building on the later work of Ostrom to explore commons of the future, including knowledge commons and digital commons (e.g. Dulong de Rosnay and Stalder, 2020). Finally, other geographers are exploring day-to-day practices of commoning and how these practices are both shaped by and shape a conception of 'personhood' or **subjectivity** that positions people not as insular individuals but as collective beings whose existence is interdependent with all those around (including the **more-than-human**) (e.g. Singh, 2017).

Discussion points

- What commons do you encounter in your everyday life? Following Ostrom, what are the evolved norms and rules which govern the use of these commons?
- Which of these commons do you think are robust and which are fragile?
- What are some examples of commons on different forms of property? Can you identify any commons on privately held property?

- Who can be involved in commoning? Explore this by using the Commons Identi-Kit (above) to analyse one of the commons you have identified.
- What commons are most under threat? Can you identify some commons within your local area as well are international commons that are under threat? What are these threats? What's needed to maintain the commons? What role might state agencies play? What role is there for other commoners?

References

Bollier, D. (2011). The commons, short and sweet, Available at https://www.bollier.org/commons-short-and-sweet (last accessed 20 February 2023).

Bresnihan, P. (2016). *Transforming the Fisheries: Neoliberalism, Nature, and the Commons*. Lincoln, Nebraska: University of Nebraska Press.

de Angelis, M. (2006). Introduction: re(in)fusing the commons. *The Commoner* 11: 1–4.

Dietz, T., Ostrom, E., and Stern, P. (2003). The struggle to govern the commons. *Science* 302(5652): 1907–1912.

Dulong de Rosnay, M., and Stalder, F. (2020). Digital commons. *Internet Policy Review* 9(4): 1–15.

Gibson-Graham, J. K., Cameron, J., and Healy, S. (2013). *Take Back the Economy: An Ethical Guide for Transforming Our Communities*. Minneapolis: University of Minnesota Press.

Gibson-Graham, J. K., Cameron, J., and Healy, S. (2016). Commoning as a Postcapitalist Politics. In *Releasing the Commons: Rethinking the Futures of the Commons*, eds. A. Amin and P. Howell. Oxfordshire: Routledge, 192–212.

Hansen, K. (2012). Discovering the Ozone Hole: Q & A with Pawan Bhartia, NASA Feature, Available at https://climate.nasa.gov/news/781/discovering-the-ozone-hole-qa-with-pawan-bhartia/ (last accessed 3 March 2024).

Hardin, G. (1968). The tragedy of the commons. *Science* 162(3859): 1243–1248.

Hardin, G. (1998). Extensions of 'The Tragedy of the Commons'. *Science* 280(5364): 682–683.

Huron, A. (2018). *Carving Out the Commons: Tenant Organizing and Housing Cooperatives in Washington, DC*. Minneapolis: University of Minnesota Press.

Linebaugh, P. (2008). *The Magna Carta Manifesto: Liberties and Commons for All*. Berkeley: University of California Press.

Ostrom, E. (1990). *Governing the Commons. The Evolution of Institutions for Collective Action*. Cambridge: Cambridge University Press.

Ostrom, E., Burger, J., Field, C. B., Norgaard, R. B., and Policansky, D. (1999). Revisiting the commons: local lessons, global challenges. *Science* 284(5412): 278–282.

Singh, N. (2017). Becoming a commoner: the commons as sites for affective socio-nature encounters and cobecomings. *Ephemera: Theory and Politics in Organization* 17(4): 751–776.

Snyder, R., and St Martin, K. (2015). A Fishery for the Future: The Midcoast Fishermen's Association and the Work of Economic Being-in-Common. In *Making Other Worlds Possible: Performing Diverse Economies*, eds. G. Roelvink, K. St Martin, and J. K. Gibson-Graham. Minneapolis: University of Minnesota Press, 26–52.

St Martin, K. (2009). Toward a cartography of the commons: constituting the political and economic possibility of place. *The Professional Geographer* 61(4): 493–507.

St Martin, K., and Hall-Arber, M. (2007). Environment and Development: (Re)connecting Community and Commons in New England Fisheries, USA. In *Participatory Action Research Approaches and Methods: Connecting People, Participation and Place*, eds. S. Kindon, R. Pain, and M. Kesby. London: Routledge, 51–59.

The Nobel Prize. (2009). Elinor Ostrom: Facts. Available at https://www.nobelprize.org/prizes/economic-sciences/2009/ostrom/facts/ (last accessed 24 February 2023).

UNOOSA (United Nations Office for Outer Space Affairs). (no date). Treaty on Principles Governing the Activities of States in the Exploration and Use of Outer Space, including the Moon and Other Celestial Bodies. Available at https://www.unoosa.org/oosa/en/ourwork/spacelaw/treaties/introouterspacetreaty.html (last accessed 3 March 2024).

van Laerhoven, F., and Ostrom, E. (2007). Traditions and trends in the study of the commons. *International Journal of the Commons* 1(1): 3–28.

Online materials

- https://www.bollier.org/—Covers news and perspectives on current commons issues.
- https://thecommoner.org/—A web-based open-access journal that has regular contributions on issues related to the commons.
- https://www.thecommonsjournal.org/—The website for the *International Journal of the Commons*, an interdisciplinary peer-reviewed open-access journal.
- https://www.onthecommons.org/—Includes the *Commons Magazine* and a range of other resources related to the commons.

Further reading

Bauwens, M., Kostakis, V., and Pazaitis, A. (2019). *Peer to Peer: The Commons Manifesto*. London: University of Westminster Press.
Explores the creation of diverse digital commons by small peer-based groups cooperating around the globe.

Bollier, D., and Helfrich, S. (eds.) (2015). *Patterns of Commoning*. Bielefeld: Commons Strategies Group.
A collection of over 50 essays by researchers, practitioners and activists that showcases examples of functioning commons the world over.

Hudson, B., Rosenbloom, J., and Cole, D. (eds.) (2020). *Routledge Handbook of the Study of the Commons*. London: Routledge.
A collection that introduces a range of analytical frameworks for studying commons in various contexts.

Linebaugh, P. (2014). *Stop, Thief! The Commons, Enclosures, and Resistance*. Binghamton: PM Press.
A classic text that examines histories of various commons that have relevance today.

Vivero-Pol, J. L., Ferrando, T., De Schutter, O., and Mattei, U. (eds.) (2019). *Routledge Handbook of Food as a Commons*. London: Routledge.
A collection of essays that tackle the challenge of reframing food as a commons rather than a commodity.

SECTION TWO

COLLABORATIONS WITH TECHNOLOGY

Big data

Benjamin Adams

Introduction

We live in an era of **big data**, where the vast scale and range of information available provides new perspectives and opportunities to understand a wide variety of phenomena. What counts as 'big' changes from one discipline to another, but generally speaking big data refers to data with the three 'V' properties: volume, velocity, and variety (Kitchin and McArdle, 2016). *Volume* refers to the size of the data, *velocity* to the near real-time speed at which data is generated, and *variety* to the different forms that data takes. The 'three Vs' are interrelated, and the promise of big data is that data with these properties allow us to find new patterns using statistics and related quantitative methods, which in turn lead us to discover new knowledge. While big data analytics can be a powerful tool, it is not a panacea and works best when interpreted alongside discipline-specific knowledge.

In geography, working with large data sets is not new. Remote sensing tools such as imaging satellites have been generating very large amounts of environmental data for decades. We have **geographic information systems** (GISs) and other tools to analyse this data to understand environmental processes and change in great detail. Prior to the early 2000s, most large geographic data sets were generated by centralised, authoritative sources such as national mapping agencies or private companies that standardised the information. However, more recently with the expansion of the Internet and new forms of user-generated content, the sources of geographic data have become much more heterogeneous. This rich landscape of new data sources represents a sea change in how we gather information about human-place processes, and this variety is usually what we are referring to when discussing *big data* in the context of human geography.

Over the last two decades a number of communities of non-experts have arisen to generate a new type of geographic data, called volunteered geographic information (VGI) (Goodchild, 2007). Just like Wikipedia developed as a bottom-up source of encyclopaedia knowledge from a vast array of individual contributors, analogous VGI platforms such as OpenStreetMap (OSM) have been extremely successful at building massive global geographic data sets from the contributions of volunteers. In addition to these sorts of community-run endeavours, online content includes a lot of passively generated geographic data as well. For example, with the everyday use of mobile devices, there has been a drastic shift in the amount of information we collect about human behaviour in **space** and over time. The forms that geographic data take have also expanded significantly. Where historically we might have characterised geographic data as being explicitly spatial—points or shapes representing longitude and latitude locations on

DOI: 10.4324/9780429265853-78

899

Earth—*geographic big data* takes a more comprehensive view, including place-based information such as online text that people write about places or photographs they take.

In the remainder of this chapter, we will discuss some examples of how big data is being used today in human geography research and some of the implications. We will highlight three main areas where big data is making an impact in human geography: volunteered geographic information with OSM as an example, mobile data and movement analysis, and data-driven models of place from unstructured data.

Summary

- Big data in human geography refers to not only a large amount of data being produced but also an increase in the speed and variety of data sources providing insight into human-place processes.

Volunteered geographic information

The most prominent example in recent years of user-generated data supplanting authoritative geographic data sets is the OSM project (Bertolotto et al., 2020). OSM is a regularly updated global data set consisting of millions of data points describing road networks, buildings, points of interest, and other geographic features. OSM was created in 2004 as a free map of the world, because in many parts of the world, high-quality map data from authoritative sources was prohibitively expensive for people to acquire. Today, the quality of OSM data is on par with that provided by national mapping agencies and is, in fact, more up-to-date in many places, because contributors can update data directly. In its first 15 years, OSM has grown to over 6 million contributors, by far one of the largest volunteer crowdsourcing endeavours ever. Although OSM data collection is not centralised and anyone can contribute, organised social structures have developed around OSM which have shaped the course of the project. For example, the Humanitarian OSM (HotOSM) team organises real-time mapping actions to support response efforts in places hit by natural disasters like earthquakes.

Despite its success, OSM has some of the same limitations as other large online crowdsourcing projects such as Wikipedia. For example, there is one version of the global map at any given time, which means that differing representations on the map cannot easily co-exist. The labels used to categorise points of interest are also fixed, which might not match well with local conceptualisations. Plus, the contributors of the data do not always include representatives of local populations, and as a result the type of coverage varies greatly in different parts of the world. All data is 'theory-laden', which means that the form data takes is dependent on a number of presuppositions imposed by the data collector about the domain and what is being measured (Longino, 1979). For example, the categories (such as: 'park' and 'amenities') used to classify map features on OSM can be interpreted to have very different meanings by different contributors. That interpretation can be based on individual background, expertise, culture, or even the circumstance under which the data is being collected (for example, an emergency response event). This also impacts which features a contributor thinks are important to be mapped in the

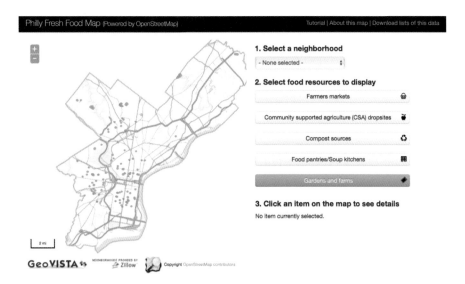

Figure 66.1

Philly food maps (http://www.gis.cwu.edu/phillyfood/) is a website that uses crowdsourced OpenStreetMap data to show access to fresh food in the city of Philadelphia

Source: http://www.gis.cwu.edu/phillyfood/

first place. In OSM (and with big data in general) the process of data creation is not homogeneous and what is represented in the data is variable, which complicates its interpretation in aggregate and when applied to new problems. In addition, although OSM started primarily as a free map, with its quality now matching other map data sources, it is used by many commercial applications. Some companies such as Facebook (Meta) are not only users but also contributors to the data, sometimes using automated machine learning tools to update data, raising questions for some members in the community about whether the project has strayed from its volunteer roots.

The representativeness (and accompanying bias) of data is an ongoing concern when working with big data, because sometimes we do not have a full picture of the population generating the data. In the case of OSM there are questions about how the data reflects the demographics of the contributor community, or even commercial interests. The relevance of these issues for human geography research is context-dependent. If you need up-to-date transportation network data from an urban area, in order to do analysis on food deserts and access to healthy food (see Figure 66.1), then OSM could be an excellent source for that. If you are interested in understanding sites of cultural importance for a group which does not actively contribute to OSM, then it might not suit the purpose. We will see the theme of representativeness of big data arise in the next two sections as well.

Summary

- Volunteered geographic information is geographic data that has been crowdsourced from volunteers and local populations. In many cases this data has replaced data that was historically provided by more centralised and authoritative data producers.

Movement data from mobile devices

In geographic research, the collection of information from the use of mobile devices is often referred to as *social sensing* (Liu et al., 2015). The devices that individuals carry not only tell us something about their mobile behaviour, but they can also act as sensors embedded and moving through the human environment. Mobile devices are uniquely personal computers; they are usually linked to one individual, and we carry them with us throughout our daily tasks. We also use them to store personal information and socially connect with others.

Although in some cases mobile data is explicitly gathered for a specific research purpose, more often than not social sensing data is the by-product of applications intended for a completely different purpose. Any geographical analysis of this information requires serious consideration of the ethics of its use as well as a nuanced understanding of the underlying population generating the data. If we are to extrapolate anything about human societies or culture from this data, then we need to carefully consider how the data is collected and contextualise any findings in terms of other geographic and sociological theories. In addition, since mobile data might be collected via opaque, proprietary systems, care must be taken in its interpretation. An artist named Simon Weckert amusingly demonstrated this when he made Google Maps display a traffic jam for a Berlin street simply by putting 99 smartphones in a handcart and walking it down the street (Figure 66.2).

Devices, such as mobile phones, which have global positioning system (GPS) receivers and wireless sensors that locate a person in space, are commonplace and can provide observational data about human movement through the environment. Movement data contains spatio-temporal signals from which we can glean information about a number of human-geographical processes (Dodge et al., 2016). When we collect this data, it can be used for analysis about past

Figure 66.2
Screenshot of the Google Maps Hacks video showing the artist walking down the street with a cart of smartphones and the resulting 'traffic jam' shown on Google Maps

Source: Simon Weckert's Google Maps Hacks video, available from https://www.simonweckert.com/googlemapshacks.html

behaviour as well as to seed simulations that can help us infer what might happen in future scenarios. There are a wide variety of domains where movement data is useful, including transportation studies, epidemiology, disaster risk and response, and for understanding human mobility.

When location data is gathered over time, it becomes a set of points that can be linked together into *trajectories*. Each trajectory represents the movement of an object through space over time. When trajectories intersect with points of interest or with other trajectories that often represents events that are meaningful for analysis. Contact tracing during the COVID-19 pandemic was a particularly salient example of how analysing trajectory data can help with social issues. Because many people carry mobile phones throughout the day, we can collect data about their movement through the environment and identify when close contacts are made which might have spread the virus (McKenzie and Adams, 2020). It can also be used to understand how well social policy messaging influences mobility behaviour. The application of mobility data in epidemiology is not limited to the interaction of people. Movement data can also be combined with other sensors, e.g. physiological sensors, which measure other health-related information, or environmental sensors that detect pollutants. When combined together with the data from other sensors, movement data provides whole new ways to better understand how individual health, behaviour, and environmental exposures are interrelated.

Time geography is an analytic method for describing the possible trajectories that an individual can take within a specific time frame and for a given geographic space (Hagerstrand, 1970). For example, there are a limited number of grocery stores that a person can reach within 20 minutes of travel time from their house. The exact answer depends on not only the road or transportation network but also the day of the week, the time of the day, and the movement of all other people in the same space. Although time geography is not a new method (see Chapter 4), big data about people's movement allows us to apply time geography methods in new ways to analyse our transportation networks in a dynamic way and simulate a variety of different hypothetical scenarios. For example, urban planners have introduced the concept of '15-minute cities', which are physical environments where people should be able to access their core needs within a 15-minute bike ride (or other target time or transportation, also known as 'x-minute' cities). Such concepts are intended to support low-carbon transportation (walking, bicycling) for a significant percentage of the population that lives there (Logan et al., 2022). Movement big data can be used to empirically test how long various transport methods will take under different conditions or future development, to see whether such targets can be met.

The flipside to all the utility derived from movement data is that what makes it extremely useful also exposes very real problems for privacy. Location-based data is one of the most sensitive types of personal data that one can gather about a person (Keßler and McKenzie, 2018). The reason for this is that it not only tells you where a person is, it tells you where they live, where they work, what activities they engage in, who else they interact with, and more. Furthermore, because our mobile behaviour tends to follow very distinct patterns—we don't randomly visit different places every day—even a small amount of location data can quickly expose a great deal of private information about a person. There have been a number of research studies which have shown that fully anonymised movement data can easily be de-anonymised when combined with other data sources, such as public home ownership records (Gambs et al., 2014). The vast amount of location data that is collected through mobile devices in an unregulated manner is truly staggering—in 2019 *The New York Times* wrote an exposé on a data set of 50 billion location pings, which although anonymised, revealed tracking of individuals on nearly every street in the

United States (Thompson and Warzel, 2019). They found it was easy to identify the complete movement of notable figures based on very little additional public information. In absence of regulation, researchers who wish to share location data need to be cognisant of the possibility of misuse of location data, even when anonymised.

Apart from the privacy issue, there is the issue of consent when using movement data for human geography research. As mentioned, telecommunication companies collect a tremendous amount of location-based information. It is possible to purchase mobility data from these companies, which they have gathered under their terms of use, but while these private companies might have the legal right to the gather the information, there is an onus on researchers to apply a higher standard of explicit consent. As an excellent example of how to ensure informed consent for mobility data studies, Kreuter et al. (2020) describe in detail the consent process used by a research study that passively collected smartphone data to examine the long-term effects of unemployment on social activity. They show that engagement in such studies is possible to achieve even when collecting fine-grained data about participants' location as well as social media interactions.

Summary

- The advent of personal mobile devices has led to the collection of fine-grained data about people's movements through the environment. This data has great utility for observing human societies but it also raises many questions about the ethics of data use in research and user privacy.

Using 'unstructured data' to learn about place

In addition to movement data, people are generating more data about their experiences of places than ever before. We take pictures and annotate them with our impressions, we write travel blogs about places we visit, we respond to current events on social media, and so on. This is often referred to as 'unstructured data' because it is not like GIS data which is stored in a specific format for spatial analysis, rather it is data that is meant for other humans to consume. This information is embedded in space and time, and it represents experiences filtered through the eyes of different individuals, potentially providing new insights into the many ways that people experience places. Increasingly, this data is feeding into new technologies that we use in our day-to-day lives, such as question-answering search engines, which analyse the data using sophisticated **artificial intelligence** algorithms.

When unstructured data comes in the form of written text or spoken language, it is often called *natural language data*. Other common types of unstructured data that tell us about places are images and videos. Often natural language text is combined with images, e.g. in social media posts. Unstructured data can be interpreted as geographic information in different ways. First, there might be some geographic *metadata* associated with the data. For example, we take an image and record the location data where the image was taken, or we post a message on social media, and it is tagged with a place name. In that case there is an association between the content and a single geographic location. In other cases, the geographic aspect might be part of content of the data. For example, a newspaper article might reference a number of named places such as cities. In that case, the association is between the place that has been mentioned and the surrounding text. It can also have information about the relationships between places.

The analysis of unstructured data has advanced greatly in recent years with the invention of new methods in artificial intelligence, which work best when applied to very large quantities of data. *Natural language processing* refers to a broad array of tools and methods which allow us to discover patterns and parse information from written text. One example of natural language processing is sentiment analysis, which categorises text by its emotional content: for example, positive or negative sentiment. Applied to geographic big data this can tell us about broad sentiment trends in a data set about different places or events. Another type of analysis is topic modelling, which can tell us what kinds of topics people are writing about in different locations or time periods. For example, the tourism industry can look at real-time social media data to analyse perceptions of a place.

A corpus is a very large collection of text that we can statistically analyse to find patterns, which can help basic research on geography and language, and also help us create new kinds of tools to explore geographic knowledge. Linguistic research on dialects and language use across geographic space traditionally relied on small survey data sets, usually focusing on a single language. Today, however, there are several multi-lingual corpuses built using web data (for example, from Twitter) that comprise billions of words. This data provides new insights into geographic variability and change in everyday language use and allows linguistics researchers to ask new questions and test existing theory.

One example application which applies statistical methods on web data to explore geographic knowledge was the Frankenplace website, shown in Figure 66.3 (Adams

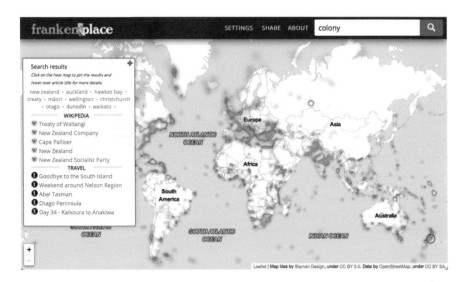

Figure 66.3
A screenshot of the search results for the keyword 'colony' on the Frankenplace website. The user has clicked on a location in New Zealand bringing up results for the Treaty of Waitangi, New Zealand Company, etc.

Source: Adams et al., 2015

et al., 2015). The Frankenplace system took over 5 million articles from the English Wikipedia data set plus several hundred thousand travel blog entries from around the world and used natural language processing to extract thousands of named places from around the globe to create a geographic search index for articles. The result was an interactive tool that allowed people to explore the relationships between places and topics. As with any big data analysis, the results shown on the Frankenplace website perhaps told us as much about bias in the English version of Wikipedia as it did about specific places or topics.

One growing area for the application of artificial intelligence to unstructured geographic data is geographic question-answering systems. Digital assistants (like Siri, Google Assistant, Copilot, Alexa) which answer questions are being integrated into many aspects of our daily lives. For example, digital assistants use personal and location data to contextualise answers for users to find a local restaurant based on personal preferences or to indicate places that one might want to visit while on vacation. All of these systems rely on big data to train, and the algorithms used are complex and opaque. In a sense, *more data* is better because it allows the system to build a model that is robust and can work in many different circumstances, but *good data* is even more important (Bender et al., 2021). If built on massive quantities of unfiltered web data, it is inevitable that an artificial intelligence model will absorb statistical relationships which reflect human biases in human language as well as uneven representations in the underlying data. One example is that the amount of English language data online vastly outweighs all other languages, potentially leading to strong cultural biases. As we hand over more and more decision-making to computers, it will be an ongoing challenge to make sure that these systems are informed by human geography. Finally, the more embedded digital assistants and artificial intelligence become in our daily lives, the more they will impact human behaviour. Thus, there will be a feedback loop where the big data we generate through our behaviour will in turn influence our behaviour. This remains a wide-open area for human geography research.

Summary

- Geographic big data today is not limited to traditionally spatially referenced data, such as maps. It also includes unstructured information, such as written text and photographs, that people share on the web about places. This data provides a view into diverse individual experiences.

Conclusion

In almost every domain we are generating greater volumes of data, at higher velocity, and in more variety of forms than ever before, and this includes human geography. For human geography some of the biggest changes in recent years have come about from new methods of gathering data, including crowdsourcing from volunteers, new types of mobile devices, and online web data, in particular social media. Combined, these new data sets provide a number of new opportunities to analyse human-geographic processes in finer detail than ever before. Despite the huge value of these types of data sets, it is important to consider how the data has been created and interrogate our assumptions about the population which created the data. Thus, effective big data analysis in human geography is careful analysis, ideally informed and substantiated by relevant theory as found elsewhere in this volume.

Discussion points

- What are some key characteristics of big data, and human geography big data in particular?
- Provide three example sources of geographic big data. What makes the data 'big'?
- What do you think about the use of your personal mobile phone data or your social media posts for big data analysis?
- In a *New York Times* interactive feature on location data privacy, Professor Paul Ohm is quoted as saying, 'D.N.A. is probably the only thing that is harder to anonymize than precise geolocation information'. Discuss why he makes this claim.
- How has geographic big data contributed to our understanding of place?

References

Adams, B., McKenzie, G., and Gahegan, M. (2015). Frankenplace: interactive thematic mapping for ad hoc exploratory search. In *Proceedings of the 24th International Conference on World Wide Web* (pp. 12–22).

Bender, E. M., Gebru, T., McMillan-Major, A., and Shmitchell, S. (2021, March). On the Dangers of Stochastic Parrots: Can Language Models Be Too Big? In *Proceedings of the 2021 ACM Conference on Fairness, Accountability, and Transparency* (pp. 610–623).

Bertolotto, M., McArdle, G., and Schoen-Phelan, B. (2020). Volunteered and crowdsourced geographic information: the OpenStreetMap project. *Journal of Spatial Information Science* 20(2020): 65–70. https://arrow.tudublin.ie/scschcomart/106/

Dodge, S., Weibel, R., Ahearn, S. C., Buchin, M., and Miller, J. A. (2016). Analysis of movement data. *International Journal of Geographical Information Science* 30(5): 825–834.

Gambs, S., Killijian, M. O., and del Prado Cortez, M. N. (2014). De-anonymization attack on geolocated data. *Journal of Computer and System Sciences* 80(8): 1597–1614.

Goodchild, M. F. (2007). Citizens as sensors: the world of volunteered geography. *GeoJournal* 69(4): 211–221.

Hagerstrand, T. (1970). What about people in regional science? *Papers of the Regional Science Association* 24: 7–21.

Keßler, C., and McKenzie, G. (2018). A geoprivacy manifesto. *Transactions in GIS* 22(1): 3–19.

Kitchin, R., and McArdle, G. (2016). What makes big data, big data? Exploring the ontological characteristics of 26 datasets. *Big Data & Society* 3(1): 2053951716631130.

Kreuter, F., Haas, G.-C., Keusch, F., Bahr, S., and Trappmann, M. (2020). Collecting survey and smartphone sensor data with an app: opportunities and challenges around privacy and informed consent. *Social Science Computer Review* 38(5): 533–549.

Liu, Y., Liu, X., Gao, S., Gong, L., Kang, C., Zhi, Y., Chi, G., and Shi, L. (2015). Social sensing: a new approach to understanding our socioeconomic environments. *Annals of the Association of American Geographers* 105(3): 512–530.

Logan, T., Hobbs, M., Conrow, L., Reid, N., Young, R., and Anderson, M. (2022). The x-minute city. measuring the 10, 15, 20-minute city and an evaluation of its use for sustainable urban design. *Cities* 131: 103924.

Longino, H. (1979). Evidence and hypothesis: an analysis of evidential relations. *Philosophy of Science* 46(1): 35–56.

McKenzie, G., and Adams, B. (2020). A country comparison of place-based activity response to COVID-19 policies. *Applied Geography* 125: 102363

Thompson, S. A., and Warzel, C. (2019). Twelve million phones, one dataset, zero privacy. *The New York Times*. https://www.nytimes.com/interactive/2019/12/19/opinion/location-tracking-cell-phone.html. Accessed online: 7 February 2022.

Online materials

- More information on Simon Weckert's Google Maps Hacks: https://simonweckert.com/googlemapshacks.html, video: https://www.youtube.com/watch?v=k5eL_al_m7Q. This website showcases Simon Weckert's creative projects that manipulate Google Maps to challenge and explore the concept of digital mapping.
- HotOSM: https://www.hotosm.org. This website is the official page of the HotOSM Team, an organisation that uses open mapping data to support humanitarian and development initiatives worldwide.
- COVID-19 Community Mobility Reports from Google: https://www.google.com/covid19/mobility/. Google's official webpage provides reports on community mobility during the COVID-19 pandemic, illustrating trends and changes in people's movement patterns based on aggregated and anonymised location data.

Further Reading

Learn more about big data and human geography.

Kitchin, R. (2013). Big data and human geography: opportunities, challenges and risks. *Dialogues in Human Geography* 3(3): 262–267. DOI: 10.1177/2043820613513388

Learn more about crowdsourced geographic information.

Capineri, C., Haklay, M., Huang, H., Antoniou, V., Kettunen, J., Ostermann, F., and Purves, R. (2016). *European Handbook of Crowdsourced Geographic Information*. London: Ubiquity Press. DOI: 10.5334/bax

Learn more about movement analysis with big data.

Dodge, S., Gao, S., Tomko, M., and Weibel, R. (2020). Progress in computational movement analysis – towards movement data science. *International Journal of Geographical Information Science* 34:12, 2395–2400. DOI: 10.1080/13658816.2020.1784425

Learn more about methods and techniques to analyse text-based big data for human geography.

Purves, R. S., Koblet, O., and Adams, B. (2022). *Unlocking Environmental Narratives: Towards Understanding Human Environment Interactions through Computational Text Analysis*. London: Ubiquity Press. DOI: 10.5334/bcs

Participatory cartographies for social change

Luke Drake

Introduction

Maps are great at telling stories about people and the world around us. But whose stories? And who is telling the stories? These are important questions for participatory cartography, because maps can be deceptively simple: a good map takes only a second to understand but can take a long time to make; the seemingly neutral and innocent world map posted in primary school classrooms around the world was a product of, and central to, European **imperialism**. New maps emerge as the world changes, other maps seem to reaffirm long-held beliefs, and other maps are retelling stories that have been stifled for a long time. Cartography is the theory and practice of mapmaking, and decisions about what to include and exclude from maps are bound up in layers of power relations. Participatory cartography is the theory and practice of involving different kinds of knowledge when mapmaking, and intentionally considering these power relations when it comes to mapmaking.

People around the world have been making maps for thousands of years, and creative mapmaking continues today. Just what *is* a map, though? Geographers often start by thinking of maps as a way to share spatial knowledge. In this way, verbal communication and oral stories about landmarks, routes, and **territories** are perhaps universal human practices since antiquity until today. We certainly think about web-based maps on smartphones as pervasive across society. But think for a moment—how many times have you simply told someone driving directions to a shop, or walking directions across campus? Even when maps are in their formal cartographic form of a digital or paper map, oral communication is still used often to understand what's on the map. You might have had the experience of looking at a university campus map or a public transportation route map posted at a train station or bus stop, helping a friend figure out how to make sense of the colourful lines—where is 'here' and how to get to 'there'.

If we think about maps in that way, they don't just stand alone but are extensions of other forms of communication about **space** and place. They link together individuals, communities, institutions, and states in myriad ways. As forms of communication, maps are one type of **discourse** alongside written texts, oral histories, songs and chants, and cultural landscapes (see Chapter 6 on 'reading' landscapes). And as many human geographers have pointed out,

DOI: 10.4324/9780429265853-79

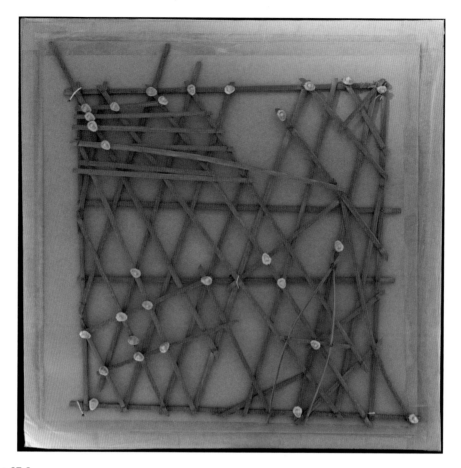

Figure 67.1
Marshall Islands Navigation Chart, undated

Source: Courtesy of University Library at California State University, Northridge. Image prepared by David Deis

discourse is bound up with complex power relations. All of this is really to help you start thinking about maps as not just a noun but also as a verb—mapping—and something that is done as part of an array of discursive practices that link people together in often unequal ways.

Take, for instance, the navigational charts developed by Indigenous Marshall Islanders (Figure 67.1). They were developed to teach and communicate complex oceanographic knowledge about the interactions between islands, currents, and swells, and they were sustainably produced using local materials such as shells and wood. Some of these maps, called *meddo* and *rebbelib* in Kajin Majel (Marshallese), represent locations of islands, but others called *mattang* visualise the concepts of wave diffraction, refraction, and reflection that enabled Marshallese navigators to find islands across vast distances. Importantly, these *mattang* maps did not aim for a spatial representation of locations, nor did they communicate oceanographic processes as standalone maps. Rather, they existed alongside the passing of knowledge from one generation to the next; they had to be talked about to be understood. They also existed relationally with the spatial practice of ocean voyaging. These maps declined from use during German and Japanese colonial occupation, as prohibitions on traditional sailing were introduced in the name of safety and to bolster the revenues of colonial trading companies. Without the voyaging, the maps dropped out of use. Mapping in this case was not only assembling the map but also the spatial practice of voyaging. The knowledge of voyaging and the knowledge of mapping were inter-dependent. The imposition of movement restrictions dissolved these mapping practices until revived decades later. This example shows how maps are extensions of an array of communica-tion and knowledge practices—and how they are right in the middle of struggles over power and discourse. **Colonisation** of the Marshall Islands depended in part on stifling those Indigenous spatial practices and spatial knowledge.

Although sharing spatial knowledge is universal, the most famous maps might be the ones that demonstrate how mapping has been tightly linked with state power. One of the earliest world maps ('world' is relative to what was known to Europe and the Near East) was made by North African cartographer Muhammad al-Idrisi in 1154, which was commissioned by Sicilian king Roger II (Figure 67.2). Mappa Mundi (literally: world maps in Italian) were produced under the direction of European theocratic leaders showing Jerusalem at the centre of the world.

It is important to see maps as a part of discourse, power, and knowledge, because it puts a critical perspective on the field of cartography—the study of map design and production. There is indeed specialised knowledge required for professional mapmaking nowadays—**map pro-jections**, colour theory, and increasingly, knowledge of database management in **geographic information systems** (GIS). Such standards are the result of the emergence over the past few centuries of a particular kind of cartography emerging from Western Europe—one where specialised training strived to accurately represent the three-dimensional Earth's surface in a two-dimensional map (see Chapter 66). This kind of cartography, rather than be satisfied with relative locations, relied on precise controls of the distortions that happen when projecting the 3-D Earth surface onto a map. Mathematical models called map projections were developed by cartographers to reduce the distortions of the shapes of countries and continents, geographical areas, distances, and directions.

Formal cartography techniques that are taught and used today were developed mainly through imperialism, and in recent years anti-colonial and **decolonial** cartography practices have emerged. The Mercator projection map, where the prime meridian centres the United Kingdom in the middle of the map, is perhaps the best example of the imperial legacy of cartography. Now seen in classrooms all around world, Gerardus Mercator developed the pro-jection in 1569 to aid ship navigation, and it thus contributed to the spread of European **colonialism**. Even today, this projection is also the basis for the Web Mercator projection, used for nearly all web-based maps today such as Google Maps. This is not to say that such maps are still actively imperialistic, rather that this legacy is embedded in many ways in every-day life. Anti-colonial mapping and decolonial mapping seek to represent and interpret the world in ways that subvert that imperial legacy and recentre Indigenous practices. Examples include reclaiming Indigenous place names, centring Indigenous relationships to the environ-ment, and reimagining the mapping process altogether (Rose-Redwood et al., 2020). While some of these efforts reject mapmaking practices that have been derived from settler colo-nialism, others reappropriate cartographic techniques in order to resist neocolonial practices (Bryan and Wood, 2015). The need to think about, plan, and create maps in new ways that reveal geographic knowledge that may otherwise go unnoticed or erased is part of a set of prac-tices called participatory cartography.

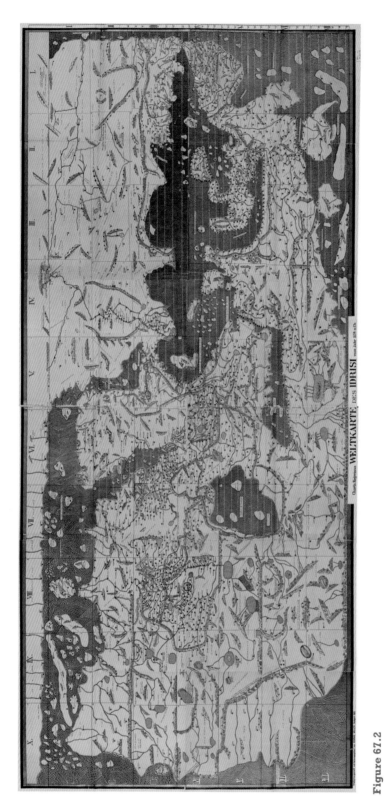

Figure 67.2

One of the maps made by Muhammad al-Idrisi in 1154 CE for the atlas known as Tabula Rogeriana

Source: Wikimedia Commons

Summary

- Maps are embedded in social, political, and economic processes.
- Although cartographers strive to accurately represent the Earth's surface and its features, decisions about what to put on a map are guided by deliberate and implicit influences.
- Different types of maps and cartography techniques have risen and declined in social contexts.
- Decolonial cartography and anti-colonial cartography are being done in response to imperial histories of cartography.

What is participatory cartography?

Most simply, participatory cartography refers to the combination of participatory research methods with formal cartography. It includes various ways that people who have received formal training and education in cartography make maps together with people who have not. In practice, the participants and the cartographers range across a wide spectrum. Participants might be a community group, staff from a non-governmental organisation, workers at a firm, or secondary school students. The cartographers could be academic staff from a university, but they might also be staff from a non-governmental organisation or even members of a community group with cartographic training. In short, there isn't one set of criteria.

People engage in participatory cartography projects for many reasons. A non-governmental organisation may want to create maps of environmental hazards, but their staff do not have the funding to purchase GIS software or have the training to use such software. A community group may want to visualise the locations of unsafe pedestrian road crossings in their neighbourhood to send to their local government representatives but lack the tools and training to make it look 'official'. A researcher who volunteers at a charity might recognise an opportunity to map the organisation's service areas in order to find out how to improve their outreach and service delivery efforts. One shared theme is that these projects seek to represent local knowledge about places and communities that is not easily accessible through secondary data sources.

Context: participatory GIS in the 1980s and 1990s

Although people have made their own maps since antiquity, participatory mapping as an academic subject started to emerge a few decades ago. Its historical context was the rise of computers in the 1980s and the emergence of GIS. At that time, geographers began a long period of debate about the role of GIS within the discipline of geography. While many of those supportive of GIS lauded its advantages—the ability to process and analyse large amounts of data tremendously quicker than analogue map analysis—critical geographers pointed out a substantial list of concerns. Privacy and geo-surveillance were some of the critiques of GIS (see Chapter 66); additionally, there was the question of whether this technology would be accessible to marginalised communities. At the time, large institutions such as government agencies, corporations, and universities were likely to be the only ones who could afford computers and have the space to house them (at the time, computers capable of GIS analysis were quite large). If the technology itself were characterised by huge social inequalities, what then would the social impacts look like? For a few years, some geographers thought GIS and critical geography were incompatible. These concerns were carefully explained in the book *Ground Truth: The Social Implications of Geographic Information Systems*, edited by John Pickles and published in 1995.

Efforts to open mapping to new ways of thinking also began to emerge in the 1990s. One publication that brought attention to this was Weiner et al. (1995), who combined Black South Africans' knowledge of landscape characteristics and experiences of apartheid with state datasets on soils. This revealed some of the ways that local knowledge can inform and stand alongside government datasets. Participatory mapping can also rely entirely on data collected by or from community participants. However, geographer Sarah Elwood (2006) has carefully pointed out that participation is not just a matter of adding maps to a community project, or adding communities to a mapping project. Ethics, equity, and distribution of burdens and benefits must be carefully considered. Some reasons for this include the risk of token participation—for example, asking for community participation without using their input when decisions are made—or shifting work burdens to communities while reaping the benefits of their work.

Why participatory cartography?

There are many reasons why a project might use participatory mapping techniques. It can be a way for community members to build and strengthen their connections to each other and to place. Working together to plan, collect data, analyse, and report findings is a social process, and gathering around maps has been done increasingly around the world (see example on participatory cartographies of fisheries in Chapter 65). Other uses include data enrichment, particularly in terms of local knowledge that is unavailable or unfitting for the data structure in secondary datasets. Government-provided data typically is quantitative and discrete data points, standardised across many locations and regions. Local knowledge about a place could be quantitative or qualitative, but it might not fit well into that kind of dataset because it often comes through intensive site visits, fieldwork, and interactions with other people. Lastly, results of participatory cartography might be actionable and taken seriously by community organisations; knowledge coming from the community about the community might have more credence than a report generated by far away civil servants.

How is technology used in participatory cartography?

With the expansion of GIS technologies, web-based geospatial tools, and mobile phone and tablet technology, the possibilities on who can be involved in these kinds of projects, and the capacity to contribute, have multiplied enormously (see Chapter 66). However, sometimes the best technology to use is the simplest—paper and pencil. Perhaps the most widely practised participatory mapping is done through face-to-face gathering of a group of people around a map printed on a piece of paper or a three-dimensional physical model. This is perhaps the image most associated with international development in the **Global South** or **Majority World**, as a way to engage communities without access to the Internet and communication technologies.

But it certainly isn't restricted to those contexts—mental maps are made by human geography students across the world.

Computer systems and mobile technologies have become a central part of cartography, and participatory methods increasingly make use of them as well. Websites such as Google Maps, OpenStreetMap, or ArcGIS Online provide various options for creating custom basemaps, placing points of interest or other features over pre-made basemaps, or as platform for data collection. Desktop software such as Quantum GIS (QGIS) or ArcGIS allows for management, processing, and analysis of large datasets, followed by map visualisation of the data. Mobile devices such as smartphones, tablets, and handheld **Global Navigation Satellite Systems** (GNSS) units, along with laptop computers, can help groups work together in field locations, across multiple locations, and in locations that are accessible to participants.

Summary

- Participatory GIS emerged from debates about the social impacts of GIS.
- There are many reasons and uses for participatory cartography.
- Technology can be used in many ways for these kinds of projects.

Collecting and mapping data about community livelihoods

I have been involved in a community mapping project for some years with a community organisation in the Pacific Island nation of Vanuatu (see Drake et al., 2022). Hango Hango Community Association was formed by Ambae Islanders from one of the country's northern provinces who were living in the capital city Port Vila, located on Efate Island in the central part of the island chain. Although their kin were located in and near each other in the same village on the home island, those living in the capital were dispersed across different neighbourhoods. The community's executive board wanted to conduct a livelihood assessment to gain a better understanding of how community members met their daily household needs and engaged in community-building activities in the capital city. Activities included mapping the locations of community members' households, and site visits to a sample of households to photograph and enter attributes about urban agriculture and agrobiodiversity of food grown at home. Mapping activities were complemented with interviews about livelihood activities such as work, participation in community activities, and food access.

The chairperson of the community association selected the households for the sample, and with some youth members, I joined them to collect data. This included marking the points of the backyards with a Bluetooth-enabled GNSS receiver that provided location data to ArcGIS Collector app. **Geo-tagged** photos were taken and attached to the GIS layer in ArcGIS Collector. These photos enabled us to save time during fieldwork by looking at the photos later to quantify how many homes had space nearby for growing food crops and which types of plants were grown. Mapping activities took place in 2017, 2018, and then again in 2023 (Figure 67.3). They

Figure 67.3
Members of the Hango Hango Community Association survey team, including a first-year University
of the South Pacific student, use ArcGIS Field Maps mobile app to enter agrobiodiversity and disaster
impact data about member households after two tropical cyclones impacted Port Vila, Vanuatu in March
2023

Source: Photo credit: Luke Drake

provided longitudinal data to the community, as well as crucial short-term change information
following evacuations from Ambae Island's volcanic eruption in 2017 that caused temporary
migration to Port Vila, and after two tropical cyclones that happened in March 2023 that damaged houses and backyard gardens (Figure 67.4).

In terms of the principles described below, this project was developed in large part through
relationships I had maintained for many years with several of the community members. Although
my formal relationship with the association was somewhat new, my relationships with some of
the members and their kin had gone back many years, which fostered trust that helped the project
to happen. Reciprocity and shared expertise were part of this work in terms of the decisions about
sampling methods, questions asked, and data collected. I offered suggestions, but the community
partners had first and final say on what data to collect and which locations to visit. After the
mapping and interviewing was done, I presented our findings at a community meeting in Bislama
language and wrote a report in English, printing several copies to distribute to the association's
executive board members along with a digital copy. Additional shared expertise was through
some members of the community who had studied GIS at university in New Zealand, and who
were able to work with some of the map data, especially in the events that happened next.

Figure 67.4
Hango Hango Community Association members use a multispectral camera and Bluetooth-enabled global positioning systems to examine disaster impacts to a food garden near Port Vila, Vanuatu. Pole aerial photography is an alternative where UAVs or drones are not feasible, and it can be a great way to engage community members

Source: Photo credit: Luke Drake

In the years following the initial mapping, we continued to update the community map and eventually completed a web-based map of all households belonging to Hango Hango Community Association. The community executive board used this in 2022 during the COVID-19 pandemic, when a lockdown spurred the community association to begin community relief efforts. Transparency was important throughout—this community knowledge was managed by the community, and not my possession—and so web links and digital materials from our mapping project were still available to the community to use, alter, and reproduce.

How was shared expertise handled in terms of technology? For my part, I used the institutional resources of my university, which provided tools such as an ArcGIS Online subscription, tablets, laptop computers, and Bluetooth-enabled handheld GNSS receivers. These resources are unavailable for many community organisations (and are discussed in the next section). However, this project was not styled as a contracted-out or consultancy, where I did the work on my own and provided the results to the partners. Rather, we worked together, with my providing technical expertise and technology equipment, and community partners providing research design and GIS experience. This is what made it participatory.

Summary

- Projects involving collaborations between university researchers and Indigenous community members relied on shared decision-making at several steps of the cartography process.
- Different partners' expertise was recognised and valued in the participatory process.
- Decisions about how to share resources were made collaboratively.
- Data and maps from these projects were shared between researcher and community members.

What are some important principles of participatory cartography?

There are different ways to do this kind of work, in terms of the types of participants, the degree of involvement by participants, and the technologies used. However, some cross-cutting themes can be applied across many contexts.

Respect and shared expertise. Geographers in a participatory project need to respect the community participants as equals. Geographers should recognise the participants' expertise they bring to a project, as well as recognise that the geographers are not experts in everything either. They are experts in their own lives, their neighbourhoods, and their communities in ways outsiders may never understand. Formal training in GIS and cartography is a great contribution, but it does not convey authority over participants. This is perhaps the first rule—do not treat community participants as if they were laboratory subjects. Western scientific practice has been filled with patterns of violence—at times, this put people in physical danger and even injury and death; at other times, participatory research was no more than a ruse to invoke harmful laws and policies under pretences that community members accepted the results. One strategy that can be successful is to find a person who can act as a liaison—someone who might understand the position of a geography student or professional geographer and who also is a trusted member of the participants' community. That person can help the researcher establish rapport with the participants.

Transparency and reciprocity. When working with a community group to gather data for a geographical research project, researcher intentions and goals should be clear to the participants, and they should not be expected to participate simply to help a researcher reach their own goals. Is the researcher trying to fulfil requirements for a thesis or a course project? This is probably going to be ok with most community groups—they know students have a job to do or a degree to complete. A researcher should also—hopefully—be genuinely interested in the participants' goals and livelihoods, but it is not necessary to pretend you are doing this work out of pure altruism with nothing to gain from it. Trust is fundamental in participatory projects, and one part of building trust is being clear about what you are doing and why.

Likewise, reciprocity is important because participatory cartography can be labour-intensive for participants. It is not participatory but exploitative if the researcher simply uses participation as a way of getting data to complete their own project. In participatory cartography, it is an equally important objective to create a product that the participants can own and use as well. Some examples include the following: a report about the project written in jargon-free, non-academic language for them to distribute as they wish; a collection of maps that the community group may freely use however they choose; community workshops on how to use mobile mapping tools, awareness of geo-privacy issues, or how to use open-source GIS software; helping the group apply for grants by finding grant opportunities or reviewing their grant proposals. Extracting data from a community group without reciprocating can follow a pattern of disempowerment and exploitation that many communities have repeatedly experienced.

Taking time to listen. A participatory project cannot run on a professional researcher's schedule, because most of the time, participants are trying to work on this project in their spare time. Many aspects of their lives may take precedence. Researchers must listen to their concerns and hear what they are experiencing, while paying attention to how the group wants the project to proceed. Would participants rather have more power in decision-making, even if it makes the project take longer—or are they interested in having you take on some of their tasks and decisions so that they can reach the end of the project more quickly? There isn't a correct answer here because it always depends on the participants' concerns and objectives.

Thinking collaboratively. Participation is a concept and a practice that requires critical reflection. Participatory cartography suggests inclusivity and shared knowledge, rather than the exclusive domain of experts. One can (and should) ask many questions about all of this. Who gains from their involvement in a project that is labelled 'participatory'? Who decides to call a mapping project participatory? Who comes up with the project's objectives? Does anyone take on more of a burden than others when doing the work? What are the benefits of a participatory project, and how are those benefits distributed? Did a project's managers simply want to convey an image of inclusivity to gain political or financial support?

Participation means decisions about any of the following steps in mapmaking:

- Deciding the purpose and audience of a map
- Collecting data
- Processing and analysing data
- Deciding which features to put on a map
- Choosing visual design and symbology for those features
- Choosing which features to label
- Deciding to use a legend and deciding which features to show in the legend
- Who 'owns' the map and can decide on its distribution (or withholding from public view)?

Summary

- Although there are diverse ways to engage with participatory cartography, some guidelines have become clear over many years.
- Respect of shared expertise includes both professional researchers and also community partners.

- It is important for geographers to be transparent in their goals when communicating about a project, so that community partners can build trust that a project is equitable. Reciprocity, relationship-building, and listening are also important.
- Participation can happen at any point in the cartography process, from research planning to the production and distribution of maps.

Conclusion

This chapter began by exploring some of the origins of participatory cartography and why it developed. It then provided some examples of participatory projects and described some guidelines for engaging in this kind of mapping. Key points included the importance of collaboration and listening. Where to next for participatory cartography? This is an exciting, dynamic time for this work. Institutions, communities, and individuals are exploring how to use conventional techniques to do unconventional things and how to move away from conventional ideas about mapping altogether. Technologies enable new kinds of remote and face-to-face interactions. New technologies will continue to be part of the conversation and debate, but how can they be used in collaborative, more equitable ways? Future directions may point to decisions about when it is appropriate to use proprietary or open-source technology. The rise of unmanned aerial vehicles or remotely piloted aircraft for aerial photography reinvigorates longstanding debates in critical GIS about privacy and imperialism, and how such technologies might be used for participatory cartography. In sum, there are many types of participation, and many ways to engage in participatory cartography.

Discussion points

- Why is participatory cartography important to the study of geography?
- What are some of the ways that cartography projects can be participatory?
- How could the principles described in the chapter be applied to emerging technologies, such as open-source software, remotely piloted aircraft, and artificial intelligence?

References

Bryan, J., and Wood, D. (2015). *Weaponizing Maps: Indigenous Peoples and Counterinsurgency in the Americas*. New York: Guilford Press.

Drake, L., Liunakwalau, H. M., and Hango Hango Community Association. (2022). Locating the traditional economy in Port Vila, Vanuatu: Disaster relief and agrobiodiversity. *Asia Pacific Viewpoint* 63(1): 80–96.

Elwood, S. (2006). Critical issues in participatory GIS: deconstructions, reconstructions, and new research directions. *Transactions in GIS* 10(5): 693–708.

Pickles, J. (ed.) (1995). *Ground Truth: The Social Implications of Geographic Information Systems*. New York: Guilford Press.

Rose-Redwood, R., Blu Barnd, N., Lucchesi, A. H. E., Dias, S., and Patrick, W. (2020). Decolonizing the map: recentering indigenous mappings. *Cartographica: The International Journal for Geographic Information and Geovisualization* 55(3): 151–162.

Weiner, D., Warner, T. A., Harris, T. M., and Levin, R. M. (1995). Apartheid representations in a digital landscape: GIS, remote sensing and local knowledge in Kiepersol, South Africa. *Cartography and Geographic Information Systems* 22(1): 30–44.

Online materials

- PPGIS.net: https://www.ppgis.net/. This electronic forum is focused on participatory use of geospatial information systems and technologies. It hosts four distinct communities, namely the global list which is Anglophone, and lists for French-, Spanish-, and Portuguese-speaking practitioners.
- Participatory mapping project in the Congo basin: https://www.mappingforrights.org/participatory-mapping/. Mapping For Rights is a set of tools and approaches aimed at putting rainforest communities on the map and promoting sustainable, transparent, and equitable governance of the Congo Basin.

Further reading

Drake, L., Liunakwalau, H. M., and Hango Hango Community Association. (2022). Locating the traditional economy in Port Vila, Vanuatu: Disaster relief and agrobiodiversity. *Asia Pacific Viewpoint* 63(1): 80–96.
Read more about the participatory project with Hango Hango Community Association.

Elwood, S. (2006). Critical issues in participatory GIS: deconstructions, reconstructions, and new research directions. *Transactions in GIS* 10(5): 693–708.
This important article describes some of the issues with participatory GIS and sets out a research agenda—how much of this have we followed, and what has changed?

Pickles, J. (ed.) (1995). *Ground Truth: The Social Implications of Geographic Information Systems*. New York: Guilford Press.
Ground Truth is the first book to explicitly address the role of geographic information systems (GIS) in their social context.

Smart cities and everyday urbanism

Prince K Guma

Introduction

'Maximum governance and control with minimum administration' has become a mantra of how technology is used by state and private actors in a number of cities all over the world. Cities are increasingly promoting different forms of new technologies, smart devices, the **internet of things** (IoT, see also Chapter 69) and **big data** (Chapter 66) approaches for improving **infrastructure** provision, urban planning and urban governance (see also Chapter 17).

The smart city **discourse** has been particularly powerful and alluring for examining such contemporary developments in the smart digital age. A large portion of contemporary studies from critical geographers and urban planners has investigated smart cities and everyday urbanism in the Global South, highlighting the local articulations and politics such processes enact amidst spatial inequalities and conditions of urban segregation and polarisation. These studies emphasise the imperative of challenging techno-managerial approaches of city making and planning processes through more nuanced and contextualised understandings of urbanism in the age of smart technologies.

This chapter addresses this topic by outlining the ideal of the smart city: its definition, use in urban design and development in the Global North and South, and different articulations in everyday urban contexts in the Global South or Majority World. It concludes with key considerations for researching smart cities and everyday life in both Minority and Majority Worlds, or Global North and South (see Chapter 9).

What are smart cities?

While there is no universal definition for 'smart cities', the concept implies a particular set of rationalities that embody the ubiquitous use of new technologies, smart devices, the IoT and big data approaches to deliver sustainable, prosperous and inclusive urban futures. Smart cities reflect an aspirational urge for a hyper-networked and technologically modern urban geography where traditional networks and services are made more efficient through smartphone apps and sensors, central control responses and automation, algorithms and heuristics, and data-driven

DOI: 10.4324/9780429265853-80

Figure 68.1
New markets and micro-economies being formed in the digital age

Source: Photo credit: Prince K Guma

governance for the benefit of urban inhabitants, business and government. Implicit in this is the incorporation of 'smarter' dimensions of governance (present in vision statements), citizenship (citizen-focused approaches), economy (technically inspired innovation, creativity and entrepreneurship), and technological infrastructure to solve urban challenges and achieve sustainable urban development and governance.

Over the last decades, smart cities have been developed by urban business and policy practitioners seeking to promote the role of information and communication technology (ICT) solutions for improving infrastructure provision, urban planning and urban governance. Across the world, different kinds of technologies are being applied in cities to deliver maximum governance with minimum government (see Figures 68.1 and 68.2). Take for instance these five examples.

1.   Aspirational cities have transformed themselves into some of the smartest and most sustainable, inclusive and integrated cities in the world. These cities include Dubai and Singapore that have integrated infrastructural and digital elements ranging from advanced sensor-centric solutions and network-connected systems to more basic IoT solutions like smart meters and smart grids, bike and car sharing, smart and electric mobility and traffic systems, and intelligent billing and crediting systems on a grand scale. They seek to realise interactive and responsive city administration and management and enhance responsiveness of public services to citizens.
2.   Ambitious smart city programmes are in progress, such as the Smart City Mission to develop 100 smart cities in India through the Smart Cities Mission Programme; Indonesia's '100 Smart Cities' programme; and China's more than 500 smart city projects. In all of these

Figure 68.2
Konza Technopolis, a large technology hub, special economic zone and futuristic city located in Kenya

Source: Photo credit: Prince K Guma

cases, the central government is integral in developing smart cities through programmes that offer a typology of smart city development prioritising smart governance, smart citizen and smart infrastructure at the policy level across a national scale.

3. Enclave infrastructure developments in the form of private investments by international ventures and real estate developers. These constitute premium network spaces including city extensions in urbanising hinterlands, wealthy enclaves, satellite cities, industrial zones and business districts supplemented by new and existing infrastructure and digital systems, ranging from smart grids to multimodal transport networks. Government-approved futuristic cities are increasingly emerging in Africa including Konza Techno City and Tatu City in Kenya, Diamniadio City in Senegal, Eko Atlantic City in Nigeria, Hope City in Ghana and Vision City in Rwanda.

4. Smart digital projects to transform specific urban services through infrastructure, including urban transport, water and energy supply, and waste management. In mega-cities like Delhi, Nairobi and Lagos, such projects include ubiquitous text-based money transfer and banking services, targeted e-payments technologies, digital media and app-based platforms, and incremental metering devices to infrastructure development and housing projects. These smart digital projects are deployed by state agencies, private companies and/or global actors and often tend to target renewal and improvement of existing infrastructures and services.

5. National- and city-level data, algorithms and **artificial intelligence (AI)** platforms. In China, tracing technology and facial recognition technology have been used for mass surveillance and everyday governance, tracking and containment of the COVID-19 pandemic and spread. These have come to constitute a new generation of smart public health systems across many cities.

Altogether, the above smart city initiatives offer technological responses to contemporary urban problems. While innovative, experimental and sought after as socially beneficial, such technological solutions and digitalisation processes can have disturbing implications for equity-seeking groups. For example, they are more likely to discriminate as they often tend to enact and re-enact existing spatial inequalities and conditions of segregation, polarisation and disfranchisement in urban regions. Ride-hailing platforms in particular – devoid of legislation from the state, social protection, job security and fair pay – tend to leave platform workers largely unprotected as employment and labour laws shift the burden of economic risk more onto workers who often are more or less freelancers (see Chapter 33). Moreover, as smart cities initiatives and processes collect too much data and information about individuals and institutions, they are sometimes more likely to invade individual privacy and to pose data privacy and security issues (see Chapter 66). This is not particularly surprising as algorithmic controls and tracking systems through which technology users are disciplined, monitored and surveilled have long been a substantial critique of smart cities and IoT devices.

Summary

- Cities all over the world are increasingly promoting new forms of technology that deliver maximum governance with minimum government.
- Smart cities are developed by urban inhabitants as well as by business and policy practitioners seeking to promote ICT-based solutions for infrastructure provision, urban planning and governance.
- While smart city initiatives offer 'smarter' responses to contemporary urban problems, they can have disturbing implications for equity-seeking groups.

Discourses of smart cities

Discourses of smart cities have been stimulated by scholarship and engagement from the Global North/Minority World. They emerged from initial conceptualisations of the relationship between ICT and cities that immediately inspired a varying nomenclature, including 'wired cities', 'computable cities', 'cyber cities', 'digital cities', 'intelligent cities'. Of note is Graham and Marvin's (1996) seminal *Telecommunications and the City*, which claimed to shift 'telecommunications from the margins to the center of urban studies' (ibid: 75). Graham and Marvin (2001) illustrate how trends in the telecommunications sector contributed to the development of networked urbanism and unequal development of cities and regions, particularly due to competition in the sector to supply telecommunications services and infrastructures to the most profitable areas, to the detriment of the less favoured ones.

Since then, the discourse has undergone significant evolution, particularly following the increased penetration of ICTs and the spiralling of vast top-down large-scale projects by public and private institutions in the larger cities. Different disciplines at the intersection of urban studies, mobility studies and critical infrastructure have examined wide-ranging aspects of digital technology networks, smart city analytics, data politics and smart city analytics, drawing attention to global circulations and local articulations (Kitchin, 2015). Research studies have explored the effects of smart technologies on the development of cities, and broad relational aspects of these technologies within urban, regional and global spheres. Greater engagement has focused on the smart city both as an ideal and practice (Madsen, 2018), and as a catalyst for urban and infrastructure development in the pursuit of smarter and more sustainable goals including the Sustainable Development Goals ratified during the UN General Assembly in September 2015.

Recent studies in both Majority and Minority World places emphasise the need for contextually informed definitions of smart cities, foregrounding articulations that are situated and located (see e.g. Datta, 2015, Shelton et al., 2015, Guma, 2021, Odendaal, 2021). With the smart city discourse increasingly gaining more traction across the world, research is increasingly more critical of technological and aspirational inscriptions for a hyper-networked city, as well as dominant dichotomies of the city as static or as an extremely relative space. A critical analysis of the smart city discourse is particularly important for examining contemporary developments of urbanisation in the smart digital age. Such an analysis offers a way of reading dominant corporate discourses on smart cities and business-led initiatives that are channelled through urban policy towards quasi-unavoidable smart, sustainable and integrated city futures. It offers a reading of the imaginaries and significations used to depict hyper-networked aspirations and motivations, particularly those aimed at translating assumedly universal and transferable models and ideals. In other words, a critical analysis shifts focus from the universal, techno-driven and top-down views of smart urbanism to give attention to the situated, continuous and context-dependent nature of such urbanism.

Thus, when examining smart cities and urban processes, it is important to focus beyond utopian and representational descriptions, labels, policies and plans, and beyond complex, homogenic and progressive processes into other ways in which cities are produced. A broader conception of smart urbanism provides a better understanding of blended approaches within the smart cities discourse. For example, examining everyday urbanism in the 'actually existing smart city' (Shelton et al., 2015) is imperative for two major reasons. Firstly, it is important to go beyond new management paradigms and governance arrangements enabled through top-down and centralised urban governance based on command and control. And secondly, an everyday urbanism goes beyond the idea of smartness as a constitution of orderly, complete and immanent systems (Guma, 2022). A broader understanding of smart urbanism is important for offering a more situated, nuanced and differentiated conception of smart urbanism, illuminating smart city projects beyond limited views of technology as future proof, universally transferable, and simply conforming to logics of **neoliberalism** or apolitical and business-as-usual trajectories. Such a broader understanding is important for further advancing a more critical research agenda and theoretical dialogue in a manner that runs contrary to technological determinism or the idea that technology develops independently of specific societal conditions. It substantiates emergent calls in urban studies to move.

Summary

- The smart city discourse has been particularly powerful and alluring for examining contemporary developments of urbanisation in the smart digital age.
- A critical analysis of the smart city discourse and broader conception of smart urbanism is particularly important for examining contemporary developments of urbanisation in the smart digital age.
- Recent studies reinforce the need for contextually informed definitions of smart cities beyond technocratic and deterministic approaches that underlie narratives of the smart city.

Smart cities and everyday urbanism in the Global South

In the Global South, studies have meticulously examined universal visions and plans for the smart city and the spiralling of top-down large-scale projects by public and private institutions. Addressing the phenomenon of 'African urban fantasies', Watson cites 'new city plans, satellite cities and large urban projects in sub-Saharan Africa' (2014: 222) that are currently being remodelled 'in the rhetoric of "smart cities"' (Watson, 2015). Watson shows how these attempts promise to modernise cities in a way that reflects a new urbanism in place. Likewise, Datta (2015) takes the case of Dholera as a 'new utopia' in India, to examine the ways in which the city is being reshaped through planning and governance processes based on new forms of technology. By doing so, Datta gives insight into a new phase of utopian urbanisation in India, examining the linkages between global models and local histories, politics and laws (2015: 12). Sometimes the 'rhetoric of urgency' regarding the problems of urbanisation is used to ignore the extant planning systems or any possibilities for public participation (Datta, 2015: 5). When this happens, the tendency is for smart city plans to be top-down, biased and generally rushed.

More recently, studies have had a significant socio-technical focus, examining everyday operations and developments of the smart city in particular places. Nairobi is a great example of a city where the smart city ideal is increasingly gaining traction. Since the early 2000s, numerous smart city projects have arisen in the city. For example, I have examined actually existing forms of smart urbanism, where the urge to become smart has triggered various technology-oriented development initiatives (Guma, 2019, Guma and Monstadt, 2021). It is therefore not surprising that Nairobi is often portrayed as a distinctive and enviable space of innovative ICTs, where IoT integration in such sectors such as water, electricity and telecommunications (Guma, 2021) has aimed at optimising the efficiency of operations and services in the city for adequate, efficient and affordable sanitation and water supply, electricity supply, urban mobility and transport, housing, and healthcare and education.

In the sanitation and water supply sector, for instance, a range of new projects offering automation of water access in Nairobi include Maji-Voice (an innovative accountability mechanism), Water ATMs (self-operated kiosks that dispense water via cash or prepaid card payments), prepaid water systems (water meters where the service is paid ahead of use), e-bills (electronically generated and delivered invoices that enable mobile payment for services) and Jisomee Mita (a mobile

Figure 68.3
Singapore aims to become the world's first smart city-state and big data connection technology is remarkably valuable in its smart city-state development

Source: Photo credit: Yang Suping/Costfoto/Sipa USA/Alamy

phone-based platform that allows customers to self-read meters, receive and pay water bills, and make queries virtually, see Figure 68.3). These platforms target (mostly but not exclusively) informal settlements and they allow service providers to provide quality water in underserved areas (or lower income groups/those in informal areas). They enable service providers to upgrade water services in low-income areas and a better mechanism to interact with customers through digital and automated smartphone apps and data-driven solutions to urban challenges to water access. Likewise, they allow customers to manage queries, invoices, prepaid payment and crediting, remote data collection, and automated billing via the mobile phone.

While most of these smart city initiatives are mundane small-scale and experimental projects that cannot be scaled up to the entire city, they seek to impose their techno dreams and fantasies of smartness upon ordinary places upon diverse urban places (see Figure 68.4). However, they are often translated in unforeseen ways: shaped not only 'from the top' but also 'from below', with local-level actors and citizens increasingly negotiating and translating them on the ground in so doing pursuing alternative forms of inclusion, participation and justice. As such, these technologies unfold and are translated, hybridised and localised in different ways as urban populations appropriate, contest and recalibrate that, by so doing, transforming smart city ideals and leading to different versions that reflect 'smartness' not only from the top but also from below.

This means that in practice, smart city initiatives have failed to work as conceived. Take for instance how in being able to get access to their rights (of water), most residents have ended up circumventing the technologies via forms of resistance from below, in fact, creating their own impact on these technologies and infrastructure systems. Jisomee Mita and Water ATMs are great examples whose prescribed technological plans and designs have continuously been remodelled

Figure 68.4
The ecological wisdom island in Nanjing, China – A smart park that consists of eight Pentagon buildings, and each building has a green roof

Source: Photo credit: tcharts/Alamy

and recalibrated by residents often in ways that reflect different social, economic and political logics at play. Not only have residents translated and hybridised these technologies through local forms of resistance such as contestation and circumvention in rather unforeseen ways but also sometimes eradicated some or all aspects of the new technological systems. Thus, these smart city initiatives draw us to how cities and people can produce novel forms of smart urbanism beyond conventional representations and manifestations of **hegemonic** designs. They highlight how smart city plans and infrastructure developments are produced not just through universal notions but also differentiated actors and processes on the ground.

In sum, the everyday articulations of smart city initiatives challenge techno-managerial approaches of city making and planning processes. They highlight the need for more nuanced and contextualised understandings of urbanism in the age of smart technologies. Thus, smart cities research needs to foreground everyday engagements, negotiations and relations, which calls not only for further rethinking of smart urbanism but also the situation of smart city research. Empirical and real-world accounts are important for providing evidence of different processes and forms of knowledge production concerning how smart city ideals are translated and applied in situated and wide-ranging contexts. They are important for situating smart city processes and articulating the nature of politics enacted by such processes amidst spatial inequalities and conditions of segregation and polarisation. They remind us that we must not always assume that citizens, cities and technologies will simply intersect through universal sensor-activated programmes but will be shaped by the realities of everyday contexts which are characterised by situated contingencies, nonlinear progressions and transient temporalities that evolve across human and **more-than-human** networks.

Summary

- A large portion of contemporary studies from critical geographers and urban planners has examined smart cities and everyday urbanism in the Global South/Majority World.
- In practice, smart city initiatives have failed to work as conceived, highlighting local articulations and politics amidst spatial inequalities and conditions of urban segregation and polarisation.
- These studies remind us to challenge techno-managerial approaches of city making and planning and turn towards more nuanced and contextualised understandings of urbanism in the smart digital age.

Conclusion

Smart cities studies provoke lively debates within geography and urban studies as they highlight hegemonic and universal visions and plans but also lived experiences or actual implications within situated urban localities. Studies from the Global South have been particularly important for challenging the hegemony of Western theorising (of the cities and infrastructures) by fronting the actuality of diverse urban settings, lived experiences and local politics. These studies opened space for alternative conceptions, illuminating how cities produce novel forms of urbanism that exceed hegemonic ideas of **modernity**. They remind us of the importance of rethinking current debates around smart cities with a contribution from the point of view of located geographies beyond the Minority World. This is important for destigmatising situated articulations of smart urbanism (particularly those that are bottom up and thus not entirely promoted by business and policy experts). It is important for understanding that while meeting basic and aspirational characterisations of smartness in their mundane and ordinary ways, situated articulations of smart urbanism might not meet the universal standards of smartness – particularly in the worlds where smartness is synonymous with hyper-networked urbanism.

The discourse on smart cities and everyday urbanism from the Global South/Majority World reminds us of the importance of revisiting qualifiers of (what constitutes) smartness: what it might mean for cities or infrastructure to be smart; and what a 'real' or 'true' smart city might actually look like (see, e.g. Hollands, 2008). It is pointless to strive for a singular 'true' or 'real' smartness, as all smartness in its varied forms can indeed be 'real' and 'true'. Instead, we need to ask why or how smart city projects may not always be future proof or universally explicable, nor completely disciplined to the logics of neoliberalism. A more nuanced and critical understanding of contemporary developments of smart urbanism brings urban spaces into a more exhaustive discussion that considers the nature of smart urbanism within diverse contexts. Such an understanding is even more critical now with newer and even more apparent socio-technical challenges and encounters affecting the world, including COVID-19 and climate and urban change increasing the surge in demand for 'smarter' solutions to urban problems.

Going forward, it is important to take on new opportunities in researching smart cities and everyday life in both the Global North and South. First, by studying and theorising through such technological developments to further illuminate and reframe the way we think about cities.

Second, by extending dynamic and broad attention to this and similar subjects, particularly those that invite us to revisit mainstream perspectives of what we think we know, or what we view as familiar or unsettling about recent urban development. And third, by examining how smart urbanism is embedded in vertical relations (e.g. to national governments, supranational organisations), in relations with international donors but also in horizontal relations with other cities (nationally and internationally, e.g. how ideas and technologies travel, how cities learn from each other).

The **postcolonial** critique of urban and technology studies is particularly imperative for raising questions about global circulations and local articulations of smart city plans and technologies. This critique reminds us of the need to depart from the tendency to view the smart city ideal as a decontextualised incident or as an entirely top-down phenomenon. This is particularly imperative as the smart city ideal is part and parcel of institutional patterns which manifest through situated processes and practices and is **embodied** and empirically grounded in social and contextual realities. Thus, in our conceptualisation, this calls for a better focus on the politics and **spatiality** of smart urbanism but even more importantly, on the relations and comparisons within, across and beyond cities of the Global North and Global South. This would continue to add more insight to contemporary debates around smart urbanism in ways that further widen theoretical pluralism in urban studies.

Summary

- The discourse on smart cities offers a way to better understand interactions between digital technologies and contemporary large-scale infrastructure systems in urban geographies.
- It is important to take on new opportunities in researching smart cities and everyday life in the Global North and South.

Discussion points

- What does the concept of smart cities mean?
- What are the emerging discourses of smart cities?
- What new forms of technology are being promoted to deliver maximum governance with minimum government in the Global South?
- How are everyday accounts (and local articulations, politics inequalities, segregation and polarisation) important for resisting dominant forms of power?

References

Datta, A. (2015). New urban utopias of postcolonial India: 'entrepreneurial urbanization' in Dholera smart city, Gujarat. *Dialogues in Human Geography* 5(1): 3–22.
Graham, S., and Marvin, S. (1996). *Telecommunications and the City: Electronic Spaces, Urban Places.* London: Routledge.
Graham, S., and Marvin, S. (2001). *Splintering Urbanism: Networked Infrastructures, Technological Mobilities and the Urban Condition.* London: Routledge.

Guma, P. K. (2019). Smart urbanism? ICTs for water and electricity supply in Nairobi. *Urban Studies* 56(11): 2333–2352.

Guma, P. K. (2021). *Rethinking Smart Urbanism: City-Making and the Spread of Digital Infrastructures in Nairobi*. Utrecht: Eburon Uitgeverij BV.

Guma, P. K. (2022). The temporal incompleteness of infrastructure and the urban. *Journal of Urban Technology* 29(1): 59–67.

Guma, P. K., and Monstadt, J. (2021). Smart city making? The spread of ICT-driven plans and infrastructures in Nairobi. *Urban Geography* 42(3): 360–381.

Hollands, R. G. (2008). Will the real smart city please stand up? Intelligent, progressive or entrepreneurial? *City* 12(3): 303–320.

Kitchin, R. (2015). Making sense of smart cities: addressing present shortcomings. *Cambridge Journal of Regions, Economy and Society* 8(1): 131–136.

Madsen, A. K. (2018). Data in the smart city: how incongruent frames challenge the transition from ideal to practice. *Big Data and Society* 5(2): 1–13. https://doi.org/10.1177/2053951718802321

Odendaal, N. (2021). Everyday urbanisms and the importance of place: exploring the elements of the emancipatory smart city. *Urban Studies* 58(3): 639–654.

Shelton, T., Zook, M., and Wiig, A. (2015). The 'actually existing smart city'. *Cambridge Journal of Regions, Economy and Society* 8(1): 13–25.

Watson, V. (2014). African urban fantasies: dreams or nightmares? *Environment and Urbanization* 26(1): 215–231.

Watson, V. (2015). The allure of 'smart city' rhetoric: India and Africa. *Dialogues in Human Geography* 5(1): 36–39.

Online materials

- CNBC Explainer: What is a smart city? https://youtu.be/bANfnYDTzxE. This short video explains what 'smart city' refers to, with some examples. It is a mostly positive take on smart cities, but how might you critique it?
- Jisomee Mita: https://youtu.be/Ng9VXtnl4BA. This short video explains how the Jisomee Mita works in Nairobi, Kenya.
- World Economic Forum on smart cities: https://www.weforum.org/agenda/2021/08/what-is-a-smart-city/. Find out what the WEA is saying about smart cities here. Do you agree? What questions might you raise about this?

Further reading

Datta, A. (2018). The digital turn in postcolonial urbanism: smart citizenship in the making of India's 100 smart cities. *Transactions of the Institute of British Geographers* 43(3): 405–419.
This article explores how the implementation of smart city initiatives in India shapes notions of citizenship and urban governance, making it relevant to geography students interested in the intersection of postcolonialism, technology and urban development.

Guma, P. K., and Wiig, A. (2022). Smartness beyond the network: water ATMs and disruptions from below in Mathare Valley, Nairobi. *Journal of Urban Technology* 29(4): 41–61.
This article examines the role of grassroots initiatives, particularly water ATMs, in challenging dominant narratives of smartness in Nairobi, providing a case study that geography students interested in bottom-up approaches to smart urbanism would find intriguing.

McFarlane, C., and Söderström, O. (2017). On alternative smart cities: from a technology-intensive to a knowledge-intensive smart urbanism. *City* 21(3–4): 312–328.
This article argues for a shift from technology-focused smart cities to knowledge-intensive urbanism, offering insights for geography students interested in alternative approaches that prioritise local knowledge and social innovation.

Odendaal, N. (2023). *Disrupted Urbanism: Situated Smart Initiatives in African Cities*. Bristol: Bristol University Press.
This book delves into the context of African cities and examines how situated smart initiatives can disrupt urbanism, appealing to geography students interested in the specific challenges and opportunities of smart city development in African contexts.

69 Ordinary technologies of everyday life

Chen Liu

Introduction

Over the last few decades, geographers have begun to track the social lives of ordinary technologies in everyday life. They do this in order to understand how changing technologies affect our living, working and leisure spaces, because the small everyday practices and spaces we engage in have larger implications in the continuous making and re-making of our living more-than-human world. Technologies are embedded in our everyday practices. In writing this chapter, I recorded my experience of using technologies on an ordinary day:

> *Before going out, I asked the voice assistant about the weather…I connected my iPhone to the car computer via Bluetooth. Then I drove to my office while listening to an album downloaded to my iPhone. After arriving at my office, I turned on the computer and started my working day by checking and replying to emails…After lunch on such a hot day, I used the smart home control hub on my iPhone to turn on the air conditioner in my living room to cool my cats. I turned on the security camera and tried to check whether my cats were comfortable remotely…In the evening, I worked out with Nintendo Ring Fit Adventure, took a shower, dried my hair, did daily laundry and vacuumed the floor as usual.*

The ordinary technologies I used that day include an office computer, an iPhone, a security camera, an air conditioner, a washing machine, a water heater, a voice assistant, a car and a car computer, a Nintendo Switch, a vacuum cleaner, a hairdryer as well as the software, wireless connection system and platforms/apps installed in these devices. My experiences with technologies overlap with other daily practices, such as working, commuting, doing household chores, maintaining social networks and taking care of pets. These experiences, while seemingly simple, result from a complex relationality and **spatiality** of things. The experiences include both unthinking habits and intentional design of everyday life (Shove et al., 2007). This chapter will focus on how human geographers have come to understand these experiences of everyday technologies and why such understandings are important (see also Chapter 68).

Scholars in geography and related disciplines have drawn on *social practice theories* to highlight how human society and technology reproduce social and cultural norms. Social practice theories provide an approach for exploring our living world through bodily movements, material

DOI: 10.4324/9780429265853-81

cultures, practical knowledge and routines. Social practice theory encourages self-understanding and connects society with personal lives (Shove et al., 2012). These theories emerge from the philosophical inheritance of Ludwig Wittgenstein and Martin Heidegger, who proposed that human activity rests on something that cannot be put into words. The basic insight of practice theories is that practices are the fundamental unit of social existence.

Social practice theorists indicate that practice is 'a routinized way in which bodies are moved, objects are handled, subjects are treated, things are described and the world is understood' (Reckwitz, 2002: 250), and an open-ended, spatial-temporal nexus of organised doings (the performing of an action) and sayings (doings in which something is said) governed by understandings of norms, rules, goals or purposes and emotions (Schatzki, 2010). It includes three elements: competences (skill, know-how and technique), meanings (symbolic meanings, ideas and aspirations) and materials (things, technologies, tangible physical entities and the stuff of which objects are made) (Shove et al., 2012: 12), which are partly autonomous and partly constituted by each other (see Figure 69.1).

In recent decades, the rapid development of new technologies has significantly contributed to the emergence and development of 'digital environments' – meaning that digital devices have become part of the material arrangements with which people's practices are entangled (Schatzki, 2019: 20). Challenging the anthropocentric tradition of social practice theories which emphasises human **performance**, Strengers and her colleagues (Strengers et al., 2019) add a 'non-human'

Figure 69.1
The three-element social practice framework

Source: Figure credit: Chen Liu adapted from Shove et al. (2012)

layer to understand the varieties of human and non-human actors – animals (pets and pests), other objects (such as plants, microbes, furnishings and decorations) and the environment – in practices. In this way of thinking, although social practices are carried, identified and interpreted by humans, they are distributed and co-performed between different types of human and non-human actors.

In this sense, the material arrangements which comprise, integrate, reproduce and dissolve practices include humans, artefacts, technologies, non-human organisms and phenomena of nature. Indeed such actors can alter arrangements on their own based on a variety of social relations among themselves (Schatzki, 2019). Practices, then, can be thought of as comprising 'human and non-human activities' (Schatzki, 2001: 102) and relations between arranged material entities (Schatzki, 2019). We might say that these practices and material arrangements are '**more-than-human**' (Chapter 7).

Considering our everyday lives with ordinary technologies as a bundle of interrelated social practices, this chapter will first use examples from and beyond human geography studies to illustrate the dynamic spatialities and temporalities of the co-evolution of the consumption of technology and other practices. Then, it will analyse the possibilities for socio-technological change and transition towards a more sustainable future in times of climate and environmental crisis.

Summary

- Technologies are both immaterial and material.
- Ordinary technologies are both an important component of social practice and active agents that make up the design of everyday life and social relations.
- The co-constitution of the social and the technological can produce and reproduce new social and cultural norms.

Situating ordinary technologies in everyday consumption

Living with technologies is about consuming the material and immaterial dimensions of technologies and situating technologies in the mundane through practices. Consuming technologies is more than the moment of acquisition of devices, and it is also about the skills and the social relations involved in the practice-related activities of using, making and doing with technologies (Shove et al., 2007, see also Chapter 32). Moreover, consumption is not just a consequence of one's individual attitude, behaviour, choice or personal preference. Consumption is an important component of social practices governed by wider social norms (such as moralities and the ideal order of society), and a process of normalising technologies in our society. In this sense, social practice theories not only 'stress the routine, ordinary, collective, conventional nature' of everyday experiences but also consider practice as a culturally and socially situated event where 'persons in different situations do the same activity differently' (Warde, 2005: 146). Everyday technologies are thus situated and located in specific places and practices (Pink, 2012).

The following two subsections will further detail how social practices shape the situated knowledge of everyday places and spaces. These practices may include walking, driving, taking photos, doing household chores and communicating, all with ordinary technologies. Our interactions with these ordinary technologies are important because they structure billions of people's lives every day and have global consequences.

Consuming technologies in public

Technologies are embedded in our everyday **encounters** with different places and our ways of experiencing these places. The development of technologies can provide us with multi-sensory experiences of place and give geographers significant insight into exploring the changing meanings of space. For example, in the late twentieth century, museums and art galleries generally adopted the audio guide which offered 'expert' interpretation. With the popularity of MP3 players in the first few years of the new millennium, a small industry was developing in creating audio trails delivered through portable media (Butler, 2007). After the 2010s, due to the development of GPS, location-based services (LBS), sensors, augmented reality (AR) and other technologies, our urban experiences have been digitally mediated (see Chapters 66 and 68). By the end of 2020, 51% of the world's population was using mobile internet, and smartphones accounted for 68% of total mobile connections[1]. Our daily interface with digital devices, in particular smartphones, is becoming influential in shaping the informational **infrastructure** of urban space and living via collective intelligence generated by billions of digital platforms (Barns, 2019).

Here, I use two examples to show how our daily practices in public are entangled with mobile technologies in the contemporary world. The first example is daily mobilities. Mobile mapping, LBS, the development of platform-based sharing economies (such as ride-hailing services and bike/car sharing) and self-tracking technologies are involved in our everyday movements. Mobile technologies, bodies and personal understandings of the self are inseparably intertwined in everyday practices of walking, riding, driving and other types of mobilities, blurring public with private, physical with virtual and 'here-and-now' with 'there-and-then' (Rueb, 2014). These technologies and their services empower people's navigational capability by providing data on routes, travel modes, travel time, 'you-are-here' and destination dots and so forth, based on their algorithms and interfaces; and in turn, people make digital maps and produce locational data by their pace, trajectory, halts and turns of their movements and their consumption of apps and platforms (Figure 69.2). In this way, algorithmic logic and computation are intimately involved in the daily mobilities of millions of people, influencing their decisions and creative activities when consuming such technologies.

However, while many of us are being shaped by such technologies, we are not entirely shaped by platforms' algorithmic logic and computation. Everyday users adapt, ignore and re-make the calculative confines of algorithms. For example, Wilmott's (2016) research on the 'small moments' of walking with mobile apps has demonstrated that walking apps have situated spatial **big data** in our everyday rhythms and paces of walking practices, through recording our locations, walking routes, speed and health conditions (such as heart rate and sweating), and incessantly interrupting and updating users. When the recorded data inserts itself into the daily walking experiences, it works between our own assessment of walking and location by providing data for us to establish, support but also *resist* the role of big data in our life. Wilmott, for example, notes that a participant situates spatial big data in her daily walking with a mobile app by gathering data from the app, looking back on it, tracking her fitness levels and speed, as well as stopping and looking at things that are not on the app (or any other) (2016: 4–5). Thus, we must notice that our public experiences are not entirely determined by digital technologies, instead, they are *co-constituted* by the design of technologies, data and various ways of using technologies.

The second example concerns changes in how people read and experience urban landscapes, increasingly via social media. Since the availability of digital cameras in the 1990s, photography increasingly meant a set of practices of taking, storing, manipulating and sharing pictures (Shove et al., 2007). After the new millennium, the proliferation of smartphones and social media sites has made digital photography a popular pursuit and an everyday habit. Nowadays, social media-driven photography has strongly influenced our ways of seeing, interpreting and experiencing our living world, creating and disseminating similar or distinctive **imaginative geographies** of people and places.

Figure 69.2

Person using a mobile map app. This photo shows a person using her smartphone to search for nearby laundry shops in her car. Her daily driving was dependent on her smartphone and map apps, because, according to her own words, she was 'an idiot driver who had just got a driving license'

Source: Photo credit: Chen Liu

The power of social media impacts how people create, select, process and share their images. People intend to use images to prove 'I was there' and show 'socially desired' images of self under the influence of the digital and networked facilitation of autonomy, self-centeredness culture and the social convention of sharing images on social media. Moreover, as LBS have become more common in the Web 2.0 era, the 'ambient visuality' of digital images in which the geographic location is overlain with the social and emotional in many cultural contexts (see, for example, Hjorth and Gu, 2012). The incorporation of geo-location into text, images and video and the growing popularity of displaying physical activities on social media platforms create what Schwartz and Halegoua (2015: 1644) define as the expressions of the 'spatial self': 'a variety of instances (both online and offline) where individuals document, archive and display their experience and/or mobility within space and place in order to represent or perform aspects of their identity to others'. That is to say, social media promotes an online practice of identity performance – people tend to create different aspects of themselves online by sharing photos with hashtags and **geo-tags**. This phenomenon requires geographers to develop new approaches to map the increasingly complex identity-making process in the digital era (see chapter 66).

Living with domestic devices

Geographers pay attention to how people live with technologies at the household scale to understand the extended **commodity** chains in home spaces. After electric devices entered private homes in the first half of the twentieth century, household labour and time involved in cleaning, heating, cooking, washing and other domestic tasks, as well as domestic care and intimacy, have been transformed (Shove, 2003). For example, fridges enabled less frequent shopping, and changes in understandings of freshness, which has changed the nature of women's domestic labour in particular (see Chapter 33). In some places, fridges have also become a central bulletin board for household organisation and children's artwork (Watkins, 2006). It thus works far beyond the kitchen to perform domestic order, rhythms and even emotional work as a service and organising space. When fridge-freezers were introduced to Chinese families, shopping and cooking routines changed. This affects the flows and routines not just of the household but also of the local fresh food markets in cities all over China.

Nowadays, domestic care and care spaces are reshaped by real-time audiovisual communication technologies, enabling a new form of distant intimacy. The daily use of communication technologies, such as video-calling and video meeting apps, can re-cast the connections between human bodies, screens, webcams, mobile devices and domestic spaces, gendered relations and responsibilities, intimacies and emotional geographies of home and family and alter family life-cycle (Longhurst, 2016). For example, in the post-pandemic period, when physical mobilities were still constrained, regular visits to family members who live apart were partly moved online. Such digitalisation of family togetherness can shift family mobilities in the physical world and postpone or advance important family events that mark the transition of a family, such as marriage registration and celebrating the birth of a new baby.

Embracing the advantages of technology, some academic and popular **discourses** have taken a **technological solutionism** view that the advances of **modernity**, **capitalism**, industrialism and contemporary technological innovations provide more time convenience to people who have obligations at home. Recently, smart home technologies are 'taking over' human tasks and practices. With smart technologies' mediation, interference and intervention in everyday life, how these technologies co-fabricate domestic experiences have gained increasing attention (Maller and Strengers, 2019), as they impact how domestic practices are performed, emerge, endure and decline. What researchers have found, however, is that this techno-utopian envision never achieves its desired outcomes (see also Chapter 68).

Domestic technologies often fail to decrease the amount of labour, especially women's time-consuming burden of housework, because they raise expectations and conventions of cleanliness, comfort, security and leisure which in turn increase household labour and disrupt everyday practices (Hargreaves et al., 2018, Nicholls and Strengers, 2019). Moreover, the acceptance and adoption of domestic technologies require a time-consuming process of learning to use new devices and getting used to new software, making people feel more harried, more time-pressured and busier. For example, I bought a smart feeder to reduce my daily burden of feeding my cats. Yet I found that this smart device increases my time and effort in taking care of pets! After plugging this device in, I downloaded an app, learned how to connect it to my smartphone and the app, and how to use the app to set my feeding plans for around half an hour. Then, I checked the app every day to ensure the feeding plan worked. It seems my cats and I have confirmed previous findings, and we also did not achieve a techno-utopia. In what follows, I illustrate the points I have made on everyday technologies with another pet-related example: the modern-day phenomenon of Roomba riding.

CASE STUDY
ROOMBA RIDING

The popular autonomous floor cleaners (or 'robovacs') can exemplify the roles of complex human-non-human interactions in the dynamic social practices of vacuuming. The traditional vacuum technologies always require a human performer or operator to complete the 'doing' of vacuuming by blowing, sucking and extracting dirt and other materials from the floor. In contrast, robovacs are designed to operate without a human operator, aside from initial purchase and setup. These robots have their own 'sayings' (built-in algorithms and programmes) and 'doings' (the automated process of vacuuming and generating data, and the practice of mediating daily interactions between humans and technologies) in completing their tasks. In the automatic vacuuming process, another type of non-human is often performing a distinctive practice: 'Roomba riding' – domesticated animals riding robotic vacuum cleaners for their own enjoyment (Strengers, 2019). New human practices, such as filming pets riding Roombas, dressing them in funny outfits, posting and watching videos of Roomba ridings on YouTube, are generated and modified by this more-than-human practice.

Therefore, the robovacs are at the same time material elements of practices performed by people, (actual or perceived) autonomous performers of vacuuming practices and elements of other non-human practices performed by animals.

Summary

- Everyday encounters with ordinary technologies produce situated knowledges of space and place. These encounters are shaped by wider social and material contexts. Understanding these encounters is important because the use of such technologies has widespread social and environmental implications.
- The complex and dynamic human-non-human interactions need more attention in studying technologies in everyday life because these interactions are fundamental components of everyday practices and spaces.

Promoting changes and transitions for a sustainable future

Our daily experiences with technologies, such as cooking, eating, cooling and heating the home, cleaning the home, clothing and our bodies, and commuting to work, are consuming energy and carrying significant environmental burdens (Evans, 2018). Moreover, the consumption of digital devices has generated a considerable amount of electronic waste, produced uneven geographies of waste trade between the Global North and Global South and created new economic **agglomerations** for recycling, repair and reuse in the developing world (Pickren, 2014).

However, centring on the social and material features of everyday sustainability, recent studies have pointed out that the development of technologies seeks to make the world 'better' in some way – that is, increase forms of well-being and health, work towards environmental sustainability, create equality of access to resources (Pink et al., 2020). Adopting a practice approach to sustainable consumption that recognises both individual agencies and systematic structures, both bottom-up and top-down dynamics of change, and influences generated by human actors, objects and technological infrastructures (Spaargaren, 2011), some studies have highlighted the co-evolution of technology-as-a-material-force and society (Evans, 2020) in making social changes and movements towards a more sustainable future.

Social movements are integrated into existing social structures and practices. The continuities between the practices of activism and everyday life are established through contemporary developments in the popularity of Web 2.0 and its potential for public communications and campaigning (Pink, 2012). The networked digital spaces can empower ordinary people to resist and re-make their living environments, making a more-than-real connection – a relational understanding of the human-technology network that defines the digital as both material and immaterial and both real and virtual (unreal) – between human, society and physical environment (McLean, 2016, 2020). One example to illustrate this more-than-real way of socio-environmental movements is the Alipay Ant Forest project. Alipay, one of China's most popular online payment platforms, launched its climate action – the Alipay Ant Forest project – in 2016.[2] This project rewards its users with 'green energy points' each time they reduce their carbon emissions, such as taking public transport and buying sustainable products. These points grow into a virtual tree on the user's Alipay app, which Alipay matches by planting a real tree or protecting a conservation area, in partnership with local NGOs.

Against this backdrop, policy interventions and studies on environmental sustainability are increasingly focused on everyday practices with technologies. Yet large-scale interventions often include the development of more efficient machines and top-down behaviour change initiatives. They often depend on techno-utopian projects or scientific models centred on smart metres, grids, homes and cities to improve and plan for a predictable sustainable future – a future imagined as a single destination unfolding exactly as planned (see Chapter 68). However, futures are multiple and complex systems entailing the evolution of society and are generated through uncertain and contingent ways in which humans and non-humans co-constitute new practices of being in the world – including in everyday practices (Nicholls and Strengers, 2019).

As such, taking practices (rather than individuals who carry them out) as the core unit of analysis makes sense to both social theory and policy. A practice orientation to policy recognises and works with and within essentially uncontrollable processes, because social practices are ever-changing, contingent and dynamic, and thereby difficult to measure or model. This argues for a cross-sectoral analysis of how various forms of policy-making influence social practices, including the texture and rhythm of daily technology/energy consumption patterns, as well as these practices' impact on planning and future infrastructure needs. It attempts to steer the direction and attention of energy futures towards diverse possibilities of future everyday scenarios. Therefore, policy interventions may support the chances of more sustainable ways of life to persist and thrive. Shove et al. (2012) identify routes through which the practice-oriented policy might occur: policymakers and other actors can influence the distribution and circulation of elements (materials, competences and meanings) and consider their role in configuring relations between practices, in shaping the careers and trajectories of practices and those who carry them, and in forging and breaking some of the links, relationships, networks and partnerships involved. Therefore, policy interventions designed to address systemic challenges only have an effect when taken up in and through practice, and such effects are never stable, being always subject to ongoing reproduction.

Summary

- Environmental and climate change policy interventions must take the daily experiences with technologies into consideration.
- Social and environmental movements are integrated into existing social practices, and these movements are concerned with everyday life as a site for social change.

Conclusion

In this chapter, I have done two things. First, I sketched out the main lines of practice-oriented studies on ordinary technologies, and their socio-environmental implications within and beyond human geography. And second, I have illustrated the advantages of practice-oriented approaches to promoting socio-environmental transitions to a more sustainable future. In a society with the rapid development of science and technology, understanding how we interact with technologies in everyday life is an ongoing interdisciplinary project. Consuming technologies exist in everyday spaces in both material and immaterial forms. As geographers, we must map the complex trajectories of these technologies, study their roles in the production of situated knowledges of our living world and remember that situated knowledges are always changing.

Discussion points

- Ordinary technologies have both 'material' and 'immaterial' features. Can you think of some examples in your own life that illustrate this?
- Ordinary technologies shape place and space. What examples can you identify in the place where you currently live?
- What is the relationship between ordinary technologies and social and environmental change and climate action? Think about both digital and material technologies.
- Why is it important to consider 'practices' when thinking about technologies? How might this help us understand and intervene in environmental and climate problems? Can a 'practice-oriented' understanding of technology offer us an alternative imaginary of the future?

Notes

1. The State of Mobile Internet Connectivity 2021, https://www.gsma.com/r/wp-content/uploads/2021/09/The-State-of-Mobile-Internet-Connectivity-Report-2021.pdf, accessed on 11 July.
2. https://unfccc.int/climate-action/momentum-for-change/planetary-health/alipay-ant-forest

References

Barns, S. (2019). *Platform Urbanism: Negotiating Platform Ecosystems in Connected Cities*. Singapore: Springer.

Butler, T. (2007). Memoryscape: how audio walks can deepen our sense of place by integrating art, oral history and cultural geography. *Geography Compass* 1(3): 360–372.

Evans, D. M. (2018). Rethinking material cultures of sustainability: commodity consumption, cultural biographies and following the thing. *Transactions of the Institute of British Geographers* 43(1): 110–121.

Evans, D. M. (2020). After practice? Material semiotic approaches to consumption and economy. *Cultural Sociology* 14(4): 340–356.

Hargreaves, T., Wilson, C., and Hauxwell-Baldwin, R. (2018). Learning to live in a smart home. *Building Research & Information* 46(1): 127–139.

Hjorth, L., and Gu, K. (2012). The place of emplaced visualities: a case study of smartphone visuality and location-based social media in Shanghai, China. *Continuum* 26(5): 699–713.

Longhurst, R. (2016). *Skype: Bodies, Screens, Space*. Oxon & New York: Routledge.

Maller, C., and Strengers, Y. (2019). *Social Practices and Dynamic Non-Humans. Nature, Materials and Technologies*. London: Palgrave.

McLean, J. (2016). The contingency of change in the Anthropocene: more-than-real renegotiation of power relations in climate change institutional transformation in Australia. *Environment and Planning D: Society and Space* 34(3): 508–527.

McLean, J. (2020). *Changing Digital Geographies*. Cham: Springer; Palgrave McMillan.

Nicholls, L., and Strengers, Y. (2019). Robotic vacuum cleaners save energy? Raising cleanliness conventions and energy demand in Australian households with smart home technologies. *Energy Research & Social Science* 50: 73–81.

Pickren, G. (2014). Geographies of e-waste: towards a political ecology approach to e-waste and digital technologies: political ecology e-waste. *Geography Compass* 8(2): 111–124.

Pink, S. (2012). *Situating Everyday Life*. London: Sage.

Pink, S., Ardèvol, E., and Lanzeni, D. (2020). Digital Materiality. In *Digital Materialities: Design and Anthropology*, eds. S. Pink, E. Ardèvol, and D. Lanzeni. London: Routledge, 1–26.

Reckwitz, A. (2002). Toward a theory of social practices: A development in culturalist theorizing. *European Journal of Social Theory* 5(2): 243–263.

Rueb, T. (2014). Restless: Locative Media as Generative Displacement. In *Mobility and Locative Media: Mobile Communication in Hybrid Spaces*, eds. A. de S. E Silva and M. Sheller. London: Routledge, 241–258.

Schatzki, T. (2001). Introduction: Practice Theory. In *The Practice Turn in Contemporary Theory*, eds. K. K. Cetina, T. Schatzki, and E. V. Savigny. London: Routledge, 10–23.

Schatzki, T. R. (2010). *The Timespace of Human Activity: On Performance, Society, and History as Indeterminate Teleological Events*. Plymouth: Lexington Books.

Schatzki, T. R. (2019). *Social Change in a Material World*. London: Routledge.

Schwartz, R., and Halegoua, G. R. (2015). The spatial self: location-based identity performance on social media. *New Media & Society* 17(10): 1643–1660.

Shove, E. (2003). *Comfort, Cleanliness and Convenience: The Social Organization of Normality*. Oxford: Berg.

Shove, E., Pantzar, M., and Watson, M. (2012). *The Dynamics of Social Practice: Everyday Life and How It Changes*. London: Sage.

Shove, E., Watson, M., Hand, M., and Ingram, J. (2007). *The Design of Everyday Life*. Oxford: Berg.

Spaargaren, G. (2011). Theories of practices: agency, technology, and culture: exploring the relevance of practice theories for the governance of sustainable consumption practices in the new world-order. *Global Environmental Change* 21(3): 813–822.

Strengers, Y. (2019). Robots and Roomba Riders: Non-Human Performers in Theories of Social Practice. In *Social Practices and Dynamic Non-Humans*, eds. C. Maller and Y. Strengers. Cham: Springer, 215–234.

Strengers, Y., Pink, S., and Nicholls, L. (2019). Smart energy futures and social practice imaginaries: forecasting scenarios for pet care in Australian homes. *Energy Research & Social Science* 48: 108–115.

Warde, A. (2005). Consumption and theories of practice. *Journal of Consumer Culture* 5(2): 131–153.

Watkins, H. (2006). Beauty queen, bulletin board and browser: rescripting the refrigerator. *Gender, Place & Culture* 13(2): 143–152.

Wilmott, C. (2016). Small moments in spatial big data: calculability, authority and interoperability in everyday mobile mapping. *Big Data & Society* 3(2): 1–16. DOI:10.1177/2053951716661364.

Online materials

- https://wp.lancs.ac.uk/socialpractice/

  The Centre for Practice Theory at Lancaster website provides resources, events and networking opportunities for the international and interdisciplinary community of researchers working with Social Practice Theories.

- https://www.sciencemuseum.org.uk/objects-and-stories/everyday-technology

  Stories of how everyday technology changes our lives collected by the Science Museum group.

- https://www.youtube.com/watch?v=dnaSMKrD6ZE

  A YouTube video called 'How Technology Is Reshaping Every Aspect of Daily Life' about the present and future use of everyday technologies.

Further reading

Shove, E. (2003). *Comfort, Cleanliness and Convenience: The Social Organization of Normality*. Oxford: Berg. Acknowledging comfort, cleanliness and convenience as contemporary consumer cultures, this book provides an insight into the interdependences between everyday practices, socio-technological devices and socio-technical systems.

Shove, E. (2007). *The Design of Everyday Life*. Oxford: Berg.
This book focuses on the intersection of the material cultures of design, technologies and consumption in the everyday context, highlighting practices as a central unit of analysis.

Maller, C., and Strengers, Y. (eds.) (2019). *Social Practices and Dynamic Non-Humans. Nature, Materials and Technologies*. Cham: Palgrave.
This interdisciplinary volume provokes discussion and advances conceptualisations of non-humans in social practice theories in the age of automation.

McLean, J. (2020). *Changing Digital Geographies. Technologies, Environments and People*. Cham: Palgrave Macmillan.
Considering digital geographies as an inflection of geographic thoughts and practices in the new era, this book offers an analysis of digital spaces as more-than-real, recognising the **affective** and emotional forces that co-produce the digital and the process of re-making digital spaces by social and environmental movements.

SECTION THREE

COLLABORATIONS WITH JUSTICE

70 Black geographies

Camilla Hawthorne

Introduction

Understanding the complexities of Black life, oppression, resistance, and radical imagination has long been a focus for Black scholars. However, these perspectives, though longstanding, have only recently received recognition within the field of geography. The establishment of the Black Geographies Specialty Group in 2016 by Dr. LaToya Eaves marked an important milestone in institutional recognition for Black Geographies. This progress has been the result of dedicated efforts by Black intellectuals, particularly Black women, to create spaces for their scholarship and political commitments within geography.

The pressing need for Black geographies is evinced in the disproportionate impacts of climate change on Black communities; the surveillance and policing of Black neighbourhoods; and the new configurations of anti-Black racism, nationalism, and xenophobia represented by the global resurgence of the far-right. The deadly entanglements of white supremacy, **capitalism**, settler colonialism, **patriarchy**, and **heteronormativity** today call for careful attention to the connections between space, place, and **power**. The emergence of new Black social movements that (in the internationalist spirit of the Black Radical Tradition) defy national borders also requires geographically attuned tools of analysis (Figures 70.1 and 70.2).

This chapter is a condensed version of an earlier paper 'Black matters are spatial matters: Black geographies for the twenty-first century' published in *Geography Compass* and re-printed here with permission. The chapter, like the paper, provides an overview of Black geographies, its intellectual and political lineages, and its contributions to the discipline of geography. Prominent interconnected themes within Black geographies are then explored: Black geographic imagination, racial capitalism, cities and policing, and racism and plantation futures. The chapter then highlights avenues for future research, including the need for studies to go beyond North America and engage with Latinx and Native/Indigenous geographies.

Situating Black geographies

Questions of praxis—the idea that theory and political practice are inextricably intertwined—are central to Black geographic scholarship. Any account of the field of Black Geographies must also take into consideration the history of the discipline of geography as well as the material conditions of possibility that shape intellectual labour in the academy. The under-representation of Black geographers in higher education institutions and the challenges faced by Black scholars in

DOI: 10.4324/9780429265853-83

Figure 70.1
Black Lives Matter mural on a boarded-up business in Minneapolis, Minnesota, listing some of the names of people killed by police violence

Source: Photo credit: Stock Photo/Alamy

a predominantly white discipline (Pulido, 2002), sit alongside a much longer disciplinary history intertwined with **colonialism**, enslavement, and **imperialism** (Livingstone, 1993, Kobayashi, 2014). The self-perception of the discipline tends to emphasise a sharp break among Eurocentric Enlightenment and Victorian geographies and the interventions of radical **Marxist** geographers studying inequality in the twentieth century. Yet these interventions are all too often heralded as part of a redemptionist narrative that cleanses geography of its racist history. Furthermore, its focus on economic structures might have touched upon racial inequalities, but it failed to develop the theoretical tools necessary to address the ongoing production of **race** and racism through spatial processes.

Black geographies as a subdiscipline challenges geography's troubled history by examining the spatial practices, struggles, and knowledge of Black communities. In the 2007 volume *Black Geographies and the Politics of Place*, McKittrick and Woods identify three central themes that cut across the study of Black Geographies:

> … the ways in which essentialism situates black subjects and their geopolitical concerns as being elsewhere (on the margin, the underside, outside the normal), a spatial practice that conveniently props up the mythical norm and erases or obscures the daily struggles of particular communities.
>
> … how the lives of these subjects demonstrate that 'common-sense' workings of **modernity** and citizenship are worked out, and normalized, though geographies of exclusion.

948

Figure 70.2
A George Floyd mural in Manchester, UK. On the 25 May 2020, George Floyd, an unarmed 46-year-old Black man, was murdered by Derek Chauvin, a white Minneapolis police officer who had pressed his knee into Floyd's neck until he stopped breathing

Source: Photo credit: Jon Super/Alamy Live News Stock Photo – Alamy

> … the situated knowledge of these communities and their contributions to both real and imagined human geographies [as] significant political acts and expressions.
>
> *McKittrick and Woods, 2007: 4*

Black geographic thought has existed (though under other names) for centuries, in formal academic environments, political struggles, and everyday practices of Black space-making. It simply has not always been legible to scholars working within the discipline of geography.

Influences

Black geographies upend the traditional canon of geography. But this does not mean that Black geographies represent an incommensurable 'outside' to white, Western geography. Rather, scholars of Black geographies emphasise the mutually constitutive relationship between what McKittrick in *Demonic Grounds* describes as Black spatial knowledge, negotiations, and resistances on the one hand, and geographies of domination—colonialism, slavery, imperialism, racial-sexual displacement—on the other (McKittrick, 2006: x). As McKittrick argues, this relationship reveals the ways in which Blackness has been central to both the production of space and to the formation of Western, Eurocentric forms of geographic knowledge. At the same time, the modes of Black geographic knowledge that have emerged in resistance to domination provide alternative pathways towards new understandings of **space** and to the undoing of violent practices of geographic organisation (McKittrick, 2006: xiv).

Black geographies also stress the power of Black **epistemological** decentrings to bring about new ways of understanding the world. In an article on diasporic epistemologies and decolonised curricula, Lewis takes on these possibilities by examining the influence of the 'colonial curriculum' on de- and anticolonial Caribbean intellectuals such as Stuart Hall and C.L.R. James. Hall and James—to the surprise of many contemporary readers—believed that their colonial education could actually serve as the basis for a radical **decolonial** intellectual project. This was because the Eurocentric canon did not completely 'foreclose freedom and liberation' (Lewis, 2018: 24). Rather, as a complex terrain of struggle, it could also be read against the grain, first to understand how Western European practices and prescriptions have ordered the world, and then to begin to dismantle these modes of European colonial thought and spatial organisation. In this way, Hall and James questioned the 'centrality of Europe in the European intellectual traditions and disciplines' (Lewis, 2018: 24). Through the work of Hall and James, Lewis foregrounds the multiple traditions that exist within that which is traditionally conceived of as the 'European intellectual tradition'—as opposed to categorising Black disciplinary contributions as secondary, separate, and supplementary. In doing so, he also makes the case for Blackness as an analytic that entails both a 'stretching' of Western modes of analysis (Fanon, 1961/2007: 5) and radically interdisciplinary modes of study.

In this spirit, Black geographies draws upon the Black Radical Tradition (Robinson, 1983/2005; see also Johnson and Lubin, 2017). This school of political thought and action emphasises the connections between Black liberation movements and the project of anti-capitalism. It also understands racism and white supremacy to be central organising principles of capitalism. Black **feminist** theory and epistemology have also been profoundly influential to the development of Black geographies. Black women scholars and activists have insisted on the analytical inseparability of race, **gender**, sexuality, and capitalism, as well as the commitments to critically engaging and transforming the power-laden category of 'human' (see Combahee River Collective, 1977/1986).

Black geographies have also been deeply informed by Black Caribbean intellectual traditions, especially the work of Édouard Glissant, C.L.R. James, and Sylvia Wynter, (1995) to radically re-orient dominant narratives about progress, modernity, and **temporality** (Thomas 2016). According to James, for instance, the racial **political economy** based around the **transnational** sugar trade thrust enslaved Black folk in the Caribbean into 'a life that was in its essence a modern life' (James, 1938/2001: 392). James' location of modernity in the particular socioeconomic relations of the seventeenth-century West Indies is central to anticolonial and **postcolonial** analyses of modernity and works to reconfigure the relationship of Black life to the West, liberalism, and capitalism. It also represents an injunction to seek out practices of resistance that are not immediately legible according to orthodox Western Marxist modes of analysis—for instance, by looking beyond the factory floor to the plantation.

Finally, Black geographies draw heavily upon modes of critical geographic thought developed within the field of Black/African **diaspora** studies. After all, diaspora is a fundamentally spatial relation. Scholars of the Black Atlantic, in particular, have developed sophisticated analyses of the spatially extended cultural politics of Blackness (for example, Du Bois, 1940/2011, Hall, 1990,

Gilroy, 1993). Theories of diaspora also entail powerful counter-narratives about the origins and conditions of capitalist modernity, by foregrounding the foundational violence of the transatlantic slave trade in their analyses.

Summary

- Black geographies challenge traditional geography by emphasising the interconnectedness of Black spatial knowledge, resistance, and geographies of domination.
- Black geographies highlight the power of Black epistemological decentrings to bring about new understandings of space and dismantle European colonial thought and spatial organisation.
- Influenced by the Black radical tradition, Black feminist theory, Black Caribbean intellectual traditions, and Black/African diaspora studies, Black geographies explore the connections among Black liberation movements, anti-capitalism, and the inseparability of race, gender, sexuality, and capitalism.

Four interconnected themes

Space-making and the Black geographic imagination

The first theme emphasises the **spatiality** of Black life and explores the spatial imaginaries, space-making practices, and senses of place within Black communities. Starting from the understanding that all social relations are grounded in spatial relations, this scholarship privileges Black world-making practices in all of their multiplicities. It challenges the notion that Black people lack geography (due to the upheaval of the trans-Atlantic slave trade) or are solely victims of geography (due to ongoing practices of displacement and spatial segregation). Taken together, these modes of analysis efface a Black sense of place (McKittrick, 2011) and perpetuate a dangerous understanding of space as transparent—of geographies as static, inert, and self-evident, and of current spatial arrangements as natural, innocent, and ahistorical (McKittrick, 2006: 5–6).

The lens of transparent space elides the relationship among racism, racialisation, or race-making, and the production of space. In response, Black geographies scholarship asserts that racism is also a spatial practice—space is not just a blank canvas upon which racist activity unfolds. Space both reflects and (re)produces racisms (Lipsitz, 2011). Indeed, one of the primary ways in which anti-Blackness functions is by positing Blackness as perpetually 'out of place' or as placeless (Domosh, 2017).

Central to this argument is an understanding that Blackness and Black knowledge, while **embodied**, are not rooted solely in the biocentric body. An over-emphasis on the Black body (even in the form of well-intentioned critiques of **scientific racism**) detracts from the study of Black life by 'singularising' and 'flattening it' into mere biology (McKittrick, 2016: 6). Similarly, an understanding of Black knowledge as necessarily tethered to such a 'violated body' denies the existence of multiple forms of Black knowledge—including spatial knowledge. Shifting the lens of analysis from the body to space and place allows for a reading of Black life as not reducible to racism, violence, and death (Woods, 2002). By de-centring the body as the primary unit of analysis, Black geographies in turn open up new avenues for the study of racism and Black resistance.

Food has been a particularly generative site of engagement, bringing traditional geographical concerns with nature, agrarian production, and political economy together with questions of Black space-making. This work studies Black spatial knowledges as they relate to food production, as well as the ways Black communities past and present craft food security and sovereignty in the face of racialised dispossession (Ramírez, 2014, McCutcheon, 2015, Reese, 2019). Scholars have also brought geographical analytics to bear on questions of diaspora, examining how Black **subjectivities** operate both within and against **hegemonic** understandings of nation, race, place, and membership (Brown, 2005). And, influenced by Black feminist and queer theory, a growing number of researchers have foregrounded the rich spatial imaginaries and space-making practices of Black queer communities (Eaves, 2017).

Geographies of racial capitalism

The second theme focuses on the intersection of capitalism and racism. Black geographies contribute important insights to political economic analysis. Specifically, Black geographies emphasise the mutual significance of the material and the symbolic, rejecting simplistic economic determinisms in which racism is understood as being of secondary importance to the means and relations of production. Robinson famously argued that capitalism and racism coevolved, such that capitalism had been thoroughly suffused with race and practices of racial differentiation since its emergence out of feudalism (Robinson, 1983/2005). Robinson's intervention was to transform the concept of 'racial capitalism' from the description of a specific system (i.e. apartheid South Africa) to the characterisation of capitalism as a whole (Kelley, 2017)—a shift that in turn centred slavery and colonialism in the history of capitalism. For geographers, then, the task is to study how capitalism's tendency to racially differentiate takes spatial form.

Gilmore argues that while there have been a range of approaches within geography for contending with racism and race, they generally share two assumptions: '(1) social formations are structured in dominance within and across scales; and (2) race is in some way determinate of sociospatial location' (Gilmore, 2002: 17). As she explains, once scholars recognise the interdependency of power and structure, it subsequently becomes necessary to untangle the ways power is distributed within a structure (Gilmore, 2007: 17). This in turn requires a finely grained, spatial analysis of the relationship between racism and capitalism.

Scholars of Black Geographies insist that racism and capitalism are fundamentally intertwined and that this relationship is both structured by and structuring of space (Bledsoe and Wright, 2018a). In Bankers and Empire, for instance, Hudson shows that the rise of finance capital was bound up with U.S. imperialism and that bankers from the United States actively 'instrumentalised' white racism in the Caribbean when experimenting with new banking projects (Hudson, 2017). Hudson's work can be situated within a broader body of literature that approaches slavery and anti-Black racism as ongoing conditions of possibility for worldwide capitalist accumulation. At a different scale of analysis, other scholars have focused on the ways identities and political struggles are mediated by experiences of racialised economic dispossession stemming from slavery, colonialism, and imperialism (Heynen, 2009).

Black geographic political economy has also engaged with the question of 'natural disasters'. This work denaturalises 'nature' without falling back upon economic determinisms to understand the unevenly distributed causes and effects of climate change, earthquakes, and hurricanes. Vergès has powerfully critiqued the notion of the '**Anthropocene**', arguing that scholars must 'write a history of the environment that includes slavery, colonialism, imperialism and racial capitalism, from the standpoint of those who were made into "cheap" objects of commerce … fabricated as disposable people, whose lives do not matter' (Vergès, 2017, see also Chapter 62). In this vein, Woods argued that the abandonment of New Orleans in the aftermath of Hurricane Katrina can only be understood as part of a longer historical trajectory stretching back to the overthrow of Radical Reconstruction. This is a history in which processes of economic development, racialised dispossession, environmental destruction, and white supremacy were inseparable (Woods, 2017b). This mode of analysis has also shaped an abiding concern in the Black Geographies literature with questions of environmental racism and environmental justice (see Chapters 40 and 44).

Cities, policing, and carceral geographies

The third theme explores the relationship among urban geography, critical surveillance/prison studies, and the experiences of Black communities. By engaging with questions of **gentrification**, displacement, **uneven development**, and spatial segregation via the mutual production of race and space, scholars have challenged the naturalisation of Black life to underserved urban spaces (Summers, 2019). This literature demonstrates that Black urban life is not wholly defined by or determined by racism. Instead, by engaging with insurgent practices of Black political ecology, community formation, political action, and artistic reappropriation, these scholars also show the richness of Black urban spatial imaginaries.

Scholars of surveillance, policing, and incarceration understand urban segregation as part of a broader, racialised continuum of control that stretches from the **ghetto** to the prison. The spatial confinement of Black communities in the United States is tied to the shifting relationship of capital to Black populations in the wake of Emancipation (Wilson, 2000). But while these processes are shaped by the workings of capitalism, they are not fully determined by them. In *Golden Gulag*, Gilmore critiques attempts to explain the disproportionate imprisonment of Black men and women as a modern plantation system designed for the extraction of unfree labour (Figure 70.3). Rather than presuming an **ontological** or naturalised condition of Black abjection, Gilmore presents a nuanced geographical rebuttal to the 'new slavery' thesis, one that understands mass incarceration as a spatial fix for the surplus land and labour generated by capitalism. Gilmore's analysis, which links together 'money, income, jobs, race and **ethnicity**, gender, lawmaking, state agencies, and the politics that propel them to act, rural communities, urban neighbourhoods, uneven development, migration and **globalisation**, hope and despair' (Gilmore, 2007: 26), provides an analytical foundation for a robust abolitionist political programme.

Beyond the institution of the prison itself, Black geographies research identifies a spatially extended carceral archipelago of racialised surveillance and control. Scholars of carceral geographies have demonstrated that policing, surveillance, architectural design, and rehabilitation programmes all collectively work to reproduce the spatial confinement of Black communities (Shabazz, 2015). These forms of capillary surveillance are by no means new, however. In *Dark Matters*, for instance, Browne constructs a counter-genealogy of surveillance that effectively

Figure 70.3
Under Jim Crow racial restrictions, African Americans faced imprisonment for petty infringements, including vagrancy, unlawful assembly, and interracial relationships. Prisoners were leased to farmers, construction companies, and lumber companies in exchange for payment, as shown in this picture from Florida in 1915

Source: Photo credit: © Alamy/D and S Photography Archives

dislodges the primacy of French theorist Michel Foucault. It instead locates modern surveillance technologies in practices that were developed to control the movements of colonised and enslaved populations (Browne, 2015). But once again, these scholars also show that Black life is not entirely determined by surveillance and control. Black Geographies research has thus directed attention to the ways Black communities resist and creatively subvert surveillance, policing, and mass incarceration.

Racism and plantation futures

The fourth theme delves into the spatialities of Black life, the plurality of Black spatial imaginaries, and the goal of unsettling racist and colonial forms of spatial organisation. As such,

Black geographies cannot be reduced to just the study of racism, as this would relegate Black subjects to the condition of being 'always already' oppressed. Yet scholars of Black geographies are still deeply concerned with the sedimentations of racist histories in contemporary landscapes (Inwood, 2011). This work is rooted in the Black studies tradition of approaching the plantation as a central organising principle through which present-day forms of capital accumulation, spatial organisation, and racialisation emerged. Clyde Woods' scholarship has been especially influential—specifically, his careful analysis of economic development and social movements in the Mississippi Delta (Woods, 2017a). In addition, the journal *Southeastern Geographer* has long been a forum for scholarship on the legacies of slavery and Jim Crow laws in the racial-spatial organisation of the U.S. South (see Chapter 55).

But while 'the plantation provides the future through which contemporary racial geographies and violences make themselves known' (McKittrick, 2011: 950), there are always fissures in these plantation futures. These cracks can be wrenched open to create transgressive spaces of rupture, intervention, and resistance. While historical patterns of socio-spatial organisation have shaped the terrain of political struggle in the present, Black spatial imaginaries can never fully be contained by racist geographies. Thus, scholars of Black geographies also consider what forms of Black life always remain in excess of the logics of racial-spatial violence, foregrounding the multiple and overlapping spatialities of Black struggle.

Summary

- Black geographies scholarship examines the spatial imaginaries, space-making practices, and resistance within Black communities, challenging notions of placelessness and highlighting the role of racism as a spatial practice.
- Black geographies scholars emphasise the intertwined nature of racism and capitalism, rejecting economic determinism and highlighting the spatial dimensions of racial capitalism.
- Scholars in the field of carceral geographies examine the interplay between cities, policing, and surveillance systems, challenging the naturalisation of Black life in underserved urban spaces while highlighting the resilience and resistance of Black communities against spatial confinement and control.
- Black geographies challenges racist spatial organisation and studies the spatialities of Black life, including the plantation as a central concept, to understand the legacies of racism while emphasising the resilience and resistance of Black spatial imaginaries.

Future collaborations

There are many possible new avenues for future Black geographies research. A sizeable proportion of the Black geographies scholarship has thus far been carried out in North America and, to a lesser extent, the Caribbean. There is an urgent need for Black geographies research that considers the spatial politics of race and Blackness in other geographical contexts and draws attention to the 'inherent pluralities' of Black geographies (Bledsoe and Wright, 2018b). This scholarship would also do the necessary work of provincialising North American understandings of race, racism, and Blackness (Wright, 2015). Scholars of Black geographies are well situated to engage with the global circulation of both racisms and the politics of Blackness, as well as the ways specific racial formations 'take place' in different historical-geographic contexts.

In particular, there is much room for an engagement with the African continent, as well as the relationship between Africa and the wider Black diaspora, in Black geographies. The persistent division between 'African studies' and 'Black studies' in academia—which often rests on the questionable assumption that, with the exception of South Africa, 'race' and 'Blackness' are not relevant categories on the African continent—has been well documented (Pierre, 2013). This intellectual division of labour, which is far too often taken for granted, could be productively challenged by scholars of Black geographies. Indeed, many researchers are already beginning to do this necessary work. For instance, Matlon (2014) studies masculinity and racial capitalism in postcolonial Côte d'Ivoire; Hagan (2017) investigates the anti-Blackness experienced by sub-Saharan African migrants in the Maghreb; Merrill (2018) highlights the oft-overlooked 'Black spaces' crafted by African migrants and their children in contemporary Italy; and Bledsoe (2017) explores the legacies of African marronage and the idea of the quilombo in Brazil (Figure 70.4 and Box 70.1).

The 'oceanic', in particular, has emerged as a rich site of engagement with global Black geographies, as an analytic frame that necessarily resists methodological nationalism. After all, as Bhimull reminds us, 'An ocean has many sides' (2017: 103). Chari's (2015) work, for instance, looks beyond the Black Atlantic to consider processes of racialisation, circuits of extraction, transnational cultural connections, and spatial imaginaries across the Indian Ocean Black diaspora. In addition, Hawthorne (2017) engages with the Black Mediterranean as a capacious analytical

Figure 70.4
Dancers at the Jongo Festival in Quilombo, São José da Serra, Rio de Janeiro State, Brazil

Source: Photo credit: Igor Alecsander/imageBROKER

BOX 70.1

QUILOMBOS IN BRAZIL

'Quilombos', which are also referred to as maroon communities, were independent settlements formed by enslaved individuals who escaped from bondage. These communities served as a permanent resistance against and a refuge from the oppressive forces of white supremacy. In contemporary times, the term 'quilombos' is embraced by Afro-Brazilian settlements that maintain a profound connection to their ancestral lands, using it as a powerful tool to combat cultural erasure, environmental destruction, and racism (Bledsoe, 2017; Figure 70.4). As of 2016, the Brazilian government had officially recognised 244 of these communities.

framework not only for studying the circumstances of Black diaspora in the Mediterranean region but also for understanding processes of racial criminalisation and racialised citizenship in southern Europe more broadly.

There are also exciting possibilities for engagements across Black geographies, Latinx geographies, and Native and Indigenous geographies (see Chapters 10, 43, and 71). Thinking across these fields can trouble longstanding disciplinary silos wherein Black Studies is tasked with questions of racism and the body (see King, 2019); Latinx studies engages with questions of borders and immigration (see Cahuas, 2019); and Native studies is preoccupied with questions of land and settler colonialism (see Coulthard, 2014). These diverse fields share a commitment to radical interdisciplinarity and anticolonial scholarship. Together, they can help to diagnose the insidious rearrangements of race and racism taking place in the twenty-first century and offer creative pathways for undoing these geographies of inequality.

Summary

- Future collaborations in Black geographies should prioritise research in diverse geographical contexts beyond North America and the Caribbean, challenging North American-centric understandings of race and Blackness.
- There is potential for fruitful collaborations between Black geographies, African studies, and the wider Black diaspora to bridge the intellectual divide and explore topics, such as masculinity, racial capitalism, anti-Blackness, and Black spaces, in different contexts.

Conclusion

Black geographies are not exclusively the study (or rather, positivist description) of Black people, nor does the concept entail the identification of some sort of reductive, non-relational 'Black space'. It is also not simply a matter of adding Black subjects to geography syllabi in a liberal multicultural project of 'add diversity and stir'. Rather, the use of 'Black' in the phrase 'Black geographies' is intended, at least in part, to serve as a radical provocation to the discipline of geography. It is a call to centre those subjects, voices, and experiences that have been systematically excluded from the mainstream spaces of geographical inquiry. It is also an invitation to consider how an analysis of space, place, and power can be fundamentally transformed by foregrounding questions of Blackness and racism. To put it another way, Black geographies asks how the analytical tools of critical human geography can be used to engage with the spatial politics and practices of Blackness, and how an engagement with questions of Blackness can in turn complicate foundational geographical categories, such as capital, scale, nation, and empire. By revealing the colonial and racist assumptions that undergird so many key concepts in geographical inquiry, Black geographies can then point the way to their eventual undoing.

Even after the legal architecture of explicit, biologically based racism has been dismantled, racialised disadvantage and exclusion persist under new guises. Insights from Black geographies also allow us to trace the many ways that racism was 'buried alive' (Goldberg, 2009), embedded into material landscapes and urban planning documents and transnational capital flows. A geographical understanding of racism provides an analytical toolkit for identifying forms of differentiation that do not explicitly invoke blood or biology but nonetheless employ essentialising logics. By shifting the focus away from race as a variable of stratification, Black geographies approach racism as a process that undergirds modern socio-spatial organisation and produces the ever-shifting 'objective reality' of race (Gilmore, 2007). But at the same time, by steadfastly refusing to equate Blackness (and specifically, the Black body) with racism, oppression, and dehumanisation, Black geographies open up possibilities for alternative, anticolonial, and liberatory forms of geographic knowledge and world-making (McKittrick, 2013).

Finally, a key aspect of the Black geographies project is recognising that theories of space are not the exclusive domain or property of disciplinary geography. Rather, there are many overlapping and intertwined genealogies of spatial thought, ways of knowing, and modes of knowledge production. These have in turn emerged from diverse disciplines, intellectual and political traditions, and geographical contexts. From Africana feminism to anticolonial philosophy to queer of colour critique, holding geography accountable to this multivocality will strengthen the discipline's ability to respond to the urgent challenges of our time. After all, the goal of Black geographies should never be full institutionalisation or 'disciplining' to conform to the normative parameters of traditional geography. The power of Black geographies research lies in its capacious interdisciplinary reach and liminal position on both the inside and the outside of geography andits radical political potential hinges on this transgressive 'unruliness'.

Discussion points

- In what ways do Black geographies offer insights into the importance of **critical thinking** and possibilities in doing geography (refer also to Chapter 2)?
- In your own studies, to what degree have Black perspectives been included in both theory, and in terms of examples and content?
- The chapter reiterates that Black geographies insists on the **agency**, capacity, and creativity of Black lives, and that Black lives are 'always in excess' of racism, violence, and structural

oppression. Take some time to reflect on the tension between representing oppressive structures, and representing agency and self-determination in scholarly practice.

- The chapter discusses the 'world-making' work of Black geographies—what does world-making mean and why might this be an important idea?

References

Bhimull, C. D. (2017). *Empire in the Air: Airline Travel and the African Diaspora*. New York: NYU Press. https://doi.org/10.18574/nyu/9781479843473.001.0001

Bledsoe, A. (2017). Marronage as a past and present geography in the Americas. *Southeastern Geographer* 57(1): 30–50. https://doi.org/10.1353/sgo.2017.0004

Bledsoe, A., and Wright, W. J. (2018a). The anti-Blackness of global capital. *Environment and Planning D: Society and Space* 37: 8–26. https://doi.org/10.1177/0263775818805102

Bledsoe, A., and Wright, W. J. (2018b). The pluralities of Black geographies. *Antipode* 51: 419–437. https://doi.org/10.1111/anti.12467

Brown, J. N. (2005). *Dropping Anchor, Setting Sail: Geographies of Race in Black Liverpool*. Princeton: Princeton University Press.

Browne, S. (2015). *Dark Matters: On the Surveillance of Blackness*. Durham: Duke University Press. https://doi.org/10.1215/9780822375302

Cahuas, M. (2019). Interrogating absences in Latinx theory and placing Blackness in Latinx geographical thought: A critical reflection. Society & Space. Retrieved May 15, 2019, from Society & Space website: http://societyandspace.org/2019/01/23/interrogating-absences-in-latinx-theory-and-placing-blackness-in-latinx-geographical-thought-a-critical-reflection/

Chari, S. (2015). African extraction, Indian Ocean critique. *South Atlantic Quarterly* 114(1): 83–100. https://doi.org/10.1215/00382876-2831301

Combahee River Collective. (1986). *The Combahee River Collective Statement: Black Feminist Organizing in the Seventies and Eighties*. Latham: Kitchen Table: Women of Color Press (Original work published 1977).

Coulthard, G. S. (2014). *Red Skin, White Masks: Rejecting the Colonial Politics of Recognition*. Minneapolis: University of Minnesota Press. https://doi.org/10.5749/minnesota/9780816679645.001.0001

Domosh, M. (2017). Genealogies of race, gender, and place. *Annals of the American Association of Geographers* 107(3): 765–778. https://doi.org/10.1080/24694452.2017.1282269

Du Bois, W. E. B. (2011). *Dusk of Dawn: An Essay Toward an Autobiography of a Race Concept*. New Brunswick: Transaction Publishers (Original work published 1940).

Eaves, L. E. (2017). Black geographic possibilities: on a queer Black South. *Southeastern Geographer* 57(1): 80–95. https://doi.org/10.1353/sgo.2017.0007

Fanon, F. (2007). *The Wretched of the Earth*. New York: Grove/Atlantic, Inc.

Gilmore, R. W. (2002). Fatal couplings of power and difference: notes on racism and geography. *The Professional Geographer* 54(1): 15–24. https://doi.org/10.1111/0033-0124.00310

Gilmore, R. W. (2007). *Golden Gulag: Prisons, Surplus, Crisis, and Opposition in Globalizing California*. Berkeley: University of California Press.

Gilroy, P. (1993). *The Black Atlantic: Modernity and Double Consciousness*. Cambridge, MA: Harvard University Press.

Glissant, É. (1997). *Poetics of Relation*. Ann Arbor: University of Michigan Press (Original work published 1990). https://doi.org/10.3998/mpub.10257

Goldberg, D. T. (2009). *The Threat of Race: Reflections on Racial Neoliberalism*. Malden: Wiley-Blackwell.

Hagan, A. (2017). Algeria's Black fear. Retrieved December 13, 2018, from Africa is a Country website: https://africasacountry.com/2017/08/algerias-black-fear/

Hall, S. (1990). Cultural Identity and Diaspora. In *Identity: Community, Culture, Difference*, ed. J. Rutherford. London: Lawrence & Wishart, 222–237.

Hawthorne, C. (2017). In search of Black Italia: notes on race, belonging, and activism in the Black mediterranean. *Transition* 123(1): 152–174.

Heynen, N. (2009). Bending the bars of empire from every ghetto for survival: the Black Panther Party's radical antihunger politics of social reproduction and scale. *Annals of the Association of American Geographers* 99(2): 406–422. https://doi.org/10.1080/00045600802683767

Hudson, P. J. (2017). *Bankers and Empire: How Wall Street Colonized the Caribbean*. Chicago: University of Chicago Press. https://doi.org/10.7208/chicago/9780226459257.001.0001

Inwood, J. F. J. (2011). Geographies of race in the American South: The continuing legacies of Jim Crow segregation. *Southeastern Geographer* 51(4): 564–577. https://doi.org/10.1353/sgo.2011.0033

James, C. L. R. (2001). *The Black Jacobins: Toussaint L'ouverture and the San Domingo Revolution*. New York: Penguin Books Limited (Original work published 1938).

Johnson, G. T., and Lubin, A. (eds.) (2017). *Futures of Black Radicalism*. London: Verso Books.

Kelley, R. D. G. (2017). What did Cedric Robinson mean by racial capitalism? Boston Review. Retrieved July 17, 2019, from http://bostonreview.net/race/robin-d-g-kelley-what-did-cedric-robinson-mean-racial-capitalism

King, T. L. (2019). *The Black Shoals: Offshore Formations of Black and Native Studies*. Durham, NC: Duke University Press.

Kobayashi, A. (2014). The dialectic of race and the discipline of geography. *Annals of the Association of American Geographers* 104(6): 1101–1115. https://doi.org/10.1080/00045608.2014.958388

Lewis, J. S. (2018). Releasing a tradition: diasporic epistemology and the decolonized curriculum. *The Cambridge Journal of Anthropology* 36(2): 21–33. https://doi.org/10.3167/cja.2018.360204

Lipsitz, G. (2011). *How Racism Takes Place*. Philadelphia: Temple University Press.

Livingstone, D. N. (1993). *The Geographical Tradition: Episodes in the History of a Contested Discipline*. Oxford, UK: Wiley-Blackwell.

Matlon, J. (2014). Narratives of modernity, masculinity, and citizenship amid crisis in Abidjan's Sorbonne. *Antipode* 46(3): 717–735. https://doi.org/10.1111/anti.12069

McCutcheon, P. (2015). Food, faith, and the everyday struggle for Black urban community. *Social & Cultural Geography* 16(4): 385–406. https://doi.org/10.1080/14649365.2014.991749

McKittrick, K. (2006). *Demonic Grounds: Black Women and the Cartographies of Struggle*. Minneapolis: University of Minnesota Press.

McKittrick, K. (2011). On plantations, prisons, and a Black sense of place. *Social & Cultural Geography* 12(8): 947–963. https://doi.org/10.1080/14649365.2011.624280

McKittrick, K. (2013). Plantation futures. *Small Axe: A Caribbean Journal of Criticism* 17(3 (42)): 1–15. https://doi.org/10.1215/07990537-2378892

McKittrick, K. (2016). Diachronic loops/deadweight tonnage/bad made measure. *Cultural Geographies* 23(1): 3–18. https://doi.org/10.1177/1474474015612716

McKittrick, K., and Woods, C. (eds.) (2007). *Black Geographies and the Politics of Place*. Cambridge, MA: South End Press.

Merrill, H. (2018). *Black Spaces: African Diaspora in Italy*. New York: Routledge. https://doi.org/10.4324/9781351000758

Pierre, J. (2013). *The Predicament of Blackness: Postcolonial Ghana and the Politics of Race*. Chicago: University of Chicago Press.

Pulido, L. (2002). Reflections on a White discipline. *The Professional Geographer* 54(1): 42–49. https://doi.org/10.1111/0033-0124.00313

Ramírez, M. M. (2014). The elusive inclusive: Black food geographies and racialized food spaces: Black food geographies and racialized food spaces. *Antipode* 47(3): 748–769. https://doi.org/10.1111/anti.12131

Reese, A. M. (2019). *Black Food Geographies: Race, Self-Reliance, and Food access in Washington*. Chapel Hill: University of North Carolina Press.

Robinson, C. J. (2005). *Black Marxism: The Making of the Black Radical Tradition*. Chapel Hill: University of North Carolina Press (Original work published 1983).

Shabazz, R. (2015). *Spatializing Blackness: Architectures of Confinement and Black Masculinity in Chicago*. Urbana: University of Illinois Press. https://doi.org/10.5406/illinois/9780252039645.001.0001

Summers, B. T. (2019). *Black in Place: The Spatial Aesthetics of Race in a Post-Chocolate City*. Chapel Hill: University of North Carolina Press.

Thomas, D. A. (2016). Time and the otherwise: Plantations, garrisons and being human in the Caribbean. *Anthropological Theory* 16(2–3): 177–200. https://doi.org/10.1177/1463499616636269

Vergès, F. (2017). Racial Capitalocene. In *Futures of Black Radicalism*, eds. G. T. Johnson and A. Lubin. London: Verso Books, 72–82.

Wilson, B. M. (2000). *America's Johannesburg: Industrialization and Racial Transformation in Birmingham*. Lanham: Rowman & Littlefield.

Woods, C. (2002). Life after death. *The Professional Geographer* 54(1): 62–66. https://doi.org/10.1111/0033-0124.00315

Woods, C. (2017). *Development Arrested: The Blues and Plantation Power in the Mississippi Delta*. London and Brooklyn: Verso Books.

Woods, C. (2017b). *Development Drowned and Reborn: The Blues and Bourbon Restorations in Post-Katrina New Orleans*. Athens: University of Georgia Press.

Wright, M. M. (2015). *Physics of Blackness: Beyond the Middle Passage Epistemology*. Minneapolis: University of Minnesota Press. https://doi.org/10.5749/minnesota/9780816687268.001.0001

Wynter, S. (1995). 1492: A New World View. In *Race, Discourse, and the Origin of the Americas: A New World View*, eds. S. Wynter, V. L. Hyatt, and R. Nettleford. Washington, DC: Smithsonian Institution Press, 5–57.

Online materials

- Geographies of Racial Capitalism with Ruth Wilson Gilmore An Antipode Foundation film (https://www.youtube.com/watch?v=2CS627aKrJI)—a short introduction to racial capitalism
- If You're New to Abolition: Study Group Guide (https://abolitionjournal.org/)—detailed resources on the prison industry complex and abolitionist alternatives
- Ruth Wilson Gilmore, Intercepted Podcast: Ruth Wilson Gilmore on Abolition (https://theintercept.com/2020/06/10/ruth-wilson-gilmore-makes-the-case-for-abolition/)
- Ruth Wilson Gilmore, Abolition Geography: Essays Towards Liberation (https://www.youtube.com/watch?v=-r0cfvvcyZs)—YouTube Ruth Gilmore provides an accessible introduction to abolitionist geography in this conversation with Chenjerai Kumanyika

Further reading

Benjamin, R. (2022). *Viral Justice: How We Grow the World We Want*. Princeton: Princeton University Press. This recent book demonstrates Black Geographies of world-making. It is available as both audio and text and covers a range of Black Geography topics made even more pressingly visible in the wake of the Black Lives Matter movement.

Gilmore, R. W. (2022). *Abolition Geography: Essays Towards Liberation*. London and Brooklyn: Verso Books. A collection of writings of Ruth Wilson Gilmore on the origins of policing and mass incarceration sets out an abolitionist framework that addresses activism, state power, and racial capitalism.

Heynen, N., and Ybarra, M. (2021). On abolition ecologies and making 'Freedom as a Place'. *Antipode* 53: 21–35. https://doi.org/10.1111/anti.12666
Rather than define communities by the violence they suffer, this paper draws attention to the coalitional land-based politics that dismantle oppressive relations of white supremacy.

McKittrick, K. (2006). *Demonic Grounds: Black Women and the Cartographies of Struggle*. Minneapolis: University of Minnesota Press.
This classic text in Black Geographies offers a powerful interpretation of Black women's geographic thought.

Wilson, B. M. (2019). *America's Johannesburg: Industrialization and Racial Transformation in Birmingham* (Vol. 46). Athens: University of Georgia Press.
A detailed examination of the links between Alabama's slaveholding order and the rise of industrial capitalism in the state.

Woods, C. (2017). *Development Arrested: The Blues and Plantation Power in the Mississippi Delta*. London and Brooklyn: Verso Books.
This book examines the impact of the plantation system and Black struggle for social and economic justice.

71 Decolonisation

Mike Ross, Rebecca Kiddle,
Amanda Thomas, Bianca Elkington,
Ocean Ripeka Mercier and
Jennie Smeaton

Introduction

He tatau pounamu
[A greenstone door]

Greenstone is highly prized by Māori because of its usefulness, beauty and permanence. In earlier times, its gifting was used to seal peace agreements and signal the desire for conflicting parties to engage in talks (Figure 71.1). Arranged marriages were also described as greenstone 'doors', an acknowledgement that it could take a generation to restore some relationships, and the birth of mokopuna (grandchildren) to enable individuals, families, communities or nations to see a shared future. This chapter touches on **colonisation** and its effects, but its aim is to be part of the intergenerational process of restoring relationships. The discussion on colonisation can be confronting as it positions the coloniser as a foreign power, who dominated and exploited another country (see Chapter 49). Dealing with the legacy of colonisation in a just and fair way moves those in conflict towards a safer, more equitable and dynamic society. It enables individuals, families, communities and nations to restore relations.

The power of colonisation and **colonialism** is often hidden from plain view by its creeping structural change over long periods of time. In the case of Aotearoa (New Zealand), colonists became regular visitors and then settlers from the late 1700s until the early 1800s. Māori welcomed the new trade and technology, adapting tribal life to take advantage of the opportunities. A treaty for peaceful settlement was signed in 1840 (see Chapter 45) and from that point mass immigration occurred, overwhelming the Indigenous (Māori) population. Estimates of settler numbers at 1 or 2% of the total population in 1840 were almost reversed in 1906 where the Māori population was 5% of the nearly 1 million New Zealanders (Stats, 2020). The influx of settlers, their physical needs to survive, an advanced military force and an attitude of superiority coupled with ignorance soon marginalised Māori people and their way of life. This has ongoing effects in contemporary society in terms of health, governance, housing, incarceration, education and more.

DOI: 10.4324/9780429265853-84

Figure 71.1
This mere pounamu is thought to have been presented to Government forces as a symbol of peace at
the cessation of hostilities by Waikato at the end of the New Zealand Wars [1863–1865]

Source: Image courtesy of Te Papa Tongarewa Museum of New Zealand, gift of W Leo Buller, 1911

Respected Māori elder and activist Moana Jackson uses the metaphor of two houses to describe
the colonising process. Each house represents a society built to provide a secure and stable shelter for the people who live in those houses. The foundations of the house include systems of
political decision-making, economies, health, education and a common language, providing the
strength of a house. These foundations are organised differently based on the occupants' beliefs,

history, environment and resources. The art traditions, etiquette, myths, stories and music are expressed in the adornment of each house and were developed by its owners over centuries, creating spaces for innovation and adaptation (Elkington et al., 2020).

The colonists arrived in Aotearoa with a kitset, ready to be built 'house'; however, it lacked the cornerstone foundation, the resource base, to sustain its existence in this new land. The process of colonisation removed resources from the Māori house and applied them to the colonisers eventually fortifying the new state of New Zealand and its Western-style government, health, education, justice systems with mainly English language and Western art traditions.

The Māori response varied but the overall erosion of Māori independence and a loss of resources led to conflict, war, subjugation, assimilation policies and the continued resistance by Māori (see also Chapter 45). The resulting marginalisation reduced the Māori house and contents to museum artefacts and cultural practices viewed as quaint tourist experiences, while any negative social issues for Māori became evidence of an inherently ignorant, or worse, 'degenerate' Māori lifestyle.

However, Māori want to be Māori, past, present and future. Māori community institutions responded to support and promote a Māori way of life and gave a focus for resistance to colonisation. These institutions include marae (communal meeting places), the Kīngitanga (the Māori King movement formed to unite Māori politically and socially), the Ratana Church (concerned with the spiritual, physical and political welfare of Māori) and others. At a family and community level, Māori resilience is demonstrated in the continued use of ceremony to mark important life events, from birthing practices (such as returning the whenua/placenta to be buried in tribal whenua/lands) to tangi (funeral rites shared with family and friends) to the first Indigenous national holiday of Matariki (celebrating the Māori lunar New Year). Although Māori have struggled to maintain these traditions and institutions in a hostile environment, they continue to survive.

When one of us spoke to a tribal elder about why he dedicated so much of his life to the physical, cultural and spiritual responsibilities of his marae community, he responded,

> My grandparents did the same thing, my parents did likewise and now it was my turn. It honours all those that gave of themselves so that we could have this place.
>
> Oscar Dixon, Chairperson & Elder, Kai-a-te-mata Marae, Ngāti Hauā
> (personal communication November 1998)

Inherent in his comment was an appreciation of wisdom passed on from one generation to the next. This wisdom was tried and tested over time, including principles for a satisfying and full life. It is an understanding that belonging to a people and place comes with responsibility; service is essential for maintaining community connections. And there is the challenge for this generation to serve and lead in the same way. A house can be rebuilt and restored to its former state.

We have started this chapter on decolonisation with a description of colonisation and resistance in Aotearoa New Zealand because decolonisation is primarily a community-led process, which is rooted in particular places while having connecting threads across context. Later in the chapter, we return to specific examples of what decolonisation looks like, but before that, it is important to discuss the role geography as a discipline has played in processes of colonisation, how geographers have grappled with this and what it would mean to decolonise geography.

In writing about colonisation and decolonisation, it's important to be explicit about where we speak from. We are a group who have worked together to understand decolonisation, especially of urban environments, in Aotearoa New Zealand. The team is led by and mostly made up of Māori but also includes Pākehā. This make-up reflects a broader principle of decolonisation – that it must be led by Indigenous people and people of colour, but it also requires the work of non-Indigenous folks.

Summary

- Learning about colonialism provides an opportunity to move on from conflict towards a fairer future.
- Colonisation has ongoing impacts on Indigenous populations. The independence of Indigenous people has been undermined; the taking of resources led to conflict, war, subjugation, assimilation policies and the continued resistance by Māori.
- Indigenous people want to live as Indigenous people. Decolonisation, a process rooted in place and community, is a way to work towards this, as well as securing fairer, more just lives for everyone.

Geography and colonialism

Colonialism describes processes and structures that attempt to dominate people and places – the undermining of the foundations of Indigenous people and places. One way of dominating is occupation of land and sea, and the imposition of economic and political systems that benefit the colonising power. As Chapter 10 on Indigeneity has noted earlier, geographers and the geography discipline were an important part of colonisation in many places.

The Geographical Society in London (later the Royal Geographical Society) was established in 1830 and, over the next decades, sponsored exploration of vast parts of the globe. The Society was attempting to establish geography as a credible science, as well as contribute to 'civilising' non-white, non-Christian populations (Barnett, 1998). White scientists were sent on missions to 'find' and 'discover' places (see also Chapter 10). We have used scare quotes here, because like so many narratives around colonial exploration and discovery, the knowledge held by Indigenous and local people is ignored and erased. In examples like Australia, the very existence of Indigenous people was erased entirely when the colonisers declared *terra nullius*, a legal term for empty and unoccupied land (see also Chapters 7, 43 and 49). Clive Barnett (1998) describes how Dr Andrew Smith reported back to the RGS in 1836 that people in Central Africa could not give him accurate directions to a lake he wanted to visit. He reported his frustration that people could not understand compass points, or how to describe the distance in terms of Eurocentric measures of time (e.g. hours) it would take to get to the lake. Barnett (1998: 245) writes that 'No room is left either for the possibility of misunderstanding or, more significantly, the possibility that what [Smith] hears is not confusion and ignorance but a different form of knowing tied to different ways of producing space'. To these RGS geographers, there was only one way of producing space. The RGS was an important institution in justifying and carrying out colonisation. These justifications were underpinned by economic opportunism, and ideas of cultural and racial superiority – white supremacism.

In 2023, the RGS-IBG website notes: 'The history of the Society was closely allied for many of its early years with colonial exploration in Africa, the Indian subcontinent, the polar regions, and central Asia'. There is no explanation on that page that this 'colonial exploration' might be problematic. As we've described above, in Aotearoa New Zealand whole ways of living and organising society were interrupted and suppressed. This omission is one small reflection of the way colonialism persists in the discipline of geography; there is a lack of recognition of how geographers have been complicit in the enormous and persistent violence that colonialism has unleashed.

It's important to note here that colonialism isn't something relegated to the past. Invasion and 'discovery' still happen; think here of West Papua, or the news stories that crop up sporadically of 'discovering' uncontacted tribes in the Amazon. Colonialism describes something more though, specifically the way oppressive **power** relations persist, the way such power relations shape who holds resources, and what is understood to be 'normal'. Places where colonisers arrived and stayed – Aotearoa New Zealand, the United States, Canada, Australia – are described as settler colonies (see Chapter 49). In settler colonies, colonial structures and institutions were imposed over Indigenous ones. To this day, Indigenous people are working to restore Indigenous ways of being, doing and knowing which are plural and diverse (see Chapters 7 and 10).

Summary

- Geography as a discipline has been complicit in colonisation in many places. For example, members of the Royal Geographical Society went on explorations to 'discover' places and 'civilise' people.
- Colonialism describes persistent power inequalities that shape what is seen as normal, and who holds resources.
- Decolonisation involves restoring Indigenous norms around knowledge, action and existing, and Indigeneity is multiple and varied.

Colonial knowledge politics

One of the ways that colonialism persists is in shaping what counts as 'knowledge'. We might also ask, whose knowledge matters? Where does knowledge come from? Above, we've described the assumptions of white explorer geographers who thought their ways of understanding space were the only right ones. Similar dynamics persist to this day, despite overwhelming evidence that understandings of space and place are culturally situated and therefore diverse.

Juanita Sundberg (2014: 34) uses the term '**Eurocentrism**' to describe the way Europe is imagined and positioned in a lot of geography literature as the 'primary architect of world history and bearer of universal values, reason, and theory' (see also Chapter 44). This is a dynamic that crops up frequently in our discipline, and others. Zoe Todd (2016: 7), an Indigenous (Red River Métis, *Otipemisiwak*) anthropologist, has described going along to a seminar by Bruno Latour, a very prominent scholar who has worked on theories of knowledge, and the relationship between science and society:

> I waited, … as I do through most of these types of events in the UK – waited to hear a whisper of the lively and deep intellectual traditions borne out in Indigenous Studies departments, community halls, fish camps, classrooms, band offices and Friendship Centres across Turtle Island (North America) right now. European and North American academies are separated, after all, by a mere pond, and our kinship relations and ongoing colonial legacies actually weave us much more closely together than geography suggests.
>
> It never came. He did not mention Inuit. Or Anishinaabeg. Or Nehiyawak. Or any Indigenous thinkers at all.
>
> *Todd, 2016: 7, see also* Chapter 64

A result of this lack of engagement has been that particular understandings of the world have dominated geography as a discipline. One example has been the way a lot of environmental geography has presumed as a fundamental truth that nature and society are two separate things (rather than being messily tangled together in complicated and mutually reliant relationships). Sundberg (2014) argues that the assumption that this is true to everyone, everywhere is representative of ongoing colonialism in geography (see also Chapter 43). Her arguments draw on **postcolonial** theory.

Postcolonial theory emerged from literary studies through the 1970s and deeply influenced geography from the 1980s onwards. Thinkers like Dipesh Chakrabarty, Edward Said and Gayatri Chakravorty Spivak were very critical of the colonial knowledge politics we've described: that Europe (or more broadly, 'the West') is the source of true, or good, knowledge. These scholars sought to put Europe in its place, so to speak, to name and identify the way power inequalities had dominated and distorted how people thought about the world. Edward Said (1979) described in detail the way the 'East' (or 'not-West') was imagined by the West – as places of romanticism, unserious, irrational. These imaginations were used to justify intervention and dominance. Postcolonialism in geography (see also Chapters 37 and 68) has questioned the development of the discipline and allows us to ask what counts as geography and why?

Decolonial scholars have built on the work of postcolonial scholars. Rather than attempting to speak back to Western knowledge, or put it back in its place, decolonial scholars have focussed on theory and action from particular places, and how knowledge and imaginations emerge from place (Radcliffe, 2017). Of course, this is not a simple binary between Western/non-Western (Radcliffe, 2017). Knowledge travels and enters conversation with people and place. But it is an effort to rebalance power and pay attention to those knowledges that have been ignored and erased. Decolonial geographies also intervene in and confront ways of thinking and acting that reinforce power inequalities (Noxolo, 2017).

Summary

- In geography and related disciplines, there has been a long-standing and ongoing lack of engagement with both theory and lived experience of Indigenous and non-white people.
- Geography has been dominated by Eurocentrism, the notion that Europe is the main actor in shaping the world, and that knowledge that comes from there is the most credible. Postcolonial scholars have shone a light on Eurocentrism and challenged it.
- Decolonial scholars have built on postcolonialism to highlight theory and action from particular places and actively address power inequalities.

Decolonising geography

At the university many of the authors of this chapter have worked at, in the building where the geography staff work, there was a prominently positioned painting of four white men standing above an apparently unpeopled Te Whanganui a Tara, the city of Wellington. These 'founding fathers' of geosciences at Victoria University of Wellington stood in an imagined landscape where they were the discoverers and conquerors. This painting made many Māori deeply uncomfortable; it sent a clear message about who belonged in the building and whose work was important. This example demonstrates the connection between knowledge and space, in particular whose knowledge is seen as part of geography and allied disciplines, and how spaces and places reflect these assumptions. No Māori were included, as the 'conquering experts', or being at all present. Māori histories – which go back many hundreds of years in Te Whanganui a Tara – were entirely erased. The politics and style of the painting seemed to reflect geosciences from 80 years ago. The first geography professor in Aotearoa New Zealand, George Jobberns, writing in the first issue of the journal the *New Zealand Geographer*, described the national geography in the following way:

> Our nation began as a British colony. Through our hundred years ... we have built up an economy... for the products of our grasslands. We have achieved a political autonomy, but most of us are still strongly colonial in outlook, and will continue so to be for a long time because our people and all our culture and traditions are of Britain. How often our intellectuals complain that we have as yet no distinctive national culture of our own!
>
> *Jobberns, 1945: 17*

As with the painting, Māori were completely erased from economy, politics and culture in Jobberns' geography. The painting was actually commissioned in 2009, reflecting that perhaps not much has changed. Esson et al. (2017: 384) write that geography is a 'discipline that may not be ready to, or even capable of, responding to the challenge of decolonisation'. By this they mean that the structures, traditions and cultures of geography may be too stubborn and resistant to change, and the nature of many of the conversations within the discipline too shallow

The experience of Māori geographer Naomi Simmonds (2021) seems to support this. Naomi's research into Māori women's maternal geographies is award-winning, and she has made significant contributions to theory and methodology in geography (e.g. Simmonds, 2014). Yet she and her work were belittled and undermined at geography conferences and in her day-to-day work in a geography department. Naomi writes that decolonising geography:

> was personally and professionally difficult. Staff and students working in this space had a lot to offer, but our energies were expended in our attempts to dismantle a system that seemed set on paying lip service to Māori knowledges, that saw it as a 'nice addition' to a relatively unchanged colonial and masculine production.
>
> *Simmonds, 2021: 135*

As a result of the resistance to decolonisation and subsequently toxic environment, she decided to leave geography. In doing so, she was led to

> a 'new' but ancient set of geographical knowledge that is always inherently about relationships to place, politics and power. These are the geographies that are grounded within the lands and waters of my ancestors; the geographies of my home, which are both critical and hopeful, decolonising and transformative.
>
> *Simmonds, 2021: 137*

Perhaps in some geography classes or textbooks, you might read about founding (normally) fathers of geography, and tracing back the first geographers to Ancient Greece. Here Naomi questions what counts as geography if it really is about 'place, politics and power' and argues for something more expansive that includes Indigenous theory.

Naomi is also arguing for a geography where she is not a lone or lonely Māori voice, where the way the space is set up, funding incentives, and behaviours of people around her uphold colonialism. James Esson and colleagues have argued that at times there may have been too much emphasis on decolonising *knowledge* within geography, rather than decolonising institutions and structures in our discipline, universities and the world around us (Esson et al., 2017). It must go further; as Eve Tuck and Wayne Yang (2012) famously wrote, 'decolonisation is not a metaphor'. There must be material changes in order for decolonisation to happen – these changes should include but go beyond things like taking down colonial paintings. Namely land and resources must be returned to Indigenous people, and for our discipline, the spaces and practices of research and teaching need to be rethought.

In what follows, we explore some examples of decolonisation in community where spaces and places are remade.

Summary

- Despite the efforts of many Indigenous people and groups, decolonising geography has been challenging and come with a big cost. There is a lot of resistance to changing the politics and power relations that dominate many geography departments.

- Indigenous geographers have questioned established narratives about what geography is and where it comes from.
- There is much more work to do to shift not only geographical knowledge but also the institutions and structures of geography, and how geographers research and teach.

What does decolonisation look like in practice?

Decolonisation is multi-faceted and may differ from context to context. Examples here in Aotearoa New Zealand, the place from which the authors of this chapter write, span from a literal returning of land to the more symbolic act of correcting place names and more.

Above, we have written about decolonisation as enabling Māori to *be* Māori, to live as Māori. To achieve this, Moana Jackson (in Elkington et al., 2020) has written about an ethic of restoration. This might look like a peeling back of colonial power inequalities to restore Māori practices and ways of organising. This might be country-wide changes, like constitutional transformation, or slow and steady changes. The slow and steady approach has also been advocated for by Sir Mason Durie, an advocate for Māori wellbeing. He proposed the restoration of Te Whare Tapawhā/the four walled house, a model for mental, physical, spiritual and social health arguing that small incremental change in each of those areas will provide the ground work for larger transformational shifts (Durie, 2019, see also Chapter 60).

Te Whare Tapawhā is now taught in schools, universities and professional organisations across the country and informs countless health practices and systems. There are many examples of similar changes aimed at addressing the position of Māori in New Zealand society, ones which position Māori language and culture as normal. Māori language use in public is mostly welcomed and expected in formal occasions. Despite this, translating a chocolate label to support Māori language week in 2023 seemed to cross the line for some people, with online vitriol and even panic prompted in some. Despite responses such as these, government organisations, educational and health providers and many private companies have Māori signage, and translations in by-lines. Māori customs are used to welcome guests, launch projects and although at times awkward, this engagement with Māori culture and language can create space for further development or strengthen a Māori position. Other visible changes in signage seek to redress previous wrongs. In the region where we live, Wellington (Te Whanganui a Tara), a street previously named Waripori Street, was corrected by way of a local council vote. A local resident learnt that the street was likely named after a famous Māori chief from the local area, Te Wharepouri, and it was understood by many that his name had been anglicised to Waripori. It wasn't until 2020 that local government politicians voted to correct the spelling of the street despite ongoing resistance to the idea from some Wellington residents (see Figure 71.2).

In nearby Porirua, Ngāti Toa Rangatira, the tribe belonging to that area unusually still live within and around one of their traditional marae (meeting place) in a village-like setting. This is unusual as when colonisation took place, most traditional settlements were subsumed into the urban fabric and Māori were dispersed. Children and teenagers from Ngāti Toa Rangatira in 2018 designed the first bilingual signs (Figure 71.3) for the area contributing to an ongoing sense of place and signalling their tribe's ongoing and long-standing presence in Porirua. In both of these

Figure 71.2
Decolonisation and push back in Wellington. The incorrect spelling of 'Waripori' was updated after
many decades to the correct spelling Te Wharepōuri

Source: Photo credit: Gradon Diprose

examples, language is reclaimed as normal, Māori history and presence are made visible, and
therefore the meaning of these places is shifted.

Perhaps more fundamentally, giving the land back beneath those signs has long been the cry
of Indigenous peoples as per Tuck and Yang's quote above, and there have indeed been some
efforts in this regard. Legislation, such as the Public Works Act 1928, and subsequent revisions
have been used to take Māori owned land both historically and in contemporary times. This,
along with a host of other historical tools (see Walker, 1990 for further reading on these), has
been fundamental to the ongoing colonisation of Aotearoa New Zealand which has centred
on the taking of land and natural resources. It has been estimated that, through official central
government avenues for recourse and compensation, the Indigenous people in Aotearoa New
Zealand have only ever received about 1% of the resources lost through colonisation (Mutu,
2019).

However, there are some examples outside of the official claim process whereby land has
indeed been given back to Indigenous peoples. For instance, in Rotorua in 2022, the local council
signed an agreement to return land to the tribe, Ngāti Kearoa Ngāti Tuara, around the Karamu
Takina spring, taken almost 100 years earlier. This took 12 years of research from the tribe and in
addition to some land back the tribe have entered into a co-governance arrangement with the
Council to manage the spring (Bargh, 2022). In another example, a white farmer on Banks

Figure 71.3
Bilingual signs in Porirua

Source: Bianca Elkington

Peninsula gave back the farmland to Wairewa Rūnanga, a group within Ngāi Tahu (a South Island tribe). According to the Wairewa chairperson at the time, Jaleesa Panirau, the farmer said 'this land is Māori land' (O'Callaghan, 2023). The rūnanga has recently formalised plans to reforest the land with native plants and, in the process, generate income through carbon credits.

Summary

- Decolonisation is not an abstract concept – communities are leading this work and reshaping places.
- Decolonisation is context-specific, can happen at all scales and can involve big structural shifts or slow and steady changes.
- Decolonisation requires removing colonial power inequalities to restore Indigenous ways of living. This can look like changes that shift or restore the meaning of places, and the return of land and resources to Indigenous people.

Conclusion

Decolonisation in practice can be slow, resource-intensive work. It is often met with racist and vitriolic responses by people who benefit from the power inequalities under colonialism. It is directly confronting those inequalities – in communities when remaking places, and within geography when trying to change a discipline – and normalising Indigenous ways of being and doing that makes decolonisation distinct from other projects.

For geographers, Esson and colleagues (2017) and Patricia Noxolo (2017) have warned us not to stop exploring power inequalities. They argue that this understanding needs to be accompanied with action and activism. This activism needs to break down colonialism.

In the meantime, decolonisation is happening all around us. Structures that sustain unequal power are being pulled down – sometimes gradually – and Indigenous and non-white people are leading this change. We would suggest that 'colonisation sucks for everyone' ultimately when society maintains inequality (see chapter in Elkington et al., 2020 for further discussion on this). For new generations of geographers, it's essential that we learn about the problems with our discipline, and its role in colonialism. But it's equally important that we accompany this with learning from the communities around us, prioritising Indigenous and non-white voices, and actively challenging colonialism where we encounter it.

The *tatau pounamu* (greenstone door) is predicated on an awareness and ownership of a problem, and then acting with generosity to move forward. In the words of Moana Jackson,

> Stories for and about transformation rely on honesty about the misremembered stories and the foresight to see where different stories might lead. That is the ethic of transformation. It offers the chance or challenge, to clutch the truth and justice for future flowerings.
>
> *Jackson, in Elkington et al., 2020: 154*

Discussion points

- Thinking about where you are from, how have processes of colonisation and decolonisation shaped the context around you?
- Thinking about big structural shifts, and also slow and steady work, as well as different parts of the world, what other examples of decolonisation can you think of?
- Thinking about your own family histories, what action can you take to support decolonisation?

References

Bargh, R. (2022). *The Long Road to #LandBack*. https://e-tangata.co.nz/history/the-long-road-to-landback/, accessed 20 Jan 2023.

Barnett, C. (1998). Impure and worldly geography: the Africanist discourse of the Royal Geographical Society, 1831–73. *Transactions of the Institute of British Geographers* 23: 239–251.

Durie, Sir Mason. (Seminar 29 July 2019, Wellington NZ) Mauri Ora – The Metrics of Flourishing with Mason Durie. Compass Seminars NZ, Wellington.

Elkington, B., Jackson, M., Kiddle, R., Mercier, O., Ross, M., Smeaton, J., and Thomas, A. (2020). *Imagining Decolonisation*. Wellington: BWB Texts.

Esson, J., Noxolo, P., Baxter, R., Daley, P., and Byron, M. (2017). The 2017 RGS-IBG chair's theme: decolonising geographical knowledges, or reproducing coloniality. *Area* 49(3): 384–388.

Jobberns, G. (1945). Geography and national development. *New Zealand Geographer* 1(1): 5–18.

Mutu, M. (2019). The treaty claims settlement process in New Zealand and its impact on Māori. *Land* 8(10): 152. Retrieved from http://dx.doi.org/10.3390/land8100152

Noxolo, P. (2017). Decolonial theory in a time of the re-colonisation of UK research. *Transactions of the Institute of British Geographers* 42: 342–344.

O'Callaghan, J. (2023). Banks Peninsula farmland to return to native forest brining carbon credit income and healing for mana whenua. *Stuff.co.nz*. Retrieved from https://www.stuff.co.nz/pou-tiaki/131207488/banks-peninsula-farmland-to-return-to-native-forest-bringing-carbon-credit-income-and-healing-for-mana-whenua

Radcliffe, R. A. (2017). Decolonising geographical knowledges. *Transactions of the Institute of British Geographers* 42: 329–333.

Said, E. (1979). *Orientalism*. New York: Vintage Books.

Simmonds, N. (2021). Ancestral Geographies: Finding My Way Home. In *Ngā Kete Mātauranga: Māori Scholars at the Research Interface*, eds. J. Ruru and L. W. Nikora. Dunedin: Otago University Press, 126–137.

Simmonds, N. (2014). Tū te turuturu nō Hine-te-iwaiwa: Mana wahine geographies of birth in Aotearoa New Zealand (Thesis, Doctor of Philosophy [PhD]). University of Waikato, Hamilton, New Zealand. Retrieved from https://hdl.handle.net/10289/8821

Stats, N. Z. (2020). *New Zealand's Population Passes 5 Million*. Retrieved from https://www.stats.govt.nz/news/new-zealands-population-passes-5-million

Sundberg, J. (2014). Decolonizing posthumanist geographies. *cultural geographies* 21(1): 33–47.

Todd, Z. (2016). An Indigenous feminist's take on the ontological turn: 'ontology' is just another word for colonialism. *Journal of Historical Sociology* 29(1): 4–22.

Tuck, E., and Yang, W. (2012). Decolonization is not a metaphor. *Decolonization, Indigeneity, Education & Society* 1(1): 1–40.

Walker, R. (1990). *Ka Whawhai Tonu Mātou: Struggle without End*. Auckland: Penguin Books.

Online materials

- Ambrose, T. (2022). Royal tour 'in sharp opposition' to needs of Caribbean people, says human rights groups. *The Guardian*. Available from https://www.theguardian.com/uk-news/2022/mar/28/royal-tour-in-sharp-opposition-to-needs-of-caribbean-people-says-human-rights-group

  In this article, the author describes the growing push back from the Caribbean against the British Crown and its role in colonialism. You could read it alongside the following article below.

- Wright, A. (2023). British slave owners' family makes public apology in Grenada. *The Guardian*. Available from https://www.theguardian.com/world/2023/feb/27/british-slave-owners-family-makes-public-apology-in-grenada

- NZ History Podcast. (2020) *Memorials, Names and Ethical Remembering*. Available at https://new-zealandhistory.podbean.com/e/memorials-names-and-ethical-remembering/

  This podcast discusses the process of changing the name of Te Wharepōuori Street.

- RNZ. (2019). Land of the Long White Cloud (Kathleen Winter, director). *RNZ*. Available from https://www.rnz.co.nz/programmes/land-of-the-long-white-cloud

  This documentary series is an exploration of the role of white New Zealanders (also called Pākehā) in challenging racism and working towards decolonisation.

- RNZ. (2021). Ake Ake Ake (Whatanui Flavell, director/producer) *RNZ*. Available from https://www.rnz.co.nz/programmes/ake-ake-ake

  This three part documentary follows a land occupation at a place called Ihumātao, on the edges of Auckland, in an effort to reclaim land taken by the Crown in the 1860s.

Further reading

Elkington, B., Jackson, M., Kiddle, R., Mercier, O., Ross, M., Smeaton, J., and Thomas, A. (2020). *Imagining Decolonisation*. Wellington: BWB Texts.
This is a short book we wrote to try and demystify decolonisation for a general audience. It is specific to Aotearoa New Zealand in many ways but covers research and thinking about colonisation and decolonisation in more depth than we are able to in this chapter.

Jazeel, T. (2012). Postcolonialism: orientalism and the geographical imagination. *Geography* 97(1): 4–11.
This article provides a useful and easy to read introduction to postcolonialism.

Kimmerer, R. W. (2013). *Braiding Sweetgrass: Indigenous Wisdom, Scientific Knowledge and the Teachings of Plants*. London: Penguin Books.
This is a beautifully written book by an enrolled member of the Citizen Potawatomi Nation and scholar. Each chapter draws on stories from place to think about knowledge, politics and power to imagine a more environmentally just world.

Said, E. (1979). *Orientalism*. New York: Vintage Books.
Orientalism is an incredibly important book in developing critiques of colonialism and understanding the nuanced impacts of it.

72 Queer geographies

Rachel Bayer and Kath Browne

Introduction

'Queer' is a word that has been (and still is) used to ridicule those who do not fit and to deride those who operate outside of the rules of heterosexuality and two-**gender**/sex. For some people, queers were and are seen as a 'problem' to be fixed, as people to be avoided, and communities to be sent to the 'bad' areas of cities. Despite these negative origins, activists, groups, and individuals have also reclaimed queer and embraced the questions that they/we pose to mainstream society. Scholars have argued against and rejected norms that say that not being straight or **cisgender** is somehow bad, evil, or dangerous. Not only this, but there is inherent hope, creativity, and joy in seeking to create 'other' places and new worlds that are more liberated, and that offer sexual and gender freedoms to make lives liveable. In this chapter, we show how human geographers have collaborated with queer thinking, queer theory, queer scholars, and queer activists to think differently about space and place, and to challenge the restrictive ways that sexuality and gender are lived. The word 'queer' is thus used in different ways: as an identity that challenges the 'normal' of heterosexuality, and also as a perspective that challenges how things like identities can come to be seen as fixed and 'normal' in problematic and inequitable ways. 'Queer' can be used in helpful and joyful ways, opening up possibilities for different kinds of societies and geographies.

We begin this chapter by discussing the idea of 'queering spaces'. We then look at how queer can be used as a perspective to explore the way norms are formed and challenged. In this section, we explore how diverse heterosexualities can also create queer spaces, through things like sex work, and how some things like same-sex marriage have been critiqued as creating new forms of '**homonormativity**' that also exclude diverse queer identities and relationships. Finally, the chapter discusses how queer has contested the academic discipline of geography and opened up what it might be. In this way, we might say that queer geographies are relevant to the discipline as a whole, since bodies, sex, sexuality, and gender are central to examining the 'human' of human geography.

Gay ghettos, straight streets: LGBT+ space

Academic geographies of sexualities began by looking at bars, clubs, and shops that marked somewhere as 'gay', specifically in US cities like San Francisco and New York. By looking at gay sites and the clustering of specific venues, including community centres, it was clear that spaces

DOI: 10.4324/9780429265853-85

were being created and 'gay **ghettos**' formed in some cities, which provided for some a sense of freedom, and some protection and visibility (Knopp, 1990). This work was further developed by discussions of lesbian spaces, such as bars and clubs, as well as neighbourhoods where lesbians clustered (Rothenburg, 1995). The existence of such spaces challenged the assumption that heterosexuality is the norm. The research into these spaces challenged human geographers to further explore people and places without presuming that everyone is straight and in a heterosexual family. Studies continue to show that lesbian, gay (and increasingly, bisexual, trans, plus) (LGBT+) spaces create moments of belonging, welcome and inclusion, as well as being somewhere to play, have fun and experiment with sexualities and genders (Lane, 2015, Turesky and Crisman, 2023).

Pride events offer a different exploration of queer joy and create spaces of acceptance (see Figure 72.1). In some places, these are annual parades/marches, parties, and associated events, where LGBTQ+ lives are highly visible and often celebrated. For one day a year, same-sex couples can hold hands, drag queens can walk down the middle of the road, and LGBT+ people can dance, play, and parade in spaces where, on other days, they would be noticed and potentially targeted and attacked. Early Pride marches were protesting police attacks and other social injustices, where people took to the streets to demand rights, inclusion, and safety. They often marched against the police, who would raid gay bars and clubs using violence and force, arresting, and seeking to scare people by threatening to reveal their identities publicly. The march for rights has in many places become a celebration that allows some to feel empowered, included, and part of a majority in ways that are impossible in the very same place the next day. Such events enabled geographers to show how space isn't *necessarily* heterosexual. Instead, heterosexual spaces are created through what we do and what is considered ordinary. Pride events therefore *queer* the streets by being against the normal (see, e.g. Bell and Valentine, 1995). From

Figure 72.1
Dublin LGBTQ pride parade 2019

Source: Photo credit: William Murphy

these beginnings, geographers of queer and other sexualities have explored the ways in which non-normative sexualities and identities are made in and through place.

Queer geographers have also used their research to challenge the inclusions/exclusions of LGBT+ spaces. This work has shown how such spaces can, in fact, be unwelcoming for bi and trans people. Bi people in seemingly 'straight' relationships can, for example, feel out of place in gay and lesbian spaces by being stopped at the door if they are with partners perceived to be of a different sex and invisiblised by the assumption that people are either gay or straight (Maliepaard, 2015). Bi people have challenged this assumption and created innovative spaces such as BiCon and BiFest that enhance visibility and provide spaces of recognition and inclusion, as well as fun (Voss et al., 2014). Alongside bi people, trans people can also be excluded from 'gay ghettos', Pride, and other LG(BT+) spaces. Studies in trans geographies have shown how cisgendered spaces, even where these are inclusive of certain forms of gay (and at times lesbian) sexualities, can directly exclude trans people and make people feel uncomfortable in what can be labelled LGBT+ space. In this way, these spaces can still be gender normative, presuming men/women and male/female. This can be particularly hard where trans people existed in, used, and developed lesbian/gay/bi spaces pre-transition. Trans people can see these spaces as theirs. It is also difficult in a **heteronormative** world, where trans people and others can believe they have found accepting and inclusive spaces only to experience transphobia (Nash, 2011). Furthermore, those who do not fit within gender normative paradigms, such as intersex, non-binary, asexual, aromantic, and agender people, may also not feel welcome or even recognised in LGBT+ spaces. Rachel's doctoral research, for example, focuses on asexual people's everyday experiences of space in Ireland, and the ways in which spaces (including LGBT+ spaces) operate under a particular set of norms and assumptions affecting who feels welcome and safe there. While some might seek inclusion into LGBT+ spaces, for others, this may not be desired as these spaces are set within specific paradigms. Instead, they seek to be empowered to create their own spaces to develop new ways of living, doing, and connecting.

Encounters with sex and gender binaries also pervade everyday spaces like work, home, and socialising (Doan, 2010). In this way, not only are people sexed (often within man/woman), but spaces are as well. This is perhaps best seen in toilet spaces, where those visibly marked as 'different' from expected gender presentations can be vulnerable (see Figure 72.2). This is usually associated with trans people who are treated as out of place in toilet spaces and changing rooms and other spaces that are sexed as man/woman. On the other hand, some trans people are very much 'in place' because they 'pass' in sexed spaces, and in this way, reaffirm their identities/bodies through using the space. This might not be the case for other cisgender women who are mistaken for men and can be challenged and subjected to abuse, violence, and **othering** (Browne, 2005). The sexing of space then affects all who use the space, either reaffirming our sex through an ease of use or questioning it through confrontation and conflict.

Researchers in queer geographies have offered extensive critiques of LGBT+ spaces with reference to other marginalised groups. Many LGBT+ spaces have disproportionately centred the lives and experiences of white, middle class, cisgendered, and able-bodied people. Studies of Black, Muslim, and Asian struggles, for example, have highlighted the challenges to such exclusions and the creation of new spaces of '**sociality**, community, desire, pleasure, support and love' (Bailey and Shabazz, 2014: 449). This includes protest events, and clubbing and music spaces for people to dance in and enjoy while decentring whiteness and settler colonial cultures. For example, Camilla Bassi (2006) looked at the survival of a monthly British Asian gay night in

Figure 72.2
All gender toilets can provide a safe space for those facing discrimination

Source: Photo credit: Ted Eytan

Birmingham to demonstrate cultural creativities in the face of a white gay commercial scene. Challenging the absence of Black lesbian/bi and queer sites, Nikki Lane (2015) has also explored parties and events that created visibility for LGBT+ people within racialised communities.

In this section, we have described a shift in geographical research from an initial focus on gay spaces, then lesbian spaces, and on to then consider some of the critiques of who is included in lesbian, gay, bisexual, and trans spaces. Recognising that the banner of LG or LGBT is limited, LGBTQIA+ (lesbian, gay, bisexual, trans, queer, intersex, asexual/aromantic/agender, plus) has now become a commonly used inclusive acronym, and many people also now use 'queer' to describe identities that fall under this umbrella. It is shorthand, and for some, that makes it quicker and easier to encompass the diverse and various ways people live outside of heterosexual/cisgender norms. However, using 'queer' in this way means that differences between LGBTQIA+ people and their experiences of space can also be overlooked. Sub-areas such as 'lesbian geographies' and 'queer Black geographies' therefore show how difference is meaningful in people's lives and the places they live, work, and play (Eaves, 2017, Browne, 2021). There are also opportunities to create solidarities across these differences recognising that these might be interlinked. For example, Luibhéid (2018) points to the ways LGBT and migration struggles in Ireland should not be disentangled in the push for spatial justice.

Alongside work on diversities within LGBTQIA+, work by Nash and Browne (2020) shows that there are some who seek to reiterate heteronormativitities (both sexualities and the binary genders that support them) in places where LGBT+ equalities and rights are in place. These geographically specific tactics travel in diverse ways, appealing to national and local cultures and concerns. **Heteroactivism** names and conceptualises these new tactics that move away from direct vilification towards promoting what they see as the rights of children and the loss of civilisation. More is needed to understand these emergent movements, including those called 'anti-gender'.

While there has been growth in discussions of trans geographies, as well as emerging work on gender variant and intersex geographies (Johnston, 2019), more work is needed in these areas. There is significant research to be done in areas that have remained largely unexplored by geographers of sexualities, such as asexual geographies or geographies of those who might be encompassed under the '+'. This requires both an examination of everyday spaces of exclusions, marginalisations, and othering, as well as considering the limits of 'queer' identities and the LGBTQIA+ umbrella in understanding and engaging people's spatial lives. However, it is also critical to empower, engage, and enthuse as well as critique. This includes continuing to collaborate to explore the hope, resistance, creativity, and communities of those who challenge and make lives in the interstices of what is possible, recognisable, and liveable.

Summary

- The discipline of geography first explored sexualities by looking at the spaces made by gay men and lesbians, including Pride events and spaces. These challenged the idea that all space is inherently heterosexual.
- These spaces can often exclude bi and trans people, and in many places in the Global North, they can also be predominantly white.
- People of colour and others can create their own spaces to enjoy, protest, seek visibility, and question what is considered normal in LGBT+ spaces.

Queer geography: thinking queerly about places, sexualities, genders

In the section above, we focused on the way LGBTQIA+ **spatialities** contest heteronormativities. But there is more to queer than this! Queer is about disruption, unruliness, contestations, and celebrations. In this way, queer thinking that disrupts ideas of a 'natural order' collaborates well with critical geographical thinking. Queer geographers understand that things are fluid across place and time, including space, place, gender, and sexuality. Conversely space, place, and time are shaped by sexuality and gender in 'normal' and 'diverse' ways (although queer thinking would question this binary).

In this section, we see queer as a *perspective*, a way of thinking about the world that challenges what many see as normal and a 'better' way of living and loving. 'Queer' can therefore also be about resisting binaries and hierarchies, where a particular kind of 'lining up' of gender and sex, sexuality, relationality, and **embodied** presentation is understood as preferable, normal, and valued more highly (Rich, 1980). These hierarchies are normalised and naturalised through relations of power (Butler, 1990). This means that certain people's lives and relationships are celebrated (for example, through state-supported weddings), while others are seen as unnatural, wrong, and at times dangerous (for example, the negative way trans athletes are often discussed across popular culture). A queer perspective likewise further contests *all* identities (including heterosexual ones) by not seeing these as fixed, innate, or 'biological' (in ways that can be termed *essentialist*). In this way, queer is not only about LGBTQIA+ lives/politics/identities (although these are often central), but also about showing how identities come to be normalised (including heterosexualities) in certain spaces, and at whose expense.

Being 'normal' is more than being heterosexual. The 'right' type of heterosexuality also needs to be attained. In many places, dominant forms of heterosexuality can be based on divisions between men and women that presume they will come together through monogamous, coupled relationships to be 'whole' (Butler, 1990). In this worldview, men/women map neatly onto male/female, and perhaps even provider/caregiver, rational/irrational, and a range of other normative binaries. In turn, there is a presumption that the 'opposite' side will be attracted to its other. **Heteronormativity** therefore refers to not only the idea that heterosexuality is inherently normal and natural, but also to a set of racialised, classed, gendered, and ableist ideals that further create a particular version of what heterosexuality is *supposed* to be (Brown and Browne, 2016). Furthermore, idealised heterosexual spaces in the Global North are often white, wealthy (or at least middle class), and able-bodied. Focusing on these spaces shows how 'normal' is reconstituted in ways that are often overlooked, for example in heteronormative family homes. Heterosexual homes are often presumed to be 'natural' sites of romance and love, and this presumption makes their normalisation invisible. Yet as Morrison (2013) has pointed out, 'home' does not simply exist as such. It needs to be 'made' by heterosexual couples in the same ways that street and public spaces are also remade to be heterosexual. Heterosexual people can also reflect, seek to attain, or reject heteronormative ideals. In this way, there is instability. If something has to be created every day, then it is not fixed or certain. Understanding sexualities and spaces as making each other through what we do is a queer way of looking at the world that invites us to consider not only that which is out of place, but also what can be considered 'in place' and how this is produced and experienced.

If heteronormativity also must be 'made', then certain forms of heterosexuality and heterosexual spaces can also be anti-normative and thus queer. Operating in opposition to heteronormativities are thus what are considered 'perverse' heterosexualities, including kink and sex work (Hubbard, 2006, Herman, 2007). Perverse/Queer heterosexualities can be hidden for fear of social stigma, as well as police or state intervention or attack. In the case of sex work, they can also be relegated to 'dangerous places' and sought to be 'zoned out' of 'family' neighbourhoods and suburbs that are presumed to be safe (Hubbard, 2006). For example, spaces like 'red light' districts are seen as 'other' and problematic to 'good society' and 'civilisation', through the visible presence of sex workers (and at the turn of the century, also gay men). Sex work, particularly before the internet and mobile phones, was spatialised into specific parts of the city and phone boxes used as a means of communicating and selling services. Since the advent of digital communications, the geographies of sex work have changed, with mobile phones and other technologies facilitating communication, location, and payment for a wide variety of services, both virtual and in person. Although most sex work is heterosexual, it contests heteronormative ideals around sex (that it should be monogamous within a couple and 'free'). In this way, some forms of heterosexuality can be queer because they challenge what is seen as 'normal' or 'natural', and these vary depending on where you are. In some places, for example, premarital sex or childless couples are non-heteronormative. In other places, gender diverse people significantly alter the ways in which heterosexuality is imagined as being between a normative man and a normative woman. Thus, the work of queer geographers is also about *queering* heterosexualities and presumptions of 'normal', such as single people's geographies of home (Wilkinson, 2014), childfree lives and non-reproduction (Wilkinson, 2019), and 'alternate' queer geographies in spaces and contexts that are traditionally seen as heteronormative (Pham, 2019).

Queer explorations also show that not all expressions of LGBTQIA+ identities, lives, and politics necessarily align with queer's anti-normative perspective. Queer thinking, for example, has critically explored the normativities of same-sex couples. This is because some same-sex sensibilities may not always contest normativity or be queer and might instead be seen as **homonormative**. Changes to legislations and cultures have meant that some (usually white, cis, middle-class, monogamous, and able-bodied) non-heterosexual people and identities have become more 'normal' in certain places (Oswin, 2008). At the start of the twenty-first century, these changes led to concerns particularly around the normalisation of monogamous, coupled relationships, and their recognition through same-sex marriage. The concept of homonormativity (Duggan, 2002) was coined to discuss the changes to 'normal' that now encompassed some lesbians and gay men who were formerly considered 'deviant' (Brown and Browne, 2016).

Homonormative spaces are seen as replicating (or seeking to replicate) heteronormative spaces. This can take various forms, including buying into **neoliberal** orders, such as engaging in **capitalist** exploitation and developing LGBT+ markets, being part of the state/army and other contexts that once rejected 'homosexuality' and continue to perpetuate abusive systems; seeking state recognition through same-sex marriage and perhaps buying into other relations of power that leave 'queers in the cold' (Sears, 2005). Queer geographers have shown that it is not possible to exist outside of all norms and structures that create places, meaning that queers are complicit in upholding power structures that privilege certain (racialised, classed, gendered, and sexed) relationships and people (Oswin, 2008). The spatial construction of hetero- and homonormativities shows how interlocking systems of power affect the lives of marginalised groups in uneven ways in different places. For example, Bacchetta et al. (2015) noted how space is co-created across sexuality, **race**, and genders in Europe in ways that see Europeanness as white and racialised subjects as 'straight' and 'cis'. Jasbir Puar (2007) created the related concept of homonationalism to describe how countries like the USA can justify going to war and other imperialist acts on the basis of 'saving gays and lesbians'. She looked at how in the early twenty-first century, some of the justification around the US War on Terror drew on ideas of such homonationalist superiority.

Queer geographers are clear that what is considered 'normal' is different in different places. Geography matters in what queer is, who does queer work, who is recognised as queer, who lives queer lives, and where they live them. For example, thinking about homonormativity was initially predominantly based on cities in the USA, and so same-sex marriage in the context of San Francisco and other North American cities has been understood as homonormative. In Ireland, however, campaigning for same-sex marriage in the 2015 referendum was undertaken by those who see themselves as queer and against the institution of marriage itself. These activists have discussed how they did so to challenge the anti-same-sex marriage politics that would make LGBTQIA+ lives more dangerous and difficult. This activism then was not homonormative, as it sought to challenge heteronormativity in ways that *queered* Irish legislations and recent histories (Neary, 2016).

Of course, the term 'queer' itself also does not simply travel to other places and keep the same meaning. For example, people in same-sex relationships in some parts of the world may not identify with 'Western' identity terms (such as gay/queer) or relationship forms (such as monogamous gay couples) but can still live various lives and relationships outside of heteronormativity. Within geography, and beyond, the term 'queer' has been critiqued as an English language one, with all the problematic associations this has with white, 'Western' and imperialist ways of thinking (Rodó-de-Zárate, 2016, Pitoňák 2019). In some places, other understandings of gender and sexuality, such as *hijra*, *takatāpui*, and *fa'afafine*, do not map straightforwardly onto the English term queer but are non-normative so could be explored using a queer perspective. Such genders and sexualities challenge the ways in which these are structured in Anglo societies. Terms such as 'two spirit' have also been criticised by some as anglifying and appropriating Indigenous North American cultures (de Vries, 2009). The meanings and usages of 'queer' have not only changed through time, but they also differ across places, languages, and cultures. This means that queer as a word and concept does not always easily translate, and when it travels to other places, it does not remain the same.

Summary

- 'Queer' as a perspective is not just LGBTQIA+, and as such, queer space cannot be defined solely through the presence of these and other sexual/gender minorities, although they might be labelled as 'queer'.
- Some heterosexual relationships, behaviours, and activities like sex work and kink can create queer spaces that challenge what is normal.
- Homonormativity is a term that names the process of assimilation by those who were once queer into what is 'normal', for example, through same-sex marriage.
- Queer is an English word, and in some places, this and other Global North terms such as LGBTQIA+ have different meanings that are linked to **colonialism**.

Queering geography: collaborating to challenge heteronormative geographies

Queer geography has played a key role in developing thinking in twenty-first century geography. 'The Geographer' was/is gendered (male) and sexualised (heterosexual). In this section, we explore how the concepts and research developed in the first two sections reshaped the discipline of geography, both by including LGBTQIA+ people, and by fundamentally shifting what was/is considered 'Geography' by queering geographical knowledge.

Queer geographers have troubled traditional understandings of what 'counts' as geography, building upon and collaborating with **feminist** geographers who challenged what 'serious' geographical scholarship should be. Queer geographers have noted geography's 'squeamishness' around sex – particularly anything outside of specific forms of procreative heterosexual sex. The absence of sex (beyond bland and seemingly sexless discussions of fertility and population) was a key critique of the discipline of geography, and this included heterosexual sex (Binnie, 1997). Yet to understand people and place in human geography, we must also understand sex practices, behaviours, and desires, alongside identities and norms around LGBTQIA+ as important to how people and places are shaped.

Troubling understandings of the world (including feminist ones) includes troubling essentialist binary divisions between men and women. Challenges to the gender binary have come from trans, intersex, and gender variant geographies, as well as more general queering and disruption of usual practices of lining up of sex, gender, sexual attraction in the discipline of geography. This has meant that as queer geographers have continued to queer geography, they have also contested the white, cis-heteropatriarchal dominance of the discipline, and the ways of thinking that are associated with such dominant groups (Oswin, 2020). In the past decade, queer challenges within geographies have included critiquing sexualities/queer geographies itself, as an Anglo-American[1] and English-speaking sub-discipline. Some of the critiques of the Anglophone cultural dominance of queer geographies have emerged from Eastern Europe and elsewhere, where there are diverse geographical temporalities with regards to 'progress' in sexual and gendered equalities. They contended that such dominance has often rendered them 'backwards' in contrast to the supposedly 'progressive' Global North or Minority World (Kulpa and Mizielińska, 2011). This meant that colonising nations such as the UK were represented as 'leading the way' and, as such, should be followed. Such a perspective fails to recognise how place plays a key role in sexualities and genders and how they are lived and experienced. It also ignores how in places that are supposedly 'progressive', heteronormativity still actively displaces those who are not heterosexual and cisgender as out of place, marginalised and excluded (Banerjea and Browne, 2023).

These discussions drew on **intersectionality** (Crenshaw, 1991), a concept created and developed in Black feminism as a framework to explore interlocking power relations – where one identity intersects with another (such as Black and queer) to produce differential and often compounding experiences of inequality. Queer of colour geographers, predominantly in the USA, have drawn attention to the whiteness of queer/sexualities geographies and noted the queer of colour critiques in broader queer theorising. Geographers have also been criticised for only paying 'lip service' to intersectionality and doing little to actually unsettle the whiteness of the discipline (Mahtani, 2014, Eaves, 2020). It is therefore important for queer geographies and geographers to critically reflect on the power relations that constitute the discipline and how our complicity can reiterate the very normativities that queer seeks to contest.

Summary

- Human geography must pay attention to sex/sexualities in order to understand people/place.
- Geography was and continues to be a discipline that assumes people are heterosexual and cisgender.
- Queer geographers have themselves been critical of the centring of white, Anglo-American Scholarship. More is needed to address the power relations that create queer geographies.

Conclusion: queer geographical collaborations

Research in human geography has worked in collaboration with queer thinking to develop new ways of considering the world and challenging dominant power relations. Human geographers need to engage with sexualities and genders to understand the processes that create people and places. Queer geography, however, does more than include LGBTQIA+ research; it challenges the ways in which geography is formed and understood, creating new ways of thinking about place, space, lives, and politics. Queer geographers reconsider space/place by looking at how they are created between people through their relations, as not fixed but recreated through what we do in relation to power dynamics that value and hierarchise. Queer geographers then challenge and create the discipline of geography and have also used geographical thinking to speak back to and 'spatialise queer' (Gieseking, 2013).

Queer geographies have explored the inclusions/exclusions of LGBTQIA+ spaces and also examined the normalisations that create our worlds in ways that are not distinguished into easy categorisations. Yet more is needed to develop engagements beyond 'the usual subjects' of sexuality and gender research. This could include exploring the spatialities of intersex and asexual people, as well as those who refuse to fit into the categories of LGBTQIA+. Queer geographies also remain white and disproportionately focused on the UK and USA. It is therefore important to amplify and support researchers that question and challenge what has become mainstream queer geographies. Future research could explore inequities and highlight cultures, resistances, and creative strategies critical to this field. This will require collaborating across places, and differences, critique and hope to continue to build on the disruptions that queer geographers started over 40 years ago.

Discussion points

- How do LGBTQIA+ people find space where you live? Where might it be less welcoming/open?
- Consider what is 'normal' around gender and sexualities where you live, work, and socialise. How is, or might this be disrupted?
- What other new areas of research might queer geographies begin to explore to work beyond what has been central to date?
- How might geography/geographers work to address the power relations that continue to define the discipline?

Note

1. Here we refer to scholars located in North America and England predominantly, but also places such as Ireland, Scotland, Australia, and New Zealand as Anglophone spaces.

References

Bacchetta, P., El-Tayeb, F., and Haritaworn, J. (2015). Queer of colour formations and translocal spaces in Europe. *Environment and Planning D: Society and Space* 33(5): 769–778.

Bailey, M. M., and Shabazz, R. (2014). Gender and sexual geographies of Blackness: new Black cartographies of resistance and survival (part 2). *Gender, Place & Culture* 21(4): 449–452.

Banerjea, N., and Browne, K. (2023). *Liveable Lives*. Bloomsbury: London.

Bassi, C. (2006). Riding the dialectical waves of gay political economy: a story from Birmingham's commercial gay scene. *Antipode* 38(2): 213–235.

Bell, D., and Valentine, G. (eds.) (1995). *Mapping Desire*. London: Routledge.

Binnie, J. (1997). Coming out of geography: towards a queer epistemology? *Environment and Planning D: Society and Space* 15(2): 223–237.

Brown, G., and Browne, K. (eds.) (2016). *The Routledge Research Companion to Geographies of Sex and Sexualities.* London: Routledge.

Browne, K. (2021). Geographies of sexuality I: Making room for lesbianism. *Progress in Human Geography* 45(2): 362–370. https://doi.org/10.1177/0309132520944494

Butler, J. (1990). *Gender Trouble.* London: Routledge.

Crenshaw, K. (1991). Mapping the margins: intersectionality, identity politics, and violence against women of color. *Stanford Law Review* 43(6): 1241–1299.

de Vries, K. M. (2009). Berdache (Two-Spirit). In *Encyclopedia of Gender and Society*, ed. J. O'Brien. Thousand Oaks: SAGE, 62–65.

Duggan, L. (2002). The New Homonormativity: The Sexual Politics of Neoliberalism. In *Materializing Democracy*, eds. C. Russ, D. N. Dana, and E. P. Donald. Durham: Duke University Press, 175–194.

Eaves, L. (2017). Black geographic possibilities: on a queer black South. *Southeastern Geographer* 57(1): 80–95.

Eaves, L. (2020). Fear of an other geography. *Dialogues in Human Geography* 10(1): 34–36.

Gieseking, J. J. (2013). A Queer Geographer's Life as an Introduction to Queer Theory, Space, and Time. In *Queer Geographies*, eds. L. Lasse, M. Aranios, F. Zúñiga-González, M. Kryger, and O. Mismar. Roskilde: Museet for Samtidskunst, 14–21.

Herman, R. (2007). Playing with Restraints: Space, Citizenship and BDSM. In *Geographies of Sexualities: Theory, Practices and Politics*, eds. K. Browne, J. Lim, and G. Brown. Aldershot: Ashgate, 89–100.

Hubbard, P. (2006). *City.* London: Routledge.

Johnston, L. (2019). *Transforming Gender, Sex, and Place.* London: Routledge.

Knopp, L. (1990). Some theoretical implications of gay involvement in an urban land market. *Political Geography Quarterly* 9(4): 337–352.

Kulpa, R., and Mizielińska, J. (2011). *De-Centring Western Sexualities.* London: Routledge.

Lane, N. (2015). All the Lesbians Are White, All the Villages Are Gay, But Some of Us Are Brave: Intersectionality, Belonging, and Black Queer Women's Scene Space in Washington, D.C. In *Lesbian Geographies*, eds. K. Browne and E. Ferreira. London: Routledge, 219–242.

Luibhéid, E. (2018). Same-sex marriage and the pinkwashing of state migration controls. *International, Feminist Journal of Politics* 20(3): 405–424.

Mahtani, M. (2014). Toxic geographies: absences in critical race thought and practice in social and cultural geography. *Social & Cultural Geography* 15(4): 359–367.

Morrison, C.-A. (2013). Homemaking in New Zealand: thinking through the mutually constitutive relationship between domestic material objects, heterosexuality and home. *Gender, Place & Culture* 20(4): 413–431.

Nash, C. J. (2011). Trans experiences in lesbian and queer spaces. *The Canadian Geographer* 55(2): 192–207.

Nash, C. J., and Browne, K. (2020). *Heteroactivism.* London: Bloomsbury.

Neary, A. (2016). Civil partnership and marriage: LGBT-Q political pragmatism and the normalization imperative. *Sexualities* 19(7): 757–779.

Oswin, N. (2008). Critical geographies and the uses of sexuality: deconstructing queer space. *Progress in Human Geography* 32(1): 89–103.

Oswin, N. (2020). An other geography. *Dialogues in Human Geography* 10(1): 9–18.

Pham, J. M. (2019). Queer space and alternate queer geographies: LBQ women and the search for sexual partners at two LGBTQ-friendly U.S. universities. *Journal of Lesbian Studies* 24(3): 227–239.

Pitoňák, M. (2019). Lessons from the 'Periphery': countering Anglo-Geographic Hegemony over geographies of sexuality and gender. *Documents d'anàlisi geogràfica* 65(3): 563–585.

Puar, J. K. (2007). *Terrorist Assemblages*. Durham: Duke University Press.

Rich, A. (1980). Compulsory heterosexuality and lesbian existence. *Signs: Journal of Women in Culture and Society* 5(4): 630–660.

Rodó-de-Zárate, M. (2016). Feminist and Queer Epistemologies beyond Academia and the Anglophone World: Political Intersectionality and Transfeminism in the Catalan Context. In *The Routledge Research Companion to Geographies of Sex and Sexualities*, eds. G. Brown and K. Browne. Oxon: Routledge, 155–164.

Rothenburg, T. (1995). 'And She Told Two Friends': Lesbians Creating Urban Social Space. In *Mapping Desire*, eds. D. Bell and G. Valentine. London: Routledge, 150–165.

Sears, A. (2005). Queer anti-capitalism: what's left of lesbian and gay liberation? *Science and Society* 69(1): 95–112.

Turesky, M., and Jae-an Crisman, J. (2023). 50 years of pride: Queer spatial joy as radical planning praxis. *Urban Planning* 8(2): 262–276. https://doi.org/10.17645/up.v8i2.6373

Voss, G., Browne, K., and Gupta, C. (2014). Embracing the 'and': between queer and bisexual theory at Brighton BiFest. *Journal of Homosexuality* 61(11): 1605–1625.

Wilkinson, E. (2014). Single people's geographies of home: intimacy and Friendship beyond 'the family'. *Environment and Planning A: Economy and Space* 46(10): 2452–2468.

Wilkinson, E. (2019). Never after? Queer temporalities and the politics of non-reproduction. *Gender, Place & Culture* 27(5): 660–676.

Online materials

- https://www.queeringthemap.com/

  Queering the Map is an interactive digital platform that allows LGBTQ+ individuals to anonymously share their personal stories and experiences tied to specific locations, creating a diverse and inclusive map of queer narratives worldwide.

- https://www.aag.org/groups/queer-and-trans-geographies-specialty-group/

  The Queer and Trans Geographies Specialty Group of the American Association of Geographers (AAG) provides resources, information, and a community for scholars and researchers interested in topics relating to queer and trans studies, gender, and sexuality within and beyond geography.

- https://ssqrg.org/

  The Space, Sexualities and Queer Research Group of the Royal Geographical Society (with the Institute of British Geographers) is a study group dedicated to the promotion and support of research, scholarship, and scholar activism regarding sexualities and queer geographies, working across interests and disciplines within academia and beyond.

Further reading

Brown, G., and Browne, K. (eds.) (2016). *The Routledge Companion to Geographies of Sex and Sexualities*. London: Routledge.

Provides a comprehensive exploration of the intersections between geography and sex/sexualities, offering insights into how space and place shape and are shaped by diverse sexual identities and experiences.

Gieseking, J. J. (2013). A Queer Geographer's Life as an Introduction to Queer Theory, Space, and Time. In *Queer Geographies: Beirut, Tijuana, Copenhagen*, eds. L. Lasse, M. Aranios, F. Zúñiga-González, M. Kryger, and O. Mismar. Museet for Samtidskuns: Roskilde, 14–21.
Presents a personal account of a queer geographer, introducing them to queer theory and its intersections with space and time, providing valuable insights into the experiences of LGBTQ+ communities in different geographical contexts.

Johnston, L. (2019). *Transforming Gender, Sex, and Place: Gender Variant Geographies*. London: Routledge. Explores the relationship between gender, sex, and place, highlighting the experiences of gender variant individuals and the ways in which spatial dynamics influence their lives and identities.

Kulpa, R., and Mizielińska, J. (2011). *De-Centring Western Sexualities: Central and Eastern European Perspectives*. London: Routledge.
Offers alternative perspectives on sexuality and space by focusing on Central and Eastern Europe, challenging the dominance of Western viewpoints, and providing a broader understanding of how cultural, social, and geographical factors shape sexualities in different regions.

73 Spiritual activism and postsecularity

Andrew Williams and Callum Sutherland

Introduction

Considering 84% of the world's population identifies with some form of religion (Pew Research Centre, 2017), it becomes crucial to understand how religious voices and worldviews can be included in progressive politics. Such a suggestion might seem incongruous to many people. After all, religion is often perceived as exacerbating injustice, and given the role played by religious values and institutions in historical and contemporary oppression, this is for good reason. But neither 'religion' nor 'secularism' are bounded or singular entities – they defy neat classification, and their variegations reflect distinct cultural, socio-economic, and political contexts.

Geographers, among other academics, have deconstructed some of the unhelpful categories that structure debates on religion, spirituality, and politics. Binary classifications of the religious (as private and concerned with the immaterial) and the secular (as public and material) have been challenged from various places: from Indigenous worldviews, growing religiosity in the Majority World, and the contested relationship between progressive approaches to inclusion and the selective deployment of 'secularism' in different parts of the world (on French secularism, see Lizotte, 2020; see Vasilaki, 2016 on bans on Islamic veiling in public places in several European countries).

The origins of secularism – as a political and philosophical project that necessitates the state to be separate from, or at least neutral on, matters of religion – are commonly linked to Christian and Enlightenment thought (Tse, 2014). However, variegations of secularism have their own complex set of histories and geographies with differing relationships to secularity and secularisation, broadly understood as the 'socio-political compartmentalization of religion' and a social process of differentiation that separates 'non-religious spheres from the authority of the religious sphere', respectively (Wilford, 2010: 328, 333). Also, secularism should not be confused with secularisation which is defined by Wilson (1966: xiv) as 'the process whereby religious thinking, practices and institutions lose their social significance'. But with the decline in religious affiliation in Western Europe bucking a global trend of rising religiosity, it is important for geographers to examine the changing relationship between secularism and religious diversity in different contexts.

To date, geographers have made key contributions to understanding religious movements, identities, and diversity in a globalised world; and to analysing how such phenomena interact with wider social, cultural, (geo)political, environmental, and economic processes, in both

DOI: 10.4324/9780429265853-86

historical and contemporary contexts (see Chapter 28). This kind of research requires a theoretical and empirical sensitivity to the divergent politics that arise from different amalgamations of religion and secularism. Critical geographies of religion must work with ambivalence and remain pluralistic: encompassing negative critique to scrutinise and challenge the power dynamics, hierarchies, and interests connected to religious phenomena whilst also experimenting with more affirming approaches to researching religion that underscore progressive possibilities.

On one hand, collusion between fundamentalist religion and conservative political factions has been shown to reinforce regressive politics of **neoliberal** welfare retrenchment (Hackworth, 2012) and foster hatred towards marginalised groups, most recently seen in areas of sexuality and **gender**-rights (Nash and Browne, 2020). Religious nationalism remains a key focus in understanding recent authoritarian turns in India (Chowdhury, 2023), Central and Eastern Europe (Lendvai-Bainton and Szelewa, 2021), as well as the right-wing populism on show in the 2021 U.S. Congress and 2023 Brazilian Congress Attacks (Gorski and Perry, 2022). Oppositional critique in this context requires unmasking the entanglements of religion in oppressive structures of power.

On the other hand, geographical research has also demonstrated the material, institutional, and spiritual resources that religious people and organisations can offer to progressive movements (Beaumont, 2008, Slessarev-Jamir, 2011, Braunstein et al., 2017). Progressivism in this chapter is understood in light of **postcolonial** and **decolonial** critiques of 'progress' (Dussel, 1995). 'Progress' has often been framed as a way of understanding and 'bettering' the world, shaped significantly by the priority of ensuring the political and economic comfort of the Minority World (Ramirez, 2023). Against this, we promote a sense of 'progress' based on rising to the contemporary challenge of working towards a world of sustainability, equality in plurality, and reparation.

Research has documented and collaborated with religiously inspired social movements focused on issues such as poverty, human rights, and environmental protection. For example, the Brazilian Landless Workers Movement (Movimento dos Trabalhadores Rurais Sem Terra, or MST), which is inspired by liberation theology (Karriem, 2009); or Islamic **feminist** movements which seek to promote gender equality within the context of Islam alongside rethinking the Eurocentric assumptions about feminist agency and religious devotion (Vasilaki, 2016). Given religion's uneven and multifaceted relationship to politics, oppositional, collaborative, and participatory stances must all be available to researchers working with religious people and organisations, though it is important to acknowledge the moral and ethical conflicts facing researchers who have to navigate tense 'insider/outsider' dynamics with participants (see Han's 2010 **ethnography** of South Korean Missionaries). Fundamentally, the choice of research design – and the ethical dilemmas faced in research – tends to reflect the way in which researchers are positioned theoretically, religiously, politically, and geographically.

Summary

- The divergent and ambivalent relationship between religion, secularity, and justice demands critical attention from geographers.
- If the Majority World is religious, how might geographers research religion and secularity in a way that amplifies and encourages politically progressive outcomes?

Postsecularity

One of the ways in which geographers have sought to comprehend the intersections of religion, secularism, and politics more broadly has been by contributing to the conceptual development of 'postsecularity'. The notion of postsecularity – as well as 'the postsecular' and 'postsecularism' – is much disputed across the humanities and social sciences (McLennan, 2007). Generally, it has been used to describe the social, cultural, and political re-emergence or new visibility of religion in contemporary society (Beaumont, 2019). Jürgen Habermas' writing on 'postsecular society' (2008) takes a normative stance on religion's increased visibility in the public sphere, advocating for political cultures that foster an ethic of reciprocity between religious and secular ways of being. Rather than understanding postsecularity as some grand epochal shift – the reversal of secularisation – or signalling a return to a pre-secular era, Cloke and Beaumont (2013) argue for a more geographical understanding of postsecularity that focuses on sites, spaces, and practices where diverse religious, humanist, and secularist subjects come together to find ways to co-operate politically and ethically and – sometimes – develop a greater appreciation for, adaptation-towards, even adoption-of, one another's differences. Postsecularity should not be conflated with anti-secularism nor does it offer a normative template for what comes 'after' secularism. Similar to McLennan (2007), Cloke et al. (2019) understand postsecularity as a 'heuristic conceptual device to question and probe the underlying assumptions of secularity, and in so doing to re-interrogate the faith-reason binary by recognising new modes of belief, new conditions for [the] enactment of belief, and new ways in which the secular and the sacred may be becoming blurred' (2019: 8). This is not simply about faith-secular partnerships in welfare or local governance, it is about the new kinds of ethics and politics produced through collaboration across faith-secular divides, and the kinds of **subjectivities** that arise as a result. These ethical values are characterised by a 'crossing-over' of religious and secular stories, practices, and actions that become visible in certain places focused on care, welfare, justice, and protest (Box 73.1; also see Cloke et al., 2016 on the Occupy movement) and in expressions and desires for greater degrees of in-commonness with others (see Cloke et al., 2019: 3).

Cities have attracted the most attention for postsecular scholars on three grounds: as sites where social marginality commonly is most visible; where the scale and organisation of faith-motivated actors are most concentrated; and as sites characterised by diverse sets of ethnic, cultural, and religious plurality that have challenged established structures of secularity and ideologies of secularism (Gorski and Altınordu, 2008). Recent scholarship, however, has begun to highlight the emergence of postsecularity in a range of other spaces, including rural places and **transnational** and global justice movements. Cloke et al. (2019) trace the emergent postsecularity in the following:

- *Spaces of care* for socially excluded groups such as homeless people, asylum seekers, victims of trafficking, and those facing indebtedness, where faith-based organisations act as practical devices for diverse religious and secular motivations to accrete around shared ethical impulse and crossover narratives.
- *Spaces of direct resistance and subversion* where different religious and secular groups come together in the most deprived and disempowered spaces of the city to politically organise or provide direct provision to contest the hostility of government policy. This can range from

BOX 73.1
THE MORAL MONDAY MOVEMENT OF CIVIL DISOBEDIENCE

The 'Moral Monday' movement of civil disobedience is another example of religious and secular rapprochement over justice (Figure 73.1). The movement began on April 29, 2013, when 17 church ministers and leaders of the National Association for the Advancement of Colored People (NAACP) were arrested inside the North Carolina General Assembly building in Raleigh for protesting the punitive welfare, education, health cuts, and racially discriminating voting-ID laws passed by the Republican administration who controlled the general assembly. In the following two months, the NAACP, organised through the churches, mobilised a state-wide campaign of nonviolent civil disobedience where over 700 people were arrested for following suit. The Moral Monday Movement and subsequent protests against North Carolina government's anti-LGBT legislation, high-profile police killings of unarmed Black citizens, and white supremacist marches in Charlottesville, Virginia, have further served to unite disparate ideologies and religious, ethnic, and sexual identities, coming together on the basis of a shared 'spirituality', a mutual ethos that allows divergence and convergence in a specific space (Phelps, 2013).

Figure 73.1
Reverend William Barber II is arrested by U.S. Capitol Police during the Poor People's Campaign Moral Monday demonstration near the U.S. Capitol in Washington, D.C. on August 2, 2021

Source: Photo credit: Bryan Olin Dozier/NurPhoto/Alamy

broad-based and interfaith community organising around immigrant worker rights to more mundane welfare and advocacy groups that work inside and outside the trappings of state control in ways that contravene or contest the **hegemonic ideology** of neoliberal social policy.

- *Spaces of ethical identity* (see, for example, fairtrade; sanctuary movement; living wage) where campaigns around particular ethical tropes at the city level reflect a range of religious and other interests brought together to express identities and values, within which lie significant points of ethical convergence between theological, **ideological**, and humanitarian concern.
- *Spaces of protest* – such as Occupy Wall Street, Taksim Gezi Park, and the Arab Spring – characterised by an explicit 'crossing over' of religious and secular narratives, symbolism, practices, and **performances** in public space.
- *Spaces of reconciliation and tolerance* where individuals and groups work across previous divides involving inter-religious, anti-religious, or anti-secular tensions. These include grass-roots programmes of interfaith dialogue to more everyday sites of co-presence that temper sectarianism.
- *Spaces of cross-subsidy and solidarity* that develop socio-spatial connections between people and places that unsettle not only perceived religious/secular boundaries but also **territorial** ones.

Cloke et al., 2019: 89–94

The progressive promise of postsecularity is that it might lend a shoulder to the formation of new kinds of political and ethical collectives at a time when reactionary politics is on the rise in the Global North. Not only are reactionary politics on the rise, but also the conditions in which progressive causes flourished – that is, the mass unionisation, visible socialist alternatives, a thriving avant-garde, and robust social security of the 1960s and 1970s – have been viciously denuded (Fisher, 2009). When the tried-and-true processes of progressive solidarities have been mercilessly beaten back, and the ground on which struggle is waged has been irrevocably altered, new ways of developing progressive coalitions are essential. Postsecularity advocates for an ethic of generosity and coalition building. It holds out for what might be called 'solidarity without similarity' (Colquhoun, 2021: 200); a figuring out of the shared ends of a diverse collective, abetted by ideological humility and an openness to the infinite possibilities of the future (Goh, 2015). Openness to the forming of new and surprising solidarities – and daring, experimental processes of forming them – is crucial, presently, given how significantly reactionaries have sought (and seek to) limit the cultural purchase of progressivism.

As well as widening the political landscape in which progressives might find partnership and common-cause, postsecularity offers insights for contemporary progressivism emerging from its analysis of the co-creation of religion and secular sensibilities. If progressives have been stripped of many material resources needed to exercise power, what role might *immaterial* power play?

In a time when it would be easy for dispossessed progressives to be melancholic and listless, immaterial resources need to be mustered in order to struggle anew and to make up for deficits in material clout. Rather than shunning spirituality due to its perceived association with immaterial or other-worldly concerns, progressives must use the spiritual resources they have – which blend material and immaterial elements and practices – to their utmost potential. The 'metapolitical' territory of convictions, belief, and passion, Krznaric (2022) argues, has been ceded almost entirely to reactionary forces, who seem much less squeamish presently about approaching the terrain of the immaterial; a terrain which is often associated with spirituality and/or religion. If progressives are willing to form what might now be classified as postsecular partnerships across the secular/ religious aisle, it may result not only in novel partnerships imbued with the ability to outflank reactionaries but also in the reinvigoration of progressive coalitions with the emotional depth and profundity that engagement of spiritual matters can offer (White, 2016, Jones, 2023). One way of conceptualising this infusing of progressive causes with immaterial power has been called 'spiritual activism', and it is this consideration to which we will now turn.

Summary

- Postsecularity denotes a co-productive relationship between secular and religious groups modelled around core commitments to solidarity, mutual hospitality, and openness to difference.
- Rather than focusing on moves from the religious to the secular, geographers bring an emphasis onto the particular sites, spaces, and practices where diverse religious, humanist, and secular voices come together dialogically and enter into a learning and experimental process in which secular and religious mentalities can be reflexively transformed.
- Spaces of postsecularity disturb boundaries between the religious and the secular but also open up alternative imaginaries and practices with a capacity to generate new ethical and political subjectivities.

Spiritual activism

One way of framing spiritual activism is as a practice of raising personal or collective awareness of forces – which may be greater than the sum of material parts – that affect (and can be affected by) the collective or individual. Spiritual activism involves the collective or subject engaging these forces and altering their orientation towards them; disentangling themselves from them, drawing on them, or transmuting their energies. A progressive form of spiritual activism is to engage this 'inner work' (Keating, 2008: 57) so as to energetically and compulsively smash through structures of oppression and cultivate more diverse and liberatory ways of living together (Ramirez, 2017). In this progressive formation, these 'powers from beyond' may include the **atmosphere** of a ritual (or set of rituals), a worldview that extends well beyond the space-time of the present, or – in more secular terms – desire. However, we must note here that these powers are not necessarily beneficent, nor does engaging with them necessarily lead to progressive outcomes. As Sendejo (2013) argues, spirituality can be co-opted 'as a means of reproducing hierarchies of power and promoting the exclusion of [the] marginalized' (p. 65), as much as constituting a site for nourishment, strengthening, and healing from 'environmental, classist, racist and sexist wounds' (p. 71). It is important to consider what kinds of 'spiritual' powers – and what modes of engaging them – geographers might explore to widen the scope of our understanding and imagination for progressive politics.

For some people, the whole idea of engaging with spiritual aspects of activism might seem unpalatable. Spirituality is often framed as other-worldly or a form of escapist introspection that is, at best, irrelevant to material struggles over injustice, and at its worst, a highly individualistic spirituality that serves as a salve for neoliberal **capitalism** (see Purser, 2019). The dualisms of spiritual/material, inner/outer, and individual/collective remain durable constructs despite attempts by poststructuralist scholars to deconstruct essentialist and binary-oppositional categories. Dismantling these categories, Chicana feminist thinker Gloria Evangelina Anzaldúa (1942–2004) was one of the first to examine gender in relation to other categories of social difference, including, religion/spirituality, **race/ethnicity**, sexuality, **class**, geography, and health (Keating, 2016). For Anzaldúa spiritual activism 'intertwines "inner works" with "public acts", private concerns with social issues. Indeed, this simultaneous attention to personal and collective issues/concerns is a vital component in spiritual activism' (Keating, 2008: 57). Anzaldúa writes:

> The struggle is inner: Chicano, indio, American Indian, mojado, mexicano, immigrant Latino, Anglo in power, working class Anglo, Black, Asian – our psyches resemble the bordertowns and are populated by the same people. The struggle has always been inner, and is played out in outer terrains. Awareness of our situation must come before inner changes, which in turn come before changes in society. Nothing happens in the 'real' world unless it first happens in the images in our heads.
>
> *Anzaldúa, 1999: 87*

Anzaldúa's politics of spirit 'demonstrates that holistic, spirit-influenced perspectives – when applied to racism, sexism and homophobia, and other contemporary issues – can sustain and assist us as we work to transform social injustice' (Keating, 2005: 56). It is not a solely individual, personal spirituality, but one that actively works to transform social hierarchies and oppression. Alongside the interdependency between self-change and social transformation, Anzaldúa offers an inclusionary politics that acknowledges the vital gains made by 'identity politics', whilst recognising that the overly rigid and restrictive divisions produced by binary-oppositional identity categories can prevent recognition of interconnections with others. Analouise Keating writes:

> The us-against-them stance we have employed in oppositional forms of consciousness seeps into all areas of our lives, infecting the way we perceive ourselves and each other. When we turn this lens against each other – as we so often do – we implode. Rather than work together to enact progressive social change, we battle each other, thus reproducing the status quo.
>
> *Keating, 2008: 65–66*

Whilst spiritual activism exists both within and beyond organised religion, Anzaldúa argues for the need to leave the patriarchal and colonial trappings of organised religion and escapist spiritualities. The fusion of spirituality, survival, and resistance has long been a feature of feminist and Latin American liberation theology and the radical activism of African Americans in the U.S., from civil rights to environmental activism (Rodriguez, 1994, McCutcheon and Kohl, 2022). Brenda Sendejo's (2013) ethnography conducted in the Texas-Mexico borderlands with 18 Tejana women highlights the ways spirituality is used to challenge gender oppression within the Catholic Church and its legacy of 'sixteenth-century spiritual colonization of indigenous peoples' (pp. 64–65). Meanwhile, van Klinken (2019) highlights how queer Kenyan Christian imaginations and refugees fleeing repressive anti-LGBTQ+ legislation in neighbouring Uganda challenge religious homophobia by reclaiming the Bible as a site of meaning, healing, and empowerment. Here dominant religio-cultural accounts of 'African homophobia' are dismantled by focusing on longer histories of African LGBTQ+ people, communities, and activism, tracing the colonial roots of homophobic legislation, and exposing the well-funded anti-LGBTQ+ religious groups often based in the Global North seeking to protect 'traditional' values from 'Western' gender ideology (Chitando and van Klinken, 2021).

Spiritual activism is also integral to Indigenous claims over sacred sites which have opened out significant local, national, and international contestations about **postdevelopment** (for links with postsecularity and secularism, see Moxham, 2017). Examples include Kraft's (2020) case study of Sámi resistance to plans for a power plant to be built at the base of Aahkansnjurhtjie, a sacred mountain in Southern Sápmi (Kjerringtind in Norway), and Estes' (2019) account of resistance to the Dakota Access Pipeline at Standing Rock (Figure 73.2). At Standing Rock, Indigenous, environmentalist, religious, union, NGO, and veteran groups formed a surprisingly diverse 'progressive coalition – one grounded in an ethic of deep social inclusion and planetary care' (Klein, 2017: 20).

As we hinted above, spiritual activism might not only offer social movements a project of 'inner work' to undergird their struggles but a re-appraised '[a]wareness of our situation' (Anzaldúa, 1999: 87); a re-reading of the terrain on which struggles are fought (Lara, 2014). Questions of spiritual activism not only foreground the issue of sourcing immaterial power amidst diverse coalition

Figure 73.2
The Standing Rock Sioux Tribe, joined by other indigenous groups and allies, march to a sacred burial ground disturbed by bulldozers building the Dakota Access Pipeline on the Standing Rock Reservation

Source: Photo credit: Getty Images/Robyn Beck/Staff

building but also more adequately delineate the severe material and psychological conditions in which this practice is being advanced. Growing geographical attention has been given to how neoliberalism works through and is sustained by an amalgam of emotion, belief, and **affect**, shaped by capitalist rhythms and regimes of immaterial labour (Anderson, 2016). Capitalism hollows out belief in its alternatives until belief itself is 'collapsed at the level of ritual or symbolic elaboration, all that is left is consumer-spectator' (Fisher, 2009: 4). Scholars, from a variety of philosophical and political commitments, have converged on this space to discern what can be described as the 'spiritual ennui' of neoliberalism – a weariness towards social change and an emptiness of hope. For example, Ann Cvetkovich (2012) notes the escalation of depression and hopelessness that characterises the toxic cultures of possessive individualism, materialism, debt, and overwork; while others have explored the **political economy** of unhappiness and **alienation** (Davies, 2011). As Tim Jensen (2011, citing Derrick Jensen, 2006: 552) explains:

'It would be a mistake to think this culture clearcuts only forests. It clearcuts our psyche as well. It would be a mistake to think it dams only rivers. We ourselves are dammed (and damned) by it as well. It would be a mistake to think it creates dead zones only in the ocean. It creates dead zones in our hearts and minds. It would be a mistake to think it fragments only our habitat. We, too, are fragmented, split off, shredded, rent, torn'. When these territories of desire and imagination are stolen, ravaged, and toxified it becomes that much easier for the theft and destruction of natural landscapes to go uncontested, unnoticed.

Jensen, 2011: np

However, by engaging in the 'inner work' outlined above by Anzaldúa, progressive spiritual activists unlock the possibility of recontextualising or revivifying these 'dead zones', drawing on, aligning with, even building new powers that exceed – or exist despite – the 'spiritual ennui' of neoliberalism. For example, Ramirez (2017) writes about the reimagined spiritualities drawn on and represented by Chicana artists in Oakland in order to inhabit, animate, and advocate for cosmologies that colonialism and capitalism have tried to wipe from the record. Through their work, these artists insist on and set in motion an alternative vision for being. Furthermore, Blencowe (2015) has argued that 'the commons' – a key concept in post-capitalist geographies (see Chapters 64 and 65) – can be conceived of beyond its material and cultural cache as a power that can be built beyond the self or collective to sustain and carry them. As De Angelis (2017) argues, the commons is a complex system sustained, in part, by practices that reproduce sharing relationships (not just shared resources and the people willing to maintain and share them). This opens up the possibility of relating to the commons also as a spiritual power enabling people to get 'outside of [themselves] by entering, and sharing, a world' (Blencowe, 2015: 187). With this in mind, the spirituality of the commons is about self-transcendence:

commons promise escape from the disenchanted iron traps of instrumentalised, privatised lives – a route to self-transcendence that is also the transcendence of nihilism, existential angst and hopelessness. Alienation and disenchantment are not, as is often thought, the symptom of an overly institutionalised or fixed formation of life. Rather, they express the absence of a shared reality, of knowing together in a common world.

Blencowe, 2015: 187

Summary

- Spiritual practices are intimately tied to politics of oppression, healing, and activism.
- Emotional and affective life in late capitalism and its patterning of desire can be key sites of spiritual activism.
- Practices of spiritual activism – and postsecularity more specifically – have the capacity to generate experiential spaces that amplify alternative values, practices, and subjectivities and cultivate an affective capacity for hopefulness and healing, hospitality and generosity, justice and equality.

Hopeful geographies?

This chapter has outlined some of the ways geographers might collaborate on issues of religion, spirituality, and justice. Whether it is challenging the entanglements of religion in unjust and exclusionary systems or participating in broad-based movements seeking justice and care, critical geographers need to remain ambivalent and pluralistic: being open to the potential for religious and spiritual involvement to lead to reactionary *and* progressive ends. Spiritual activism and postsecularity are two ways in which geographers might rethink the dominant narrative around sacred/secular, spiritual/material, inner/outer, and individual/collective. In these movements beyond religious and secular fundamentalism, there is a hopeful space emerging that amplifies practices of reciprocity, in-commonness, and solidarity across lines of religious and secular difference. Geographical work can explore the curation of these progressive openings and their spatial variegations, including the diverse sources of nonhuman powers and collective rituals that can animate activism.

Discussion points

- How do global religions intersect with issues of social and environmental justice, and what challenges and opportunities does this present for structures of secularity and religion?
- In what ways has religion been used as a tool for social and economic oppression and resistance across different geographical contexts?
- What is postsecularity and how can it help galvanise our thinking about spiritual activism?
- How does spirituality play a role in contemporary movements fighting against white supremacy, corporate power, and state violence?
- How does activism help us expand our definition of spirituality, and how does an engagement with spirituality expand our understanding of what activism is?

References

Anderson, B. (2016). Neoliberal affects. *Progress in Human Geography* 40(6): 734–753.
Anzaldúa, G. (1999). *Borderlands/La Frontera: The New Mestiza*. San Francisco: Aunt Lute.
Beaumont, J. (2008). Introduction: faith-based organisations and urban social issues. *Urban Studies* 45(10): 2011–2017.

Beaumont, J. (ed.) (2019). *The Routledge Handbook of Postsecularity*. London: Routledge.

Blencowe, C. (2015). The Matter of Spirituality and the Commons. In *Space, Power and the Commons: The Struggle for Alternative Futures*, eds. S. Kirwan, L. Dawney, and J. Brigstocke. Abingdon and New York: Routledge, 197–215.

Braunstein, R., Fuist, T. N., and Williams, R. H. (eds.) (2017). *Religion and Progressive Activism*. New York: NYU Press.

Chitando, E., and van Klinken, A. (2021). *Reimagining Christianity and Sexual Diversity in Africa*. London: Hurst & Co.

Chowdhury, S. (2023). Economics and politics under Modi government: a synoptic view. *Human Geography* 16(2): 146–161.

Cloke, P., Baker, C., Sutherland, C., and Williams, A. (2019). *Geographies of Postsecularity: Re-Envisioning Politics, Subjectivity and Ethics*. London and New York: Routledge.

Cloke, P., and Beaumont, J. (2013). Geographies of postsecular rapprochement in the city. *Progress in Human Geography* 37(1): 27–51.

Cloke, P., Sutherland, C., and Williams, A. (2016). Postsecularity, political resistance, and protest in the Occupy movement. *Antipode* 48(3): 497–523.

Colquhoun, M. (2021). *Egress: On Mourning, Melancholy and Mark Fisher*. London: Repeater Books.

Cvetkovich, A. (2012). *Depression: A Public Feeling*. Durham and London: Duke University Press.

Davies, W. (2011). The political-economy of unhappiness. *New Left Review* 71: 65–80.

De Angelis, M. (2017). *Omnia Sunt Communia: On the Commons and the Transformation to Postcapitalism*. London: Zed.

Dussel, E. (1995). *The Invention of the Americas: Eclipse of 'the Other' and the Myth of Modernity*. New York: Continuum.

Estes, N. (2019). *Our History Is the Future: Standing Rock Versus the Dakota Access Pipeline, and the Long Tradition of Indigenous Resistance*. London and New York: Verso Books.

Fisher, M. (2009). *Capitalist Realism: Is There No Alternative?* Ropley, UK: John Hunt Publishing.

Goh, I. (2015). *The Reject: Community, Politics, and Religion After the Subject*. New York: Fordham University Press.

Gorski, P., and Altınordu, A. (2008). After secularization? *Annual Review of Sociology* 34: 55–85.

Gorski, P. S., and Perry, S. L. (2022). *The Flag and the Cross: White Christian Nationalism and the Threat to American Democracy*. Oxford: Oxford University Press.

Habermas, J. (2008). Notes on post-secular society. *New Perspectives Quarterly* 25(4): 17–29.

Hackworth, J. (2012). *Faith-Based: Religious Neoliberalism and the Politics of Welfare in the United States*. Athens and London: University of Georgia Press.

Han, J. H. J. (2010). Neither friends nor foes: thoughts on ethnographic distance. *Geoforum* 41(1): 11–14.

Jensen, T. (2011). On the emotional terrain of neoliberalism. *Journal of Aesthetics and Protest* 8. Available from http://joaap.org/issue8/jensen.htm (last accessed 07/07/18).

Jones, G. (2023). *Red Enlightenment: On Socialism, Science and Spirituality*. London: Watkins Media Limited.

Karriem, A. (2009). The rise and transformation of the Brazilian landless movement into a counter-hegemonic political actor: a Gramscian analysis. *Geoforum* 40: 316–325.

Keating, A. (2005). Shifting perspectives: spiritual activism, social transformation, and the politics of spirit. *EntreMundos/AmongWorlds: New Perspectives on Gloria E. Anzaldúa*, 241–254.

Keating, A. (2008). 'I'm a citizen of the universe': Gloria Anzaldúa's spiritual activism as catalyst for social change. *Feminist Studies* 34(1/2): 53–69.

Keating, A. (2016). Gloria Evangelina Anzaldúa (1942–2004). In *Fifty-One Key Feminist Thinkers*, ed. L. Marso. London: Routledge, 10–15.

Klein, N. (2017). *No Is Not Enough: Defeating the New Shock Politics*. London: Penguin UK.

Kraft, S. E. (2020). Spiritual activism. Saving Mother Earth in Sápmi. *Religions* 11(7): 342. https://doi. org/10.3390/rel11070342

Krznaric, R. (2022). How to be a good ancestor. *Novara Media*. https://novaramedia.com/2022/06/23/ novarafm-how-to-be-a-good-ancestor-w-roman-krznaric/

Lara, I. (2014). Sensing the Serpent in the Mother, Dando a Luz la Madre Serpiente: Chicana Spirituality, Sexuality, and Mamihood. In *Fleshing the Spirit: Spirituality and Activism in Chicana, Latina, and Indigenous Women's Lives*, eds. E. Facio and I. Lara. Tucson: University of Arizona Press, 113–134.

Lendvai-Bainton, N., and Szelewa, D. (2021). Governing new authoritarianism: populism, nationalism and radical welfare reforms in Hungary and Poland. *Social Policy & Administration* 55(4): 559–572.

Lizotte, C. (2020). Laïcité as assimilation, laïcité as negotiation: political geographies of secularism in the French public school. *Political Geography* 77: 102121.

McCutcheon, P., and Kohl, E. (2022). Introduction: Divinely Inspired Spaces and African American Environmentalism. In *Symposium – 'Let Justice Roll Down Like Waters': The Role of Spirituality in African American Environmental Activism in the US South*. Antipode Online. https://antipodeonline. org/2019/05/21/let-justice-roll-down-like-waters-the-role-of-spirituality-in-african-american-environmental-activism-in-the-us-south/

McLennan, G. (2007). Towards postsecular sociology? *Sociology* 41: 857–870.

Moxham, C. (2017). Postdevelopment and nonsecularism in an officially secular state: faith-based social action in the Philippines. *Journal of International Development* 29: 370–385.

Nash, C. J., and Browne, K. (2020). *Heteroactivism: Resisting Lesbian, Gay, Bisexual and Trans Rights and Equalities*. London: Zed Books.

Pew Research Centre. (2017). *Report: The Changing Global Religious Landscape. The Changing Global Religious Landscape*. Pew Research Center.

Phelps, H. (2013). *Resonating Moral Monday. Political Theology Network 11 July 2013*. Available from www.politicaltheology.com/blog/resonating-moral-monday/ (last accessed 22/07/18).

Purser, R. (2019). *McMindfulness: How Mindfulness Became the New Capitalist Spirituality*. London: Repeater.

Ramirez, M. M. (2017). Decolonial ruptures of the city: art-activism amid racialized dispossession in Oakland. PhD Thesis: University of Washington.

Ramirez, M. M. (2023). World-making, desire, and the future. *Dialogues in Human Geography* 13(1): 133–136.

Rodriguez, J. (1994). *Our Lady of Guadalupe: Faith and Empowerment Among Mexican American Women*. Austin: University of Texas Press.

Sendejo, B. (2013). The cultural production of spiritual activisms: gender, social justice, and the remaking of religion in the borderlands. *Chicana/Latina Studies* 12(2): 59–109. http://www.jstor.org/ stable/43943329

Slessarev-Jamir, H. (2011). *Prophetic Activism*. New York: New York University Press.

Tse, J. K. (2014). Grounded theologies: 'religion' and the 'secular' in human geography. *Progress in Human Geography* 38(2): 201–220.

van Klinken, A. (2019). *Kenyan, Christian, Queer: Religion, LGBT Activism, and Arts of Resistance in Africa*. University Park, PA: Penn State University Press.

Vasilaki, R. (2016). The politics of postsecular feminism. *Theory, Culture & Society* 33(2): 103–123.

White, M. (2016). *The End of Protest*. Toronto: Knopf Canada.

Wilford, J. (2010). Sacred archipelagos: geographies of secularization. *Progress in Human Geography* 43(3): 328–348.

Wilson, B. (1966). *Religion in Secular Society*. London: C.A. Watts and Co.

Online materials

- Series of films about Standing Rock protest *Awake the film* (2017) and *End of the Line: The Women of Standing Rock* (2021)
- Documentary 'Kenyan, Christian, Queer' (2020) https://www.youtube.com/watch?v=bsU6QROlfzs

Further reading

Blencowe, C. (2015). The Matter of Spirituality and the Commons. In *Space, Power and the Commons: The Struggle for Alternative Futures*, eds. S. Kirwan, L. Dawney, and J. Brigstocke. Abingdon and New York: Routledge, 197–215.
A slightly more advanced text that gives an excellent account of politics underpinning spirituality and the progressive potential of the commons.

Cloke, P., and Beaumont, J. (2013). Geographies of postsecular rapprochement in the city. *Progress in Human Geography* 37(1): 27–51.
A foundational text on postsecularity that draws on case studies about faith-based organisations and welfare provision in Europe.

Keating, A. (2008). 'I'm a citizen of the universe': Gloria Anzaldúa's spiritual activism as catalyst for social change. *Feminist Studies* 34(1/2): 53–69.
A good introduction to Anzaldua's theory of spiritual activism and its importance for feminist and liberatory struggle.

PART FIVE

AFTERWORD

Afterword: Going forward with human geography

In the Preface at the very beginning of the book, we used the metaphor of a travel guide to describe how the book is intended to accompany and guide you as you find your way around the discipline of human geography. We hope you have enjoyed that journey and have come to appreciate the rich and varied terrain that the discipline covers. We know that for most of you, much more of that terrain still lies ahead, and we hope that you will occasionally dip back into the book as you chart your own route through human geography and find the areas of the subject that inspire and enthuse you. As you do so, we would urge you to remember what we said at the end of Chapter 2 – that doing human geography is about more than just learning a university subject – it is also about preparing yourself for contributing to both people and planet in a range of different ways. We've tried to help you with that preparation, not just by introducing you to the varied subject matter of human geography but also by taking a very deliberate approach to the subject which has stressed **critical thinking** and the diversity of voices, perspectives and knowledge systems that you can draw on. For this reason, certain themes have run through the book – those to do with social and environmental justice, **feminist** and Indigenous geographies, diverse economies and the **pluriverse**.

But we want to end the book by referencing another theme which we've tried to emphasise throughout the book, that of hope. For where do you find hope when faced with a catalogue of injustices? These include global environmental destruction; persistent racism and socio-economic inequalities; **patriarchy** and transphobia; post-political pessimism, far-right populism and resurgent authoritarianism. Injustice seems to abide everywhere. At times injustice appears to take on a gorgon quality – to comprehend or even look upon the magnitude of planetary challenges turns us to stone. Perhaps, when reading this book, you found inspiration in existing struggles that challenge what is possible and tear up unfair scripts crafted by those with vested interests. From Indigenous rights activists and landworker movements fighting against displacement, corporate power and state violence; movements against racist and **gender**-based violence; and **transnational** solidarities over labour conditions or autonomous geographies, there are numerous movements that affirm the possibility of re-ordering, of restoring, or, at very least, of imagining different worlds.

Geography has an enduring and increasing relevance in these times, not least in helping us reflect critically and ethically on our own geographical worlds. As the discipline continues to evolve in relation to new turns (digital, **decolonial**) and planetary challenges (heatwaves, droughts, flooding, displacement, resource conflicts), our desire is that readers will be inspired

DOI: 10.4324/9780429265853-88

to break through the malaise of hopelessness to reveal possibilities for social and environment justice. As graduates of human geography, you will be equipped with a particular set of skills; skills that you will acquire through meticulous analysis and engagement with the world; skills that make you a nightmare for laissez-faire attitudes. As Raymond Williams (1989: 172) writes in *Resources of Hope*, the roots of any radical transformation lie 'in making hope practical, rather than despair convincing'.

We wrote in the acknowledgements about the influence of Paul Cloke – not just on this book but also on the subject matter of human geography. Among the many things that Paul inspired us to think about was the interchangeability of love and justice. In his classic paper *'Deliver us from evil?'* (2002) published in *Progress in Human Geography*, Paul discussed the difficulties of living out the human geographies of ethics and justice, rather than just talking and writing about them. As he put it, 'we can envision a human geography in which living ethically and acting politically can be essentially intertwined with a sense for the other in a sensitive, committed and active approach to the subject' (p. 602). Over 20 years on, that challenge to live ethically and act politically remains ever more pertinent. Living out the human geographies of ethics and justice that we write about continues to be a struggle inside the university and beyond. Nevertheless, cultivating our personal and academic lives in relationship to those on the margins offers one way of sustaining a committed 'sense for the other' and a hopeful politics of how the world could – and will – be. After all, to paraphrase Cornel West, justice is what love looks like in public.

As you go forward in your geographical learning, we invite you to continue to bring yourself to geography, to reflect critically and ethically on your own geographical worlds and to bring the geographies of justice, ethics and hope to your own future journeys.

Andrew Williams, Kelly Dombroski, Mark Goodwin and Junxi Qian

The editors, June 2023

References

Cloke, P. (2002). Deliver us from evil? Prospects for living ethically and acting politically in human geography. *Progress in Human Geography* 26(5): 587–604.

Williams, R. (1989). *Resources of Hope: Culture, Democracy, Socialism*. London: Verso.

Glossary

This glossary provides short, elementary definitions of key terms used but not explained fully in the course of this collection's chapters. For more in-depth definitions, there are a number of more comprehensive resources, such as *International Encyclopedia of Human Geography, Concise Encyclopedia of Human Geography, The Dictionary of Human Geography* or *Keywords in Radical Geography*. The terms listed in the glossary are marked in bold when first used in a particular chapter. Cross-referencing between entries is facilitated by capitalising terms that are separate glossary entries in their own right.

Actor-Network Theory: sometimes shortened to ANT, Actor-Network Theory is an approach that emerged from the sociological study of science and technology, and which became widely influential within human geography during the 1990s. Two key features can be identified: (a) ANT questions traditional foci on the 'social' in the social sciences and the 'human' in human geography, arguing for the inclusion of non-human entities (animals, plants, technologies, objects and so on; (b) ANT views the world as comprising networks of 'associations' involving these entities. For ANT it is the nature of these associations that produce different forms of POWER and AGENCY.

aesthetics: whilst the term might be colloquially associated with beauty, appearance or high art, it is not limited to such uses. It has roots in the Greek term *aesthesis* meaning 'perception' or 'sense perception', referring to the capacity of the senses to receive and respond to stimuli in the external world.

affect, affective: the study of affect has been promoted by an 'affective turn' across the social sciences and humanities, and within Human Geography, by the influence of NON-REPRESENTATIONAL THEORIES. In that context, affect is associated with scholarship that emphasises EMBODIMENT and the experience of life as it is lived. More specifically, the notion of affect refers to: (a) a change in bodily state, which can increase or decrease that body's capacity to act; (b) how this change comes from ENCOUNTERS between various sorts of bodies and things; and (c) the existence of affecting forces beyond any individual human subject/body.

agency: the capacity to 'act' of humans and MORE-THAN-HUMANS, or, in effect, to have an impact and shape the world. Human geographers have widely debated the character, sources and locations of agency. These debates have included the issue of whether HUMAN AGENCY is exclusively human, or whether it emerges from networks of relations between people, other forms of life and non-living things (see also HUMAN AGENCY, NON-HUMAN AGENCY and ACTOR-NETWORK THEORY).

agglomeration: the clustering together of economic and social activities and institutions. Agglomeration is often understood as a driving force of urbanisation for it enables divisions of labour, economic specialisation, social collaboration, efficiencies in production and distribution, sharing and imitation, infrastructural development and economic growth.

alienation: a term with two interrelated meanings, the second being a more specific formulation of the first. First, alienation refers to a sense of estrangement or lack of POWER felt by people living in the MODERN world. In this respect it is often used to describe the experience of modern urban living, in which traditional forms of social cohesion and belonging supposedly break down. Second, and drawn from MARXIST social thought, alienation refers more particularly to the separation of labour from the means of production under CAPITALISM, where workers have no control over their productive lives, how production is organised, what is produced, what the product is used for and how they relate to other workers.

anarchist, anarchism: a political philosophy that opposes the state, any form of authority, hierarchy and domination. Anarchist thinkers propose a society based on voluntary cooperation, mutual aid and individual autonomy, aiming to create a world free from oppression, exploitation and domination.

Anthropocene: a proposed new geological epoch covering the most recent period of geological history in which humankind has been the dominant planetary influence on Earth systems and environments. This influence has often been negative, as manifested through anthropogenic climate change and various forms of pollution (see also Chapter 62).

artificial intelligence (AI): the simulation of human intelligence processes (perceiving, synthesising and inferring information) by machines, especially computer systems.

assemblage: a collection of things (e.g. machines, organisations, technologies, plants, people) which through their relationships give human and non-human entities agency, that is the capacity to act and influence the social world.

atmosphere: a concept used to understand how specific sites have a characteristic AFFECTIVE quality. We might say, for example, that a room is welcoming or a park is relaxing. Atmospheres are ambiguous: they surround and envelop particular sites, cannot be definitively located, but are present in that people may 'feel' an atmosphere. Atmospheres emanate from the collections of people and things that make up particular sites, without being reducible to any one element.

big data: data sets that are too large or complex in nature to be dealt with by traditional data-processing application software.

bio-power: a term formulated by Michel Foucault which refers to techniques of disciplinary control (usually by the NATION-STATE) to manage the behaviour of large populations. Foucault looked at the regulation of public health and sexual behaviour, as well as at the surveillance and self-regulation required by the emergence of the factory system in the eighteenth and nineteenth centuries. Human geographers have drawn on the term to study RACE and COLONIALISM as well as demography and migration.

capitalism, capitalist: an economic system in which the production and distribution of goods are organised around the profit motive and characterised by marked inequalities in the social division of work and wealth between private owners of the materials and tools of production (capital) and those who work for them to make a living (labour) (see also CLASS).

cisgender: having a GENDER identity that aligns with the sex one is assigned at birth.

cis-heteronormative: a pervasive system of thinking and belief (on individual, systemic and IDEOLOGICAL levels) that being cisgender and heterosexual (straight), with associated ways of being in the world (life-path, material desires, family/kinship structures, political/social goals and so on) are the assumed default and considered 'normal'.

class: a collection of people sharing the same economic position within society, and/or sharing the same social status and cultural tastes. The precise ways in which one's economic position – for example as a worker, a CAPITALIST or a member of the land-owning aristocracy – is related to one's social status or cultural tastes has been much debated. However, human geographers have studied class and its geographies from all these perspectives: as an economic, social and cultural structuring of society.

closet: a spatial metaphor to explain the state of being secretive about one's authentic GENDER identity and/or sexual identity. A person may feel compelled to be closeted in order to keep a job, housing situation, family/friends or to stay safe. Many queer and trans individuals are 'out' in some situations and 'closeted' in others.

co-becoming: a term embracing relationships and relationality, recognising that everything is constantly emerging together in relationship with other people and things (see also ACTOR NETWORK THEORY and ASSEMBLAGE).

colonialism, colonisation, coloniality: the domination and/or dispossession of an Indigenous (or enslaved) majority by a minority of invaders or colonisers. This domination is established and maintained through political structures and military force but may also shape economic and cultural relations. This in turn results in the rule of a NATION-STATE or other political power over another, subordinated people and place (see also NEO-COLONIALISM and IMPERIALISM). See Chapter 49 for a longer consideration of these terms and also Chapters 37 and 71).

commodity: something that can be bought and sold through the market. A commodity can be an object (a car, for example) but can also be a person (the car production worker who sells their labour for a wage) or an idea (the design or marketing concepts of the car). Those who live in CAPITALIST societies are used to most things being commodities, though there are still taboos (the buying and selling of children or body parts for example).

consumptive countryside: rural areas as spaces for consuming goods and services, either individually or collectively (e.g. tourism, recreation, housing, GENTRIFICATION).

cosmopolitan: a person, organisation or thing that belongs to the world, without the limitation or prejudice of any political IDEOLOGIES, cultures or interests.

Country: Country is an Australian Aboriginal English term which encompasses a known and deeply loved place, a TERRITORY, homeland and a web of relationships. Country is land and sea and sky, Country is animal and plant and insect, wind and tide, cloud and current, Country is concrete and wires, road and rail tracks. Country is ancestors and future generations. Country is human beings. Country is MORE-THAN-HUMAN as it embraces humans as part of Country yet decentres human authority.

creative destruction: the economist Joseph Schumpeter defined the term as the 'process of industrial transformation that continuously modernises the economic structure from within, constantly destroying the old one, unceasingly establishing a new one'. In human geography, David Harvey has drawn attention to how such destruction has spatial as well as temporal components.

critical race theory: a theoretical framework that analyses RACE and racism, emphasising that race is not a natural or biologically determined category but a social construct interwoven with POWER structures, everyday practices, institutions and policies.

critical thinking: is an open and curious approach to thinking, bringing a degree of scepticism to any topic, questioning the underlying assumptions and the logical coherence of any argument or framework.

culture: in geography culture is understood in an inclusive manner, beyond the narrow focus on traditions and high cultures. It is defined as the ways in which we make sense of the meanings, symbols, REPRESENTATIONS, values and ethics that shape our everyday experiences.

decolonial, decolonisation: these terms have two meanings: (a) the ending of formal colonial rule by one power over another (see COLONIALISM); (b) the departure of a settler population from a colonised TERRITORY. In both cases, however, processes of decolonisation are, in fact, likely to be far less of a 'clean break' than these definitions suggest. Legacies from, and new forms of, colonialism are still central to POSTCOLONIAL experiences (see also Chapter 71). More recently there have been calls to decolonise human geography itself, which means opening up teaching, learning and research to previously marginalised and silenced groups. In other contexts, decolonisation refers to reforming systems of governance to make space for Indigenous governance institutions in settler colonial states (see Chapter 71).

devolution: a process (rather than a single event) describing the transfer of political powers to more local levels of government, often associated with the formation of local and regional assemblies. This can take place at many scales: within the European Union, for example, POWER can be devolved to individual nations, or to regions; within a nation, power can be devolved to regions and localities; and within a city, powers can be devolved to neighbourhoods.

dialectics, dialectical: a process through which two opposites are generated, interrelated and eventually transcended. This process can be purely intellectual, in so far as it is a process of thought, where two opposing views are reconciled through argument, or it can be identified as part of the wider world. An example would be the combination in a COMMODITY of both use value and exchange value, in which these opposites become wrapped up together in the commodity form.

diaspora: the dispersal or scattering of people from their original home. As a noun it can be used to refer to a dispersed 'people' (hence the Jewish diaspora or the Black diaspora). However, it also refers to the actual processes of dispersal and connection that produce any scattered, but still in some way identifiable, population. In this light it also can be used as an adjective – diasporic – to refer to the senses of home, belonging and cultural identity held by a dispersed population.

discourse, discursive: drawing on the work of Michel Foucault, human geographers define discourses as ways of talking about, writing about or otherwise representing the world and its geographies (see also REPRESENTATION). Discursive approaches to human geography emphasise the importance of these ways of representing. They are seen as shaping the realities of the worlds in which we live, rather than just being ways of portraying a reality that exists outside of language and thought. More specifically, human geographers have stressed the different ways in which people have discursively constructed the world in different times and places and examined how it is that particular ways of talking about, conceptualising and acting on people and places come to be seen as natural and common-sensical in particular contexts. Moreover, because these discourses are SOCIALLY CONSTRUCTED by individuals, groups and institutions, they can operate to produce inclusions and exclusions of people and things from different spaces and places.

ecology, ecological: a way of studying living things (plants, animals or people) that emphasises their complex and dynamic interrelationships with each other and the environment. As well as their use in Biogeography, ecological theories about competition for resources, invasion and distribution have also been applied in other areas of geography.

embodied, embodiment: suggests that the self and the body are not separate, but rather that the experiences of any individual are, invariably, shaped by the active and reactive entity that is their body – irrespective of whether this is conscious or not. The argument, then runs that the uniqueness of human experience is due, at least in part, to the unique nature of individual bodies. Geographers writing on embodiment have emphasised experience (memory, perception, emotion, imagination) and bodily action (social habits, gestures, practices, routines) and have built on FEMINIST perspectives on the body. Here embodiment is shown to be complex and formed through a combination of material and cultural dimensions and a product of specific social-spatial-temporal conditions.

encounters: the coming together of two or more things in an event that might result in something new being produced. What is produced in an encounter cannot be accounted for by reference to any of the participants on their own. For this reason, the concept of the encounter privileges the relation between entities. Societies are made up of innumerable encounters; between two friends who unexpectedly happen across one another in a street; between an individual and an idea; between a person and a building; between one crowd and another crowd etc.

epistemic: relates and refers to knowledge, systems of knowledge and ways of knowing. In human geography there is growing recognition of diverse epistemic traditions and how these shape the way we come to know.

epistemology, epistemological: the study of knowledge, particularly with regard to its methods, scope and validity. This technical term from philosophy refers to differing ideas about what it is possible to know about the world and how it is possible to express that knowledge. Different academic disciplines, and indeed different general approaches within a discipline, are marked by distinctively different epistemologies, Human geographers are interested in the epistemological questions raised by the geographical knowledges held both by academics and by the population at large. In studying these epistemological questions, human geographers seek to connect questions of content (what kinds of things people know) with structures of belief (how and why they claim to know) and issues of authority (how and why these knowledges are valued and justified).

ethnicity: a criterion of social categorisation that distinguishes different groups of people on the basis of inherited cultural differences. Ethnicity as a term is therefore associated with belonging to a cultural group, and aspects of ethnicity are generally understood to include religious traditions, language use, belief systems and cultural practices (such as culinary and musical traditions) but can also be understood as overlapping with ancestry. There are a wide variety of definitions of ethnicity, and in popular usage ethnicity often overlaps with, or may become a synonym for, RACE. However, race differentiates people on the grounds of physical characteristics and ethnicity on the grounds of learned cultural differences.

ethnography, ethnographic: research processes that use qualitative methods to provide in-depth explorations and accounts of the lives, interactions and 'textures' associated with particular people and places. Through being present in the research context (sometimes for substantial amounts of time) researchers are able to collect data through a variety of techniques which include observation, participant-observation, conversation, various forms of interaction and interviews.

Eurocentrism: the notion that Europe is the main actor in shaping the world, and that knowledge that comes from there is the most credible.

expatriate, expatriation: in principle, an expatriate, or 'expat', is simply a person who resides outside her or his native country. However, the term is often more specifically used to refer to professional elites taking positions outside their home country, either independently or sent abroad by their employers.

extractive capitalism: a type of CAPITALISM built on the depletion of resources in order to extract wealth and value from nature and people. The phrase was used by Saskia Sassen to explain how the extraction of precious stones, rare-earth metals and other materials from particular places during the recent phase of CAPITALISM is leaving behind dead land and dead water leading to the gradual exhaustion of all possible resources from these areas.

feminist, feminism: a series of perspectives, which together draw on theoretical and political accounts of the oppression of women in society to show how GENDER and POWER relations are interconnected (see also PATRIARCHY).

financialisation: the growing importance of money and finance within the economy. It is a multi-faceted phenomenon that can be measured through deeper links between the international financial system and household economies; a growing reliance on the financial services sector for economic growth; and increased pressure on firms to respond to, and meet, the demands of the international financial system and their shareholders in particular.

foreign direct investment (FDI): an investment made in a foreign country (usually by a firm in productive facilities). This can include a direct investment in an existing firm and its productive capacity (classically, for example, a factory or a mine). However, it is always distinct from indirect investment, such as buying shares in a foreign company.

gated communities: residential developments which restrict access by non-residents, often containing a controlled entrance and a closed perimeter of walls and/or fences. Sometimes called walled communities.

gender: a criterion of social organisation that distinguishes different groups of people on the basis of femininity or masculinity. In any one location, many masculinities and femininities interact. As a concept, gender has been used in human geography in distinction to that of sex (i.e. femaleness and maleness) in order to emphasise the SOCIAL CONSTRUCTION of gender roles, relations and identities for men, women and non-binary people. Human geographers' accounts of the world have always been shaped through understandings of gender (see MASCULINISM), but explicit analyses of the geographies of gender and the gendering of geographies are associated with the growth of feminist geography (see FEMINISM).

gentrification: a geographical process commonly taken to have two main attributes. The first is the invasion (or replacement) of traditional working-class residential areas by middle-class in-migrants; the second is the upgrading, improvement and renovation of existing housing, whether done by the new residents or by developers. Commercial gentrification refers more specifically to the replacement of older, traditional, low-rent, retail and other uses by new, stylish, fashionable boutiques, cafés, bars and other retail outlets.

geo-tagged, geo-tags: a computer file with metadata containing geographic coordinates.

geographic information systems (GIS): abbreviated as GIS, this refers to computer-assisted systems for storing, processing and analysing geographic data.

ghetto, ghettoisation: a spatially concentrated area, typically in a city, where a specific disadvantaged group, usually racialised, is involuntarily confined and isolated. It differs from other kinds of urban enclaves where people choose to congregate for economic, social, political and cultural development.

global navigation satellite systems: the use of satellites to identify a geographic position; also referred to as satellite navigation or GPS.

global value chain (GVC): the distributed activities associated with the production of a good or service that can be monetised. These typically include invention, design, production, marketing and distribution. A global value chain can be constructed and managed by one or more firms.

globalisation: the economic (see Chapter 35), political, social and cultural processes whereby: (a) places across the globe are increasingly interconnected; (b) social relations and economic transactions increasingly occur at the intercontinental scale (see TRANSNATIONAL); and (c) the globe itself comes to be a recognisable geographical entity. As such, globalisation does not mean everywhere in the world becomes the same. Nor is it an entirely even process; different places are differently connected to the world and view that world from different perspectives. Globalisation has been occurring for several centuries, but in the contemporary world, the speed, scale and extent of social, political, cultural and economic connection appear to be qualitatively different to international networks in the past.

hegemony, hegemonic, hegemon: hegemony is an opaque power relation relying more on domination through consensus than coercion. In this way, domination takes place through the permeation of ideas rather than through force or the threat of violence. For instance, concepts of hegemony have been used to explain how 'the ruling ideas are the ideas of the ruling class'. Hegemonic is the adjective attached to the institution or group that possesses hegemony – under CAPITALISM, for instance, the bourgeoisie are the hegemonic CLASS. Hegemon is a term used when the concept of hegemony is applied to the competition between NATION-STATES: a hegemon is a hegemonic state, as in the case of the USA in the mid-twentieth century.

heteroactivism: activisms that seek to reiterate, reinforce and reinstate HETERNORMATIVITY, including CISGENDERED heterosexual families as 'best for society, best for children'.

heteronormativity: a system of organised beliefs between narrow GENDER dualisms (male/female) that regulates and provides support to the symbolic REPRESENTATION and PERFORMANCE of gender in Western societies. Heteronormativity uncritically accepts such dualism as the 'natural' conception and construction of sex/GENDER.

homonormativity: a critique of the normalisation of 'homosexuality' through things like same-sex marriage. Critiques assimilation into white, CISGENDERED, monogamous, NEO-LIBERAL orders by same-sex couples and others.

historicity: to recognise the historicity of human geographies is to recognise their historical variability. This involves both an emphasis on historical specificity – on how historical periods differ from each other – and on historical change – on how human geographies are re-made and transformed over time.

human agency: usually indicates self-conscious, purposeful action. Geographers have used this term to stress the freedom and capacity of people to generate, modify and influence the course of every day and world events (see also AGENCY).

humanistic geography: a theoretical approach to human geography that concentrates on studying the conscious, creative and meaningful activities and experiences of human beings.

Coming to prominence in the 1970s, humanistic geography was in part a rebuttal of attempts during the 1950s and 1960s to create a law-based, scientific human geography founded on statistical data and analytical techniques (see SPATIAL SCIENCE). In contrast, it emphasised the SUBJECTIVITIES of those being studied and, indeed, the human geographers studying them. Human meanings, emotions and ideas with regard to place, SPACE and nature thus became central.

hyper-separation: a term used by Val Plumwood to describe the operation of separations associated with European/Western understandings of human SUBJECTIVITY and place in the world. Hyper-separations form the basis of extractivist, colonial and exceptionalist logics, the idea that humans are separate from or have somehow risen above nature. See also ALIENATION.

ideological: a meaning, idea or thing is ideological in so far as it helps to constitute and maintain relations of domination and subordination between two or more social groups (CLASSES, GENDERS, age groups etc.).

ideology: a meaning or set of meanings that serve to create and/or maintain relationships of domination and subordination, through symbolic forms such as texts, landscapes and spaces.

imaginative geographies: REPRESENTATIONS of place, SPACE and landscape that structure people's understandings of the world and in turn help to shape their actions. In the work of Edward Said, the term refers to the projection of images of identity and difference onto geographical SPACE in a way that sustains unequal relationships of POWER.

imperialism: a relationship of political, and/or economic, and/or cultural domination and subordination between geographical areas. This relationship may be based on explicit political rule (see COLONIALISM) but need not be. An unequal human and TERRITORIAL relationship involving the extension of authority and control of one state or people over another.

infrastructure: the physical and organisational structures that enable resources and goods to be produced and distributed (e.g. roads, railways, bridges, power stations, telecommunications, oil pipelines, sewage systems). Currently a vibrant focus of geographical research and debate, infrastructure has been shown to involve systems which are at once material, technical, social and legal, and they profoundly impact equality and well-being in urban environments.

international division of reproductive labour: a term developed by Rhacel Parreñas to refer to the international transfer of care work from more privileged women to less privileged women in the global economy.

international financial centre: an area, often a district within a city, in which financial services are concentrated in order to take advantage of the AGGLOMERATION benefits that stem from being co-located with other financial services firms. These benefits include: being able to share technological innovations; learning about competitor activities; the ability to work with other forms on transactions; and the opportunity to share and develop new financial knowledge through personal networks.

Internet of Things (IoT): a network of physical objects that are embedded with sensors, processing ability, software and other technologies for the purpose of connecting and exchanging data with other devices and systems over the internet or other communications networks.

intersectional, intersectionality: an analytical framework for understanding how different properties or processes combine with each other to create overlapping and strengthened modes of discrimination and privilege. A term coined by Kimberle Crenshaw to emphasise that black women faced legal discrimination based on being black and being female, and sometimes through a combination of the two. Now, more widely used to describe how an individual's multiple characteristics, such as RACE, GENDER, CLASS and sexuality 'intersect' and interact with one another to potentially compound the disadvantage that might arise from any one of these characteristics alone.

map projection: a systematic method for transforming the curved Earth's surface into a flat plane.

Marxist, Marxism: social and economic theories influenced by the legacy of the nineteenth-century economist and political philosopher, Karl Marx. Highly influential in the framing of radical and critical geography from the early 1970s onwards, these theories focus on the organisation of CAPITALIST society and the social and environmental injustices that can be traced to it. See also CAPITALISM, ALIENATION and CLASS.

masculinism, masculinist: masculinist is a form of knowledge production that, while claiming to be universal and impartial, actually understands the world in ways associated with men's (often straight, CISGENDER, white and able-bodied) experiences and concerns. Many FEMINIST geographers have argued that human geography has traditionally been masculinist.

migrant division of labour: the way in which the labour market is differentiated by the immigration status of workers, complicating segmentation patterns that reflect long-established divisions based on GENDER and ETHNICITY.

milkarri: when Yolŋu women cry or keen the SONGSPIRALS. Milkarri is an ancient song, an ancient poem, a map, a ceremony and a guide but it is more than all this too. Milkarri is a very powerful thing in Yolŋu life. It is very complex and there are limits to what non-Yolŋu can understand.

modern, modernity, modernism: ideas of the modern are most commonly defined through their opposition to the old and the traditional. In this light, the adjective 'modern' is synonymous with 'newness'; 'modernity' refers both to the 'post-traditional' historical epoch within which 'newness' is produced and valued, as well as to the economic, social, political and cultural formations characteristic of that period; and 'modernism' applies more narrowly to artistic, architectural and intellectual movements that centrally explore ideas of 'newness' and develop 'new' AESTHETICS and ways of thinking to express these. Modernity has been most commonly located in Euro-American societies from the eighteenth century onwards and associated with their characteristic combination of capitalist economies (see CAPITALISM), political organisation through NATION-STATES, and cultural values of secularity, rationality and progress. However, increasingly, human geographers are recognising that modernity is a global phenomenon that has taken many different forms in different times and places.

more-than-human: refers to non-human beings and species, environmental processes, technologies and ECOLOGIES. Unlike 'non-human', however, it can also include humans as part of the relational webs which sustain us and connect us with other species, ecologies and things.

multifunctional agriculture: the notion that agricultural activity may also have several other functions beyond its role of producing food and fibre – such as renewable natural resource management, landscape and biodiversity conservation and a contribution to the socio-economic viability of rural areas.

multifunctional countryside: implying the shifting and multiple roles of the contemporary countryside across production, consumption and protection (e.g. agricultural production, environmental conservation, landscape management, heritage preservation, economic development etc.).

multispecies justice: an emergent term used to trouble and repair persistent tensions across and between social, environmental and ECOLOGICAL justice. First introduced by Donna Haraway, it emphasises the differential and coalitional thinking in multiple worlds, key to aspirations for justice for humans and Earth others.

nation-state: a form of political organisation that involves (a) a set of institutions that govern the people within a particular TERRITORY (the state) and (b) that claims allegiance and legitimacy from those governed, and from other states, on the basis that they represent a group of people defined in cultural and political terms as a nation. Hence, the 'nation' refers to a degree of cultural uniformity, and the 'state' refers to a combination of centralised political authority, territorial boundaries and the right to use physical force to keep its people secure. (See also Chapter 48.)

neo-colonialism: economic and political ties continuing after formal independence between colonising countries of the Global North and the colonised nations of the Global South, that work to the benefit of the North (see also COLONIALISM, and Chapter 49).

neoliberalism, neoliberal: pertaining to an economic doctrine that favours free markets, the deregulation of national economies, decentralisation and privatisation of previously state-owned enterprises (e.g. education, health, utilities). Many geographers have argued that this is a doctrine which favours the interests of the powerful against the less powerful (see also Chapter 52).

new international division of labour (NIDL): the reshaping of the division of labour such that various components of the production process are located in multiple countries. This concept emerged in the context of debates about the impact of GLOBALISATION, especially in the 1970s when production was being relocated from Europe and North America to Asia and Latin America to take advantage of cheaper labour costs. NIDL is also facilitated by technological change (e.g. container shipping).

non-conscious: a broad term to designate a range of phenomena that occur below the threshold of conscious awareness. The negative – non – does not designate a lack, nor does it designate a dimension of experience that is completely separate from conscious acts of thinking. Rather, conscious and non-conscious processes are intertwined with one another. The nature of the relation between the two is a key concern of the research that has emerged in relation to NON-REPRESENTATIONAL THEORIES.

non-human agency: while traditionally geographers have used the term AGENCY to stress the freedom and capacity of people to generate, modify and influence the course of every day and world events, increasingly they are affording comparable levels of agency to non-human animals, organisms, technologies, machines and hybrid kinds of ASSEMBLAGE or apparatus.

non-representational theories: an umbrella term for a group of theories that attempt to attend to life as it happens. What is shared between them are three questions; how do sense and significance emerge from on-going practical action? How, given the contingency of orders, is practical action organised, and how to attend to events and the chance of something different that they open up? The plural – theories, rather than theory – is important: for there are now a range of non-representational theories that respond to these three starting problematics. Rather than denying the importance of REPRESENTATIONS, non-representational theory has sought to resist an undue obsession with them through a direct focus on actions, events, moments and things.

ontology, ontologies: a classic philosophical consideration that asks fundamental questions and offers contested propositions about the very nature of existence. Geographers have traditionally been concerned with these questions of 'being' in terms of human existence, though recently have extended their enquiries to wonder at all manner of living organisms, as well as objects, things and technologies, in the changing make-up of life. A new frontier of ontological politics has resulted, represented in a shift in philosophical thought, away from what is (beings) towards what emerges (becomings).

Orientalism, Orientalist: derived from Edward Said's pioneering book *Orientalism* (1981), which considered how regions such as the Middle East were consistently imagined and represented by Western authors and texts as exotic, mysterious and/or dangerous (see IMAGINATIVE GEOGRAPHIES).

other, otherness: an Other is that person or entity supposed to be opposite or different to oneself. Otherness is the quality of difference which that Other possesses. Potentially applicable at various scales, these terms have been used in human geography to highlight how the Other is often defined in relation to the Self – as everything the Self is not – rather than in its own terms. The terms were popularised in Said's book on ORIENTALISM where it is used to describe the Western tradition of categorising the Western Self against the exotic Other through binary categorisation, such as civilised/savage and advanced/primitive. Geographers have stressed how ideas of otherness have also been applied to a variety of groups within contemporary society.

out: to be 'out' is when LGBTIQ+ people recognise and accept their sexual orientation, sexuality and/or GENDER identity and expression. There is no one way of 'coming out' and experiences differ across places and communities.

participatory geographies: a way of doing academic research and theory based on the co-production of knowledge with participants. Although there are different forms and levels of participation, in general, participatory research is animated by the principle that research should be developed with and for participants and the desire that research should be beneficial to those participants.

patriarchy: a harm-inducing hierarchy that elevates some men and masculinities over other men and masculinities, and all men and masculinities over women and femininities. Patriarchy is oppressive to people of all GENDERS, not just girls and women.

performance: the EMBODIED, material actions through which SUBJECTIVITIES, spaces and worlds are made. Performances are always situated in both SPACE and time and are able to connect across multiple sites and scales of activity. Although performances may be repetitive and socially taught, they can also be intuitive, spontaneous and unexpected. This creativity and originality often link performance to the subversion of existing power relations and the opening up of new forms of collaboration and co-production. It also draws attention to a colloquial understanding of performance as a product of the performing arts.

performativity: the repetitious acts through which bodies produce identities and bring them into being. These acts constitute rather than reflect identity. However, these performances emerge from the workings of POWER; they are the product of DISCURSIVE constraints, or socially sanctioned codes, that enable identity and necessitate that it is continually repeated. Performativity thus links bodily action to the re-enactment of social norms including inherited understandings, symbolic codes and modes of comportment. Although these repeated actions consolidate the norms of identity practice, they also provide possibilities for slippage and subversion because an act is never identical in its repetition.

pluriverse: often used to emphasise alternatives to dominant narratives of MODERNITY, GLOBALISATION, state formations and CAPITALIST economic development in ways that challenge universal and hetero-patriarchal conceptualisations of humans, nature, time, economy and society. Emergent narratives and movements for non-human personhood and the rights of nature, which recognise non-humans as sacred and sentient beings, are aligned with pluriversal thinking, which are often led by Indigenous peoples.

poetics: put broadly, a concern with how to write. In more complex terms, poetics raises questions about how to represent the world through writing and signals that words are not just straightforward mirrors of the world. Instead, poetics stresses the complexity of language and the importance of social POWER and cultural norms in conveying particular meanings.

political economy, political-economic: the study of how economic activities are socially and politically structured and have social and political consequences. Political-economic approaches in human geography have paid particular attention to understanding CAPITALIST economies and their geographical organisation and impact (see MARXISM). Central to such analyses have been questions concerning the CLASS-based nature of the human geographies of CAPITALIST societies.

positionality: the personal experiences, beliefs, identities and motives of the human geographer, which influence her or his work and the way in which her or his knowledge is situated

postcolonial, postcolonialism: the historical, psychological, economic and political complexities resulting from colonial experience; also used to refer to a social criticism that reveals unequal processes of REPRESENTATION from such experience. Sometimes used to describe a particular post-colonial era, i.e. the historical period following a period of COLONIALISM (see also DECOLONISATION) or particular political, cultural and intellectual movements and their perspectives, which are critical of the past and ongoing effects of European and other COLONIALISMS (see also Chapter 49).

postdevelopment: a set of practices and theories that seeks to move beyond the universalising dominance of Western prescriptions of development programmes and instead promotes more diverse ONTOLOGIES and ECOLOGIES of knowledge, economies and life worlds.

post-Fordism: refers to the forms of production, work, consumption and regulation that emerged out of the crisis of mass, standardised forms of CAPITALIST production (Fordism) during the 1970s. In terms of production and work, post-Fordism turns on the importance of flexibility in work and other institutional forms of productive organisation. Accompanying these changes in production are changes in consumer demand (the centrality of quality over standardisation), in labour markets, in finance and legal structures and in the broad social contract that characterised post-war Fordism

postmodern, postmodernity, postmodernism: used to suggest a move beyond 'modern' society and culture (see MODERN, MODERNITY, MODERNISM). More specifically: (a) postmodern is an adjective used to describe social and cultural forms that eschew 'modern' qualities of order, rationality and progress in favour of 'postmodern' qualities of difference, ephemerality, superficiality and pastiche; (b) 'postmodernity' is the epoch, after a period of 'modernity', in which such postmodern forms supposedly predominate, an epoch characterised both by the loss of an overall sense of social direction and order and by the triumph of the media image over reality; and (c) 'postmodernism' refers more narrowly to a collection of artistic, architectural and intellectual movements that promote postmodernist values, AESTHETICS and ways of thinking.

post-productivist transition: a transition in rural policy that includes and aims to tackle broader rural (i.e. TERRITORIAL) development concerns, rather than simply agricultural/farming interests (i.e. sectoral).

power: the capacity to get something done, exercised at all scales from the individual household to the entire global economy. Geographers work with three conceptions of power: (a) as something possessed by an individual, group or organisation or power 'over' others; (b) as a resource or capacity, or power 'to' achieve desired outcomes; and (c) power as strategy or technique. The interest of human geographers partly stems from the fact that the exercise of power often has a spatial component, and indeed state power is almost always geographically bounded (see TERRITORY).

producer services: intermediate service inputs to improve, expand and develop other production activities, typically with a high knowledge content. Management consultancy and accountancy are typical examples of producer services.

productivism, productivist: the belief that the accumulation of material goods and the expansion of production should be the central focus of society, it values the production and consumption of goods and services as the primary drivers of economic growth and societal well-being.

race: implies that there exist discrete and measurable biological groups that can easily be distinguished from one another. It is now widely accepted by social scientists and human geographers that racial categories, while having very real consequences for people's lives, cannot simply be assumed as biological realities, having instead to be recognised as SOCIAL CONSTRUCTIONS. Genetically race has been proven not to exist, but often social understandings of race reflect older biological understanding and lead to discriminatory practices as a result.

regionalisation: active measures promoting regional capacity often through new governance arrangements and practices in the field of the economy and public service provision.

regionalism: a political or cultural movement which seeks to further regional interests. Traditionally intended as the focus of decentralised national-state policies, 'regionalism' has developed into a POLITICAL-ECONOMIC approach to strengthening and supporting regional capacity.

reification: the act of transforming human properties, relations and actions into properties, relations and actions that appear to be independent of human endeavour. It can also refer to the transformations of human beings into 'thing-like' beings. Reification is therefore a form of ALIENATION.

representation: the cultural practices and forms by which human societies interpret and portray the world around them and present themselves to others. In the case of the natural world, for instance, these might range from prehistoric cave paintings to the media images and scientific models that shape our imaginations today. Representations were often taken at face value prior to the 1970s, but by the 1980s, the 'politics of representation' was gaining traction which called into question the idea that representations somehow mirror the world. Such concerns led to the so-called crisis of representation in the late 1980s, which saw representations not as more or less faithful reflections of the world but as 'creatures of our own making' that are invariably shaped by those doing the representing (see also DISCOURSE and Chapter 8).

romanticised: a stereotypical understanding based on assumptions of an idealised reality.

rural restructuring: referring to radical transformations in rural areas and their impacts on rural economy and society (e.g. declining role of agriculture, growing rural settlements as people move from cities, rural GENTRIFICATION trends, new environmental concerns and challenges, land use conflicts about the regulation and use of rural space etc.).

scientific racism: based around the collection of physical anthropological data, including body measurements such as cephalic index, cranial capacity, height and pigmentation to support arguments that races could be classified and split into hierarchies based on physical and mental capacities. This approach has now been completely discredited, but these pseudo-scientific arguments were given legitimacy through publication in key scientific journals in the late nineteenth and early twentieth centuries.

social construction, socially constructed: refers to the idea that the social context and environment in which any individual is situated shapes their understandings of the world – and indeed the world's understanding of them. Rejects the idea that identity categories are essentialist (fixed, and never changing), so that RACE, ETHNICITY, GENDER, CLASS or other forms of identity are understood as categories that shift and change over SPACE and time. This means (a) that the things, situations and ideas that surround us are the product of social forces and practices that themselves require explanation; and (b) they are not inevitable, instead being open to the possibility of critique and change.

sociality: socialities can be thought of as the connections, relationships and interactions between people. These can be not only interpersonal relations (as in work colleagues, families, Facebook friends) but also relations in which unknown people are connected across spaces (as in in ethical imaginings of distant OTHERS connected through one's consumption practices). In recent years, geographers have demonstrated the importance of non-human things in the establishment, maintenance and dissolution of socialities (e.g. animals, plants, photos, food, environments and technologies).

songspirals: are often called songlines or song cycles. In the work of Bawaka Country (see Chapter 43), they are called songspirals because they spiral in and out, go up and down and around forever. They are a song that moves in many directions and is not a straight line. They are a map to follow through COUNTRY as they connect to other clans.

sovereignties: the ability, the right, the obligation to make decisions and to govern. The term is pluralised to highlight that with the AGENCY of MORE-THAN-HUMANS comes multiple sovereignties, the ability, the right, the obligation of more-than-humans to make decisions and agreements and to govern themselves. These relations are underpinned by Indigenous sovereignties – relationships of land, law/lore and people.

space: the simultaneity of multiple trajectories in which contemporaneous relations between people and non-human things are arranged. Space has often been understood as abstract, while place is more specific. Space (which geography was said to analyse) has also often been understood as distinct from time (which is what the discipline of history was thought to analyse). However, geographer Doreen Massey's influential work reimagined space as multiple and relational and always contextual.

spatial science: an approach to human geography that became influential in the 1950s and 1960s by arguing that geographers should be concerned with formulating and testing theories of spatial organisation, interaction and distribution. The theories were often expressed in the form of models – for instance, land use, settlement hierarchy, industrial location and city sizes. If validated, these theories were then accorded the status of universal 'laws'. Through this manoeuvre, the advocates of spatial science claimed that human geography had been shifted from an essentially descriptive enterprise concerned with the study of regional differences to a predictive and explanatory science. Critics claim that in its attempts to formulate universally applicable laws, spatial science ignored the social and economic context within which its spatial variables were located.

spatiality: the spatial arrangements of relations between people and non-human things. This involves the production of SPACE emphasising how places are socially and materially created, reconfigured and experienced in the context of the changing economic, political and cultural relations between other places, people and things. A consideration of spatiality also includes the effects spaces have on these relations and the POWER relations associated with this.

spectrality: a condition or experience of SPACE, place and the self where something that is seemingly present (something that is *there*) is disturbed or haunted by something that is absent (something that is not *there*). This disturbance can lead to feelings of ambiguity and undecidability as we seek to understand geography.

structure of feeling: a concept developed by Raymond Williams to describe the 'felt sense of the quality of life at a particular place and time'. A structure of feeling conditions what is and can be felt by individuals or groups and reminds us that what might appear to be most ephemeral – feelings – are organised and patterned.

structural adjustment policies: sometimes called structural adjustment programmes (SAPs), these are a package of economic policies adopted by, or imposed upon, countries of the Global South by the International Monetary Fund and the World Bank as conditionality for loans to address balance of payments deficits and long-term economic decline. Many Global South countries depended on exporting primary commodities and faced a steep decline in their international prices relative to industrial products through the 1980s, as well as rapid currency depreciation. At the same time many governments had huge debt burdens, having been persuaded to take substantial loans from Western banks and the World Bank. The package of policies designed to help address these challenges focussed on reducing state expenditure and encouraging private investment and free trade to stimulate economic growth, but often led to austerity and rising poverty. Recognising these negative effects, stronger social and poverty reduction elements were added in later programmes.

subaltern: those excluded and marginalised, often due to colonial and/or HEGEMONIC power relations.

subjectivity, subjectivities: a complex term, referring to our understandings of ourselves and our capacity to act. Sometimes this relates to our knowledge of the world (as when we speak of subjective knowledge based on individual experience); sometimes to the very status of what makes us a human individual (as when the philosopher Descartes associated human subjectivity with thought: 'I think, therefore I am'). Human geographers draw on a range of theories of subjectivity, but generally these emphasise how our individual and collective subjectivity is fashioned through wider social forces.

super-diversity: used to indicate that present-day levels of population diversity are significantly higher and more complex and stratified than before.

super-gentrification: the conversion of prosperous, already gentrified and solid upper-middle-class neighbourhoods into much more expensive and exclusive enclaves.

technological solutionism: a 'problem-solving' framework which refers to using technologies to optimise and solve social and environmental problems.

teleology, teleological: the idea that events can be accounted for as stages in the movement towards a pre-ordained end. This approach was often used to 'explain' the different stages of economic development experienced by different countries, as they were all seen to be progressing towards an advanced industrial endpoint, albeit at different rates.

temporality: socially produced time. This term is used by human geographers to emphasise how time is SOCIALLY CONSTRUCTED and experienced, rather than being an innate back-drop to social life (see also Chapter 4).

territory, territorial, territoriality: a more or less bounded area over which an animal, person, social group or institution claims control. Territorial is the adjective referring to attempts to impose and enforce that control, while territoriality refers to the assignment of persons and social groups to discrete areas using boundaries, whether through popular acceptance or enforcement (see also Chapter 47).

time-space compression: coined by the geographer David Harvey, this phrase has been widely used to express (a) the transformations in TEMPORALITY and SPATIALITY produced in a world of ever more rapid turnover and even quicker forms of communication; and (b) the subjective experience of these changes.

topophilia: from the Greek 'topos' and 'philia', meaning love of place. Popularised by the geog-rapher Yi-fu Tuan, the term describes the strong emotional attachment and affection that people can feel for a certain place or a certain landscape. This can be combined with a sense of cultural identity.

transnational: an adjective used to describe human geographical processes that have escaped the bounded confines of the NATION-STATE. These have been identified in the realms of the economy through transnational corporations; in politics (for instance, through the politi-cal agency of groups in relation to a nation-state they do not reside in); and in culture (for example through the identification of 'transnational communities' that have dispersed from an original homeland into a number of other countries but that also have strong linkages across this DIASPORA).

uneven development: refers to the geographically unequal distribution of resources, POWER and wealth across different regions and communities. This unevenness results in the cre-ation of geographical spaces of inequality, where some regions and communities experience growth and prosperity while others experience economic decline. With MARXISM becom-ing a key theoretical force within human geography in the 1970s and early 1980s, a concern for uneven development came to the fore.

urban-rural continuum: the proposition that urban and rural SPATIALITIES co-exist in the settle-ment pattern, merge and even overlap, contrary to the notion of an 'urban-rural dichotomy'.

urban sub-proletariat: the proletariat is the social CLASS of wage-earners whose only means of subsistence is to sell their labour power for a wage. The sub-proletariat describes a social level below the proletariat. In Keith Hart's pioneering study of informal economies in Ghana, urban sub-proletariat is used to describe the urban migrants who earn their living not by wage employment but by self-employment and other non-wage economic activities.

vital materialism: a belief that matter itself has vitality and life, leading human geographers to recognise the influence of non-human objects and the spaces in which humans live and move through (see also NON-HUMAN AGENCY and MORE-THAN-HUMAN).

Index

Note: Page numbers in *italics* and **bold** refer to figures and tables, respectively.